23581

W9-AIA-631

WITHDRAWN

Short Story
Criticism

Guide to Gale Literary Criticism Series

For criticism on	Consult these Gale series
Authors now living or who died after December 31, 1959	*CONTEMPORARY LITERARY CRITICISM (CLC)*
Authors who died between 1900 and 1959	*TWENTIETH-CENTURY LITERARY CRITICISM (TCLC)*
Authors who died between 1800 and 1899	*NINETEENTH-CENTURY LITERATURE CRITICISM (NCLC)*
Authors who died between 1400 and 1799	*LITERATURE CRITICISM FROM 1400 TO 1800 (LC)* *SHAKESPEAREAN CRITICISM (SC)*
Authors who died before 1400	*CLASSICAL AND MEDIEVAL LITERATURE CRITICISM (CMLC)*
Black writers of the past two hundred years	*BLACK LITERATURE CRITICISM (BLC)*
Authors of books for children and young adults	*CHILDREN'S LITERATURE REVIEW (CLR)*
Dramatists	*DRAMA CRITICISM (DC)*
Hispanic writers of the late nineteenth and twentieth centuries	*HISPANIC LITERATURE CRITICISM (HLC)*
Native North American writers and orators of the eighteenth, nineteenth, and twentieth centuries	*NATIVE NORTH AMERICAN LITERATURE (NNAL)*
Poets	*POETRY CRITICISM (PC)*
Short story writers	*SHORT STORY CRITICISM (SSC)*
Major authors from the Renaissance to the present	*WORLD LITERATURE CRITICISM, 1500 TO THE PRESENT (WLC)*

ISSN 0895-9439

Volume 23

Short Story Criticism

Excerpts from Criticism of the
Works of Short Fiction Writers

Margaret Haerens
Drew Kalasky
Editors

Jeff Hill
Marie Rose Napierkowski
Mary K. Ruby
Christine Slovey
Lawrence J. Trudeau
Associate Editors

GALE

DETROIT • NEW YORK • TORONTO • LONDON

STAFF

Margaret Haerens, Drew Kalasky, *Editors*

Marie Rose Napierkowski, Christine Slovey, Lawrence J. Trudeau,
Associate Editors

Debra A. Wells, *Assistant Editor*

Marlene S. Hurst, *Permissions Manager*

Margaret A. Chamberlain, Maria Franklin, Kimberly F. Smilay, *Permissions Specialists*

Diane Cooper, Edna Hedblad, Michele Lonoconus, Maureen Puhl,
Susan Salas, Shalice Shah, *Permissions Associates*

Sarah Chesney, Jeffrey Hermann, *Permissions Assistants*

Victoria B. Cariappa, *Research Manager*

Laura Bissey, Julia C. Daniel, Tamara C. Nott, Michele P. Pica,
Tracie A. Richardson, Norma Sawaya, Cheryl L. Warnock, *Research Associates*

Mary Beth Trimper, *Production Director*
Deborah L. Milliken, *Production Assistant*

C. J. Jonik, *Desktop Publisher*
Randy Bassett, *Image Database Supervisor*
Mikal Ansari, Robert Duncan, *Scanner Operators*
Pamela Hayes, *Photography Coordinator*

Margaret Haerens, Drew Kalasky, Christine Slovey,
Lawrence J. Trudeau, *Desktop Typesetters*

Library of Congress Catalog Card Number 88-641014
ISBN 0-7876-0755-X
ISSN 0895-9439

Printed in the United States of America
10 9 8 7 6 5 4 3 2 1

Contents

Preface vii

Acknowledgments xi

Preface

A Comprehensive Information Source
on World Short Fiction

S *hort Story Criticism (SSC)* presents significant passages from criticism of the world's greatest short story writers and provides supplementary biographical and bibliographical materials to guide the interested reader to a greater understanding of the authors of short fiction. This series was developed in response to suggestions from librarians serving high school, college, and public library patrons, who had noted a considerable number of requests for critical material on short story writers. Although major short story writers are covered in such Gale series as *Contemporary Literary Criticism (CLC), Twentieth-Century Literary Criticism (TCLC), Nineteenth-Century Literature Criticism (NCLC),* and *Literature Criticism from 1400 to 1800 (LC),* librarians perceived the need for a series devoted solely to writers of the short story genre.

Coverage

SSC is designed to serve as an introduction to major short story writers of all eras and nationalities. Since these authors have inspired a great deal of relevant critical material, *SSC* is necessarily selective, and the editors have chosen the most important published criticism to aid readers and students in their research.

Approximately eight to ten authors are included in each volume, and each entry presents a historical survey of the critical response to that author's work. The length of an entry is intended to reflect the amount of critical attention the author has received from critics writing in English and from foreign critics in translation. Every attempt has been made to identify and include excerpts from the most significant essays on each author's work. In order to provide these important critical pieces, the editors sometimes reprint essays that have appeared elsewhere in Gale's Literary Criticism Series. Such duplication, however, never exceeds twenty percent of an *SSC* volume.

Organization

An *SSC* author entry consists of the following elements:

- The **Author Heading** cites the name under which the author most commonly wrote, followed by birth and death dates. If the author wrote consistently under a pseudonym, the pseudonym will be listed in the author heading and the author's actual name given in parentheses on the first line of the biographical and critical introduction.

- The **Biographical and Critical Introduction** contains background information designed to introduce a reader to the author and the critical debates surrounding his or her work.

- A **Portrait of the Author** is included when available. Many entries also contain illustrations of materials pertinent to an author's career, including holographs of manuscript pages, title pages, dust jackets, letters, or representations of important people, places, and events in the author's life.

- The list of **Principal Works** is chronological by date of first publication and lists the most important works by the author. The first section comprises short story collections, novellas, and novella collections. The second section gives information on other major works by the author. For foreign authors, the editors have provided original foreign-language publication information and have selected what are considered the best and most complete English-language editions of their works.

- **Criticism** is arranged chronologically in each author entry to provide a useful perspective on changes in critical evaluation over the years. All short story, novella, and collection titles by the author featured in the entry are printed in boldface type to enable a reader to ascertain without difficulty the works discussed. Also for purposes of easier identification, the critic's name and the publication date of the essay are given at the beginning of each piece of criticism. Unsigned criticism is preceded by the title of the journal in which it appeared.

- Critical essays are prefaced with **Explanatory Notes** as an additional aid to students and readers using *SSC*. An explanatory note may provide useful information of several types, including: the reputation of the critic, the intent or scope of the critical essay, and the orientation of the criticism (biographical, psychoanalytic, structuralist, etc.).

- A complete **Bibliographical Citation,** designed to help the interested reader locate the original essay or book, precedes each piece of criticism.

- The **Further Reading List** appearing at the end of each author entry suggests additional materials on the author. In some cases it includes essays for which the editors could not obtain reprint rights. Boxed material following the further reading list provides references to other biographical and critical sources on the author in series published by Gale.

Beginning with volume six, *SSC* contains two additional features designed to enhance the reader's understanding of short fiction writers and their works:

- Each *SSC* entry now includes, when available, **Comments by the Author** that illuminate his or her own works or the short story genre in general. These statements are set within boxes or bold rules to distinguish them from the criticism.

- A **Select Bibliography of General Sources on Short Fiction** is included as an appendix. This listing of materials for further research provides readers with a selection of the best available general studies of the short story genre.

Other Features

A **Cumulative Author Index** lists all the authors who have appeared in *SSC, CLC, TCLC, NCLC, LC,* and *Classical and Medieval Literature Criticism (CMLC),* as well as cross-references to other Gale series. Users will welcome this cumulated index as a useful tool for locating an author within the Literary Criticism Series.

A **Cumulative Nationality Index** lists all authors featured in *SSC* by nationality, followed by the number of the *SSC* volume in which their entry appears.

A **Cumulative Title Index** lists in alphabetical order all short story, novella, and collection titles contained in the *SSC* series. Titles of short story collections, separately published novellas, and novella collections are printed in italics, while titles of individual short stories are printed in roman type with quotation marks.

Each title is followed by the author's name and corresponding volume and page numbers where commentary on the work is located. English-language translations of original foreign-language titles are cross-referenced to the foreign titles so that all references to discussion of a work are combined in one listing.

Citing *Short Story Criticism*

When writing papers, students who quote directly from any volume in the Literary Criticism Series may use the following general forms to footnote reprinted criticism. The first example pertains to material drawn from periodicals, the second to material reprinted from books:

[1]Henry James, Jr., "Honoré de Balzac," *The Galaxy* 20 (December 1875), 814-36; excerpted and reprinted in *Short Story Criticism,* Vol. 5, ed. Thomas Votteler (Detroit: Gale Research, 1990), pp. 8-11.

[2]F. R. Leavis, *D. H. Lawrence: Novelist* (Alfred A. Knopf, 1956); excerpted and reprinted in *Short Story Criticism,* Vol. 4, ed. Thomas Votteler (Detroit: Gale Research, 1990), pp. 202-06.

Comments

Readers who wish to suggest authors to appear in future volumes, or who have other suggestions, are invited to contact the editors by writing to Gale Research Inc., Literary Criticism Division, 835 Penobscot Building, Detroit, MI 48226-4094.

Acknowledgments

The editors wish to thank the copyright holders of the excerpted criticism included in this volume and the permissions managers of many book and magazine publishing companies for assisting us in securing reprint rights. We are also grateful to the staffs of the Detroit Public Library, the Library of Congress, the University of Detroit Mercy Library, Wayne State University Purdy/Kresge Library Complex, and the University of Michigan Libraries for making their resources available to us. Following is a list of the copyright holders who have granted us permission to reprint material in this volume of *SSC*. Every effort has been made to trace copyright, but if omissions have been made, please let us know.

COPYRIGHTED EXCERPTS IN *SSC*, VOLUME 23, WERE REPRINTED FROM THE FOLLOWING PERIODICALS:

The American Spectator, v. 28, November, 1995. Copyright © The American Spectator 1995. Reprinted by permission of the publisher.—*The Antigonish Review*, ns. 81-82, Spring-Summer, 1990 for "A Good Grandmother Is Hard to Find: Story as Exemplum" by Sheldon Currie. Copyright 1990 by the author. Reprinted by permission of the publisher and the author.—*The Atlantic Monthly*, v. 174, December, 1944 for "The Simple Act of Murder" by Raymond Chandler. Copyright 1944, renewed 1972 by The Atlantic Monthly Company, Boston, MA.—*AUMLA*, n. 63, May, 1985. Reprinted by permission of the publisher.—*Ball State University Forum*, v. XXIII, Winter, 1982. Copyright © 1982 Ball State University. Reprinted by permission of the publisher.—*Book Forum*, v. VI, 1982 for "Chandler in the Thirties: Apprenticeship of an Angry Man" by Roy Meador. Copyright © 1982 by The Hudson River Press. Reprinted by permission of the author.—*Book World--The Washington Post*, February 9, 1986. Copyright © 1986, Washington Post Book World Service/Washington Post Writers Group. Reprinted with permission.—*British Book News*, July, 1984. Copyright © British Book News, 1984. Courtesy of British Book News.—*Chicago Sunday Tribune Magazine of Books*, March 18, 1962.—*The Christian Science Monitor*, v. 57, September 30, 1965, April 23, 1970. Copyright © 1965, 1970 The Christian Science Publishing Society. All rights reserved. Reprinted by permission from The Christian Science Monitor.—*The Comparatist*, v. XII, May, 1988. Copyright © 1988 by the Southern Comparative Literature Association. Reprinted by permission of the publisher.—*Colloquia Germanica*, v. 14, 1981 for "Heinrich Boll's 'Die verlorne Ehre der Katharina Blum' as Novelle" by Margit M. Sinka. Copyright © A. Francke AG Verlag Bern, 1981. All rights reserved. Reprinted by permission of the author.—*The Denver Quarterly*, v. III, Autumn, 1968 for "Miss Flannery's Good Man" by Marion Montgomery. Copyright © 1968 by the University of Denver. Reprinted by permission of the author.—*English Studies in Canada*, v. XIV, December, 1988 for "Cats, Crime, and Punishment: The Mikado's Pitti-Sing in 'A Good Man Is Hard to Find'" by J. Peter Dyson. Copyright © Association of Canadian University Teachers of English 1988. Reprinted by permission of the publisher.—*The Flannery O'Connor Bulletin*, v. VII, Autumn, 1979. Reprinted by permission of the publisher.—*German Life & Letters*, v. XXXIV, July, 1981. Reprinted by permission of the publisher.—*The Hudson Review*, v. IX, Autumn, 1956. Copyright © 1956, renewed 1984 by The Hudson Review Inc. Reprinted by permission of the Literary Estate of William Arrowsmith./ v. XL, Winter, 1988. Copyright © 1988 by The Hudson Review, Inc. Reprinted by permission of the publisher.—*Hispania*, v. LXXIV, May, 1991 for a review of "Goodbyes and Stories" by George R. McMurray. Copyright © 1991 The American Association of Teachers of Spanish and Portuese, Inc. Reprinted by permission of the publisher and the author.—*Journal of the Short Story in English*, n. 16, Spring, 1991. Copyright © Universite d'Angers, 1991. Reprinted by permission of the publisher.—*Latin American Literary Review*, v. II, Fall-Winter, 1973. Reprinted by permission of the publisher.—*The Massachusetts Review*, v. XIV, Winter, 1973. Copyright © 1973. Reprinted from The Massachusetts Review, The Massachusetts Review, Inc. by permission.—*The Michigan Academician*, v. XIV, Summer, 1981. Copyright © The Michigan Academy of Science, Arts, and Letters, 1981. Reprinted by permission of the publisher.—*Mississippi Quarterly*, v. XXVIII, Fall, 1975. Copyright 1975 Mississippi State University. Reprinted by permission of the publisher.—*MLN*, v. 102, March, 1987. Copyright ©1987 by The Johns Hopkins University Press. All rights reserved. Reprinted by permission of the publisher.—*Modern Fiction Studies*, v. XXIV, Autumn,

Heinrich Böll
1917–1985

(Full name Heinrich Theodor Böll; also transliterated as Boell) German short fiction writer, novelist, poet, playwright, essayist, translator, and editor.

INTRODUCTION

A recipient of the 1972 Nobel Prize for Literature who has often been deemed "the conscience of the German nation," Böll is best known for satires and moral tales in which he delineates the problems of post-World War II German society. Noted for their concise and simple style, varied narrative voices, and nonconformist themes, Böll's works marked an abrupt departure from the propagandist fiction of Nazi Germany. His short fiction is usually set during and after World War II and dramatizes the plight of the victim in order to stress the need for compassion, tolerance, and social reform.

Biographical Information

Böll was born in Cologne into a family of devout Catholics. Because Cologne was the site of numerous Nazi demonstrations in the 1920s and 1930s, Böll grew up with a strong dislike of Germany's new political structure; when asked to join Adolf Hitler's Youth Corps, he refused. After graduating from a local secondary school in 1937, Böll became apprenticed to a bookseller in Bonn and then served in Hitler's compulsory labor program. He enrolled in the University of Cologne in 1939 intending to study philology and literature, but his studies were interrupted when he was drafted into the German army. Forced to serve on the French and Russian fronts, Böll grew resentful and quickly became an outspoken critic of the German military. In 1945 he deserted from the German army and was later interned in an Allied prisoner-of-war camp. After the war Böll returned to Cologne to resume his writing career, only to discover that his early writings had been destroyed. He published his first short story, "Die Botschaft" ("Breaking the News"), in 1947 and his first novella, *Der Zug war pünklicht* (*The Train Was on Time*), in 1949. Böll became actively involved in politics, denouncing German capitalism as well as rearmament in the 1950s and calling for a social system that valued and protected basic human rights. Because his political views often contradicted government policy he was frequently placed under police surveillance after 1974. He died in 1985.

Major Works of Short Fiction

Böll's earliest works—such as his novella *The Train Was on Time* and his first short story collection, *Wanderer,*

kommst du nach Spa . . . (*Traveller, If You Come to Spa,* 1950)—are set during World War II and focus on individuals who are confronted with an awareness of their own mortality and the senselessness of war. Although Böll's first published story "Breaking the News," is also set during the war, this piece introduces themes that would preoccupy Böll in his later works, particularly the sense of loss and guilt experienced by the German people following the war. "Nicht nur zur Weihnachzeit" ("Christmas Every Day," 1952), a satirical story often considered a classic work of postwar literature, similarly focuses on the problem of guilt in the postwar era, specifically the attempts of many Germans to deny that atrocities were committed during World War II. Much of Böll's short fiction also chronicles Germany's attempts to rebuild in the years after the war. In such stories as "Der Wegwerfer" ("The Thrower-Away") and "An der Brücke"—which lampoon capitalism, the work ethic, and Germany's *Wirtschaftwunder*, or economic miracle—the government creates inane jobs for its citizens in order to curb unemployment. Through his stark depiction of the economic hardships of postwar Germany Böll implies that individuals who are accustomed to being deprived of food, drink, and shelter are unable to move beyond their physical needs and engage in meaningful relationships.

Critical Reception

Because Böll was of Catholic ancestry and his fiction advocates individual rights and a return to Christian ethics, some critics have described him as a Catholic writer. Others have compared Böll to Hemingway and Kafka, referring favorably to his vivid but economical evocations of scenes and characters and to his sometimes nightmarish sense of satire. When Böll's writing is faulted, it is for the occasional clichéd story ending, or for being overly sentimental or reductive.

PRINCIPAL WORKS

Short Fiction

Der Zug war pünktlich [*The Train Was on Time*] (novella) 1949
Wanderer, kommst du nacht Spa . . . [*Traveller, If You Come to Spa*] 1950
Nicht nur zur Weihnachtzeit [*Christmas Every Day*] 1952
Das Brot der frühen Jahre [*The Bread of Those Early Years*] (novella) 1955
So ward Abend und Morgen 1955
Unberechenbare Gäste 1956
Abenteuer eines Brotbeutels, und andere Geschichten 1957
Doktor Murkes gesammeltes Schweigen, und andere Satiren [*Dr. Murke's Collected Silences and Other Satires*] 1958
Der Bahnhof von Zimpren 1959
Der Mann mit den Messern: Erzählungen 1959
Die Waage der Baleks, und andere Erzählungen [*The Balek Scales and Other Stories*] 1959
Als der Krieg ausbrach; Als der Krieg zu Ende war: Zwei Erzählungen 1962
Die Essenholer, und andere Erzählungen 1963
1947 bis 1951 1963
Entfernung von der Truppe [*Absent without Leave*] (novella) 1964
18 Stories 1966
Ende einer Dienstfahrt [*End of a Mission*] (novella) 1966
Children Are Civilians Too 1970
Erzählungen, 1950-1970 1972
Die verlorene Ehre der Katharina Blum; oder, Wie Gewalt entstehen und wohin sie führen kann [*The Lost Honor of Katharina Blum: How Violence Develops and Where It Can Lead*] 1974
Du fährst zu oft nach Heidelberg, und andere Erzählungen 1979
Gesammelte Erzählungen. 2 vols. 1981
Der Angriff: Erzählungen, 1947-1949 1983
Die schwarzen Schafe: Erzählungen, 1950-1952 [*The Black Sheep: Stories*] 1983
*Die Verwundung, und andere frühe Erzählungen [*The*

Casualty] 1983
Veränderungen in Staech: Erzählungen, 1962-1980 1984
The Stories of Heinrich Böll 1986

Other Major Works

Und sagte kein einziges Wort [*Acquainted with the Night*] (novel) 1953
Haus ohne Hüter [*Tomorrow and Yesterday*] (novel) 1954
Irisches Tagebuch [*Irish Journal*] (travelogue) 1957
Billard um halb zehn [*Billiards at Half-past Nine*] (novel) 1959
Ein Schluck Erde (drama) 1962
Ansichten eines Clowns [*The Clown*] (novel) 1963
Gruppenbild mit Dame [*Group Portrait with Lady*] (novel) 1971
Missing Persons, and Other Essays (essays) 1977
Fürsorgliche Belagerung [*The Safety Net*] (novel) 1979
Was soll aus dem Jungen bloss werden?; oder, Irgendwas mit Büchern [*What's to Become of the Boy? or, Something to Do with Books*] (autobiography) 1981
**Der Vermächtnis [*A Soldier's Legacy*] (novel) 1982
Frauen vor Flusslandschaft: Roman in Dialogen und Selbstgesprächen (novel) 1985
Heinrich Böll als Lyriker (poetry) 1985

*The stories collected here were written between 1946 and 1952.

**This work was written in 1948.

CRITICISM

Kurt Vonnegut, Jr. (essay date 1965)

SOURCE: "The Unsaid Says Much," in *The New York Times Book Review*, September 12, 1965, pp. 4, 54.

[*Vonnegut is an American writer of darkly comic fiction which reflects his essential compassion for humanity and his complete pessimism. He rose to prominence during the 1960s with such works as* Cat's Cradle *(1963),* God Bless You, Mr. Rosewater *(1965), and* Slaughterhouse Five *(1969), which is considered his best novel to date. His novels and short stories, which frequently contain elements of science fiction, satirize human stupidity, short-sightedness, and brutality, assailing in particular humanity's tendency towards warfare and the worship of automation. In the following review, he praises the incomplete quality of the two novellas comprising* Absent without Leave.]

Disturbing, queer things these—two unconnected novellas ["**Absent without Leave**" and "**Enter and Exit**"] in one thin volume—tales told in the first person by German males who, like the author, were of military age during World War II. The reader must bring to each his own understanding of Germans and the war, for the principal materials used by Heinrich Böll are blanks and holes.

He uses the qualities of nothingness as a modern sculptor does, which sounds like a rotten idea, but he makes it work like a dream. Take the second of the tales, **"Enter and Exit."** It begins with the first day of the war, and ends with the day of the narrator's return to peace. There is not one word about what happened between those two days. Hey presto! Do what you will with the missing six years.

"Enter and Exit" is easy reading. The two days are odd but natural. The other novella [**"Absent Without Leave"**] which has the same title as the whole book, is a royal pain, a mannered, pretentious, patronizing, junky sort of *Notes From the Underground.* It seemed a sophomoric piece of work to me. I couldn't imagine the narrator, even though he did his best to tell me wry, funny, warm stories about himself in the war. He was apparently a yardbird, a foul-up, a Sckweik, a coward and a fool in the Nazi scheme of things, but he didn't amuse me much.

What burned me up especially was his explicit refusal to tell me this or that, things that would be interesting to know. "The pastor's words at her graveside were so embarrassing," he said of his mother's funeral, "that I prefer not to repeat them." He refused to say what she looked like, too. On his relationship with his wife he said, "It is neither my purpose nor within the scope of my capabilities even to try and describe, let alone explain, the power of love," and so much for that.

The suspicion might be too easily aroused that his work is anti-militarist or even pro-disarmament or anti-armament. "Oh no," he said a little farther on, "I am concerned with something much more exalted. . . . with love and innocence." I thanked heaven that he had at last told me something mildly useful, but then he booted *that* by asking, "Who can describe innocence? Not me. Who can describe the happiness and ecstasies of love? Not me." He refused to try.

So I threw the book across the room. And then I understood: The narrator was being so absurd and evasive, his story was so full of holes because there were so many things he dared not let himself remember. What were they? Who knows? Each reader has to guess. So we had another story built mainly of nothing—not a nothing sandwich like **"Enter and Exit,"** but a very airy and stale Swiss cheese.

I approve. Does anybody really need to go over the nauseatingly familiar details of World War II yet again? Why not call the era "X," or do what Böll has done, which is to leave a blank, and then go on to the more profound business, as Böll does, of what the effects of "X" or blank were on various human souls?

"I urge everyone to go absent without leave." On the basis of skimpy clues, I hazard the guess that he attempted rather ineffectually to get out of serving in the war, was severely humiliated and punished for it and finally decided that he might as well do what everybody else was doing, which was serve in the war.

He recommends desertion to the young of today, with this warning: "But watch out when they start shooting! There are some idiots who aim to hit!" In other words, the alternative to dishonor is frequently death. And, from the way the narrator fails to tell his story, the young of today can also learn that the results of service in a bad cause, voluntary or involuntary, can be holes in the memory and a half-dead soul.

Donald Heiney (essay date 1965)

SOURCE: "The Irreverent Germans," in *The Christian Science Monitor,* Vol. 57, No. 259, September 30, 1965, p. 11.

[*Heiney is an American educator, novelist, and critic. In the following favorable review, he examines stylistic aspects of Böll's* Absent without Leave.]

The new wave of young German writers, led by Günter Grass and the 47 Group, has finally arrived. Germany, which recovered physically from the war so quickly, has taken much longer to recover culturally and intellectually. It was only with Grass's novel *The Tin Drum* in 1959 that the German literary world showed some real signs of vitality. Even today German writers are still preoccupied—one can almost say obsessed—with the war, long after American writers, the British, French, even the Russians have gone on to write about something else.

But now that the new German writing has finally appeared it is vigorous, highly talented, and totally original while remaining totally German. These are the literary sons of Hermann Hesse and Thomas Mann. Like all children, they resemble their parents and yet don't resemble them; they are themselves and not mere facsimiles of their fathers.

These writers—Grass, Uwe Johnson, Heinrich Böll, and the two Swiss authors Dürrenmatt and Max Frisch, who resemble them in many ways—are all basically ironic in attitude and anti-realists in style. If there is one term to sum them up—and it seems a strange word to apply to Germans—it is irreverence for authority. They are sarcastic about the State, the family, German culture, religion, the literary forms of the past. They were fed so much hot air during the Nazi period when they were children that they can no longer take any idea—or any ideal—seriously and because they can't take anything seriously they are basically humorists, or at least satirists.

Heinrich Böll was born in 1917 and was therefore just old enough to receive the full impact of the war. He fought on both fronts, was wounded and captured, and repatriated to his shattered country only after the war was over. Everything he has written so far is about the war, or at least dominated by the traumatic memory of the war experience. He achieved his first success with a novel called *Billiards at Half-Past Nine,* and went on to write another best-seller in *The Clown.*

This latest book, **Absent Without Leave,** consists of two long rambling tales or novellas. The first, the title story, somewhat resembles the work of Frisch, especially "I'm Not Stiller." The narrator Wilhelm, a middle-aged citizen of Cologne, rambles on in a confused manner about his war experiences but by hook or crook succeeds in never telling the whole story, or at least in concealing the essential parts from us. One thing is clear: that by "absent without leave" Wilhelm means going AWOL from everything—home, society, nation—and he advises the reader to do the same. Insofar as Böll has a philosophy this is it.

But the real merit of this tale is not philosophical; it is technical or stylistic. At one point Wilhelm explains his story-telling method, which is also the literary credo of Böll himself: a story should be told like those drawing-books where pictures are indicated by dots, and the reader can fill in and color to suit his own taste. "There is no question about it: a few outlines, given a certain direction by a few skillfully scattered dots, permit of much greater freedom than the yearned for absolute freedom, for this absolute freedom is at the mercy of the imagination of the individual who, as we all know, has no ideas at all, none whatever, and in whom a blank sheet of paper can provoke just as much despair as that empty hour when the television set is out of order."

If this is not clear, it is as clear as the rest of the tale. Visible in the blur are some striking scenes of life in the German army just before the outbreak of the war, also Wilhelm's relatives and in-laws. At the end—final irreverence—there is even a set of discussion questions for students, ending with, "The narrator is concealing something. What?"

The second tale, **"Enter and Exit,"** actually consists of two brief fragments, **"When the War Broke Out,"** related by a rather bumptious adolescent German soldier, and **"When the War Was Over,"** told by the confused and traumatized cynic the young man has become. In between the war has taken place, but this is a blank. The German writer—even the anti-Nazi—can discuss the war only by distorting it profoundly, by turning it to grotesque humor, or by not discussing it at all, which is in itself a kind of a comment.

Perhaps this is the answer to the question "The narrator is concealing something. What?" Could the "what" be that the Nazis systematically slaughtered millions of people, and that all Germans, even the anti-Nazis, must bear part of the guilt? This book is worth reading not only for what it says but for what it doesn't say.

Dieter Baacke   (essay date 1965-1966)

SOURCE: "The Short Stories of Heinrich Böll," in *Studies in Short Fiction,* Vol. 3, No. 1, Fall, 1965-66, pp. 89-103.

[*In the following essay, Baacke provides a thematic analysis of Böll's short fiction.*]

The principal theme of Böll's short stories up until approximately 1951 is the war. Only very rarely, however, does he show actual fighting; his stories take place in areas where the battle has not yet begun or has just ended: at the station where soldiers board a train for the front; in the dugout or infirmary where the wounded prepare to die. That the narrator is himself involved is shown most clearly by his usually appearing as "Ich." He not only portrays the horror but takes part in it himself. In the story **"Wiedersehen mit Drüng,"** he awakens critically wounded "in einer niedrigen Bauernstube, deren Decke wie der Deckel eines Grabes aus grünem Dämmer sich auf mich herabzusenken schien." Eventually he discovers someone next to him, lying motionless on a stretcher. He determines with amazement that it is his former classmate Drüng, a quiet, rather homely person whom he has not seen for years. A meager candle situated between them burns its remaining wax. After the operation, when the narrator is again lying in the room of the farmhouse, Drüng, upon whom the notation "Exitus" was long since to be found, speaks comfortingly to the other. The scene becomes unreal because here we find a dead man speaking to one who is dying. By this time the candle had long since burned out, but when Drüng "die zuckende Hand hochnahm, schwamm immer noch der Docht, war immer noch Licht da, und ich blickte durch das Loch in Drüngs Bauch auf einen hellen gelben Flecken an der Wand hinter ihm." There is still light, and the two dead men follow the apparition of the nurse Dina, "die durch die verschlossene Tür zu uns getreten war, und wir wussten, dass wir nun lächeln durften. . . ." Similarly an "Ich" relates his own death in **"Die Essenholer"** or **"Wiedersehen in der Allee."** A striking feature is that death is never something terrible. Torture and pain are only briefly depicted. The climax of the story lies in an intermediate zone beyond reality, that of death itself. The mess attendants, who already carry a dead man with them, are torn apart by a grenade. The narrator awakens after the first state of stupor, but it is no longer this life into which he steps.

> Ich ging muting nach vorne in den Trichter hinein, aber ich fiel nicht und sank nicht; weiter, weiter ging ich, immer wieder auf wunderbar sanftem Boden unter dem vollendeten Dunkel des Gewölbes . . . bis der grosse, gelbe, glänzende Stern vor mir aufstieg und sich am Gewölbe des Himmels festpflanzte. . . . Da wusste ich, dass ich an einem anderen Ziele war. . . .

Only now does the reader, confused by the mysterious, suggestive language, understand. He feels that the "andere Ziel" is no longer the food-provision station but God himself, with whom the dead once again find themselves. The severity of war is mitigated through such endings; indeed, it is no longer taken completely seriously because the horror is not the final stage. It is here that Böll the Catholic speaks, attempting to reestablish death (on earth without meaning) as something meaningful. After all suffering, man receives a kind of new paradise, peace in the presence of God.

Such mystical consonances contradict Böll's own conception of the short story, the language of which is supposed to be "kühl und klar." In his better works such consonances are not to be found. The portrayal of an airplane crash in **"Wir Besenbinder"** ends considerably less edifyingly. "Ich sah nichts mehr ausser Licht und Feuer, den verstümmelten Schwanz der Maschine, einen Zerfressenen Schwanz wie ein schwarzer Stummelbesen, auf dem eine Hexe zu ihrem Sabbat reiten mochte. . . ." Here reality is not abandoned until the very end, and through the comparison of the fuselage of the airplane with a witch who looks towards her Sabbath, Böll shows with cruel irony the absurdity and ugliness of the destruction. However, the stories closing with no explanation or evaluation of any kind have met with the most success. In **"Lohengrins Tod"** a boy, while stealing coal at the end of the war, is caught in a train and seriously injured. He lies dying in the room of a large hospital. The doctors are busy and the nun cannot help the boy, who is writhing with fever delirium. When the doctors enter the room "lachend," the narrator verifies—and it is his last sentence—"Lohengrin war tot." This sobriety without commentary, intensified through the contrast between the laughing men and the dead boy, finds its effectiveness in its brevity and needs no supplement.

Two further important motifs occurring in the body of war themes are those of loneliness and strangeness. Pandemic violence throws man out of his established order in which he found protection. Those who love him are far away; moreover, the world in which he finds himself alone remains without consolation. So it is in the story **"Die Botschaft."** The narrator travels to one of those "Drecknester, wo man sich vergebens fragt, warum die Eisenbahn dort eine Station errichtet hat." His task is to report to a young woman the death of her husband. This woman, however, is with another man, whom she now pushes away from her. But she knew that her husband had been killed and is therefore innocent, in spite of her unfaithfulness. The scene takes place in an "engen Stube, die mit ärmlichen Möbeln vollgepfropft war und worin der Geruch von schlechtem Essen und sehr guten Zigaretten sich festgesetzt hatte." The narrator is glad when he has completed his assignment. "Unheimlich vorsichtig," he feels his way through the darkness back to the station. He waits in the drafty, tiny lobby, until the "Mann mit der roten Mütze" reports that the train is late. Now the narrator is definitely and inescapably submitted to isolation and despair. The setting of this narrative is ugly and petty; Böll banishes anything of beauty from it. There is no escape, and thus is the tone of the narrative melancholy from beginning to end. The story **"In der Finsternis"** reduces the dimensions of fear of the apocalypse (already alluded to in the title) to the dimensions of a dugout. A younger and an older soldier lie next to one another. It is raining outside; furthermore, it is dark. "Mach jetzt die Kerze an," says the older to the younger, who is trying to fall asleep and cannot. "Sein ganzes Kindergesicht war beschmiert, fast überall an den Rändern der verfilzten Haare klebten Brotkrümel." The vision of destruction disappears in the banality and repulsiveness of this trench community, before which death and loneliness—outside a corpse robber is shot—already stand. At the end,

the loneliness is complete. The boy must rise to stand at his post; the older soldier is alone as is the other, whom he had to send away. ". . . und er blies die Kerze aus und lag in völligem Dunkel ganz allein in der Erde. . . ."

The postwar situation brings new themes. The soldiers have returned home to the destroyed cities, in which men are searching for a new order. It is necessary in this world to come to terms with one another. For the first time, clearly satirical elements appear in Böll's short stories, for example in **"Mein Onkel Fred."** He "kam an einem Sommernachmittag aus dem Kriege heim, schmucklos gekleidet, als einzigen Besitz eine Blechbüchse an einer Schnur um den Hals tragend sowie beschwert durch das unerhebliche Gewicht einiger Kippen. . . ." This uncle terrifies the not yet fully grown child with his enormous appetite that causes apprehension that there will be nothing left for the others. He lies for weeks inactive on the sofa, an embodiment of laziness. Then suddenly he becomes active and provides himself with some zinc buckets in order to start a florist business. Contrary to the expectations of his relatives, he is successful. Again and again new subsidiaries are opened; Uncle Fred is a "gemachter Mann" and the narrator likewise, because he is named heir and is to study economics "um die steuerliche Betreuung des Unternehmens schon vor Antritt der Erbschaft übernehmen zu können." The affected business style of the passage quoted betrays the parodistic element of this story whose narrator, provided with a "Bildung, die längst komplett ist," presents himself as the typical "Wohlstandsbürger." Similar is the story **"Geschäft ist Geschäft,"** which opens with the sentence "Mein Schwarzhändler ist jetzt ehrlich geworden," whereby this honesty proves itself more remorseless than the externally unlawful business of the black-marketeer. The stress on social criticism is not to be overlooked and makes itself more and more felt, for example, in "Mein teures Bein."

Böll removes himself considerably from that which, to the German Republic, is reality. He is on the side of the outsider, who is neither able nor desires to adapt himself to the existing conditions. The theme found in many of his stories is the unusual profession which does not conform to the ordinary, and, therefore, calls for disapproval. The story **"An der Brücke"** begins, "Die haben mir meine Beine geflickt und haben mir einen Posten gegeben, wo ich sitzen kann: ich zähle die Leute, die über die Brücke gehen." The outsider is left with a war injury which renders him unsuitable for a normal civil occupation. But the modern welfare state takes care of everyone. The narrator has a post "wo ich sitzen kann." Böll gives no character a name. The critical attitude towards the representatives of a seemingly well ordered world is clearly indicated by the introductory "Die." The narrator smiles at them: "Es macht ihnen ja Spass, sich ihre Tüchtigkeit mit Zahlen zu belegen, sie berauschen sich an diesem sinnlosen Nichts aus ein paar Ziffern, und den ganzen Tag . . . geht mein stummer Mund wie ein Uhrwerk, indem ich Nummer auf Nummer häufe, um ihnen abends den Triumph einer Zahl zu schenken." Thus it is the outsider who is the actual giver. "Die" are dependent upon him. Moreover he does not even bother to be accurate. The narrator does not include in his count his little girl friend, who crosses the bridge twice daily. She is too good for statistics because human relations are independent of, indeed free from "denen da."

The story that brought Böll in 1951 the award of the *Gruppe 47* states the theme of the outsider already in the title: **"Die schwarzen Schafe."** These are family members who almost ruin the reputation of their relatives because they cannot decide upon a profession; they are charming people who merely have the unpleasant fault of borrowing money from their relatives. Nevertheless they have the sympathy of the narrator, who considers himself "ein schwarzes Schaf." Children love them and Lady Luck, as well, because it is the very black sheep himself who wins first prize and bequeaths a considerable sum—naturally, after having paid all pending debts—to the next black sheep of the family.

"Wenn ich nach meinem Beruf gefragt werde, befällt mich Verlegenheit," reports a man who has become a "Lacher." "Das Lachen Amerikas ruht in meiner Brust, das Lachen Afrikas, weisses, rotes, gelbes Lachen—und gegen ein entsprechendes Honorar lasse ich es erklingen, so wie die Regie es vorschreibt." Another story deals with the "Bekenntnisse eines Hundefängers," a kind-hearted man, exact and reliable in his task, which is to track down all dogs which have not been reported for the purpose of taxation. Only his own dog, a mongrel, does he conceal from the tax office—just as the narrator on the bridge does not count his girl friend. Then again someone surprises his acquaintances (who believe him, the learned doctor, to be appointed to a higher profession) with his occupation, which is merely to announce through the loudspeaker at the train station, "Hier ist Tibten," a job which, moreover, completely satisfies him. He does not comprehend "dass man diese Arbeit meiner für unwürdig hält." However, he directs the travelers to the object of greatest interest in the city, the grave of Tiburtius, a Roman youth who out of lover's grief threw himself one day into the lead mine in Tibten. On his grave are to be admired "Figürchen aus elfenbeinfarbenem Stoff; zwei Elefanten, ein Pferd und eine Dogge." Of course the announcer had long ago replaced these much admired originals with some figures that a margarine firm distributes with its product. It is not the greed of possession which has prompted him to this; he himself no longer can recognize the genuine animals among his huge collection of margarine figures. Here again a profession is pursued with "Demut und Sorgfalt" and obviously still not taken completely seriously.

In all of these short stories, the theme of the buffoon appears again, the clever Till Eulenspiegel modernized. Through their behavior, all outsiders protest an administrated world where everything moves "wie am Schnürchen," and there is no room for that which is genuinely human. From this point there is only a short distance to satire, the form with which Böll is probably at his best. His satires lack the pathos which had a painful effect in the earlier stories; the aggression of society does not occur as an indictment but as a caricature. **"Im Lande der Rujuks"** concerns a supposedly very fruitful special research that is long since of no importance. In **"Der Bahnhof von Zimpren"** the passion for prosperity in economics and in the civil service is made to appear ridiculous and questionable. Here we reach the border of our consideration, as satire is no longer a theme but a literary form in itself. It is a variation of the short story, being even older than this form.

The late Nobelist Heinrich Böll is as popular in Russia as he is in the West, and small wonder: not since Remarque has anyone written about war quite so convincingly. Böll's war is that of the infantryman, not the armchair general and not the Hollywood director.

—*A review of* The Casualty, *in the* Virginia Quarterly Review, *Autumn, 1987*.

G. Ralph Smith, II (essay date 1966-1967)

SOURCE: A review of *18 Stories,* in *Studies in Short Fiction,* Vol. 4, No. 1, Fall, 1966-67, pp. 355-57.

[*In the following essay, Smith explores the childlike aspects of Böll's short fiction.*]

Most of [*18 Stories*] show conflicting interpretations of the world. One set of characters, usually children or childlike adults, is concerned with natural forces and events, no matter how old. The opposing characters are wiser in the ways of the world. They are more concerned with the devious procedures and protective screens used by civilized people to protect themselves from life than with life itself. For example, in **"Like a Bad Dream,"** the narrator (who has "married into the excavating business") is introduced by his wife to a simple method of bribery. Although he catches on only slowly ("perhaps I failed to grasp what was happening at the time"), he learns quickly enough that by the end of the story he can increase his profit on his own. In spite of his success, he seems a bit dismayed at the turn his life has taken. At the end of the story his wife avoids him for a time, and he reflects: "I knew what she was thinking; she was thinking: he was to get over it, and I have to leave him alone; this is something he has to understand." He concludes, however, by saying, "But I never did understand. It is beyond understanding."

In both **"The Balek Scales"** and **"The Thrower-Away,"** the central character not only sees through an accepted but wasteful or dishonest procedure of his society, but he also helps others to do the same thing. In **"The Balek Scales,"** a child discovered and revealed that the scales of the Balek family, the landowners, on which the herbs and mushrooms of the peasant children were weighed before sale to the Baleks, were dishonest. Böll perhaps strains too hard for a universal symbolism here. The situation is made to resemble that of divine law: "One of the laws imposed by the Baleks on the village was: no one was permitted to have any scales in the house. The law was so ancient that nobody gave a thought as to when and how it had arisen, and it had to be obeyed, for anyone who broke it was dismissed."

"The Thrower-Away" is as farfetched but logical as some of Poe's lesser-known stories. A man who strives to seem like everyone else (he says that he looks like "a citizen who has managed to avoid introspection") is hired to destroy junk mail. Both he and the child in **"The Balek Scales"** see through an aspect of their culture that everyone else has accepted without question, and they try to protect others from the crime or nuisance of that aspect.

Another conflict between appearance and reality appears in **"This is Tibten!"** Eighteen hundred years ago Tiburtius, a Roman youth, killed himself for love of a local girl. Buried with him were some small carved animals. These animals and the boy's tomb are the major tourist attractions of the town of Tibten, where the narrator of the story is a train announcer. He reveals that he has secretly stolen the ancient carved animals and substituted for them some identical toys from margarine boxes. He then takes the real artifacts home and mixes them with more of the margarine-box toys so that not even he can distinguish the one from the other. In effect, the suicide of Tiburtius had some meaning, but that which tries to perpetuate the meaning does not. As in most of these stories, we find that we must go beyond the accepted and respected to find any real meaning.

Probably the best story in the collection is the longest, **"In the Valley of the Thundering Hooves."** It treats different responses to guilt, or, more specifically, to the guilt feelings associated with the sexual awakening of a young boy and girl. The girl, Katherine, is growing into her teens and out of her sweaters, thereby evoking the lascivious attention of several older men, most boys, and especially of Paul, the fourteen-year-old central character of the story. The responses are essentially different for the adults and the young people. When Katherine unbuttons her blouse in front of Paul, his mother becomes angry and forbids their being together again. Katherine's mother's response is to send the girl away for a time to live with her father with the advice, "Never do what they think you've been doing." The adults are motivated by the desire to prevent a recurrence of what they consider a sinful episode, preferably by avoiding its possibility. The problem of the young people is that they are involved and therefore must face more intimately the problem..Katherine vows that she will eventually return, implying that the adult attempt to deny some aspect of the human situation will fail.

The case of Paul is more complex. Early in the story he says that he would rather die than sin. He apparently believes that he *has* sinned, but he flees from church before going to confession. Believing that Paul would

prefer death to unrelieved guilt, the reader expects the first (of many) references to pistols to foreshadow the boy's suicide. Böll, however, turns to a use of the pistol, and such objects as jam-pots and tennis balls, which a reading of Freud or his followers probably suggested. The extent to which he over-uses the phallic and other symbols and the occasional artificiality with which he uses them tend to mar an otherwise sensitive story by distracting the reader from what is probably the major theme. The young people are moved by natural and powerful force and are disturbed by it, but the adults are involved in artificial, mundane affairs. Paul's father hides his pistol, the phallic symbol, under "checkbooks and ledger sheets"; Katherine's mother is seen by the daughter as a "monument"; and, at the end of the story, when Paul has fired the pistol at a beer sign and been seized by a policeman who knows him and where he lives, the policeman nevertheless *asks* the boy where he lives, probably because he thinks the by-standers expect this of him. (Incidentally, there is a minor flaw in the translation from the German here. In answer to the policeman's question Paul says, "My God, you know very well where I live." The translation reads "Hell . . . you know where I live." Reading only the translation, one is not sure whether "Hell" is merely an expletive or whether Böll makes Paul reveal his feelings about the kind of life he has led in the past.)

The world of the adults, as well as being routine and artificial, is also devoted to destruction, the denial of life forces. This is evident, not only in Paul's mother's anger and the exile of Katherine, but also in a thrice-seen newspaper headline the visible part of which reads "Khrush-chev" and then "open grave." The reference may be to Khrushchev's "We will bury you" speech. At any rate there is at the international level the same kind of threat of uncomprehending and insensitive negation that exists at the family level for Böll's young people.

The major flaw in these stories is a sense of strain. Böll has tried too hard for a meaning or an effect. As a result, the reader feels either that the author has done too much for him, as in **"In the Valley of the Thundering Hooves"** and **"The Balek Scales,"** both of which are replete with various kinds of symbols, or that he has tried too hard to let events speak for themselves and thereby omitted something meaningful, as in **"Unexpected Guests."** In this story we find a household consisting quite casually of dogs, cats, baby chicks, rabbits, Gottlieb, "the baby hippopotamus we keep in our bathtub," Wally the elephant and Bombilus the lion. We can see some of the childlikeness found in others of Böll's stories in the human and animal characters of this story, but the fact that the story simply presents a situation, (and such a situation) with no real development, leaves the reader feeling mocked or cheated.

J. P. Bauke   (essay date 1966)

SOURCE: "Watcher on the Rhine," in *The New York Times Book Review*, October 16, 1966, pp. 4-5.

[*In the following review, Bauke lauds* 18 Stories, *maintaining that "it is a measure of Böll's insight and wisdom that his stories, despite their intensely local color, have universal application."*]

Heinrich Böll is one of the most significant writers in contemporary Germany. Though he has never been so extravagantly praised as Günter Grass or Jakov Lind, his reputation has grown steadily over the years. In the late forties, when his countrymen turned to rebuilding their towns and their industry and started to forget the Nazi interlude, Böll established himself as the spokesman of those who remembered. His early novels, full of passionate pacifism, captured the mood of a generation that wanted peace at any price and won for their author audiences in more than a dozen languages. A decade later, Böll castigated the materialism and the spiritual vacuity of the new Germany in *Billiards at Half-past Nine,* and, more recently, took a brilliant swipe at the German upper classes in *The Clown.*

Now approaching 50, Böll is generally acknowledged as the moralist among his country's novelists, the man who looks for authentic humanity in a society thriving on ersatz. He is a kind of one-man Der Spiegel, grimly determined to expose what's foul on the banks of the Rhine. While a number of German critics are increasingly irritated by Böll's insistence on focusing on the darker side of the economic miracle, reviewers in this country usually find their suspicions about the Germans confirmed with every new book from his pen. Mistaking Böll's satiric distortions and ironic exaggerations for realistic description, they regard Böll as a voice of reason and humanity in a morass of Teutonic perversion. They sometimes overlook that Böll is primarily an artist.

This new collection of stories, [*18 Stories*] written over 15 years, is Böll's eighth book to appear in translation. There are no new or unexpected themes here, but Böll's admirers will not be disappointed. The stories encompass the whole range of the author's concerns, from the memories of war (**"The Post Card," "A Case for Kop"**), to loving portraits of German Holden Caulfields (Böll translated Salinger into German) and savage invective against the flourishing *Kultur* business of Germany.

The English version, by Leila Vennewitz, an experienced hand at translating Böll, flows naturally and is almost flawless. One could wish, however, that the publishers had given the dates of the original publication of the stories. **"Bonn Diary,"** kept by a general of Prussian persuasion, reads like an oblique commentary on recent headlines about Bonn's military establishment. Apparently Böll has a touch of the prophet.

At his best, Böll creates satiric close-ups of unsurpassed power. In my favorite, **"Murke's Collected Silences,"** Böll evokes the venal atmosphere of the broadcasting stations whose influence and power are far greater in Germany than in this country. A typical radio star is Bur-Malottke, "who had converted to Catholicism during the religious fervor of 1945, had suddenly . . . felt he might be blamed for contributing to the religious overtones" in broadcasting, and now decides to omit mention of God "who occurred frequently in both his half-hour talks on The Nature of Art and [replace] him with a formula more in keeping with the mental outlook which he had professed before 1945." The *trahison des clercs* may be a familiar theme, but the opportunism of German intellectuals has never been pilloried as ruthlessly as in the 30 pages of this Swiftian exercise.

"Action Will Be Taken" is a take-off on the vaunted economic miracle that, in Böll's telling, is worked by people who only by a strong effort of will keep "from singing away all day long." No one cares what Wunsiedel's factory produces as long as it runs full speed. The laziest employee survives the frantic pace and is designated to carry a wreath of artificial flowers behind his boss's coffin. In the end he joins a funeral home to become a professional mourner. His counterpart is the professional laugher, who laughs "mournfully, moderately, hysterically . . . like a streetcar conductor or a helper in the grocery business," exactly as requested. His own laughter has never been heard.

The mourner and the laugher are cut of the same cloth as the protagonist of **"This Is Tibet!,"** a cicerone with credits from five universities and two doctorates. Decent people, Böll leaves no doubt, are clowns or court jesters in a world run by the wicked and the rich. As in all of Böll's work, in these stories goodness is where the heart is: left of center. Sometimes Böll's art is made to serve the ends of this naive belief, as in **"The Balek Scales,"** a preachy tale of a wicked landlord who cheats his tenant farmers.

But Böll is not Brecht; his assault is directed against the indolence of the heart, not the social order. Hence the slightly smug attitude of his non-heroes who feel good because they are good. It is better to throw away the mail, as **"The Thrower-away"** actually does, than to participate in a communications racket where the "envelopes are worth more than the contents."

These 18 stories are not those of an innovator. Unlike his younger colleagues, Böll makes no attempt to exploit the form for experiments and new perspectives. More in the tradition of Hemingway than Thomas Mann, he casts a poetic glow over the commonplace and lovingly characterizes the dropouts of the Volkswagen and Mercedes society. It is a measure of Böll's insight and wisdom that his stories, despite their intensely local color, have universal application. The present collection proves once again that Böll is a master storyteller.

The Times Literary Supplement (essay date 1966)

SOURCE: "Jeep Thrills," in *The Times Literary Supplement,* No. 1028, November 10, 1966, p. 1028.

[*In the following review, the critic commends the diverse range of characters in Böll's novella* Ende einer Dienstfahrt.]

On the eve of his demob (and return to the family furniture-making business) a private in the Bundeswehr is sent on an extended jeep ride. The ostensibly absurd, but administratively tenable, object of this exercise is the "clocking up" of a certain mileage in time for the next vehicle inspection. Rather than wear out long stretches of Autobahn the driver heads straight for home, parks the jeep without switching off the engine, and a few sawdust-shrouded days later the milometer indicates the desired figure (minus the distance back to camp). But the return journey is never completed; in full public view father and son pour petrol over the jeep and set it alight, compounding temporal dereliction with a spiritual affront by intoning the Litany as accompaniment to their auto-da-fe.

Exuding beatific nonchalance they are arraigned before a court benightedly unfamiliar not merely with the orthography of the word "happening" but with its very meaning. The ensuing trial is as startlingly mock-serious as the offence. Herr Böll manages to depict the various incidents in and around the court-room as somehow highly plausible and quite inconceivable at one and the same time, and the reader grows so inured to this bifocal vision that the arsonists' *acte gratuit* soon assumes attributes of inevitability. After all, how are a village Chippendale up to his ears in debt to the Inland Revenue and his equally gifted son, disoriented beyond measure by the ennui of army life, to abreact their despair at the absurdity of the cosmos other than via the art-form explicitly created to render the absurd meaningful—namely a "happening"?

This is the central idea that Herr Böll allows to proliferate with a free-wheeling insouciance that occasionally teeters on the edge of whimsy, but never plunges irretrievably downwards. He uses the happening theme as a slow circuitous fuse that flares up by fits and start to illuminate the same landscape—the small Rhineland town in which the trial takes place—from every angle. In this way the legal proceedings serving as narrative simultaneously compose the identikit picture of a whole community; a community ingrown and musty yet wreathed in an aura of bonhomie that reveals the author (for all his ironic distancing devices) as susceptible to the idyllic fallacy.

One would have expected the narrow compass of an *Erzählung* to preclude such a panoramic approach, but Herr Böll manages to deploy a luxuriant range of characters and their interrelationships without straining his chosen format. An annotated cast-list seems indicated at first but on closer inspection even the figures in the middle distance emerge as so variously delineated that any reader ought to be able to cope.

What splendid collector's items they all are: the octagenarian priest exhaling a rich blend of ecumenism and pipe-tobacco, the long-service corporal who values the interminable boredom of barrack-room routine as a source of increased sexual potency, the blue-stockinged with-it Catholic barrister's wife nicknamed "Pillen-Else" on account of her Malthus syndrome, the guild-master whose pride in a fellow carpenter's (Ulbricht's!) career earns the court's severe reprimand, the Amtsgerichtrat too preoccupied with

what size tip would both reflect his status and look reasonable on an expense-form to enjoy his restaurant meal, &c., &c.

And yet in the last resort it remains problematical whether **Ende einer Dienstfahrt** can be accounted a wholly successful essay in marrying serenity to dialectic, and miniaturization to *la condition humaine*. The tone is just that much too tranquil, the *oratio* just that degree too *obliqua*, the total ambiance just that shade too idyllic. Even so there can be little doubt that it constitutes a noteworthy extension of its author's range. What is more, the tired cliché about *Galgenhumor* being the only form of humour natural to Germans cannot long survive Herr Böll's vertical take-off into fantastication and wit.

Edward M. Potoker (essay date 1966)

SOURCE: "At the Fringes of the Miracle," in *The Saturday Review,* New York, Vol. XLIX, No. 50, December 10, 1966, pp. 50, 55.

[*Potoker is an American educator and critic. In the following favorable review, he examines themes common in Böll's short fiction.*]

Heinrich Böll, whose prose is remarkable for its vitality, lucidity, and color, now enjoys a reputation, well and scrupulously earned, as one of contemporary Europe's most influential writers. Achieving international recognition in the immediate postwar years, Böll was hailed as the analyst—indeed, the laughing vivisectionist—of the German generation that promoted and somehow accommodated Hitler. With an integrity that must have been painful to sustain, he scrutinized Germany's so-called "undigested past," in the process rendering it clear but by no means more digestible. In his probe of the modern German condition he uncovered the quirks that lay, like noxious organisms, beneath Germany's values and social institutions, and uncovered as well the dangerous illusions which Germans cherished about these quirks.

Böll has always been a moralist in the sense that Kafka and Camus were, but his artistry, like theirs, generally triumphs over the occasional excesses of his moral passion. His novels, especially *Billiards at Half-past Nine* and *The Clown,* received high critical acclaim in this country, and his readership has been growing steadily since 1962. However, since Böll began his career with short stories and continues to write them, it is gratifying to have finally available a representative collection of his work in that form.

18 Stories, written over a period of nearly two decades, shows the imaginative range, power, and wit that we expect of Böll. More important, these pieces, in a shrewd and skillful translation by Leila Vennewitz, allow us to perceive easily that Böll is a master of short prose, even if all the stories included are not masterpieces. For the most part, Böll's techniques are conventional: his narratives tend to be straightforward and realistic. Because he can write stories that are cogent, dramatic, and immediate, he seems to eschew experimental methods.

There are, unfortunately, no convenient rubrics in this collection, dates are not provided, and the order of presentation is haphazard. Nevertheless, from the satirical masterpieces scattered throughout the book a central theme emerges, one that deals with the indignities and absurdities of making a living in postwar Germany. Böll's protagonists, naïve or clownish or both, hover at the fringes of the German economic miracle, sufficiently alienated from the efficient burghers whom they mock. These protagonists frequently stem from the lower middle class, to which Böll is somewhat romantically attached, but they are not, in the inelegant speech of sociologists, "upward mobile." On the contrary, they are weirdly static. Their grotesque confrontations with higher middle-class values and occupations provide the cutting edges of these stories and much marvelous buffoonery.

"Action Will Be Taken," subtitled "An Action-Packed Story," has as its anti-hero a nameless narrator who gets a job in a factory renowned for efficiency and furious activity. His frantic boss constantly goes about shouting, "Let's have some action!" The required reply from all employees is, "Action will be taken!" One day the narrator hesitates in answering the boss's unchanging invocation, thereby shocking him to death. At the funeral he receives an offer from a firm of undertakers to join their staff as a professional mourner. Easily persuaded that he is a "born mourner," he happily pursues his true vocation, in which pensiveness is essential and inactivity his duty.

> This volume, *18 Stories,* which contains only a few examples of Böll's sporadic gaucherie, is about as distinguished and satisfying as any collection of short stories can be.
>
> —*Edward M. Potoker*

"The Thrower-Away" is about a complex stooge whose activity is devoted entirely to destruction: he throws away. Employed by a large insurance company, he uses an elaborate system for sorting first-class mail from the oppressive junk that threatens to inundate every business enterprise. Travel folders, brochures from political parties and religious sects, notifications from charities and lotteries he gleefully throws away. Suspected of nihilism, he knows that his punch-card file in the City Hall contains the symbols for "mental case" and "anti-social." These symbols are the price he must pay for his chosen activities.

The tactics in both pieces, of course, are those of Kafka, who, like Böll, was a master cultural pathologist. However, Böll's work is never as depressing as Kafka's. There is a dash of Fielding in him that always mitigates the

effects of his paranoia, a gusto and vigor that enable him to envision, eccentrically but firmly, human order as well as ordure.

Although many of these stories have political overtones, most are not overtly political. The chief exception is "**Bonn Diary,**" which does in twelve pages what Kirst did in *The Night of the Generals.* The German military caste and its post-war re-emergence are mordantly satirized. General Erich von Machorka-Muff, a forthright soldier and to his old superiors an "idealist," sees his pet project become a reality: the Bonn Government, with special prodding from the Ministry of Defense, has decided to erect an "Academy for Military Memoirs, where every veteran from the rank of major up is to be given the opportunity of committing his reminiscences to paper." The General delivers the Academy's first lecture, fittingly entitled "Reminiscence as a Historical Duty." He is especially pleased that his dream came to pass in a democracy. "A democracy in which we have the majority of Parliament on our side," confides a high-ranking bureaucrat from the Defense Ministry, "is a great deal better than a dictatorship."

Inevitably, such a large collection has its duds. When Böll writes about the sexual problems of adolescents ("**In the Valley of the Thundering Hooves**") or the religious anxieties of adulterers ("**The Adventure**") he is sentimental and unconvincing. Nevertheless, this volume, which contains only a few examples of Böll's sporadic gaucherie, is about as distinguished and satisfying as any collection of short stories can be.

William J. Schwarz (essay date 1970)

SOURCE: A review of *Children Are Civilians Too,* in *The Saturday Review,* New York, Vol. LIII, No. 13, March 28, 1970, pp. 38-40.

[*In the following essay, Schwarz asserts that most of Böll's early stories depict the dreariness of war.*]

Heinrich Böll has written short stories, *Novellen,* novels, radio plays and drama, but his true talent lies in telling stories. His first "novel," *Adam, Where Art Thou,* is really a series of terse short stories, held together by a theme—the little man in war—rather than by central characters. In Böll's radio plays several stories are usually told by a commentator to amplify the dialogue. His *Irish Journal* likewise consists of a sequence of stories about life in Ireland.

Much less convicting than these early works are Böll's ambitious novels, *Acquainted with the Night, Billiards at Half-Past Nine,* and *The Clown.* Here Böll revels in contrived symbolism and in monotonous attacks on German nationalism and chauvinism. These are the works, of course, for which he won the widest acclaim behind the Iron Curtain, where he is celebrated as the foremost West German representative of the so-called Critical Realism; by 1962 more than 800,000 copies of his books had been sold in Communist countries. Unfortunately, the literary appeal of his writing is all too often diminished by the uncompromising hatred of the capitalist society in the Federal Republic that Heinrich Böll reiterates in his novels. The author here plays the fatal role of the *Praeceptor Germaniae,* the moralist and prophet of his nation, the Nestor of our century. Böll's last two major publications, ***Absent Without Leave*** and ***End of a Mission*** are tendentious in an obtrusive manner, leaving little to the imagination in their overzealous criticism of West German militarism.

None of this is detectable in ***Children Are Civilians Too***. Here speaks a true teller of tales, Böll at his best. These short sketches appeared between 1947 and 1951, when the author was trying to come to terms with the experiences of the Second World War. Böll is a devout Catholic—not an orthodox adherent of the official church doctrine, but an unwavering disciple of Christ. The six long years he was forced to fight in Hitler's war were against his inner convictions, certainly, yet he never openly took issue with Nazi despotism and crime. This contradiction, a prevalent one among the rank-and-file soldiers of the former German *Wehrmacht,* is reflected in most of Böll's early stories.

Twenty-six of them have been selected and well translated by Leila Vennewitz; together they present a valid testimony of the situation of those who do not really act in wartime, but are acted upon. Two of the stories do not actually belong to the collection. One of them, **"My Sad Face,"** is a somewhat lame farce about modern totalitarianism, written in the parable form of the Kafka tradition. The second, **"Black Sheep,"** is a humorous exploration of the artist's existence. For **"Black Sheep,"** incidentally, Böll received, in 1951, the Gruppe 47 prize, which established his reputation as a writer in Germany and abroad. All twenty-six stories, originally conceived in the laconic, careless speech of the ordinary German, are impressive for their precise settings, firm structure, and forceful, pregnant dialogue.

In his presentation of war Heinreich Böll never depicts the real fighting; he never confronts the reader with gruesome pictures of human suffering as did Theodor Plievier and others. It goes without saying that any glorification of war in the fashion of Ernst Jünger is excluded from his writings. Böll prefers to show the monotony of war, the waste of time and effort—he talks of dirt and lice and boredom and of the little yet utterly frustrating privations. He describes the war from the perspective of the plain soldier who worries about finding a slice of bread or a cigarette. Böll places his anti-heroic heroes into sick bays, crowded trains, drafty railway stations, and destroyed cities. His characters are rootless, homeless figures that fight a day-to-day battle for survival. They are preoccupied with their petty problems to such a degree that they find no time to reflect on the larger issues of the war.

Böll's stories give a gray, grim picture of wartime and postwar Germany, but few of them are completely without light and hope. **"My Pal with the Long Hair"** ends with the significant phrase: "We have been together ever since—in these hard times." In the title story, **"Children Are Civilians Too,"** Böll writes: "The snow fell on her fine blonde hair, powdering her with fleeting silver dust; her smile was utterly bewitching." A glance, a smile that two people exchange breaks the isolation and solitude in a strange, hostile world. It is in the encounter of two human beings that the miseries of war and after-war are overcome. And if there is no soul to communicate with, man still is not left in the cold because there is always God. In **"Candles for the Madonna"** a man reflects after a visit to the church: ". . . my heart was lighter than it had been for a long time." Böll's figures are weak—every one a sinner in his own way—but they are, at the same time, believers who know where they can find an answer to their anguish.

Donald Heiney (essay date 1970)

SOURCE: "Böll—'A Miniature Dante'," in *The Christian Science Monitor,* Vol. 62, No. 125, April 23, 1970, p. 12.

[*Heiney is an American educator, novelist, and critic. In the following review, he provides a positive assessment of* Children Are Civilians Too.]

It may very well be that "national voices" in literature, as they used to be known, are disappearing. In the time of Dostoevski and Tolstoi people talked about the "Russian Soul." The German tone of Hesse and Mann, the Scandinavian mood of Hamsun and Selma Lagerlöf, the Frenchness of Paul Bourget, are unmistakably linked with their national origins. There was an "American voice" in fiction that began with Twain and Melville, and was still recognizable in the writers of the '20s and '30s.

But this is no longer so, or not to the degree that it used to be. It is a common-place to say that technology is making us all alike, making the world into a single nation, and it is evident that this law applies in literature too. These stories [***Children Are Civilians Too***] of Heinrich Böll, concerned with the war and the confusion of the postwar period, could easily be by any American writer of the parallel generation, an Irwin Shaw or a Norman Mailer.

The immediate reaction of the American reader is to imagine he has detected an influence. But this is too easy. We are dealing with an "international style" that was really no more caused by Hemingway than freeways were caused by the invention of cement. As with freeways, you can like it or dislike it, but there is nothing much you can do about it. It is what is happening in the world these days.

Böll writes very well. And, having suffered the war a great deal more deeply than the average Shaw or Mailer, he writes about it a little more profoundly. The best of the war tales, in this book of 26 stories, is probably the first, **"Across the Bridge"**—a simple anecdote turning around a fragmentary memory of the war, an image seen through a train window, "a spindly little girl of about nine or ten holding a large, clean doll and frowning up at the train." The precision and vividness of this phrase are so powerful, and yet it is so simple, that you wonder how it is done. It is done with very great skill, and a lot of hard work; it is not as easy as it looks.

This story manages to be plotless and yet have a surprise ending. A unique achievement in the history of fiction.

The war stories tend to be gloomy and horrifying; the ones set in the period after the war tend to the grotesque. Many of them are about economic difficulties: **"The Man With the Knives,"** for instance, in which the narrator is delighted and yet terrified to get a circus job as a knife-thrower's assistant—". . . all I needed to do was stand still and dream a little. For twelve or twenty seconds"—while the knives thud into the wall around him. Or **"My Sad Face,"** in which the hero is arrested first for looking happy and then, after a change of government, for looking sad—a Kafkaesque scenario with Charlie Chaplin in the lead. The motto of the imaginary society of the future, in this story, is "Joy and Soap." All of Böll's precision, and all his sarcasm, is in this phrase.

The stories date over a period from 1947 to 1951, and they are rather diverse in tone, in length, and even in quality. By working your way through them you can see the process working in Böll that operates in so many writers: he begins as a realist, then gradually acquires complexity, an idiosyncratic style, and a penchant for the fantastic or imaginative.

These are not pleasant stories. But it is a well-known paradox that art may give us pleasure even dealing with experiences that give us pain. This has been true at least since Dante, and Böll serves as a kind of miniature Dante of our time. He has no Virgil to guide him, and gets along without Beatrice; like most Germans of his generation, he has learned to mistrust authorities.

Gabriele Annan   (essay date 1977)

SOURCE: A review of *The Bread of Those Early Years,* in *The Times Literary Supplement,* No. 3911, February 25, 1977, p. 201.

[In the following negative review, Annan finds The Bread of Those Early Years *typical of Böll's work.]*

Walter Fendrich, a washing-machine maintenance man, is the first-person hero of this novella [*The Bread of Those Early Years*]; twenty-three, Catholic, a virgin, and engaged to his employer's daughter, Ulla Wickweber. The story takes place in Cologne on a Monday in March during the early 1950s. Walter's father, a schoolteacher in a small town, has asked him to find a room for the daughter of a colleague who is coming to the city to train as a teacher. The moment Walter sees Hedwig he falls in love with her, both sexually and ontologically. In a semi-mystical flash he realizes that she represents an alternative way of life—

less tough and less materialist than life with Ulla. By the end of the day and after various vicissitudes, including Walter's farewell interview with Ulla, Walter and Hedwig are ready to fulfil their destiny by going to bed together—without the blessing of the Church, although Hedwig is also a practising Catholic. Why they cannot wait to get it is never quite explained, but their hurry is made to seem somehow existential.

Böll has always been anti-clerical and anti-establishment: not a very startling position for a German Catholic, even in 1955 when this book first appeared, and it is obvious that the sexual act the novel leads up to but does not include is a rite in what J. P. Stern (*TLS,* January 30, 1976) called "selfconscious Roman (or rather Rhenish) Catholicism, a weird spirituality". *The Bread of Those Early Years* is a textbook example of Böll's work. An examination candidate having to answer a question on his themes, Weltanschauung and symbolism would not need to read much else. First, there is the typical petty bourgeois milieu with built-in alienation. Then want: Walter is doing well in the early years of the post-war economic recovery; but flashbacks reveal a childhood and early youth of deprivation—he was always hungry and the thought of bread obsessed him until bread eventually became an addiction. Now he cannot pass a baker's shop without going in to buy some. But bread is not just the counter-symbol to want, it is also a sacrament: there is a symbolic scene when Walter offers Hedwig a roll and watches her break it. In fact, there is so much bread about that one is inclined to agree with Ulla when she says: "Please don't say the word 'bread' again."

Ulla and her family stand for the acquisitive society in the black market years just after the war when the strong and wily exploited the weak. In later works Böll's target shifts towards the consumer society; here the Wirtschaftswunder is only just beginning: in both cases society is selfish and materialist. The weak are not only exploited but killed. The landscape of Walter's memory is littered with corpses, especially young corpses—another favourite theme of Böll's. Walter's mother dies of tuberculosis, an unattractive spotty girl in Wickweber's factory from a nutritional deficiency disease. The poorest boy in Walter's class is drowned, and that too because of poverty: his mother had made his swimming trunks from an old petticoat of hers, and he was so ashamed of them that he went to bathe as far as possible from the other boys. Finally there is Walter's fellow apprentice with whom in the days of shortages he and Ulla went hunting for metal scrap: he dies when the floor of a bombed building collapses under him, and Walter watches Ulla cross his name off the pay sheet.

Ulla and her father are the only two "bad" characters; or more accurately "least good", because Böll sees some goodness in everyone. Goodness is what interests him and it comes in various packages and strengths: Ulla's brother is a decent, loyal, well-meaning fellow; Walter's landlady—called Frau Brotig, which would, if it were a word, mean "bready"—is generous, warm, and speaks gently to her child; his distant cousin Clara is a nun (Böll always puts in a nun when he can), another selfless giver of bread;

his father is a low-key saint; and Hedwig represents Böll's *ewig Weibliche,* later to turn into Katharina Blum and the Lady in the Group Portrait: a streak of Raskolnikov's Sonya in her, but more mysterious, much more attractive, and much keener on sex, so long as it is suffused with spirituality (see Professor Stern above). Walter himself is the holy fool whom critics have spotted in other works of Böll's.

Professor Stern was sorry that Böll won his Nobel Prize for literature rather than for his "immense decency". His moral stance, he said, was impeccable but unoriginal, and artistically he was unadventurous, even "quietist". True, but the same accusation—of being a *guter Mensch aber schlechter Musikant*—could equally well be levelled at Solzhenitsyn: perhaps it is something to do with the Nobel Prize. Böll may turn out to be one of the overrated writer's of the century. Still, he is not despicable and far from unreadable: his bread goes down easily, even though in this particular work he adopts a hushed religious tone throughout—mitigated by the translation which (mercifully perhaps) is not quite faithful in this respect. Whether the book merits a new translation (Mervyn Savill made one in 1957) is another matter, although it exhibits some of Böll's special gifts: he is wonderful at creating atmosphere and describing smells, sounds, and, of course, tastes, as well as sights. His metaphors are unexpected and illuminating, and he can draw out the *lacrimae rerum* better than almost anyone. Too well perhaps, but his books are getting steadily dryer, and this early one is a reminder of how far the process has gone.

Margit M. Sinka (essay date 1981)

SOURCE: "Heinrich Böll's *Die verlorene Ehre der Katherina Blum* as Novelle," in *Colloquia Germanica,* Vol. 14, No. 2, 1981, pp. 158-74.

[*In the following essay, Sinka summarizes how* Die verlorene Ehre *has been classified (variously as a novella, novel, and political pamphlet) and explores how genre-based perceptions affect interpretations of Böll's work.*]

Reader response to Heinrich Böll's *Die verlorene Ehre der Katharina Blum,* accessible thus far mainly from interviews and media coverage, focuses on Böll's characterization of Katharina and on the interpretation of her deed—that of killing the newspaper reporter Tötges. In the course of pondering whether or not Katharina is a credible figure, critics either reject her as an anarchist or sanctify her as a heroine. Equating the author with his main character, they either criticize Böll for advocating terrorism or praise him for justifying concrete action to counter dehumanizing attacks of the state and the media against the individual.

Yet Böll considers it a grave mistake to equate an author with his main character. Just as he has insisted on divorcing himself from the character of Leni in *Gruppenbild mit Dame,* from her noninvolvement, he insists on separating himself from Katharina. Painstakingly, again and again,

Böll rejects especially the canonization of Katharina. Correcting reader responses, Böll asks critics to take a much closer look at how he actually characterized Katharina: she is a "tüchtige Konformistin", a "durchaus angepaßte Figur, die das Wirtschaftswunder mitmacht, überzeugt davon ist", and she is a "vollkommen konventionelle, konforme Person unserer . . . materialistischen Gesellschaft". Böll simply fails to understand how he might have created a character imbued with saintly attributes.

Misunderstanding between Böll and his readers also extends to the structure of the narrative. Tiring of comments vigorously comparing *Die verlorene Ehre* with *Gruppenbild* on the basis of superficial similarities (the main character in both works is a female and the compositional technique of both depends on research and gathering details to explain the main characters), Böll argues that his purpose for *Die verlorene Ehre* was entirely different from his purpose for *Gruppenbild,* implying thereby that the divergent purposes created different artistic forms which, in turn, should elicit dissimilar interpretations.

In *Gruppenbild,* Böll attempted to treat a long line of developments extending over a time span of 40 years. There his main concern was indeed the major character, Leni. Through her, he tried to create, to make real instead of symbolizing, a totally un-iconographic figure—one who is German but fits no stereotypes of Germans—one who is non-political but causes those around her to become political. In an interview with Manfred Durzak, barely hiding his irritation, Böll emphasizes in regard to *Gruppenbild*: "Das dürfen Sie nicht vergessen . . . Das ist ein Roman." *Die verlorene Ehre,* on the other hand, is "ein Pamphlet in Form einer Reportage, order wie man's nennen soll, die einen ganz anderen Anspruch hat. Das ist doch eine legitime Ausdrucksform, die man mögen mag oder nicht, aber es ist doch ein politisches Pamphlet. . . . Man muß die Intention—die kann mißglückt sein—sehen, das muß die Voraussetzung sein, daß es ein plakatives Werk ist, eine Streitschrift."

Implicit in Böll's comments is the stance adopted by Roman Ingarden in the debate regarding the famed hermeneutic circle, i.e., that the understanding of the whole conditions the understanding of the parts *before* the understanding of the parts causes comprehension of the whole. Evidently, misunderstandings between Böll and his readers (Durzak being representative of others) have developed because the concepts of the whole underpinning their interpretations are norms based on different genre constructs. Böll entitled *Die verlorene Ehre* an *Erzählung,* but he also called it a political pamphlet (as with Durzak) and at yet another time a *Kriminalgeschichte.* The readers, however, emphasizing character and the organizing role of the narrator, tend to approach *Die verlorene Ehre* from the construct of the novel, illustrating Robert Scholes' observations: "In the middle of the twentieth century, our view of narrative literature is almost hopelessly novel-centered. The expectations which readers bring to narrative literary works are based on their experience with the novel. Their assumptions about what a narrative should be are derived from their understanding of the novel."

Can an interpretation of *Die verlorene Ehre* based on the novel as norm—an interpretation so diametrically opposed to Böll's as is Durzak's—possibly have validity? Even while recognizing, of course, that an author's viewpoint is one-sided and that a work may have many implications unintended by the author, a critic should not, as a consequence, banish the author from his text altogether.

Authors do present their works as gifts to readers, Böll admits, but he maintains that the reader, in turn, must prove himself worthy of a gift: "indem er sich zwingt, indem er gezwungen wird, die Form zu durchschauen oder sie anzunehmen, die Zumutung der Form und des Inhalts." It is thus the reader's responsibility to choose a genre construct adequate for both the text *and* its author.

That "all understanding of verbal meaning is necessarily genre-bound"—to quote a well-known statement by E. D. Hirsch—and, moreover, that the first generic construct chosen by a critic is seldom relinquished willingly becomes evident in the way Durzak disputes Böll's classification of *Die verlorene Ehre* : "Sie erwähnen: Pamphlet. Aber das ist im Grunde eine theoretische, tagespolitische Streitschrift, politische Tagesjournalistik." Almost exasperated, Böll attempts to puncture Durzak's rigid normative generic concepts even more: "Das Pamphlet in Form einer Erzählung ist vielleicht eine noch nicht so recht praktizierte Form." To Durzak's renewed objections, Böll replies: "Ich rege nur an."

What genre critics advocate, Böll practices: "If a reader ignores or despises genre, or gets it wrong, misreading results", he should be reminded of the fruitfulness of genre concepts or be urged to change the inappropriate genre construct. Such change may be in order, for an interpretation ought not be "helplessly dependent on the generic conception with which an interpreter happens to start", even though it "is dependent on the last, unrevised generic conception with which he starts".

To declare genre as the departure point for interpretation need no longer imply acceptance of rigid prescriptive norms that determine the value of a work. Rather, descriptive genre concepts (emphasizing what *is* or what *was* instead of what *should be*) enable the critic to view genres as "historical families", comprised—in the words of Hans Robert Jau—"von Werken, die durch eine kontinuitätsbildende Struktur verbunden sind und historisch zutage treten, eine Gruppe bilden und gattungsgeschichtlich beschrieben werden". A genre concept based on understanding developed descriptively may allow the critic to understand the nature of an individual work, precisely because of its departure from the norm. Thus one ought not dismiss genre-based interpretation, as Benedetto Croce does, merely because "Jedes wahre Kunstwerk hat eine festgelegte Gattung verletzt", for clearly, again in the words of Jau, "die Kongruenz zwischen Theorie und Praxis ist nie vollständig erreichbar." The absence of total congruence, moreover, does not give one the right to blithely disregard theory altogether. Does one not, by so doing, contribute to the faulty scholarship that Cleanth Brooks regards as the result of "abundant signs of poor literary theory or no

literary theory at all"? Rather than discarding theory entirely, the critic should adopt concepts broad enough to accommodate change and yet not so broad as to eliminate useful constructs of expectation. Thus genre may be the mechanism, as Claudio Guillen tells us, to "incite the questioning of literary works."

With respect to *Die verlorene Ehre,* Böll has shown himself willing to consider various generic assumptions for interpretation, as long as they are not novel-centered and do credit him with a purposeful choice of form. In Böll's view, especially a *Germanist* can interpret his work knowledgeably, for he approaches a narrative in the same way an author does: "nicht mit Vorurteilen, aber mit bestimmten Erwartungen, Vorstellungen von literarischen Entwicklungen, generellen, speziellen." A *Germanist* can therefore readily apply a generic construct to *Die verlorene Ehre* different from those already mentioned—that of the *Novelle,* particularly if he is aware of Böll's insistence that he is Kleistian rather than Schillerian.

Whether or not the horizon of expectations evoked by the *Novelle* will indeed be helpful for interpreting Böll's narrative may provide arguments for answering yet another question: Has the *Novelle* as a genre sputtered to a halt, Böll's *Die verlorene Ehre* providing merely another example confirming the death of the genre, or does the genre continue to assert itself in our stage of the twentieth century—to be sure, expanded in its generic function but not stretched so widely that its generic label becomes meaningless?

Just what are the expectations evoked in a *Germanist* by the term *Novelle?* All too often they are merely the elements forming the famous checklist (*Rahmen, deutliche Silhouette, Falke, Wendepunkt, eine sich ereignete unerhörte Begebenheit,* etc.). How could these elements, irate critics have protested, possibly serve to characterize the *Novelle,* since they are to be found abundantly in other literary forms? Eliminating items from the checklist thus became a favored critical activity. Yet, somehow, the items so vigorously banned have just as vigorously marched back to their places, reconstituting the checklist. Why else is it necessary for John Ellis, in a relatively recent work, to once again sweep away the items which Karl Polheim and others (e.g., W. Pabst, Manfred Schunicht, Emil Staiger) previously had sought to eliminate, and with painstaking care? Can Ellis' arguments (e.g., artistic concentration is not peculiar to the *Novelle,* since all art deals with material "that is rather more concentrated than everyday life") really convince those checkpoint adherents who already have been subjected to far more stringent iconoclastic criticism of the individual components?

That all of the elements in the list of *Novelle* components may also occur in other literary forms cannot be disputed. But defenders of the structural components for the *Novelle* maintain that in each particular *Novelle* they tend to occur together—if not all of the time, then most of the time. How many elements, though, can be left out before a work loses its status as *Novelle?* Nino Erné goes so far as to conclude—and he by no means stands alone—that only the *sich ereignete unerhörte Begebenheit* constitutes the dominant as well as indispensable element: "Wo dieser Kern fehlt, ist das Gebiet der Novelle zu Ende."

To reduce a *Novelle* definition to the *unerhörte Begebenheit* seems, however, just as inadequate as insisting on a more extensive list of disparate elements. Not only the existence of the components but *how* they are mixed, i.e., the delicate balancing of the elements with each other, expressed by a concept such as Henry Remak's *Das Novellistische,* proves to be a far more convincing argument in favor of retaining the elements for *Novelle* theory. But the problem of appropriate blend again raises the question of boundaries—that is, what types of mixtures would burst the confines of the genre? The *Novelle* as a genre, and this is stated explicitly or implicitly by all theoreticians who still believe in the genre construct, must create unity from its material of disparate elements. Thus one of the most persistent criteria used for literary evaluations in general (from Schiller's times to our own)—the concept of the organic whole—applies to the *Novelle* in particular.

Much of the most recent work on the *Novelle* concentrates, therefore, on a unitive element—on the element of tension evident in nineteenth and early twentieth century *Novellen* and on the resolution of the tension. When we read, for instance, Manfred Schunicht's conclusion that the *Novelle* is a bilateral structure in which objective reality and subjective artistry create a unique form or Judith Leibowitz' theory that the generic goal is "intensity and expansion" (compressing the material while also expanding its implications), we recognize the difference from arguments such as Fritz Lockemann's in which the traditionally accepted *Novelle* components function as historical ordering principles seeking to bridge the gap between "chaos and order", but we also recognize the similarity of these standpoints in their common stress on the element of tension and the need to resolve it. This is, moreover, the area of investigation that has proved to be so fruitful for Martin Swales' *Novelle* study. Under his careful scrutiny, even the much maligned checklist elements gain new vitality because he views them with regard to the tensions they express.

Since not only the ability but even the attempts to resolve tensions seems to have disappeared in our times, the predictions for the *Novelle* as a viable genre for the present and future are dismal. In Helmut Prang's view, for instance, old nineteenth century form and new twentieth century psychological and sociological contents jar so much that reconciliation in a unity is impossible. For Fritz Martini, who emphasizes the crisis-ridden, problematic, even tragic realm of the nineteenth century *Novelle,* the twentieth century world has become so fragmented, the crises so numerous and dispersed, that there is no longer a way to unify. It is this abdication of an attempt to resolve the opposites in life, whether or not such an attempt succeeds, which Josef Kunz views as proof that full-length *Novellen* can no longer be written. Or, in Martin Swales' words, modern authors no longer undertake the "interpretative risk", the "gamble", which results in a *Novelle*.

Yet the "complex and reflective relationship" to events considered by Swales the hallmark of the *Novelle* is still very evident in Böll's *Die verlorene Ehre*. The narrator in Böll's work obviously wants to interpret. But, what? Because of his article, "Will Ulrike freies Geleit?" critics frequently assumed that Böll wrote his narrative in direct response to the Baader-Meinhof events in Germany. Denying this emphatically, as well as the assumption that his tale is concerned with countering the practice of manipulative journalism, Böll insists that his narrative is exactly about what his subtitle states: "Wie Gewalt entstehen und wohin sie führen kann."

Böll wishes to highlight *one* specific problem so that it may serve representatively for other cases, thus fulfilling what F. Th. Vischer regards as the essence of the *Novelle*: "Die Novelle zeigt ein Stück aus einem Menschenleben, das . . . uns durch eine Gemüths- und Schicksalswendung mit scharfem Accente zeigt, was Menschenleben überhaupt ist." Stressing in addition that he was concerned with what happens to an individual without recourse to the weapons of language and fame when maligned by the organs of society (press, police, etc.), Böll clearly demonstrates that the element of conflict and an attempt at its resolution motivate him just as they had *Novelle* authors of the past.

Böll also complies with *Novelle* expectations of explicating an event that had already occurred. Instead of "richten" like the *Zeitung,* his narrator intends to "berichten." The modern American author Cynthia Ozick would consider this factor alone to have conditioned a novella form: "If the novella is the most captivating short form of all, it is because there is nothing more interesting than beginning with the end, nothing more mysterious than heading out to seek your fortune with your destination . . . in your pocket." The compact *sich ereignete unerhörte Begebenheit* with which Böll opens his tale provides the requisite aspect of "completion" at the outset: "Am Mittwoch, dem 20. 2. 1974, am Vorabend von Weiberfastnacht, verläßt in einer Stadt eine junge Frau von siebenundzwanzig Jahren abends gegen 18.45 Uhr ihre Wohnung, um an einem privaten Tanzvergnügen teilzunehmen. Vier Tage später . . . gegen 19.04 –, klingelt es an der Wohnungstür des Kriminaloberkommissars Walter Moeding . . . und gibt dem erschrockenen Moeding zu Protokoll, sie habe mittags gegen 12.15 in ihrer Wohnung den Journalisten Werner Tötges erschossen."

While the occurrence of an extraordinary event is a generic expectation associated with the *Novelle,* it is not the event itself but the problem of its explicability—precisely because it seems so logical and illogical at the same time—that motivates a *Novelle* narrator. Attending a harmless carnival party leads, in Böll's tale, to murder. This event *is* unusual, but it receives its "unheard-of" texture only in the course of Böll's work. It is highly contingent on the personality of Katharina herself—a personality pieced together from her various actions and utterances, from the opinions others have of her, and from the attitudes they demonstrate toward her. What is perhaps most inexplicable at the outset is that Katharina, who was not noted for her spontaneity, should fall in love so quickly with Götten, indeed after spending only one evening and night with him. This is the Katharina who repeatedly rejects the advances men make, the Katharina who found even her husband "zudringlich", who decides to leave employment in a physician's house because the doctor too became "zudringlich", the Katharina who rejects the handsome and well-regarded Sträubleder, and the woman who is happy to have her own car so that she can escape from the advances men make toward her. This same Katharina unconditionally accepts and returns Götten's affection—in direct opposition to what society (press and police) expect of her.

In other respects, however, Katharina has accepted societal values. Katharina is "fast prüde", "planmäßig", "kühl", and "nüchtern". She trusts the police and is exacting as she insists on a totally correct transcription of her account; she records her income and expenditures in an extremely orderly way (Chapter 24). She is goal-oriented, saving carefully to complete payments on the apartment she had bought in the complex "Elegant am Strom Wohnen". Having sought to further her own education, she is "was die ästhetische Seite betreffe, aufs beste gebildet und ausgebildet." She too is influenced by the media, in particular the movies. Her love is "love at first sight", basically a romantic love depicted in movies. Helping Götten escape seems to her a "Räuber- und Banditengeschichte." When she shoots Tötges (does she not perhaps also have this idea from the movies?), she remarks: "Und er guckte mich noch 'ne halbe Sekunde oder so erstaunt an, so wie im Kino, wenn einer plötzlich aus heiterem Himmel erschossen wird."

The problem in Böll's narrative arises when Katharina, who has accepted all other values of society, cannot accept society's judgment about Götten: "Da fängt ihre Verstrickung an, fängt auch die Unerklärlichkeit an . . . Liebe ist nicht gerecht und nicht moralisch. Diese . . . erotische und sexuelle Bindung ist nicht moralisierbar." The tragic "Verstrickung" Böll speaks of develops as the representatives of societal institutions (police, press) become angry at Katharina's refusal to stop defending Götten, at her refusal to relinquish her affection. Critics often overlook the fact that Katharina did act in a reprehensible way: Blorna and Frau Woltersheim do let Katharina know that she transgressed against society's laws by helping Götten escape. In Böll's mind, too, there isn't much integrity in hiding a criminal and letting him escape. Nonetheless, it is the spontaneity which Katharina allows in only one sphere of her life—affection—which becomes her downfall. Because of her love, irreversible on the basis of her character, Katharina must inevitably come into conflict with society.

In a sense, Katharina's development is depicted so emphatically to show the strength of her character, to show that she never did tolerate violations of her personal territory: she blushed in school when the others teased her for being "rötlich"; she escaped from the coarseness of her family, from that of her husband; she did not allow men's advances; she resented her husband and his friends making her drunk; she did not like the coarseness and loudness of discos. When the police and the *Zeitung* relentlessly attack the very essence of her being, "Treue und Stolz", Katharina is driven to her limits. As Böll relates, "dieses Getriebenwerden in eine bestimmte Ecke . . . das ist das Entscheidende dabei". Böll did depict this process, as well as the personality of Katharina, credibly. The events are indeed, as the narrator remarks in his opening comments, "nicht unerklärlich, sogar fast logisch", and yet it remains impossible to explain the entire affair. In this instance too, Böll's narrative confirms the horizon of expectations associated with the *Novelle*.

Authors do present their works as gifts to readers, Böll admits, but he maintains that the reader, in turn, must prove himself worthy of a gift. . . . It is thus the reader's responsibility to choose a genre construct adequate for both the text *and* its author.

—*Margit M. Sinka*

Another problem containing *Novelle*-type tension in Böll's work pertains to the political sphere, i.e., how does a totally unpolitical person become political? Inherently, Katharina is certainly not political: working long hours, not even taking vacations, she barely has any free time: she rarely receives mail; she does not have a T. V. to keep her abreast of political events; in her book collection, the books of her own choosing are four romances, three mysteries, two biographies (the rest were sent by a book club), and not even her pamphlets are political—rather, they treat such topics as "Verwendung von Sherry in Soßen". The only circles in which Katharina is well-known are gastronomical ones. Her only excess seems to be buying boxes of chocolate occasionally (but, she doesn't even waste the boxes, saving them for letters and photographs). A more unlikely candidate for "Person der Zeitgeschichte" can hardly be imagined (other than her mother who also becomes a "Person der Zeitgeschichte", although she does nothing but lie passively in the hospital). That Katharina became a "Person der Zeitgeschichte" nonetheless is entirely due to forces beyond her control. Even her most harmless actions, such as trips in the car merely for the sake of driving, seem to have political consequences in the eyes of police and press. Ironically, while she defends herself, she actually implicates Götten. Yet Götten is not a terrorist but an army deserter. The conspiracy against the state, of which Katharina and Götten are accused, is actually a conspiracy between the police and press against innocent individuals—an irony contributing to the tension of the entire narrative.

All efforts on Katharina's part to remain unpolitical fail. She starts to read *all* her mail (something rarely done by unpolitical citizens), finding out that she is considered a "Kommunistensau", "rote Wühlmaus", "Kreml-Tante".

Later, throwing bottles of alcohol at her *makellose* living room walls, sauce bottles at the kitchen walls, and make-up bottles at the bathroom walls, Katharina sullies her surroundings—the symbols of middle class life she had spent so much time to build—just as her own honor had been sullied. Lashing out at society by lashing out at her own life created in society's image, though in the orderly fashion consistent with her character, Katharina demonstrates that she has indeed become political.

As a sign of her increased politization, Katharina keeps reading the *Zeitung,* losing interest in most other matters. She starts to read analytically instead of emotionally. And, as her belief in the ability of words to depict the truth evaporates, her readiness for action without words increases. At the police station, she had still controlled "mit erstaunlicher Pedanterie jede einzelne Formulierung", insisting—for example—on "gütig" rather than "nett" and affirming "es sei genauso, wie sie angegeben habe". Toward the end of the narrative, however, she has lost faith in verbal weapons: "Wer würde ihr schon glauben, daß sie einem Menschen wie Sträubleder widerstehen würde?" When she steals a copy of the *Zeitung,* probably for the first time ever—in her instance signifying a major transgression against society, she sets into motion a future act against society. The same day on which she steals the newspaper, she also "steals" Konrad's gun—i. e., she takes it without his knowledge.

Unlike Dr. Heinen who was going to sue the *Zeitung* for having published Tötges' interview with Katharina's mother and who did not do anything, unlike Katharina's father, who constantly whined against authorities but flattered them in their presence, unlike Trude Blorna who merely makes an anonymous angry phone call consisting of two phrases and who later fights only with the uninfluential Mrs. Sträubleder, unlike Blorna who punches Sträubleder at an art exhibit—much later than he first intended—and causes only a few drops of blood to flow from his nose, unlike Frau Woltersheim who controls herself "mit Gewalt" not to throw bowls of potato salad at buffet guests—unlike all these people venting their anger at the "system" ineffectively, Katharina refuses to be victim any longer and retaliates because of the violence that has been committed against her. Step-by-step, Böll shows how logical it was for Katharina to indeed become politicized, to indeed resort to action. Yet he still does not erase the enigma of why everything happened as it did—the enigma of the irrational love that caused her conflict with society.

To reconstruct the events leading to Katharina's deed is possible—but where, exactly, did the *Wendepunkt* occur? With 19th and early 20th century novellas, this question can be answered relatively unproblematically. Though readers might not form a consensus, there is certainly more agreement than disagreement, with the areas of speculation being limited. Why the attempt, though, to locate the *Wendepunkt* at all when it has so often been pronounced a fruitless, pedantic activity?

As the surprise element of the *Novelle,* the *Wendepunkt* provides much of its aura of mystery. The ability to pin-

point it and to understand it helps one to explain the event itself. Perhaps it is the *Wendepunkt* that is the secret, the secret to which Todorov refers when he states that it constitutes the essence of the novella. Certainly for Böll's narrator, to find the *Wendepunkt* would mean the ability to unmask the secret: At exactly which point does violence ensue, at exactly which point can a maligned individual no longer suffer without retaliating?

No matter how much he tries, however, Böll's narrator is unable to locate the *Wendepunkt.* Did Katharina begin to have thoughts of murder when she read the first article in the *Zeitung,* as she herself maintains when Blorna is planning her defense? Was it actually the last *Zeitung* article, the one appearing on Sunday morning—not long before she killed Tötges, which motivated her action? Did she already decide to kill Tötges when she invited him for an interview? Did she already know on Saturday night, when she asked for Konrad's apartment key, that she would take Konrad's gun in order to use it on Tötges? Was a murder plan firmly established in her mind when she decided to make her own sheik costume? Or, did she decide to murder, as she herself mentions, only when she could not find Tötges in the Journalist Club and was unable to formulate a realistic image of him as a human being? How much of a role did the actual meeting in her own apartment play?—a meeting in the wake of a deep realization that the apartment had become "verschmiert und verdreckt". Or, was her decision to kill made only when she actually pulled her gun out, right after Tötges suggested to her: "ich schlage vor, daß wir jetzt erst einmal bumsen".

Finding it impossible to pinpoint when Katharina decided to commit her extraordinary act, impossible to locate the *Wendepunkt,* the narrator thwarts a major generic expectation associated with the *Novelle.* As a consequence, there is no relaxation of tension, none of the *Entladung* after which the traditional *Novelle* again assumes the properties of a secret which also the concept of an "organic whole" entails. Instead of decreasing tension in regard to the interpretability of the event, the narrator increases it steadily. He shares his rising frustrations with the reader; he seeks to elicit the reader's sympathy for his problem of determining the value of isolated bits of information. He compares himself to phone tappers who must also experience difficulty with sifting facts. Do they think that "Palatschinken mit Mohn" and "Erdbeeren mit Sahne" are codes to be interpreted? These phone tappers, whose identity remains anonymous just as the narrator's—are they simple people? How do they live—they who are gathering information like he and trying to make sense of it? Do they, like the narrator, suffer from the information they gather?

Drawing attention to his inability to find the *Wendepunkt* and thus to his predicament of ever attaining interpretation of the events, Böll's narrator no longer interrupts the horizon of expectations to the degree necessary for pleasurable reading experiences to occur at all, as Jauâ has suggested, but interrupts it so frequently that the result of the excessive interruptions becomes indeed the danger foreseen by Wolfgang Iser: frustration. Relinquishing any hope of finding resolution of the tensions, the reader becomes just as frustrated as the narrator. And frustration is certainly not a reaction associated with *Novelle* reading. The *Novelle* does illuminate a problem, but in the end, it leads the reader to reflect, to ponder. It causes scrutiny—not frustration, not failure.

How does the "Ordnungsvorgang" which the narrator perceives as his function—a task comparable to the interpretative reflection of the event stressed by Kunz and Swales—lead to his failure to achieve understanding, cohesion, unity? To find an answer, the narrator's procedure must be contrasted to that of the police and press. After all, the police and press had also highlighted problems that were, for them, "unheard-of": the escape of a suspected criminal under their watchful eyes, the prudish nun-like Katharina's falling in love upon a first meeting, the unexplained mileage of her car when she was so careful with recording other data, and many others. This is material that makes headlines. Yet the police and press are able to solve their own *unerhörte Begebenheiten* in rapid succession. Convinced that all events are attributable to conspiracy against the state, they alone are able to perform the *Ordnungsaufgabe* associated with the traditional narrator unproblematically. Ironically, they are the ones who act in a *Novelle* manner, using only those facts from Katharina's life useful for their purposes (e. g., her brother's misdemeanors, her mother's drinking, her father's harmless pronouncement on socialism, the *Herrenbesuch*). They, who should investigate *all* sources, have no difficulty being selective. Yet their selectivity renders their account subjective when it should have been objective.

In contrast, the narrator hopes to achieve greater objectivity by choosing to be far less selective. But his course too jeopardizes objectivity. It jars with the role traditionally expected of a narrator, leading to an inability to create order at all, to an inability to be objective in any respect. Even the narrator's potentially useful information has no "Zeugniskraft" or "Öffentlichkeitswert": resting on shaky grounds, much of it on hear-say, it fails to convince even him. His relativism becomes so pervasive that he doubts what others have not only "nachgewiesen, sondern sogar . . . zugegeben". The more information he gathers, the less the narrator can decide what is pertinent and what is superfluous. He reacts like the programmer to the computer whose lights inexplicably start to blink all at once; seeking to pay attention to all of them individually and collectively, he loses control entirely.

The events cannot be reconciled with each other. The narrator's sources, as opposed to those of the police and press, do not flow together unproblematically. Thus even the metaphor chosen by the narrator to unify his tale— the puddles that lead nowhere, the sources of water that refuse to merge despite efforts to drain them, to reroute them to another level or to link them by channels—turns out to be an image resisting unification.

With his superb command of irony (something Böll feels is neither practiced nor appreciated by Germans), Böll's narrator refuses to make concessions to the traditional form of narration. As Roland Barthes has stated, the traditional book "is an object which connects, develops, runs, and flows . . . Sympathetic metaphors of the book are . . . water flowing, flour to be milled, paths to be followed". Obviously sarcastic about reader expectations such as these, which also imply that the "'flow of words' should be in the service of an event or an idea which 'makes its way' toward its denouement or its conclusion", Böll selects an antipathetic metaphor, telling the reader in his second chapter: "Wenn der Bericht . . . hin und wieder als 'fließend' empfunden wird, so wird dafür um Verzeihung gebeten: es war unvermeidlich." What he wants is not a steady flow but a type of drainage or "Trockenlegung" of puddles. Instead of proceeding effortlessly, spontaneously, or even with necessity (as a *Novelle* author might), Böll's narrator performs with conscious effort his "unvermeidliche Kanalarbeit". Whenever possible, he avoids the work, indulging his *Spieltrieb* instead. Only afterwards does he return "reumütig" to his *Kanalarbeit,* to the task of seeking unity. But he repeatedly warns of "Stauungen", "Stockungen", "Versandungen", "mißglückte Konduktionen", as he had warned of "Verstrickung, Verwicklung, Befaßtheit, Befangenheit" at the outset of his report. Just as the muddy puddles, Katharina's "undurchsichtige" past causes problems; just as the waters refuse to flow, Katharina is "verstockt" and "verweigert Aussage".

The narrator's metaphor nonetheless succeeds in unifying his basic theme: form is impossible, unity is impossible. Surely Böll deserves credit for using form to metaphorically state the impossibility of form—a delicate endeavor indeed. In like manner, the narrator's flashbacks, generally used in cinema and literature to explain the present by means of the past (to create unity), function as blockages to unity. When the narrator explicates the first two days of the four which the narrative intends to cover (hardly a lengthy period) by means of a flashback from the third day and frequently informs the reader of the status of the flashback (at what stage it is, how much longer it will last), he again creates disunity on purpose, ironically labeling it "überflüssigen Spannungsstau." Still, the disunity aggravated by the flashbacks also shows that intended content and conscious form again overlap. They are, in fact, unified.

That critics so far have had no sympathy for the narrator's predicaments regarding form and unity and have failed even to discuss his irony indicates how strongly embedded in the horizon of expectations a *Novelle* type denouement still is. Aware of this, the ironic narrator directs contrite comments to the general reader that would suit *Novelle* adherents in particular: his tale is too "handlungsstark," containing "lauter Dingeund Leute, die einfach nicht synchronisierbar sind und dauernd den Fluß . . . stören." Later he ruefully admits: "Nicht Integration, Konfrontation hat sich ergeben." Wondering at the result, the narrator seeks to gain last-minute control, recapitulating the events in comprehensible, one-by-one succession, in capsule form. Before he is aware of it, though, he is again digressing (e. g., Frau Blorna's possibilities for jobs), proving his own assertion that "so wenig Harmonie mitgeteilt und nur sehr geringe Hoffnung auf solche gemacht werden kann." The question, moreover, of how matters will end—what Erné calls the "echte Novellenfrage"—is treated ironically in Böll's work. After Blorna has gathered all his facts (though he doesn't know that he may be barred from being the defense attorney), the narrator wailingly asks:" Was soll daraus werden, wie soll das enden?"

While a *Novelle* frequently contains irony, the irony of Böll's narrator pertains not to the event itself but to its lack of interpretability and extends to all other areas of the work as well (e. g., both the avuncular Beizmenne and Katharina are happy over one telephone conversation Katharina has with Götten; the suspected criminal, Götten, is not costumed and does not seek to hide, while the policemen dress up as sheiks and try to hide their identities). Frequently, no matter how enjoyable it may be, the irony exists for its own sake, always emphasizing the lack of unity—intentionally, to be sure, but nonetheless in a way that constantly punctures the construct a *Germanist* may expect from a *Novelle*.

Even though Böll's narrative obviously contains many of the checklist elements associated with the *Novelle* as a genre, they refuse to be blended into the requisite unified mixture that constitutes a *Novelle*. The police and press in Böll's work succeed in attaining unity because they eliminate disparities, but the *Novelle* mix achieves unity not at the expense of removing contradictions—rather, the unity is more significant because the contradictions, though disappearing from the surface, remain alive in entities such as the Novelle's *Dingsymbol*.

The disproportionately important function of Böll's narrator and his failure to reach any conclusions at all, however tentative, concomitantly the escalation of tension instead of its reduction, and ultimately the justification of formlessness—these factors place Böll's **Die verlorene Ehre** beyond the confines of the *Novelle* as perceived even by those critics who concentrate on tension and interpretative attempt. It seems, therefore, that the *result* of the interpretative reflection of the event—not merely that such reflection is attempted (as Kunz and Swales have maintained)—becomes crucial for the generic construct of the *Novelle*.

Yet modern genre theory, clearly descriptive, as Warren and Wellek state, "doesn't limit the number of possible kinds and . . . supposes that traditional kinds may be 'mixed' and produce a new kind." It is thus still too early to tell whether or not, in the perspective of history's descriptive genre investigations, Böll's narrator will have caused the work to stray into a generic category other than the *Novelle,* in the process having helped to mark the *Novell*'s boundaries, or have induced a new category composed of elements from other genre sources also, or actually have expanded the genre concept of the *Novelle*. At the very least, though, viewing Böll's work from *Novelle* perspectives has not only widened interpretation possibilities but has also enabled interpretation to reflect, even if not mirror, authorial intention.

Robert C. Conrad (essay date 1981)

SOURCE: "Heinrich Böll's Political Reevaluation of Adalbert Stifter: An Interpretation of Böll's 'Epilog zu Stifters "Nachsommer" '," in *The Michigan Academician,* Vol. XIV, No. 1, Summer, 1981, pp. 31-9.

[*In the following essay, Conrad determines the influence of Adalbert Stifter's novel* Der Nachsommer *on Böll's story* "Epilog zu Stifters 'Nachsommer'," *and asserts that* "although [the story] reads as an entertaining spoof, on close analysis it reveals Böll's serious social concerns at the beginning of the seventies."]

Böll's work has never been without its moral dimension, but in the five years between the novels **End of a Mission (Ende einer Dienstfahrt,** 1966) and *Group Portrait with Lady (Gruppenbild mit Dame,* 1971), while Böll's public life and his essays became more political, his prose fiction seemed to grow less so. The stories of this half decade, a mere three short pieces, appear to confirm this conclusion. "Er kam als Bierfahrer," 1968, retells the myth of Taurus and Europa. "Veränderungen in Staech," 1969, satirizes mildly—one could almost say affectionately—the cloistered monastic life, youthful protests of the sixties, and life in the capital. And **"Epilog zu Stifters 'Nachsommer,'"** 1970, experiments with the epilogue as a short story form. Although this latter piece reads as an entertaining spoof, on close analysis it reveals Böll's serious social concerns at the beginning of the seventies.

This satire is not easily understood, however, without knowing the book on which it is based, "the greatest of totally unread novels," as one critic calls *Der Nachsommer* ("The Indian Summer"), and without knowing something of Böll's attitude to Adalbert Stifter before 1970.

Stifter's *Der Nachsommer* (1857) is a utopian *Entwicklungs-* and *Bildungsroman,* a first-person narrative of Heinrich Drendorf, son of a wealthy businessman, lifelong student of nature, art, and literature, an ideal human being and perfect spouse of a perfect young woman of sensibility, beauty, intelligence, and modest charm. The work is a culmination of the German romantic-classical tradition of bourgeois humanism: showing respect for life, art, nature, and people, illustrated by self-control, confidence in friendship, patience with one's emotions, and resignation to the world as it is. Restraint is the characteristic trait of the narrative. The book moves unhurriedly, harmoniously, and tranquilly through the stages of Drendorf's life. Only near the very end of the novel does Heinrich reveal his own name and Natalie's (his fiancée's) family name. The characters of the novel live in an intimate world of friendship and family, where children always strive to please their parents, and friends are always considerate of one another. It is a private world of perfection in which the passage of years is measured less by the calendar than by growth of intellect and character, a world in which time is spent immersed in art, nature, and the beautiful. The narration concerns detailed descriptions of flowers, cacti, paintings, dramas, statues, furniture, and stone collections. The novel's pace is set by sentences that come in slow rhythmic breaths. The mood is always quiet, calm, mild, peaceful, gentle, humane, civil. Goethe's *Wilhelm Meister* and Novalis' *Heinrich von Ofterdingen* hover over the book like protecting angels. The youthful lovers, Heinrich and Natalie, live in total submission to the will of their parents; there is no generation gap. Parents and adults represent the noble image in which the children are formed. Love is abundant but sex absent from this bourgeois utopia. Even in the engagement scene in which Heinrich and Natalie profess their eternal devotion to one another, sexual delight does not enter their minds and hearts. They even agree never to see one another again if any elder objects to their union. On the day of Heinrich and Natalie's wedding, the joy of the bride and groom is to witness the blooming of the rare cactus *cereus peruvianus,* the symbol of the uniqueness and beauty of their love and marriage. It is a novel of perfection and purity, the ideal utopian dream of Stifter's "sanftes Gesetz" ("gentle law").

In his summer lectures of 1964 at the University of Frankfurt in which he attempts to develop an aesthetic of the humane, Böll praises *Der Nachsommer* as the "grandest model for living in German literature." In the course of the third lecture Böll contrasts a long passage from *Der Nachsommer* describing beautiful inlaid furniture to the poem "Inventory" by Günter Eich written about life in a POW camp after World War II ("This is my cap, / this is my coat, / here my shaving things / in a linen bag. . . . ") in order to illustrate the inability of postwar German literature to find roots in the traditional values of home and family. A nostalgia runs through Böll's lectures for the soundness of a civilized, pre-Auschwitz past, which, however, in no way advocates an escapist literature of inwardness. Because of his double longing for a healthy world and a committed literature, Böll has mixed feelings about the unreal quality of Stifter's masterpiece. He calls it a "desperate dream of permanence, learning, and living" yet, he concludes:

> The only person after Goethe who found continuity was Stifter. It is from his work, as from Jean Paul's, that one can glean an aesthetic of the humane. . . . The profit for me from my occupation with Stifter consists in the rediscovery of his hidden fullness and modernity under his prudish language—which means to me actuality of means. I believe he could become the father of a new humane realism, could stand as sponsor for attempts, not at closing the chasm between statistical reality and reality as described in literature, not at bridging the chasm, but perhaps at slowly filling it in.

As the sixties progressed, Böll became more concerned with current German politics as his essays on the enacting of the Emergency Laws, the socialist experiment in Prague, and the founding of the West German Writers' Union amply attest. Inherent in these essays were a growing sensitivity to socialist criticism and a growing awareness of a socialist economic point of view against which, in 1970, he reevaluated Stifter's novel.

Der Nachsommer appeared in 1857 nearly a decade after the revolutionary events of 1848. The historical setting of the novel, however, despite all of Stifter's attempts at timelessness, is as he states in a letter of 1857: "not in our time, but over thirty years ago," i.e., in the 1820s. Thus, the action of the novel predates, and the writing of the novel postdates, the March Revolution of 1848. Although the novel takes place in the period before the uprisings of the middle of the century, nowhere in the work does Stifter touch upon the problems which caused the revolutions: industrialization, expanding capitalism, and the frustrated longings of the middle class for political equality. They are purposely disregarded in his dream world of the leisure life in which persons seek self-fulfillment, unfettered by a profession, unhindered by work, unhampered by material worries. Despite the enormous expense in pursuing a life such as Heinrich Drendorf and his friends lead— paying private tutors, enjoying unrestricted travel, investing in scientific studies, building homes and laying out gardens, purchasing jewels, statues, and works of art, supporting servants, buying good food, clothing, and furniture, giving presents, paying generous wages, and treating employees with dignity—nowhere is there any indication that such a life is possible for any but the wealthy few. Stifter's dream of each man's developing to his potential is, under the conditions presented in the book, a false dream for humanity. Stifter's dream is not an ideal based on character or ability. It is merely a social construct for a wealthy elite despite all effort on the part of the author to pass off his vision of education as a possibility for all who seek it. Heinrich's leisurely road to maturity is for those who can live according to the advice of Heinrich's father: "Be always certain of your basic investment" ("Sei immer deines Grundvermögen sicher") and for those who, like Heinrich, can count on "an increase of wealth" ("eine Vermehrung eures Eigentums").

Heinrich's father justifies the system under which they live with the belief: "We all stand in the hand of God." "God directs the world in such a way that talents are properly distributed, so that every kind of work is done which has to be done on earth, and so that there will never be a time when all men are architects." And Natalie's mother promotes their way of life by instilling in her daughter and in Heinrich a belief in "the highest power that orders everything that exists." Such a faith is for them not only a religion but a social philosophy. God for them is a protector of a social system rather than a creator of a changing universe. Since religion, per se, is absent as a theme from the novel, the world that is in order, controlled by God, perfect as it is, is the social order which guarantees the interest on Heinrich's investments and increases the value of his property.

This artificial utopia, this world which hides poverty, exploitation, and evil, ignores sickness, suffering, death, and class struggle, this world which avoids the negative, the harsh, the bitter, this world of distorted ethics is what Böll satirizes in his epilogue.

The manner in which Böll comes to terms with the other side of Stifter's *Der Nachsommer* derives from Böll's considerations of Tolstoi's *War and Peace,* especially his criticism of the epilogue, which Tolstoi set eight years after the end of the novel. Böll agrees with the critics who judge the epilogue's final family scene, in which all the main characters are married with children and settled into a life of bourgeois responsibility, as a weakening of the artistic structure of the novel. But Böll argues that its weakness lies not in the surprising philistine conclusion, but rather in the inability of the reader to believe in or trust the artificially happy denouement. Böll feels that Tolstoi's entire novel casts doubt on marriage as a happy institution; too many broken and unhappy marriages in the novel speak against marriage as a happy state. He asserts that conjugal fidelity has too often been betrayed for the reader to trust the status of Tolstoi's epilogue: André had loved Natasha while he was married to another; after his wife's death and his engagement to Natasha, she eloped with an attractive scoundrel; Pierre's first marriage was to a woman more courtesan than wife, who provided him with years of misery; André's old father railed frequently against women and marriage. All the unhappiness and suffering which came through marriage is too vivid in the reader's memory, Böll maintains, for the reader to put much confidence in Tolstoi's epilogue.

Böll wrote his essay on *War and Peace* in 1970, in the same year he wrote the epilogue to Stifter's *Der Nachsommer*. The sociological and aesthetic considerations which he treats in the Tolstoi essay also form the basis of his reevaluation of the Austrian classic. Böll's epilogue does far more than demonstrate the problems in Heinrich and Natalie's marriage and does more than show it to be a union reduced to habit and convention. The epilogue is a full attack on the social values represented by Heinrich Drendorf and embodied in Stifter's novel. In the epilogue, Heinrich becomes an adulterer and shows himself an opportunist, a manipulator, a militarist, and a self-satisfied hypocrite. Böll manages to compact in his nine-page conclusion the sociological aspects of life ignored or minimized by Stifter: economics, politics, class differences, and the danger of conjugal routine. In the epilogue Böll scrutinizes the increase in Heinrich's wealth and the growth of his inheritance since his marriage. He details the disposition of the business of Heinrich's father, refers to Austria's political relations with Russia and Prussia, and comments on the sexless relationship of the wise old Risach with Mathilde, Natalie's mother.

To summarize the lives of several characters in a few pages and to continue Stifter's form of first-person narration, Böll employs in the epilogue a unique temporal structure whose time span is a mere thirty minutes. In this short period before the beginning of his twelfth wedding anniversary, Heinrich recollects events since his marriage. The first section of the thirty-minute epilogue covers eighteen minutes of revery as Heinrich surveys his own life and the lives of his children, his wife, and his friends. The second section relates the actual remaining twelve minutes immediately before the anniversary festivities, when Heinrich visits the greenhouse to see once again the blooming *cereus peruvianus* and there becomes involved in a spontaneous adulterous relationship with the gardener's grandchild, ironically named Natalie after his wife. The epilogue concludes with Heinrich returning to his family on the balcony to observe the fireworks opening the celebration.

The epilogue has several levels of parody. Heinrich's flashback of his past twelve years has its parallel in the novel in Risach's flashback account of his sad courtship with Natalie's mother. But whereas Risach's reminiscence serves as a lecture to Heinrich on the wisdom of patience, moderation, self-control, and submissiveness to parents, Heinrich's flashback serves merely to reveal his snobbishness, social ambition, and careerism. The parody continues with reference to Natalie's superstitious attachment to the number twelve which Böll uses as a leitmotif in the epilogue (her six children born at regular two-year intervals, their twelfth anniversary, and Heinrich's unfaithfulness twelve minutes before the beginning of the anniversary celebration). But most effective in the parody is Böll's use of language: an accurate imitation of Stifter's style, diction, tone, and sentence structure, varied with crass modernisms and up-to-date expressions (*Präzision, Experimenten, Praxis, das Fleischliche, Sensibilitätssystem*) to suggest the change in Heinrich's character.

For example, in the opening paragraph Böll indicates Heinrich's snobbishness and class attitude with his use of the word *Gesinde* when referring to the servants, an expression which evokes in the reader the diminutive form *Gesindel,* meaning rabble. Stifter himself never uses the word *Gesinde*; instead the servants are referred to as *Diener* (servants), *Mägde* (maids), or by their occupation: *Hausverwalter* (stewarts), *Gärtner* (gardeners), or most often by name. In the household of Heinrich's father the servants even eat with the family and the employees in the father's business share the same food and wine as the family. The tone of Heinrich's epilogue indicates that he no longer follows this democratic practice. Although Heinrich's father was a successful and wealthy businessman, it was clear in the novel that he spent many hours at work. Heinrich, however, never had to work because of his inheritance; he was granted the leisure to pursue the educational ideal of "free development" (*"freie Entfaltung"*). It is this "ideal" education made possible by the labor of others that Böll puts in question. With his vast knowledge of science and art, Heinrich has become a cartographer, appropriately an artist-scientist, but not a person who uses his skills and insights to increase man's knowledge of the earth; his expertise is put at the disposal of the Kaiser's army. The free unfolding of his talents which was to satisfy his growing intellect and lead naturally to service of society bestows no benefit on mankind. Heinrich makes this adjustment in his educational goal in order to rise socially, to satisfy his egotism, and to acquire aristocratic advantage. As cartographer on the general staff for military planning, he receives an appointment to colonel, is raised to the nobility, and is eventually promoted to general. The tenor of the epilogue in the section which records these events is no longer in the language of Stifter, but that of Böll's **"Bonn Diary" ("Hauptstädtisches Journal,"** 1957) in which the militarist Machorka-Muff recounts his political maneuvers and sexual conquests in his advancement to general. Furthermore, Heinrich's desire to enter the nobility recalls Böll's early story of another Austrian family, the exploiting Baleks ("**The Balek Scales,**" 1951), who, indeed, treat their social inferiors as *Gesindel* and who, like Heinrich, are favored with aristocratic franchisement because of their wealth and loyal support of a feudal system.

The key sentence in Böll's satire is Heinrich's conclusion that: "The main subject of my interests and research [will be to investigate] the limits, the domains and the border transgressions between art and artificiality (Kunst and Künstlichkeit), or to express it more practically [to investigate] the possibilities of the artifice (Möglichkeiten der Verkünstlichung)." "The possibilities of artifice" is the theme of the satire. Böll's epilogue shows the magnificent world of Stifter to be "artificial" and deceptive. In their Indian summer old Risach and Mathilde have "raised [their lives] above the sexual (*Fleischliche*) and the passionate"; their lives now proceed with such "precision" that the narrator compares them to figures in a clockworks; they have ceased to be people and have become "automatons." Heinrich's marriage has fared even worse than the arid union of Risach and Mathilde. In the final chapter of the novel Stifter recounts Heinrich and Natalie's wedding day and their visit to the greenhouse to see the rare bloom of the *cereus peruvianus*. In the epilogue Böll has Heinrich go to the greenhouse alone to see the exquisite cactus and there witness the false Natalie plucking the flower before their spontaneous liaison. Thus, on returning to the house Heinrich can only offer his wife an expensive, artificial porcelain replica of the symbol of their marriage. When he says, "Between my dear wife and me there was no visible disharmony," the emphasis falls on the word visible. The disharmony is there. The marriage has become like the porcelain *cereus peruvianus,* an imitation cased in gold.

Heinrich's life, too, has become an artifice, a perversion of what it was intended to be—a model of human intellectual development which strove first to fulfill itself and thereby serve society. Heinrich's father argues in the novel against the concept that man must first strive to be useful to others: "Man is not on earth for the sake of society, but for his own sake. And when each person lives the best way he can for himself, then he lives also for society." Böll's epilogue shows how easy it is to deceive one's self, how almost inevitable it is that a person reared in the philosophy of Heinrich's father, a person educated as Heinrich has been, educated to follow his inclinations (*Neigungen*) in the belief that the fulfillment of self will *automatically* benefit society, will turn out as Heinrich does in the epilogue. Böll's satire reveals how a person educated to pursue all of his intellectual pleasures is likely to become a person who lives selfishly. Heinrich has become in Böll's epilogue what he should not have become according to Stifter's bourgeois theory of liberal education. He has become an adulterer, not a faithful husband; a snob, elitist, and aristocrat, not a benefactor of society; a deceiver of self and others, not an honest man; a self-satisfied egotist, not a modest person. Böll's epilogue in its ironic, satirical manner challenges the premise of Stifter's dream that underlies the novel. It is Böll's reeval-

uation of Stifter as a model for a humane society. The epilogue indicates that Stifter's *Humanitätsideal* has in it the basis of its opposite: *Inhumanitätsgesellschaft.*

Der Nachsommer was intended by Stifter as a model fulfillment of his *"sanftes Gesetz,"* which he defines in the "Vorrede" to *Bunte Steine* as "the law of justice, the law of morality, the law which would that every person be respected and honored, that he stand next to his neighbor without fear, that he be able to pursue his highest human career, that he win the love and admiration of his fellow man, that he be treated as a precious stone, for every man is a precious stone for all other men." Stifter explains further where this "gentle law" most clearly manifests itself: "It lies in the love of spouses for each other . . . in the work which sustains us, [and] in the activity which one does for his circle, for the future, and for mankind . . ."

Böll's epilogue does not question the goal of Stifter's *"sanftes Gesetz."* It only questions whether the goal is, indeed, realizable according to the conditions presented in *Der Nachsommer.* Böll's epilogue exposes with satiric and ironic means how Heinrich has failed in those spheres of life in which Stifter's ideal of the *"sanftes Gesetz"* was to reveal itself best: in family, work, and society.

Yvonne Holbeche (essay date 1981)

SOURCE: "The Rhenish Foxes: An Approach to Heinrich Boll's *Ende einer Dienstfahrt,*" in *German Life & Letters,* Vol. XXXIV, No. 4, July, 1981, pp. 409-14.

[*In the following essay, Holbeche examines Böll's interpretation of the relationship between "the artist as social critic and the state" as evinced in his* Ende einer Dienstfahrt.]

Like so many of Böll's works, *Ende einer Dienstfahrt* has sharply divided critical opinion. For some, mostly Eastern European critics, the Gruhls' 'happening' is an act of resistance against the West German state, and Birglar society a refuge of those humanistic values which are lacking on higher social and political levels. Some Western critics on the other hand have claimed that in presenting their action as a purely aesthetic one the Gruhls render it quite harmless—as Manfred Durzak has put it [in *Der deutsche Roman der Gegenwart,* 1979]: 'Statt Aufsprengung der Sinnlosigkeit steht am Ende Verharmlosung durch Verniedlichung der moralisch gemeinten Tat als Kunstwerk'—and have also found the village idyll too utopian to be credible as a microcosm of contemporary society. This striking divergence of views reflects not only the different ideological assumptions of the two groups, but also, more importantly, the fundamental ambiguity and 'hintergründige Ironie' of the novel itself, which have on the whole not been sufficiently recognized by critics. In fact only one of those cited, Hans Joachim Bernhard, appears to appreciate that Böll is not, despite his own comments, expressing a straightforward 'Aufforderung zur Aktion', but exploring both the possibilities and the limitations, or, to use Bernhard's terms, the 'Macht und Ohnmacht' of art as a form of social and political protest, and that the Gruhls' apparent 'Verharmlosung' or 'Verniedlichung' of their action is a manifestation of the cunning of what are essentially 'Schelm' figures who are as concerned with self-preservation as they are with exposing the mechanisms of the state and its bureaucracy [*Die Romane Heinrich Bölls,* 1970].

As far as the small-town setting is concerned, it has not generally been realised that its idyllic, 'humanistic' features are seriously undermined, indeed shown to be naive and ineffectual, by the numerous indications that the state is deliberately exploiting these elements from behind the scenes for its own political purposes, specifically to prevent the Gruhls' action from arousing wider public interest. The emphasis placed by critics on the charming social foreground has led not only to an underestimation of the role of the state but also to a failure to comprehend its essential nature in the novel. For the state is just as much a 'Schelm' or trickster as the Gruhls themselves—in fact there are several important hints that its most powerful representatives are to be viewed as modern variants of one of the classic rogues of European literature, Reynard the Fox, most notably Prosecutor Kugl-Egger's exasperated reference to his superiors as 'diese[n] rheinischen Füchse[n]'. As this article aims to show, it is only in the light of the parallelism between what are in essence two opposing groups of Rhenish foxes—a parallelism that is reflected in Frau Stollfuss's ambiguous allusion to 'diese Füchse' when she, like her husband, realises what both the Gruhls and the state are up to—that Böll's central concern in the work, the problematic relationship of the artist as social critic and the state, can be fully understood.

Böll provides some useful, though by no means altogether reliable clues to this relationship in his 'Einführung in "Dienstfahrt"', where he neatly, if rather ironically, summarizes the ambiguous position of the artist vis-à-vis society in general and the state in particular (hinted at by the metaphor of the 'Irrenhausdirektor'). On the one hand, Böll suggests, society's bland and genial reception of art amounts to the artist's relegation to a kind of padded cell where he is at best humoured. At the same time, the realisation, prompted by public response to the 'Provos' in Amsterdam and to 'happenings' generally, that all forms of art are taken seriously by society led him to the conclusion that society may be tricked by an art which is on the surface innocuous but in reality serious social criticism into accepting its subversive kernel, so that, as a result, 'Kunst, also auch Happening, eine, vielleicht die letzte Möglichkeit sei, die Gummizelle durch eine Zeitzünderbombe zu sprengen oder den Irrenhausdirektor durch eine vergiftete Praline ausser Gefecht zu setzen'. In this way the resourceful artist can perhaps break out of his 'padded cell' and even have some political impact on the state itself.

The central incident of ***Ende einer Dienstfahrt,*** the burning of an army jeep, represents just such a combination of time bomb and 'vergiftete Praline'. The most noteworthy aspect of this incident, which is in fact an act of sabotage, is that it is staged as a multi-faceted work of art by the Gruhls. And indeed, at the subsequent trial (reminiscent of the 'Gerichtstag' in the Reynard tradition), whose proceedings constitute the body of the work, the Gruhls' action, in the course of which they had sung a litany and beaten out a rhythm with their pipes, '"seelenruhig" und "mit offensichtlicher Genugtuung"', is described by a professor of art, Büren, as a 'Kunstwerk' embodying five dimensions: 'die Dimension der Architektur, der Plastik, der Literatur, der Musik . . . und schliesslich tänzerische Elemente, wie sie seines Erachtens im Gegeneinanderschlagen der Tabakpfeifen zum Ausdruck gekommen seien'. The testimony of the waggish Büren, who delights in stressing his status as a 'Beamter', puts the official seal of approval on the Gruhls' own presentation of their action as a happening, rather than a political protest. This act of trickery on their part enables them to protest with relative impunity against what they perceive as the wastefulness of an absurd military system and the society of which it is symptomatic, and to expose it to ridicule.

The exposure is achieved not by the burning of the jeep itself, which is incomprehensible to most of those who witness or hear about it, but by the ensuing trial, which has no doubt been anticipated by the Gruhls and which they seem to regard as a continuation of the happening itself, as their behaviour in court suggests—for example, their constant amusement at the proceedings and the evidence given, made possible by their apparent indifference to the outcome of the trial. It is characteristic of their cunning that they remain by and large reticent, particularly about the motives behind the happening. It is left to the witnesses to draw the social, legal and political implications of their action and in the course of so doing, in keeping with the spirit of the Reynard satire, to provide a damning indictment of a whole range of abuses in contemporary West German society. This is all the more telling since it emerges particularly from the testimony of a number of so-called experts in their respective fields, even though some of them clearly present their evidence tongue-in-check.

For the older Gruhl the incident is the culmination of a lifelong opposition to militarism and state bureaucracy going back to his period of service with the army in France during the Second World War, where he saw action on the 'Möbelfront', as he describes it, restoring antique furniture for German officers. The incidents which are reported from this period reveal the same guile and healthy sense of self-preservation as are manifested in the happening and its aftermath. This is exemplified especially by his denial of any political motivation following his arrest for clandestine activities on behalf of the French resistance and his claim that he had acted merely out of friendship for his acquaintance Heribault. The same attitude also comes out at a later stage when he falls victim to what another subversive figure, the tax-expert Grähn, calls the merciless tax system, for which, as an independent craftsman, Gruhl is a ridiculous anachronism. In order to survive he displays considerable cunning in evading taxation and escaping the clutches of the bailiff and thus outwitting the state bureaucracy, whose relationship to the individual citizen is described by Grähn and the bailiff, Hall, in terms of the metaphor of the hunter and his prey, which is clearly an elaboration of the underlying allusion to the state as a Reynard figure, an elaboration which in this case hints at the more brutal and rapacious aspects of Reynard's behaviour.

The younger Gruhl's motivation in staging the happening can be found in an alarmingly similar experience to that of his father in the army (a point that Böll is at pains to stress in order to attack postwar West German rearmament by implying a fatal continuity of the German military tradition). *His* artistic skills were also exploited during his period of military service when he had been obliged to make bar-fittings for the officers' mess. However, whereas his father had been prepared to exploit the corruption of the officer corps for his own benefit by subtly blackmailing his superior into giving him promotion, the son had suffered intensely under the weight of the tedium and wastefulness of military life, which had come to a head for him in the absurd 'Dienstfahrt' of the title. Indeed, it is his awareness of the favouring of unproductivity over creativity, the contrast between the senselessness and emptiness of the military routine and the parlous financial situation of his highly talented and industrious father, the feeling of impotence in the face of the military and bureaucratic machine, which result in the display of anarchism revealed in the jeep-burning incident of which the son is the instigator and in which the father is a willing collaborator.

The Gruhls' insistence on the purely aesthetic quality of their act of protest provides them with a kind of 'Narrenfreiheit'. At the same time, however, it has decided disadvantages. The artistic form which their action assumes plays into the hands of the state which, while clearly recognizing its subversive potential, cunningly defuses the issue in a number of ways: by charging the Gruhls not with sabotage but merely with 'grober Unfug' and 'Sachbeschädigung', by having the army forgo its jurisdiction over the son on the basis of a technicality, by having the Gruhls brought to trial before an elderly judge, Stollfuss, who is renowned for his light sentences, by holding the trial in the provincial setting of the Gruhls' home town, Birglar, where sympathies run strongly in their favour, and by exerting pressure on the press not to give the affair publicity.

Through Judge Stollfuss, who is only too willing to accept the Gruhls' aesthetic interpretation of their protest, the state is able to absorb their criticism and ensure that its significance does not become apparent beyond a small clique of Birglar initiates who know how to read the work of art as an act of protest. The judgement which Stollfuss hands down at the end of the day's proceedings reflects the ambiguity and the irony which lie at the heart of the work, for while it represents in some respects a victory for the Gruhls, the outcome is really an even more satisfactory one for the state. On the one hand the sentence of six weeks' imprisonment which the Gruhls receive does not amount to any real punishment, particularly as it has in fact already been served during their 'Untersuchungshaft'.

Indeed, so idyllic was their period in custody that it could well be seen as a reward. On the other hand, however, the leniency of the sentence, which has been so cleverly engineered by the state, virtually rules out the possibility of the incident having further judicial repercussions or attracting wider publicity. The game of wits between the subversive artist and the state thus ends in a kind of stalemate—primarily because the state does not prove gullible like the King in the Reynard tradition but shows itself to be in every way as skilful a trickster as its opponents.

The state's trickery has of course been just as fraught with danger as that of the Gruhls. The strategy adopted by its more highly placed representatives who are the real manipulators of the trial, President Grellber and an unidentified parliamentarian, of remaining behind the scenes and exercising their power by proxy, notably through Judge Stollfuss, places the political interests of the state in the hands of a man who proves in his own way to be just as much a rebel as the Gruhls themselves. Although not officially initiated into Grellber's strategy, Stollfuss realises the role he is intended to play in the trial after hearing his wife's reports of her telephone conversations with her superior. During the proceedings he does of course in some respects serve the interests of the state, for example, by defending its right to insist on a closed court for the hearing of the military witnesses. At the same time, however, he reveals considerable independence of spirit, for instance, in his defence of the witness Horn, whose description of Gruhl's relations with the taxation office—'er befand sich im natürlichen Zustand der Notwehr'—is rejected as outrageous by the state prosecutor. More importantly, in his summing-up in this, his final case, Stollfuss steps completely out of his role of judge (symbolised by his removal of his cap) and dispenses advice to the Gruhls (advice they of course hardly need) which, coming from a public official, can only be regarded as subversive, in the sense that he seems to be advocating the behaviour of a Reynard as the only appropriate strategy in present-day society:

> . . . sie sollten sich unabhängig vom Staat machen, indem sie ihm—das betreffe die Steuerschuld des Angeklagten Gruhl sen.—gar keine Möglichkeit gäben, sie in ihrer Freiheit einzuschränken, und sie sollten, wenn sie diesen Tribut entrichteten, schlau wie die Füchse sein, denn es sei hier von einem Wissenschaftler, der als kompetente Kapazität gelte, die Gnadenund Erbarmungslosigkeit des Wirtschaftsprozesses geradezu bescheinigt worden, und einer gnadenlosen, erbarmungslosen Gesellschaft dürfe man nicht ungewappnet entgegentreten.

Like the Gruhls' protest, however, this act of rebellion on the part of Stollfuss is qualified by the fact that it is witnessed by only a handful of people and is thus hardly likely to undermine the state. Indeed, Böll subsequently draws attention again to the sinister power of the state in the second last episode of the novel by having Bergnolte, Grellber's observer at the trial, report in person to his superior, who notes the names of certain witnesses for further investigation. The power of the state, although nowhere else as explicit as in this particular incident, is in fact a constant presence throughout the work and provides a threatening backdrop to the trial, making it clear that the humanitarianism of the village has little bearing on the political decisions which determine the inhabitants' lives and is no more than a cosy facade which can easily obscure the realities of genuine political power and manipulation.

In the conflict between the state and that form of art which calls the state and its institutions into question, it is the state that has the last word. While the Gruhls achieve a substantial moral victory, enjoying the satisfaction of having taken on a much more powerful opponent in the state, of having exposed its essential nature and having forced it on to the defensive, the state is ultimately able to control and limit their protest. In a sense the Gruhls have emerged from the 'Gummizelle' of art, since they have clearly shown that art can pose a threat to the political interests of the establishment. At the same time, however, it is precisely the aesthetic nature of their protest which enables the state to deal with it so effectively and which thus prevents it from having any lasting consequences—there is certainly no question of it putting the 'Irrenhausdirektor' out of action, in other words, of subverting the state, which, though demonstrated to be hopelessly inadequate in other important respects, is eminently adept at preserving its own power.

The novel is thus considerably more sceptical and, one is tempted to say, more realistic than Böll's comments on the function of art in the 'Einführung in "Dienstfahrt"', which, in view of this, are perhaps best interpreted not as a description of his original intention but as a retrospective correction of the 'Verharmlosung' of the work by its first critics.

William S. Sewell (essay date 1982)

SOURCE: "'Konduktion and Niveauunterschiede': The Structure of Böll's *Katharina Blum,*" in *Monatshefte,* Vol. 74, No. 2, Summer, 1982, pp. 167-78.

[*In the following essay, Sewell analyzes the form of Böll's novella* Die verlorene Ehre der Katharina Blum, *describing it as "a structure which threatens to slip into chaos, but paradoxically does not."*]

If critics have by and large directed their energies towards the content of Böll's work, they have been seduced into doing so, as Rainer Nägele points out [in *Heinrich Böll: Einführung in das Werk und die Forschung,* 1976], by the very nature of the work itself:

> Es liegt allerdings zum Teil an Bölls Werk selbst, wenn das Interesse an formalen Aspekten oft in den Hintergrund getreten ist; denn im Gegensatz etwa zur experimentellen Literatur bleibt das Formale bei Böll eher unauffällig, während das emotionale Engagement sich viel deutlicher aufdrängt.

In the case of the "Erzählung" *Die verlorene Ehre der Katharina Blum* there is no doubt that the "emotional commitment" does clamor for the immediate attention of the critic, intimately connected as it appears to be not only with Böll's own treatment at the hands of the Springer press after his intercession on behalf of Ulrike Meinhof, but also—as he himself has insisted—with the "Rufmord" of other individuals, specifically Professor Peter Brückner of Hannover. Accordingly, in the limited body of secondary literature which is concerned with *Katharina Blum,* the emphasis has been on the social and moral questions raised by the work. [In *Heinrich Böll: Einführung in das Werk und in die Forschung,* edited by Hanno Beth, 1975], Hanno Beth, for example, analyzes the portrayal of the fomentation of violence by the "Boulevardpresse" and is able to sum up the latter's methods in Plutarch's maxim: "Audacter calumniare, semper aliquid haeret." [In *The Writer and Society: Studies in the Fiction of Günter Grass and Heinrich Böll,* 1976] Charlotte W. Ghurye brings to the fore the dimension of "social prejudice against women in a male dominated society." [In *Böll: Untersuchungen zum Werk,* edited by Manfred Jurgenson, 1975], Günther Wirth takes the very self-evident step from the private violence endured and meted out in the "Erzählung" to "jener Gewalt in der kapitalistischen Gesellschaft, die von den Banktresoren und den Zentralen der psychologischen Kriegsführung ausgeht." [And in *Heinrich Böll,* 1978] Jochen Vogt discerns in this story a variation of Böll's continuing pre-occupation with the "gestörte Idylle," where the destructive power of "die unfaßbare Schicksalsmacht Krieg" in earlier works is replaced by "der gesellschaftlich konkretisierte Mechanismus *struktureller Gewalt* in Form des Sensationsjournalismus."

Despite the critical emphasis on the themes of *Katharina Blum,* however, there has been a useful discussion of the language employed by Böll: with its marked contrast between the sensitive precision of Katharina's insistence on a word such as "gütig" and the harsh vernacular of the police and the "ZEITUNG," the language is said to show the all-pervading nature of "strukturelle Gewalt." This was pointed out in an early review by Dorothee Sölle [in *Merkur,* 1974], who highlighted two levels of language in the "Erzählung"—"Vulgäre, lange Zeit nicht literaturfähige Sprache" and "vergessene, traditionelle Sprache"—and claimed that "dem Verlust an Ehre für das Individuum entspricht der Verlust an Sprache für die Gesellschaft." More recently, Sölle's argument appears to have been echoed by Rainer Nägele, who considered that the work "thematisiert ausdrücklich die Sprache in ihren dystopischen und utopischen Aspekten, dargestellt in der Konfrontation von journalistischer Sprachmanipulation und der Sprachsensitivität der Heldin."

Less attention has been devoted, on the other hand, to Böll's very conscious attempt to provide a comprehensive structure by means of introducing an "intentionale Erzählhaltung," i.e., a narrative perspective which reflects the very act of narration. Yet it is evident that the structure plays as important a role in underpinning the work's thematic substance as does the language, for it too reflects a contrast: between the desire of the narrator to bring the story to a satisfactory conclusion and the awareness that Katharina's act is, at the most, of individual significance and ultimately futile. The result is a structure which threatens to slip into chaos, but paradoxically does not. The narrative structure has been cursorily examined by Rolf Michaelis, who in an otherwise positive review [in *Die Zeit,* 1972] decried the "Ubermaß an Konstruktion" and the "kokette Struktur, spielerische Verschachtelung, zwinkernde Röck- und Vorblenden," and by Zipes [in *New German Critique,* 1977], who concludes that the narrator's "scruple about finding the right word to describe the process for putting together his data, and his admission that he might not be able to bring everything together are signs of openness which allow us as readers to share in his discoveries with a critical eye." But only Manfred Durzak has paid any detailed attention to the question of narrative perspective.

In two articles Durzak compares *Katharina Blum* with Böll's earlier novel *Gruppenbild mit Dame* (1971). In the first [which was published in *Die subversive Madonna: Ein Schlüssel zum Werk Bölls,* edited by Renata Matthaei, 1975], concerned with the political significance of both works, the private protests of the central protagonists are criticized as being no more than "eine subjektive momentane Befreiung"; in the second, entitled "Entfaltung oder Reduktion des Erzählers? Vom 'Verf.' des *Gruppenbildes* zum Berichterstatter der *Katharina Blum,*" Durzak investigates the role of the narrator. If a principal characteristic of contemporary German narrative prose is the author's allowing or compelling the reader to assemble the work for himself from a number of disparate parts, then *Katharina Blum* and *Gruppenbild* seem to reflect epic traditions of the past. For in these two works the reader is guided from beginning to end by a narrator whose personality and attitude are articulated to a greater or lesser degree. There is little to add to Durzak's characterization of the narrator in *Katharina Blum,* but certain factors will be summarized here, since they form a useful basis for the discussion which follows. First, he maintains that the narrator is to a great extent an "abstraktes Konstruktionsvehikel," functioning as a "Personen-Maske des realen Erzählers, der sich dahinter verbirgt," by which one assumes he is referring to the author himself; at any rate, the contours of the narrator's personality are not so clearly defined as in *Gruppenbild.* Secondly, Durzak speculates—rather wildly—as to the identity of the narrator, ranging from the reasonable assumption that he is "als Person in der Umgebung des Rechtsanwaltes Blorna und des Staatsanwaltes Hach zu suchen" to the supposition that he is "ein juristisch gebildeter Journalist," for which there is no evidence. Thirdly, the narrator is said to be "allwissend," which is true to the extent that, unlike the "Verf." in *Gruppenbild,* the former is aware of the outcome of the events from the beginning of his narrative; but it must also be emphasized that the narrator in *Katharina Blum* knows only as much as his sources have revealed and is therefore reduced to an "eingeschränkte Erzählposition." Finally, Durzak points out the important fact that the narrator is at pains to produce an "erzählerisch effektvolle Aufbereitung des Stoffes," particularly in the extended metaphor of "Dränage oder Trockenlegung," but is unable in view of the facts to bring about an "epische Harmonisierung." Despite these instructive observations, however, Durzak omits to give a thorough demonstration of the formal

mechanisms by which the narrator/author organizes his material, and it is to this end that my study is specifically directed.

The major structural element in the "Erzählung" is that ostensibly devised and developed by the narrator. It is a structure of some transparency, the existence of which is brought about through the narrator's desire to impose an aesthetic harmony on facts and events which essentially cannot be harmonized. Throughout the work there are strong indications that the narrator has such artistic pretensions, and reflections of this kind are often intimately connected with the extended image chosen by the narrator to embody the structure. This image derives from the literal meaning of the terms "Quellen" and "Nebenquellen," which are introduced, naturally enough, in the first chapter, where the narrator names his sources. The discovery is made that the associations arising from these terms afford an appropriate metaphor for describing the shape of the narrative, which is frequently "fließend" in nature. The second chapter is therefore devoted to an exposition of this metaphor, which reads:

> Wenn der Bericht—da hier soviel von Quellen geredet wird—hin und wieder als "fließend" empfunden wird, so wird dafür um Verzeihung gebeten: es war unvermidlich. Angesichts von "Quellen" und "Fließen" kann man nicht von Komposition sprechen, so sollte man vielleicht statt dessen den Begriff der Zusammenführung (als Fremdwort dafür wird Konduktion vorgeschlagen) einführen, und dieser Begriff sollte jedem einleuchten, der je als Kind (oder gar Erwachsener) in, an und *mit* Pfützen gespielt hat, die er anzapfte, durch Kanäle miteinander verband, leerte, ablenkte, umlenkte, bis er schließlich das gesamte, ihm zur Verfügung stehende Pfützenwasserpotential in einem Sammelkanal *zusammenführte,* um es auf ein niedrigeres Niveau ab-, möglicherweise gar ordnungsgemäß oder ordentlich, regelrecht in eine behördlicherseits erstellte Abflußrinne oder in einen Kanal zu lenken. Es wird also nichts weiter vorgenommen als eine Art Dränage oder Trockenlegung. Ein ausgesprochener Ordnungsvorgang! Wenn also diese Erzählung stellenweise in Fluß kommt, wobei Niveauunterschiede und -ausgleiche eine Rolle spielen, so wird um Nachsicht gebeten, denn schließlich gibt es auch Stockungen, Stauungen, Versandungen, mißglückte Konduktionen und Quellen, die "zusammen nicht kommen können," ausserdem unterirdische Strömungen usw. usw.

The rationale behind this extended metaphor is that the events in *Katharina Blum* cannot be reproduced in a neat, consecutive fashion; instead, because the narrator is confronted with a multiplicity of disparate sources, he is of the opinion that it is preferable to communicate each body of information with regard to its respective internal connections, rather than to strict chronological order. Each item of information may be considered a tiny "Pfütze," which is collected with other related "Pfützen" in a larger "Pfütze," until a particular area has been exhausted or "drained," at which point the combined volume of information is stored, while the process is resumed elsewhere. Eventually, each body of information is released into the "Sammelkanal," which corresponds to the principal direction of the narrative. However, by marking carefully the points at which material is stored or released, the narrator is able to maintain considerable control over the time, which, far from lapsing into chaos, reveals in fact a clear symmetrical pattern. It can thus be seen that a major function of the extended metaphor is to provide an alternative time sequence. Two other, less critical functions are also indicated: in the term "Niveauunterschiede" there is an aesthetic as well as a temporal dimension; and "unterirdische Strömungen" signifies the hidden connections between one item or body of information and another, which in this context assume a social dimension. Finally, it should be noted that this "drainage" metaphor is also an oblique expression of the narrator's distaste for much of the material he is handling: he literally wishes to "flush it away."

As far as the temporal function of the metaphor is concerned, its most important facet is contained in the word "Stauungen," for it is with this term in particular that the narrator maintains the apparatus outlined in Chapter two through the course of the "Erzählung." In order to appreciate how this operates, it is necessary to divide the work into a number of independent sections—seven in all—over and above the division into chapters:

1. The first section (Chapters 1-3) is purely introductory in nature, giving the sources, the structural logic and also, in a skeleton form, the bare facts of the case: "Das sind also die Fakten." Although it represents the narrative present, it is clearly removed from the time-scheme of the rest of the "Erzählung" and requires no further discussion here.

2. Chapters 4-7 represent a "Vorblende" or anticipation of events after the shooting of the journalist Tötges: the discovery of the photographer Schönner's body on Ash Wednesday, the funerals of Tötges and Schönner. This "Vorgriff" is motivated by the desire to exclude Katharina from the outset from any involvement with the photographer's murder, which occurs in a purely coincidental fashion.

3. With this section (Chapters 8-23), a chronological order is followed from the Wednesday afternoon (20 February 1974), through the events of the next day—Götten's escape from Katharina's apartment, her interrogation by the police—to a sudden switch of location and "acceleration" of time in focussing on the Blornas, from their first full day at the skiing resort (Thursday, 21 February) to their return on Saturday morning (23 February). Such an "acceleration" of time would seem to correspond to the image "in Fluß kommen," for by concentrating on the situation of the Blornas the narrator has to bypass for the present the events occurring on Friday (22 February) in the city. This temporary emphasis on the Blornas represents therefore the collection and release of a certain volume of information, which need not now interfere on a future occasion.

4. However, it does necessitate what the narrator calls a "Rückstau," comprising Chapters 24-37, in order to give full attention to the omitted important events of the Fri-

day: "Hier muß eine Art Rückstau vorgenommen werden, etwas, das man im Film und in der Literatur Rückblende nennt. . . ." The narrator thus extends the metaphor of Chapter two to express the device of the "flashback." But he also makes an apology in Chapter 25 for having to operate with such "Stauungen":

> Gewisse Stauungen, die man auch Spannungen nennen kann, sind ja unvermeidlich, weil nicht alle Quellen mit einem Griff und auf einmal um- und abgelenkt werden können, so daß das trockengelegte Gelände sofort sichtbar wird.

Indeed, he even introduces in the same chapter—which concerns Katharina's intimate telephone conversation with Götten—the term "Nebenpfützenstau," thus establishing further the extreme complexity of the task before him. Since much occurs on the Friday, this "Rückstau" is a lengthy one, the end of which is delayed on two occasions. Already at the opening of Chapter 34 we find the statement: "Hier sollte erkannt werden, dass der erste Rückstau fast beendet ist, man vom Freitage wieder zum Samstag gelangt. Es wird alles getan werden, weitere Stauungen, auch überflüssigen Spannungsstau zu vermeiden." But we are many pages away from its conclusion. Again at the beginning of Chapter 37 the qualification is made: "Bevor der Rückstau endgültig als beendet betrachtet werden . . . kann . . .", and even at the very end the "Rückstau" is abandoned only with reluctance, it seems: "In diesem Augenblick kann der Rückstau für vorläufig beendet erklärt werden. . . ." It is as if the narrator has little confidence in his mastery of the material and is anxious lest he has inadvertently excluded something of importance.

5. Chapters 38-49 return to the orthodox chronological order of my section 3, resuming with the arrival of the Blornas on Saturday morning and proceeding to noon of the following day, when Katharina leaves the journalists' bar "Zur Goldente" for her fateful interview with Tötges. This section does not unravel entirely smoothly, since there is one lengthy chapter devoted to a "technische Zwischenbemerkung" (131), which interrupts the narrative, but does not disturb the time sequence unduly.

6. The sixth section (chapters 50-57) consists of the second "Vorblende," anticipating events after the shooting of Tötges: Blorna's investigations on behalf of Katharina, the subsequent professional difficulties of both Blorna and his wife, and the incident at the opening of Le Boche's exhibition. This "flash-forward" in fact reaches on occasions into the narrative present—for example, in the description of Blorna's physical appearance during the period leading up to Katharina's trial—thus complicating even further the time sequence. However, the unity of this section is not thereby subverted, since it remains a simple "Vorblende" in terms of the overriding movement of the narrative.

7. The anticipation of subsequent events, most of which show the effects of "Gewalt" on the Blornas—and also on Else Woltersheim (Chapter 55)—allows the narrator to

close with Katharina's account of the circumstances of the murder (Chapter 58). It is significant that at this point the narrator abdicates his position entirely, reproducing her account verbatim and neglecting even to add any concluding comments of his own. In terms of the time structure of the "Erzählung," her statement may be regarded as a "Rückstau," even though it is made subsequently to the span of Wednesday to Saturday which comprises the focal point of the work. Concluding the narration as it does, it gives Katharina's plight a certain immediacy and thus elicits the sympathy of the reader for her.

Summarizing these sections briefly, it can be seen that a symmetrical pattern of sorts emerges: the "Erzählung" operates primarily on the time continuum Wednesday 20 February 1974 to Sunday 24 February 1974 (sections 3-5); but at each end of the work we encounter "Vorblenden" (sections 2 and 6) and in the middle a lengthy "Rückstau" (section 6); it is prefaced by an introduction, which stands apart from the time-scheme, and concluded by a "Rückstau" released by a different narrator.

The major structural element in *Katharina Blum* is that ostensibly devised and developed by the narrator. It is a structure of some transparency, the existence of which is brought about through the narrator's desire to impose an aesthetic harmony on facts and events which essentially cannot be harmonized.

—*William S. Sewell*

Although the terms "Niveau" or "Niveauunterschiede" obviously have some bearing on the time structure of *Katharina Blum,* in that the narrator alternates, as we have just witnessed, between differing levels of time, they tend to be employed instead as a reflection of the narrator's aesthetic pretensions. As early as Chapter three this function of the terms is indicated, where the narrator attempts to distance himself from the portrayal of murder in the popular media, and here the use of "Niveauunterschiede" quite clearly has nothing whatever to do with time:

> Es soll hier nicht so viel von Blut gesprochen werden, denn nur *notwendige* Niveauunterschiede sollen als unvermeidlich gelten, und deshalb wird hiermit aufs Fernsehen und aufs Kino verwiesen, auf Grusi- und Musicals einschlägiger Art; wenn hier etwas fließen soll, dann nicht Blut.

This statement stands by no means in isolation: it is echoed on at least three other occasions in the course of the "Erzählung." At the beginning of Chapter seven, for example, we find: "Gehen wir von diesem äußerst niedrigen

Niveau sofort wieder auf höhere Ebenen. Weg mit dem Blut"; in Chapter 39: "Es soll hier . . . möglichst wenig Blut fließen . . ."; and finally, in Chapter 51, the narrator excuses himself from reporting what the "ZEITUNG" prints after the murder:

> Das soll hier nicht alles erwähnt oder zitiert werden. Gewisse Niveauverletzungen oder -verlassungen sollen nur dann vorgenommen werden, wenn sie notwendig sind, und hier sind sie nicht notwendig, weil man ja inzwischen die ZEITUNG wohl kennt.

The other significant aesthetic utterance of the narrator is revealed in Chapter 41, the "technische Zwischenbemerkung," in which he complains bitterly about the difficulty of assembling the material in a satisfying fashion. For one thing: "In dieser Geschichte passiert zu viel. Sie ist auf eine peinliche, kaum zu bewältigende Weise handlungsstark: zu ihrem Nachteil"; and in addition he is troubled by "lauter Dinge und Leute, die einfach nicht synchronisierbar sind und dauernd den Fluß (bzw. den linearen Handlungsablauf) stören. . . ." This would seem to imply that, despite the positive start with the metaphor of "Konduktion," the narrator's confidence in his ability to relate the events as conscientiously as possible is becoming severely shaken; and in the "Zwischenbemerkung" he is showing irritation and at the same time excusing his apparent incompetence. Thus, when in Chapter 57 he makes the apologetic remark:

> Es ist natürlich äußerst bedauerlich, daß hier zum Ende hin so wenig Harmonie mitgeteilt und nur sehr geringe Hoffnung auf solche gemacht werden kann. Nicht Integration, Konfrontation hat sich ergeben.

he is referring not only to the unsatisfactory outcome of the plot, but also to the lack of formal harmony.

Before we leave the metaphor which dominates the structure of *Katharina Blum,* the question of the "unterirdische Strömungen" must be resolved. There is no doubt that it is these which are partly responsible for the narrator's structural difficulties: those hidden connections within society which render his task that much more complex. He comments in the "technische Zwischenbemerkung": "Nun, es geschieht so vieles im Vordergrund—mehr noch im Hintergrund." Then he proceeds to give the example of the "ZEITUNG'S" close links with Sträubleder's business associate, Lüding, links confirmed earlier in Sträubleder's first interview with Blorna, in which the former claims: "Alles, was wir wissen, wissen wir von der ZEITUNG, zu der Lüding zum Glück gute Beziehungen hat." Another, perhaps more sinister, hidden connection is that which exists between the "ZEITUNG" and the police. The first evidence for this is provided when Katharina is escorted back to her apartment by Moeding, after her interrogation on Thursday, and he advises her: "Lassen Sie die Finger vom Telefon und schlagen Sie morgen keine Zeitung auf," indicating that certain details have already been leaked to the press. This link is corroborated when Beizmenne admits that certain particulars of his investigation—such as the fact that Else Woltersheim's mother resides voluntarily in the GDR—he owes to the reporters of the "ZEITUNG," the publishing house belonging to it and "mit diesem Haus verbundene Organe,"

> die nun einmal lockere und nicht immer konventionelle Methoden hätten, Einzelheiten zu erfahren, die amtlichen Rechercheuren verborgen blieben.

A clandestine arrangement of mutual benefit to the police and the "ZEITUNG" is thus clearly suggested. From these two examples it can be perceived that the "unterirdische Strömungen" represent an attempt on the part of the narrator/author to extend the field of "Gewalt" beyond the private sphere, by revealing the complicity of social institutions and commerce. However, the widening of scope in this manner is not developed sufficiently to be fully convincing, since by concentrating largely on a single case Böll is operating in his usual fashion, as Zipes comments, with a "moralist and individualistic approach"; consequently, "the origins of violence become too personalized for us to gain a clear picture of the power relationships of the political reality in the Bundesrepublik."

Notwithstanding the dominance of the extended metaphor introduced in Chapter two, there are three other structural links in the "Erzählung" which should not be overlooked. These are not explicitly inserted by the narrator in asides to the reader, but arise from the actual plot of the "Erzählung," over which the narrator has less control, although he is of course at liberty to arrange and include or discard its components as he sees fit. Such links represent the author's attempt to reinforce in a rather more subtle manner the overt linking mechanism devised by the narrator. The first example appears in two particular instances of the wounding of Katharina's "Sprachsensitivität," each occurring at critical junctures in the story. After the police under Kommissar Beizmenne storm Katharina's apartment on the morning of Thursday, February 21st, Beizmenne is rumored to have asked Katharina, with reference to the wanted Ludwig Götten: "Hat er dich denn gefickt?" Her reaction is to blush and reply proudly: "Nein, ich würde es nicht so nennen." For the narrator this exchange is of crucial importance, since it establishes from the outset the very tense relationship between the policeman and Katharina, who is said to be "in sexuellen Dingen äußerst empfindlich, fast prüde." It is possible that this initial encounter produces an antagonistic attitude in Katharina, thus setting off the chain of reaction which results in her shooting of the journalist Tötges. For the episode early in the "Erzahlung" where Beizmenne offends her sensibility is mirrored at the very end by the crude proposition which Tötges makes to her when he arrives at her apartment for his interview: ". . . ich schlage vor, daß wir jetzt erst einmal bumsen." This is immediately connected in Katharina's mind with the gun in her handbag through the double meaning of "bumsen": ". . . und ich dachte: 'Bumsen, meinetwegen,' und ich hab die Pistole rausgenommen und sofort auf ihn geschossen." Beizmenne has thus unwittingly set in motion a process which ends in murder; and the link is cemented in the synonyms "ficken" and "bumsen."

Another link is to be found in the references to "moderne Malerei," again at early and late points in the narration. This is associated in the first instance with the effect of the blood drawn by the pistol-shots on Tötges's "improvisiertes Scheichkostüm, das aus einem schon recht verschlissenen Bettuch zurechtgeschnitten war . . ." The narrator then makes a comparison between this effect and modern art, the revolver having become a kind of "Spritzpistole." The image here is paralleled in the scene towards the conclusion in which Blorna strikes Sträubleder and the blood from the latter's nose is caught on a piece of blotting-paper by the artist Frederick Le Boche and subsequently dubbed a "One minute piece of art" with the title "Ende einer langjährigen Männerfreundschaft." The function of the link in this example is twofold: first of all to underline the futility of both Blorna's and Katharina's actions; and secondly, to express the fact that the commercial potential of contemporary art tends to minimize its function as a medium of social protest—a state of affairs not without some relevance to *Katharina Blum* itself. For Le Boche donates his "creation" to Blorna, in order to help alleviate the latter's financial embarrassment, to which the narrator adds the ironic comment: "Man sollte an dieser letzterwähnten Tatsache sowie an den eingangs beschriebenen Gewalttätigkeiten erkennen dürfen, duss die Kunst doch noch eine soziale Funktion hat."

The final and perhaps most important set of corresponding events arises from Katharina's relationship with the "ZEITUNG." It differs from the first two examples in that the events occupy a rather more central position in the narrative instead of being confined to early and late stages. After Katharina reads the Friday editions of the "ZEITUNG," she at first restricts her reaction to asking whether it is possible for the state to protect her and restore her "lost honor." Not until the Saturday morning does she retaliate in any way, and this expresses itself in the trivial gesture of stealing the latest edition of the "ZEITUNG". However, the manner in which this incident is related makes it clear that its inclusion is by no means gratuitous: ". . . [sie hat] eine Art Sakrileg begangen, denn sie hat das VERTRAUEN der ZEITUNG mißbraucht, indem sie eine ZEITUNG herausnahm, ohne zu bezahlen!" The capitalization of "Vertrauen" and the exclamation mark indicate the narrator's sympathetic irony; but it would also seem that at this point, in formal terms, the concept "Vertrauen" is to the newspaper what "Ehre" is to Katharina: by abusing their trust, albeit in a very minor way, she restores some measure of her personal integrity. The process does not end here, however, for in the Saturday "ZEITUNG" Katharina discovers that a reporter has gained admittance to her dying mother. But it appears to be not so much this outrage as the insinuation printed in the "SONNTAGS-ZEITUNG" that she is responsible for her mother's death which, as Blorna surmises, drives her to the murder of Tötges. Thus the stealing of the newspaper can be seen as an intermediate stage in Katharina's dealings with the "ZEITUNG," and the implication is that had it not persisted in hounding her, she might have been satisfied with this harmless gesture.

In Durzak's eyes *Katharina Blum* is doubly condemned. As a "politisches Pamphlet" it fails, because it is able to offer no realistic solutions: Katharina's protest is essentially private and does not significantly impair the "Boulevardpresse" or its questionable practices. It also fails because the "auktoriale Überlegenheit," with which the "Erzählung" commences, is forced to capitulate in the face of such a glaring lack of harmony in both the content and the formal construction—to the point, one may add, that the task of narration is relinquished at the end to the main protagonist herself. However, Durzak fails to do justice to both Böll's intentions and to his artistry. It must be asked, for instance, whether realistic solutions can be legitimately expected from the work, not only because the durability of the "ZEITUNG" is underlined in the very plot, but also because of Böll's subsequent comments on the work. Successors to both Tötges—an Eginhard Templer, "der . . . eine Art Fortsetzung von Tötges betreibt"—and to the photographer Schönner, "ein gewisser Kottensehl"—are explicitly mentioned, both engaged on aspects of the Blum/Blorna case. Moreover, in his interview with Christian Linder Böll himself casts doubts on the efficacy of Katharina's violent action, questioning even whether she is able to regain her lost honor: ". . . aber wenn man weiterdenkt, und das müssen wir, dann kann man natürlich nicht durch einen Mord, und wäre es ein Mord am schlimmsten Schwein, seine Integrität wiederherstellen." As Balzer rightly asserts [in the forward to *Werke: Romane und Erzählungen 1*, 1977] the work is in fact "ein Dokument des Scheiterns," in which the "Nicht-Integrität" of Katharina is made explicit. Under these circumstances it would seem that whereas the theme of "Gewalt" finds its most subtle expression in the very language, the theme of "Ehre," or rather the lack of it, is ingeniously reflected in the disharmonious structure. The narrator seems to lose control of his material precisely because there can be no satisfactory outcome: while Katharina's individual protest may provide a temporary catharsis, it reduces even further her hard-earned social integrity and is politically futile. Having come to this conclusion, however, there remains one problem. We have seen that, despite the somewhat cumbersome, even confused presentation of events, a time structure of almost symmetrical proportions emerges and firm connections are deliberately built into the plot. Thus there is in the structure at least some evidence of a paradoxical harmony in disharmony. Perhaps this constitutes a sly hint that Katharina has after all restored a quantum of her lost honor. But it seems more likely that, while on one level the disharmony in the structure articulates the lack of a meaningful political solution, on a second level the harmony underlines the message of the work's subtitle— "Wie Gewalt entstehen und wohin sie führen kann"—in that it hints at the logical and systematic workings of "strukturelle Gewalt."

Yvonne Holbeche (essay date 1985)

SOURCE: "Carnival in Cologne: A Reading of Heinrich Böll's *Die verlorene Ehre der Katharina Blum*," in *AUMLA*, No. 63, May, 1985, pp. 33-42.

[*In the following essay, Holbeche explores the significance of the carnival in* Die verlorene Ehre der Katharina Blum.]

Criticism of Heinrich Böll's *Die verlorene Ehre der Katharina Blum* has only briefly addressed the question of the significance of the carnival which provides such a suggestive backdrop to this melodramatic tale. Traditionally a period of gaiety and frivolity preceding Lent, whose origins, although still a subject of some dispute, can be traced to ancient Greek, Roman, Germanic and Celtic mid-winter and spring festivals and fertility cults, the carnival has long been celebrated with processions and parades, masquerades and street theatre. For a brief period of time the social order is turned upside down as the donning of masks or costumes enables individuals to step outside their usual roles and to enjoy an unaccustomed familiarity with one another. The clearest expression of this topsy-turvy world, of the carnival as 'die umgestülpte Welt', as Michail Bachtin puts it, is provided by the customary crowning of a person of humble social origins as 'Karnevalskönig' or in some cases as another figure of authority, for example as a priest, bishop or pope.

The traditional features of the carnival such as masks, costumes and general merry-making are central to Böll's story, whose action, set in a 'fröhliche[n] Stadt' (presumably Cologne), spans a period of four days from the evening of Wednesday, 20 February, 'am Vorabend von Weiberfastnacht', when Katharina attends a party at her godmother's flat, to the following Sunday evening, when she visits police-officer Moeding at his home to give herself up for the murder of the journalist Werner Tötges. The surface gaiety of the carnival is, however, not only a colourful background and an ironic foil for the destruction of Katharina's hitherto ordered existence which occurs during the four days in question. More importantly, it provides a potent metaphor for the discrepancy between appearance and reality, for the fact that many characters are not what they seem. Moreover, the general confusion of the carnival, the blurring of identities and relationships, can be paralleled with the impenetrable 'Netz von Beziehungen' between the 'ZEITUNG', various bureaucratic authorities and certain shadowy individuals, all of whom participate in an intrigue for which Katharina proves no match and which threatens to engulf her. Finally, it will be seen that the development which Katharina undergoes in the course of the four days of the action, a development which is sparked by her meeting with Ludwig Götten, is presented in what can be described as carnivalesque terms.

In the most significant contexts in which the motif occurs, the donning of a costume does not necessarily imply participation in a carnival party or ball, rather the wearing of a disguise for the purpose of deception. This is illustrated most clearly by the fact that the police pursuing Götten use a variety of disguises to provide a 'Tarnung', not only the most popular costume during that particular carnival, 'the costume of the new aristocracy', that of a sheik, but also cowboy and Spanish dress as well. The wearing of masks and costumes which hide an individual's true identity creates an ambivalent, even uncanny atmosphere, and it is not by chance that Böll introduces a central theme of the novel, that of trust and its abuse, in the context of the carnival—in Chapter 5 'Ein hoher Karnevalsfunktionär, Weinhändler und Sektvertreter' rather cynically expresses his satisfaction at the fact that the murders of Tötges and his colleague Schönner became known only after the carnival was over: 'So was am Anfang der frohen Tage, und Stimmung und Geschäft sind hin. . . . Ausgelassenheit und Frohsinn brauchen Vertrauen, das ist ihre Basis'. This remark is, of course, an ironic comment on Böll's part on the commercialization of the carnival. More importantly, however, the functionary's claim that the use of 'Verkleidungen' for criminal activities is an abuse of the trust which is the basis of the festive atmosphere, is the author's indirect way of indicting the undercover tactics of the police, the best example of which is provided by the police-officer Karl, likewise in sheik costume who, in order to continue 'tailing' Götten, strikes up a conversation with Hertha Scheumel and Claudia Sterm in the Café Polkt and invites himself to Frau Woltersheim's party.

Not only the police resort to such ruses in the course of their professional activities but representatives of 'die ZEITUNG' as well. A crass disregard of fundamental human values is displayed by the journalist Tötges, who claims that, by disguising himself as a painter, he had managed to gain access to Katharina's mother in hospital where she was recovering from an operation for cancer. Although this claim cannot be substantiated by the narrator, he later accepts it at face value and consequently holds Tötges and 'die ZEITUNG' responsible for the subsequent death of Katharina's mother. This action parallels the 'Rufmord' which the journalist perpetrates upon Katharina and thus further justifies the ominous name, Tötges, which Böll has given him. It is of the utmost significance that in the fateful encounter between Tötges and Katharina in her apartment, which culminates in the shooting of the journalist, he is wearing for the only time in the novel 'ein improvisiertes Scheichkostüm', a most fitting garb in this context as it underscores his participation in the general duplicity and also suggests that Katharina's target is not only this specific tormentor but the overall intrigue of which she has been a victim. An ironic parallel is provided by the killing of 'den ebenfalls als Scheich verkleideten' photographer Adolf Schönner who is, however, as the narrator remarks sarcastically, not an 'Opfer seines Berufes' but probably 'das Opfer eines Eifersuchtsdramas', having presumably met his death at the hands of 'einer als Andalusierin verkleideten jungen Frauensperson' with whom he had been seen on the day he was killed. All of these incidents highlight a recurring theme of the work which was touched upon by Rolf Michaelis in an early review, namely the baroque contrast of 'Lebenslust und Todesqual' which is played out against the carnival background.

Whether the murder of Tötges is to be seen as an act of self-defence or an act of revenge on Katharina's part, it signals the final destruction of her personality which the narrator carefully documents in his 'Bericht'. It is significant that Böll uses carnival imagery in order to illustrate this process. In view of the overtones of guile and deception associated with the wearing of costumes in most of the cases that have been commented on so far, it is noteworthy that Katharina does not wear a carnival costume when she attends Frau Woltersheim's party on the eve of 'Weiberfastnacht': ' . . . sie war weder als Beduinenfrau noch als Andalusierin verkleidet, sondern lediglich mit einer roten Nelke im Haar, in roten Strümpfen und Schuhen, in einer hochgeschlossenen Bluse aus honigfarbener Honanseide und einem gewöhnlichen Tweedrock von gleicher Farbe', an outfit which seems appropriate for someone whose prudishness has earned her the nickname 'Nonne' amongst her friends, though, of course, the carnation and the red stockings and shoes indicate a certain willingness to enter into the spirit of things. In general, however, her lack of a carnival costume suggests an openness, even the 'Unschuld' of character to which Blorna refers, and above all a dangerous vulnerability. (In an interesting carnivalesque reversal, the suspected criminal on the run, Götten, is also not 'verkleidet' and unlike his pursuers, does not attempt to hide his identity, a situational irony to which Margit Sinka has recently drawn attention [in *Colloquia Germanica*, 1980–1981].)

Böll's presentation of Katharina (and Götten) in this crucial context is typical of his largely idealized characterization of her which has so often been commented upon by critics. Although Böll himself has rejected this interpretation, insisting that Katharina is 'ein lädierter Engel, der sehr durchschnittlich ist', 'eine durchaus angepasste Figur, die das Wirtschaftswunder mitmacht', whose actions in hiding Götten and allowing him to escape can only be described as criminal, it is not her 'durchaus fragliche Züge' that are played up by the narrator, who, for example, allows Blorna's (and Frau Woltersheim's) admiration for the tenacity with which Katharina had overcome the disadvantages and disappointments of her earlier life to shape the reader's attitude to her, indeed who seems to share this admiration to the extent that he professes his belief in her innocence in the affair with Götten and glosses over the crimes of which they both are guilty. This partisan approach is, of course, also reflected in the contrasting 'sprechende[n] Namen' of the novel's main characters, the diabolic and one-dimensional Tötges and the abrasive Kriminalhauptkommissar Beizmenne on the one hand, Katharina, 'die Reine', and the Messianic Götten (who, as Durzak has pointed out, is presented virtually from Katharina's point of view), on the other.

The fact that Frau Woltersheim's 'Hausball' takes places 'am Vorabend von Weiberfastnacht', indeed was originally planned for the 'Weiberfastnacht' itself, is significant, for Böll is clearly drawing on the traditional associations of this specifically Rhenish carnival day, which was one of a number of special 'Frauentage' in February when women reigned supreme and had the freedom to do as they pleased without fear of recrimination. Despite her reluctance to participate in carnival activities and her disapproval of Hertha Scheumel and Claudia Sterm's expressed intention of going to the Café Polkt in order to pick up two young men to take to the party, it is ironic that Katharina unconsciously takes advantage of the 'Weiberfastnacht' tradition herself when she invites Götten home with her from the party after only a casual meeting, having recognized that ' . . . er war es eben, der da kommen soll'. However, the personal fulfilment which the relationship promises is overshadowed by the harrowing situation into which she is immediately catapulted as a consequence of this apparently quite uncharacteristic action. In the events that follow, the search of her flat on the Thursday morning ('Weiberfastnacht') and her interrogation on the Thursday and the Friday, her personal vulnerability makes it impossible for her to cope with the quite brutal treatment to which she is subjected by Beizmenne and his associates.

This vulnerability expresses itself particularly in the 'sprachliche Sensibilität' that she exhibits during the two days of interrogation and which makes her especially sensitive to verbal attack. Thus, in a variation of an important theme of the novel, the narrator speculates that a 'Vertrauensverhältnis' did not develop between Katharina and Beizmenne because of the latter's alleged use during the house search of an all too explicit and vulgar term to describe Katharina's brief affair with Götten. The initial lack of trust between Katharina and Beizmenne is subsequently reinforced by Beizmenne's attempts to find evidence to implicate Katharina in the 'Verschwörung' in which he is convinced Götten is involved. The suggestion of covert activities behind a mask of bourgeois respectability provides another variant of the carnival metaphor, which has its ironic counterpart in the mysterious channels of communication operating behind a facade of bureaucratic propriety between the 'ZEITUNG', the police, the 'Staatsanwaltschaft' and the 'Innenministerium' on the one hand, and between the businessmen Sträubleder and more particularly Lüding, and the newspaper and the 'Innenministerium' on the other.

> **Viewed in the light of its traditional associations, the carnival in *Die verlorene Ehre der Katharina Blum* has a much more significant function than that of simply providing a colourful setting for the story.**
>
> —*Yvonne Holbeche*

However, a more important variant is found in the treatment of Katharina by the press. The reports about Katharina in the three editions of the paper to which Böll specifically refers result in the creation of a fictitious persona which bears no relationship to the real Katharina, thus ironically paralleling the disguised and unrecognizable figures of the carnival. For these reports all involve exaggeration and distortion of the information provided to the paper, even information clearly supplied by the police or based on police transcripts (in particular, the reference to the 'Herrenbesuch' and to Beizmenne's conspiracy theory). For example, the police maintain that Götten is 'ein lange gesuchter Bandit . . . des Bankraubes fast überführt

und des Mordes und anderer Verbrechen verdächtig' and are confident of securing a conviction for bank theft. But they have no real proof that Götten has committed the murder, an allegation which is in fact eventually shown to be false. The newspaper goes even further, and refers to Götten as a 'Bandit und Mörder' and to Katharina as 'Mörderbraut' and 'Räuberliebchen'. Further insinuations of criminal activity, political unreliability and sexual promiscuity are reinforced by crude misrepresentations of statements made by Katharina's relatives, friends, acquaintances and employers.

The verbal assault upon Katharina which was initiated by the police and the press is moreover continued by obscene phone calls to her flat and to that of Frau Woltersheim, and by unsolicited mail containing either sexual innuendo, political abuse or religious admonitions, all of which contribute to the change which occurs in Katharina's attitude to the 'Eigentumswohnung' for which she had worked so hard and which comes to suggest something like the integrity of her personality. The police search of Katharina's flat, while no doubt necessary and justifiable under the circumstances, probably sets this process in train. What is, however, of crucial importance here is Katharina's relationship with her neighbours. Until the house search, Katharina appears to have led a relatively anonymous life in the apartment block where she lived. However, the questioning of her neighbours, who are the source of the term 'Herrenbesuch', and most especially an anonymous obscene telephone call from a man claiming to be a 'Hausbewohner', which causes her to flee her flat, lead to Katharina's total loss of interest in the 'Wohnung. This attitude is reinforced by her experiences when she returns to her flat on the Friday afternoon after the final interrogation, having asked Frau Woltersheim and Konrad Beiters to accompany her because of her fear: 'Sie habe Angst, sogar Angst vor dem Telefon'. That this fear is justified is demonstrated most clearly by the situation which arises when they are forced to share the lift with two 'Hausbewohner': 'Ein . . . als Scheich verkleideter Herr, der sich in offensichtlicher Distanzierungsqual in die Ecke drückte, . . . und eine . . . als Andalusierin verkleidete Dame, die, durch eine Gesichtsmaske gedeckt, keineswegs von Katharina abrückte, sondern direkt neben ihr stehenblieb und sie aus "frechen, harten, braunen Augen" dreist und neugierig musterte'. The reappearance of the carnival world underscores the sense that Katharina's private sphere has now been invaded and highlights the destruction of what was earlier a 'heile Welt' for her, the loss of her anonymity and the alienation from her 'Mitbewohner' who either shrink from contact with her or exhibit a morbid curiosity in her. As a result the 'Verstörtheit' in Katharina's personality, to which Frau Woltersheim had drawn attention earlier in the day during her interrogation at police headquarters and which she had linked even then with her godchild's loss of interest in the apartment, comes to a head and finds concrete expression in Katharina's despoliation of her own flat. In view of the time and the energies she had invested in it, this act is equivalent to a kind of suicide.

Bachtin has drawn attention to the ambivalent nature of many carnival customs and figures: 'Sie vereinigen in sich alle Polaritäten des Wechsels und der Krise: Geburt und

Tod. . . .' Certainly, the carnival from its earliest origins as a festival celebrating the end of winter and the coming of spring has symbolized death and rebirth, a symbolism we of course also associate with Easter which it precedes. This symbolism can be applied as well to Katharina's development in both a positive and a negative sense. Katharina's description of Götten as 'der, der da kommen soll', echoing John the Baptist's enquiry of Christ, suggests that the crucial meeting with Götten may be seen as signalling a new beginning in her life as a consequence of which she can turn her back on unhappy personal experiences in the past and, even while she is preparing for her trial at the end of the novel, look forward to a reunion with her lover many years hence. While this future perspective appears to give the conclusion of the novel an optimistic note, this is overshadowed by the generally negative development which Katharina undergoes in the course of the work. For in a grimly ironic variation of the carnival theme of death and rebirth, the experiences to which she is subjected during the four days of the action lead to the destruction of the old naive, trusting and innocent Katharina and the emergence of a Katharina who is open to corruption. Katharina's despoliation of her flat is not merely an indicator of the incipient breakdown of the integrity of her personality but may indeed be viewed as a turning-point in this process. It is no coincidence that the narrator speculates in the very next chapter (Chapter 36) on when Katharina entertained 'die ersten Mordabsichten' or indeed conceived 'den Mordplan' and that he then in Chapter 37 notes Katharina's decision (on the Friday evening after the visit to her flat) to make a carnival costume in the popular 'Scheichmode' in which she intends (as she expresses it in a veiled way) 'selbst am Samstag oder Sonntag als Beduinenfrau "loszuziehen"'.

The motif of 'Vertrauen' recurs in this chapter as well when the narrator documents the fact that Katharina had stolen out of Frau Woltersheim's flat early on Saturday morning in order to obtain a copy of 'die ZEITUNG', adding the ironic comment: '. . . sie hat das VERTRAUEN der ZEITUNG mißbraucht, indem sie eine ZEITUNG herausnahm, ohne zu bezahlen!' This scene has aroused some interest amongst critics. Although overlooking the overall significance of 'Vertrauen' in the novel, William Sewell sees this incident as having a positive aspect in the sense that by abusing the newspaper's trust, 'albeit in a very minor way, [Katharina] restores some measure of her personal integrity'. At the same time, he links this 'harmless gesture' with the murder of Tötges, viewing it as 'an intermediate stage in Katharina's dealings with the "ZEITUNG"'. Margit Sinka too interprets the stealing of the paper as a setting into motion of 'a future action against society', drawing attention as well to the theft of Konrad's gun on the following morning.

What should be emphasized here, however, is that the references to the 'Mordabsichten' and the 'Mordplan', the numerous allusions to the preparation of the bedouin costume, the mention of the abuse of trust involved in the theft of the paper and of the gun all suggest the gradual corruption of an initially innocent and intact personality which culminates in the meeting in the despoiled flat between Katharina 'als Beduinenfrau verkleidet', and the likewise costumed Tötges, with its fateful outcome. By wearing a costume and resorting to deception and violence, Katharina is merely responding in kind to the experiences of the previous four days. It can be said that she has become 'eiskalt und berechnend', having adopted the persona that has been created for her, thus taking the carnival theme to its ugly extreme. The wearing of the costume can be seen as a further sign of the disintegration of her original self. For whereas, when she had earlier met Götten, there had been no need for a disguise, after her 'Rufmord' by the 'ZEITUNG' Katharina too needs a costume, not only, as has been pointed out, 'to evade her journalistic notoriety' but to protect what is left of herself.

Viewed in the light of its traditional associations, the carnival in *Die verlorene Ehre der Katharina Blum* has a much more significant function than that of simply providing a colourful setting for the story. The principal features of the carnival which Böll exploits—not only disguised identity but also the ancient ritual of death and rebirth—help to point up essential aspects of the novel's theme: the duplicity and corruption of the representatives of powerful public and private institutions, and the gradual corruption of the vulnerable and initially innocent central figure, who, far from emerging from the tragic sequence of events untainted, is herself reduced (albeit out of desperation) to the treacherous and violent level of her oppressors. Like Böll's previous novel, *Ende einer Dienstfahrt,* with its repeated references to Reineke Fuchs, *Die verlorene Ehre der Katharina Blum,* ostensibly realistic and contemporary, subtly draws on a venerable literary and cultural tradition which adds a rich dimension of allusion to the novel, thus helping to make it, notwithstanding its occasional clumsiness, into a sophisticated work of fiction rather than the angry topical polemic which readers and critics have so often seen it to be.

S. S. Prawer (essay date 1986)

SOURCE: "Modern Germany's Master Storyteller," in *Book World—The Washington Post,* February 9, 1986, p. 4.

[*Prawer is a German-born English critic and educator specializing in German literature, particularly the work of Heinrich Heine. In the following review of* The Stories of Heinrich Böll, *he analyzes the strengths and weaknesses of the short fiction comprising the collection.*]

This generous selection [*The Stories of Heinrich Böll*] from the late Heinrich Boll's shorter and medium-sized fictions forms an ideal introduction to one of the world's master storytellers. No German author has managed so consistently to arrest attention by a striking opening sentence, and few have so successfully cultivated the kind of short story which makes a strong point in just a page or two. Arranged in roughly chronological order, these tales add up to an inner history of Germany from the 1940s to the late 1970s, seen from a sharply defined point of view.

The sufferings brought on Germans as well as those they oppressed and invaded in Hitler's wars; the misery of defeated soldiers returning home to devastated and beggared cities; the black market which slowly but inevitably gives way to more "normal" trade; economic recovery, culminating in the much-discussed economic "miracle" after currency reform; sharp social divisions, in which some of the least admirable citizens shoulder their way to the top; the threat and reality of urban terrorism, and overreaction to it, including the denial of employment to those who help the victims of fascist regimes abroad—all these are brought before the reader, not abstractly, but transformed into convincing scene and story. The point of view from which we are made to see these phenomena is that of the underdog rather than the man in control; the Catholic who takes his stand on the Sermon on the Mount rather than on dogmatic territory occupied by the Church establishment.

Capable of conveying, movingly, the plight and grief of the dispossessed, Boll is at his best when he can indulge his pawky Rhineland humor—when he casts a sardonic eye on posturing establishment figures in Church and State and dramatizes the discrepancy he perceives in German society between human possibility and social opportunity, between what is necessary for full emotional and intellectual development and what it takes to succeed in the world of Organization Man. He unites Dostoevskian sympathies with the insulted and injured, Swiftian satire, and a spareness of narration that recalls, again and again, the Hemingway of "A Clean, Well-Lighted Place."

From the wealth of realistic detail with which Boll evokes his world, recurrent symbols emerge: the railway station and railway journeys; the gift of bread; the mass of papers, the avalanche of junk mail, fit only to be thrown away; the tape-recorder and what it feeds into the airwaves . . . But realism is frequently heightened into fantasy which (as in the world of Kafka) illuminates the life we all know: as when a broadcasting expert collects, splices together, and listens to moments of silence snipped from the tapes he edits; or when a character suddenly forces her all-too-compliant family to celebrate Christmas every day of the year.

No German author has managed so consistently to arrest attention by a striking opening sentence, and few have so successfully cultivated the kind of short story which makes a strong point in just a page or two.

—S. S. Prawer

The collection exhibits Boll's weaknesses along with his strength. **"The Train was on Time"** contains a brothel idyll, complete with Beethoven on the piano and golden-hearted tart doubling as spy, which becomes intolerably

cloying. Presentation of Jewish victims of the Nazis, well-intended though it is, is vitiated by Boll's compulsion to Catholicize his sympathetic Jewish women—a tendency taken to ridiculous lengths in *Where Were You, Adam?* The sharp division Boll constantly makes between his petit-bourgeois or proletarian heroes and those who administer their lives or rise in their society may have a good deal of justification, but he allows far too little room for compromise and for the give-and-take possibilities of democratic politics. Boll's frequent presentation, however, of the possibilities of tenderness and mutual commitment between human beings, and of the way in which these are thwarted by social climbers and unfeeling bureaucrats, is genuinely moving because of its concrete, unrhetorical embodiment in convincing characters and situations. Behind the narrators whom Boll deploys with such art, the reader constantly glimpses the concerned human being who seeks to show what places are still left for kindness, tenderness, and fully committed love.

The volume here reviewed surprises by the absence of some of Boll's most celebrated shorter pieces: notably **"In the Land of the Rujuks"** (1953) and **"Metropolitan Journal"** (1957). It does, however, include several longer works originally published in a volume of their own, as well as one splendid and representative story, **"A Soldier's Legacy,"** which has escaped the anthologies that have popularized Boll's work in his native Germany.

In Leila Vennewitz Boll has found a congenial translator, who discovers convincing equivalents for his jokes and etymological games, and reserves his shifts of style, even if she occasionally gets a detail wrong (the "Fackeln" mentioned in **"My Father's Cough"** are paper-lanterns, not torches) or neglects such fine distinctions as that between the word *Sie,* which opens **"My Expensive Leg,"** and the more dismissive and alienating *Die,* which opens **"At the Bridge."** For most of the time these versions remain faithful to Boll without ever falling into translationese. They are bound to win new friends for a compassionate and humorous storyteller who shows in concrete instances, again and again, what tragedy can result from insensitivity as well as wickedness in a fallen world, but who is able, at the same time, to convey to his readers some of his own faith in the redeeming kindness, and the capacity for love, which reside in ordinary, unheroic and unostentatious men and women.

D. J. Enright   (essay date 1986)

SOURCE: "When They Were Wrong They Were Right," in *The New York Times Book Review*, February 23, 1986, p. 42.

[Enright is an English man of letters who has spent most of his career abroad, teaching English literature at universities in Egypt, Japan, Berlin, Thailand, and Singapore. His critical essays are frequently marked by sardonic treatment of what he considers the culturally pretentious in literature. In the following favorable review, he exam-

ines the plots, characters, and major themes of the stories collected in The Stories of Heinrich Böll.]

Born into a liberal Roman Catholic family in Bonn in 1917, and the least military of men, Heinrich Böll was drafted into the German army in 1939 and eventually taken prisoner by the Americans. His first novel was published in 1949, and in 1972 he was awarded the Nobel Prize in Literature for a body of work that, in its emphasis on life and a positive vision, fulfilled the ideals the prize is meant to honor. Possibly his sense of noblesse oblige induced him to serve as the quasi-official conscience of postwar Germany—who else was anything like as eligible?—and this function, one may surmise, proved a burden to him. How could so private a person, the ironic champion of the outsider and the lone wolf, feel comfortable as a spokesman on public issues and for large and sometimes simple-minded causes?

Böll became an advocate and arbiter, someone from whom decent, balanced appraisals were expected, someone who was obliged—or who obliged himself—to see both sides of every question, including the Berlin Wall. In his collection of essays, *Missing Persons,* he felt it necessary to correct Aleksandr Solzhenitsyn's "unworkable" preference (expressed passingly in his *Gulag Archipelago*) for the Gestapo over the Soviet M.G.B., predecessor of the K.G.B.; again, he felt he had to explain, in connection with the Soviet invasion of Czechoslovakia in 1968, that both the population and the Soviet soldiers were victims, "both devout, both deeply wounded in their trust," the one side unable to halt their tanks, the other unable to offer tea and bread and the use of their toilets. The present generous volume [*The Stories of Heinrich Böll*] is a memorial to the far more subtle-minded author that he was; and also a tribute to Leila Vennewitz, his faithful English-language translator of more than 20 years.

Böll's characters fall into three categories: the ill-treated near-saint; the reprobate who is good at heart; and the plain villain, more commonly a hypocrite or a bully than a monster of iniquity. The second category has always been a favorite of fiction writers, of course; its most famous exemplar in English is Fielding's Tom Jones, who falls into error and commits peccadilloes but is honest and endowed with "natural" virtue. The boundary between the first category and the second isn't always firmly defined. Margret Schlömer, a minor character in Böll's richest novel, *Group Portrait With Lady,* is suffering from a peculiarly advanced form of venereal disease: "tears might come out of her nipples and urine out of her nose." She is not a prostitute, we are told, but a "woman forever tangled in certain masculine desires," and she caught the infection from a visiting statesman in whom, on official instructions, she sought to inspire a "treaty mood." That is, she worked for the benefit of society, a society that wants to know nothing about the sacrifices made on its behalf. She dies not of the disease but of blushing, for in reality she was a modest woman.

The reference to "certain masculine desires" sounds like a failed euphemism. And here and elsewhere resistance may set in on the part of the reader, who senses a loading of the scales to the advantage of pet characters, although the author might argue that it was only fair to go easy on those on whom an "achievement-oriented" society has borne down hard.

Margret was a modest and sweet-natured woman and a sacrificial victim, but scarcely a saint. She allowed herself to be used; she was not sufficiently independent in spirit. A more complete Böllian hero is Hans Schnier in that fine albeit slightly overinsistent novel, *The Clown.* Schnier, a talented mime, is a man of honor and integrity, lacking worldly power: he will always be out of step. People with dubious pasts are doing nicely in postwar Germany; Schnier's mother, for instance, once keen on driving "Jewish Yankees" from "our sacred German soil," is now active in reconciliation work and gives lectures on the remorse of German youth. Schnier could himself make a good living were it not that reality keeps getting in the way. He gives up his successful number, "The General," when he is visited by a little old woman, the widow of a general killed in battle. In East Germany his satiric "Board Meeting" would go down splendidly, as would his "Party Conference Elects Its Presidium" in West Germany; but he wants to do the latter in Leipzig and the former in Bonn. Perverse of him, to aspire to be effective rather than simply to poke fun harmlessly and lucratively!

Schnier epitomizes Böll's way of thinking and feeling. A similar situation is evoked in the novella *Absent Without Leave,* published in 1964, a year after *The Clown.* Here, the narrator's admired mother-in-law says the rosary with the children of one son, a leftist and atheist, and encourages obstinate rebelliousness in the children of a pious, "churchy" son. She is instinctively religious, as opposed to mechanically or expediently so. And in her habit of commenting "Then all I can say is, the Pope was wrong," she reminds us of Schnier's animus against the Catholic Church, whose agents have persuaded his beloved to marry "one of them." Despite his bitterness, Schnier accepts that there are Catholics who are good men; it is Catholic*ism* he objects to, the party line, the ganging up, and equally athe*ism* German*ism,* social*ism* and any other institutionalized ism or ology. It is the individual who matters; for Böll, more consistently so than for Brecht, the truth was concrete.

As one would expect, his stories are less schematic or calculated than his novels, and also less inward in the presentation of character and its quiddities. Some of them are agreeably lighthearted, close to fantasy or not far from farce. **"Recollections of a Young King"** tells how the ruler of Capota runs away to join a circus as its cashier. **"The Staech Affair"** concerns a celebrated Benedictine abbey, a showpiece for prominent visitors from abroad, whose monks are frequently absent with or without leave, attending writers' conferences or studying Bavarian baroque, so that on ceremonial occasions young demonstrators have to be brought in off the streets to substitute for them, in return for 40 marks and a solid meal. Life's little idiocies are exposed in brief anecdotes: one man makes a living as a thrower-away of circulars, another counts the people crossing a newly constructed bridge, a third has knives thrown at him in a vaudeville act ("a profession where all I needed to do was stand still and dream a little"). A more pointed anecdote tells of a well-meaning, camera-carrying tourist who urges a lazy fisherman to catch more fish so he can buy a second boat, then a whole fleet, then a pickling factory, and grow rich enough to doze in the sun without a care. But he was doing exactly that, the fisherman retorts, before the tourist's clicking camera woke him up.

Like the novella *And Where Were You, Adam?* (answer: in the middle of a world war), the earlier stories of wartime concern people whose present life is not their life but who (sustained by tobacco and cheap drink, and sometimes sex) have to behave as if it were. One of them reflects, "Our patriotic literature has no room for reality": reality, or the absurdity of what passes for it, was exactly the author's subject. These sad and bitter, often harrowing, stories are relieved only by imaginative touches; for example, in his first publication, *The Train Was on Time,* antiaircraft searchlights are thought of as fingers groping for a bedbug, "a tiny bug in the cloak of the night." Or by moments of stoical humor: in **"A Case for Kop"** a consignment of sugar tongs finds its way to a Russian village. But there is no sugar. You could use the tongs for pinching yourself in the behind, says a man. If you still had one, a woman replies. Well then, the children could play with them. And they all laugh, for there are plenty of children around.

Not surprisingly in so firmly principled an author, the preoccupations of the novels reveal themselves fleetingly in the stories. **"On Being Courteous When Compelled to Break the Law,"** which construes a bank robbery, undertaken for good reasons and conducted in an amiable spirit, as a "forced loan," bears a family resemblance to the novel *The Lost Honor of Katharina Blum.* The latter is an animated tract against the gutter press and its readers' taste for what the 19th-century British historian Macaulay termed "periodical fits of morality." The crime of Katharina's "gangster" sweetheart is merely to have deserted from the army along with the regimental pay. In his small way he is a Tom Jones figure, as is Katharina herself.

In another story a man is sent to prison for displaying a happy face and later, political circumstances having altered, imprisoned again for displaying a sad one. Böll's characters have the gift of always being in the wrong— which proves they are right. (This, it must be admitted, makes for a certain predictability, but perhaps no more than resides in reality.) In the novel *Billiards at Half-Past Nine,* the anti-Nazi Schrella escapes to the Netherlands, where he is jailed for uttering threats against a Dutch politician who maintains that all Germans should be killed. When the Germans enter the country they free him under the impression that he is a martyr. They soon discover their mistake, and he flees to England, where he is jailed for threatening a British politician who contends that nothing should be preserved of Germany but its works of art.

Ironies of a more up-to-date kind feature in Böll's last novel, *The Safety Net.* Protection against terrorism is itself a form of terrorism: privacy ceases to exist, phones are tapped and rooms bugged, minor offenders against the conventions of society are inadvertently caught in the "safety net," and the daughter of the protected household has virtually no choice but to fall in love with the security guard assigned to her. As for the terrorists, somewhat rosily represented here as bunglers, they succor capitalism by burning and blowing up cars, and then they blow themselves up.

My own favorite among the stories is **"Murke's Collected Silences."** A young broadcasting editor, working on the cultural side, is sorely oppressed by the pretentious rubbish he handles, in particular the outpourings of a "spiritual thinker" who, having experienced a fashionable change of heart, insists that all his references to "God" should be replaced by the phrase "that higher Being Whom we revere." This operation lengthens the two talks by half a minute each and entails rescheduling; so it is fortunate that the word "art," which Murke notices occurs 134 times, is left untouched. He snips out the rare moments on tape when speakers have paused to take breath, splices them together, and preserves his sanity by playing them back, at home, in the evenings. This story, like that of the mime, epitomizes beautifully its author's thought and sensibility.

Böll died in July 1985. We may hope that he too found comfort, and some relief from his public persona, in a collection of saving silences.

Lynton Lesserday (essay date 1986)

SOURCE: A review of *The Casualty,* in *Punch,* Vol. 291, No. 7607, October 8, 1986, p. 72.

[*In the following posive review, Lesserday compares Böll's early war stories to those of Ernest Hemingway.*]

How surprising it is that *The Casualty,* this little book of early (1946 to 1952) stories by the German Nobel Prize winner, Heinrich Böll, has never been published in English before. But then they were not published in German until 1983, two years before Böll's death. One can perhaps see why the Germans would feel uncomfortable with these tales of the 1939-45 war. They are raw, straightforward, brutal stories told without any frills. They are rather like that Solzhenitsyn story "We Never Make Mistakes", in the way the brutality of the Nazis is presented in such an off-hand manner. Indeed, one story **"Cause of Death: Hooked Nose"** is practically a twin of the Solzhenitsyn story, but the Böll one is far more horrible. In it the Nazi death squads are shooting Jewish men, women and children (the babies are kicked to death) behind the lines in Russia. In Solzhenitsyn it was only one man who was mistaken for a spy. Here the deaths are in the thousands. A young German lieutenant attempts to save the Russian whose house he is billeted in. The man has been taken away because he has a hooked nose.

The title story of the book is brutal in a different way: full of whores, drunken soldiers and many corpses of men and horses. And an arrogant German officer actually says "We never make mistakes." The unnamed hero, a private soldier is deliriously happy because he has been wounded by a grenade fighting the Russians outside Jassy in Rumania and reckons he will be sent home.

There is some marvelous stuff, like young Ernest Hemingway, describing the soldier taking a tramcar back from the front and being unable to pay for a ticket—the Rumanians are Germany's allies so, he thinks, he must pay. In the town he gets drunk with another soldier who has paid to have himself shot in the arm. There is some tough, black humour as a drunken corporal asks if he can buy the grenade wound from the soldier.

In the sordid mess of a train full of wounded, many of them seriously, one suddenly learns that this hard combat soldier we have been following is only 18 years old and that Hubert, the soldier with the "store bought" wound, is an old-timer of 25. We then learn that this is June 6, 1944 and that the British and Americans have landed at Normandy.

The news is read to the wounded. "In this solemn hour, comrades," an officer says, "when the cowardly liars are finally confronting us, we will not fail to utter a threefold Sieg Heil!" But one of the wounded shouts "Hurrah!" at the news—the men are happy because they know the war will soon be over, "What's that supposed to mean, Kramer?" the officer asks. "Sir," the soldier says, "because at last they're confronting us, you see—that's why I'm shouting hurrah."

The train is in Hungary by then and the soldiers go to a café and celebrate with the Hungarians.

Later, just as in those wonderful early Hemingway stories, the story ends, not with a twist, but with a dying fall, with the young soldier remembering putting his finger on a map of Hungary in a geography class at school and thinking, "who would ever have thought that one day you'd be swaying, swaying so quickly and quietly on your way to Debrecen, in the middle of the night."

This is marvelous stuff, done by Böll when he was only 25 and the horrors of war were still something that only happened yesterday.

Russell A. Berman (essay date 1987)

SOURCE: "A Language to Live In," in *The New York Times Book Review,* August 23, 1987, p. 27.

[*In the following mixed review, Berman contends that the stories in* The Casualty *are vivid but not as accomplished as Böll's later works.*]

In one of Heinrich Böll's most famous stories, the narrator, a young soldier just wounded in the final days of World War II, describes a makeshift military hospital. From his stretcher he sees enough of the hallways to recognize that the building formerly served as a high school, a classical *Gymnasium,* for the walls are adorned with busts of Cicero and Caesar, paintings of Prussian kings and imposing portraits of Friedrich Nietzsche and Adolf Hitler.

Yet not until he reaches the drawing room, now converted into an operating room, does he realize that this is his own erstwhile school, which he had left only weeks before. Penmanship had been taught in the drawing room, and he catches sight of his own handwriting on the blackboard, the scrawled phrase that gives the story its title: **"Traveller, if You Come to Spa . . ."**; it is the epitaph of the Spartans who fell at Thermopylae, broken off in the middle of a word. And just as he reads the truncated verse, the surgeon amputates the hands with which he had written it, in an allegory of the writer in postwar Germany, for whom national history led directly to a destruction so cataclysmic that it thoroughly discredited the cultural tradition.

It was henceforth more plausible to assert that literature itself had become impossible than to imagine culture proceeding as it had in the past, from Cicero to Nietzsche and Hitler: or, in the words of one of Böll's unlikely critical admirers, Theodor W. Adorno, "writing poetry after Auschwitz is barbaric."

That allegorical writer is of course Böll himself, who commenced his literary career with an adamant rejection of the political fantasies and cultural pretenses that had led to the catastrophe that was Nazi Germany. The result was not, however, a simple tendentiousness. On the contrary, Böll avoids political exhortations and the "heroic realism" of fascist writing. Instead he opts for material from everyday life—stories of common soldiers, inhabitants of the bombed-out cities, and later the population of the West German *Wirtschaftswunder,* struggling with the problems of a new and sometimes labile democracy. Chronicling that society, he judges it, since, as he put it in his Frankfurt lectures on poetics in 1964, "morality and esthetics turn out to be congruent and indivisible."

Other authors, like Günter Grass, translated this moral urgency into activism for the Social Democrats. Böll shied away from such partisanship, since his whole literary identity entailed a moral commitment to the "search for an inhabitable language in an inhabitable country." His initial concentration on antiwar themes therefore led in the 1950s to a critique of the conservatism of the Roman Catholic Church (while his own ethical passion derives largely from the radicalism of Catholic social teaching). Later he befriended East European dissidents and West German radicals hounded by a tabloid press not concerned with the niceties of due process. Because he defended civil rights, he was accused of supporting terrorism; such attacks probably contributed to a sense of resignation in the last years before his death in 1985. His opponents labelled him pejoratively a *Sympathisant,* which translates roughly as "bleeding heart"; it does indeed point to a core of Böll's work, the capacity for human sympathy.

The 22 stories collected in *The Casualty,* written between 1946 and 1952, were not published in Germany until 1983. None of them measures up to the best of Böll's early fiction. The young author seems not yet in full control of his material. Some texts, like the title story, wander and lose their impact, while others sound overstated and hollow. Yet precisely this lack of polish makes the collection interesting, shedding light on the emergence of the major voice in West German literature. One can watch Böll explore the several literary languages that suddenly become available after 1945: fragments of Expressionist prose from Weimar Germany, Surrealist turns of plot from the European avant-garde and some of the hard-nosed realism of the American short story. Usually he was read, with reference to that last component, only as the German heir to Faulkner and Hemingway, but this early work transforms one's understanding of the later, mature fiction, in which the moments of fantasy, the grotesque and the uncanny take on a new significance: the chronicler Böll turns out to be the modern E. T. A. Hoffmann.

These stories, translated by Leila Vennewitz in a fine rendering, as always, of Böll's German, vividly present the two overriding concerns of the young Böll: the impact of the war on the individual soldier and the experience of poverty in the immediate postwar period. In fact, the war material assumes an uncharacteristically violent shape in two stories, **"The Murder"** and **"Vive la France,"** which both describe enlisted men who, just trying to survive, assassinate their officers. It is an irony of West German history that the author who provided such compelling accounts of mutinies in the Nazi army would be accused 30 years later of aiding and abetting terrorists. Many of the postwar stories display a fundamental structure of Böll's ethical thought, the tension-alienated structures of social organization and a utopian realm of genuine human interaction, "the humanity bred by misery." The philosopher Jürgen Habermas in his work addresses much the same conflict between institutional systems and the life and world of communities, and Böll's fiction turns out to be social theory in disguise, a theory of the difficulties of German democracy and of the possibilities of human community in the modern world.

Tom Wilhelmus (essay date 1988)

SOURCE: "Nothing Pretentious about Life and Art," in *The Hudson Review,* Vol. XL, No. 4, Winter, 1988, pp. 669-76.

[*In the following excerpt, Wilhelmus offers a mixed review of* The Casualty.]

Böll, well known to American audiences, resembles Hemingway in his blunt, uncompromising portrayal of the brutality of war, its occasional absurdity, its desperate humor, and its dehumanizing effects.

[*The Casualty,* a collection of stories] written between 1946 and 1952 (when Böll was between the ages of 29 and 35),

clearly predict the successful career to follow. In conception as well as execution they are journeyman pieces intended to establish the writer's credentials: his social consciousness and serious demeanor, his right to be considered in the same company as Brecht and Kafka, and—as a former soldier—his right to speak with bitter irony. Missing as yet is the more refined social comedy and thoughtful observation that will later shape stories like **"Christmas Every Day"** and novels like *Group Portrait With Lady.*

The collection divides into roughly two equal halves, one describing experiences of everyday soldiers leading up to the surrender, the other describing the depressing conditions of the immediate postwar period. Apart from the title story, I prefer the later tales. For one thing, there is a depressing similarity in the stories that writers of any nationality tell about combat: the soldier who ironically lives when his comrade dies; the private who shoots his inhumane officer out of boredom, bitterness, or despair; the wounded man who searches for the nurse whom he has once kissed. All these clichés and others may of course truly reflect the actual nature of war, but if so, their repeatability is ample reminder that war is no longer glorious (if it ever was) and we would prefer to avoid it.

Therefore, stories like **"Beside the River,"** about a young man who has lost his family's ration stamps and who is saved from suicide by an American, command more interest because they present a less familiar side of postwar experience and because of the precise way in which Böll captures the mannerisms of the American's speech. Even briefer sketches, like **"The Rain Gutter"** and **"Autumn Loneliness,"** are more like Picasso drawings, elegant and eloquent despite their being about brutal circumstances. Some stories are surrealistic—like **"The Waiting Room"** with its heavily laden title, about a man who trades his hat for bread. Others are comic or even make a brush with metafiction, like **"An Optimistic Story."** All of them are startlingly fresh and memorable.

Nonetheless, the centerpiece is **"The Casualty"** itself. Occupying forty-five of the whole book's 181 pages of text, it traces the experiences of a young casualty as he travels from the front to an uneasy peace in the rear—a plot that provides a suitable metaphor for the whole book. My sense is that **"The Casualty"** will be read on many levels as a statement of what book jackets like to call "the spiritual condition of mankind in the twentieth century." In this case, such a statement might even be true.

Charlotte Armster (essay date 1988)

SOURCE: "Katharina Blum: Violence and the Exploitation of Sexuality," in *Women in German Yearbook,* Vol. 4, 1988, pp. 83-95.

[*In the following essay, Armster examines the issue of sexual exploitation in* Die verlorene Ehre her Katharina Blum.]

In 1974, Heinrich Böll's then recent novel *Die verlorene Ehre der Katharina Blum* was serialized in the West German magazine *Der Spiegel*. The appearance of the novel in the news magazine was notable, as it marked the first time that *Spiegel* published a literary work in its entirety. The novel's literary merit was not, however, the reason the editors chose to make an exception to their usual policies regarding what they print. Instead, Böll's short novel was viewed as having actual news value in that it possessed a direct tie to immediate political events in Germany. In *Spiegel*'s own words: "Eine denkwürdige publizistische Affäre—Bölls Kontroverse mit 'Bild' über dessen Baader-Meinhof-Berichte—hat ein aktuelles belletristisches Nachspiel: In einer Erzählung mit dem Titel *Die verlorene Ehre der Katharina Blum oder: Wie Gewalt entstehen und wohin sie führen kann* attakiert der Kölner Literatur-Nobelpreisträger 'gewisse journalistische Praktiken. . . .'"

To *Spiegel* editors, the publication of *Die verlorene Ehre der Katharina Blum* was seen as the continuation of a bitter public confrontation between Böll and the Springer-controlled press. In January 1972, Böll had written an article for *Der Spiegel* entitled "Will Ulrike Meinhof Gnade oder freies Geleit?" It was in part a response to an earlier story in the *Bild,* and its main point was to call into question the role which the Springer press had in escalating the violence exhibited by both the German police and such radical groups as Baader-Meinhof. *Bild,* and similar publications such as *Quick,* immediately targeted Böll for public vilification. In their pages he was repeatedly denounced and accused of latent and intellectual complicity with terrorist groups. The stories had an effect. On June 1, 1972 the police surrounded and searched Böll's country house in the Eifel region, believing it to be a possible hide-out for Ulrike Meinhof.

Other news articles, including ones in *Die Zeit* [by Wolf Donner, October, 1975] and *Süddeutsche Zeitung* [August 10-11, 1974], tended to stress the political aspects of the novel. Böll himself, within the structure of the novel, seemed to invite interpretations which concentrated attention on the relationship between his narrative content and actual political events. "Sollten sich bei dieser Schilderung gewisser journalistischen Praktiken Ähnlichkeiten mit den Praktiken der 'Bild'-Zeitung ergeben haben," reads in part an ironic disclaimer at the beginning of the novel, "so sind diese Ähnlichkeiten weder beabsichtigt noch zufällig, sondern unvermeidlich." With these words, a comparison between the fictional world of the novel and Böll's actual experiences with the Springer press became inevitable.

In light of the political climate at the time, it is not surprising that many initial interpretations of *Die verlorene Ehre der Katharina Blum* were primarily concerned with obvious connections to the external world. Such an approach, however, obscured the sexual exploitation depicted in the novel (which is integral to the entire plot development) and concentrated almost solely on the political reality of West Germany. This is most readily apparent in the fact that these interpretations emphasized the importance of the subtitle: "How violence develops and where it can lead"—and neglected the importance of the primary

title: "The lost honor of Katharina Blum." The sexual nature of "lost honor" and its connection to violence, as implied by the interplay between title and subtitle, was simply overlooked.

In the few early interpretations where sexual aspects of the novel's structure were noted, their significance was completely downplayed. Rainer Nägele, for example, criticized the ambiguity of Katharina's use of her vulgar word *bumsen* with the argument:

> Offenbar wollte Böll hier den Zusammenhang von Wort und Gewalt in Wortspiel zur Unmittelbarkeit verdichten. Das ist ihm einerseits zwar gelungen, jedoch mit bedenklichen Kosten: denn was das Wortspiel symbolisch verdichtet, löst es im Kontext der Handlung auf, indem es die Motivation verwirrt und den Schuß zur Reaktion auf eine sexuelle Attacke macht, womit die von der Recherche mühsam aufgebauten Motivationszusammenhänge gefährlich in Frage gestellt werden [*Heinrich Böll: Einführang in das Werk und die Forschung,* 1976].

In fact, the motivation for killing Tötges is not confused in the sense that Nägele believes. From the beginning, a misuse of sexual innuendo and sexual terms provides the basis for the subsequent violence in the novel.

The most extreme example of an interpretation which disregards the importance of sexual aspects in the novel was that of Marcel Reich-Ranicki [published in *Frankfurter Allgemeine,* August 24, 1974]. According to him, any sexual problems present in the story arose from the fact that Katharina Blum is frigid. ("Sie leidet . . . an ihrer Frigidität.") For him, sexuality was totally irrelevant to the political concerns of the novel.

The concern with the political nature of *Die verlorene Ehre der Katharina Blum* has continued, but as events which related to the novel have passed, some literary critics have finally begun a more intrinsic examination of the work. Most frequently, these analyses have focused on structural aspects, including narrative perspective, genre form, and such elements as the symbolic significance of character names. Yet, even these less political approaches to the novel have failed to explore in detail the sexual exploitation of the heroine. When the sexual tones dominant throughout the work have been touched, they have generally been relegated to minor significance. The notion of "lost honor" is viewed as "old-fashioned," or the characterization of Katharina Blum as a "prude" is accepted at face value, or her behavior is termed "romantically idealistic."

The repeated attempt to exclude or to reduce the importance of the sexual implications in *Die verlorene Ehre der Katharina Blum* has meant that the political—and not the sexual—qualities of the novel are still generally considered to be primary to the novel's meaning. The fact that sexual stereotypes motivate much of the political action has simply been isolated from the novel's overall meaning. Yet, Katharina Blum, whose name is central to the title, is not simply an arbitrary figure made to serve the text as a convenient vehicle through which a political message is revealed or exemplified. Instead, her character as a woman is crucial for an understanding of the novel. "Lost honor"—referred to in the primary title—is a concept which denotes a loss of virginity or something sexual when applied to women. And it is this "woman's honor" which first must be comprehended in order to discern the connection with violence mentioned in the subtitle.

The reader learns almost nothing about Katharina Blum, including her honor, in a direct manner. Almost all information about her is derived from a variety of documents—newspaper articles, police reports, interviews—and these in turn are transmitted through a seemingly objective narrator who gathers facts much the way a journalist might. To a certain extent, the narrator (presumably male) serves as a counterweight to the actual journalist Tötges, from whom the slanderous newspaper accounts originate.

In part, Böll's use of this narrative structure serves to provide the text with a type of control against which the varying "fact-gatherers" in the novel are to be measured. Journalists and police, for example, supposedly serve as public fact-gatherers, and it could be assumed that their portrait of Katharina Blum would be based on the objectivity of facts. Yet, the factual evidence presented by the narrator makes clear that the supposed objectivity of the journalist Tötges and the police is distinctly biased. Their reports are deliberately distorted and serve interests other than objective fact-finding.

Despite the narrator's role as counterbalance to Tötges and the police, his presentation of the facts is not without bias. His own anger surfaces in ironic comments. "Hier ist endlich ein Gebiet, wo Kirchen und Gewerkschaften zusammenarbeiten könnten," he writes after a critical passage on the practice of tapping telephones. "Man könnte doch mindestens eine Art Bildungsprogramm für Abhörer planen. Tonbänder mit Geschichtsunterricht. Das kostet nicht viel." Elsewhere, when mentioning Katherina Blum's organizational talents, he remarks that these abilities are received "als Schreckensnachricht durch alle haftanstalten. Man sieht: Korrektheit, mit planerischer Intelligenz verbunden ist nirgendwo erwünscht, nicht einmal in Gefängnissen, und nicht einmal von der Verwaltung."

Interestingly, the narrator's most open irony is directed toward bureaucratic targets. When presenting descriptions of Katharina Blum, there is no mockery—although the possibility exists. The categories used by others to describe Katharina Blum—the sympathetic as well as the hostile ones—are invariably sexual. The narrator makes no comment on this, but simply reproduces both in a seemingly objective manner. His supposed objectivity is a limited perspective, which does not allow him to comprehend fully the sexual nature of the conflict. Like many of the critics, his eyes are focused on the political implications.

From the moment the police storm Katharina Blum's apartment, the fact that she is a woman provides a special vulnerability. In an attempt to humiliate her in order to extract a confession, the police immediately categorize her night spent with Ludwig Göttens in the most vulgar of terms: "Beizmenne (the police inspector) soll die aufreizend gelassen an ihrer Anrichte lehnende Katharina nämlich gefragt haben: 'Hat er dich denn gefickt,' woraufhin Katharina sowohl rot geworden sein wie in stolzem Triumph gesagt haben soll: 'Nein, ich würde es nicht so nennen'." It was a fleeting triumph, as verbal sexual abuse became the method by which Katharina Blum was attacked.

What the police began, the journalist Tötges continued and expanded. The discrepancy between the newspaper's statements about Katharina Blum and the facts which the narrator uncovers is readily apparent. Tötges altered, for example, the characterization of Katharina Blum as "eine sehr kluge und kühle Person" to read that she is "eiskalt und berechnend." The testimony "Wenn Katharina radikal is, dann ist sie radikal hilfsbereit, plannvoll und intelligent" is transformed into the quote: "Eine in jeder Beziehung radikale Person, die uns geschickt getäuscht hat." Her mother's lament—"Warum mußte das so enden, warum mußte das so kommen?—is changed to: "So mußte es ja kommen, so mußte es ja enden." Other alleged facts presented by Tötges are similarly falsified: her father is labeled a communist, her mother an alcoholic, and Katherina herself is said to be fully capable of committing a crime.

Tötges's distortions are obvious when viewed in light of the documentation provided by the narrator. In order to create a sensational story which will sell well, Tötges manipulates, falsifies, and even fabricates facts and quotes. What is not immediately apparent, however, is that the success of his slander depends upon specific public stereotypes of women. Before the labels of "radical" and "communist" assume emotional significance for readers of the newspaper, Katharina Blum must be degraded sexually and made into "that kind of woman" who would do anything. As with the police, Tötges's attack begins with verbal sexual abuse.

Eiskalt und berechnend is Tötges's first characterization meant to undermine Katharina Blum's reputation by attacking her sexuality. To label a woman "ice-cold and calculating" implies that she is someone without feelings who will do anything to achieve her ends, including using her own sexuality. To malign her further, Tötges then speaks (as do the police) of *Herrenbesuche*, intimating that she is a prostitute. In fact, everything Tötges writes about Katharina Blum presents the image of a woman of questionable virtue. By questioning publicly her sexual purity, he undermines her character in all respects so that readers will view her as a criminal with questionable political beliefs.

The direct connection between questionable sexuality and criminal behavior is made by Tötges when he writes about Katharina Blum's reputed long-term relationship with Ludwig Götten. He calls her a "Räuberliebchen" and a "Mörderbraut." A characterization is again made in sexual terms, but now in combination with criminal labels. Of course, Katharina Blum is neither a "robber" nor a "murderer." Her ostensible "crime" is being sexually involved with a "criminal." By associating sexuality with criminality in this way, Tötges succeeds in discrediting Katharina Blum doubly. Questioning her sexual virtue lent credence to the public depiction of her as a criminal. To discredit her politically then becomes easy.

That a woman's honor, and not a man's, can be attacked by sexual innuendo is underscored in the text by the figure of Alois Sträubleder. A prominent industrialist, Sträubleder functions as a minor counterpoint to Katharina Blum. In contrast to Katharina Blum, whose reputation depends upon her sexual virtue, Sträubleder indicates that public knowledge of illicit romance could not harm him. "Eine romantische Frauengeschichte bringt mich höchstens privat in Schwierigkeiten, nicht öffentlich. Da würde nicht einmal ein Foto mit einer so attraktiven Frau wie Katharina Blum schaden," he says. He even implies that his reputation as a man might be enhanced by a sex-linked scandal. His only worry is that such a story might suggest an association with criminals. Sexuality for Sträubleder is a private matter, not subject to public dishonor.

Because Tötges succeeds in dishonoring Katharina Blum by exploiting her sexuality in the public sphere of politics and journalism, it appears that she seeks revenge and kills him. On the surface, the motif of "lost honor" and revenge seems to establish the connection between the title of the novel and the violence referred to in the subtitle. This motif, however, functions largely as cliché or stereotypical theme, masking the fact that a different, more lethal type of violence other than Katharina Blum's act of murder relates to honor within the framework of the novel. As Wolfram Schutte wrote in an early review: "Die Gewalt, von der die Rede ist, geht von der Presse aus, und führt Katharina Blum zum Mord" [*Frankfurter Rundschan*, August 10, 1974].

The violence which permeates the novel is foremost a violence committed through the medium of language. Violence occurs through the use of words as weapons rather than guns. Words and language create a story based on lies, innuendo, and misrepresentation. The world is ordered linguistically in such a way that it is destructive to the individual, and therein lies its inherent violent quality. By the misuse of words, the sanctity of the individual is violated.

Although language can be made to impart a quality of violence, it is not language per se which is violent. Tötges does not succeed in his attack on Katharina Blum solely because he distorts facts or misuses language. The images he creates of Katharina Blum, though bound by a certain inner consistency, do not have intrinsic meaning. Instead, they gain their meaning from a set of rigid sexual stereotypes embedded in societal consciousness. To have meaning, his characterization of Katharina Blum is in need of these specific referents. His images do not represent any form of pure linguistic or artistic invention, but are inventions in the form of distortions—and these distortions are meant only to give expression to a distorted, yet widely accepted view of reality in which women and men are characterized and judged in terms of sexual stereotypes and gender role expectations.

The connection between language and reality is underscored by Böll's disclaimer which prefaces the novel. His disclaimer is purposefully unsubtle, as it points a finger at the actual publishing concern of Axel Springer. The reader is made aware of a real situation outside the text, even if unaware of West Germany's political climate. The result is a parody of what has become a standard literary form—that is, a pro forma denial that the fictional reality of a particular book is in any way based on actual characters and events. For Böll, the connection between fictional reality and our social reality is implicit. Tötges and his manner of reporting are not meant to be singular to him as a particular (and in this case fictionalized) individual. Instead, his reporting is representative of a whole type of journalism. And the success of this reporting depends on preconceived gender expectations, which prepare the reader to accept as fact certain sexual stereotypes.

In the case of Katharina Blum, for example, her secure financial situation is "explained" (by both the police and Tötges) by the supposition that she works as a prostitute. Her long solitary drives are first seen as trips to "gentlemen visitors," then as journeys to "case" a villa for her lover. Her divorce is reported as caused by adultery. Her mother's death is attributed to shock at her "loose" ways. And her reactions are consistently described as "analytical" rather than "emotional"—a characterization for a woman which immediately implies she is hardened and deceptive. This reduction of reality to sexual stereotypes—conveyed through language—is the initial violence in the novel.

Once a woman has "lost" her sexual "honor," there exists no possibility to reverse or halt the process which judges and condemns her. The terms used to censure and describe her are locked into place, and she is tainted for life. If the individual seeks recourse, revenge is the only choice. Katharina Blum's act of physical (i.e., "real") violence appears to form a part of this unvarying circle. In conformity with clichéd expectations, a woman's lost honor is avenged by the murder of the man who besmirched her reputation. The only break with the stereotype is the fact that Katharina Blum does not remain a passive female, dependent upon a man to revenge her honor. She herself becomes her own agent of revenge. Yet her act alters nothing. By killing Tötges, she becomes an outcast as a convicted criminal. This does allow her to join the world of her lover, but the reunion is only symbolic. Her violence is nothing more than an act of defiance, but not a genuine alternative.

But does Katharina Blum kill Tötges to avenge her lost honor? Although both title and plot seemingly portray the familiar theme of lost honor revenged, Katharina Blum is actually motivated to commit murder for reasons apart from a sense of lost honor. She shoots Tötges to protect the integrity and sanctity of her own inner world, rather than to defend a stereotypical idea of honor in which she does not believe. For her, a woman's honor is something other than her sexual purity.

Within the novel, a contradiction exists between the public image of Katharina Blum and her own private self-conception. Töges and the police contribute most to the creation of the public image. As already noted, this image does not rest on actual facts, but is based on a set of sexual stereotypes. Katharina Blum's efficiency, thriftiness, and modest lifestyle—all of which enable her to buy her own apartment—are overlooked as qualities uncharacteristic for a woman. Instead, the assumption is made that a wealthy "customer" (or "customers") supports her.

The repeated attempt to exclude or to reduce the importance of the sexual implications in *Die verlorene Ehre der Katharina Blum* has meant that the political—and not the sexual—qualities of the novel are still generally considered to be primary to the novel's meaning.

—*Charlotte Armster*

This conception of Katharina Blum relegates her to a dependent position, similar to that of a child. At the first police interrogation, her sense of independence goes completely unnoticed. Commissioner Beizmenne, at first harsh and authoritarian, adopts a "fatherly" tone and condescendingly reassures her that it is acceptable for a woman in her position to receive "gentlemen visitors" (*Herrenbesuch*). Later, one of the policemen also suggests that she (the potential criminal) is in need of protection and should be jailed for her own safety.

It is this public portrait of Katharina Blum, based on repeated factual distortions and sexual stereotypes, for which the concept "lost honor" has meaning. Publicly, her sexual behavior is placed into question, thereby dishonoring her. Within her own private world, however, there is never a loss of honor in the same sexual sense. At no time does she understand her relationship with Ludwig Götten in terms of lost honor. Instead, she gropes for other categories to define her sexual relationships. Important to her is *Zärtlichkeit* as opposed to *Zudringlichkeit*.

Katharina Blum does not develop these categories. They remain private and personal, and are not understood in the public sphere. Nevertheless, they do point to an attempt on her part to define her sexuality in terms other than those implied in such stereotypes as "lost honor." And it is this attempt to articulate her own understanding of sexuality which creates conflict when she is confronted with established norms.

To a large extent, Katharina Blum is unable to make publicly clear her private values because they remain an unconscious part of herself. She in no way regards herself as different, although in reality she lives a life which is quite different from others. The life which she has created mirrors that of an average single woman. Her taste in books, her leisure activities, her condominium, and her friends

are all evidence of a basically middle-class mentality. Yet, behind this seemingly average existence is something which makes her stand out. She possesses an unusual independence, as is made clear by her financial arrangements with the Blornas, her divorce, and her refusal to engage in meaningless sexual relationships. It is this uniqueness which the police and Tötges are unable to comprehend, as it does not conform to their preconceived stereotypes.

Honor in its conventional sense bears little real meaning for Katharina Blum. By maintaining her own private values, her personal sense of honor remains intact, even while she suffers a public loss of honor. But rapidly, the sexual stereotypes used to characterize her begin to undermine and threaten her private world. In a number of ways, the public smear campaign initiated by Tötges intrudes on Katharina Blum's private sphere. Obscene phone calls and sexual solicitations by unknown neighbors become common. Her private world is attacked, and is in no way protected—not even by her friends and close acquaintances. They, too, essentially perceive her in terms of sexual stereotypes.

The manner in which Katharina Blum's friends view her does differ from that of the police and Tötges, yet their characterizations are also primarily sexually based. Her employer and friend Hubert Blorna, for example, cannot describe her without sexual reference. Although he on occasion speaks of her modesty and efficiency, equally important to him is her physical attractiveness and what he considers her sexual prudishness. In his eyes, she is a helpless and vulnerable female.

The belief that Katharina Blum is sexually prudish is shared by most of her acquaintances, who repeatedly refer to her as "the nun." The image of Katharina Blum as a nun is interesting, because it is diametrically opposed to the one formed by the police and Tötges. Despite the contradictory nature of the two images, neither presents an accurate portrait of Katharina Blum. Neither recognizes in any way her private set of values or her personal identity, and both represent extremes frequently used to characterize a woman—a whore or a nun. Her values are consequently distorted by both, as she is perceived only in terms of sexual stereotypes. In the case of Tötges, her aloofness, which originates from the desire to find someone *zärtlich*, is misconstrued negatively in such as way as to depict her as *eiskalt und berechnend*. For friends and acquaintances, this same quality is endearingly understood as sexual prudishness.

The fact that close acquaintances, similarly to the police and Tötges, view Katharina Blum only in terms of sexual stereotypes means that her private values and ideals receive no public recognition or articulation. Her defense is to kill Tötges. Nevertheless, she does not shoot him to gain revenge. Instead, as the conclusion demonstrates, she shoots Tötges only when he acts in such a way as to threaten what remains of her private world:

> Er sagte "Na, Blümchen, was machen wir zwei denn jetzt?" Ich sagte kein Wort, wich ins Wohnzimmer zurück, und er kam mir nach und sagte: "Was guckst du mich so entgeistert an, mein Blümelein—ich schlage

vor, daß wir jetzt erst einmal bumsen." Nun, inzwischen war ich bei meiner Handtasche, und er ging mir an die Kledage, und ich dachte: "Bumsen, meinetwegen", und ich hab die Pistole rausgenommen und sofort auf ihn geschossen.

Ja, nun müssen Sie nicht glauben, dass es was Neues für mich war, daß ein Mann mir an die Kledage wollte—wenn Sie von Ihrem vierzehnten Lebensjahr an, und schon früher, in Haushalten arbeiten, sind Sie was gewohnt. Aber *dieser* Kerl—und dann "Bumsen", und ich dachte: Gut, jetzt bumst's.

Ich dachte natürlich auch an den Erschossenen da in meiner Wohnung. Ohne Reue, ohne Bedauern, er wollte doch bumsen, und ich habe gebumst, oder?

As these passages make clear, Katharina Blum shoots only when Tötges attempts to violate her personally. He is, in accordance with her personal values, *zudringlich*. To allow him to violate her in this manner would mean that he had finally destroyed her private sense of honor as well as her public honor. In actuality, then, Katharina Blum's act of violence is not so much revenge for a public loss of honor, as it is a defense of private integrity.

In the end, Katharina Blum's private definition of honor remains inaccessible to others, making it impossible for those around her to understand her motivations. Realizing that Tötges, as a man, is able to render sex an act of violence, Katharina Blum, in the only way possible for a woman, responds in kind by equating the sexual act with a violent one ("ich habe gebumst"). Her defense, however, ultimately remains unsatisfactory. An act of violence cannot redeem her public name, nor can it challenge the sexual stereotypes which have been used to undermine her individual values. Like her attempts to define herself in terms other than sexual stereotypes, her defense remains locked and isolated within a private world. As an act of rebellion, the shooting of Tötges does not challenge the rigid stereotypes, nor does it free her from them.

Russell A. Berman   (essay date 1993)

SOURCE: "The Rhetoric of Citation and the Ideology of War in Heinrich Böll's Short Fiction," in *Cultural Studies of Modern Germany: History, Representation, and Nationhood,* The University of Wisconsin Press, 1993, pp. 147-58.

[*In the following excerpt, Berman analyzes the semiotic aspects of Böll's short story "When the War Began."*]

Böll's 1961 story [**"Als der Krieg ausbrach" ("When the War Began")**)] presents itself as a personal recollection of a historical moment, linking objective and subjective dimensions by eliding the title—"When the war began" with the initial sentence, "I lay in the window, sleeves rolled up, looking out the window to the telephone office . . ." Grand history and individual experience evidently run into

each other, collide, and generate the existential scenario typical of much of Böll's work: the living individual in conflict with hierarchies of power, be they political, social, military, or ecclesiastic. Approaching the text in this manner, one ends up asking only whether it should be treated as primarily a subjective, nearly impressionistic remembrance, more than twenty years after the fact, or, on the other hand, as above all an attempt at a definitive, i.e., objective account of the fact itself, the historical moment, "als der Krieg ausbrach."

Yet even if the opening of the text stages the collision of person and history, subject and object, the course of the text demonstrates nothing if not the inadequacy of either account in isolation. For the I who, at the outbreak of the war, is lying at the window never achieves much substantial particularity, and all the purportedly personal memories are strikingly devoid of any nuance or idiosyncrasy that might indicate a concrete individuality. That is, if the text is about personal memory, it is also about the dissolution of personhood. A similar dialectic undermines any naively objectivist reading as well. The title's insistence on temporal specificity is irreparably undercut by the ambiguities of the text: does the war break out at the beginning or the end of the story? The narrator, at least, refuses to accept the notion of the war's having commenced at all, even when he learns of his friend Leo's death, i.e., the moment named by the title remains frustratingly elusive, and the pretext of the story, the promise of chronological accuracy, turns out to be highly labile, with presumably far-reaching consequences for any historiographic project.

If the text is neither purely autobiographical nor naively historiographic, subjective or objective, it is evidently about the relationship—or disjunction—between the two, i.e., it is not an untroubled unity of subject and object but a staging of their separation, their unity as separated, at a specific conjunction in time. The figure who initially lies at the window in a posture of seclusion, recognizably romantic no matter how deflated—indeed he is waiting to call his lover, even if this eroticism is extraordinarily arid— this latter-day romantic ego of the outset is, by the conclusion, marching in a column of soldiers singing "Muss i denn" ("For I must go"), the crucial citation in the text and the announcement of both compulsion (a far cry from "Kein Mensch muss müssen") and separation: the fate of the *Schatz* left behind, never articulated as such in the text but, like the concluding line of the popular song, precisely therefore all the more prominent.

The text records the process by which the prone ego is gotten up out of bed and integrated into the mobilized masses, but this apparent integration of the individual into society remains an unfree and therefore false sublation precisely because it depends on the compulsion and separation named by the citation. Compulsion: at stake is an arbitrary order, the establishment of an arbitrary code that lacks any referential legitimacy vis-à-vis a rapidly vanishing life-world. The code depends on the production of differences and, consequently, of separations. To talk about the text as an account of a reorganization of meaning and social structure would be wrong precisely because it investigates something like the enforced organization of meaninglessness and the painfully felt absence of society, i.e., a genuine or adequate human society. A natural order, traditionalism, is present only as memory—what Leo and the narrator used to do; it is replaced by arbitrary signification and the laceration of community, semiotics and alienation (names for the dual absence of meaning and society).

The objection that this relatively simply story cannot support an examination in terms of semiotics and alienation (in other words: structuralism and Marxism) can be easily countered with reference to the frequency with which the text itself foregrounds the problem of signification (and social division as well; more on that later). The point therefore is not to produce a semiotic reading of **"Als der Krieg ausbrach"** but to note that **"Als der Krieg ausbrach"** is already a critical reading of semiotics. For the story itself thematizes the status of signs and the proliferation of certain sorts of sign systems as constitutive of the moment of the outbreak of war. Thus the story commences with an account of a sign language: the narrator "waited for my friend Leo to give the agreed-upon sign," and the text proceeds immediately to describe the act of signification: "coming to the window, taking his cap off and putting it on again." This seemingly absurd act is dependent on an arbitrary difference—"Leo alone wore a cap, and only in order to take it off to give me a sign." That is, he is not a lover of caps or a mysteriously formal dresser but rather an element within a system dependent on abstract differentiation.

The initial description of the sign system is surrounded by two questions, each inquiring into the relationship between the system and specific social or political terrains. First we are told that although the system is itself only conventional—what Leo has on his head is meaningful only within the code—it does have an extrasystemic goal: to alert the narrator to the fact that at certain points in time he can use a telephone to call a girlfriend for free. Is there any tighter relationship between the semiotic code and the communicative act (indeed the communication between lovers)? The answer is yes, but it is, counterintuitively, not the relationship suggested by the opening scene. Instead of an elaboration of sign systems augmenting communication, the opposite transpires; as codes proliferate, the connection between the narrator and his lover snaps— their sole conversation is one in which he admonishes her not to come for a visit (as if signifying chains were incompatible with marriage bonds). Yet this marginalization of the woman, or her repression, is itself part of a code of patriarchal separation that is inscribed in the unwritten continuation of the leitmotific citation: "Aber du mein Schatz bleibst hier" ("But you my dear stay here").

If a dimension of communicative authenticity, eros, and woman is left, so to speak, behind the expansion of a semiotic system, does the system—this is the second question—run up against another border too, i.e., what is outside the system? "I suddenly noticed that the rhythm of plugging and unplugging had changed; the arm motions

lost their mechanical character, became imprecise, and Leo threw his hands over his head three times: a sign we had not agreed upon but which told me something extraordinary had happened." It appears that the system has broken down, that the code has come to an end, and that war amounts to the end of the semiotic order. But the sentence goes on and, in a stunning reversal, keeps the question open. Is war located subsequent to the semiotic scene, or is it, in contrast, the outcome and expansion of semiosis? Is signifying order concluded by the disorder of war, or is the system which produced arbitrary distinction and the repression of communication the sine qua non of war? Thus the text proceeds: "then I saw how one telephone operator took his helmet from the closet and put it on; he looked ridiculous, sitting there, sweating in an undershirt, his tag around his neck and a helmet on his head-but I couldn't laugh, since I recalled that putting on a helmet meant something like 'battle-ready' and I was afraid." If the *Stahlhelm* is not the *Mütze*, they are after all both hats, and the difference between them can be accounted for easily within the same binary paradigm of hat-on and hat-off, i.e., the basic system of signification has not changed at all. Is the system itself implicated in the war that is just now breaking out?

> **"Als der Krieg ausbrach" entails by no means solely a report on the past, the war, and the origins of divided Germany, but something like its redemption and therefore also an imagination of an obliteration of artificial differences and borders: between classes, genders, and states as well.**
>
> **—*Russell A. Berman***

Böll's text is centrally concerned with a political critique of the economy of the sign. The initial example of Leo's covered or uncovered head is quickly expanded by a different difference, i.e., the difference between a soldier with or without a helmet. This sort of pattern pervades the story; we read of differentiations between military ranks, discussion topics, and social groups, between Poles and Germans, Protestants and Catholics, open collars and buttoned ones. Meaning constructed in this manner is a function less of reference than of difference, and the production of difference is complicitous in that outbreak of agonistics called war.

Consider a further example: "Once there came a field kitchen. We got lots of goulash and few potatoes, and real coffee and cigarettes we didn't have to pay for. It must have been in the dark, since I remember a voice saying: real coffee and free cigarettes, the surest sign of war; I don't remember the face that went with the voice." The "surest sign of war" is therefore identifiable as such not because of any subjective involvement; it is after all a disembodied, faceless voice that speaks, and the agency distributing the wares disappears into the anonymity of the *Feldküche.* Neither sensuous enjoyment nor intentional consciousness is at stake but solely the difference between cigarettes and coffee for free and another state of affairs where one would have to pay for them, i.e., the difference is an absence, costlessness, *umsonst,* in other words, nothing at all, which nevertheless makes all the difference between war and peace. What is the form of social organization that prevails in the bureaucratic context of signification via arbitrary difference?

It is a society of alienation, characterized by an estrangement between groups that is as emphatic as it is absurd: the rank and file soldiers divide into opposing cliques, the foot soldiers face the officers, the Germans confront the Poles, and everyone goes to war. Because of differential semiosis, not only 1939 but also 1949, hot war and cold war ensue, both dependent on the differences. The text suggests a linkage between a specific mode of signification, alienated society, and belligerence. Is this an ontological claim? Does Böll, in his glorious existentialist abstraction, suggest that meaning necessarily means war? Not at all, since the problematic is relativized by a historicizing reference which, on its own, would be rather unconvincing, were it not simultaneously bound to the central question of repression and patriarchy. When Leo reports the news—of full mobilization—he immediately adds that it would be a long time before the two could again bicycle in the countryside, to which the narrator appends the parenthetical comment: "(In our free time, we bicycled through the country, out in the fields, and we had peasant women make us fried eggs with bread)." The figure of a utopian return to nature—which is also a return to women—of rustic simplicity and sensuous pleasure, is bracketed between parentheses and relegated to an unretrievable past (although of course even its merely parenthetical presence in the text disrupts the postromantic normalcy of the present). That remembered travel into a gendered world of *Bauersfrauen,* a life-world of preconceptual experience, is now proscribed by a semiotic order that disallows precisely such material experience—subjectivity doesn't count—while it marks women, arbitrarily, as an alterity to be repressed. In place of the journey to the peasant women, the narrator breaks with Marie and moves off from her, represses her, as the repressed verse itself recommends: "Aber du mein Schatz bleibst hier." That is, the world constructed in terms of a proliferation of differentiation is simultaneously both alienated and patriarchal, and it is also a world of universal necessity, general mobilization, and compulsion: "Muss i denn."

Is this world of unfreedom describable as society? Barely, for as the narrator puts it: "I needed company and had none." A stranger in his own land because it is a land of universal estrangement and encoded difference, he finds no society—society, or companionship, sinks into the past of the bicycle trip with Leo. A different mode of organization prevails; instead of society, signifying chains: "this time we loaded detergent cartons, piled in a gym . . . we made a chain, and carton after carton passed through my hands . . ."

Significatory order is associated with an authoritarian organization of mechanical labor, i.e., the same principle of compulsion announced by the title of the song. The system of formal difference that excludes subjective consciousness is not just a guarantor of meaning but also a foundational element in the system of domination that depends on an ideology of compulsion. "Sometimes we met or passed soldiers singing 'Muss i denn.' There were three bands and everything was quicker. It was later, after midnight, when we finished the last cartons—and my hands remembered the number of pots and noted little difference between cartons of detergent and cooking pots." Labor, difference, and intractable necessity are brought into a proximity defining the authoritarian structure at the outbreak of war.

Yet Böll's text does not only delineate this structure and explore the resonance between semiotic order and alienated society; it also articulates a critique in the course of the final scenario of the narrative. The structure of this final scenario is such that it repeats features of the opening; the narrator is again lying on his bed, his comrades are quibbling over minor points, and an interpretive event transpires: the signs of general mobilization in the first scene are paralleled now by the announcement of Leo's death. This death, however, is presented as a consequence of the system of differentiation: only now is the narrator distinguished by being addressed with a formal *Sie,* only in death does Leo become a person with a last name. Death intervenes as the ultimate differentiation, between the living and the dead, and the point where, after all, everything is the same, since nothing matters any longer, which is why the narrator protests and refuses the news. His rejoinder to the report that Leo Siemers had become "der erste Gefallene des Regiments" repeats the congruence of history and individuality evidenced in the first sentence of the story. For Leo cannot have become a *Gefallene,* since there has been no declaration of war—that is the objective argument—and Leo, too, his personal friend, with his disregard for military order, is not one to have sought a hero's death: "Leo doesn't die in battle, not him . . . you know it."

The comment on the "surest sign of war," which figured importantly in the investigation of the structure of the sign, was pronounced by an invisible speaker, and the story might well be read as a subtle record of the disappearance of speech: crossed telephone wires giving way to an arbitrary sign system, proceeding finally to the death notice brought, tellingly enough, by a writer, the *Kompanieschreiber,* as if the vocality of the outset (the telephone call) were displaced by the silence and epitaphic writing of the end. The story that records the loss of a life-world and viable communication simultaneously suggests the privileging of writing, a sort of backhanded self-reflection of the author Böll, for whom writing is about its own impossibility or, which is to say the same, will always verge on the obituary.

That a story about the outbreak of the war might be primarily morbid is hardly surprising. Is it only morbid? Preserving Leo's memory, the narrator also rescues him, i.e., the same Leo who enfigured a sort of resistance to division, disregarding the separations of telephone lines and bringing lovers together. The text thereby suggests an alternative to the strategy of difference and control, divide and conquer, the bureaucratic-administrative repression of the life-world whose mode of operation Böll so cogently dissects. **"Als der Krieg ausbrach"** entails by no means solely a report on the past, the war, and the origins of divided Germany, but something like its redemption and therefore also an imagination of an obliteration of artificial differences and borders: between classes, genders, and states as well.

FURTHER READING

Biography

Reid, J. H. *Heinrich Böll: A German for His Time.* Oxford: Berg Publishers Ltd., 1988, 245 p.

    Critical biography.

Criticism

Conrad, Robert C. *Heinrich Böll.* Boston: Twayne Publishers, 1981, 228 p.

General critical study of Böll's life and career that includes three chapters on his short fiction.

Kuschel, Karl-Josef. "The Christianity of Heinrich Böll." *Cross Currents* XXXIX, No. 1 (Spring 1989): 21-36.

    Examines the nature of Böll's Christianity and how his Catholic faith is reflected by his writings.

Ley, Ralph. "Making It in the Big Apple: Heinrich Böll in the New York Press, 1954–1988." In *The Fortunes of German Writers in America: Studies in Literary Reception*, edited by Wolfgang Elfe, James Hardin, and Gunther Holst, pp. 249-75. Columbia: University of South Carolina Press, 1992.

    Discusses the critical reception to Böll's short fiction by the American press. Ley includes a list of Böll's works and the New York publications in which they have been reviewed to 1988.

Schwarz, Wilhelm Johannes. *Heinrich Böll, Teller of Tales: A Study of His Works and Characters*, translated by Alexander and Elizabeth Henderson. New York: Frederick Ungar Publishing Co., 1969, 123 p.

    Explores the major characters featured in Böll's writing.

Additional coverage of Böll's life and career is contained in the following sources published by Gale Research: *Contemporary Literary Criticism*, Vols. 2, 3, 6, 9, 11, 15, 27, 39, 72; *Dictionary of Literary Biography*, Vol. 69; *Dictionary of Literary Biography Yearbook: 1985*; and *World Literature Criticism.*

Raymond Chandler
1888–1959

American short story writer, novelist, essayist, screenwriter, poet, and critic.

INTRODUCTION

Along with Dashiell Hammett, Chandler elevated the genre known as the hard-boiled detective story into an American art form still imitated in literature, television, and motion pictures. Chandler's short fiction, following the formula writing required by the genre, is marked by lurid violence and action but displays his wisecracking wit, knack for dialogue, and love of metaphor and simile. The stories feature alienated middle-aged male characters—often private eyes—with high ideals who work against great odds to right wrongs. Unlike contemporary English mystery writers, who employed intricate plotting and puzzle-solving, and portrayed stereotypical characters and events, Chandler placed more emphasis on developing his characters and their motivations and used a sophisticated literary style that was uncommon in the pulp detective genre. In addition, his works, set primarily in Los Angeles in the 1930s, represent to many the essence of southern California: the superficialities of Hollywood, crime and vice glossed over with wealth, the cult of glamor, and a certain enduring mystery that eludes precise definition.

Biographical Information

Chandler was born in Chicago. When he was seven years old, his parents divorced and he was taken by his mother to live in England. While there he received a thorough education in the classics and displayed a strong interest in languages. As a young man Chandler wrote poetry, reviews, and essays for *The Academy* and *The Westminster Gazette*. When he returned to the United States at the age of 24, however, he settled in California and opted for a career as a businessman in the oil industry. After losing his job many years later, he began to study the pulp detective magazines such as *Black Mask*, and familiarized himself with the narrative devices of such successful authors in the genre as Erle Stanley Gardner—creator of Perry Mason—and Dashiell Hammett. Chandler developed a mastery of the American language in its slang and idiom, later commenting that he preferred it to the language spoken in England because of its vitality and versatility. Ultimately, he brought his highly original talent for characterization and description to the market with considerable success. A slower and more methodical worker than most of his fellow detective-fiction writers, his alcoholism and the long-term illness of his much-older wife, Cissy, affected his ability to produce much work toward the end of his life, though the writing he left behind after his death in 1958 continues to generate interest and debate, as well as to inspire imitators.

Major Works of Short Fiction

Chandler's initial efforts in fiction were short stories written for pulp detective magazines such as *Black Mask* and, later, *Dime Detective*. In the beginning, he had little experience with mystery stories, either as a reader or a writer. He taught himself the tough-guy form by rewriting plots that appeared in the magazines and in 1933 he submitted his first story, "Blackmailers Don't Shoot," to *Black Mask*. This dark tale of extortion and racketeering contains all the hard-boiled genre's conventional tropes: violence, corrupt officials, gangsters and gun molls, and a detective with a fast gun and a code of ethics. In the next five years Chandler published sixteen short stories of the same ilk, mostly in *Black Mask*. They feature early prototypes of his hero, detective Philip Marlowe, and display Chandler's growing adeptness with dialogue, characterization, thematic development, and the voice and viewpoint of the detective figure. In these early pieces, Chandler experimented with style and narrative technique, eventually finding the most success with the first-person point of view. His private-eye heroes are essentially the same in each work—grizzled and alienated romantics who hold to an ideal of gallantry. By the late 1930s Chandler was feeling limited by the short story form and turned his attention to novels. The greater popularity of these works allowed the publication of his collected short stories. *Five Murders* appeared in 1944, five years after his first major novel, *The Big Sleep*, was published. Other short story collections surfaced routinely after that, though the stories were primarily written prior to the period in which Chandler wrote his novels. The collections include *Five Sinister Characters* (1945), *Red Wind* (1946), and *Pearls Are a Nuisance* (1953). From these stories he created the plots for his early novels through a process he termed "cannibalizing"— a method in which he reworked several previously published pieces of short fiction into a sustained story.

Critical Reception

Many modern-day critics see Chandler's short stories as a training ground for his novels. While some commentators have described these early works as formula pieces, poorly plotted, overly talkative, and contrived, others have observed that the crisp, declarative style, terse characterization, wit, and ominous tone of Chandler's novels can be discerned in his stories, which served as a training ground for the author. Chandler himself said that if he had written too well for the pulp magazines, he would not have been published. His writing style and several opening scenes in his novels and short stories still elicit considerable admiration. Nevertheless the hard-boiled detective type and Chandler's use of metaphors and similes have been more often parodied than praised. The majority of critics acknowledge that Chandler's use of simile is somewhat overdone and that his writing is occasionally marred by sentimentality but most also note that his work has a literary sophistication, which some critics have remarked elevated the genre to the level of an art form. Throughout his career, critics have noted his weak plotting and narrative structure, pointing out that he preferred to develop character and style. Overall, it is for these latter two qualities, as well as for an arresting and gritty portrayal of southern California in the 1930s, that Chandler's works of short fiction are chiefly praised.

PRINCIPAL WORKS

Short Fiction

Five Murders 1944
Five Sinister Characters 1945
Red Wind: A Collection of Short Stories 1946
Spanish Blood 1946
Finger Man and Other Stories 1947
The Simple Art of Murder 1950
Trouble Is My Business: Four Stories from "The Simple Art of Murder" 1951
Pick-Up on Noon Street 1952
Pearls Are a Nuisance 1953
Killer in the Rain 1964

The Smell of Fear 1965
Smart-Aleck Kill 1976

Other Major Works

The Big Sleep (novel) 1939
Farewell, My Lovely (novel) 1940
The High Window (novel) 1942
The Lady in the Lake (novel) 1943
The Little Sister (novel) 1949
The Long Goodbye (novel) 1953
Playback (novel) 1958
Raymond Chandler Speaking (letters, essays, short story, and unfinished novel) 1962
Chandler Before Marlowe: Raymond Chandler's Early Prose and Poetry, 1908-1912 (poetry, essays, and criticism) 1973
The Notebooks of Raymond Chandler and "English Summer: A Gothic Romance" (notebooks and short story) 1976
Selected Letters of Raymond Chandler (letters) 1981

CRITICISM

Raymond Chandler (essay date 1944)

SOURCE: "The Simple Art of Murder," in *The Atlantic Monthly*, Vol. 174, No. 6, December, 1944, pp. 53-9.

[*In the following essay, Chandler describes what he believes is good mystery fiction.*]

The detective story, even in its most conventional form, is difficult to write well. Good specimens of the art are much rarer than good serious novels. Second-rate items outlast most of the high-velocity fiction, and a great many that should never have been born simply refuse to die at all. They are as durable as the statues in public parks and just about as dull.

This fact is annoying to people of what is called discernment. They do not like it that penetrating and important works of fiction of a few years back stand on their special shelf in the library marked "Best-sellers of Yesteryear" or something, and nobody goes near them but an occasional shortsighted customer who bends down, peers briefly, and hurries away; while at the same time old ladies jostle each other at the mystery shelf to grab off some item of the same vintage with such a title as *The Triple Petunia Murder Case* or *Inspector Pinchbottle to the Rescue*. They do not like it at all that "really important books" (and some of them are too, in a way) get the frosty mitt at the reprint counter while *Death Wears Yellow Garters* is put out in editions of fifty or one hundred thousand copies on the newsstands of the country, and is obviously not there just to say good-bye.

To tell you the truth, I do not like it very much myself. In my less stilted moments I too write detective stories, and all this immortality makes just a little too much competition. Even Einstein couldn't get very far if three hundred treatises of the higher physics were published every year, and several thousand others in some form or other were hanging around in excellent condition, and being read too.

Hemingway says somewhere that the good writer competes only with the dead. The good detective story writer (there must after all be a few) competes not only with all the unburied dead but with all the hosts of the living as well. And on almost equal terms; for it is one of the qualities of this kind of writing that the thing that makes people read it never goes out of style. The hero's tie may be a little out of the mode and the good gray inspector may arrive in a dogcart instead of a streamlined sedan with siren screaming, but what he does when he gets there is the same old futzing around with timetables and bits of charred paper and who trampled the jolly old flowering arbutus under the library window.

I have, however, a less sordid interest in the matter. It seems to me that production of detective stories on so large a scale, and by writers whose immediate reward is small and whose meed of critical praise is almost nil, would not be possible at all if the job took any talent. In that sense the raised eyebrow of the critic and the shoddy merchandising of the publisher are perfectly logical. The average detective story is probably no worse than the average novel, but you never see the average novel. It doesn't get published. The average—or only slightly above average—detective story does. Not only is it published but it is sold in small quantities to rental libraries and it is read. There are even a few optimists who buy it at the full retail price of two dollars, because it looks so fresh and new and there is a picture of a corpse on the cover.

And the strange thing is that this average, more than middling dull piece of utterly unreal and mechanical fiction is really not very different from what are called the masterpieces of the art. It drags on a little more slowly, the dialogue is a shade grayer, the cardboard out of which the characters are cut is a shade thinner, and the cheating is a little more obvious. But it is the same kind of book. Whereas the good novel is not at all the same kind of book as the bad novel. It is about entirely different things. But the good detective story and the bad detective story are about exactly the same things, and they are about them in very much the same way.

I suppose the principal dilemma of the traditional or classic or straight deductive or logic and deduction novel of detection is that for any approach to perfection it demands a combination of qualities not found in the same mind. The coolheaded constructionist does not also come across with lively characters, sharp dialogue, a sense of pace, and an acute use of observed detail. The grim logician has as much atmosphere as a drawing board. The scientific sleuth has a nice new shiny laboratory, but I'm sorry I can't remember the face. The fellow who can write you a vivid and colorful prose simply will not be bothered with the coolie labor of breaking down unbreakable alibis.

The master of rare knowledge is living psychologically in the age of the hoop skirt. If you know all you should know about ceramics and Egyptian needlework, you don't know anything at all about the police. If you know that platinum won't melt under about 3000° F. by itself, but will melt at the glance of a pair of deep blue eyes if you put it near a bar of lead, then you don't know how men make love in the twentieth century. And if you know enough about the elegant *flânerie* of the pre-war French Riviera to lay your story in that locale, you don't know that a couple of capsules of barbituric acid small enough to be swallowed will not only not kill a man—they will not even put him to sleep if he fights against them. And so on and so on.

Every detective story writer makes mistakes, of course, and none will ever know so much as he should. Conan Doyle made mistakes which completely invalidated some of his stories, but he was a pioneer, and Sherlock Holmes after all is mostly an attitude and a few dozen lines of unforgettable dialogue. It is the ladies and gentlemen of what Mr. Howard Haycraft (in his book *Murder for Pleasure*) calls the Golden Age of detective fiction that really get me down. This age is not remote. For Mr. Haycraft's purpose it starts after the First World War and lasts up to about 1930. For all practical purposes it is still here. Two thirds or three quarters of all the detective stories published still adhere to the formula the giants of this era created, perfected, polished, and sold to the world as problems in logic and deduction.

These are stern words, but be not alarmed. They are only words. Let us glance at one of the glories of the literature, an acknowledged masterpiece of the art of fooling the reader without cheating him. It is called *The Red House Mystery,* was written by A. A. Milne, and has been named by Alexander Woollcott (rather a fast man with a superlative) "one of the three best mystery stories of all time." Words of that size are not spoken lightly. The book was published in 1922 but is timeless, and might as easily have been published in July, 1939, or, with a few slight changes, last week. It ran thirteen editions and seems to have been in print, in the original format, for about sixteen years. That happens to few books of any kind. It is an agreeable book, light, amusing in the *Punch* style, written with a deceptive smoothness that is not so easy as it looks.

It concerns Mark Ablett's impersonation of his brother Robert, as a hoax on his friends. Mark is the owner of the Red House, a typical laburnum and lodge gate English country house. He has a secretary who encourages him and abets him in this impersonation, and who is going to murder him if he pulls it off. Nobody around the Red House has ever seen Robert, fifteen years absent in Australia and known by repute as a no-good. A letter is talked about (but never seen) announcing Robert's arrival, and Mark hints it will not be a pleasant occasion. One afternoon, then, the supposed Robert arrives, identifies himself to a couple of servants, is shown into the study. Mark goes in after him (according to testimony at the inquest). Robert is then found dead on the floor with a bullet hole in his face, and of course Mark has vanished into thin air.

Arrive the police, who suspect Mark must be the murderer, remove the debris, and proceed with the investigation—and in due course, with the inquest.

Milne is aware of one very difficult hurdle and tries as well as he can to get over it. Since the secretary is going to murder Mark, once Mark has established himself as Robert, the impersonation has to continue on and fool the police. Since, also, everybody around the Red House knows Mark intimately, disguise is necessary. This is achieved by shaving off Mark's beard, roughening his hands ("not the hands of a manicured gentleman"—testimony), and having him use a gruff voice and rough manner.

But this is not enough. The cops are going to have the body and the clothes on it and whatever is in the pockets. Therefore none of this must suggest Mark. Milne therefore works like a switch engine to put over the motivation that Mark is such a thoroughly conceited performer that he dresses the part down to the socks and underwear (from all of which the secretary has removed the maker's labels), like a ham blacking himself all over to play Othello. If the reader will buy this (and the sales record shows he must have), Milne figures he is solid. Yet, however light in texture the story may be, it is offered as a problem of logic and deduction.

If it is not that, it is nothing at all. There is nothing else for it to be. If the situation is false, you cannot even accept it as a light novel, for there is no story for the light novel to be about. If the problem does not contain the elements of truth and plausibility, it is no problem; if the logic is a chimera, there is nothing to deduce. If the impersonation is impossible once the reader is told the conditions it must fulfill, then the whole thing is a fraud. Not a deliberate fraud, because Milne would not have written the story if he had known what he was up against. He is up against a number of deadly things, none of which he even considers. Nor, apparently, does the casual reader, who wants to like the story—hence takes it at its face value. But the reader is not called upon to know the facts of life when the author does not. The author is the expert in the case.

Here is what he ignores:—

1. The coroner holds formal jury inquest on a body for which no competent legal identification is offered. A coroner, usually in a big city, will sometimes hold inquest on a body that *cannot* be identified, if the record of such an inquest has or may have a value (fire, disaster, evidence of murder). No such reason exists here, and there is no one to identify the body. Witnesses said the man said he was Robert Ablett. This is mere presumption, and has weight only if nothing conflicts with it. Identification is a condition precedent to an inquest. It is a matter of law. Even in death a man has a right to his own identity. The coroner will, wherever humanly possible, enforce that right. To neglect it would be a violation of his office.

2. Since Mark Ablett, missing and suspected of the murder, cannot defend himself, all evidence of his movements before and after the murder is vital (as also whether he has money to run away on); yet all such evidence is given by the man closest to the murder and is without corroboration. It is automatically suspect until proved true.

3. The police find by direct investigation that Robert Ablett was not well thought of in his native village. Somebody there must have known him. No such person was brought to the inquest. Why? (The story couldn't stand it.)

4. The police know there is an element of threat in Robert's supposed visit, and that it is connected with the murder must be obvious to them. Yet they make no attempt to check Robert in Australia, or find out what character he had there, or what associates, or even if he actually came to England, and with whom. (If they had, they would have found out he had been dead three years.)

5. The police surgeon examines a body with a recently shaved beard (exposing unweathered skin) and artificially roughened hands, but it is the body of a wealthy, soft-living man, long resident in a cool climate. Robert was a rough individual and had lived fifteen years in Australia. That is the surgeon's information. It is impossible he would have noticed nothing to conflict with it.

6. The clothes are nameless, empty, and have had the labels removed. Yet the man wearing them asserted an identity. The presumption that he was not what he said he was is overpowering. Yet nothing whatsoever is done about it.

7. A man is missing, a well-known local man, and a body in the morgue closely resembles him. It is unbelievable that the police should not eliminate the chance that the missing man *is* the dead man. Nothing would be easier than to prove it. Not even to think of this is incredible.

The detective in the case is an insouciant amateur named Anthony Gillingham, a nice lad with a cheery eye, a nice little flat in town, and that airy manner. He is not making any money on the assignment, but is always available when the local gendarmerie loses its notebook. The English police endure him with their customary stoicism, but I shudder to think what the boys down at the Homicide Bureau in my city would do to him.

There are even less plausible examples of the art than this. In *Trent's Last Case* (often called "the perfect detective story") you have to accept the premise that a giant of international finance, whose lightest frown makes Wall Street quiver like a chihuahua, will plot his own death so as to hang his secretary, and that the secretary when pinched will maintain an aristocratic silence—the old Etonian in him, maybe. I have known relatively few international financiers, but I rather think the author of this novel has (if possible) known fewer.

There is another one, by Freeman Wills Crofts (the soundest builder of them all when he doesn't get too fancy), wherein a murderer, by the aid of make-up, split-second timing, and some very sweet evasive action, impersonates the man he has just killed and thereby gets him alive and distant from the place of the crime. There is one by Dorothy Sayers in which a man is murdered alone at night in his house by a mechanically released weight which works because he always turns the radio on at just such a moment, always stands in just such a position in front of it, and always bends over just so far. A couple of inches either way and the customers would get a rain check. This is what is vulgarly known as having God sit in your lap; a murderer who needs that much help from Providence must be in the wrong business.

And there is a scheme of Agatha Christie's featuring Hercule Poirot, that ingenious Belgian who talks in a literal translation of schoolboy French. By duly messing around with his "little gray cells" M. Poirot decides that since nobody on a certain through sleeper could have done the murder alone, everybody did it together, breaking the process down into a series of simple operations. This is the type that is guaranteed to knock the keenest mind for a loop. Only a halfwit could guess it.

There are much better ones by these same writers and others. There may be one somewhere that would really stand up under close scrutiny. It would be fun to read it, even if I did have to go back to page 47 and refresh my memory about exactly what time the second gardener potted the prize-winning tea-rose begonia. There is nothing new about these stories and nothing old. The ones I mentioned are all English because the authorities, such as they are, seem to feel that the English writers have an edge and that the Americans, even the creator of Philo Vance, only make the Junior Varsity.

This, the classic detective story, has learned nothing and forgotten nothing. It is the story you will find almost any week in the big shiny magazines, handsomely illustrated, and paying due deference to virginal love and the right kind of luxury goods. Perhaps the tempo is a wee bit faster and the dialogue a little more pert. There are more frozen daiquiris and stingers and fewer glasses of crusty old port, more clothes by *Vogue* and decors by *House Beautiful,* more chic, but not more truth. We spend more time in Miami hotels and Cape Cod summer colonies and go not so often down by the old gray sundial in the Elizabethan garden.

But fundamentally it is the same careful grouping of suspects, the same utterly incomprehensible trick of how somebody stabbed Mrs. Pottington Postlethwaite III with the solid platinum poignard just as she flatted on the top note of the "Bell Song" from *Lakmé* in the presence of fifteen ill-assorted guests; the same ingénue in fur-trimmed pajamas screaming in the night to make the company pop in and out of doors and ball up the timetable; the same moody silence next day as they sit around sipping Singapore slings and sneering at each other, while the flatfeet crawl to and fro under the Persian rugs, with their derby hats on.

Personally I like the English style better. It is not quite so brittle and the people as a rule just wear clothes and drink drinks. There is more sense of background, as if Cheesecake Manor really existed all around and not just in the part the camera sees; there are more long walks over the downs and the characters don't all try to behave as if they had just been tested by MGM. The English may not always be the best writers in the world, but they are incomparably the best dull writers.

But there is a very simple statement to be made about all these stories: they do not really come off intellectually as problems, and they do not come off artistically as fiction. They are too contrived, and too little aware of what goes on in the world. They try to be honest, but honesty is an art. The poor writer is dishonest without knowing it, and the fairly good one can be dishonest because he doesn't know what to be honest about. He thinks a complicated murder scheme which baffled the lazy reader, who won't be bothered itemizing the details, will also baffle the police, whose business is with details.

The boys with their feet on the desks know that the easiest murder case in the world to break is the one somebody tried to get cute with; the one that really bothers them is the murder somebody thought of only two minutes before he pulled it off. But if the writers of this fiction—much loved and much admired as I know it is—wrote about the kind of murders that happen, they would also have to write about the authentic flavor of life as it is lived. And since they cannot do that, they pretend that what they do is what should be done. Which is begging the question—and the best of them know it.

In her introduction to the first *Omnibus of Crime,* Dorothy Sayers wrote: "It [the detective story] does not, and by hypothesis never can, attain the loftiest level of literary achievement." And the reason, as she suggested somewhere else, is that it is a "literature of escape" and not "a literature of expression." I do not know what the loftiest level of literary achievement is: neither did Aeschylus or Shakespeare; neither does Miss Sayers. Other things being equal, which they never are, a more powerful theme will provoke a more powerful performance. Yet some very dull books have been written about God, and some very fine ones about how to make a living and stay fairly honest. It is always a matter of who writes the stuff, and what he has in him to write it with.

As for "literature of expression" and "literature of escape"—this is critics' jargon, a use of abstract words as if they had absolute meanings. Everything written with vitality expresses that vitality: there are no dull subjects, only dull writers. All men who read escape from something else into what lies behind the printed page; the quality of the dream may be argued, but its release has become a functional necessity. All men must escape at times from the deadly rhythm of their private thoughts. That is part of the process of life among thinking beings. It is one of the things that distinguish them from the three-toed sloth; he apparently—one can never be quite sure—is perfectly content hanging upside down on a branch, not even reading Walter Lippmann.

I think what was really gnawing at Miss Sayers's mind was the slow realization that her kind of detective story was an arid formula which could not even satisfy its own implications. It was second-grade literature because it was not about the things that could make first-grade literature. If it started out to be about real people (and she could write about them—her minor characters show that), they must very soon do unreal things in order to form the artificial pattern required by the plot. When they did unreal things, they ceased to be real themselves. They became puppets and cardboard lovers and papier-mâché villains and detectives of exquisite and impossible gentility.

The only kind of writer who could be happy with these properties was the one who did not know what reality was. Dorothy Sayer's own stories show that she was annoyed by this triteness; the weakest element in them is the part that makes them detective stories, the strongest the part which could be removed without touching the "problem of logic and deduction." Yet she could not or would not give her characters their heads and let them make their own mystery. It took a much simpler and more direct mind than hers to do that.

In *The Long Week End,* which is a drastically competent account of English life and manners in the decades following the First World War, Robert Graves and Alan Hodge gave some attention to the authors of detective stories, whose books sold into the millions, and in a dozen languages. These were the people who fixed the form and established the rules and founded the famous Detection Club, which is a Parnassus of English writers of mystery. Its roster includes practically every important writer of detective fiction since Conan Doyle.

But Graves and Hodge decided that during this whole period only one first-class writer had written detective stories at all. An American, Dashiell Hammett. Traditional or not, Graves and Hodge were not fuddy-duddy connoisseurs of the second-rate; they could see what went on in the world and that the detective story of their time didn't; and they were aware that writers who have the vision and the ability to produce real fiction do not produce unreal fiction.

How original a writer Hammett really was it isn't easy to decide now, even if it mattered. He was one of a group— the only one who achieved critical recognition—who wrote or tried to write realistic mystery fiction. All literary movements are like this; some one individual is picked out to represent the whole movement; he is usually the culmination of the movement. Hammett was the ace performer, but there is nothing in his work that is not implicit in the early novels and short stories of Hemingway.

Yet, for all I know, Hemingway may have learned something from Hammett as well as from writers like Dreiser, Ring Lardner, Carl Sandburg, Sherwood Anderson, and himself. A revolutionary debunking of both the language and the material of fiction had been going on for some time. It probably started in poetry; almost everything does. But Hammett applied it to the detective story, and this,

because of its heavy crust of English gentility and American pseudo-gentility, was pretty hard to get moving.

I doubt that Hammett had any deliberate artistic aims whatever; he was trying to make a living by writing something he had firsthand information about. He made some of it up; all writers do; but it had a basis in fact; it was made up out of real things. The only reality the English detection writers knew was the conversational accent of Surbiton and Bognor Regis. If they wrote about dukes and Venetian vases, they knew no more about them out of their own experience than the well-heeled Hollywood character knows about the French Modernists that hang in his Bel-Air château or the semi-antique Chippendale-cum-cobbler's bench that he uses for a coffee table. Hammett took murder out of the Venetian vase and dropped it into the alley; it doesn't have to stay there forever, but it looked like a good idea to get as far as possible from Emily Post's idea of how a well-bred debutante gnaws a chicken wing.

Hammett wrote at first (and almost to the end) for people with a sharp, aggressive attitude to life. They were not afraid of the seamy side of things; they lived there. Violence did not dismay them; it was right down their street. Hammett gave murder back to the kind of people that commit it for reasons, not just to provide a corpse; and with the means at hand, not hand-wrought dueling pistols, curare, and tropical fish. He put these people down on paper as they were, and he made them talk and think in the language they customarily used for these purposes.

He had a literary style, but his audience didn't know it, because it was in a language not supposed to be capable of such refinements. They thought they were getting a good meaty melodrama written in the kind of lingo they imagined they spoke themselves. It was, in a sense, but it was much more. All language begins with speech, and the speech of common men at that, but when it develops to the point of becoming a literary medium it only looks like speech. Hammett's style at its worst was as formalized as a page of *Marius the Epicurean;* at its best it could say almost anything. I believe this style, which does not belong to Hammett or to anybody, but is the American language (and not even exclusively that any more), can say things he did not know how to say, or feel the need of saying. In his hands it had no overtones, left no echo, evoked no image beyond a distant hill.

Hammett is said to have lacked heart; yet the story he himself thought the most of is the record of a man's devotion to a friend. He was spare, frugal, hard-boiled, but he did over and over again what only the best writers can ever do at all. He wrote scenes that seemed never to have been written before.

With all this, Hammett did not wreck the formal detective story. Nobody can; production demands a form that can be produced. Realism takes too much talent, too much knowledge, too much awareness. He may have loosened it up a little here, and sharpened it a little there. Certainly all but the stupidest and most meretricious writers are more conscious of their artificiality than they used to be. And he demonstrated that the detective story can be important writing. *The Maltese Falcon* may or may not be a work of genius, but an art which is capable of it is not "by hypothesis" incapable of anything. Once a detective story can be as good as this, only the pedants will deny that it *could* be even better.

Hammett did something else; he made the detective story fun to write, not an exhausting contenation of insignificant clues. Without him there might not have been a regional mystery as clever as Percival Wilde's *Inquest,* or an ironic study as able as Raymond Postgate's *Verdict of Twelve,* or a savage piece of intellectual double-talk like Kenneth Fearing's *The Dagger of the Mind,* or a tragi-comic idealization of the murderer as in Donald Henderson's *Mr. Bowling Buys a Newspaper,* or even a gay Hollywoodian gambol like Richard Sale's *Lazarus #7.*

The realistic style is easy to abuse: from haste, from lack of awareness, from inability to bridge the chasm that lies between what a writer would like to be able to say and what he actually knows how to say. It is easy to fake; brutality is not strength, flipness is not wit, edge-of-the-chair writing can be as boring as flat writing; dalliance with promiscuous blondes can be very dull stuff when described by goaty young men with no other purpose in mind than to describe dalliance with promiscuous blondes. There has been so much of this sort of thing that if a character in a detective story says "Yeah," the author is automatically a Hammett imitator.

And there are still a number of people around who say that Hammett did not write detective stories at all—merely hard-boiled chronicles of mean streets with a perfunctory mystery element dropped in like the olive in a Martini. These are the flustered old ladies—of both sexes (or no sex) and almost all ages—who like their murders scented with magnolia blossoms and do not care to be reminded that murder is an act of infinite cruelty, even if the perpetrators sometimes look like playboys or college professors or nice motherly women with softly graying hair.

There are also a few champions of the formal or classic mystery who think that no story is a detective story which does not pose a formal and exact problem and arrange the clues around it with neat labels on them. Such would point out, for example, that in reading *The Maltese Falcon* no one concerns himself with who killed Spade's partner, Archer (which is the only formal problem of the story), because the reader is kept thinking about something else. Yet in *The Glass Key* the reader is constantly reminded that the question is who killed Taylor Henry, and exactly the same effect is obtained—an effect of movement, intrigue, cross-purposes, and the gradual elucidation of character, which is all the detective story has any right to be about anyway. The rest is spillikins in the parlor.

But all this (and Hammett too) is for me not quite enough. This is the point at which I begin to talk a little above myself, but it can't be helped. The realist in murder writes of a world in which gangsters can rule nations and almost rule cities, in which hotels and apartment houses and celebrated restaurants are owned by men who made their money out of brothels, in which a screen star can be the fingerman for a mob, and the nice man down the hall is a boss of the numbers racket; a world where a judge with a cellar full of bootleg liquor can send a man to jail for having a pint in his pocket, where the mayor of your town may have condoned murder as an instrument of money-making, where no man can walk down a dark street in safety because law and order are things we talk about but refrain from practicing; a world where you may witness a holdup in broad daylight and see who did it, but you will fade quickly back into the crowd rather than tell anyone, because the holdup men may have friends with long guns, or the police may not like your testimony, and in any case the shyster for the defense will be allowed to abuse and vilify you in open court, before a jury of selected morons, without any but the most perfunctory interference from a political judge.

It is not a fragrant world, but it is the world you live in, and certain writers with tough minds and a cool spirit of detachment can make interesting and even amusing patterns out of it. It is not funny that a man should be killed, but it is sometimes funny that he should be killed for so little, and that his death should be the coin of what we call civilization. All this still is not quite enough.

In everything that can be called art there is a quality of redemption. It may be pure tragedy, if it is high tragedy, and it may be pity and irony, and it may be the raucous laughter of the strong man. But down these mean streets a man must go who is not himself mean, who is neither tarnished nor afraid. The detective in this kind of story must be such a man. He is the hero; he is everything. He must be a complete man and a common man and yet an unusual man. He must be, to use a rather weathered phrase, a man of honor—by instinct, by inevitability, without thought of it, and certainly without saying it. He must be the best man in his world and a good enough man for any world. I do not care much about his private life; he is neither a eunuch nor a satyr; I think he might seduce a duchess and I am quite sure he would not spoil a virgin; if he is a man of honor in one thing, he is that in all things.

He is a relatively poor man, or he would not be a detective at all. He is a common man or he could not go among common people; he has a sense of character, or he would not know his job. He will take no man's money dishonestly and no man's insolence without a due and dispassionate revenge; he is a lonely man and his pride is that you will treat him as a proud man or be very sorry you ever saw him. He talks as the man of his age talks—that is, with rude wit, a lively sense of the grotesque, a disgust for sham, and a contempt for pettiness.

The story is this man's adventure in search of a hidden truth, and it would be no adventure if it did not happen to a man fit for adventure. He has a range of awareness that startles you, but it belongs to him by right, because it belongs to the world he lives in. If there were enough like him, the world would be a safe place to live in, without becoming too dull to be worth living in. Such is my faith.

J. B. Priestley (essay date 1962)

SOURCE: "Close-up of Chandler," in *New Statesman,* Vol. LXIII, No. 1618, March 16, 1962, pp. 379-80.

[*In the following review of* Raymond Chandler Speaking, *Priestley assesses Chandler's story-telling skills and his efforts to turn murder mysteries into literature.*]

Raymond Chandler Speaking offers us various unpublished pieces, including several chapters from the novel he left unfinished at his death, and a large number of letters written to his publishers, agents, fellow writers and various friends. It is a rather more solid book than it would first appear to be, and Chandler's many admirers will find it good value. Young writers chiefly concerned with the novel of action and violence should not miss it, for Chandler, at his best a master of this kind of fiction, has much to say that deserves their attention.

Though I make no appearance in these pages, I was in fact among the first over here to praise him in print. (Like many good American writers, he was properly appreciated here before he was given any serious consideration in his own country, as he himself points out.) After exchanging several letters with him, I accepted an invitation, early in 1951, to break my journey from Mexico to Santa Monica and spend a few days with him at La Jolla, a small seaside town not far from San Diego. It is the setting of his last completed novel, *Playback.*

He met me at the airport in Tiajuana, and as he drove me up to La Jolla he explained that as his wife was ill he was putting me up in an hotel. (It was a pleasant hotel though I seemed to be the only guest there under 80.) But we had some talk, among other places, in his library, filled with good books that were not there for show. He was in fact extremely well-read, though he was capable of pretending not to be. He was even less like his Philip Marlowe, or any other tough, brash private eye, that I am; and seemed rather shy, ruminative and mumbling round his pipe, more English in manner than American, not unlike a boffin character in an Ealing film. . . .

Between 1919 and 1932 he tried a variety of jobs in Southern California, finally helping to run a number of small oil companies but not, as an executive, surviving the depression. Then he began writing for the detective story 'pulps', especially *Black Mask.* There is a photograph in this book of a dinner group of *Black Mask* writers, in which we see Chandler, still looking thin-faced, scholarly and a refugee from the *Academy* and the *Westminster Gazette,* standing in a line that has at the end of it the towering though rather ghostly figure of Dashiell Hammett. (It was the only time they met.) How good Hammett had been as a private eye, we do not know, but what is certain is that in American

fiction he was a powerful originator to whom full justice has not been done. It is a mistake, in my opinion, to think of him in terms of the films made out of his *Maltese Falcon* and *Thin Man.* He is strongest and most original in *The Glass Key,* not simply another 'mystery story' but a genuine novel of violence and city politics in the gangster era.

Chandler, whose first full-length story, *The Big Sleep,* came out in 1939, owed something to Hammett but not very much. His qualities and his whole approach were quite different. Hammett, arriving by way of Pinkerton's, wanted the reader to share a kind of experience he himself had known; his flat, hard style (his own, not borrowed from Hemingway) and laconic manner of narration drove at realism. 'This is how it was,' he is saying. But Chandler, altogether more self-conscious, really a literary man and not a story-teller shaped and hardened by experience, approached the novel of action and violence from the other end. Deliberately he developed and experimented with it as a literary form. If there should be any doubt about this, a glance at these letters will immediately remove it.

As he freely confesses, Chandler was not a natural story-teller, a fertile plotter. This is proved by his habit, astonishing to me, of making use in his full-length novels of earlier short stories. Moreover, he has not the forward movement, the natural follow-through, of the born story-teller. The novels in the new *Second Chandler Omnibus—The Little Sister, The Long Goodbye* and *Playback*—seem to me badly constructed, weak narratives on the 'murder-mystery' level. Nevertheless, though generally inferior to the novels in the *First Omnibus,* they can be read and, after an interval, re-read with pleasure if you have, as I have, a taste for this writer's sharp flavour.

Consider, for example, *The Little Sister,* which Chandler himself, as we learn from these letters, did not like too well. The underlying story pattern seems to me a complete failure. It leaves one neither knowing nor caring. But many of its episodes, as scenes, are astonishingly good. And what are perhaps the best—those in the film agent's office and in the studio—add little or nothing to the story line. They exist in their own right. Here is the key to Chandler, who was not really writing 'murder mysteries' at all. He accepted a mediocre form—it is his own phrase—and made something like literature out of it.

He put together mosaics of brilliant scenes. He took that *Black Mask* and worked over it in bright enamels. He turned the American 'mystery story' into a kind of private theatre, almost as artificial in its way as Restoration Comedy. He was a highly self-conscious novelist who would not venture on a novel. (This explains the uneasiness and touchiness displayed in these letters; when we are sharp with everybody we are criticizing ourselves.) In a sense he was like those dons who dare not come out into the open as novelists and so write elaborate detective-puzzles under false names. He did not write that kind of story—and his 'Simple Art of Murder' contains a devastating criticism of it—but he did cling to the murder-and-detection rigging when he could have done without it, as some of us told him. He had to have, like a frame for the mosaic, the gunmen and the menacing whispers over the telephone, the night club gambling, the grilling by the cops, the ice-cold whisky and the hot-tongued blondes.

Because such material is cheap and easy we must not imagine that what he made out of it is cheap and easy too. To any reader with an eye and an ear Chandler's scores of imitators have never come near the edge and brilliance of his scenes. Behind this talent of his for writing dialogue, description (sometimes overdone), social comment, was an odd character with an odd mixture of experience. He was an American educated in England. He began writing in the London of Saki and the *Westminster*. He was a man with a literary temperament and training who, when he started writing again, hammered out tough tales for the 'pulps'. Rather late in life he acquired the persona of a sardonic professional storyteller, ready to take Hollywood and the big money in his stride, but he remained at heart—in the better sense of this term—an amateur of letters. There are two photographs in this book, one taken in 1958 (all persona), the other perhaps 35 years earlier; it is hard to believe they are of the same man.

He did not go to Southern California to write but to earn any kind of living, all the way from picking apricots to running oil companies. An immense variety of experience went into his fiction. This explains why to some of us, not unacquainted with the region, he is not simply the wittiest of the 'murder-mystery' writers but the man who comes nearest yet to being the novelist of Southern California. Its scene is being dazzlingly illuminated by the searchlight flashes of his scenes. And this is no Deep South, a lingering survival, alien to most of us. Here in Southern California is a much-admired, widely-imitated section of our western society, the filmgoer's dreamland, the teenager's Mecca. Its antics and values today will be our antics and values tomorrow. And it is here that Chandler, while shaping and colouring his mosaics for our entertainment, points his torch and makes his comment.

There are so many sharp comments here in these letters that I have marked too many passages and now, when I have space for only a few, may miss the best. But here are some for us writers:

> I know you publishers. You send the proofs off by air express and I sit up all night correcting them and send them back the same way. And the next thing anybody hears about you, you're sound asleep on somebody's private beach in Bermuda. But when anybody else has to do something, it's rush, rush, rush . . .

> The publisher could justify himself perhaps, but he won't give any figures out. He won't tell you what his books cost him, he won't tell you what his overhead charge is, he won't tell you anything. The minute you try to talk business with him he takes the attitude that he is a gentleman and a scholar, and the moment you try to approach him on the level of his moral integrity he starts to talk business . . .

> . . . The very nicest thing Hollywood can possibly think of to say to a writer is that he is too good to be only a writer . . .

> . . . I have done everything from giving would-be writers money to live on to plotting and re-writing their stories for them, and so far I have found it to be all waste. The people whom God or nature intended to be writers find their own answers, and those who have to ask are impossible to help. . . .

> . . . It is not enough for a critic to be right, since he will occasionally be wrong. It is not enough for him to give colorable reasons. He must create a reasonable world into which his reader may enter blindfold and feel his way to the chair by the fire without barking his shins on the unexpected dust mop. The barbed phrase, the sedulously rare word, the high-brow affectation of style—these are amusing but useless. They place nothing and reveal not the temper of the times. The great critics, of whom there are piteously few, build a home for the truth . . .

After comparing two kinds of novelists, the solid practitioners and the rare artists, he goes on:

> Not that I class myself with any of these people. I really don't class myself at all, nor greatly care about it. I'm still an amateur, still, psychologically speaking, perfectly capable of chucking writing altogether and taking up the study of law or comparative philology . . .

He wrote that in 1949, when he had already entered his sixties, and it is the truth about one side of him. Like most good writers he was very much a divided man. The opposites in him can be found in this volume, generously displayed. And for my part I am glad Dorothy Gardiner and Kathrine Sorley Walker edited it, and Hamish Hamilton published it.

Wilson Pollock (essay date 1962)

SOURCE: "Man with a Toy Gun," in *The New Republic,* Vol. 146, No. 19, May 7, 1962, pp. 21-2.

[*In the following review of* Raymond Chandler Speaking, *Pollock describes Chandler's writings in light of significant events in his life.*]

Following in Dashiell Hammett's footsteps, Raymond Chandler brought a new vigor to detective fiction. His books sold in the millions but they were detective stories not serious literature, and so he was never invited to join the Boys in the Back Room, not even for a short beer. He died in La Jolla, California, March 26, 1959, at the age of 70. *Raymond Chandler Speaking* is a collection of excerpts from letters to friends, publishers, agents, and others during the forties and fifties. It also contains an unpublished short story, two articles, and the opening chapters of a new Philip Marlowe novel called *The Poodle Springs Story* which he did not live to finish.

Chandler began writing seriously in the thirties after losing a job with a California oil company. He wrote for money from the very beginning and he sold stories with titles like **"Blackmailers Don't Shoot," "Nevada Gas,"** and **"Guns at Cyrano's"** to magazines with names like *Black Mask* and *Dime Detective Monthly*. In 1939 he published his first full-length book, *The Big Sleep,* and in 1943 he went to Hollywood. No one could accuse him of selling out.

He was no intellectual and although some of his work might seem to reveal a political conscience it wasn't there. "There was even a bird," he writes, "who informed me I could write a good proletarian novel; in my limited world there is no such animal, and if there were, I am the last mind in the world to like it, being by tradition and long study a complete snob." He merely believed that society was corrupt, that the only god was the fast easy buck, and that there was not very much any one could do about it. "The only difference I can see [between American big business and Russian Communism] is that in Russia when you begin to slip a little they either shoot you or send you to a forced labor camp, whereas in the United States they ask you for your resignation or else force you to give it without being asked by humiliating you beyond endurance." He accepted Hollywood's big money without feeling anything like guilt; he seems to have liked the movies if not necessarily the men who made them. In one of the articles included here, "Writers in Hollywood" he tells the well-known story of the hamstrung screenwriter. "The impulse to perfection cannot exist where the definition of perfection is the arbitrary decision of authority. That which is born in loneliness and from the heart cannot be defended against the judgement of a committee of sycophants." He was in the thick of the celluloid at the time, but the tone was detached. "My agent was told by the Paramount story editor that it [the article] has done me a lot of harm with the producers at Paramount." He is not impressed. "Charlie Brackett said: 'Chandler's books are not good enough nor his pictures bad enough to justify that article' . . . I would reply to Mr. Brackett that if my books had been any worse I should not have been invited to Hollywood and that if they had been any better, I should not have come . . ."

He thought occasionally about writing serious novels, stories, and toward the end, a serious play, but he never did very much about it. The serious story included here is about a couple of people who slowly and painfully come to realize that they are not writers. It is like the work of a bright young man trying to break into the little magazines. Chandler wrote it when he was 63 and it is no wonder that it was never published. It was too late.

Drugstore literature of the kind he wrote is consumed by juvenile delinquent and dowager alike and Chandler knew it. It was pretty raw stuff sometimes, but he was never one of those "writers of comic strips like Mickey Spillane." Auden, in an article on the detective story called "The Guilty Vicarage" said that Chandler was "interested in writing serious studies of a criminal milieu." Chandler's comment on this was: "So now I look at everything I put down and say to myself, Remember, old boy, this has to be a serious study of a criminal milieu. Are you serious? No. Is this a criminal milieu? No, just average corrupt living with the melodramatic angle overemphasized, not because I am crazy about melodrama for its own sake, but because I am realistic enough to know the rules of the game."

In a letter to one of his readers who wants to know more about Philip Marlowe he writes about his detective-hero as if he were a very good friend. He describes Marlowe's education, smoking and drinking habits, attitudes toward women, the lay-out of his apartment. Then in another letter he writes, ". . . if being in revolt against a corrupt society constitutes being immature, then Philip Marlowe is extremely immature. If seeing dirt where there is dirt constitutes an inadequate social adjustment, then Philip Marlowe has an inadequate social adjustment. Of course Marlowe is a failure and he knows it. He is a failure because he hasn't any money. A man who without physical handicaps cannot make a decent living is always a failure because their particular talents did not suit their time and place. In the long run we are all failures or we wouldn't have the kind of world we have." It comes as a letdown when Chandler writes, "But you must remember that Marlowe is not a real person. He is a creature of fantasy. He is in a false position because I put him there. In real life a man of his type would no more be a private detective then he would be a university don."

Chandler was interested in everything but what he cared about most was his wife Cissy who was 18 years older than he was and died five years before he did. "She was the beat of my heart for 30 years. She was the music heard faintly at the edge of sound. It was my great and now useless regret that I never wrote anything really worth her attention, no book that I could dedicate to her. I planned it. I thought of it but I never wrote it. Perhaps I couldn't have written it." And three years later ". . . I wasn't faithful to my wife out of principal but because she was completely adorable, and the urge to stray which afflicts many men at a certain age, because they think they have been missing a lot of beautiful girls, never touched me. I already had perfection."

Chandler attempted suicide in 1955, a little more than a year after his wife's death. According to the editors of this book one of Chandler's friends described it as being "the most inefficient effort at suicide on record." He writes about it frankly here in one of these carefully edited letters. Too carefully edited. Chandler may not have been as hardboiled as Marlowe but he had guts, and it doesn't seem right that guts should be represented in a man's last work by three dots.

He knew the language of the underworld the way Ring Lardner knew the language of baseball. "How do you tell a man to go away in hard language? Scram, beat it, take off, take the air, on your way, dangle, hit the road, and so forth. All good enough. But give me the classic expression used by Spike O'Donnell (of the O'Donnell brothers of Chicago, the only small outfit to tell the Capone mob

to go to hell and live). What he said was, 'Be missing'."
And in the same letter Chandler says he is sure that O'Neill
borrowed the phrase "the big sleep" for *The Iceman
Cometh* thinking that it was an underworld expression.
But Chandler had made it up.

It is only natural that Hemingway's name should come up.
Chandler defends *Across the River and Into the Trees* against
what most people were saying about it at the time and are
still saying. "Candidly, it's not the best thing he's done, but
it's still a hell of a sight better than anything his detractors
could do." Chandler and Hemingway had more in common
than Humphrey Bogart. "The Killers" could almost be a
Black Mask story except that the ending would probably
have cost the author a rejection slip. *To Have and Have
Not* is not very much better than *Farewell, My Lovely*. The
biggest difference is that Hemingway also wrote *A Farewell to Arms*. It's too bad that Chandler and Hemingway
never got together. But maybe they didn't have to.

Philip Durham (essay date 1963)

SOURCE: "The Tale-Teller," in *Down These Mean Streets
a Man Must Go: Raymond Chandler's Knight,* The University of North Carolina Press, 1963, pp. 22-30.

[*In the following essay, Durham examines Chandler's
published short stories, praising his evocative descriptions of character and the city of Los Angeles.*]

Thousands of ghost-like flimsy wooden derricks were
standing throughout the Los Angeles Basin, the Dabney-
Johnston Oil Corporation (soon to move to tiny quarters
at 620 West Olympic Boulevard with only one company,
the South Basin, remaining) was still operating, but Raymond Chandler, in 1933, was no longer in the oil business. His separation from business, although primarily for
economic reasons, was hardly less abrupt than was Sherwood Anderson's a few years before.

When Anderson decided to leave the world of business,
he did it (so he said) in dramatic fashion. In his factory
office he turned to his secretary, saying, "My feet are
cold, wet and heavy from long wading in a river. Now I
shall go walk on dry land." Going through the door, a
"delicious thought" came to him: "Oh, you little tricky
words, you are my brothers. It is you, not myself, have
lifted me over this threshold. It is you who have dared
give me a hand. For the rest of my life, I will be a servant
to you." So thinking, he went out of the town, out of that
phase of his life.

Raymond Chandler left no such romantic account of his
farewell to the business world. The former oil executive
went only a few blocks westward, to home and Cissy [his
wife]. But from that time on words were indeed his brothers. And from that time on he was "a tale-teller." The
youthful interest in writing, suppressed for many years,
came suddenly to the surface through the phenomenon of
a devastating economic depression.

A number of alphabetical groups designed to provide work
were being instituted in the nation's capital, but Chandler
did not apply. Instead he set about on his own to learn the
craft of fiction. In 1933 he listed himself as merely a
"writer." Write he undoubtedly did, but the published
results were contained in only one eighteen-thousand-word
story, **"Blackmailers Don't Shoot,"** which he sold to *Black
Mask* for one cent a word.

The *Black Mask* had been founded in New York thirteen
years earlier by Henry L. Mencken and George Jean
Nathan. Within a few issues after its founding, the *Black
Mask* began to emerge as a distinctive pulp magazine,
primarily through the stories of Carrol John Daly. Daly's
hero, Race Williams, became the prototype for the widely
used American private eye. By 1923 the *Black Mask* was
publishing Dashiell Hammett's detective stories, and the
magazine had developed a following.

When Captain Joseph Shaw assumed the editorship of the
Black Mask in 1926, he decided to make it a magazine in
which Hammett's style would predominate, so he sought
manuscripts from those authors who could write in the
"hard-boiled" manner. Shaw published the early short stories of Horace McCoy, and he printed, serially, many of
Dashiell Hammett's novels, including *The Maltese Falcon*
and *The Glass Key*. It was to this magazine that Chandler
sent his first story.

The December, 1933, issue of *Black Mask* that carried
Chandler's story also had contributions from Tom Curry,
Eugene Cunningham, Raoul Whitfield, and Erle Stanley
Gardner, the perennial *Black Mask* writer. In the year in
which Chandler published his first tale, Gardner published
The Case of the Velvet Claws, his first of more than one
hundred novels. In Chandler's **"Blackmailers Don't
Shoot"** his original private eye went from Chicago—during the Century of Progress Exposition—to Los Angeles,
where for twenty-two stories and seven novels he was to
remain. At the age of forty-five Chandler left his career as
a successful oil executive to begin what was to be an even
more successful one as a writer.

Raymond Chandler's first story is competent. The plot
and theme are conventional; characterization and setting
are the most interesting. From the beginning Chandler used
the technique of minute, detailed description to create
character. As the story began, the reader knew nothing
about Rhonda Farr, except what was publicly implied in
the person of a Hollywood movie queen. In a few descriptive sentences, however, Chandler separated Rhonda from
the fuzzy public image by giving her an individual personality. "Rhonda Farr was very beautiful. She was wearing,
for this occasion, all black except a collar of white fur,
light as thistledown, on her evening wrap. Except also a
white wig which, meant to disguise her, made her look
very girlish. Her eyes were cornflower blue, and she had
the sort of skin an old rake dreams of. . . . She held up her
hand, the one with the cigarette holder, looked at it, posing. It was a beautiful hand, without a ring. Beautiful hands
are as rare as jacaranda trees in bloom, in a city where
pretty faces are as common as runs in dollar stockings."

This kind of description was to become a Chandler trademark, especially as he made more frequent use of images. One character in **"Blackmailers Don't Shoot"** had to be satisfied with a terse description, but he could not thereafter be mistaken for anyone else. He had "a ludicrous big bulbous nose, no eyebrows at all, hair the color of the inside of a sardine can."

> Raymond Chandler's first story ["Blackmailers Don't Shoot"] is competent. The plot and theme are conventional; characterization and setting are the most interesting. From the beginning Chandler used the technique of minute, detailed description to create character.
>
> *—Philip Durham*

In this first story Chandler began recreating the city of Los Angeles for his purposes. As a painter fills in his scene, the writer added his streets, buildings, trees, flowers, birds, and hills: "The car went past the old well that stands in the middle of La Cienega Boulevard, then turned off on to a quiet street fringed with palm trees. . . . They went casually through a red light, passed a big movie palace with most of its lights out and its glass cashier's cage empty; then through Beverly Hills, over interurban tracks. The exhaust got louder on a long hill with high banks paralleling the road." The car arrived in front of a house "which stood well back from a wide curve. It had a lot of tiled roof, an entrance like a Norman arch, and wrought iron lanterns lit on either side of the door. By the sidewalk there was a pergola covered with climbing roses." In a Westwood Village apartment "the carpet was a mess of fat green and yellow lozenges," and the "bile-colored davenport" was "spotted with angry-looking red squares." In another part of the city there stood a frame house behind which "the gaunt shapes of a couple of derricks groped towards the sky. . . . A gravel driveway led along to a shed without a door. There was a touring car parked under the shed. There was thin worn grass along the driveway and a dull patch of something that had once been a lawn at the back. There was a wire clothes line and a small stoop with a rusted screen door. The moon showed all this." From story to story Chandler continued to add the small details until the city eventually emerged as a completed mosaic.

In 1934 the Chandlers moved from 4616 Greenwood Place to 1639 Redesdale Avenue, nine moves in ten years. All of these residences, incidentally, were unpretentious in either middle-class or lower middle-class neighborhoods. The constant moving about did not come from Chandler's rise in the business world but must have been the result of restlessness. "People live so comfortably and easily here that one can appreciate why Los Angeles has been and still is one of the most reactionary cities," wrote Oswald Garrison Villard in *The Nation* of March 21, 1934. Chandler was pretty conservative, but if he was now living comfortably it must have been on money left over from the oil days because he certainly was not living high as a result of the only two stories he published that year: **"Smart-Aleck Kill"** and **"Finger Man,"** in the July and October issues of *Black Mask*.

In **"Smart-Aleck Kill"** Chandler continued working with detailed description, achieving at times the quiet objective reporting made so prominent by Hemingway. "It was a big room with walls paneled in diagonal strips of wood. A yellow Chinese rug on the floor, plenty of good furniture, countersunk doors that told of soundproofing and no windows. There were several gilt gratings high up and a built-in ventilator fan made a faint, soothing murmur. Four men were in the room. Nobody said anything." The same unemotional method was used to describe violent death. "Derek Walden was slumped almost casually in the brown and gold chair. His mouth was slightly open. There was a blackened hole in his right temple, and a lacy pattern of blood spread down the side of his face and across the hollow of his neck as far as the soft collar of his shirt. His right hand trailed in the thick nap of the rug." The fact that Derek Walden's shirt had a soft collar and the rug a thick nap was as important as any other detail to the writer learning to use the objective technique; startling it was, however, that Chandler should have learned it so well in his second story.

The second and third stories, **"Smart-Aleck Kill"** and **"Finger Man,"** had a limited audience, but not so for *The Postman Always Rings Twice*, the Southern California novel by James M. Cain which also came out in 1934. And being an observant man to whom Los Angeles was thematic—a way of life—Chandler was probably noting that while Cain's book was a sensation in fiction, the once fabulous oil man C. C. Julian had just committed suicide "during a glittering dinner party with a woman in the Astor House Hotel in Shanghai" and that to the many "I am" religious cults in Los Angeles was added "Mankind United."

Los Angeles in the middle thirties provoked one citizen to say, "This isn't a city; this is a goddam conspiracy. It isn't interested in anything except selling vacant lots and cures for consumption." It also abounded in characters, one of whom was a newly-rich movie star who wired a New York book collector to "Send me one hundred seven rare books by air mail." But all of this was material for the author who had increased his writing tempo and published eight short stories during 1935 and 1936, seven in *Black Mask* and one in *Detective Fiction Weekly*. These stories, among them some of Chandler's good ones, used the city through which he had moved and the people with whom he had been associated or known about during the previous fifteen years. The big Pittsburgh steelworker, in **"Killer in the Rain,"** who had become a wealthy oilman by being in the right place at the right time was drawn from reality. Violence and gambling, used in **"Nevada Gas,"** were a part of Los Angeles. The seven murders in **"Spanish Blood"** may have been excessive for one short story, but were not excessive for Los Angeles. (Chandler threatened to write a detective story without a single murder, but the threat was never carried out.) The theme of **"Guns at Cyrano's"** had been repeated in the city many times: the man who must live with his conscience while also living on the money his father had made from various crooked schemes. When the private detective in **"The Curtain"** left General Winslow's home he looked at a scene completely familiar to the author: "Beyond the estate the hill sloped down to the city and the old oil wells of La Brea, now partly a park, partly a deserted stretch of fenced-in wild land. Some of the wooden derricks still stood. These had made the wealth of the Winslow family and then the family had run away from them up the hill, far enough to get away from the smell of the sumps, not too far for them to look out of the front windows and see what had made them rich." One element of society—the chiseler—found the atmosphere of Los Angeles a delightfully thriving one. He was frequently described in fact and fiction, including Chandler's **"Goldfish."** "You can wear the cops down. . . . You can wear the insurance company down and even the postal men. . . . But you can't wear the chiselers down. They'll never lay off. There'll always be a couple or three with time enough and money enough and meanness enough to bear down."

In the late 1930's the Chandlers lived for a year or two on Hartzell Avenue in the Pacific Palisades, the suburban area lying at the farthest western edge of Los Angeles, just north of Santa Monica. For a time Chandler thought of building and settling down in the Palisades, but he did not because, he later said, it was too windy. During this period his writing was slow and deliberate, for he was still learning his trade; only **"Try the Girl"** and **"Mandarin's Jade"** were published in 1937, and 1938 saw only **"Red Wind," "The King in Yellow,"** and **"Bay City Blues."** There was, however, an additional sharpness and at times a brilliance in the style, the delineation of character was frequently distinguished, and the atmosphere was breathing. Often in the years since its publication readers and critics have praised the manner in which Chandler created atmosphere in **"Red Wind"** by allowing the desert wind to permeate and motivate the story. The wind not only set the stage for murder but left its trail across the city: along Sunset Boulevard "gardens were full of withered and blackened leaves and flowers." **"Mandarin's Jade"** and **"Bay City Blues"** made extensive use of the Pacific Palisades and Santa Monica, with so much effect that the reader not only sees but also feels the streets, houses, trees, hills, canyons, and shore line.

By this time Chandler's achievements in the short story had gone almost as far as they were to go. He had used the form to develop his setting, to create his detective-hero, and more or less to master the style he had originally chosen. Although, with the exception of a limited number of pulp readers, his work was completely unknown, he was ready and anxious to try his skill in the big arena.

Philip Durham (essay date 1963)

SOURCE: "The Technique," in *Down These Mean Streets a Man Must Go: Raymond Chandler's Knight,* The University of North Carolina Press, 1963, pp. 106-29.

[*In the following essay, Durham analyzes Chandler's narrative technique, noting his lively prose, elegant expression, and belief that style was more important than plot.*]

In England early in 1954 Ralph Partridge, in *The New Statesman and Nation,* wrote that although there was a "jarring note of sentimentality" in *The Long Goodbye,* the "crusading" Marlowe was, nevertheless, a "remarkable creation"—"the perpetually crucified redeemer of all our modern sins." Almost alone among the reviewers, Partridge commented on Chandler's writing technique: "Mr. Chandler's style by now can be regarded as fixed . . . [his] language has lost none of its impetus, the rhythm of his prose is superb, and the intensity of feeling he packs into his pages makes every other thriller-writer look utterly silly and superficial." With the publication of *The Long Goodbye,* it was well that Mr. Partridge looked to what he considered Chandler's "fixed" style, for although no one knew it at the time Chandler had only one more book to write, and from that book much of the style had fled. "In the long run," Chandler once wrote, "however little you talk or even think about it, the most durable thing in writing is style, and style is the most valuable investment a writer can make of his time."

In the pages of the *New Yorker,* back in the autumn of 1944, Edmund Wilson took off on the authors of detective stories as being writers of a very low breed indeed. Wilson thereby joined the twentieth-century battle between the irrepressible admirers and the irreverent disclaimers of detective stories, both groups capable of being irresponsible. From his easy chair in *Harper's,* Bernard De Voto advised the "cosmically cockeyed" Wilson, "If distinguished prose is what Mr. Wilson wants, let him try Mr. Raymond Chandler." Wilson did try Chandler, and—at the insistence of his readers—several other detective story writers. Then he answered his readers and the "umbrageous Bernard De Voto," saying that what he had read had not caused him to change his mind. Of the fifty-two writers recommended, the only one who had the gift of story-telling was Raymond Chandler; and of the sixty-seven books suggested, "*Farewell, My Lovely* is the only one of the books I have read all of and read with enjoyment." A kind of qualified acceptance of Chandler was the only point on which Wilson and De Voto could agree.

Writing in the *Nation* in 1960, George P. Elliott raised the question of whether Chandler would ever be elected into literary history. "The odd thing is that he is known and enjoyed by those who have the power to vote him in—critics, writers, scholars, literary historians—and even so it begins to look as though his nomination for membership may not be seconded." Assuming that Chandler's work is up for consideration before the great committee, on what basis should it be fairly considered before he is elected or voted down? It should be on his use of literary techniques, his style; on his ability to handle the language, its preciseness, imagery, poetry and flow, and sense of pace; on his awareness of sentence structure and syntax; on his consistency in maintaining an effective viewpoint with a careful manipulation of the objective technique; and on his development of plot structure. His traditional literary hero and his theme—man in search of truth and justice—have already been discussed as part of a mainstream in American fiction.

In reviewing another's book, Raymond Chandler once wrote that "by literature I mean quite simply any sort of writing at all that reaches a sufficient intensity of performance to glow with its own heat." This simple definition of art is, of course, not simple, but it does point up Chandler's demands on writing—it must have "magic," it must "glow," or it must "burn." "There must be some magic in the writing after all," he once said, "but I take no credit for it. It just happens, like red hair. But I find it rather humiliating to pick up a book of my own to glance at something and then find myself twenty minutes later still reading it as if someone else had written it." One test of a piece of writing was whether he would want to reread it. Applying a concept of style to his own genre, he thought a good detective story was one which would be read even if the end were missing. Unlike many detective writers who build their stories on clues and gimmicks in order to hold the reader to the end, Chandler's approach to writing was analogous to the Greek dramatists who wrote for an audience that had known the stories since childhood. The test was whether the author could bring new magic to an old story.

One way to make writing glow is to understand fully and to utilize completely the possibilities and limitations of the language in which one is writing. Chandler insisted that he wrote American English as distinct from British English. He studied first and then wrote in what H. L. Mencken called "the American language." For Mencken, the common American speech was the best possible vehicle "for the terse and dramatic presentation of ideas"; so it was for Chandler.

In 1937 Chandler had been offended by the style and tone of a piece in a little Los Angeles paper called *The Fortnightly Intruder* and wrote to the editor to express irritation: "Your essay on flower arrangement is priceless . . . but to what audience in heaven's name do you address yourselves? You are precious, you write in a dead language. . . . You are of a pretty wit and a soothing yet deadly irony. . . . Who, except those by life already defeated and wasting in the twilight, has any taste for such writing as yours?" The editor objected to "violent" writers, and Chandler wrote again two weeks later: "The best writing done in English today is done by Americans, but not in any purist tradition. They have roughed the language around as Shakespeare did." When interviewed by Cyril Ray, Chandler said that when he first settled down in America he "felt himself a foreigner at first in a country where language was fascinating, vigorous, alive; almost Elizabethan in its freshness; wasn't stylized; hadn't be-

come a 'class' language like literary English." This is to say that Shakespeare wrote in the language of his time, and Chandler believed in writing twentieth-century language in the twentieth century. In Germany, Fritz Wölcken also found in Chandler the colorful, precise expression reminiscent of Shakespeare and the English Renaissance, and he illustrated his observation with a quote from Chandler: "She was completely outfitted with hills and valleys, impossible to improve upon."

Writing a lively prose did not mean for Chandler a sloppy, violent, inelegant expression. When he used such words and phrases as "concatenation," "frowst," "insouciant amateur," "spilikins in the parlor," "futzing around," or "the logic is a chimera," he used them with preciseness and appropriateness. If he allowed himself, on occasion, a French word such as "flânerie," it was because he knew French, and in an essay such a word was expressive. He also knew enough and thought enough of the language to make such distinctions as the difference between "imply" and "infer." In "The Simple Art of Murder" in 1944 he wrote the following sentence: "It seems to me that production of detective stories on so large a scale, and by writers whose immediate reward is small and whose meed of critical praise is almost nil, would not be possible at all if the job took any talent." Two years later an editor, whose knowledge of the language was not up to Chandler's, changed or allowed to be changed *meed* to *need*. In reprinting the essay in 1950, Chandler caught the "correction," so it became *meed* once more.

In later life Chandler maintained that there were two things he would have chosen for a career, had he been free to choose; one was law, the other was comparative philology. When he became the "proud possessor" of *British and American English Since 1900,* he wrote to Eric Partridge, the author, a discussion of the expression *anymore* used in the sense of *now*. To Bergen Evans, master of ceremonies for the television program "The Last Word," he wrote a letter on the correct and incorrect use of *everyone*. In many letters, to Hamish Hamilton, Dale Warren, Edward Weeks, and others, he wrote long discussions of the proper and improper uses of dozens of different but specified words, not only for the linguistic correctness but for emotional effectiveness. "How do you tell," for example, "a man to go away in hard language? Scram, beat it, take off, take the air, on your way, dangle, hit the road, and so forth. All good enough. But give me the classic expression actually used by Spike O'Donnell (of the O'Donnell brothers of Chicago, the only small outfit to tell the Capone mob to go to hell and live). What he said was: 'Be missing.' The restraint of it is deadly."

Long before he began to write fiction, and on occasions throughout his life, Chandler had a try at poetry. His is only passable, being too sentimental and without the vigor that one finds in the poetic passages of his prose. Along with other hard-boiled writers, Chandler is frequently classed in the group that writes the "poetry of violence." Be that as it may, there is a distinctive poetic flavor in Chandler's work which is more tender than violent: "A dead moth was spread-eagled on a corner of the desk. On the window sill a bee with tattered wings was crawling along the woodwork, buzzing in a tired remote sort of way, as if she knew it wasn't any use, she was finished, she had flown too many missions and would never get back to the hive again." The blend of nature, man, and the city expressed in a rhythmical flow of words is a Chandler trademark: "The wind had risen and had a dry taut feeling, tossing the tops of trees, and making the swung arc light up the side street cast shadows like crawling lava. I turned the car and drove east again. . . . I was hungry and hollow inside. I went over to Vine to eat, and after that I drove downtown again. The wind was still rising and it was drier than ever. The steering wheel had a gritty feeling under my fingers and the inside of my nostrils felt tight and drawn. The lights were on here and there in the tall buildings. The green and chromium clothier's store on the corner of Ninth and Hill was a blaze of it. In the Belfont Building a few windows glowed here and there, but not many. The same old plowhorse sat in the elevator on his piece of folded burlap, looking straight in front of him, blankeyed, almost gathered to history." One need not strain to feel the rhythm and poetic quality of these lines:

> The wind had risen
> [with] a dry taut feeling,
> tossing the tops of trees,
> making the swung arc light
> up the side street
> cast shadows like crawling lava.
>
> The steering wheel had a gritty feeling
> under my fingers . . .
> the inside of my nostrils
> felt tight and drawn.
> The same old plowhorse
> sat in the elevator
> on his piece of folded burlap,
> looking straight in front of him,
> blankeyed,
> almost gathered to history.

Chandler sometimes complained of the "flat-footed" style of those who seemed unaware "that the artistic use of language has been going on for a couple of thousand years."

In his essay "The Great Detective Stories," Willard Huntington Wright declared that there is no place in the detective story for a "literary" style, "replete with descriptive passages, metaphors, and word pictures, which might give viability and beauty to a novel of romance or adventure." Subsequent critics do not agree, at least when considering Chandler's work. *Time* magazine reported that he "wrote fresh crackling prose and it was peppered with newly minted similes. . . ." According to George Elliott, the special quality of Chandler's style is its "rhinestone brilliance." No American since Mark Twain, added Elliott, has invented as many wisecracks as the "British-educated classicist." The most effusive praise came from D. C. Russell who remembered that he resisted for some time the pressure of friends who insisted that he read Chandler, but he finally succumbed. With a taste, he became an addict. He found that Chandler had "artistry of craftsman-

ship and a realism that can rank him with many famous novelists. In his hands, words do become beautiful and wonderful things, operating with economy and precision. What a delight it is to come upon a writer who tosses off a good image on almost every page. . . . Chandler is prodigal in his imagery. If they seem more wise-cracks than high-flown literary similes, I will point out that Chandler writes the characteristic American humor. In doing this he comes closer to literature than other writers who disdain the native brand of thought and language." His writing has "a beauty which shows that Chandler cannot be pigeonholed merely as an expert in tough language."

Some of Chandler's similes and metaphors are used to describe his characters. By seeing a face, for example, one may be looking at a whole personality. This might be said of the bouncer whose face had "nothing to fear. Everything had been done to it that anybody could think of." Then there were the hoofers with good legs, but "their faces were as threadbare as a bookkeeper's coat." The psychosomatic Carmen Sternwood could at times reveal a face "like a scraped bone." And there was the man whose countenance was a curse: "The upper part of his face meant business. The lower part was just saying goodbye."

Jessie Florian had "weedy hair of that vague color which is neither brown nor blonde, that hasn't enough life in it to be ginger, and isn't clean enough to be grey." She was a quite different person from Mrs. Murdock who had "pewter-colored hair set in a ruthless permanent." And they were both unlike the blond whose hair was "as artificial as a nightclub lobby." They all, however, had at least some advantages over the woman with a "mouth made for three-decker sandwiches."

Eyes can also tell a story: "large cowlike eyes with a peasant dullness in them"; "small sharp eyes with urchin greed in them"; eyes that become "narrow and almost black and as shallow as enamel on a cafeteria tray"; eyes that have "as much expression as the cap on a gas tank"; or eyes that "held an expression of indifferent dislike."

Billy Wilder said that Chandler was particularly wonderful at creating mood and milieu, and he suggested the setting in the orchid greenhouse in *The Big Sleep* as an example. When Chandler described the scene he almost literally created the heat that filled the air. Creating atmosphere by the use of imagery was a frequently used technique. There are, for example, the room that "was hot and heavy with a disaster that could no longer be mended"; the room in which the "smell of old dust hung in the air as flat and stale as a football interview"; the one that "was suddenly full of heavy silence, like a fallen cake"; or "On the air of the room a rather heavy perfume struggled with the smell of death, and lost. Although defeated, it was still there." And there was the elevator that "had an elderly perfume in it, like three widows drinking tea."

In Marlowe's town one could look down on the remains of poor old Morningstar—"Fuzz grew out of his ears, far enough to catch a moth." Listen carefully to Red's thoughtful expression as he "spoke slowly and what he said had

After publishing his first short story in 1933, Chandler became a star contributor to Black Mask.

wisps of fog clinging to it, like beads on a mustache." Stare at the legs with "ankles long and slim and with enough melodic line for a tone poem." See the girl who "looked as if she would have a hall bedroom accent," or the man who spoke "softly, in the manner of a sultan suggesting a silk noose for a harem lady whose tricks had gone stale." Avoid the racket beer that is "tasteless as a roadhouse blond," and run for shelter when "suddenly the rain let go in big splashing drops and the sky was as black as Carrie Nation's bonnet." Above all one should beware of "a house dick whose standard of ethics would take about as much strain as a very tired old cobweb."

Time can be an unfortunately boring element in the life of a detective. All too often he must watch and wait for someone else to make the next move. How does he do it? He waits while minutes go "by on tiptoe, with their fingers to their lips," or while minutes drop "silently down a well." Waiting while "another army of sluggish minutes dragged by," he could listen to "the sunshine burn the grass." There is also lost time, when "yesterday was a hundred years ago, something crystallized in time, like a fly in amber."

Somerset Maugham said that Chandler wrote "a nervous colloquial English racy of the American soil." Not knowing which, if any, particular passage Maugham had in mind, I have chosen my own racy example: "The eighty-five cent dinner tasted like a discarded mail bag and was served to me by a waiter who looked as if he would slug me for a quarter, cut my throat for six bits, and bury me at sea in a barrel of concrete for a dollar and a half, plus sales tax."

A favorite image for many readers is from the short story **"Goldfish"**: "There were long slim fish like golden darts and Japanese Veiltails with fantastic trailing tails, and X-ray fish as transparent as colored glass, tiny guppies half an inch long, calico popeyes spotted like a bride's apron, and big lumbering Chinese Moors with telescope eyes, froglike faces and unnecessary fins, waddling through the green water like fat men going to lunch." All Peter Forster could say—after quoting this passage in an article in *John O'London's Weekly*—was "I wish I could write like that."

How to use the American idiom to its fullest was constantly in Chandler's vision; to do but not overdo, to squeeze out all the good juice but not the pulp, to be realistic without sacrificing artistic prerogatives. What he wrote in praise of Ian Fleming's *Dr. No* was his own writing formula: escape the forced pretentiousness of the language, have an "acute sense of pace," know "how far to go, when to stop, when to destroy a mood and when to regain it, when to write a scene on a postcard and when to write richly and with leisure."

The literary use of slang, thought Chandler, was a study in itself, and there were only two kinds that were useful: "slang that has established itself in the language, and slang that you make up yourself. Everything else is apt to be passé before it gets into print." Making up one's own language was permissible if one recognized the hazards, he decided, and he gave as an example the occasion on which Knopf's printers had a difficult time reconciling

themselves to a sentence that read, "a guy's there and you see him, and then he ain't there and you don't not see him." This is not unlike the line used in the Kansas City *Star* during the days when young Hemingway was one of the cub reporters: "He hit the girl he was engaged to's brother."

As it has for many, Chandler believed that the style in which he wrote—the American language—was a part of his heritage and belonged to everyone. James M. Cain discovered that the style in which he wrote was the speech he heard in California. This American language, according to Chandler, allowed Dashiell Hammett to say things "he did not know how to say, or feel the need of saying." Chandler knew the extent to which one could copy speech, for all "language begins with speech, and the speech of common men at that, but when it develops to the point of becoming a literary medium it only looks like speech." With Hemingway, Chandler adopted the principle of the iceberg: write one eighth and imply the rest. Also with Hemingway, Chandler knew that it isn't what the character says but what the reader thinks he says that passes for reality.

In the *Saturday Review* version of "The Simple Art of Murder," Chandler expressed himself pretty clearly on those "who regard detective fiction as sub-literary on no better grounds than that it does not habitually get itself jammed up with subordinate clauses, tricky punctuation, and hypothetical subjunctives." It was not so much the difficulties of syntax that cause poor writing, he once told an interviewer, but the lack of feeling for the weight of words. Punctuation was not a static thing, but a matter of style, varying with scene and situation. In *The Long Goodbye* the man from the New York publishing house was a "guy who talked with commas, like a heavy novel." Chandler could measure his prose without weighing it. When he wrote an article on Hollywood for *The Atlantic*, an unimaginative assistant "corrected" the copy, bringing forth Chandler's full and expressive thoughts on the matter: "By the way, would you convey my compliments to the purist who reads your proofs and tell him or her that I write in a sort of broken-down patois which is something like the way a Swiss waiter talks, and that when I split an infinitive, God damn it, I split it so it will stay split, and when I interrupt the velvety smoothness of my more or less literate syntax with a few sudden words of barroom vernacular, this is done with the eyes wide open and the mind relaxed but attentive."

Fortunate is the writer who has but little difficulty in handling narrative viewpoint, and lucky is the one who can move back and forth from the first to third person narration without any noticeable difficulty. Most writers experiment with both, hoping to discover that they can use either, depending on the approach and effect they intend to achieve in a given piece of prose. Henry James (to Chandler he was "my revered Henry James") could not, so he thought, master the use of the first person, and grew old lamenting the fact because he felt that the first person viewpoint could have given him the kind of objectivity he sought and admired in Tolstoy. Chandler, like other writers hoping to master the craft, experimented. Beginning with his earliest story he used the third person; working back and forth, the pattern is as irregular as it should be— the first two stories are in the third person, the next two are in the first, the next three are in the third, the next uses the first again, and so on. In his twenty-two stories (excluding the two fantasies **"The Bronze Door"** and **"Professor Bingo's Snuff,"** both of which use the third person) Chandler used the first person narration fourteen times and the third person eight. Experimenting with the narrative viewpoint decided for him, apparently, the approach he thought most effective, at least for his longer fiction. In his novels he used only the first person narrator. The twenty-two short stories suggest another interesting result in the development of the narrative viewpoint for Chandler. Sixteen of the stories used a private investigator, and all but the first two of these are in the first person. The other eight used such assorted heroes as a gambler or hotel dick, and these stories are written with the third person narrator. Each of the seven novels has the same first person narrator, Philip Marlowe, the private investigator.

Although a mastery of the objective technique is a frequently sought-for accomplishment, the best writers also recognize the limitations of purely objective writing. Hemingway's early work is predominantly objective, but halfway through his career he sought a wider horizon and began to add the subjective element. Objectivity focuses on one person, who must be a man of action. No thoughts or feelings can be implied by characters other than the narrator or third person so designated; no expressions of the author can come except through his spokesman. The omniscient one has no place. This works well for the author who is concerned only with the man of action, the man who is never off the scene, and around and through whom everything takes place. The exclusive use of the objective technique, however, hampers the writer who wants to develop opinions and attitudes toward such things as politics, religion, and philosophy. Chandler, who had no special interest in politics, religion, and philosophy, was uninhibited by the objective technique. "Of course I am prejudiced," he once said, and "I know it. I am committed as a writer to a point of view; namely, that the possibilities of objective writing are very great and they have scarcely been explored. The unfortunate thing about it is that objective writing is very easy to fake. All the 'I-was-there' boys who try to write like Hemingway get very tiresome." As far as I know, Chandler tried the subjective style only in one or two minor pieces.

Editor Shaw in his introduction to *The Hard-Boiled Omnibus* described the objective manner in which the *Black Mask* authors wrote. Their style was both "constrained and restrained." They "observed the cardinal principle in creating the illusion of reality; they did not make their characters act and talk tough; they allowed them to. They gave the stories over to their characters, and kept themselves off the stage. . . . They did not themselves state that a situation was dangerous or exciting; they did not describe their characters as giants, dead-shots, or infallible men. They permitted the actors in the story to demonstrate

all that to the extent of their particular and human capabilities." Chandler, one of the leading contributors to *Black Mask,* belonged especially within Shaw's definition.

In "The Simple Art of Murder" Chandler twice referred to those writers who have a "certain" or "cool spirit of detachment." We call this objectivity, Mark Twain called it deadpan, and some think of it in terms of stage drama. It was with this spirit that Chandler wrote. Theoretically, at least, the author tells us nothing; the only person in the novel from whom we can learn anything is Marlowe. If we receive knowledge of any other character it is only if and when Marlowe wants us to have it. What we know about Los Angeles is what Marlowe tells us or allows others to tell us. The detached author is not on the stage, and we are not even sure he is in the wings. The burden is always on the author never to let us know how he feels, never to give us any "dear reader" asides, and never to tell us how his characters feel; the characters must tell us everything we know about them by their own actions and expressions.

When Marlowe walked into a scene it was not with such comments as "My God, what a mess" or "That poor girl was too young to die" or "I'm damn glad that guy got his." The "I" looked around a room with almost as much detachment as the nonexistent author and described it like a camera. It was a wide room with a low-beamed ceiling, brown plaster walls, and low bookshelves. There was "a thick pinkish Chinese rug in which a gopher could have spent a week without showing his nose above the nap." There was a broad low divan of old rose tapestry with a wad of clothes on it, including lilac-colored silk underwear. There was a black desk with carved gargoyles at the corners. On a high-backed teakwood chair sat Carmen Sternwood, wearing only a pair of long jade earrings. On the floor lay Geiger, wearing Chinese slippers with thick felt soles, black satin pajamas, and a Chinese embroidered coat. He was dead. True, the choice of words is subjective and the gopher image has subjective implications, but as Marlowe described in detail each item in the room, he made no distinctions among such items as bookshelves, underwear, carved gargoyles, a naked girl, and a dead man. If the reader wants to react to any one of the items, he may take his choice. His emotions are getting a certain amount of directing, but they are not being pulled around by the nose. What interested Marlowe, although he did not let the reader know, may have been the dead man. The slippers with the thick felt soles may intrigue a particular reader, and because no one has told him how to feel about any one of the items, his special interest is his own business, quite legitimate and not interfered with. Peter Forster wrote of Chandler's work, "Everything is described, nothing is explained. It is a technique which perforce depends on the ability of the writer to present a continually vivid and intriguing visual picture; I should say that Raymond Chandler is the best describer (if there is not such a word there should be!) alive to-day [1953]."

Chandler once said that there is nothing more difficult to manage than an explanation, and if explanation is used it must be accompanied by action. He was wise enough not to try to explain how his characters talk. Occasionally there is a "he answered" or "she shrieked," but his pattern (followed generally by writers using the objective technique) is simply "I said," "she said," "he said." We are supposed to know enough about the characters so as to make an explanation of their manner of conversation unnecessary. How they say what they say should be implicit. A Chandler blond never speaks with a sad sob and a quivering tear in her thin voice.

The very nature of a detective story necessitates a kind of standard plot in which there must be a crime or unhealthy condition for the detective to solve or correct. Yet this need not mean, argued Joseph Wood Krutch, that detective stories are sub-literary because they follow a formula. Preferring to call the formula a *form,* Krutch believed this form may be a good thing, especially at a time "when the novel, always rather loose, so frequently has no shape at all." For Chandler, however, paying conscious attention to form was a nuisance that hindered him from concentrating on style and characterization. He refused to be committed in advance to a rigid outline, preferring to begin with a general idea and to let the style develop the plot. In "The Simple Art of Murder" he wrote that the "technical basis of the *Black Mask* type of story . . . was that the scene outranked the plot, in the sense that a good plot was one which made good scenes." This is not to say that his stories were without structure, but rather that they had form in preference to formula. Chandler's work in general is made up of sharply written scenes tied together by the ever-present Marlowe. To insure for his scenes the sharpness he demanded of them, he developed a home-made crutch; he wrote on half sheets, 51/2 by 81/2, requiring of himself that each half sheet (125-150 words) contain some detail, description, or action that contributed to the scene and the forward movement of the story. This device kept him from becoming prolix.

Almost all writers re-use their material, especially by working short stories into novels. In his novels Chandler included scenes, situations, and characters—reworked and developed—from eight previously published short stories, which he called "cannibalized": **"Killer in the Rain," "The Man Who Liked Dogs," "The Curtain," "Try the Girl," "Mandarin's Jade," "Bay City Blues," "The Lady in the Lake,"** and **"No Crime in the Mountains."** On occasion he used a small bit from a story not included in the cannibalized list. The principal uses are as follows:

The Big Sleep:
    "Killer in the Rain"
    "The Curtain"
    "Finger Man" (small bit)
    "Mandarin's Jade" (small bit)

Farewell, My Lovely:
    "The Man Who Liked Dogs"
    "Try the Girl"
    "Mandarin's Jade"
    "Trouble Is My Business" (small bit)

The High Window:
    "The King in Yellow" (small bit)

The Lady in the Lake:
    "Bay City Blues"
    "The Lady in the Lake"
    "No Crime in the Mountains"

The Long Goodbye:
    "The Curtain" (small bit)

An analysis of *The Big Sleep* can serve to show Chandler's technique of borrowing and enlarging scenes, his over-all method of narration, his development of plot or form, and his adapting and adding characters to fit the more sustained form.

The plot of **"Killer in the Rain,"** in brief, concerns Dravec, a big Serbian steelworker, who was sitting on top of a dome in California when an oil boom started underneath him. With too much money and no moral sense, his thumb-sucking daughter Carmen became involved with several of society's trash. The private eye tried to eliminate some of the social evil and protect Dravec from a little heartache. In **"The Curtain"** General Winslow's psychopathic little grandson killed his stepfather, but to protect the family the mother had the body disposed of and left the impression that her husband had pulled down the curtain. The private eye discovered the true situation and continued to protect the family. The plots of **"Mandarin's Jade"** and **"Finger Man"** are not relevant because only isolated scenes were used from these two stories in *The Big Sleep.* In this novel Chandler drew from **"The Curtain"** for Chapters 1-3, 20, 27-32; from **"Killer in the Rain"** for Chapters 4, 6-10 (small part), 12-16; from **"Mandarin's Jade"** a small part of Chapter 11; from **"Finger Man"** Chapter 22 and a small part of 23; Chapters 5, 17-19, 21, 23 (small part), 24-26 are added. Roughly, one third of the novel drew from **"The Curtain,"** one third from **"Killer in the Rain,"** and one third was entirely new. A considerable portion of the first half of *The Big Sleep* was built around **"Killer in the Rain,"** and as such the novel came to a climactic end with Chapter 19. But with Chapter 20 Chandler picked up the plot thread from **"The Curtain"** by having Marlowe go in search of the missing Rusty Reagan. Throughout the novel these two story plots are intricately woven into a unified whole.

There is no definite pattern in Chandler's re-use of his earlier material. In the example of **"Killer in the Rain,"** he took only those elements he thought particularly useful. With this method he left out much and added more; he built a sentence into a paragraph and a paragraph into several pages; on occasion he lifted a line verbatim, but more often he reworked the portion he borrowed. A sample passage will illustrate the borrowing technique.

"Killer in the Rain"	*The Big Sleep*
No more cars came up or down the hill. It seemed to be a very quiet neighborhood.	No more cars came up the hill. No lights went on in the house before which I was parked. It seemed like a nice neighborhood to have

Then a single flash of hard white light leaked out of Steiner's house, like a flash of summer lightning.	bad habits in. At seven-twenty a single flash of hard white light shot out of Geiger's house like a wave of summer lightning.
As the darkness fell again a thin, tinkling scream trickled down the darkness and echoed faintly among the wet trees. I was out of the Chrysler and on my way before the last echo of it died.	As the darkness folded back on it and ate it up a thin tinkling scream echoed out and lost itself among the rain-drenched trees. I was out of the car and on my way before the echoes died.
There was no fear in the scream. It held the note of a half-pleasurable shock, an accent of drunkenness, and a touch of pure idiocy.	There was no fear in the scream. It had a sound of half-pleasurable shock, an accent of drunkenness, an overtone of pure idiocy. It was a nasty sound. It made me think of men in white and barred windows and hard narrow cots with leather wrist and ankle straps fastened to them.
The Steiner mansion was perfectly silent when I hit the gap in the hedge, dodged around the elbow that masked the front door . . .	The Geiger hideaway was perfectly silent again when I hit the gap in the hedge and dodged around the angle that masked the front door.

This rather extreme case of more or less faithful borrowing is intended only to show how the author reworked a passage by changing a single word or adding a sentence in an attempt to intensify the mood. An average example is the use of the greenhouse scene which was rewritten from 1100 words in **"The Curtain"** to 2500 words in *The Big Sleep*. The other extreme can be illustrated by the use of the "shiny black bug with the pink head and pink spots" in *Farewell, My Lovely*. As an introduction to Chapter 9 of **"Trouble Is My Business,"** Chandler used the bug only as a minor detail in a scene. Later, in *Farewell, My Lovely*, the same bug became a symbol and was used to indicate man's struggles and frustrations, man's feebleness in a social order backed by power. But as Chandler did at almost every opportunity, the bug also served to show the value of human feelings and compassion.

As Chandler borrowed scenes and situations from his short stories, so did he borrow characters. Of the twenty-one characters in *The Big Sleep*, seven were drawn directly from **"The Curtain,"** six from **"Killer in the Rain,"** four were composites from the two stories, and four new characters were added. The composites are technically the most interesting. Philip Marlowe, of course, is the private eye from the two short stories; Eddie Mars is the gambling-club owner from both (and also from **"Finger Man"**); General Guy Sternwood is the General Dade Winslow of **"The Curtain"** and Dravec of **"Killer in the Rain."** The twenty-year-old Carmen Sternwood is the truly frighten-

ing combination of the pathetic Carmen Dravec of **"Killer in the Rain"** and the sadistic eleven-year-old Dade Winslow Trevillyan of **"The Curtain."** Carmen Dravec was relatively passive, while Dade Trevillyan was pathologically active. Together in Carmen Sternwood they formed a psychoneurotic character who created the basic motivation for the novel, and this motivation is more realistic in the longer work than it had been in either of the two short stories.

It is no good arguing that Chandler was a writer who should have chosen the "serious" novel rather than the detective form. The fact is that there is sufficient evidence to deem him a good technician who could tell an excellent story and who set about creating fictional art in a sensible manner. It was most appropriate that Mr. Partridge should choose to point out that "Mr. Chandler's style by now can be regarded as fixed" at a time when the novelist sorely needed, and fortunately was receiving, dividends from his "investment in style."

Philip Durham (essay date 1964)

SOURCE: An introduction to *Killer in the Rain*, by Raymond Chandler, Hamish Hamilton Ltd., 1964, pp. vii-xi.

[*In the following essay, Durham discusses Chandler's efforts to develop his short detective stories into serious novels concerned with themes of social injustice.*]

During his lifetime Raymond Chandler published twenty-three short stories. Yet of this relatively small output only fifteen are generally known to the reading public. For a quarter of a century the remaining eight have lain buried in the crumbling pages of old pulp magazines. And these eight stories are among his finest.

For one who became, with Dashiell Hammett, a leading writer of 'the poetry of violence', it is odd indeed that Chandler should have published his first story at the age of forty-five. When this first story, **'Blackmailers Don't Shoot'**, appeared in December 1933, Chandler was only one of the many good writers of the old *Black Mask* school. But when he died in 1959 he had been translated and published in eighteen countries and his work was sought throughout the world by those who recognized a good story and appreciated artistry in detective fiction.

Born in Chicago in 1888, Raymond Chandler went, as a small boy, to England with his mother. There he grew up and received his education, excelling in the classics at Dulwich College. Shortly after reaching his majority he returned to the United States, from where he went on to Canada to join the Gordon Highlanders. After serving in England and France in 1917-18, he returned again to America to begin a business career in Los Angeles. By the early 1930s he had become an executive in five oil companies, and had it not been for the great depression, it is probable that he would be unknown today—buried in forgotten records as a writer of oil reports. For not until the depression caused the oil business to collapse did Chandler abruptly become a writer of fiction.

In 1950 Chandler published his 'official' collection of short stories under the title **The Simple Art of Murder,** but that volume does not include any of the eight stories of this collection [*Killer in the Rain*]. Although all eight had been published, the author excluded them because they had been 'cannibalized'.

When Raymond Chandler published *The Big Sleep,* his first of seven novels, in 1939, he did what multitudes of writers had done before him: he re-used some of his earlier material. Unlike most writers, however, re-using previously published stories left him with an uneasy feeling. Once a story was used in a novel it became—to use his word—'cannibalized'. Therefore he could justify this writing method only by leaving such stories buried, virtually unknown in the pages of the rapidly disappearing pulp magazines. The stories in this volume, then, were not collected during the author's lifetime. Since his death, however, there have been very many requests that they should be reprinted and there no longer seems any good reason why, provided their origin is clearly explained, they should be denied to the many thousands of Chandler's readers. Apart from the pleasure Chandler's audience will derive from the stories themselves, it is further hoped that his readers will realize that only a skilled craftsman could turn eight separately conceived short stories into three excellent novels.

A substantial part of Chandler's first novel, *The Big Sleep* (1939), was made from **'Killer in the Rain'** (*Black Mask,* January 1935) and **'The Curtain'** (*Black Mask,* September 1936); the second novel, *Farewell, My Lovely* (1940), made extensive use of **'The Man Who Liked Dogs'** (*Black Mask,* March 1936), **'Try the Girl'** (*Black Mask,* January 1937), and **'Mandarin's Jade'** (*Dime Detective Magazine,* November 1937); and the fourth novel, *The Lady in the Lake* (1943), relied on **'Bay City Blues'** (*Dime Detective Magazine,* November 1937), **'The Lady in the Lake'** (*Dime Detective Magazine,* January 1939), and **'No Crime in the Mountains'** (*Detective Story Magazine,* September 1941).

Turning short stories into cohesive novels tested the extent of Chandler's skill. It meant combining and enlarging plots, maintaining a thematic consistency, blowing up scenes, and adapting, fusing, and adding characters.

To illustrate Chandler's method of combining and enlarging plots, one can see in *The Big Sleep,* for example, how the author drew from **'The Curtain'** for Chapters 1-3, 20, 27-32 and from **'Killer in the Rain'** form Chapters 4, 6-10, 12-16. With the exception of small bits borrowed from **'Mandarin's Jade'** and **'Finger Man'**, Chapters 5, 11, 17-19, 21-26 were added. Ten chapters were drawn from **'The Curtain'**, eleven were taken from **'Killer in the Rain'**, and eleven were almost all new material. The twenty-one borrowed chapters, however, were expanded considerably beyond their original state in the short stories.

In 'The Curtain' Dade Winslow Trevillyan killed Dudley O'Mara, his stepfather, but to shield the family Dade's mother had O'Mara's body disposed of, leaving the impression that the missing man had pulled down the curtain. In 'Killer in the Rain' young Dade's counterpart is Carmen Dravec; both are psychopathic. In *The Big Sleep* young Dade Trevillyan and Carmen Dravec are fused into Carmen Sternwood, the twenty-year-old girl who had 'little sharp predatory teeth, as white as fresh orange pith and as shiny as porcelain'. Carmen Sternwood, the thumb-sucking psychopath, committed the murder which had been performed in 'The Curtain' by Dade Trevillyan. The central portion of the novel, largely added, linked the two short stories together, but throughout the novel the plots of the two stories were neatly woven into a unified whole.

At times Chandler lifted whole passages, changing only a word here and there to improve the syntax or vary a mood. More frequently, however, he blew up scenes for the novel. An example is the greenhouse scene, which accounts for approximately 1,100 words in 'The Curtain', but is enlarged to 2,500 words in *The Big Sleep*.

In miniature, the transformation developed as follows: forty-two words from 'The Curtain',

> The air steamed. The walls and ceiling of the glass house dripped. In the halflight enormous tropical plants spread their blooms and branches all over the place, and the smell of them was almost as overpowering as the smell of boiling alcohol.

became eighty-two words in *The Big Sleep,*

> The air was thick, wet, steamy and larded with the cloying smell of tropical orchids in bloom. The glass walls and roof were heavily misted and big drops of moisture splashed down on the plants. The light had an unreal greenish colour, like light filtered through an aquarium tank. The plants filled the place, a forest of them, with nasty meaty leaves and stalks like the newly washed fingers of dead men. They smelled as overpowering as boiling alcohol under a blanket.

Both passages are intense and vivid. The selection from 'The Curtain' achieves its effectiveness through terseness, while the selection from the novel allowed the author to create a mood through the use of hyperbole and striking similes.

When Chandler converted short stories into a novel he needed a greater array of characters for the longer form. The manner in which he adapted, fused, and added characters for *The Big Sleep* was again a test of the author's literary ingenuity. Of the twenty-one characters in *The Big Sleep,* seven were drawn directly from 'The Curtain', six were taken from 'Killer in the Rain', four were composites from the two stories, and four were new creations.

The fusing of Dade Trevillyan and Carmen Dravec into Carmen Sternwood, and the fusing of General Dade Winslow of 'The Curtain' and Tony Dravec of 'Killer in the

Rain' into General Guy Sternwood of *The Big Sleep* are examples of technical competence.

More important, however, was Chandler's development of the detective-hero. Philip Marlowe, the consistent hero throughout all of his novels, first appeared in *The Big Sleep* in 1939. But he had been conceived in 'Blackmailers Don't Shoot' in 1933. The evolution of the character is a point of interest in the eight stories of this volume.

When Chandler published 'Killer in the Rain', his fourth story, in 1935, he was still experimenting with his principal character, a nameless first person narrator. In the next of these three stories the detective operated under the name of Carmady, and in the following three he was John Dalmas. By 1941 in 'No Crime in the Mountains' he appeared as John Evans, but in the meantime he had become the Philip Marlowe of Chandler's novels.

> The thematic difference between what Chandler called the standard detective story and his own stories is that his hero was motivated less by the desire to solve the mystery of a murder than by the compelling necessity to right social wrongs.
>
> —*Philip Durham*

Throughout these stories it is always obvious that Chandler's protagonist is much more concerned with helping people than he is with making money. He protects the helpless whether or not they have money. In 'Try the Girl' Carmady moved in to clean up a messy social situation, after making it clear to the police that he, a free and independent man, had to do a job they could not accomplish. John Dalmas in 'Mandarin's Jade' was passionately ethical, one who would not think of accepting money until he had more than earned it. And in 'Bay City Blues' the hero exhibited the kind of courage normally found in heroes of the frontier and the Far West.

In each of these stories the hero is 'a man fit for adventure'. He is a knight whose mission in life is to protect the weak and to make sure that justice is done. It was in the stories in this volume that Chandler developed his detective-hero, the man he wrote about so eloquently in his essay, 'The Simple Art of Murder'. 'He is the hero; he is everything. He must be a complete man and a common man and yet an unusual man. . . . He must be the best man in his world and a good enough man for any world.'

It is at this point that the mission of the hero becomes the thematic core of all these stories. Chandler once wrote that 'the emotional basis of the standard detective story was and had always been that murder will out and justice will be done'. He added, however, that justice will not be done 'unless some very determined individual makes it his business to see that justice is done'.

The thematic difference between what Chandler called the standard detective story and his own stories is that his hero was motivated less by the desire to solve the mystery of a murder than by the compelling necessity to right social wrongs. There is murder in these stories, to be sure, but the detective risked his life and reputation to correct social injustices of any nature: to protect the weak, to establish ethical standards, to ease pain, or to salvage whatever might be left in fragile human beings. That the murderer was eventually caught and punished was not at all as important as the main theme.

In this sense, with this ever-present theme, Chandler went beyond the scope of what is normally thought of as an ordinary detective story. Because the concern for murder, in these stories, was a minor one, and the concern for human misery was a major one, Chandler was using an important theme of what we choose to call 'serious' literature.

Now, after a quarter of a century, Raymond Chandler's 'cannibalized' stories have been rescued for those readers who did not share the excitement of reading the *Black Mask* and other pulp magazines of the 1930s.

[*Killer in the Rain* contains] eight stories in which one finds suspense, violence, tragedy, and a knight who cared about human lives. And one sees the city of Los Angeles—sometimes 'a big dry sunny place with ugly homes and no style, but good-hearted and peaceful' and sometimes 'a hard-boiled city with no more personality than a paper cup'—vividly spread out there in Southern California, just as Raymond Chandler saw it.

E. M. Beekman (essay date 1973)

SOURCE: "Raymond Chandler & An American Genre," in *The Massachusetts Review*, Vol. XIV, No. 1, Winter, 1973, pp. 149-73.

[*In the following essay, Beekman maintains that Chandler's writings transcend the ordinary limitations of mystery-detective fiction through the author's acute consciousness of style and expert use of simile, metaphor, and characterization.*]

The Traditional Detective Novel is not a novel at all but an intellectual game on the level of acrostics or checkers. Like any other game it answers to certain strict rules and such injunctions have been legislated by such early practitioners as Dorothy Sayers, S. S. Van Dine, Freeman Wills Crofts, not to mention scores of articles and histories of the genre. As in the nature of games, one is either addicted to whodunits or one despises them.

A famous supporter is W. H. Auden who, in a fascinating essay written with a pen dipped in Holy Water, not only openly confesses to addiction ("like tobacco or alcohol") and enjoins strictures as moral as Scripture and as interdictory as Aristotle (Aquinas would have been proud of the performance), but also expels one particular writer from this innocent Eden of crime and punishment.

> Actually, whatever he may say, I think Mr. Chandler is interested in writing, not detective stories, but serious studies of a criminal milieu, the Great Wrong Place, and his powerful but extremely depressing books should be read and judged, not as escape literature, but as works of art.

Edmund Wilson is the most famous champion of the detractors. In three acerbic articles Wilson records his dislike for this kind of fiction. "You cannot *read* such a book, you run through it to see the problem worked out; and you cannot become interested in the characters, because they never can be allowed an existence of their own even in a flat two dimensions but have always to be contrived so that they can seem either reliable or sinister, depending on which quarter, at the moment, is to be baited for the reader's suspicion." But just as in Auden's case there is an exception and Wilson also speaks of a writer who, he feels, does not belong among his rejects and whom he saves from his critical slop bucket:

> The gift for telling stories is uncommon, like other artistic gifts, and the only one of this group of writers . . . who seems to me to possess it to any degree is Mr. Raymond Chandler. His *Farewell, My Lovely* is the only one of these books that I have read all of and read with enjoyment. . . . It is not simply a question here of a puzzle which has been put together but of a malaise conveyed to the reader, the horror of a hidden conspiracy that is continually turning up in the most varied and unlikely forms. To write such a novel successfully you must be able to invent character and incident and to generate atmosphere, and all this Mr. Chandler can do. . . .

The reason that these two critical antagonists praise the same author comes from the fact that Raymond Chandler's books are novels which use elements of a particular fictional tradition, and in so doing either amplify or destroy established constrictions, not for malice but from a superior artistic imagination.

Like other excellent writers who use the genre of crime fiction, Chandler is more often than not a victim of a kind of literary snobbism. In this country, crime fiction begs in vain for serious attention, for, whenever one of these authors does receive critical praise, scores of hecklers are quick to howl "Intellectualization!" In Europe, however, these crime authors are measured as writers first and secondly as exemplars of a genre. Even in England, as Chandler found out to his surprise, he was for the first time in his life reviewed as a novelist. "Over here [in London] I am not regarded as a mystery writer but as an American novelist of some importance. . . . A thriller writer in England, if he is good enough, is just as good as anyone else. There is none of that snobbism which makes a fourth-rate serious novelist, without style or any real talent, superior by defi-

nition to a mystery writer who might have helped recreate a whole literature."

The Thirties saw another renegade of some importance, the American author Dashiel Hammett (1894-1961), whose first book was published in 1929. With the debut of Hammett the "pure" tale of detection was dead and it seems unlikely that it shall ever be fully resuscitated. Many histories of the genre are available which will provide the reader with the details. The most recent and one of the best is *Mortal Consequences: A History from the Detective Story to the Crime Novel* by Julian Symons.

The rebellion in crime fiction started in fact with Dashiel Hammett. From *Red Harvest* (1929) to *The Thin Man* (1934), his books used the hero as a man who was not far removed from the criminal elements he combatted. No fancy pants, he was ready to shoot or hit and to use illegal means to finish a case. Solutions were less important than the need to settle a job: that's what he got paid for. Nor was this an intellectual mandarin outwitting the stereotypical dumb police, but a professional of crime who knew that the police are—seriously—either incapable of solving certain crimes because of the orthodoxy of their methods or unwilling to solve them for political reasons. Organized crime became part of the world of fiction so that the miscreant was no longer a peculiar individual with even remote socially acceptable motives, but a faceless cog in a large machine which used violence with a ruthless neutrality.

The writing itself changed. Hammett's style is bare and terse, with a delivery that is direct and to the point, while the tone is cynical. Action and style support each other: both have a relentlessness which makes events seem inevitable. Though the detection puzzle remained, there was now more emphasis on atmosphere and characterization. This was the saving grace of the particular development, variously called the "thriller," "private-eye fiction," the "hardboiled school of writing," or the "crime novel." In terms of literature it made something mandatory which only talent can provide: style.

> **Like other excellent writers who use the genre of crime fiction, Chandler is more often than not a victim of a kind of literary snobbism. In this country, crime fiction begs in vain for serious attention, for, whenever one of these authors does receive critical praise, scores of hecklers are quick to howl "Intellectualization!"**
>
> **—E. M. Beekman**

As a matter of fact there are those who would make the puzzle, the problem, and nothing else a requirement, lest superlative writing get in the way of their problem-solving. But when the ingenuity of the mystification becomes secondary, a book depends a great deal more on the creation of atmosphere and character—and those cannot be written with the butt end of the pencil. So as a writer Hammett showed his superiority to anyone who had written tales of detection before, with the exception of Poe and Conan Doyle.

The setting also changed permanently. The hardboiled story is a metropolitan genre. The big city is its beat and the depiction is democratic in that it shuttles back and forth with (cynical) ease from the slums to the penthouses of the rich. The hardboiled hero is an inmate of the jungle of concrete so that he is totally out of place in rustic surroundings. Here was another major departure from the Arcadian detective novels; besides, clean air would probably kill the new "detective." This aspect connects the hardboiled novel with Dickens and Balzac for whom the city was also a disease they could not live without. The representation of society becomes more inclusive because the metropolis houses every strata, showing humanity stripped of all its various disguises. Finally, there is nothing ingenious about a corpse lying on a sidewalk: death is then and there a dirty fact of life and no longer an Arcadian anachronism.

Some will think it ironic that the genre which saved crime fiction from a ludicrous death was nurtured in the pulp magazines of the Twenties and Thirties, particularly *Black Mask Magazine* which, under the editorial reign of J. T. Shaw became the best of its kind. *Black Mask* published Hammett, Chandler, Erle Stanley Gardner and many other writers who became subsequently famous.

These pulps were literate comic strips. Everything in the stories printed was subordinated to action and realism. Soon it became hackwork and the style standardized. The impetus for this kind of writing was summarized in Chandler's famous phrase: "When in doubt, have a man come through a door with a gun in his hand." But in order to be fair one has to remember that these stories were written for money and that the writers were paid as long as the magazine was lucrative. Most magazines still make a profit from certain editorial formulae, and when a writer ignores them the blue pencil of the editor still carves him ruthlessly back into line.

Yet there was something about these stories that was different from the classical tale of detection, something that could be developed into a major fiction. Recalling the period from 1920 to roughly the beginning of the Second World War, Chandler gave the following explanation for that difference:

> Possibly it was the smell of fear which the stories managed to generate. Their characters lived in a world gone wrong, a world in which, long before the atom bomb, civilization had created the machinery for its own destruction and was learning to use it with all the moronic delight of a gangster trying out his first machine-gun. The law was something to be manipulated for profit and power. The streets were dark with something more than night.

From these perishable magazine-pages emerged a kind of fiction which belongs nominally to crime literature but which finally gave a chance to writers of talent so they could write mature works of fiction in a medium that would earn them a living and which was to establish itself as a genuine American genre.

It was Hammett and Chandler who made the hardboiled crime novel an inimitable American genre. The detective story *per se* could be imitated, as was shown by the success of British and Continental writers, but it is practically impossible to copy the style, the wit and the settings of the hardboiled novels. The attitude toward violence is different in Europe. Despite its wars, Europe does not have the same quotidian familiarity with violence and guns as we do. To shoot a man, particularly with a handgun, in, say, London, Paris or Amsterdam is still a shocking event there. In our nation it is more a matter of course, as events keep on proving to anyone still naïve enough to doubt it. In Europe one does not see private vehicles riding around with gunracks behind the driver's seat—you may see such trucks in New England, not exclusively in the South and West. In Europe a father does not put on his red jacket to go teach his son autumn hunting, because he would have no weapon, would not be able to get one, nor be able to find a place to kill game. The weapons in Europe are in the hands of the authorities and the privileged classes, and perhaps here is the reason for Europe's strong fascination for the American hardboiled novel—which shows, after all, a lone man stubbornly pursuing the powerful trinity of money, politics and police. In Europe, Chandler's Philip Marlowe would have to be a popular uprising.

In any case, the new crime novel set the tale of detection free to develop meaningful and exciting alternatives to the game of hygienic evil. The hardboiled novel develops from scene to scene and pays less attention to plot. Its gritty quality allows more realistic developments, and its heroes are simpler men than the noble paper tigers of yore. And so, no matter what historians of the genre care to propose, I would insist that the hardboiled detective story, in its rapid development from the pulps to Hammett and Chandler, is responsible for today's novels which describe the police at work in a realistic manner, for the so-called "thriller," for the crime novel and, finally, for the spy story, though I feel that the latter has developed into an important form in its own right and should not be classed so readily as it often is with tales of detection. Hammett and Chandler are the godfathers of Simenon's Maigret, Nicolas Freeling's Van der Valk (a Dutch police officer created by an Englishman), and Sjöwall and Wahlöö's Martin Beck (a Swedish policeman), to mention only three nationalities. These writers are not direct heirs of Conan Doyle or Dorothy Sayers; their books are novels of great power which can be read as such and do not need the bait of detection to be memorable. With such authors it should be obvious that relegating their work to wholesale reviewing in a "mystery column" is a crime of judgment and a pointless snobbism on the part of critics.

. . . . .

When a book, any sort of book, reaches a certain intensity of artistic performance it becomes literature.

That intensity may be a matter of style, situation, character, emotional tone, or idea, or half a dozen other things. It may also be a perfection of control over the movement of a story similar to the control a great pitcher has over the ball.

When Raymond Chandler (1888-1959) wrote this in 1946, he had published three novels and a number of stories, all categorized under the rubric of mystery fiction. But according to his own formula, the novels were literature when tested for such matters as style, situation, emotional tone and idea. He is the greatest creator of the hardboiled detective novel, a greater writer than Hammett, who invented the genre, and a writer of such stature that he should be included in any account of modern American literature.

Chandler came late to the profession of writing. When he was eight his mother took him with her to England and educated him there. Later Chandler studied for a year on the continent in France and Germany, worked in the British Civil Service, and made a living as a journalist in London. During the First World War he enlisted in the Canadian Armed Services, fought in France, and in 1918 joined the RAF. In 1919 he was back in California and in 1924, after the death of his mother, Chandler married a woman seventeen years his senior. It is another remarkable instance of the power of the imagination that Chandler, who became famous for writing tales of tough men and fast women, remained very much in love with the same woman for thirty years. When she died in 1954 after a long illness, Chandler was heartbroken and tried to commit suicide.

Before earning his living from writing Chandler had all sorts of jobs, such as picking apricots ten hours a day, stringing tennis rackets for a sporting goods store and teaching himself bookkeeping (which gave him a start in business). He gradually worked himself up to the position of director of half a dozen independent oil corporations. "The depression finished that. Wandering up and down the Pacific Coast in an automobile, I began to read pulp magazines, because they were cheap enough to throw away and because I never had had at any time any taste for the kind of thing which is known as women's magazines. This was in the great days of the *Black Mask* (if I may call them great days) and it struck me that some of the writing was pretty forceful and honest, even though it had its crude aspect. I decided that this might be a good way to try to learn to write fiction and get paid a small amount of money at the same time."

He was forty-five when his first story was published in *Black Mask* (1933). Six years later his first novel, *The Big Sleep,* appeared. When he died in 1959 Chandler had published seven novels, twenty-three stories, several essays, and had written a number of scripts for Hollywood including *Double Indemnity, The Blue Dahlia* and *Strangers on a Train.* His fiction has also been used for the screen. During his lifetime *Farewell, My Lovely, The Big Sleep* (starring Bogart, with dialogue by Faulkner), and *The Lady in the Lake* were filmed. Since his death, unlikely actors have attempted to portray Philip Marlowe: James

Garner was terrible in *Marlowe* (based on *The Little Sister),* and at present Elliott Gould is making a dubious attempt at Chandler's hero in the screen version of *The Long Goodbye.*

Most of his personal experiences are reflected in his books, but Chandler was in person far from the tough character of a private investigator. The world of his novels is a world of the imagination: a particular, highly individual creation. Chandler did not have the practical experience of Hammett, who had been a Pinkerton operative, nor did he have the savage delight in blood and guts of Mickey Spillane. He is superior to both as a writer, and the labels of "tough," "violent," and "hardboiled" which were liberally pasted onto his work only show how successful Chandler was in pleasing a general audience while doing much more than just telling a tough tale.

The violence in his work is the commonplace of our general habitat, while the toughness is really one of mind. The physical variety is mostly stubbornness and an expression of the constitutional durability of his hero. For contrast, the degenerate mindlessness of Spillane's books—and their preposterous success—show what many people really want in order to satisfy sado-masochistic fancies, while another commercial success, *No Orchids for Miss Blandish* by James Hadley Chase, instantly indicates what lack of intelligence and talent can do to the same vehicle Chandler used. This novel of Chase's has a bland morbidity which actually manages to make depraved violence as routinely vulgar as pornography. Chandler said that he had made the form respectable for another generation. If this is true—and I see only a modest advance in our acceptance of this illegitimate child of American literature—it is primarily due to his stature as a writer and not because the ingredients in his work were more shocking than in that of anyone before him.

Chandler's output was remarkably small for an author of popular fiction. Age seems to have little to do with it. At 54, John D. MacDonald has written more than 60, and at 37 Donald E. Westlake has published over 65 books. Spillane sold over 40,000,000 copies of more than 20 books, and "Ellery Queen" has written almost 40 crime stories. The list is long: Edgar Wallace, Oppenheimer, Fleming. . . .

Chandler published only *seven* novels because he worked slowly and carefully. He cared about the choice of words, the rhythm of a sentence, the building of a paragraph, the architecture of a scene and the composition of a novel. Evidence for his concern with his craft can be found in his remarks on writing, included in *Raymond Chandler Speaking,* a collection of letters and drafts. Unfortunately this volume is out of print and it behooves Houghton Mifflin Company to reissue it if only to complement their recent anthology of Chandler's work (containing two of his best novels, four stories and the famous essay "The Simple Art of Murder"). This book of letters which a contemporary German author, Alfred Andersch, has called "one of the finest books on the art of writing," reveals Chandler struggling with practical and theoretical problems of style and consciously attempting to create a new hybrid from trivial *and* mentally stimulating literature.

This was a difficult task, and he knew it. Throughout his letters Chandler shows an honesty which made him admit that the mystery novel was more often than not badly written, that the conventional rules were silly and irrelevant, and that his real problem was whether two entirely different kinds of intellect (the analytical one which devises the puzzles and the imaginative one which cares about style) can be combined—if, indeed, he wondered, this is even necessary. Quite obvious is his irritation at being subjected to critical denunciation which is really directed at the genre he had chosen to remodel. All Chandler wanted was that a critic would have a discerning eye which could sift the wheat from the chaff.

> There is no top-drawer critical writing about the murder or mystery novel, factually based or otherwise. Neither in this country nor in England has there been any critical recognition that far more art goes into these books at their best than into any number of fat volumes of goosed history or social-significance rubbish. The psychological foundation for the immense popularity with all sorts of people of the novel about murder or crime or mystery hasn't been scratched . . . And if you have to have significance . . . it is just possible that the tensions in a novel of murder are the simplest and yet most complete pattern of the tensions on which we live in this generation.

He summarized the problem he faced as well as the achievement of his own work, when he said that "the real problem for a writer now is to avoid writing a mystery story while appearing to do so."

Such a performance is a difficult balancing act, but Chandler had trained well. The letters contain a disquisition on the genre's critical terminology, a discussion of the relative merit of British and American-English as stylistic phenomena, a knowledgeable report on the derivation of American slang, and remarks on a wide range of writers from the classics to the mundane. The volume furthermore has fascinating things to say about the practical aspects of writing, about working in Hollywood, about agents and publishers, rounding off with Chandler's remarks on his own work and with autobiographical statements (of which his letters concerning his wife are the most moving, and those admitting his passion for cats the most charming). Chandler comes alive as an urbane, educated and witty man who, nevertheless, remains a puzzle. He was an honest and an angry man, a writer of great power and insight who was forced to campaign to get his fiction accepted by the critics, yet realistic enough to be bitter about the results.

> A good story cannot be devised; it has to be distilled. In the long run, however little you talk or even think about it, the most durable thing in writing is style, and style is the most valuable investment a writer can make with his time.

That is precisely what Chandler did. One familiar with all of his work can see that he used his stories as the raw material for his novels. Very little went to waste; even his last published novel, *Playback* (1958), was based on a filmscript never used.

The intricate plots of the novels result from interlocking totally different stories. Characters from various tales were fused into a single new one, the separate plot lines were skillfully joined into an alternative story, individual scenes were enlarged, so that everything was reordered for consistency with the new material he had written. His first novel, *The Big Sleep* (1939) uses the stories **"Killer in the Rain," "The Curtain,"** and **"Fingerman"**; his second novel, *Farewell, My Lovely* (1940), uses **"The Man Who Liked Dogs," "Try the Girl," "Mandarin's Jade," "Pearls are a Nuisance,"** and **"Trouble is my Business"**; *High Window* (1942), the third novel, uses elements from **"The King in Yellow"**; *Lady in the Lake* (1943), his fourth novel, "cannibalized" (as Chandler called his own practice) the stories **"Bay City Blues," "The Lady in the Lake,"** and **"No Crime in the Mountains."**

And all this fictional carpentry was performed with an enviable technical dexterity. The stories were what the sketchbook is to the painter, but the finished canvas is far superior to the brief notations. Such an examination can also undermine the common notion that mystery fiction is best represented by the short story; this is only true if one wants nothing more than a puzzle plot, but it will simply not hold if the writer wants to develop a character, a scene, or a thematic motif.

Chandler's method can be more immediately examined by comparing the story **"The Curtain"** and his novel, his sixth, *The Long Goodbye* (1953), which was recently reprinted in *The Midnight Raymond Chandler*. The germ for the novel (his longest) lies in the first five pages of the story. Larry Batzel, sketched briefly in the opening pages of the story, becomes the complex and intriguing character Terry Lennox of *The Long Goodbye*. The comparison illustrates Chandler's method of amplifying a brief sentence or short scene into an elaborate description or into an entire chapter. The action of the first five pages of **"The Curtain"** is expanded, as a jazz musician builds a solo from a single melody line, into five chapters of the novel. The story starts:

> The first time I ever saw Larry Batzel he was drunk outside Sardi's in a secondhand Rolls-Royce. There was a tall blonde with him who had eyes you wouldn't forget. I helped her argue him out from under the wheel so that she could drive.

That very first sentence alone becomes a paragraph in the book:

> The first time I laid eyes on Terry Lennox he was drunk in a Rolls-Royce Silver Wraith outside the terrace of the Dancers. The parking lot attendant had brought the car out and he was still holding the door open because Terry Lennox's left foot was still dangling outside, as if he had forgotten he had one. He had a

young-looking face but his hair was bone white. You could tell by his eyes that he was plastered to the hairline, but otherwise he looked like any other nice young guy in a dinner jacket who had been spending too much money in a joint that exists for that purpose and for no other.

The simple description of the girl in the story's second sentence becomes more precise:

There was a girl beside him. Her hair was a lovely shade of dark red and she had a distant smile on her lips and over her shoulders she had a blue mink that almost made the Rolls-Royce look like just another automobile. It didn't quite. Nothing can.

The third quoted sentence from **"The Curtain"** becomes 800 words of description and dialogue in the novel.

Chandler's diction is a mixture of colloquial and poetic language, producing a style which is never purely realistic yet always concrete—Chandler seldom apostrophizes abstraction. This is a hallmark of the American style, of course, from Melville to Hemingway: a direct style of communication which is clear and precise without sacrificing poetic beauty. Such precision can etch a person or a scene very sharply and can create similes or metaphors which are startling either in their beauty or their wit.

Many reviewers have attacked Chandler's "tough-guy similes" which were so cleverly parodied by S. J. Perelman in "Farewell my Lovely Appetizer," but they forget that Chandler intended them to be witty and, more importantly, that he had devised not all of them for humorous purposes only, though humor is very much a part of his work. At times his figurative language is as sharply apt as that of Dickens or Conrad, two authors with whom Chandler has something in common. The stylistic devices look easy enough, but their realization is more difficult. Most often Chandler yokes two incongruous subjects to achieve a startling and fresh observation. Samples:

1)—I could see, even on that short acquaintance, that thinking was always going to be a bother to her.

2)—The plants filled the place, a forest of them, with nasty meaty leaves and stalks like the newly washed fingers of dead men.

3)—A few locks of dry white hair clung to his scalp, like wild flowers fighting for life on a bare rock.

4)—The General spoke again, slowly, using his strength as carefully as an out-of-work showgirl uses her last good pair of stockings.

5)—There were low bookshelves, there was a thick pinkish Chinese rug in which a gopher could have spent a week without showing his nose above the nap. There were floor cushions, bits of odd silk tossed around, as if whoever lived there had to have a piece he could reach out and thumb.

6)—Hair like steel wool grew far back on his head and gave him a great deal of domed forehead that might at a careless glance have seemed a dwelling-place for brains.

7)—Under the thinning fog the surf curled and creamed, almost without sound, like a thought trying to form itself on the edge of consciousness.

8)—I was as empty of life as a scarecrow's pockets.

9)—He looked about as inconspicuous as a tarantula on a slice of angel food.

10)—It was a blonde. A blonde to make a bishop kick a hole in a stained-glass window.

11)—I lit a cigarette. It tasted like a plumber's handkerchief.

12)—The house itself was not so much. It was smaller than Buckingham Palace, rather grey for California, and probably had fewer windows than the Chrysler Building.

13)—[A bug crawling over a desk] It wobbled a little as it crawled, like an old woman carrying too many parcels.

14)—Its color scheme was bile green, linseed poultice brown, sidewalk grey and monkey-bottom blue. It was as restful as a split lip.

15)—Grayson put his bony hand out and I shook it. It felt like shaking hands with a towel-rack.

16)—[The elevator] had an elderly perfume in it, like three widows drinking tea.

17)—Bright moonlight lay against its wall like a fresh coat of paint.

18)—I belonged in Idle Valley like a pearl onion on a banana split.

19)—It would have depressed a laughing jackass and made it coo like a mourning dove.

Most often the vehicle negates the tenor of the comparison implying the abjuratory world of Chandler's fiction. (See items 2, 3, 4 above.) There is a comic fierceness in the hyperbole which often relies for its effect on the creation of an outrageous grotesquerie so that it becomes similar to surrealism or "black humor." (See 9, 10, 18, 19.)

It seems to me that critics have denigrated these similes simply because they don't expect to find them in this genre of fiction. But I would venture to say that they are no less fittingly-preposterous than Pope's in "The Rape of the Lock," Dickens' famous descriptions, or such similes as Conrad's in *The Secret Agent*: ". . . the Chief Inspector went on peering at the table with a calm face and the slightly anxious attention of an indigent customer bending over what may be called by-products of a butcher's shop with a view to an inexpensive dinner." The Inspector, by the way, is examining a pulverized corpse.

Yet Chandler could also get his point across with irony (see 1, 6), just as there are similes of simple poetic beauty which are not so immediately obvious (see 7, 8, 13, 17). How difficult it would be to emulate Chandler's hyperbolic sarcasm can be seen in the work of the many epigones of the hardboiled school of writing, such sorry tradesmen as Spillane, Cheyney, Chase, *et al.*, and in a recent pastiche by a British writer (*Gumshoe,* also made into a film) which only passes muster because the hero is deliberately presented as a bad stand-up comic.

But Chandler's mastery of style is better observed in more expanded rhetorical devices. In chapter 31 of *Farewell, My Lovely,* the aforenoticed little bug crawls across the desk of the investigating police officer and falls to the floor. Throughout a conversation about murder Marlowe keeps track of the little bug which is trying to find a way out. When he is leaving, Marlowe picks the bug up and carries him down eighteen floors to put him gently among some vegetation. By referring indirectly to the helplessness of the insignificant insect as a counterpoint to the brutality of the conversation, Chandler implies the inhumanity of the world Marlowe inhabits and, in the final act of off-handed tenderness, he depicts Marlowe's concern for life much better than could many pages of discursive prose. It is a chivalrous act, just a touch insane, since anyone else in that room would have squashed the bug, not necessarily with malice but simply because it would be bothering somebody.

In the same novel Chandler gives a description of a calendar which serves as an indirect metaphor for his gritty, seedy world, and for his hero who will not bow to its malice.

> They had Rembrandt on the calendar that year, a rather smeary self-portrait due to imperfectly registered color plates. It showed him holding a smeared palette with a dirty thumb and wearing a tam-o'-shanter which wasn't any too clean either. His other hand held a brush poised in the air, as if he might be going to do a little work after a while, if somebody made a down payment. His face was aging, saggy, full of the disgust of life and the thickening effects of liquor. But it had a hard cheerfulness that I liked, and the eyes were as bright as drops of dew.

This is a description that becomes a metaphor for the fictional world and also nicely delineates Chandler's faith in the indomitable spirit of man (and artist), no matter how we are forced to live. The description echoes his remarks elsewhere about Shakespeare.

> Shakespeare would have done well in any generation because he would have refused to die in a corner; he would have taken the false gods and made them over;

he would have taken the current formulae and forced them into something lesser men thought them incapable of. Alive today he would undoubtedly have written and directed motion pictures, plays and God knows what. Instead of saying "This medium is not good," he would have used it and made it good. If some people called some of his work cheap (which some of it is), he wouldn't have cared a rap, because he would know that without some vulgarity there is no complete man. He would have hated refinement, as such, because it is always a withdrawal, a shrinking, and he was much too tough to shrink from anything.

This, with a bow to himself as the writer who had "to accept a mediocre form and make something like literature out of it."

In *The High Window* another nonhuman detail is used antithetically as a leitmotiv. A little garden statue of a black boy reoccurs throughout the novel as a symbol of decency and camaraderie which is lacking in the society Marlowe is embroiled in. Such technical devices and the constancy of the hero carry Chandler's novels from scene to scene. They have a unity which is both technically and poetically "right." The technical contrivances of plot, energized by the conventions of the genre are admirably achieved but they are also subservient to a larger design. Chandler's is a poetry of evil which keeps each book pacing relentlessly to an inconclusive end—certainly a major departure from the melioristic endings of traditional detective fiction. And so one can see that, from the fundamentals of sentences, tropes, rhetorical devices, paragraphs and scenes, a web of fiction is fabricked which is more than the sum of its parts.

The Big Sleep is a good example. In the second chapter of that novel Philip Marlowe goes to call on a very wealthy, retired general. The interview is conducted in a hothouse where orchids are cultivated. An arresting notion. But Chandler makes the scene a complex metaphor which suggests the entire novel and echoes the theme(s) of the book. The precise details and the striking similes become poetry, metaphors for a claustrophobic artificiality and for a life that is a parasitic death. The flowers are cultivated in an artificial heat where they thrive in profusion. The plants form a jungle of sinister proliferation which surrounds the dying general, who is paralyzed, confined to a wheelchair, brittle, unnaturally cold and barely a living organism. The plants which viciously resemble human flesh, abound in energy and the human being, dried out like a withered leaf, can enjoy life only by proxy; the general can do no more than approximate satisfaction of his vices by greedily watching another man enjoying them for him. Claustrophobia and perversion are enhanced by images of moisture and of the sickroom. Life is a travesty here and the contradictions continue. General Sternwood fathered two daughters at an age when incipient parenthood is not the norm. His children are perverse and ruthless; the only member of his family he ever liked was a son-in-law who was a gangster and who turns out to have been murdered. The scene has a Baudelairean touch in the exuberance of the vice described, while the oppressive mood recalls Faulkner who, incidentally, collaborated on the screenplay based on Chandler's book.

These themes of corruption and sinister inversion are mercilessly pursued. The artificial jungle of the hothouse grows into that of a perverse society of sex, money, murder, immorality and betrayal. There is no escape from it, just as there is no escape from a narcosis. The only awakening possible is into the "big sleep" of death, and death is cynical in its democracy. It is a nocturnal book and the bleakness of the world depicted is underscored by a persistent rain. All that was intimated in the scene in the hothouse has been developed into a powerful evocation of evil which taints everything, from people to climate, and which is further disclosed in a gallery of brilliantly created characters and through a style of forceful poetry.

This book, and the six other novels by Chandler, are in the tradition of a negative romanticism which is perhaps the dominant mode of American literature from Hawthorne to our contemporary black humorists—that power of darkness which Hawthorne, Poe and Melville explored, which Mark Twain could not laugh away, and which created a mythical landscape in Faulkner. Poe's "The Fall of the House of Usher" can be regarded as the rehearsal for the saga of the Sartoris-Compson-Sutpen families in Yoknapatawpha County. And the predecessor of Chandler's Californian nightmare had his hero Dupin "be enamored of the night for her own sake." But where Poe brought inductive light to moral darkness, Chandler refuses to cheat his vision in like manner. When Marlowe has solved a dilemma, he has not explained the enigma. All of Chandler's books end on a note of dissatisfaction. The purported solution does not tidy things up since there is no end to a waking nightmare.

This dark vision has lost none of its power today. The excess of violence of which Chandler has been needlessly accused is now hardly noticeable, nor was it lovingly attended to for shock effect, but rather described because life is simply that cheap in this truly egalitarian society: literally, a matter of fact. And so Chandler does not laud death with the lyrical mesmerism of Hemingway, nor does he play metaphysical games with it in Sartrean ingenuity. A death is a waste of life.

A corrupt universe can house no justice or, inversely, justice would be an embarrassing intruder. The forces of authority in Chandler's world are part of an eroding fabric. Justice is a matter of chance and the law a mechanism. As a lawyer in *The Long Goodbye* puts it: "The law isn't justice. It's a very imperfect mechanism. If you press exactly the right buttons and are also lucky, justice may show up in the answer. A mechanism is all the law was ever intended to be." Nevertheless, the parts of this mechanism have power and will grind people down who happen to get stuck in them. The enforcers of the law often look like the machinery they serve and Chandler emphasizes their frightening neutrality, as machines are wont to be.

> They had the calm weathered faces of healthy men in hard condition. They had the eyes they always have,

cloudy and grey like freezing water. The firm set mouth, the hard little wrinkles at the corners of the eyes, the hard hollow meaningless stare, not quite cruel and a thousand miles from kind. The dull ready-made clothes, worn without style, with a sort of contempt; the look of men who are poor and yet proud of their power, watching always for ways to make it felt, to shove it into you and twist it and grin and watch you squirm, ruthless without malice, cruel and yet not always unkind. What would you expect them to be? Civilization had no meaning for them.

> *(The Little Sister)*

In *The Long Goodbye* Chandler describes the environment they operate: it is society as a house of detention.

> In the corner of the cell block there may be a second steel door that leads to the show-up box. One of its walls is wire mesh painted black. On the back wall are ruled lines for height. Overhead are floodlights. You go in there in the morning as a rule, just before the night captain goes off duty. You stand against the measuring lines and the lights glare at you and there is no light behind the wire mesh. But plenty of people are out there: cops, detectives, citizens who have been robbed or assaulted or swindled or kicked out of their cars at gun point or conned out of their life savings. You don't see or hear them. You hear the voice of the night captain. You receive him loud and clear. He puts you through your paces as if you were a performing dog. He is tired and cynical and competent. He is the stage manager of a play that has had the longest run in history, but it no longer interests him.

The population which inhabits the grid of the night captain is dead in a different sense.

> We've got the big money, the sharp shooters, the percentage workers, the fast dollar boys, the hoodlums out of New York and Chicago and Detroit—and Cleveland. We've got the flashy restaurants and night clubs they run, and the hotels and apartment houses they own, and the grafters and con men and female bandits that live in them. The luxury trades, the pansy decorators, the Lesbian dress designers, the riff-raff of a big hardboiled city with no more personality than a paper cup. Out in the fancy suburbs dear old Dad is reading the sports page in front of a picture window, with his shoes off, thinking he is high class because he has a three-car garage. Mom is in front of her princess dresser trying to paint the suitcases out from under her eyes. And Junior is clamped on to the telephone calling up a succession of high school girls that talk pidgin English and carry contraceptives in their make-up kit.

> *(The Little Sister)*

Chandler made metropolitan California into a metaphor of America in a manner which has the same harsh clarity as the paintings of Edward Hopper. His fictional world has an unremitting gloom: injustice and the seven deadly sins are paramount and decency is something of a vice.

But, like Faulkner, Chandler fostered a negative heroism. This bleak world is illuminated by the stubborn endurance of his hero, Philip Marlowe, a man who insists on a private code which is not so much one of justice as one of *humanitas*. Marlowe is not a bright shiny volunteer for a superlative of good. He is an angry and bitter man, tainted by the world he invades in his violence, his gallows humor and his melancholy—a melancholy which is at times close to despair since he knows that his efforts are so futile. But he is a man who must endure and who must persist in his defiance against the forces of coercion—a sad man since he realizes the futility; and a noble man because he will not be vanquished.

Marlowe, who was described by Marshall McLuhan as "Chandler's echo of Christopher Marlowe's supermen Tamburlaine and Dr. Faustus," is in a long line of Romantic heroes. He is an outsider, a loner, a man who will not fit the pattern, a character who must not toe the line. If Marlowe were an archetype he would be a somber knight on a never finished quest, recharging his faith by adversity. A Romantic Hero, to be sure, but one who has been mired in reality. As an outsider, in his preference for solitude, in his stubborn defiance and power to endure, Marlowe is very much the archetypical hero of American fiction, from Melville's Ishmael and Bartleby to Hemingway's Frederic Henry and Robert Jordan. In Chandler's novels Marlowe is the only figure with warmth and compassion, but there is a constant infiltration of the autumnal mood, of weariness and futility. That is why these novels are not simply crime fiction: at their close little has been resolved despite the fact that the murderer has been found. All of them end on a note of dissatisfaction.

Marlowe is thus not a simplistic creation. In fact, he is quite subtle and ambiguous. In this character there is a fierce grief which has little opportunity to be assuaged— a grief for a loss, perhaps a primeval Eden, perhaps a community of decent men. Not a grief, however, simply for a loss of innocence, but a bitter frustration about the fact that things *are* as they are though they shouldn't be that way. There is a revulsion for this world yet also a distaste for his own defiant nobility, a nobility very much like a pawned code of honor. In all these particulars Marlowe is a reflection of the most typical American fictional hero, and I think that not enough emphasis has been put on his furious grief which can only escape through a tenuously controlled pathos or through the painfully blasphemous fury of, for example, Frederic Henry at the end of Hemingway's *A Farewell to Arms*. Exiles ever, these characters are not destined to join their fellow men.

In Chandler's angriest and yet saddest novel, *The Long Goodbye*, the conventional vehicle of murder is almost irrelevant. It is basically a novel about friendship and the emotional combat of human relations. Marlowe's affection for Terry Lennox is one of those baffling emotional frauds life is fond of putting over on us. Despite his better judgment, despite the negative qualities of Lennox, despite the trouble this man is fated to visit upon anyone associated with him, Marlowe feels a strong bond and defends him against preposterous odds of circumstantial misfortune. Lennox is weak, cynical, apparently resigned to his fate, yet, though reluctantly, Marlowe finds himself

enticed into a bond of fellowship with a man who is a counterfeiter of life in need of protection. This kinship of exile has one flaw: Lennox has no profound relationship left in him to spend. He is a burned-out case fitted with a new exterior by money and modern medicine. Lennox is Marlowe's negative double, and if Marlowe had given in to his feelings he would have had to admit his own defeat at trying to maintain a precarious balance on that edge between despairing ruthlessness and an anger born from a tenuous faith.

Yet Lennox is kin, and it is appropriate that Marlowe pays a silent tribute to this ghostly friendship when he is alone. It is a moving passage, written with superb control of language and emotion, showing how Chandler could handle that most difficult task of the novelist: to create pathos that never gibbers into sentimentality. Marlowe has just finished reading a letter from Lennox who has fled into voluntary exile in Mexico. The letter contained a five-thousand-dollar bill and Lennox asks him to perform a few commemorative gestures.

> I sat there and looked at it for a long time. At last I put it away in my lettercase and went out to the kitchen to make that coffee. I did what he asked me to, sentimental or not. I poured two cups and added some bourbon to his and set it down on the side of the table where he had sat at the morning I took him to the plane. I lit a cigarette for him and set it in an ashtray beside the cup. I watched the steam rise from the coffee and the thin thread of smoke rise from the cigarette. Outside in the tecoma a bird was gussing around, talking to himself in low chirps, with an occasional brief flutter of wings. Then the coffee didn't steam anymore and the cigarette stopped smoking and was just a dead butt on the edge of an ashtray. I dropped it into the garbage can under the sink, I poured the coffee out and washed the cup and put it away. That was that. It didn't seem quite enough to do for five thousand dollars.

It is no accident I am sure, that the book deals not only with a counterfeit friendship but also with a counterfeit writer who has prostituted his talents, and with a counterfeit love. Nor is it an accident that most of the book takes place in an idyllic valley settled by the very rich. But in modern American fiction every Eden turns out to be a fraud—the only reality is that of the city, and it is one that sours.

In Chandler's work there is Fitzgerald's tone of disenchantment and cynicism, Nathaniel West's exaggerated humor and rueful tenderness, Hemingway's melancholy and brooding, and Faulkner's decadence and stubborn endurance. But unlike Hemingway's heroes, Chandler's Marlowe is not passive. Marlowe pushes against a recalcitrant existence with the quixotic energy of a Bartleby's "I prefer not to." For a man who felt intellectually like a displaced person, at home on neither continent, Chandler wrote a superlative chapter of the American myth.

Blinded by Hemingway's terseness, commentators have praised Dashiel Hammett's spare staccato style in, for example, his first novel *Red Harvest*. But a re-examination has convinced me that the book is little more than a literate comic strip with neither nuance nor depth of language, character or scene. Because of its plot, which hinges on pitting rival against rival, with the private eye as a catalyst for an almost comically hyperbolic violence, it seems to have been the shooting script for Kurosawa's film *Yojimbo*. Hammett's second novel, *The Dain Curse,* is an embarrassment, even as a tale of detection, while its use of occultism is a gothic gone flat. The acclaim for the characterization in *The Maltese Falcon* is, as far as I can judge, clouded by the superlative film and little more than a fond *nostalgie de primeur*. Nor does *The Glass Key,* considered Hammett's masterpiece, favorably compare with Chandler's novel on a similar theme of friendship, the far more subtle and complex *The Long Goodbye*. Only *The Thin Man,* with its blend of cynicism, wit and vitriolic characters, can withstand repeated scrutiny. Let us grant Hammett the honor of having been the founder of the hardboiled school of writing, but that does not automatically confer excellence.

The legacy of Chandler's work is soon traced. Ross MacDonald has directly modeled his novels on Chandler's fiction. Their locale, Southern California, is the same, and MacDonald's hero, Lew Archer, is clearly a descendant of Marlowe: humane, brooding, and exilic. Another feature in common is that MacDonald's alleged crime novels are, like Chandler's, everything else *but* whodunits. Several historians of the genre have asserted that Sophocles' Oedipus was the first detective. If this were true, then MacDonald's twenty-odd novels are so many variations on the Greek theme because most of them deal with an oedipal search for family and identity. Like Chandler, MacDonald relies on characterization and theme, and his style is graceful and ingenious.

Chandler once remarked that he had made literature out of the crime novel and that he had made the genre respectable. His struggle bore fruit: MacDonald's work has been seriously considered and critically applauded in lengthy reviews by such commentators as William Goldman and Eudora Welty. The latter two were correct, yet such serious consideration is still rare. It baffles me how the majority of honest critics can fantasize profundity in Norman Mailer's potboiler, *An American Dream,* but refuse a similar investigation of Chandler's work, or plead intellectual hemophilia when they do encounter serious attention given to crime novelists. An example is Geoffrey Hartman's review of MacDonald's latest novel, *The Underground Man,* in *The New York Review of Books*. Mr. Hartman cannot forgive Chandler and MacDonald for being so brazenly serious when they should merely be entertaining. He considers the genre of crime fiction not serious, yet these two writers appear to be so, hence *they* are wrong because the genre is not serious. He finds their characters "too understandable," which is a crime, of course, since the complexities of Mailer, Malamud, and Mary MacCarthy defy comprehension. "Neither writer [Chandler and MacDonald] puts much emphasis on problem-solving, on finding out who killed Roger Ackroyd. But in spite of their claims for the honesty, morality, and the authentic qualities of the detective novel one cannot overlook the

persistence in their work of the old problem-solving formula." Obviously his logic fails Mr. Hartman here. He furthermore finds it disconcerting that criminality comes from the familiar world; but I would like to know where else it should come from, or is this a peculiar capitalism of crime? He dislikes similes as well as images that "flash all around us like guns."

After dumb parodies, fraudulent metaphysics ("we don't ever learn who is paying off the inner Marlowe or Archer"[!]), the critical stalwarts are brought out: negative comparisons. How futile is such a statement as "they lack a Jamesian reticence." Of course they do: neither Chandler nor MacDonald like to get caught in an embarrassing profusion of clausal circumlocutions.

Critics of Mr. Hartman's ilk can accept violence and death from just about any other literary source, but it is somehow improper when they are used by crime novelists. "There is something erotic, even pornographic, in this need to see justice done, which draws us into one false hypothesis of flashy scene after another." Mr. Hartman with many others believes that content comes before style and that content, if concocted with the proper stuff of accredited seriousness, is what fiction is all about. As Chandler once put it to James Sandoe:

> [Nothing] changes the essential irritation to the writer, which is the knowledge that however well and expertly he writes a mystery story it will be treated in one paragraph, while a column and a half of respectful attention will be given to any fourth-rate, ill-constructed, mock-serious account of the life of a bunch of cotton pickers in the deep south. The French are the only people I know of who think about writing as writing. The Anglo-Saxons think first of the subject matter and second, if at all, of the quality.

In the crime novels of the black writer, Chester Himes, Chandler's blend of realism and exaggeration is exuberantly developed. His series of novels paints life in Harlem, including all levels of society from the pimps to the rich, in a direct, brusque style which is so very American that it is amazing Himes' reputation had to be particularly established in France (where he is considered the "Balzac of Harlem"). Himes likes grotesque exaggeration, and his gallows humor is very vitriolic indeed. But despite their humor, their superb dialogue and poetic realism, these crime novels are angry books. Violence has a quality of grim delight here, born of a barely repressed hatred. In his explosive ferocity, Himes has an authenticity that a paper-shredder like Spillane completely lacks and for which Chandler did not have the personal motivation. I am surprised that Himes is so little appreciated in his own country while in Europe he is well known and seriously appreciated—surprised because his work is a pioneering document of black experience which, in many ways, is far more incisive than some recent autobiographical statements on the subject.

Donald E. Westlake seems to have taken Chandler's liberation of the genre for granted and has developed Chandler's dry wit into a series of very funny variations on the theme of the tainted innocent becoming involved against his will in a lethal situation. For Westlake the story is more important than the detection—a position Chandler would have appreciated.

That side of Chandler which observes with a coolly realistic eye has been brought to its logical conclusions (not forgetting the European authors mentioned previously) in a recent novel by George V. Higgins, *The Friends of Eddie Coyle*. This book comes very close to being the slice-of-life-realism Zola was once famous for. Chandler's deliberate fictions have been discarded, the style has been stripped of its poetry and wit, and descriptions are at a minimum. Higgins' book reaches back to Hemingway in its simplicity of expression and its technique of building characters from dialogue—except that his dialogue sounds as though it has been dictated straight from a tape recording. With Higgins' novel we are equally far removed from the traditional detective novel as from Chandler: it is far superior to the first but it has lost the magic of the second.

Julian Symons (essay date 1981)

SOURCE: "Raymond Chandler: An Aesthete Discovers the Pulps," in *Critical Observations,* Ticknor & Fields, 1981, pp. 156-65.

[*In the following essay, Symons traces stylistic developments in Chandler's works and characterizes the author as a romantic aesthete primarily concerned with the literary quality of his writings.*]

> Fairyland is Everyman's dream of perfection, and changes, dream-like, with the mood of the dreamer. For one it is a scene of virgin, summery Nature undefiled by even the necessary works of man . . . For another it is a champaign, dotted with fine castles, in which live sweet ladies clad in silk, spinning, and singing as they spin, and noble knights who do courteous battle with each other in forest glades; or a region of uncanny magic, haunting music, elves and charmed airs and waters.

That is Raymond Chandler writing in 1912 for *The Academy.*

> The man in the powder-blue suit—which wasn't powder-blue under the lights of the Club Bolivar— was tall, with wide-set grey eyes, a thin nose, a jaw of stone. He had a rather sensitive mouth. His hair was crisp and black, ever so faintly touched with grey, as by an almost diffident hand. His clothes fitted him as though they had a soul of their own, not just a doubtful past. His name happened to be Mallory.

That is the opening paragraph of Raymond Chandler's first story for the pulps, **'Blackmailers Don't Shoot'**, which appeared in *Black Mask,* December 1933.

Between the two pieces lay twenty-one years in time and the Atlantic in distance, but they had a common emotional basis. The Chandler who wrote for the pulps was still a man who dreamed of fairyland. As I have said elsewhere it is emblematically right that in this first story the detective should be named Mallory, echoing the *Morte d'Arthur.* His carapace of iron (only iron could survive those frequent assaults with cosh and blackjack) conceals a quivering core, and whether his name is Mallory, Carmady, Dalmas or Philip Marlowe, he is truly a knight errant. Chandler's stories about criminals and a detective carried over into an alien field the literary aestheticism of his youth.

Raymond Chandler became a writer for the pulp magazines because he was broke, not because he wanted to write for the pulps. 'Realism and Fairyland' was one of the last pieces he published in England before he gave up the hope of making a literary living there, and he printed nothing in America until 1933. In between he had a variety of jobs, lived with his mother, married a woman eighteen years older than himself as soon as his mother died (his wife Cissy knocked ten years off her age for the marriage register), became vice-president of a group of oil companies, drank hard, had affairs, was eventually sacked. At the age of 44 he had no money and no prospects. At this point he listed himself as a writer in the Los Angeles directory, and began to study the pulp magazines. It struck him, as he said, that he might get paid while he was learning.

He was not likely, as he must have known, to get paid very much. The pulp magazines, so called because they were printed on wood pulp, began in the nineteenth century with the publication of the Nick Carter stories. The *Nick Carter Weekly* first appeared in 1891 and, like Sexton Blake in England, was the product of multiple authors. The chief of them, the bearded Frederic Dey (that is, Frederick Marmaduke Van Rensselaer Day) produced a 25,000 word story every week for years, and did not get rich. In 1929 he shot himself in a cheap New York hotel. Nick Carter's fame endured, and indeed endures, so that when *Detective Story Magazine* began publication in 1915 its editor was named as Nicholas Carter. *Black Mask,* in which most of Chandler's early stories appeared, was founded in 1920 by H. L. Mencken and George Jean Nathan, but did not take on its true character until Captain Joseph Shaw became editor in 1926. During the decade of Shaw's reign the magazine published stories that moved sharply away from the conventional detective story aspect of earlier pulp fiction (Edgar Wallace was one of the stars of *Detective Story Magazine*) to reflect the violence of American society and the vivid colloquialisms of American speech.

Chandler's approach, his background and his age made him a very unusual figure among the pulp writers. Most of them were hacks, although they would have called themselves professionals. They were hard-working, sometimes hard-drinking men who wrote fast and wrote for the money. To make a fair living they had to write a great deal, for the basic rate of one cent a word meant that you had to write a million words to make $10,000 a year. Many of them, like Erle Stanley Gardner, used several names, and some wrote romances and Westerns as well as crime stories. Such a literary netherworld exists in England now, although because there are no magazines its inhabitants write books, turning out ten or a dozen a year to make a reasonable living. In America during the Depression years similar writers worked mostly for the pulp magazines. Few of them had the specialized knowledge of Dashiell Hammett, who had been a Pinkerton agent, but most had familiarized themselves with some aspects of the law and crime, and knew a good deal about firearms. Many of them appeared to write with an ink-dipped cosh rather than a pen.

Chandler resembled them very little. He had read only three or four detective stories when he set out to make a living in the field, and he learned the technique of the crime story in the spirit of a young artist copying masters in the Louvre. He read everything he could find, in particular Hammett, but also Gardner and other pulp writers. He made a detailed synopsis of a Gardner story, rewrote it, compared the result with the original, rewrote it again, and then apparently threw it away. He took what he was doing seriously, because if he had not done so he could not have justified doing it. He was writing for *Black Mask* and *Dime Detective Magazine,* and he knew that what he did was hack work, but he gave to this hack work the care he had devoted to the literary pieces produced for English magazines long ago.

He knew little about the technical aspects of crime, and never bothered to learn, relying instead on textbooks. From the beginning he sensed that for a writer like himself such things were not important, and that any success he won would come through sharpness of language and observation rather than through expert knowledge. In a battling introduction to a collection of his short stories published in 1950, when he had become famous, he defended the pulp crime story by saying that 'even at its most mannered and artificial [it] made most of the fiction of the time taste like a cup of lukewarm consommé at a spinsterish tea-room.' He said also that he wished the stories being republished were better, but that the distinction of the imprint meant that he need not be sickeningly humble, even though 'I have never been able to take myself with that enormous earnestness which is one of the trying characteristics of the craft.' In fact he took himself very seriously indeed, and strongly resented adverse criticism from others, although he was prepared to make it himself. He also made claims for the form in which he was working that must seem over-stated. 'The aim is not essentially different from the aim of Greek tragedy, but we are dealing with a public that is semi-literate and we have to make an art of language they can understand.' The aim may be similar but the results, as he should have seen, are so different that the comparison is absurd.

Chandler remained by temperament a romantic aesthete. His feebly literary early essays and poems are full of either/ors like sciences and poetry, romance and realism. Are we to be saved 'by the science or by the poetry of life'? That, he said, 'is the typical question of the age',

and he came down on the side of poetry as opposed to science and of romance against realism. Or rather, of realism seen romantically, so that 'any man who has walked down a commonplace city street at twilight, just as the lamps are lit' would see that a true view of it must be idealistic, for it would 'exalt the sordid to a vision of magic, and create pure beauty out of plaster and vile dust'. The phrases echo Chesterton, and also look forward to the famous peroration of 'The Simple Art of Murder' which runs: 'Down these mean streets a man must go . . .' It was Chandler's strength, and his weakness, that he brought this basically sentimental aestheticism to the crime stories, so that they had increasingly to be about a romantic hero whose activities gave the novels at least 'a quality of redemption' so that he could think of them as art. That was the weakness. The strength lay in the fact that by treating seriously everything he did Chandler achieved even in his early stories for the pulps more than his fellow practitioners.

To talk about Chandler as a romantic aesthete may make him sound like an intellectual, but in fact he disliked intellectuals and the magazines for which they wrote. In the few meetings I had with him near the end of his life, it was possible to sense his distrust. Was this another of those damned critics trying to get at him? He was fond of using big words like art and redemption, but shied away from such things when they moved from the general to the particular. He could be deeply imperceptive and philistine. 'I read these profound discussions, say in the *Partisan Review,* about art, what is it, literature, what is it, and the good life and liberalism and what is the definitive position of Rilke or Kafka, and the scrap about Ezra Pound getting the Bollingen award, and it all seems too meaningless to me. Who cares?' he wrote to his English publisher Hamish Hamilton. He got on well with fellow pulp writers, partly because they regarded him, as one of them put it, as 'a professorial type, more of an intellectual than most of the other pulp writers I knew'. He was the oldest of them, a year older than Gardner and six years older than Hammett. They respected him, and so made him comparatively at ease. In general he avoided places and people through which he might be involved in literary discussion, preferring to talk to garage men and postal clerks. Other writers, and his opinions of them, he preferred to put on paper.

Second only to romantic aestheticism in giving his work its colour and character was his loneliness. He seems to have been from youth a shy person who found it hard to make friends, and this shyness was accentuated by his marriage to a woman so much older than himself. In these years also they were poor. For a decade Chandler scraped a living, writing for the pulps and publishing crime novels that received critical praise but were far from being best sellers. They moved from place to place, had few friends, went out little. Out of this loneliness, now and later, Chandler created his best work. When he began to write for films and became involved in the social life of the studios he wrote little, and that little was usually not very good. Shut up in an apartment, with Cissy in the next room and with 'life' making no demands, he sparkled on paper.

The third important element in Chandler's writing was its Anglo-American character. He had been brought up in England, he longed to return (and on the whole was not disappointed when he came), and the delighted disgust with which he saw California came partly from the contrast between its brash newness and English good taste. When he read Max Beerbohm he felt that he too belonged to an age of grace and taste from which he had been exiled. 'So I wrote for *Black Mask*. What a wry joke.' No doubt he would have felt hopelessly out of place in an age of grace (if such an age ever existed) and would have written ironically about it, but that is not the point. The flavour of his stories is individual partly because, even though, as he said, all the pulp writers used the same idiom, his is filtered through an English lens.

The very intelligent notes on English and American style which he put down in his notebook end with a striking observation of differences in verbal tone:

> The tone quality of English speech is usually overlooked. This tone quality is infinitely variable and contributes infinite meaning. The American voice is flat, toneless and tiresome. The English tone quality makes a thinner vocabulary and a more formalized use of language capable of infinite meanings. Its tones are of course read into written speech by association. This, of course, makes good English a class language, and that is its fatal defect. The English writer is a gentleman (or not a gentleman) first and a writer second.

Most of these distinctions seem to me very good ones, but in any case they were important to Chandler. Once he began to write, he became absorbed in the verbal problems involved, in particular the problem of giving an English variability to the 'flat, toneless and tiresome' pattern of American speech. The best of his work is witness to his triumphant success.

Chandler was not a prolific writer. He wrote in all twenty stories for the pulps, at the rate of two, three or four a year. It is true that almost all of them were much longer than the usual story, and that they might almost be called short novels, but even so the output was small. It has been said already that he was poor in the decade after he started to write crime stories. His average yearly earnings during the late 1930s and early 1940s were between one and two thousand dollars. In truth, there was no way of making a reasonable living by writing for the pulps unless you published ten or twelve stories a year. It is a mark of Chandler's integrity as a writer that he refused to do this, or was incapable of doing it, as later he refused to do what he was told in Hollywood when he was employed there at a salary gloriously or ludicrously large compared with his earnings at the time from stories and novels.

About the pulp stories considered as stories there is little to say except that they are not very good. 'Everybody imitates in the beginning,' as Chandler said himself, and the writer he imitated most was Hammett. The young blond gunman in **'Blackmailers Don't Shoot'** is obviously derived from Wilmer in *The Maltese Falcon*, the sadistic thug in **'Pick-**

Up on Noon Street' is based on Jeff in *The Glass Key*, and there are other echoes. Standard scenes and characters appear in most of the stories. There will be at least one night-club scene, a variety of villains will appear in every story, and some of them will be gangsters or gamblers who own the night clubs. The hard men who hit the detective over the head will be exceptionally stupid, and the gangsters will be only just a little smarter beneath their veneer of sophistication. The police will be tough, cynical, and occasionally corrupt. There will be a lot of shooting, with an Elizabethan litter of corpses piled up by the end. At the heart of the trouble there will be a girl, and she is almost never to be trusted, although she may have 'the sort of skin an old rake dreams of' (Rhonda Farr in **'Blackmailers Don't Shoot'**) or hair that is 'like a bush fire at night' (Beulah in **'Try the Girl'**) or even hair that 'seemed to gather all the light there was and make a soft halo around her coldly beautiful face' (Belle Marr in **'Spanish Blood'**). The women in the short stories are not as deadly as they become in the novels, but they are dangerous enough.

These standard properties are used in a standard way. The detective himself is not much more than a man whose head is harder and whose gun is faster than his rivals'. This is true of Marlowe, who appeared first in 1934, as much as of Mallory or Carmady. But the basic defect of the stories is that the length to which they were written did not fit Chandler's talent. The weakness of his plotting is more apparent in the stories than in the novels. The demand of the pulps, he said later, was for constant action, and if you stopped to think you were lost. 'When in doubt, have a man come through a door with a gun in his hand.' The novels gave more space for the development of situations and the creation of an environment. One of Chandler's great merits was his capacity to fix a scene memorably. He sometimes did this in a phrase, but he could do it even better in a paragraph or a page. The stories did not give him time to create anything of this kind. Everything that did not carry forward the action was excised by editors.

If we read these stories today it is for occasional flashes of observation that got by the blue pencil, and for the use of language. Chandler's ear for the rhythms of speech was good from the beginning, but it developed with astonishing speed. The stories written in the later 1930s, like **'Killer in the Rain'**, **'The Curtain'**, **'Try the Girl'** and **'Mandarin's Jade'** are often as well written as the novels, where the early tales are full of clichés. **'Smart-Aleck Kill'** (1934) has eyes that get small and tight, eyes with hot lights in them, eyes that show sharp lights of pain. There are cold smiles playing around the corners of mouths, and mirthless laughter. But within a very few years these have almost all disappeared, and we recognize the sharp cleverness of the novels when we are told that the garage of a modernistic new house is 'as easy to drive into as an olive bottle' or that a smart car in a dingy neighbourhood 'sticks out like spats at an Iowa picnic'.

It was these later and better stories that Chandler cannibalized, to use his own word, to make three of the novels.

This was an extraordinary process. Other writers have incorporated early material in a later work, but nobody else has done it in quite this way. Most writers who adapt their earlier work take from it a particular theme or character and jettison the rest. Chandler, however, carved out great chunks of the stories, expanded them, and fitted them into an enlarged plot. Where gaps existed, like spaces in a jigsaw, he made pieces to fit them. It meant, as Philip Durham has said, adapting, fusing and adding characters, blending themes from different stories, combining plots. Much of his first novel, *The Big Sleep,* was taken from two stories, **'Killer in the Rain'** and **'The Curtain',** plus fragments from two other stories. About a quarter of the book was new material, but the passages from the two principal stories used were much enlarged. There could be no better proof of the limitation Chandler felt in being forced to work within the pulp magazine formula.

Almost all of the enlargements were improvement. They added details of description, vital touches of characterization, or they were simply more elegantly or wittily phrased. They also helped to make the stories more coherent. In **'The Curtain'** the detective does not call on General Winslow in his orchid house until chapter three. In the novel Chandler, realizing that this was a splendid starting point, begins with it. (He economically kept chapter one for use years later in *The Long Goodbye.*) The difference in the effectiveness of the two scenes is startling. What was no more than adequate in the story has become memorable in the novel, with the old half-dead General emerging as a genuinely pathetic figure. One would need a variorum text to show exactly how Chandler did it, but here are one or two significant changes. The General is telling Marlowe to take off his coat in the steaming hot orchid house. In **'The Curtain'** he says:

> 'Take your coat off, sir. Dud always did. Orchids require heat, Mr Carmady—like rich old men.'

In *The Big Sleep* this becomes:

> 'You may take your coat off, sir. It's too hot in here for a man with blood in his veins.'

It is the last sentence that gives real flavour to the bit of dialogue, telling us more about the General than would half a dozen descriptive phrases. And, freed from the blue pencil, Chandler let his love of simile and metaphor run free. The smell of the orchids is not just like boiling alcohol as it was in the story, but like boiling alcohol under a blanket. In the story the General just watches the detective drink, but now 'The old man licked his lips watching me, over and over again, like an undertaker dry-washing his hands.' These are samples from thirty similes or metaphors brought into the scene. Is some of it a little too much? That is obviously partly a matter of taste, but the exuberance of it, the sense of a man using his own talent in his own way for the first time, cannot be anything but enjoyable. This 50-year-old colt is kicking up his heels in sheer pleasure. And Chandler now is on the look-out for clichés. In **'The Curtain'** the General has 'basilisk eyes'. Now they just have a coal-black directness.

The famous, and at the time rather daring, pornographic books passage in *The Big Sleep* appeared first in **'Killer in the Rain'**. This too has been transformed. In the story the detective knows in advance of the pornographic book racket, while in the novel suspense is created by our learning with Marlowe the meaning of 'Rare Books'. In the book store he meets a girl with silvered fingernails. A comparison of texts shows the value of Chandler's enlargements.

> She got up and came towards me, swinging lean thighs in a tight dress of some black material that didn't reflect any light. She was an ash blonde, with greenish eyes under heavily mascaraed lashes. There were large jet buttons in the lobes of her ears; her hair waved back smoothly from behind them. Her fingernails were silvered.
>
> She gave me what she thought was a smile of welcome, but what I thought was a grimace of strain.
>
> **('Killer in the Rain')**

> She got up slowly and swayed towards me in a tight black dress that didn't reflect any light. She had long thighs and she walked with a certain something I hadn't often seen in bookstores. She was an ash blonde with greenish eyes, beaded lashes, hair waved smoothly back from ears in which large jet buttons glittered. Her fingernails were silvered. In spite of her get-up she looked as if she would have a hall bedroom accent.
>
> She approached me with enough sex appeal to stampede a businessmen's lunch and tilted her head to finger a stray, but not very stray, tendril of softly glowing hair. Her smile was tentative, but it could be persuaded to be nice.
>
> *(The Big Sleep)*

The hall bedroom accent and the businessmen's lunch are the phrases that principally lift this from the commonplace to something hallmarked Chandler, and the elaboration of the scene from one page to three, with a client coming in to change a book, add a lot to its effectiveness.

The blonde reappears, both in story and novel, as the companion of a gangster named Marty (in the book Joe Brody). In both versions the detective gets a gun away from her, she sinks her teeth into the hand with the gun in it, and he cracks her on the head. A couple of grace notes are added in the novel. 'The blonde was strong with the madness of fear,' it says in the story. The sentence is rhetorical, and somehow inadequate. In the book it becomes: 'The blonde was strong with the madness of love or fear, or a mixture of both, or maybe she was just strong.'

The final touch is not in the story at all. After Brody has handed over some compromising photographs from which he was hoping to make money, the blonde complains of her luck. 'A half-smart guy, that's all I ever draw. Never once a guy that's smart all around the course. Never once.'

'Did I hurt your head much?' Marlowe asks.

'You and every other man I ever met.'

It is a perfect pay-off line, marvellously done.

One could go through the whole book, and through the other novels that have a basis in the stories, showing how, passage by passage, Chandler converted the mechanical effects of the stories into something unique in style and delivery. He discovered his own quality as a writer through the freedom given him by the form of the novel.

The pulp magazines had shaped him, but once he had learned the trade they were a restriction. The novels enabled him to burst the bonds and to express the essential Raymond Chandler: a romantic aesthete and a self-conscious artist, an introvert with the power of catching the form, the tone, the rhythm, of American speech supremely well on paper. In its kind Chandler's mature dialogue is perfect. One cannot see how it could be better done. The stories are not much in themselves, but without them perhaps we should never have had the novels.

Jerry Speir (essay date 1981)

SOURCE: "The Raw Material: The Short Stories," in *Raymond Chandler*, Frederick Ungar Publishing Co., 1981, pp. 85-104.

[*In the following essay, Speir discusses how Chandler's short stories evolved into novels and argues that the pulp stories were an essential stage in Chandler's development as a novelist.*]

Chandler's novels, of course, followed his noteworthy career as a writer of short stories for popular "pulp" magazines. A survey of those stories gives evidence of considerable experimentation in subject matter, style, point of view, and detective types which contributed to the novels' later success. Some of the stories were "cannibalized," as Chandler put it, into the novels, and a close look at that process allows us the unusual opportunity of observing the writer at work, transforming his own earlier, simpler material into the broader vision of the later books. But even the stories that weren't cannibalized have much to teach us about Chandler's development as a writer, and it seems appropriate here to look back at those stories for the deeper appreciation they may give us of the novels and the novelist.

From a purely artistic perspective some of these twenty-two detective/mystery short stories are considerably more successful than others. All, we should bear in mind, were written for a very specific market with rather rigorous demands for violence. Some meet that demand in a fairly standard manner; others manage considerable innovation within that framework. That innovation, of course, and the alterations which occurred between the stories and the novels, are our primary interests.

The Big Sleep, Farewell, My Lovely, and *The Lady in the Lake* are the novels which owe most of their plots to the stories. *The Big Sleep* evolved primarily from **"Killer in**

the Rain" and "The Curtain," with minor borrowing from **"The Man Who Liked Dogs."** *Farewell, My Lovely* combines elements from **"Try the Girl"** and **"Mandarin's Jade."** And *The Lady in the Lake* draws largely on **"Bay City Blues"** and **"The Lady in the Lake"** while borrowing a few details from **"No Crime in the Mountains."** The other four novels are, with minor exceptions, completely original creations.

Initially, Chandler's system of "cannibalization" worked well. *The Big Sleep,* for example, was completed in only three months. But *The Lady in the Lake* required over four years to produce. The slow pace at which it was developed can be attributed partly to disturbances in the world and within Chandler's own life; the war, for example, was a powerful distraction. But, it also seems likely that technical problems encountered in combining the stories for this novel may have contributed to that slow development and persuaded Chandler, finally, to abandon the cannibalizing technique. A comparison of the novel with its source stories highlights the difficulties.

The short story **"The Lady in the Lake"** (January 1939) tells only that part of the novel's story that occurs at Little Fawn Lake. It is a much simpler tale and the motives which direct it are decidedly different from those of the novel. The detective in the short story, John Dalmas, is hired by a man named Howard Melton (cf. Derace Kingsley in the novel) to find his wife who has disappeared from their lake cabin. At the cabin, Dalmas meets Bill Haines (cf. Bill Cross) and, shortly, a body presumed to be Haines's wife Beryl is discovered in the lake. Dalmas has already discovered the dead body of Lance Goodwin (cf. Chris Lavery) with whom Mrs. Melton was supposed to have disappeared. Cleverly, Dalmas tricks Melton and the female killer into appearing at Goodwin's at the same time. The woman is Beryl Haines—who has evidently been in league with Melton all along to help him get rid of his wife and claim her wealth. Melton hired Dalmas because he needed the body positively identified to legitimize the inheritance. The mechanics of this plot obviously resemble that part of the novel involving the body in the lake and the resulting confusion of identities. The characters also have recognizable analogues in the novel. But it is, finally, a rather simple story of a stock type: a man has attempted to rid himself of his wife and cover the deed with a case of mistaken identity.

"Bay City Blues" (June 1938) is the source of the other half of *The Lady in the Lake.* It is a story of dope, jealousy, and murder surrounding a Dr. Austrian (cf. Almore), "a guy that runs around all night keeping movie hams from having pink elephants for breakfast." Dr. Austrian's wife is found dead, presumably of carbon monoxide poisoning, much as Mrs. Almore is in the novel. The person who is evidently responsible for her death is Helen Matson, Dr. Austrian's nurse (cf. Mildred Haviland). But the doctor covers for his nurse, evidently because of his romantic involvement with her, and the police, who are obviously being paid off, cover for the doctor. That cover-up falls apart, though, because of the combined monetary and frustrated romantic interests of two other men closely associated with Helen, and because of the competition for control between the local political and racketeering circles. When Helen Matson is herself murdered later and the detective, Johnny Dalmas, is framed for it, the story begins to make sense to him. He is left, as he mockingly describes himself, "a miracle man. . . . the great American detective—unpaid" to explain the tale all "from a pinch of dust, just like the Vienna police."

Part of the "pinch of dust" that allows him to unravel the case concerns two identical pairs of green velvet slippers, which also appear in the novel. But another factor in the resolution involves Dalmas' inferences from a scene of viciousness unlike anything in the novels. A tough cop named DeSpain (cf. Degarmo) beats up a politico-rackets figure called Big Chin in a protracted display of sadism that weaves in and out of the narrative for seven pages. The very theatrical nature of this brutality finally persuades Dalmas that DeSpain is the real killer trying to cover his own guilt with another man's forced confession. By making this cruelty and violence serve as an essential clue in the plot's resolution, Chandler does manage—barely—to avoid the charge that such scenes are totally gratuitous. But the savagery was also, he recognized, a virtually mandatory ingredient of stories intended for the "pulp" market. Another example of Chandler's acquiescence to such demands, also from **"Bay City Blues,"** is Dalmas' description of Harry Matson, the victim of another beating, just before his death: "One of his temples was a pulp, . . . The one straining finger that wasn't white had been pounded to shreds as far as the second joint. Sharp splinters of bone stuck out of the mangled flesh. Something that might once have been a fingernail looked now like a ragged splinter of glass." Such grotesque scenes are most common in the early short stories, become less frequent in the later ones, and are generally avoided in the novels.

But Chandler's transformation of these two stories into a novel involve considerably more than rendering the violence less explicitly. **"The Lady in the Lake,"** though it uses the mistaken identity ploy on which the novel so heavily depends, is essentially a straightforward story of misguided love and murder for profit. **"Bay City Blues,"** with its inclusion of decadent dope doctors preying on the artificial wealth of Hollywood, along with the story's confusion of love, political, and racketeering interests, comes closer to the complexity of the novel but still lacks much of the novel's intricacy and mystery.

The basic device which Chandler employed to combine these stories was, of course, entangling the lives of the central female characters from each story. . . . Though much of the plotting of the novel is evident in the stories, this collision of the lives of two women from different parts of California's corrupt society allows Chandler to develop the larger theme of coincidence and the fate of bit players in a villainous and alien world. The novel is also able to expand its scope to include the real war in progress at the time, using it not only as background and commentary but also, finally, to bring the tale to its just and provocative end. A character consumed by his own petty lusts for power meets his death because of his refusal to comprehend the larger struggle of which his own is only a minuscule reflection.

Frank MacShane has argued that Chandler's "experience with the pulps was an essential stage in his development as a novelist, for it taught him to mistrust the mind of the short story writer, which, he later acknowledged, 'gets by on an idea or a character or a twist without any real dramatic development.'" The creation of *The Lady in the Lake* lends credence to that argument. The short story **"The Lady in the Lake"** gets by on the mistaken identity twist; **"Bay City Blues"** gets by on the almost satanic character of Lieutenant DeSpain. Such techniques are simply not sufficient to sustain the longer work. Though the novel relies on the stories for basic plot lines, it, like all of Chandler's novels, is concerned with plot only to the extent that plot functions as a frame for his "dramatic development" of character and motivation and for his experiments in style. Character, motivation, and style, we must never forget, were his central interests.

Chandler's stylistic experiments and his keen awareness of language are particularly evident in a comparison of specific scenes which occur in both the short stories and the novels. *The Big Sleep* offers many such opportunities for comparison. To begin with one very brief example, Marlowe says of Vivian Sternwood at their last meeting in the novel, "She was in oyster-white lounging pajamas trimmed with white fur, cut as flowingly as a summer sea frothing on the beach of some small and exclusive island." In **"The Curtain,"** the sentence reads, "She was in an oyster-white something, with white fur at the cuffs and collar and around the bottom." To say that she is dressed in an "oyster-white something" may, in fact, suggest this woman's essential nebulousness, but to specify "oyster-white lounging pajamas" and to include the idyllic "frothing sea" simile renders both her appearance and her state of mind with far greater precision. The casually romantic flair of her dress and carriage bespeak a desire to divorce herself from the harsh, imperfect world in which she is trapped. Her clothes suggest a certain escapism in the face of cruel facts. From just this tiny bit of elaboration we garner a sense of the warring elements at work in this woman's psyche. It is the kind of descriptive detail which the detective short story, with its demand for constant action, does not readily allow.

The scene of Marlowe's first meeting with Vivian demonstrates similar differences between Chandler the writer of short stories and Chandler the novelist. In **"The Curtain,"** we read:

> This room had a white carpet from wall to wall. Ivory drapes of immense height lay tumbled casually on the white carpet inside the many windows. The windows stared towards the dark foothills, and the air beyond the glass was dark too. It hadn't started to rain yet, but there was a feeling of pressure in the atmosphere.

In *The Big Sleep*, the paragraph has been expanded:

> This room was too big, the ceiling was too high, the doors were too tall, and the white carpet that went

Chandler's first detective story as it appeared in the December 1933 edition of Black Mask.

from wall to wall looked like a fresh fall of snow at Lake Arrowhead. There were full-length mirrors and crystal doodads all over the place. The ivory furniture had chromium on it, and the enormous ivory drapes lay tumbled on the white carpet a yard from the windows. The white made the ivory look dirty and the ivory made the white look bled out. The windows stared towards the darkening foothills. It was going to rain soon. There was pressure in the air already.

The first paragraph only describes the stark contrast between the white interior and the darkness outside. The second, while retaining that essential contrast, expands to comment on the paradoxical core of the Sternwood family: the material excess that is incapable of disguising their moral vacuity. Even their decorative attempt at purity looks phony and bled out by the contrasts in white. And no amount of decoration can deny the gathering darkness on the other side of the windows. This "bled out" image is echoed near the very end of the novel when Vivian says: "I knew Eddie Mars would bleed me white, but I didn't care. I had to have help and I could only get it from somebody like him." The General has already supplied a context for interpreting that remark when he told Marlowe early on that neither of his children "has any more moral sense than a cat. Neither have I. No Sternwood ever had." In such a world, devoid of the moral sense, being "bled white" in exchange for "help" is only what one expects. And though we may, in fact, develop a certain sympathy for Vivian and her plight, the literal description of her colorless life implies a figurative colorlessness which, we begin to understand, dooms her to an unceasing commerce with Eddie Mars or men like him. The contrast between the two paragraphs demonstrates both the flexibility of the novel format in comparison with the strict limits of the pulp short story and also Chandler's knack for exploiting that flexibility.

The greater restrictions of the short story were responsible, especially in his early stories, for limiting Chandler's subject matter as well as his style. His first story, **"Blackmailers Don't Shoot"** (December 1933), explores a theme common to many of Chandler's early efforts. Its fury arises from the internal struggles of rival racketeers and its social comment from the close connection between the rackets and the "authorities"—police, lawyers, and politicians. **"Blackmailers Don't Shoot"** is, in fact, one of Chandler's better early stories. It complicates the organized crime story with a young movie starlet, Rhonda Farr, who, in her attempt to adapt to the wickedness of the town and profession in which she finds herself, contrives a public relations stunt which backfires. The initial captivation of the story derives from the rather curious circumstance that the detective, Mallory, appears to be one of the blackmailers. But Mallory's act proves to be only part of a game which he is playing for his employer, a minor rackets figure named Landrey. The object of the game is, evidently, to revive the lost romance between Landrey and Rhonda Farr, the starlet. Finally, as is typical of Chandler even in this very first story, the facts of the matter are decidedly unclear. We are left with the police explanations, which are self-satisfying and internally consistent, but which we, and Mallory, know to be false.

In its obscuring of the truth, indeed in its suggestion that the truth is hopelessly elusive, the story establishes a pattern evident throughout the Chandler canon. Mallory here, as Marlowe frequently does in the novels, constructs several alternative possibilities for why things happened the way they did. None of them are totally satisfying. And yet we sense in this story motivations basic to human nature and not overly complex. Mallory speaks of Landrey's motives in these simple, if oblique, lines: "He crossed everybody up and then he crossed himself. He played too many parts and got his lines mixed. He was gun-drunk. When he got a rod in his hand he had to shoot somebody. Somebody shot back." It is a tale of cunning, self-deception, and a random violence directed only at "somebody" in a mysterious world where that "somebody" can shoot back.

The story is decidedly Chandlerian—in its refusal to offer a simple resolution, in its choice of subject matter and suggestion of a general corruption, and in its flashes of descriptive power and brilliant dialogue. But, given the stylistic excellence which the novels have led us to expect, there are also lapses here which startle the ear. Two such shortcomings occur on the story's first page. In the opening description of Mallory, we read: "His hair was crisp and black, ever so faintly touched with grey, as by an almost diffident hand." The word *diffident* calls undue attention to itself as rather exaggerated for the context. And our first look at the starlet begins: "Rhonda Farr was very beautiful." It is the kind of flat abstraction which we do not expect of Chandler and which rarely recurs after this first effort.

Chandler's art:

In the detective story, as in its mirror image, the Quest for the Grail, maps (the ritual of space) and timetables (the ritual of time) are desirable. Nature should reflect its human inhabitants, *i.e.,* it should be the Great Good Place; for the more Eden-like it is, the greater the contradiction of murder. The country is preferable to the town, a well-to-do neighborhood (but not too well-to-do—or there will be a suspicion of ill-gotten gains) better than a slum. The corpse must shock not only because it is a corpse but also because, even for a corpse, it is shockingly out of place, as when a dog makes a mess on a drawing room carpet.

Mr. Raymond Chandler has written that he intends to take the body out of the vicarage garden and give murder back to those who are good at it. If he wishes to write detective stories, *i.e.,* stories where the reader's principal interest is to learn who did it, he could not be more mistaken; for in a society of professional criminals, the only possible motives for desiring to identify the murderer are blackmail or revenge, which both apply to individuals, not to the group as a whole, and can equally well inspire murder. Actually, whatever he may say, I think Mr. Chandler is interested in writing, not detective stories, but serious studies of a criminal milieu, the Great Wrong Place, and his powerful but extremely depressing books should be read and judged, not as escape literature, but as works of art.

> *W. H. Auden, "The Guilty Vicarage," in*
> Harper's Magazine, *May, 1948.*

His next two stories, **"Smart-Aleck Kill"** (July 1934) and **"Finger Man"** (October 1934), are very similar to **"Black-**

mailers Don't Shoot" in their subject. Both chronicle a series of struggles within the rackets organizations and highlight the involvement of an important political figure in those organizations. But because they lack some of the complications of **"Blackmailers"**—the confused and confusing starlet, the bizarre love interest as catalyst—these are rather slight stories by comparison.

But Chandler's fourth story, **"Killer in the Rain"** (January 1935), marks a new direction in which organized crime is no longer the central motif. The first story to be "cannibalized" (for *The Big Sleep*), it concerns Carmen and the smut-lending business of a man named Steiner (cf. Geiger). The story ends with a shootout at Joe Marty's apartment which is similar to, but more violent than, the scene at Joe Brody's in the novel. But, though the story shares many features of the novel, its most curious twist is in the handling of the father. Carmen's father here is a "former Pittsburgh steelworker, truck guard, all-round muscle stiff" who wandered to California and blundered into a fortune when oil was discovered on his property. A curious touch is added to the story when he confesses, "Carmen—she's not my kid at all. I just picked her up in Smoky, a little baby in the street. She didn't have nobody. I guess maybe I steal her, huh?" And the strange quality of the tale is compounded when he asserts further that he is now in love with her and wants to marry her. His concern is that she has developed an interest in this Steiner character, and he wants help in ending it.

Though there is still an element of organized crime lurking in the shadows, the story focuses on this bizarre romance which leaves the detective, in anticipation of Marlowe, wondering "why I had taken the trouble" and feeling "tired and old and not much use to anybody." Curiously, the detective is never given a name in this story; he is just an anonymous first-person narrator.

Throughout his career as a short-story writer, Chandler was obviously searching for the ideal detective and the ideal narrative stance. His next story, **"Nevada Gas"** (June 1935), attempts to bridge the gap between first- and third-person narration. It opens with a powerful scene of vindictiveness which a first-person detective narrator could not describe—simply because he could not have been on the scene. But once the detective, Johnny DeRuse, enters the story, he is followed very closely—in the manner of a first-person narration. Chandler was here striving to fuse the objectivity of the third-person point of view with the subjectivity of the first person. The dichotomy was one which he toyed with throughout his early career. First-person narration, of course, limits an author to the perceptions and experiences of his narrator. Third-person narration, on the other hand, denies the author the immediacy of his detective's sensibilities and reactions. The objectivity of the third person obviously appealed to Chandler early; six of his first nine stories are written from that point of view. But then a string of first-person stories reversed that pattern, and eleven of his last thirteen detective stories have first-person narrators. Chandler's final resolution of this subjective-objective problem in the novels, of course, was to create a first-person narrator, Marlowe, with a very objective narrative style. His very "objectivity," then, provides a veil for what are obviously very intense subjective responses to the events of the novels, and Chandler is able to achieve some of the virtues of both points of view.

Much as objectivity, or the illusion of objectivity, is one of Chandler's focal interests, also paramount is his concern for truth and illusions which pass for truth. His next story, **"Spanish Blood"** (November 1935), addresses that issue. Superficially, it seems yet another rackets and political corruption story, but, by its conclusion, we have reason to question such assumptions. A unique feature of the story is that its investigator is a policeman, Detective Lieutenant Sam Delaguerra. The end of the story reveals two clear—and clearly different—explanations for the murder, the one we and Sam know to be true and the one the police hierarchy believes. For his own reasons, Sam lets the "official" version stand, and we, as readers, are left with one of Chandler's most explicit statements on the subject of illusion and the sinister reality only barely beneath its surface.

"Guns at Cyrano's" (January 1936) also plays upon the now standard mobsters and corrupt politicians theme, but it offers a new twist in the introduction of Ted Carmady, a detective who reappears in several subsequent stories. Carmady describes himself "grimly" as "the All-American sucker. . . . A guy that plays with the help and carries the torch for stray broads." He is a man who "used to be a private dick" but who has avoided the profession of late. Unlike Marlowe, he doesn't need the money. As he explains to Jean Adrian, his girlfriend in the story, he has rather an ambivalent attitude toward the "dirty money" he lives on:

> My dad made it out of crooked sewerage and paving contracts, out of gambling concessions, appointment pay-offs, even vice, I daresay. He made it every rotten way there is to make money in city politics. And when it was made and there was nothing left to do but sit and look at it, he died and left it to me. It hasn't brought me any fun either. I always hope it's going to, but it never does. Because I'm his pup, his blood, reared in the same gutter. I'm worse than a tramp, angel. I'm a guy that lives on crooked dough and doesn't even do his own stealing.

Carmady is thus set apart from Chandler's typical characters by the guilt at the root of his motives, a guilt which will not allow him to continue in his father's greedy footsteps. He is also set apart by the relationship he develops with Jean Adrian, herself less than noble, which finally promises at least the possibility of their future happiness together. In its holding out even the chance of an optimistic, romantic future, this is indeed a rare story for Chandler.

Chandler's other short-story detectives continue to display idiosyncrasies in social position and professional background. Walter Gage, for example, also has money and a beautiful girlfriend; Pete Anglich is an undercover narcotics agent who also "used to be" a private investigator. But

these rather superficial differences between them and the later Philip Marlowe are less striking than their similarities. All exhibit some degree of alienation; all are committed to high ideals against great odds; and, as the stories progress, they increasingly manifest more of the wisecracking wit that so distinguishes Marlowe in the novels. Though the detective is not called Marlowe until *The Big Sleep,* it is obvious, as Chandler himself said, that "he certainly had his genesis in two or three of the novelettes." Some of the short-story detectives are so like Marlowe, in fact, that their names were changed to Marlowe in reprinted editions without doing much damage to his character except making him appear more violent. But these were not Chandler's changes. Rather, he attributed them to "a base commercial motive" on the part of publishers.

This violent streak of the stories is particularly evident in the next one, **"The Man Who Liked Dogs"** (March 1936). But the style in which the violence is handled has a far greater ambition than simply to shock or to titillate. Consider this scene:

> The machine gun began to tear the door apart as I bawled into the ear of a bored desk sergeant.
>
> Pieces of plaster and wood flew like fists at an Irish wedding. Slugs jerked the body of Dr. Sundstrand as though a chill was shaking him back to life. I threw the phone away from me and grabbed Diana's guns and started in on the door for our side. Through a wide crack I could see cloth. I shot at that.

The description is highly visual and objective. Verbs, with support from a few aptly-placed similes, drive the action long. Adjectives and adverbs are rare. The terror of the scene is balanced by the simplicity of its telling, and the net effect is of a world of mayhem and madness passing for normalcy.

The story ends with a similar scene in which the narrator, Ted Carmady, tells us:

> The gun in my hand felt large and hot. I shot the dog, hating to do it. The dog rolled off Fulwider and I saw where a stray bullet had drilled the chief's forehead between the eyes, with the delicate exactness of pure chance.

The tale itself has a kind of "delicate exactness" not unlike the stray bullet squarely between the chief's eyes. But this is not an "exactness of pure chance"; rather, it is the studied exactness of a man absorbed by the mysteries and ironies of language. And Chandler's extraordinary power in using a simple language and a simple form to suggest the mysterious depths of human activity is the chief source of his narrative richness.

"Pickup on Noon Street" (May 1936) resembles Chandler's first story, **"Blackmailers Don't Shoot."** It is another tale of an ill-conceived, Hollywood publicity stunt which backfires and embroils the principal characters in yet another rackets power struggle. Its chief distinction lies in its further experimentation with street slang. The story opens with a man and woman walking past the Surprise Hotel. After the man's rather forceful attempt to pick her up, the woman replies: "Listen, you cheap grifter! . . . Keep your paws down, see! Tinhorns are dust to me. Dangle!" Such dialogue manifests Chandler's attentive ear and anticipates some of the speech patterns of the novels. But, beyond this, the story shows little innovation.

Chandler's next story, **"Goldfish"** (June 1936), takes several new tacks. For one thing, it forsakes the Southern California setting for a trip to Olympia, Washington, and, finally, to Westport, the westernmost point in the U.S. For another, it is a story of a crime from the past and the power of gossip, ultimately, to uncover it. Wally Sype spent fifteen years in Leavenworth for theft of the famous Leander pearls. The pearls were never recovered. But Wally made the mistake of talking about the job to his cellmate once; when the cellmate got out, he talked; and the string of talk finally leads to the literal end of the West where Sype, now in hiding, worries out his old age playing with goldfish. They're "like people," he says, "They get things wrong with them. . . . Some you can cure . . . and some you can't."

Both the comparison of the fish with people and the setting of this story at the limits of the West serve to give this tale a symbolic value which is new for Chandler. By the end of the tale, we have reason to wonder that if the fish are "like people," may it not be in their confined existence and their subjugation to powers outside their own tiny frame of influence? As the stories and novels develop, this theme of fate, coincidence, and a general helplessness in the face of imponderable forces will take on greater significance.

Elements of Chandler's next story, **"The Curtain"** (September 1936), have already been discussed in relation to the novel, *The Big Sleep,* which grew from it. The plot of the story has much in common with the novel, but, as usual, it is the differences which are most intriguing. The story opens, in fact, with a scene closely parallel to the opening of *The Long Goodbye* where Marlowe meets Terry Lennox. But the focus quickly shifts to an open concern for the whereabouts of Dud O'Mara (cf. Rusty Regan), a story always in the background in *The Big Sleep.* The figure in this story who later became Carmen in the novel is a child, Dade Winslow Trevillyan, son of the character who later becomes Vivian. The impetus of his actions is pure hatred, and precisely because of such simply characterized motivations, the story fails to maintain our interests. Though rather pedestrian in itself, this story, combined with **"Killer in the Rain,"** constitutes the humble origins of one of Chandler's better novels.

His next two stories, **"Try the Girl"** (January 1937) and **"Mandarin's Jade"** (November 1937), were "cannibalized" to create *Farewell, My Lovely.* The two stories offer striking contrasts in their resolutions. **"Try the Girl"** is essentially the story of Steve Skalla's (cf. Moose Malloy) search for Beulah (cf. Velma). In the end, a central question is: Who killed Dave Marineau? Both Steve and Beu-

lah seem intent on taking the blame. Beulah claims to have killed him because "he roughed me up and tried to blackmail me into something and I went and got the gun." But she bears no bruises or torn clothes to verify her version of the events. To simplify matters for the police, the detective (Ted Carmady again) roughs her up, waits for the bruises to set and darken, then takes her downtown where the police, because of her appearance, "didn't even think of holding her or checking her up." The ending is one of expediency rather than strict justice and, again, what the world is willing to accept as "truth" is, in fact, something less than that.

"Mandarin's Jade," on the other hand, contrives its ending considerably more neatly than does *Farewell, My Lovely,* which incorporated much of its story line. Here we have the story of the jade necklace being ransomed, but in this case, there is a much closer and more apparent relationship between Lindley Paul (cf. Lindsay Marriott) and Soukesian the Psychic (cf. Amthor). Soukesian is the brains and Paul is the finger for a high-class jewel ring— a relationship which is suggested in the novel but which is never proven and which remains obscured in the haze of possible causes for the book's actions. Here, the explanation of the crime is simplified; in the novel, precise causes remain mysterious.

This plot transformation, though, is only one aspect of the interest of **"Mandarin's Jade."** We also witness here a *style* in transition from the blood-and-gore, purely action-oriented early stories to the more pensive manner of the novels. For instance, when John Dalmas sits looking at Soukesian's card, he tells us:

> I had a rough idea what his racket would be and what kind of people would be his customers. And the bigger he was the less he would advertise. If you gave him enough time and paid him enough, he would cure anything from a tired husband to a grasshopper plague. He would be an expert in frustrated women, in tricky, tangled love affairs, in wandering boys who hadn't written home, in whether to sell the property now or hold it another year, in whether this part will hurt my type with my public or improve it. Even men would go to him—guys who bellowed like bulls around their own offices and were all cold mush inside just the same. But most of all, women—women with money, women with jewels, women who could be twisted like silk thread around a lean Asiatic finger.

The passage exhibits the brooding, almost cynical detective stance characteristic of the novels—he already has "a rough idea what his racket would be"; he's seen all this before. And it also demonstrates Chandler's attempt to find a way to get beyond the genre's demand for mayhem, to find a forum for commenting on the state of the world. Here, Dalmas makes the comment for him. He analyzes the society's problems as a general weakness of both men and women—an inability to deal intelligently with love and money, and a susceptibility to the illusions of people like Soukesian. It is the kind of passage on which the novels thrive, but which, in the short stories, runs the risk of appearing simply as excess baggage.

"Red Wind" (January 1938), in its dialogue, its tone, its descriptions, and its provocative implications, is another story that has many stylistic affinities with the novels. Its opening paragraph is one of Chandler's best:

> There was a desert wind blowing that night. It was one of those hot dry Santa Anas that come down through the mountain passes and curl your hair and make your nerves jump and your skin itch. On nights like that every booze party ends in a fight. Meek little wives feel the edge of the carving knife and study their husbands' necks. Anything can happen. You can even get a full glass of beer at a cocktail lounge.

The wind establishes an atmosphere of general foreboding. The empathy which that wind evokes in people suggests their general frailty and the irrationality just beneath the illusion of order. The last line then undercuts the weightiness of the mood just created and makes it palatable. Such quizzical humor is characteristic of Marlowe in the novels and helps relieve his brooding cynicism. It is his humor which allows him to broach serious subjects obliquely.

In keeping with the ominous atmosphere established by the wind, the story involves some great and grave coincidences and is another which suspects the world of being well out of control. Its language asserts the point. After the cop has been told the story of the tale's first shooting three times, he says: "This dame interests me. And the killer called the guy Waldo, yet didn't seem to be anyways sure he would be in. I mean, if Waldo wasn't sure the dame would be here, nobody could be sure Waldo would be here." The narrator can only respond: "That's pretty deep." The language proves too imprecise to penetrate the essence of matters, a general failing that is, of course, another motif which emerges more forcefully in the longer works.

The story also exhibits the mocking tone characteristic of the novels. At one point, when we think the story is beginning to resolve itself, the central female character brings up the subject of her pearls. The narrator is taken aback:

> I might have jumped a little. It seemed as if there had been enough without pearls. . . .
>
> "All right," I said, "Tell me about the pearls. We have had a murder and a mystery woman and a mad killer and a heroic rescue and a police detective framed into making a false report. Now we will have pearls. All right—feed it to me."

The paragraph recapitulates all the standard plotting devices on which this and so many other mysteries depend. It calls attention to its own formula, ridicules it, but then accepts it and proceeds. In so doing, it also forces the reader to recognize the author's own self-consciousness about the stylized simplicity of his tale.

The story's finale also anticipates the endings of the novels. Although the pearls finally prove to be an essential element of the plot, they are not real. The real ones were evidently sold by one of the story's crooks who then substituted imitation ones. The detective (called Marlowe in most of the reprints of the story) has imitations made of the imitations and returns this second-generation set of fakes to their owner. The first set of fakes he takes with him to the beach. There he sits tossing the pearls one by one into the water, watching the splashes and the seagulls, contemplating the vegetation burned by the hot wind and the ocean that "looked cool and languid and just the same as ever," and thinking of Stan Phillips, the man who first purchased the original pearls and made a gift of them to Lola, setting the plot in motion. It is an ending with a definite Marlovian touch; the stories are beginning to find their meaning in the effect they have on the detective. His musing synthesizes all the appearance vs. reality motifs which have arisen in the story: the pearls have now been twice bastardized; the newspaper accounts of the action of the story aren't even close to the truth; and a police lieutenant has been framed by his own enthusiasm into taking credit for an arrest he didn't make and which later recoils against him.

The narrator accepts it all as quite believable. But he also needs the time alone with the "cool and languid and . . . same as ever" ocean to restore his sense of equilibrium. And it is in the contrast of his ability to cope and his obvious sense of loss and futility that the stories make their emotional impression on the reader. We feel, with the man tossing fake pearls into the ocean, the profound absurdity of the modern world, but we also sense with him the necessity and the possibility of carrying on. It is an experience not unlike catharsis.

"The King in Yellow" (March 1938) may seem less typical of Chandler because it avoids centering on the sentiments of the detective in the manner of **"Red Wind"** and so many other of Chandler's better stories. Rather, it examines a relationship between two brothers and a sister, the brothers being out to revenge their sister's death. Eventually, one brother tires of killing and the ever-widening circle of death which the first death set off and he puts an end to it, paradoxically, by killing his brother and committing suicide. But the story simply ends. Its third-person narration—one of Chandler's last uses of the third person—is incapable of the kind of emotive power which his first person narrators can convey. It is a flat ending to a comparatively slight story.

Chandler's next two stories, **"Bay City Blues"** (June 1938) and **"The Lady in the Lake"** (January 1939), have already been discussed as the sources for *The Lady in the Lake*. The story which followed them, **"Pearls Are a Nuisance"** (April 1939), is a fine example of Chandler's linguistic experimentation within the detective form and one of his better treatises on male camaraderie, a subject which was later to form the basis for *The Long Goodbye*. Walter Gage, the detective here, is a man with money, a beautiful girlfriend, and a formal diction which allows Chandler to achieve new heights of humor. He says things to people like, "Have the kindness to unlock the door," "I cast no aspersions . . . , I now suggest we repair to my apartment," and "The sunset hour is nigh. . . . and the morning glories furl themselves in sleep." Such language offers a dramatic contrast with the street slang of Henry Eichelberger, who is given to remarks like, "Bugs completely is what the guy is," or "Here's some mug finds out Lady Penruddock has a string of oyster fruit worth oodles of kale, and he does hisself a neat little box job and trots down to the fence."

"Pearls Are a Nuisance" is one of Chandler's funniest stories, and its humor is largely a result of this startling juxtaposition of languages. Moreover, these languages express two very diverse personalities whose interaction is the center of the comedy. Gage is a man of wealth and aristocratic pretensions; Eichelberger is a big, brutish chauffeur. Gage initially suspects Eichelberger of the pearl theft, but, in a series of brawls and heroic drinking bouts, the two become fast friends. Their friendship, in fact, is finally responsible for making the culprit "too soft to go through with the deal," and the story ends with what in comparison to the other stories is almost a general rejoicing. It argues well that Chandler had his lighter moments when he was truly able to divorce himself from the world's malaise and allow his sense of language play and the comedy of human relationships to have full rein.

His next story, **"Trouble Is My Business"** (August 1939), is another competent but slight story which plays upon the standard themes of blackmail, greed, and murder. Curiously, the villain here is another chauffeur who, this time, has a Dartmouth education. But the story displays little innovation. It is typical of the genre and evidence that Chandler could also, occasionally, be content with tried and true formulas.

But **"I'll Be Waiting"** (October 1939), which followed, is a curious piece of experimentation that mimics the romantic exploit of a knight in shining armor rescuing a tower-bound lady in distress. The knight in shining armor in this case is a "short, pale, paunchy, middle-aged man" named Tony Reseck who is the house dick at the Windermere Hotel. The lady in distress is a red-haired, violet-eyed, has-been nightclub singer named Eve Cressy who has "a tower room" in the hotel and who hasn't been outdoors in the five days since her arrival. Around her, but just outside her field of awareness, a rackets war is developing among the males of her world. Her ex-husband, Johnny Ralls, whom her testimony helped convict of manslaughter, is back in town. And his mob friends are after him for money which he presumably beat them out of. One of the mobsters suggests that Eve be moved from the hotel. But the detective Reseck has a sentimental attachment to her. He arranges, instead, to play the mobsters off against each other, getting people killed in the process. But Eve never knows what happened. And the last we see of her, she is asleep, curled up motionless, listening to the radio in a room off the lobby which is a private, little, mock-Edenic haven for this curious pair of platonic lovers. On one level, the story is a mock romance. But on another, the story argues that such sentimentality is a powerful shaper of life—even among these people who hardly fit the romantic stereotypes. That we are all, at bottom, motivated to

some extent by such sentiments is one of Chandler's central tenets.

"No Crime in the Mountains" (September 1941) switches to a more topical theme. It is, in a sense, a war story. A German and a Japanese have set up a counterfeiting and smuggling operation at Puma Point in order to finance an Axis intelligence operation. John Evans, the detective, almost gets tipped off about it, but his informer is killed before they can talk. Evans is thus left to figure it out for himself and to stumble onto a number of other strange happenings in the process. He gets a lot of help from the local constable, a man named Barron, who is virtually a carbon copy of Tinchfield in **"The Lady in the Lake"** and Jim Patton, a central figure in the novel version of that story. But aside from Barron's countrified humor and the plot's wartime concerns, this too is a fairly standard story.

Eighteen years separate the publication of **"No Crime in the Mountains"** and that of Chandler's last detective short story, **"The Pencil"** (April 1959). In a brief introductory note to it, he explained that he had

> persistently refused to write short stories, because I think books are my natural element, but was persuaded to do this because people for whom I have a high regard seemed to want me to do it, and I have always wanted to write a story about the technique of the Syndicate's murders.

Marlowe is the detective here. His client is "a slightly fat man with a dishonest smile" named Ikky Rosenstein. He claims to be on the run from the mob because he's been penciled. As Marlowe later explains the term, "You have a list. You draw a line through a name with a pencil. The guy is as good as dead. The Outfit has reasons. . . . It's bookkeeping to them." As he also later explains, "I neither believed him nor disbelieved him. I took him on. There was no reason not to." The voice is decidedly Marlowe's—calm, detached, seen-it-all, a surface placidity masking a deeper trepidation—and it is Marlowe's voice that gives the story what distinction it has. It is a voice still capable of hilarious self-mockery, as we see when Marlowe tells us at one point:

> I bought a paperback and read it. I set my alarm watch for 6:30. The paperback scared me so badly that I put two guns under my pillow. . . . Then I asked myself why I was reading this drivel when I could have been memorizing *The Brothers Karamasov.*

But it is also a tired voice, telling a tired story, almost a cliché, as if filling out a form, walking the familiar tightrope between burlesque and sentimentalism and falling, finally, in the direction of the latter.

One of the story's most curious sentimental lapses concerns its resurrection of Anne Riordan, the wonderfully competent, too-good-to-be-true character from *Farewell, My Lovely.* In one conversation between them, she becomes perturbed by Marlowe's distant attitude and asks, straightforwardly, "How come I'm still a virgin at twenty-eight?" Marlowe's response is: "We need a few like you. . . . I've thought of you, I've wanted you, but that sweet clear look in your eyes tells me to lay off. . . . I've had too many women to deserve one like you." And as he walks out, he is thinking, "The women you get and the women you don't get—they live in different worlds. I don't sneer at either world. I live in both myself." The exchange is perplexing and finally unsatisfying. Marlowe is here defeated by his own romantic idealism. He is trapped within his own code. Anne is "too good" for him, he is "too shop-soiled" for her, and the story retreats from complication into stereotypes.

As a group, the stories display for us the mind of a technician in the midst of honing his craft. The crisp declarative style, plain descriptions, terse characterizations, sardonic wit, and ominous mood can all be seen here in their formative stages. But it is only in the novels that all those elements so characteristic of Chandler achieve their maturity. The difference is partly a matter of space—space to allow for dramatic and character development and to get away from the requisite, slavish devotion to plot. And it is partly a matter of the creation of the voice of Marlowe who, though he may appear in the stories in prototype, is only realized completely in the longer works. The novels, unlike the short stories, consistently make their impression upon the reader through the sympathy they evoke for this endearing, nobly motivated detective.

Roy Meador (essay date 1982)

SOURCE: "Chandler in the Thirties: Apprenticeship of an Angry Man," in *Book Forum*, Vol. VI, No. 2, 1982, pp. 143-53.

[*In the following essay, Meador discusses Chandler's early writing career, tracing the development of his use of language and his social attitudes, while also describing the creation of his chief fictional hero—Detective Philip Marlowe.*]

Los Angeles in the 1930s was not a sleepy village as Marlowe describes it in *The Little Sister*. The city he sentimentally recalls there is adrift somewhere in the past, kept alive through the remembering words of Raymond Chandler:

> I used to like this town. A long time ago. There were trees along Wilshire Boulevard. Beverly Hills was a country town. Westwood was bare hills and lots offering at eleven hundred dollars and no takers . . . Los Angeles was just a big dry sunny place with ugly homes and no style, but goodhearted and peaceful. It had the climate they yap about now. People used to sleep out on porches.

In this passage, Chandler's memory was turning back a calendar of decades rather than years to early in the century. The Los Angeles of hustle and threat that Marlowe faced in the 30s was rather different. *Colliers* reported in 1938 that Los Angeles had 600 brothels, 300 gambling houses,

1,800 bookies, and 23,000 one-armed bandits. It was a city with ample work for Marlowe and the tough Chandler detectives who prepared the way for him in the 1930s pulps: Mallory, Johnny DeRuse, Carmady, John Dalmas, Steve Grayce, Pete Anglich. These were the tough and harassed protagonists of Chandler's pulp apprenticeship in the 30s.

Why the pulps? They were ubiquitous, popular, and greedy for stories from any competent writers who could help satisfy the national appetite by the 1930s for approximately 200 million words annually. The typical pulp had 120 pages, 7 x 10 inches in size, with showy covers and long stories written to a formula that emphasized brisk action, gripping suspense, and an atmosphere of violence and peril. Over a thousand pulp writers, a third of them in Manhattan, wrote fast to meet deadlines and earn their penny a word. Pulp specialists such as Erle Stanley Gardner churned out stories in a few days and often published under pseudonyms. Chandler's output was minuscule compared with such fiction speed demons. From the start he worked painstakingly. He had something more than immediate income as an objective.

The pulps in the 1920s and 1930s provided a valuable training ground for many writers, especially the major pulp alumni led by Dashiell Hammett and Raymond Chandler. After assessing the pulp field, Chandler selected *Black Mask* as his model and target. This proved his taste and literary savvy. *Black Mask,* founded by H. L. Mencken and George Jean Nathan to earn capital for *Smart Set,* under editor Captain Joseph T. Shaw began demonstrating in the 1920s that literature can happen on wood pulp paper as well as slick paper.

Black Mask ran Dashiell Hammett's first story in 1922 and the September 1929-January 1930 issues contained *The Maltese Falcon,* featuring Marlowe's deadly and distinguished forerunner in the private eye vocation, Sam Spade. Chandler wrote of this seminal creation, "an art which is capable of it is not 'by hypothesis' incapable of anything. Once a detective story can be as good as this, only the pedants will deny that it *could* be even better."

Chandler analyzed the work of Hammett and others with the fidelity scholars typically reserve for erudite prospecting in the pages of a Shakespeare or Joyce. In 1932 when he started, Chandler was a 44-year old undergraduate attending *Black Mask* university with that magazine's hardboiled contributors as the faculty. Chandler rewrote stories in his own words and compared with the originals. He told Erle Stanley Gardner about his results with a Gardner novelette: "In the end I was a bit sore because I couldn't try to sell it. It looked pretty good."

Chandler's synopses and annotations tutored him in the methods and tough manners of pulp detective stories. George Eliot called popular fiction "spiritual gin," but little could be labeled spiritual about the pulps, though gin was perhaps apropos. Chandler wrote that "the demand was for constant action; if you stopped to think you were lost. When in doubt have a man come through a door with a gun in his hand."

When he was ready to stop "playing the sedulous ape," after laborious writing and rewriting, Chandler finished and submitted his first story, **"Blackmailers Don't Shoot."** Captain Shaw promptly acknowledged its quality and published the novelette in the December 1933 issue of *Black Mask.* The payment of $180 worked out to a rate of about $1 per day. Chandler needed to sell at least ten such stories annually to come within nibbling distance of an austere living, but he continued to write as if each story was not an ephemeral pulp but an overture to literature. He exercised care that was an unheard of luxury among pulp professionals. Obstinate rewriting was an epicurean affectation for writers trying to make a living.

Chandler sold one story in 1933, two in 1934, three in 1935, five in 1936, two in 1937, three in 1938, and five in 1939. The three stories sold to *Dime Detective* in 1938 earned $1,275. During part of 1938, Chandler worked on *The Big Sleep,* an essential investment in the future but no immediate help as a source of funds. By contrast, across town in the film colony, Fred Astaire's 1937 salary was $271,711, Marlene Dietrich's was $370,000, and Louis B. Mayer's was $1,161,753.

When he completed *The Big Sleep,* Chandler worked several months on a second novel, only to scrap the results. A December 1939 letter states:

> I had to throw my second book away, so that leaves me with nothing to show for the last six months and possibly nothing to eat for the next six. But it also leaves the world a far far better place to live in than if I had not thrown it away.

> *(Selected Letters of Raymond Chandler)*

Scrapping work that might have produced income underscores Chandler's stubborn integrity as a writer even before he was established. As the Depression decade ended and the 40s began, Chandler labored with that familiar occupational torment of authors—the second novel. In April 1940, he finished *Farewell, My Lovely* which broodingly portrays the Los Angeles scene of the 1930s insistently and poetically. Later, as he had thrown away an early version of his second novel, Chandler in a sense also threw away the city that spawned his detective and gave direction to his private vision.

After the 30s, wartime boom and postwar growth transformed Southern California into a plush megalopolis Philip Marlowe would never quite fit or call home. Marlowe's true city is always Los Angeles with a 1930s frown, venal, sweaty before air conditioning, dangerous. In *The Long Goodbye,* a disillusioned Marlowe realizes "there aren't any safe places" left in "the big angry city" where "twenty-four hours a day somebody is running, somebody else is trying to catch him. Out there in the night of a thousand crimes . . . A city no worse than others, a city rich and vigorous and full of pride, a city lost and beaten and full of emptiness."

Chandler demonstrated that it is not essential to admire a place to write about it memorably. A 1939 Chandler letter complains that there is a touch of the desert about everything in California and the minds of the people. "I'm sick of California and the kind of people it breeds," he wrote. Such statements could also signal weariness with a rough decade and hanging on until better days arrived. Those days came in the 1940s, and Chandler used screenwriting profits to buy a house in La Jolla. He claimed not to miss the city, but Marlowe showed the loss. In *Playback* (1958), Marlowe is a shadow image of himself without the city as a dynamic, mobile stage for his performance. He is a man whose significance depends on a specific place which seems to have been misplaced. In a 1956 letter Chandler acknowledged the city's importance:

> I know now what is the matter with my writing or not writing. I've lost any affinity for my background. Los Angeles is no longer my city . . . To write about a place you have to love it or hate it or do both by turns, which is usually the way you love a woman. But a sense of vacuity and boredom—that is fatal.

> *(Selected Letters of Raymond Chandler)*

Chandler's attitude in the 30s was ambivalent. Then he both loved and loathed the city, which can be a potent mixture of emotions for creating the special tensions of literature. From the start, Los Angeles served Chandler as a vital backdrop. His first detective, Mallory in **"Blackmailers Don't Shoot,"** comes to Los Angeles from Chicago on a case and stays. Mallory's successors including Marlowe keep Los Angeles their permanent beat.

Chandler needed to sell at least ten . . . stories annually to come within nibbling distance of an austere living, but he continued to write as if each story was not an ephemeral pulp but an overture to literature.

—Roy Meador

A parallel Chandler concern from the start was to get the most from the American language, which he claimed to learn as a foreign language after returning to the country of his birth with a British education. Captivated by the possibilities of the American language, Chandler insisted it "could say almost anything."

> All I wanted to do when I began writing was to play with a fascinating new language, to see what it would do as a means of expression which might remain on the level of unintellectual thinking and yet acquire the power to say things which are usually only said with a literary air. . . . I wrote melodrama because when I looked around me it was the only kind of writing I saw that was relatively honest and yet was not trying to put over somebody's party line.

> *(Raymond Chandler Speaking)*

In stories and novels, Hemingway had vividly illustrated the special power of this "new language." James M. Cain had also revealed its possibilities for mystery and suspense fiction in his 1934 novel set in Southern California, *The Postman Always Rings Twice*, whose narrator Frank Chambers is a primitive Marlowe ancestor in language if not character. Following Hemingway's large-booted lead, Chandler used ordinary American slang and vernacular with extraordinary skill to achieve graceful, robust, unexpected effects. Though a disciple of Hammett, Chandler noted Hammett's failure to venture far with the language and its flexible potential. In "The Simple Art of Murder," Chandler wrote, "The American language . . . can say things he did not know how to say, or feel the need of saying. In his hands it had no overtones, left no echo, evoked no image beyond a distant hill." In a letter to John Houseman, Chandler spoke late in life about his fun with the language and his severed connection with the city:

> I could write a bestseller, but I never have. There was always something I couldn't leave out or something I had to put in . . . I have had a lot of fun with the American language; it has fascinating idioms, is constantly creative, very much like the English of Shakespeare's time, its slang and argot is wonderful, and so on. But I have lost Los Angeles. It is no longer the place I knew so well and was almost the first to put on paper. I have that feeling, not very unusual, that I helped create the town and was then pushed out of it by the operators. I can hardly find my way around any longer.
>
> (From a Memoir by John Houseman included with *The Blue Dahlia, A Screenplay*)

Chandler in the 30s sought to make both language and locale accurate and appropriate for his stories. These 1930s pulp efforts are fast-paced, sport a tough milieu, and obey the tradition of laying on the violence; but they contain many early intimations of the simile-rich Chandler style that distinguishes the Marlowe novels and elevates them from escapist thrillers to art. Frank MacShane in *The Life of Raymond Chandler* calls it a miracle, considering the author's financial straits, that from 1933 to 1938 his work steadily improved.

His pulps of the 30s eventually proved to be astute investments of time and effort. The stories have been resurrected from their wood pulp archives and reprinted. Many of them served as raw materials for the Marlowe novels. In *The Big Sleep*, Chandler used material from the 1935 and 1936 *Black Mask* stories, **"Killer in the Rain"** and **"The Curtain."** He displayed similar frugality with his literary capital from the Depression years by skillfully metamorphosing other pulp novelettes into Marlowe novels, all prominent today among the small group of mysteries hailed as important and accepted as literature.

Style, language, and site are important in mystery stories, but the detective is the prime mover in the equation. Chandler's detectives from the 1933 Mallory through Marlowe show a pattern of evolution from pulp-primitive to Marlowe-sophistication; but Chandler's men have certain character traits in common, especially a commitment to ethical and professional work, loyalty to clients, sympathy for underdogs, and a day's work for a day's pay ($25 per day and expenses plus eight cents a mile in Marlowe's early cases). Chandler's detective returns the fee if he can't deliver. He stubbornly applies his author's British public school principles as he painfully lives up to what are no doubt the most famous lines ever published and republished about a private eye:

> Down these mean streets a man must go who is not himself mean, who is neither tarnished nor afraid . . . He must be, to use a rather weathered phrase, a man of honor—by instinct, by inevitability, without thought of it, and certainly without saying it. He must be the best man in his world and a good enough man for any world.
>
> ("The Simple Art of Murder")

Chandler's detective is committed to social justice because social injustice was a grim fact of American life in the 1930s. When Tom Joad says goodbye to Ma, telling her that he will be wherever there's a fight so hungry people can eat, it seems not implausible that Tom Joad, on the run, changes his name to Philip Marlowe and opens an office in Los Angeles. Both men are crusaders, and Steinbeck's saga of the Okies and *The Big Sleep* appeared about the same time early in 1939. Two other lasting California documents appeared that year: Huxley's *After Many A Summer Dies the Swan* and West's *The Day of the Locust*. Among these four 1939 books with a claim on the present, *The Big Sleep* is probably familiar to more people than the three other classics combined. It has established as permanent a toehold in American culture as Bogart's twitch. Marlowe in *The Big Sleep* is, of course, the definitive Chandler detective, encompassing the others and reaching out to new dimensions. Marlowe is the archetypal private eye, a knight-errant equipped to cope with 20th century urban dragons. The same as Hamlet, he occupies a world badly out of joint and has the nontransferrable duty to set it right.

Marlowe is a loner, as dedicated and nearly as celibate as an Irish priest. He is a man of the 30s in his thirties, a graduate student of hard times. He works all hours and greets beatings or bullets as occupational hazards. Examine Edward Hopper's 1942 painting, "Nighthawks," showing a city lunch counter at midnight. A man and woman drink coffee. Another man, alone in the heart of loneliness, sits with his back to us, rehashing a dangerous day. That man could be Marlowe. He goes home eventually to his bachelor apartment, *i.e.,* monastic cell. If his bed is occupied by a corrupt female such as Carmen Sternwood, he throws her out and remakes the bed with clean sheets. "This was the room I had to live in. It was all I had in the way of a home . . . I couldn't stand her in that room any longer." At the soul's dark hour of three a.m., he drinks alone and plays a solitary game of chess. Soon with the new day, new problems. They won't be easy.

Marlowe, Los Angeles knight of the 30s, must be a special man, because his jobs are far outside the safe and tame boundaries of the normal. In the 1930s, failure and fear suddenly became avenues of life in America for people who had never met such strange enemies before. Raymond Chandler sent Marlowe to battle them. If he cannot right now turn social defeat into victory, Marlowe brings the consolation that there are worse things than defeat, and tomorrow is another day for another try. In the 1930s, something had gone awry, and the times called for a combination Zorro-Lochinvar-Shadow to cauterize public evil. Chandler gave Marlow the assignment. He must keep honest and aloof, refuse to compromise with corruption, battle gangsters and police, remain "a lonely man, a poor man, a dangerous man," while polishing up the American dream. "Marlowe is a failure," Chandler admitted. "In the long run I guess we are all failures or we wouldn't have the kind of world we have." Chandler knew his detective-crusader could not win, not permanently. The cities of America in the 1930s were not programmed for automatic happy endings. Police Captain Gregory in *The Big Sleep* tells Marlowe:

> I like to see the law win . . . That's what I'd like. You and me both lived too long to think I'm likely to see it happen. Not in this town, not in any town half this size in any part of this wide, green, and beautiful U.S.A. We just don't run our country that way.

Marlowe sees no reason to argue, but he keeps trying to make it happen, perpetually quixotic. Chandler made his detective responsible for an impossible moral struggle and a modern Crusade in the homes, offices, alleys, and streets of Los Angeles. Marlowe calls it a place dedicated to the principle that "law is where you buy it." We have scant reason to wonder that Chandler's man goes to bed "full of whiskey and frustration" and sometimes feels "as empty of life as a scarecrow's pockets." "I don't like it," says Marlowe, "but what the hell am I to do? I'm on a case. I'm selling what I have to sell to make a living. What little guts and intelligence the Lord gave me and a willingness to get pushed around in order to protect a client."

From his first pulp story, Chandler hoped to transcend the conventional mystery format and to write scenes that would "leave an afterglow." Defining a classic as writing that surpasses the possibilities of its form, Chandler believed no such classics of crime and detection had been written, "which is one of the principal reasons why otherwise reasonable people continue to assault the citadel."

He was never satisfied with his own results in the 30s or later, but he granted the power of stories in the *Black Mask* tradition. Though primitive and predictable, they packed a wallop and generated "the smell of fear."

> Their characters lived in a world gone wrong, a world in which, long before the atom bomb, civilization had created the machinery of its own destruction, and was learning to use it with all the moronic delight of a gangster trying out his first machine gun. The law was something to be manipulated for profit and power. The streets were dark with something more than night.

> (Raymond Chandler, 1950 Introduction to
> *Trouble Is My Business*)

When the 30s ended, so did Chandler's apprenticeship. He was ready for his Marlowes of the 40s, for Hollywood, for Depression's end. In 1945 he paid income taxes of nearly $50,000. "Pretty awful for a chap who was gnawing old shoes not too many years ago." In the 30s he found what he wanted to do and learned how to do it. Now we go to Chandler to gauge the look, meaning, and symptoms of the 30s in urban places. These lessons have value. They explain human responses to trouble through the insights, truth, and singular beauty of literature by a writer who traveled beyond a distant hill and leaves an afterglow. "Pulp paper never dreamed of posterity," wrote Chandler, but his 30s struggles bestowed on his own pages the birthright of long life.

Edward Margolies (essay date 1982)

SOURCE: "Raymond Chandler: The Smell of Fear," in *Which Way Did He Go?: The Private Eye in Dashiell Hammett, Raymond Chandler, Chester Himes, and Ross MacDonald,* Holmes and Meier Publishers, Inc., 1982, pp. 33-52.

[*In the following essay, Margolies presents an overview of Chandler's career, commenting on his themes, style, and characters, as well as placing his works in their cultural and historical contexts.*]

Raymond Chandler was [Dashiell] Hammett's principal successor—his melancholy, tough-talking hero, Philip Marlowe, is one of the best-known and widely imitated popular heroes of the 1940s. Marlowe is a six-foot-tall, thirty-eight-year-old bachelor who works for himself because he is too much of an individualist to take orders from others. He is not very successful financially—his office is somewhat shabby and his living quarters spare—not because he cannot find clients but because he can be neither bought off nor scared off by the rich, the police, or by gangsters. He respects courage and physical endurance and tells us he has no use for homosexuals. His integrity and his laconic wit are his armor, but in a corrupt world he can be very lonely. The vulnerabilities with which his creator endowed him were Chandler's own, and are among the things that make him attractive.

Chandler's is a curious case. Although we like to think of him as writing quintessentially American stuff, his outlook was far more English than might ordinarily be supposed. His detectives, for all their presumed toughness, entertain Victorian notions of honor and self-sacrifice that Hammett's Op would have found amusing. Chandler was the more sophisticated stylist, although he did not possess Hammett's storytelling logic. For Chandler, scene and atmosphere were far more important than plausibility; Hammett, on the other hand, regarded plot as the most essential element of his fiction and seldom sacrificed narrative for melodramatic moments. The differences in the educational backgrounds of the two men are also striking. If Hammett was largely self-taught—accruing thereby certain primitive literary strengths—Chandler attended schools in England and France from whose formalities he may have suffered as much as he benefited. Hammett's education or lack of it contributed to more hardbitten, pragmatic attitudes. In his pre-Marxist writing years . . . he toyed with the idea of a senseless universe governed by jungle ethics, but Chandler, whose English schooling imbued him with a sterner sense of purpose, ultimately rejected such a view as nihilistic. Consequently Chandler was the more compassionate of the two, betraying greater concern for the bittersweet in human relationships. As children, both lacked strong male figures with whom they could identify, and in their adult years they enjoyed reputations as womanizers, whether merited or not. Both drank so heavily they required medical attention. Oddly, their paths crossed only once—at a reunion dinner for *Black Mask* writers in 1936. Although Chandler was an admirer of Hammett, neither spoke much to the other. One suspects they both were too shy.

Chandler was born in Chicago in 1888, two years after the wedding of his parents. His father, Maurice, a railroad engineer, was born of Quaker and Irish-American stock, but his Anglo-Irish mother, née Florence Dart Thornton, had only recently come to America from Waterford, Ireland. The Chandlers lived for several years in a small town in Nebraska, but the marriage did not take, and in 1896 Mrs. Chandler returned to Europe with her young son in tow. For the next fifteen years Raymond and his mother lived with his aunt, Ethel, and his maternal grandmother, Annie, in genteel but far from fashionable sections of London—a source of never-ending irritation to his grandmother who had known better days as an upper-class Protestant living in Ireland. Chandler remembered Annie more than fifty years later as a "stupid and arrogant" snob who worshipped wealth. Yet some of that snobbery may have rubbed off on her grandson who in 1955 described some of the first Americans he met on his return to the States as "canaille." Philip Marlowe's loathing of the phoney rich as well as the coarse and vulgar lower classes may also owe something to Chandler's grandmother.

Young Raymond passed his summer holidays in Waterford where one of grandmother Annie's sons still flourished, and here Chandler gained first-hand experience in the delicate arrangements governing Irish Catholic/Protestant relationships. (One apparently did not ask one's Catholic playmates to tea.) As an outsider—neither wholly American, English, or Irish—Raymond observed these rites with some objectivity. He was also made acutely aware of the nuances of social distinctions, an awareness he would later bring to his Los Angeles fiction. During these years his grandmother rarely allowed her daughter to forget the disgrace of her failed American marriage, arousing in Raymond the counter desire to protect and defend his mother. Florence herself no doubt reinforced her son's chivalric impulses by telling him about his American father's brutality toward her. Afterwards Chandler would speak of his mother as a "saint" and his father as an alcoholic "swine," but he may have internalized an image of his father in the philandering alcoholism of his own married years.

Perhaps Chandler's distressed heroines and violent villains are fantasy projections of his mother and father. But one must wonder whether the numerous predatory women who inhabit his fiction also reveal other attitudes towards his mother. Natasha Spender, one of Chandler's English friends of the mid-1950s, suggests that Chandler's mother made intense emotional demands on him in return for her approval. As we shall see, Chandler himself practiced a kind of emotional blackmail when, towards the end of his life, he would call his friends and tell them he would commit suicide if they did not come and minister to him at once. Interestingly, several of Chandler's short stories deal with blackmail as do all but one of his novels, but in Chandler's fiction his blackmailers are despicable—which may have been Chandler's way of expressing what he disliked about himself.

As a young man, Chandler's Galahad image of himself was probably strengthened by a class-oriented Victorian education. From 1900 to 1906 he attended Dulwich College, a preparatory school where he studied classics but also read as part of the curriculum Tennyson's Arthurian poetry and Matthew Arnold. Young scholars at Dulwich were expected to be manly, disciplined, self-sacrificing, and honorable—the same qualities of character Philip Marlowe displays some thirty years later. It was at Dulwich too that Chandler was pressed to write short sentences devoid of cumbersome adjectives under the aegis of one of the masters. Upon completing his course of studies, Chandler studied business education briefly in France and Germany (the Thorntons having determined that they could not afford to send the bookish Raymond to university). A short stint in the Civil Service (the Admiralty) and a few faint forays into journalism, book reviewing, and poetry writing rounded out Chandler's remaining English years. At the age of twenty-four he headed back to the States.

It is not clear why Chandler chose to return. He was obviously no resounding success as a writer or civil servant and America may have represented another chance. Perhaps he entertained some romantic notion of rediscovering his father. Or perhaps, as one of his 1932 poems suggests, he wanted to flee a painful love affair. On his arrival in America he took odd jobs, first in St. Louis and later in Nebraska where he visited his mother's relatives. But life in the Midwest was not to his liking, and he moved on to Los Angeles where he rejoined the Lloyd family, shipboard friends whom he had met coming to America. After further desultory employment in Los Angeles, he attended three weeks of business college and with the help of the Lloyds found work as a bookkeeper in a creamery. The elder Lloyd, a lawyer and Yale Ph.D., often entertained small circles of intellectual friends at his home, and here Chandler met his future wife, Mrs. Julian Pascal (Cissy), eighteen years his senior and married at the time to a concert pianist. In 1916 Chandler's mother came to live with him. The following year he enlisted in the Canadian army. As a noncommissioned officer he led a brigade in battle and witnessed some of the carnage in France—he was the only man in his platoon to survive a German artillery barrage. Later he tried to join the Royal Air Force but the war ended and he returned to Canada where he was mustered out. According to his biographer, Frank MacShane, Chandler seldom alluded to his battle experiences afterwards. He said it was a nightmare he'd rather forget, and aside from a short unpublished sketch he wrote about a soldier under fire, there is no evidence he ever attempted war fiction. He may have transferred the fear and the horror he had known in battle to the more manageable context of the detective story, or possibly the courage and cool detachment of a platoon commander in combat are qualities not very different from those that a hardboiled detective must display under duress. In a 1957 letter recalling the war, Chandler wrote, "As a platoon commander many years ago I never seemed to be afraid, and yet I have been afraid of the most insignificant risks. If you had to go over the top somehow all you seemed to think of was trying to keep the men spaced, in order to reduce casualties."

When Chandler returned to Los Angeles in 1919 he resumed his friendship with Cissy Pascal. They had corresponded while he was away but their letters were probably platonic. When they realized they were in love, they consulted their friends and Cissy's husband (whom she claimed she still loved but not as much as she loved Raymond) and decided it would be best if Cissy obtained a divorce. This would be her second divorce—she had been married once before to a Boston businessman. In 1920 the divorce decree was granted but Chandler's mother's objections prevented their marriage. In March 1924 Chandler's mother died and two weeks later he married Cissy. Despite her age Cissy at fifty-three was still a remarkably youthful and attractive looking woman. Nonetheless the difference in years was significant and rocky times lay ahead.

Four years before his marriage, Chandler, again with the aid of the Lloyds, had obtained a minor administrative post in one of the new California oil companies. Very quickly he worked his way up to what might be termed a vice-presidency so that by the time he wed Cissy he was earning a sizable salary. He was, it appears, a rather effective executive and a stickler for principle. He went out with Cissy when circumstances demanded, but after a few years she no longer felt comfortable being seen with a man who looked so much younger, and Chandler took to making social rounds on his own. For a period the marriage appeared to founder. Chandler began drinking excessively and having affairs with some of the young women who worked in his office. He was on occasion an extremely ebullient and self-pitying drunk who once threatened to kill himself when an infuriated associate wanted to throw him out of his house for annoying his wife.

Chandler's business capabilities were inevitably affected by the changes that had come over him. Was he disenchanted with his aging wife? Given his romantic spirit, did he find his business success tedious and unfulfilling? Today it would be said that he faced a "mid-life crisis." There were days he simply did not appear at his office. He was warned. He persisted. In 1932 he was fired. Afterwards he would claim he was let go because of office politics, and at the height of his popularity as a writer he told interviewers he was fired because of the depression. His colleagues knew otherwise.

In an essay he wrote in 1950, Chandler thought back on the pulp fiction of the decades before the War. Its "power," he proposed, lay in "the smell of fear"—a curious phrase that manages to transpose an abstract emotion into something almost physical. Probably Chandler was correct, but he may well have been describing the purgative effect of pulps on his own state of mind at the start of his career. Soon he would be writing about middle-aged detectives who, like their author, perceived themselves as isolated outsiders in a hostile world. Palpable fear was not of course peculiar to Chandler's heroes or to heroes of pulps generally. Fear as a fictional theme said something about the nature of the times as well.

Nineteen thirty-three, the year Chandler's first published short story appeared, was also a year jittery Americans were observing the spread of fascism abroad and economic depression the world over. Political movements of both the extreme right and left seemed to many to be taking root on American soil, while the violence, sadism, and ruthlessness of criminal gangs seemed all too similar to the behavior of fascists abroad. Some of the political fiction of the time, such as Sinclair Lewis's *It Can't Happen Here* and Nathaniel West's *A Cool Million* dealt with the emergence of American fascism. E. E. Cummings' *him* (1927) portrays European dictators as American gangsters; Cummings suggested that hidden homosexual elements lay behind the tough-guy veneer of his fascists and their hatred of "fairies." Neither Chandler nor Hammett portrayed their tough homosexual-baiting detectives as fascists or as being anything but masculine, but despite Hammett's and Chandler's democratic proclivites, the violent private eye who possesses little faith or patience with democratic and judicial processes has something of a vigilante mentality. (Gershon Legman in *Love and Death,* 1949, goes further and describes Chandler's Philip Marlowe as both a latent homosexual and necrophile.)

Anxiety so pervaded the nation that in his inaugural address, the new American president tried to reassure the public that the only thing they needed to fear was fear itself. Western Americans were particularly susceptible. For rootless and jobless Californians like Chandler, the sudden mass influx of Okies and other out-of-state depression victims aggravated anxieties. Hollywood meanwhile, the nation's dream factory, as Chandler once bitterly observed, continued churning out images further and further removed from the kind of life people knew.

One of the ways Americans coped with their amorphous fears was by becoming vicarious participants in what the mass circulation newspapers, magazines, and movies termed "the war against crime." In all probability the crime rate of the depression years was not much higher than in previous decades, but to an uneasy populace crime was visible, tangible, and above all comprehensible. Abolish crime, it was said, and a more secure order would be restored. Thus alert police forces or an FBI could cite "public enemies," and by picking them off, one by one, give Americans the sense that *something* was being done.

On a fantasy level, pulp detective stories also helped. By eliminating crooks and injustices (often by illegal means), the private detective in a few short pages relieved the reader of the perceived causes of his discontent. But for Chandler the pulps did not simply provide wish-fulfillment; they also served as a metaphor for the larger world. In an "Introduction" for a collection of his short stories, he commented:

> Their characters lived in a world gone wrong, a world in which long before the atom bomb, civilization had created the machinery for its own destruction and was learning to use it with all the moronic delight of a gangster trying out his first machine gun. The law was something to be manipulated for profit and power. The streets were dark with something more than night.

The Depression years for Chandler were trying ones—one is tempted to say sobering, since he had evidently curtailed his drinking and begun taking his marital responsibilities seriously. It was obviously not the easiest time for a middle-aged ex-alcoholic with an English accent to pick himself up and start over. Cissy remained loyal, but the straitened circumstances of their lives required that they periodically move from one Los Angeles house to another. Perhaps Chandler's sensitivity to the mood and feel of lower middle-class life comes as much from these peregrinations as they do from his penurious youth.

He apparently determined again to try his hand at writing—or perhaps he had never given up the dream—but it is ironic that he decided to write for the lowly pulps, since one of the reasons he says he left England was that an English editor, "a suave Cantabrigian in a cutaway coat," had suggested to him that he write newspaper serials. Chandler was so affronted at "having to write what then appeared to me the most appalling garbage . . . [that] I gave him a sickly smile and left the country." Yet some twenty years later Chandler, who had evidently been studying American pulps closely—especially Hammett's work—submitted his first story, **"Blackmailers Don't Shoot,"** to *Black Mask.* Its editor, Joseph Shaw, was so impressed that he thought him a "genius." Within the next six years Chandler would publish twenty additional stories, half of these in *Black Mask.* In most respects they followed the general formula although they clearly reveal Chandler as a cut or two above his colleagues in matters of style and character. One suspects too that for Chandler the rattling good tale existed for making some melancholy points about human nature.

Part of his melancholy may be attributed to a nostalgia for England. Time and distance had magnified her attractions, which he now evidently associated with a frustrated love affair. The bittersweet tone of Chandler's prose is prefigured in an unpublished poem written in 1932 in which he recalls England's unparalleled beauty and an unknown woman as "the promise of an impossible paradise." America, by contrast, is the "bright and dismal land of my exile and dismay." Paradoxically, the attitudes of Chandler's immediate influences, Hammett and Hemingway, may also have encouraged him in his melancholy. One does not ordinarily think of two of America's most hardboiled authors as contributing to a third author's *langueurs,* but

underneath the tough exterior of their prose lay an unmistakeable *weltzschmerz* that Chandler seems to have imbibed.

Chandler drew what he needed from his contemporaries and wedded their values to his own peculiarly Victorian outlook. (Chandler wrote a rather good, but never published, parody of Hemingway at about the time he was beginning to publish his detective stories. He also names one of his typically simple-minded, tough characters in his second novel, *Farewell My Lovely,* Hemingway. The title of that book, incidentally, suggests Hemingway's own second novel, *A Farewell to Arms.*) From Hammett Chandler learned not only the main ingredients of formula but how to express a sense of resignation about ever discovering rational order in this world—a fashionable post-World War I affectation that Chandler probably never fully accepted, given his Victorian upbringing. Yet in his stories there is more than a touch of the meaninglessness of events that his detectives obsessively try to make sense of. From Hemingway he learned not only how to pare his sentences and toughen his dialogue but how to communicate his heroes' private dignity in the presence of death. (Shades of Matthew Arnold and Kipling.)

The stoic behavior of Chandler's heroes—a stoicism Chandler himself was not always capable of—may say something about the displacement value of literature. One thinks, for example, of the grotesque ex-convict in Chandler's short story **"Try the Girl"** who after seven years' absence relentlessly but hopelessly seeks out an old girl friend who has all but forgotten him. Could Chandler have been thinking of his own long absence from the English woman he once loved? What sticks about the story is not the murder mystery that attaches itself to the con's search, but the mystery of his curious idealism, his obsessive love that causes him to kill, and yet still makes him strangely sympathetic. Indeed the moral ardor of the story is directed against one of the girl's employers who wants to keep the convict away, not in order to protect her but to use her for his own selfish ends. This, as we shall see, is a theme to which Chandler would return in subsequent works: how the rich and socially powerful use and manipulate others less strong than they, as if their humanity meant nothing.

Chandler's biographer, Frank MacShane, thinks Chandler's antagonism toward the rich stems in part from his resentment of his wealthy employer at the oil company, and we know as well that Chandler despised his snobbish Irish grandmother, upon whom both he and his mother were so dependent. The theme of emotional exploitation by the rich and socially successful was of course also a notion of F. Scott Fitzgerald with whom Chandler later felt an affinity. But Chandler's class anger was more moral than political despite the fact that he used conventional symbols of social injustice—brutal police, corrupt officials, venal lawyers, and so on. What he objected to was not so much the "system," as persons who use the system to intimidate others. Some of Chandler's characters blame society for their own moral weaknesses, but the very presence of Chandler's unsullied heroes represents a rebuke in itself.

Justice in Chandler is not so much "legal" as poetic. Bad guys often die not for their crimes but for their lust and their avarice. Conversely, some of Chandler's characters, including his detectives, literally get away with murder if the murder seems deserved (**"Spanish Blood,"** 1935) or if the murderer is not psychologically responsible for his actions (**"The Curtain,"** 1936). In each of these short stories, the detective's role is not simply to solve crimes, but to protect the weak and the troubled—often at his own expense—and to make sure, insofar as it is possible in an imperfect world, that justice is done.

Although Chandler would later claim that the ideal detective was a poor but honest man, this was not always the case in his own first writings. In one story (**"Guns at Cyrano's,"** 1936) the detective's father had once "owned" the town, and in another (**"Pearls Are a Nuisance,"** 1939), the hero takes a rather condescending view of the lower classes. As a rule, though, Chandler's early detectives emerge as undeveloped versions of Philip Marlowe, conforming both to Hammett's hardboiled archetype and to Chandler's evolving chivalric code. If their adventures tax belief, this too is partially convention. Action is primary, plausibility secondary. Chandler often extricates his detectives from sticky situations by having the bad guys kill one another off in one climactic scene. The story is told that Joseph Shaw, the editor of *Black Mask,* once advised his writers that if ever they were stymied for plot, they might have one or two thugs come through the door with guns in their hands; such persons do make occasional appearances in Chandler's apprentice fiction.

Yet Chandler's tales are so fast-paced his readers have little time to remark on their absurdities. Actions unfold in terse hard sentences characterized by simple monosyllabic words:

> Marty didn't like that. His lower lip went in under his teeth and his eyebrows drew down at the corners. His whole face got mean.

> The buzzer kept on buzzing.

> The blonde stood up quickly. Nerve tension made her face old and ugly.

> Watching me, Marty jerked a small drawer open in the tall desk and got a small, white-handled automatic out of it. He held it out to the blonde. She went to him and took it gingerly, not liking it.

> "Sit down next to the shamus," he rasped. "Hold the gun on him. If he gets funny feed him a few."

> The blonde sat down on the davenport about three feet from me, on the side away from the door. She lined the gun on my leg. I didn't like the jerky look in her green eyes.

Likewise gore and death are described almost clinically with few, if any, encumbering phrases that might decelerate the story.

> Braced to the door frame by eight hooked fingers, all but one of which were white as wax, there hung what was left of a man.

> He had eyes an eighth of an inch deep, china-blue, wide open. They looked at me but they didn't see me. He had coarse gray hair on which the smeared blood looked purple. One of his temples was a pulp, and the tracery of blood from it reached clear to the point of his chin. The one straining finger that wasn't white had been pounded to shreds as far as the second joint. Sharp splinters of bone stuck out of the mangled flesh. Something that might once have been a fingernail looked now like a ragged splinter of glass.

Lightning changes in the hero's precarious fortunes produce the principal effects of these stories—that smell of fear. Sometimes the detectives merely fear for their lives. But what Chandler seemed really to be aiming for was a larger sense of fear, an undefined malaise that hangs over events before they happen, a fear the more terrifying because, he suggests, sudden death lies as much in the familiar as in the unknown. Thus an atmosphere of threat hovers over Chandler's city streets, shabby offices, and rented rooms. By the time he came to write his first novel Chandler would be much more successful in putting all of these elements together.

The Big Sleep was published by Knopf in 1939. The following year *Farewell My Lovely* appeared. There was no question now that Chandler's star had risen. Hollywood bought both novels, the first of which would become a 1946 film classic, directed by Howard Hawks and featuring Humphrey Bogart, formerly Hammett's Sam Spade in *The Maltese Falcon.* Other books followed at longer intervals: *The High Window* (1942), *The Lady in the Lake* (1943), *The Little Sister* (1949), *The Long Goodbye* (1953), and *Playback* (1958). All but *Playback* were made into movies, most of which were produced under different titles; *Farewell My Lovely,* for example, was called *The Falcon Takes Over* (1941) and *Murder My Sweet* (1945).

From 1942 to 1946 Chandler wrote plot synopses and screenplays for Paramount and in 1950 he worked with the director, Alfred Hitchcock, on Patricia Highsmith's novel, *Strangers on a Train.* Suddenly, well into his fifties, he had become a celebrated figure. Yet judging from his letters and the few personal essays he wrote dealing with Hollywood, literature, and his own aspirations, he was not very uplifted by his fame. Chandler resumed drinking heavily, which on one occasion led to his being taken off an assignment. Despite his frequent complaints that Hollywood was false, corrupt, and commercial, one suspects that what he hated most was how attracted and vulnerable he was to the very tawdriness he deplored. Studio work brought him once again into close contact with young women and again he had affairs—but Cissy forgave him.

Like his predecessor, Hammett, Chandler remained a loner. After 1945 neither Cissy nor Chandler was seen about much. Cissy was said to be more self-conscious than ever about her age, and Chandler was embarrassed by a skin allergy he had developed. They made few friends, but as if to compensate, Chandler wrote numerous letters to readers, publishers, agents, and acquaintances about himself, his wife, his cat, and his work. One of his correspondents was S. J. Perelman who thought no one wrote better accounts of Southern California. In 1946 the Chandlers moved to the fashionable outlying town of La Jolla presumably to get away from the hurlyburly of Hollywood. But although the quiet new community pleased him at first, he did not especially like the rich and elderly retired people who lived there. "It's for old people and their parents," he wrote one correspondent, and to another he spoke of "arthritic billionaires and barren old women." Less than three years after the move, he told of feeling "dull and depressed . . . too often."

Chandler, as he put it, "cannibalized" his short stories to write *The Big Sleep*. Several of his other novels were written the same way: he took ideas, themes, characters, and sometimes whole passages from his pulp writing and incorporated them into his longer fiction. He did not of course imagine that anyone would ever seek out the magazine origins of these books, but if the Chandler scholar wants to discover some of his sources they are not hard to find. It should not be supposed though that Chandler's borrowings are the consequence of an arrested imagination. His novels considerably improve upon his short stories by sharpening, condensing, and meshing them. The cannibalized parts constitute only small portions of the novels and are often employed for entirely different purposes than they were in their original spots. For example, although the main plot ideas of *The Big Sleep* come from two earlier pieces, **"The Curtain"** (1936), and **"Killer in the Rain"** (1935), the solution to the mystery lies outside these stories. He changes characters as well. In *Farewell My Lovely,* a woman who was treated sympathetically in her pulp origins, **"Try the Girl"** (1937), reemerges in the novel as a heartless calculating killer. In fact, she too is an amalgam, derived in part from the villainess of another story, **"Mandarin's Jade"** (1937).

The Big Sleep opens with Philip Marlowe's summons by a General Sternwood who asks his help in exposing an unknown blackmailer. While trying to do this, Marlowe unearths several blackmailing schemes bit by bit, and in so doing discovers venality, guilt, and shame wherever he turns. To be sure, there are exceptions, including the private "soldierly" virtues of the ancient dying General Sternwood, whose values, we are given to feel, are about to die with him. The General possesses an unflinching honesty about himself and his daughters, and a towering loyalty to his son-in-law, a former fighter for Irish freedom, who has unaccountably vanished. The General's loyalty is matched by that shown by Harry Jones, a shabby, low-level crook, who remains faithful to his grasping, self-serving sweetheart. Rather than betray her, Harry dies horribly of cyanide poisoning. Finally Marlowe's own compassion for the General results in attempts to rescue reluctant ladies in distress.

As knight errant in a nonchivalric world, Marlowe saves himself from the absurdity of his role by a wry sense of humor.

The main hallway of the Sternwood place was two stories high. Over the entrance doors, which would have let in a troop of Indian elephants, there was a broad stained-glass panel showing a knight in dark armor rescuing a lady who was tied to a tree and didn't have any clothes on but some very long and convenient hair. The knight had pushed the vizor of his helmet back to be sociable, and he was fiddling with the knots on the ropes that tied the lady to the tree and not getting anywhere. I stood there and thought that if I lived in the house, I would sooner or later have to climb up there and help him. He didn't seem to be really trying.

Nonetheless Marlowe takes his job seriously; from time to time we see him alone in his apartment pushing a knight across a chessboard as he muses about what to do next. At one point he describes himself as "painfully" honest in what one of the General's daughters describes as "this rotten crime-ridden country" and despite the fact that he is at constant odds with both criminals and police (most of whom are cynical, brutal, or resigned to corruption), he carries on courageously and alone. Above all he is an individualist, suspicious of all social institutions, who insists on doing "my thinking myself."

In reaction to his realization that greed and lust lie behind the crimes he investigates, Marlowe is also something of an ascetic. He scarcely makes a living at "twenty-five dollars a day and expenses" and seems to take a rather dim view of sex. He loathes "pansys" (one of whom is a murderer and another a pornographer and blackmailer), but although he claims he is as "warmblooded as the next guy," he rejects, for no discernible reason, the blandishments of the Sternwood daughters. When he finds the younger, Carmen, awaiting him naked in his bed one night, he equates her carnality with evil. "A hissing noise came tearing out of her mouth." Perhaps the key is that her presence threatens his insularity.

> I didn't mind what she called me. . . . But this was the room I had to live in. It was all I had in the way of a home. In it was everything that was mine, that had any association for me, any past, anything that took the place of a family.

He throws her out and slowly drinks a glass of whiskey, then tears "the bed to pieces savagely." Afterwards he writes, "You can have a hangover from other things than alcohol. I had one from women. Women made me sick."

Men and women rarely respect one another in Chandler's works. At best they make tenuous and temporary alliances for what they regard as mutual gain—but betrayal is always imminent. In *The Big Sleep* the only true positive relationship is the one that existed between the General and his vanished son-in-law, for whom Marlowe, in a sense, becomes the substitute. Not until *The Long Goodbye* (1953) would Chandler again allow his hero to express such intense feelings toward other human beings.

In retrospect we begin to suspect that much of the terror that lies at the root of Chandler's novels and makes his tough guys *act* tough is a morbid fear of sexuality. For example, Carmen, whose name suggests Bizet's femme fatale, is described as having "predatory teeth." Even the vegetation in the General's hothouse possesses a kind of moribund carnality: "The glass walls and roof were heavily misted and big drops of moisture splashed down on the plants. . . . The plants filled the place, a forest of them, with nasty meaty leaves and stalks like the newly washed fingers of dead men." In an image reminiscent of Eliot's "Prufrock," Marlowe writes: "Under the thinning fog the surf curled and creamed, almost without sound, like a thought trying to form itself on the edge of consciousness." Indeed even when Chandler's imagery is less explicitly sensual, danger lurks everywhere in the vibrancy of nature, however much men may attempt to domesticate it: "[The] bright gardens had a haunted look, as though small wild eyes were watching me from behind bushes, as though the sunshine itself had a mysterious something in its light."

For Chandler, the tangible and real portend the mysterious, and the familiar often betokens fear of the unknown. A typical passage in *The Big Sleep* begins: "It was a wide room the whole width of the house. It had a low beamed ceiling and brown plaster walls decked out with strips of Chinese embroidery and Chinese and Japanese prints in grand wood frames." Five sentences follow, each beginning with "There" or "There were," listing the contents of the room, its furnishings, its color and the odd paraphernalia scattered about in it. The last sentence, however, shifts swiftly from the visual to the olefactory implying violence, death, and perversity.

> The room contained an odd assortment of odors, of which the most emphatic at the moment seemed to be the pungent aftermath of cordite and the sickish aroma of ether.

At his best, Chandler was surely one of the masters of the American language. Events in *The Big Sleep* are recounted with great economy, and suspense and atmosphere are fused into what might best be termed Los Angeles gothic. Here and there, he will follow pulp conventions and torture a simile: An empty house is "as dismal as a lost dog"; a woman's hat "looked as if you could have made it with one hand out of a dark blotter" and people who patronize pornography shops are "as nervous as a dowager who can't find the rest room." But he is a master at using dialogue to identify both social class and character. Eddie Mars sardonically addresses Marlowe as "soldier"—which he is, in a manner of speaking. And here is Harry Jones, "a three for a quarter grifter" who wants to sell Marlowe information about the General's son-in-law.

> I knew Rusty myself. Not well, well enough to say "How's a boy?" and he'd answer me or he wouldn't, according to how he felt. A nice guy though. I always liked him. . . . High strung. Rusty wouldn't get along with [his rich wife]. But Jesus, he'd get along with her old man's dough, wouldn't he? That's what you think. This Regan was a cockeyed sort of buzzard. He had long-range eyes. He was looking over into the next

valley all the time. He wasn't scarcely around where he was.

Chandler's second book, *Farewell, My Lovely* (1940), was even more popular than his first. Created in part from cannibalizations of his earlier story **"Try the Girl,"** *Farewell* deals with Marlowe's pursuit of an ex-con who is searching for his former sweetheart. In the course of his quest, the con, a giant named Moose Malloy, kills the manager of a Negro social club and Marlowe promises to help a demoralized detective lieutenant find him. Nulty, the lieutenant, complains to Marlowe that nobody in the police or newspapers really cares about "shine killings." In some respects the novel is more of a social statement than Chandler's first. A crooked cop tells Marlowe: "Cops don't get crooked for money. . . . They get caught in the system. . . . You gotta play the game dirty or you don't eat." His suggestion for making the world over, however, is Moral Rearmament.

Marlowe's adventures lead him from the very bottom to the top strata of Los Angeles society, whose foibles he denounces in acid tones. He visits the eerie home of a fashionable Southern California "psychic consultant" (not unlike the one in which Hammett's Op found himself in *The Dain Curse*), and a sanatorium that is really a hideout for wanted criminals. In both of these, Marlowe is taken prisoner and given the ritual beating that private detectives must take before they are allowed to carry on.

Nearly everyone he meets, regardless of social class, is hardened and corrupt, but the streets and houses of lower middle class neighborhoods may also convey the resignation and despair of their inhabitants.

> 1644 West 54th Place was a dried-out house with a dried-out brown lawn in front of it. There was a large bare patch around a tough-looking palm tree. On the porch stood one lonely wooden rocker, and the afternoon breeze made the unpruned shoots of last year's poinsettias tap-tap against the cracked stucco walls. A line of stiff yellowish half-washed clothes jittered on a rusty wire in the side yard.

The moneyed classes on the other hand link themselves to criminals when they feel it is to their advantage, and buy and sell politicians and the police; yet despite their power, they are almost as fearful and unhappy as anyone else. And because they believe in nothing, they clutch desperately at anything to secure their precarious identities. Here in splendid Americanese, Marlowe speaks of the unhappy rich who consult Jules Amthor, the Charlatan psychic consultant.

> Give him enough time and pay him enough money and he'll cure anything from a jaded husband to a grasshopper plague. He would be an expert in frustrated love affairs, women who slept alone and didn't like it, wandering boys and girls who didn't write home, sell the property now or hold it for another year, will this part hurt me with my public or make me seem more versatile. . . . A fakeloo artist, a hoopla spreader, and

a lad who had his card rolled up inside sticks of tea, found on a dead man.

In his fashion Chandler had declared Southern California to be as much a spiritual wasteland as Eliot's London.

Marlowe feels self-disgust on more than one occasion when he is forced to do disagreeable things in the line of duty. At one point he plies an alcoholic widow with liquor to glean more information from her, and at another feels as "nasty" as if "he had picked a poor man's pocket," when he is discovered by a Mr. Grayle just as he is about to kiss the elderly gentleman's wife. He knows he is not all that good at his job; at one point, he is hired as a bodyguard, only to have his client murdered in his presence.

Still, it is not all self-hatred. Earlier on in the book he describes a "smeary self portrait" of Rembrandt on a calendar. Marlowe might well have been describing himself. The "face was aging, saggy, fully of the disgust of life and the thickening effects of liquor. But it had a hard cheerfulness . . . and the eyes were as bright as dew." And indeed Marlowe displays a certain zest for life and is not always so moralistic towards his antagonists. Several of his exchanges with Nulty are truly funny and he expresses some sympathy for the isolated, love-lorn, and grotesque, even when they kill. Perhaps this was because he was beginning to feel a kinship with them.

Chandler's books of the war decade are something of a mixed bag. In two of them he appears to be taking himself overseriously while at the same time making fun of himself. *The High Window* (1942) and *The Little Sister* (1949) were probably intended partially as self-parodies and partially as hints of Chandler's mixed feelings about himself both as an artist and as a commercial success. By poking fun at himself, Chandler seems to be saying: "You see, I don't take this sort of writing as anything more than a bit of fun." But segments of these novels are tense, suspenseful, and moralistic, as if Chandler were somehow afraid to commit himself entirely to satire for fear of losing his mass audience.

The High Window is probably the best of his post-*Farewell* books of the 1940s. (Chandler thought it his worst.) It begins almost as a parody of *The Big Sleep* with Marlowe calling on a rich, crotchety, domineering, old woman who in certain respects is the female counterpart of General Sternwood. She wants him to track down a rare coin she believes stolen from her collection. Here, Marlowe does not identify himself with a knight, as he did in *The Big Sleep,* but with an absurd painted statue of a Negro on the lawn, dressed in riding gear, and wearing a sad, discouraged expression on his face as if he had been waiting too long. On the block at his feet, there is an iron hitching ring. Marlowe pats the Negro on the head and says, "You and me both, brother."

There are one or two other passages that imply Marlowe's social consciousness; one is a description of a rundown outlying town called Bunker Hill (an ironic allusion to America's revolutionary glory?). Marlowe tells of its declining neighborhoods and streets, the flyblown restaurants, the rooming houses with their lost and desperate inhabitants:

> In the tall rooms, haggard landladies bicker with shifty tenants. On the wide cool front porches, reaching their cracked shoes into the sun, and staring at nothing, sit the old men with faces like lost battles.

A verb or a phrase may say all. Somewhere "a radio is blatting a ball game." In an alley stand "four tall battered garbage pails in a line with a dance of flies in the sunlit air above them."

These images have the feel of Eliot's "Preludes" or passages from "Prufrock," but the novel as a whole hearkens back to Chandler's Fitzgeraldian theme of how the rich and powerful use those less fortunate than they. In contrast to the present-day exploitative West Coast, Chandler has a vision of a simpler, more honest America that existed in the past and perhaps lives on still in the Midwest. As the novel ends, the chivalrous Marlowe takes the depleted heroine back to her Kansas home for spiritual and emotional renewal, not unlike the narrator of Gatsby who plans to return to his Midwestern home for the same reasons.

The plot and characters in *The High Window* are artificial; on one occasion Marlowe complains that everyone he meets behaves as if he were playing a role in a B movie. In places, the novel pokes fun at elite critics who derided Chandler's stuff, as when Marlowe tells a startled customer in a drugstore whom he thinks is "sneering" at him over a copy of the *New Republic,* "You ought to lay off that fluff and get into something solid, like a pulp magazine." Walking away, he hears someone say, "Hollywood's full of them."

Chandler's next book, *The Lady in the Lake* (1943), represents a departure of sorts from his earlier work. Much of the action takes place not in the city but in the mountains east of Los Angeles, and here Chandler moves from the argot of the streets to a stylized version of rural speech. There are no extremes of wealth and poverty, nor are there professional gangsters. Possibly America's mood of wartime unity dictated playing down class differences and the menace of organized crime.

The Little Sister (1949) was published six years later but nonetheless looks like a hurry-up job. It appeared after Chandler had for the most part given up studio work and was probably intended as a "Hollywood novel." There are several lively depictions of Hollywood types—talent agents and their hacks, unemployed actors, and so on. There is a wonderful scene on a Hollywood lot where Marlowe meets a film mogul whose incontinent boxer dogs pee and root about while the mogul complains to Marlowe that everyone in the movie business is up to his neck in sex, and the more mistakes one makes, the more money one gets. Chandler reverses many of his earlier themes. The "bad guys" come from the "pure" Midwest to exploit and extort money from a Hollywood movie actress. The seemingly naive heroine who supplicates Marlowe for help is really a ruthless blackmailer, the police are sometimes sympathetic, and the rich and powerful seem sometimes quite bewildered.

But as a whole, *Little Sister* is really not much of an achievement, lying somewhere between intended and, one suspects, unintended burlesque. Hot-blooded females throw themselves at the impervious Marlowe who meditates unhappily about soul-destroying materialism. Perhaps by now the times had passed Chandler by. The war was over and machismo and the stiff upper lip—that nice blend of very English and very American stoicism that Chandler brought to his earlier writings—no longer seemed applicable. In some ways he may have sensed this.

The last ten years of Chandler's life are a sad mix of success and degradation. These were years in which he would write his most ambitious and perhaps interesting book, *The Long Goodbye* (1954), and his most uneven, *Playback* (1958). They were years in which he made several triumphant returns to England (the first with Cissy) but responded to his welcome with ambivalence. In the 1940s he had had a large following in England, both among intellectuals and less educated readers—his last three books were published first in England—but on his visits he feared the admiration was condescending and reacted irritably. Possibly he was responding to the snubs he had received in his youth or perhaps he himself deeply felt, despite his protestations to the contrary, that mystery writing was not quite respectable. In any case his reactions were a source of puzzlement to his hosts who for the most part were Chandler aficionados like Stephen and Natasha Spender, Ian Fleming, and J. B. Priestly.

In 1954 Cissy, now in her eighties, died of fibrosis of the lungs. Chandler was beside himself with grief. Several times he called friends and threatened suicide—and once indeed shot off a gun in his bathtub, probably by accident. He had begun drinking heavily again, so heavily in fact that on a number of occasions he required hospitalization. When he was not drinking, he often seemed to be playing out the dreams he had hitherto confined to his writing. From time to time he assumed the Philip Marlowe role of protector and defender of helpless women. As a consequence he sometimes found himself in peculiar situations. At one point he almost married a fan who had written to him, and at another, he made his troubled Australian secretary the beneficiary of his will. He evidently thought better of both intentions later.

In his five remaining years Chandler made a number of other trips to England. His behavior in England was not much different from what it had been in California. His friends write that he liked to think of himself as enormously attractive to the young English women to whom he was introduced, although there is very little evidence that he was. One of the women who took him seriously was Helga Greene, a literary agent. Helga probably had few illusions about him, but after several years of spotty courtship she agreed to marry him.

In March of 1959 Chandler entrained to California from New York where he had just been inaugurated president of the Mystery Writers of America. Later he planned to rejoin Helga in London. On the way, he fell ill with pneumonia. Once more he began to drink, and once more he was taken from his La Jolla quarters for hospitalization. Several days later he died. Seventeen people attended his funeral. Scarcely any of them had more than a passing acquaintance with the deceased. . . .

How do we account for the continuing popularity of Chandler with his present-day audience? Several possibilities suggest themselves. He was a superb storyteller, and while we may occasionally be amused at Marlowe's tough sentimentality, more significantly we are drawn to Marlowe because he is decisive and self-possessed in a perplexing, threatening, indifferent world. In some ways it is a world not unlike our own, fraught with tensions, terror, wars, and economic crisis. As Chandler observed in his famous essay, "The Simple Art of Murder" (1944), his hero is a poor man, unafraid of "mean streets," and above all "a man of honor." Thus, unlike the antiheroes or "survivors" of contemporary letters, Marlowe carries forward the tradition of the true democratic hero, the uncommon commoner, certain of his values.

It is thus clear that Marlowe would not have had very much sympathy for Sam Spade's startling perception of a world without meaning, although on several occasions Marlowe himself very nearly succumbs to despair. Near the end of *Playback* Marlowe says of himself: "Wherever I went, whatever I did, this is what I would come back to. A blank wall in a meaningless room in a meaningless house." Fortunately a phone call from Linda Loring lifts him from his despondency, but a better answer arrives earlier in the novel when Marlowe meets an old man in a hotel lobby wearing gloves (as Chandler did) because "my hands are ugly and painful." The old man refuses to despair and suggests to Marlowe that meaning may derive from the very nature of one's struggle to discover meaning. Surely this is what Chandler would have liked to believe. Possibly this is what his books are really about.

> How strange it is that man's aspirations, dirty little animal that he is, his finest actions also, his great and unselfish heroism, his constant daily courage in a harsh world—how strange that these things should be so much greater than his fate on earth. That has to be somehow made reasonable. Don't tell me that honor is merely a chemical reaction or that a man who deliberately gives his life for another is merely following a behavior pattern. Is God happy with the poisoned cat dying alone by convulsions behind the billboard? . . . There is no success where there is no possibility of failure, no art without the resistance of the medium. Is it blasphemy to suggest that God has his bad days when nothing goes right, and that God's days are very, very long?

William Marling (essay date 1986)

SOURCE: "Looking for a Knight: The Short Stories," in *Raymond Chandler*, Twayne Publishers, 1986, pp. 51-72.

[*In the following essay, Marling surveys Chandler's short stories, addressing issues of plot, character, and style in each.*]

Before he invented Philip Marlowe in *The Big Sleep*, Chandler created prototypes in gambler Johnny De Ruse, policeman Sam Delaguerra, vice detective Pete Anglich, hotel dick Steve Grayce, and man-about-town Ted Malvern. His best effort was a private detective named Mallory, after the author of *Le Morte d'Arthur*. Later Chandler changed his name to Carmady, and finally to John Dalmas.

Mallory appears in Chandler's first story, **"Blackmailers Don't Shoot"** (*Black Mask*, December 1933). While the story is primitive compared to his later efforts, and flawed by clichéd dialogue, motiveless actions, and pointless turns of plot, it was relatively polished by *Black Mask* standards.

Private detective Mallory comes to Los Angeles from Chicago, Chandler's birthplace, at the request of a gambler named Landry. His love letters to former girlfriend and film star Rhonda Farr have been stolen. The blackmail becomes kidnapping when a gang of crooked cops, politicians, and crooks, led by her own lawyer, snatch Farr and Mallory. He escapes, turns the tables by kidnapping the lawyer, then frees Farr while the gang members kill each other. In the resolution Mallory learns that Farr set everything in motion; her contract was expiring and she wanted publicity. That fed Landry's vindictiveness and her attorney's greed; they conspired against her with the gang. At the story's end, a policeman tells Mallory that Eclipse Films needs a detective.

Blackmail and kidnapping became Chandler's favorite plots. Blackmail threatens the public image of a person, which is usually a charade anyway, and kidnapping removes the actual person, putting his worth to others in question. The motive for both crimes is money, the desire for which causes all evil in Chandler's early work. He also experimented with the captivity of the heroine or detective, a time-tested device of American melodrama that originated in Puritan narratives of captivity among the Indians. In this early work the Indians are clearly criminal. Later on, the tendrils of drugs and gambling lead from the criminals to Hollywood, providing Chandler with a canvas that encompasses society and giving his detective grounds for sweeping moral judgments.

This first story also employs a plot pattern to which Chandler turned repeatedly: a triangle in which two men love one woman who manipulates both of them. One of the men hires or is a friend of the detective; in this man's demise the detective sees his fate if he had loved the woman. In later work the detective himself becomes part of the triangle.

Chandler featured Mallory, renamed Dalmas in later editions, in his second story, **"Smart-Aleck Kill"** (*Black Mask*, July 1934). Now employed by Eclipse Studios, Mallory tries to help smut director Derek Walden find out who is blackmailing him. Two thugs kidnap Mallory and by the time he returns, Walden is dead, an apparent suicide. He learns that Walden liked liquor and supplied himself, during Prohibition, by smuggling booze from Ensenada. This left him open to blackmail by gangsters; he turned for protection to a gang run by Councilman John Sutro and racketeer Gay Donner. Sutro kills Walden, then Donner, and is killed in turn by his wife for having had an affair.

Why does Sutro kill Walden? Loose plot ends and improbable motives mar this story. It uses Prohibition-era settings and rationales, but Prohibition (1920-33) ended before it was published. Most of the characters are stereotyped, their lines predictable, and their reactions mere generic conventions. Some minor touches are notable, such as the portrait of Helen Dalton, first in a series of blonde bitches, and the dialogue sometimes reveals an acute ear, such as Denny's line: "I don't what you call know him." There are also indications, such as Mallory's "We gotta find out all about it before the cops even know Walden is dead. . . . Like they do in the movies," that Hollywood was not just a setting for Chandler, but an influence and a goal from the start. According to the editors of *Black Mask*, their magazine was "regarded by the biggest motion picture companies as one of the important sources of new story material. . . . three of our series heroes are very much in the mind of the film producers at this time."

Like his first two efforts, **"Finger Man"** (*Black Mask*, October 1934) involves a corrupt politician who deals in influence and blackmail. "I'm tough and I get what I want," says Frank Dorr. Chandler's now nameless detective unravels the fabric of politics and crime behind Dorr's organization, but the story lacks significant tensions and female characters. Nevertheless, Chandler felt that he hit his stride with this story.

These three stories indicate that Chandler was determined to make sham and facade his theme from the beginning. The superficiality extends from actors to gangsters and politicians, a tableau spanning American life. Unfortunately, the Prohibition era, so convivial to the theme, was over, though in blackmail and kidnapping Chandler found serviceable substitutes. Money was his universal motive. What he lacked was a knight to unmask sham and deal justice while protecting innocence. Mallory had an appearance, but no ethos, interests, or thoughts. In fact, in the first story he appeared most concerned with his pay, just like other *Black Mask* detectives.

"KILLER IN THE RAIN"

Chandler discovered the first-person point of view in his fourth story, **"Killer in the Rain"** (*Black Mask*, January 1935). By giving his narrator the freedom to describe what he saw, Chandler was able to avoid some of the stereotypes and conventions that plagued detective fiction. The narrator could also tell the reader something about his feelings, usually through simile and hyperbole, which Chandler found he liked.

For

JOSEPH THOMPSON SHAW

with affection and respect, and in memory of
the time when we were trying to get murder
away from the upper classes, the week-end house
party and the vicar's rose-garden, and back
to the people who are really good at it.

Chandler's first three short story collections, published between 1944 and 1947. Chandler's first collection, Five Murders, *was dedicated to the editor of* Black Mask.

This story became the basis of Chandler's first novel. Anton Dravec hires the nameless detective to free his daughter Carmen from porn dealer Harold Steiner. Everyone is in love with Carmen: chauffeur Carl Owen, a "guy named Joe Marty," even Dravec, who reveals that he adopted her. The detective finds a drugged Carmen posing nude before the camera of Steiner, who is dead. But his body and her negative disappear after the detective takes Carmen home. He discovers Joe Marty transferring Steiner's porn books to his apartment, then chauffeur Carl Owen turns up dead. The detective makes a deal with Marty for the negative, but Carmen shows up with a gun. Then Dravec breaks down the door. After Marty and Darvec kill each other, the detective destroys the negative.

Chandler cited "*Carmen* as Merimée wrote it," rather than Bizet's opera, as one of his favorite stories. Although Chandler's Carmen is a vulgar imitation of the original, she elicits the same jealousy and murder that doomed Merimée's hero, José Navarro. She refuses to marry Carl Owen after eloping with him, like her namesake preferring the pleasure of many lovers. Chandler retained the character of the original Carmen, but interpreted her independence as promiscuity; in the place of Merimée's narrator, who loves Carmen and hears of her death from Navarro, Chandler put his detective, who hears Carmen's story from Dravec (a lover) and is himself sexually attracted to her. The tensions that could be generated within a triangle were considerable, as Chandler knew by having won Cissy from Julian Pascal.

In this story Chandler also discovered weather and colors as symbolic motifs. He made it rain in sunny Los Angeles: "I stared at the window, watched the rain hit it, flatten out, and slide down in a thick wave, like melted gelatin. It was too early in the fall for that kind of rain." This aspect of the ballyhooed California climate corresponds to Steiner's porn world, where the nether side of human desire reigns. Chandler also began to use colors in symbolic schemes from which he varied little for the rest of his career. Green is the color of lust, of sensuality; Carmen dresses in a green and white coat, and wears green jade earrings. Red is the color of action and confirmation, while shades of gray and white ("scraped bone" or "putty colored") describe morally empty characters. If blonde may be deemed a color, it becomes clear in this story that no blonde woman is to be trusted: this was already a convention of the genre, but Chandler applied it with a new brutality.

The sex and sadism, overt and implicit, of **"Killer in the Rain,"** broke new ground. Under "Cap" Shaw's direction, *Black Mask* had kept its heroines chaste. It featured a married detective and a couple who worked as a team, but aside from a kiss upon rescue for the hero, most of the sex occurred offstage. Hammett changed that, and Chandler had sufficient technique to make the pulp story leer. He saw that, when the description of sex had gone as far as permitted, a symbolic representation of sex followed by a graphic depiction of death could provide a comparable sensation. Here his detective finds Carmen:

> She was wearing a pair of long jade earrings, and apart from those she was stark naked.

I looked away from her to the other end of the room.

Steiner was on his back on the floor, just beyond the edge of the pink rug, and in front of a thing that looked like a small totem pole. It had a round open mouth in which the lens of a camera showed. The lens seemed to be aimed at the girl in the teakwood chair.

. . . . .

Steiner was wearing Chinese slippers with thick white felt soles. His legs were in black satin pajamas and the upper part of him in an embroidered Chinese coat. The front of it was mostly blood. His glass eye shone brightly and was the most lifelike thing about him. At a glance none of the three shots had missed.

In this scene and another later the detective slaps women. The circumstances are carefully justified and the reader invited to enjoy the necessity of this misogyny. Carmen, for example, is drugged: "The tinny chuckling was still going on and a little froth was oozing down her chin. I slapped her face, not very hard. I didn't want to bring her out of whatever kind of trance she was in, into a screaming fit."

GAS, BLOOD, AND GUNS

Three of the next four stories that Chandler wrote used rainy weather as a motif. **"Nevada Gas"** (*Black Mask,* June 1935) reverts to a third-person narrator and finds a new hero in tough-guy gambler Johnny De Ruse. He uncovers the murder/extortion plot of George Dial, his rival for Francine Ley. After killing his own boss, Dial has De Ruse kidnapped and taken for a ride in a cyanide gas car, from which De Ruse escapes. Patient legwork and information from gamblers Zapparty and Parisi lead De Ruse back to Dial, who dies when he attempts to run off with the wife of his dead boss.

The strong points of the story are the settings and the characterization of amoral types George Dial, Francine Ley, and De Ruse. The romance between Ley and De Ruse is one of the most complex male-female relationships that Chandler ever attempted, owing much to Hammett's portrayal of Nick and Nora Charles in *The Thin Man* (1935). The story introduces the gambling club, a setting that Chandler used increasingly, and employs abandoned stucco houses in the La Crescenta flood plain to amplify the rain motif wonderfully. But the story fails, despite the innovations, because of loose plot ends and the hero's lack of mythic resonance.

Chandler's plots often frayed at the ends because he was building scene by scene, refusing to discard good scenes that did not fit. Instead he adjusted the ending. The method he worked out was to abut dissimilar scenes, forcing the reader to absorb new characters and conflicts rather than permitting him to solve the story's "mystery." The source of this technique is revealed by a sentence describing the Club Egypt: "The balcony was high and the scene down below had a patterned look, like an overhead camera shot." He discovered that narrative transitions could not only be left out, with the reader/viewer inferring them, but that this gave the story a sense of the texture of modern life. In a genre dominated by plot conventions, in which readers were accustomed to trying to guess what the author/hero would do next, Chandler became the most unpredictable, and thus interesting, by omitting transitions and simply abutting his best scenes.

When he began to write, Chandler admitted, he had read only one or two detective novels. His sixth story, **"Spanish Blood"** (*Black Mask,* November 1935), shows that he was studying the work of Dashiell Hammett. Chandler's hero shares the first name of Hammett's Sam Spade, and the story's depiction of big-city political bosses owes to Hammett's *The Glass Key* (1931). That novel's theme of a man's loyalty to his best friend in spite of their love for the same woman appealed to Chandler's sense that he had not wronged Julian Pascal. This story also pays tribute to Hammett's stoolies in Joey and Max Chill, to his drug addicts in Stella La Motte, and to his Filipinos in Cefarino Toribo. These were staples of Hammett's Op stories.

In spite of its debts **"Spanish Blood"** is exceptionally well done. It has a credible hero with a code and a past: Sam Delaguerra's *Californio* grandfather was one of the country's first sheriffs. "My blood is Spanish, pure Spanish. Not nigger-Mex and not Yaqui-Mex," Delaguerra tells a white politician. His name ("of the war") gives him mythic stature. When he is pulled off the murder of his longtime friend Donegan Marr ("We used to carry the torch for the same girl") by an Inspector who suspects his objectivity, Delaguerra investigates on his own, finding at Marr's cabin the body of the suspected assassin, Assistant District Attorney Imlay. Through stoolies and underworld contacts, Delaguerra learns that the political bosses, in league with Police Commissioner Drew, wanted Imlay off their election ticket. Only Delaguerra and Commissioner Drew survive the meeting in which the hero confronts the bosses with the truth. Drew proposes to credit himself with an undercover investigation that exposed the corruption. A realist, Delaguerra agrees. The story concludes with a twist when he visits Belle Marr and reveals that she, in fact, killed her husband. But since Marr covered up for her, intending that no one know, Sam says he will respect his friend's wish.

The story is well constructed and paced, the ending neither predictable nor overblown. The low-life characters are nearly as authentic as those of Hammett, but, what is more important, Chandler manages to make the desire for justice, which is the motive force, broad enough to accommodate both the idealism that drives Delaguerra to vindicate his dead friend and the cynicism of his realistic deal with Commissioner Drew.

The substance of **"Spanish Blood"** came from an actual incident that drew considerable press coverage. Charles Henry Crawford, the crime boss of Los Angeles, was gunned down 20 May 1931. Everyone's candidate for the rap was Guy McAfee, who had joined the L.A.P.D. after seeing a policeman roll a drunk and had risen through the vice squad to control Los Angeles casinos and gambling.

But it turned out that the killer was an exceptionally good-looking Deputy District Attorney and candidate for judge known as Handsome Dave Clark.

In **"Guns at Cyrano's"** (*Black Mask,* January 1936) Chandler continued his search for a persona and a hero. Told in the third person, this story introduces Ted Malvern (Ted Carmady in later editions.) He attempts to free blonde Jean Adrian and boxer Duke Targo from extortion by racketeers, but discovers that they in turn are blackmailing a local politician. The unexpectedly moral politician shoots the crime boss who uses him and then commits suicide. Since neither Targo nor Adrian garner any reader sympathy, the plot falls flat. In the resolution Chandler shot himself in the foot by explaining why one of the hirelings hadn't killed Jean in the opening scene.

Nevertheless, **"Guns at Cyrano's"** is an important story. Chandler worked hard to give his hero some humanity. Malvern pays attention to the lives of "little people," such as elevator operators, cigar-counter girls, and doormen. He gives the bellboys in his hotel five-dollar bills when they imply they're hungry. "Malvern the All-American sucker," he says of himself, "a guy that plays with the help and carries the torch for stray broads." As a hero Malvern fails because of such obvious pandering, and because Chandler makes him the scion of a fortune accumulated through political corruption. Saddled with wealth, Chandler's original sin, Malvern can't possibly become a democratic hero.

Chandler's mastery of repartee and ability to stretch the accepted generic limits of sex and violence had also advanced. Malvern's best lines are unpredictable. "I see our next trip is all arranged for," he says to his kidnapper when they pass a hearse. As in **"Killer in the Rain,"** Chandler finds new ways to substitute death for sex. When Malvern reports the bellboy's death to Jean, he uses its shock value as part of his seduction technique. "There's something horrible about you!" says Jean. "Something—satanic. You come here and tell me that another man has been killed—and then you kiss me. It isn't real." In a clever manipulation of archetypal plot situation and sexual nuance, Chandler has Malvern rephrase this charge: "There's something horrible about any man that goes suddenly gaga over another man's woman." When Jean exclaims "I'm not his woman," she justifies, in the masculine code, a seduction technique of kisses and death that even Chandler recognized as macabre.

The first seven stories have a similarity in plot deeper than their details. In his first story Chandler discovered the traitorous woman who causes her lovers' deaths in her quest for fame or money. He used variations on this type over and over, not because he was misogynic but because the type set up intense reactions among the men Chandler arrayed around her. He did not pretend to be able to write about women; men were the readers and principal characters of *Black Mask* stories. Once he discovered that this type solved all his plot problems, Chandler stuck with what worked, since by his own admission he was inept with narrative structure.

Resolving the relationship of the detective to the femme fatale was not as easy. Ideally the detective should have a love relation with her so that the reader felt the hero's life was threatened. In **"Spanish Blood"** and **"Nevada Gas"** Chandler made his detective the present or former lover of a woman who has been or may be won by another man. This detective, like Merimée's Navarro, is part of the triangle. But when Chandler allowed his detective to seduce the traitorous female in **"Guns at Cyrano's"** the triangle posed formula problems. Sentimental himself, Chandler couldn't end his detective's liaison in other than maudlin fashion.

Hammett did not offer Chandler any clues here. In "The Girl with the Silver Eyes" Hammett had sent Jean Delano (the model for Jean Adrian and "Silver Wig," Mona Mesarvey) to prison; at the end of *The Maltese Falcon* he sent Brigid O'Shaughnessy to probable death. But as Chandler's hero developed, sentimentality became his distinguishing feature; without it he had no special generic identity. The solution was to create a love triangle or circle (in the case of Carmen Dravec) in which one male was an analogue for the detective, who would be threatened symbolically. In **"Killer in the Rain"** Chandler hit on the first part of the solution with Carmen and her attraction to the detective, but not until **"The Curtain"** did he have his detective repeat the steps that led to Dud O'Mara's death at the hands of his stepson. These two subplots lay in loose relation until Chandler united them in *The Big Sleep*.

"The Man Who Liked Dogs"

Although the influence of Hammett reappears, Chandler soon passed from his sway to that of Ernest Hemingway, whose reliance on nouns and verbs, and short simple sentences connected by "and" are evident in **"The Man Who Liked Dogs"** (*Black Mask*, March 1936). Told in the first person, this story concerns detective Ted Carmady, whom the reader meets engaged in the humble work of checking veterinarians to find a dog: "There was a brand-new aluminum-grey DeSoto sedan in front of the door. I walked around that and went up three white steps, through a glass door and up three more carpeted steps. I rang a bell on the wall. Instantly a dozen dog voices began to shake the roof. While they bayed and howled and yapped I looked at a small alcove office with a rolltop desk and a waiting room with mission leather chairs and three diplomas on the wall, at a mission table scattered with copies of the *Dog Fancier's Gazette*."

Carmady's code is an honest day's work for an honest dollar: when Chief Fulwider and Galbraith discuss the $1,000 reward on Farmer Saint, Carmady says, "You cut me out. . . . I'm on straight salary and expenses." Resistance to monetary corruption and sympathy for small people define Chandler's detective distinctly for the first time. He looks for a lost girl, Isobel Snare; bawls out Chief Fulwider ("You cleaned the town up once and you can do it again"); befriends ex-cop Red Norgard, and sympathizes with Diana and Jerry Saint.

Hemingway's code of courage is evident in the unreal amount of punishment that Carmady absorbs, though the way he shakes off the effects of morphine and alcohol still owes to Hammett (see "The Temple of the Holy Grail" in *The Dain Curse*). But dominating these influences is the sense of place and contemporary interest that Chandler imparts to this story. Not only is Bay City based on Santa Monica, but Chief Fulwider is a civic booster of the sort that dominated Los Angeles in the 1920s, much to Chandler's disgust: "Our little city is small, but very, very clean. I look out of my west window and I see the Pacific Ocean. Nothing cleaner than that. On the north Arguello Boulevard and the foothills. On the east the finest little business section you would want to see and beyond it a paradise of well-kept homes and gardens." Other details, from the "disused interurban right of way, beyond which stretched a waste of Japanese truck gardens" to the gambling ship *Montecito* and its water taxis, are authentic. Beginning with the *Johanna Smith* and *Monfalcone* in 1928, gambling ships operated beyond the two-mile territorial limit off Long Beach. Chandler was probably most impressed by the July 1935, storming of the *Monte Carlo,* when six men with automatic weapons seized the boat, chained the crew, and stole $35,000 in cash and jewels from passengers.

So confident was Chandler in this story that he began to experiment with his tone. There are jokes in Spanish: the sanitarium where Carmady is drugged, imprisoned, and shot at is on Descanso ("rest") Street. There are topical references: the namesake of the gambling ship *Montecito* is a community north of Los Angeles with many millionaires. And there are multiple similes: "His eyes stuck out like peeled eggs. A thin trickle of saliva showed in the fat crease at the corner. He shut his mouth with all the deliberation of a steam shovel." Chandler wrote later that "to break the mood of the scene with some completely irrelevant wisecrack without entirely losing the mood—these small things for me stand in lieu of accomplishment. My theory of fiction writing is that the objective method has hardly been scratched, that if you know how to use it you can tell more in a paragraph than the probing writers can tell in a chapter."

For his first story outside *Black Mask* Chandler created another hero, perhaps wishing to keep Carmady within the pages of the magazine that nurtured him. Undercover vice-squad detective Peter Anglich appears only in **"Noon Street Nemesis,"** later retitled **"Pickup on Noon Street"** (*Detective Fiction Weekly,* May 1936.) A less interesting hero, he seems to exist to let his author into the black flophouses and "cheat spots" of the Central District. These hovels are supposed to be as much part of the fabric of crime and fraudulence as Trimmer Waltz's Juggernaut Club and actor John Vidaury's Hollywood suite.

As in **"Smart-Aleck Kill"** and **"Blackmailers Don't Shoot,"** the plot depicts the blackmail of a Hollywood figure by a racketeer. Again it turns out that the actor arranged the threats in order to revive his career. The subplot concerns Anglich's efforts to return a bedraggled girl named Token Ware to decent society. The sketches of the cook at the Bella Donna Diner, the clerk at the Surprise Hotel, and Rufe, Trimmer Waltz's bodyguard, were homework for Chandler's return to Central in **"Try the Girl."** The settings and social classes it surveys make this an interesting story, but the scenes are so disjunctive, united only by the denouement, that the reader struggles to make sense of them.

CARMADY RETURNS

With **"Goldfish"** (*Black Mask,* June 1936) Chandler wrote the first of three stories in a row concerning Carmady, the detective of **"The Man Who Liked Dogs."** There are new elements: the story takes place in Olympia, Washington, and Westport, California, and the crime has already occurred. Wally Sype was caught stealing the famous Leander pearls and told his cellmate about the unrecovered loot. As the story is told, the cellmate is hiding because he knows too much, comforted only by the goldfish of the title, which becomes a symbol for humanity.

In **"The Curtain"** (*Black Mask,* September 1936) Chandler returned to the first-person point of view and his favorite plot. This time he set the love triangle of Larry Batzel and Dud O'Mara for Mona Mesarvey at one remove from Carmady, allowing him to avoid the sentimental excess that marred the end of **"Nevada Gas."** In the death of Batzel, which opens the story (repeating the male loyalty theme of **"Spanish Blood"**) and his subsequent discovery that O'Mara is probably dead too, Carmady sees the fate that awaits him if he also succumbs to the temptations of **"Silver Wig"** Mona Mesarvey.

The hero of this story is basically the Marlowe of *The Big Sleep,* for which this story provided the basic plot. He is a working detective who calls on General Dade Winslow (the model for General Sternwood) and affirms the primacy of his code by turning down Winslow's offer of $1,000. He reveals his other important quality, sentimentality, when he takes the job of finding Dud O'Mara, whom he suspects is dead, though he does not want to tell the General. He likes the General, his pioneer heritage, and his love of O'Mara. Earlier, tougher versions of Chandler's private eye could have cared less. But Chandler, certain of his discovery now, made Marlowe quick to defend this feeling. When Lieutenant Roof snubs his effort to protect the General from news of O'Mara's death, Carmady responds "Maybe I'd go pretty far to attend to that sentiment."

In spite of improbabilities such as Carmady shooting accurately with his hands cuffed behind him, this story ranks among Chandler's best efforts. The repartee is crisp and unpredictable. Like Francine Ley and Jean Adrian, Mona Mesarvey is a strong, independent woman able to match Carmady's wisecracks. It is important, in the convention of the "blonde" that Chandler exploited, for her platinum wig to fall off at the moment of truth, revealing her honest brunette heart. Chandler united his best motifs, from the rain to the oil boom, with a theme that he carried through the story from start to end: money corrupts. From the General's initial offer to the detective's discovery that Dade Winslow Trevillyan is "a little lad that likes money," Chandler pursues the sickness of wealth.

For **"Try the Girl"** (*Black Mask,* January 1937) Chandler added new facets to Carmady's character: a past on the police force and a dash of self-criticism. Cruising the Central district, he meets Steve Skalla, a white version of the giant Rufe. Skalla involves him in the death of the owner of Shamey's bar, where Skalla goes in search of his old flame Beulah. Skalla flees, but Carmady traces Beulah through interviews with decrepit Violet Shamey and Dave Martineau, studio manager at KLBL radio, where Beulah hosts the Jumbo Candy Bar program. Before he reaches Beulah, he accidentally tips Mrs. Martineau to her husband's infidelities: when Martineau turns up dead in Beulah's bed, Carmady suspects his wife, but Skalla arrives and says he committed the murder earlier. Mrs. Martineau shoots him, but when Beulah arrives Carmady finds that actually she killed Martineau. In a finale borrowed from **"Spanish Blood,"** Carmady helps cover up Beulah's crime.

This story again stretched the generic conventions with regard to sex. To justify Beulah's claim of self-defense, Carmady beats her and tears her clothes to simulate an attack. "I hadn't even kissed her," he notes. "I could have done that at least. She wouldn't have minded any more than the rest of the knocking about I gave her." The sexual tension thus generated is dissipated with highly symbolic action, followed by death: "We rode the rest of the night, first in separate cars to hide hers in my garage, then in mine. We rode up the coast and had coffee and sandwiches in Malibu, then on up and over. . . . He died at two-thirty the same afternoon. She was holding one of his huge, limp fingers, but he didn't know her from the Queen of Siam."

This is a more refined technique than he used in **"Killer in the Rain,"** but Chandler shows in **"Try the Girl"** that he can manipulate these leers for humor too, as when he portrays Violet Shamey: "She got up out of the chair, sneezed, almost lost her bathrobe, slapped it back against her stomach and stared at me coldly. 'No peekin,' she said, and wagged a finger at me and went out of the room again, hitting the side of the door casement on her way."

Such a scene is balanced by a new self-critical element in Carmady's character. After he gets Violet Shamey drunk to obtain information, he feels badly: "I was a nice boy, trying to get along. Yes, I was a swell guy. I liked knowing myself. I was the kind of guy who chiseled a sodden old wreck out of her life secrets to win a ten-dollar bet."

Chandler was also finding new ways to avoid the clichés and stereotypes of the genre. From Hemingway he learned to understate the real emotion: "She began to laugh. Then she went over to the mirror and looked at herself. She began to cry." His similes and hyperboles, though growing from the fad for "wisecracks," became ways to avoid clichéd descriptions. Chandler wrote that "except for the motor horns, the distant hum of traffic up on Sunset Boulevard wasn't unlike the drone of bees." If he had written that the hum of traffic was like the drone of bees, readers would have yawned. By employing the cliché in a double negation, he ironically indicates both its utility and emptiness. The horns make the distant traffic *completely* unlike the drone of bees. Chandler's famous similes begin in this simultaneous dependence on and desire to burlesque conventional description: "The silence of that house was what made me go in. It was one of those utterly dead silences that come after an explosion. Or perhaps I hadn't eaten enough dinner. Anyway I went in."

Once he began to mock the conventions, it was logical for Chandler to extend the burlesque by intruding on his narrator's thoughts. He tried it in the last scenes of **"Try the Girl."** Hearing Mrs. Martineau's confession of how her husband's trysts led to her attempt to kill him, Carmady remarks:

> "The story," I said: "I know how you felt. I've read it in the love mags myself."

> "Yes, Well, he said there was something about Miss Baring he had to see her about on account of the studio and it was nothing personal, never had been, never would be—"

> "My Gawd," I said, "I know that too. I know what he'd feed you. We've got a dead man lying around here. We've got to do something, even if he was just your husband."

A writer who can move smoothly from such satire to the sentimental conclusion of **"Try the Girl"** has clearly mastered the nuances of tone.

CHANDLER LEAVES *BLACK MASK*

"Try the Girl" was Carmady's last appearance. Along with several other writers, Chandler stopped submitting to *Black Mask* when its new owners fired editor "Cap" Shaw. Chandler continued the character under the name of John Dalmas in *Dime Detective*, where he published **"Mandarin's Jade"** in November 1937. An excellent story, which Chandler used in *Farewell, My Lovely*, this piece features an exemplary cast of minor characters.

Lindley Paul hires Dalmas to help ransom a jade necklace, but Paul is beaten to death by thugs. Dalmas meets Carol Pride, a police chief's daughter turned journalist, whose contacts turn up most of his leads. Her imperfections ("an upper lip a shade too long and a mouth more than a shade too wide"), like those of Steve Skalla, mark her as a serious character, unlike the standard types of the genre. Dalmas tells her, "You've got the sweetest set of nerves I ever met on a woman," and Chandler notes that she "held her light as steadily as any tough old homicide veteran." Like most positive female characters in Chandler, she holds her own in repartee; in several places she initiates double entendres: "I saw your little light flickering around down in the hollow and it seemed to me it was pretty cold for young love—if they use lights." Chandler so enjoyed setting these two wits in opposition that he sometimes let Carol dominate an exchange. It provided him with an occasion for authorial intrusion, as when Carol remarks: "Now you've got me doing the wisecracks."

Equally memorable are such minor characters as Second Planting, a Hollywood Indian whom Chandler surely saw in the streets of Los Angeles when he arrived, and his boss, Soukesian The Psychic, who represents the cultism of Los Angeles. Soukesian's cult fills the function of fraudulence that Chandler usually assigned to Hollywood: "I had a rough idea of what his racket would be and what kind of people would be his customers. . . . He would be an expert in frustrated women, in tricky, tangled love affairs, in wandering boys who hadn't written home, in whether to sell the property now or hold it another year, in whether this part will hurt my type with my public or improve it."

Chandler's detective is by this point such a flexible vehicle, ranging from tough to sentimental, that he can make witty observations on his own poverty: "I unlocked the communicating door, which looked better than just kicking the lock lightly—which had the same effect—and we went into the rest of the suite, which was a rust-red carpet with plenty of ink on it, five green filing cases, three of them full of California climate, an advertising calendar showing the Dionne quintuplets rolling around on a sky-blue floor, a few near walnut chairs, and the usual desk with the usual heel marks on it and the usual squeaky swivel chair behind it."

The plot of **"Mandarin's Jade,"** when unraveled, is a variation on the love triangle. Mrs. Prendergast has been playing her two lovers, Soukesian and Paul, against each other to get her necklace back. If one or both were killed, that simply eliminated blackmail. She seeks to draw Dalmas into the same pattern, asking him to investigate a bar near the Hotel Tremaine; when he does, he's sapped and nearly killed except for Carol's intervention. The teetotaling Carol stands as a dramatic foil to the drunken Mrs. Prendergast, giving a greater variety of female characters and more complexity of plot than Chandler had previously managed with the triangle.

"Red Wind" (*Dime Detective*, January 1938) is a lesser effort, despite its reputation. Having had success with unseasonable rain as a setting, Chandler set this story during the rasping hot Santa Ana winds of May, thought to promote irritability and crime. As in the previous story, the story centers on a stolen necklace and blackmail. Chandler acknowledges his source in an authorial intrusion: "I suppose you've read that story. About the wife and the real pearls and her telling her husband they were false?" "I've read it . . . Maugham," says Dalmas, alluding to Somerset Maugham's story "Mr. Know-all."

In the story Dalmas witnesses a murder in a bar, then in his apartment house runs into a woman described by the victim. Lola Barsaly wanted to buy back her pearls from the dead man because they were a present from an old love. Dalmas's work on her behalf leads him to confront tough cops Copernik and Ybarra and eventually to her husband, whom Dalmas finds with his mistress. The dead man had been blackmailing both Barsalys. Dalmas sets everything straight with everybody; he even has a cheap set of pearls made for Lola, hiding the fact that the originals, as in Maugham, were quality imitations. Such excess sentiment, present throughout, torpedoes the tale.

Chandler set aside Dalmas to try a different kind of detective in **"The King in Yellow"** (*Dime Detective,* March 1938). The hero is smoother and the plot capitalizes on contemporary interests. Hotel detective Steve Grayce loses his job when he throws out a famous jazz trombonist named King Leopardi, so he becomes a private detective. When the musician turns up dead in the bed of old girlfriend Dolores Chiozza, Grayce takes on the task of clearing her. It turns out that the murder avenges the suicide of a girl mistreated by Leopardi years earlier. Her brothers planned to kill him in the room where their sister died, but Grayce unwittingly interfered, so they killed him at Chiozza's apartment. In the resolution one brother kills the other, and Grayce allows the survivor to escape in return for a signed confession. The survivor commits suicide by running his car off the mountain highway, a finale Chandler reused in *The Lady in the Lake.*

While a competent piece of craftsmanship, **"The King in Yellow"** does little more than demonstrate Chandler's knowledge of music and tour the Bunker Hill shabbiness that he had already described so well. The plot has the usual holes: Why did the brothers send Leopardi a ransom note asking for $10,000? What is Jumbo Walters's function in the story? The story does not represent any advance in technique or theme.

With **"Bay City Blues"** (*Dime Detective,* June 1938) Chandler returned to Dalmas and a first-person narrator. This story had so much action and so many interesting characters that it begged to be developed; it became Chandler's fourth novel, *The Lady in the Lake.* The story grew from a new plot idea, the murder of one woman by another who is a vicious bitch with a history of using and discarding men. Dr. Leland Austrian's wife is murdered by his nurse Helen Matson, a "red-haired man-eater with no looks but a lot of outside curves." When Dalmas meets Matson she is at a gambling club, trying to blackmail the owner because Mrs. Austrian was his mistress and died after leaving his club. Helen is independent, audacious, and imperfect, like Chandler's positive female characters. But she is a redhead and the convention for the type prevails. She has already dumped Harry Matson, the colleague who ensnared Dalmas in the case, as well as Al De Spain, a demoted Bay City homicide detective modeled on Galbraith in **"The Man Who Liked Dogs."**

De Spain is a brutal sadist, whose beating of "Big Chin" Lorenz is often cited by critics as the most violent scene in Chandler's work. He cannot adequately be explained as an expansion of the genre's limits on violence. Despite Chandler's efforts to justify the scene through Dalmas's protest that "I felt sick at my stomach," most readers finish the two pages of close detail feeling they have witnessed something very foul. De Spain also commits the brutal execution and simulated rape of Helen, his old flame, for which he frames Dalmas. Incredibly, at the story's end Dalmas says, "The hell of it is I liked De

Spain. He had all the guts they ever made." Insofar as the story justifies De Spain, it puts Chandler uncomfortably close to Mickey Spillane, whom he professed to detest. The designation of De Spain as the villain in *The Lady in the Lake* suggests that Chandler realized his error in the short story.

Minor characters are developed in more detail than usual in Chandler's stories. Dr. Austrian turns out to have complex reasons for covering up his wife's murder; he shares the propensity of Donegan Marr (**"Spanish Blood"**) and Steve Skalla (**"Try the Girl"**) for protecting guilty lovers. Newsman Dolly Kincaid is a nice thumbnail portrait, as is De Spain's sidekick Shorty. Portrayed for the first time is Los Angeles homicide detective Violets McGee, a frequent source of cases for Chandler's detectives, so named because of his fondness for violet-scented breath mints.

Chandler set several of his stories at Big Bear Lake in the San Bernardino Mountains, a summer retreat that he and Cissy enjoyed. It appears in scenes of **"Spanish Blood"** and **"The King in Yellow."** With **"The Lady in the Lake"** (*Dime Detective,* January 1939) he set most of a story in the mountains. That the lake invigorated him is shown by the crisp, detailed descriptions of the scenery and the crowds of tourists: "Hundred-foot yellow pines probed at the clear blue sky. In the open spaces grew bright green manzanita and what was left of the wild irises and white and purple lupine and bugle flowers and desert paintbrush. The road dropped to the lake level and I began to pass flocks of camps and flocks of girls in shorts on bicycles, on motor scooters, walking all over the highway, or just sitting under trees showing off their legs. I saw enough beef on the hoof to stock a cattle ranch."

Chandler also enjoyed creating Deputy Sheriff Tinchfield, who is an expansion of house detective Kuvalich in **"Nevada Gas."** In contrast to his urban representatives of law Chandler made Tinchfield the apotheosis of justice and diligence. Chandler's ear for accents and colloquialisms played with the opportunities Tinchfield afforded. "You wait here, son. I'll be back in a frog squawk," he says, and later "Where at are you stayin', son?"

In plot, however, **"The Lady in the Lake"** repeats **"Bay City Blues."** A vicious redhead kills another woman and gets two men, Howard Melton and Bill Haines, to be her saps. Like De Spain, Melton seems to square with Dalmas, but he too has killed his wife. This similarity permitted Chandler to unite the plots in *The Lady in the Lake.* There are new motifs, cosmetics and doubling, but they are not much exploited. Howard Melton is a cosmetics executive, and Beryl Haines has hair "a dark red color with glints of blue in the shadows—dyed." She applies her rouge roughly, leaving prominent red blotches, and a guest at Goodwin's house uses a lipstick called "Carmen." Julia Melton and Beryl Haines look like sisters and are similarly promiscuous; Dalmas is not sure which is which in photos at first. But Chandler did not follow up the possibilities of these motifs.

PLANNING GREATER THINGS

As this succession of stories suggests, Chandler was enjoying a period of quality production. He began to plan *The Big Sleep* in 1938, and in March 1939 wrote out a schedule for other books. "Since all plans are foolish," he wrote, "let us make a plan." He described what became *Farewell, My Lovely, The High Window,* and a third novel never written. These were to support him as he wrote a "short, swift, tense, gorgeously written" drama called **"English Summer"** and "a set of six or seven fantastic stories," among which he listed **"The Bronze Door"** and **"The Disappearing Duke."** The novels were to "make enough money for me to move to England and to forget mystery writing," he wrote. As he embarked on this plan, Chandler cleared his desk of manuscripts and in new stories ventured from his usual material.

"Pearls are a Nuisance" (*Dime Detective,* April 1939) is one of his strangest and funniest stories. On the one hand, it is a satire in which Chandler pits the English and American mystery schools against each other and lampoons the conventions of all detective fiction. On the other hand, as several critics have noted, its scenes are blatantly homoerotic.

The story is told by a first-person narrator, Walter Gage, who speaks the King's English: "I cannot seem to change my speech. . . . my father and mother were both severe purists in the New England tradition, and the vernacular has never come naturally to my lips, even while I was in college." Pushed by his prim fiancée Ellen Macintosh, Gage tries to recover a dowager's fake pearl necklace (a satire on **"Mandarin's Jade"** and **"Red Wind"**). This leads him to her recently departed chauffeur, Henry Eichelberger. The two fight, drink, argue, wake up in the same bed, and decide to cooperate in solving the case; they are Natty Bumppo and Chingachgook, Huck and Jim, in the storied land of male camaraderie. It turns out that the pearls are real, given by an admirer who could afford them but didn't want the dowager to worry (a twist on Maugham's "Mr. Know-all.") The admirer ransoms them, and the heroes engage in a round of carousing. At last the apparently naive Gage turns up Henry, who had the pearls all along.

Through the interleaving of formal and vernacular speech Chandler makes several technical points about dialogue. On the whole it is a successful piece of humor, the only pure comedy among Chandler's stories, but it has provided fuel for critics, such as Gershon Legman, who argue that "Chandler's Marlowe is clearly homosexual—a butterfly, as the Chinese say, dreaming that he is a man."

Less interesting is the widely anthologized **"Trouble is My Business"** (*Dime Detective,* August 1939), told by John Dalmas in the first person. He is hired by Anna Halsey for a difficult case involving heir Gerald Jeeter and his lover Harriet Huntress, a friend of gangster Marty Estel. Jeeter's father wants Huntress to vanish. Dalmas investigates and finds that the previous detective on the case died; then he's held up by two thugs, one of whom takes a shot at him and is later killed by the Jeeters' chauffeur. Dalmas is warned off the case by gangster Estel, but solves it when he finds Gerald dead in Harriet's closet, killed by the chauffeur. It's an unsatisfying plot and hardly anything in Chandler's repertoire of wisecracks, femmes fatales, or brutality seems to click. It has a weariness that suggests he just wanted it off his desk.

Chandler finally succumbed to the "slicks" when he wrote **"I'll Be Waiting"** (*Saturday Evening Post,* 14 October 1939). The plot is a mishmash of earlier stories. Hotel detective Tony Resick is a tubby Steve Grayce (**"The King in Yellow"**). He finds Eve Cressy (Eve Millar) listening to Benny Goodman in the lobby (where Grayce listened to Leopardi). She's waiting for her ex-husband, whom she "put in a bad place" (like Beulah in **"Try the Girl"**). Tony's hoodlum brother arrives and tells Tony that the "trouble boys" are waiting for her ex-husband because he welshed on a gambling scheme. But he is already in the next room, unknown to Eve, so Tony sneaks him out without Eve learning that he came. Later he hears that both his brother and her ex-husband are dead and returns to Eve, one of Chandler's tough/tender women, to revel in his bittersweet knowledge. Like **"The King in Yellow,"** this story has informed appreciations of jazz and classical music. It was a powerful, successful piece for the *Post,* yet Chandler disliked it: "It was too studied, too careful. I just don't take to that sort of writing. The story was all right, but I could have written it much better in my own way, without trying to be smooth and polished, because that is not my talent. I'm an improviser, and perhaps at times an innovator."

Chandler wrote two more short stories about his detective, but only one is of consequence. **"No Crime in the Mountains"** (*Detective Story,* September 1941) uses the Big Bear Lake setting of **"The Lady in the Lake"** and was incorporated into the novel. The portrait of Sheriff Baron repeats that of Tinchfield, and his assistant Andy is a development of Tinchfield's helper Paul Loomis. Detective John Evans, telling the story in the first person, is called to Puma Lake to see Fred Lacey, only to find him dead. An Oriental named Charlie saps Evans and spirits away his body. The rest of the plot explains how the five hundred real dollars that Lacey stuffed in the toe of his wife's shoe turned into five hundred counterfeit dollars. The answer is that the Japanese Charlie and Nazi Frank Leuders are counterfeiting U.S. currency to weaken the economy. The plot is so bad that one critic suggests Leuders should have shot the narrator instead of himself. There are a few good scenes in the resort town of Indian Head, but the story is most notable for its World War II hysteria.

The other short detective story was written in the late fifties, when Chandler had lost his powers but Philip Marlowe was a known name. It has several titles: **"Marlowe Takes on the Syndicate," "Wrong Pigeon," "Philip Marlowe's Last Case,"** and most commonly **"The Pencil."** It is an awful pastiche of dated tough-guy dialogue, modern revelations about the Cosa Nostra, and predictable plotting. Chandler fans should avoid it.

FANTASTIC STORIES

As his work plans reveal, "the fantastic genre" tempted Chandler in the late 1930s when he was bored by the detective story. Although he was highly critical of science fiction, he was fascinated by the idea of characters who could disappear. **"The Bronze Door"** (*Unknown*, November 1939) and **"Professor Bingo's Snuff"** (*Park East*, June/August 1951) combine this mildly supernatural motif with mystery plots. The second, more interesting story concerns a man who kills his boarder, after the latter sleeps with the man's wife and strangles her. He doesn't care about his wife; he simply takes advantage of the invisibility afforded by Professor Bingo's Snuff to carry out his fantasies. His tendency to make himself invisible in bathrooms and to meet strong men strengthens the Legman school of analysis.

There is also an unfinished Marlowe story titled **"The Poodle Springs Story,"** which details the married life of Marlowe and Linda Loring after *Playback*. They move to a thinly disguised version of Palm Springs, trade backchat, and become parodies of themselves: "I browsed on her eyebrows and her lashes, which were long and tickly," says Marlowe. He runs into gangster Manny Lipshultz, but the manuscript ends just when the reader has reason to hope that Lipshultz will bump off this travesty of the once-noble Marlowe.

"ENGLISH SUMMER"

"English Summer: A Gothic Romance" is a longish story that Chandler mentioned in his writing plan of 1939, but did not finish until the mid-fifties. First-person narrator John Paringdon tells the story, set in the English country cottage of Edward Crandell. The visiting narrator had a longstanding, unreciprocated crush on Millicent, Crandell's wife, so every encounter is pregnant with a Jamesian delicacy of meaning and unexpressed emotion. They joke mildly about her swaggering husband; the narrator apologizes for his American expressions and habits. Indeed, he sounds a bit like Marlowe.

Down at the lake, the narrator meets Lady Lakenham, a temptress on a black stallion whose sexual significance is obvious to everyone but the author. The first chapter ends on their kiss. Almost immediately they arrive at her shambling estate; the exterior is woolly with vines, the interior ravaged. The second section ends with the pair in bed.

When he returns, Millicent asks Paringdon if he ever has loved her. He says yes, and on his way upstairs decides he must leave. Coming back down, he announces his decision and they have tea. Millicent says Edward is drunk; he had a quarrel with Lady Lakenham, and she lashed him with her crop and ran him down with her stallion. Paringdon realizes he is in the middle of a triangle, but when he goes to get his bag, he finds Crandell dead.

Here the plot line breaks. Paringdon becomes a detective; his first thought is to save Millicent by framing Edward. But she responds that she killed him because he was being

"cheap" and "a little more brutal than usual." Paringdon engineers a suicide scene and departs, intending never to see Millicent again.

For three weeks he hides, but a constable and a Scotland Yard man catch up with him. It's clear from their questions they know what happened. Paringdon sees Millicent at the inquest, but doesn't speak to her. Later he meets Lady Lakenham by Green Park in Piccadilly; she's still a man-eater and wants him to come see her in her rooms the next day. He agrees, knowing that he is leaving before then. The story ends: "I stood there for what seemed a long, long time, looking after nothing. There was nothing to look after."

The story shares many features of *The Long Goodbye*, such as the taking of tea with the murderess, and it would be interesting to know if these were in the 1939 sketch or added later. While intriguing, the story is seriously flawed by the break in tone and Chandler's inability to control the sexual motif. Unfortunately, this was as close as he came to his dream of escaping the detective genre.

James Wolcott (essay date 1995)

SOURCE: "Raymond Chandler's Smoking Gun," in *The New Yorker*, Vol. LXXI, No. 29, September 25, 1995, pp. 99-102, 104.

[*In the following essay, Wolcott discusses Chandler's works in light of current literary tastes.*]

Lined up on the shelves in their glossy black jackets, the books constituting the Library of America resemble tiny, shiny coffins. Modelled on the portable French Pléiades editions of classic authors, the Library of America is the final resting place for writers—where they receive their induction into the canon and a chance for rediscovery by the common reader, assuming there are any left. Until now, the authors whom the Library has chosen have been mostly safe and genteel—illustrious pilgrims in what Alfred Kazin has called "the American procession." With the induction of Raymond Chandler, the American procession sidesteps to fetch its latest recruit. The creator of Philip Marlowe and the man who brought a chin stubble of maturity to the cheeky face of cheap prose, Chandler is not only the first detective writer to be inaugurated into the hall of fame but the first outright popular-fiction practitioner—a genre artist. (Edgar Allan Poe, the original psychic astronaut in the spheres of science fiction, horror, and mystery, practiced metaphysical witchcraft using his skull as the bubbling pot, and was too oddball-baroque to be strictly categorized as a genre writer.) Chandler is also a bit of a reach for the Library of America roster because an American is what he didn't feel himself deep down to be. "I always feel like a phoney when I say 'we Americans' because basically I never have and never will feel quite a native," he wrote his London publisher, Hamish Hamilton, in 1954. His sensibility was transatlantic, a marriage of English taste and American mobility, the mental finery of Henry James hooked up to an exhaust pipe. An expatriate in his own country, Chandler spiritualized the smog.

Born in Chicago in 1888, Chandler was taken to England by his mother after his parents divorced. He was educated in Greek and Latin at Dulwich (the same school as P. G. Wodehouse), his young mind gold-leafed with the glory of chivalry. His alter ego Philip Marlowe was first named Mallory, an allusion to "Le Morte d'Arthur." Like Marlowe, Chandler prided himself on being an inside outsider—a sensitive toughie possessing school-of-hard-knocks know-how about the workings of the real world, and lonesomely alienated from society at large. (To Marlowe, the rich are risen scum.) After serving with distinction during the First World War, Chandler returned to America and lived in California with his mother. Employed in the oil industry, he saw the shady side of business, and sometimes burst loose in drunken binges. In 1924, after his mother died, he married Cissy Pascal, a much older woman, to whom he was as slavishly devoted as Dr. Johnson was to his beloved Tetty.

Chandler was also an inside outsider as a writer, jimmying loose the iron-jawed formulas of pulp magazines like *Black Mask* and using the detective genre for his own artistic ends. Reading most pulp writers of that period, you could hear the slug of hot type and the rip of cheap panties. Chandler added a slash and splash of pictorial power. In "The Country Behind the Hill," Clive James observed, "When Chandler wrote casually of 'a service station glaring with wasted light' he was striking a note that Dashiell Hammett had never dreamed of." He also wrested the mystery novel away from the raised pinkie of the Lord Peter Wimsey tearoom set. Like Hemingway, whom Chandler admired and defended (though he couldn't resist taking a poke at him in *Farewell, My Lovely*: "'Who is this Hemingway person at all? A guy that keeps saying the same thing over and over until you begin to believe it must be good'"), he elevated a stiff manner to a stoic code. And, like Hemingway, he put a high premium on style, believing it the best investment a writer could make for posterity. Some styles endure. Others dry to a thick, cracked coat.

In recent years, Chandler's status as the neoclassical daddy of the *roman noir* has come under scrutiny for reasons that have nothing to do with prose. His political incorrectness has made him suspect. For every academic text analyst diagramming Chandler's tactics on a grid, one can find a jury of socially conscious types doing a sensitivity checklist on Chandler/Marlowe and finding him guiltier than H. L. Mencken. He is cited for bias against Jews, blacks, homosexuals, and Indians with hygiene problems ("His smell was the earthy smell of primitive man, and not the slimy dirt of cities."—*Farewell, My Lovely*). His women are faulted for being either playmate pinups or pathological nuts. Either way, they drain a man dry. Underlying the leftward tilt of these complaints against Chandler is the extreme individualism he lionized in the Marlowe novels. His famous credo from the essay "The Simple Art of Murder"—"But down these mean streets a man must go

who is not himself mean, who is neither tarnished nor afraid"—privileges the lone cowboy at the expense of group supervision. That way lies vigilantism. (A mean street plus a mean streak equals Mickey Spillane.)

What irks even some of Chandler's fellow-novelists is that Marlowe never came off his high horse. They find his attitudinizing annoying. Kingsley Amis complains, "There is . . . a moral pretentiousness whereby Marlowe is now and again made the vehicle for criticizing the sordid lives of Hollywood's denizens: the perverted producers, the writers drowing in bourbon and self-hatred, the chicks who will do absolutely anything to get a part—all that. Most of this comes ill from a private eye, even a comparatively honest one." James Ellroy, who considers the dominance of the great white hope a great white hoax, told *The Armchair Detective,* "My L.A. Quartet and 'American Tabloid' are designed to give crime fiction and violent intrigue back to the men who would really have perpetrated it—and they are *men* and they are *white men.* I see hardboiled crime fiction as a heavily ritualized transit horseshit and largely spun off of Raymond Chandler. Chandler is a very easy writer to imitate, which is why so many people have been able to adapt his formula with such success, but I hate that formula, and I hate its sensibility."

Chandler's strong presence on the page also accounts for the raft of revisionist versions (Robert Altman letting Elliott Gould out of the kennel to amble through *The Long Goodbye*) and parodies (from S. J. Perelman's "Farewell, My Lovely Appetizer" to the movie *Dead Men Don't Wear Plaid*), which over time have jumbled into kitsch pastiche—a cartoon of smoldering intrigue. The value of the Library of America edition is that it takes you back to those Los Angeles parlors when the varnish was new and the characters were speaking their lines for the first time.

The Library of America's collected Raymond Chandler runs a total of two thousand two hundred and seventy-five pages, in two volumes. It contains all his complete novels, a chunk of his pulp stories, his best-known essays, including "The Simple Art of Murder" and "Writers in Hollywood," the screenplay of James M. Cain's *Double Indemnity,* and some of his letters. Posterity may approve of all the devotion, but I think paying this much homage to that much wordage has done him a disservice. Given that Chandler's novels are all still available in paperback, installing such inferiorities as *The High Window* and *The Little Sister* on the permanent shelf is profitless, ditto publishing the screenplay of *Double Indemnity* which, minus the urgent smack of Billy Wilder's direction and Barbara Stanwyck's platinum finish, loses its zing. The five hundred and eighty pages of Chandler's stories for *Black Mask* and other pulp mags is even more wasteful. Aside from the bravura opening of **"Red Wind,"** the stories are generally no more interesting than the magazine garbage that Theodore Dreiser ground out between obstinate masterpieces. "Conant's face was a mask of fury. He balled his fist, took a jerky step forward. 'Why you—damn louse—.'" That is a typical moment from a story entitled **"Guns at Cyrano's."**

Chandler's first Marlowe novel, *The Big Sleep* (1939), is the one betraying the least rust and sounding the loudest heartbeat of animal vitality. Like Ian Fleming, with whom he corresponded, Chandler came late to writing novels—the pulp stories were tuning-up exercises for a mind that had ripened. James Bond and Philip Marlowe were both life-size fantasy molds. Indeed, Chandler was reluctant to release publicity photos of himself, fearing that readers might be put off at finding that the tough guy they thought wrote the books was in fact an older, milder owl. Maturity aside, the chief advantage that Chandler had over the pulp hacks was his mastery of the establishing shot. He wrote an opening scene as if he were looking through a wide-angle lens. The description of the Sternwood mansion, with which *The Big Sleep* begins, still holds its spell: "Over the entrance doors, which would have let in a troop of Indian elephants, there was a broad stained-glass panel showing a knight in dark armor rescuing a lady who was tied to a tree and didn't have any clothes on but some very long and convenient hair." So does Marlowe's interview with General Sternwood in the greenhouse, a fungus palace where the pale stalks suggest "the newly washed fingers of dead men" and the orchids smell like prostitutes.

As everyone knows, the story in *The Big Sleep* is bumpy with potholes (Chandler himself couldn't keep track of all the body traffic), but it doesn't matter; the novel barrels along on the nervous energy of a writer who has found his way out of hack formula and into his own personal terrain. Like Howard Hawks' 1946 film version, which remains the best adaptation of a Chandler novel (*The Long Goodbye* is more Altman than Chandler), the novel has the roomy ease and confidence of improvised jazz, free of the world-weariness that barbiturated the genre later, when the private eye became a stand-in for the existentialist living in a place without order, honor, or decent coffee. *The Big Sleep* also has a frisky air, with Marlowe establishing his credentials as a leg man ("The calves were beautiful, the ankles long and slim and with enough melodic line for a tone poem") and dishing out wisecracks ("Her face fell apart like a bride's pie crust") as if dealing from a fresh deck. The warning signals of self-caricature are sounded in the clever banter, where one can hear the dentures click:

"Cute, aren't I?" she said.

I said harshly: "Cute as a Filipino on Saturday night."

The Big Sleep was followed, in 1940, by *Farewell, My Lovely,* which was almost called "'Zounds, He Dies," forsooth. Another novel with outstanding set pieces (like the chapter beginning "The room was full of smoke," where Marlowe's concussion conjures a trance state), *Farewell, My Lovely* was the one mystery novel that Edmund Wilson singled out for stingy praise in his famous essay "Who Cares Who Killed Roger Ackroyd?" (first published in *The New Yorker*). Even so, when he came to the end of *Farewell, My Lovely* he experienced the diminuendo effect he felt with all mystery novels: "Because here again, as is so often the case, the explanation of the mysteries,

when it comes, is neither interesting nor plausible enough. It fails to justify the excitement produced by the picturesque and sinister happenings, and I cannot help feeling cheated."

In an era in which Patricia Cornwell conducts autopsy reports so thorough that the dead function as data banks, Elmore Leonard tattoos sleaze in the tropical colors of Hawaiian shirts, James Ellroy competes with Oliver Stone as the leading conspiracy theorist of late capitalism, Ed McBain turns the Eighty-seventh Precinct into Hieronymus Bosch, and Walter Mosley squires us (in his Easy Rawlins novels) through the Negro neighborhoods of postwar Los Angeles which lay on the outskirts of Marlowe's world, Wilson's complaints about the pinched focus of the detective novel sound fuddy-duddy. These days, we're less likely to feel cheated than overwhelmed by the wild variety of what the detective novel can do. Where Chandler insisted in his essay "Notes on the Mystery Story" that "the murderer must not be a loony," we've become accustomed to sociopaths and psychopaths pruning the populace as serial killers. Kinky sadism has become part of the everyday. The skullduggery in Chandler's novels seems admirably devoid of sick kicks compared with the hip nihilism of *Pulp Fiction* and *American Psycho*. He wrote as though pain hurt and life mattered.

But if Wilson's complaints about the detective novel have been outstripped by research-and-development in the field, that doesn't mean he was wrong about Chandler's limitations. Rereading *Farewell, My Lovely* and its successors, one shares Wilson's vision of dying quail as Marlowe's guided tour of the life styles of the rich and shameless narrows into a concern with cracking the case so that he can lumber back to his lonely office and do his jaw-firming exercises. The beautiful, deep-dyed descriptive passages of buildings, botanical life, rainfall, and car drives at night which one remembers best from Chandler are almost detachable from the logistical labor of getting Marlowe from Point A to Point B. Closing the case invariably involves talky explanations, and the dialogue seems rattled off from crib notes: "You didn't tell me about Brunette or the cards that were in those reefers or Amthor or Dr. Sonderborg or that little clue that set you on the path of the great solution," Anne Riordan, the sex interest in *Farewell, My Lovely* babbles in the novel's penultimate chapter. Although *Farewell, My Lovely* was only Marlowe's second outing, his persona is already being discussed in terms of the quixotic. After he answers Riordan's query about the cards in the reefers, etc., she mocks him in that special mocking way women have:

"You're so marvelous," she said. "So brave, so determined and you work for so little money. Everybody bats you over the head and chokes you and smacks your jaw and fills you with morphine, but you just keep right on hitting between tackle and end until they're all worn out. What makes you so wonderful?"

"Go on," I growled. "Spill it."

Anne Riordan said thoughtfully: "I'd like to be kissed, damn you!"

Everything in Chandler is aimed right at the kisser.

The novel that is Chandler's most overt fumble for truth and his most earnest effort to bend the prison bars of the genre is *The Long Goodbye*, published in this country in 1954. Written while his wife, Cissy, was dying, *The Long Goodbye* took more out of him than any other book. "I watched my wife die by half-inches and I wrote my best book in the agony of that knowledge," he confided in a letter. After Cissy's death, he drank even more heavily than usual and, in this depression, attempted suicide. Although another novel (*Playback*) followed, *The Long Goodbye* carries the parchment seal of a last testament. The novel is a study in loyalty and betrayal, its object lesson being an alcoholic named Terry Lennox, whose surgically repaired face is a shattered mirror of Marlowe's (and Chandler's). Indeed, *The Long Goodbye* is a double mirror, its other reflection belonging to Roger Wade, a mountain-size novelist whose creative powers have crumbled. Like Lennox and Chandler, Wade is a heavy boozer. The novel thus dramatizes Chandler's fear of being a broken-down drunk and a spent force. It's also his way of confronting his place in the American canon, Terry Lennox being an F. Scott Fitzgerald boy-angel, beautiful and damned, while Roger Wade compares himself to Fitzgerald but behaves like Hemingway. (In Altman's version, Wade was played by Sterling Hayden, in full Papa beard.) *The Long Goodbye* requires more psychological insight than earlier Marlowes. In the past, Marlowe could play off cheap hoods and classy dames as if they were bumpers in a pinball machine. Here Chandler has to create foes and allies that have a rounded existence independent of Marlowe's.

He isn't up to it. Of the two alter egos, Wade is the more clumsily realized—a deflated blowhard spouting about what a fraud he is, like a ham actor holding court. The novel is marred by the kind of rhetorical posturing from Marlowe that miffed Kingsley Amis. While cooling his heels at the Wade estate, Marlowe reflects, "I might even have got rich—small-town rich, an eight-room house, two cars in the garage, chicken every Sunday and the *Reader's Digest* on the living room table, the wife with a cast iron permanent and me with a brain like a sack of Portland cement. You take it, friend. I'll take the big sordid dirty crooked city." Many consider *The Long Goodbye* Chandler's autumnal masterpiece, but the only part I enjoyed reading this second time was a funny riff that Marlowe does on the different categories of blondes—an instant lecture in pop anthropology which recalls the unforced momentum of *The Big Sleep*. After doing justice to alcoholic blondes and perky blondes, Marlowe muses:

> There is the pale, pale blonde with anemia of some non-fatal but incurable type. She is very languid and very shadowy and she speaks softly out of nowhere and you can't lay a finger on her because in the first place you don't want to and in the second place she is reading "The Waste Land" or Dante in the original, or Kafka or Kierkegaard or studying Provençal. She adores music and when the New York Philharmonic is playing Hindemith she can tell you which one of the six bass viols came in a quarter of a beat too late. I hear Toscanini can also. That makes two of them.

The paragraph closes like a clasp. After *The Long Goodbye*, there wasn't anything left to do with Marlowe but pair him off with a marriageable woman and watch him squirm. Chandler's last completed novel, *Playback* (the posthumous *Poodle Springs* was completed by Robert B. Parker), is a halfhearted effort in which he goes sentimental on us with love scenes too goopy to quote, yet it's somehow gratifying that Marlowe remains a leg man to the end: "Still satisfied with my legs?" his future fiancée, Linda Loring, asks dreamily, and although Marlowe makes a flip reply, you know he's thinking, Yes, yes, a million times yes. When Marlowe deflects her proposal of marriage by saying, "I'm a tired hack with a doubtful future," it's clear who's really doing the talking. A year after *Playback* was published, Raymond Chandler died in California, on March 26, 1959.

The Library of America edition concludes with a selection of Chandler's letters. When a book of Chandler's complete letters, edited by Frank MacShane, was published, in 1981, the critic and mystery maven Julian Symons praised their lively touches but said that no one who read them would think the better of Chandler himself afterward. The letters, he said, tar Chandler as coarse, competitive, and anti-intellectual. To me, they had a tonic effect. Far from being disillusioning, the letters portray Chandler as an old pro taking a breather in the corner between rounds. Alternately belligerent and touchingly generous, he surfaces in his correspondence as an appealing sorehead, touchy about his turf, fretful of his status, proud of his flair for the verbal jugular. The writer he most reminds me of is John O'Hara, another pugnacious workhorse. (O'Hara's defiant boast "I don't consult dictionaries, dictionaries consult me" finds its echo in Chandler's "When I split an infinitive, God damn it, I split it so it will stay split.") Many of the letters that offended Symons with their slurs are excluded from the Library of America edition—no great loss. It would be unfair and mistaken, though, to leave the impression that Chandler was a one-man defamation league. A grim wisecrack like "Los Angeles has nothing for me anymore. It's only a question of time until a Gentile has to wear an armband there" is balanced by wry, worldly comments on Jews and other minorities which bear no resemblance to hate talk. More sorely missed are the passing shots Chandler took at the passing scene, such as his putdown of *A Place in the Sun* ("They ought to have called it 'Speedboats for Breakfast'") and his horror at what passes for elegance in La Jolla ("Puce dinner jackets!").

The letters that are included in the Library of America edition mostly concern issues of craft and style, with an occasional outburst against those who deny that the private-eye genre has both. Of *The Maltese Falcon* Chandler wrote, "Frankly, I can conceive of better writing and a more tender and warm attitude to life, and a more flowery ending; but by God, if you can show me twenty books written approximately 20 years back that have as much guts and life now, I'll eat them between slices of Edmund Wilson's head." The last letter expresses Chandler's bewilderment over a comment made about a rival, John Dickson Carr—that Carr was good at plotting a book but hated the actual writing. "A writer who hates the actual writing, who gets no joy out of the creation of magic by words, to me is simply not a writer at all," Chandler exclaims. "The actual writing is what you live for. The rest is something you have to get through in order to arrive at the point. How can you hate the actual writing? . . . How can you hate the magic which makes of a paragraph or a sentence or a line of dialogue or a description something in the nature of a new creation?" In the best pages of the Marlowe novels, you can feel Chandler's creative pleasure; the lawns wet with rain seem minted in Heaven. In the worst pages, the mean streets that Marlowe walks echo with the hollow footsteps of a movie back lot. The bad pages may outnumber the good, but it's the good pages that stick, if you're lucky. Raymond Chandler was lucky.

Donald Lyons (essay date 1995)

SOURCE: A review of *Raymond Chandler: Stories & Early Novels* and *Later Novels & Other Writings,* in *The American Spectator,* Vol. 28, No. 11, November, 1995, pp. 78-9.

[*In the following review, Lyons favorably critiques the Library of America's two-volume edition of Chandler's collected writing.*]

The Library of America has just issued a two-volume edition of Raymond Chandler—pulp fiction on Olympus! When word came to Chandler in the Elysian Fields that he was to report for a meeting with Emerson and Melville, he must have felt, somewhat like his hero Philip Marlowe:

> It was about eleven o'clock in the morning, mid October, with the sun not shining and a look of hard wet rain in the clearness of the foothills. I was wearing my powder-blue suit, with dark blue shirt, tie and display handkerchief, black brogues, black wool socks with dark blue clocks on them. I was neat, clean, shaved, and sober, and I didn't care who knew it. I was everything the well-dressed private detective ought to be. I was calling on four million dollars.

Thus begins Chandler's first novel, *The Big Sleep.* At the time of its publication in 1939, the art of detective fiction had only half-emerged from the chrysalis of the cheap magazines. Dashiell Hammett was his only weighty predecessor, and Chandler gave Hammett full marks for breaking away from the genteel school of detecting exquisites, the likes of Lord Peter Wimsey and Hercule Poirot. As Chandler wrote in his essay "The Simple Art of Murder," included here, Hammett gave "murder back to the kind of people that commit it for reasons."

But Chandler sought to do more than his predecessor, whose language, he thought, had "no overtones, no echo," and whose "mean streets" lacked the normative moral presence of a man "who is not himself mean, who is neither tarnished nor afraid." In Philip Marlowe he created such a man. First came a name: He had started out calling

his detectives things like Carmady, John Dalmas, and Walter Gage. Disastrous! Names for cops or insurance salesmen. He struck gold when he decided to echo the double trochee of his own name. Then a first-person voice. Then a place: Depression-scarred Los Angeles, a town of dirty money, sadistic cops, and dangerous dames. Marlowe's L.A. is a Hobbesian terrain of dry greed and joyless pleasure and, above all, a place of melancholy and loneliness:

> I walked to the windows and pulled the shades up and opened the windows wide. The night air came drifting in with a kind of stale sweetness that still remembered automobile exhausts and the streets of the city. I reached for my drink and drank it slowly.

This is from *The Big Sleep;* by the third book, *The High Window,* Chandler had perfected this vein of nocturnal ode (Marlowe is in his office):

> It was getting dark outside now. The rushing sound of the traffic had died a little and the air from the open window, not yet cool from the night, had that tired end-of-the-day smell of dust, automobile exhaust, sunlight rising from hot walls and sidewalks, the remote smell of food in a thousand restaurants, and perhaps, drifting down from the residential hills above Hollywood—if you had a nose like a hunting dog—a touch of that particular tomcat smell that eucalyptus trees give off in warm weather.

Chandler also made Marlowe a man of his populist and cranky times, with a drawerful of crotchets to prove it: "You can have a hangover from other things than alcohol. I had one from women. Women made me sick." "To hell with the rich. They made me sick." "A pansy has no iron in his bones, whatever he looks like." These attitudes go with the territory, and God knows contemporary detective fiction is correcting Marlowe's sexual and racial attitudes with a vengeance. The rich, though, and the cops—especially big-city cops—have remained the villains of the genre; the politically correct moral landscape of pulp fiction is now a tiresome and self-defeating cliché.

Born in Chicago in 1888, Raymond Chandler was taken to England at age seven by a strong mother who wanted to get the boy away from his alcoholic father. (Both of these elegant volumes include a useful and discursive chronology of his life.) He studied classics at Dulwich College, and came back to America in 1912; on the return voyage he made the acquaintance of a member of the rich Los Angeles Lloyd family. Chandler headed for L.A., and in 1917 joined the Canadian Army, with which he saw action, and was wounded, in France. Back in L.A. in 1919, he began an affair with Cissy Pascal, an older married woman who divorced in 1920 but did not marry Chandler until after the death of his disapproving mother.

He worked as an auditor for the Lloyd-owned South Basin oil company, and was fired in 1932 for "drunkenness and absenteeism." After a separation and reunion with Cissy, he was re-hired by the Lloyds, who gave him a generous stipend to devote himself to writing. Thereafter his life fell into the familiar pattern of acclaim, frustration (especially in screenwriting), and drink. But it was the early, pre-writing experiences that bear pondering when we look back from the perspective of the novels. . . .

Behind Chandler's rich language lie Hemingway's invention of a laconic American vernacular, Fitzgerald's sad urban romanticism, and a native wisecrack tradition going back at least to Twain. Some of it has not dated well, especially the patter of smart similes—"as shallow as enamel on a cafeteria tray," "empty as a headwaiter's smile." But as his best Chandler created a substantiated verbal and moral world.

And what of Chandler's numerous progeny? His immediate, embarrassingly close follower was Ross MacDonald, who in the 1960s attenuated Marlowe into the arty brooder Archer, adding little to the geography of Chandler's Southern California except for some chic ecological worrying. MacDonald specialized in improbable plots involving generations of familial crime; once taken very seriously, he is now perhaps underrated.

His other California heirs include the likable Sue Grafton, whose Kinsey Millhone is easily the best of the new breed of women PIs, though without anything like Chandler's palette. Walter Mosley brings a black PI voice to his period L.A. When we read the opening of his *Devil in a Blue Dress,* "I was surprised to see a white man walk into Joppy's bar," we know where we are—in a re-imagined *Farewell, My Lovely.*

Chandler's one successor who has truly brought something new to the genre is John D. MacDonald. His Florida of the 1960s is what his predecessor's L.A. had been—a paradise threatened and going under. Travis McGee, that maritime philosopher of very un-Marlovian sex, is a perfect lens to focus MacDonald's world. The Travis McGee books, which all have a color in the title, are being reissued in snazzy, gaudy, color-coordinated paperbacks. Not the Library of America just yet, but welcome all the same.

These superbly edited volumes present the seven Marlowe novels, as well as thirteen earlier stories from the magazine pages of *Black Mask* and *Dime Detective.* Also included is the screenplay that Chandler and director Billy Wilder co-wrote in 1944 from James M. Cain's *Double Indemnity,* and a bouquet of essays and letters—in all, a selection that amounts to a charter for this kind of fiction, which even today needs justifying as much as it did back when Edmund Wilson attacked it.

FURTHER READING

Bibliography

Bruccoli, Matthew J. *Raymond Chandler: A Descriptive Bibliography.* Pittsburgh: University of Pittsburgh Press, 1979, 146 p.

Thorough primary bibliography with a selection of secondary materials.

Biography

MacShane, Frank. *The Life of Raymond Chandler.* New York: Dutton, 1976, 306 p.

Definitive source on Chandler's life, beliefs, and writings.

Criticism

Elliott, George P. "Raymond Chandler." In *A Piece of Lettuce: Personal Essays on Books, Beliefs, American Places, and Growing Up in a Strange Country,* pp. 50-65. New York: Random House, 1957.

Explores Chandler's value as a literary writer and his moral views.

Gross, Miriam, ed. *The World of Raymond Chandler.* London: Weidenfeld and Nicolson, 1977, 189 p.

Important collection of critical and biographical essays on Chandler—some written by close friends of the writer.

Hamilton, Cynthia S. "Raymond Chandler." In *Western and Hard-boiled Detective Fiction in America: From High Noon to Midnight,* pp. 146-71. Iowa City: University of Iowa Press, 1987.

Discusses Chandler's detective stories and novels as examples of American adventure fiction.

Highsmith, Patricia. "A Galahad in L. A." *The Times Literary Supplement,* No. 3875 (18 June 1976): 733.

Discussion of Chandler's life and body of work, occasioned by a review of Frank MacShane's biography of Chandler.

Jameson, Fredric. "On Raymond Chandler." *Southern Review* 6, No. 3 (July 1970): 624-50.

Examines Chandler's view of American life as seen through his fiction.

Knight, Stephen. "'. . . a hard-boiled gentleman'—Raymond Chandler's Hero." In *Form and Ideology in Crime Fiction,* pp. 135-67. Bloomington: Indiana University Press, 1980.

Analyzes Chandler's style and method of characterization, while comparing his writing to that of Dashiell Hammett.

Lott, Rick. "A Matter of Style: Chandler's Hardboiled Disguise." *Journal of Popular Culture* 23, No. 3 (Winter 1989): 65-75.

Argues that Chandler worked to take his detective fiction beyond the limits of the genre by adding literary style.

Martin, Stoddard. "Raymond Chandler." In *California Writers: Jack London, John Steinbeck, the Tough Guys,* pp. 161-84. New York: St. Martin's Press, 1983.

Overview of Chandler's writings discussing theme, plot, technique, and style, often drawing comparisons to works by fellow Californian writers such as Hammett and Cain.

Maugham, W. Somerset. "The Decline and Fall of the Detective Story." In *The Vagrant Mood: Six Essays*, pp. 91-122. London: William Heinemann Ltd., 1952.

Critiques the detective-mystery story and discusses Chandler's contributions to the genre.

Reck, Tom S. "Raymond Chandler's Los Angeles." *The Nation* 221, No. 21 (20 December 1975): 661-63.

Describes Chandler's presentation of Los Angeles as a city symbolic of evil.

Ruhm, Herbert. "Raymond Chandler: From Bloomsbury to the Jungle—and Beyond." In *Tough Guy Writers of the Thirties*, pp. 171-85. Carbondale and Edwardsville: Southern Illinois University Press, 1968.

Assesses Chandler's writing style and briefly recounts his life.

Sissman, L. E. "Raymond Chandler Thirteen Years After." *The New Yorker* XLVIII, No. 3 (11 March 1972): 123-25.

Critiques Chandler's literary style, commenting on the limitations of his plots and formulaic devices, but praising his "almost tactile vision of Los Angeles" and "sometimes tremendous characterizations."

Wilson, Edmund. "Who Cares Who Killed Roger Ackroyd? A Second Report on Detective Fiction." *New Yorker* XX, No. 49 (20 January 1945): 52-4, 57-8.

A harsh critic of detective and mystery stories praises Chandler's *Farewell, My Lovely*, calling Chandler the only writer in this genre with a talent for telling stories.

Additional coverage of Chandler's life and career is contained in the following sources published by Gale Research: *Contemporary Authors*, Vols. 104, 129; *Concise Dictionary of American Literary Biography, 1929-1941*; *Dictionary of Literary Biography Documentary Series*, Vol. 6; *Major 20th-Century Authors*; and *Twentieth-Century Literary Criticism*, Vols. 1, 7.

"The Garden Party"
Katherine Mansfield

(Born Kathleen Mansfield Beauchamp; also wrote under the pseudonym Boris Petrovsky) New Zealand short story writer, critic, and poet.

The following entry presents criticism of Mansfield's short story "The Garden Party," first published in 1922 in *The Garden Party, and Other Stories*. For an overview of Mansfield's short fiction, see *SSC*, Volume 9.

INTRODUCTION

During her brief career Mansfield helped shape the modern short story form with her innovative literary style. In such influential stories as "The Garden Party," "Bliss," and "Prelude," Mansfield perfected her meticulous craft, examining the human condition in restrained and deceptively everyday prose. Her avowed intention was to intensify "the so-called small things so that everything is significant." In "The Garden Party," for example, the description of sunbeams playing on an inkwell is the kind of detailed observation that lends an almost hallucinatory visual acuity to this celebrated tale. In her attention to the "the so-called small things," Mansfield was in the forefront of those writers who treated ordinary life rather than momentous events, and, according to H. E. Bates, many followed her "in squeezing the significance out of the apparently commonplace, trivial behavior of their fellow men." Working on the fringes of British Modernism, Mansfield developed the use of stream-of-consciousness technique, earning the admiration—and rivalry—of a contemporary, Virginia Woolf. Like Woolf, Mansfield emphasized the importance of incident over conventional narrative, and thus, in "The Garden Party" Laura's impressions dictate the shape of a story drawn from Mansfield's own childhood memories.

Plot and Major Characters

Set in colonial New Zealand, "The Garden Party" falls into two clearly differentiated parts. Most of the story concerns the preparations and aftermath of a garden party, ostensibly organized by Laura, Meg, and Jose, the daughters of the privileged Sheridan family. As dawn breaks, Laura goes into the Sheridan's exquisite garden to inspect the proposed site for the marquee. Her encounter with three workers hired to raise the tent is awkward and confused, as she finds herself torn between snobbery and her developing sense of moral responsibility. Back at the house preparations continue: a florist delivers several trays of pink lilies; Mrs. Sheridan fusses over the sandwiches; and Meg rehearses a comically inappropriate song. A delivery man brings an order of delectable cream puffs—and news of the accidental death of a local carter, a nearby neighbor of the Sheridans. Laura immediately proposes the cancellation of the party, much to the amusement, and then irritation, of Jose and Mrs. Sheridan. Neither sees any need to consider the feelings of their impoverished neighbors. Ultimately Laura herself is distracted from compassion by her mother's spur-of-the-moment gift of a pretty black hat decorated with gold daisies. Startled by the sudden revelation of her own beauty, she slips effortlessly into the role of party hostess, promising to remember the tragic accident later. The garden party passes in a blur of pleasure, and a delightful afternoon slowly ends. As the Sheridans gather under the deserted marquee, Laura's father re-introduces the subject of the dead carter. To Laura's discomfort, Mrs. Sheridan brightly suggests that her daughter bring some party leftovers to the grieving widow. Laden with cream puffs and still dressed in her party clothes, Laura self-consciously crosses the broad road which divides the Sheridan's property from the mean, cramped dwellings of the poor. Down a narrow, dark lane she finds the carter's home and is led by the widow's sister to view the body. Alone with the dead man, Laura is unexpectedly overwhelmed by the peaceful beauty of the corpse and absurdly sobs, "Forgive my hat." Outside the house she meets her brother Laurie, with whom she shares a special empathy. She struggles to convey the feelings that she just experienced, but is at a loss for words.

Major Themes

The central theme of "The Garden Party" is commonly perceived to be the contrast between life and death. The Sheridan's garden is a place of thoughtless pleasure and burgeoning energy, where young people resemble brilliant butterflies and arum lilies bloom with an almost frightening vitality. In contrast, the home of the dead carter is dark and oppressive, guarded by an aged crone and surrounded by a shadowy crowd. Mansfield deliberately exaggerates the difference between these two locations in order to emphasize her theme. That life and death are part of the same continuum is suggested by the temporal structure of the story, which begins at dawn and ends in a gathering dusk. As many critics have noted, Laura's journey to visit the bereaved family has strong mythic overtones and resembles the tale of Proserpina, a goddess who was abducted by Hades into the underworld. Laura's moment of epiphany testifies to a kind of knowledge unavailable in the sunny world of the garden party. In this way, her journey also has the quality of an initiation rite, in which a naive young girl achieves emotional and moral maturity.

Critical Reception

Much of the critical discussion about "The Garden Party" has centered on the story's structure. Sparking considerable debate, Warren S. Walker contended that the conclusion of "The Garden Party" is flawed by Laura's ambiguous response to the carter's corpse. Robert Murray Davis, Donald S. Taylor, and Adam J. Sorkin have all responded to Walker's misgivings, arguing that the story's central oppositions (life and death, dream and reality, youth and maturity, beauty and ugliness) result in artistic unity and satisfying thematic tension. Another commentator, Ben Satterfield, found the ambiguity of "The Garden Party" consistent with the irony that he detected throughout the story. In recent years attention has centered on such issues as the characterization of Laura and the author's representation of social classes. From the perspective of psychoanalysis, feminist critics, such as Kate Fullbrook and Mary Burgan, have interpreted "The Garden Party" as the story of a young girl's attempt to establish her own identity.

CRITICISM

Warren S. Walker   (essay date 1957-58)

SOURCE: "The Unresolved Conflict in 'The Garden Party,'" in *Modern Fiction Studies,* Vol III, No. 4, Winter, 1957-58, pp. 354-58.

[*In the following essay, Walker finds the conclusion of "The Garden Party" ambiguous.*]

The most frequently anthologized of Katherine Mansfield's works, **"The Garden Party,"** has long enjoyed a reputation for near-perfection in the art of the short story. Its characters are deftly drawn with quick Chekhovian strokes; its action moves along at a vigorous pace; its central situation, richly textured, suggests both antecedence and aftermath; its dialogue, especially the internal debate, is psychologically apt and convincing. And yet, for all its undeniable strength and beauty, **"The Garden Party"** often leaves readers with a feeling of dissatisfaction, a vague sense that the story somehow does not realize its potential. The difficulty, I think, is a structural one: the conflict has a dual nature, only part of which is resolved effectively.

"The Garden Party" is a story concerning the most common form of character development, if not the easiest to portray: the process of growing up. Viewing the changing reaction of the protagonist to an incident that threatens to upset an upperclass social occasion, one is aware that throughout the whole story there is a groping toward maturity, and that at the end Laura is indeed more mature than she is at the opening. The incident is the accidental death of a relatively unknown man, but for Laura it brings the first real consciousness of the phenomenon of death. Shocked at first, she comes eventually to see life and death in a new perspective in which death is not as unlovely as she had imagined. One aspect of the conflict, then, and seemingly the more important one, is the struggle between fear of and acceptance of death. That death is different from what she had anticipated, that it is beautiful in one respect is the new awareness, and this, climaxing a story about a young person, can be considered a maturing experience.

But there is another aspect of the conflict that immediately engages the attention of the reader, one which is less fundamental but surely not unimportant: the clash of basic social attitudes represented by Laura and by her mother. This adds a dimension of irony to the story, for on the surface Laura attempts to ape her mother socially by taking charge of the arrangements for the party; she even affects the mannerisms of Mrs. Sheridan, "copying her mother's voice" when she first addresses the workmen and trying "to look severe and even a bit short-sighted" as she comes up to them. Beneath such trivia, however, there is a profound difference. The sensitivity of Laura for the suffering of others is set over against the callousness of Mrs. Sheridan, and the two attitudes struggle for dominance in the child's mind. What she strongly feels to be right is pronounced wrong by the person she imitates, and Laura wavers and is understandably perplexed. Open hostility between the two forces breaks out over the propriety or impropriety of going ahead with plans for the party after it is learned that a near neighbor has been killed. Laura insists that the noisy affair—a band has been employed for the event—must be cancelled. The mother, at first amused ("She refused to take Laura seriously"), finally loses all patience with her daughter. Mrs. Sheridan implies that Laura is being immature and calls her "child" in the argument that ensues. Here, then, is another criterion for maturity, one in the realm of human rather than cosmic considerations.

Whether it is maturity that is involved or something else, the reader, from the opening paragraphs, identifies himself with Laura, is sympathetic toward her point of view, and is himself antagonized by the values of Mrs. Sheridan. This is true even before the accidental death of Scott, a carter, brings the issue to a crisis. When, for example, Laura realizes that laborers are really fine people after all and remarks, in the internal dialogue, on their "friendliness" and on the "stupid conventions" that have kept her from seeing this before, the reader is less amused at the ingenuousness of her observations than annoyed at the parents responsible for a social orientation that would make necessary such an elementary discovery. It is even more true when mother and daughter argue, and the reader's passive agreement with Laura's humane stand turns into empathic support. Mrs. Sheridan is hopelessly alienated from the reader, and everything she says makes her appear worse. In an attempt to soften the incontrovertible fact that one of the indigent cottagers is dead, she remarks, with heartless logic, "'I can't understand how they keep alive in those poky little holes.'" In refutation of Laura's statement that the party should be postponed out of deference to the bereaved survivors, she says, "'People like that don't expect sacrifices from us.'" It is with no surprise that we learn that the Sheridan children have been brought up to scorn the cottages of the laborers:

> They were the greatest possible eyesores, and they had no right to be in that neighborhood at all. They were little mean dwellings painted a chocolate brown. In the garden patches there was nothing but cabbage stalks, sick hens, and tomato cans. The very smoke coming out of their chimneys was poverty-stricken. Little rags and shreds of smoke, so unlike the great silvery plumes that uncurled from the Sheridans' chimneys.

The Sheridans, who see this rural slum adjacent to their estate as "disgusting and sordid," apparently never make any effort to alleviate the condition of the wretches living there, or even to extend moral support to them. Laura, on the other hand, overcoming the snobbery of her upbringing, is acutely concerned about their feelings.

A resolution of this second aspect of the conflict seems to be suggested obliquely by the use made of hats—hats in general, and one hat in particular. Hats are used functionally in the plot and acquire symbolic value within the framework of the story as they come to represent the whole social milieu of the Sheridan class with its leisure, its conspicuous consumption, and its caste distinctions. In an opening scene, "Father and Laurie stood brushing their hats ready to go to the office." Immediately after this mention of male headwear, Mrs. Sheridan tells Laura to ask Kitty Maitland, with whom Laura is talking on the telephone, to be sure "'to wear to the party that sweet hat she had on last Sunday.'" When Laura is badly upset by the death of the carter, Mrs. Sheridan diverts her attention from the tragedy by giving her a bright jewel from her glittering social world, a "black hat trimmed with gold daisies and a long black velvet ribbon." Laura is thus enticed, for the time being, from her better feelings. One last spark of humane concern flares up that afternoon when

Laura encounters her brother Laurie, home from work now. Perhaps Laurie, who of all the family is the only one who even begins to understand Laura, will agree with her on the undesirability of going on with the party. In her confused state she relies on Laurie to provide an ethical touchstone for testing the validity of her opinion.

> She wanted to tell him. If Laurie agreed with the others, then it was bound to be all right. And she followed him into the hall.
>
> "Laurie!"
>
> "Hallo!" He was half-way upstairs, but when he turned round and saw Laura, he suddenly puffed out his cheeks and goggled his eyes at her. "My word, Laura! You look stunning," said Laurie. "What an absolutely topping hat!"
>
> Laura said faintly "Is it?" and smiled up at Laurie, and didn't tell him after all.

Her last resistance overcome now, the spell of society is upon her, and Laura does not escape its influence throughout the ritual of the party.

She is the official hostess, according to plan, thus assuming the position the mother would ordinarily have held, welcoming guests, helping them solicitously to refreshments, and receiving their compliments—for her hat. Finally, the party over and the guests departed, the Sheridans sit down to rest, and Mr. Sheridan contributes to the conversation what he mistakenly thinks will be news to the family: the information about the carter's death. His wife, secretly exasperated at the necessity for renewing a debate she had thought won, rallies with "one of her brilliant ideas." Still completely unmoved by the plight of the widow and her five children, Mrs. Sheridan realizes that now Laura will have to be placated on the issue, and so she suggests that they gather up a basketful of the left-overs from the party and send them to the grieving family, much as one might pick out scraps for a pet sow that had hurt its foot. Laura, quite appropriately, is appalled to think that this is the best they can do for people in trouble, but she goes along with her mother's suggestion, the only concession she has been able to gain. She starts for the cottage of the deceased with the basket, and only when it is too late to turn back realizes how inappropriate is her hat, which by now has become an emblem of the mother and her hard-shelled world. "If only it was another hat!" she admonishes herself. Then comes the incident in the Scott cottage, during which Laura sees something quite peaceful and serene in death. But, significantly, the only thing she says to the dead man is "'Forgive my hat.'" She has not, it seems, succumbed permanently to the enchantment of her mother's world after all.

Here at the climax of the story, then, a decisive stage has been reached in the respective struggles between two sets of opposing forces: 1) youthful fear of death vs. some kind of acceptance of death, and 2) Laura's social attitude vs. her mother's. There is no doubt about the resolution of the first issue:

There lay a young man fast asleep. . . . He was given up to his dream. What did garden-parties and baskets and lace frocks matter to him? He was far from all those things. He was wonderful, beautiful. . . . All is well, said that sleeping face.

About the second part of the conflict, however, there is considerable doubt, for the problem is suddenly dropped, and no further reference is made to it. Does Laura now switch to her mother's view of the matter, and does she now feel that her previous concern about the cotter's family was as unwarranted as the fear of death that accompanied it? Or has her plea "Forgive my hat" indicated her irrevocable commitment to a position opposed to that of Mrs. Sheridan? If so, will she not now have to reorient her feelings toward her family? We never find out, for no hint of an answer to this dilemma is to be found in the conclusion.

To make matters still more vague at the end, in comes Laurie, who she thinks will understand her. He had failed to sense her difficulty before the party, however, when she had depended on him to do so, for he too had made the social genuflection to the sanctity of the hat. Now Laura hopes that he will grasp intuitively the feelings she is unable to articulate. But does he? The scene at the cottage was "wonderful, beautiful . . . this marvel" to her, but Laurie seems to think that it must have been otherwise. "'Was it awful?'" he asks. And then a moment later when she says, "'Isn't life . . .'" (mysterious, or surprising, or something else), he answers, "'Isn't it, darling?'" Does he really understand what she is talking about? One wonders. One wonders whether he even understands the significance of the death to her; one is morally certain that he never suspects the inner turmoil she has undergone in defending to herself, as well as to the family, her benevolent sensibility.

Donald S. Taylor (essay date 1958-59)

SOURCE: "Crashing the Garden Party: A Dream—A Wakening," in *Modern Fiction Studies,* Vol. IV, No. 4, Winter, 1958-59, pp. 361-62.

[*In the following essay, Taylor examines the pattern of dream and reality in "The Garden Party."*]

Laura states the conflict in **"The Garden Party"** and reveals her instinctive loyalties when she says to her unsympathetic sister Jose, "But we can't possibly have a garden-party with a man dead just outside the front gate." The garden party epitomizes the dream world of the Sheridan women, a world whose underlying principle is the editing and rearranging of reality for the comfort and pleasure of its inhabitants. Its war is with the real world, whose central and final truth is death. In the course of the story Laura wakes to reality from the dream to which her sex, her class, and particularly her mother, custodian of the dream, would confine her.

The story's first paragraph introduces the dream. The Sheridans order nature—lawns are mowed and swept and flowers bloom on schedule in delineated beds. In this garden, Mrs. Sheridan plans to give her daughters the illusion of maturity, thus keeping them within the dream. "I'm determined to leave everything to you children this year." And yet her disposing hand is everywhere—ordering lilies, planning the food, deciding what people shall wear. At the end of the story she tries still to keep up the illusion. "Why," she asks, "will you children insist on giving parties?"

Throughout the first half of the story Laura is quite caught up in this charming dream, which reaches its apotheosis in the delightfully arranged garden party. "Ah, what happiness it is to be with people who are happy, to press hands, press cheeks, smile into eyes." Within this dream the sorrows of the real world are the stuff of prettily melancholy songs: "This Life is *Wee*-ary, / A Tear—a Sigh. / A Love that *Chan*-ges, /. . . . And then . . . Goodbye!" And yet Jose's empty song holds the key to the story: "A Dream—a *Wa*-kening."

Early in the story occurs a mock engagement between the two worlds. Workmen come to put up the marquee and Laura finds them "extraordinarily nice" and decides that only "absurd class distinctions" separate her from them. Thus is introduced the social conflict which Mr. Walker finds unresolved, but the treatment here is largely comic. The first genuine attack from the real world penetrates the great house, significantly enough, through a back door. A delivery man tells of the accidental death of a carter, a resident of the gloomy lane of working-class cottages just below the Sheridan's house. Laura immediately insists that the party be cancelled, but Jose defends the dream. "You won't bring a drunken workman back to life by being sentimental,' she said softly." Laura is enraged at the comforting falsehood so slyly introduced and goes to her mother. In Mrs. Sheridan's reaction the conflict is again epitomized:

> "Mother, a man's been killed," began Laura.
>
> "Not in the garden?" interrupted her mother.

Mrs. Sheridan's strategy in this scene is to pretend to be amused with Laura, then to reason with her, finally to bribe her with one of her own hats. Laura is angry at first, but a charming glimpse in the mirror persuades her that she has been extravagant. Temporarily, at least, she accepts her mother's view with her mother's hat.

> Just for a moment she had another glimpse of that poor woman and those little children, and the body being carried into the house. But it all seemed blurred, unreal, like a picture in the newspaper. I'll remember it again after the party's over, she decided. And somehow that seemed quite the best plan. . . .

Thus, reality, within the dream, becomes unreal. After the shocked awakening, the sleeper has been persuaded to return to the pleasant dream, which can exorcize insistent reality by incorporating it.

After the "most successful party," reality again asserts itself, this time through the father, who mentions the death.

Mrs. Sheridan fidgets at her husband's tactlessness, but counterattacks brilliantly—Laura shall carry a basket of party scraps to the widow. The charity which suffereth not and is kind is, for Mrs. Sheridan, the only possible link between her dream and reality. Though there is danger in this strategy—Laura may see the dead man—Mrs. Sheridan decides that forbidding this sight would be poor tactics: ". . . better not put such ideas into the child's head."

Laura departs through the garden gates, but she cannot shake off the dream. ". . . it seemed to her that kisses, voices, tinkling spoons, laughter, the smell of crushed grass were somehow inside her. She had no room for anything else." But she crosses the road, finds the dark cottage, and is brought, almost against her will, to the deathbed. And there, quite suddenly, she moves from the darkness of the lane into the light of truth. Death is the real dream. "He was given up to his dream. What did garden-parties and baskets and lace frocks matter to him. . . . He was wonderful, beautiful." Laura understands now that she had, earlier, let herself be bribed from this truth. When she sobs, "Forgive my hat," she rejects at last the meaningless dream of the garden party and stands now on the threshold of the real world, sinister at first, but now transmuted into beauty by the dream of death.

As for the story's social implications, we note that in the ugly lane lived "a man whose housefront was studded all over with minute bird-cages." Are the cottages (where "men hung over the palings") to the Sheridan house what these cages are to his house? And Laura is expected in the lane, much as though the party scraps are the rich's necessary acknowledgment that it is the inescapable reality of the poor which supports their dream. But both this possible social statement and Mr. Walker's clash of social attitudes are subordinate to the larger struggle within Laura. And for her the dream world of the garden party flies before death, the real dream, the final fact which gives beauty and significance to man's real life on earth.

Daniel A. Weiss (essay date 1958-59)

SOURCE: "Crashing the Garden Party: The Garden Party of Proserpina," in *Modern Fiction Studies,* Vol. IV, No. 4, Winter, 1958-59, pp. 363-64.

[*In the following essay, Weiss views Mansfield's "The Garden Party" as a tale of mythic initiation.*]

Can **"The Garden Party"** get along without resolving Laura's social attitude? It can, if one accepts the premise that the class differences in the story are a subordinate component of the primary theme—Laura's discovery of death, and its coextensiveness with life.

I have no wish to still the lively music of Katherine Mansfield's style into some measured archetypal cadence, but much in the story, dealing as it does with a primordial theme, lends it the quality of a myth, the initiation of a novice into mysteries.

There is, to begin with, the element of election. Laura's older sister is outside the mysteries. She knows the facts of life and death, but, in Shelley's words, she cannot "imagine" what she "knows." Laura qualifies in her novitiate because she is the "artistic one." Her sensibilities are at work in anticipation of her ordeal, prefiguring her vision, when she realizes that the workingmen are "extraordinarily nice," and that class distinctions are "absurd."

Laura's thoughts on class distinctions would write her off (along with her creator) as an unconscious snob rather than a sensitive neophyte, if it were not for the fact that **"The Garden Party"** is dealing with life and death in the classical mode, as entities, with local habitations and names, a geography as absolute as the garden of Proserpina and the mouth of Pluto's underworld. The garden, especially with a party going, is all life without death—and the cottages are all death, without life. What prevents these equivalences from being distasteful is that the story uses social attitudes and class distinctions, garden parties and cottages, as a sociological pun upon the natures of life and death. They are presentations in Laura's initiation. The lower classes represent—by being "lower," by living "in a lane to themselves at the very bottom of a steep rise that led up to the [Sheridan] house," by providing Laura with her first vision of death itself—the land of the dead.

Laura exploits the pun when she denies her sense of class distinctions early in the story. In life democracy is the great leveller; in death it is Death. Her unconscious acknowledgment of this second fact leads her in her initiation to commit what might be called the judicious error. She proposes an impossible conundrum. How can life and death *be* simultaneously? Death has come into the world. How can life continue? Call off the party.

Her sister's rejection of the proposal is based, not on a more perfect knowledge, but upon ignorance. Jose knows nothing; even the song she sings about Life is an expression of thoughtless banalities. Laura's mother, while she also rejects Laura's impossible plea, injects another quality into her reply. She speaks from a knowledge, perhaps from a memory of an almost forgotten initiation into the same mystery. She answers Laura's question.

> "If someone had died there normally—and I can't understand how they keep alive in those poky little holes—we should still be having our party, shouldn't we?"
>
> Laura had to say "yes" to that, but she felt it was all wrong.

Death, then, can *be* simultaneously with life. But now that Death has been allowed another question arises: what is Death like? what does it ask of Life? Mrs. Sheridan does not answer these questions. Instead she gives Laura her beautiful hat, whose first property is its ability to reconcile Laura to the garden party.

The last step in Laura's initiation is accomplished at the instigation of Mrs. Sheridan at the end of the party at the going down of the sun. Carrying a basket of broken breads (the lilies are rejected at the last moment; flowers grow on the earth, not under it) Laura makes her descent into Avernus, past Cerberus and across the "broad road" that divides her world from this one like a river.

A moment before this her mother has enclosed in an ellipsis the very heart of the mystery that Laura is about to encounter. "And Laura!"—her mother followed her out of the marquee—"don't on any account—" Finished, the sentence must read, "Don't on any account look at the dead man!" It is like Demeter's warning her daughter that she must not eat anything in the land of the dead. Mrs. Sheridan anticipates the culmination of Laura's search, the answer to her questions, and with the answer the end of Laura's innocence.

At the door of the dead man's house Laura breathes a prayer, "Help me, God," and enters. And at last, by a second judicious error, a wrong turning, she is face to face with the mystery. Life and death are coextensive dreams. She and the young man are peers in equally felicitous, classless states, mutually and benignly indifferent to one another. Her acknowledgment of this truth reveals the second property of the mother's hat. It is talismanic. Not only did it reconcile Laura to life in the presence of death; it allows her, like the magical garments of mythical heroes, to intrude in the land of the dead. "Forgive my hat" is in effect to say "Forgive me for being alive." Or, to speculate on the fascination the young man holds for her (Proserpina *did* become the queen of the dead), Laura is saying, "I love you, but I am committed to life now."

On her return she tries to communicate her new knowledge to her older brother. She cannot voice it, but he understands. He has also been initiated. Had they not both been there already, equipped with the insatiable curiosity of children who will not rest until they betray their sense of immortality, and with it their childhoods? "Laura and Laurie on their prowls sometimes walked through. It was disgusting and sordid. They came out with a shudder. But still one must go everywhere; one must see everything. So through they went."

"The Garden Party"'s appointed task is to leave Laura at this pristine moment, on the other side of her childhood. To ask whether she will become ultimately like her mother or "reorient her feelings toward her family," is like asking what finally happened to Snow-White or Catskin. It is asking for another story.

Don W. Kleine (essay date 1963)

SOURCE: "'The Garden Party': A Portrait of the Artist," in *Criticism,* Vol. V, No. 4, Fall, 1963, pp. 360-71.

[In the following essay, Kleine discusses Laura's imaginative shaping of experience in "The Garden Party."]

"The Garden Party" is generally, and with justice, regarded as one of the most nearly flawless short stories in the language. Young Laura Sheridan's discovery of death in life is itself discovered with poetic truth and technical purity, and Miss Mansfield's work deserves the small, enduring place it has won in the history of modern fiction. Writes the author less than year before her own death:

> And yes, that is what I tried to convey in **"The Garden Party."** The diversity of life and how we try to fit in everything, Death included. That is bewildering for a person of Laura's age. She feels things ought to happen differently. First one and then another. But life isn't like that. We haven't the ordering of it. Laura says, "But all these things must not happen at once." And Life answers, "Why not? How are they divided from each other?" And they *do* all happen, it is inevitable. And it seems to me there is beauty in that inevitability.

If there is beauty in that inevitability, there is lasting pertinence in Katherine Mansfield's sensitive portrayal of Laura's young bewilderment before the mystery, and her final acceptance.

While it would accord with many readers' understanding of **"The Garden Party,"** Miss Mansfield's statement seems nevertheless, on closer inspection, a little misleading. Is it, after all, her story's primary effect to convey a sense of "the diversity of life?" Does she really show how "we try to fit in everything?" Rather, if one would be accurate, the story conveys Laura's *realization* of life's diversity; it shows how *she* finally fits in everything. To be sure, the young girl's perception of the oneness of happy parties and tragic deaths is true to our adult awarenesses; and thus it appears natural for a reader to subordinate the youthful perceiver to her perception. Yet the fact remains that—in the story—the perception is Laura's alone. To overlook this fact is, I think, to overlook not only the dramatic structure of **"The Garden Party,"** but also its total symbolic meaning. Miss Mansfield's artistic intention is even more complex than her statement would indicate. Her heroine is not a mere function of an ultimate issue. In revealing that issue she too is reciprocally revealed, and quite as ultimately. That reciprocity is, to my view, a central though secret subject of **"The Garden Party,"** and a key to the work's persisting veracity and power.

If Laura's dramatic role appears deceptively modest, so does the story itself. Its seemingly commercial surface polish, and lightness of tone, almost belie its poignance and narrow profundity. During much of the piece, Miss Mansfield's attitude toward her materials seems so airy as to be hardly serious. Before the workmen who set up a marquee for the party, Laura poses hopefully, trying to be everything at once. She blushes, she scowls; she invokes class distinctions and almost in the same mental breath damns "stupid conventions"; she wills a childish piece of bread-and-butter out of her hand and moments later takes "a big bite . . . just like a work-girl." It is a dreadful tableau of everyone's adolescence; yet, colored with Miss Mansfield's amused affection, it impresses one as straightforwardly comic and nothing more. Laura's mother too, flighty and forgetful, but much more efficient than she seems, resembles a stock character in a family magazine, or a situation comedy. She cannot read her own writing: "'It looks like mice. It can't be mice, can it?'" At times the author's wit appears broad to the point of frivolity. Laura and her sister Jose, "too grown-up to really care" about cream puffs, are two minutes later "licking their fingers with that absorbed inward look that only comes from whipped cream." Lightheartedly, Miss Mansfield notes a profusion of domestic trifles: a girl sips coffee with her freshly-washed hair in a green towel; two men brush their hats and hurry off to work; women chatter of egg and olive sandwiches, broken meringue shells and black hats trimmed with gold daisies. The narrative is stunningly deft, often charming, always authentic. But hardly, up to the point when Laura hears of the poor neighbor's death, does it resemble the stuff of serious fiction.

What accounts for this apparent levity of touch? Remarks Sylvia Berkman in her incisive critical biography: "'**The Garden Party'** juxtaposes social gaiety and sudden death to reveal the bewildering shock a young girl suffers at the knowledge that in life such incongruities can coexist." Miss Berkman's observation, like those of the story's other commentators, implicitly exalts Laura's discovery over Laura herself. Clearly the bright, almost frivolous tone with which Miss Mansfield depicts the preparations for the party does afford sharp contrast with "sudden death" in the poor neighbor's cottage. But why does the author dwell at such length on the preparations, and so briefly on the social gaiety itself? Most obviously, she does so in order to develop Laura's joyous expectations toward a "bewildering shock"; less obviously, to develop an ample sense of a woman's world. The woman to whom the world belongs is Laura's mother. In Mrs. Sheridan's world, the tradesmen are always punctual, the daisy plants shine on signal from the gardener, and the husbands and sons who make it all possible glide in the background like discreet ghosts. Nothing really can be serious in a house filled, like the Sheridans', with tinkling pianos, canna lilies and cream puffs. The tragic accident, in short, is juxtaposed not merely with the social gaiety of the garden party but, more pointedly, with Mrs. Sheridan's safe unserious way of life.

When Laura reads "All is well" in a dead workman's face, her discovery and inner acceptance effect her passage out of the mother's snug, evasive world, and into the larger adult world. The story's most recent interpreters, Donald Taylor and Daniel Weiss, have both noted this fact. They differ, however, as to the medium through which she undergoes her maturing release. Mr. Taylor sees this medium as a metaphorical awakening from the "dream" the mother has spun about her children, an awakening presaged by Jose's earlier song ("'A dream—a *Wa*-kening'"). Mr. Weiss sees the medium as myth: in the last part of the story a series of ritual accidents draw the acolyte into ultimate mysteries. The text, of course, sustains both readings, since any discovery is a sort of awakening, and since Miss Mansfield's heroine obviously does get initiated. Mr. Taylor and Mr. Weiss seek the

story's meaning outside of Laura, however, and neither reading provides the work with a principle of *cumulative* dramatic revelation.

A more profitable strategy, it seems to me, would be to seek the story's meaning in terms of the medium through which all its events are concretely defined: the ardent, entranced sensibility of the young girl herself. Despite its abruptness, Laura's discovery of unity between the vulnerable living and their inviolable dead is an imaginative perception. She is not awakened to womanhood wholly from without, as by an alarm clock. Rather, examination of the text reveals that her own consciousness has been inexorably ticking toward just such an "accident" from the beginning of the story. It reveals, too, that she is not a purely passive acolyte of ritual mystery (though sensitivity does fit her to receive the secret); throughout the story she is progressively refined for that mystery by an increasingly bitter inner debate. In a very real sense, Laura earns her adulthood.

When she figuratively exorcises childhood by apologizing to the dead man for her festive party hat, the act is intrinsically moral, not only as an assertion of human solidarity, but also because it projects her beyond her mother's way of life. For it is not fanciful to remark that in the story Mrs. Sheridan's "dream" is meant to be, quite literally, immoral. To exist in it one must deny death and, in denying death, Laura's mother denies life, experience, to her young daughters. She has substituted for life a smoothly-tailored Good Life. To coin a fairly accurate metaphor: she presides, as a benevolent Acrasia, over a sexless Bower of Bliss, a realm of matronly artifice designed solely for the delight and safety of its enthralled inhabitants. (The pathetic blankness of this Acrasia is cloaked in lovable muddle, but the reader has already seen her, gone rather dead behind the eyes, glaring from a thousand society pages.) An aspect of Mrs. Sheridan's life-denying immorality is her cultivated indifference to the savage social basis on which her world rests. Mrs. Sheridan sees the neighboring cottagers as "poor creatures," whose surprising ability to "keep alive in those poky little holes" is more impudent than admirable; indeed, the adulthood which Laura earns is partly identified with transcending class barriers, and the childhood she escapes is partly identified with staying inside them.

To arraign social differences is not Katherine Mansfield's primary intention, however, for the workmen and the Sheridans' servants are always rendered either as faceless or as functions of Laura's attitude toward them. Rather, the story's focus—and central dramatic impulse—is the young girl's secret struggle to grow up. Laura, who suspects it no more than the rest of her family, is only a nominal citizen of the Bower of Bliss. Unlike her smug sister Jose, she is a healthy child, impatient for adulthood, for experience. But something sets her apart from other healthy children as much as from her unhealthy sister. Laura is "the artistic one," and the healthy child's hunger for experience becomes with her the hunger not just for an adult role, but for imaginative rapport with adult experience, and for the moral selfhood which such rapport can achieve. It is appropriate, then, that the story's events should be conveyed exclusively through Laura's own naive impressions, since only thus can Miss Mansfield objectify her character's movement toward self-fulfillment.

Mrs. Sheridan lets her daughters play hostess at a garden party which she covertly monitors to the last detail. To "the artistic one" whose sensibility is forthwith ignited, the party does seem, for a time, a truly important experience: her imagination makes it so. Inasmuch as Laura feels that by playing hostess one automatically becomes a grown-up, she is deluded; the particular party on the Sheridan lawn is only another childhood diversion. Yet insofar as Laura senses in the party a harbinger of adult experience, she is not deluded at all; her delight in the party predicts the fusion of parties and deaths at the end, predicts her own self-realization.

It is hard to grow up out of Mrs. Sheridan's world. Jose, though older than Laura, has not yet done so, and probably never will. To win the adulthood of which she senses an augury in the party, Laura must overcome the childhood within her, and also strive outwardly with her mother and sister. The two-fold struggle involves the young girl's very identity as a human being. On neither level can she define the struggle or its stakes.

Indeed, Laura's childlike unawareness conceals from a reader her importance to the story's total meaning: by definition, such innocence cannot define itself. She lacks social authority; things happen to her. Yet, while it is true that Laura is outwardly passive to events, it is also true that her pristine sensibilities continually qualify and shape events. Her inner struggle, for all her unawareness, accounts in large part for the story's poignance, style and structure. Only in terms of this implicit struggle, I believe, can the explicit action of the *whole* story be adequately explained. The flying rhythms of Miss Mansfield's prose reflect not only Laura's impulse to fly to experience, but to fly from it as well. Throughout the narrative this opposition is identified with her age: she is a child-adult. The action moves in accord with Laura's inner debate until, in an imaginative resolution, she gains herself.

> And after all the weather was ideal. They could not have had a more perfect day for a garden-party if they had ordered it. Windless, warm, the sky without a cloud.

As Laura gazes out the window during breakfast, her ecstatic view of the garden, the unclouded sky, is also, implicitly, a perception of life's wondrous possibilities. But the perception is fragmentary. The garden, like Laura's youth, is too perfect, too well tended. She must be proved. So when the workmen come with the marquee it is fitting that she is the one who goes forth to meet them on the garden path. Her success in this first encounter with real experience outside her mother's world is a qualified one. Laura's problem lies in not knowing

who she is. Childishly encumbered with a piece of bread-and-butter, she practices adult faces:

> She blushed and tried to look severe and even a little bit shortsighted as she came up to them.

But there is only one adult face in her repertory: "'Good morning,' she said, copying her mother's voice." Unlike her mother and sister, Laura cannot comfortably wear the affected mask of social superiority; so momentarily she reverts to childhood:

> But that sounded so fearfully affected that she was ashamed, and stammered like a little girl . . .

Then, impulsively, she would share her excitement with the workmen: "How very nice workmen were! And what a beautiful morning!" But she cannot do that either: "She mustn't mention the morning; she must be businesslike. The marquee." There is more of her mother in her than she suspects; she begins to wonder if her friends are "quite respectful."

For the moment, in fact, her pursuit of experience seems baffled. The workmen are strangers after all:

> "H'm, going to have a band are you?" said another of the workmen. He was pale. He had a haggard look as his dark eyes scanned the tennis-court. What was he thinking?

A glance at the nearby karaka trees suggests the illusory alternative of an isolation which will secure her release from childhood, yet avoid adult commitment:

> They were like trees you imagined growing on a desert island, proud, solitary, lifting their leaves and fruits to the sun in a kind of silent splendour.

Instantly this fancy is dispelled when one of the workmen sniffs a flower, and "she forgot all about the karakas in her wonder at him caring for things like that." Laura has unexpectedly gained the clue to this entire encounter; ardent receptivity like hers transcends class barriers; she *is* sharing the pleasures of her garden. But, falsifying this clue which anticipates her communion with the dead man, she rushes to a romantic fallacy: "Why couldn't she have workmen for friends rather than the silly boys she danced with and who came to Sunday night supper?" Though she exults in this inverse snobbery, it actually confirms her childhood.

Laura had flown to the lawn in hope of adult connection, but her attempt was premature. Betrayed by inexperience, the thrust toward experience falters. Laura's imaginative impulse toward the larger world outside her family has been made evident (she would share the morning with workmen). But the conflict between that impulse and her mother's world, reflected in Laura's own reactions, has been made equally evident.

Now she is recalled to the house, her joy in the party enhanced by the fancied victory on the garden path. She tries to impart it to her brother Laurie, a sympathetic intermediary between their mother's hothouse and the outside world, but he is in a hurry and cannot listen. Her feeling persists after Laurie has gone. The very sounds of the house echo her delight. A thudding door, a flutter of wind, a spot of sunlight on an inkpot possess unutterable promise. Two trays of canna lilies arrive; Mrs. Sheridan has ordered them secretly:

> Nothing but lilies—canna lilies, big pink flowers, wide open, radiant, almost frighteningly alive on bright crimson stems.

The "frighteningly alive" flowers hint that, for all Laura's delight, real experience still lies ahead.

She joins Jose, who has been directing the re-arrangement of the drawing-room.

> Jose loved giving orders to the servants, and they loved obeying her. She always made them feel they were taking part in some drama.

A strategist like her mother, Jose's attitude toward life is essentially theatrical and, like her mother's, immorally shallow. Her thespianism stems from a defect, not an excess, of imagination. Jose believes people (especially servants) are a game you play and, despite her undeniable skill at the game, she cannot respect people, since to play the game at all you must make them into dolls. In the story, she is Laura's anti-type. Her bogus rapture is a counterpart of Laura's real rapture:

> "I have never seen such exquisite sandwiches," said Jose's rapturous voice. "How many kinds did you say there were, cook? Fifteen?"

Jose does not believe in her mother's garden party. Unlike Laura, Jose is not innocent, because to her all experiences are equally unreal. But neither, for the same reason, will she ever be adult. Predictably, then, Jose is wholly consecrated to the upper middle-class Good Life. She expresses the reality which it denies in a silly refrain:

> "This Life is *Wee*-ary,
> A Tear—a Sigh.
> A Love that *Chan*-ges,
>   This Life is *Wee*-ary,
> A Tear—a Sigh.
> A Love that *Chan*-ges,
> And then . . . Good-bye!"

Muffled, as if heard in a womb, outer reality in Jose's song is distorted, made innocuous: her face mocks the words she sings.

That real life which Jose had mocked now appears at the kitchen door. A delivery man tells that a young carter from the cottages below the Sheridans' house has been killed in an accident. For Laura the shock is profound. The garden, seen through a window, suggested life's radiant possibilities, not life's single certainty. And simply because she had

felt the impending party so intensely up to now, Laura for the time being suspends belief in it:

> "But we can't possibly have a garden-party with a man dead just outside the front gate."

In effect, she has decided that she cannot live with death, that she cannot live *and* die. Yet Laura's abrupt relinquishment of what had seemed adulthood has drawn her a stage closer to it: for the first time, she detects a contradiction at the heart of reality. The imaginative insight is simultaneously a moral one:

> "And just think of what the band would sound like to that poor woman," said Laura.

Instantly it flings her against an immoral *status quo*. Appropriately, the initial defender of the *status quo* is Jose, Laura's anti-type:

> "You won't bring a drunken workman back to life by being sentimental," she said softly.

Jose views the contradiction of death in life unimaginatively, and so to her there is no contradiction at all: ". . . Don't be so extravagant." Jose is right, for the wrong reason. Laura is wrong, for the right reason.

Childishly, she flies to Mrs. Sheridan for support.

> "Mother, a man's been killed," began Laura
>
> "*Not* in the garden?" interrupted her mother.
>
> "No, no!"
>
> "Oh, what a fright you gave me!" Mrs. Sheridan sighed with relief.

To Laura, there really is a corpse in the garden:

> "Of course, we can't have our party, can we?" she pleaded.
>
> "The band and everybody arriving. They'd hear us, mother; they're nearly neighbors!"

But for her mother there is no such thing as a neighbor:

> "You are being very absurd, Laura," she said coldly. "People like that don't expect sacrifices from us."

Childhood itself has suddenly turned on Laura, and for the moment there is nowhere left to go—except to her bedroom, remarking significantly, "'I don't understand.'"

Mrs. Sheridan had tried to placate her daughter with sham adulthood: her own charming hat, in which Laura looks "'such a picture.'" A chance glimpse in the mirror confirms her mother's compliment. The grown-up hat falsely appeases Laura's yearning for experience, and enables her to half-willingly will suspension of disbelief in the garden party:

Just for a moment she had another glimpse of that poor woman and those little children, and the body being carried into the house. But it all seemed blurred, unreal, like a picture in the newspaper. I'll remember it again after the party's over, she decided. And somehow that seemed quite the best plan.

It is another lapse into childhood (the hat, like Jose's song, blurs the fact of death); yet Laura has learned too much to permanently forget the picture of the widow. Indeed, when Laurie arrives just before the party, "She wanted to tell him. If Laurie agreed with the others, then it was bound to be all right." But she cannot resist his distracting admiration of her hat, and she "didn't tell him after all."

The party begins, and magically it seems to fulfill all expectations.

> Wherever you looked there were couples strolling, bending to the flowers, greeting, moving on over the lawn. They were like bright birds that had alighted on the Sheridans' garden for this one afternoon, on their way to—where? Ah, what happiness it is to be with people who are all happy, to press hands, press cheeks, smile into eyes.

Like the bright birds, Laura herself is bound for a strange place, her journey certified by the entranced sensibility which has been predicting it since morning. Intimations that this passage will be intrinsically moral persist even during the party:

> She ran to her father and begged him. "Daddy darling, can't the band have something to drink?"

Just a few lines earlier, the band had appeared to a friend of Laura's in a different light:

> "My dear!" trilled Kitty Maitland, "aren't they too like frogs for words? You ought to have arranged them round the pond with the conductor in the middle on a leaf."

Like Jose or Mrs. Sheridan, Kitty sees the poor as sub-human objects.

"And the perfect afternoon slowly ripened, slowly faded, slowly its petals closed." The bright and frightening lilies start Laura at last on her errand of discovery. When the final guests have gone, her father reopens the subject which he had promised herself to remember. Now, however, she doesn't "want to be teased about it." The intervening hours have sufficed to show that stopping the party would indeed have been "extravagant." Mrs. Sheridan, who had hoped the subject closed for good, "fidgeted with her cup"; but then she has "one of her brilliant ideas." Laura will go with the party leftovers. The impertinent condescension of such charity is evident to Laura alone:

> Again, how curious, she seemed to be different from them all. To take scraps from their party. Would the poor woman really like that?

But go she must, the lilies added to the food because "'people of that class are so impressed by arum lilies.'" At the last moment the flowers are called back lest they ruin her dress, and Mrs. Sheridan tells her daughter "'don't on any account—'"; she leaves unfinished the warning not to look at the body in the cottage.

As Laura passes out of the garden into the dusk, it seems that she should have left behind not only the lilies, but also her happiness:

> Here she was going down the hill to somewhere a man lay dead, and she couldn't realize it. Why couldn't she? She stopped a minute. And it seemed to her that kisses, voices, tinkling spoons, laughter, the smell of crushed grass were somehow inside her. She had no room for anything else.

Laura still cannot reconcile the garden party to death, or realize that the impulsive sympathy toward the workmen on the lawn, and the skirmish with her mother and sister, were themselves symptoms of the party inside her.

Once she literally crosses "the broad road" which divides the Sheridans' estate from the working class lane, childhood dreads, hidden before, are awakened: "A big dog ran by like a shadow." The lane, with its vital and disorderly poverty, seems ominously "dark." Almost at the carter's door she wonders if it is too late to turn back. But the house is reached. The widow's sister, a sinister "little woman in black," meets Laura at the door. In the kitchen they confront the widow herself. Terrible with grief, she glares blindly at her visitor. Laura presents the basket. Then, muddled with pity and shame, she exits into the dead man's room, pursued by the sister:

> "Don't be afraid, my lass . . . 'e looks a picture. There's nothing to show."

The picture is not blurred like one in the newspaper:

> His head was sunk in the pillow, his eyes were closed; they were blind under the closed eyelids. He was given up to his dream. What did garden-parties and baskets and lace frocks matter to him? He was far from all these things. He was wonderful, beautiful. While they were laughing and while the band was playing, this marvel had come to the lane.

Laura, at last fully awake, can abandon herself to a dream of her own, the dream death makes of life. The intuition instantly draws her beyond class and childhood. Yet she must make a final amends for blunders perpetrated on the way to this moment. So, with a "loud childish sob," she exclaims, "'Forgive my hat,'" and rushes into the night. There she meets Laurie, and tries to impart what she has learned.

> "It was simply marvelous. But, Laurie—"

> She stopped, she looked at her brother.

"Isn't life," she stammered, "isn't life—"

But what life was she couldn't explain.

It is noteworthy that Laura's naive and fervent receptivity should be associated with extreme youth; at the end of the story she is ready for adult life, but she has not yet begun to live it. Yet the childlike freshness and spontaneity of Laura's responses, despite their limitations, *have* enabled her to sense, albeit vaguely, the manifold opportunities of existence. Gifted in vision, she is qualified, both because of and in spite of her youth, to discover what her mother and sister have always known, yet never known. The true subject of **"The Garden Party,"** then, is not only the ultimate reality we perceive but, equally, the way an artistic one perceives it. Laura, a sensitive young romantic, is the appropriate heroine of what might be termed an educational romance in miniature, a parable of innocence as discovery.

In short, to subordinate the heroine of **"The Garden Party"** to her discovery is to miss the story's central meaning. Laura is not merely "a young girl." Rather, she is The Young Girl, a prototypical figure in many of Katherine Mansfield's stories. But nowhere is this figure so consummately realized as in **"The Garden Party."** A main reason for the work's continuing vitality is Laura who, as the story recedes, persists in the memory as the symbol of a certain state of heart:

> She blushed and tried to look severe and even a little
> bit short-sighted as she came up to them.

Her exit from childhood, a first death poetically associated with the last, is true to a reader's experience because Laura herself is. She contains the party.

Robert Murray Davis   (essay date 1964)

SOURCE: "The Unity of 'The Garden Party,'" in *Studies in Short Fiction*, Vol. II, No. 1, Fall, 1964, pp. 61-5.

[*In the following essay, Davis reveals symbolic and narrative consistency in "The Garden Party."*]

In view of Katherine Mansfield's statement that the meaning of **"The Garden Party"** is "the diversity of life, and how we fit in everything, Death included," one would expect the structure and symbols of the story to be at the same time complex and finally resolvable into a unity. However, Warren S. Walker's "The Unresolved Conflict in 'The Garden Party'" began a trend in which either the complexity or the unity is exaggerated. One way of avoiding this distortion is to examine carefully the symbols and images of the story and their place in the basic pattern. By this means, one can perceive both the diversity and unity that Mansfield mentioned, can place the conflict within Laura alone and thus see its unity, and can restore Laura to her proper place as a character with whom the reader sympathizes because she doubts her mother's values at the

same time that he recognizes her inability, until the very end of the story, to distinguish between sensitivity and sentimentality.

The incidents of **"The Garden Party"** repeat in varying degrees of complexity one basic situation as a framework for the symbols, parallels, and contrasts. At the core of most scenes is Laura's attempt first to deal with other people or with experience on a mature level in a style—whether verbal or physical—learned from her mother; then her loss of confidence in that style; and finally her retreat to childish responses. The first challenge, dealing with the workmen come to erect the marquee, establishes this situation most clearly: "'Good morning,' she said, copying her mother's voice. But that sounded so fearfully affected that she was ashamed, and stammered like a little girl, 'Oh—er—have you come—is it about the marquee?'" She attempts briefly to maintain the adult role, avoiding mention of the morning's beauty because "she must be business-like" and wondering, because of her upbringing, "whether it was quite respectful of a workman to talk to her of bangs slap in the eye." But with her admission that "she did quite follow him" comes a release from the stiffness of the adult role she has learned from her mother. She is now free to wonder what the workmen are thinking; in the pre-sexual curiosity of childhood, she can contrast the workman's sensitivity to the lavender sprig with the silliness of her dancing partners; and, taking a bite of the piece of bread and butter which had spoiled her portrayal of a mature woman, she is able to feel "just like a work-girl," matey and comfortable with the workmen.

It is as a child that Laura hugs her brother, speaks on the telephone, and, with a child's impulsive sentimentality, responds to the "darling little spots" of sunlight, "Especially the one on the inkpot lid. It was quite warm. A warm little silver star. She could have kissed it." But it is as a girl on the verge of physical and emotional maturity that she responds to the lilies:

> Nothing but lilies—canna lilies, big pink flowers, wide
> open, radiant, almost frighteningly alive on bright
> crimson stems.

> "O-oh, Sadie!" said Laura, and the sound was like a
> little moan. She crouched down as if to warm herself
> at that blaze of lilies; she felt they were in her fingers,
> on her lips, growing in her breast.

These flowers are also the basis of Laura's renewed contact with her mother. At the beginning of the story, Mrs. Sheridan's garden is full of roses: "You could not help feeling that they understood that roses are the only flowers that impress people at garden parties; the only flowers that everybody is certain of knowing." It is with this view of flowers as socially useful that the workman's spontaneous appreciation of the lavender is contrasted. Now, confronted with the lilies that her mother has bought on impulse and her mother's admission that she is not logical, that is, not wholly governed by her conventional views, Laura accepts her mother on a deeper level. In the first episode, she tried on her mother's verbal style and physical mannerisms like a little girl scuffling along in mother's high heels; now she has discovered a shared enthusiasm, a sympathy, so that she is not merely imitating but becoming.

When Laura and Jose learn of the accident, their ensuing quarrel about canceling the party descends to childish irrelevance.

> [Jose] looked at her sister, just as she used to when they were little and fighting together. "You won't bring a drunken workman back to life by being sentimental," she said softly.

> "Drunk! Who said he was drunk?" Laura turned furiously on Jose. She said, just as they had used to say on those occasions, "I'm going straight up to tell mother."

Laura's attack on Jose's irrelevance, an excuse for not sympathizing with the dead man, masks the weakness in strict logic of her own position: drunk or not, the workman cannot be brought back to life by sentimentality, true sympathy, or anything else. But although her inarticulateness and appeal to authority are childish, her sympathy is not, even though she cannot defend it vocally.

In her confrontation with her mother, Laura is also rendered speechless by her mother's logic: hearing about the death is itself accidental and should therefore make no difference; furthermore, Laura's prating about sympathy is itself unsympathetic, Mrs. Sheridan implies, to the only people that matter. Having made sympathy seem childish, Mrs. Sheridan bestows on Laura the hat which temporarily reconciles her to the party and to the social, logical view of life. Walker identifies the hat as a symbol of "the spell of society" and notes that its immediate effect is to block communication with Laurie. Further examination reveals an even more complex set of meanings. For one thing, it presents Laura with a new life-style: as a "charming girl" Laura is bemused by the hat because it represents not merely social position or rank—which she need not accept at her mother's valuation, though she does not yet know it—but also her transformation from child to woman, a condition she cannot avoid. Therefore, the hat is difficult for her to reject because it meets her own needs and even, as the scene with the lilies shows, her latent desires. Yet the style is for her unsatisfactory; though she "looks a picture" (a key phrase), it is the picture of a woman in her mother's image; and it is to this altered version of his sister rather than to the sensitive child—who despite her hat and her new role still needs sympathetic human contact—that Laurie responds.

Laura's acceptance of the role imposed by her mother persists until she begins to descend the hill into the darkening lane of cottages. In the darkness, dressed in white lace and "the big hat with the velvet streamer," she feels cut off from the "dark people" around her. A second reference to the hat ribbon, which Laura nervously tosses over her shoulder, underlines the contrast between the encounter with the workman in the golden haze of the morning—"His smile was so easy, so friendly that Laura recovered."—and that with the dark people in the lane, when a woman's queer smile and reply disconcert her. As in the morning episode, where she felt like a workgirl, she wishes to assume a disguise, "to be covered up in anything, one of those women's shawls even," but she can no longer dismiss class distinctions because here she is different.

Critics have assumed that Laura's response to seeing the dead workman indicates a new maturity or an accession of knowledge. That this is by no means certain is clear when we examine the language of the episode in the context of the whole story. When Em's sister leads Laura towards the body, she reassures Laura with the words "'e looks a picture. There's nothing to show." The language recalls Mrs. Sheridan's use of "picture" to describe Laura and Laura's thoughts, after seeing herself in the hat, "of that poor woman and those little children, and the body being carried into the house. But it all seemed blurred, unreal, like a picture in the newspaper." Even if one does not accept the argument that the term "picture" has become synonymous with "untrustworthy, unreal, artificial," the description of Laura's response to the body indicates that she is once again retreating from the real world:

> There lay a young man, fast asleep—sleeping so soundly, so deeply, that he was far, far away from them both. Oh, so remote, so peaceful. He was dreaming. Never wake him up again. His head was sunk in the pillow, his eyes were closed; they were blind under the closed eyelids. He was given up to his dream. What did garden-parties and baskets and lace frocks matter to him? He was far from all these things. He was wonderful, beautiful. While they were laughing and while the band was playing, this marvel had come to the lane. Happy . . . happy. . . . All is well, said that sleeping face. This is just as it should be. I am content.

The insistent repetition and sentimental metaphors indicate the childishness of her thoughts, and the detail about the pillow, combined with Em's sister's "There's nothing to show" and the earlier description of the head injury as the cause of death, is sufficient evidence that Laura is once more attempting to retreat, to escape harsh reality through childishness, this time through a sentimentality that, ignoring or incapable of seeing the injury, projects into the corpse the girl's own desire to escape the complexity and ambiguity of life. For it should be noted that just as the thought of the worker's wife and children fades as Laura looks at herself in the mirror, so here the view of "this marvel [that] had come to the lane" blots out for Laura her glimpse of the wife: "Her face puffed up, red, with swollen eyes and swollen lips, looked terrible."

Yet Laura has in a way matured, in a way reconciled herself to her situation and to life. When she says, with "a loud childish sob," "Forgive my hat," she becomes more mature than her mother and Jose ever can be. She has earlier feared and retreated from her mother's kind of maturity—the only kind she knows—because it insists upon a view of life that carefully restricts sympathy and almost precludes it. Yet her own childish position, impulsive and thoughtless, cannot suffice because it cannot endure. It is in subconscious recognition of these facts that she says "Forgive my hat." Not "the hat," as it had been when she first entered the dark lane, but "*my* hat."

In accepting the hat—it is "a black hat trimmed with gold daisies"—she accepts intuitively its symbolic components: the blackness representing the fact of death and suffering and division of humanity which in the morning she had rejected; the gold the beauty that there is in life, in light, even in garden parties where one can "be with people who are all happy, to press hands, press cheeks, smile into eyes"; the flowers not the roses or the arum lilies that are socially impressive, but the daisies that had been displaced (as unworthy the company of roses?) at the story's beginning, which like the canna lilies symbolize necessary and instinctive maturing. The way lies open for her to accept maturity without accepting her mother's version of it.

All of this is, of course, implicit, for at the end of the story she stammers, as she had after her first attempt to play an adult role. This time, however, she is not ashamed, but awed, and her recognition of the complexity of experience is her first step towards maturity.

Nariman Hormasji (essay date 1967)

SOURCE: "Chekhov and Katherine Mansfield," in *Katherine Mansfield: An Appraisal,* Collins, 1967, pp. 106-16.

[*In the following excerpt, Hormasji studies the influence of the Russian writer Anton Chekhov on Mansfield and compares "The Garden Party" to Chekhov's story "After the Theater."*]

Whatever Mr [John Middleton] Murry might have said to the contrary, Katherine Mansfield, the chief exponent and craftsman of the short story, was the first English woman to be influenced by the works of Anton Chekhov. The modern English short story would not have developed out of the Wellsian fantasy. It would have remained in the hot-house of Kipling and the wooden boxes of Hardy. In other words, it would never have become earthbound.

From a combination of Chekhov's example and her own genius, Katherine Mansfield anticipated the emancipation of the short story. She took it out of the hands of the nineteenth century writers.

In which particular year of her life Miss Mansfield began to read Chekhov, it is difficult to say. "As for Chekhov, translations of his tales began to appear in the 1890s, and as early as 1909, Arnold Bennett was writing about him enthusiastically in the *New Age.*" It is likely that Miss Mansfield had read his tales before the Garnett translations. In 1910 **"The Child Who Was Tired"** was published in the *New Age* and its intimate relationship to Chekhov shows that she was already, in that year, under his influence.

No artist feels genuine love and admiration for another artist unless there are elements of his own temperament and sensibility that attract him. Throughout her short life she went on accumulating impressionistic scenes in Chekhov's manner and, at times, recording them in her *Journal* and *Scrapbook*. Whenever an occasion arose, she withdrew them from the stock, made use of "random details, casual incidents, unconscious gestures and remarks".

Though there are obvious resemblances to her master's treatment, theme, situation and tone, she lacked his depth of wisdom and his comprehensive understanding of human nature. Having no aptitude for understanding man in his social environment and man's relation to nature, her studies often remained superficial. Hence we find often in her stories such flaws as sentimentality, parochialism, and preciosity.

As a physician, Chekhov came in contact with women in the grip of passions, in the pain of separation and disease, of the crises of life; men with intent to commit murders and subject to the pressure of neuroses and mental strain. He saw humanity in a seething cauldron of pain and sorrow, rarely in joy and ecstasy, more often in the final stage of disintegration. "I have reasons for believing that the training a medical student has to go through is to a writer's benefit," he wrote. "He acquires knowledge of human nature which is invaluable. He sees it at its best and at its worst. When people are ill, when they are afraid, they discard the mask which they wear in health. The doctor sees them as they really are, selfish, hard, grasping, cowardly; but brave too, generous, kindly and good. He is tolerant of their frailties, awed by their virtues."

How could Katherine Mansfield have come into similar contact with ailing humanity? When she might have had the chance, she was practically confined to bed, or in voluntary exile and self-sought seclusion. In her stories, therefore, she could rarely scratch beneath the skin; she never saw blood coming out of any human body except her own. What a tragedy it was that she should confine herself to the ordinary visions of humanity in the ordinary crises of life! She had so few contacts with different kinds of people that she had no opportunities for enlarging the sphere of her observation.

Yet there was one thing in common between Katherine Mansfield and Chekhov. It was this: In their art they "tend to fasten upon certain moments, certain moods, certain apparently trivial incidents as possessing a special significance—moments that he knows will reveal not the stereotyped but the unique personality" [Dorothy Brewster and Angus Burrell, *Modern Fiction,* 1934].

There is no doubt that she was nearer to Chekhov in technique than to any other writer. "Their sensitiveness of perception is similar, their grasp of significant detail, their sense of quiet pattern, and their insistence on poetic quality of simple homely familiarities" [E. O'Brien, *Dictionary of National Biography, 1922-1930,* 1937].

Katherine Mansfield, like A. E. Coppard, was then remarkable for imbibing the Russian influences in her work and consequently transmitting those influences to the next generation of writers. As Somerset Maugham has pointed out, if the technique of modern short-story writers of today differs from that of the masters of the nineteenth century, it is to a great extent the result of her influence.

Let us compare Chekhov's "After the Theatre" with Katherine Mansfield's **"The Garden Party"**.

In the portrayal of Laura, Katherine Mansfield excels her acknowledged master. Chekhov's Nadya, quivering with *joie de vivre* and with her body emotionally moved by physical love, exhibits the characteristics of a young woman in love. She has all the subtleties of youth, all the imagination of a young woman in love, all the capacity to feel the warmth of love. Though she lacks depth of maturity and wisdom, she is not incapable of forming a judgment about the stupidity of an irresponsive love. With the sudden dawn of the realisation, she stops writing a letter to her lover which had begun with the words, "I love you" . . . ending with, "my God, how interesting, how fascinating men are!" As a susceptible girl she sinks into a reverie, bringing forth irrelevant images of her mother and rural surroundings.

Katherine Mansfield's Laura has similar characteristics and capacities for feeling the joy of the world, but her mind is more complex and given to philosophising. She goes to the length of questioning the wisdom of God in creating the world.

Like Nadya, she falls into a reverie and is soon disturbed.

"'Laura, Laura, where are you? Telephone, Laura!' a voice cried from the house. 'Coming.' Away she skimmed, over the lawn, up the path, up the steps, across the veranda and into the porch. . . ."

This is not Laura alone; millions of girls of her age in any part of the world behave, talk, and romp exactly as she does.

When her brother Laurie asks her to see if his coat needs pressing, she says, "I will" and "suddenly she couldn't stop herself. She ran at Laurie and gave him a small, quick squeeze. 'Oh I do love parties, don't you?' gasped Laura."

Thus immense joy fills her with yearning. Emotions quiver on her lips and her heart is bursting with joy at the preparation of the garden party.

"The house was alive with soft, quick steps and running voices." The piano is being moved. "Little faint winds were playing chase in at the tops of the windows, out at the doors. And there were two tiny spots of sun, one on

the inkpot, one on a silver photograph frame, playing too."

Godber's cream puffs were brought in and looking at them, Laura says, "Don't they carry one back to all one's parties?"

In a flash she is carried back to the days of her childhood. As she is not alone, she is pulled back and within a few seconds Laura and Jose "were found licking their fingers with that absorbed inward look. . . ."

Death intrudes upon her inner sanctuary where a few moments ago all was joy. Someone had died of an accident.

> "Dead!" Laura stared at Godber's man.

> "Dead when they picked him up," said Godber's man with relish. "They were taking the body home as I came up here."

She thinks of stopping the party and reminds her mother, "'The band and everybody arriving. They'd hear us, mother; they are nearly neighbours!'"

In her heart of hearts she felt it was wrong to have a party.

> "Mother, isn't it really terribly heartless of us?"

> "You are being very absurd, Laura," she said coldly. "People like that don't expect sacrifices from us . . ."

These little phrases bring out delicate shades of character.

The party is nearly over. Katherine Mansfield writes: "And the perfect afternoon slowly ripened, slowly faded, slowly its petals closed."

Her mother sends Laura with a basket of food to the stricken family.

> On that late afternoon, Laura was led into the room where lay a young man, fast asleep—sleeping so soundly, so deeply, that he was far, far away from them both. Oh, so remote, so peaceful. He was dreaming. Never wake him up again. His head was sunk in the pillow, his eyes were closed; they were blind under the closed eyelids. He was given up to his dream. What did garden parties and baskets and lace frocks matter to him? He was far from all those things. He was wonderful, beautiful. While they were laughing and while the band was playing, this marvel had come to the lane. Happy . . . happy . . . All is well, said that sleeping face. This is just as it should be. I am content.

Thus it is shown that for Laura death does not create feelings of terror but makes her wonder what life is. She is unable to explain the philosophical meaning of life and death. Yet she *understands* well that the demarcation line between the two is thin and that death walks hand in hand with life.

The juxtaposition of the grace of living and the disgrace of existing, of living joy and mocking death, of opulence and poverty, of laughter on the one hand with dishes sprawling into the dustbins and of tears shed and unshed going to waste on a face that once laughed is the highlight of **"The Garden Party"**.

One among many human beings was destined to feel the contrast; the only one who was sensitive to her surroundings and who had any love for the dead and the bereaved. That one was Laura. To have accepted such maladjustments in existence was Laura's destiny. Though they were near to one another physically, Laura was a thousand miles apart emotionally, intellectually, socially, from the dead young man: one was on the highest rung of the social ladder, the other at the bottom; though they were strangers to one another, Laura felt bound to the young man by a new awareness of their common humanity, which death had revealed to her.

Miss Mansfield discovered for herself that to live, her art had to be distinctive and not imitative; that the stories which she wrote had to be governed by principles she herself evolved. Her gradual development of critical taste is reflected in her letters. She had enough strength to detach herself from any extraneous influence. For her immediate English predecessors and contemporaries, she had no use. But it is clear that she sharpened her poetic sensibility by reading Shakespeare and Keats.

Some critics have accused her of triviality—a charge which she herself recognised in her *Journal*. But few have been prepared to endorse this self-criticism, impressive though it is. Such an analysis arose not so much out of modesty as out of dissatisfaction with her own achievement. It was honest and searching and directed wholly towards improving her style, her technique and her means of transmitting her vision.

It was her high sense of literary values, her deep honesty and her concept of her ultimate goal that made her self-conscious about her "trivial" achievement. Endowed as she was with a critical sense, she anticipated that some day critics would find fault with her stories. Hence she would not permit the reprinting of her earlier stories; hence she stopped writing when she found no more inspiration, when she was drifting in strange waters she could not chart.

Anders Iversen (essay date 1968)

SOURCE: "A Reading of Katherine Mansfield's 'The Garden Party,'" in *Orbis Litterarum*, Vol. 23, 1968, pp. 5-34.

[*In the following essay, Iversen offers a comprehensive account of mythological, structural, and autobiographical aspects of "The Garden Party."*]

There is a short story "Two Worlds" ("To Verdener") by the Danish writer I. P. Jacobsen (1847-85). Its imagery offers points of similarity with Katherine Mansfield's story **"The Garden Party"**, and though I do not postulate any influence from I. P. Jacobsen on Katherine Mansfield, yet a glance at Jacobsen's story will help to bring out the main theme of **"The Garden Party"**.

The scene of "Two Worlds" is laid in a poor village on the river Salzach. The story opens with a telling meiosis: "The Salzach is not a cheerful river, and there is a little village on its eastern bank which is very dreary, very poor, and strangely quiet." A sick and lonely woman from the village tries to transfer, by means of magic, her illness to a healthy young woman passing by in a boat with a group of friends. The magic does not work, and a year later the poor suffering woman drowns herself just as the other woman happens to be passing by a second time; she is now on her honeymoon. The two women belong to different worlds, and not even magic suffices to bridge the gulf between them.

What is of importance here is the way in which I. P. Jacobsen describes the two worlds. The houses of the village are "like a miserable flock of stunted beggars", their "black, dull window panes" scowling spitefully at "the happier houses" belonging to the other world, beyond the river, in a green plain stretching far away into the golden haze. The poor houses, huddling together, are shrouded in "oppressive gloom and silence", the only sound being the inexorable murmur of the slow, languid, "strangely absent-minded" river.

The sick woman is in keeping with this world of misery: her figure is "weak, emaciated", her hand "almost transparent", her face "waxen", her eyes "despairing" and anxious, her mouth "tired", her smile "strangely feeble-minded". "For long, long years she had been suffering from a painful disease, from which she never obtained any relief".

The party of travellers in the boat belong to the other world, the rich world across the river. The sunlight, golden and glittering, is focused upstream on the river around the boat, which "seemed to be sailing on a mirror of gold". The young woman at the helm looks the very picture of youthful strength and happiness. She and her companions are unaware of the existence of the sick woman and her world. The boat is a self-contained world, floating past. The carefree, flippant attitude of its passengers is indicated by the snatches of talk overheard: "happiness" and "blessedness" are words bandied about in the game of polished conversation; though, on the occasion of the second passing, there are hints of the inconstancy of happiness. It is the theme of a sentimental but beautiful song sung by the bride: her present happiness is enhanced by the memory of how she had yearned for such happiness. She proposes a toast:

> I drink to Happiness *before* it was mine,
> To the poverty of mere hoping,
> I drink to dreams!

The main point of the story is the contrast between the two worlds: one described in words signifying brilliant colours, happy noises, motion, active enjoyment; the other in words conveying the ideas of darkness, drabness, silence, decay, and suffering. One is life, the other death.

In **"The Garden Party"** we find much the same contrast. Katherine Mansfield creates two worlds, juxtaposing and opposing the Garden (life) and the lane (death). But Katherine Mansfield's starting-point is that of the rich world, and her story differs from I. P. Jacobsen's also in that some sort of contact is established between the two worlds.

"The Garden Party" can be read on several levels: as a social comedy with satirical sketches of Mrs. Sheridan, etc., developing into a serious discussion of the relations between two social classes (the author sympathizing with the underdog); as a penetrating psychological study; as a pattern of archetypal images (the Garden of Eden; the journey to the nether world); and like most of Katherine Mansfield's stories it can be read for its autobiographical interest. The various planes, of course, are not like water-tight compartments; they intersect. Yet it is worth while to keep them in mind as the analysis progresses.

The social comedy is obvious from the outset. The preponderantly feminine world of the Sheridans is an enclave, almost isolated from the outside world. In the garden one may conveniently forget that there *is* a world outside, until some day, perhaps, one is rudely awakened. In an early poem (1912) Katherine Mansfield writes:

> There was a child once.
> He came to play in my garden;
> – – –
> I led him down each secret path,
> Showing him the hiding-place of all my treasures.
> – – – – – On tiptoe we walked among the deepest
>   shades;
> We bathed in the shadow pools beneath the trees,
> Pretending we were under the sea.
> Once—near the boundary of the garden—
> We heard steps passing along the World-road;
> Oh, how frightened we were!
> I whispered: "Have you ever walked along the
>   road?"
> He nodded, and we shook the tears from our eyes . . .

Mrs. Sheridan and her daughters move and have their being in a world of sunshine, wealth, and ease, prattling about dresses, hats, and hair-dos, with no major practical problems—all except Laura ("the artistic one"), who has a questioning mind ("how curious, she seemed to be different from them all"). She is the only one who reaches out beyond that world. (Her father and brother do not really count, as they are only briefly *in* the Garden, and very partially *of* it.)

> When the Sheridans were little they were forbidden to
> set foot [in the lane with the mean little cottages]—
> But since they were grown up, Laura and Laurie on

their prowls sometimes walked through. It was disgusting and sordid. They came out with a shudder. But still one must go everywhere; one must see everything. So through they went.

One is reminded of Katherine Mansfield's own quest for "experience". She was, says William Orton (in *The Last Romantic*), "one of the few people in whom the 'thirst for experience' is a genuine thing, indicating a genuine need."

The Garden, as Katherine Mansfield describes it, is a place of brilliant colours, gay noises ("tinkling spoons, laughter"), birdlike movements. The weather is "ideal", the day "perfect", "windless, warm, the sky without a cloud. Only the blue was veiled with a haze of light gold." There is an abundance of nature everywhere, and amid such plenty a heightened sense of being alive. The Garden of the Sheridans is like the Garden of Eden.

> Hundreds, yes, literally hundreds [of roses], had come
> out in a single night; the green bushes bowed down as
> though they had been visited by archangels.

> . . . . .

> And [the karaka trees] were so lovely, with their broad,
> gleaming leaves, and their clusters of yellow fruit. They
> were like trees you imagined growing on a desert island,
> proud, solitary, lifting their leaves and fruits to the sun
> in a kind of silent splendour.

There is a primeval quality about the Garden: everything is in its prime ("a perfect morning" "in early summer"). The freshness and splendour of this world are reminiscent of what Katherine Mansfield says about her native New Zealand: "in the early morning there I always remember feeling that this little island has dipped back into the dark blue sea during the night only to rise again at gleam of day, all hung with bright spangles and glittering drops" [*The Letters of Katherine Mansfield,* Vols. I & II, 1928].

As if this natural abundance was not enough, Mrs. Sheridan has ordered more flowers from the florist's. Characteristically, what is a wild extravagance (not "logical") and looks like a mistake, only serves to make perfection more perfect: "—a wide, shallow tray full of pots of pink lilies. No other kind. Nothing but lilies—canna lilies, big pink flowers, wide open, radiant, almost frighteningly alive on bright crimson stems". A profusion of canna lilies, "another whole tray", is carried in. Passing the shop the day before, Mrs. Sheridan had "suddenly thought for once in my life I shall have enough canna lilies. The garden-party will be a good excuse". Here they are, a "blaze of lilies" just inside the front door. And we may note in passing that the door "that led to the kitchen regions" is a green baize door. Verdure surrounds the Sheridans on all sides.

In such a world young girls do not walk; they rather fly: "Away Laura flew"; "Away she skimmed, over the lawn, up the path, up the steps, across the veranda and into the porch"; and Jose is called "the butterfly". They are brightly coloured birds: Kitty Maitland is to wear a white dress, and Laura's frock "shone". And there are other birds of the same feather. The guests at the garden party "were like bright birds that had alighted in the Sheridans' garden for this one afternoon, on their way to—where?" We remain on the wing with Mrs. Sheridan's voice which "floated down the stairs", and with Kitty's: she "trilled". Even the cream puffs "look beautifully light and feathery."

Everything, indeed, seems airy, alive, astir.

> [The canna lilies were] almost frighteningly alive on bright crimson stems. "O-oh, Sadie!" said Laura, and the sound was like a little moan. She crouched down as if to warm herself at that blaze of lilies; she felt they were in her fingers, on her lips, growing in her breast.
>
> . . . . .
>
> All the doors in the house seemed to be open. The house was alive with soft, quick steps and running voices. The green baize door – – – swung open and shut with a muffled thud. – – – But the air! If you stopped to notice, was the air always like this? Little faint winds were playing chase in at the tops of the windows, out at the doors. And there were two tiny spots of sun, one on the inkpot, one on a silver photograph frame, playing too. Darling little spots. Especially the one on the inkpot lid. It was quite warm. A warm little silver star. She [Laura] could have kissed it.

Logic being a mundane quality, "a logical mother" is not called for in the Garden. Mistakes do not matter. They are remedied at once (the flags for the sandwiches), or turn out to be not mistakes at all but means to make things even more perfect (the canna lilies). The garden is 'out of the world', so to speak; beyond the bounds of time and space. It is appropriate that Mrs. Sheridan should seem to be no older than her daughters. Change and death (i.e. time) are unheard of in the Garden except as something happening to strange creatures outside, or as empty words to be sung with "a brilliant, dreadfully unsympathetic smile".

One may venture to carry the Paradise image further. GOD-ber's man comes as an angel of death. Acting through cook he tempts Laura and Jose to eat of the forbidden cream puffs. That eating is the moment of supreme happiness: "two minutes later Jose and Laura were licking their fingers with that absorbed inward look that only comes from whipped cream". But it is followed immediately by a disturbing new knowledge of good and evil. It upsets Laura, not Jose, who remains innocent in more than one sense of the word. "Something had happened"; and Godber's man tells them about the accident in which a young man, Scott, from one of the neighbouring cottages, had been killed that morning.

Laura senses that the Scott family are "nearly neighbours", and that it would be "terribly heartless" not to stop the garden party. But against the lack of understanding of

Jose and her mother she cannot yet prevail. She is tempted (her mother popping a big black hat on her and making her a present of it) to forget about the poor man's death for the time being ("I'll remember it again after the party's over, she decided"). That is her sin of omission.

The hat charms not only herself, but also her brother Laurie, and evokes many compliments at the party: she looks "striking", "quite Spanish", etc. Tinged with a knowledge of death, her beauty is more interesting, more dramatic. It is heightened, as it were, by means of the black hat (symbol of sin).

Between the Garden and the outside world there is just enough contact for Laura to be conscious of its existence and for the others to ignore it.

The first confrontation of the two worlds is when the workmen come to put up the marquee. It is left to Laura, "the artistic one", to deal with them, because the others are in various degrees of Paradisiacal undress. The workmen look like friendly lumbering animals, bears perhaps ("we won't bite"). Laura is conscious of the difference and distance between them and herself, but too self-conscious to be quite sure how to address them. She begins by speaking condescendingly to them, but fails. The workmen, however, are "so easy, so friendly", so "nice" that she at once "recovered". She realizes, or thinks she realizes, the absurdity of class distinctions, which are as involved (with loops, etc.) as the syntax in which they are described:

> It's all the fault, she decided, as the tall fellow drew something on the back of an envelope, something that was to be looped up or left to hang, of these absurd class distinctions.

Then she rushes into generalization, sentimentalizing workmen:

> Oh, how extraordinarily nice workmen were, she thought. Why couldn't she have workmen for friends rather than the silly boys she danced with and who came to Sunday night supper? She would get on much better with men like these.

From being less than ordinary human beings they have now become more than human.

If this is a wrong view Laura at least errs on the generous side, unlike her mother and sister. The idea of another species inhabiting the world outside is more or less explicit in Jose's words about "a drunken workman" and about the "absurdity" and "extravagance" of Laura's suggestion that they should stop the garden party; and also in Mrs. Sheridan's words:

> "Mother, a man's been killed," began Laura.
>
> "*Not* in the garden?" interrupted her mother.
>
> "No, no!"

"Oh, what a fright you gave me!" Mrs. Sheridan sighed with relief – – –

"But listen, mother – – – Of course, we can't have our party, can we?" she pleaded. – – –

"But, my dear child, use your common sense. It's only by accident we've heard of it. If someone had died there normally—and I can't understand how they keep alive in those poky little holes—we should still be having our party, shouldn't we?"

The same note is struck, unwittingly, by Kitty, when she says about the "green-coated" band: "aren't they too like frogs for words?"

Sympathy and *tact,* as the words occur and recur in Mrs. Sheridan's and Jose's vocabulary, only apply to people of their own class:

"You are being very absurd, Laura. – – – People like that don't expect sacrifices from us. And it's not very sympathetic to spoil everybody's enjoyment as you're doing now."

Mrs. Sheridan can pretend that she does not like parties, and a moment later she will blame Laura for having suggested that they should put off the party. She considers it "very tactless" of her husband to mention the fatal accident. Perhaps the least attractive side of her character, her callous egoism, is adequately summed up in her "brilliant" idea of sending the crumbs from her own rich table down to the widow.

To Jose and Mrs. Sheridan Laura's behaviour must no doubt appear absurd and extravagant. Laura's sympathy is *extravagant* in the precise etymological sense of the word: it wanders beyond the bounds of the garden. For Laura the day is a crisis and a turning-point. One period of her life is drawing to a close with the knell sounding the end of the party: "And the perfect afternoon slowly ripened, slowly faded, slowly its petals closed".

When Laura sets out on her descent into the world of the dark lane, the archetypal element becomes more marked. She is entering a place which is in every respect the opposite of the Garden. It is dark, drab, silent, with slow-moving forms; a realm of shades.

The colours are all dark. The houses are "painted a chocolate brown". They are "in deep shade". The lane is "smoky and dark", and the very smoke coming out of the chimneys is "poverty-stricken. Little rags and shreds of smoke, so unlike the great silvery plumes that uncurled from the Sheridans' chimneys". Only "a flicker of light" is seen in some of the houses. Inside Mrs. Scott's house the passage is "gloomy", and there is "a wretched little low kitchen, lighted by a smoky lamp".

The people, appropriately, are as dark and sombre as their surroundings Mrs. Scott's sister is dressed in black, and outside the house there is "a dark knot of people". One may notice the contrast between this group of people (who stop talking and draw aside as Laura approaches) and the gaily rotating couples at the garden party.

Here "down below in the hollow" everything is so "quiet" after the afternoon with its "kisses, voices, tinkling spoons, laughter". Only "a low hum" is heard from "the mean little cottages". We are told that "children swarmed", and that they "played in the doorways", but on the occasion of Laura's visit they are very quiet children. We scarcely hear them, if at all. If the lane is rich in offspring, it seems to be poor in everything else. The houses are repeatedly called "little mean dwellings", or "those poky little holes". They are "the greatest possible eyesore". It is a "disgusting and sordid" world.

There are gardens, or rather "garden patches", but how unlike the Sheridans' garden! There is no superabundance of nature here: no flowers, "nothing but cabbage stalks" and "tomato cans". Nor is there any birdlike movement, no flying or skimming, though birds there are—namely "sick hens"—and bird-cages: one "house-front was studded all over with minute bird-cages". One old woman has to use a crutch, and shadows are seen to move "crab-like" across windows. The creatures who "hurry by" or "hang over the palings" are not the bright birds of the garden party, but people with dirty jobs like sweeps and a cobbler and washerwomen.

They have no surplus energy for flirtation and compliments. Indeed, their world is almost sexless. Women wear "shawls and men's tweed caps", and men are seen hanging "over the palings", literally and figuratively, but are otherwise conspicuous by their absence. Like the Garden, this is a predominantly feminine world: the men are on the sidelines only. (For a similarly devitalized atmosphere, see Katherine Mansfield's description of the inmates of the pension L'Hermitage, at Mentone, who "looked exactly as though they were risen from the dead – – – They are still sexless, and blow their noses in a neuter fashion—neither male nor female blows", *Letters*).

No wonder that the language used in the lane should sound "revolting" to delicate Sheridan ears; and it is in keeping with the otherness of this lower world that we do not find bright and brisk names like Kitty and Jose, but only the name *Em*, an almost inarticulate sound, like a plaintive noise, not a name so much as an anonym.

Time and change and death, however, are stark realities here. There are old and decrepit people: "an old, old woman with a crutch sat in a chair". And some people look ugly, e.g. the widow sitting in her kitchen at the fire: "Her face, puffed up, red, with swollen eyes and swollen lips, looked terrible. She seemed as though she couldn't understand why Laura was there".

This confrontation in the "wretched little low kitchen" is another of the many well-balanced contrasts of the story. It should be compared with the kitchen scene in the Sheridans' house: the culmination of happiness, followed by the knowledge of death, but death by hearsay only, something that Laura could decide to forget till the party was over, because "it all seemed blurred, unreal, like a picture in the newspaper"—unlike the present face-to-face encounter.

From the kitchen Laura proceeds to the bedroom, without wanting to, without knowing where she is going or why. Since she entered the lane, there has been something inevitable about her progress: she seems to have been caught up in some slippery machinery that carries her along. The people are not figures in the round, but shadows rather, almost parts of the machinery: the "dark knot of people" outside Mrs. Scott's house "parted", as Laura approached. "It was as though she was expected as though they had known she was coming here". One of the women smiles "queerly", and Mrs. Scott's sister, who acts as cicerone in the House of Death, does not answer Laura's questions (she "seemed not to have heard her"). She leads her on, with her "oily voice" and "oily smile". Later her voice "sounded fond and sly".

Laura has, indeed, ventured outside her own world, and not only in social terms. Like Aeneas she is "walking in the darkness, with the shadows round her and night's loneliness above her, through a substanceless Empire" (see W. F. Jackson Knight's translation of the *Aeneid* in the *Penguin Classics*, 1964). This Empire is situated "at the very bottom of a steep rise", and its houses are "in a lane to themselves". To get there one has to cross "a broad road", which "gleamed white", while "down below in the hollow the little cottages were in deep shade". As if to remind us whither Laura is bound "a big dog ran by like a shadow".

As Laura makes her way into this world of crab-like scuttling and listless hanging-about, dusk and darkness close in on her. The passage becomes narrower and narrower, the claustrophobic feeling more and more intense. From the narrow lane she passes through a gate and "up the tiny path", invoking God ("She actually said, 'Help me, God'") as she walks up to the house. There she is "shut in the [gloomy] passage", and next finds herself in "a wretched little low kitchen, lighted by a smoky lamp". The confrontation here with the "terrible" face of grief, with which there is no communicating, marks the penultimate stage of her ordeal. She is momentarily back in the passage, and then walks "straight through into the bedroom", the chamber of Death.

As it turns out, the final confrontation here, which is the real goal of her journey, is not terrible or "awful", but "wonderful, beautiful", "simply marvellous". Death is *young* and beautiful; "'e looks a picture":

> There lay a young man, fast asleep—sleeping so soundly, so deeply – – – Oh, so remote, so peaceful. He was dreaming. Never wake him up again. – – – He was given up to his dream. – – – He was wonderful, beautiful. While they were laughing and while the band was playing, this marvel had come to the lane. Happy . . . happy . . .

Laura, deeply moved by the peacefulness and beauty of death, responds with a silent echoing of the young man's "message": an acceptance of death. "Happy . . . happy

Portait of Mansfield, 1918.

. . . All is well, said that sleeping face. This is just as it should be. I am content".

On top of such an experience Laura's "Forgive my hat" may seem pathetically weak, but it is psychologically true that she cannot boil down what she has just gone through to a neat formula, and take her leave with a quotable envoy, just as, a few minutes later, she gropes in vain for words to express to Laurie what life is. It is worth noting, too, that "Forgive my hat" is a more pregnant remark than may at first sight appear from the context (an apology for the tactlessness of wearing such a hat and dress). It was the hat that had tempted her to forget about the young man's death earlier in the day. If it is true that she has experienced a break-through into a fuller understanding of life, her words may be interpreted: "Forgive the insensitiveness of my old self."

Now that her task is accomplished, Laura is strong enough to walk by herself: "this time she didn't wait for Em's sister. She found her way out – – –". Laurie meets her half-way: he is closer to her than any of the other Sheridans and instinctively understands her. She returns to her own world, a sadder and a wiser girl, but also strangely happy. She has escaped out of the narrowness of Paradise into the fullness and richness and sadness of mortal life.

What has happened to Laura can be summarized thus: She leaves her own people to walk in the valley of the shadow of death; after a narrow passage through the nether world she returns to the upper world, but changed, reborn as it were.

This pattern of images I take to be a symbol of her growing-up. Not that she was a child in the morning and is now an adult, but she has taken a decisive step on the road—the broad World-road—leading through experience to maturity. The Garden thus comes to represent the paradise of childhood and innocence, and the Two-Worlds imagery is a means of making the psychic process of growing-up more manifest, of giving it a local habitation and a name.

The two worlds of the garden and the lane may be taken as an instance of the Paradise-Hades archetype, as it is discussed in Maud Bodkin's *Archetypal Patterns in Poetry*. (I am concerned here only with archetypes as patterns of images found in imaginative literature, not with the Jungian implications of the archetypes, their mode of existence, etc.) The Paradise-Hades pattern can be considered in its spatial aspect, as was done above, but also in a temporal aspect as the Rebirth archetype (including "the night journey"); or if the two archetypes are not identical, they are at least closely related.

This brings us to the idea of initiation. Maud Bodkin calls attention to the parallels between the underworld journey of Aeneas and the initiation rites of mystery cults. And it may be suggested that Laura's journey in **"The Garden Party"** can be profitably regarded as a rite of initiation, not into a mystery cult but into the adult world.

To throw light on this initiation one can turn from Miss Bodkin to another "pattern-monger", Arnold van Gennep, who in his *Rites de passage* (1908) studied the rites pertaining to man's transition from one age group or status to another (birth, initiation, marriage, etc.), and found a typical pattern recurring in all the so-called *rites of passage*. Such transition is very often symbolized by means of "a territorial passage" as of a man passing from his own country or territory into another country, wavering for a certain length of time between two worlds (van Gennep, *The Rites of Passage*, translated by M. B. Vizedom and G. L. Caffee, 1960).

In the chapter dealing with initiation rites van Gennep dwells particularly on rites at puberty, distinguishing between physical puberty and social puberty, and concentrating on the latter to the exclusion of the former, which he finds unimportant from his point of view. If we narrow down the field of vision even further, focusing on the psychological aspect of puberty, we shall find van Gennep's pattern illustrated in **"The Garden Party"**. It is even possible to apply his subdivisions of the category of *rites of passage* to Laura's career through the story. The rites of passage, according to van Gennep, can be subdivided into *rites of separation, transition rites,* and *rites of incorporation,* though the "three subcategories are not developed to the same extent by all peoples or in every ceremonial pattern". Laura's altercations with her mother

and Jose before and after the party would constitute the separation rites, her visit to the lane the transition rites, and the first stage of the incorporation (into a new group) would be marked by Laurie's coming to meet her at the corner of the lane.

Several of Katherine Mansfield's stories are about girls at the age of puberty, who are faced with such "facts of life" as death, birth, and sexual maturity. A case in point is Sabina, the very young and naïve servant girl in **"At Lehmann's"** (from *In a German Pension*). She is confronted at once with the mystery of birth and the first stirrings of love: her mistress, fat ugly Frau Lehmann, is in labour upstairs, while a young man, who frequents the café, makes love to Sabina downstairs. **"At Lehmann's"** is an early and somewhat crude story, but it catches vividly the period of transition between childhood and adult age ("Look here," [the young man said to Sabina], "are you a child, or are you playing at being one?"), with its puzzled and puzzling realization that birth and death and love, beauty and ugliness, somehow all exist side by side.

One of the salient features of the experience of adolescence seems to be a new awareness of time. One is at the beginning of everything, and it suddenly occurs to one that what has a beginning must also have an end. Hence alternating feelings of self-congratulation and self-pity (sometimes pity for others). This is felt by the young couple in **"Honeymoon"** (from *The Doves' Nest*), though they are presumably a few years older than Laura and Sabina. Listening to and old man's singing, she, Fanny, thinks: "Is life like this too? – – – There are people like this. There is suffering. – – – Had she and George the right to be so happy? Wasn't it cruel? – – – But George had been feeling differently from Fanny. The poor old boy's voice was funny in a way, but, God, how it made you realise what a terrific thing it was to be at the beginning of everything, as they were, he and Fanny!"

Another illustration of this theme will be found in **"Her First Ball"**, in the same collection as, and in some respects a companion piece to, **"The Garden Party"**. Leila, an 18-year-old country-cousin of the Sheridans', accompanies Meg, Jose, Laura, and Laurie to a ball. She can hardly contain her expectation. Everything seems to be dancing along, and there is the same birdlike motion as in **"The Garden Party"**. To Leila it all seems heavenly, "simply heavenly!" "Her first ball! She was only at the beginning of everything". But in this heavenly harmony there is a jarring note. One of her partners is quite unlike the others: old fat, bald; "he ought to have been on the stage with the fathers and mothers". Dancing with him is "more like walking than dancing". His words are also sadly different from the usual teen-age ball-room conversation. For one thing, he has "been doing this kind of thing for the last thirty years", and for another his purpose seems to be to force Leila to look ahead a similar span of years.

> "Of course," he said, "you can't hope to last anything like as long as that. No-o, – – – long before that you'll be sitting up there on the stage, looking on, in your nice black velvet. And these pretty arms will have

turned into little short fat ones – – – And your heart will ache, ache – – – because no one wants to kiss you now."

This soft-voiced parading of the disillusioning realities of time, change, and death before Leila in her moment of bliss gives her pause:

> Was it—could it all be true? It sounded terribly true. Was this first ball only the beginning of her last ball, after all? At that the music seemed to change; it sounded sad, sad; it rose upon a great sigh. Oh, how quickly things changed! Why didn't happiness last for ever? For ever wasn't a bit too long.

> "I want to stop," she said in a breathless voice. – – – [She tried] smile. But deep inside her a little girl threw her pinafore over the head and sobbed. Why had he spoiled it all?

However, on this occasion, "a soft melting, ravishing tune, and a young man with curly hair"—her partner for the next dance—prove stronger than the fat man's intimations of mortality: "In one minute, in one turn, her feet glided, glided. The lights, the azaleas, the dresses, the pink faces, the velvet chairs, all became one beautiful flying wheel." And when later she bumps into the fat man, she does not even recognise him again.

It will probably be granted that Laura in **"The Garden Party"** receives a less fleeting impression of the reality of time and change than does Leila, and also that **"The Garden Party"** is richer in tone and significance than the other "teen-age" stories. The heroine is a young girl, and the problem she grapples with is typical of adolescence, but the "moral" of the story, the solution Laura is moving towards, is of universal application, and it can lead to a discussion of Katherine Mansfield's mature philosophy of life.

The moral, in brief, is this: we must *accept* everything, death included; and there is beauty in such acceptance. Katherine Mansfield herself says as much in a letter to William Gerhardi (March 13, 1922):

> – – – that is what I tried to convey in **"The Garden Party"**. The diversity of life and how we try to fit in everything, Death included. That is bewildering for a person of Laura's age. She feels things ought to happen differently. First one and then another. But life isn't like that. We haven't the ordering of it. Laura says, "But all these things must not happen at once." And Life answers, "Why not? How are they divided from each other." And they *do* all happen, it is inevitable. And it seems to me there is beauty in that inevitability.

(Letters II)

The idea of acceptance is often mentioned in her letters, as a principle or a confession of faith, sometimes as a *cri de cœur*. Beauty and ugliness exist side by side, but one can reach the point where one accepts ugliness and feels that it no longer mars beauty; indeed, there would be no

beauty in the usual sense without ugliness. Suffering, too, must be accepted, "bodily suffering such as I've known for three years", she writes in October, 1920. It has changed everything, but she dwells not on what has been taken away but rather on what has been added: "there is something added. *Everything has its shadow.* Is it right to resist such suffering? Do you know I feel it has been an immense privilege. Yes, in spite of all". Only the writer who has "—in the profoundest sense of the word—*accepted life*" can create worthwhile literature, and life is relationship, not fastidious isolation. In a letter of March 1, 1921, she warns an unnamed correspondent against blaming parents too much! "We *all* had parents." And she goes on:

> One is NEVER free until one has done blaming somebody or praising somebody for what is bad and good in one. – – – Don't think I underestimate the enormous power parents can have. I don't. – – – But like everything else in life—I mean all suffering, however great—we have to get over it—to cease from harking back to it—to grin and bear it and to hide the wounds. More than that, and far more true is we have to find the *gift* in it. We can't afford to waste such an expenditure of feeling; we have to learn from it—and we *do,* I most deeply believe, come to be thankful for it. By saying we can't afford to . . . waste . . . feeling! I sound odious and cynical. I don't feel it. What I mean is. *Everything must be accepted.*

Such is the "philosophy" upon which **"The Garden Party"** is based. Part of it, as also suggested by Middleton Murry (*Katherine Mansfield and Other Literary Studies,* 1959), is summed up in Keats's "Beauty is truth, truth beauty", if we dare to disregard the warnings of Cleanth Brooks (*The Well Wrought Urn*) and others against detaching this ambiguous statement from its dramatic context. The philosophy, as here distilled from letters, remains vague, which is not surprising, but perhaps enough quotations have been given to hint at its tenor and give some definition to even such a saying as the following: "It seems to me that the *secret* of life is to *accept* life" (*Letters* II). Katherine Mansfield's philosophy grew out of her experiences, and she did not use words like *accept* glibly.

All these ideas, of course, are not explicit in Laura's words or thoughts, but as I interpret the story they are there implicitly. Laura wins through to accepting death and the ugliness and suffering she has been confronted with as inevitably part of life. She cannot formulate this experience in words, and has the good sense not to take refuge in inadequate words. And it is worth remembering that earlier, before her visit to the lane, her "absurd" uneasiness had found expression in "extravagant" sympathy, whereas the Song of Innocence here may be said, a little fancifully perhaps, to be the "dreadfully unsympathetic" "This Life is Wee-ary".

It is no more strange that archetypal elements should appear in Katherine Mansfield's work than in the work of contemporaries like Lawrence, Virginia Woolf, Eliot, and Joyce. She was steeped in English literature from Chaucer to Joyce and Eliot, her special favourites being her "divine Shakespeare" and the Romantic poets. She also kept her weather eye open, watching the intellectual currents of her own time closely and critically, and one need not have been a student of Jung at this early stage to come across archetypes. Indeed, such ideas may have come "natural" to her, or been absorbed from her early reading. In several of her early poems (from the years 1909-11) there are personifications of the heavenly bodies and the forces of nature, and she often tries her hand at a little myth-making.

But it is remarkable that for once it is possible to locate Paradise and Hell. Paradise is to be found, not, as was once surmised, in a fabled country of the Orient, nor on some western Isles of the Blest, but in the South Seas, in Thorndon, a suburb of Wellington, New Zealand, at 75 Tinakori Road to be precise; and Hell, or Hades, awkwardly, is on a neighbouring piece of ground. Tinakori Road, on which more than one of Katherine Mansfield's childhood homes were situated, ran down the hill, towards Lambton Quay and the windy Esplanade (cf. **"The Wind Blows"** in *Bliss*). The topography offered dramatic contrasts here. Close to the road there was a deep rift, a gorge cutting towards the harbour.

No. 75, to which the family moved when Katherine was in her tenth year, is described, in her *Journal,* as a big, white-painted house, standing high and dry, hidden away in a wildish garden, which sloped away in terraces down to a stone wall. Unfortunately, the neighbourhood was very mixed. It was "a little trying to have one's own washer-woman living next door", and "beyond her 'hovel', as Mother called it" there lived other strange creatures. And then to descend into the pit: "just opposite our house there was a paling fence, and below the paling fence in a hollow, squeezed in almost under the fold of a huge gorse-covered hill, was Saunder's Lane" [*Journal of Katherine Mansfield,* 1936].

Little manipulation or landscaping was necessary to make this locality into the scene of **"The Garden Party"**. A Tinacori Road setting is found in other stories, even—somewhat incongruously—with German names in **"A Birthday"** (from *In a German Pension*) with the house overlooking a windswept gully like the one behind No. 11 Tinakori Road, the house in which Katherine Mansfield was born. Her childhood surroundings gave her all the components needed for the setting of **"The Garden Party"**, from the green baize door, which "swung to with a 'woof'" to "an endless family of halfcastes who appeared to have planted their garden with empty jam tins and old saucepans and black iron kettles without lids"; and the most precious gift of all was the Garden, one among several luxuriant gardens in her life and her stories.

"The Garden Party" belongs to what might be called the Beauchamp cycle of Katherine Mansfield's work, the group of stories in which she took her own family, the Beauchamps, as the models of many characters, recreating aspects of her childhood world with fond precision and a vividness that often seems magical. In some stories the whole family come alive, and it could be argued that a knowledge of Katherine Mansfield's biography, though

extrinsic, adds something of value to the appreciation of stories like **"Prelude"** and **"At the Bay"**. It would also be possible to study autobiographical elements in **"The Garden Party"** and find the source of many incidents and characters in her own life. Such study, besides throwing light on the author at work, might help to elucidate the intimacy between Laura and Laurie, the fictional counterparts of Katherine Mansfield and her beloved brother Leslie (cf. again **"The Wind Blows"**), but otherwise it would add little to an understanding of **"The Garden Party"**, less, at any rate, than to the understanding of some of her other stories.

Her purpose in writing **"The Garden Party"** seems to have been, not primarily to recall and re-create a day in the life of her family, as in **"At the Bay"**, but rather to focus on a dramatic moment in a young girl's life, and in so doing to illustrate, almost to discuss, an "idea". The story may be less "simple, open" than the stories she proposed to write after her brother's death, though it is not a "problem story" in the nineteenth-century sense of the term. The "idea", to be clearly presented, calls for a unity of action not found in episodic stories like **"Prelude"** and **"At the Bay"**, and this explains why she was more selective in the use she made of her own family as models for **"The Garden Party"**. (I realize that with Katherine Mansfield the characters and scenes undoubtedly came before the "ideas", but I am not retracing the process of writing the story here.)

What is particularly admirable in **"The Garden Party"** from a technical point of view is the way in which the story moves at once on several planes; how it holds together, containing both intimacy and universality, both 75 Tinakori Road and Paradise, with their annexes. This is done with great economy and without straining, and it is worth while to examine the technique in some detail.

The unity of the story is preserved through the use of several devices, chief among which is the keeping of Laura at, or very close to, the centre of consciousness throughout the story. The *point de vue* is important in most of Katherine Mansfield's stories. They contain little straight-forward narrative, objective description, or authorial comment. In her best stories nearly everything is seen and registered through the eyes of the characters, but not, except in a few cases like **"The Lady's Maid"** (in *The Garden Party*), the eyes or stream-of-consciousness of any one character. The stories unfold by means of a technique of hovering consciousness, that is to say a consciousness hovering above the story and alighting now in one, now in another character. This method can be studied in **"At the Bay"**.

That story describes a day in the life of the Burnell family in a summer colony at the bay, beginning early in the morning and ending late at light. As the consciousness or point of view shifts through the story, the reader moves into each of the characters in turn, seeing with his or her eyes, sometimes even through the eyes of a dog or a cat. In a few descriptive passages—occurring at the hours when one notices and marks the passage of time: at dawn, noon, sunset—it may be difficult to decide who is the bearer of the consciousness at a given moment. Thus the opening, with "the whole of Crescent Bay" emerging out of the misty dawn, cannot very well have been observed by anybody except an omniscient author, unless one wants to postulate a collective "Bay" or Burnell consciousness awake and at work even while all the Burnells and their neighbours are still asleep. (Some of the observations, but not all, might be ascribed to the shepherd driving a flock of sheep past the colony.) Again, there is a certain ambiguity at the end of the day when we have a feline registration of nightfall: "She [the Burnells' cat Florrie] looked content, as though she had been waiting for this moment all day. 'Thank goodness, it's getting late,' said Florrie. 'Thank goodness, the long day is over.' Her greengage eyes opened". Florrie's thinking aloud here may be explained as an extrapolation of Linda's thoughts: the point of view seems to be Linda's both before and after the interlude with Florrie.

But apart from these ambiguous passages, where it sometimes *is* hard to tell whether we are inside this or that character, or whether perhaps the author interferes unobtrusively with a little stage-managing, it is fairly easy to decide in which character the consciousness of the story has for the moment alighted. In section II it moves from Stanley Burnell to Jonathan Trout. In section III we go in to breakfast with Stanley, and the point of view veers between him and Beryl; then on to old Mrs. Fairfield (Grandma) and Kezia; and back to Stanley and Beryl—all within less than four pages. Towards the end of the section Beryl's consciousness (her feeling of relief at having the man out of the house is shared by the other women and by the children) merges with old Mrs. Fairfield's and even the servant girl Alice's into a kind of collective female viewpoint.

Sometimes we move by fine gradations from the consciousness of one of the characters (or the author) into that of another, so that it may be impossible to say precisely when the shift is made. At other times one can locate the exact place where the points of view overlap or interlock, ["Yes, she was thankful", "It was the old woman's turn to consider", and "But no, Beryl was unfair"]. . . . In these cases one consciousness answers another, entering into a conversation that runs smoothly throughout the story.

The advantages of this method of shifting points of view are obvious: it makes the narrative both supple and subtle; the story moves along with great ease. But there is also the danger of vagueness and a certain sameness of diction; the writing may become, not only fluent, but fluid and diffuse. If that danger is avoided in **"At the Bay"**, it is not only because Katherine Mansfield handles the method with consummate skill, but also because the theme of the story—a day in the life of the Burnell family—makes it relatively unimportant whether the point of view is Linda's or Stanley's or Kezia's or Beryl's. There are differences of age, temperament, and outlook between them, but they all move within one frame of reference. Thus one can perhaps accept, in a somewhat

modified form, the idea of a collective Burnell consciousness.

But the method of hovering consciousness, if carried to the same extreme as in **"At the Bay"**, would have been disastrous in **"The Garden Party"**, because there the tension between the generations is potentially and actually greater (the children are grown up or fast growing up). Laura and her mother have no common frame of reference; they are worlds apart.

Throughout **"The Garden Party"** Laura is on the stage, and the point of view is hers except for two or three short passages, and even there she is a participant in the dialogue. The first nine pages offer no difficulties; the drawing-room scene, with Jose giving orders for the moving of the furniture, can easily have been overheard by Laura from the hall. . . . [However], with the long paragraph beginning "That really was extravagant, for the little cottages were in a lane to themselves", the point of view becomes Jose's; but since this is in the middle of the heated discussion between Laura and Jose, the shift signifies no more than a carrying on of the conversation without speeches, as it were, for a few lines.

In the description of the lane, as it is mentally surveyed by Jose, there is nothing that would not have been familiar to Laura, who may be supposed to share, to a great extent, her sister's view of it. The two of them must have picked up many of Mrs. Sheridan's opinions and prejudices, and for all Laura's sentimentalizing of workmen she is also the girl who would try to look "a little bit short-sighted" at them, and "wonder for a moment whether it was quite respectful of a workman to talk to her of bangs slap in the eye". She is without the harshness and narrowness that characterize Jose and Mrs. Sheridan, but there is no reason to postulate a revaluation of all values in her *social* universe. At any rate, before the end of the paragraph we are looking through Laura's eyes once again, as she and Laurie "on their prowls" sometimes walked through the lane, and the shifting of the point of view from Jose to Laura is scarcely perceptible. Thus, if for a dozen lines Laura is not the centre of consciousness, at least she is not far away.

The same is true . . . [when], in the course of the family reunion after the party, the point of view veers and backs for a few seconds between Laura and her mother. Mr. Sheridan has mentioned the "beastly accident", and "An awkward little silence fell. Mrs. Sheridan fidgeted with her cup. Really, it was very tactless of father . . .". Mrs. Sheridan's unspoken thought ("very tactless", etc.) could have been inferred by Laura from her general knowledge of her mother and from watching her on this occasion, but it is natural to take Mrs. Sheridan as the bearer of the consciousness of the story here, as also in the following paragraph, where she has "one of her brilliant ideas". It must be gratifying to Mrs. Sheridan to have such ideas, but the word "brilliant" is ambivalent in that an ironical light is thrown back on it by Laura's next speech: "But, mother, do you really think it's a good idea?" It may be justifiable, then, to say that both points of view, Mrs.

Sheridan's and Laura's, are present in the sentence "She had one of her brilliant ideas".

By the middle of the page Laura is again the centre of consciousness, and she remains so to the end of the story, except for the few seconds when her mother sends her off on her pilgrimage. Mrs. Sheridan follows her out of the marquee to stress the importance of the warning: "don't on any account—", and the reader may supply the missing words (presumably: "go in and see the dead man"), but Laura, though she is very perceptive, could not! Mrs. Sheridan stops herself short: "No, better not put such ideas into the child's head! 'Nothing! Run along'." This seems to me to be the only place where we are clearly beyond Laura's ken. The sentence "No, better not put such ideas into the child's head!" is the only "remark" in the story that Laura could have neither overheard nor inferred. But since the consciousness of the story does alight for some moments in Jose and Mrs. Sheridan, we, too, had better stop short before we consign to limbo a remark that does not square with our own pedantic measure of consistency.

One more sentence deserves brief notice: "And the perfect afternoon slowly ripened, slowly faded, slowly its petals closed". This I take as a piece of discreet authorial time-keeping, to be compared with several (longer) passages in **"At the Bay"**.

The relative singleness of vision helps to keep the disparate elements of the story together. With Laura we move easily from the surface level with its wealth of detail and feminine fluency (e.g. the telephone conversation) to deeper levels with their few simple configurations (archetypes) and the limit of words ("Isn't life—").

Another device used to unify the story is the carefully balanced system of parallels and contrasts. Many contrasts have been noted between the two worlds and their inhabitants, and contrast is also a principle of composition, the way in which scene follows scene. Thus immediately after Laura has "felt just like a work-girl", she is absorbed in the safely upper-class telephone conversation with Kitty; and a little later the blissful moments of eating the cream puffs are followed at once by the news of the "horrible accident". Attention was drawn above to the parallels (and contrasts) between the two kitchen scenes, and it is worth comparing also the postmortem of the party (the Sheridans gathered in the marquee with the leftovers from the party) with another post-mortem: the grief of the Scott family. The party is the culmination of the day, until Laura finds that while they were giving their noisy party, a "marvel had come to the lane".

Moving from the larger units of scenes to the smallest units, the individual words, we find basically the same system of parallels and contrasts. Many words and phrases echo through the story. It is not surprising to find two "layers" of adjectives to describe the two worlds; on the one hand, words like *perfect, ideal, happy/happiness, success(ful)*; on the other hand, words like *horrible, dreadful, terrible, awful*; and finally the blessing of the other world with words like *wonderful, beautiful, marvel(lous)*. More remarkable are the changes rung on a number of key words and phrases: *look a picture, brilliant, absurd, extravagant, (un)sympathetic*.

"The Garden Party" naturally falls into three parts:

I Before the party: 11 ½ pages

II The party: 3/5 of a page

III After the party: 4 ½ pages

The party, in other words, may be regarded as the dividing line between parts I and III, between two worlds.

That the first part should take up two-thirds of the whole story is reasonable enough, since it includes the setting of the scene and the introduction of the *dramatis personae* and the "problem", besides taking the action through the first crisis on to a point of relative calm: the party. The noisy party, "the fray", actually marks a point of peace and calm, the suspension of hostilities between Laura and her mother and sister for the time being. After the party the scenes are shorter and full of drama, and with the last part of the story comprising less than one-third of the whole, the story never drags.

"The Garden Party" affords good illustrations of the economy and tidiness that characterize Katherine Mansfield's art. The very first word carries the reader *in medias res*: "And after all the weather was ideal", and he is soon swept along at a brisk pace. There are quick transitions from scene to scene. . . . [We] are wafted along with Laura ("over the lawn, up the path, up the steps, across the veranda and into the porch") from the workmen to the telephone, and [later] there is a lightning movement from the kitchen regions to Mrs. Sheridan's room. We are there almost before we know where we are! Jose and Laura are having their hot dispute just outside the green baize door, and Laura says:

"I'm going straight up to tell mother."

"Do, dear," cooed Jose.

"Mother, can I come into your room?" Laura turned the big glass-door knob.

"Of course, child."

The writing of the flags for the sandwiches serves the compositorial purpose of sending Laura off to the important kitchen scene, but the little scene with Mrs. Sheridan ordering everybody about and trying in vain to make out her own handwriting, is also an impressionistic atmosphere piece in its own right: it paints vividly both the busy preparations of the household for the party, and the at once comical and exasperating helplessness of the mistress of the house. The actual writing of the flags is deftly telescoped in the description: "cream-cheese and lemon-curd" and one or two more items: enough for us to feel that we have been present at the whole process of hunting for the envelope and shooing away the mice.

The same economy is apparent in the telephone conversation. The right details are selected both to set the tone of the feminine Sheridan world and to add something to the characterization of Laura and Kitty *and* Mrs. Sheridan. It should also be noted how few words suffice to demonstrate the relationship between Laura and Laurie, who are seen together only in two or three short scenes. An impulsive gesture, and "Laurie's warm, boyish voice" saying, "Dash off to the telephone, old girl"; and a dumb show with a dozen words thrown in—this is enough to establish their intimacy so that the reader is prepared for their wordless understanding in the last scene.

It is this power of choosing the telling details which makes it possible for Katherine Mansfield to fill her canvas, without overcrowding it, with a surprising number of characters. Without counting the guests at the party, the hired waiters and the band, and the dead man's neighbours, we can discern about twenty people in **"The Garden Party"**. Several of them are very minor *dramatis personae,* it is true, but even some of the dumb, or all but dumb, characters have a certain individuality, though seen only for a few seconds. A case in point is "good little Hans", who appears briefly on two occasions. Sadie is seen going about her work in the proper self-effacing maid-servant manner, whereas cook is described rather more fully: she "did not look at all terrifying", she "smiled broadly", and her short speeches, said "in her comfortable voice", are sprinkled with "my girl" (to Sadie) and "my dears" (to Laura and Jose). Thus briefed one can appreciate the snapshot of the group . . . :

> Something had happened.
>
> "Tuk-tuk-tuk," clucked cook like an agitated hen. Sadie had her hand clapped to her cheek as though she had toothache. Hans's face was screwed up in the effort to understand. Only Godber's man seemed to be enjoying himself; it was his story.

The four workmen constitute another group. One of them is tall and lanky, another "a little fat chap". The portrait of the tall workman is memorable, but no more is heard or seen of the little chap, and the contrast in physique between them is less important than the contrast between the "easy", "friendly", "extraordinarily nice" tall fellow with his blue eyes (the positive aspect of the Workman) and the third workman (who represents the negative aspect): "He was pale. He had a haggard look as his dark eyes scanned the tennis-court. What was he thinking?" Perhaps he was thinking too much. The fourth workman is never even mentioned as an individual, but he also serves, namely to indicate the golden mean or grey average of the group. To keep the workmen as a group in their place, to prevent them from blossoming out too much, it is appropriate that one or two of them should not be too conspicuous.

The same balance is found in the group of the three sisters: Laura represents the positive value, Jose the negative value, and Meg is an absolutely neutral quantity, a foil to the other two. Of Meg we learn only one thing: she "had washed her hair before breakfast, and she sat drinking her coffee in a green turban, with a dark wet curl stamped on each cheek"; of the inside of her head, her character, etc.—not a word! But there is a good reason for this. To have had Meg mixed up in the quarrel would only have blurred the outlines. As it is, there is a neat pairing of the antagonists: Laura seconded by Laurie *versus* Mrs. Sheridan and Jose.

Every reader of **"The Garden Party"** probably feels the genuineness of the atmosphere of the party. Katherine Mansfield has measured the temperature and the pressure, and conveys her findings to the reader by means of a little description and some snatches of conversation: a few compliments ("Darling Laura, how well you look!"), kindnesses ("Won't you have an ice?"), and then the good-byes ("Never a more delightful – – –").

The party is a conveniently limited field to go botanizing in. Strolling about with the couples, bending to flowers, perhaps we can pick up a few syntactic specimens from the one paragraph of description, the eight lines which are *not* devoted to the bits of conversation just referred to.

The first two lines contain three unlinked main clauses, or simple sentences, all with the verb in the simple past tense. They describe (and demonstrate) how the garden is rather suddenly invaded by crowds of people, by sounds of music, and by the busy activity of waiting on the guests ("Soon after that people began coming in streams. The band struck up; the hired waiters ran from the house to the marquee.").

In the next two lines we seem to stand back a few steps to look more leisurely at the guests moving about the garden ("Wherever you looked there were couples strolling, bending to the flowers, greeting, moving on over the lawn."). We have got used to the music and talk, indeed in this sentence and the following one we are not aware of any sounds at all. The more leisurely tempo is due to the succession of present participles, while the absence of any conjunction (not a single little talkative *and*) makes the syntax rather formalized; this, however, goes well with the somewhat artificial movements of the strolling couples: bending, greeting, moving on—almost like mechanical toys.

In the next sentence the guests are said to be "like bright birds that had alighted in the Sheridans' garden for this one afternoon, on their way to—where?" With this Whither-goest-thou question, which is a favourite motif in Katherine Mansfield's work, we rise for a moment above the party. We are briefly reminded of the problems worrying Laura (and Katherine Mansfield), but are not allowed to start on a metaphysical flight. In the last two lines we are back again in the middle of the throng of guests ("Ah, what happiness it is to be with people who are all happy, to press hands, press cheeks, smile into eyes."). The most characteristic feature of this sentence is the string of infinitives, also without any connecting links. They excellently suggest the conventional, sometimes forced, cordiality of such parties, just as the tautology of the happiness of being with people who are happy may sum up a great deal of the conversation.

Thus in eight lines there are three conspicuous examples of asyndeton. It is obvious that the syntax helps to suggest the crowding of people at the party; it is a real get-together. It becomes even more obvious if, for contrast, one turns to the scenes between Laura and Laurie and studies the correspondence between the syntax and the relaxed intimacy there.

Katherine Mansfield "*adored* the English language". "People have never explored the lovely medium of prose. It is a hidden country still—I feel that so profoundly" (*Letters*). She herself helped to explore the resources of the language, creating "a kind of *special prose*" (*Journal*), and her mastery of English prose is the firm foundation of her stories. She would struggle with the language until it had the precision, the buoyancy, and evocative character she desired. Nothing was too small to claim attention: the choosing and placing of every single word, the minutiae of punctuation. In this as in other respects she was very much the craftsman, and took a keen intellectual interest in the *craft* of writing. She was not all imagination but had her fair share of cool reason. She knew that "the sub-conscious element" in an artist's work, his inspiration, is "a sort of divine flower to all his terrific hard gardening".

Some of the effects she gets in her stories came no doubt to her unconsciously, as flowers to her terrific hard gardening, but generally she seems to have been well aware of what she was doing and how she was gaining her effects. The sentence about the perfect afternoon which slowly ripened, slowly faded, has been mentioned twice already . . . , but it will not be amiss to have the author's own comment on it:

> *And* the reason why I used the 'florid' image was that I was writing about a garden party. It seemed natural, then, that the day should close like a flower. People had been looking at flowers all the afternoon, you see.
>
> (*Letters* II)

She had a passion, not only for flowers and gardens, but also for technique: "I have a passion for making the thing into a *whole* if you know what I mean. Out of technique is born real style, I believe. There are no short cuts". And she knew true delight and value in detail: "Do you, too, feel an infinite delight and value in *detail*—not for the sake of detail but for the life *in* the life of it" (*Letters* I).

It is not to be expected that an artist should be a reliable judge of his own work, and Katherine Mansfield is no exception despite her technical know-how. The impressions she jotted down immediately upon finishing some of her best stories sometimes reflect the fatigue following a spell of hard work rather than the achievement of the finished product. Still, it is worth taking into account what she had to say about **"The Garden Party"**.

While she was writing **"At the Bay"**, she was completely "possessed" by that "very long seaweedy story" (*Letters* II), and it took her nearly a month to "recover" from it. "But now I am not at all sure about that story. It seems to me it's a little 'wispy'—not what it might have been. The *G.P.* [**"The Garden Party"**, which she had just finished] is better. But that is not *good enough*, either . . ." (*Journal*; the entry dated October 16, 1921). Three days earlier she had written: "Oh, I am in the middle of a nice story", and at the end of the manuscript of **"The Garden Party"**: "This is a moderately successful story, and that's all. It's somehow, in the episode at the lane, scamped" (*ibid.*).

Was she thinking of the sudden fluency of Laura's thoughts at the sight of the dead man? That crucial passage cannot truly be described as scamped but perhaps after Laura's dreamlike progress through the nether world on might be surprised that her state of mind manifests itself so readily. However, the "eloquence" of her thinking can be explained by the sudden relief after long anxiety. Her pent-up emotion, released at one stroke, issues forth in a flow of emotional words ("wonderful", "beautiful", "marvel", "happy"), first breathlessly (short, isolated sentences), then in longer rhythms.

If the passage is less compelling than the rest of the story, the reason is rather that here Katherine Mansfield does not follow the advice she gave Arnold Gibbons, a young writer who had sent some stories to her. She advised him to express himself "more *in*directly" (*Letters* II): "how are we going to convey these overtones, half tones, quarter tones, these hesitations, doubts, beginnings, if we go at them *directly?*" Perhaps the "moral" of **"The Garden Party"** becomes too apparent in the paragraph we are discussing. It finds a better, because more indirect, expression in the few words that are exchanged between Laura and Laurie when he comes to meet her, and in their pauses and silences.

Whether this passage is felt as a slight blemish or not, **"The Garden Party"** remains one of Katherine Mansfield's finest stories. It can be taken as a good example of the happy balance between mind and soul which she was always aiming at; a precarious balance, as she knew too well, but a prerequisite of great art.

> It seems to me that what one aims at is to work with one's mind and one's soul *together*. By soul I mean that 'thing' that makes the mind really important. I always picture it like this. My mind is a very complicated, capable instrument. But the interior is dark. It *can* work in the dark and throw off all kinds of things. But behind that instrument like a very steady gentle light is the soul. And it's only when the soul *irradiates* the mind that what one does matters . . . What I *aim* at is that state of mind when I feel my soul and my mind are one. It's awfully, terribly difficult to get at.
>
> (*Letters*)

Katherine Mansfield's demands on art and on behalf of art were equally exacting. But then, she knew that "Good work takes upon itself a Life—bad work has death in it" (*Letters*). In the end, perhaps, such optimism as is found

in **"The Garden Party"** derives less from Laura's revelation than from the quality inherent in a finished work of
art.

Marvin Magalaner (essay date 1971)

SOURCE: "The Legacy of Fiction," in *The Fiction of
Katherine Mansfield,* Southern Illinois University Press,
1971, pp. 74-119.

[*In the following excerpt, Magalaner views "The Garden
Party" as an attempt to reconcile dream and reality.*]

One of the stories on which Katherine Mansfield's reputation as an artist chiefly rests is **"The Garden Party,"**
which she completed on October 14, 1921. Aside from its
merits as fiction, it provides an opportunity for its author
to be at once her satirical earlier self, the gentle recorder
of her New Zealand childhood, and the new, transfigured
personality whose view of life is complex, warm, and
utterly philosophical. Without self-consciousness, she
writes to William Gerhardi in 1922 that she has tried to
express in the story

> the diversity of life and how we try to fit in everything,
> Death included. That is bewildering for a person of
> Laura's age. She feels things ought to happen
> differently. First one and then another. But life isn't
> like that. We haven't the ordering of it. Laura says,
> "But all these things must not happen at once." And
> Life answers, "Why not? How are they divided from
> each other?" And they *do* all happen, it is inevitable.
> And it seems to me there is beauty in that inevitability.

Perhaps it is unfortunate that critics of **"The Garden
Party"** have dwelt so extensively on this excerpt from
Mansfield's letter, for they have generally tended to see
the story almost exclusively as a reconciliation of Death
and Life: that is, the parenthetical "Death included" has
been read as though it were "Death especially." Rather,
the attempt is equally to reconcile reality and the dream,
innocence and experience, and, with great concern, levels
of society. That Mansfield could even hope to carry out so
ambitious an enterprise within the limitations of the short
story is testimony to the increasing self-confidence that
she felt during the last year of her life.

The story itself seems simple, childishly unsophisticated,
even obvious, but this view proves untenable. The narrative involves preparations for a garden party—Laura's first
grown-up affair; a glimpse of the party itself; and the
aftermath which describes an impulsive attempt to give
the party leftovers to the bereaved family of an accident
victim. Mansfield's "selective camera" centers upon Laura,
a young and well-meaning girl trying to establish her own
values in a world carefully arranged for her by the women
in her family: her mother Mrs. Sheridan and her two older
sisters. The camera follows Laura as she adopts the ways
of her mother in talking to the workmen or to her friend
Kitty; as she helps with the sandwiches; and as she con-

fronts the insensitivity of her elders to the death which has
happened nearby. The reader notes her wavering allegiance
to the attitude of the family and, on the other hand, to her
instinctive youthful sense of proportion and good taste that
assumes the cancellation of the party out of respect for the
other family's grief. The devices employed to divert Laura
from her independent point of view and to set her firmly
once again in the Sheridan orbit are described. The story
ends with her visit to the home of the dead man bearing the
party leftovers and with her enchantment with the appearance of death as she views the body. Her final "Isn't life
. . . isn't life" represents not nearly as ambiguous and inconclusive an ending as has been charged to the author, but
a deeper look at the story is necessary to demonstrate this.

Mansfield's choice of a garden party as the focus of action
and attitude is obviously meaningful. No less than Joyce,
who praised Ibsen for using "never a superfluous word or
phrase," Katherine Mansfield insists on the inevitability of
all elements in a successful story. (Her remarks on the writing
of "Miss Brill" are particularly relevant here.) Clearly, a
garden party offered the author a many-faceted symbol.
Thus it may represent the Sheridan way of life: showy,
superficial, upper class, ephemeral (almost before final
preparations are made for the affair comes a description of
its aftermath), and with little more substance than the cream
puffs that are served. In a wider sense, the garden party is
life itself, the brief moment men enjoy between cradle and
grave. Perhaps this is why Mansfield required a party in the
garden rather than in the drawing room of the Sheridan
home. For a garden implies nature and natural development, a developing and growing into maturity, and, inevitably too, a withering and dying. It is no accident either
than Laura's own name has associations with a growing
plant or that, when the florist delivers a profusion of lilies
to augment the attractions of the garden flowers, Laura "felt
they were in her fingers, on her lips, growing in her breast."

Employment of the garden as a symbol of life, of natural
growth and development, permits Mansfield to play upon
the perversion of the natural too—whether with respect to
nature or to man. Thus, in the first paragraph of the story,
before the reader is introduced specifically to any character
or to details of plot, the point of view of the opening description suggests the unnaturalness of what is to occur in
a "natural" setting. Probably at Mrs. Sheridan's suggestion,
the gardener has been "mowing the lawns and sweeping
them" until the grass "seemed to shine." This attempt to
"methodize" nature and bring it under control is implicit
also in the line: "They could not have had a more perfect
day for a garden-party *if they had ordered it*" [italics mine],
in which climatic conditions are reduced to a matter of
commercial transaction. Further, perhaps the height of perversity is reached in the turn of mind which conceives of
roses blooming precisely in time for the party because they
are the flowers most likely to "impress people at garden-
parties" and the roses know it. The horror is that the point
of view here must be attributed to the young and innocent
Laura, though the reader quickly senses that the hands
guiding the strings are the hands of the mother. Similarly,
later in the story young Kitty Maitland's plans for the "green-
coated band" bespeak the insensitivity of the older gener-

ation: "Aren't they too like frogs for words? You ought to have arranged them round the pond with the conductor in the middle on a leaf."

This afternoon affair is Laura's coming-out party—the first social occasion on which she is to play an adult role. It is, as others have pointed out, her initiation into the mature world. If she has hitherto been merely a bud on the parent stem, on this day she will have her opportunity to blossom. The question is, of course, whether she will grow into a simple, natural flower or whether, like her mother, she is doomed to artificiality, insensitivity, and falseness. The restricted view of the world that she and her sisters have been permitted by their mother has already made inroads into her spontaneity and natural freshness, as the first paragraph abundantly proves. Without a dramatic widening of horizons to force a reevaluation of basic elements, Laura's path, following in the footsteps of Meg and Jose and her mother, is clearly predictable.

Death makes the difference and, at least temporarily, forces Laura to see in the older women in her family the crystallized and hardened views which in herself are still vague and indefinite imitations of adult models. The most final of all human activities makes her own growth and development less certain than it was that morning. Knowledge of death means an end to innocence but it also heralds the possibility of a new kind of life. The death of Scott the carter postpones maybe forever the death of the heart in Laura—a death already suffered by the other Sheridan women.

Yet if the death itself and the subsequent reactions to it of the Sheridans can accomplish this new healthy growth for Laura, why does Mansfield bother to include the last section of the story? Is it necessary for Laura to see a corpse in order for the meaning of the day's lesson to sink in? Or can Mansfield not resist the emotional value of a child's confrontation with the physical presence of death? The answers to these questions require examination of the story from another point of view.

On the day of the party, Laura loses her innocence and her parent-fostered narrowness in more ways than one. The development of her attitude toward class distinction accelerates as the day advances, further widening the gap between her and the other Sheridan women. The progress of the development is put by Mansfield in terms of Laura's increasing difficulty in generalizing about the working-class group of whose lives she knows almost nothing as the story opens. Subtly, Mansfield encourages the reader to accept Laura's stereotyped impression of the workmen who have come to put up the marquee:

> Four men in their shirt-sleeves stood grouped together
> on the garden path. They carried staves . . . and they
> had big tool-bags slung on their backs. They looked
> impressive.

Through the repetition of "they," through the monotony of sentence structure and word order, and through her underlining of the fact that these shirtsleeved men were "grouped together," Mansfield reinforces the generalization almost schematically, as though picturing on a social studies graph the distribution of laborers in the locality. And, though Laura welcomes contact with this rarely encountered group, she embraces the generalization enthusiastically. If *a* workman has nice eyes, the corollary is "How very nice workm*en* were" [italics mine]. When an individual workman uses slang in conversing with her, she wonders whether such talk is quite respectful of *a* workman. When one smells a sprig of lavender, she approves of all workmen at the expense of all "the silly boys" of her own class at dances. And when in the garden she takes a bite of bread-and-butter, she feels "just like a work-girl."

Death, the Great Leveller, succeeds in making Laura wary of generalizations. Suddenly the girl who in the garden that morning could react only on that level discovers that in her elders' resort to generalization is a method of avoiding unpleasant confrontations, mental or physical—and her natural honesty is shocked into an awareness of the immorality of the process. To her sister's "You won't bring a drunken workman back to life by being sentimental," she counters, "Drunk! Who said he was drunk?". She is similarly outraged when her mother speaks nebulously of not understanding how "they" keep alive "in those poky little holes."

But to Laura, if not to her family, a dead workman cannot be generalized away. In bringing the news of the accident, Godber's man has been deliberately particular. Though the dead man is hardly a character in the story, the protagonist and the reader are given his name, his profession, the nature of the accident, the name of the street on which it occurred, the location of the wound, his marital status, and the number of his children. Such detailed categorization is essential to the breaking down in Laura of the vague barrier between class and class. Now it is easier to see why Laura must make the post-party trip to Scott's cottage and look upon the carter not as just another dead workman to be subtracted from census statistics, but as an individual being. It becomes clear why Laura must ask the woman who opens the door at Scott's home whether she is Mrs. Scott and why she must discover that the woman is not. Identities count now, even among workpeople.

The final step in Laura's development on this day is her reaction to the dead Scott. He now transcends class. As Laura had lived in a different world from workmen hitherto, Scott inhabits a dream realm which removes him, in a sense, from his own former slum world and from her world too. His is the classless world of death to which Mrs. Sheridan and Mrs. Scott and Jose and Laura—everyone—must eventually come. It is no wonder that Laura's response to this new "marvel" should be a tearful, "Forgive my hat."

Hats had dominated the story as one image followed another from the beginning: the turban Meg wears, Laurie and his father brushing their hats, the carelessly worn hats of the workmen, Kitty Maitland's hat, and finally the hat of Laura's mother, hastily "popped" on her head by Mrs. Sheridan to make Laura forget the dead man and her opposition to holding the garden party. When the mother thus presents her daughter with her own party hat in typical coronation fashion, she is symbolically transferring to Laura the Sheridan heritage of snobbery, restricted social views, narrowness of vision—the garden party syndrome. It is not surprising that when Laura first sees herself in a mirror wearing the hat, she hardly recognizes "this charming girl" who stares back at her. Certainly the hat is, as her mother tells her, "made for" her, but she is not at all sure that she wishes to acquire her rightful legacy. In the presence of Scott, the realization of the discrepancy between what the hat indicates and what Laura in her own dawning maturity is tending toward evokes the involuntary cry. Laura has had her vision.

As several critics have shown, Mansfield has prepared the reader for this epiphany through earlier introducing the "This Life is Weary" song, whose tragic burden evokes only a "brilliant, dreadfully unsympathetic smile" from the singer herself. The final line, "A Dream—a Wa-kening," is echoed in the description of Scott at the end of the story: "He was dreaming. Never wake him up again." In a sense, Laura has through contact with death wakened from her dream-life, the existence of garden parties and Sheridan exclusivity. And Scott has, in her eyes, awakened through death to a life infinitely more desirable than that of the Sheridans. Both have a knowledge that puts them above class.

It is almost as though Katherine Mansfield dangles obscurely before the reader the dim symbol of another garden—a false Eden this time—a dream world of artificial delight and false security. The inhabitants of this fools' paradise tend the garden, "order" the appropriate weather, and regard themselves as the center of the universe. Only when Laura is expelled from the garden does she trade innocence for knowledge. Now she can see death in the world and "all our woe," unwarned not to resist by the "archangels" who Mansfield tells us had visited the garden on the evening before the party. Yet the confrontation with death is to the awakened Laura not only not frightening: it is positively an ecstatic experience. For her protagonist at least, Mansfield has been able to demonstrate that life and death may indeed coexist and that their common existence in one world may be beautiful.

The final scene with Laurie appears much less ambiguous than critics have allowed. The fairylike Laura who had, before the fact of death entered her life, dealt with life largely in terms of comfortable generalizations, finds herself speechless now to sum up the complexity that the deeper view affords. When she stammers, "Isn't life—?" the generalizing predicate adjective will not come, for no single word can encompass it. It would not matter, in this regard, whether the question were completed by "good" or "bad," "ugly" or "beautiful," "sad" or "happy." What matters is that no one word suffices in a world that encompasses, though it may not always reconcile, all of them.

The unspoken communication here between Laura and Laurie is interesting. Laurie "quite understood" although she "couldn't explain." Mansfield chooses to associate brother and sister closely not only in their ages ostensibly, but in Laurie's sympathy for his sister's point of view and his apparent humanity when contrasted with the female Sheridans' coldness. Furthermore, by calling them Laura and Laurie, the author establishes an obvious similarity. It may be that they are intended to be male and female aspects of the same personality and that, therefore, their reactions would be identical. It is not necessary, though it is possible, to believe with one critic that Laurie had earlier been initiated into knowledge of death and thus can empathize with the new initiate.

Katherine Mansfield considered **"The Garden Party"** "moderately successful," but had reservations about the quality of the ending. She had worked on parts of it during a period of at least five months, as her *Scrapbook* shows, though the episode given there in an earlier form survives in **"The Garden Party"** as the song "This Life is Weary" and as very little else. Called **"By Moonlight"** in the *Scrapbook,* the episode of the song is treated discursively for over three pages as the focal point for a view of the Sheridans: "Mother," "Father," Meg, Laura, Laurie, and Francie (the Jose of the later story). Since there is no garden party and no dead man in the sketch, the significance of the song is considerably less, its employment being confined to pointing up attitudes of those who hear it. "Mother" especially is revealed as she deplores the trend toward the "tragic" and the "depressing" in contemporary lyrics. She states her preference for "songs about primroses and cheerful normal birds and . . . [ellipsis marks Mansfield's] and spring and so on." Thus the morbid and the lower class are excluded from her world here as they will be later in the "Garden party" story. As for Meg, she finds the song "fascinating." But to the reader, the fascination is in seeing how Mansfield surrounds the song with meaning in the later version as she is unable to do a few weeks earlier.

Adam J. Sorkin   (essay date 1978)

SOURCE: "Katherine Mansfield's 'The Garden Party': Style and Social Occasion," in *Modern Fiction Studies,* Vol. XXIV, No. 3, Autumn, 1978, pp. 439-55.

[*In the following essay, Sorkin sees a creative tension between realism and symbolism in "The Garden Party."*]

Attending the Sheridan's garden party with Katherine Mansfield and her protagonist Laura, we are at once escorted into a richly textured and vividly suggestive world. This is the universe of the author's sensibility, her strong sensitivity and playful delight in imagery which are shared with her receptive, fanciful young heroine. The opening paragraph of the story is as much an exposition of mood and method as of time and place. Its initial words—"And after all . . ."—thrust us not *in medias res* but in the middle of a feeling, a relieved, satisfied expectation that the first requirement for an exceptional day has been fulfilled. The shining garden and the perfect morning weather, the sympathetic roses and the helpful archangels suggest an impressionistic concentration, an emotional intensity, and a psychological particularity that take us to the heart of the author's method in **"The Garden Party,"** one of Mansfield's most highly respected and widely anthologized works.

Throughout the story, Mansfield renders mimetic detail through a highly emotional, sensuous style, subtly manipulating both point of view narration and authorial diction. Inherent in the rendering of Laura's day from morning to evening, and of the unanticipated intrusion of a fatal accident into it, is what is most clearly understood as an aesthetic duality. The story develops within a tension, a dynamic balance and slowly developing shift of emphasis between two modes: the social and realistic, relying on concrete verisimilitude and representative typicality, on manners, morals, and material actuality; and the symbolic and lyrical, a tendency towards stylization deriving from verbal play and imagistic evocation. One of the story's major effects is a give-and-take between these two strains of artistic emphasis which are, as well, complementary perceptual emphases in apprehending the world. This duality, which functions as a doubleness in the aesthetic context of any given element in the story, ultimately creates the story's particular sense of unity, a unity of effect, standing behind and shaping the story's rich complexity, indeed evoking it as a consistent and controlled impression.

This impression of texture and multiplicity is important. **"The Garden Party"** achieves its power as fiction by eliciting for us a sense of a complex, especially an emotionally and morally complex world and then portraying, through Laura, how a sensitive and appealing human personality apprehends and faces both the richness and the stark realities of human life. Katherine Mansfield herself wrote that what she "tried to convey" in the story was "the diversity of life and how we try to fit in everything, Death included." *How* we try: the concern with unifying life's intricacies into a mature comprehension is underscored. The comment pertains most directly to Laura's bewilderment and her attempt to accept life's inevitabilities, particularly change and mortality. But it also pertains to the artistic means by which Mansfield assimilates and shapes her material. The method by which the author of **"The Garden Party"** herself tries to fit in everything and unite the diverse strands of her technique is primarily through her style as it enfolds and transforms the social realism and circumstantial specificity of the story.

This transformation of social occasion by means of active stylistic mediation between reader and fictional world has often been seen less as an effective unifying device than as a divisive ambivalence of effect. The sophisticated verbal artistry of the author is one of her most immediate attractions for us and has repeatedly been admired as an isolated beauty rather than (as I am suggesting) an integral component of her method as a whole. In consequence, it has been the story's thoroughly realistic basis, its fabric of involvement with social attitudes, class differences, and economic actualities—which is often seen as its social theme—that has troubled its admirers most. Mansfield's

social theme in isolation is, critically speaking, the other side of the coin to her poetical style taken in isolation. The problem is a telling one. A unified reading of the story must, however, begin with the realistic social representation that lies beneath and informs the verbal surface of the story.

If far less immediately compelling than the story's verbal brilliance and imagistic overlay and if in no sense an explicit theme (the story is neither the portrait of a rich young lady nor an analysis of New Zealand character, for instance), the social aspects of **"The Garden Party"** are, nonetheless, fundamental to Mansfield's method in three important ways.

For one thing, Mansfield's socio-economic consciousness is a determinant of her selection and concrete embodiment of her narrative material. The characterization and outlook of the central character, Laura Sheridan, are class based in Mansfield's conception; Laura takes life for us first as a recognizable class type. Whatever her personal psychological makeup, the heroine is definitively the privileged daughter of her monied class. The basis of Mansfield's conception of Laura is expressive in such attitudes as her self-consciousness with the workmen and such important clusters of emotions and symbolic objects as the fascination and deep-seated fear intermingled in her view of the alien, nearby cottage district. Similarly, it is often through conspicuously fetishistic objects and social institutions, as in her excess of delight at the new hat or the expensive party, that she expresses herself and articulates her desires and values. Moreover, the most crucial actions—first Laura's anticipation of her wealthy family's garden party and wholehearted delight in its extravagance and then her intense reaction to the death of the poor worker—are deeply involved with social and economic realities. Thus despite the generalized, abstract qualities of Laura's final perceptions about life and the beauty of death and despite her creator's poetic effects and metaphorical emphases, we must recognize as basic the story's unflagging realistic precision.

The story is involved with society and class in a second crucial sense in that it can be said to begin in what we accept, by and large, as a traditional modality of social realism. The reader watches a domestic social comedy in a woman's world as Laura contends with the workmen about the marquee and talks to a girl friend on the telephone, appreciates her mother's expensive caprice of buying a profusion of canna lilies and hears her sisters practice a song, helps her mother label the fifteen kinds of sandwiches ("Egg and. . . . It looks like mice. It can't be mice, can it?"), and goes with her sister Jose to help "pacify cook" who sneaks them each a cream puff. This beginning of the story's development in social realism is all the more evident if we momentarily ignore the breathless tonality and impressionism of its opening paragraph, which in any event are quickly modulated and soon seem part of the mild comedy when we discover them to be a young girl's gush of overexcitement. The story ends, however, in the artistic realm hinted at by the emotionalism of the opening which of course we cannot ignore, a realm defined more by authorial stylization and symbolic suggestiveness than external lifelikeness.

The realistic treatment of social and economic actuality also enters into the story's basic conception in a third major way: as an essential constituent of its structure. The upper class garden party focuses the social and psychological realism as a primary emphasis in the plot and is itself informed by what the realistic method achieves. One view of the story's architecture arranges the action, in echo of the work's underlying aesthetic doubleness, around dual poles, the first of which is the Sheridans' party. Although it is not the culmination of the action, the party provides a deceptive climax that is in the foreground of two thirds of the story and then acts as a fulcrum in the development, turning thematic concern from human social artificialities, which it expresses, towards deeper psychological and symbolic realities, which it contains through Laura's recognition of the transitoriness of the illusory, albeit intense, pleasures of worldly delight. For much of the story, Laura's conscious hope is the simple expectation of a rich, sheltered young girl for a successful afternoon, but about the fashionable party also coalesce Laura's attempts to grow up socially and her naive but instinctively right placing of value on social occasions, on the rituals of human community. Thus the story leads up to the fashionable party but continues beyond it, pushing it to the background (and with it, social illusions of human conviviality which represent real human needs and desires that we actualize in our lives through such institutions as garden parties).

It is, therefore, no accident that the party to which we are invited by the author is given considerable stress in the story's development and its structure, but our attendance at it seems surprisingly brief, consisting of highly selective summary and hinting snatches of conversation. The plot finally brings Laura, going to the dead carter Scott's house on a social errand of artificial charity, to the story's second structural pole and its climax: as an isolated individual, she comes to a knowledge much more deeply disturbing and also fundamentally asocial. This is the theme of (as Mansfield's letter capitalized it) Death, the story's deep interest in Laura's worried fascination with the simultaneity of life and death and her efforts to come to terms with the mixed aspects of existence. This second architectural focus provides the dramatic and emotional climax of the story's denouement and thus underlies the ending's casualness with realistic social actuality while it raises the pitch of our involvement to its most intense and serious level. What we had thought at first was the dramatic crisis, the party, an event threatened by the suspenseful counteraction of the carter's death and Laura's worries, itself turns out to be a mistaken emphasis on the reader's and the heroine's part. The celebration of life and social community becomes a relatively superficial—which is not to say unimportant—attitude and, with exceptional economy on Mansfield's part, a device of narrative retardation in the development of the work's most powerful revelation.

But social concerns and the story's concrete specification of the external world in terms of implicit social and economic categories are in no way abandoned. If the dramatic crux of the party turns out to be a mistake in emphasis, it is not because it is an unimportant event; rather, it reveals an incomplete perception of life. The story's involvement with social and economic actualities, which is not a theme but is basic to all aspects of it, is finally problematic only if we assume such realities must take a realistic expression. As we shall see in detail, the author's transmutation of her story from primarily social, mimetic art to something more like a symbolic fairy tale involves the social material and its necessary configurations. The social and economic realities of Laura's world enter forcefully not just into the characterization and the external givens of the action as social narrative but also into the imaginative conception of the plot as structure of signification. Within the verbal artifice of the author, social reality informs the story at a primary narrative level, that of plot itself. Mansfield's style, then, as it were encircles, seems to enclose the story on the outside (her side and our side) of the action. At the story's center is Laura, to whose social and physical reality as the imaginative focus of the concrete world within that circle we shall now turn.

Mansfield's reader is fundamentally drawn into the story by a susceptibility to Laura's attraction. If early detached by the mild social satire of the Sheridan household and the gentle comedy of Laura's ingenuous problems of propriety and deportment in relation to workers and cream puffs, the reader nevertheless remains committed and indeed grows in emotional closeness to her throughout her day. On a very human level, Laura's youth, sensitivity, vivaciousness, imagination, even her innocent girlish flightiness as well as her childlike irresponsibility and class-reinforced insouciance win her a sympathetic understanding, a loyal if somewhat bemused affection. Sheltered physically by her family and morally and psychologically by her mother's spiritual myopia, insulated by her social status, she is seriously limited to her protected girlhood in a domestic world. Yet she is also atypical of her family and more admirable, "the artistic one," "different from them all" as she herself senses. Moreover, the action of the story presents an intrinsically meaningful twentieth-century occasion, a ritually significant moment in our culture: the modern, well-to-do, well-brought-up girl's first important steps towards adult maturity. This is an event deceptively customary and, therefore, barely stressed by Mansfield's dramatically restrained presentation. Mansfield's reticence about the thematic and conceptual importance of Laura's initiation is reinforced by her rendering the experience through Laura's limited center of consciousness. But the importance is, of course, implicit in the author's very choice of dramatic material. The action, Laura's growth, is hardly ordinary as well as ominously symbolic in its content of gain and loss commingled.

Thus if understated, the significance of the action is crucial nonetheless. Furthermore, the sense of a ritual passage into adulthood extends past the party to its experiential culmination in Laura's further initiation, frighteningly in the background until the party and then fatefully in the foreground after it, as the story builds to its climax. Laura's initiation into knowledge of death is neither social nor cultural but a universal occurrence in the life of the individual. These thematic elements intrinsic in the plot draw forth the concern of the involved reader, who anticipates the crisis of the ending as soon as the party is over. The inevitability of Laura's viewing the dead carter's body, figuratively the occasion of her new, disturbing perception of the nature of human life, is foreseen from Mrs. Sheridan's unstated warning, an ellipsis which the reader (but not the heroine) is put in the position of filling in:

"And, Laura!"—her mother followed her out of the marquee—"don't on any account——"

"What, mother?"

No, better not put such ideas into the child's head! "Nothing! Run along."

To the lighthearted girl we meet at the beginning of the story, the child who loves parties, skims across lawns, and, though "far too grownup to really care about such things," relishes with an "absorbed inward look" of satisfaction the trifling naughtiness of eating cream puffs "so soon after breakfast," life is a garden party. Laura's is the world of the Sheridans' wealthy illusion, all the green world money can buy, a pastoral world of weather as "ideal" as if "they had ordered it," of manicured and swept lawns, of gardeners, servants, workers, and cooks, an organized life in which even roses seem to understand their status ("the only flowers that impress people") and bloom by the sacred magic of visitations "by archangels." Lilies appear in profusion at the door by Mrs. Sheridan's whim: "I suddenly thought for once in my life I shall have enough canna lilies," she explains to Laura, yet it is clear that neither the occurrence nor the sense of the purchase of power over nature is unusual to their household. Indeed the Sheridans, especially Laura's mother, seem to confuse status and reality, class and morality, money and life. Mrs. Sheridan callously complains to Laura about the poor laborers who live in the district—the "eyesore"—in the nether-region below the Sheridan eminence: she "can't understand how they keep alive in those poky little holes." Later she fixes a basket of what seems to Laura "scraps from their party" in order to be "sympathetic" to the dead laborer's widow: perceiving that the leftovers are "going to be wasted," she decides to "send that poor creature some of this perfectly good food. . . . What a point to have it all ready prepared." Before the garden party, when Laura wonders if it weren't "really terribly heartless" of the Sheridans to have the party with the dead man's family so near, her mother answers her—most fittingly—with a new hat. The story catalogues for us the salient advantages of wealth: the florist's lilies and Godber's cream puffs; the made-to-order marquees and charming grown-up new hats; the parties and "perfect" afternoons with the "kisses, voices, tinkling spoons, laughter, the smell of crushed grass" that together fill Laura "somehow inside her" so that "She had no room for anything else"; and the means of casually having charity and fellow-feeling "all ready prepared" to load into a basket. The material objects privileged to Laura's class speak in the story directly to, and through, the heroine's feelings. In the face of the powerful appeal of such things, the image of the widow and her children

with her dead husband's body seems to Laura "blurred, unreal, like a picture in the newspaper."

It is wealth's particular psychological effect to blur poverty and death and likewise to distance and ritualize mortality until it seems unusual news from elsewhere, certainly (as is the case) from outside the false paradise of the garden. Yet Laura is not "heartless." If anything, she is oversensitive, perhaps because of death's foreignness; most of us would agree in calling her "extravagant," as accused by her family, in her overreaction to the death. We do not stop parties because someone within hearing, otherwise unknown to us, has accidentally been killed. Mrs. Sheridan's knowledge of life, or at least of its customs, is more proper, despite her lack of feeling; we may recognize her "common sense," as she calls it, while despising its tone: "People like that don't expect sacrifices from us." Indeed, part of what Laura is trying to grow up to learn in the story is precisely the assurance and social poise of her mother. That her daughters learn this, in fact, is implicitly the reason that Mrs. Sheridan has her girls play at arranging the party. "I'm determined to leave everything to you children this year," she tells them near the beginning of the story, although later, when the lilies arrive and Laura accuses her of interfering, Mrs. Sheridan asks, "My darling child, you wouldn't like a logical mother, would you?" Her impulsiveness is within comfortable bounds, however. Ironically, had Laura her mother's social knowledge, she would never have gone into the Scotts' house or viewed the body. Her naïveté and indeed her shelteredness conspire with her emotional directness, her keen curiosity and sensitivity, to grant her important experiences that change and enrich her. Adult *savoir faire* insulates and protects; Laura is specially privileged in her ingenuousness. In any case, neither social experience nor carelessness about logic and morality are finally a substitute for real humanity. Laura, in her sense of distance from her mother and her sister Jose, is coming to recognize this. She is literally extravagant, then, in where she is going: outside of class domesticities and family world-views, indeed to deeper symbolic realms.

Laura's internal experience in the story is manifold: she senses she is growing up socially and physically, psychologically and morally. Early in the day, when the men arrive to put up the marquee, she puts on her mother's mannerisms in an attempt to be grown-up, unfearful, businesslike. Yet she romanticizes the workers—"how extraordinarily nice workmen were"—when the tall one sniffs the lavender, and she pretends to be "just like a work-girl" as she bites her bread-and-butter. She believes she would get on with them as friends, concluding (the formulaic phrases suggest the inverted snobbery and false sophistication; the arching, drooping, delayed syntax ironically undercuts her assertion): "It's all the fault, she decided, as the tall fellow drew something on the back of an envelope, something that was to be looped up or left to hang, of these absurd class distinctions. Well, for her part, she didn't feel them. Not a bit, not an atom. . . ." Later she hears of the carter Scott's accident from Godber's delivery man while on her way to look again at the "awfully nice" workmen.

Moreover just as the reality of death enters the house with the cream puffs (appropriately through the back door, we might add), the subjective reality, the warming flush of growing up to physical womanhood, arrives with the lilies: "wide open, radiant, almost frighteningly alive" to her, a "blaze" to which she crouches "as if to warm herself," Laura "felt they were in her fingers, on her lips, growing in her breast." Soon afterward, Laura sees herself anew, suddenly a "charming girl." When her mother wins Laura's docility by giving her her own new hat, Laura accidentally passes a mirror: "Never had she imagined she could look like that." Even to her mother, she is changed: "I have never seen you look such a picture." The black hat trimmed with gold daisies is perhaps emblematic of the youthful flowering of vitality and maturity in Laura, her soon-to-be-gained perception of life and death commingled, a natural growth of light and festive brightness against the dark background, the black of life's sufferings and death's mysteries. But the hat is also an expensive and fashionable contrast to the shawls of the women of the lane. Its daisies are gold. In the story's opening paragraph, the gardeners had only recently removed the daisy plants from "the dark flat rosettes" of the garden, as it were (it turns out) to this very hat. Ultimately, it is as if a newly grown-up Laura is putting on her social heritage with this hat from her mother, a hat whose expensiveness denotes life and spiritual vitality in the cultural idiom of her family. No wonder, later, when viewing the dead man, she immediately exclaims, "Forgive my hat." If we feel then that her instincts are good, her heart in the right place, it is because she has been created to win our sympathy. It would be blindness not to see as well that this sympathy is partially based on social admiration for her class and her particular type. She is positively as sensitive and receptive an individual as, given the right human material, wealth—class—can create.

Laura's psychological and moral growth are interconnected with her new perception of death, to which, as if to the end of a quest, she finally comes after her late afternoon journey to the anonymous lower class world down the hill below the Sheridans' house. Her growing up in the story is a bittersweet experience. Death, she learns, is ordinary, concurrent with life and parties, and extraordinary, final, a magic (or reality) beneath and beyond class, money, and dreams. Her awe at this discovery, her inability to articulate her response, is a measure of her family self-deception, the corollary of wealth's illusion, as well as a sign of the intensity of her reaction. She discovers what she had instinctively felt earlier; as she goes on a mission of charity to the proletarian regions of death, she realizes that money and advantages, parties, clothes, and cream puffs, are not life, nor what is more important about it. She reacts to this intuitively gained knowledge ecstatically, as a deeply liberating experience. Here at the end of the story, for a second time alone with a worker (the scene is parallel to the conversation about the marquee in the beginning), she still romanticizes: the dead worker is a "marvel" of serenity, a "wonderful" token of the world's rightness. Yet her reaction simultaneously indicates how far she has come towards accepting her shared humanity and mortality and towards gaining maturity, as well as

how far she has to go. To idealize is to accept, rather than reject; as a stereotyped mode of meeting experience, if no less a cliché, her reaction is a contrast to her mother's scorn and her family's distaste for the working class and their lives and houses and unpastoral "garden patches" of "cabbage stalks, sick hens and tomato cans." Laura's response to the dead man is likewise a pointed contrast to the banal, sentimental song which Jose rehearses, looking "mournfully and enigmatically," before the party:

This Life is *Wee*-ary,
Hope comes to Die.
A Dream—a *Wa*-kening.

Laura accepts death as enigmatic, a kind of dreaming from which there is no awakening, yet which in part is an awakening to contentment, to repose, to the metaphysical order and rightness of life. In her drive to accept and assimilate life, including life's struggles and doubts, she apprehends death as something that is consoling and beautiful and moving rather than abstractly mournful, the content of a drawing-room song sung by a singer beaming with "dreadfully unsympathetic" pride.

Laura's journey takes place as it is "growing dusky." As she descends out of the garden to "the hollow" where "the little cottages were in deep shade," the story most emphatically shifts to the intensely suggestive mode that we have noted is the work's stratagem for transforming sharply observed detail into narrative interiority and symbolism. Laura's outward journey, no less specific and concrete in its strikingly forceful details than the events of the opening sections of the story, is now foremost a metaphor for an inward progress, a movement shared indeed by both Laura and the closely sympathetic reader. This process of deepening perception, of approaching the depths of the psyche where our sense of self is inseparable from our sense of our mortal limitation, is parallel to Laura's quest for a grown-up, experiential knowledge of human life, the immediate object of which is the cottage where death lives. Both the symbolic psychological process and the pattern of narrative action are deeply threatening, and it is as an omen of fear for reader and heroine alike that, on the way to the quiet, dark, smoky region, "a big dog ran by like a shadow." In contrast to the Sheridan Eden of wealth and leisure, out of the harshness and drabness of the workers' lives Mansfield creates a geography of death. This alien region asserts itself as a concrete physical actuality—their squalid, chocolate brown houses and mean, scraggly gardens are truly sordid—and in that we see it from without, from Laura's unsympathetic point of view, also an illusory, socially scornful, snobbish perception of working class realities. Laura's imagination views the lower class district at the foot of the hill as literally a lower world, the land of the dead. To us this district of death-in-life complements Laura's youthfulness and there is a rightness about the ritual inexorability with which Laura approaches Mrs. Scott's house, walks through the "dark knot of people" who part "as though she was expected," questions the woman with the queer smile so unlike the easy, friendly smiles of the workmen at the beginning, enters despite herself (invoking God's protection), and—by an accident that is no accident at all in terms of plot impetus and symbolic schematism—turns into the bedroom where the body lies.

The whole movement of the story impels Laura from the bright, broad lawns of the opening out of the garden gates to the dingy, narrow lane, then to the "tiny path" to the Scotts' door, and finally to the narrower, claustrophobic "gloomy passage" inside the house, through the "wretched little low kitchen" with its smoky lamp and the woman before the fire, her face "swollen" and "terrible," and to the dead laborer. "Don't be afraid, my lass, . . ." the widow's sister tells Laura, "'e looks a picture," an ironic echo of Mrs. Sheridan's admiring compliment to her daughter in her new hat and also of Laura's inability, after catching sight of herself in the mirror, to realize the Scotts clearly save as an indistinct news photo. Here Laura's view is scathingly real, "a bang slap in the eye" far more jarring to her "upbringing" than the tall workman's colloquialism; this is the story's climactic scene. Life and death are united dramatically; Laura comes to the dead man. "You'd like a look at 'im, wouldn't you?" Em's sister asks. It seems almost impertinent to observe that the basic conceptualization of life is a rich, pretty, sensual young woman and of death, a poor worker whom she views as a handsome, remote, dreaming man. Seeing the dead worker transformed into a beautiful marvel, no longer does Laura play at being work-girl. Perhaps she is overawed by death, the great leveler of classes, but we should not be: it is the laborer who dies, and it is the sheltered, leisure class girl who imagines him as "happy." Then Laura, fearful of poverty's deathly regions and further repelled by the mourning rituals of the poor, quickly flees "those dark people."

The imagistic overtones, however, vibrate not with economics and sociology, but with Mansfield's conjoining of mythic allusion, religious miracle, and fairy tale magic. Like the roses of the opening paragraph, this worker, too, has been visited by the supernatural, the angelic—an angel of death. Mrs. Scott's sister uncovers the body, and we hear, in a passage of highly emotional interior monologue, Laura's unusual sensibility:

> There lay a young man, fast asleep—sleeping so soundly, so deeply, that he was far, far away from them both. Oh, so remote, so peaceful. He was dreaming. Never wake him up again. His head was sunk in the pillow, his eyes were closed; they were blind under the closed eyelids. He was given up to his dream. What did garden-parties and baskets and lace frocks matter to him? He was far from all those things. He was wonderful, beautiful. While they were laughing and while the band was playing, this marvel had come to the lane. Happy . . . happy. . . . All is well, said that sleeping face. This is just as it should be. I am content.

The scene is in strong contrast to the fearful ugliness, drabness, and tawdriness surrounding it. Laura's abstract vision of contentment amidst death and the gathering of mourners—both are counterpointed against the life and convivial gaiety of the afternoon's party—is an intuitive acceptance of much that is basic to the human situation. No reaction is commensurate with such knowledge.

There is unspoken recognition of this depth in the heroine's sensitivity to social occasion, her constrained realization in the paragraph immediately following that she must speak to him and "had to" cry. Mansfield's instincts in this paragraph are unerring. In Laura's act of humility, despite the clumsiness of her words, "Forgive my hat," and in the similar consistency of her expression of personal sympathy, her "loud childish sob," Laura rises to her experience as best she can with inarticulate reliance on social ritual, on symbolic gesture—a response comparable in kind to her creator's emphasis on verbal gestures, the mythic and symbolic elements foregrounded here at the end of the story. We admire Laura for what we would like to believe she intends.

But just as the party is summarized rapidly and thus effectively placed for us in the story's structure, so, too, is Laura's development placed by her nearly bathetic immediate reaction, an impression given us directly by the verbal surface as the paragraph begins: "But all the same. . . ." Likewise, Laura's childish cry is an explicit indication, along with her social awkwardness, that she develops only to the brink of transition to adulthood, which of course is no sudden metamorphosis in anyone. But her girlishness is now counterbalanced by her capacity to assimilate the experience at least through the simple acceptance of deeper realities and so to make her own way. Mansfield embeds this in the scene. "She found her way out" of the house—as with our sense of the initiation into experience, we see one of its results, a barely suggested composure, conceptualized in the dramatically understated action. Though there is a hint of terror, Laura no longer blunders wrongly. Fleeing the darkness, she then meets her brother Laurie on the way home as he steps from shadow. She is crying. "It was simply marvellous," she tells him, moved by her mixed bewilderment and fright, recognition and ecstacy. She "looked at her brother"—the contrast to her looking at the body is explicit in both word and image: "'Isn't life,' she stammered, 'isn't life——' But what life was she couldn't explain."

Laura's first reaction when she meets her brother is far less ambiguous, however; "She took his arm, she pressed up against him." Earlier Mansfield describes the party as a gathering of "bright birds that had alighted in the Sheridans' garden for this one afternoon, on their way to—where? Ah, what happiness it is to be with people who all are happy, to press hands, press cheeks, smile into eyes." Though the sensibility here may be Laura's, the voice is detached from the point of view in its brisk, set-piece qualities (most evident in the scene as a whole) and its summary diction as well as its implicit vantage point as that of a literally distant, outside onlooker who is able to see patterns of people coming "in streams" and compose the couples "wherever you looked . . . strolling, bending, . . . greeting, moving on over the lawn" into the imagistic grouping of the flock of splendid birds. The image, technically Laura's, is exotic and powerful in itself and is reinforced by the authorial presence. Having sensed death, then, and despite having seen in it a calm beauty, Laura grasps life, which is no exotic passage and, if a brief flight on the way to—ah, death, is all the more important as something to feel, to touch, to press against. The general-ized qualities of Laura's final impressions of life and death are in her phrasing, not her actions. The experience turns almost to a sensual one for Laura, who, as we see when she playfully bites her mother's ear in appreciation for the lilies, is a creature of touch. The emotional impact of Laura's experience is complex, haunting, and enigmatic.

Just as the carter's widow (who "seemed as though she couldn't understand. . . . What did it mean?"), but without the personal cost, Laura has discovered death's mystery: which is the reality? the happiness to press against others in life's garden of earthly delights? the happiness to be given up to death's detachment and contentment? Or are these dreams beside life's poverty, a death-in-life, or illu-sions deriving from wealth's confusing morality of warmth and shelter that obscure death's blind finality? The enig-ma is also life's mystery, our flight on our "way to—where?" In its deep structure the story is ultimately a garden party of gestures and images, a gathering of some of the bewilderments and consolations of life's diversity, ambi-guity, perplexity, and contradiction.

Laura's growth, one that the reader perhaps comes to perceive and understand better than the heroine, is an inward maturation. It is a shadowy and only vaguely dis-criminated development towards adulthood, as indistinct but, we feel, as inevitable as the nightfall soon to follow the dusk that pervades the final scenes of the story. This nascent maturity in Laura, however, is the conclusion of a plot heavily freighted with Katherine Mansfield's verbal poetry and emotional power. Her style, we observed, func-tions to raise the dramatic events and the characters above their realistic socio-economic being—the external dimen-sion of literature, its mimetic context—into that special realm definitive of literature's inner mechanisms of evoc-ative, myth-making, symbolizing power. In **"The Garden Party,"** this process is created as much by authorial me-diation as by anything else. It is a literary stylization of experience that translates material to an intense level of the stylization of human emotion and desire, a realm of significant metaphor and also of unnaturalistic detail and fairy tale magic.

The story's world abounds with supernatural and animis-tic details. This world's things suddenly play unexpected roles. Angels visit roses. Flowers understand people. Dai-sies move from gardens to hats. People order the weather. Laura skims and flies across her parents' lawns like a fairy child. A dog passes Laura like a nightmare as she starts out on her errand with the basket of goodies and, strangely, she seems expected at the Scotts'. There are talismans and omens, a witch-like creature and a magic hat, impossible foreknowledge and unavoidable fate. Much like Daphne, who became a laurel, that tree's namesake Laura assumes the lilies into herself; like Proserpine, she descends from a world of flowers to the world of death and returns from it (though unlike Demeter's daughter, she returns by her own powers). We view a garden and witness a departure from it, learn of a knowledge (death) that commences with a temptation (cream puffs, a temp-tation frightening in its human banality). Various more or

less magical transmutations pervade the story: for instance, the plausible, life to death; half-plausible (metaphoric), death to miraculous beauty; and implausible (petty, com-ic, and mock pastoral), a green-coated band to frogs. For Laura, too, the experience is one of metamorphoses: of herself, a girl becoming a woman, and of her self-percep-tion and perception of life. Finally, then, the combination of Laura's sensibility and Mansfield's authorial presence in the emotionally charged language of the story infuses the reader's experience with significances that transcend the surface dramatic actuality.

The authorial overlay, in its allusiveness, its suggestion of significant patterns implicit in the story's world, invites us to extrapolate further symbolic meanings. It is difficult to make the interpretive leap without at the same time feel-ing we are allegorizing a story that is solidly grounded in the experiences of a character and her social reality. None-theless, the plot of **"The Garden Party"** can also be seen as fairy tale, modern literary myth. Laura, the heroine, is rich and beautiful, the daughter of royal wealth if without royal rank. No charming, deserving lover appears for her at the party, her ball, but soon afterward she meets her prince. He is "wonderful, beautiful," but in an inversion of the sleeping beauty motif, it is he who is in a death-like trance. Laura herself, sensitive and receptive, is fully awakened to the stark realities of life by his presence: he is, in fact, dead. Ironically, Laura's prince is a lower class worker who has been killed in an industrial mishap, a carter who is the hapless victim of a machine; his steed shied at a traction engine, and he was killed.

We observed earlier that Mansfield does not altogether leave behind the social realities of the story's world as she raises its pitch of symbolic intensity. Instead, the social forces and economic necessities play a powerful determi-nant role in the structure of the fable, just as they influ-enced the characterization of its heroine. Like garden parties and modern short stories, fairy tale plots are im-plicitly social occasions. The realities of money and class in **"The Garden Party,"** which concomitantly remains a fundamentally character-based, concretely realistic story and, therefore, resists too thorough a dissolution into the metaphorical and archetypal, also take the form of a per-vasive irony in the plot, one that is inherent in its out-come. In short, the fairy princess cannot marry her prince because of his class. Thus there is no love story or only an abstract one—Laura in love with life—and the prince is dead when Laura meets him. He is beyond the real world, a sleeping beauty who indeed is idealized precisely as such by Laura's imagination. Furthermore, the difficult moral and psychological maturity toward which Laura has been struggling would be irrelevantly rewarded by a mar-riage, even were the match perfect in social or personal terms. Laura's ritual trial is an individual one, expressive of an age that believes preeminently in human potential-ity, in uniqueness, self-sufficiency, and inner growth, in a sense in unlimited personal possibilities and concomitant-ly unattainable fulfillments that are, must be (since their range is without definition), just beyond the end of any endeavor. In this perspective, the fairy tale is a fully modern one. Its plot ironies are the result of twentieth-century social and economic exigencies; and its plot structure, a process of growth begun, the completion of which is beyond the end of the story (if at all possible in an ideal sense), is symptomatic of twentieth-century uncertainties. The story formally accepts and unites these elements in the same way that Laura's "All is well" accepts her new, mixed knowledge of life.

Finally, in uniting its various strains of perception and experience, the story as story implicitly throws its emphasis on what values are immanent in the life it realizes. Laura's sensitivity, her receptivity, and emotional vitality, her just blossoming physical beauty, and her shelteredness and nurtured ingenuousness, in short, the full mixture of her characteristics as personal individual and social-economic type—all these appealing qualities which Mansfield grants her heroine are held inextricably together by the achieved solidity, the rendered validity of her presence in the story. There is no way to separate the elements of Mansfield's fundamentally dual imaginative conception of her protagonist. This very conceptualization in another sense defines why the story, in precisely the way that we have seen, informs its simple plot pattern of a young girl's first important steps towards adult maturity. Poised dialectically between the narrative world of vivid realistic clarity and specificity—the social and economic actuality of human life—and a symbolic, internalized world of metaphorical perception implicit in human reactions to everyday reality, Laura synthesizes the story's modalities and its dual emphases at the very most basic level. In the inseparability of these social and personal, aesthetic and perceptual patterns, that Laura is rich means that she is better than anyone outside her class, and that she is imaginative, sensitive, and receptive means that she is better than anyone in it. Similarly, the lyrical and symbolic technique that transforms the harsher realities of poor workers and human impermanence during this day of Laura's awakening to life and death is finally of much greater appeal than the diurnalities which it absorbs. The open-ended conclusion, emotionally effective and thematically appropriate, is indeed the only conceivable closing for the story as character-centered modern short story, as fairy tale pattern, and as radically ambiguous lyrical structure. The conceptualization of Laura is nothing other than the stylized human correlative of the story's essential unity as richly complex and deeply moving construction of conjoined dualities—intensive symbolic signification and mimetic representation, lyricism and narration, style and social occasion.

Clare Hanson and Andrew Gurr (essay date 1981)

SOURCE: "The Stories 1921-22: Sierre and Paris," in *Katherine Mansfield*, St. Martin's Press, 1981, pp. 95-139.

[*In the following excerpt, Hanson and Gurr place "The Garden Party" in the context of Mansfield's stories about the Sheridan family.*]

The Burnells of '**At the Bay**' and '**The Doll's House**' are an extended family group who appear mostly in domestic situations. Kezia is small and just beginning to open her eyes on the possibilities of the world which the adults, Linda and Beryl especially, foreshadow in their own problems. All the Burnell stories are about discovery and the growth of that kind of awareness which belongs to the intense, singular perspective of the small child. For the later stage of growth, the stage of adolescent self-consciousness and its social adjustments, Katherine Mansfield invented another family, the Sheridans.

Like the Burnells, the Sheridans are a Wellington family who live in Tinakori Road, the place from which in "**Prelude**" we see the Burnells moving to live in Karori. There is no grandmother and no small child in the Sheridan family, only the two parents with three adolescent girls and a younger boy. Katherine Mansfield had spent the years from five to ten in Karori, and moved back to Tinakori Road where she was born, in 1898, to a new house, much larger than her birthplace, the house displayed with some precision in '**The Garden-Party**'.

She had more difficulty with the Sheridan stories than the Burnell stories. They lacked the impetus of the *Karori* concept, the idea of knitting all the Burnell stories into a discontinuous but cohesive novel. The process of discovery which is basic to both cycles was more straightforward in the Burnell group, since the focus was on objects or incidents seen as isolated phenomena in the present moment of the child's wide-eyed perspective. The Sheridan stories are more concerned with human relationships, the impact of local conditions on the developing personality and how the present affects the past and future. In a letter written in March 1922 Katherine Mansfield described the Sheridan preoccupations as 'the diversity of life and how we try to fit in everything, Death included'. The Burnell stories deal with involuntary change and development, while the Sheridan stories are concerned with conscious change.

Partly as a result of this difficulty she completed little of the projected Sheridan cycle. Ian Gordon includes sixteen pieces, dated between 1915 and 1922, in the Sheridan stories printed in *Undiscovered Country*, including '**Maata**' and '**The Wind Blows**'. But only the last five seem to have been designed specifically as a Sheridan cycle. A fragment called 'A Dance' which appears in the *Journal*, tentatively dated 1920, was reconstructed as the first Sheridan story, '**Her First Ball**', in July 1921. '**By Moonlight**', which was never finished, was written in September 1921, and the only major Sheridan story, '**The Garden-Party**', in October 1921. A further piece, called 'The Sheridans', was begun in May 1922 probably with the idea of developing the stories into a complete cycle on the *Karori* model for publication in *The Sphere*. Nothing else was set down, however, before she gave up writing altogether.

Of this group only '**The Garden-Party**' is a masterpiece. There was no pillar to provide underpinning of the kind that "**Prelude**" gave to the Burnell cycle. Katherine Mansfield wrote in the manuscript of **'Her First Ball'** that it was only playing on the borders of the sea (the sea of adolescent discovery), and a month later she wrote of **'By Moonlight'**, giving as her reason for abandoning it that 'This isn't bad, but at the same time it's not good. It's too easy.' So to take up the Sheridan family again for **'The Garden-Party'** was a risk and a challenge.

It was a challenge partly because the subject, an adolescent encounter with death, demanded a more orthodox narrative structure than **'At the Bay'** or **'The Daughters of the Late Colonel'**. The **'Garden-Party'** is told as a single character's story in a straightforwardly sequential narrative. It is not divided into scenes or sections or 'cells' and Laura, the central figure, is the consciousness through which everything is observed throughout the day's events. This tighter unity was necessary because the story is more narrowly than the Burnell stories an account of adolescent discovery, and of Laura's recognition, through confrontation with death, of the distance which is beginning to develop between her and her family.

The development of Laura's differences from her family is shown in a number of ways. Her growth as an adolescent is implied, for instance, in the affinity she feels for the men of the story as much as it is shown by her divergence from her mother and sisters. Her father and her brother both respond to the news of the death down the lane more sympathetically and therefore more as Laura does than any of the female Sheridans. Laura feels a precise affinity with her brother at the end of the story, the same kind of affinity that she tells herself she feels for the workmen in her garden at the beginning. The dead man's widow and sister-in-law make little impression on her, for all their swollen faces, compared with the peaceful sleep of the dead man. Laura's world is beginning to stretch beyond the narrowly feminine confines of family and garden.

At the outset of the story her distance from her mother and sisters is only a matter of inclination. She is sent to tell the workmen where to erect the marquee because 'you're the artistic one'. In the middle, when news of the death down the lane is first delivered, the fact that she reacts in the opposite way to her sister and her mother is linked to her sense of comradeship with her brother.

> When the Sheridans were little they were forbidden to set foot [down the lane] because of the revolting language and of what they might catch. But since they were grown up, Laura and Laurie on their prowls sometimes walked through. It was disgusting and sordid. They came out with a shudder. But still one must go everywhere; one must see everything. So through they went.

Near the end, after Laura's first impulse to stop the party because of the death has been diverted by her mother's diplomacy, and the party has gone its delightful course, Laura is drawn into her mother's belated impulse to send a basket of party left-overs to the dead man's family, but now feels much more distinctly alone.

Again, how curious, she seemed to be different from them all. To take scraps from their party. Would the poor woman really like that?

Her journey down the dark lane among the dark people with the incongruous relic of the day is an adventure she takes on her own, out of her family's protection. It is her first real voyage of discovery. It is an encounter with a world which has been hitherto a male preserve, where knowledge of death is a necessary part of reality.

Mrs Sheridan will have nothing to do with such adventures. Although she uses the party as a ritual of initiation into adulthood for her children ('I'm determined to leave everything to you children this year'), her vision of the adult world does not extend beyond the garden.

> 'Mother, a man's been killed,' began Laura.
>
> '*Not* in the garden?' interrupted her mother.
>
> 'No, no!'
>
> 'Oh, what a fright you gave me!' Mrs Sheridan sighed with relief, and took off the big hat and held it on her knees.

She is an adroitly diplomatic stage-manager, allowing her children to think they are in complete control of the party, redirecting Laura by means of the beautiful hat into what she sees as the normal channel of adolescent conduct, with enough success to ensure that Laura is standing 'side by side' with her on the porch to farewell the guests after the party has ended. Only the male reminder of the death down the lane, what Mrs Sheridan feels to be her husband's distinctly tactless remark, renews her distance from her daughter. She is the perfect mother for childhood and the sheltered butterfly life of the Sheridan house and garden. Laura's divergence from her signals a departure from childhood.

The distance is also marked by that feature of the story which has troubled so many commentators, the element of social class. New Zealand critics tend to feel it is overstated, a British intrusion on their classless society. Other critics feel it is overstated because the contrast with the elegiac beauties of the garden party inside the Sheridan gates is melodramatised. Both kinds of objection put too high a priority on external realism and see the social setting in terms of its independent existence, not in relation to Laura and her growth which is the focus for the whole story.

Laura herself of course calls the social element 'these absurd class distinctions', and refuses to recognise them. To her mother they are second nature. She does not like having to deal with the lower classes. Laura is sent in her place to negotiate with the workmen over the placing of the marquee, Jose is sent to be diplomatic with the cook, and Laura is dispatched with the basket to the dead carter's family. Mrs Sheridan keeps her distance from workmen just as she enjoins her children to keep away from their cottages in the dark lane. But Laura ventures among the workmen just as she had ventured with her brother among the cottages. She rejects her mother's aversion because 'one must go everywhere'. She feels initially a warmth for the workmen with the marquee in an unconsciously patronising manner which is only a small shift away from her mother's aloofness. She is in a different world from them.

> 'H'm, going to have a band, are you?' said another of the workmen. He was pale. He had a haggard look as his dark eyes scanned the tennis-court. What was he thinking?

> 'Only a very small band,' said Laura gently. Perhaps he wouldn't mind so much if the band was quite small.

The dark eyes do not belong with bands and parties and all the attendant brightness.

Laura's sister Jose is more like her mother: 'Jose loved giving orders to the servants, and they loved obeying her. She always made them feel they were taking part in some drama.' But Laura, the artistic one, has begun her journey in a different direction.

> Oh, how extraordinarily nice workmen were, she thought. Why couldn't she have workmen for friends rather than the silly boys she danced with and who came to Sunday night supper? She would get on much better with men like these.

It is a direction which culminates in her visit to the dead carter, a visit which measures not only her distance from her family but the leap she has been forced to make from her own childish assumptions about nice workmen.

This kind of measurement is the basic feature of the story and the prime reason for its more orthodox narrative structure. Laura makes a single journey through the events of the day in sequence, concluding with the real journey she goes on out of her garden and down the dark lane. The structure follows that sequence in time and with the cohesion of the single viewpoint. It is a mildly comic paradox that this sequential structure should have produced the chief complaints about the story, its disunity. The contrast between the glorious perfections of the party and the misery of the dead man's home has produced several protests about the violence of the disjunction. And yet the whole story is built on it. The transition from bright morning to dark evening and the related patterns of contrast are the essential accompaniments to Laura's process of discovery.

The contrasts are numerous and exact. The transition of time from the morning's discoveries through the afternoon party to the evening's discoveries is gradual, but the details at either end form a pattern of sharp contrasts. The Sheridans' garden, with its roses, its lily-lawn, its tennis-court and the grove of karaka trees, contrasts with the cottages.

> They were little mean dwellings painted a chocolate brown. In the garden patches there was nothing but cabbage stalks, sick hens and tomato cans.

The cream puffs bought for the garden party appear before and after. Before, they are sampled with guilty delight by Laura and Jose; after, they are scraps loaded into the basket for the poor: 'All those sandwiches, cakes, puffs, all uneaten, all going to be wasted.' And lilies, the pink cannas which are delivered on the morning of the party like the cream puffs, and the arum lilies, the white funeral flower, which are only withdrawn from the gift of leftovers because they would stain Laura's frock, likewise appear before and after. Cream puffs and lilies are first delivered to the bright Sheridan property by the workers, the baker's man and the florist, and then are delivered by Laura to the dark property of the workers as leftovers. The 'blaze' of canna lilies and the bright cream puffs, together with all the main images of light, the morning, the colourful garden, are transmuted into images of dark, the 'deep shade' of the lane, the 'dark knot' of people at the garden gate where the dead body is housed, the 'gloom' of the cottage and in the end Laurie stepping out of the shadows. In the first part of the story people are all coming into the light, entering the glories of the Sheridan garden bringing gifts for the party. In the second half Laura goes out of the brightness on an antithetical journey carrying gifts from the party into the darkness of the lane.

Two images in particular stand out in this pattern of contrasts, and link the imagery explicitly with the central subject, the encounter with death. The beautiful hat with which Mrs Sheridan distracts Laura's mind before the party, is black, a 'black hat trimmed with gold daisies, and a long black velvet ribbon'. Like the lilies, it makes a dazzling show for the party, but like the white arum lilies which Mrs Sheridan wants Laura to take down the lane it is also a version of the trappings conventionally taken to funerals. Laura does not recognise it as such. The hat belongs with the party, and therefore is an embarrassment when she hurries down the lane with the basket of cream puffs.

> How her frock shone! And the big hat with the velvet streamer—if only it was another hat!

Finally she is taken to view the body. Dazed by its stillness she is forced to apologise to it for her misconceived symbol.

> There lay a young man, fast asleep—sleeping so soundly, so deeply, that he was far, far away from them both. Oh, so remote, so peaceful. He was dreaming. Never wake him up again. His head was sunk in the pillow, his eyes were closed; they were blind under the closed eyelids. He was given up to his dream. What did garden parties and baskets and lace frocks matter to him? He was far from all those things. He was wonderful, beautiful. While they were laughing and while the band was playing, this marvel had come to the lane. Happy . . . happy . . . All is well, said that sleeping face. This is just as it should be. I am content.

> But all the same you had to cry, and she couldn't go out of the room without saying something to him. Laura gave a loud childish sob.

> 'Forgive my hat,' she said.

The hat is her cream puff, the relic of gaiety she carries with her from the party. When she had shut the gates of the Sheridan garden behind her, she was filled with the party: 'It seemed to her that kisses, voices, tinkling spoons, laughter, the smell of crushed grass were somehow inside her.' Now it is outside her, incongruously shining on her head, the device intended to shine in the very process of giving her shade from the brightness. And for this display of childish pleasures she must now apologise.

The other and even more direct contrast linking the party with death is Jose's song.

Pom! Ta-ta-ta *Tee*-ta! The piano burst out so passionately that Jose's face changed. She clasped her hands. She looked mournfully and enigmatically at her mother and Laura as they came in.

> This Life is *Wee*-ary,
> A Tear—a Sigh.
> A Love that *Chan*-ges,
>   This Life is *Wee*-ary,
> A Tear—a Sigh.
> A Love that *Chan*-ges,
> And then . . . Good-bye!

> But at the word 'Goodbye', and although the piano sounded more desperate than ever, her face broke into a brilliant, dreadfully unsympathetic smile.

> 'Aren't I in good voice, mummy?' she beamed.

> This Life is *Wee*-ary,
> Hope comes to Die.
> A Dream—a *Wa*-kening.

In the middle of the preparations for the party the song seems merely ludicrous. The reality, with its explicit echo in Laura's reaction to the sight of the body ('He was dreaming. Never wake him up again'), is a contrast which measures Laura's advance in awareness over Jose, while at the same time marking her desperate romanticising of the corpse. She views the body as if she were in a fairy tale. The dead carter is a sleeping prince whom she has braved many terrors to reach. And when she sees him she sees his stillness as a peaceful sleep from which he must never be awoken. Instead of the sleeping princess to be roused with a kiss there is a sleeping prince to be left in peace. He is happy. All is well. He suffers none of the pains of life and parties and incongruous hats. So she can return from the darkness with the bright image from its centre, the magical awakening hers alone, and her magical brother's.

> Laurie put his arm round her shoulder. 'Don't cry,' he said in his warm, loving voice. 'Was it awful?'

> 'No,' sobbed Laura. 'It was simply marvellous. But, Laurie—' she stopped, she looked at her brother. 'Isn't life,' she stammered, 'isn't life—' But what life was she couldn't explain. No matter. He quite understood.

> '*Isn't* it, darling?' said Laurie.

And there the story ends. It is a cycle of growth. The roses open their petals for the morning of the party; the afternoon 'slowly ripened, slowly faded, slowly its petals closed'. At the end the corpse lies like a closed flower in the night, and Laura feels she has seen life through its full cycle of blossoming and closure.

Laura's learning process in the course of the day is radical, though it is also far from complete. The ending, the inexpressible discovery about life, marks her encounter with the fact of death rather than her assimilation of its full significance. The positiveness she voices to Laurie at the conclusion is in its immature confidence, and the assurance that Laurie '*quite* understood', a signal of the distances her journey still has to cover. Death is still more melodramatic to her than real. Her sleeping prince is marvellous because he reveals the completion of the cycle of life blossoming rather than the finality of death as a denial of life. Some such thought may have been in Katherine Mansfield's own mind when she wrote at the end of her manuscript, 'This is a moderately successful story, and that's all. It's somehow, in the episode at the lane, scamped.' Life is stronger in **'The Garden-Party'** than death. Those critics who approve it for its elegiac evocation of the beautiful life shy away from the dark side of the pattern of contrasts and from the transition between light and dark. But since Laura does not leave the Sheridan property for the lane until more than four-fifths of the way through the story they can claim some support for their view, both in the space given to the one over the other, and in the author's own verdict.

It is, however, a quantitative assertion which underrates the central function of Laura herself, and the gradual nature of the process which takes her away from the world of Mrs Sheridan's values. Laura is a chrysalis—Jose has already emerged as a butterfly like her mother ('Jose, the butterfly, always came down in a silk petticoat and a kimono jacket')—and the story rests on the brief intrusion of death into the butterfly world. Laura's own emergence is only beginning. The garden party is a growth point, and it is rightly portrayed as a brilliant, idyllic setting for the incipient butterfly. The final emphasis on Laura's emergence from her protective cocoon cannot cancel the idyllic glories of the butterfly world of the Sheridan garden. But the butterfly garden is also incomplete without the recognition that it can hatch creatures possessing a greater sense of engagement with life than the butterflies.

Ben Satterfield (essay date 1982)

SOURCE: "Irony in 'The Garden Party,'" in *Ball State University Forum*, Vol. XXIII, No. 1, Winter, 1982, pp. 68-70.

[*In the following essay, Satterfield contends that "irony is the keynote" for understanding "The Garden Party."*]

All of the writing on Katherine Mansfield's most anthologized story recognizes or implies that **"The Garden-**

Party" is a fable of initiation. The general interpretation argues that Laura goes from her Edenic world to one in which death exists, and that archetypally she loses her innocence, thereby acquiring knowledge and reaching a point of initiation. Laura has a great discovery, true; but because of her inability to make any kind of statement about it that would serve to clarify its meaning, critics disagree on whether she will go on to learn more about life and death or whether she will retreat into the sanctuary of the garden world. Much of the disagreement can be resolved, I believe, by a close examination of the irony—which has been largely ignored—and the function and effect of that irony upon the events of the story. Also, **"The Garden-Party"** contains *two* types of initiation, a fact mostly overlooked, and the initiations are not compatible, as the details of the story make evident.

Irony is the keynote. The central character of **"The Garden-Party,"** Laura Sheridan, is protected from the exigencies of life and is unable to view reality (even death) except through the rose-tinted glasses provided by a delicate and insulated existence. Laura's world is a world of parties and flowers, a pristine world of radiant, bright canna lilies and roses, a precious and exclusive world. Laura's sister, Jose, is early described as a butterfly—and what creature is more delicate than a butterfly? That Jose chooses to sing a song about a weary life, obviously something she is unacquainted with, has to be ironic: in the Sheridan family, weariness and sorrow are merely lyrics to be mocked.

Mansfield's exquisite use of imagery is as telling as her irony. For example, the flower imagery throughout the story serves to keep the reader reminded of the delicacy of Laura's world. The flowers are splendid, beautiful, and—what is not stated—short-lived. Laura, too, is beautiful, radiant, flower-like. But even the afternoon is likened to a flower: "And the perfect afternoon slowly ripened, slowly faded, slowly its petals closed." Laura, her vision attuned to the superficial, can see only the beauty and not the dying of the flower, and she cannot see that, in many ways, she is very much like a flower herself.

The symbolism of Laura's hat as well as her name (from *laurel,* the victory crown) is apparent. Marvin Magalaner adroitly sums up the significance of both: "When the mother thus presents her daughter with her own party hat in typical coronation fashion, she is symbolically transferring to Laura the Sheridan heritage of snobbery, restricted social views, narrowness of vision—the garden party syndrome." Surely this is the case, although Laura may not be aware of it. Hence here is an initiation that is true and subtle.

But the strong irony of this story results from the contrast between the way Laura sees herself and the way the reader is led to see her. Laura has very little—if any—insight, a fact made manifest throughout **"The Garden-Party."** Her dealings with the workmen illustrate her lack of awareness: she sees them as "extraordinarily nice," apparently not realizing that their "niceness" is more than likely due to their roles as subordinates, mere hirelings. Laura does not even seem to realize that what to her is a delightful party is simply toil to the workmen. Self-absorbed and narcissistic, she takes the superficial at face value because both she and her perceptions lack depth. "She felt just like a work-girl" is stingingly ironic because the reader knows that Laura has absolutely no concept of the life of a work-girl, just as she has no idea of what lies behind the friendly veneer of the workmen. For her to imagine that she would "get on much better with men like these" rather than the "silly boys" who come to her parties is an indication of how little general comprehension and self-understanding she possesses.

The other obvious contrast in the story is between the gaiety on the top of the hill and the sorrow below. The death of a man intrudes upon Laura's affected sensibilities and she discusses the possibility of canceling the party, but, as we suspected, her conscience is easily assuaged (and by the symbolic hat, a distraction that serves to fix Laura permanently in her world). Nothing, positively nothing, is permitted to spoil the party; even the weather is described as "ideal"—a "perfect day for a garden-party."

In the Sheridan world, suffering and misery cannot take precedence over well-ordered but mundane social functions, and will not be allowed to interfere. Consequently, Laura, with uncommon self-centeredness, blots out the death of a common man until a more convenient time: "I'll remember it again after the party's over, she decided." But even then, for her to realize that she is actually going to the house of the dead man is difficult because "kisses, voices, tinkling spoons, laughter, the smell of crushed grass were somehow inside her. She had no room for anything else." Unmistakably she has room for little else than parties, and the closer she comes to the house of the dead man the more she realizes her mistake, for here is a reality she does not want to face: it is so much easier to commiserate from the top of the hill—and then to go on with one's fun. When she actually views the dead man, she can see him only as she sees death, as something remote, far, far away. (In addition, she has no more understanding of why she is there than does the dead man's wife.) Death is so removed from Laura's insular life that it is unreal; it cannot really be experienced, much less coped with, so she sees it as she sees everything else, as something marvelous and beautiful. Just as Laura is unable to pierce the facade of the workmen, she is equally unable to see beyond the face of death, the stark reality of which is transformed into dream, and she sees the dead man as sleeping, happy, content.

Any initiation into the mystery of life and death is incomplete, whereas the installation of Laura into the Sheridan tradition is certain. That Katherine Mansfield could present two types of initiation, one profound and the other shallow, is a tribute to her consummate skill: the fact that the protagonist opts for the shallow in no way detracts from her art but serves to increase the poignancy of her tale and to mark its realism.

Laura is not without sensitivity, but her sensitivity is subordinated to the comforts and trappings of the Sheridan way of life. She is young and inexperienced, and she has been shielded from the harsher aspects of existence. Even after facing the reality of death, however, she is unable to view it realistically and transforms it into a dream, into something wonderful and happy, something that will fit into the tableau of her resplendent world. The ironic tone has been too clearly established for the reader to take Laura's encounter as profoundly affecting. In this regard, **"The Garden-Party"** asserts itself as not just another story of the loss of innocence, but an alteration of a mythic pattern.

The intimations of mortality are only vaguely perceived, and the story closes on a final note of irony: Laura apparently thinks that she has discovered something new about life, not an awesome truth, but something deep and ineffable, something she attempts to explain to her brother, but cannot. Unlike the emperor Augustus, who would sometimes say to his Senate, "Words fail me, my Lords; nothing I can utter could possibly indicate the depth of my feelings," Laura seems more confused than moved, and her inability to articulate her feelings to her brother is a result of her failure to understand, her inability to grasp the full significance of what she has witnessed. "No matter. He quite understood." That is, he understood as much as Laura. They both will in all likelihood remain in the refuge of their bright house on the hill and continue giving expensive, gay parties and toying with the surface of things until the petals of their own lives are closed.

C. A. Hankin (essay date 1983)

SOURCE: "Haunted by Death," in *Katherine Mansfield and Her Confessional Stories,* St. Martin's Press, 1983, pp. 235-47.

[*In the following excerpt, Hankin examines the subject of social class in "The Garden Party."*]

In the months following her brother's death, Katherine Mansfield had dedicated the remainder of her life to recreating and immortalising both him and the world they had shared. 'The next book will be yours and mine', she had promised in February 1916. No longer 'concerned with the same appearance of things', her writing would be 'changed utterly' in form. It would be changed because writing had become an almost religious mission, and changed because she at last had someone to write to and for: 'It is the idea . . . that I do not write alone. That in every word I write and every place I visit I carry you with me.'

In fact, it was not until her own death was imminent that the sister finally made good her promise. For, with the exception of **'The Aloe'**, revised as **'Prelude'**, Katherine Mansfield wrote almost nothing between 1916 and 1921 which centred either on her brother or their life at home in New Zealand. In the period generally reckoned as the most fruitful of her life, however, between July 1921 and February 1922, she wrote the group of stories based on

her memories of New Zealand which at once fulfilled her vow and established her literary reputation. In over half of them the idea of death is of crucial importance, and in over half Katherine Mansfield included, virtually for the first time, a character who was modelled on her brother. Leslie Beauchamp appears as the baby boy in **'At the Bay'**, as Leila's cousin Laurie in **'Her First Ball'**, as the favoured son 'Harold' in **'An Ideal Family'**, as Laura's brother Laurie in **'The Garden Party'** and as the boss's dead soldier son in **'The Fly'**.

Katherine Mansfield completed **'At the Bay'** in September 1921. A month later she wrote the story for which she is probably best known, **'The Garden Party'**. A journal entry dated March 1916 indicates that the genesis of this work lay in the trains of thought and recollection which had preoccupied her in the months following Leslie's death. 'Tinakori Road was not fashionable; it was very mixed', Katherine wrote about the Wellington neighbourhood in which she had lived. 'There was no doubt that the land would become extremely valuable, as Father said. . . . But it was a little trying to have one's own washerwoman living next door . . . and further along there lived an endless family of half-castes . . . and below . . . in a hollow . . . was Saunders Lane.'

Hardly bothering to change names, Katherine Mansfield recreates in **'The Garden Party'** the physical location of her late girlhood: the 'big, white-painted square house', the lily-pond in the garden, and Saunders Lane, the street which was a direct continuation of the Beauchamp's front path. In this street there actually did live a carrier named Scott who had a fatal accident; next door to the Beauchamps was Kitty Marchant (called Kitty Maitland in the story); and Godbers was a well-known Wellington catering firm. This much of **'The Garden Party'** and certain characteristics of the Beauchamp family, Katherine Mansfield drew from life. One important alteration is the change made in the age of the brother. Leslie Beauchamp was six years younger than Katherine: in the narrative he is transformed into Laurie and made to appear so close in age and sensibility to Laura that, as the name suggests, he might almost be her twin.

'The Garden Party' and **'The Fly'** are Katherine Mansfield's most anthologised stories, and dozens of interpretative articles have been written about them. It is a tribute to the complexity and appeal of these works that critics continue to be fascinated by their meaning and form. Most commentators have concentrated upon the philosophical significance of **'The Garden Party'**. They have variously discussed it from the mythic point of view, seeing echoes of the Garden of Eden as well as the Classical myth of Demeter and Persephone; they have seen it as a story of initiation from youth into adulthood; they have examined the thematic juxtapositions of innocence and experience, of beauty and ugliness, of life and death. But, while they have noted, too, the work's social implications, they have not seen that these are central to an understanding of **'The Garden Party'**.

Katherine Mansfield's journal entry suggests that her initial idea for the story developed out of the close proximity she had observed between the houses of the rich and the poor. The paradox that she presents us with is that, in spite of this physical closeness, the two social groups inhabit quite distinct and separate worlds. Laura's progress in the course of the narrative may be the philosophical one from innocence to experience; but in a very real sense it is the girl's instinctive attempt to find out for herself the extent and validity of the differences separating people like the Sheridans from people like the Scotts. The idea of class distinction, then, provides the thematic framework for **'The Garden Party'** as well as informing its verbal structure and patterning.

Into her narrative, Katherine Mansfield weaves a series of contrasts and parallels which unobtrusively carry forward her theme at the same time as they unify the different elements of the story. **'The Garden Party'** is a great story and a complex one because in it, as in **'At the Bay'**, we are presented simultaneously with several distinct yet interlocking levels of meaning. There is the social meaning provided by the real-life framework; the emotional and psychological overtones of the events in which Laura plays a central part; and the broader, philosophical significance of the total experience Katherine Mansfield lays before us.

The fact that the rich can avoid (or attempt to avoid) the unpleasant realities of human existence, even summon up beauty and elegance at will, is conveyed in the very first paragraph of the story. This opening paragraph is redolent of the fullness and richness of life, indeed of birth, since the rose bushes are bowed down as if 'visited by archangels' in the night. At the same time, there is an unreal, artificial quality to this beauty which the personification of the roses underlines. And so the scene is set for the contrast which is integral to the patterning of the narrative: the contrast between the essentially artificial, almost unreal world of the Sheridans and the quite different but real world of the Scotts. While the Sheridans' money brings them life in its fullness, the Scotts' lack of money confers on them only hardship and death.

The world of the Scotts dominates the ending of the story, the world of the Sheridans the first part. Rich and poor alike have their social rituals, and the ritual being celebrated by the Sheridans is the garden party, which at once allows them to display their wealth and fulfil the obligations of hospitality. Convention governs the attitudes, the behaviour and even the voices of the Sheridan women. Laura's conscious attempt to copy her mother's voice, followed by her realisation that she sounds 'so fearfully affected', indicates the artificiality of the Sheridan manner of talking. Laura, who despises 'stupid conventions', cannot act a role; but her mother and sisters do. Jose, for example, delights in the artificial. She loves 'giving orders to the servants' and making them feel that 'they were taking part in some drama'. Emotion is something she simulates but does not feel. Practising her song, 'This Life is *Wee*-ary, / Hope comes to Die', Jose sings of a tragic feeling only to break into a 'brilliant, dreadfully unsympathetic smile'. Behaviour is learned, not something spontaneous, in this sheltered world of wealth; and the Sheridan

reaction to events taking place outside the family circle is dictated by what is expected. Thus Laura's instinctive feeling that the garden party should be cancelled because a death is being mourned nearby is rejected by her mother and sister in virtually identical words. Jose tells Laura, 'nobody expects us to', and this is echoed by Mrs Sheridan: 'People like that don't expect sacrifices from us.'

It is principally through Laura's perceptions that we glimpse the quite different world of the workmen. The distinguishing characteristic of these ordinary people is their naturalness and spontaneity. Whereas feelings are assumed, disguised, or restrained by the Sheridan women, they are expressed freely by the working class. Instinctively, Laura is attracted to the warmth and friendliness of the working men who come to erect the marquee; and the sensitivity shown by the man who smells a sprig of lavender makes her compare these men and the boys of her own social class. 'How many men that she knew would have done such a thing', she thinks. 'Why couldn't she have workmen for friends rather than the silly boys she danced with and who came to Sunday night supper?' Laura is searching for an identity of her own when she inwardly voices her dislike of the 'absurd class distinctions' and 'stupid conventions' which pervade the Sheridan world and prevent her from having friendships with such men. She tries to legitimise her attraction to the workmen by pretending to be 'just like a work-girl'. But the class barriers cannot be broken down, and it is with her brother, Laurie, that she shares her own warmth. 'Suddenly she couldn't stop herself. She ran at Laurie and gave him a small, quick squeeze.' Responding in a 'warm, boyish voice', Laurie echoes the warm voices of the workmen.

Tension in the story is generated by the underlying conflict between Laura, who cannot fully accept the artificial Sheridan conventions, and her mother. Because she is close to the natural world, the girl empathises with the feelings of the working people who are themselves part of that world. With Laurie, Laura had explored the forbidden territory where 'washerwomen lived in the lane. . . . It was disgusting and sordid. . . . But still one must go everywhere; one must see everything.' If Laura is something of a rebel, out of tune with her mother and sisters because she needs to include knowledge of the real, outside world in her perception of life, she is also set apart because she is 'the artistic one'. So long as her imagination functions usefully in the context of the Sheridan life-style, all is well. But when she imaginatively experiences the horror of the working man's death and, forgetting the distinctions between the different social worlds, wants to stop the garden party, she is condemned as 'extravagant'.

Laura's inner division is central to the working out of **'The Garden Party'**. On the one hand her naturalness draws her to find out about life as it is lived outside the confines of the Sheridan household; on the other her artistic temperament causes her not only to respond to beauty but to cast over it a special imaginative colouring. The world of illusion is as precious to her, although for different reasons, as it is to her mother and sisters. It seems to be Laura who feels that roses 'understood that [they] are the only flowers that impress people at garden-parties', who registers the noise of the piano being moved as a 'long, chuckling, absurd sound', who imagines that 'little faint winds were playing chase' and that 'two tiny spots of sun . . . [were] playing too'. Knowingly, Mrs Sheridan appeals to the imaginative side of her daughter's personality when she cleverly distracts the girl by placing her own hat on her head. 'I have never seen you look such a picture', she says admiringly. As Laura gazes at her own beauty in the mirror and decides to forget the death until after the party, the attractions of illusion triumph over the demands of reality. And for the duration of the party, illusion holds sway.

But the magical perfection of the garden party, indeed the whole story, is enclosed within a philosophic framework which reminds us that everything has its opposite. There is a hint of birth in the opening paragraph; in the final section death asserts its presence. In contrast to the frivolous party given by the Sheridans, the gathering at the Scotts' is for the funeral rite of death. Instead of the artificial drama enjoyed by Jose, a real-life drama must be endured in Saunders Lane. And, while sadness and deeply-felt emotion are kept at bay by the Sheridan women, the dead man's wife mourns, her face 'puffed up, red, with swollen eyes and swollen lips'.

Emphasising the gulf between the rich and the poor is the descriptive language of the story. Words such as 'perfect', 'delicious', 'beautiful', 'splendour', 'radiant', 'exquisite', 'brilliant', 'rapturous', 'charming', 'delightful', 'stunning' convey the outward beauty of the Sheridans' life—and its artificiality. In striking contrast are words describing the working people and Saunders Lane: 'haggard', 'mean', 'poverty-stricken', 'revolting', 'disgusting', 'sordid', 'crab-like', 'wretched'. In the domain of the Sheridans, mutability can be warded off so long as the outwardly beautiful appearance of things is preserved. This unattainable ideal of permanence, or stasis, is symbolised by the word 'picture'. In their ordered perfection, the garden, the roses and the canna lilies resemble pictures. When Mrs Sheridan places her hat on Laura's head and says, 'I have never seen you look such a picture', she is in effect framing the young girl's beauty, giving it the semblance of permanence. There is a different kind of picture which Laura briefly visualises: that of the poor woman in the lane and her dead husband. 'But it all seemed blurred, unreal, like a picture in the newspaper.'

Laura is the central character in **'The Garden Party'**, from whose point of view the story is essentially told; and it is she who bridges the contrasting worlds of the Sheridans and the Scotts. Her personal dilemma is that she must reconcile a sympathetic understanding of the poor, and an awareness of reality, with an imaginative attachment to the almost unreal, magical beauty which sweetens the lives of the rich. Her ordeal comes at the end of the story when she must physically cross the boundaries between her house and Saunders Lane, and in doing so face up to that other, 'blurred, unreal' picture. When she enters the cottage of the dead man, the story comes full circle. Just as she had done previously, the girl emphathises emotionally with the working people and echoes their grief with a sob. Earlier in the day, her emotional identification with the workmen had been deflected towards her brother: again, it is Laurie who 'put his arm round her shoulder. "Don't cry", he said in his warm, loving voice.' Laurie, whose warmth links him with the workmen, helps his sister emotionally to transcend the barriers between the classes. The unchanging love of brother and sister, moreover, makes bearable the cruelty of life, the heartlessness of human beings, the 'Love that Changes' of Jose's song, and the knowledge of mutability—of the inevitable ending of a 'perfect afternoon', and the ending of life.

But the crucial philosophical problem in **'The Garden Party'**, the problem that Laura shares with all sensitive human beings, is how to encounter ugliness and death yet retain a personal vision of beauty and hope. In this closing scene, Katherine Mansfield contrives an answer. She brings together the contrasting pictures of beauty and ugliness in a picture whose beauty appears truly permanent, 'a marvel'. The sister-in-law of the dead man tells Laura that ''e looks a picture'; and Laura, the artistic one, agrees that he is indeed 'wonderful, beautiful'. Imaginatively, she is able to forget the suffering inflicted by his death and think only that, 'while they were laughing and while the band was playing, this marvel had come to the lane'. In her writing, Katherine Mansfield, too, has come full circle. Nothing, in her youthful stories, tempered a young girl's initiation into the harshness of adult life. At the ending of **'The Garden Party'** she allows Laura to retain her illusions. If we are left with the uneasy feeling that she has let her character off too lightly, we nevertheless accept the emotional rightness of the ending. For there is a sense in which Katherine Mansfield has granted us, too, a reprieve; has assuaged both our guilt about social inequalities and our haunting anxiety about death.

Hubert Zapf (essay date 1985)

SOURCE: "Time and Space in Katherine Mansfield's 'The Garden Party,'" in *Orbis Litterarum,* Vol. 40, No. 1, 1985, pp. 44-54.

[*In the following essay, Zapf analyzes the structure of "The Garden Party."*]

It has generally been noted in Mansfield criticism that **"The Garden Party"** must be regarded not only as her most popular but also as one of her most skilfully constructed stories. Her literary technique has often been compared to that of Chekov, implying a reduced importance of the plot and a shifting of the centre of interest from the dramatic presentation of extraordinary events and unique occurrences to the illumination of inconspicuous, seemingly insignificant episodes, i.e. from the direct, action-centred surface of the text to a more indirectly organised subsurface of meaningful connections and connotations. This detail-orientated, highly suggestive style has been associated with an "impressionist" dimension in her writing, which again indicates nothing else than that the data of sensory experience are assembled in such a way that their coherence is only gradually and indirectly to be discovered in the apparently random sequence of perceptions and observations.

In spite of the general tribute to the artistic achievement of **"The Garden Party,"** however, the problem of its structural unity has been one of the recurring themes of criticism ever since Warren S. Walker questioned this unity in his well-known article, "The Unresolved Conflict in 'The Garden Party.'" Walker maintained that the social level of the story, i.e. the "clash of social attitudes," is insufficiently connected with the existential level, i.e. Laura's encounter with death. In answer to Walker's challenge, various attempts have been made to defend the structural coherence of the text. I do not propose to take up this question directly here, nor do I aim at an overall interpretation. Instead, I should like to examine two elements of the story's formal structure, time and space, elements which have been discussed sporadically in different contexts but, to my knowledge, have not yet been dealt with as separate aspects, although they can be shown to contribute substantially to the subsurface coherence of the text. Specifically, they illuminate the dialectic nature of the story's composition and are employed by the author not only to support, but actually to embody an essential part of the story's theme.

The temporal frame of **"The Garden Party"** has clear symbolic connotations. The story takes place in early summer, at a time when the roses are in full bloom, i.e. at the height of the life cycle of the year. And it takes one single day of narrated time to be completed. Ranging from dawn to dusk, from the morning to the evening of that day, the story's action symbolically performs, on a smaller scale, the whole cycle from birth to death within the seasonal climax of the year. In this, the symbolic time frame resembles the situation of Laura and the other characters who, celebrating a magnificent, life-throbbing garden party, are confronted simultaneously with the death of a workman from the nearby village. And while the party itself takes place in broad daylight, Laura's encounter with death at the end of the story occurs, suggestively, in the dusk—twilight, of course, representing a highly symbolic state of ambiguity, of transition between day and night, life and death.

The age of the characters corresponds to this pattern. First of all, people of all ages appear in the story. But age does not seem important during the party, except that the events are coloured by Laura's youthful perspective. Although children seem to dominate the scene, they are children imitating the roles of adults. The party is neither organized *by* the children (but by Mrs. Sheridan), nor especially *for* the children, but is a semi-official social occasion with primarily adult guests of unspecified ages. Age is, however, specifically accentuated at the end of the story. After Laura leaves the scene of the party and walks down to the village, she meets an "old, old woman with a crutch" who is sitting beside the gate of the dead workman's house Laura is about to enter. As in the opposition of morning

to evening defining the time span of the story's events, the life cycle is embodied here in the opposition of the two female characters, confronting, at this crucial point in the story, youth with old age. The age of the dead worker, who was married and had five little children, lies between these two opposite stages of life. It is not an old man who dies but a man in the prime of his life, underlining the story's theme of the implicit presence of death in the midst of life.

As to the actual handling of time in the narrative process, two major phases can be distinguished. The first phase, comprising the party preparations from morning till lunchtime, takes up about 11½ of the 16½ pages of the story and thus the longest stretch of 'narrative time,' in which we are told the events of half a day of 'narrated time.' The party itself requires only about half a page of narrative time to summarise the events of the whole afternoon; it is presented in a very general, transitory sort of manner, being disposed of in a few passing remarks. What follows is the aftermath, the "postmortem" of the party, leading to Laura's visit to the dead man's house. This second major phase of the story takes up about 4½ pages, i.e. about one third of the story's narrative time but not more than a few minutes of narrated time.

What can we conclude from this formal observation? First of all, that **"The Garden Party"** is in fact not about the garden party itself but about the time *before* and *after* the party. Or, to put it another way, the party becomes an insignificant episode, a *quantité négligeable* in the greater flux of time in which it is situated. Its temporal presence seems to dissolve between expectation and retrospection, between past and future; it gains no real importance or substance in itself. Secondly, the lengthening of narrative time in reference to narrated time in the second phase creates the impression of time being drawn out or slowed down in comparison with the first phase—a significant change in the story's time rhythm, emphasising the increased importance and different quality of the related experience as the story approaches its existential climax.

Indeed, if we take a closer look at the story, we discover that the narrative pace, corresponding to the different nature of the narrated events, is quite different in the two phases. The morning's events are not related in the sense of a coherent, continual temporal process but of an irregular succession of moments in time passing by as if in high speed, of a series of snapshots of various scenes drawn in a few quick, incomplete strokes and following upon each other with interruptions and time lapses of varying lengths—note the repeated use of phrases such as "Breakfast was not over yet before," "Already the men had," "And now," "And the moment after," "And now," "But at that moment," "But now," "Now, Laura," etc. The action here is characterised by hectic movement, sudden changes of scene, place, and character—although remaining always within the region of the house—, creating the impression of quick, incessant, feverishly busy motion as we witness the party preparations. There is a conspicuous accumulation of words denoting accelerated motion in the first phase of the story. In the scene, for example, where Laura is called away from the workmen to the telephone, exchanges a few rapid words with Laurie on the way, and afterwards talks alternately to her friend Kitty on the telephone and to her mother upstairs, we find, within about ¾ of a page: "skimmed," "very fast," "ran," "quick," "gasp," "dash," "one moment," "flung," "quickly." Or witness the sense of hectic acceleration conveyed by Mrs. Sheridan's way of organising the party:

> "Now, Laura," said her mother quickly. "Come with me into the smokingroom . . . Meg, go upstairs this minute and take that wet thing off your head. Jose, run and finish dressing this instant . . . And—and, Jose, pacify cook if you do go into the kitchen, will you?"

Even when the news of the workman's death arrives, it is soon absorbed into the time-consuming pace and superficial sensationalism of the party preparations: while Godber's man "wasn't going to have his story snatched from under his very nose," relishing the opportunity to impress the others with the news, Laura's initial shock—she relates the accident "breathless, half-choking" to her mother—quickly dissolves when she sees herself in the mirror with her new black hat. She decides to postpone further thoughts on the matter till after the party; there is no 'time' for them now, and death becomes as unreal in the artificial context of the party activities as anything else that threatens their social success.

> Just for a moment she had another glimpse of that poor woman and those little children, and the body being carried into the house. But it all seemed blurred, unreal, like a picture in the newspaper. I'll remember it again after the party's over, she decided. And somehow that seemed quite the best plan . . .

The images of the mirror and the newspaper nicely illustrate how reality is turned upside down here: the insubstantial self-duplication in the mirror supersedes the substantial reality of death, which is at the same time reduced to its unreal duplication in the newspaper. The thought of death becomes one "moment" only in the quick, hectic succession of moments which characterises the party activities: It is the effect of feverish movement, of breathtaking mobility, i.e. of swift, but essentially superficial *change* that is created in this first phase of the story.

What is emphasised in this use of time, ironically, is the transitoriness of these activities, reintroducing the central theme of the transitoriness of life on the temporal level of the story even as it is eliminated from the consciousness of the characters. Time, indeed, is shown to gain obsessive importance in the world of the garden party, an importance inversely proportionate to the attempt to exclude the reality of time—as manifested in the death in the village—from its one-dimensional, organised happiness. The temporal structure thus implies an ironic undercutting of this attempt, illuminating the illusionary quality of the garden party, and in this respect, it assumes a function similar to the other means of ironic undercutting and foreshadowing in the first part of the story, e.g. the ambiguous meaning of the lilies that are brought to the party, Jose's song, the black hats and black clothes.

Manuscript of "The Garden Party."

In contrast to the accelerated pace of the first phase, the second phase of the story—the time after the party—shows a gradual deceleration of the narrative pace. The first sign of this gradual arrest of mobility is the family's sitting down at one of the tables after the guests have left. The death of the workman is mentioned again, whereupon "an awkward little silence fell", a significant counterpoint to the noisy atmosphere of the party preparations. Briefly, the quick, erratic motion of the first phase revives once more on a smaller scale when Mrs. Sheridan "suddenly" has another one of her "brilliant ideas," namely, to send Laura with a basket full of leftovers from the party down to the family of the dead man: she "jumped up," while Laura, if only after some hesitation, "ran for the basket" which is "heaped by her mother." But the upstrung, unnatural quality of this motion is gradually transformed into a more concentrated, almost magical sort of motion when Laura leaves the house. Twilight is setting in, the sharp contours of the party scene dissolve. And although the hectic pace of the party is, in a way, still going on inside of Laura, she is confronted with an altogether different, tranquil mood outside which increasingly takes hold of her as she descends into the valley, slowing down her motion the nearer she comes to the house of the dead man. When she sees the cottages from above, which "were in deep shade," she already senses the different dimension of time she is about to enter: "How quiet it seemed after the afternoon." Torn between her still vivid memory of the party and the uncertain expectation of her new, strange experience, she "stopped a minute." Her movement, quickening once again as she "bent her head and hurried on", becomes still more arrested when she arrives at her destination.

> This was the house. It must be. A dark knot of people stood outside. Beside the gate an old, old woman with a crutch sat in a chair, watching. She had her feet on a newspaper. The voices stopped as Laura drew near. The group parted. It was as though she was expected, as though they had known she was coming here.

In contrast to the vocabulary denoting quick, active motion, dominant in the first part of the story, we have here an accumulation of words designating passivity and immobility on the side of the group apparently expecting Laura: "was," "stood," "sat," "watching," "had," "stopped." And on Laura's side the vocabulary designates hesitation and compulsively slowed down motion: she "drew near," and, afterwards, she "walked up," "knocked," "followed," "found herself in . . . ," "was . . . standing," "walked," "came". The wife of the dead worker, to whom Laura is led as if with irresistible force by her sister, is sitting before a fire. There is a nightmarish slowness to the behaviour and communication of the two old women, doors seem to open by themselves, until Laura finally stands before the workman's deathbed, losing herself in the strangely beautiful sight of the dead man. All movement is arrested now. It is as if time itself, for a moment, has come to a standstill.

> There lay a young man, fast asleep—sleeping so soundly, so deeply, that he was far, far away from them both. Oh, so remote, so peaceful. He was dreaming. Never wake him up again. His head was sunk in the pillow, his eyes were closed; they were blind under the closed eyelids. He was given up to his dream. What did garden-parties and baskets and lace frocks matter to him? He was far from all those things. He was wonderful, beautiful. While they were laughing and while the band was playing, this marvel had come to the lane. Happy . . . happy . . . All is well, said that sleeping face. This is just as it should be. I am content.

Thus the story moves from the feverish, artificial activism of the garden party, from which death is apparently excluded, to the transcendent tranquillity of the death scene which, paradoxically becomes the medium for Laura's insight into life. The flux of time seems totally arrested in this crucial moment as Laura is confronted, in the shape of the dead man, with a deeper reality that encompasses both life and death. There is, significantly, no mention in the text that the dusk which sets in when Laura begins her walk changes to darkness during her visit; thus we get an impression in the final scene of continual twilight as some sort of timeless, half-real, half-mythical state of arrest which embodies the contradictory sides of human existence. And although afterwards, when Laura leaves the house, Laurie tells her that "Mother was getting anxious," confronting her anew with the temporal pressure, the tension and

restlessness of the party scene, she does not hurry back, but now goes at her own pace, still full of her new experience.

If the technique of temporal acceleration in the first part of the story reminds one of the time-lapse camera in film, the technique of temporal deceleration in the second part could be compared with the slow-motion camera; gradually adopted toward the end, it concentrates on the scene of Laura's encounter with the dead man.

The spatial structure of **"The Garden Party,"** parallel to the two phases of the temporal structure, is built around two poles, representing the two opposing worlds that are confronted and, in the figure of Laura, momentarily connected in the action of the story. Indeed, as has often been noted, the spatial opposition between the magnificent house of the Sheridans with its attributes of wealth and luxury and the shabby cottages of the workmen already carries part of the story's theme. The Sheridans' house and garden represent an upper-class world which is not, as Jens Iversen suggests, a perfect, paradisiacal scene "beyond the bounds of time and space" but an imperfect, ostentatious pseudo-paradise where nature is ordered and "methodized," being turned into a place where "flowers bloom on schedule in delineated beds." The garden's function is to be impressive, like the marquee for the party which is as conspicuous as to give the viewer a "bang-slap in the eye." In contrast, the sight of the "little mean dwellings" of the workmen represents to those looking down on them from the house "the greatest possible eyesore." The village appears as a counter-world, a taboo-zone which embodies everything that is suppressed, feared, despised in, and shut out from the world of the Sheridans.

> When the Sheridans were little they were forbidden to set foot there because of the revolting language and of what they might catch. But since they were grown up, Laura and Laurie on the prowls sometimes walked through. It was disgusting and sordid. They came out with a shudder. But still one must go everywhere; one must see everything. So through they went.

There are overtones of class arrogance and of sexual repression as well as of a general abhorrence of the more unpleasant, negative manifestations of life in this attitude. Since, however, it is from that very region that the Sheridans' wealth comes—from the labour of the villagers—this suppression appears as a suppression of the reality itself on which their superior life-style—and, thus, their magnificent house—is built.

The sharp spatial opposition of above and below, of an upper and a lower sphere which visually enforces the sense of social difference—the cottages "were in a lane to themselves at the very bottom of a steep rise that led up to the house"—again contains some hidden irony. For beyond the overt sociological connotation it also implies the opposition of superficial vs. deeper levels of consciousness and existence, thus undermining the self-appointed superiority of the upper sphere even as it seems to emphasise it: The two worlds are not, as the Sheridans' ideology has it, mutually exclusive, but dialectically interrelated. Although their separation is objectified in the "broad road" that "ran between"—while they are connected only by an inconspicuous lane—, there is, at the same time, a strong visual connection in that the one is always confronted with the sight of the other. For as the village is clearly seen from above, appearing, to the taste of the Sheridans, "far too near", the house, we can conclude, is likewise clearly seen from below. There is also an acoustic connection, the band playing at the party is as loud as to be heard down in the cottages, illustrating once more the showy predominance of the party scene and its indifference to the quite opposite, mournful scene in the village.

With the two poles of the story's setting, two different kinds of movements in space are correlated. If we try to follow these movements in the first part of the story we get, in correspondence to the hectic, accelerated pace on the temporal level, an impression of chaotic disconnectedness, of a simultaneity of different aims and directions. There is a constant moving about of the people as well as of the objects connected with the party (the marquee, the piano, the tables, etc.). The reader is taken in all possible directions at the same time: between the various rooms, between upstairs and downstairs, between the house and the garden. What is thereby created is no sense of spatial unity but of a labyrinth of different rooms, levels, and directions. But importantly, all of these movements are confined to the domain of the house and thus, although suggesting a multitude of spatial possibilities, are in fact limited to the narrow sphere which is defined by the social implications of the garden party.

Again, as with the deceleration and growing continuity in time, the story gains a clear aim and direction in space in the second phase. The chaotic variety of simultaneous, disconnected movements in the first phase is concentrated here into one single dominating movement, that of Laura going down from the house to the cottage of the dead man. Following this downward line, Laura transcends the narrow limitations of the house and symbolically transgresses the borderline between the two worlds. "The road gleamed white, and down below in the hollow the little cottages were in deep shade." The party world accompanies her into this 'underworld' in the shape of her conspicuously shining lace frock and extravagant black hat (which, though on a more superficial level, mirror in their colours once again the story's central opposition), keeping up the visual contrast between the two worlds as they are being connected. "How her frock shone! And the big hat with the velvet streamer—if only it was another hat!" But the force connecting them has become stronger now than the force that separates them. Although Laura wants to turn back, i.e. withdraw into separation, there appears to be no resistance possible any more to the manifestation of this connection, this existential synthesis. It all seems to happen by itself, without conscious effort or active will; it is as if space itself has become the active force of the movement, leading Laura into the timeless moment of her initiation. Instead of the aimless, self-centred *circulus-vitiosus*-pattern of the first phase, then, we have in the second phase a clear, irresistible line of spatial movement

and direction, symbolically linking the two worlds in Laura's 'transcendent' experience.

If we return from here to the initial question of the relationship between the social and the existential theme of **"The Garden Party"**—which is mainly the question of the relationship of the story's two parts—, analysis of the time-space-structure shows that the two aspects are not to be separated from each other but dialectically interrelated. The social theme of the first part is conveyed in such a way that the temporal-spatial form implies an ironic comment on the content, undermining the self-centred, pseudo-paradisiacal exclusiveness of the party scene, and implicitly relating it to the more general anthropological reality from which it tries to dissociate itself. Thus the first part structurally prepares the way and defines the conditions for the existential experience of the second part. At the same time the latter, transcending the temporal obsessions and spatial limitations of the party scene, and confronting us with precisely that dimension of authentic human reality which is shown to be excluded from the social world of the garden party, contains a fundamental criticism of the premises on which this world is based.

Kate Fullbrook   (essay date 1986)

SOURCE: "Late Fiction," in *Katherine Mansfield*, The Harvester Press, 1986, pp. 86-128.

[*In the following excerpt, Fullbrook offers a feminist account of Laura's struggle to establish identity.*]

As in **'Bliss'**, Katherine Mansfield sets up a situation [in **'The Garden Party'**] in which a woman is suddenly displaced from a frenetic social whirl that supposedly defines the totality of her being. The Sheridans in the story are a variant of the Burnells [in **'The Doll's House'**]; the setting is New Zealand and the characters prototypical colonials.

The Sheridan children, all young adults, are giving a party. The excited, happy narrative sees what they see in the terms that they see it—their fine house on a hill, bustling in preparation for the party, full of good things to eat, lovely things to wear, wonderful, expensive flowers to enjoy. The background is crammed with people to order about; the servants 'loved obeying'; friendly workmen swarm in the garden putting up a marquee; deliveries are made from shops; a band has been hired to put the finishing touches on the pleasures of the afternoon. The confident description is soaked in the values of middle-class authority as the genteel bourgeoisie prepares to play and enjoys every minute of the preparation. The pleasures at hand are both material and aesthetic, and even the perfect weather seems to endorse everything the Sheridans stand for. But the narration, insidiously, also undercuts its own exuberance with irony. Here, for example, is one of the daughters, Jose, practising for the display of her musical talents at the party:

Pom! Ta-ta-ta *Tee*-ta! The piano burst out so passionately that Jose's face changed. She clasped her hands. She looked mournfully and enigmatically at her mother and Laura as they came in.

This Life is *Wee*-ary,
A Tear—a Sigh.
A Love that *Chan*-ges,
 This Life is *Wee*-ary,
A Tear—a Sigh.
A Love that *Chan*-ges,
And then . . . Good-bye!

But at the word 'Good-bye,' and although the piano sounded more desperate than ever, her face broke into a brilliant, dreadfully unsympathetic smile.

'Aren't I in good voice, mummy?' she beamed.

Katherine Mansfield mocks Jose's 'female accomplishments' in the same ironic manner and for the same reasons as Jane Austen does in *Pride and Prejudice*. Just as Mary bored the company in 1813, displaying her vanity rather than her love for music, so Jose produces the same eminently false effect in **'The Garden Party'** of 1921. It is something of a shock to recognise the same device working so effectively in this twentieth-century story. Katherine Mansfield's attack on the inadequacy of the education of 'the daughters of educated men' is deepened by the story's account of the suffering taking place in the workmen's cottages just below the Sheridans' privileged hill. The false sentiment of Jose's song echoes the emotional disaster near at hand. The worker's world, which 'mummy' does not fully recognise (though the story emphasises the fact that she and her children live by and through their control of that world), is the scene of a casual tragedy. A workman has been killed in an accident; the news arrives during the preparations for the party. And the question of what is to be done in response to the news arises for only one character.

The character is Laura, a vaguely mutinous Sheridan daughter who, in the course of the story, acts as an intermediary between the two worlds—that of privilege and gaiety, and that of hardship, death and sorrow—and in the process is forced, if only momentarily, into the role of outsider.

We see Laura first in that most typical of middle-class occupations—romantic identification with an idealised working class. Laura, 'who loved having to arrange things', is assigned to direct the workmen who erect the marquee. Actually she directs nothing; the workmen know their job and choose the best site for the marquee in spite of her alternative suggestions. Laura's class loyalties vie with her sense of adventure; as she deals with the men their ease finally overcomes her slightly wounded dignity when they do not treat her with the deference afforded to a middle-class matron. Looking over the plan the foreman has hastily drawn, Laura dips her toe into rebellion:

Oh, how extraordinarily nice workmen were, she thought. Why couldn't she have workmen for friends

rather than the silly boys she danced with and who came to Sunday night supper . . . It's all the fault, she decided . . . of these absurd class distinctions. Well, for her part, she didn't feel them. Not a bit, not an atom . . . Just to prove how happy she was, just to show the tall fellow how at home she felt, and how she despised stupid conventions, Laura took a big bite out of her bread-and-butter as she stared at the little drawing. She felt just like a work-girl.

This is, of course, transparent affectation, but it is also a potentially significant masquerade, small as the gesture of taking a bite of bread-and-butter might be. What the significance might be is suggested when the news of the death reaches the Sheridans. Laura, still influenced by her thoughts about the workmen, wants to stop the party, but her mother simply cuts her off:

'You are being very absurd, Laura,' she said coldly. 'People like that don't expect sacrifices from us. And it's not very sympathetic to spoil everyone's enjoyment as you're doing now.'

'I don't understand,' said Laura, and she walked quickly out of the room into her own bedroom.

Several truths of unequal significance operate in this passage. Death *cannot* be conquered by stopping a party. Pleasure *is* rare enough to deserve protection. The workers do *not* have any expectations. And Laura really does have no idea what she is doing. (That her mother damns herself and her class goes without saying, but at the same time *any* life that paused with every death would soon be unliveable).

Laura's knowledge of the workmen is almost nonexistent. Their lane was forbidden territory in her childhood and since she has 'grown up' she has only walked through it once with her brother (and *alter ego*), Laurie. On the walk she sees the lane as 'disgusting and sordid. They came out with a shudder. But still one must go everywhere; one must see everything.' Laura in no way connects herself with the lane. But this distanced social voyeurism turns into something very immediate with the news of the death, and just for a moment, at the centre of the story, Laura steps outside her class and circumstances into a confrontation with the equality of all humanity in the face of mortality. What Laura 'sees' at this point is far more important than what she has 'seen' during her educational tour of a working-class habitat. For a moment, the social vocabulary of her tribe fills Laura with disgust.

But only for a moment. What draws Laura back from the isolation of her response to death is another confrontation, this time with her own face framed by a lovely hat that itself is the image of the pleasures of life that only youth and privilege provide. What she sees in a mirror, walking away from her mother, is her identity:

the first thing she saw was this charming girl in the mirror, in her black hat trimmed with gold daisies and a long black velvet ribbon. Never had she imagined she could look like that. Is mother right? she thought. And now she hoped that her mother was right.

It is an extraordinary moment of conscience callousing over, with the lovely black hat repeating the colour of death. Katherine Mansfield's characteristic attention to detail allows her to conflate conscience and consciousness, beauty and vanity, bodily and mental satisfaction as Laura's politics turn on a glimpse of herself in the mirror. Giving up her chance for a public display of her beauty would be sacrificial; Laura slips easily back into the frivolity of the garden-party. On the next page she is afraid of being 'teased' about even thinking of making her egalitarian gesture.

Since Laura's class complacency is safe and the party is over, Mrs Sheridan gives her daughter a lesson in 'proper' charity. She sends her to the dead man's cottage with scraps from the party. In her stunning hat, her mind filled with the delights of the party, Laura self-consciously walks into the cottage with her basket and into the ceremonies of death. The two social rituals—the celebrations of the rich family, and the solemnity of death for the poor one—stress the discontinuity of experience. The man's wife, huddled like some primitive wounded thing by the fire, looks up at Laura, 'Her face, puffed up, red, with swollen eyes and swollen lips, looked terrible'. Laura, ashamed and embarrassed, blunders into the room with the dead man, and as the corpse is exhibited to her with tender, ritualistic pride, her response remains in the aesthetic mode of the party: 'he was wonderful, beautiful', a 'marvel', much better, in fact, in terms of beauty than her hat for which she now blurts out an excuse. The reader must recall the earlier significance of the hat and all that it has meant for Laura's conscience to understand the meaning of that apology. The story ends with Laura's confusion as she tries to express her feelings to Laurie and the meaning she has drawn from this encounter with death.

'The Garden-Party' is radically inconclusive. It is especially interesting in its portrayal of simultaneous but opposing goods, and in its treatment of the confusion of motivations and principles in life as opposed to the clarity of abstract ideas. Katherine Mansfield stressed this aspect of the story in a letter to William Gerhardi:

> And yes, that is what I tried to convey in **'The Garden Party.'** The diversity of life and how we try to fit in everything, Death included. That is bewildering for a person of Laura's age. She feels things ought to happen differently. First one and then another. But life isn't like that. We haven't the ordering of it.

Katherine Mansfield's writing does, however, impose an order. It rejects the one that Laura accepts when she allows her aesthetic and class assumptions to dominate her at the moment when another kind of response was available to her. Laura only tastes the solitude that is the main diet of the women in many other stories, but the easiness with which a character can be thrust from full membership of a community to absolute exile in an instant, and the

way in which such exile depends upon individual consciousness, underscores Katherine Mansfield's insistence on the fragility of identity.

Barbara Currier Bell (essay date 1988)

SOURCE: "Non-Identical Twins: Nature in 'The Garden Party' and 'The Grave,'" in *The Comparatist,* Vol. XII, May, 1988, pp. 58-66.

[*In the following essay, Bell finds significant differences between the views of nature in "The Garden Party" and Katherine Anne Porter's story "The Grave."*]

From certain points of view **"The Garden Party"** and "The Grave" are so alike as to be all too easily confused. Even their authors can be mistaken for each other. Katherine Mansfield and Katherine Anne Porter, besides having similar names, led circumstantially similar lives. Their careers overlapped in time, although Mansfield died young; they shared relatively privileged backgrounds; they came from outlands to the centers of culture after breaking with their families; they had unstable relationships with men; they traveled widely; they gave steady outputs of fiction but received unsteady inputs of acclaim. Mansfield was British, Porter, American; yet they can frequently be found mentioned together, as if they were literary sisters or cousins. Porter undoubtedly furthered that opinion by her admiration for Mansfield's talent. Still, I am not aware that a detailed comparison has been made between any two stories by these writers, and have found none between two stories that are among their works most often discussed as individuals: **"The Garden Party"** and "The Grave." Indeed, no work by either author has been accorded much attention along the particular thematic lines that **"The Garden Party"** and "The Grave" seem to me to invite so especially.

Briefly summarized, **"The Garden Party"** is about the experiences of a young girl, Laura, on the day her family is giving a garden party. During the preparations, she learns that an accident has just happened in which a young man who lived in a lane for poor working people at the bottom of the hill from her "big house" has been killed. She wants to stop the party out of sympathy, but her mother and sister persuade her that she's "being absurd." The party itself takes up only a few lines of the story. The climax comes after the party, when Laura's mother suggests she take a basket of leftovers and some flowers down the hill to the dead man's family. Laura does so, is invited into the cottage to view the body, feels at first acutely uncomfortable in the poor surroundings, then strangely comforted by the peaceful look on the dead man's face, and leaves crying. At the end, she tries to explain to her brother that she has learned something important about life, but cannot find the words.

"The Grave" is a "framed" story, actually a memory about her childhood as experienced vividly by an adult woman,

Miranda, during a trip to a marketplace in a strange city. She remembers how she and her brother Paul went one day to play in some abandoned graves at their family cemetery and found there an engraved wedding ring and a coffin ornament, a silver dove, which they kept as treasures. On the way home, Paul shot a rabbit, and, skinning the carcass, the children discovered it was pregnant. Both were moved and troubled by the sight of the unborn rabbits, and an understanding about life began to grow in Miranda, but Paul swore her to secrecy, and she did not reach a full emotional integration of the day's events until her memory, twenty years later.

Both of these stories appeared at about the same time: **"The Garden Party"** in 1922 and "The Grave" in 1935. Both are less than 5000 words and seem brilliantly simple, condensed. Both have young female protagonists of about the same ages and the same sensitivies, (in both cases, an autobiographical character), and in both stories, this main character is paired with an older brother who plays a supportive role. Both draw on the Christian myth of the Fall. The main plot event matches in the stories: it is the experience of a death, a death that is relatively anonymous and that happens in otherwise undisturbing, one might say "innocent," circumstances. Correspondingly, the themes match. Both stories express a recognition of "the meaning of life"; both of the protagonists grow up.

Despite their extensive similarities, however, the stories leave the reader with strikingly different feelings and contain different messages about the meaning of life. The key to these differences lies in the different senses of nature the two stories convey—with nature to be understood most concretely as the natural environment; more generally as the natural world, or the opposite of human society; and most abstractly as the forces beyond human control that underlie all of organic life.

"And after all the weather was ideal." The first sentence of **"The Garden Party"** establishes a placid natural environment which, the reader soon comes to see, is also domesticated. The lawns are mowed, the flowers well-tended. It almost seems too perfect, this setting, as if the natural world were unnatural, and indeed the imagery seems at the least anthropomorphic: at the most sacramental. The rosebushes are said "to [bow] down as though they had been visited by archangels"; the karaka trees are imagined proudly to "lift their leaves and fruits to the sun in a kind of splendour"; and the most dominant forms of nature in the story are canna-lilies, associated more with greenhouses and altars than with the great outdoors.

While the first pages of **"The Garden Party"** are occupied with the natural setting, they are the only ones. Just as workmen bring a marquee to hide the karaka trees, human beings, along with their shelter, dress and food, dominate the scene as the story proceeds. Laura at one point sees a workman smelling a sprig of lavender and respects him for that, but for the most part the natural surroundings are of limited importance.

Contrasting with the controlled and limited appearance of the natural environment in **"The Garden Party"** is that in "The Grave." The heat is burning on the day that Miranda and Paul go out to play, and the garden where the reader sees the two—also the family cemetery—is wild. It is "neglected," its rose bushes "tangled," its grass "uncropped." The children are unkempt themselves, and plainly more used to living outdoors than in. They are compared with animals. Then, the death on which the story centers is that of an animal. The skinning and gutting of the rabbit are given in precise detail. At other points in the story, too, material aspects of nature become important and are realistically described. Overall, the natural surroundings dominate setting and plot more consistently in "The Grave" than in **"The Garden Party"**; they are less stylized; and they are more extreme.

Nature in the sense of the natural world as opposed to human society is also presented differently by the two stories. Garden parties are social events. In the Mansfield story, society predominates over nature. Its description of social relationships starts with those in the large, unified, upperclass family, moves outwards to enclose the family's servants, next surrounds the family's guests, and finally extends to the working-class people living at the bottom of the hill. All of these groups are well-rooted in their place and in society. This is to say not that society is harmonious, but only that the social world is where the action is. Thematically, social class becomes an important issue, and the importance of society is represented by, among other methods, frequent and sensitive dialogue. At the story's end, the feeling of social cohesion is underlined by the closeness between brother and sister, whose names are analogues.

In "The Grave," the natural world dominates. Its title suggests as much, for death is one of the main forces of nature. The story scarcely even shows society. The family is the only social unit that figures importantly, but it is isolated. For instance, the extended family is rootless, as the opening paragraph establishes.

> The grandfather, dead for more than thirty years, had been twice disturbed in his long repose by the constancy and possessiveness of his widow. She removed his bones first to Louisiana and then to Texas as if she had set out to find her own burial place, knowing well she would never return to the places she had left. In Texas she set up a small cemetery in a corner of her first farm, and as the family connection grew, and oddments of relations came over from Kentucky to settle, it contained at last about twenty graves. After the grandmother's death, part of her land was to be sold for the benefit of certain of her children, and the cemetery happened to lie in the part set aside for sale. It was necessary to take up the bodies and bury them again in the family plot in the big new public cemetery, where the grandmother had been buried.

Also, the nuclear family in the story is fragmented because it is motherless and set apart from the local community: the children's father is relatively poor and seems scandalous to his neighbors and gossipy crones. At the end of the story the family even has disappeared, for Miranda is all alone in a strange city. With one or two exceptions, no social issues are brought up by the story, and although Miranda is said to have a "powerful social sense," it gets nowhere near the exercise that Laura's does. The thematic absence of society in "The Grave" is mirrored formally by the story's having very little dialogue. After all, the operative characters number only two. The relatively empty social stage of "The Grave" forces the reader to become more aware of the natural world by contrast.

Nature in the sense of forces underlying life appears severally in both stories, and may be analyzed to show the deepest meanings, the deepest differences. For a start, let us take a relatively simple example of nature in this sense, namely sex. **"The Garden Party"** does not emphasize the raw power of sex. The paragraphs above illustrating how Mansfield depicts nature perhaps have already said as much. Part of Laura's experience in the story is her growing awareness of her sexuality, but that takes polite forms. For instance, she, like all the males and females in the story, follows gender stereotypes important to society. Males earn money, whether commuting to the city, carrying heavy loads, or driving carts, while females uphold social order, whether giving garden parties, cooking, or presiding at wakes. One way of interpreting Laura's day is to say it involves her growing ability to recognize and accept the responsibilities of the female role. For another instance, the main representative of Laura's emergent sexuality is her new hat: looking at it, the other characters and Laura herself remark on how pretty its wearer has become, and the message gets across without drawing attention downward to the lower areas of the body that are really at stake. If so in **"The Garden Party,"** sex is secondary and social.

In "The Grave," on the other hand, sex is primary and natural. The wedding ring is the first hint. Of course, weddings in general can be as social as garden parties or hats, but the wedding ring Miranda and Paul find is connected directly to nature. On one level, Miranda's reactions to the ring are rather characteristic of Laura—"she wanted to go back to the farmhouse, take a good cold bath, dust herself with plenty [of her sister's] violet talcum powder, . . . put on the thinnest, most becoming dress she owned, with a big sash, and sit in a wicker chair under the trees": these are inspired by her attention to the decorativeness of the ring and to its being made of gold. At a deeper level, the one tapped by the flashback, however, the ring establishes an entirely different context for Miranda's sexuality than Laura's hat does for hers. It comes out of a wild, natural setting and is engraved with "intricate flowers and leaves." Flowers and leaves are age-old signs of fertility; they connote the physical coupling decreed by nature more than the legal, moral or spiritual vows decreed by society.

Still, the most important and primitive emphasis on sex comes through Miranda and Paul's discovery of the unborn rabbits, which are symbols of fertility. Reproduction is here seen as carnally as possible, and its strong impact

is conveyed not only in Miranda's agitation on the spot, but in the overall structure of the story, which parallels the Freudian pattern of repression and recall, a process wholly associated with primitive sexual material. Miranda's thoughts at the moment she sees the babies, moreover, are in the context of a situation where the social sex roles so prominent for Laura have been explicitly suspended, since Miranda dresses and acts like a boy. The sugar-plums of sash and social stereotype disappear. It is hard, almost savage, for Miranda to see that she is, will be like the pregnant rabbit. That sex belongs more to the world of nature than to society is made explicit in the last scene, where the candy rabbits triggering Miranda's memory are connected with "raw flesh and wilting flowers."

The subject of sex opens into the further meanings of nature in these two stories and a final understanding of what each seems to express as "the meaning of life." Both are the same in showing that the meaning of life is bound up with the meaning of death: the point is obvious, but great literature often brings the obvious home, and the stories show with force and poignancy that these two most basic natural conditions are connected inseparably. **"The Garden Party"** and "The Grave" differ, however, in their versions of what exactly the connection is.

"The Garden Party" shows the connection to be paradoxical: it is a juxtaposition that is a juncture. When Laura goes down the hill she sees death quietly, modestly, even beautifully co-existing with life and at the same time interrupting life, just as the lower-class characters in the story quietly, modestly, even peacefully co-exist with the gentry on the hill, at the same time challenging their privilege. The "justice" of death in life or of upper-class dominance over the poor is not particularly at issue. Stressed instead is the surprising fact of the situation. One well-known expression of the puzzle appears in a letter Katherine Mansfield wrote to a friend:

> . . . that is what I tried to convey in **"The Garden Party"**. The diversity of life and how we try to fit-in everything. Death included. That is bewildering for a person of Laura's age. She feels things ought to happen differently. First one and then another. But life isn't like that. We haven't the ordering of it. Laura says, 'But all these things must not happen at once.' And Life answers, 'Why not? How are they divided from each other?' And they do all happen, it is inevitable. And it seems to me there is beauty in that inevitability.

Life/Death. The life-death connection in **"The Garden Party"** has a static and symmetrical yet vulnerable quality much like that between marriage partners or the opposite poles of a magnetic field. Such is the feeling of unstable pairedness at the root of nature for which **"The Garden Party"** finds words, even though Laura does not.

"The Grave" presents a view of life and death that may at first appear to be like the one in **"The Garden Party,"** but is not. In "The Grave," the connection between life and death is dynamic. Instead of life and death being ever-present with each other, one *becomes* the other: the two are separate phases of the same process. Life *is* death: nature is not paradoxical but unified.

Consider what Laura and Miranda learn from what they see. Laura learns the necessity of accepting death in life, accepts its paradoxical sense. The nonparadoxical parts of her life, functions within society, seem all the more significant by comparison. Miranda learns the necessity of playing her part in the life-death cycle and, for her, natural functions become all the more significant. There is a feeling of ceremony in **"The Garden Party,"** a feeling of biology in "The Grave."

Certainly, the tone of "The Grave" reflects more suffering. An interesting confirmation about the way the two stories treat nature may be found in the extent to which each employs Christian symbolism. Both rely on the Garden of Eden parallel to help convey their female characters' movement from innocence to knowledge. **"The Garden Party"** establishes this metaphor in its title and its early sacramental imagery, already quoted, not to mention its plot, while "The Grave" establishes it less directly in the title but similarly through initial descriptions of the scene and also its plot. "The Grave," however, carries the symbolism much farther. The theme of sexuality, for instance, follows the Christian track in "The Grave" but not in **"The Garden Party."** Also, the silver dove Miranda and Paul find is a Christian symbol and assumes a great deal of importance at the end. Detailed interpretations of Christian meaning in "The Grave" have already appeared, however, and need not be repeated here. The relevance to this essay of Porter's greater attention to the Christian message is simply that Christianity is consistent with the view of nature presented in "The Grave" but inconsistent with that presented in **"The Garden Party."** The Christian message is nothing if not dynamic: death redeems life; corruption and sin are the tragic necessities of life's general immortality. The Christian message is violent, too, like the wasteful lust and carnage of "The Grave," like the wasteful lust and carnage of nature. By contrast, **"The Garden Party,"** with its climax in the peaceful expression of the young man lying dead, counters nature's power, seeming to speak for a religion of contemplation.

So striking and revealing are the differences between **"The Garden Party"** and "The Grave" in terms of their views of nature that it is tempting to conclude this essay along the lines of the standard comparative theory on the subject. Briefly, the conventional wisdom about differences in American and British literature regarding nature starts out observing that American writers spend a great deal of time describing or thinking about nature, that they tend to display or consider it in extreme forms, and that they deem it more important than society. Then, the typical American identity is seen as formed against a natural backdrop, and a typical story line for American literature is said to be the retreat to nature for purification or enlightenment. (Sometimes this retreat is more of an assault, as D. H. Lawrence argued in *Studies in Classic American Literature*.) These ideas have been the subjects of books and articles too numerous and familiar to list here, but two comments out of a multitude may be regarded as summary.

. . . the American, or at least the American artist, cherishes in his innermost being the impulse to reject completely the gospel of civilization, in order to guard with resolution the savagery of his heart. [Perry Miller, "Nature and the National Ego," in *Errand into the Wilderness,* 1956]

The individual in America has usually taken his start outside society; and the action to be imitated may just as well be his strenuous efforts to *stay* outside as his tactics for getting inside; and if he does get inside, it makes a difference whether he is walking into a trap or discovering: the setting in which to realize his own freedom. [R. W. B. Lewis, *The American Adam,* 1955]

The reason theory gives for these features of American literature is the literal or figurative lay of the land in America. The British sense of nature, by inference, is regarded roughly as the opposite of the American.

Certainly, what has been shown here about **"The Garden Party"** and "The Grave" is that they support all the comparative theory's particulars. They are its ideal examples— so ideal that they could be taught as a mini-introduction to nature in British and American literature. That conclusion alone, however, could seem a tautology. More interesting than the two stories' agreement with the theory is the captivating fact that their relevance to the theory hardly comes clear at all until they are paired. A "twin study" in literary criticism, then, may be as revealing as it has proved to be in psychology.

Rhoda B. Nathan (essay date 1988)

SOURCE: "The New Zealand Cycle: A Bildungsroman," in *Katherine Mansfield,* Continuum, 1988, pp. 13-50.

[*In the following excerpt, Nathan views "The Garden Party" as a tale of moral and artistic maturation.*]

[In **"The Garden Party"**], as in **"The Doll's House,"** the community is mixed, and the grand houses are uncomfortably adjacent to the hovels of washerwomen, carters, tenant farmers, and the other assorted rural poor who are a fixture of the countryside. In **"The Garden Party"** the family is somewhat more insulated from the harsh facts of poverty because the poor live a good distance below the large house on the hill. If their children attend the same public school as the children of the affluent families, the Sheridans would not know, because unlike the Burnells [of **"The Doll's House"**], who were obliged to attend the same school as the dreadfully common little Kelveys, they were beyond grade-school age. The girls are nearly grown up, and the single son is already apprenticed into his father's business.

"The Garden Party" could be called **"The Doll's House,"** part 2. It is very much an enchanted kingdom, and, until the climax of the story, its inhabitants are entirely engaged in play, or in this case, playacting. Their artifice is so natural to their station, their expectations, and customs, that the reader is gulled into empathy by the very charm of their lives. It is not until ugliness intrudes and provokes some uncharming reactions that one is aware of just how much falseness is embedded in their nature.

The story begins on a charmed note: "And after all the weather was ideal." One of Mansfield's great narrative gifts is her ability to set a tone, plunge the reader into the heart of the event, and at the same time imply that the action has been building for a great while. After the heady title, **"The Garden Party,"** with its implications of ethereal and lighthearted entertainment, Mansfield has the wit to begin her tale with the conjunction "and." All the anxiety and prayer preliminary to the lawn party are implicit in that "And after all," which phrase miraculously dissipates them. "Ideal" is the perfect description for the jumbled impressions in the next pages. Blue skies, gold haze, red roses, deep velvet lawns, and the "broad gleaming leaves" of the karaka trees with their "clusters of yellow fruit" dominate this bourgeois Eden. A marquee raised for the band is taken for granted; pots of pink canna lilies are banked by the florist in careless profusion outside the porch doors, although the house is blessed with a lily lawn of its own; cream puffs and fancy sandwiches appear as if by magic from the town caterer and the capable hands of the resident cook. The servants are praised, the cook for her dependable calm, and "good little Hans" for his manly efforts to move the grand piano.

These are charming people. They are not whipped into a vulgar frenzy of delight by the bounty that pours forth from their cornucopia. They are used to it. Mrs. Sheridan justifies her extravagance of the purchased lilies by declaring to her only sensitive daughter: "For once in my life I thought I would have enough lilies," while still another flat is brought in. So relaxed is she in her idleness that she is charming even when she forgets the only task she is required to complete—to write the names of the sandwiches on their decorative little flags. Her two eldest daughters are equally unruffled. Jose, "the butterfly," exotic in a Japanese kimono that unfits her to do anything by way of preparation for the party, moves placidly to the piano to rehearse a "tragic" ballad, just in case she should be called upon to perform. When she finishes her rendition, a piece with the lugubrious title "This World Is Weary," her smooth face breaks into a "brilliant, dreadfully unsympathetic smile." Knowing Mansfield's propensity for irony, one may be sure that this insignificant episode will have reverberations later on. No gesture in this economical narrative is irrelevant to its outcome.

The adolescent Laura Sheridan, a grown-up Kezia, and the "artistic" one in the family, is as guilty of playacting as her philistine mother and sisters at the outset. Having no experience of life apart from the shelter of her community, she mimics those role models familiar to her. When inviting her friend Kitty to lunch, she coos in her socially adept mother's voice. When sent out to supervise the laborers who have come to put up the marquee, she takes a big bite of her bread and butter just like a real "working girl." More sensitive than the others, she falls naturally

into the rhythms of those she wishes to please. Romanticizing the workmen, she is enchanted by their lingo, the way they call each other "matey" so democratically. She finds herself wishing she could have them for friends instead of the "silly" boys at dancing school. But her high-mindedness is still untested; she could go either way.

Laura is at a particularly impressionable and formative stage of adolescence. Even in her sentimentalizing of the working class she betrays the heightened sensitivity that will soon mark her as an outsider in her own family. She finds herself apologizing for the luxury and excess of the party to a particularly pale and worn laborer; it will only be a very small band, she assures him, suddenly uneasy. Her guilt is in marked contrast to her friend's cavalier allusion to the musicians as "frogs" in their little green coats. She is moved by the sight of a workman inhaling a sprig of lavender from the vast lawn, and indulges in a reverie of a better world in which there are no "absurd" class distinctions. She has more trouble giving orders than her imperious sisters. Although she is still pretending at this stage of the story, there is a hint of her special quality at the very beginning. "You're the artistic one," her sister tells her, and Laura's reactions to her immediate environment document her shrewd observation. She "notices" things: the quality of the very air on the morning of the party; the "tiny spots of sun" playing on the household ornaments; the dark blue of the workman's eyes that contrast so with his pallor. It is Laura's gift of noticing that will change her life in just a few hours.

An accident, casually reported and overheard, alters the focus of the story and leads to a rite of initiation for the immature Laura. The crisis takes place offstage, as in Greek tragedy. An unfortunate event that just might mar the cloudless day is circulated through the servants' quarters. A young carter who lives in a hovel down the lane has been killed in a collision. The news is conveyed through the man who has brought the cream puffs from the caterer— a fitting irony carried by the perfect symbol of frivolity— and is disregarded by all the Sheridans save Laura, who insists the party be canceled in respect for the dead man. Argumentative and seemingly intractable, she is finally seduced by her clever mother with a bribe of a large straw hat to wear to the party. "I have never seen you look such a picture," her manipulative mother assures her. Laura, catching a glimpse of her enchanting reflection, showing her pretty face haloed in the decorative hat, is deflected from her austere purpose. Her conscience slumbers for the rest of the glorious golden afternoon.

Laura's party hat is the leitmotif for the remainder of the narrative. It is the vehicle for her false values, and it becomes the vehicle for her true self, even for her salvation. Mansfield is careful to describe the hat in all its seductive detail. It is large and round and ornamented with a wreath of artificial gold daisies, finished off with a streamer of black velvet ribbon. It is notable for its extravagance, reminding us that her sister had scolded her for her "extravagance" in insisting that the party be canceled. Laura's mother is cast as the serpent in the garden, tempting the young Eve into forgetting her higher purpose. The artificial gold daisies are appropriate to the artificial values Mrs. Sheridan is holding out to her corruptible daughter. It is noteworthy that Mansfield has prepared us for the false daisies—and the false values—at the beginning, when she describes the velvet lawn denuded of its real daisy plants, which have been dug up to make room for party paraphernalia. Those humble real flowers have been discarded for the false daisies on the seductive hat.

When the long perfect day has "ripened" and drawn to a close, Laura is dispatched by her inventive mother with a basket of party goodies for the bereaved widow and orphans. Congratulating herself on her "brilliant" idea, Mrs. Sheridan is barely restrained from sending an armload of lilies as well on the grounds that "people like that are so impressed with arum lilies." Laura, laden with party scraps, again feels "different" from the others. A sense of vulgarity haunts her, but, pliant as ever, she does as she is bidden. She is desperately self-conscious in her gleaming dress and huge festive headgear.

In the monograph *The Art of Katherine Mansfield,* Mary Rohrberger concludes that Laura has not learned much from her descent into the depths. She claims that Laura has "idealized death" as she has "romanticized" everything else in her short life. That she is still wearing the hat when she returns from her unhappy mission is, in Rohrberger's judgment, indisputable evidence that she is going back to her privileged world. If that were all, then her analysis would be unassailable. But she neglects the most significant aspect of Laura's education. The hat, which had been a symbol of vanity and shallowness at the beginning, has now become an emblem of penance. Laura must wear it as she would a hair shirt. Gazing at the dead young man dreaming his eternal dream, Laura sobs, "Forgive my hat." She then wears it home as she has done all afternoon, bringing the leitmotif to its proper thematic conclusion. In a moral sense, the hat is the vehicle that has carried Laura from heedless girlhood to maturity, from her vague "artistic" sensibility that found its only outlet in choosing the most aesthetic spot for the party tent, to the true humanity that must underlie true art. Her remorse about her festive headgear is a burst of comprehension and agonized repentance for her sin of triviality. When the old crone in the hovel leads the hatted Laura to the unmarred corpse, assuring her that "'e looks a picture," she is unconsciously imitating the callous Mrs. Sheridan, who only a few hours earlier had assured Laura that *she* looked a "picture" in her party hat.

The hat has done its work. It is a changed Laura who attempts to define the meaning of life to her brother Laurie, who shares her name and her nature. No longer smug about life's verities and certitudes, Laura has given up playacting. She asks a tentative and inchoate question: "Isn't life . . . ? Isn't life . . . ?" Her brother, a male replica of her questing, merely repeats the question, emphasizing the "isn't" and thus rendering the question an unspoken affirmation. Laura requires no further confirmation of her lesson. She has been initiated into the mystery of life through exposure to death. The little girl who a few

minutes earlier had been agonizing about the inappropriateness of leftover cream puffs to a mournful occasion has experienced an epiphany and has begun to understand the complex life outside her high protective gates.

This narrative leaves no loose ends. It turns out that life is indeed "weary," although people like Jose, the "butterfly," will go on singing about it and never comprehend its meaning. Laura has learned it, at second hand at least, from the puffy lips and swollen eyes of the young widow and the specter of the five orphaned tots. She has begun to realize that there are other "pictures" besides her young face framed in an enormous party hat. She has learned also that, in the words of the old woman in the dark shadow of the dead man's dwelling, there's nothing to be afraid of, and her morbidity and anguish may now be converted into creativity. The very inconclusiveness of her beloved brother's answer to her rhetorical question about life provides an open end for experiment and conclusion.

J. F. Kobler (essay date 1990)

SOURCE: "Stories of Young Girls," in *Katherine Mansfield: A Study of the Short Fiction,* Twayne Publishers, 1990, pp. 76-86.

[*In the following excerpt, Kobler emphasizes the limitations of Laura's moment of insight in "The Garden Party."*]

As forced thoughts of her own inevitable death momentarily intrude on Leila's happiness in **"Her First Ball,"** so, too, does a real death slightly upset the Sheridan family's garden party and result in the exposure of Laura Sheridan to death in such a highly dramatic and personal way that most readers leave **"The Garden Party"** believing that young Laura has been permanently affected and will not so easily be able to return to the dance of life. Her closing assertion or question, "Isn't life—" (which her brother, Laurie, understands), can be seen to resemble Hopkins's equally tantalizing words about how the young girl of his poem can come, in some mysterious way, to know that humans are born for death: "Nor mouth had, no nor mind, expressed / What heart heard of, ghost guessed".

Laura's mind cannot create the words for her to say aloud what truths about life this experience has brought to her, but Mansfield suggests that some spiritual connection between brother and sister does exist. As a matter of fact, some spiritual connection exists between Mansfield and many of her readers: We call it **"The Garden Party,"** a story whose message about human life and death is perfectly clear until we try to capture all that it says in a sentence or even a whole bundle of sentences. Although we readers may feel good that Laura is able to "suffer" such an emotional encounter, just as we may feel good that we are able aesthetically to enjoy her suffering, we should not believe that Mansfield is saying Laura has learned some lifelong and life-changing lesson, anymore than we can possibly believe that we have accomplished anything major for ourselves in "feeling" the story. If Laura and we readers have experienced something resembling a Joycean epiphany, that fact alone is good, but we must be aware of the impending antiepiphany or simply the mundane quotidian that will inevitably follow. Neither Joyce nor Mansfield in the short stories, however, does more than create the epiphanies. Only in his novels does Joyce have the scope to reveal the ordinary life that a Laura Sheridan, Gabriel Conroy, or John Hammond faces up to the next day. Mansfield, unfortunately, was not able to complete a novel.

"The Garden-Party" is a superior story to "Her First Ball," at least in part, because the development of Laura's inherent ability to be affected by the experience begins early in the story. Admittedly, Leila's experience with the fat man at the ball in no way emotionally resembles Laura's encounter with the death of the carter; however, if we can project Leila's character into "The Garden Party," we can see, I believe, that she would not have been capable of going down the hill to the other house. Leila's ability to shrug off the fat man's words is more like Jose Sheridan's ability to say to Laura "You won't bring a drunken workman back to life by being sentimental" than it is like Laura's feeling that the garden party cannot go on. My contention is that the slightness of "Her First Ball" rests not just on the activity involved but also on the character taking part in it. Even if Mansfield had inserted a death into the ball, she could not have achieved what she attains in "The Garden Party" without major changes in Leila's character, to make her more nearly resemble Laura. Put another way, I am arguing that character, which reacts to and ultimately gives shape to the setting and meaning to the plot, is of greater significance than those other two factors, without which, of course, there may be no story. Leila and Laura define themselves through their actions, but what in them causes diverse actions remains the great mystery.

Laura Sheridan is apparently born with the same kind of inherent moral seismograph that Huckleberry Finn possesses. Whatever it is that causes Huck to help the slave Jim escape to freedom, thereby going against all the teachings of his religious, social, and political world, also causes Laura to want to stop the garden party upon news of the nearby death. Laura's similarity to Huck and her differences from her mother and sisters are developed from the beginning of the story, as Laura has "natural" reactions that go contrary to what her social and family environment says is right and proper. Laura's first reaction in the story is an environmentally induced guilty feeling that she should not appear before the workmen eating bread and butter, but she sets out to deal with them with the food naturally in her hand. Her first words to the workmen are "Good morning," in which she copies "her mother's voice. But that sounded so fearfully affected that she was ashamed." Again, Laura's effort to use the "proper" voice in talking to workmen goes against something that she knows internally is right. One workman is not affected but has such an "easy" and "friendly" smile for Laura that she recovers her natural self. She knows from her social lessons that she "must be businesslike." When one of the

workmen gives advice on where to erect a marquee, saying it should be put "somewhere where it'll give you a bang slap in the eye, if you follow me," Laura wonders because of her "upbringing" "whether it was quite respectful of a workman to talk to her of bangs slap in the eye. But she did quite follow him."

Obviously, Laura has an easy, natural relationship with these men and is terribly uncomfortable trying to sustain the proper, inculcated one. This quality inherent in Laura's very being is established within the first two pages of the story and prepares the reader to accept as "right" her romantic and entirely impractical need (in her family's eyes) to do something about the dead man.

Mansfield, however, is as careful to keep Laura a believable human being, a mixture of the good and bad, as Mark Twain is to depict Huck, through Huck's own words, as a "real" fourteen-year-old. Huck can tell lies, when necessary, and rationalize his and Jim's need to steal food, and so Laura is pictured as going too far with her emotions in thinking that "she would get on much better" with a workman who takes a few seconds out to appreciate "the smell of lavender" than she does with the "silly boys" at the dances. Mansfield balances the account on Laura by causing her childishly "to take a big bite of her bread-and-butter" right in front of the workmen to demonstrate how she "despised stupid conventions." When Laura gives her brother "a small, quick squeeze" and gasps, "Oh, I do love parties, don't you?" she further demonstrates that she is still very young and very much a part of her society, whatever the nature of her built-in, sensitive moral seismograph.

Mansfield's point in developing, so successfully, a complex character in Laura is to show the contrast between the dogmatic self-righteousness and moral insularity of the comfortable rich and the open-minded girl on whom the facts of lives and deaths may still have some effect. As the author gives Laura a verisimilitude and a balance between being naive and understanding, so too, does she avoid piling sentimental notions on the heads of the poor carter's family down the hill. Their miserable physical existence does stand in stark contrast to the garden party of the Sheridans', but their confusion about life and death resembles Laura's. The widow of the dead man is described as not knowing why a strange girl is "standing in the kitchen with a basket," as wondering, "What was it all about?" But if Mansfield cannot in honesty credit the poor with knowing what life is all about and will not make Laura utter a platitude about it after her experience, she does develop in Mrs. Sheridan a character who has all the wrong answers about it: "People of that class are so impressed by arum lilies."

In this story Mansfield seems tacitly to forgive the poor because they are so busy just staying alive that they have no time to discover some other things that life can be; her censure is reserved for those who have apparently had money for such a short time that they have not even developed the sense of noblesse oblige that allegedly and traditionally accompanies the really rich. Mrs. Sheridan demonstrates her lack of it when she says to Laura, "People like that don't expect sacrifices from us."

But what is to be done? Nothing. Like her fellow fiction writer Chekhov, Mansfield knew that nothing is to be done about the human condition through art except to show honestly how it is and maybe sometimes to cry out against the corruption. On her way down to the dead man's house, Laura stops a moment to think about how she is so filled up with the "kisses, voices, tinkling spoons, laughter, the smell of crushed grass" from the party that "she had no room for anything else." Clearly, she does have room for a great deal more, even if she thinks she does not. Mansfield's best stories, such as **"The Garden Party,"** create a condition in which we readers have the opportunity to make room for some things from the world around us other than those that occupy our daily lives. What we do with them, of course, is our own business.

Mary Burgan (essay date 1994)

SOURCE: "'They discuss only the food': Body Images," in *Illness, Gender, and Writing: The Case of Katherine Mansfield,* The Johns Hopkins University Press, 1994, pp. 21-39.

[*In the following excerpt, Burgan provides autobiographical and psychoanalytic interpretations of the body imagery of "The Garden Party."*]

The reality of Mansfield's own alienation from her family . . . was, for one thing, founded upon the humiliation dealt by maternal disfavor that centered on her physique. A witness recalled Annie Beauchamp's chilly emphasis on Mansfield's weight as she distributed her greetings to the family after one of her travels: "Finally it was to Kathleen she spoke first, for everyone to hear. 'Well, Kathleen,' she said, 'I see that you are as fat as ever.' And in my first glimpse of Kathleen I saw her eyes flash, and her face flush with anger as she turned away with a toss of her ringlets" [unpublished memoir by Marion C. Ruddick].

That body weight should have been a major issue between Katherine Mansfield and her mother refocused in latency and adolescence the oral issues of Mansfield's infancy. The demand of Annie Beauchamp that Mansfield control her weight was at variance with the daughter's positive self-identity gained through interaction with her grandmother—that intimate confirmation of bodily existence attained through being held and fed. In "Mary," a memoir of childhood published in *Harper's Monthly Magazine* in 1910, Mansfield proudly attributed her childish plumpness to her grandmother: "I was a strong, fat little child who burst my buttons and shot out of my skirts to grandmother's entire satisfaction." The dietary prohibitions of the mother denied the value of this "strong" identity by rejecting its manifestation in Mansfield's flesh. Furthermore, Annie Beauchamp's intolerance of her daughter's body seemed especially wounding because it contrasted sharply with her acceptance of the appetitive body of her husband. Accordingly, it was within this paradox of fleshiness forbidden for females while accepted for males that Mansfield's Oedipal crisis was transacted.

The mother's denial of Mansfield's body in latency superimposed upon this dichotomy [a] set of self-contradictions. Built upon the images of fat versus thin initiated in the psychic setting of mother/daughter antagonism, these contradictions designated body weight as a marker between the inner and the outer self. And so contending body images inform a string of associated oppositions in Mansfield's self-presentation—the self that belongs to the heavy father versus the self that belongs to the slight mother, the masculine self versus the feminine self, the spontaneous self versus the role-playing self, the loving self versus the rejecting self, and—finally and decisively—the healthy self versus the diseased self. Such a network of self-oppositions would be evoked in dialogue with a whole series of "mirror faces," recorded in Mansfield's journal and dramatized in many of her stories of confused young women.

The imagination of the obese body as a patriarchal construction is best seen in Mansfield's delineations of [her father] Harold Beauchamp—in her journal and letters and then fictionalized in a series of fathers in her stories. In most of her early descriptions, she emphasizes his stoutness, his hairiness, and his bulging eyes. The hair signals sexuality, and the gaze indicates a voracity not only for food but for control of his daughter's behavior. Sexuality and power are, moreover, inscribed in the father's orality—the feature of the male which most repelled Mansfield. The intensity of her adolescent formulation of this repulsion erupted in Mansfield's remarkable description of her parents' behavior on board the ship that returned her and her two elder sisters to New Zealand in 1906 at the conclusion of their three years at school in Queen's College in London:

> They are worse than I had even expected. They are prying and curious, they are watchful and they discuss only the food. They quarrel between themselves in a hopelessly vulgar fashion. My Father spoke of my returning as damned rot, said look here, he wouldn't have me fooling around in dark corners with fellows. His hands, covered with long sandy hair, are absolutely cruel hands. A physically revolted feeling seizes me. He wants me to sit near. He watches me at meals, eats in the most abjectly, blatantly vulgar manner that is describable. He is like a constant offence, but I cannot escape from it, and it wraps me in its atmosphere. When I pass him the dishes at the table, or a book or get him a cushion, he refrains from thanking me. *She* is constantly suspicious, constantly overbearingly tyrannous. I watch him walking all the deck, his full hideous speckled trousers, his absurdly [illegible] cap. He is like a cat sometimes, I think—except that his eyes are not like a cat's eyes, they are so full, so frightfully offensive, when he is astonished or when he eats anything that pleases him, I think they must start from his head. He watches the dishes go round, anxious to see that he shall have a good share. I cannot be alone or in the company of women for half a minute—he is there, eyes fearful, attempting to appear

unconcerned, pulling at his long drooping red-grey moustache with his hairy hands. Ugh!

[*Journals of Katherine Mansfield,* 1927]

Clearly at this stage of her young life, Mansfield had moved from the situation of a vulnerable, confused child like Pearl Button [in **"How Pearl Button Was Kidnapped"**] to that of the sharp diagnostician of body forms and their implications. The furtiveness of childhood sequestration in hapless chubbiness is exchanged for the aggressive self-definition of a late adolescence in reaction against the body conformations of her parents. The enmity centered on her father's fixation on feeding as a measure of control seems also a rejection of her mother's strictures against Mansfield's weight. The mother's service of this father's gluttony is here rendered as a vicious form of feminine hypocrisy: "They discuss only the food."

According to classic Oedipal theory, the adolescent Mansfield should have transferred desire for her mother to her father, or (in Nancy Chodorow's influential version [presented in *The Reproduction of Mothering,* 1978]) she should have turned *partially* to the father as relief from her primary identification with the mother. Such accounts of the Oedipal resolution of gender presuppose, however, a conventional triadic mother/father/daughter field of psychic force; they feature the transfer of identifications in a romance of primary parent-child anxieties and affiliations. . . . Mansfield's Oedipal situation was more complicated—marked by the tenuousness of any pre-Oedipal identification with her mother. Moreover, she possesses a precocious awareness of her mother's revulsion against the father's sexuality which precluded her own competition for it; the seductiveness in the father upon which an Oedipal turn is supposed to be based was therefore negatively charged. Mansfield thus identifies the mother and father as combined in league against her. Annie Beauchamp is the phallic mother who appropriates her husband's power with a vengeance; even as she rejects his sexuality, she is the leading accomplice of the father's harsh law.

A late sketch in Mansfield's journal suggests the pathology of her mother's complicity in confusing Mansfield's self-image by rejecting the father and thereby trivializing herself as a creature of fathers. The mother presented a blank rather than a mirror that might reflect back to the daughter a usable identity. Mansfield remembers the vivacious Annie Beauchamp confiding the regrets of her life in an intimate moment; she explains that she had always wanted to be an explorer, adventuring through the "Rivers of China": "Then she said 'If Father hadn't died I should have travelled and then ten to one I shouldn't have married.' And she looked at me dreamily—looked through me, rather" [*Journals of Katherine Mansfield,* 1927]. Characteristically, here Mansfield sympathizes with the mother's sense of loss; the echo of refined slang in the phrase "ten to one" and the extravagant fantasy of the "Rivers of China" are both comic and endearing. But embedded in the sketch, it is clear—for the narrator goes back to notice accurately—the daughter has disappeared: "she looked . . . through me, rather." Thus, just as in her infancy Mansfield was left behind to make her mother's travels possible, so

her adolescent presence is nullified by the mother's regrets about the limitations of having had children. Mansfield often sought to rationalize this kind of self-involvement by viewing her mother as the child and herself as the more knowledgeable parent, translating her mother's indifference into an attractively childish idiosyncracy. Charming and beautiful women did not need to grasp the kind of stable feminine identity which could mirror the daughter's self back to her in a collaboration of identity formation. Annie Beauchamp was absolved of this parental mandate by her sense of the injustice of her own feminine fate. Thus, rather than recognizing her child, she could "look through" her.

D. W. Winnicott's essay on the mirror stage in identity formation designates the mother's face as the child's first reflection: "When the average girl studies her face in the mirror she is reassuring herself that the mother-image is there and that the mother can see her and that the mother is *en rapport* with her" [*Playing and Reality,* 1989]. This insight may help to interpret the transaction recorded in Mansfield's memory: a mother who is unable to define her own life cannot assure her daughter of a self-image. The daughter's reaction to this lack may be the construction of a false self—created in compliance with the mother's depression or need. The daughter's inability to see her true self in the mother's mirror image and her tendency to try to make up for its blankness are often featured in the mirror episodes of Mansfield's fiction.

The challenge of sorting through the mirrored identities proffered to the adolescent girl by the mother within the confines of the bourgeois family is laid out most clearly in Mansfield's famous story **"The Garden-Party."** Here the autobiographical "Sheridan" family is defined as a locus of conspicuous consumption of food and of social power: indeed, the occasion of the story is its public celebration of itself with feasting. That story has had many interpreters, but none has been able to make a convincing explanation for the significance of the heroine's young brother, Laurie, who appears at the end of the story to help her make an inconclusive comment upon the meaning of her confrontation with "life." Reading the plot, however, as engaging Oedipal confusions that seek parental allegiances in dealing with the confusions of body imagery, it is possible to view Laura Sheridan's brother as the last-resort sibling accomplice in her negotiation of a new code of feeling beyond the narrow ethos of her family.

The story opens with Laura Sheridan's morning survey of the forthcoming garden party. As the "artistic" one of the family, she is given the job of deciding where the marquee should be placed on the lawn. Her mother has delegated all of the supervisory roles to her daughters, announcing: "I'm determined to leave everything to you children this year. Forget I am your mother. Treat me as an honoured guest." With the family power thus transferred, Laura self-consciously approaches the workmen she is supposed to direct—unsure of her own gender and class status, idealizing their working-class camaraderie, and seeking to join it. Naive as she is, the only way she can show her fellow feeling is through the small gesture of taking a bite out of the piece of her breakfast bread and butter in their company: "Just to prove how happy she was, just to show the tall fellow how at home she felt, and how she despised stupid conventions, Laura took a big bite of her bread-and-butter. . . . She felt just like a work-girl." Here, as in **"How Pearl Button Was Kidnapped,"** eating is imagined as an activity of solidarity. But it is also an activity circumscribed by familial prohibition; in taking the bite, Laura has transgressed something.

Abundance of food within a circumscribed, though public, familial setting is a class signifier in the economy of the garden party. The menu includes fifteen kinds of sandwiches as well as the paradisal cream puffs mentioned earlier. These are not so much tokens of the mother's prodigality of nurture as they are tokens of the father's success and the family's ability to engage cooks and maids and workmen and delivery boys in service to it. It is in the kitchen, however, that the baker's man delivers news that a laborer who lived down the lane from the Sheridans' house has just been killed in an accident.

As yet not totally absorbed in the family's enclosed identity, Laura moves immediately to cancel the party. Her older sister responds with a proclamation of class isolation: "Of course we can't do anything of the kind. Nobody expects us to. Don't be so extravagant." Laura's next appeal is to her mother. But Mrs. Sheridan is as self-protective as the sister: "People like that don't expect sacrifices from us. And it's not very sympathetic to spoil everybody's enjoyment as you're doing now." In the process of rejecting her sensibility, both senior women in the family tempt Laura with an image of the family as so defined in its absolute identity that it is removed from judgment or blame by its distance from the working classes. Indeed, this distance is emphasized geographically by the steepness of the descent from the Sheridan mansion to the little cottages of the working people right below. And these "lower" people have been seen not only as totally separate from the privileged family but off-limits for the Sheridan children because of their low morals and their diseases—"the revolting language and . . . what they might catch."

One strategy of the women in distracting Laura from her anxiety about the tragedy in the lane is to quarantine her as "extravagant" or "absurd." But her departure from the family pattern has, in a manner of speaking, immunized her from such interdictions already. She has ventured into the lane with her brother earlier on the principle that "still one must go everywhere; one must see everything." Her artistic sensibility has been indulged in this infraction, as in the assignment of deciding about the marquee, but it is not so decisively valued that it can challenge the family's solidarity. Instead it marks Laura off as an eccentric who must be isolated or brought around.

Mrs. Sheridan's manner of bringing her daughter around involves changing the child's self-image by offering an alternative that embodies her own sense of the essential female self. This she does by ending the debate about canceling the garden party by giving Laura her own hat to wear. At first Laura can't "look at herself; she turn[s]

aside." But after she goes into her own room, she has an encounter with her own mirror which transforms her from the authentic Laura of her original instincts into the Laura fabricated by her mother: "There, quite by chance, the first thing she saw was this charming girl in the mirror, in her black hat trimmed with gold daisies, and a long black velvet ribbon. Never had she imagined she could look like that. Is mother right? she thought. And now she hoped her mother was right." Laura attends the party in the trance of this new identity, deflected from any further impulse to question it. Even when she begins to confide in her brother, she is thwarted by his comment on her looks in the new hat. Laboring under the compliments of the guests, she does her best to minister to their wants by playing at being a woman—offering tea and ices and making sure that the members of the band get something to drink.

Laura's diminishing hold on her identity is maintained by care for sharing food with the guests, and so it seems appropriate to send her down the lane with a basket of leftover food when the question of the laborer's death arises after the party is over. Significantly, perhaps, it is the father who mentions the accident, bringing some news from the outside world into the enclosed family circle. And the mother, now somewhat abashed, at last takes action by gathering food for the widow and her children. Laura worries about the sensibilities of the poor family but is overwhelmed by her mother a second time and so delivers the basket of party food to the dead man's cottage. At the revelation of death itself, especially in the presence of the corpse of the young workman, Laura's fragile self is totally obliterated. She cannot think how to respond to the powerful negation and beauty of the man's dead body: "What did garden-parties and baskets and lace frocks matter to him: He was far from all those things. He was wonderful, beautiful." Unable to find anything to say to this vision of selflessness, Laura sobs out one sentence, "Forgive my hat," before she flees.

Her comment is at once trenchant and hopelessly confused. The episode leaves Laura with an indeterminate sense of herself and of how she fits into the scheme of human bodies that die. She has no authoritative guidance from her family, and so she turns to her brother, who has come to meet her in the lane. She wants to ask a question: "'Isn't life,' she stammered, 'isn't life—'." But Laura cannot complete the query, and Laurie is little help, merely echoing her question with a class accent: "'*Isn't* it, darling?' said Laurie." Thus **"The Garden-Party"** enacts an Oedipal and familial betrayal by substituting for Laura's best, real self a socially constructed reflection of uncaring femininity. As in the fairy tale, the young girl has been seduced by the mirror image offered by a false mother. And there is no male rescuer to wake her up from her sleep of appearances. . . .

[Mansfield's] sorting out of paternal and maternal bodies in terms of their external form, and her regular staging of eidetic confrontations in her stories of adolescent girls engage her sense of identity formation as involving a vital dialectic between a hidden, inner "real" self and the outer manifestations of false personae. This conflict between her often satirical unveiling of surface "subjects" and her celebration of the hidden self—perhaps available in its transcendent beauty only in death—can be framed in terms of the issues of identity which preoccupy current critical discourse. For the comforting notion of the purposive ego in search of a familiar "self," for example, Lacanian theory hypothesizes a more distanced and confused "construction" based on mirror reflections that structure the preconscious "I" as an always unstable site for the obscure movements of desire. The collection of psychic motions so created—so acted upon—Lacan calls the "subject." The possibility of any inner revelatory agency has no place in a theory that accents the subject's determined "misrecognition" of inner drives. Even in the early, maternal register of the imaginary, the instability of fragmentary images bars direct knowledge of the self.

The satirical strain in Katherine Mansfield's fiction illustrates her recognition of some of the features of subjectivity as modeled by Lacan: she is a connoisseur of constructed selves, especially of feminine selves that have been made up in the image of the social expectations instituted by patriarchy. As in **"The Garden-Party,"** she frequently uses the encounter with mirrors to portray the ordeal of the self as it confronts a reflection that presents neither ontological reassurance nor psychological integration.

And as Mansfield frequently shows, the mirror image can emphasize the transparency of its own source—putting the empirical sensations of spatial stability and temporal sequence into terrifying disarray as the perceiver confronts the splitting of mirror images as an aspect of her inner split. Thus although Mansfield's insistence on self-discovery as the essential issue in her fiction is better understood in the light of the therapeutic (or adaptive) notions of the self such as Winnicott's, Lacan's formulations about the refracted and misrecognized formation of the subject in the "mirror stage" may illuminate Mansfield's satire.

Indeed, the bodily contrasts of thin versus fat in constituting identity contributed a kind of graveyard humor in Mansfield's imagination at times during her last years of illness when she fearfully watched her body dissipate in disease. Her diet had become a matter of excruciating concern, the intake of warm milk (which she seems to have despised) the main tonic prescribed to return her to health. Indeed, tuberculosis ravaged her breasts, the main feature of her femininity, and she wrote ruefully to a friend referring to a buxom governess, "I wish Mamselle could spare me a little tiny bit of her *front*. Mine has *gone*." She also maintained her caustic attitude about the absurdity of male health as reflected in body weight. She wrote to the same friend about John Middleton Murry's robust body during a bout of flu: "I shall have him photographed in his singlet soon, lying on a mat, you know, a-goo-gooing with REARED FROM BIRTH ON SUET PUDDINGS written underneath." Thus Mansfield's experience of the body colored her final battle with an emaciating disease. As the imagery of the gendered body of the thin mother and the plump father encroached upon her awareness of herself, however, she retained enough of the conviction of the essential fragmentariness of subjectivity to turn from the melodramatic

and sentimental imagination of death to the macabre and tough-minded recognition of the somatic reality of her condition.

Mansfield finally addressed the issue of body weight as disease wryly in a surreal narrative of the deaths of two opposite children, sketched in a very late entry in her journal. The first child was a chubby figure who didn't want to think about things: "At last she became so adorably chubby, so ridiculously light-hearted, that she fell down the stairs, and they made her a heavenly funeral, and the most warming little grave you can imagine." The second was a thoughtful, "thin little girl" who "became so disgustingly thin, so preposterously wretched, that she fell up the stairs, and they threw her into the darkest, moistest little hole you can imagine." The plots of death by surfeit and death by emaciation pay grotesque tribute to the irony of Mansfield's fated "wasting" illness; though rich in the characteristic sensory evocations of death as warmth and embrace for the chubby child, death is terrifyingly claustrophobic for the thin one. This reenactment of the body-image fractures of her childhood thus manifests Mansfield's final rejection of the ideal of rational body control which so often drives anorectics to kill themselves with dieting. Instead, she plays on an ironic confrontation of the existential horror of dying through starvation with the serenity of plenitude, even in death. There could not be a more decisive rejection of her mother's preferred body image, nor a more playful acceptance of her own.

FURTHER READING

Biography

Alpers, Antony. *The Life of Katherine Mansfield.* New York: The Viking Press, 1980, 466 p.
  Views Mansfield's life and works in the context of early British Modernism.

Crone, Nora. *A Portrait of Katherine Mansfield.* Ilfracombe, England: Arthur H. Stockwell Ltd., 1985, 348 p.
  Presents a standard account of Mansfield's life from her New Zealand childhood to her death at Fontainebleu.

Gordon, Ian A. *Katherine Mansfield.* London: Longmans, Green & Co., 1954, 36 p.
  Concise discussion of Mansfield's life and works.

Meyers, Jeffrey. *Katherine Mansfield: A Biography.* New York: New Directions, 1978, 306 p.
  A literary account of Mansfield's life, with special attention to her relationships with D. H. Lawrence and John Middleton Murry.

Criticism

Daly, Saralyn R. "Trains of Thought." In her *Katherine Mansfield,* pp. 91-3. New York: Twayne Publishers, 1994.

Comments on "The Garden Party" in the context of other Mansfield stories about children.

Kaplan, Sydney Janet. *Katherine Mansfield and the Origins of Modernist Fiction.* Ithaca, N.Y.: Cornell University Press, 1991, 233 p.
    Examines Mansfield's role in the development of British Modernism, with brief reference to "The Garden Party."

Kleine, Don W. "An Eden for Insiders: Katherine Mansfield's New Zealand." *College English* XXVII, No. 3 (December 1965): 201-09.
    Discusses the motif of the Young Girl in Mansfield's fiction, with reference to "The Garden Party."

Morrow, Patrick D. "The Garden Party." In his *Katherine Mansfield's Fiction,* pp. 74-6. Bowling Green, Ohio: Bowling Green State University Popular Press, 1993.
    Focuses on the contrast between life and death in "The Garden Party."

Nathan, Rhoda B., ed. *Critical Essays on Katherine Mansfield.* New York: G. K. Hall & Co., 1993, 236 p.
    Various essays included here contain references to "The Garden Party."

Robinson, Roger, ed. *Katherine Mansfield: In from the Margins.* Baton Rouge: Louisiana State University Press, 1994, 209 p.
    A collection of recent revisionary critical essays on Mansfield, with scattered references to "The Garden Party."

Rohrberger, Mary H. "Point of View." In her *The Art of Katherine Mansfield,* pp. 73-95. Ann Arbor, Mich.: University Microfilms International, 1977.
    Discusses point of view in Mansfield's fiction. Rohrberger considers "The Garden Party" to be one of the stories written from the "multipersonal view," in which "the narrator hovers just outside the consciousness of the characters, shifting from one to another and sometimes to a composite consciousness, causing the reader to become familiar not only with a central character or characters but also with a host of minor characters. This method, of course, enlarges the scope of the stories."

Van Gunsteren, Julia. "Narrative Methods: Restriction in Parallax." In her *Katherine Mansfield and Literary Impressionism,* pp. 96-100. Atlanta: Rodopi B. V., 1990.
    Argues that Laura is effectively the narrator of "The Garden Party."

Additional coverage of Mansfield's life and career is contained in the following sources published by Gale Research: *Contemporary Authors,* **Vols. 104, 134;** *DISCovering Authors;* *Short Story Criticism,* **Vol. 9;** *Twentieth-Century Literary Criticism,* **Vols. 2, 8, 39; and** *World Literature Criticism.*

"A Good Man Is Hard to Find"
Flannery O'Connor

(Full name Mary Flannery O'Connor) American short story writer, novelist, and essayist.

The following entry presents criticism of O'Connor's story "A Good Man Is Hard to Find," first published in her 1955 collection *A Good Man Is Hard to Find, and Other Stories*. For an overview of O'Connor's short fiction, see *SSC*, Volume 1.

INTRODUCTION

Considered one of O'Connor's best short stories, "A Good Man Is Hard to Find" depicts the callous murder of a family by a group of escaped convicts led by a notorious killer called The Misfit. The story is noted for its religious aspects, in particular O'Connor's penchant for depicting salvation through a shocking, often violent experience undergone by characters who are spiritually or physically grotesque. Commentators have praised "A Good Man Is Hard to Find" for O'Connor's effective use of local color and the rich comic detail of her Southern milieu, as well as her ability to record with a keen ear the idiosyncratic dialect of characters such as the grandmother and The Misfit.

Plot and Major Characters

The opening scene of "A Good Man Is Hard to Find" introduces us to an unappealing family: a vain and manipulative grandmother, her taciturn son Bailey, his passive wife and baby, and their difficult children, June Star and John Wesley. The family plans to travel on vacation from their home in Georgia to the state of Florida. Alarmed by newspaper accounts of an escaped convict, The Misfit, the grandmother attempts to persuade the family to change their vacation destination away from the vicinity of the fugitive. Derided for her concern, she responds by concealing her cat in the car against her son's wishes. During their long trip through Georgia the grandmother relates the story of a nearby plantation house with a secret panel. The story fires the children's interest, consequently forcing Bailey to take a unplanned detour down a rough dirt road in search of the house. Suddenly, the grandmother realizes that her memory has deceived her. In her acute embarrassment, she involuntarily releases the cat from its hiding place, causing Bailey to lose control of the car. As the family members struggle to free themselves from the ensuing wreck, three men in an ominous black car appear on the horizon. The grandmother's blurted recognition of The Misfit seals her family's fate and, in spite of her desperate attempts to win the convict's confidence, each is taken separately into the woods and shot. Left alone with The Misfit, the grandmother tries to bargain for her life by calling on him to pray. He responds by complain-

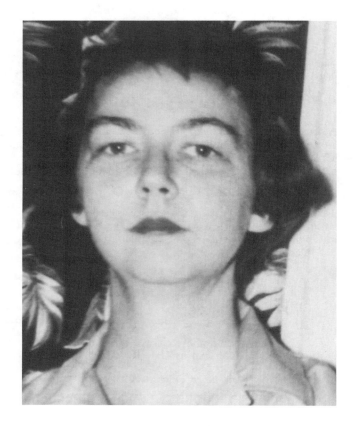

ing that Jesus offers him no choice between blind faith or violent nihilism, and his pain unexpectedly moves the grandmother to a feeling of kinship. As she reaches out to touch him, however, he reacts by shooting her three times in the chest.

Major Themes

With rare, but significant, exceptions most critics accept O'Connor's description of "A Good Man Is Hard to Find" as a tale of redemptive grace in a fallen world. The story's religious concerns are expressed through a series of motifs and emblems, cleverly muted by O'Connor's superficially naturalistic style. Critics point to the disastrous detour into the dark woods of error, for example, as a traditional theme in Christian exempla, from Dante's *Divine Comedy* to Bunyan's *Pilgrim's Progress*. The Misfit himself typifies the existential despair and guilt of the fallen sinner. As many commentators argue, the grandmother's epiphanic recognition of her kinship with the desperate figure belatedly redeems her from a life that has been petty, materialistic, and selfish. Her child-like expression as she collapses with crossed legs into her own grave has been suggested as a symbol of her sudden accession to Christian grace.

Critical Reception

"A Good Man Is Hard to Find" is regarded as one of O'Connor's best stories and has drawn much critical attention. Most discussions of "A Good Man Is Hard to Find" have focused on the story's extreme violence. O'Connor herself justified the use of terror to shock spiritually complacent modern readers: "To the hard of hearing you shout and for the almost blind you draw large and startling figures." While many critics accept this rationalization, others are less comfortable with the story's abrupt descent into brutality. For some commentators, the jarring shift from comedy to tragedy takes unfair advantage of a group of characters whose depiction verges on caricature. More recent interpretations of the tale range from structural and political analysis to an examination of its classical and medieval literary influences.

CRITICISM

Flannery O'Connor (essay date 1963)

SOURCE: "A Reasonable Use of the Unreasonable," in *Mystery and Manners: Occasional Prose,* Farrar, Straus & Giroux, 1969, pp. 107-14.

[*In the following lecture given at Hollins College, Virginia, on October 14, 1963, O'Connor discusses the function of violence in "A Good Man Is Hard to Find."*]

Last fall I received a letter from a student who said she would be "graciously appreciative" if I would tell her "just what enlightenment" I expected her to get from each of my stories. I suspect she had a paper to write. I wrote her back to forget about the enlightenment and just try to enjoy them. I knew that was the most unsatisfactory answer I could have given because, of course, she didn't want to enjoy them, she just wanted to figure them out.

In most English classes the short story has become a kind of literary specimen to be dissected. Every time a story of mine appears in a Freshman anthology, I have a vision of it, with its little organs laid open, like a frog in a bottle.

I realize that a certain amount of this what-is-the-significance has to go on, but I think something has gone wrong in the process when, for so many students, the story becomes simply a problem to be solved, something which you evaporate to get Instant Enlightenment.

A story really isn't any good unless it successfully resists paraphrase, unless it hangs on and expands in the mind. Properly, you analyze to enjoy, but it's equally true that to analyze with any discrimination, you have to have enjoyed already, and I think that the best reason to hear a story read is that it should stimulate that primary enjoyment.

I don't have any pretensions to being an Aeschylus or Sophocles and providing you in this story with a cathartic experience out of your mythic background, though this story I'm going to read certainly calls up a good deal of the South's mythic background, and it should elicit from you a degree of pity and terror, even though its way of being serious is a comic one. I do think, though, that like the Greeks you should know what is going to happen in this story so that any element of suspense in it will be transferred from its surface to its interior.

I would be most happy if you had already read it, happier still if you knew it well, but since experience has taught me to keep my expectations along these lines modest, I'll tell you that this is the story of a family of six which, on its way driving to Florida, gets wiped out by an escaped convict who calls himself the Misfit. The family is made up of the Grandmother and her son, Bailey, and his children, John Wesley and June Star and the baby, and there is also the cat and the children's mother. The cat is named Pitty Sing, and the Grandmother is taking him with them, hidden in a basket.

Now I think it behooves me to try to establish with you the basis on which reason operates in this story. Much of my fiction takes its character from a reasonable use of the unreasonable, though the reasonableness of my use of it may not always be apparent. The assumptions that underlie this use of it, however, are those of the central Christian mysteries. These are assumptions to which a large part of the modern audience takes exception. About this I can only say that there are perhaps other ways than my own in which this story could be read, but none other by which it could have been written. Belief, in my own case anyway, is the engine that makes perception operate.

The heroine of this story, the Grandmother, is in the most significant position life offers the Christian. She is facing death. And to all appearances she, like the rest of us, is not too well prepared for it. She would like to see the event postponed. Indefinitely.

I've talked to a number of teachers who use this story in class and who tell their students that the Grandmother is evil, that in fact, she's a witch, even down to the cat. One of these teachers told me that his students, and particularly his Southern students, resisted this interpretation with a certain bemused vigor, and he didn't understand why. I had to tell him that they resisted it because they all had grandmothers or great-aunts just like her at home, and they knew, from personal experience, that the old lady lacked comprehension, but that she had a good heart. The Southerner is usually tolerant of those weaknesses that proceed from innocence, and he knows that a taste for self-preservation can be readily combined with the missionary spirit.

This same teacher was telling his students that morally the Misfit was several cuts above the Grandmother. He had a really sentimental attachment to the Misfit. But then a prophet gone wrong is almost always more interesting than your grandmother, and you have to let people take their pleasures where they find them.

It is true that the old lady is a hypocritical old soul; her wits are no match for the Misfit's, nor is her capacity for grace equal to his; yet I think the unprejudiced reader will feel that the Grandmother has a special kind of triumph in this story which instinctively we do not allow to someone altogether bad.

I suppose the reasons for the use of so much violence in modern fiction will differ with each writer who uses it, but in my own stories I have found that violence is strangely capable of returning my characters to reality and preparing them to accept their moment of grace.

—*Flannery O'Connor*

I often ask myself what makes a story work, and what makes it hold up as a story, and I have decided that it is probably some action, some gesture of a character that is unlike any other in the story, one which indicates where the real heart of the story lies. This would have to be an action or a gesture which was both totally right and totally unexpected; it would have to be one that was both in character and beyond character; it would have to suggest both the world and eternity. The action or gesture I'm talking about would have to be on the analogical level, that is, the level which has to do with the Divine life and our participation in it. It would be a gesture that transcended any neat allegory that might have been intended or any pat moral categories a reader could make. It would be a gesture which somehow made contact with mystery.

There is a point in this story where such a gesture occurs. The Grandmother is at last alone, facing the Misfit. Her head clears for an instant and she realizes, even in her limited way, that she is responsible for the man before her and joined to him by ties of kinship which have their roots deep in the mystery she has been merely prattling about so far. And at this point, she does the right thing, she makes the right gesture.

I find that students are often puzzled by what she says and does here, but I think myself that if I took out this gesture and what she says with it, I would have no story. What was left would not be worth your attention. Our age not only does not have a very sharp eye for the almost imperceptible intrusions of grace, it no longer has much feeling for the nature of the violences which precede and follow them. The devil's greatest wile, Baudelaire has said, is to convince us that he does not exist.

I suppose the reasons for the use of so much violence in modern fiction will differ with each writer who uses it, but in my own stories I have found that violence is strangely capable of returning my characters to reality and preparing them to accept their moment of grace. Their heads are so hard that almost nothing else will do the work. This idea, that reality is something to which we must be returned at considerable cost, is one which is seldom understood by the casual reader, but it is one which is implicit in the Christian view of the world.

I don't want to equate the Misfit with the devil. I prefer to think that, however unlikely this may seem, the old lady's gesture, like the mustard-seed, will grow to be a great crow-filled tree in the Misfit's heart, and will be enough of a pain to him there to turn him into the prophet he was meant to become. But that's another story.

This story has been called grotesque, but I prefer to call it literal. A good story is literal in the same sense that a child's drawing is literal. When a child draws, he doesn't intend to distort but to set down exactly what he sees, and as his gaze is direct, he sees the lines that create motion. Now the lines of motion that interest the writer are usually invisible. They are lines of spiritual motion. And in this story you should be on the lookout for such things as the action of grace in the Grandmother's soul, and not for the dead bodies.

We hear many complaints about the prevalence of violence in modern fiction, and it is always assumed that this violence is a bad thing and meant to be an end in itself. With the serious writer, violence is never an end in itself. It is the extreme situation that best reveals what we are essentially, and I believe these are times when writers are more interested in what we are essentially than in the tenor of our daily lives. Violence is a force which can be used for good or evil, and among other things taken by it is the kingdom of heaven. But regardless of what can be taken by it, the man in the violent situation reveals those qualities least dispensable in his personality those qualities which are all he will have to take into eternity with him; and since the characters in this story are all on the verge of eternity, it is appropriate to think of what they take with them. In any case, I hope that if you consider these points in connection with the story, you will come to see it as something more than an account of a family murdered on the way to Florida.

With the serious writer, violence is never an end in itself. It is the extreme situation that best reveals what we are essentially, and I believe these are times when writers are more interested in what we are essentially than in the tenor of our daily lives.

—*Flannery O'Connor*

W. S. Marks III (essay date 1966)

SOURCE: "Advertisements for Grace: Flannery O'Connor's 'A Good Man Is Hard to Find'," in *Studies in Short Fiction,* Vol. IV, No. 1, Fall, 1966, pp. 19-37.

[*In the following essay, Marks analyzes "A Good Man Is Hard to Find" as religious allegory.*]

As a narrative stylist, Flannery O'Connor belongs, however peripherally, to a Pauline or Augustinian tradition extending from Langland to Bunyan and Hawthorne. Her tastes for gothicism, allegory, and regional setting derive from that special admiration for *The House of the Seven Gables* evident in so many important Southern writers from Faulkner to Truman Capote. The mingled scorn and sorrow with which Hawthorne faced the decline of New England, his ambivalent attitude towards Puritanism, and his dubious hopefulness about America's spiritual future find echoes throughout Miss O'Connor's stories of Evangelical awakening amid the scattered ashes of plantation Georgia. In "The Fiction Writer and Her Country," she makes this statement about writers in the South:

> The anguish that most of us have observed for some time now has been caused not by the fact that the South is alienated from the rest of the country, but by the fact that it is not alienated enough, that every day we are getting more and more like the rest of the country, that we are being forced out, not only of our many sins, but out of our few virtues.

Further isolated from most of her contemporaries by virtue of her staunch Catholicism, Miss O'Connor reminds us less, perhaps, of Hawthorne than of Orestes Brownson, the apostate from Transcendentalism who was converted to Rome, to Calhoun, and to the notion that only a Catholic block could stem the tide of Democratic progress which was sweeping from the land all its traditional and spiritual values.

Temperamentally, Miss O'Connor displays more in common with such lay preachers of the New Left as LeRoi Jones and James Baldwin than with any specifically Southern or Catholic reaction. Similar to Baldwin's, her gripe against white liberalism grew out of a sense of estrangement from its ultimate and unannounced purpose: the homogenizing of all racial, regional, and religious cultures into one uniform and godless civilization. Her increasing frustration with this unholy prospect produced a formula: 'Were it not for the diabolic anodynes of secular liberalism man would at once recognize his hopeless depravity and degradation, repent, and be saved from the hell of this world; out and out demonism, because it openly declares man's sinful nature, must on the other hand be regarded as salutary and even admirable.' Behind this philosophy is a fascination with Dostoyevsky easily discoverable too in the Negro radicals of her generation.

Not incidentally, many of the figures in Miss O'Connor's personal pantheon have Calvinist backgrounds. It is, finally, with Evangelicalism and with the more eschatologically preoccupied varieties of religious existentialism that her work reveals its deepest affinities. Through a humorousness notably lacking in Baldwin, she speaks just as fondly of the wrath to come. "God's grace burns," she tells her readers, excusing the characteristic violence of her plots as pious metaphor. An author's consistent choice of metaphors nevertheless has inevitable implications beyond pure technique. There is, moreover, a distinction to be made between grace (which can also fall as the morning dew) and mere metaphysical evil. Miss O'Connor's further anxiousness to demonstrate the irresistibility of this grace reduces her characters to hollow recipients of divine impulse. Like rudely carved figures in some cosmic marionette show, they twitch on their wires as the indifferent spirit moves them—either to bizarre acts of criminal insanity or to equally incredible decisions for Christ. While virtue consists in conversion, sin lies in the deplorably human tendency to cut oneself loose from the puppet master, to become independently articulate. The apocalyptic terrors she visits on those who follow this atheistic course, either from bucolic ignorance or false academic sophistication, are awful to behold.

Favoring an older and more romantic mode, Flannery O'Connor rejected literary realism for much the same temperamental reasons that led her to despise other aspects of contemporary American culture. A college generation presently repudiating the liberalism of their ancestors will scarcely fail to appreciate her dogged efforts to caricaturize and deflate this public wisdom. The rare and incurable disease that crippled her and eventually took her life doubtless encouraged her to question the very basis of liberalism: the naive faith that among them democracy, free enterprise, and science hold both the explanation and permanent cure for human suffering. Because the riddle of man's incurable mortality, his subjection to physical and metaphysical torment, could not be separated from moral evil and original sin, the Freudian *Aufklärung* that had sought to evaporate these mysteries was a blasphemous lie. The mental disturbances that, along with club feet, amputated legs, myopia, and various other bodily disorders, distinguish a host of O'Connor characters, their author quaintly conceives as a species of demonic possession. Christ, who makes foolish the wisdom of her fictional world, is its only true physician. In the Raskolnikovian analysis of The Misfit, one of the more lethal and sadistic of her anti-heroes: "Jesus was the only one that ever raised the dead, . . . and he shouldn't have done it. He thrown everything off balance. If He did what He said, then it's nothing for you to do but throw away everything and follow Him, and if He didn't, then its nothing for you to do but enjoy the few minutes you got left the best way you can—by killing somebody or burning down his house or doing some other meanness to him. No pleasure but meanness." One of Miss O'Connor's chief delights was to parody worldly wisdom through an ironic emphasis on the clichés and advertising slogans that summarize it. Frequently stock expressions—The Life You Save May Be Your Own, A Good Man Is Hard To Find—constitute disguised advertisements for the spirit. Truth, it is thus pointed out, is only hidden from the wise. For those who will hear Him, Christ speaks even from billboards. For those who won't, Miss O'Connor reserved an audience with Death and the Devil, two of her most persuasive spokesmen.

In **"A Good Man Is Hard To Find,"** one of the most characteristic and frequently anthologized of her pieces, these allegorical figures fool old Grandma Worldliwise with plausible Southern accents that may, however, give them away to the constant reader. Nominally set in back-woods Georgia (A "romantic precinct" on the order of Hardy's Wessex or Faulkner's Yoknapatawpha) the action of the story expands parabolically into a narrative of modern man's general sin-sickness. In bare outline, the plot concerns the tragi-comic destruction of some Florida-bound Georgians, chiefly through the senile offices of a grandmother who craftily, if unintentionally, detours her son and his family into the hands of a homicidal maniac called the Misfit. The main business of the plot, a plea-sure trip to the Sunshine State, neatly optimizes Ameri-ca's commercialized dream of happiness. Although each member of the family cherishes his own peculiar means of self-gratification, they are united in a common pursuit of pleasure. Enjoyment, we notice, becomes increasingly vi-carious with each succeeding generation. The needs of little John Wesley and June Star are for the most part answered by Coca-Colas and, less immediately, by the promised excitement of strange new places. Mother spends her extra nickels on the juke box, which obliges her fancy with "The Tennessee Waltz"—perhaps the most popular tune ever recorded. Sadly, but necessarily, Grandmother depends on the flattering distortions of an indifferent memory. Naturally placed in a weak and unfavorable position, she is the most resourceful and least scrupulous in attaining her ends. The old woman has lived longer than her family only to develop its distinguishing trait of vain self-regard into a case of fatal hubris. The fabrication which the grandmother uses to implement her scheme of detouring Bailey Boy past the scene of badly confused girlhood memories is eagerly swallowed by John Wesley and June Star only because it serves to promote their own craving for spurious adventure.

Florida, land of the fabled fountain of youth, remains beyond the horizon, just as Grandma's romantic planta-tion house (which is not where she remembered it) also proves elusive. Man is the victim of irreversible time. Thus the "ACCIDENT" that prevents this arrival and is occa-sioned by the sudden and expressly forbidden presence of Grandma's cat, may also fall into the categories of moral or metaphysical necessity. Still the plot leans heavily and deliberately on chance, and especially on the absurdity of accidental death. In Miss O'Connor's existential universe all events, including whatever acts of poetic justice the reader may happen to see, are essentially unpredictable, beyond human control, and, in a strict sense, accidental. It is only death, however, that speaks loudly enough to con-vince man of his foolish self-deceptions. "She was a talk-er, wasn't she?" says Bobby Lee, as the Misfit concludes his massacre of Bailey Boy's family by firing three slugs into its senior member. Underlining the major theme of the story, the Misfit rebukes his lieutenant: "Shut up, Bobby Lee. . . . It's no real pleasure in life."

Coming early in the story, the grandmother's anecdote of her dead beau Mr. Edgar Atkins Teagarden announces this theme of the vanity of human wishes and foreshadows the family's disastrous end:

> She said he was a very good-looking man and a gentleman and that he brought her a watermelon every Saturday afternoon with his initials cut in it, E.A.T. Well, one Saturday, she said, Mr. Teagarden brought the watermelon and there was nobody at home and he left it on the front porch and returned in his buggy to Jasper, but she never got the watermelon, she said, because a nigger boy ate it when he saw the initials, E.A.T.! This story tickled John Wesley's funny bone and he giggled and giggled but June Star didn't think it was any good. She said she wouldn't marry a man that just brought her a watermelon on Saturday. The grandmother said she would have done well to marry Mr. Teagarden because he was a gentleman and had bought Coca-Cola stock when it first came out and that he had died only a few years ago, a very wealthy man.

The watermelon, which neither Grandma nor Mr. Teagar-den ever got to enjoy, and instead was inadvertently de-voured by the Negro boy, symbolizes the sensual and specifically sexual gratifications allowed the Negro but denied the virtuous white man under the peculiar dispen-sations of the Protestant ethic. Her attitude of holding out for more than watermelon suggests June Star has been corrupted at an even earlier age than Pamela, while John Wesley's laughter punctuates Miss O'Connor's rather broad and heavy irony. Coca-Cola (as opposed to watermelon, an artificial gratification), which furnishes the basis of Mr. Teagarden's wealth, also provides a transition to the scene at Red Sammy's roadside barbecue-and-soft-drink tower that follows.

The irresistible hint that Red Sammy is the Devil or his agent gives the key both to his character and that of The Misfit, who to this point has remained only a sinister ru-mor. By pretending a flattering allegiance to the grand-mother's radical and disastrous prejudice in favor of the past, Red Sammy is no mean contributor to the family's downfall. He is full of platitudes, lies, and diabolical half-truths. "These days you don't know who to trust," he says ironically, all the while calculating his take at the till. While a manifestly mercenary motive would explain this cajoling of his customers, hints of a darker purpose are plentiful. At its bottom reaches—and Red Sammy's is cer-tainly that—both the physical exterior and psychological workings of capitalistic enterprise reveal its true ugliness and depravity. There is no need of a deeper hell or pro-founder hellishness. Sammy's wife says she wouldn't be surprised if The Misfit attacked their cash register. Taking up this suggestion of a harrowing of hell, the reader may prepare himself for the catastrophic and apocalyptic events that bring the story to its predicted conclusion.

The coming of The Misfit, which like the coming of Antichrist heralds the Last Day, is first rumored by the newspaper Grandma is reading as the narrative opens. Like Sammy's wife, the other characters pay religious lip service to the proximity of this terror partly to make topical conversation and partly to exorcise a real fear for their individual safety. They think of The Misfit as they think of death; and that indeed is one of the things he represents. Admirably designed as an agent of divine wrath, The Misfit is also, and less plausibly, presented as an existential Everyman. "I been most everything," he confides. "Been in the arm service, both land and sea, at home and abroad, been twict married, been an undertaker, been with the railroads, plowed Mother Earth, been in a tornado, seen a man burnt alive oncet . . . but somewhere along the line I done something wrong and got sent to the penitentiary. I was buried alive. . . ." Playing shrewdly on the religious meanings of *penitentiary,* the story draws a Kafkaesque comparison between The Misfit's unremembered crime and original sin. When the grandmother placatingly suggests he might have been brought up on false charges, he declares: "Nome. It wasn't no mistake. They had the papers on me." *Papers,* in this metaphorical instance, means Scriptural as well as legal proof. After scorning the old woman's further suggestion that his crime has been theft (the apple myth literally interpreted), he proceeds with his allegorical confessions: "It was a head doctor at the penitentiary said what I had done was kill my Daddy but I known that for a lie. My Daddy died in nineteen ought nineteen of the epidemic flu and I never had a thing to do with it. He was buried in the Mount Hopewell Baptist churchyard and you can go there and see for yourself." No doubt a psychoanalyst, the head doctor in question seems to have been imbued with Freud's theory that primitive man thought of original sin as parricide. While Freud announced this idea in "Totem and Taboo," its refinement in "Dostoevsky and Parricide" has greater relevance to the portrait of The Misfit, which is remarkably like Freud's subject in this latter essay.

According to Freud: "Dostoyevsky's condemnation as a political prisoner was unjust and he must have known it, but he accepted the undeserved punishment at the hands of the Little Father, the sin [a death wish] against his real father." Like Dostoyevsky, who made "use of his sufferings as a claim to be playing a Christlike role," The Misfit also identifies himself with Jesus, claiming: "It was the same with him as with me except he hadn't committed any crime and they could prove I had committed one because they had the papers on me." Both the Freudian Dostoyevsky and The Misfit are depicted as sado-masochists, unable either to escape or wholly to accept their guilt; and both stoically refuse to allow science to explain it away. Attempting to case further suspicion on the genuineness of Dostoyevsky's penitential experience in Siberia, Freud cites the novelist's sympathy with the criminality of his fictional characters, a feeling that "goes far beyond the pity which the unhappy wretch might claim, and reminds us of the 'holy awe' with which epileptics and lunatics were regarded in the past." For Dostoyevsky a criminal is "almost a Redeemer," Freud observes, "who has taken on himself the guilt which else must have been borne by others." This last remark, which might apply to Stavrogin, Raskolnikov, or Dmitri Karamazov, serves equally well to describe Miss O'Connor's dramatic conception of The Misfit.

The intellectual quarrel between science and religion, allegorized in the anecdote of The Misfit's difference of opinion with the prison psychiatrist, can be resolved only by the individual's (prisoner's) flight from this world (the prison break) and his spiritual alienation. Isolated, even outlawed, he will either direct the violent longings of his soul inward (under conversion) or he will direct that violence, as The Misfit does, against others. The danger of secularism (the prison's psychiatrically oriented rehabilitation program) is that it attempts to rationalize man's inherent spiritual drives out of existence, rather than acknowledging and providing for them. Secularism makes war (the story contains several strategic reminders that World War II has not been long concluded) inevitable, for the psychology of nations or masses of people is identical with that of the individual in his search for spiritual—and sexual—release. As we have already seen from the example of Edgar Atkins Teagarden, capitalism sees to it that even man's baser needs (for watermelon) are not really satisfied. Psychoanalysis is thus on a par with Coca-Cola as an index of the ersatz character of modern civilization.

We now have to deal with Act Five, The Misfit's shooting of the grandmother, an incident that fits in with the desperate and perverse imitation of Christ we have noticed earlier. Having ordered the murder of Bailey Boy, whose unneeded shirt he now wears, The Misfit understandably reminds the dazed and fear-stricken old woman of her son: "Why you're one of my babies," she cries. As she reaches to touch him, The Misfit kills her. To his warped but alert intelligence, the grandmother's embrace represents an ancient threat to his identity. He is not Bailey Boy (the Old Adam), despite the fact that he is wearing Bailey's yellow shirt, decorated with blue parrots to indicate man's animal nature. Wearing the shirt means, emblematically, putting on the flesh, becoming incarnate. This final act of seemingly incomprehensible cruelty recalls Raskolnikov's nausea at his mother's physical approach as well as certain echoes from the Gospels. By killing the old woman—again the reminder of *Crime and Punishment*—The Misfit asserts his spiritual independence from Dame Nature or Mother Earth. He is, emphatically, not one of her babies. Where the alternative to nonadjustment is Bailey Boy, one may agree that man does well to remain a "misfit."

Flannery O'Connor was, it is almost needless to say, an incorrigible allegorist, but one who was wise enough to see, as Hawthorne had, the necessity of rooting allegory in history. Her interpreter needs at the outset, therefore, a good firm grip on the obvious and literal significance of her plots before launching into an analysis of their symbolic aspects. The reader must equally go in fear of seeing too little as of finding too much in often very detailed physical descriptions of character. For example: Are the glasses The Misfit wears a "silent parable" that says in effect, We see through a glass darkly? Wherever such motifs recur through her work, as this one does, the initiate may exercise something like a confident judgment. Although doubtless familiar with the literary methods of Dante and of James Joyce, Miss O'Connor was very much her own writer. An insistence on paradigms, such as the four-fold manner of allegorical interpretation, as the key to her fiction will certainly lead to distortion rather than illumination. Any doctrinaire approach is likely, first of all, to neglect one of the major virtues of her style—the brutal satire one discovers so abundantly in **"A Good Man Is Hard To Find."** One safe rule of allegorical conduct is to remember that the true emblem participates in the reality its meaning temporarily transcends. We see through a glass darkly only where there is real glass, and real darkness.

The blackness that Flannery O'Connor detected in the American soul, and that Hawthorne had found a century before, was in neither case mere literary invention. Despite her indebtedness to Hawthorne, as well as to Kafka and Joyce, she had, however, none of their moral uncertainty, and very little of the psychological insight that would induce such a skepticism. A graver deficiency or limitation of her work is that lifelessness of characterization that Hawthorne recognized as a frequent flaw in his own early productions. As Hawthorne further saw, it was only when the plight of his brainchildren touched their author's heart as well as his moral imagination that they took on the roundness and reality of the living flesh. It is not brilliance of invention one misses in **"A Good Man Is Hard To Find,"** but something of real human dignity and "the mere sensuous sympathy of dust for dust."

Marion Montgomery   (essay date 1968)

SOURCE: "Miss Flannery's 'Good Man'," in *The Denver Quarterly,* Vol. III, No. 3, Autumn, 1968, pp. 1-19.

[*In the following essay, Montgomery explores the spiritual aspects of "A Good Man Is Hard to Find."*]

> *And if Christ is not risen, then is our preaching vain, and your faith is also vain*
>
> > I. Corinthians 15:14

> *I'm going to preach there was no Fall because there was nothing to fall from and no Redemption because there was no Fall and no Judgment because there wasn't the first two. Nothing matters but that Jesus was a liar.*
>
> > Hazel Motes, in *Wise Blood*

> *The Dragon is by the side of the road, watching those who pass. Beware lest he devour you. We go to the Father of Souls, but it is necessary to pass by the Dragon.*
>
> > Epigram to **"A Good Man Is Hard to Find,"** from St. Cyril of Jerusalem

In an interview at the Vanderbilt Literary Symposium in April, 1959, speaking of the technical difficulties she had as a fiction writer, given the handicap that is hers as a Christian writer, Flannery O'Connor remarked:

> I think it is easier to come out with something that is

negative because it is just nearer fallen nature. You have to strain for the other, strenuously, too.

The positive "other" is, specifically, the terror of mercy, which is what she builds toward as the denouement of a story, choosing to start with the "something negative" that she associates with man's fallen nature. On her skillful uses of fallen nature, it is a tribute to her art, though a particularly narrow-lensed one, when Professor Oscar Cargill says in a memorial statement that she "reported faithfully the message life of her region and its obvious social decay because these were the things her wide-angled lens took in." Thus, her use of "fallen nature" seems a species of "naturalism."

On the whole, Cargill's plumbing of Flannery O'Connor's fiction is on the same level as that of a housewife I know who, after reading **"A Good Man Is Hard to Find,"** swore never again to feed her infant from a babyfood jar because of the repulsively effective description in the story. Flannery O'Connor is no Erskine Caldwell nor James T. Farrell, as most of her readers are now prepared to admit. She does not account for evil through naturalism, with its implications of man's rescue from misfortune through education or rehabilitation within behaviorist and environmental programs. She repeatedly rejects evil as historical accident, insisting that evil's hideousness is truly seen only in relation to another grotesqueness that carries its horror too. As she writes in her "Introduction" to *A Memoir of Mary Ann,* "Few have stared at [good] long enough to accept the fact that its face too is grotesque, that in us the good is something under construction." The shocking aspect of that second horror, the good "under construction," is much more difficult to project in art than its absence; for the objectively acceptable existence of that implacable "terrible mercy" that Tarwater, in *The Violent Bear It Away,* announces, is suspect to contemporary audiences. Ours is an age, as Flannery O'Connor repeatedly indicates, that tends to see life as only temporal and transient, we being more concerned with saving our bodily lives on the highway than with rescuing the spirit which in her view mere accident cannot destroy. Yet that sharp division of our world which Jacques Maritain calls Manicheian provides Miss O'Connor her ironic materials. Just what those materials are, Maritain can help us see. Having lost what, in *The Peasant of the Garonne,* he calls the "pre-philosophy of common sense," we are given over to an abandonment of an accumulated wisdom that grew out of that common sense. The modern world's philosophers would make us "hear the plantiff ballade of a being which is not being and a knowledge which is not knowledge," until finally "What such a world can offer is the magnificent ersatz of the science of Phenomena, and along with it, power over matter; a dream of complete domination of all visible things (even the invisible) and also the abdication of the human mind, renouncing Truth for Verification, Reality for Sign."

Thus speaks the Thomist philosopher. To say the same thing, Miss O'Connor writes **"The Life You Save May Be Your Own,"** starting from that marvelously ironic National Safety Council slogan. Through Mr. Shiftlet's reflections on the skill of science in revealing the "invisible," she displays the falseness of our supposed domination of the invisible.

> "There's one of these doctors in Atlanta that's taken a knife and cut the human heart—the human heart . . . out of a man's chest and held it in his hand," and he held his hand out, palm up, as if it were slightly weighted with the human heart, ". . . and lady, . . . he don't know no more about it than you or me."

Signs are indeed taken for wonders, signifying only further signs. The "pre-philosophy of common sense" in such people as Mr. Shiftlet, and Flannery O'Connor herself, might well make the one protest and the other chuckle at the latest of our spectacular exhibits of life saving, the heart transplant.

Mr. Shiftlet would protest the new presumption of putting a new motor in an old chassis, while doing just that if occasion arose to his benefit. Miss O'Connor would be interested in both but disturbed by neither. In resolving this distinction between her reaction and a Shiftlet's lies the clue to the problem of Miss O'Connor's use of the devil and his works, part of the negative from which she makes her positive vision. Now the suspicion is abroad, directly stated to her by John Hawkes, that Miss O'Connor is on the devil's side. (She denied it emphatically.)

Let us say rather that, true to her understanding of herself as made in the image of God, she attempts through her talents to bring good out of evil through her creations. As artist, she is detached. But it is a detachment neither out of Hawthorne's "fastidiousness" (the word and application are Flannery O'Connor's) nor with that grand indifference in the name of art that Stephen Dedalus proposes. Hers is rather a recognition of the dangers to the artist of directly attempting a construction of the good. "What is written to edify," she says in the "Introduction" to *A Memoir of Mary Ann*, "usually ends by amusing." She means that such a work amuses through its failure as art. For whereas the philosopher such as St. Thomas Aquinas, in whose tradition Miss O'Connor writes, defines evil as it has reference to a good already defined (that is, evil as a deprivation, a negative), the artist starts with the complicated reality of the world in which the negative is more immediately arresting. The existence of a petty con man such as Mr. Shiftlet, or of an escaped murderer such as the Misfit terrifying the populace, strikes the reader as both immediate and dramatic, two appropriate considerations to the fiction writer. The writer who does not choose to "strain" himself "strenuously" in pursuit of that grotesque called the good is tempted to an easy reliance on homiletics or allegory in treating the facts of his own encounters with the world, such as con men and murderers. But the time for such homiletics is out of joint.

Since there is no myth to which a modern literary audience gives a general consent of faith, the uses to which allegory may be put by the modern writer seem to allow only the pleasures of correspondence. That is, allegories such as Faulkner's *Fable* or Updike's *Centaur* are of interest to the extent of their being perfected and self-contained metaphors. And even so, that concession to the "poetic" by the modern mind has been tenuously possible to the artist only through the persuasiveness of Coleridge's appeal to our suspension of disbelief. Meanwhile, we witness a widening of the gap between poet and audience, between poetry and what his potential, reluctant audience calls "real life." This is the history of the poet in society, since the eighteenth century at least. The visionary reality which Dante praises in his allegory is of scant importance to the modern world, which is why we tend to justify a reading of him as an entertainment of the mind separate from any reality of spirit, particularly in that anagogic dimension. (As psychological reality, well enough, but save us from the spiritual!) Occasionally as with Eliot there is a progression toward Dante's high reality, from Prufrock's teaparty to the *Cocktail Party*.

But Miss O'Connor chooses to approach her vision not through allegory such as Dante's (noting Hawthorne's failures) nor through the metaphor's command of intellect such as Eliot's (Eliot's approach turned his audience more to the academy than to the church). She chooses to keep fiction anchored in the literal world throughout. Her pilgrims remain in those dark woods which is Dante's starting point. It is increasingly apparent from her work that she was very conscious of the difficulties she faced in a modern audience, in contrast to Sophocles' audience or Dante's. Her letters and essays are full of that awareness, as Robert Fitzgerald illustrates in his introduction to *Everything That Rises Must Converge,* but one may see it subtly present in the comic version she presents of Dante and Virgil's descent into Hell, **"The Artificial Nigger."** She is remarkable in her art for her ability to transfer Dante's distorted souls out of their eternal static condition in Hell and make them believable in the dark pine woods of Georgia or even in the streets of Atlanta. The mark of her success is that a reader does not have to set aside his disbelief. That this is a stratagem through which "naturalism" is enlarged toward a spiritual dimension is apparent to one who analyzes her imagery in relation to Dante's, particularly her use of the pine woods, the sky, the sun, or the *Hell* images and movements in such a story as **"The Artificial Nigger."** Her intention is not like Rilke's—to change the nature of her reader through art; it is, rather, like Dante's—to lead him toward a state of bliss.

Miss O'Connor's procedure is to start with her negatives and remove from them all modern justifications of evil as an accident of existence. And who may better defend himself as more real than accident than the prince of active perversion? And in the absence of a common belief or even a common myth, how better than through the most basic common denominator of natural fallen man, the latent "pre-philosophy of common sense"? It is precisely this natural gift that is the effective weapon of the Bible salesman in **"Good Country People"** when he gets the better of that female Ph.D devoted intellectually to "the plaintive ballade of a being which is not being." It is Shiftlet's gift and Greenleaf's and Rufus Johnson's, and that of the city boys in **"A Circle of Fire."** And of course it is a gift almost perfect in its negation in the figure of the Misfit.

What these characters from Miss O'Connor's fiction have in common is an element of the diabolic. Miss O'Connor tells us that her reader "will find that the devil accomplishes a good deal of ground work that seems to be necessary before grace is effective." Grace, about which much has been written in relation to Miss O'Connor's fiction, becomes operative when that groundwork is finished. "Those moments . . . are prepared for—by me anyway—by the intensity of the evil circumstances." Grace touches her fiction with a mystery difficult to explicate, but clearly at points in a story that we would call technically a climax. It does so with an *implication* of the possibility of good, which she leaves suspended as only possibility. (Whether Tarwater successfully escapes Hell as he goes about waking the children of God is an open question.) The result is that one has the use of epiphany in her stories with a meaning at once given to the reader by Joyce and given to mankind by the New Testament. For if she insists on the real and actively malign presence of a particular evil in the world dedicated to man's destruction through a willing perversion of common sense, even more she insists upon a real and actively healing intervention of grace in the presence of that same common sense when it wilfully resists its own perversion. When she says that she is interested in the old Adam, who only happens to talk Southern because she is Southern (that is, particularized by a history and geography in which she participates but to which she is not limited) she is stating a battleground in the individual on which meet Christ and Satan.

O'Connor is remarkable in her art for her ability to transfer Dante's distorted souls out of their eternal static condition in Hell and make them believable in the dark pine woods of Georgia or even in the streets of Atlanta.

—Marion Montgomery

The devil she presents in her fiction is the devil Christ came to oppose, made articulate in a world largely given to him. Her devil is not merely a static symbol of evil, of absolute evil such as Dante images at the bottom of his Hell, but active in the world. He is, as she sees him (and as in Milton's intentions in his great fiction), an agent of good though he intends no good. (Milton, too, has been accused of being on the devil's side.) Thus it is that in her fiction her diabolic character repeatedly underlines the fundamental issue she proposes to us. For instance, the Misfit, the devil's surrogate, in **"A Good Man Is Hard to Find,"** is at large in the world, enlarged toward the legendary by his nickname. To the sophisticated reader, the mythical overtones in the figure of the Misfit are increased by the talk of people like Red Sammy and his wife, though the grandmother and her family are at first as unconvinced of any danger as they would have been had Red Sammy talked of a centaur loose in the wood.

The grandmother, it is true, has been the first to introduce the Misfit into the story, from newspaper accounts, but only because she doesn't want to go to Florida, the direction taken by the Misfit in his escape. "I wouldn't take my children in any direction with a criminal like that aloose in it. I wouldn't answer to my conscience if I did." On its first appearance, her argument is on the same level as the one that immediately follows it—that the children have already been to Florida once and might better profit from a trip to Tennessee. But it is a statement that becomes much enlarged upon as we see the grandmother coming finally to face her conscience. One might note also that the Misfit is a self-imposed title, picked up for its sensationalism by the newspapers, who are not likely to allow as more than myth the figure of that ultimate misfit of Christian orthodoxy, Satan. For the present, however, the Misfit is far less demanding of her interest than the cat Pity Sing. Yet the reader is aware through the scene at Red Sammy's "Tower" of ominous overtones, even though the comedy performed by the characters distracts him. A reader's attention to the human antics in the story is tempted to remain on the same level as the children's attention to Red Sammy's monkey, which is still possessed of enough of what Maritain calls the "pre-philosophy of common sense" to climb a tree beyond the reach of June Star and John Wesley.

The comedy of names, in this story as in others, is a calculated delight, though a tricky one. Here, for instance, the children are named for a movie star and that evangelist so important in the history of southern Protestantism. Such playful disparity is suggestive of the spiritual chaos in the world these characters inhabit, a chaos which they more shrewdly see than their elders, as witness their easy manipulation of those elders, accompanied by ill manners. That chaos, particularly spiritual chaos, as a concern of the story is thus underlined. But there are more subtle implications of names and the particulars of time and place that call for attention. It is almost noon as the family stops for lunch, and Red Sammy's Tower is "just outside Timothy." One cannot but remark Paul's words *in* Timothy, concerning the "last days" which the Grandmother and Red Sammy agree are descending upon us:

> . . . perilous times shall come. For men shall be lovers of their own selves, covetous, boasters, proud, blasphemers, disobedient to parents, unthankful, unholy,
>
> Without natural affection, truce-breakers, false accusers, incontinent, fierce, despisers of those that are good,
>
> Traitors, heady, highminded, lovers of pleasures more than lovers of God; Having a form of godliness, but denying the power thereof. (Chapter 3, verses 1-5)

The comic correspondences in the story to this passage are remarkable, but they are also deadly serious, carrying in them that voice of prophecy which Miss O'Connor saw as suitable to the poet and fiction writer. For if she takes an impish delight in private jokes, as when she calls Atlanta "Taulkinham" in *Wise Blood,* those jokes become less than private and certainly more than jokes as one penetrates the stories. Concerning the comedy of prophecy she herself remarks: "There is the prophetic sense of 'seeing through' reality and there is the prophetic function of recalling people to known but ignored truths. Certainly none of these precludes Comedy—" And just as certainly, the serious commitment of Paul, that New Testament Misfit, buttresses this story. Rather innocently, then, the reader laughs at the comedy of the grandmother asking her son to dance with her to *The Tennessee Waltz* or at June Star's ugly exchange with Red Sammy's wife, who in turn takes a caustically dim view of Red Sammy's estimate of himself as a good man.

A few pages later one's attention is seized away from the comedy of the automobile accident by the appearance of "a big black battered hearse-like automobile." The description seems to promise more than we are at first given. When we are at first directly confronted by the Misfit he seems unusual, but hardly deserving of the newspaper's honorific article. (He is *the* Misfit and Miss O'Connor sometimes in her letters calls him "The Misfit".) He is an "older man" whose hair is "just beginning to gray." His silver-rimmed spectacles give him a "scholarly look," a suggestion at first comic since he has on no clothes except bluejeans that are too small for him and sockless shoes. In one hand he politely carries a black hat. But the smile a reader is tempted to is a tentative one: in the other hand he has a gun. Even so, this is hardly a startling or impressive figuring of the old dragon as the Misfit stands looking down from the roadside at his victims in this Georgia bolge. The uneasy concern the grandmother exhibits in trying to save her life has, at this point, only mild spiritual overtones. She nevertheless has "the peculiar feeling that the bespectacled man was somehow someone she knew. His face was as familiar to her as if she had known him all her life but she could not recall who he was."

Indeed, one of the most unsettling aspects of the Misfit is his manners, which contradict the legend out of the newspapers. He has removed his hat in the presence of the two ladies, and he continues most polite as he directs the multiple executions. ("Lady, . . . would you and that little girl like to step off yonder with Bobby Lee and Hiram and join your husband? . . . Hep that lady up, Hiram.") As his manners are praiseworthy, so too is he resolute for the truth. Unlike the old woman's son Bailey, he pays close attention to what she says, treating her as a person worthy of attention, as no other character in the story does. Initially the grandmother cries excitedly "We turned over twice!" He corrects her: "Oncet . . . we seen it happen." From this point on he attempts with great care to keep the record straight. (He is a believer in records: society "had the papers" on him.) Patiently he rejects the modern excuses for that record of evil that is his, excuses which the grandmother proposes desperately in an attempt to save her life. But he will not allow her to excuse his hideousness by admitting, as Red Sammy has earlier managed to do so transparently, that he is a good man. Nor is his wickedness to be explained as his having fallen on bad luck, the victim of society's mistakes and so a fit candidate for the mercies of the sociologist or psychologist or

psychiatrist. Speaking with an evenness of tone throughout, as if with an immortal pain, he shows that he is something more ominous than simply an escaped killer.

The basic point which The Misfit insists upon is that "Jesus thown everything off balance."

> "If He did what He said [i.e., raised the dead, including Himself], then it's nothing for you to do but thow away everything and follow Him, and if He didn't, then it's nothing for you to do but enjoy the few minutes you got left the best way you can—by killing somebody or burning down his house or doing some other meanness to him. No pleasure but meanness . . ."

One might set beside the Misfit's argument one from a book by C. S. Lewis, *The Problem of Pain,* (in which book he considers the problem Miss O'Connor addresses so cogently in her "Introduction" to *A Memoir of Mary Ann*):

> There was a man born among these Jews who claimed to be, or to be the son of, or to be "one with," the Something which is at once the awful haunter of nature and the giver of moral law. The claim is so shocking—a paradox, and even a horror, which we may easily be lulled into taking too lightly—that only two views of this man are possible. Either he was a raving lunatic of an unusually abominable type, or else He was, and is, precisely what He said. There is no middle way.

C. S. Lewis and Flannery O'Connor affirm that He is what He said. The grandmother *says* Christ was what He said He was. But one knows already from her own duplicity in trying to turn the trip north instead of south, and her "treachery" to her son Bailey in smuggling the cat Pity Sing along, that her words are no more dependable than her affections. Her entertainment of the children, including her anecdotes and jokes, are empty rituals such as are historically expected of a grandmother. In short, the grandmother's position is one in which we see that her manners are without substance, a revelation that comes to her also in the last instance. And one must conclude that, unless one take "meanness" to be exhibited only through such physical acts as the Misfit catalogues, the grandmother's whole family is devoted only to meanness. That their meanness is exhibited in petty acts of rudeness against each other and the strangers encountered does not obscure its corrosive presence, which has an effect in the story of conjuring up the devil. What one begins to see is that the Misfit is apparently not unlike the grandmother and her family, but that his similarity is at first obscured by his polite manners and his scrupulous insistence upon being honest about his condition.

Because he was not there when Christ raised the dead, the Misfit can act only as if Christ were one historical man. That is, he assumes Christ a lunatic. "Listen Lady," he says, "if I had of been there I would know and I wouldn't be like I am now," being out of his misery either because dead in history or alive in Christ. Cursed by his scholarly awareness of alternatives and so unable to act upon what

Lewis calls the "horror" of that "shocking paradox" of God made man, he reacts, turning downward. The Misfit has made himself indeed "a lunatic of an unusually abominable type," whose ultimate figuring is the antithesis of the Son of Light.

The root meaning of *abominable,* a word Lewis carefully chooses, with its Biblical uses relative to outer darkness, makes it an apt description of the Misfit. His words, setting the alternatives to which there is no middle way, come at the very instant the grandmother recognizes just what an ill omen he is. At first she has thought him familiar through the newspaper accounts of him; now at the moment of her death, she sees through him the dark abyss and must conclude, as Miss O'Connor would have us conclude, that the devil is not simply a metaphor for an adornment of fiction, whether that in a story by Miss O'Connor or a story in an Atlanta paper, which prefers the term *The Misfit* to apply only on a social level. The devil's active pursuit of non-being is no gimmick to facilitate an illusion of action in Miss O'Connor's story. He turns out also to be more than a sentimental naming of evil in a natural or social environmentalist philosophy, through which we prefer to pursue a state of innocence. She insists that

> We lost our innocence in the fall of our first parents, and our return to it is through the redemption which was brought about by Christ's death and by our slow participation in it. Sentimentality is a skipping of the process in its concrete reality and an early arrival at a mock state of innocence which strongly suggests its opposite.

Evil exists, and in its pained torment cannot do otherwise than put things directly in antithetic action to good, between which there is no middle way despite the illusion which sentimentality provides as alternative. Our pretense grows in the circumstance of these "last days" such as St. Paul spoke of in *Timothy,* in which we are overcome by what Maritain calls that "magnificent ersatz of the science of Phenomena" whose spectacle overwhelms our common sense till we renounce "Truth for Verification, Reality for Sign."

Insofar as evil is presented as an absolute negation, it expresses a more shocking Manicheism than the comfortable, sentimental devotees to secular phenomena can tolerate. In man, to be hypocritical is to attempt to substitute a lesser for a greater good so that one may rest comfortably in the substitution by a deliberate refusal of reason to employ common sense. It is a false means toward a false end. But the devil's hypocrisy does not involve self-deception as does man's; it is a means toward wilfully and knowingly making the lesser the greater, the ancient stratagem in the conflict with Light. The devil, of necessity, is a confirmed Manicheian. To set the alternatives boldly before the unthinking is effective if, as with Hawthorne's sentimental Goodman Brown, both good and evil are rejected. For the devil enjoys a singular triumph in that conversion, being the prince of negation.

In this light, we may at last see just how shocking the grandmother's final words to the Misfit truly are. When she says "Why you're one of my own babies. You're one of my own children," she has reached an extremity of attempts to save her life through denial. (She specifically denies Christ.) At this point there is a glimmer of recognition of her failure. And for the first time in the story there is coming into existence a being at once repulsive to and frightening to the force of evil. When she says the words, touching the Misfit's arm, he draws back in terror "as if a snake had bitten him" and then shoots her "three times through the chest." Whether that dawning recognition of participation in evil, through grace which enters the story to lift the scales from the grandmother's eyes, is sufficient to rescue the grandmother is perhaps a moot question, beyond our concern as is Tarwater's subsequent history after his terrifying experience with another of the agents of darkness. As Miss O'Connor says, "Judgment is separate from vision" as God is separate from man, and the grandmother's visionary reaction to the Misfit is here the center of our concern.

Miss O'Connor, while she avoids strict allegory, is constantly hinting at analogue. Hers is not a formal, point by point structural use, such as Joyce's in *Ulysses.* Her suggestiveness, through the careful selection of details, gives her fiction a continuity out of Biblical history. Thus in **"A Good Man Is Hard to Find"** one is taken back to man's first disobedience, and to the first fruits of that disobedience as presented in the third and fourth chapters of Genesis. For if one consider the grandmother here in her aspect as The Grandmother (that is, as Eve [i.e., the "mother of all living" Genesis 3:20]) as we have considered the misfit as The Misfit (that is, as Satan), interesting overtones result from the details. The Misfit bears the mark of Cain (on the level of the story in which the literal murder is, he is, as I have said, the devil's surrogate). Cain is the child of Eve's ambition. For wishing to be equal to the gods through a knowledge of good and evil, she gained not an equality but a limited specialization for mankind. The gods, as the serpent presents the case in Genesis, have the power of life and death. Man through his fall gains the power of death in an absolute sense, that of negation. Its first fruit is the death of Abel, out of that incurable questioning of the gods. In our story the Misfit, the questioning child of Eve, recalls his father (of the generation of the grandmother, by the way) who recognized his particular curse:

> ". . . Daddy said, 'It's some that can live their whole life out without asking about it and it's others has to know why it is, and this boy is one of the latters.'"

His father has called him "a different breed of dog" from his brothers and sisters. Miss O'Connor's wit may also be involved in this respect in the minor character of the child John Wesley, named after the Protestant evangelist to Georgia. The child is described as if a miniature version of The Misfit. Like the Misfit, he wears glasses, but more important he is interested in getting behind the appearance of things. When the grandmother builds her false Eden, the old mansion with its rose arbors, out of her childhood,

John Wesley begins to plunder it in his imagination, getting into its secret passages. The grandmother's false Eden is also conjured again in her vain attempt to save her life, in her arguments for the Misfit's innocence, the plea that he might settle down somewhere "and have a comfortable life and not have to think about somebody chasing you all the time." But the Misfit knows that, as God told Cain, he is destined to be "a fugitive and a vagabond . . . in the earth." Even the Misfit's words, against calling on Jesus for help ("I don't need no hep") are an inversion of Cain's "Am I my brother's keeper." And he knows too that "Everyone that findeth me shall slay me." Thus to prolong his misery that seems to be life he must destroy these witnesses of a chance encounter. The grandmother's false version of Eden is, I take it, changed by the time of her death. That is, she comes to see that Eden cannot be regained, but also that she is responsible for its loss. That is part of what happens as the Misfit puts on Bailey's yellow shirt, with the bright blue parrots. (The popular American version of Eden is usually thought of as off Florida's coast.) At first the grandmother "couldn't name what the shirt reminded her of." But it clearly reminds her of much more than simply her son Bailey when she reaches out to touch the Misfit and says "Why you're one of my babies! You're one of my own children!" We are all the children of Adam and the parents of both Cain and Abel. To acknowledge Cain is a first step toward that place where the soul may settle down and not worry about somebody chasing it all the time.

In any event, we may make one final observation about the mystery that settles upon the story. We do notice that our final image of the grandmother, seen through the eyes of the gunmen, is that she

> half sat and half lay in a puddle of blood with her legs crossed under her like a child's and her face smiling up at a cloudless sky.

It is a picture of innocence in bodily death and suggests a victory the three gunmen are excluded from understanding. And we notice that the colloquy between the grandmother and the Misfit that climaxes with her death carries itself through a distorted version of the confessional, in which the grandmother occupies the role of priest, with the Misfit as penitent. She literally stands above him during the crucial exchange. The story is in the beginning deliberately comic (the comic irony residing in the pretended measure of the true by the false characters): the characters in the first part of the story say generally true words to which they are not committed, as in the grandmother's first arguments against going to Florida and Red Sammy's analysis of the decline of civilization. The forms necessary to the comic continue in that final examination of evil, with the grandmother intent upon explaining away evil, while the Misfit clings insistently to his evil as his own. It is only at the moment of climax that the grandmother recognizes her own participation in evil, with the beginnings of an entry into what in the final words of another story is called "the world of guilt and sorrow."

The story's climactic scene then is a black confessional, analogues to Hawthorne's black mass, but acted out under the full sun rather than in Goodman Brown's dream of a night confrontation with the devil. Neither the Misfit nor the grandmother looks up to discover the sun they both state as missing from the sky, though in the grandmother's final posture, the sun shines full upon her face. When the grandmother makes her gesture of hand and words to acknowledge her estate, the roles become reversed. It is an act freely made by her, a sacrifice on which point Miss O'Connor once said:

> My view of free will follows traditional Catholic teaching. I don't think any genuine novelist is interested in writing about a world of people who are strictly determined. Even if he writes about characters who are mostly unfree, it is the sudden free action, the open possibility, which he knows is the only thing capable of illuminating the picture and giving life. So that while predictable predetermined actions have a comic interest for me, it is the free act, the acceptance of grace particularly, that I always have my eye on as a thing which will make the story work. In the story **"A Good Man Is Hard to Find,"** it is the grandmother's recognition that the Misfit is one of her children.

The Misfit, on the other hand, as if fearing exorcism, leaps back from that recognition and shoots the grandmother. If in the tragic, one has a reverse of the comic, that is if one has a measure of the false by the true (the aspect we call tragic irony), then we may see triumph in that final picture of the grandmother sitting like a child, smiling up into a cloudless sky. For either the Misfit is right that Christ was a fake, and hence the grandmother's death carries no meaning beyond the fact that she has reached the end of what the Misfit calls "the few minutes" allowed natural man. Or the grandmother's arguments about Christ are true, even when not truly taken by her until by implication in her last moment. If Christ was what He said, we see the tragedy of waste in the lives of the characters of this story. And we see also the appropriateness of our attention being turned back to the Misfit in the final sentences of the story. He is that agent of evil which, in a Christian reading of tragedy, is the cause of all tragedy. We may conclude from the skill with which Miss O'Connor manages her conclusion something of what she meant when she said, in acknowledging her kinship to Hawthorne, that she writes "tales" in the sense Hawthorne wrote them, though she trusts she does so "with less reliance on allegory." The Misfit's final position, like Goodman Brown's, is maintained in emptiness. But there is not even bitterness in his final word, only what I have called an immortal pain in that worldly darkness as immediately present as pine trees and a bright blue cloudless sky. So long as one inhabits this world only, "It's no real pleasure in life."

Josephine Hendin (essay date 1970)

SOURCE: "Flannery O'Connor and Southern Literature," in *The World of Flannery O'Connor*, Indiana University Press, 1970, pp. 147-51.

[*Hendin is an American educator and critic. In the fol-*

lowing excerpt, she compares The Misfit to other violent characters in Southern literature.]

While, from a statistical point of view considering annual income, national origin, and religion, some of O'Connor's heroes could wander into [Faulkner's fictional setting of] Yoknapatawpha, one senses they would find it totally alien. Faulkner and Styron build their countries out of the South's greatest literary virtue: its ability to lag behind the rest of America in giving up the romantic sense of the hero and of history. O'Connor and Capote have abandoned the South's most distinctive concerns. Whether by choice or default, they write out of the mainstream of the American consciousness, In their murder scenes, a framework of meaning, if it exists at all, has receded into so remote a distance that it provides no scale of value. While [Faulkner's] Christmas and [Styron's] Turner transcend a life of ambivalence and ambiguity, make of their murders and death a resolution of significance to them and to us, the fate of [O'Connor's] the Misfit and Motes, of [Capote's] Smith and Hickock, remains irrelevant in a larger sense, even to them.

Smith, Motes, and the Misfit can connect nothing with nothing. They are so estranged from themselves, so out of touch with their own feelings that they only know them from external signs or infer them from their own actions. Like the Misfit who speaks most honestly with his gun, or Motes, whose most potent part is his car, they come closest to connecting with objects, things which magically fulfill their fantasies of destruction. Looming about O'Connor's vivid acts of violence is an immense and total silence. It is the silence that engulfs the Misfit's polite speech as he shoots the grandmother. It is in this silence that Flannery O'Connor becomes most eloquent. Like a painter with a genius for using negative space, O'Connor says most about human feeling when she says nothing. In both her murder scenes it is what is left out that says most.

O'Connor clearly intended **"A Good Man Is Hard to Find"** to *be* tragedy and *Wise Blood* to burlesque it. But the two are oddly alike. Missing in both is a sense of human death, human life or directly felt passion. Both the story and novel convey a feeling of undifferentiated life—of there being few distinctions between living and dying. O'Connor conveys a sense of consuming meaninglessness. If Faulkner was obsessed with the power of memory, the power that let Virginia Du Pre make myths, O'Connor is obsessed with the power of forgetfulness. As the Misfit observes, "you can do one thing or you can do another, kill a man or take a tire off his car, because sooner or later you're going to forget what it was you done and just be punished for it." He cannot remember his own crime because "they never shown me my papers."

Like Motes's Essex, the Misfit's papers, kept by the Authorities, would explain why he was imprisoned, would anchor him to reality and give some direction to a mind that gropes to make his crime—which he has forgotten—equal his punishment—which seems to be his life. Although the Misfit thinks a lot about the Authorities and even the miracles of Christ, what he affirms is not the existence or nonexistence of either. He affirms the sameness of all events, the difficulty of telling the difference between murdering a man or stealing his tire. Where the deaths of Christmas and Margaret float endlessly significant, no death has much meaning for the Misfit.

What frees the Misfit from total emptiness is his gun. Solid and enduring in his otherwise blank universe, the gun expresses the Misfit's unfathomable rage. Its "voice" is far more authentic than the polite phrases he uses to address the family before he has them exterminated. The gun is his most "animal" part, a potent extension of himself. When the grandmother touches him, her touch is like a snakebite. And for the first time in this story where he has behaved like the politest of backwoods gentlemen, he answers that snakebite touch with an instinctual, immediate gunshot.

> **Looming about O'Connor's vivid acts of violence is an immense and total silence. It is the silence that engulfs the Misfit's polite speech as he shoots the grandmother. It is in this silence that Flannery O'Connor becomes most eloquent.**
>
> **—*Josephine Hendin***

The grandmother's gesture of "tenderness"—her claim that he is one of her babies—is ambiguous and ironic. All her babies that we know of are dead, killed, in a sense, by her own manipulation of their trip and her desire to keep their wills infantile and subjected to her own. In likening him to one of her dead babies, she may be reminding him of his own mortality. Her tenderness diminishes, infantilizes him, minimizing his power as a murderer. Suggesting that he is as helpless as a baby, she implies that she can somehow cure his misery like Asbury's mother in "The Enduring Chill," who convinces her son that she can overpower death. She resembles all those indefatigably optimistic, powerful mothers in O'Connor's fiction. Sitting in her blood like a smiling child, she seems an earlier Mrs. Chestny who has spent her life looking for the past and reverts to her childhood in death. At a moment when she is surely the Misfit's victim, as Mrs. Chestny was the victim of the Negro woman's "emancipation," she tries to be his redeemer. Like Mrs. Chestny, who tried to put the Negro woman in her place with a bright new penny, the grandmother tries to buy off the Misfit's revenge with a gesture. Like Mrs. Chestny, she is attacked in the heart, shot three times in the chest. Although the Misfit's voice is on the verge of breaking as he laments his absence at the miracles of Christ—perhaps he cries as his red-rimmed eyes imply—he shoots her quickly and, cleaning his glasses, restores his perspective on life as he orders her thrown with the other bodies.

O'Connor probably intended her Misfit hero to be a kind of Christ. But the grandmother who tries to be his mother also tries to be his redeemer, his Christ. Beneath the veneer of kindness and gentility, it is clear that these two Christs are crucifying *each other*. The most powerful crucifixion for O'Connor is the one you live out daily for a lifetime, the constant agony involved in human contact, human needs, and human striving. It is, in large part, the agony of being part of the human chain, of having a grandmother who wants to "care" for you. For O'Connor, it is the horror she sees at the core of family life. Almost predictably, the only one who can survive this family outing is the cat, Pitty Sing, who rubs herself pleasurably against the Misfit's leg.

A cause of the accident and the murders, the cat who jumps when the grandmother moves her knees, jumps at random. The cat is too slender a figure to carry much symbolic weight. The cat's leap is not one that seems the result of an accumulation of history or of a lifetime of mingled hatred and desire. It seems no expression of some ultimate cosmic force. The meaning of the cat seems to derive precisely from its symbolic thinness. That a pet, a cat, leaping at random for no great reason, should cause the destruction of an entire family expresses the randomness, the pointlessness of the murders. That the cat's name is Pitty Sing suggests O'Connor's attitude toward violence. In the *Mikado,* it is Pitti Sing who remarks in a sprightly way, "Well, dear, it can't be denied that the fact that your husband is to be beheaded in a month does seem to take the top off it, you know." It does indeed.

Like O'Connor, Pitti Sing sings without pity, a precursor of doom without human compassion. The murders in **"A Good Man Is Hard to Find"** are of no particular importance to the cat, or to the Misfit. They are not the stuff romantic legends are made of. Only a cat and a Misfit survive the human wreck as detached observers of the scene.

C. R. Kropf (essay date 1972)

SOURCE: "Theme and Setting in 'A Good Man Is Hard to Find'," in *Renascence,* Vol. XXIV, No. 4, Summer, 1972, pp. 177-80, 206.

[In the following essay, Kropf surveys the major themes of "A Good Man Is Hard to Find."]

The Criticism of Flannery O'Connor's work has failed to throw any considerable light on one of her most popular stories, **"A Good Man Is Hard to Find."** To a large extent critics of Miss O'Connor have been preoccupied with the religious meaning of her symbols and the relation of her stories to Catholic doctrine. To a degree such a preoccupation is obviously valid; Miss O'Connor's own comments in "The Fiction Writer and His Country" to the effect that "I see from the standpoint of Christian orthodoxy" have encouraged commentators on her works to bring to their task the assumption, rarely qualified or ex-

plained, that as Thomas A. Lorch has written "Flannery O'Connor was a Catholic writer, and she expressed her religious vision in her art" [*Critique,* 1968]. The reader of such criticism, however, is led to the unfortunate conclusion that her religious vision is all that Miss O'Connor's art contains. This specialized doctrinaire approach I take to be responsible for the critical failure to appreciate the complexity of Miss O'Connor's artistic achievement in her works as a whole, and in **"A Good Man"** in particular, which as the title story of the volume in which it appears would seem to have been high in Miss O'Connor's regard. For this and other reasons which will appear in the following discussion, it lends itself especially well to a broader sort of critical analysis I believe could be used to advantage to supplement the standard doctrinaire approach.

The critical pronouncements on **"A Good Man"** are a good example of the limitations of an excessively specialized approach. Commentaries always deal primarily with the final scene or the final conversation in the story, one between a psychotic killer and a preoccupied grandmother, neither of whom is in very firm contact with reality. The final scene is no doubt a crucial one, but the story is full of vivid details for which such discussions fail to account. The riot of carefully described color, the numerous events before the final one, the trite anecdotes Grandmother tells, the presence of Red Sammy Butts all pass unmentioned as the typical critic hastens on to unfold the religious implications of the final scene. Miss O'Connor's working methods and her advice to young writers would suggest that more attention to details is justifiable. She advised aspiring young authors of fiction that a good author "makes his statements by selection, and if he is any good, he selects every word for a reason, every detail for a reason, every incident for a reason, and arranges them in a certain time-sequence for a reason." And later in the same address, recently reprinted in *Mystery and Manners,* she asserted that detail "has to be controlled by some overall purpose, and every detail has to be put to work for you."

If Miss O'Connor's theory bears any relation to her practice, critical attention to details is likely to furnish significant clues to the broader concerns of theme and structure in her stories, and at least in the case of **"A Good Man"** the setting appears to be one of the important details. Miss O'Connor's remarks to an audience at Hollins College at a reading of **"A Good Man"** imply that the setting deserves more than casual attention. This story, she said, "certainly calls up a good deal of the South's mythic background, and it should elicit from you a degree of pity and terror, even though its way of being serious is a comic one." She then goes on to associate this mythic background with her religious concerns by remarking that the assumptions underlying the story "are those of the central Christian mysteries." The combination of Southern history with religious matters recalls a similar comment Miss O'Connor made on another occasion in a discussion of the position of the Southern author. The Civil War in Southern history, she suggests, is analogous to the Fall of Adam in human history, and the Southern author is "doubly blessed, not only in our Fall, but in having a means to interpret it," provided by the South's strong Christian tradition. The association on both of these occasions of Southern history with the Christian mysteries indicates that the two were blended in Miss O'Connor's thinking and in her fiction, a fact Robert Drake implies when he writes that "literally rural Georgia was Miss O'Connor's true country, man's encounter with Jesus Christ her true story." In other words one cannot separate the religious theme of her works from their Southern setting and its historical implications without the risk of seeing only a part of the meaning of her stories. Only if the critic draws on both of these traditions can he appreciate the extent to which, as Caroline Gordon has remarked in "Heresy in Dixie," "her stories are soundly constructed," or see her as an artist instead of a knowledgeable Catholic [*Sewanee Review,* 1968]. The synthesis of Christian morality and Southern myth so that the two comment upon each other appears to inform nearly all of her works, but it dominates **"A Good Man"** and is the theme itself of the story. To that extent **"A Good Man"** is a thematic statement of what Miss O'Connor tried to achieve in her art.

Early in **"A Good Man"** it becomes clear that Grandmother and her family are at odds over more than superficial opinions. While the family wants to visit Florida, a desire typical of modern middle-class Americans, Grandmother wants to visit her "connections" in Tennessee. The family dresses casually for the trip, but Grandmother dresses like "a lady" and insists that things were not like this in the old days. She has the inevitable story of the wealthy suitor who has grown rich on the inevitable Coca-Cola stock and whose trite gift of a watermelon is mistakenly consumed by the inevitable ignorant servant boy. Her allusion to *Gone with the Wind,* the official handbook of ante-bellum myths, and her reaction to the grinding poverty of the Negro family as a pretty picture all mark her as one who is attracted by and would gladly return to the mythic past. The antagonism between Grandmother and the family goes much deeper than matters of dress and children's respect for their elders; it extends to values. She agrees with Red Sammy Butts on the deplorable state of morality while the modern family remains apathetically silent, and she maintains all the prim and proper concerns of conventional morality. She laments, in Miss O'Connor's terms, the loss of that prelapsarian innocence so obviously missing in present society and so easily attributed to the mythic past.

The conflict between the past and present, and metaphorically between the values they represent, becomes more overt when in the midst of its typically modern activity the family is interrupted by Grandmother's idealized recollection of a plantation house with all the appropriate trimmings of columns, towering oaks, arbors, garden, and suitor. With the aid of a carefully placed lie, the past, in the form of Grandmother, wins. Bailey must turn around both literally and figuratively, backtrack, and leave the modern paved highway for a little-traveled dirt road. The symbolic interpretation of these events as a turning away from the present and toward the past is inescapable in light of the conflict the author has carefully set up previous to their occurrence. That the past to which the old

lady is trying to return is largely mythical is indicated by the fact that the house, its six columns corresponding to the six occupants of the car, is not there.

Up to this point **"A Good Man"** is similar in theme to **"A Late Encounter with the Enemy"** in which Sally Poker Sash blindly regards her grandfather, a lecherous and senile Confederate Veteran, as a symbol of the past and its values. In **"A Good Man"** the old lady is not only blind to the evils of the past; she attributes to it virtues which, Miss O'Connor implies, it never had. The conclusion of the story suggests that the attempt to live in an idealized past leads to death and destruction, and this conclusion the author prepares us for by the careful selection of detail. Grandmother is a confused and exasperating character, but she is not evil; she is certainly not to be regarded as the witch (complete with cat) some readers had supposed her to be, much to the author's amusement. What the old lady believes and stands for, however, is clearly ominous; it is the function of Red Sammy Butts in the story to identify it as such. The ironic title phrase "a good man (woman)" is applied only to Red Sammy, Grandmother, and the Misfit; the color red is associated only with them; and all three are linked with animals. All three of these details first appear together in the visit to Red Sammy's. It is a visit with a devil figure in a metaphorical hell. Red Sammy lives in a Tower, reminiscent of the Tower of Dis, and presides over his "famous barbecue" and a "burnt-brown" wife. Outside the Tower he keeps chained a monkey, a grotesque travesty of fallen man. Once the title phrase, the color red, and the animals have been associated with impending evil, many of the rest of the story's details fall into place. As the family drives along the dirt road to its doom, the pink dust swirls up to envelop their car just as Grandmother's ideals have enveloped their attention. The Misfit, with his red-rimmed eyes and red ankles, slowly destroys the family, and finally even Grandmother lies dead in a pool of her own red blood. The Misfit's last act in the story is to pick up the old lady's cat which has been rubbing itself affectionately against his leg.

In the confrontation between the Misfit and Grandmother the two major themes of the story, the nature of the mythic past and the problem of sin, combine and form comments on each other. As the story has made clear, Grandmother is a misfit in her own right; at the moment of her death she recognizes the Misfit as her own son and understands that they are alike in more profound ways than their alienation from current society. Most basically both are confused about the past and its proper relation to the present. The old lady is convinced that her own romanticized memories furnish a perfect code of conduct; the Misfit believes that in the present uncertain state of things "meanness" is the only answer. He is most disoriented when he thinks about the past and remarks that "if I had of been there" at Christ's resurrection "I would of known and I wouldn't be like I am now." From the first sight of him Grandmother has been vaguely aware of a feeling that "she had known him all her life," and his statement of doubt about the resurrection confirms her feelings and triggers her insight into their relation. Miss O'Connor's analogy between the Fall of Adam and the Civil War is operative here. In doubting the historicity of the resurrection of Christ, the Misfit of necessity doubts the possibility for divine mercy to forgive original sin. If man's condition is one of such hopeless sin, then meanness is the only answer, and there can be no joy in life.

Grandmother is likewise concerned with the sinful state of man and society, but for her the crucial historical moment is the Civil War, analogous to the Fall, and the possibility of eradicating its effects by returning to the past. But as the story as shown, the past as Grandmother conceives it is mythical and its values are more likely to be represented by a Red Sammy Butts than an arisen Christ. In the last analysis Grandmother is as merciless in her regard to the Negro family as the Misfit is in regard to hers. Both are confused about the nature of right and wrong, the definition of which lies at the heart of Christian morality. In the terms of the analogical reasoning which informs this merging of themes, the Misfit is Grandmother's son, and her salvation lies in her recognition of that fact immediately before her death.

The two themes which appear in **"A Good Man"** never merge and comment on each other in quite the same way in any two stories, but in one form or another they appear and interact again and again throughout Miss O'Connor's works. It is probably of more than passing significance, for example, that the title story of *All That Rises Must Converge* treats the same themes as that of **"A Good Man."** Here Julian's mother, in her attitudes toward race, dress, and social mores in general, is reminiscent of Grandmother and her values. But in this case it is Julian's system of values which receives the ironic comment; it is to him that the revelation comes. These two stories, one early and one late in Miss O'Connor's career, and both in dominant positions in their collections, are strong indications that Miss O'Connor's true country is more than a spiritual abstraction. Perhaps the central fact of life in her fiction is the religious experience, but that life cannot be divorced from the soil of the deep South.

Martha Stephens (essay date 1973)

SOURCE: "Belief and the Tonal Dimension," in *The Question of Flannery O'Connor*, Louisiana State University, 1973, pp. 18-36.

[*Stephens is an American critic. In the following excerpt, she examines the abrupt shift from comedy to tragedy in "A Good Man Is Hard to Find."*]

"A Good Man Is Hard to Find" divides, in terms of the time it encompasses, into two parts. The opening page of the story describes the grandmother's attempt to get the family to go to Tennessee instead of Florida on their vacation; this serves as a kind of brief prologue to the rest of the tale, all of which takes place the following day as the family begins its fatal trip to Florida. The trip itself then divides into two parts of its own. The first part—the

morning ride through middle Georgia with the grandmother and children reacting to the sights along the roadside and the grandmother entertaining the children with stories of her girlhood—is climaxed by a highly entertaining scene at Red Sam's Barbecue. The second part of the story may be said to begin, as the family starts out again after lunch, with the grandmother's suggestion, clamorously taken up by the children, that they turn off the highway onto a certain dirt road which leads to an old plantation house the grandmother had visited in her youth. Or—even better—let us say that this scene in which the aggravated father finally agrees to take the turn onto the dirt road to the old house, serves as a transition between the two parts. For just off the dirt road, the grandmother's cat, secretly smuggled into the car in a basket, leaps onto Bailey's back and makes him wreck the car. The car overturns into a deep ditch alongside the road, and as the occupants are pulling themselves together, the "hearse-like" car of the Misfit appears on the road overhead. The major break in the story comes with the following passage: "The road was about ten feet above and they could see only the tops of the trees on the other side of it. Behind the ditch they were sitting in there were more woods, tall and dark and deep. In a few minutes they saw a car some distance away on top of a hill, coming slowly as if the occupants were watching them." Our easy enjoyment of the domestic comedy of this very ordinary family excursion begins at this point sharply to subside. Here the story clearly takes a much more solemn turn than we had expected it to—just *how* solemn we are not yet sure. The Misfit and his two mates now appear on the scene with drawn guns; they are as sinister a trio as they could well be, and the main concern, surely, of any reader from this point on is with what is going to happen to the family in the hands of the convicts.

The final scene will need to be studied in detail, but one may stop at this point to ask: what kind of story do we have up until the major tonal shift which occurs with the words *tall and dark and deep* in the above passage?

Plainly it is a comic view of the family that we get in the first half of the story—and it is rich comedy indeed. The comedy issues, as it often does in O'Connor, from the author's dry, deadpan, seemingly unamused reporting of the characters' hilarious actions and appearance. Like many good modern comedies, the story is, in other words, all the funnier for not appearing to be told in a funny way. The grandmother, of course, is the largest and funniest figure, and she is the character from whose point of view the tale unfolds.

Like so many O'Connor vignettes, the opening scene is remarkable for what it accomplishes in a brief space; the vivid visual picture is etched in with swift, deft strokes, and the speech of the grandmother and the children (in this tableau-like scene the parents are silent) is also deftly, wittily done, so that even at the end of the first page we have a sharp sense of the personalities involved and a feeling for the kind of family life that is in question.

What is particularly impressive here is the way the visual image—the image of the family gathered in the living area of the house on what is perhaps a Sunday afternoon—takes shape from the ever-widening lens of the eye of the story. The opening sentence presents no image but tells of the grandmother's desire to go to Tennessee: "The grandmother didn't want to go to Florida. She wanted to visit some of her connections in east Tennessee and she was seizing at every chance to change Bailey's mind." Then we see, not the grandmother, but Bailey, sitting at the table over the *Journal*; and in the next sentence the grandmother herself comes into view behind the son, rattling at his head a piece of newspaper: "Here this fellow that calls himself The Misfit is aloose from the Federal Pen and headed toward Florida and you read here what it says he did to these people. Just you read it. I wouldn't take my children in any direction with a criminal like that aloose in it. I couldn't answer to my conscience if I did."

The grandmother gets no response from her shut-mouthed son, and as she wheels around to face the mother, the eye of the story widens again so that the mother, her face "as broad and innocent as a cabbage," is allowed to come into view sitting on the sofa silently feeding the baby his apricots. "You ought to take them somewhere else for a change so they would see different parts of the world and be broad. They never have been to east Tennessee," urges the grandmother. But the voice that replies comes from John Wesley, "a stocky child with glasses," and the eye of the story moves back again to bring into view the two older children reading the funny-papers on the floor.

> "If you don't want to go to Florida, why dontcha stay at home?". . .
>
> "She wouldn't stay at home to be queen for a day," June Star said without raising her yellow head.
>
> "Yes and what would you do if this fellow, The Misfit, caught you?" the grandmother asked.
>
> "I'd smack his face," John Wesley said.
>
> "She wouldn't stay at home for a million bucks," June Star said. "Afraid she'd miss something. She has to go everywhere we go."
>
> "All right, Miss," the grandmother said. "Just remember that the next time you want me to curl your hair."
>
> June Star said her hair was naturally curly.
>
> The next morning the grandmother was the first one to the car, ready to go.

During the trip the next day we continue to relish the comical side of the grandmother's character: her busybody backseat driving—which so infuriates her ill-natured son Bailey ("He didn't have a naturally sunny disposition like she did."); her awful humor ("'Where's the plantation?' John Wesley asked. 'Gone with the Wind,' said the grandmother."); the inevitable childlike recounting of her early courting days ("She would have done well to marry

Mr. Teagarden because he was a gentleman and had bought Coca-Cola stock when it first came out.").

The grandmother's costume for the trip is carefully etched in, detail by tiny detail:

> The old lady settled herself comfortably, removing her white cotton gloves and putting them up with her purse on the shelf in front of the back window. The children's mother still had on slacks and still had her head tied up in a green kerchief, but the grandmother had on a navy blue straw sailor hat with a bunch of white violets on the brim and a navy blue dress with a small white dot in the print. Her collar and cuffs were white organdy trimmed with lace and at her neckline she had pinned a purple spray of cloth violets containing a sachet. In case of an accident, anyone seeing her dead on the highway would know at once that she was a lady.

Now this business of being a lady, of doing *right* ("In my time . . . children were more respectful. . . . People did right then."), of being nice, begins rather early in the story to suggest the superficiality of the old lady's sense of good and evil, of what is right and good in the world. It is the grandmother who, when Red Sam of the barbecue palace says to her, "These days you don't know who to trust," delivers the crowning turn on the title line, "A good man is hard to find":

> People are certainly not nice like they used to be.

When Red Sam complains of his own misplaced trust in his fellow man—why did I let them fellers charge the gas they bought?—the grandmother is ready: "Because you're a good man!"

This conversation with Red Sam and his wife—the latter is perhaps the choice comic figure of the story—certainly prefigures the climactic dialogue, with its "good man" theme, between the grandmother and the Misfit at the end. In the final scene the utter absurd comedy of the grandmother's values is pointed up by her belief that "a good man" wouldn't shoot "a lady"! The grandmother's pathetic strategy, even early on in the fatal encounter with the Misfit, comes to no more than that. When the grandmother says, "You wouldn't shoot a lady, would you?" the Misfit replies, "I would hate to have to," and the old lady blunders on with her grotesque appeal to the escaped murderer's sense of "niceness": "'Listen,' the grandmother almost screamed, 'I know you're a good man. You don't look a bit like you have common blood. I know you must come from nice people!'"

But for all the grandmother's innocence and absurdity, one's feelings about her are by no means totally negative. If she is not endowed with insight into the eternal scheme of things—well, what of that? It is certainly possible to feel affection for the grandmother—though one may not be sure, as he reads, whether against the grain of the story or not. And yet surely there are lines and passages where the story is designedly setting our sympathies astir. The grandmother has a liveliness, curiosity, and responsiveness that the others seem to lack. Her true delight in telling stories ("she rolled her eyes and waved her head and was very dramatic") and in watching June Star dance ("the grandmother's eyes were very bright . . . she swayed her head from side to side") does not cast her in an ugly light. And the tone of such a passage as this, for instance, where she plays with the baby, is hardly ambiguous: "The grandmother offered to hold the baby and the children's mother passed him over the front seat to her. She set him on her knee and bounced him and told him about the things they were passing. She rolled her eyes and screwed up her mouth and stuck her leathery thin face into his smooth bland one. Occasionally he gave her a faraway smile." It is the grandmother, moreover, who sees the beauties of the Georgia landscape—the "blue granite," for instance, "that in some places came up to both sides of the highway; the brilliant red clay banks slightly streaked with purple; and the various crops that made rows of green lace-work on the ground." About the sentence that follows, "The trees were full of silver-white sunlight and the meanest of them sparkled," one may well ask: who sees the trees in this way? This line, it may be recalled, is the one singled out by Robert Fitzgerald, in his preface to *Everything That Rises Must Converge,* as evidence of O'Connor's "sense of natural beauty and human beauty" (even the meanest of her characters, Fitzgerald argues, can be said "to sparkle" as well). But are we to take the line as an aside of the author, or is it, in fact, strongly implied that the grandmother herself sees the trees in this way?

The Misfit is a figure that seems, one must say to the story's credit, to have fascinated more readers than any other single O'Connor character, and it is by contrast with the tormented spiritual state of this seeming monster that the nature of the grandmother's futile values becomes evident.

—Martha Stephens

However that may be, one thing, I think, is clear: all in all, the comedy of the grandmother's portrait is not wholly without warmth, is not totally abusive and satiric. Certainly one cannot view the grandmother as one whose malignity of soul is such that one can welcome—be amused by, or, let us say, accept in a comic spirit—her fatal comeuppance at the hands of the Misfit. There is not, in other words, such heavy stylization, such gross distortion, in the characterization of the old lady that one's distance from her is great enough to preclude any pain that her tortured death might bring. Indeed, there is everywhere in the first part of this story the most scrupulous comic realism. It is the averageness, the typicality of this old grandmother that is so nicely caught by the story.

The story's careful realism is nowhere better seen than in the lunch scene at Red Sam's barbecue palace. Red Sam's memorable helpmate, for instance, is closely drawn on the cheerless, complaining, vacant-eyed, fish-wife of the country Georgia road-stop. Bringing in the family's barbecue plates, this wife delivers herself of another variation of the good-man-is-hard-to-find motif:

> "It isn't a soul in this green world of God's that you can trust," she said. "And I don't count nobody out of that, not nobody," she repeated, looking at Red Sammy.

> "Did you read about that criminal, The Misfit, that's escaped?" asked the grandmother.

> "I wouldn't be none surprised to see him. If he hears it's two cents in the cash register, I wouldn't be atall surprised if he . . ."

> "That'll do," Red Sam said. "Go bring these people their Co'Colas. . . ."

Much of the charm of this comic characterization one may certainly lay to O'Connor's gift for folk speech. (Ben Jonson's injunction to a hypothetical character—"Language most shows the man—speak! that I may see thee!"—was one O'Connor would have fully appreciated.)

Just before the descent of this story into the much darker and grimmer world of Part Two, the domestic comedy peaks again in the scene in which the father is tormented into making the turn down the dirt road to the plantation. The ritualistic rhythm, for instance, of the following scene is altogether too familiar for there to be any question of the reader's not being drawn into the experience of the family:

> The children began to yell and scream that they wanted to see the house with the secret panel. John Wesley kicked the back of the front seat and June Star hung over her mother's shoulder and whined desperately into her ear that they never had any fun even on their vacation, that they could never do what THEY wanted to do. The baby began to scream and John Wesley kicked the back of the seat so hard that his father could feel the blows in his kidney.

> "All right!" he shouted and drew the car to a stop at the side of the road. "Will you all shut up? Will you all just shut up for one second? If you don't shut up, we won't go anywhere."

> "It would be very educational for them," the grandmother murmured.

> "All right," Bailey said, "but get this: this is the only time we're going to stop for anything like this. This is the one and only time."

> "The dirt road that you have to turn down is about a mile back," the grandmother directed. "I marked it when we passed."

> "A dirt road," Bailey groaned.

What we have, in other words, up until the moment when the grandmother, startled by the sudden embarrassed realization that memory has played a foul trick on her and that the old plantation is not on this road at all and not even in this state, jolts the basket and frightens Pitty Sing into springing with a snarl onto Bailey's shoulder, causing him to overturn the car—what we have is a skillful and richly entertaining domestic comedy of a not very lighthearted if not totally abusive kind. And if we have happened to read the inscription on the fly-leaf of *A Good Man Is Hard to Find,* on the page in fact facing this title story, we have certainly forgotten it—so little apropos does it seem to this funny family tale:

> The dragon is by the side of the road, watching those who pass. Beware lest he devour you. We go to the father of souls, but it is necessary to pass by the dragon.
>
> —St. Cyril of Jerusalem

No trace of a devouring dragon here! And though this epigrammatic dragon ought, perhaps—critically speaking—to be dealt with (is it the Misfit himself who plays the part in this story of a dragon by the side of the road?), if it crosses our minds, as we read, to wonder at all where the story is heading (and because O'Connor always *seems* to have her tales so well in hand, usually it doesn't cross our minds), the actual appearance of a death-dealing Misfit does not seem a very likely possibility. Some final sumptuous comic irony—harmlessly or indirectly involving, perhaps, the real or an imagined Misfit—is probably what one half-consciously expects.

Then the story breaks in two. Behind the wrecked family, sitting paralyzed with fear and shock in the ditch, the woods, which seen a few hours ago from the highway were full of silver-white sunlight, are now described as "tall and dark and deep." After the arrival of the convicts, the line of woods behind them will be said in fact to *gape* "like a wide open mouth"; and when the first member of the family is taken off to the woods and shot, the wind will seem to the grandmother "to move through the tree tops like a long satisfied insuck of breath." A very different story indeed!

With the accident, then, and the appearance of the armed convicts, the reader is much taken aback. "Why this is not at all the kind of story I thought it was going to be," he may feel—somewhat pleasurably; and he is much affected by the terrifying situation the family finds itself in and is suddenly hypersensitively alert to the slightest detail of the action which follows. Other stories of sudden disaster, when all had seemed to be going normally and well, may occur to him: Richard Wright's "Big Boy Leaves Home," for instance, a story similar to **"A Good Man Is Hard to Find"** in the perfectly gratuitous nature of the suddenly descending misfortune—that is, the sudden appearance of the hysterical white woman at the edge of the swimming hole where the naked black boys are playing on a summer day.

In **"A Good Man Is Hard to Find"** it is true that in a trivial sense everything that happens is the grandmother's fault: it was she who urged the turn-off onto the dirt road, she who stowed Pitty Sing away in the basket and who startled him into making Bailey wreck the car, and it is she who finally dooms them all by recognizing the Misfit and saying so: "You're The Misfit!" she shrieks; "I recognized you at once!"; and any sense the reader might have had that the story could continue in the comic mode is shattered by the Misfit's reply: "Yes'm, but it would have been better for all of you, lady, if you hadn't of reckernized me."

It is within the consciousness of the grandmother that we continue to experience the action of the story, even though the suffering of the mother and father is perhaps even more affecting than hers for being witnessed from the outside. The mother is shown from time to time sitting in the ditch, her left arm dangling helplessly and holding with the other the baby (who—a horrifying and somehow totally characteristic O'Connor detail—has gone to sleep). When the Misfit politely asks her if she would like to "step off yonder" into the woods with the killers, she replies "faintly": "Yes, thank you." Let a reader who feels that one can take this story too seriously ponder that detail—and with it the image, early on, of the father walking to his death with his son, holding the boy's hand.

But in any case it is to the author's purpose that the parents can credibly be made to remain for the most part dumb with shock. The grandmother has consistently been shown as "a talker," as the killer Bobby Lee puts it, and the effect of the situation on her is to make her try to talk her way out of it. The Misfit is a talker too, and the grandmother's insistence that he is really "a good man" who comes from "nice people" incites him to a long, querulous, rambling, rather absentminded reflection on the course of his life—his upbringing, his real or alleged wrongdoing, and the vexed (to say the least) state of his soul. What is of course the chief horror of the whole massacre scene is the way in which his casual discussion of these matters is punctuated by his polite commands for the execution of the other members of the family. The grandmother grows dizzier and dizzier as the murders are carried out, and finally, she seems, in a sequence that has been given as many as half a dozen conflicting interpretations, to take leave of her tortured senses altogether: "[The Misfit's] voice seemed about to crack and the grandmother's head cleared for an instant. She saw the man's face twisted close to her own as if he were going to cry and she murmured, 'Why, you're one of my babies. You're one of my own children!' She reached out and touched him on the shoulder. The Misfit sprang back as if a snake had bitten him and shot her three times through the chest." The Misfit begins to clean his glasses, and this is the way the story ends:

> Hiram and Bobby Lee returned from the woods and stood over the ditch, looking down at the grandmother who half sat and half lay in a puddle of blood with her legs crossed under her like a child's and her face smiling up at the cloudless sky.

> Without his glasses, The Misfit's eyes were red-rimmed and pale and defenseless-looking. "Take her off and

Flannery O'Connor

A criminal who took pleasure in killing
A neglected little boy who seeks love
A wife who is shocked when she becomes pregnant
A Bible salesman who steals a girl's wooden leg

These are a few of the colourful, conniving, well-intentioned or evil people you will meet in this extraordinary collection of short stories by a brilliant young American writer

'She understands her country and its people so well that in her hands they become all humanity'—New York Herald Tribune

'Highly unladylike . . . a brutal irony, a slam-bang humour and a style of writing as balefully direct as a death sentence'—Time

'A Southern writer who has something to say and the good courage and sense to say it in her own way without imitating anyone'—New York Times

FLANNERY O'CONNOR **was born in Savannah, Georgia, in 1925. Her first novel, Wise Blood, has already been published by The New English Library. A GOOD MAN IS HARD TO FIND first appeared in 1955 and Miss O'Connor was awarded a Ford Foundation fellowship in creative writing in 1959. THE VIOLENT BEAR IT AWAY, her latest book, will be published later in the Four Square series.**

A GOOD MAN IS HARD TO FIND

A FOUR SQUARE BOOK
Published by The New English Library Ltd.

The front and back covers of the 1962 edition of A Good Man Is Hard to Find.

thow her where you thown the others," he said, picking up the cat that was rubbing itself against his leg.

"She was a talker, wasn't she?" Bobby Lee said, sliding down the ditch with a yodel.

"She would of been a good woman," The Misfit said, "if it had been somebody there to shoot her every minute of her life."

"Some fun!" Bobby Lee said.

"Shut up, Bobby Lee," The Misfit said. "It's no real pleasure in life."

Thus the mean tonal snarl the story has wound itself into. What *is* the reader to think or feel about anything in the massacre scene? There is pain and shock but much that mocks that pain and shock—the heavy comedy, for instance, indeed one might say the almost burlesque treatment, of the three killers. There is the feeling that though we cannot help but pity the tormented family, the story continues to demand our contempt for them. One feels that somehow the central experience of the story—in spite

of the affecting, the chilling details surrounding these deaths, in spite even of the not altogether abusive treatment of the grandmother in Part One—will elude anyone who gives way to these feelings of pain and pity. If the writer's task is, as Conrad said, to make us "see," what is here to be seen? Surely not that life is wholly senseless and contemptible and that our fitting end is in senseless pain.

Looking at the narrative skeleton of the story again, having corrected our original notion of it after reading the final half, what now do we have? An ordinary and undistinguished family, a family even comical in its dullness, ill-naturedness, and triviality, sets out on a trip to Florida and on an ordinary summer day meets with a terrible fate. In what would the interest of such a story normally lie? Perhaps, one might think, in something that is revealed about the family in the way it meets its death, in some ironical or interesting truth about the nature of those people or those relationships—something we had been prepared unbeknownst to see, at the end plainly dramatized by their final common travail and death. But obviously, as regards the family as a whole, no such thing happens. The family is shown to be in death just as ordinary and ridiculous as before. With the possible exception of the grandmother, we know them no better; nothing about them of particular significance is brought forth.

The grandmother, being as we have seen the last to die, suffers the deaths of all her family while carrying on the intermittent conversation with the Misfit, and any reader will have some dim sense that it is through this encounter that the story is trying to transform and justify itself. One senses that this conversation—even though our attention is in reality fastened upon the horrible acts that are taking place in the background (and apparently against the thrust of the story)—is meant to be the real center of the story and the part in which the "point," as it were, of the whole tale lies.

But what is the burden of that queer conversation between the Misfit and the grandmother; what power does it have, even when we retrospectively sift and weigh it line by line, to transform our attitude towards the seemingly gratuitous—in terms of the art of the tale—horror of the massacre? The uninitiated reader will not, most likely, be able to unravel the strange complaint of the killer without some difficulty, but when we see the convict's peculiar dilemma in the context of O'Connor's whole work and what is known of her religious thought, it is not difficult to explain.

The Misfit's most intriguing statement—the line that seemingly the reader must ponder, set as it is as the final pronouncement on the grandmother after her death—is from the final passage quoted above: "She would of been a good woman if it had been somebody there to shoot her every minute of her life." Certainly we know from the first half of the story that the grandmother has seen herself as a good woman—and a good woman in a day when good men and women are hard to find, when people are disrespectful and dishonest, when they are not nice like they used to be. The grandmother is not common but a lady; and at the end of the story we know that she will be found dead just as we know she wanted to be—in the costume of a lady. She was not common, and the Misfit, with his "scholarly spectacles," his courtly apology for not wearing a shirt, his yes ma'ams and no ma'ams, was not common either—she had believed, wanted to believe, or pretended to believe. "Why I can see you come from good people," she said, "not common at all." Yet the Misfit says of her that she *would* have been a good woman if somebody had been there to shoot her all her life. And if we take the Misfit's statement as the right one about the grandmother, how was she a good woman in her death?

A good woman, perhaps we are given to believe, is one who understands the worthlessness and emptiness of being or not being a "lady," of having or not having Coca-Cola stock, of "being broad" and seeing the world, of good manners and genteel attire. "Woe to them," said Isaiah, "that are wise in their own eyes, and prudent in their own sight." The futility of all the grandmother's values, the story strives to encapsulate in this image of her disarray after the car has overturned and she has recognized the Misfit: "The grandmother reached up to adjust her hat brim as if she were going to the woods with him but it came off in her hand. She stood staring at it and after a second she let it fall on the ground."

The Misfit is a figure that seems, one must say to the story's credit, to have fascinated more readers than any other single O'Connor character, and it is by contrast with the tormented spiritual state of this seeming monster that the nature of the grandmother's futile values becomes evident. We learn that the center of the Misfit's thought has always been Jesus Christ, and what becomes clear as we study over the final scene is that the Misfit has, in the eyes of the author, the enormous distinction of having at least faced up to the problem of Christian belief. And everything he has done—everything he so monstrously does here—proceeds from his inability to accept Christ, to truly believe. This is the speech which opens the narrow and emotionally difficult route into the meaning of the story:

> "Jesus was the only One that ever raised the dead," The Misfit continued, "and He shouldn't have done it. He thown everything off balance. If He did what He said, then it's nothing for you to do but thow away everything and follow Him, and if He didn't, then it's nothing for you to do but enjoy the few minutes you got left the best way you can—by killing somebody or burning down his house or doing some other meanness to him. No pleasure but meanness," he said and his voice had become almost a snarl.

The Misfit has chosen, at least, whom he would serve—has followed the injunction of the prophet in I Kings 18:21: "And Elijah came unto all the people, and said, How long halt ye between two opinions? if the Lord be God, follow him: but if Baal, then follow him." The crucial modern text for the authorial view here, which belongs to a tradition in religio-literary thought sometimes referred to as the sanctification of the sinner, is T. S. Eliot's essay on Baudelaire, in which he states: "So far as we are human, what we do must be either evil or good; so far as we do evil or good, we are human; and it is better, in a paradoxical way, to do evil than to do nothing; at least, we exist. It is true that the glory of man is his capacity for salvation; it is also true to say that his glory is his capacity for damnation."

Thus observe how, in the context of these statements, **"A Good Man Is Hard to Find"** begins to yield its meaning. What O'Connor has done is to take, in effect, Eliot's maxim—"It is better, in a paradoxical way, to do evil than to do nothing"—and to stretch our tolerance of this idea to its limits. The conclusion that one cannot avoid is that the story depends, for its final effect, on our being able to appreciate—even to be startled by, to be pleasurably struck with—the notion of the essential moral superiority of the Misfit over his victims, who have lived without choice or commitment of any kind, who have in effect not "lived" at all.

But again, in what sense is the grandmother a "good woman" in her death, as the Misfit claims? Here even exegesis falters. Because in her terror she calls on the name of Jesus, because she exhorts the Misfit to pray? Is she "good" because as the old lady sinks fainting into the ditch, after the Misfit's Jesus speech recorded above, she mumbles, "Maybe he didn't raise the dead"? Are we to see her as at last beginning to face the central question of human existence: did God send his son to save the world? Perhaps there is a clue in the dead grandmother's final image: she is said to half lie and half sit "in a puddle of blood with her legs crossed under her like a child's and her face smiling up at the cloudless sky." For Christ said, after all, that "whosoever shall not receive the kingdom of God as a little child shall in no wise enter herein."

To see that the Misfit is really the one courageous and admirable figure in the story; that the grandmother was perhaps—even as he said—a better woman in her death than she had ever been; to see that the pain of the other members of the family, that any godless pain or pleasure that human beings may experience is, beside the one great question of existence, *unimportant*—to see all these things is to enter fully into the experience of the story. Not to see them is to find oneself pitted not only against the forces that torture and destroy the wretched subjects of the story, but against the story itself and its attitude of indifference to and contempt for human pain.

Now as it happens, **"A Good Man Is Hard to Find"** was a favorite story of O'Connor's. It was the story she chose to read whenever she was asked to read from her work, and clearly it held a meaning for her that was particularly important. Whenever she read the story, she closed by reading a statement giving her own explanation of it. (One version of that statement can now be read in the collection of O'Connor's incidental prose edited by Robert and Sally Fitzgerald titled *Mystery and Manners*.) She had come to realize that it was a story that readers found difficult, and she said in her statement that she felt that the reason the story was misunderstood was that the present age "not only does not have a very sharp eye for the almost imperceptible intrusions of grace, it no longer has much feeling for the nature of the violences which precede and follow them." The intrusion of grace in **"A Good Man Is Hard to Find"** comes, Miss O'Connor said, in that much-discussed passage in which the grandmother, her head suddenly clearing for a moment, murmurs to the Misfit, "Why, you're one of my babies. You're one of my own children!" and is shot just as she reaches out to touch him. The grandmother's gesture here is what, according to O'Connor, makes the story work; it shows that the grandmother realizes that "she is responsible for the man before her and joined to him by ties of kinship which have their roots deep in the mystery she has been merely prattling about so far," and it affords the grandmother "a special kind of triumph . . . which we instinctively do not allow to someone altogether bad."

This explanation does solve, in a sense, one of the riddles of this odd story—although, of course, one must say that while it is interesting to know the intent of the author, speaking outside the story and after the fact, such knowledge does not change the fact that the intent of the narrator manifested strictly within the story is damagingly un-

clear on this important point. And what is even more important here is that O'Connor's statement about the story, taken as a whole, only further confirms the fact that the tonal problem in this tale is really a function of our difficulty with O'Connor's formidable doctrine. About the Misfit, O'Connor's says that while he is not to be seen as the hero of the story, yet his capacity for grace is far greater than the grandmother's and that the author herself prefers to think "that the old lady's gesture, like the mustard-seed, will grow to be a great crow-filled tree in The Misfit's heart, and will be enough of a pain to him there to turn him into the prophet he was meant to become." The capacity for grace of the other members of the family is apparently zero, and hence—Christian grace in O'Connor, one cannot help noting, is rather an expensive process—it is proper that their deaths should have no spiritual context whatever. O'Connor goes on to say (and here I am quoting from a version of the statement read at the University of Georgia and included in the O'Connor papers recently given to the Georgia College library by the author's mother):

> **"A Good Man Is Hard to Find"** has been written very baldly from the orthodox Christian view of the world. I think we seldom realize just how deliberately we have to change our sights to read such a piece of fiction. It is a view of the world which is offensive to modern thought and particularly to modern feeling. It is a view of the world which sees the life of the body as less important than the life of the soul, and the happiness of the individual as secondary to his observance of truth and his practice of charity.

This, in fact, is rather mildly put. A statement in the former version makes the reader's harsh dilemma even clearer: "in this story you should be on the lookout for such things as the action of grace in the Grandmother's soul, and not for the dead bodies."

Michael O. Bellamy (essay date 1979)

SOURCE: "Everything Off Balance: Protestant Election in Flannery O'Connor's 'A Good Man Is Hard to Find'," in *The Flannery O'Connor Bulletin,* Vol. VII, Autumn, 1979, pp. 116-24.

[In the following essay, Bellamy determines the role of Protestantism in "A Good Man Is Hard to Find," maintaining that "it is difficult to explain the crucial event in this story, the sudden and abrupt conversion of the grandmother, without reference to evangelical Protestantism."]

Robert Milder's article "The Protestantism of Flannery O'Connor," [which was published in *The Southern Review,* Vol. II, 1975] is based on two essential aspects of Protestantism he finds in O'Connor's so-called Catholic fiction: "The first is an insistence upon the absolute and irremediable corruption of the natural man, and consequently upon the necessity of divine grace for every good work; the second is an exaltation of private religious experience at the expense of the sacraments and the institutional Church." Late in his essay, Milder mentions that **"A Good Man Is Hard to Find"** is one of O'Connor's more Catholic stories. I would like to take issue with Milder, not because of his association of O'Connor's writings with Protestantism, but rather because, at least in the case of **"A Good Man,"** he does not go far enough. It is difficult to explain the crucial event in this story, the sudden and abrupt conversion of the grandmother, without reference to evangelical Protestantism. Moreover, the Misfit, the other major character in **"A Good Man,"** is a visible manifestation of the theological contradictions which Milter describes in his discussion of O'Connor: much like his author, the Misfit is a Bible Belt Fundamentalist in spite of himself. Thus, we can learn something significant about this story in particular, as well as its author's more generally significant religious beliefs, by considering the extent to which **"A Good Man"** reveals the conflict between Flannery O'Connor's avowed Catholicism and her tendency to view religious experience in the context of Protestant Election.

On the most general level, the story has resonances of the typical spiritual allegory of the Protestant pilgrim. Once this overall similarity to the situation in, say, *Pilgrim's Progress,* is established, specific differences stand forth. The family in O'Connor's story is on a journey, but unlike the pilgrim in Bunyan's book, they are literally, and spiritually, on vacation; it is appropriate that they get lost, for, though they are headed for Florida in a sense, they are really going nowhere. O'Connor's story also differs from Bunyan's in that the entire family comes along; given the incessant bickering of the family in **"A Good Man Is Hard to Find,"** it is obvious, in retrospect, why the pilgrim in *Pilgrim's Progress* who hopes to succeed must leave his family behind. The accident that ends with the automobile "in a gulch off the side of the road" is reminiscent of the "slough of despond" that temporarily interrupts the quest in *Pilgrim's Progress.* The crucial difference is that the family does not survive. Their executor, the Misfit, appears on the road above them in his "hearse-like" automobile, an Anti-Christ in his chariot, announcing the apocalypse. The Misfit's role as an Anti-Christ is subsequently maintained by other ironic inversions of divine characteristics. Unlike Christ, who suffered little children to come unto Him, the Misfit shuns John Wesley and June Star, for children make him "nervous." His reference to the fact that he "was a different sort of dog" from his brothers and sisters is similarly indicative of his satanic nature, for "dog" is, of course "God" spelled backwards, and demonology is based on inverting the sacred.

This set of inversions is consistent with the Misfit's entire personality, for he is a sort of Protestant exegetical scholar *manqué.* Temperamentally, he is suited for the kind of profound, sustained curiosity that motivates the biblical scholar. His father used to describe this trait in a down-to-earth way: "It's some that can live their whole life out without asking about it and it's others has to know why it is, and this boy is one of the latters. He's going to be into everything." The Misfit even looks like a scholar: "His hair was just beginning to gray and he wore silver-rimmed

spectacles that gave him a scholarly look." Like many literal interpreters of the Bible, he has an inordinate respect for the written word. He does not, for example, question that he is guilty of the crime for which he was originally sent to prison, though he confesses he cannot recall exactly what he did. But never mind, he tells the grandmother: "It wasn't no mistake. They had the papers on me." For the original, but impossible, goal of tracking down his original sin, he has substituted the rectitude of keeping good records:

> He [Jesus] hadn't committed any crime and they could prove I had committed one because they had the papers on me. That's why I sign myself now. I said long ago, you can get a signature and sign everything you do and keep a copy of it. Then you'll know what you done and you can hold up the crime to the punishment and see do they match and in the end you'll have something to prove you ain't been treated right.

His interpretation of the prison psychiatrist's oedipal diagnosis is similarly indicative of exaggerated faith in the literal word. His literal understanding of Freud is but a secular correlative of a Fundamentalist reading of the Bible:

> It was a head-doctor at the penitentiary said what I had done was kill my daddy but I know that for a lie. My daddy died in nineteen ought nineteen of the epidemic flu and I never had a thing to do with it. He was buried in the Mount Hopewell Baptist churchyard and you can go there and see for yourself.

The Misfit is the man from Missouri who believes only in what he has seen; thus we learn immediately the difference between the grandmother's hypocrisy and his fidelity to his own experience when he corrects her version of the accident, stating that the car actually only turned over "Oncet," for he had seen it happen. All he lacks is faith, for had he been there when Jesus "raised the dead," he would have immediately and radically changed his life:

> Jesus was the only One that ever raised the dead . . . and He shouldn't have done it. He thrown everything off balance. If He did what He said, then it's nothing for you to do but throw away everything and follow Him, and if He didn't, then it's nothing for you to do but enjoy the few minutes you got left the best way you can—by killing somebody or burning down his house or doing some other meanness to him. No pleasure but meanness.

The central message of the Misfit's sermon, for a sermon is what his remarks amount to, is a familiar one in Flannery O'Connor's fiction; there is no middle ground between absolute belief in Christ's messianic function and a belief that life is nasty, brutish, and short. In fact, since the Misfit lacks faith in Christ's resurrection, he actually sees it as his duty to make life nastier, shorter, and more brutish. Implicit in the Manichean reduction of life to two antithetical alternatives is the Protestant insistence on man's total depravity without God's saving grace. The Misfit describes this belief as it applies to himself: "I found out the crime don't matter. You can do one thing or you can do another, kill a man or take a tire off his car, because sooner or later you're going to forget what it was you done and just be punished for it." The Misfit not only assumes that man is inherently guilty; he also assumes men are individually responsible for Original Sin. Given this congenital depravity, man is utterly incapable of doing anything to effect his own salvation. To do so would be roughly equivalent to pulling himself up by his own bootstraps. Here we have the surest sign of Protestantism: the absolute necessity of faith and, as a corollary, the belief that good works are at most merely a sign of God's favor.

The Misfit must be given credit for acting in conformity with his nature. We cannot say as much for the grandmother, for she is, until the moment of her death, a thorough hypocrite. It is of crucial importance that her election occurs at the very moment when she is at her most hypocritical. She has, in fact, just conceded—she will do anything to survive—that "maybe He [Christ] didn't raise the dead" after all. The moment of her election merits quoting at length:

> "Maybe He didn't raise the dead," the old lady mumbled, not knowing what she was saying and feeling so dizzy that she sank down in the ditch with her legs twisted under her. . . .

> "I wasn't there so I can't say He didn't," the Misfit said. "I wisht I had of been there," he said, hitting the ground with his fist. "It ain't right I wasn't there because if I had of been there I would of known. Listen lady," he said in a high voice, "if I had of been there I would of known and I wouldn't be like I am now." His voice seemed about to crack and the grandmother's head cleared for an instant. She saw the man's face twisted close to her own as if he were going to cry and she murmured, "Why you're one of my babies. You're one of my own children!" She reached out and touched him on the shoulder. The Misfit sprang back as if a snake had bitten him and shot her three times through the chest. Then he put his gun down on the ground and took off his glasses and began to clean them.

> Hiram and Bobby Lee returned from the woods and stood over the ditch, looking down at the grandmother who half sat and half lay in a puddle of blood with her legs crossed under her like a child's and her face smiling up at the cloudless sky.

It is clear that the grandmother is a better woman at the moment of her death than she had been at any time heretofore; or, as the Misfit puts it, "She would of been a good woman if it had been somebody there to shoot her every minute of her life." The grandmother's salvation occurs when "her head cleared for an instant"; thus her legs, earlier described as "twisted" under her, are, subsequent to her salvation, "crossed under her like a child's." Similarly, for the first and only time, she imitates the rhetoric of the New Testament, not for her own selfish purposes, but because she actually feels a maternal concern for the Misfit as one of her own children.

The extraordinary thing about the grandmother's story is the radical discontinuity between her behavior and her redemption. In fact, this discontinuity is most apparent during the moments that immediately precede her conversion. How could the irrelevance of good works for salvation be more effectively demonstrated? How could there be any relationship between good works and election when it is the confrontation with death that brings about the moment of grace? Clearly, the grandmother will not be around for any good works, since her death is the occasion for her conversion.

There is another more explicit indication of the paradoxical relationship between merit and outcome in **"A Good Man"**: the Misfit's very name is itself indicative of his inability to discover how his punishment fits his crime. This discontinuity is but the converse of the discrepancy between the grandmother's behavior and her extraordinary fate. If Christ has, in fact, "thrown everything off balance" by overcoming death, His offer of salvation through grace has also disturbed the balance of the scales of justice. Again, broadly speaking, the imbalance implicit in the irrelevance of good works and the emphasis on the gift of faith are Protestant. The Misfit accepts this imbalance as the only conceivable interpretation of Christianity, even as he agonizes over the injustice of his own damnation. For without the gift of faith, the Misfit is inevitably unable to establish whether or not Christ actually rose from the dead: "It ain't right I wasn't there because if I had of been there I would of known. . . . Listen Lady, if I had of been there I would of known and I wouldn't be like I am now." Where, he asks, is the justice in a world in which grace is a gift, a gift he feels temperamentally incapable of receiving? Where is justice when the word "grace" actually means "favor"? For surely, by the very definition of the word, some people are "favored" or "gifted" and some are not.

This radical discontinuity between man's efforts and the divine gift of grace is the most obvious, and the most important, aspect of Flannery O'Connor's Protestantism. Again, the discontinuity is apparent in fates of both of the main characters in **"A Good Man"**: The Misfit is genuinely concerned—in fact he is obsessed—with the ultimate issues of the human condition, while the grandmother, up to the very instant of her election, is a nauseating hypocrite. Thus, the Misfit's sincere efforts to investigate his place in the universe are to no avail, while the grandmother seems to stumble into salvation. Milder's comments on Protestantism are illuminating with respect to the fate of both characters. The attempt of the Misfit to understand his condition is bound to fail, for total depravity decrees "that man's reason has become so obscured since the Fall and his nature so debased that he is wholly incapable of virtue in his unregenerate state." On the other hand, Milder's remarks on the grandmother are revealing to the extent that they tend to distort her experience. He sees **"A Good Man"** as one of O'Connor's more Catholic works in that the grandmother's election demonstrates "a free acceptance of grace," an aspect of the episode that Milder sees as "one of the few remaining doctrinal points which . . . [links Flannery O'Connor] to the Catholic tradition." In the first place, it is obvious that "acceptance," free or otherwise, is not a very active word to describe the grandmother's role in the episode. Even at that, her will is barely apparent in what looks like a gratuitous gesture that is utterly antithetical to everything else in her life. In fact, her attempt to touch the Misfit is much like the existentialists' gratuitous act in its radical discontinuity from what went before. Given the doctrine of total depravity, election must be gratuitous, which is to say a gift given out of the context of the receiver's life. Thus, the grandmother is suddenly converted by an overwhelming infusion of grace, an experience much like St. Paul's abrupt enlightenment at the moment of his fall from his horse. What we have, in short, is Protestant election.

There are obvious aesthetic advantages to this kind of abrupt turn-about through a direct confrontation with God. The experience of election, as Milder perceptively points out, is far more likely to be dramatically moving than gradual spiritual improvement through the mediation of the sacraments or the practice of good works. But what is missing from the stunning conversion of the grandmother is the sense of balance, the sense of justice, so central to what Thomas Acquinas called the *via media,* or the middle way. Acting in good faith is not, in this context, acting according to a specific body of doctrine, but rather the sort of endeavor the Misfit describes. He feels this kind of effort ought to be sufficient, but he does not believe it actually is. Conversely, the world in which the grandmother seems to be so arbitrarily saved, so far off the beaten track, or what we might call a middle way, does seem off-balance. The grotesque element that so many people have noted in O'Connor's fiction is in great part a result of this puzzling void between the few who seem to be somewhat arbitrarily saved, and just about everybody else, the depraved. This void is also a major feature of the surrealistic element in O'Connor's fiction, that nightmarish quality that pervades the allegorical landscapes in which her grotesque figures engage in Manichean struggle. But if we step back from the works and view them in the context of their author's avowed beliefs, the most significant struggle is not this Manichean battle between good and evil, but rather the conflict between Flannery O'Connor's tendency to conceive of the human condition in terms of stark polarities, and the tendency, infrequently fulfilled but implicit in her Catholicism, to view mankind in the context of a middle way. It is because of this second attitude that the world of her fiction appears to the Misfit, to the Catholic humanist in Flannery O'Connor, and no doubt to many readers as well, as off-balance, almost at times in fact, as grotesque.

Kathleen Feeley (essay date 1982)

SOURCE: "The 'New Jesus'," in *Flannery O'Connor: Voice of the Peacock,* Fordham University Press, 1982, pp. 69-76.

[*Feeley is an American author and educator with a special interest in the work of Flannery O'Connor. In the* following excerpt, she views "A Good Man Is Hard to Find" as a clash between "a romanticist creating her own reality and an agnostic cut off from spiritual reality."]

A romanticist creating her own reality and an agnostic cut off from spiritual reality come into violent conflict in the title story of the first collection of O'Connor short stories, *A Good Man Is Hard to Find.* One of her most perfectly wrought artifacts, it relates the meeting of a vacation-bound grandmother and her family with the Misfit, a psychopathic killer. A piece of comic realism, the story explores the characters' apprehension of reality—both natural and supernatural. The grandmother dominates the first half of the story; through its events one sees that her inability to grasp reality truly alienates her from its spiritual extensions. When the Misfit enters, he brings a different kind of alienation: he has an absolutely honest conception of reality which embodies all reason and no faith. His agnosticism cuts him off from the supernatural world. The violent conflict of these two views marks the advent of grace. About this violence, the author stated:

> I suppose the reasons for the use of so much violence in modern fiction will differ with each writer who uses it, but in my own stories I have found that violence is strangely capable of returning my characters to reality and preparing them to accept their moment of grace. Their heads are so hard that almost nothing else will do the work. This idea, that reality is something to which we must be returned at considerable cost, is one which is seldom understood by the casual reader, but it is one which is implicit in the Christian view of the world.

Violence moves into the story when a grey-haired man with "silver-rimmed spectacles that gave him a scholarly look" slides down the gully to the scene of the family's car accident, and the grandmother shrieks, "You're the Misfit!"

Up to this point, the structure and details of the story have given vivid life to an ordinary family, starting on their annual vacation. Through the action, each member of the family displays his attitude toward reality. A self-centered romantic, the grandmother arranges reality to suit herself when she can, and indulges in fantasy when she cannot. Her false gentility precludes any honest reaction to life: the naked Negro child whom they see in a doorway is "a cute little pickaninny" that she'd like to paint; the tombstones in the cotton field are remnants of a grandiose plantation. To Bailey, her son, bending over the sports section of the paper or over the steering wheel of the car, reality is a heavy weight. The world is real for him—too real. He faces it stolidly until his automobile accident attracts the Misfit. Then, eye-to-gun with his destiny, he can only reiterate, "We're in a predicament." His wife, called "the children's mother" all through the story, is alienated from reality by her passivity. She exhibits no will; she acquiesces to everyone. In the lunchroom, "June Star said play something she could tap to and the children's mother put in another dime"; in the gully the Misfit asks her if she'd like to join her husband who has just been led away to his death and she replies dazedly, "Yes, thank you." Her one statement of assertion concerning her son's exploring the old house—"We'll all stay in the car"—seems to signal her attitude toward life.

Only the children respond honestly (if brattishly) to reality. They fade out of view when the Misfit takes over the scene with his devastating honesty. But while they, with the grandmother, hold the center of the story, they are foils for her gentle deviousness. They listen to her trying to persuade their parents not to go to Florida. To Bailey she speaks of the danger of meeting the Misfit; to his wife she extols the educational advantages of travelling to new places, and they had all been to Florida. The boy, John Wesley, faces the truth: "If you don't want to go to Florida, why dontcha stay at home?" On the trip, when the grandmother exclaims over the Negro child, June Star comments flatly, "He didn't have any britches on." The story seems to imply that the children instinctively see the visible world truly, and are therefore open to invisible reality.

When the family stops for lunch at The Tower, the scene points up a subtle contrast between man's penchant for closing his eyes to reality (a form of alienation) and an animal's immediate apprehension of it. When the family approaches the lunchroom, the children run toward "a grey monkey about a foot high, chained to a small chinaberry tree." The monkey responds by climbing to the highest limb of the tree. He knows how to deal with the world realistically. During lunch, the grandmother shows her tenuous grasp of reality. As the juke box plays, she pretends that she is dancing in her chair; to Red Sammy, the owner of The Tower, she presents her view that "Europe was entirely to blame for the way things were now." Even though she watches Red Sammy treat his wife as a menial, she calls him "a good man." She seems completely incapable of dealing with the real world. As the group leaves the lunchroom, they notice the monkey dealing effectively with reality; he is "catching fleas in himself and biting each one carefully between his teeth as if it were a delicacy." The two references to the monkey which frame the family's visit to the lunchroom seem to imply a comparison between man's power to deal subjectively with reality, and an animal's instinctive objective response.

As the trip progresses, the pace of the story quickens. The grandmother erroneously remembers an exciting old mansion slightly off their route; the children badger their father to make a detour; clouds of pink dust rise from the dirt road onto which the grandmother directs her son; Pitty Sing, the cat, springs out of the grandmother's hiding place and onto Bailey's shoulder, precipitating the accident. So real are the events of the story that one can accept the metaphysical turn which the story takes when the Misfit enters. With his appearance, two attitudes toward reality converge. The Misfit apprehends visible reality honestly; the grandmother rearranges visible and invisible reality to suit herself. The first conflict concerns the accident: "We turned over twice!" said the grandmother. "Oncet," the Misfit corrected. "We seen it happen." The conflict then moves rapidly to the center of supernatural reality: the

Redemption. For the Misfit, it *mattered* whether or not Christ was God: if He was, then all lives were His; if He was not, then life was meaningless. For the grandmother, it really did not matter. She could adjust supernatural reality to her own liking—"Maybe He didn't raise the dead"—just as she could readjust natural reality—"not telling the truth but wishing she were." Although she talked religion—"If you would pray, Jesus would help you"—it is evident that Christ has no reality in her life. The author phrases this ambivalence succinctly: "Finally she found herself saying 'Jesus, Jesus,' meaning Jesus will help you, but the way she was saying it, it sounded as if she might be cursing."

One thing about the grandmother is clear: she believes she is a Southern lady. From her appearance at the beginning of the trip in her navy blue sailor hat to her genteel statement, "I think I have injured an organ" as she sits down in the ditch, the grandmother is a weak, plebeian version of the gentility of the Old South. But as her confrontation with the Misfit becomes more intense, more *real,* the gentility is stripped away. This is symbolized by the fate of her hat, the true sign of a lady: as the Misfit invites Bailey to his death, "the grandmother reached up to adjust her hat brim as if she were going to the woods with him but it came off in her hand. She stood staring at it and after a second she let it fall to the ground." Gradually her concern becomes more oriented to someone other than herself. Although she begins by begging for her life, she ends by pleading with the criminal to save himself. She tells him over and over to pray. It is a strange phenomenon for a person on the edge of death to tell her captor to pray rather than pray herself. Throughout the final dialogue, her concern is obviously with his conversion for her sake. But in a final moment of absolute reality, all pretense is over and vision fills the void: "the grandmother's head cleared for an instant," and her heart embraces the criminal in a movement of perfect charity. The Misfit's comment, "She would of been a good woman . . . if it had been somebody there to shoot her every minute of her life," indicates that he understands the impact of violence which has ended her alienation by returning her to reality and transformed her from a "lady" to a "good woman." The distance which the grandmother travelled after the speedometer registered 55,890 is the distance from her vacuous comment, "look at the cute little pickaninny" to her amazed realization of the bonds of humanity—"Why, you're one of my babies." The story's moment of grace is extended by the description of the dead woman "with her legs crossed under her like a child's [reborn in an act of selfless love] and her face smiling up at the cloudless sky."

The Misfit explains his philosophy clearly, and its echoes can be heard in the voices of Albert Camus, Martin Heidegger, and other alienated agnostics of our time. Because he "wasn't there," and he couldn't "know," he refused to open his mind to belief. Some writers might have made him an existential hero, but Flannery O'Connor portrays the moral sterility of his world. The Misfit describes the world of the agnostic, forced to meaningless suffering in a world beyond his understanding, when he describes the penitentiary: "Turn to the right, it was a wall. . . . Turn to the left, it was a wall. Look up it was a ceiling, look down it was a floor." Symbolic of the Misfit's spiritual condition is the sky which overhangs the scene of the six passionless murders. He calls attention to it as he stands, seemingly embarrassed, in front of his captives. "Ain't a cloud in the sky," he remarked, looking up at it, "Don't see no sun but don't see no cloud either." While describing his walled existence, he looks up again at "the cloudless sky." As he faces the last of his victims, "there was not a cloud in the sky nor any sun." The sun suggests divinity, and clouds suggest rain, a biblical symbol for grace. The blankness of the sky suggests the Misfit's spiritually unlighted, unnourished world.

"A Good Man Is Hard to Find" leaves open the possibility that the grandmother's mysterious action of love will open the Misfit's mind to the reality of mystery.

—*Kathleen Feeley*

Yet the Misfit is a "good man" in many respects. The author draws him with compassion and puts him far ahead of Bailey and Red Sammy in gentleness and politeness. With his clear conception of the significance of Redemption, what bars him from belief? The story indicates that pride in his self-sufficiency blocks his apprehension of spiritual reality. An interesting theological corollary of this idea appears in Joseph Peiper's *Belief and Faith*. Peiper quotes from Cardinal Newman, whose influence on Flannery O'Connor seems evident from the number of books concerning him in her library, and her references to him in her essays and lectures. O'Connor marked this passage, in which Peiper says:

> If a man becomes aware of certain teachings, or of certain data which purport to be the Word of God— then he cannot possibly assume the right to remain "neutral for the present." This is a point to which John Henry Newman repeatedly adverts. Men, he says, are greatly inclined to "wait quietly" to see whether proofs of the actuality of revelation will drop into their laps, as though they were in the position of arbitrators and not in that of the needy. "They have decided to test the Almighty in a passionless judicial fashion, with total lack of bias, with sober minds." It is an error as common as it is fatal, says Newman, to think that "truth may be approached *without homage.*"

That homage is a mental attitude foreign to the Misfit seems immediately evident. His father had said of him when he was a child that he would have to know the "why" of everything. This complete dependence on reason excludes any apprehension of that which the mind of man cannot encompass. Coupled with his complete reliance on reason is the Misfit's self-sufficiency. In a wry repudiation of the crime of theft, he asserts that "nobody

had nothing I wanted." That he also repudiates any reaching out toward supernatural reality becomes evident when he answers the grandmother's question, "Why don't you pray?" with the dogmatic assertion, "I don't want no hep; I'm doing all right by myself."

The books in Flannery O'Connor's library give strong evidence of her concern with this type of pride, which is the cause of spiritual alienation. Among her marked or signed books which reflect this interest are James Collins's *The Existentialists*; Martin Heidegger's *Existence and Being*; Gabriel Marcel's *The Mystery of Being*; Henri De Lubac's *The Drama of Atheist Humanism*; Ignace Lepp's *Atheism in Our Time*; and Martin Buber's *The Eclipse of God*. In this last volume, O'Connor marked a passage which seems to explain theologically the Misfit's state of mind:

> All religious reality begins with what Biblical religion calls the "fear of God." It comes when our existence between birth and death becomes incomprehensible and uncanny, when all security is shattered through the mystery. This is not the relative mystery of that which is inaccessible only to the present state of human knowledge and is hence in principle discoverable. It is the essential mystery, the inscrutableness of which belongs to its very nature; it is the unknowable. Through this dark gate (which is only a gate and not, as some theologians believe, a dwelling) the believing man steps forth into the everyday which is henceforth hallowed as the place in which he has to live with the mystery. He steps forth directed and assigned to the concrete, contextual situations of his existence. That he henceforth accepts the situation as given him by the Giver is what Biblical religion calls the "fear of God."

The Misfit is standing in the "dark gate" of the unknowable, and has been standing there during his adult life— a misfit because he belongs neither with the complacent nor with the believers. This gate has become for him "a dwelling" because movement through it demands faith: "the believing man steps forth." Faith implies an acceptance of mystery, which, for the Misfit, is impossible, because he has to know "why." The story leaves open the possibility that the grandmother's mysterious action of love will open the Misfit's mind to the reality of mystery. The grandmother both reaches this gate and steps through it in a single action. Throughout her life she has been estranged from "religious reality" because her existence has never seemed "incomprehensible" or "uncanny" to her. Living only on the surface of life, she is unaware of its depth. She does not discern life's mystery; the Misfit does not accept it. Their conflict brings both face to face with religious reality. The grandmother embraces it, and the Misfit's response is deliberately ambiguous.

Victor Lasseter (essay date 1982)

SOURCE: "The Genesis of Flannery O'Connor's 'A Good Man Is Hard to Find'," in *Studies in American Fiction*, Vol. X, No. 2, Autumn, 1982, pp. 227-31.

[*In the following essay, Lasseter explores the real-life incidents that probably inspired O'Connor's "A Good Man Is Hard to Find."*]

Flannery O'Connor's **"A Good Man Is Hard to Find"** begins as Bailey reads the sports section of the *Atlanta Journal* (the evening edition of the *Constitution*). The tableau is appropriate: a study of the genesis of **"A Good Man"** shows that from 1950 to 1952 O'Connor found substantial pieces of her short story in the Atlanta newspaper; her transformation of newspaper clippings into a tale of theology and violence on a Georgia back road provides insights into her creative process.

O'Connor frequently used newspaper accounts as source material for her fiction. Harvey Klevar has shown how O'Connor used advertisements and news articles from the *Milledgeville Union Recorder* for **"A Late Encounter with the Enemy,"** **"The Displaced Person,"** and for parts of *Wise Blood*. Like the woman in **"Greenleaf"** who collects morbid stories from the newspaper, O'Connor delighted in sending friends clippings of Hadacol advertisements, odd names from birth announcements, and such human interest stories as the report of Roy Rogers' horse attending church in California or the seven-year-old who won a talent contest singing **"A Good Man Is Hard to Find."** Commenting on her fascination with such miscellanea, O'Connor wrote: "I live in a rat's nest of old papers, clippings, torn manuscripts, ancient quarterlies, etc., etc., etc."

O'Connor's letters, collected in *The Habit of Being,* show that she was a fairly regular reader of the *Constitution* while she was working on **"A Good Man,"** which she could have begun as early as 1950 and which she sold in 1953. O'Connor no doubt relied on newspapers as well as correspondence to communicate with the world outside Milledgeville after the first attacks of lupus put her in the hospital and made travel difficult. By the end of 1950, O'Connor was hospitalized in Milledgeville; in January, 1951, she was taken to Emory University Hospital in Atlanta, where she also spent much of the summer of 1951. She was able to travel to Connecticut in the summer of 1952, but when she returned she was increasingly slowed down by her illness. During this summer, however, the Milledgeville paper gave her the idea for **"A Late Encounter with the Enemy."** In the fall, she read the *Constitution* closely while following the Eisenhower-Stevenson race. During this period she found several newspaper articles that inspired **"A Good Man Is Hard to Find."**

O'Connor may have clipped some stories from the *Constitution* as early as winter, 1950; these stories closely parallel some of the details in **"A Good Man."** Two other items in the fall of 1952 would provide O'Connor with the ideas for the dangerous escapees, the name of The Misfit, and the character of the polite killer who discusses theology at gunpoint. On February 15, for instance, the paper ran a front page account of a New Orleans man and his children whom burglars held captive for three hours. The two bandits showed unusual courtesy in fetching comic books for the boys and spirits of ammonia for the father,

earning themselves this headline: "Two Gentle People Win Dad's Praise as Kindliest Bandits He Ever Met." On February 22, O'Connor may have noticed the story of Jack Ellis Vines, who had been sentenced to one hundred twenty years in prison for thirty armed robberies. As part of his rehabilitation for parole, Mr. Vines announced that he would be ordained into the ministry. Certainly the idea of the robber-preacher would have caught O'Connor's attention, adding a religious dimension to the character of the kindly bandit. In the same issue, O'Connor probably saw this more violent story: a woman testified secretly in Raleigh, North Carolina, about her flogging by the Ku Klux Klan. Since The Misfit in **"A Good Man"** has "even seen a woman flogged," perhaps this violent image began to transform the simple idea of the kindly bandit into something more complex and disturbing. Another kindly bandit story appeared on June 15, 1951, the summer of O'Connor's hospitalization at Emory. When three escaped convicts released their hostages, they gave the mother of two children sixty cents. The victim remarked that the convicts were "very considerate."

A character was growing in O'Connor's mind; his religious side took on new importance as O'Connor read (on July 11, 1951) about a thirty-year-old evangelist involved in an armed robbery. While his older brother (Bernie Lee) and another accomplice fatally wounded an Atlanta grocer during a hold-up, the evangelist prayed on his knees in the getaway car. In contrast to the comic incongruity of the preacher-robber, a report of a violent crime appeared in the August 4, 1951 *Constitution*. In this story, a fourteen-year-old boy admitted arguing with his father over money for a rifle. In the argument, the boy shot his father. Two days later, the *Constitution* reported another patricide. And in the same month, the paper featured two items about dangerous prison escapees. By now, O'Connor had in her "rat's nest" of clippings a kindly bandit, a robber-preacher, a flogging, several dangerous prison escapees, and a patricide.

Before leaving for Connecticut in the summer of 1952, O'Connor doubtless noticed another flogging story (June 2), this time about a public flogging of a wife beater in Delaware. She may have also read in August of the robber who blamed his crime on headaches: "Sometimes I don't know what I'm doing, I guess. I don't know what gets into me." Here is a source for the introspective but violent Misfit who patiently tries to explain his motives: "I forget what I done, lady. I set there and set there, trying to remember what it was I did and I ain't recalled it to this day."

The Habit of Being shows that O'Connor was following the Eisenhower-Stevenson race in the fall of 1952 closely enough to comment on some of John Crowe Ransom's letters to the editor. One can be almost certain, therefore, that she followed the sensational news of James Francis ("Maniac") Hill, which broke on the front page of the October 25 edition. This frightening report of criminals terrorizing innocent citizens supplied a major increment in the character of The Misfit. The story described "one of the largest police searches in the history of the South" for a "three-man gang led by a self-styled madman." (Hill was later committed to an insane asylum.) The report went on to identify the most recent of Hill's kidnapping victims, who had been forced to drive the Hill Gang from Tennessee to Atlanta. After kidnapping a Tennessee hunter and locking his companion in his car trunk, Hill gave his victim eight dollars so he could go back and release his friend.

The story of "Maniac" Hill, the politely insane kidnapper, competed with news of the presidential election. On the eve of the election, November 1, 1952, Hill made the front page again. A photograph shows a young man (twenty-nine) whose wire-rimmed spectacles and graying hair give him a look of age, wisdom, and kindliness. His photograph resembles O'Connor's description of The Misfit: "His hair was just beginning to gray and he wore silver-rimmed spectacles that gave him a scholarly look." The man who called himself a "three gun maniac" said that he would have gone down shooting at the Florida roadblock had he not felt kindly toward the young couple he took as hostages.

The November 1 issue of the *Constitution* gave more details about Hill. He had only recently been released from prison in Florida when he made the first of twenty kidnappings in a "two-week rampage" that "advanced him from an obscure hoodlum to top billing as a public enemy." When asked why he did it, Hill said that after the first kidnapping "I faced more time than I could make anyway, so I decided I might as well have some fun"; in **"A Good Man,"** Bobby Lee thinks that killing is "some fun!" A Florida prison superintendent's comment on Hill suggests a further parallel: Hill, he said, "apparently was just one of those adventurous kids who has to lead." O'Connor's criminal quotes his father as saying, "'It's some that can live their whole life out without asking about it and it's others has to know why it is, and this boy is one of the latters. He's going to be into everything!'"

Up to this point, newspaper articles had suggested to O'Connor the character of a gentle, polite, but dangerous criminal who kidnapped "for fun." Another article gave her an idea that transformed the front page criminal into an archetypal O'Connor character, The Misfit. On November 6, 1952, a headline in the *Constitution* read "'The Misfit' Robs Office, Escapes with $150." The brief story told of a thirty-year-old male who walked into an Atlanta Federal Savings and Loan Office and handed the teller a bag with this message: "Put $150 in here and don't say anything. I have a gun, and I am 'The Misfit.'" This small-time criminal, his very name the equivalent of "Hard Luck" tattooed across the knuckles, suggested to O'Connor not only a social but also spiritual outlaw. O'Connor needed another party to the back road confrontation; she found her in a brief November 19 item about a pious sixty-year-old woman who survived five days in her car which had overturned in a ditch. "I just knew the Lord would send someone," the woman said. From these front page beginnings, O'Connor created her story of spiritual rebellion colliding with spiritual complacency.

O'Connor's creation of fiction from the newspaper confirms what she has written about her own creative processes. A recurring theme in her letters is that her fiction begins with an external stimulus: "I have to have a 'story' in mind—some incident or observation that excites me and in which I see fictional possibilities—before I can start a formal piece." As an example, **"The Artificial Nigger"** began on a trip with her mother to buy a cow (surely one of the most homely origins in American literature). When her mother stopped to ask directions, a farmer told her that she couldn't miss the place because "it was the only house in town with an artificial nigger." O'Connor was so intrigued by that comment that she said "I made up my mind to use it." The provocation for her fiction often came, then, from casual encounters, observation, anecdote, and newspapers. She remarked once that she had "one of those food-chopper brains, that nothing comes out the way it went in."

Of course, O'Connor was an artist who knew that a memory and a pair of scissors do not make art. One of her most important statements about fiction emphasizes the dimension that art adds to life: "Fiction is not a case history or a reported incident . . . because it has an extra dimension and I think the dimension comes about when the writer puts us in the middle of some human action and shows it illuminated and outlined by mystery." Like thousands of other readers, Flannery O'Connor read the *Constitution*'s human interest items and accounts of criminals who were polite, religious, and mad. But out of these newspaper materials O'Connor fashioned a fiction with a mystery at the center: out of "Maniac" Hill and the Atlanta Misfit she created a symbol of the modern anti-Christ; out of the pious accident victim, a symbol of the modern infidel. She was attracted to these news accounts less by their sensationalism than by their fictional possibilities and ironic suggestions; her genius transformed these "human interest" stories into ironic and profound metaphors of modern disbelief.

Madison Jones (essay date 1984)

SOURCE: "A Good Man's Predicament," in *The Southern Review,* Vol. XX, No. 4, Autumn, 1984, pp. 836-41.

[*In the following essay, Jones offers an alternative to O'Connor's interpretation of the controversial conclusion of "A Good Man Is Hard to Find."*]

Flannery O'Connor's **"A Good Man Is Hard to Find"** has been for the past decade or more a subject of virtually countless critical readings. Any brilliant work of fiction resists a single interpretation acceptable to everyone, but judging by the variousness and irreconcilability of so many readings of **"A Good Man"** one might conclude, as R. V. Cassill does, that like the work of Kafka the story "may not be susceptible to exhaustive rational analysis." The suggestion, I believe, would be quite apt if applied to a good many O'Connor stories. Not this one, however. If there are in fact authorial lapses, moments when the reader's gaze is led a little awry, they are simply that, lapses, instances of O'Connor nodding.

Much has been made of O'Connor's use of the grotesque, and the vacationing family in **"A Good Man"** is a case in point. The family members are portrayed almost exclusively in terms of their vices, so much so, it would seem, as to put them at risk of losing entirely not only the reader's sympathy but even his recognition of them as representatively human—a result certain to drain the story of most of its meaning and power. Such is not the result, however. What otherwise must prompt severity in the reader's response is mitigated here by laughter, the transforming element through which human evil is seen in the more tolerable aspect of folly. The author laughs and so do we, and the moral grossness of the family becomes funny to us. This is what engages and sustains our interest in them and, through the effect of distance that humor creates, makes possible our perception of their representative character.

What we see portrayed is increasingly recognizable. Here embodied in this family are standard evils of our culture. Indeed the term "family" is itself a misnomer, for there is no uniting bond. It is each for himself, without respect, without manners. The children, uncorrected, crudely insult their grandmother, and the grandmother for her own selfish ends uses the children against her surly son. The practice of deceit and the mounting of pietisms are constants in her life, and her praise of the past when good men were easy to find degrades that past by the banality of her memories. Even such memories as she has are not to be depended on; in fact, it is one of her "mis-rememberings" that leads the family to disaster.

But this portrait of unrelieved vulgarity is extended, and by more than implication only, to suggest the world at large. This is the function of the interlude at Red Sammy's barbecue joint where the child June Star does her tap routine and Red Sammy bullies his wife and engages with the grandmother in self-congratulatory conversation about the awfulness of the times and how hard it is to find a "good" man these days. It is hard indeed. In a world unleavened by any presence of the spiritual—a world portrayed, incidentally, in scores of contemporary TV sitcoms—where is a good man to be found? Nowhere, is the answer, though in one way the Misfit himself comes closest to earning the description.

The Misfit is introduced at the very beginning of the story by the grandmother who is using the threat of him, an escaped convict and killer, as a means of getting her own way with her son Bailey. After this the Misfit waits unmentioned in the wings until the portrait of this representative family is complete. His physical entrance into the story, a hardly acceptable coincidence in terms of purely realistic fiction, is in O'Connor's spiritual economy—which determines her technique—like a step in a train of logic. Inert until now, he is nevertheless the conclusion always implicit in the life of the family. Now events produce him in all his terror.

The Misfit comes on the scene of the family's accident in a car that looks like a hearse. The description of his person, generally that of the sinister red-neck of folklore, focuses on a single feature: the silver-rimmed spectacles that give him a scholarly look. This is a clue and a rather pointed one. A scholar is someone who seeks to know the nature of reality and a scholar is what the Misfit was born to be. As the Misfit tells the grandmother:

> "My daddy said I was a different breed of dog from my brothers and sisters. 'You know', Daddy said, 'it's some can live their whole life without asking about it and it's others has to know why it is, and this boy is one of the latters. He's going to be into everything!'"

And in the course of his life he has been into everything:

> "I was a gospel singer for a while," the Misfit said. "I been most everything. Been in the arm service, both land and sea, at home and abroad, been twict married, been an undertaker, been with the railroads, plowed Mother Earth, been in a tornado, seen a man burnt alive oncet," . . . "I even seen a woman flogged," he said.

Life and death, land and sea, war and peace, he has seen it all. And his conclusion, based on his exhaustive experience of the world, is that we are indeed in the "terrible predicament" against which Bailey, who is about to be murdered for no cause, hysterically cries out. "Nobody realizes what this is," Bailey says, but he is wrong. The Misfit knows what it is: a universal condition of meaningless suffering, of punishment that has no intelligible relationship to wrongs done by the victim.

> "I call myself the Misfit," he said, "because I can't make what all I done wrong fit what all I gone through in punishment." . . . "Does it seem right to you, lady, that one is punished a heap and another ain't punished at all?" . . . "No, lady," . . . "I found out the crime don't matter. You can do one thing or you can do another, kill a man or take a tire off his car, because sooner or later you're going to forget what it was you done and just be punished for it."

Now the Misfit signs everything and keeps a copy. That way:

> "you'll know what you done and you can hold up the crime to the punishment and see do they match and in the end you'll have something to prove you ain't been treated right."

The Misfit, of course, makes reference here to one significant experience not included in the catalogue previously quoted, but this experience was probably the crucial one. He was sent to the penitentiary for a crime—killing his father—of which he has no memory. In fact he is certain that he did not do it. But they had the papers on him. So, without any consciousness of the crime for which he was being punished, he was "buried alive," as he says. And his description of his confinement, with walls every way he turned, makes an effective image of the Misfit's vision of the world.

The penitentiary experience, however, has a further important thematic significance. It is the very figure of a cardinal doctrine of Christianity, that of Original Sin. Man, conscious or not of the reason, suffers the consequences of Adam's Fall. Guilt is inherited, implicit in a nature severed from God's sustaining grace and submitted to the rule of a Prince who is Darkness. Hence a world deprived of moral order, where irrational suffering prevails: the world that the Misfit so clearly sees with the help of his scholarly glasses. Here, he believes, are the facts, the irremediable facts, of the human condition.

"A Good Man Is Hard to Find" is perhaps Flannery O'Connor's finest story—coherent, powerfully dramatic, relentless, and unique. In essence it is a devastating sermon against the faithlessness of modern generations, man bereft of the spirit.

—Madison Jones

What the Misfit cannot see, or cannot believe in, is any hope of redress for the human condition. He may be haunted, at times tormented, by a vision of Christ raising the dead, but he cannot believe it: he was not there. All that he can believe, really believe, is what his eyes show him: this world without meaning or justice, this prison house where we are confined. Seeing this, what response is fitting? Says the Misfit:

> "then it's nothing for you to do but enjoy the few minutes you got left the best way you can-by killing somebody or burning down his house or doing some other meanness to him. No pleasure but meanness," he said and his voice had become almost a snarl.

It is like the response of Satan himself, as Milton envisions it:

> Save what is in destroying; other joy
> To me is lost.

But release for hate of an unjust creation is at best an illusory pleasure. "It's no real pleasure in life," the Misfit says, after the carnage is complete.

What has driven the Misfit to his homicidal condition is his powerful but frustrated instinct for meaning and justice. It may be inferred that this same instinct is what has produced his tormenting thoughts about Christ raising the dead, making justice where there is none. If only he could have been there when it happened, then he could have believed.

> "I wisht I could have been there," he said, hitting the ground with his fist. "It ain't right I wasn't there

because if I had of been there I would of known. Listen lady," he said in a high voice, "if I had of been there I would have known and I wouldn't be like I am now."

It is torment to think of what might have been, that under other circumstances he would have been able to believe and so escape from the self he has become. In light of this it is possible to read the Misfit's obscure statement that Jesus "thowed everything off balance," as meaning this: that it would have been better, for the world's peace and his own, if no haunting doubt about the awful inevitability of man's condition ever had been introduced. In any case it could only be that doubt has made its contribution to the blighting of the Misfit's soul.

But doubts like this are not enough to alter the Misfit's vision. In the modern manner he believes what he can see with his eyes only, and his eyes have a terrible rigor. It is this rigor that puts him at such a distance from the grandmother who is one of the multitude "that can live their whole life without asking about it," that spend their lives immersed in a world of platitudes which they have never once stopped to scrutinize. This, his distinction from the vulgarians whom the grandmother represents, his honesty, is the source of the Misfit's pride. It is why, when the grandmother calls him a "good" man, he answers: "Nome, I ain't a good man," . . . "but I ain't the worst in the world neither." And it is sufficient reason for the violent response that causes him so suddenly and unexpectedly to shoot the grandmother. Here is what happens, beginning with the grandmother's murmured words to the Misfit:

> "Why, you're one of my babies. You're one of my own children." She reached out and touched him on the shoulder. The Misfit sprang back as if a snake had bitten him and shot her three times through the chest.

Given the Misfit's image of himself, her words and her touching, blessing him, amount to intolerable insult, for hereby she includes him among the world's family of vulgarians. One of her children, her kind, indeed!

This reason for the Misfit's action is, I believe, quite sufficient to explain it, even though Flannery O'Connor, discussing the story in *Mystery and Manners,* implies a different explanation. The grandmother's words to the Misfit and her touching him, O'Connor says, are a gesture representing the intrusion of a moment of grace. So moved, the grandmother recognizes her responsibility for this man and the deep kinship between them. O'Connor goes on to say that perhaps in time to come the Misfit's memory of the grandmother's gesture will become painful enough to turn him into the prophet he was meant to be. Seen this way, through the author's eyes, we must infer an explanation other than my own for the Misfit's action. This explanation would envision the Misfit's sudden violence as caused by his dismayed recognition of the presence in the grandmother of a phenomenon impossible to reconcile with his own view of what is real. Thus the Misfit's act can be seen as a striking out in defense of a version of reality to whose logic he has so appallingly committed himself.

Faced with mutually exclusive interpretations of a fictional event, a reader must accept the evidence of the text in preference to the testimonial of the author. And where the text offers a realistic explanation as opposed to one based on the supernatural, a reader must find the former the more persuasive. *If* the two are in fact mutually exclusive. And *if,* of course, it is true that the acceptability of the author's explanation does in fact depend upon the reader's belief in the supernatural. As to this second condition, it is a measure of O'Connor's great gift that the story offers a collateral basis for understanding grace that is naturalistic in character. This grace may be spelled in lower case letters but the fictional consequence is the same. For sudden insight is quite within the purview of rationalistic psychology, provided only that there are intelligible grounds for it. And such grounds are present in the story. They are implicit in the logic that connects the grandmother and the Misfit, that makes of the Misfit "one of my own children." In the hysteria caused by the imminence of her death, which strips her of those banalities by which she has lived, the grandmother quite believably discovers this connection. And so with the terms of the Misfit's sudden violence. His own tormenting doubt, figured in those preceding moments when he cries out and hits the ground, has prepared him. Supernatural grace or not, the Misfit in this moment sees it as such, and strikes.

These two, the author's and my own, are quite different explanations of the Misfit's sudden violence. Either, I believe, is reasonable, though surely the nod should go to the one that more enriches the story's theme. *If* the two are mutually exclusive. I believe, however, that they are not. Such a mixture of motives, in which self-doubt and offended pride both participate, should put no strain on the reader's imagination. And seen together each one may give additional dimension to the story.

"A Good Man Is Hard to Find" is perhaps Flannery O'Connor's finest story—coherent, powerfully dramatic, relentless, and unique. In essence it is a devastating sermon against the faithlessness of modern generations, man bereft of the spirit. This condition, portrayed in the grossness of the vacationing family, barely relieved by the pious and sentimental prattle of the grandmother, produces its own terror. The Misfit enters, not by coincidence but by the logic implicit in lives made grotesque when vision has departed. He, O'Connor tells us, is the fierce avenger our souls beget upon our innocent nihilism.

Carter Martin   (essay date 1987)

SOURCE: "'The Meanest of Them Sparkled': Beauty and Landscape in Flannery O'Connor's Fiction," in *Realist of Distances: Flannery O'Connor Revisited,* edited by Karl-Heinz Westarp and Jan Nordby Gretlund, Aarhus University Press, 1987, pp. 147-55.

[*Martin is an American author and educator with a special interest in O'Connor's work. In the following excerpt, he examines moments of epiphanic beauty in "A Good Man Is Hard to Find."*]

"'We've had an ACCIDENT,'" the children cry gleefully. "'But nobody's killed,' June Star said with disappointment." Within a few minutes, June Star is dead, and so is the rest of her family. This extraordinary irony informs the story in several ways. Like Eliot being surprised that so many have crossed the bridge or Ransom's characters being astonished at a child's death, we as readers of "A Good Man Is Hard to Find" are awed by the swiftness and finality of the six deaths effected by The Misfit. I think we come back to the story time and again to experience this awe and to inquire into it. We are, in this, somewhat like Mrs. Greenleaf, who clips stories of grotesque deaths and bizarre suffering so that she can wallow in the dirt and pray over them. There is a medieval quality about the centrality of death in O'Connor's fiction.

There are, however, other dimensions to the irony of "A Good Man Is Hard to Find," specifically, that the automobile accident and the swift deaths following it constitute an opening up, a movement of this fiction to a moment when Flannery O'Connor shows us, as she so often does, the landscape of eternity. Rather than showing us, as Eliot does, "Fear in a handful of dust," she shows us *beauty* in the most horrible of human experiences. This journey of the imagination from the horrible to the truth of God's grace has been an important response often noted by O'Connor's readers. Nevertheless, there is a wallowing in the dirt about it all, for we too often assume that it is only through the ugly and the grotesque, through suffering and pain, through loss and death that the grand truths of the universe emerge from *Wise Blood, A Good Man Is Hard to Find, The Violent Bear It Away,* and *Everything That Rises Must Converge.* However, O'Connor presented the beauty of this world as vividly as sunlight through the stained-glass window of a Gothic cathedral or the brilliant icons of the churches of Byzantium. It is this beauty I want to show in its importance in the total perception of O'Connor's fiction. It is one reason for her popularity—not just among academics but among readers everywhere of every persuasion and personal circumstance.

In his introduction to *Everything That Rises Must Converge,* Robert Fitzgerald took issue with those who complained that O'Connor's fiction "lacked a sense of natural beauty and human beauty." In refutation, Fitzgerald cites a line from a beautiful story, which is actually also O'Connor's most notoriously violent story, "A Good Man Is Hard to Find." The line reads: "The trees were full of silver-white sunlight and the meanest of them sparkled." More generally but relevant to this passage, Fitzgerald says: "Beyond incidental phrasing and images, beauty lies in the strong invention and execution of the things, as in objects expertly forged or cast or stamped, with edges, not waxen and worn or softly moulded." For this quality he uses the term *ascesis* because of its economy, its spareness and brevity. Further, he contends that the wife in "A Good Man Is Hard to Find" carries out a beautiful action when she politely says "Yes, thank you," to her murderer, as he leads her away into the woods. Such actions, he contends, are beautiful, "though as brief as beautiful actions usually are."

In spite of Fitzgerald's pointing the way, too little has been written about the very real beauty to be found in O'Connor's fiction. She herself does not use the word often, but in her nonfiction she makes it clear that beauty is very important to her view of the world. In a letter to "A" she states: "I am one, of course, who believes that man is created in the image and likeness of God. I believe that all creation is good. . . ." And when reviewers failed to see that there was (according to her) no bitterness in her stories but a cherishing of the world, she took their failure to be a moral one and tantamount to "what Nietzche meant when he said God was dead." She admits that her stories in **A Good Man Is Hard to Find** contain ". . . many rough beasts now slouching toward Bethlehem to be born," but contends that reviewers have "hold of the wrong horror." She insists that "you have to cherish the world at the same time that you struggle to endure it."

I want to demonstrate in several of O'Connor's works a pattern of beauty which I take to be an important part of the rhetorical structure of her fiction. These patterns happen to be at one with the narrative structure, and they are at one with her own statements in regard to what the works are "about." She once complained in a letter to Sister Mariella Gable that critics too often do not see what is really there, and she invoked Gerard Manley Hopkins' notion of "inscape" to explain what she meant. Her method is at one with so many other writers who have, like Hopkins, written in 'Pied Beauty' about:

> All things counter, original, spare, strange;
> Whatever is fickle, freckled (who knows how?)
> With swift, slow; sweet, sour; adazzle, dim; . . .

It is a method of indirection that nevertheless is especially about the beautiful. One thinks of Emily Dickinson, who spoke of this matter in one of her poems:

> Tell all the truth but tell it slant—
> . . . The truth must dazzle gradually,
> or every man be blind—

She carries out what Robert Browning's painter "Fra Lippo Lippi" claimed was one of the artist's functions:

> . . . We're made so that we love
> First when we see them painted, things we have
>   passed
> Perhaps a hundred times nor cared to see;
> . . . Art was given for that; . . .

O'Connor was herself a visual artist as well as a literary one. Robert Fitzgerald describes some of this graphic art: "They are simple but beautiful paintings of flowers in bowls, of cows under trees, of the Negro house under the bare trees of winter." Her literary work is also highly visual, and when this visualization is specifically beautiful it often constitutes a special form of punctuation that gives rhythm and shape to the structure of her narrative. One

must look carefully to appreciate this aesthetic, for it is similar to what Auden perceives about Breughel and the old masters in his poem "Musée des Beaux Arts": Those painters understood, he says, the human position of suffering,

> . . . how it takes place
> While someone else is eating or opening a window
>   or just walking dully along,
> . . . That even the dreadful martyrdom must run its
>   course
> Anyhow in a corner, some untidy spot
> Where the dogs go on with their doggy life and the
>   torturer's horse
> Scratches its innocent behind on a tree

The beauty in O'Connor's stories is that way: it occurs casually, is understated, characterized by the spareness of *ascesis,* and is usually surrounded by ugliness, banality, or violence. The result, however, is not necessarily an impression that beauty is chimerical or accidental but instead that it is the reality that informs the entire structure of the affective world she portrays. "For the almost blind," she wrote, "you draw large and startling figures." Which is to say that she, like Dickinson, doubted the capacity of her audience to look directly and consistently upon the beauty that she herself perceived in the universe. Breughel's "The Blind People," portrays in the foreground a single file of stumbling, wildly disoriented blind men; but in the background landscape is the church. The rhetoric could not be simpler or clearer. In his "The Fall of Icarus" the rhetoric is similar; the great tragic drowning is proportionately minuscule in comparison to the coarse farmer, his ox and plow cutting fresh furrows in the foreground. In "The Hunters in the Snow" Breughel creates unusual beauty from a severe, colorless and cold landscape by investing it with meaning that comes from the shape of life and activity and the sense of returning home or coming into the open. The village and the frozen lake lie below the men and their slender dogs.

O'Connor's use of such forms of beauty is found throughout her work. . . . In **"The Life You Save May Be Your Own,"** we find what might be called a brief conceit of grotesque beauty: "A fat yellow moon appeared in the branches of the fig tree as if it were going to roost there with the chickens." The poetic adequacy of this sentence is as fully realized as Ezra Pound's poem, "In a Station of the Metro":

> The apparition of those faces in the crowd;
> Petals on a wet, black bough.

O'Connor's sentence achieves what Pound himself claims for his poem and his concept of *Imagisme* and vorticism: that the image when presented directly transforms an outward and objective thing "into a thing inward and subjective," but he goes on to say that "the image is not an idea. It is a radiant node or cluster, . . . a *vortex,* from which, and through which, and into which, ideas are constantly rushing." Pound quotes Thomas Aquinas, *Nomina sunt consequentia rerum,* that is, names are the consequence of things. O'Connor's sentence permits the reader to find beauty where it would not have been perceived without the intervention of art; she permits the beauty and objective propriety of the moon/fig tree/chickens image to emerge. The entire matter illustrates the meaning of a passage she underlined in her copy of Croce's "A Breviary of Aesthetics": "Art is an ideal within the four corners of an image." In this case the ideal is linked with the actual and is made flesh by the linking of heavenly bodies with earthly ones—a converging of actualities in one plane of perception. Another fleeting but beautiful image in an unlikely context is Mrs, Lucynell Crater's perception of the evening sun in **"The Life You Save May Be Your Own"**: it "appeared to be balancing itself on the peak of a small mountain." Mrs. Crater sits "with her arms folded across her chest as if she were the owner of the sun." The sun, from her perspective, is indeed on the mountain, and as seen from her porch it is indeed her sun. Just as she is confident that *her* chickens are roosting in *her* fig tree, so the moon *must* be there and be hers. Her literal-mindedness and simplicity are counterbalanced by Mr. Shiftlet's mechanical rationality and calculatingly evil opportunism. The flashes of beauty, brief though they may be, enable the reader to understand the wholeness of the world portrayed by O'Connor—its depth and its contradictions and its multiple realities.

When a reader enters an O'Connor story by looking through such windows that open onto beauty—particularly when he feels that the narrative house from which he looks is filled with darkness and terror and malignity—he is experiencing what Martin Heidegger referred to as "coming into the open." Heidegger asserts that "meaning is . . . not a property attaching to entities, lying 'behind' them, or floating somewhere as an 'intermediate domain.'" It is the field upon which "something becomes intelligible as something." Heidegger contends that the poet experiences the abyss (the "default of God," he calls it) and causes readers to reach into the abyss to discover divine radiance shining "in everything that is" and also to realize that absence is presence, "the ancient name of Being." In "What are Poets For?" Heidegger says that they "sense the trace of fugitive gods" and trace for others the way toward the turning. In the midst of the unholy, he claims, the songs of the venturesome poets (those who take dangerous risks) turn "our unprotected being into the Open."

A reader's experience of coming into the open by way of O'Connor's punctuation of beauty is more elaborately realized in one of her most violent and disturbing stories, **"A Good Man Is Hard to Find."** The pattern of this story is a series of scenes in confined space which are seen in the context of unbounded space—light, sky, clouds, and woods seen from above so that they stretch out as the blue tops of trees. The story moves from the unpleasant circumstances of three-generational family life to the awesome absence of the lives so recently present. Yet this movement is one that leads us from the beauty of the world to the beauty of death or perhaps to the beauty of grace attendant upon death. The key lines form an image cluster that controls this meaning. Significantly, the perception originates with the grandmother, just as the pres-

ence of grace is understood only with reference to her at the time of the mass murder. When the family is setting out on their Florida trip, the grandmother tries to share the beauty she sees with the ill-tempered children, Wesley and June Star:

> She pointed out interesting details of the scenery: Stone Mountain; the blue granite that in some places came up to both sides of the highway; the brilliant red clay banks slightly streaked with purple; and the various crops that made rows of green lace-work on the ground. The trees were full of silver-white sunlight and the meanest of them sparkled.

All of these images are patently beautiful: the mountain, the granite, the red clay, the crops, the trees, the sunlight, and in the combination that O'Connor places them, they are poetic and constitute a potential vortex, a radiant node or cluster into which the meaning of the story eventually enters. Only five of the twenty-one pages of the story do not contain cognate imagery. Even though we do not perceive it as beauty as it casually occurs, this imagery represents the macrocosm of the story and permits the reader to come into the open thematically on what O'Connor calls elsewhere "the true country." The fleeting signs of the reality of that country are in this story the woods filled with light, beginning with the grandmother's paean and moving through the chinaberry tree at Red Sammy Butts', the "blue tops of trees for miles around," trees that look down on the family car, "woods, tall and dark and deep," "woods [that] gaped like a dark open mouth," and the woods that relentlessly devour the family before the awestruck grandmother: "Alone with The Misfit, the grandmother found that she had lost her voice. There was not a cloud in the sky nor any sun. There was nothing around her but woods." At this point the story has moved from the circumstantial beauty of the affective world to the ideal and permanent beauty of the action of grace that paradoxically informs the irrational gesture in which the grandmother reaches out to touch The Misfit, anagogically accepting him as her own, as Christ accepted sinners.

This remarkable conclusion to the story has been explained by O'Connor herself in terms of grace and its focus on the grandmother, but her explanation is not easy for many readers who see in the foreground a homicidal maniac carrying out a mass murder. However, if the reader examines the structure of the story, the affirmation of this reading is more available, even to the reader who may be unfamiliar with O'Connor's explanation. The pattern already described is enhanced by its contrapuntal movement with reference to the imagery of enclosure. The grim, threatening quality of the story begins before the appearance of The Misfit and is associated with the microcosm of the family, specifically as they are presented enclosed and entrapped, so confined and relentlessly bound to each other's presence that, except for the grandmother, they are unable to look out to the larger world or to conceive of the possibility that they may come into the open, enter a larger, freer, more beautiful world.

The first of these enclosures is the home itself. Only one and one-half pages long, it is a tightly blocked stage setting which conveys the maddening intimacy of family life. Bailey, the father, is unsuccessfully trying to escape by immersing himself in the sports section of the *Journal*. The garrulous grandmother is invading everyone's space by fatuously claiming a role as wise elder, warning the family of The Misfit and trying to change the plans for the trip to Florida; that she is expressing her desperate lack of belonging, of being an unwanted outsider is borne out by the cruel remarks of the children, who are lying on the floor reading the funny papers: ". . . why dontcha stay at home?" one of them asks. The mother, "whose face was as broad and innocent as a cabbage," sits on the sofa in quiet desperation, feeding apricots to the baby. The terrible proximity of them all creates an atmosphere of hysteria, and the reader's inclination is to scream and flee. This first instance of enclosure is brief and quite intense.

The enclosure in the automobile is similarly cloying because of the quite raw conflicts between the generations: a lonely and silly old woman trying to be cheerful and agreeable, children who are by turns ill-mannered or sullenly oblivious, and parents who are almost stupefied and overtaxed by their role as the responsible adults. They are caged and baffled in a rolling domestic zoo, objectified with satire and irony by the grandmother's stories, the children's cloud game, the baby being passed to the back seat, and occasional glimpses of the quickly passing stable world outside the car, one of which, the Negro child, the grandmother would like to bring into stasis: "If I could paint, I'd paint that picture," she says. The overwhelming irony of the boredom and tension is that the end of it in the affective world is not reconciliation or a coming into love and harmony but sudden death.

The same ironic pathos informs the details of the third objectification of the existential enclosure of life in the countryside or the fallen world. Red Sammy Butts' restaurant, "The Tower was a long dark room with a counter at one end and tables at the other and dancing space in the middle." The discontent and hostility continue: Bailey glares at his mother when she asks him to dance, June Star insults Red Sammy's wife, he tells his wife "to quit lounging on the counter and hurry up with these people's order." The conversation is premonitory and pessimistic in its concern with The Misfit and the degeneration of mankind in general. It is a relief when "The children ran outside into the white sunlight and looked at the monkey in the lacy chinaberry tree."

The next narrative block returns to the enclosure of the automobile. It is at this time that the grandmother awakens "outside of Toombsboro" (note the extension of the irony and the imagery) with her plan to visit an old plantation, the venture that leads them to their encounter with The Misfit. The children are eager to get out of the car. The imagery of the secret panel and hidden silver and the sudden emergence of the cat from its basket foreshadow the sudden and catastrophic opening up of the narrative and of the six lives.

With the grandmother, the reader is awed by the ten-page conclusion to the story, more than one-third of its length. O'Connor protracts this event. She has prepared us for it carefully, so that when we see the hearselike car on the hill and look down upon the family spilled out from their banal entrapment into the big world, we know the terrible outcome at once. Thus we must participate in the moment of dying, with horror, outrage, and finally with wonder. This narration is somewhat like the medieval drama *Everyman* in which the protagonist's moment of death is expanded artistically and dramatically to include his realization, his pleading, his acceptance, and his receiving the sacraments and God's grace. A similar effect is achieved by Tolstoy in "The Death of Ivan Ilyich" and by William Faulkner in his treatment of the death of Joe Christmas in *Light in August*. To stand for so long before the mystery of death enables the reader to realize the irrelevance of the banality, the tension, the petty egotism and pride which constitute the ordinary life in physical and metaphysical confinement. This we are made aware of by the events at large and by passages of humbly apocalyptic beauty: "There was a pistol shot from the woods, followed closely by another. Then silence. The old lady's head jerked around. She could hear the wind move through the tree tops like a long satisfied insuck of breath. 'Bailey Boy!' she called."

That the grandmother's action of reaching out to The Misfit signifies the moment when grace is manifest is a received truth about the story. It is not, however, a surprise ending. Her identity with grace occurs early and at several points before this conclusion. Coming into the open is clearly part of the story's structure and imagery, and part of the grandmother's character. We see this, for example, after the others have been taken away; she is alone with The Misfit and O'Connor confirms in this penultimate moment her having come into the open: "There was not a cloud in the sky nor any sun. There was nothing around her but woods. She wanted to tell him that he must pray. She opened and closed her mouth several times before anything came out. Finally she found herself saying, 'Jesus, Jesus,' meaning Jesus will help you. . . ." Again the imagery of clouds, sky, sun, and trees objectifies beauty, spare and stark though it be; the end thus returns to the beginning image of the meanest trees filled with light.

J. Peter Dyson (essay date 1988)

SOURCE: "Cats, Crime, and Punishment: *The Mikado*'s Pitti-Sing in 'A Good Man Is Hard to Find'," in *English Studies in Canada*, Vol. XIV, No. 4, December, 1988, pp. 436-50.

[*In the following essay, Dyson explores the links between The Mikado and "A Good Man Is Hard to Find," maintaining that "both works explore thematically the significance of the mysteriously arbitrary design by which characters and situations are moved despite themselves."*]

If the grandmother is, as she appears to be, the "good man" who is so hard to find in Flannery O'Connor's story,

"A Good Man Is Hard to Find," then who or what, one wonders, is Pitty Sing, the grandmother's cat? Her namesake is of course one of the "Three Little Maids from School" who come tripping on-stage early in Act 1 of Gilbert and Sullivan's operetta *The Mikado*. The connection between Pitti-Sing and Pitty Sing might not appear to be worth following up but for two reasons: the first is the nature of the fiction O'Connor was writing at this stage of her career; the second, growing out of the first, is that O'Connor herself seems clearly to reinforce the connection of the names by making one of the key utterances in her tale a clear echo of the best-known sentence from W. S. Gilbert's sardonic libretto. The Mikado explains himself and his conception of justice to his subjects by announcing, "My object all sublime / I shall achieve in time— / To let the punishment fit the crime— / The punishment fit the crime." The Misfit attempts to explain *himself* and the way, in his view, justice functions, to the bewildered grandmother by saying: "I call myself The Misfit because I can't make what all I done wrong fit what all I gone through in punishment."

Few commentators on the story have had anything to say about Pitty Sing, and those that have have been less than helpful. Puzzlement is the usual response; ignorance of, or generalized comment on, the connection with *The Mikado* character the norm. Josephine Hendin, the major commentator to date on Pitty Sing, may be taken as representative of how far interpretation of the cat's function in the tale has gone. "The meaning of the cat," she writes [in *The World of Flannery O'Connor,* 1970], "seems to derive precisely from its symbolic thinness. That a pet, a cat, leaping at random for no great reason, should cause the destruction of an entire family expresses the randomness, the pointlessness of the murders." Life, and indeed cats, may be random, but O'Connor as a writer, especially at this stage of her career, was emphatically not. Reading *Wise Blood*, written about the same time though published a year earlier, one feels that if it has a fault as a novel it is the almost excessively logical density of its symbolic texture. Only an insensitive reader could miss the precisely crafted significance of individual props (for example, Haze's Jesus-seeing hat, the potato-peeling machine, or, indeed, the mummy, revealed in the fullness of time and plot as the new Jesus of the Church of Christ without Christ) and the ingenious intricacy of the roles these props are called on to play or the interlocking system of character-doubling which underpins, with almost too cerebral a clarity, the fictional structure. "Symbolic thinness," "random," and "pointless" are inappropriate terms to apply to O'Connor's fictional technique in this tale which shares many of *Wise Blood*'s characteristics.

I am less interested in "proving" sources than in following up some of the numerous and complex *Mikado* echoes in "A Good Man Is Hard to Find," letting them throw what light they can; the fact that the light is considerable is less surprising than one might suppose. The priorities of this paper preclude an extended discussion of Gilbert's libretto, the best-known of course among many, but, to a reader familiar with both, it is obvious that important aspects of its technique—the hardness of its intellectual

structure and its witty brilliance—are manifest in O'Connor's early fiction. Utilizing the major elements of wit—paradox, reversals of language and action—both works explore thematically the significance of the mysteriously arbitrary design by which characters and situations are moved despite themselves. But while Gilbert's all-powerful Mikado figure is deployed along his happily despotic way for purposes of social satire, the vagaries of human pretension are exploited by O'Connor as the material for a blackly comic exploration of the terrifying nature of Providence. A clue to that nature is provided by the epigraph to the volume *A Good Man Is Hard to Find,* a feature of the story to which I shall return.

The primary usefulness of Pitty Sing, the connector between the two works, is to illuminate the roles of The Misfit and the grandmother in the O'Connor story; nevertheless, it is more useful to begin with a broader perspective. The best starting-point for seeing how the road coming out of the town square of Titipu leads structurally to the back roads of Georgia is the Mikado himself. Five minutes into the first act we learn that this supreme, arbitrary law-giver had paradoxically begun his reign by introducing a law with a purportedly educative purpose. Intended as "A plan whereby / Young men might best be steadied," it has succeeded in nothing but handing the kingdom over to absurdity and reducing the idea of law to a mockery. The "crime" is flirting, the punishment, beheading: "Our great Mikado, virtuous man, / When he to rule our land began, / Resolved to try / A plan whereby / Young men might best be steadied. / So he decreed in words succinct, / That all who flirted, leered or winked / (Unless connubially linked), / Should forthwith be beheaded."

The absurd law begets a correlatively absurd response, reductive in nature, from the affected townspeople: "And I expect you'll all agree / That he was right to so decree. / And I am right / And you are right, / And all is right as right can be!" The law is a great leveller since everyone in Titipu is equally affected, but it is the young who suffer most: "The youth who winked a roving eye, / Or breathed a non-connubial sigh, / Was thereupon condemned to die—/ He usually objected."

Well might the youth of Titipu cry out with the voice of The Misfit, "I call myself The Misfit because I can't make what all I done wrong fit what all I gone through in punishment." However, The Misfit's perception of the irrationality of punishment is more thoroughgoing since it draws out the Mikado's logic one step further: If the severity of punishment is pushed beyond all logical correlation, then all crimes take on the same moral weight. His reply to the grandmother's question about what he did to get sent to the penitentiary the first time makes the point unmistakably: "I forget what I done, lady. . . . I found out the crime don't matter. You can do one thing or you can do another, kill a man or take a tire off his car, because sooner or later you're going to forget what it was you done and just be punished for it."

The final stanza of the song about the Mikado's law introduces a new character, Ko-Ko, whose career finds an astonishing echo in that of The Misfit. The townspeople of Titipu had taken counter-action against the threat of near-universal decapitation: "And so we straight let out on bail, / A convict from the county jail, / Whose head was next / On some pretext / Condemned to be mown off, / And made *him* Headsman, for we said, / 'Who's next to be decapited / Cannot cut off another's head / Until he's cut his own off.'" Ko-Ko, the "cheap tailor," released in order to be appointed headsman, becomes thereby a paradox: through the townspeople's recognition of their mutual vulnerability, he becomes his own next victim—the lowest man in the kingdom, the condemned man—simultaneously with the highest (since the rank of Lord High Executioner is the highest next to that of the Lawgiver himself). Ko-Ko thus points towards both The Misfit's paradoxical Jesus "who thown everything off balance" by becoming simultaneously the lowest and the highest, the all-powerful Being who allows himself to be put to death, and towards The Misfit himself, who is the condemned-man-turned-executioner of the grandmother and her family.

The Mikado, accepting the logic underlying the townspeople's stratagem, extends it by adopting a moral stance which links Titipu structurally with Georgia. Pooh-Bah explains: "Our logical Mikado, seeing no moral difference between the dignified judge who condemns a criminal to die, and the industrious mechanic who carries out the sentence, has rolled the two offices into one, and every judge is now his own executioner." O'Connor follows the pattern by rolling the two offices into one, requiring The Misfit to act as both "judge" and "mechanic."

However, the *OED* [*Oxford English Dictionary*] distinguishes two principal meanings of the verb "judge": 1. "To try or pronounce sentence; to condemn"; and 2. "To form an opinion about; to estimate; to appraise." The first meaning is the more relevant to *The Mikado,* but it is The Misfit's interest in the second that leads to his carrying out the first. "My daddy," he confides to the grandmother, "said I was a different breed of dog from my brothers and sisters. 'You know,' Daddy said, 'it's some that can live their whole life out without asking about it and it's others has to know why it is, and this boy is one of the latters. He's going to be into everything!'" The Misfit is moved to pass sentence on individual cases by his impulse to philosophize on the nature of the circumstances which produce the individual cases: Since Jesus "has thown everything off balance . . . then it's nothing for you to do but enjoy the few minutes you got left the best way you can—by killing somebody or burning down his house or doing some other meanness to him. No pleasure but meanness." The fruits of this considered judgement are the decision to kill the family. The execution of Bailey together with his wife and children he delegates to Hiram and Bobby Lee; the execution of the grandmother he reserves—for reasons of narrative strategy suggested by *The Mikado*—for himself.

That the unanticipated, though very logical, corollary of the Mikado's "object all sublime"—the ironic transformation of victim into judge and executioner—helps account for O'Connor's conception of The Misfit should now be clear, but, as a matter of fact, the character in whom the judge-executioner pattern occurs most startlingly is not The Misfit but the grandmother herself. It is her case which is dramatized in the story; it is she whom O'Connor makes act out—for the most part unwittingly—the pattern of crime-punishment-victim-judge-executioner before the reader's disbelieving eyes. Indeed, she exhibits the pattern with a good deal more subtlety and complexity than The Misfit himself does. But The Misfit, as his name suggests, is a special case, while the grandmother is the average person who, by means of the savage logic of paradox (both *The Mikado*'s and O'Connor's), is turned into the opposite of what she intended to be. Let us trace the pattern first, then, as she exhibits it.

The grandmother is established, in the story's abrupt opening sentence ("The grandmother didn't want to go to Florida") in terms of her "wants"—characteristically negative—and of the destinations she either rejects or aims at. She immediately begins to manipulate to achieve her goal of getting to Tennessee rather than to Florida, pointing out to her son Bailey with an air of self-satisfaction that an escaped convict is headed towards Florida: "I wouldn't take my children in any direction with a criminal like that aloose in it. I couldn't answer to my conscience if I did." The course of action she embarks on develops according to a Titipu logic unperceived by herself or those accompanying her to lead to an end other than that which she envisages: by sending the family mistakenly down the abandoned road, she unwittingly leads her child and his children in precisely the direction in which the criminal is "aloose"; by starting up suddenly in the car when she realizes her mistake—that she has led them down the road to her not-yet-abandoned "want" to go to Tennessee—she lets the concealed denizen of Titipu, the cat Pitty Sing, "aloose" among them to cause the accident; by voicing her recognition of The Misfit, she seals her fate, sending them all to their ultimate destination.

Bizarre as it sounds, her "crime" is nothing more than to want to go to Tennessee rather than to Florida, and to engage in manipulation to get there; her punishment is that she has to "answer to [her] conscience" for leading her family to their deaths and to lose her own life. The disproportion is scarcely less absurd than that of being decapitated for flirting. The logic, therefore, by which the grandmother becomes victim and executioner is easy enough to trace; it is perhaps more difficult to see her as "judge." Nevertheless, it is the handling of the "judge" aspect that reveals most clearly O'Connor's reworking of the *Mikado* material into something extraordinarily original. Understanding it requires turning to another character from *The Mikado,* one who has bequeathed to the grandmother her most notable characteristic, her defining of herself by her gentility.

This is Pooh-Bah, the courtier who sets out the Mikado's logic in combining the offices of judge and executioner. Pooh-Bah relates that when Ko-Ko, the condemned man, was released from prison to be made Lord High Executioner, all the great officers of state resigned in a body because they were too proud to serve under a former criminal. Pooh-Bah thereupon allowed himself to be persuaded to accept all their various offices to become Lord High Everything Else, an act which required him to mortify his family pride since, as he disarmingly confesses, "I am, in point of fact, a particularly haughty and exclusive person, of pre-Adamite ancestral descent. . . . my family pride is something inconceivable. I can't help it. I was born sneering."

Pooh-Bah is invited, in the course of Act 1, to take on one more office, Lord High Substitute, which means putting his head on the block in place of Ko-Ko for whom a substitute victim is required. Pooh-Bah predictably declines, but the reasons he gives are instructive for understanding O'Connor's conception of the grandmother. He advances family pride as the reason why he is simultaneously obliged both to accept and decline the honour: "I am so proud, / If I allowed / My family pride / To be my guide, / I'd volunteer / To quit this sphere / Instead of you, / In a minute or two." Family pride must be "mortified," however; humility forbids him to make such a straightforwardly heroic gesture.

Family pride has two sides according to Pooh-Bah: the first is the *noblesse oblige* dimension which inspires man to rise magnanimously to heroic challenges; the second is the exploitative dimension which tempts man to use his gentility merely to avoid unpleasantness. Pooh-Bah achieves the second by paying lip-service to the first; in the very act of acknowledging that *noblesse* does oblige him to put himself forward as voluntary victim, he parodies the obligation by ironically turning it into self-promotional capital—advancing it as a reason why he should *not* have to die.

The grandmother's conception of gentility is altogether shabbier; that *noblesse* should oblige her to anything does not enter her head, although she is as quick as Pooh-Bah to lay the obligation on others. For her, gentility is a pure and simple defence against unpleasantness. "Does it seem right to you, lady," The Misfit asks the grandmother, "that one is punished a heap and another ain't punished at all?" The grandmother's response—the exchange takes place between the off-stage shootings of her daughter-in-law and of her two remaining grandchildren—is to use both The Misfit's gentility and her own as the reason why *she* should not have to die. "'Jesus!' the old lady cried. 'You've got good blood! I know you wouldn't shoot a lady! I know you come from nice people! Pray! Jesus, you ought not to shoot a lady.'" She advances *his* gentility as the reason he should not kill her; *hers* as the reason she should not have to die.

O'Connor has been careful to establish this pattern back in the very first exchange between The Misfit and the grandmother, precisely at the point at which the old lady voiced her recognition of the stranger *as* The Misfit:

> "You wouldn't shoot a lady, would you?" the grandmother said and removed the clean handkerchief from her cuff and began to slap at her eyes with it.

> The Misfit pointed the toe of his shoe into the ground and made a little hole and then covered it up again. "I would hate to have to," he said.

The mordancy of The Misfit's answering gesture in this opening joust indicates how very mistaken the grandmother is in advancing her gentility as a defence against the threat he represents. Indeed, the futility of reliance on her shabbily self-interested conception of gentility has already been signalled by the flimsiness of the genteel paraphernalia with which she has equipped herself for the journey—the "clean handkerchief," accessory to the "navy blue straw sailor hat" and the "navy blue dress with a small white print," worn so that "in case of an accident, anyone seeing her dead on the highway would know at once that she was a lady"—and by the emptiness of her defensive slapping gesture.

Unfortunately for her, however, *noblesse* carries no more sense of obligation for him than it does for her:

> "Listen," the grandmother almost screamed, "I know you're a good man. You don't look a bit like you have common blood. I know you must come from nice people!"

> "Yes mam," he said, "finest people in the world."

The grandmother's threadbare genteel vocabulary—"lady," "good," "common," "nice," "fine"—stands in need of redefinition, which the tale proceeds to give it. Lacking any glimmer of the magnanimity or generosity inherent in true gentility, she is pushed by the pressure of events towards a perception of the terrifying demands of gentility in its root meaning, which the *OED* gives as from "L. *gentilis,* of the same *gens* or race." The moment at which the old lady makes the breakthrough to this level of understanding is, though she is scarcely aware of it, clearly marked for the reader as a moment of vision:

> The grandmother's head cleared for an instant. She saw the man's face twisted close to her own as if he were going to cry and she murmured, "Why, you're one of my babies. You're one of my own children!" She reached out and touched him on the shoulder. The Misfit sprang back as if a snake had bitten him and shot her three times through the chest.

The grandmother, at this moment when her "head clear[s]," becomes the "good man" who is so hard to find, precisely because she abandons her hold on gentility as a defence, a means of keeping the unpleasant "other" at a distance. *Noblesse oblige*: she acknowledges her kinship with, her motherhood of, The Misfit. That the grandmother should be executed at the very moment she becomes "good"—indeed *because* she has become "good"—is the final link in the paradoxical chain of logic. Having been made the inadvertent executioner of her family, she transcends the threat posed by The Misfit by reaching a new, altruistic level of judgement about him, the consequence of which is death. In her momentary clarity of vision, the grandmother judges The Misfit and herself to be members essentially of the same race—the human—and reaches out to seal the kinship with an embrace. The Misfit ratifies his name by his violent repudiation of the kinship. Yet the kinship *is* there, and a glance back at Pooh-Bah in *The Mikado* will help illuminate its nature. Pooh-Bah is haughtily exclusive because he considers himself to be of "pre-Adamite ancestral descent." The grandmother, having set herself apart from "common" man, learns now that The Misfit is one of her "own," that they are both children of Adam. As Pooh-Bah would have died at the hands of Ko-Ko, the executioner whose place he would be taking had he followed the demands of gentility, so the grandmother dies at the hands of The Misfit in answer to his question, "Does it seem right to you, lady, that one is punished a heap and another ain't punished at all?" All the children of Adam are born to be punished by suffering and death; the grandmother's acknowledgement—however muddled—of this mystery of kinship earns her the right to the title, "lady."

But now it is time to return to the prototype, Pitty Sing, who suggested all these connections, and trace the geometrically precise role O'Connor has assigned to him. Although mentioned early in the story, he does not enter the action properly speaking until he is inadvertently released from his hiding-place in the car and causes the accident. He then disappears again until just after the grandmother's death, when he returns to offer himself to The Misfit who, surprisingly, responds by picking him up.

The sequence, however, can be described from a quite different perspective: the grandmother (we may say) initiates the action by bringing Pitty Sing with her; Pitty Sing, accidentally made a free agent, initiates a specific sequence of events and disappears while The Misfit completes the sequence; Pitty Sing reappears, identifies with The Misfit, an identification which The Misfit accepts. The cat, therefore, begins by being identified with the grandmother; having helped bring about the grandmother's death, he then identifies with her murderer. Clearly, the relationship of both cat and convict to the grandmother is primarily structural; the clue to how it works lies with Pitti-Sing, the prototype.

The original Pitti-Sing is one of two companions of Yum-Yum, the heroine of *The Mikado*. The grouping of the girls as a threesome—they introduce themselves rather insistently in their opening trio as "Three little maids from school"—suggests a model for O'Connor's gangster trio as they step out of their "hearse-like" automobile and arrange themselves around their "scholarly" leader in front of the shaken family.

The primary note associated with the girls throughout the operetta is mockery. They begin, on their entry, by attacking the pretensions of Pooh-Bah (the incarnation of virtually every aspect of the status quo) to gentility, and his condescension towards their youth ("Go away, little girls. Can't talk to little girls like you. Go away"), a condescension echoed by the grandmother ("In my time children were more respectful of their native states and their parents and everything else").

Ko-Ko, the Lord High Executioner, oscillating ambivalently between his roles as society's victim and its sanctioned exterminator, participates in the mockery of Pooh-Bah in a way which provides a pattern for The Misfit's ambiguous gallantry towards the grandmother. "Don't laugh at him, he can't help it," Ko-Ko explains in an aside to the girls; "Never mind them, they don't understand the delicacy of your position," he reassures Pooh-Bah *sotto voce*. The Misfit apologizes for Bailey's outburst of profanity at his mother. "Lady, don't you get upset. Sometimes a man says things he don't mean. I don't reckon he meant to talk to you thataway," and then, as he sends Bailey off to be shot, he apologizes without a hint of a smile for not having a shirt on before the "ladies."

Any member of the trio of school-girl mockers might perhaps have made a natural prototype for the cat who will permanently end the grandmother's pretensions to gentility, but what presumably caught O'Connor's attention about Pitti-Sing is the fact that, of the three, she alone is witness to an execution. The *Mikado* execution (Act II) is, to be sure, not real but fictional. It is fabricated by Ko-Ko, Pooh-Bah, and Pitti-Sing to appease the Mikado who, arriving unexpectedly, wants to hear the details of all recent executions. None having taken place, they invent one. The fictional *Mikado* execution provided O'Connor with a number of features which she incorporated into her handling of the grandmother's death. I would now like to trace those.

Ko-Ko, the prototype for The Misfit, sings the first stanza, setting out, in the *persona* of the executioner, the preparations for the decapitation: "The criminal cried, as he dropped him down, / In a state of wild alarm—/ With a frightful, frantic, fearful frown, / I bared my big right arm. . . . Oh, never shall I / Forget the cry, / Or the shriek that shrieked he, / As I gnashed my teeth, / When from its sheath / I drew my snickersnee!"

Two moments in this narration find an echo in **"A Good Man."** The first, the threatening menace of the executioner in the opening quatrain causing the criminal to "[drop] him down," reappears in the climax of The Misfit's apologia just before he kills the grandmother: "'. . . then it's nothing for you to do but enjoy the few minutes you got left the best way you can—by killing somebody or burning down his house or doing some other meanness,' he said and his voice had become almost a snarl."

In the state of "wild alarm" produced by this theological onslaught, the grandmother squirms, struggles, and mumbling, "Maybe He didn't raise the dead," sinks down in the ditch.

The second, more emphatic, echo from Ko-Ko's narration ("Oh, never shall I / Forget the cry . . .") produces one of the most electrifying moments in the dialogue between the old lady and her killer. The second group of shots—those killing her daughter-in-law and her two remaining grandchildren—is heard from the woods:

> There were two more pistol reports and the grandmother raised her head like a parched old turkey hen crying

for water and called, "Bailey Boy, Bailey Boy!" as if her heart would break.

"Jesus was the only One that ever raised the dead," The Misfit continued.

The grandmother's crying-out signals a crucial change of direction for her on the road out of Titipu. She cries out to/for her son who is in fact already dead, killed by the first pair of shots. The poignancy of the moment comes in part from the homeliness of the parched turkey hen metaphor; its significance lies in her calling out not on behalf of herself but for another person. The breaking of her heart moves her towards the disinterested maternal love that becomes both her nemesis and her glory. The Misfit's sardonic response—"Jesus was the only One that ever raised the dead"—cannot halt her approaching readiness, almost in spite of herself, to offer The Misfit a place to "fit," the place of the Bailey Boy he has just murdered.

The second stanza of the execution narration, belonging to Pitti-Sing, I will return to in a moment. Pooh-Bah describes, in the final stanza, what happens immediately after the victim has been executed: "Now though you'd have thought that head was dead / (For its owner dead was he), / It stood on its neck, with a smile well-bred, / And bowed three times to me! / It was none of your impudent off-hand nods, / But as humble as could be; / For it clearly knew / The deference due / To a man of pedigree!"

This underpins the grandmother's reliance on her own gentility as *the* quality which will see her through safely into the next world ("anyone seeing her dead on the highway would know at once that she was a lady"). The smile Pooh-Bah discerns on the corpse acknowledging his pedigree is echoed on the grandmother's dead face: "Hiram and Bobby Lee returned from the woods and stood over the ditch, looking down at the grandmother who half sat and half lay in a puddle of blood with her legs crossed under her like a child and her face smiling up at the cloudless sky." The fact is, her gentility *has* seen her through; however, it is gentility now made authentic, as I suggested a moment ago, by its disinterested acknowledgement of kinship with The Misfit, acceptance of his pedigree as one of her "own children." Her smile is now directed towards that "cloudless sky" which is, in effect, the sky of *Wise Blood,* carrying on above the unseeing eyes of Hazel Motes and the inhabitants of Taulkinham its "vast construction work that involved the whole order of the universe and would take all time to complete."

The stanza Gilbert assigns Pitti-Sing narrates the moment of execution: "He shivered and shook as he gave the sign / For the stroke he didn't deserve; / When all of a sudden his eye met mine, / And it seemed to brave his nerve . . . / As the sabre true / Cut cleanly through / His cervical vertebrae! / When a man's afraid, / A beautiful maid / Is a cheering sight to see; / And it's oh, I'm glad, / That moment sad / Was soothed by the sight of me!"

The primary point of connection between the two Pitti-Sings is that each is a witness to and implicated in an execution. The two moments made to stand out in Gilbert's version—when the victim's eye suddenly meets Pitti-Sing's and the moment "sad" when the victim is "soothed" by the sight of her—are particularly helpful in clarifying the intricacies of the role relationships among the grandmother, The Misfit, and the cat. Understanding Pitty Sing's role in the action from the beginning will clarify his role in the grandmother's execution.

Essentially, Pitty Sing functions as a double of the grandmother (much the way Enoch Emery, Solace Layfield, and others act for Hazel Motes in *Wise Blood*), expressing a dimension of her self of which she is largely unaware. The nature of that aspect, pointed to by the *Mikado* prototype, becomes clear when we trace the operation of the double. The morning of the trip, the grandmother is "first one in the car, ready to go." The first mention of the cat follows immediately: "[The grandmother] had her big black valise that looked like the head of a hippopotamus in one corner, and underneath it she was hiding a basket with Pitty Sing, the cat, in it." The point of the oddly incongruous "head of a hippopotamus" image is twofold: "hippopotamus" obviously suggests the size, colour, and shape of the valise, but the relevance of the "head" emerges only—if at all—with the announcement of the cat's name and the reader's retroactive realization that the cat's prototype appears in a work dominated by the threat of decapitation. The cat is a concealed, forbidden presence in the car. The grandmother's reason for bringing the cat against her son's wishes—her fear that, left on his own, Pitty Sing might unwittingly bring about his own death—ironically figures forth the direction her own life is about to take because of her insistence on bringing Pitty Sing with her on the journey.

The grandmother's other reason for not wanting to leave Pitty Sing behind ("because he would miss her too much") suggests both the symbolic identification between the two and the grandmother's ignorance of Pitty Sing's true nature. The ground underlying both these reasons is her narcissistic wilfulness ("*She didn't intend* for the cat to be left alone") which opposes itself to Bailey's wishes ("*He didn't like* to arrive at a motel with a cat" [emphases added]). Pitty Sing functions essentially as an extension of the grandmother's wilfulness.

The journey begins; Pitty Sing remains quiescent while the grandmother takes "cat naps." The grandmother continues to pursue her own will by "craftily" manipulating the children ("Not telling the truth but wishing she were") to "yell and scream" until their father agrees to take them to the house which represents the imperfectly remembered desires of her youth. Bailey unwittingly underlines the portentousness of the decision: "All right, . . . but get this: this is the only time we're going to stop for anything like this. This is the one and only time." When the grandmother suddenly realizes as they drive down the abandoned road that she has led them in the wrong direction, her startled reaction frees Pitty Sing to act out her—the grandmother's—wilfulness without any hindrance. The result is the car crash, after which Pitty Sing disappears.

The passage in which Pitty Sing makes his startlingly graphic entry into the tale as an active agent repays close analysis:

> The road [to the grandmother's remembered plantation] looked as if no one had travelled on it in months.

> "It's not much farther," the grandmother said and just as she said it, a horrible thought came to her. The thought was so embarrassing that she turned red in the face and her eyes dilated and her feet jumped up, upsetting her valise in the corner. The instant the valise moved, the newspaper top she had over the basket under it rose with a snarl and Pitty Sing, the cat, sprang onto Bailey's shoulder.

The grandmother's "thought"—the sudden realization that she has been betrayed by the determined, narcissistic "wanting" which has dominated her since the story's opening sentence—triggers off a series of reactions in which the parts of her body and her suitcase take on an identity and life of their own (like the head of the hippopotamus or the head which "bowed three times" to Pooh-Bah) and act out, independently, the meaning and consequences of the perception she has just had: "her eyes dilated . . . her feet jumped up. . . . the valise moved, the newspaper top . . . rose with a snarl," climaxing in "and Pitty Sing, the cat, sprang."

The cat's spring metamorphoses into another grotesque decapitation image: "Bailey remained in the driver's seat with the cat . . . clinging to his neck like a caterpillar." The causal connection between the grandmother's "thought" and the accident having been established ("The horrible thought she had before the accident was that the house she had remembered so vividly was not in Georgia but in Tennessee"), Bailey "removed the cat from his neck with both hands and flung it out the window against the side of a pine tree." While Bailey is still "in the driver's seat," he violently rejects the cat, real and symbolic, and steps out onto the road, unaware that he is in a landscape controlled by the logic of *The Mikado*; his own and his family's execution thereby become inevitable. Inevitable because, although Pitty Sing has vanished, the grandmother is about to meet and be driven by her impetuous wilfulness to recognize the agent destined to continue the process of destruction set in motion by Pitty Sing. Or, to put it in literary terms, The Misfit is about to take over Pitty Sing's role as double to the grandmother.

Many readers of **"A Good Man"** have been puzzled by the grandmother's initial reaction to The Misfit: "The grandmother had the peculiar feeling that the bespectacled man was someone she knew. His face was as familiar to her as if she had known him all her life but she could not recall who he was." Identifying him a few minutes later as The Misfit, she cries, "I recognized you at once!" What is clear to the reader is that she didn't recognize him as something (or someone) who has always been present in her life but as something or someone she cannot yet put a name to; she recognizes him as that aspect of herself which has been present since the first sentence, that aspect which has till now found its symbolic expression in Pitty

Sing. Bailey having flung Pitty Sing temporarily out of the action, The Misfit takes over and extends Pitty Sing's function until Pitty Sing himself returns to endorse what has transpired in his absence.

The links between the cat and The Misfit are many, beginning with the cat's change of sex from female to male. The verbal associations are powerful. For example, The Misfit's first appearance is in the newspaper the grandmother is holding as the story opens, "rattling" it at Bailey, the same paper which makes its reappearance at the moment Pitty Sing is inadvertently turned loose by the grandmother. A quick reading of the passage might suggest that Pitty Sing springs up from *under* the "newspaper top" which conceals him—as in actuality he would—but the language embodies a more precise suggestion: "The instant the valise moved, the newspaper top she had over the basket under it rose with a snarl and Pitty Sing, the cat, sprang." That is to say, the decapitated head of the hippopotamus gets out of the way, the newspaper containing The Misfit rises with a snarl, and Pitty Sing springs to send the car into the ditch. The "snarl" emanating from the "newspaper top" recurs at that crucial moment of the story when The Misfit reaches the climax of his frighteningly logical deductions from the proposition that Jesus "thown everything off balance": "'No pleasure but meanness,' he said and his voice had become almost a snarl."

The re-entry of Pitty Sing into the story as The Misfit orders his men to "Take [the grandmother] off and thow her where you thown the others" is no more accidental, structurally speaking, than any other aspect of his role; neither is his cosily domesticated overture to The Misfit, nor The Misfit's acceptance of the offered identification. The shocking juxtaposition of The Misfit's answering gesture to the cat—picking it up—with his brutality to the grandmother—shooting her three times "through the chest" merely because she touched him—is a typical O'Connor procedure in this story, but it should not divert us from seeing that, primarily, the function of this final gesture is to express the oneness of Pitty Sing with The Misfit.

The two aspects of the *Mikado* execution emphasized by Gilbert's Pitti-Sing, the moment at which the victim's eye met hers and the sense that her presence "soothed that moment sad" for the victim, are both thematically relevant to and intertwined with **"A Good Man Is Hard to Find."** Since the grandmother reaches the same eye-level as The Misfit only when she sinks to the ground under his snarling "No pleasure but meanness," it is then that, her "head clear[ing]," she sees "the man's face twisted close to her own," and reaches out to him compassionately. As in *The Mikado,* the victim looks at the executioner: the expression on his face ("as if he were going to cry") precipitates the gesture which in its turn precipitates the shot. But if the grandmother's touch prompts The Misfit to kill her, it is what he has not been able to *see* that is at the root of his reaction: "'I wasn't there so I can't say [Jesus] didn't [raise the dead],' The Misfit said. 'I wisht I had of been there,' he said, hitting the ground with his fist. 'It ain't right I wasn't there because if I had of been there I would of known. . . . and I wouldn't be like I am now.'" Not knowing because he wasn't there to see, he shoots her.

That the limitations on his vision are implicit in the Pitti-Sing perspective is clear from the careful juxtaposition O'Connor makes between the two gestures she now gives The Misfit. He puts away his glasses as a prelude to picking up the cat:

> Then he put his gun on the ground and took off his glasses and began to clean them. . . . Without his glasses, The Misfit's eyes were red-rimmed and pale and defenseless-looking. "Take her off and thow her where you thown the others," he said, picking up the cat that was rubbing itself against his leg.

The glasses, in conjunction with the return of Pitty Sing, help chart The Misfit's spiritual course in the last moments of the story. The "scholarly look" they endowed him with on his first appearance established his connection with the *Mikado* schoolgirl whose function is to mock; removing the glasses, he removes the mocking perspective, allowing him to look as "defenseless" as the old lady now lying in the ditch with "her legs crossed under her like a child's." The last thing O'Connor would do, however, is sentimentalize this moment of vulnerability; indeed, the removal of the glasses enables The Misfit to see and pronounce a very hard truth—a sardonic version of Pitti-Sing's "sooth[ing] that moment sad" for her victim and the only eulogy the grandmother will enjoy: "She would of been a good woman . . . if it had been somebody there to shoot her every minute of her life." Cold comfort, the reader may well feel; but O'Connor is merely being relentlessly—albeit characteristically—precise. The eulogy is "sooth[ing]" to the exact degree allowed by the compassionate ferocity, the paradoxical theological perspective, expressed in the excerpt from St. Cyril of Jerusalem which O'Connor chose as the epigraph to the collection in which **"A Good Man"** figures as the title-story: "The dragon is by the side of the road, watching those who pass. Beware lest he devour you. We go to the father of souls, but it is necessary to pass by the dragon."

The ironically sentimental tableau made by Pitty Sing and The Misfit—the killer cuddling the pussy-cat—represents, in structural terms, the grandmother's apparent defeat at the hands of her "dragon." While the obvious dragon waiting by the side of the road may indeed have been The Misfit, it was Pitty Sing who, in an immediate sense, brought her to the rendezvous. However, what is even clearer is that both these dragons are, as symbolic extensions of the grandmother's own inadequacies, interiorized dragons. The grandmother's rendezvous on her way to "the father of souls" is, in the last analysis, with herself.

The tale's closing moment is a tableau in which Pitty Sing and The Misfit, joined by Bobby Lee, recreate the schoolgirls' opening trio, while refining the nature of the sardonicism their predecessors expressed. The girls sang:

YUM-YUM: Everything is a source of fun! (*Chuckle*).

PEEP-BO: Nobody's safe, for we care for none! (*Chuckle*).

PITTI-SING: Life is a joke that's just begun! (*Chuckle*).

"Some fun!" is Bobby Lee's verdict, echoing Yum-Yum as he "slid[es] down the ditch" with a "yodel" instead of a "chuckle." The Misfit, for his part, has made it a clean sweep—"Nobody's safe"—by finishing off the family in the person of the grandmother. Nevertheless, with glasses off and Pitty Sing in his arms, The Misfit is moved to stretch his vision beyond the restrictions of his own earlier perspective ("No pleasure but meanness"). Bobby Lee's facile enjoyment is curtly dismissed ("Shut up, Bobby Lee"); Pitti-Sing's "Life is a joke!" has gone sour. Facing up to the implications of the epigraph, he utters a disclaimer that is also the bottom line: "It's no real pleasure in life."

Mary Jane Schenck (essay date 1988)

SOURCE: "Deconstructed Meaning in Two Short Stories by Flannery O'Connor," in *Ambiguities in Literature and Film,* edited by Hans P. Braendlin, The Florida State University Press, 1988, pp. 125-34.

[*In the following excerpt, Schenck offers a deconstructionist analysis of "A Good Man Is Hard to Find."*]

Many contemporary theories of criticism address problems of meaning based on philosophies of language and the aesthetics of reception, so we worry less today about the author's conscious intentions than in previous times. Nevertheless, interpreting works of an author who has commented extensively on his or her own art may still be considered presumptuous. When the author has offered religious interpretations, counterarguments may seem to border on the heretical. Such are the risks for critics attempting to discuss how the fiction of Flannery O'Connor creates meanings in addition to or in contrast with what she herself said about her work.

O'Connor frequently commented on the Catholic faith, which she insisted formed her work, and most critics accept her own exegetical interpretations of her bizarre and troubling stories. Although the stories seem too brutal to be illustrations of Christian doctrine, at least as we conventionally conceive of it, O'Connor was able to justify her preoccupation with the ugly and grotesque by insisting on the writer's role as a prophet who must shake the reader and open his complacent eyes to reality and the need for grace. She was quite emphatic about the didactic function of the narrated events for both characters and readers, though the complications of interpreting her stories arise from the fact that they are not straightforward narratives like parables or exempla. Her texts are thoroughly ironic, and her use of irony creates ambiguities that undercut her own interpretations, even suggesting opposite ones, as other critics have suggested.

What I would like to do is consider the ironic language of the texts in light of what Baudelaire in "De l'Essence du Rire" and Paul de Man in "The Rhetoric of Temporality" have revealed about this figure. For Baudelaire, comedy results from a doubling of spectator and laughable object or person. The heightened form of comedy, called irony, is in part an internalized doubling; it is a capacity to be at once self and other. As de Man explains:

> The *dedoublement* thus designates the activity of a consciousness by which a man differentiates himself from the non-human world. . . . The reflective disjunction not only occurs *by means* of language as a privileged category, but it transfers the self out of the empirical world into a world constituted out of, and in, language. . . . Language thus conceived divides the subject into an empirical self, immersed in the wold, and a self that becomes like a sign in its attempt at differentiation and self-definition.

What de Man says of the ironic consciousness accurately depicts the method by which characters are created and create themselves in O'Connor's fiction. In **"A Good Man Is Hard to Find"** . . . characters consciously or unconsciously use both written and oral language as well as pictorial "texts" to create a doubled self to escape an empirical one. To the extent that they succeed, they illustrate the performative quality of language, momentarily creating reality rather than reflecting it. But most of O'Connor's characters fail to understand the performative and arbitrary nature of their language. The disastrous climaxes so characteristic of her fiction are created in part by the conflict between the two selves as well as the conflict between characters who all may be doubled. The ironic doubling leads to a complete disintegration of the self at the moment when the character must confront the absence of grounding behind the linguistic self. As de Man explains, this process is not a finite or affirmative one. It is a radical process of deconstruction leading to madness. In a statement that well could have been written about the ironic process in O'Connor's fiction, de Man says:

> Irony is unrelieved *vertige,* dizziness to the point of madness. Sanity can exist only because we are willing to function within the conventions of duplicity and dissimulation, just as social language dissimulates the inherent violence of relationships among human beings. Once this mask is shown to be a mask, the authentic being underneath appears necessarily as on the verge of madness.

As we will see in the following discussion, the unmasking of language in O'Connor's stories leads very precisely to violence, if not madness.

"A Good Man Is Hard to Find" presents a masterful portrait of a woman who creates a self and a world through language. From the outset, the grandmother relies on "texts" to structure her reality. The newspaper articles about The Misfit mentioned in the opening paragraph of the story is a written text which has a particular status in the narrative. It refers to events outside and prior to the primary *récit,* but it stands as an unrecognized prophecy of the events which occur at the end. For Bailey, the newspaper story is not important or meaningful, and for the grandmother it does not represent a real threat but is part of a ploy to get her own way. It is thus the first one of her "fictions," one which ironically comes true. The grandmother's whole personality is built upon the fictions she tells herself and her family. Although she knows Bailey would object if she brought her cat on the trip, the grandmother sneaks the cat into the car, justifying her behavior by imagining, "he would miss her too much and she was afraid he might brush against one of the gas burners and accidently asphyxiate himself." She also carefully cultivates a fiction about the past when people were good and when "children were more respectful of their native states and their parents and everything else." As she tells Red Sam at the Tower when they stop to eat, "People are certainly not nice like they used to be."

The grandmother reads fictional stories to the children, tells them ostensibly true stories, and provides a continual gloss on the physical world they are passing. "Little niggers in the country don't have things like we do. If I could paint, I'd paint that picture." Lacking that skill, the grandmother nevertheless verbally "creates" a whole universe as they ride along. "'Look at the graveyard!' the grandmother said, pointing it out. 'That was the old family burying ground. That belonged to the plantation.'" She creates the stories behind the visual phenomena she sees and explains relationships between events or her own actions which have no logic other than that which she lends them.

Her most important fiction is, of course, the story of the old plantation house which becomes more of an imperative as she tells it. The more she talks about it, the more she wants to see it again, so she does not hesitate to self-consciously lie about it. "'There was a secret panel in this house,' she said craftily, not telling the truth but wishing she were. . . ." At this point we see clearly the performative quality of the grandmother's language. At first it motivates her own desire, then spills over onto the children, finally culminating in their violent outburst of screaming and kicking to get their father to stop the car. The performative quality of her language becomes even more crucial when she realizes that she has fantasized the location of the house. She does not admit it, but her thoughts manifest themselves physically: "The thought was so embarrassing that she turned red in the face and her eyes dilated and her feet jumped up, upsetting her valise in the corner." Of course, it is her physical action which frees the cat and causes the accident. After the accident, she again fictionalizes about her condition, hoping she is injured so she can deflect Bailey's anger, and she cannot even manage to tell the truth about the details of the accident.

The scene with The Misfit is the apogee of the grandmother's use of "fictions" to explain and control reality, attempts that are thwarted by her encounter with a character who understands there is no reality behind her words. When the grandmother recognizes The Misfit, he tells her it would have been better if she hadn't, but she has *named*

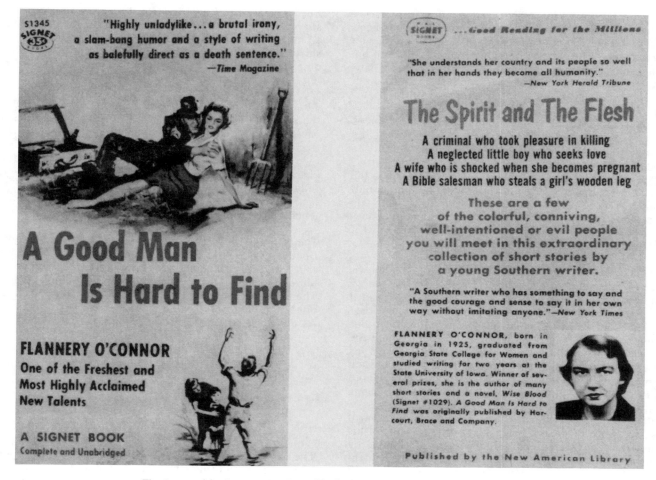

The front and back covers for the 1956 edition of A Good Man is Hard to Find.

him, thus forcing him to become what is behind his self-selected name. In a desperate attempt to cope with the threat posed by the murderer, the grandmother runs through her litany of convenient fictions. She believes that there are class distinctions ("I know you're a good man. You don't look a bit like you have common blood"), that appearance reflects reality ("You shouldn't call yourself The Misfit because I know you're a good man at heart. I can just look at you and tell"), that redemption can be achieved through work ("You could be honest too if you'd only try. . . . Think how wonderful it would be to settle down . . ."), and finally, that prayer will change him ("'Pray, pray,' she commanded him").

In contrast to the grandmother, whose flood of questions, explanations, and exhortations accompany the sequence of murderous events, the mother and Bailey react only physically. Deprived of language, they are barely more than props in the drama unfolding around them. Even the grandmother soon starts to lose her voice, the only mechanism that stands between her and reality. When she does try to tell The Misfit he must pray, her language has become fractured; all that comes out is the end of a sentence. "She wanted to tell him that he must

pray. She opened and closed her mouth several times before anything came out. Finally she found herself saying, 'Jesus, Jesus,' meaning, Jesus will help you, but the way she was saying it, it sounded as if she might be cursing." She finally loses control of her language and the myths they provide: "'Maybe He didn't raise the dead,' the old lady mumbled, not knowing what she was saying and feeling so dizzy that she sank down in the ditch with her legs twisted under her."

When she reaches out to touch The Misfit and says, "Why you're one of my babies. You're one of my own children," she either has uttered her final fantasy, having lost touch with reality as she confuses The Misfit (who is now wearing Bailey's shirt) with her own child, or she is attempting a last ingratiating appeal for his sympathies. O'Connor's interpretation of this line is that at this moment the grandmother realizes, "even in her limited way, that she is responsible for the man before her and joined to him by ties of kinship which have their roots deep in the mystery she has been merely prattling about so far." This is one possible reading of the scene and in some quarters the accepted one, but we could also say that the grandmother simply is wrong again, and her comment provokes The Misfit into shooting her. Surely we witness here the moment when a clash of language creates the vertiginous movement of irony into violence and madness. The Misfit rejects her interpretations of his being and refuses to provide a grounding for that language. Her fictions are proven to be "just talk" and both her empirical and linguistic self are destroyed.

In counterpoint to the grandmother's slow destruction as each verbal system she has created fails to reflect the reality around her, The Misfit uses language literally to relate events, at the same time recognizing the dangerous power of words. His language accurately describes the accident scene: "'We turned over twice!' said the grandmother. 'Oncet,' he corrected. 'We seen it happen.'" He is the only one who seems to know that sometimes language fails utterly: "He seemed to be embarrassed as if he couldn't think of anything to say."

His understanding of himself is grounded not in a knowledge of the events of his empirical self but in the recognition that language has created him. His father provided him an essence by describing him as "a different breed of dog." He knows that he has been or done various things in his life, but he is curiously unclear about the crime which sent him to jail. Nevertheless, he says his punishment is no mistake for two reasons—a written document says he committed it and a psychiatrist told him so. Even though he maintains it was a lie, he accepts the power of words to define his existence, and he knows that he should get things in writing in order to control his life. Since he cannot make sense of the events of his empirical self, he quite consciously creates a double by remaining himself The Misfit and living out its violent implications. The phenomenon of a character acquiring a new identity by using a new name is common to both stories we are discussing, and it is the most explicit indication of the linguistically doubled self so crucial to the irony of the texts.

"A Good Man Is Hard to Find" presents a masterful portrait of a woman who creates a self and a world through language.

—*Mary Jane Schenck*

We might believe that The Misfit through his ironic vision has at least created a self that copes with the empirical world when he says, "It's nothing for you to do but enjoy the few minutes you got left the best way you can—by killing somebody or burning down his house or doing some other meanness to him. No pleasure but meanness." But in the very last line of the story, he deconstructs even this doubled self: "'Shut up, Bobby

Lee,' The Misfit said. 'It's no real pleasure in life.'" His strange alternations between polite talk and cold-blooded murder and his last statement demonstrate the radical shifting back and forth between selves that cancel each other figuratively as he has literally cancelled the shifting consciousness of the grandmother. . . .

At the conclusion of ["**A Good Man Is Hard to Find**"] the reader is left with a vision of destruction of human life both literal and figurative that is absurd rather than tragic because the victims are not heroic figures reduced to misfortune. They are ordinary, even unsympathetic characters who meet a grotesque fate. But they are not villains either, so it is difficult to accept the outcome as justified in any way by their conduct, no matter how much we may dislike the grandmother. . . .

The difficulty in "reconstructing meaning," to use Wayne Booth's term, is that the central characters with whom we should identify or from whom we hope to grasp some sense of meaning dissolve before our eyes into non-beings. The frightening moment occurs when we witness the fictional self confront a challenge to the reality of that self. As de Man and Baudelaire have pointed out:

> The movement of the ironic consciousness is anything but reassuring. The moment the innocence or authenticity of our sense of being in the world is put into question, a far from harmless process gets underway. It may start as a casual bit of play with a stray loose end of the fabric, but before long the entire texture of the self is unraveled and comes apart.

The personalities of [O'Connor's] characters are created by language, and this language fails them in one of two circumstances. They either are confronted by the natural world whose laws mock their interpretations, or they are confronted by a character who understands that language is mere convention. If the conventions are not shared, the encounter will lead to devastating physical or emotional violence. Seen from this perspective, the events which may seem absurd at first now appear to be well motivated by language. All types of language—names, Bible stories, daydreams, myths, sermons, and newspaper articles—function to create characters and events. The people are separated from each other and their world through this language, but at the outset the alienation is merely a tension inhibiting communication. By the end, when the language of the doubled selves has been unmasked, the characters behind it are totally deconstructed and no longer exist. Kierkegaard refers to "the infinite elasticity of irony, the secret trap door through which one is suddenly hurled downward, not like the schoolmaster in *The Elfs* who falls a thousand fathoms, but into the infinite nothingness of irony." In spite of her intentions to the contrary, at the end of O'Connor's stories we feel a sudden shock of recognition as we witness the unraveling of the characters' personalities. Like the characters' fictional selves, our own experience with the text is deconstructed as we sense ourselves "fall through the trap door," uncertain of where, or if, we will land on any firm ground of meaning.

Sheldon Currie (essay date 1990)

SOURCE: "A Good Grandmother Is Hard to Find: Story as Exemplum," in *The Antigonish Review,* Nos. 81-2, Spring-Summer, 1990, pp. 143-55.

[*In the following essay, Currie examines "A Good Man Is Hard to Find" as a religious exemplum.*]

Near the end of **"A Good Man Is Hard to Find,"** The Misfit's henchmen Hiram and Bobby Lee shoot the grandmother's son, Bailey, the two grandchildren, and the children's mother. After she exhausts her repertoire of verbal manoeuvers, in a desperate effort to save herself, the grandmother reaches out and touches The Misfit on the shoulder. He responds with three pistol shots to the chest, aborting a promising encounter between two people who have much in common. Then:

> Hiram and Bobby Lee returned from the woods and stood over the ditch, looking down at the grandmother who half sat and half lay in a puddle of blood with her legs crossed under her like a child's and her face smiling up at the cloudless sky.

This is the second mention of her legs, first as twisted, now as crossed. Critics seem agreed the author intends the reader to understand crossed legs as a sign of Christ's cross implying that the grandmother, at the last moment, accepts the gift of grace and is redeemed. Before the shots, before she reached to touch The Misfit on the shoulder, "She saw the man's twisted face close to her own as if he were going to cry and she murmured, 'Why you're one of my babies. You're one of my own children!'" Critics take her act to be of the same kind as the Ancient Mariner's blessing the slimy sea creatures and consequent lifting of the curse; the grandmother opened herself to God, God made the offer of grace, she accepted.

I think a deathbed conversion, a standard piety, is probably the farthest thing from O'Connor's mind at the end of this gruesome comedy [as Kathleen Feeley writes in *Flannery O'Connor: Voice of the Peacock,* 1982]:

> Flannery O'Connor despised sentimentality, a quality [she defined] as "giving to any creature more love than God gives it." She saw sentimentality as an attempted short cut to the grace of Redemption which overlooks its price.

The author disapproves of both The Misfit and the grandmother, although she is easier on the grandmother than many readers are. Indeed, the reader is unwittingly led to condemn her genteel, middle-class values; unwittingly, because no character in O'Connor more resembles the genteel reader than this grandmother does, particularly the reader who presumes to espouse Christian values. The alert reader should recall T. S. Eliot's reminder of Baudelaire's caution to the reader in *Les Fleurs du Mal:* "Hypocrite lecteur,—mon semblable,—mon frère!" On the other hand, readers who are prepared to disparage the grandmother's values are often quick to accord the Misfit a grudging

admiration. O'Connor intends and approves of this grudging admiration. But the question remains: who is the good man and who is the bad man in **"A Good Man Is Hard to Find"**?

Like Hazel Motes and Enoch Emery in *Wise Blood,* The Misfit and the grandmother are contrary aspects of the same problem. A close look at T. S. Eliot's influence on O'Connor's work will help us understand how these unlikely spiritual twins resemble one another and how they differ. Sally Fitzgerald has demonstrated that Eliot's *Wasteland* was a major influence on *Wise Blood,* and it is difficult now not to think of the wounded knight of the grail legend seeking the chapel perilous, as Hazel Motes carries his mysterious war wound up and down the streets of Taulkinham.

It would be interesting to know when O'Connor read Eliot's essay on Baudelaire, because a serious O'Connor student who reads it will soon be reminded of Hazel Motes and The Misfit. Here is Eliot on Baudelaire's relationship to christianity:

> He is discovering christianity for himself; he is not assuming it as a fashion or weighing social or political reasons, or any other accidents. He is beginning in a way at the beginning; and being a discoverer, is not altogether certain what he is exploring and to what it leads; he might almost be said to be making again, as one man, the effort of scores of generations. His christianity is rudimentary or embryonic, . . . His business was not to practice christianity, . . . [but] more important for his time—to assert its necessity.

Eliot's later statement about Baudelaire's dissatisfaction with "post-Voltaire France" could well serve as a description of Hazel Motes' or The Misfit's attitude toward the world, and by implication the world Flannery O'Connor so sharply criticizes for its lack of attention to significance:

> . . . the recognition of the reality of Sin is a New Life; and the possibility of damnation is so immense a relief in a world of electoral reform, plebiscites, sex reform and dress reform, that damnation itself is an immediate form of salvation—of salvation from the ennui of modern life, because it at least gives some significance of living.

"Baudelaire's notion of beatitude certainly tended to the wishy-washy," Eliot says, but (like Motes and The Misfit) he had a firm conviction that a perception of the importance of sin is essential for an adequate perception of the significance of human life. Eliot later encapsulates his own idea of what a human life is all about, and what a Christian life is all about. We can easily imagine O'Connor running her pencil under these lines:

> So far as we are human, what we do must be either evil or good; so far as we do evil or good, we are human; and it is better, in a paradoxical way, to do evil than to do nothing: at least, we exist. It is true to

say that the glory of man is his capacity for salvation; it is also true to say that his glory is his capacity for damnation. The worst that can be said of most of our malefactors, from statesmen to thieves, is that they are not men enough to be damned. Baudelaire was man enough for damnation . . .

Although Eliot disapproves of much in Baudelaire's life and work, he can't help according him a grudging admiration, just as the genteel reader accords the same to The Misfit. Eliot, with Dante, accorded the same grudging admiration for Anthony and Cleopatra whose sins were enormous, but at least they were important sins, committed with passion, unlike the pathetic transgressions of the typist and the young man carbuncular, home at the violet hour for a can of beans and a bit of hanky-panky, and unlike the mild mannered passivity of J. Alfred Prufrock. These people are not sinners. A social worker might stretch a point and put them down as slightly maladjusted; they have their problems, but they are not in the arena with lions.

In Flannery O'Connor's economy, as Hazel Motes might say, if you are not in the arena with the lions, then like Eliot's "malefactors," you are not man enough to be damned. Eliot lamented the fact that few who still accept Baudelaire's message: "La vraie civilisation . . . est dans la diminuition des traces du péché originel." Certainly O'Connor would agree. For her a sign of progress would not be the introduction of an enlightened penal code to accommodate the misfits of society, for example, as useful as such a code might be; but if the penal code were based on the assumption that every human being has a great potential for evil, which can be transformed into a great capacity for good, then true progress might be possible. For O'Connor "la diminuition des traces du péché originel" is not a question of social reorganization, but of a transformation of individuals from sinners to saints, as in the cases of St. Paul and St. Augustine.

Many other writers from Chaucer to Hemingway would agree with Baudelaire and have declared themselves in their work. For them, evil, or sin, the religious name for it, makes human life significant, and therefore interesting. A complete list might start with Chaucer, whose friar figured out he could have a more comfortable and fun-filled life if he could collect money from widows rather than hand it out to them. But many modern writers would impress Eliot, Baudelaire and O'Connor with their vision of how human beings behave at their best and worst.

Nathaniel Hawthorne, for whom O'Connor expressed admiration, displays a sense of humor more gentle, civilized, less raucous, less violent than hers, but based on the same perception of lost opportunity in the moral arena, and on the enormous discrepancy between the courageous and significant behavior people are capable of, and the timid, insipid, insignificant ways they often settle for.

Hawthorne is too civilized, perhaps too sensitive, to laugh out loud at Young Goodman Brown, who, like many of O'Connor's fictional people, is a cartoon character and the butt of the author's subtle humor. Hawthorne won't laugh at this sad young man, a Calvinistic caricature, but he smiles at his refusal to understand, that like his wife, Faith, and his neighbors, and his father and all his ancestors, he can only live a significant life by taking a chance on damnation. He won't understand that God didn't pick two teams, the good guys and the bad guys. He won't realize that there are only, on the one hand the bad guys, like his father and his wife, who are capable of transforming themselves into good guys, and on the other hand, guys like himself, who won't play, and therefore in any significant sense, never join the game, the human race.

Another young man of Hawthorne's invention, Robin, in "My Kinsman Major Molineux," manages better with the help of a guide. After crossing the water to pick up a job he presumes is saved for him by his kinsman, Robin discovers that Major Molineux no longer enjoys the power he wielded under the old dispensation. Now the young man will have to find his own place, brave the dangers, or get back on the boat. Hawthorne tries to identify and define political and spiritual freedom, and the price that must be paid. The price is danger. He smiles at spiritual adolescents who naively believe that freedom, spiritual, political or economic, is a gift handed out to nice people by a benign forefather, so they won't have to worry and can devote their lives to feeding their cats and teaching Sunday school. As O'Connor pointed out in her introduction to *Wise Blood,* a person's integrity lies in what he is not able to do. Dignity and freedom lie not in what has been settled once and for all, but in what has not yet been settled. It is essential to have something to settle. Without weakness there can be no strength, without sin no salvation.

> In Flannery O'Connor's moral economy there are two levels of being and acting. Some characters belong to a moral aristocracy. The Misfit and the grandmother belong to this group. But not every aristocrat is aware of the significance of his position or the responsibilities that go with it.
>
> —*Sheldon Currie*

Flannery O'Connor barely nodded to Ernest Hemingway in her letters; and her only reference to him in *Mystery and Manners* is in an enigmatic sentence on page 161 in which she also mentions Kafka, Gide and Camus, and the spirit of the times, which, she implies, they represent, and which she does not. But a close look reveals that O'Connor and Hemingway have a significant interest in common. It is true that Hemingway looks at the world as unbeliever, but he is a most reluctant unbeliever. Jake Barnes, in *The Sun Also Rises,* agonizes because he has not been a good Catholic and because the opportunity to become one is lost. Jake, another wounded knight, understands that his task, in the absence of a Christian blueprint, is to find, or create, in the void, a mode of behavior, a way for a human being to act with dignity. He tolerates the superficial behavior of his friends, who are expatriates like himself, aliens in the spiritual as well as political sense of the word. Their meaningless behavior is understandable in the circumstances, like playing solitaire in a bomb shelter, waiting for the siren to sound the all clear. But Jake knows there will be no siren, and he wants a real solution, not a "truce with mediocrity." At the end of the novel, Jake has not found the way, but he refuses to allow his thinking or feeling about it to degenerate into either sentimentality or rationality: "the world would be a nice place if only . . ." or "life is nothing but . . ." When Brett offers such a bromide, Jake replies, "Isn't it pretty to think so." A keen ear could almost hear O'Connor's silent applause.

Similarly, the author, the reader, and the older waiter in "A Clean Well Lighted Place," accord grudging admiration to the old man who can think of no other way to cope with the collapse of the universe, having failed at suicide, than to drink brandy until he can sleep, to try to hold himself in abeyance, to sit in a circle of cleanness and light in the middle of the spiritual and physical rubble that used to be Spain, while the sympathetic waiter chants parodies of the old praises, "Our Nada, who art in Nada, . . . Hail Nada, full of Nada". The old man refuses the truce with mediocrity; he will have dignity, or he will have nothing; or he will have dignity and nothing.

"The Short Happy Life of Francis Macomber" will bring us back to Eliot, Baudelaire, Flannery O'Connor, The Misfit and the grandmother. In Hemingway's most clear visioned morality, Francis Macomber, on safari with his wife Margot and guide Wilson, fails miserably in the lion hunt. He shoots and wounds the lion, then panics and runs while Wilson and his men kill the lion which is now under cover and dangerous. Macomber is in disgrace. That night his wife sneaks from their tent and goes to bed with Wilson: small consolation in an imperfect world. Good whisky. Good sex. Waiting for the siren. But the following day Macomber overcomes his fear and stands up to a buffalo. While he is killing the buffalo, however, Margot raises her rifle and kills him. An accident? Was she aiming for the buffalo? Was it a subconscious act? We don't know, but no matter, the act is symbolic and is only significant at the symbolic level. Macomber, by virtue of courage, has raised himself to a new level of existence. His years of spiritual subsistence are nothing compared to his few moments of real, rich life. Wilson and Margot accord him a grudging admiration. After the mess is cleared up they'll have some good whisky. They will be consoled. It is more comfortable not to be in the arena with the lions, better, as Binx Bolling suggests in *The Moviegoer,* to be consoled with "the sad little happiness of drinks and kisses, a good little car and a warm deep thigh." But the wounded knight is not consoled. Macomber's integrity, like Hazel Motes', stems from what he is not able to do.

In Auden's poem, "Musee des Beaux Art," Icarus ignores his father's advice and flies his wax and feather wings too high. The heat of the sun melts the wax and Icarus plunges nose first into the sea, thus finding out how far he can go by finding out how far he can't go, and demonstrating that he too would not settle for a truce with mediocrity as his father advised him to do. Auden is pointing out that such bold behavior has a price, and the price is suffering, and when you are suffering, you are out there, or up there, all by yourself. Suffering is individual, which is why a good man is hard to find.

A good man *is* hard to find, and an evil man is hard to find, because as Eliot put it, man is a moral being and if he is not good or evil, he is nothing, he does not exist as a human being. In **"A Good Man Is Hard to Find"** the henchmen, Hiram and Bobby Lee, do not count, they are nobodies, they do their evil acts unthinkingly, as a dog might run off with his master's sirloin steak, inadvertently dropped on the kitchen floor. The steak is just as gone as if the dog were a moral being, and you are just as dead no matter who shoots you, Hiram and Bobby Lee or The Misfit; the physical evil is the same, but the moral evil adheres only to The Misfit. Hiram and Bobby Lee are moral morons, no more capable of committing sin than an idiot is capable of writing **"A Good Man Is Hard to Find."** In Eliot's economy, in O'Connor's economy, in Baudelaire's, Hiram and Bobby Lee don't exist. The Misfit, however, as his daddy recognized, is "a different breed of dog from [his] brothers and sisters." The Misfit is a moral thoroughbred with a curious and active nose. ". . . it's some that can live their whole life without asking about it and it's others has to know why it is, and this body is one of the latters. He's going to be into everything." So says The Misfit's father, and so says the grandmother: "You're not common," she tells him, ". . . You don't look a bit like you have common blood." And how does she know? Another old saying might have been as apt a title for this story: "It Takes One To Know One."

The Misfit first appears in the story as a "scholar," wearing silver-rimmed spectacles and a black hat, a rabbi, perhaps, in spite of his shirtless torso, ill-fitting blue jeans, and gun in hand. Contradictions in his appearance alert the reader who should know, if this is not his first trip through O'Connor county, that the author is introducing another "different breed of dog." The grandmother too is alerted: "His face was as familiar to her as if she had known him all her life but she could not recall who he was." This comment is metaphorical and is intended to set up the grandmother's comment on the next page, so that her recognition is not simply a recollection of his description from the radio broadcast of the escape; and it is only two pages later that The Misfit's forgotten crime and subsequent imprisonment recapitulates the doctrine of man's forgotten fall from grace and imprisonment in original sin. The subtext is allegorical, more subtle, but no less concrete than the adventures of Una and The Redcross Knight in Spenser's Faerie Queene, "pricking across the plain," searching to free Una's parents who had been imprisoned by the evil demon Orgoglio. O'Connor's mind was informed by the medieval in form as well as in substance.

The best way to understand how the grandmother is like The Misfit is to note the contrast between her and the children's mother:

The old lady settled herself comfortably, removing her white cotton gloves and putting them up with her purse on the shelf in front of the back window. The children's mother still had on slacks and still had her head tied up in a green kerchief, but the grandmother had on a navy blue straw sailor hat with a bunch of white violets on the brim and a navy blue dress with a small white dot in the print. Her collars and cuffs were white organdy trimmed with lace and at her neckline she had pinned a purple spray of cloth violets containing a sachet. In case of an accident, anyone seeing her dead on the highway would know at once she was a lady.

A lady! The grandmother is frequently criticized for the mediocrity of her values, but O'Connor often reminds the reader that she does have values, like The Misfit, who feels there should be criteria for human behavior, and unlike the children's mother, whose passivity is so complete she even thanks The Misfit for sending her off with Hiram and Bobby Lee to be shot. It is important not to underestimate the grandmother's vanity (not a virtue but a close enough imitation to be often taken for one). It indicates a recognition of the need for virtue, that is, the habit of acting and being according to criteria. O'Connor's description of The Misfit and the grandmother identify them as Lord and Lady, part of a moral aristocracy which does not include the children's mother, Bailey, Red Sam's wife, Hiram and Bobby Lee. Eliot and Baudelaire would not count them as moral, therefore human in their strict meaning of the term.

Unlike the children's mother, the grandmother is active, even, in her genteel manner, aggressive. When she looks after the children she tells them stories, or curls June Star's hair, or bounces the baby on her knee and talks to it or sings, stimulating it rather than holding it and hoping it will go to sleep. At The Tower restaurant she tries, to no avail, to get Bailey to dance to "The Tennessee Waltz," she scolds the children for their unpatriotic remarks about several southern states, she won't let them throw their garbage out the window. She encourages them to play games, and she tries to transform their vacation into more than a boring ride down the road by associating it with a search for an enchanting plantation with a secret panel somewhere inside the house. The children's mother, on the other hand, spends her time in silence and/or asleep. When O'Connor introduces her she describes her metaphorically as a cabbage and a rabbit, the proletarians of the plant and animal kingdoms.

The Misfit and the grandmother are identified also by their mutual interest in decorum. Like her, he is very careful to be polite in conversation and takes care to apologize for the impropriety the clothing circumstance has forced upon him. But though he recognizes the need of social criteria, it is something he has gone beyond to a deeper need, that is, for moral criteria against which to measure behavior.

"If [Jesus] did what He said, then it's nothing for you to do but throw away everything and follow Him, and if He didn't, then it's nothing for you to do but enjoy the few minutes you got left the best way you can—by killing somebody or burning down his house or

doing some other meanness to him. No pleasure but meanness," he said and his voice had become almost a snarl.

The leap beyond the social to the moral level, the human level in Eliot's terms, is the significant difference between the grandmother and The Misfit. Both have the potential to rise to the moral level. The Misfit made the leap, the grandmother did not. Leaping to the moral level does not mean becoming a good man, it may just as easily mean becoming an evil man. "'Nome, I ain't a good man,' The Misfit said after a second as if he had considered her statement carefully, . . ." He is correct. He is a moral man but not a good man. But at this point in the story The Misfit no longer matters. We know that he, à la Baudelaire, is man enough to be damned. The question is: is the grandmother woman enough to be damned? Because if she is not woman enough to be damned, then she is not woman enough to be saved. The grandmother is obviously not a bad woman. The question is: is she a good woman? And the answer is no. We have the author's word for it, through the mouth of The Misfit: "She would of been a good woman, . . . if it had been somebody there to shoot her every minute of her life."

And we have the author's word for it through some weather imagery. Early in the story the grandmother advances the information that it is a good day for a drive, "neither too hot nor too cold, and she cautioned Bailey that the speed limit was fifty-five miles an hour . . ." We might be reminded here of Christ's caution against caution: "Be ye either hot or cold; if you are lukewarm, I will vomit you from my mouth." And we might be reminded of Eliot's "awful daring of a moment's surrender which an age of prudence can never retract." It may be stretching a point to try to extract too much meaning from such a simple reference to the weather. However, there is more. "'Ain't a could in the sky,' he remarked, looking up at it. 'Don't see no sun but don't see no could neither.'" A cloudless, sunless sky can be a metaphorical fact, but is an astronomical impossibility between sunrise and sunset. What can this metaphor mean? Chances are it does mean something because the author, with her usual generosity, repeats it four pages later: "There was not a cloud in the sky nor any sun." And at the end the grandmother is dead and "lay in a puddle of blood with her legs crossed under her like a child's and her face smiling up at the cloudless sky." The woman is still a child. The sky is neutral; there is nothing in it. If what Eliot said is to be taken seriously, that man's glory is his capacity for salvation and for damnation, then it seems that in this story, only The Misfit qualifies.

The next question might be: did the grandmother, at the last minute, in a moment of grace, make the leap, become a good woman? But this question cannot receive an answer. In real life no one can answer such a question because no one can know the answer. In fiction, the question is irrelevant, because life is over and fiction cannot go beyond life, and in this particular fiction there is nothing to indicate that the grandmother is up to anything but an understandable, desperate attempt to save her skin, even to the extent of denying her professed Christian belief: "'Maybe he didn't raise the dead,' the old lady mumbled . . ." The grandmother's denial of Christ's power is a bit inconsistent with her alleged deathbed conversion.

But the eventual disposition of the grandmother's soul is not finally relevant to the meaning of the story, for ultimately the story is an exemplum, and the reader must stand in the grandmother's place. The Misfit (always capitalized by O'Connor) is the cartoon character, the caricature, the "large and startling figure" drawn to shock the reader into recognition; The Misfit is the reader, distorted, almost beyond recognition; or at least he is a twisted version of one possibility of the reader's self. The grandmother too is the reader, undistorted, equipped to make the leap to the moral level of existence, where action and being are measured against moral criteria, but not likely to do so without some sort of metaphorical gun pointed at the bridge of the nose.

Lest the reader be tempted to feel superior to the grandmother, as he accords grudging admiration to The Misfit, and perhaps even to himself, he should note that he and The Misfit have a decided advantage over the grandmother, for she does not get her needed shock until too late, if, indeed it was too late. Neither The Misfit nor the reader has that excuse.

Like Parker in "Parker's Back," The Misfit has experienced the shock of fortune. He has seen the world and it has given him pause, and reason to reflect:

> 'I was a gospel singer for a while,' The Misfit said. 'I been most everything. Been in the arm service, both land and sea, at home and abroad, been twice married, been an undertaker, been with the railroads, plowed Mother Earth, been in a tornado, seen a man burnt alive once . . . I even seen a woman flogged,' he said.

Like Mr. Shiftlet in **"The Life You Save May Be Your Own,"** The Misfit, wounded by the spear of experience, has developed a "moral intelligence." He knows there is more to life than chit-chat and wearing clean underwear in case you're found dead on the road. But the grandmother, like Julian's mother in **"Everything That Rises Must Converge,"** is a moral innocent. She has lived in a cocoon and is whacked into death before she can emerge as a butterfly, or its moral opposite.

> 'Oh, look at the cute little pickaninny!' she said and pointed to a Negro child standing in the door of a shack. 'Wouldn't that make a picture now?' she asked and they all turned and looked at the little Negro out of the back window. She waved.

> 'He didn't have any britches on,' June Star said.

> 'He probably didn't have any,' the grandmother explained.

> 'Little niggers in the country don't have things like we do. If I could paint, I'd paint that picture,' she said.

A few pages later the grandmother offers the opinion that "Europe was entirely to blame for the way things were now." It is obvious that the grandmother's mindless blaming the victims of tragedy is not because she lacks generosity or is indifferent to the need for justice, but because she is innocent. Her political as well as her moral intelligence is dormant. Whether or not a person of her curiosity, intelligence and age has a right to such an innocence is another question. The fact is, she is innocent. She must be excused, rather than forgiven.

But in real life, the grandmother does not matter any more. The story is over. In real life, the reader, who now wears the grandmother's shoes, can not plead innocence. If he had not been shocked into knowledge before he read the story, then the story should be his education. If formerly he thought poverty was cute and that the rest of the world was corrupt but none of it was his responsibility; or if he thought, like Young Goodman Brown, that evil was part of other people's lives, not his, then the three shots in the grandmother's chest should teach him the knowledge he needs, and perhaps gratitude that he didn't have to be shot in the chest, or gassed in an oven, or starved in a ghetto just to lose his adolescent innocence.

In Flannery O'Connor's moral economy there are two levels of being and acting. Some characters belong to a moral aristocracy. The Misfit and the grandmother belong to this group. But not every aristocrat is aware of the significance of his position or the responsibilities that go with it. Note Marie Larish and other notables in *The Wasteland,* who didn't bother to mind the store and whose carelessness Eliot blames for the disintegration of European culture and civilization. Some aristocrats are themselves a menace and others do damage simply by default. What distinguishes the grandmother from The Misfit is that she, though a spiritual aristocrat, is spiritually still a child, at best an adolescent, and like Belinda at a party for Queen Anne, she is powerless to deal with the corruption surrounding her because she is unaware of it. Unfortunately, the grandmother stays adolescent until the day she dies.

Some O'Connor characters belong to what might be called the moral mediocracy, characters like the children's mother, who seem to be totally unaware that anything is happening but time. Such characters are not bad and not good, but moral morons. Just as some people can't compete in track and field because they are physically crippled, and others cannot become teachers or lawyers or plumbers because they are mentally crippled, these characters cannot operate in a moral world because they are spiritual cripples. If such people exist in real life, they could be Christians only in a nominal sense, since Christianity presupposes an ability to distinguish between good and evil and insists on the exercising of fortitude to decide on one or the other, not between one of them and nothing, which is no choice at all.

Whether or not moral nonentities exist in the world, they serve a function in O'Connor's fiction. Just as she presents us with large and startling figures, The Misfit, Mr. Shiftlet, and Hulga, she similarly presents us with small and unprepossessing figures like the children's mother who, with her cabbage face and rabbit ears, is as much a cartoon character as her opposite, The Misfit.

Real life, of course, is not a cartoon. In reality people are not characters, but people, and few if any resemble either The Misfit or the children's mother, except, perhaps, in the minds of their enemies. In reality people are like the grandmother, and of course the reader, and it behooves each one, before he gets shot to death in a ditch, to decide whether or not he is going to measure his acts and his being against moral criteria, every day, morning, noon, and night, in sickness and in health, because it isn't going to be someone to shoot him (us) every minute of his life.

Robert Donahoo (essay date 1991)

SOURCE: "O'Connor's Ancient Comedy: Form in 'A Good Man Is Hard to Find'," in *Journal of the Short Story in English,* No. 16, Spring, 1991, pp. 29-39.

[*In the following essay, Donahoo analyzes the influence of Dantean and Aristophanean comedy on "A Good Man Is Hard to Find."*]

More than any other short story in the Flannery O'Connor canon, **"A Good Man Is Hard to Find"** has attracted the attention of commentators, not the least of whom is the author herself. Both in letters and lectures, O'Connor found herself explaining the story, trying to recover it from the grasp of symbol hunters and allegory explicators, by ending a frustration perhaps summarized by her description of an exchange with an "earnest" young teacher seeking to know why the Misfit's hat was black. "Anyway," O'Connor wrote to Dr. Ted Spivey, "that's what's happening to the teaching of literature."

Perhaps this explains why, in a lecture to English teachers, O'Connor attacked what she saw as the usual ways literature is taught and called for "attention, of a technical kind." She elaborates:

> The student has to have tools to understand a story or a novel, and these are tools proper to the structure of the work, tools proper to the craft. They are tools that operate inside the work and not outside it; they are concerned with how this story is made and with what makes it work as a story.

> In the act of writing, one sees that the way a thing is made controls and is inseparable from the whole meaning of it. The form of a story gives it meaning which any other form would change, and unless the student is able, in some degree, to apprehend the form, he will never apprehend anything else about the work, except what is extrinsic to it as literature.

In emphasizing the importance of form and mechanics to the search for meaning, O'Connor clearly places herself in the modernist critical tradition sketched out by such predecessors as Eliot and Pound, both of whose work she claimed to know and appreciate. Moreover, O'Connor's emphasis on form goes beyond the critical sense; it undergirds her best work and points to levels of meaning commonly sought in the work of more prestigious figures but ignored in the fictions of this isolated Southern lady. In fact, her form, as it appears in **"A Good Man Is Hard to Find,"** is not an idiosyncratic creation but a définite patterning of her work according to classical models whom Eliot and Pound would surely have approved: Dante and Aristophanes.

Of the two writers, Dante's importance to O'Connor's work seems the least surprising. His *Divine Comedy,* with its foundations in Catholic theology, particularly the thought of Augustine, provides an obvious model for any writer interested in combining orthodox faith and "serious" art. And, as Kinney's research in O'Connor's personal library shows, O'Connor certainly had access to the great Italian's poetry—an access her own private writings argue she used. "For my money," she wrote to "A" in 1955, "Dante is about as great as you can get." More importantly, in her essay "The Grotesque in Southern Fiction," she directly refers to Dante as a model even as she hints as to how that model will be reflected in her own work:

> I am told that the model of balance for the novelist should be Dante, who divided his territory pretty evenly between hell, purgatory, and paradise. There can be no objection to this, but also there can be no reason to assume that the result of doing it in these times will give us the balanced picture that it gave in Dante's. Dante lived in the thirteenth century, when that balance was achieved in the faith of his age. We live now in an age which doubts both fact and value, which is swept this way and that by momentary convictions. Instead of reflecting a balance from the world around him, the novelist now has to achieve one with a felt balance inside himself.

The key here is form—a Christian comic form which places individual narrative events into a particular perspective. Moreover, as John Freccero has well pointed out, Dante's form is built around his idea of conversion, "a death and resurrection of the self" dramatized in the journey of "gradual illumination." Looking at **"A Good Man Is Hard to Find"** with an awareness of Dante's views begins to resolve some of the basic questions which critics have long argued. Instead of counting the bodies or the jokes, explaining the symbolic hats and cats, or even discerning the good guys from the bad, an awareness of O'Connor's modeling of Dante frees the reader to watch for signs of this illuminating journey—as well as for signs of what Freccero calls "the journey that fails," "the journey without a guide" in which the pilgrim seeks ultimate reality through his own intellect. Certainly, journeys, both literal and figurative, abound in O'Connor's text; indeed everyone in this story is moving. Recognizing Dante's presence behind the text pushes the reader to judge each motion in the light of his sense of comedy and to see why O'Connor herself was adamant about her tale's comic nature.

The opening sentences of the story reveal the two most overt journeys, one that will be taken and one that won't: "The Grandmother didn't want to go to Florida. She wanted to visit some of her connections in east Tennessee and she was seizing at every chance to change Bailey's mind." The family is planning a trip to the exotica of Florida, America's vacation wonderland, the Mecca of a tired middle-class looking for an inexpensive place to relax. It could almost be seen as a trip to paradise, except for the fact that by the 1950s Florida was already scarred by the line of neon-lit motels stretched along its beaches. Traveling there provides no pilgrimage toward illumination but an escape from reality. Moreover, as the Grandmother points out, "'The children have been to Florida before'"; rather than discovering unknown territories, the family is only continuing in its comfortable rut. In fact, the family has little interest in traveling at all. Bailey, at his best, is a nervous driver, and the children dislike scenery ("'Let's go through Georgia fast so we won't have to look at it much,' John Wesley said." They would all be much happier to just be there—to be translated, as it were, from the living room of their Atlanta home to a Florida beach.

The Grandmother's purposed journey—her wish to travel to Tennessee—is hardly closer to the Dantean comic ideal. For, she desires not pilgrimage onward, but a return to her "connections." Moreover, her East Tennessee has no more reality than neon-orange Florida; it is largely the creation of her own romantic memory, complete with a courting prince (Mr. Teagarden) and a castle with secret panels (the plantation house). Like the family, she seeks no revelation; instead, she wants a solipsistic world with everything in its place, be they good men or pickaninnies.

But there is a third literal journey here, one that hardly seems important at first, but one which alters completely both the Grandmother's and the family's travel plans. This, of course, is the journey of The Misfit. Initially, his journey seems to parallel the one the family desires: an escape from Georgia to Florida. Drawing from the information in the newspaper, the Grandmother announces, "Here this fellow that calls himself The Misfit is aloose from the Federal Pen and headed toward Florida and you read here what it says he did to these people. Just you read it. I wouldn't take my children in any direction with a criminal like that aloose in it." However, the direction The Misfit is headed is not really *toward* any particular place or thing; it's merely *from*. In fact, such movement *away* has defined his entire life's journey, despite its division into two distinct parts by his time in prison. Rather than construct anything in his life, he has moved from experience to experience. He describes his early life this way: "'I was a gospel singer for a while. . . . I been most everything. Been in the arm service, both land and sea, at home and abroad, been twict married, been an undertaker, been with the railroads, plowed Mother Earth, been in a tornado, seen a man burnt alive once . . . ; I even seen a woman flogged. . . . I never was a bad boy that I remember of . . . but somewheres along the line I done something wrong and got sent to the penitentiary.'" In images striking for their relation to what is to come, he describes prison as being "buried alive," a time when he tried to

realize "what I done," only to discover that he can't remember anything. In the sense of Dante's journey of illumination, of his having learned anything capable of redirecting his life, this memory is accurate. For though The Misfit seeks illumination, he searches for it as a form of information—a form "in" which, according to Dante's poem, it does not have. Thus, he resembles Dante's Ulysses, of whom Freccero writes, "Just as the ancients equated knowledge and virtue, so too Ulysses seems to equate them, making no provision in his calculations for the journey within, the personal askesis upon which all such attempts at transcendence must be based. The distinction between Ulysses' journey and the journey of the pilgrim is not in the objective, for both are directed toward that mountain in the southern hemisphere, but rather in how the journey is accomplished." Seen in this light, it is not surprising that the Misfit has sometimes been mistakenly admired as a hayseed Byronic hero and the story twisted to show him in a positive manner. Nevertheless, for O'Connor, committed to the model of Dante's comedy, his very Byronic nature makes him damnable. And just as her model did not hesitate to place his misguided hero in hell, O'Connor clearly embeds her Misfit in a hellish morass of evil—in his own words, "'it's nothing for you to do but enjoy the few minutes you got left the best way you can—by killing somebody or burning down his house or doing some other meanness to him. No pleasure but meanness.'"

These are the literal journeys in the story, none of them illuminating, none comic. Were **"A Good Man Is Hard to Find"** merely the record of these movements, it would offer a dark vision indeed. However, an unacknowledged, spiritual journey is going on within the character who dominates this tale: the Grandmother. This journey has led her to the dark wood of her present self, to a danger she cannot immediately sense, and it will be altered, detoured, rescued only by an encounter with a guide she neither wants nor expects. Though, in many ways, her journey parallels the movement of The Misfit, it has that one crucial variation: the obtaining of a guide to whom she loses control.

As many critics have pointed out, the Grandmother begins the story as a self-centered, self-conscious representative and exploiter of genteel Southern-ness. She tries to assert her will over the family in the choice of a vacation spot; she smuggles the cat, the cause of the accident, onto the trip; she points out the "cute little pickaninny," enjoying the picturesqueness of his poverty; she ignores Red Sam's sloth and rudeness to his wife; and she deliberately lies about the "secret panel" in order to force a detour in the family's trip. The catalog of these events differs only in externals from the list of The Misfit's pre-prison activities; both are equally banal and unconstructive. But whereas he entered the crucible of prison and was left alone, her crucible comes in the confrontation with him, a guide from hell who takes her on a journey of illumination through loss.

Though The Misfit may seem an unlikely Virgil, he does share with Dante's guide one essential quality: an awareness of his situation, an awareness of what he does not have. What he lacks is Virgil's penitent nature, his hell-gained acceptance of his condition. Instead, like a good empiricist, he defines his essential problem as his inability to have first-hand information, an inability to have certainty about history, the past, the supernatural world. In his own words, "'[Jesus] thown everything off balance. If He did what He said, then it's nothing for you to do but thow away everything and follow Him, and if He didn't, then it's nothing for you to do but enjoy the few minutes you got left the best way you can. . . . I wasn't there so I can't say He didn't [raise the dead]. . . . I wisht I had of been there. . . . It ain't right I wasn't there. . . . because if I had of been there I would of known. Listen lady, . . . if I had of been there I would of known and I wouldn't be like I am now.'" Clearly, The Misfit believes he lacks information, and, by blaming his lack of information for his actions, he again links himself to the pre-Christian idea of equating knowledge and virtue. Considered from the Christian perspective, however, his problem could be seen, not as a lack of information, but a rejection of the possibility of ordering life by faith.

At this point, The Misfit and the Grandmother show their fundamental similarity. Like him, the Grandmother also bases her life on what she can see, though she seems well aware that what is seen may be mere appearance, not reality. After all, she has dressed for her journey so that "anyone seeing her dead on the highway would know at once that she was a lady." At the same time, her social position (dependent upon a son's charity) and her regional origins in rural East Tennessee hardly coincide with those of the gentility. Far from being a "lady," she is a pretentious, middle-class woman.

The difference between the two characters lies in their words. The Misfit's statements are as harsh as his vision; the Grandmother disguises her vision beneath traditional Christian pieties. In fact, she disguises it so well that even she is unaware of its true nature—until forced to view it in the mirror of The Misfit. When she does, she begins to change, to unify her words and actions, her medium and message—something that happens in what many view as an instantaneous conversion—an occurrence which Dante's form would seem to reject.

The writer's problem which O'Connor's situation on the highway presents is how in a limited physical situation to realize Dante's gradual illumination. Certainly, a reader could claim some sort of vague psychological journey—the kind of eternity-experienced-in-a-single-instant which not only stood Ambrose Bierce in good stead but has since provided fodder for such post-modernists as Barth and Borges. However, O'Connor is not interested in such literary tricks. Instead, she turns to a second, even more ancient, model for a comic form that suggests great action within a limited space: the comic form of Aristophanes.

Any suggestion of a link between O'Connor and the king of ribald fifth-century Greek comedy must, at first, seem odd. However, such a connection is more than possible. Robert Fitzgerald has noted the influence of Sophocles'

Oedipus plays upon the composition of *Wise Blood,* and O'Connor herself seems to confirm this report in a 13 February 1954 letter to Ben Griffith: "At the time I was writing the last of [*Wise Blood*], I was living in Connecticut with the Robert Fitzgeralds. Robert Fitzgerald translated the Theban cycle with Dudley Fitts, and their translation of the *Oedipus Rex* had just come out and I was taken with it. Do you know that translation? I am not an authority on such things, but I think it must be the best, and it is certainly very beautiful. Anyway, all I can say is, I did a lot of thinking about Oedipus." Moreover, this chance encounter was not the limit of her contact with ancient Greek literature. As might be expected of the housemate and close friend of a Greek translator—if not a Georgia recluse—O'Connor shows in her letters a familiarity with the work of Euripides and Homer. Also, Kinney's study of her library reveals a volume of plays by Aeschylus and translations of two plays by Aristophanes—the two comedies, significantly, translated by Fitzgerald's co-worker on the Oedipus translation: Dudley Fitts. Admittedly, from this point, any further connection becomes tenuous, and it is not the argument advanced here that O'Connor consciously drew upon Aristophanes as a model. Nevertheless, the biographical evidence suggests that she knew at least some of Aristophanes' plays, while the text of **"A Good Man Is Hard to Find"** offers striking parallels to his comic structure.

Francis MacDonald Cornford, in providing one of the major discussions of that structure, explains that in the comedies of Aristophanes there exists a "definite section" "referred to in the text as 'the *Agon*'." Although he disagrees with those critics who see it as "the whole play," Cornford labels it "the first moment in the action" and "the chief and critical moment." He further describes the *Agon* this way:

> In some plays, it is less a debate than a criminal trial, and less like a trial than a duel, with the two half-Choruses acting as seconds and the Leader as umpire. It is several times preceded by an actual fight with fists or missiles, which is somehow arrested in order that the flushed combatants may have it out with their tongues instead. Though the victory is finally won by argument— a term which must include all the arsenal of invective— the *Agon* is no mere 'dramatised debate'; it ends in the crisis and turning-point of the play, reverses the situation of the adversaries, and leads not to an academic resolution, but to all the rest of the action that follows. Above all, it is, as we have said, organically related to the final marriage in which the victor is bridegroom, the triumph of the new God or the new King.

He also describes the major players in the *Agon* as follows:

> First there are the two Adversaries (as we shall call them). For the sake of convenience, we shall distinguish them as the 'Agonist' and the 'Antagonist.' The Agonist is the hero, who is attacked, is put on his defense, and comes off victorious. The Antagonist is the villain, who is in the stronger position at first, but is worsted and beaten from the field.

With these definitions and descriptions in mind, O'Connor's paralleling of them in **"A Good Man Is Hard** to Find" becomes apparent. The dialogue between the Grandmother and The Misfit serves as "the chief and critical moment" in the story, and clearly, it consists of a debate which develops elements of both trial and duel. The question at hand involves "goodness": is there a good man present in the situation—the *"accident,"* as the children refer to it—who can redeem or save those involved in it?

The course of this debate provides much of the story's black humor. The Misfit opens the proceedings and takes the offensive by aligning himself with the negative in his hints of the evil to come: "'it would have been better for "all" of you, lady, if you hadn't of reckernized me.'" The Grandmother counters by asserting the positive, using as the basis of her reasoning the evidence of appearance: "'I know you're a good man,'" she tells The Misfit, who is pointing a gun at her. "'You don't *look* a bit like you have common blood.'" The Misfit answers her with a direct denial—"'Nome, I ain't a good man'"—even as he emphasizes his good appearances by apologizing, like a gentleman, for being shirtless. Meanwhile, he orders his henchmen to take Bailey and John Wesley into the woods where they will be shot. Round one goes to The Misfit. This defeat forces the Grandmother to move on to another point of argument: the familiar forms of her religion. "'You could be honest too if you'd only try,'" she tells him, and then she asks, "'Do you ever pray?'" Obviously, the Grandmother imagines prayer as a kind of vending machine, and she sees goodness as some sort of necessary consumer item, part of the "comfortable life" she touts. At first, the Misfit replies by denying his materialism. "'Nobody had nothing I wanted,'" he tells her. However, in light of his story about borrowing clothes, this argument seems blatantly untrue, and, sensing a weakness, the Grandmother presses her point: "'If you would pray . . . Jesus would help you.'" Here The Misfit admits she is telling the truth— "'That's right'"—but then destroys her point by showing that it is not germane: "'I don't want no hep . . . I'm doing all right by myself.'" Round Two goes to The Misfit. Her second point vanquished, the Grandmother moves onto a third position, a rather surprising one given her previous certainty but one, perhaps, dictated by the dire nature of events: the Grandmother presses her case on the basis of the mystery of Jesus. In seeing "Jesus" as both possible help and curse, as paradox, she moves toward the position her opponent claims: "'Yes'm . . . Jesus thown everything off balance.'" The truth of this statement in Christian doctrine is that by his existence Jesus demonstrated that humans could not justify themselves, that God does not run a good/credit, evil/debit accounting system. Instead, orthodoxy holds that "goodness" is not dependent upon human action but upon a faith which participates in the death/resurrection pattern Jesus established. In short, goodness stands in relationship to the paradoxical pattern St. Paul describes when he writes, "I am crucified with Christ: nevertheless I live; yet not I, but Christ liveth in me: and the life which I now live in the flesh I live by the faith of the Son of God, who loved me, and gave himself for me." By his statements, the Misfit responds to the Grandmother's use of the mystery of Jesus by claiming that it supports, not her case, but his.

At this point, The Misfit appears to have won the Agon, a sign that he is the "hero" of this tale; however, he then admits that he does not hold the position that he has described. He will not claim the argument of Christ's mystery because he lacks empirical evidence and refuses to accept on faith the possibility of Christ's action: "'I wasn't there so I can't say He didn't [raise the dead]. . . . I wisht I had of been there. . . . It ain't right I wasn't there because if I had of been there I would of known. Listen lady . . . if I had of been there I would of known and I wouldn't be like I am now.'" The winning argument is now up for grabs, and the Grandmother advances to it. Having earlier admitted the impossibility of certainty—"'Maybe He didn't raise the dead'"—she begins symbolically to enact the death St. Paul speaks of, despite uncertainty. The text describes her as sinking "down in the ditch with her legs twisted under her." She then rises, not to argue that someone else is a good man, but she rises as a good man— justified, in the eyes of orthodoxy, by faith. More importantly, the discerning reader justifies her as well—not because of an unseen faith but due to an overt act. The Grandmother stops merely showing good manners by her words and, instead, shows love to her enemy by an act. "'Why you're one of my babies. You're one of my children'," she says, followed by a small but undeniable act of compassion: a touch. Such argument is unanswerable; the Grandmother wins the *Agon,* a fact the Misfit's wordless, mindless murder of her seems to admit.

In picturing the Grandmother's "change" as a Greek *Agon,* O'Connor manages to avoid giving her an instantaneous conversion and instead has her conform to the Dantean pattern of comic illumination achieved through a descent into a hell. In combining the two comic forms, she achieves in her art an illustration of the idea Emmanuel Mounier expressed in a passage which O'Connor marked in his book *Personalism*: ". . . life is a struggle against death; spiritual death is a struggle against the inertia of matter and the sloth of the body. The person attains self-consciousness, not through some ecstasy, but by force of mortal combat; and force is one of its principal attributes. Not the brute force of mere power and aggression, in which man forsakes his own action and imitates the behavior of matter; but human force, which is at once internal and efficacious, spiritual and manifest."

Still, this is not the end of the story, or of O'Connor's paralleling of Greek comedy. Cornford notes the tendency in the Sacrifice/Feast/Wedding portions of the plays for "elderly heroes" to "throw off the slough of sour and morose old age, and emerge at the end carrying their youthful behavior to the point of scandal"—a pattern especially clear in *Wasps.* In **"A Good Man Is Hard to Find,"** the final image of the Grandmother displays her not only as sacrificial victim, but also as strangely rejuvenated, her position "like a child's." Moreover, in the face of so much "serious" horror, "her face [is] smiling up at the cloudless sky."

The modern reader may be tempted to shiver at the thought of a smile in the face of so much blood—just as we shiver at horrors which the protagonist of Dante's poem encounters in hell. Moreover, unlike Dante, O'Connor does not mitigate her picture of suffering by allowing the reader to follow The Grandmother beyond the river of death into purgatory or paradise. Her focus remains plainly on this world, not the next. In Dante, however, the vision of *Inferno* changes because, as Freccero points out, we finally see it from the view of paradise. "In a sense," Freccero writes, "the purpose of the entire journey is to write the poem, to attain the vantage-point of Lucy, and of all the blessed, from which to perceive the *figura* and the coherence in life, and to bear witness to that coherence for other men."

The loss of faith in modern times, the difference O'Connor noted between Dante's age and her own, makes such a vantage point and such a coherence seem a fantasy—an obvious fiction unacceptable within the bounds of "realism." "Happily ever after" exists only in the province of fairy tales; O'Connor dare not claim it as "real." Instead, she can only make use of forms which imply it—the forms of comedy as it was known in ancient times.

Thomas Hill Schaub (essay date 1991)

SOURCE: "Christian Realism and O'Connor's 'A Good Man Is Hard to Find'," in *American Fiction in the Cold War,* The University of Wisconsin Press, 1991, pp. 125-36.

[*Schaub is an American educator and critic. In the following excerpt, he examines "A Good Man Is Hard to Find" in the context of the revisionary liberalism of the 1950s.*]

The idea of "the South" and of "southern writing" also helps to situate O'Connor's [*A Good Man Is Hard to Find*], for during the fifties specific political and cultural meanings were attributed to the southern experience. When Walker Percy won the National Book Award in 1961 for *The Moviegoer,* he was asked why the South was contributing so many fine writers. He answered, "Because we lost the War." O'Connor gave her interpretation of Percy's meaning in an essay she contributed to *Esprit*: "He didn't mean by that simply that a lost war makes good subject matter," O'Connor wrote. "We have gone into the modern world with an inburnt knowledge of human limitations and with a sense of mystery which could not have developed in our first state of innocence—as it has not sufficiently developed in the rest of our country." This is a summary identical to those we can find in the writing of Hartz, Niebuhr, and Vann Woodward—all of whom used the experience of the South as a source of directives for United States foreign policy.

There is some evidence that O'Connor's interpretation of Percy's comment paraphrased C. Vann Woodward's thesis in "The Irony of Southern History." O'Connor wrote to "A" on May 25, 1963, "I have taken up with reading C. Vann Woodward. Have you ever read this gentleman— *The Burden of Southern History* is what I have but I in-

tend to order off after more. Southern history usually gives me a pain, but this man knows how to write English." Though O'Connor apparently did not read Vann Woodward's essay until 1963, he delivered the lecture in 1953 as an elaboration of Reinhold Niebuhr's thesis in *The Irony of American History,* published the year before.

One of the architects of postwar foreign policy, George Kennan, had defined this irony in terms similar to Niebuhr's. In the forward to *American Diplomacy,* Kennan described the ironic aura of the Allied victory: "one had the inescapable fact that our security, or what we took to be our security, had suffered a tremendous decline over the course of the half-century. A country which in 1900 had no thought that its prosperity and way of life could be in any way threatened by the outside world had arrived by 1950 at a point where it seemed to be able to think of little else but this danger."

The thesis of Vann Woodward's lecture, given in 1953, was part of a widespread conviction in the intellectual community that American foreign policy must recognize its limitations. One reads this in Schlesinger's *The Vital Center,* and in Louis Hartz's *The Liberal Tradition in America* (1955), which asserts the "innocence" (and unconsciousness) of American liberalism, and argues that cold war conflicts may force Americans to understand "liberalism" as but one ideology among others: "which is to say that America must look to its contact with other nations to provide that spark of philosophy, that grain of relative insight that its own history has denied it."

Vann Woodward's essay first restated "the ironic incongruities of our position" and then explored this irony in light of southern history. In Vann Woodward's opinion, the southern historian can bring a special point of view and experience to these national ironies, and therefore is capable of making "a special contribution to the understanding of the irony of American history." For "the historian of the South can hardly escape the feeling that all this has happened before." The point of vantage for the southern historian, of course, is established by the South's having lost the Civil War, an experience setting it apart from the national experience: never having "known what it means to be confronted by complete frustration" has led to ideas of American invincibility and a vague belief that "history is something unpleasant that happens to other people." In sharp contrast, the South has something in common with Europe that the rest of the country does not. Hartz drew a similar lesson from southern history, though he focused upon the failure of the North to learn anything from the "Reactionary Enlightenment." Vann Woodward makes explicit the regional assumptions informing O'Connor's fiction, assumptions which she herself later articulated in terms evolved from cold war discourse.

Vann Woodward's essay helps historicize or situate a pervasive southern conviction within a specific postwar context. The irony of O'Connor's antiliberalism is the success of her vision, its marvellous coincidence with dominant discourses of cold war liberalism. One may be perfectly willing to grant the ahistorical legitimacy of

O'Connor's religious objections to the modern temper—without, in doing so, ignoring the historical discourses which O'Connor's language intersects and reinforces. O'Connor's good fortune, it may be said, was to be working at a time when her own objections to liberal thought were widely shared by the liberal audience that would have to make up her readership, if she was to have one at all. She and they shared for a time the emphasis upon "realism," innocence, evil, ambiguity, limitation, tragedy, and so forth. I think it fair to say that once we array this discourse beside O'Connor's work of the early fifties, there are many places at which the liberal self-critique and O'Connor's critique of liberalism overlap. This historicizing allows us to read aspects of her work with an enlarged sense of their cultural dialogue.

Revisionist liberalism is not so explicitly inscribed within the title story of *A Good Man Is Hard to Find* as in O'Connor's satire of Joy-Hulga in **"Good Country People."** The qualities that make this story so identifiable with the postwar era are more complex, powerfully embedded in ironic reversals and the themes they accentuate. This is especially clear if we read the fiction through its allusions to Margaret Mitchell's *Gone with the Wind,* which bring the irony of southern history to bear upon the Grandmother and her son's family.

In the story **"A Good Man Is Hard to Find,"** the Grandmother's desire differs from her son's: instead of vacationing in Florida, she wants to visit her "connections" in east Tennessee. Her son and his family seem to be interested only in comics, in the "funny papers" and the sports page; they have no eye for beauty in the landscape, no respect for family relations. As in so many of O'Connor's stories, the character who is going to take the hardest fall—here the Grandmother—is made to look good by contrast with her son and his family. Bailey is a bald, taciturn father, wearing a Hawaiian shirt with parrots on it. The mother, who is virtually mute, has a face "as broad and innocent as a cabbage" and a kerchief on her head with "two points on the top like rabbit's ears." The children are disobedient brats who speak in screams and shrieks. In this context, the Grandmother's vitality, her interest in things, however shallow, is refreshing. If we smile at her, we also feel the family line has degenerated a bit. She is stuck with a pretty slow crew. Their lives are a vacuity, they are always on "vacation," and they are headed for Florida, then beginning to incarnate the emptiness and deregionalization of American culture.

The Grandmother is so taken up with her desire to visit her relations that during the ride she begins to associate the scenery they are passing through with her girlhood landscapes, and this association is a recollection at once of her past and of the Old South before the Civil War. When they pass a cotton field with an "island" of graves in the center she says, "that was the old family burying ground. That belonged to the plantation." Her son's boy, John Wesley, asks where the plantation is and the grandmother makes a joke: "Gone With the Wind," she laughs. O'Connor left the words capitalized in order to emphasize their reference to Mitchell's novel and the film adaptation that won an Academy Award for best picture in 1939.

Like the fact that she has named her cat "Pitty Sing" after a character in Gilbert and Sullivan's *The Mikado,* the grandmother's reference to *Gone with the Wind* further identifies her as a character whose consciousness is in some degree manipulated by the kitsch of democratic-liberal culture. Though the Grandmother elaborates her harmless allusion no further, her joke participates in a complex system which O'Connor extends throughout the rest of the story and which dramatizes the serious consequences of mass cultural representation. The allusion at once tells a truth and refers to the transformation of southern history into representation, into writing and film—sign of that history's having lost its substantial meaning, of its conversion now to a diluted, glorified sentimentality. O'Connor herself had little interest in or patience with the South's antebellum nostalgia or with the war itself. She asks one of her correspondents, "What you want to read *A Stillness at Appomattox* for? Buy it for me but don't send it to me. I never was one to go over the Civil War in a big way. . . ." The literal representation of history was of less interest to O'Connor than the ahistorical and spiritual truths which the Grandmother's nostalgia overlooks.

For John Wesley to ask "where's the plantation?" is to ask where is the South? Where is its wealth and pastoral, Edenic promise? The past as a time when men were gentlemen and children respected their elders is a constant theme of the old woman. To quiet the children, the Grandmother tells them a story of her youth "when she was a maiden lady . . . courted by a Mr. Edgar Atkins Teagarden." Clearly, O'Connor wants us to understand the old lady's revery as a dream of lost paradise: her gentleman caller is named for the very "garden" that has been lost, and his initials—E.A.T.—are clearly meant to remind us of the story of the Fall. Mr. Teagarden was in the habit of leaving the Grandmother a watermelon with his initials carved on it. The old lady doesn't read the spiritual fact within the accidental name, and identifies her loss with the money Teagarden made from his Coca-Cola stock.

In many ways, **"A Good Man"** is a story about eating, about appetites and the Garden of Eden, and about nature's appetite, which swallows rich and poor alike. In fact, the children have just finished the lunch the grandmother has made for them when the family stops for barbecued sandwiches at Red Sammy's. While Sammy and the Grandmother discuss "better times" and complain about the Marshall Plan ("the way Europe acted you would think we were made of money," she tells Red Sammy), the children watch a monkey in the chinaberry tree outside, who is "busy catching fleas on himself and biting each one carefully between his teeth as if it were a delicacy."

O'Connor further elaborates the Civil War allusion in the scene which follows, describing the soporific car ride after lunch and the confused recollection the Grandmother has of "an old plantation that she had visited in this neighborhood once when she was a young lady. She said the house had six white columns across the front and that there was an avenue of oaks leading up to it and two little wooden trellis arbors on either side in front where you sat down with your suitor after a stroll in the garden." To induce her son to look for this old house she invents a lie that elaborates and projects her antebellum nostalgia: "'There was a secret panel in this house," she said craftily, not telling the truth but wishing that she were, "and the story went that all the family silver was hidden in it when Sherman came through but it was never found.'" The "secret panel" idea is a hit with the kids and Bailey is forced to capitulate.

The "secret panel," like the memory generally, is a facile representation of an undefiled South, a secret access to a recoverable past. But as with the explicit reference to *Gone with the Wind,* O'Connor turns the Grandmother's nostalgic allusions against her. For the woods, beside which their overturned car finally comes to rest, are (from Frost) "tall and dark and deep", and once the Misfit and his gang appear—outside "Toombsboro" in a "big black battered hearse-like automobile"—the woods become even more threatening: "behind them the line of woods gaped like a dark open mouth." The family's mindless, animal appetites here reemerge as instances of nature's appetite, red in tooth and claw, ready to consume. The ironic allusions to Mitchell's novel find their fulfillment in the pistol shots announcing the death of her son Bailey and the boy John Wesley, for the Grandmother "could hear the wind move through the tree tops like a long satisfied insuck of breath." Bailey and his son are gone with the wind, and this is no joke, but the irony of southern history.

The language of this scene implies not only a malign and unforgiving nature, but also the spiritual inadequacy of the "Liberal approach" based upon naturalist beliefs, such as that articulated by John Dewey and Sidney Hook in their "Failure of Nerve" essays: that the world of natural human history and society is a sufficient amphitheater for human aspiration, reason, and perfection. The two major players in the final scene of the story—its last third—are the Grandmother and the Misfit, both of whom are struggling within and coming to recognize the limitations of this "modern idea." Certainly the Misfit is more aware of this than is the Grandmother, whose "liberalism"—if we may ascribe such to her—is a watered-down set of mass cultural "banalities." She keeps a record of their mileage, encourages an aesthetic appreciation of the countryside, prattles on about education and the need to be "broad," and imagines a time when there used to be "good men." The lack of good men follows from a decline in culture or politics ("Europe was entirely to blame for the way things were now," she tells Red Sammy), instead of following from the idea—as O'Connor expressed it to Cecil Dawkins—that "man has fallen and that he is only perfectible by God's grace."

The Misfit, too, bears traces of "the Liberal approach." His "silver-rimmed spectacles" give him a "scholarly look," and he turns out to be a precise, literal man, outraged by the incommensurability of his crimes and punishments. He, too, is a record keeper, ready to acknowledge the claims made upon him by "papers" and accounts. "That's why I sign myself now," he tells the Grandmother. "I said long ago, you get you a signature and sign everything you do and keep a copy of it. Then you'll know what you done

and you can hold up the crime to the punishment and see do they match and in the end you'll have something to prove you ain't been treated right." This language is as close as O'Connor comes to acknowledging the song which gave her story its title. The Misfit is a man who hasn't been "treated right." The love he lacks, one supposes, is God's love, which his rigid rationalism prevents him from receiving. The Misfit's accounting house tropes may remind us of liberalism's origins in the rise of the middle class, as well as of the Grandmother's regret that she failed to marry into Teagarden's Coca-Cola wealth.

But cold war discourse denied that the bookkeeping of capitalism, its ideas of fairness and contracts, had any basis in the truth of human nature or social and political history. In his lecture "Diplomacy in the Modern World," Kennan argued the deficiencies of the "legalistic approach"—expecting the world's nations to subscribe to a common law and judicial process—especially because of "the inevitable association of legalistic ideas with moralistic ones" and the military indignation that follows from a conviction of moral superiority. "It is a curious thing," he wrote, echoing Lionel Trilling's conclusion to "Manners, Morals, and the Novel," his Kenyon talk on the novel, "that the legalistic approach to world affairs, rooted as it unquestionably is in a desire to do away with war and violence, makes violence more enduring, more terrible, and more destructive to political stability than did the older motives of national interest." On this subject there was a marvellous consistency to the discourse of the liberal center. Niebuhr's language echoes Trilling's even more perfectly: "Our moral perils are not those of conscious malice or the explicit lust for power. They are the perils which can be understood only if we realize the ironic tendency of virtues to turn into vices when too complacently relied upon. The ironic elements in American history can be overcome, in short, only if American idealism comes to terms with the limits of all human striving, the fragmentariness of all human wisdom, the precariousness of all historic configurations of power, and the mixture of good and evil in all human virtue." Niebuhr goes on to cite Kennan's book, which appeared the year before Niebuhr's, drawing a moral-religious lesson from history rather than stopping short with one of "national self-interest."

The Misfit's violence, of course, is a form of moral indignation that his experience and his morality do not "match," and his inability to remember his first crime suggests that the Misfit is human rationality itself, unable to comprehend the affront of mortality as a punishment for man's original "fall." "I done something wrong and got sent to the penitentiary. I was buried alive," he tells the Grandmother. In the "Liberal approach" there is no escape hatch from this mortality, and our natural environment becomes a prison house. "'Turn to the right, it was a wall,' The Misfit said, looking up again at the cloudless sky. 'Turn to the left, it was a wall. Look up it was a ceiling, look down it was a floor. I forget what I done, lady.'"

The Misfit's symbolic penitentiary reveals how thoroughly O'Connor has invested her story with images of enclosure: the "black valise" imprisoning the Grandmother's cat, Pitty Sing; the gravestones the family sees at the beginning of their trip; the name Toombsboro; the "black, battered, hearse-like automobile"; the prison walls which enrage the Misfit; the dark open mouth of the woods. Even the name of the Grandmother's son, "Bailey," means the outer wall of a castle or the court enclosed by it. These are all images of enclosure producing the violence of history: as when Pitty Sing "rose with a snarl" from the valise and "sprang onto Bailey's shoulder"—causing the accident and the family's extinction. This movement is repeated later when the Misfit asks his sidekick for Bailey's Hawaiian shirt: "the shirt came flying at him and landed on his shoulder." Clothing himself in "Bailey"—as it were—the Misfit imprisons himself in the false paradise of the natural world. For him there is "no pleasure but meanness," and "his voice had become almost a snarl." The fiction itself operates as a place of punishment and retribution, imprisoning its characters in the straitjacket of moral reality.

At the same time, to see them as images only of enclosure is to misread the natural text—as the Grandmother misreads the initials carved on Teagarden's watermelon—for these images participate in a vast ironic reorganization of meaning, accessible to us through another image of enclosure, the Grandmother's fictive "secret panel." She imagined that inside this nonexistent panel they would find the "family silver," and family silver is exactly what she does find. The Misfit's hair is "silver-gray," he is wearing "silver-rimmed glasses," and one of his accomplices has a "silver stallion" embossed on his sweatshirt. (Now and then O'Connor ended her letters with the closing, "hi yo silver.") Readers may recall that the "trees" earlier in the story "were full of silver-white sunlight and the meanest of them sparkled." This is also "family" silver because when the imminence of death "cleared her head for an instant" she recognizes the Misfit as "one of my own children!"—though not one of the "connections" she wanted to make in east Tennessee. When she touches "him on the shoulder"—in the second repetition of the cat's escape from prison—the Misfit recoils and shoots her three times in the chest. The Misfit here is a kind of black Lone Ranger, a mixture of good and evil, whose (phallocentric) "meanness" saves the Grandmother's life by killing her: "She would of been a good woman," he tells Bobby Lee, "if it had been somebody there to shoot her every minute of her life." In the religious register of the story, the secret panel has become a doorway to the kingdom of heaven.

The stress this ending places upon the family is the culmination of the story's thorough reorganization of natural accident into the design of a spiritual parable. O'Connor repeatedly insists upon the family's belief in the power of accident: the Grandmother has taken the cat along because she is afraid he will "accidentally asphyxiate himself"; she dresses formally for the trip so that "in case of an accident, anyone seeing her dead on the highway would know at once that she was a lady"; when the car overturns, the children scream "We've had an ACCIDENT!" in a "frenzy of delight." They shout this three times, perhaps as a sign of the spiritual denial their lives represent. Just as their vacation is revealed to be an antipilgrimage,

and the digressive sidetrip down the dirt road becomes a spiritual journey taking them into the same woods in which Dante lost his way, so here the Grandmother's sense of familial connection is entirely and radically altered under the pressure of the Misfit's presence. One system is displaced and reorganized into another as O'Connor's irony converts a world of reason without ground to an irrational world grounded in Christ.

The Grandmother's recognition of the Misfit as one of her own children, uniting the world's people beyond the bonds of blood and locality, signifies two central assumptions of revisionist liberalism—human depravity and the universality of human circumstance. In his essay on *The Family of Man* photographic exhibit at the Museum of Modern Art in the 1950s, Eric J. Sandeen described the collected images as an "elaborately conceived argument for the validity of the photograph as a persuasive document, as well as for the liberal sentiment that 'mankind is one.'" When Steichen invited photographers to submit their work, he told them, "It is essential to keep in mind the universal elements and aspects of human relations and the experiences common to all mankind rather than situations that represented conditions exclusively related or peculiar to a race, an event, a time or place." Sandeen offers this contextualization of those directives: "Like the liberal historians of the '50s, [Steichen and Miller] assumed that culture worked to bring humans together rather than to differentiate them. . . . Steichen believed in the psychic unity of mankind and used qualities of life, accessible to a mass audience, to get at this deeper level of confluence."

Such displacement of racial and class differences by a universalizing perspective was one of the more conservative implications of the new liberalism. Of course for O'Connor this subordination of race and class to the family of man was consistent with her religious focus and her Agrarian belief in the organic development of culture. "The South has to evolve a way of life in which the two races can live together with mutual forbearance." she told an interviewer in 1963. "You don't form a committee to do this or pass a resolution: both races have to work it out the hard way." O'Connor's fiction represents the relations of race and class in the South, but always as a means of demonstrating the universalism of the human condition. Several of the stories in the *Good Man* collection end with this reminder of universality: Mr. Head and his grandson "could both feel [the artificial Negro] dissolving their differences"; Mrs. Cope's face, at the end of **"A Circle in the Fire,"** "looked as if it might have belonged to anybody, a Negro or a European or to Powell himself"; and the old black man in **"The Displaced Person"** tells Mrs. McIntyre, "Black and white . . . is the same."

Reviews of *A Good Man Is Hard to Find* often praised O'Connor's characters as "part of the human tragicomedy." The *New York Herald Tribune* reviewed the book on page 1 of its book review section and praised O'Connor for her "use of the regional to communicate the universal" ("Flannery O'Connor: A New Shining Talent"). The *Commonweal* reviewer noted that "here, in rural miniature, are the primary intuitions of man." Certainly O'Connor herself thought in just these terms. She wrote Ben Griffith about her story **"The Artificial Nigger"** that she meant "to suggest with the artificial nigger . . . the redemptive quality of the Negro's suffering for us all"; nine months later, when she recalled the story's origin, O'Connor gave the statue a more specific cultural and historical significance: "It's not only a wonderful phrase but it's a terrible symbol of what the South has done to itself."

We needn't forget that O'Connor's demonstration of universality was rooted in Christian mystery, but this point of view not only had some currency within the postwar liberal community but also supplied a foundation for the social responsibility indigenous to "liberal sentiments." O'Connor's explanation of what happens at the end of **"A Good Man"** suggests how her story might easily be read within the terms of the liberal narrative: "Her head clears for an instant and she realizes, even in her limited way, that she is responsible for the man before her and joined to him by ties of kinship which have their roots deep in the mystery she has been merely prattling about so far."

Within the postwar context the Misfit is really a double figure: on the one hand he is a defenseless liberal intellectual, guilty of what Trilling said was liberalism's tendency "to organize the elements of life in a rational way"; on the other he is the reality of violence and evil for which the liberal is unprepared. He is the reality of "history" itself—Stalin, Hitler, European evil showing up on the red dirt back road of the Georgia countryside—indeed, he is the greater evil that results from the astonished innocence of liberalism. His is the violence of a simplifying reason imposing its punitive logic upon the recalcitrant complexities of human nature and history.

Before encountering the Grandmother, the Misfit had developed a logic by which he could live, but it was a logic that required disbelief: if Jesus didn't raise the dead, he explains to her, "then it's nothing for you to do but enjoy the few minutes you got left the best way you can—by killing somebody or burning down his house or doing some other meanness to him." The possibility that Jesus might have raised the dead throws "everything off balance" and destroys the logic of his behavior. The Grandmother's gesture testifies to her belief, and it is for this reason that the Misfit is described springing back "as if a snake had bitten him." The Grandmother's gesture violates the consistency of the Misfit's protective logic and removes his last line of defense against the mystery of existence: "The Misfit's eyes were red-rimmed and pale and defenseless-looking."

Understood in this way, **"A Good Man Is Hard to Find"** turns out to enact one of the central parables of cold war thinking and the "end of ideology"—that the naive rationality of liberal idealism produces a greater violence than a belief which recognizes the reality of evil in human behavior. Introducing this story to her audience at Hollins College in Virginia (1962), O'Connor told them, "I have found that violence is strangely capable of returning my characters to reality and preparing them to accept their moment of grace." This is Christian realism with a vengeance.

The true authority of this story resides within the narrative action itself, which brings its characters and readers to a perception of human mortality and depravity—that is, to a perception of the silent authority of reality, presented here in the relentlessness of the criminal, and engineered throughout by O'Connor. Indeed, all the stories in *A Good Man Is Hard to Find* may be read as depictions of the "family of man" in need of its "father." The collection's title reminds us that there are almost no fathers in any of the stories, and none who exert authority. In **"A Good Man,"** the Misfit is a man who has lost his father, Bailey is an ineffectual father, and we hear nothing at all of the Grandmother's husband, alive or dead.

The need for authority is one she herself felt. "If you live today you breathe in nihilism," she told one correspondent. "If I hadn't had the Church to fight it with or tell me the necessity of fighting it, I would be the stinkingest logical positivist you ever saw right now." Similarly, to another she wrote, "I know that [baptism] had to be given me before the age of reason, or I wouldn't have used any reason to find it." The Misfit appears to be her imagination of how mean she could be without the faith. At the same time her faith seems to permit her the violence she wreaks upon her characters.

Inscribed within that violence was one of the repeated admonitions of revisionist liberalism—that we must return to "reality"—just as it was part of the liberal narrative (the story told by many liberals) that history ("all the lessons of modern history," Schlesinger wrote) had violently alerted them to the simplifications of liberal ideology. Despite O'Connor's expressed alienation from liberal culture, the "ugly words" of her fiction reproduce in another register the recurring injunctions of cold war discourse. All seemed to agree: it's time to establish a new realism, a less idealistic approach to domestic culture and foreign affairs, because a good man is hard to find.

Frederick Asals (essay date 1993)

SOURCE: An introduction to *A Good Man Is Hard to Find*, by Flannery O'Connor, Rutgers University Press, 1993, pp. 3-9, 17-24.

[*Asals is an American educator and critic. In this excerpt, he lauds thematic and stylistic aspects of "A Good Man Is Hard to Find," praising, in particular, the significant role of the grandmother in the story.*]

"A Good Man Is Hard to Find" is probably now, as during her lifetime, the single story by which Flannery O'Connor is best known. She herself may have had something to do with this: when she was asked to give a reading or a talk to students, **"A Good Man"** was the story she usually proposed. As she wrote to John Hawkes, she preferred a reading with commentary to a lecture because "It's better to try to make one story live for them than to tell them a lot of junk they'll forget in five minutes and that I have no confidence in anyhow." It was not, she claimed, her favorite among her stories (that honor she accorded **"The Artificial Nigger"**); she chose **"A Good Man"** for public readings (or so a friend told me) because it was the only one she could get through and not "bust out laughing."

Whatever force these readings had in establishing the story, she had already singled it out by making it the title piece of her first collection, published in 1955 (*A Good Man Is Hard to Find and Other Stories*). That alone might not have sufficed to give it preeminence (when the collection was published in England it bore, without authorial permission, the title *The Artificial Nigger*). In 1960, however, her friends Allen Tate and Caroline Gordon selected it for inclusion in the second edition of their enormously influential anthology, *The House of Fiction,* and thus began the history of **"A Good Man"** as a favorite of anthologizers. Its only rival among her work at the time was, once more, **"The Artificial Nigger,"** which had been anthologized earlier, but in less powerful places. By 1966, W. S. Marks III could speak casually of **"A Good Man"** as "one of the more frequently anthologized of her pieces." More recently, other stories, including those from her second collection, *Everything That Rises Must Converge,* have displaced it as an inevitable choice of anthologists, but it was established for long enough to remain the single tale most immediately associated with Flannery O'Connor.

That eminence is not entirely arbitrary or accidental. Its quality aside, the story probably makes available more rapidly and obviously than anything else she ever wrote the unsettling mix of comedy, violence, and religious concern that characterizes her fiction. Other stories may, arguably, be funnier, subtler, more moving, more resonant, but **"A Good Man"** brings before the reader, with a powerful shock, the main features of O'Connor's fictive world. Perhaps its place in her career helps explain why it seems to capture within its borders some essence of her vision.

"A Good Man Is Hard to Find" was first published in Avon's *Modern Writing 1* in late September 1953. It was the last of the four stories she published that year, a group which, in turn, comprised her first crop of mature stories, works that she would consider worthy of putting between hard covers. Her master's thesis for the University of Iowa's Writer's Workshop had been comprised of a half-dozen stories, but these she clearly viewed as apprentice pieces, and a section cut out of her novel-in-progress and published independently in 1949 would get heavily rewritten and retitled (**"A Stroke of Good Fortune"**) before its later admittance to her collection. O'Connor rarely sat on completed work—her usual practice was to send a story out for responses from trusted friends, make any revisions in light of their commentary, then send it on to her agent—and her letters suggest that all the stories published in 1953 (**"A Late Encounter with the Enemy," "The Life You Save May Be Your Own,"** and **"The River"** were the others) were written in 1952 or early 1953. It is unlikely any were written earlier, as 1951 was taken up almost entirely with two occupations: surviving the lupus

erythematosus that had suddenly struck her down in December 1950 and preparing for publication the manuscript of her first novel, *Wise Blood.*

At first glance, *Wise Blood* (1952) seems radically different from **"A Good Man Is Hard to Find."** It is a severely stylized novel, populated by the grotesque denizens of a nightmarish urban landscape who engage in ironically rendered verbal and physical violence while approaching their absurd or dreadful ends. At its center is Hazel Motes, grandson of a fundamentalist preacher, so desperate to be rid of Jesus that he devises and preaches a backwoods version of nihilistic existentialism with a ferocious intensity usually reserved for more orthodox creeds. As Robert Fitzgerald has pointed out, existentialism was the "last word in attitudes . . . when Flannery O'Connor began to write," and it provides a thematic link between novel and story. Its postures reverberate in the rolling-stone experience of **"A Good Man"**'s Misfit: "I been most everything. Been in the arm service, both land and sea, at home and abroad, been twict married, been an undertaker, been with the railroads, plowed Mother Earth, been in a tornado, seen a man burnt alive oncet. . . . I even seen a woman flogged." Existentialist accents sound even more clearly in his metaphysical questionings of "why it is"—why some suffer and others do not, why punishment and crime never match, why the very earth itself seems both devoid of significance and a prison. If The Misfit's stance of interrogation differs from Hazel Motes's blasphemous defiance, both postures are nonetheless assumed on a similar basis—the basis of the apparent meaninglessness of human existence in a neutralized cosmos from which the divine is absent. It is little wonder that echoes of "existentialist" writers from Dostoyevsky to Camus have been detected in The Misfit's speeches.

But if The Misfit glances back toward *Wise Blood,* his antagonist in the story, the grandmother, has no real predecessor there. She is the first of many O'Connor figures to ground the work (as *Wise Blood* never is grounded) in what Flannery O'Connor referred to as the realm of "manners," an everyday worldliness concerned with such matters as family relations, dress and appearance, etiquette, economic and social status. Complacent and self-satisfied, these characters—and they are usually women—may well pay lip service to conventional Christianity, but their eyes are fixed firmly on the imperatives of this world. Murderously polite criminals evolved out of O'Connor's imagination working on the more sensational news of the day . . . ; genteel ladies she had known since childhood. If The Misfit seems to emerge from the wildness that produced *Wise Blood,* the grandmother looks forward to the many stories that are rooted in a recognizable Southern social milieu, and their long confrontation, both comic and violent, in the second half of **"A Good Man"** may be what makes this seem *the* quintessential O'Connor story.

Whenever O'Connor worked on the story, it was virtually complete by late March or early April of 1953 when she sent it off to her friends Sally and Robert Fitzgerald for their response. Apparently she got one, but it seems not to have survived, and on June 7 she wrote to inform them she had sold it to the *Partisan Review Reader*. Like all her fiction, the story bears the discernible traces of its time of composition, most of which were more local in time and place than The Misfit's existential musings. The advertising for Red Sammy Butts's short order house, "filling station and dance hall" includes the patriotic claim that the proprietor is a veteran (a role he plays right down to his "khaki trousers"), a reminder that the reverberations of World War II were still to be felt in the early fifties. These were the years of the Marshall Plan of aid to war-ravaged Europe, but in the xenophobic South, this policy was likely to produce the kind of conversation that takes place between Red Sammy and the grandmother.

> He and the grandmother discussed better times. The old lady said that in her opinion Europe was entirely to blame for the way things were now. She said the way Europe acted you would think we were made of money and Red Sam said it was no use talking about it, she was exactly right.

The fifties are detectable in other touches as well: in June Star's tap dance lessons and her reference to the popular show of the fledgling medium of television, "Queen for a Day"; in the slacks and head-kerchief of the children's mother; in the country and western tune popularized nationwide by Patti Page, "The Tennessee Waltz." Perhaps the atmosphere of the times is nowhere more powerfully, if indirectly, expressed than in the following passage:

> "In my time," said the grandmother, folding her thin veined fingers, "children were more respectful of their native states and their parents and everything else. People did right then. Oh look at the cute little pickaninny!" she said and pointed to a Negro child standing in the door of a shack. "Wouldn't that make a picture, now?" she asked and they all turned and looked at the little Negro out of the back window. He waved.
>
> "He didn't have any britches on," June Star said.
>
> "He probably didn't have any," the grandmother explained. "Little niggers in the country don't have things like we do. If I could paint, I'd paint that picture," she said.

The grandmother's complacency, her reduction of the moral to the picturesque (poverty as aesthetic category?), and the brilliant non-sequitur of the verb "explained"—the old lady's explanation of course illuminates nothing but the imperviousness of her kind—all expose the automatic racism of the postwar South in those years immediately preceding the civil rights movement. It is frequently noted that O'Connor virtually never made the South's racial situation her central fictional subject; it is less frequently noted that virtually every story contains at least one trenchant passage like this one that epitomizes that situation. She knew what she was about: as she wrote a friend about a pending public appearance. "I am going to read **'A Good Man Is Hard to Find,'** deleting the paragraph about the little nigger who doesn't have any britches on. I can write with ease what I forbear to read."

The local appears in other ways as well. The reference to "The Tennessee Waltz" not only fixes the temporal period of the action, but connects with the entire "Tennessee motif" in the story, which is itself part of a larger, typically Southern nostalgia. It is the note on which **"A Good Man"** opens: "The grandmother didn't want to go to Florida. She wanted to visit some of her connections in east Tennessee." When the song plays on the nickelodeon at Red Sammy's, the grandmother "swayed her head from side to side and pretended she was dancing in her chair"; shortly thereafter, she will "pretend" so successfully that she knows a plantation with white columns, twin arbors, and an avenue of oaks where, behind a secret panel "the family silver was hidden . . . When Sherman came through," that she will fool even herself. Not only does her deception lead the family down the fatal dirt road, but a sudden "horrible thought" produces the spasmodic reaction that precipitates the accident that leaves them all at the mercy of The Misfit—a chain of causation with the inflexibility of iron links. "The horrible thought she had had before the accident was that the house she had remembered so vividly was not in Georgia but in Tennessee."

That house, as the grandmother has joked about another antebellum plantation, is truly "Gone With the Wind. . . . Ha. Ha." The South's nostalgia for its own supposed glorious past, its glamorous lost cause is, in O'Connor's view, a form of sentimentality that is far from harmless, that can precipitate car accidents and is not divorced from a perception of poor black children as picturesque. Born in Savannah, Georgia, she had grown up there and in Milledgeville, and had spent a half-dozen of her adult years outside of the South, yet even when she was living elsewhere—in Iowa, New York, or Connecticut—it was her native region that occupied her and provided the material of her fiction. Unlike Faulkner and other southern writers of a previous generation, she was not fascinated by the Civil War, but she was fascinated by the South's own fascination (that fascination is the subject of another of the 1953 stories, **"A Late Encounter with the Enemy"**). The ultimate result of this sentimental backward-looking, **"A Good Man"** implies, is such a figure as The Misfit, a man thrust into the moral and metaphysical vacuum that results in part from self-serving nostalgia. One of the story's nicer ironies is that down this road in an imagined "Tennessee," the grandmother has indeed come face to face with one of her "connections.". . .

[Her lecture delivered at Hollins College in 1963 offers] two of O'Connor's own anecdotes about the reactions of undergraduate students to **"A Good Man,"** [and] it may not be inappropriate to add a third. Granted, these were not Southern students like those O'Connor was sure "all had grandmothers or great-aunts just like [the story's protagonist] at home"; my students were Canadian, and they were not at all convinced that this "old lady . . . had a good heart." They found this central female character not only "a hypocritical old soul," but the possessor of assorted juicy sins unforgivable to the minds of nineteen-year-olds—garrulous, insensitive, underhanded, pretentious, manipulative, self-serving, morally obtuse, out of touch with "reality," and so on. In short, they *judged* the grandmother, and they did so in part because they felt, and not incorrectly, that the story invited such judgment; they sensed, even if they could not always articulate it, the narrator's ironic tone, the element of caricature in the presentation (nor were they blind to the bratty children, the lumpish mother, the sullen father in this family). And if they were puzzled by the import of her last words to The Misfit and somewhat shaken by the wholesale massacre in the final part of the story, they did not find this old lady's demise entirely without moral justification. The wind moving through the trees "like a long satisfied insuck of breath" as the gunshots go off seems an expressive summation of their response.

The eminence of "A Good Man Is Hard to Find" is not entirely arbitrary or accidental. Its quality aside, the story probably makes available more rapidly and obviously than anything else O'Connor ever wrote the unsettling mix of comedy, violence, and religious concern that characterizes her fiction.

—Frederick Asals

Surely an important part of the story's effectiveness, of the pleasure we are able to take in what, outlined, would seem merely grim tabloid material, comes from such stylization, from the ironic comedy which distances the reader from this family and particularly from its chief member, the grandmother. Nevertheless, she is the "chief member" only because the story has so presented her, privileging her point of view over that of the others. Within the family itself, she is clearly a marginal figure, ignored (as we see in the opening scene) by her son and daughter-in-law, freely insulted by her grandchildren, powerless before all. If she is all the things my students claimed, surely that is because she has to be: her comically desperate attempts to assert a self that is denied by all around her, no less by the parents' silence than by the children's diminishing taunts ("She has to go everywhere we go"), testify to her lack of any essential role in the only context which age, sex, and widowhood have left open to her.

Failing to produce even a reconsideration of family vacation plans, she apparently capitulates with absurd rapidity: "The next morning the grandmother was the first one in the car, ready to go" (as the children claim, she is not about to be left behind, and she doubtless considers promptness a cardinal virtue). Nonetheless, the hidden presence of her cat, Pitty Sing, suggests a more complex response. Her reasons for taking the animal expose both her sentimentality and that melodramatic imagination which has already drawn her to newspaper reports of The Misfit—"he would miss her too much and she was afraid he might brush against one of the gas burners and accidentally asphyxiate himself"—but the paragraph's final sentence, which concerns not the inclusion but the secreting of Pitty Sing, hints at something more. "Her son, Bailey, didn't like to arrive at a motel with a cat" presents the animal as agent of rebellion, the grandmother's private refusal to acquiesce without at least a token of revolt against an order that denies her. If she has her way, Bailey *will,* like it or not, "arrive at a motel with a cat."

No such destination, of course, is ever reached, but the cat nevertheless plays a key role in the story's action. By that time, however, it has become a more problematic locus of possibilities. The grandmother has spun her tale of the plantation house, and for once, backed by the children (who first said grandparents and grandchildren naturally gravitate together to face a common enemy?), she has apparently finally got her way, moved the family in the direction of her desires. That archetypal Southern mansion both has and is a pseudo-secret—the grandmother knows there is no hidden panel in the house, and she is about to discover there is no house at all down that road—and with the sudden revelation to her of the truth, she uncovers the genuine secret of the cat. "The thought was so embarrassing that she turned red in the face and her eyes dilated and her feet jumped up, upsetting her valise in the corner. The instant the valise moved, the newspaper top she had over the basket rose with a snarl and Pitty Sing, the cat, sprang onto Bailey's shoulder." The cat, like The Misfit, identified through their common "snarl," will not be contained by the newspaper, and as a result the car flips over into a ditch.

This is the turning point of **"A Good Man,"** the "ACCIDENT" that occurs precisely at the story's half-way mark. It is the moment in the tale that novelist T. Coraghessan Boyle recently approved [in *The New York Times Magazine,* December 9, 1990] because it "violate[s] the familiar comic balance": "It's very powerful when the safety net drops away from the comic universe where nothing can go wrong, and there's this overpowering, terrible violence." The sudden, unpredictable quality of the car accident is essential to the effect and implications of **"A Good Man,"** yet so is the recognition that it has been precipitated, however obliquely, by the grandmother. But if her original smuggling aboard of the cat suggested her underground revolt against the family's suppression, the uncovering of that secret seems to imply a different focus of dissatisfaction. Despite the fact that Pitty Sing springs directly at Bailey, patriarch of the new order that diminishes her, the grandmother's release of the cat results from her visceral acknowledgement of her *own* failure, of the falsity of that sentimental symbol of the old order she believes she believes in, the plantation house. The cat thus comprehends the rejection of *both* social orders, the old and the new, as somehow inadequate; both Florida and the plantation house fail as possible destinations. If the story provides no justification for the grandmother's sentimental concern that the cat "would miss her too much" (note its final appearance in the closing paragraphs), it abundantly justifies her belief in a fatally melodramatic world where "he might *accidentally* asphyxiate himself" [italics added].

That world is most fully defined in the story by The Misfit, whom the accident seems to conjure up, as if the very incarnation of such a universe. His self-chosen title, he tells us, proclaims both his recognition of this world and his place in it, a paradoxically inevitable existence of radical contingency where "one is punished a heap and another ain't punished at all." I have argued elsewhere that while The Misfit claims to have lived this experience, the story in its very structure demonstrates it, breaking its action with the car accident and bringing down on all members of this family, even to the infant, the same lethal "punishment." Yet, in her heart of hearts, the grandmother recognizes this world too, even to the point of absurdly dressing for it. She is carefully groomed so that "In case of an *accident,* anyone seeing her dead on the highway would know at once that she was a lady" [italics added]. In short, the gap between the grandmother and The Misfit, which closes with her fatal recognition of him as "one of my babies . . . one of my own children," is never as great as it may at first appear.

Nevertheless, the action of the story is precisely designed to uncover this awareness in her, to apply such pressure that all her unquestioned assumptions will be gradually denied until her physical collapse in the ditch manifests the loss of her accustomed inner supports. It is The Misfit's stripping away of her "social" ("good blood," "nice people"), materialistic ("You must have stolen something"), and conventionally religious (If you would pray . . . Jesus would help you") values that brings the grandmother to her moment of recognition, yet both the presence of the cat and the occasion of its catastrophic leap imply her readiness to undertake and respond to this cathartic process: the purging of the values both of a contemporary world which allows her no role and a nostalgic one which has built for her only a hollow, inauthentic self.

Meanwhile, her male antagonist is undergoing an analogous process whereby his apparent self-sufficiency and command is gradually revealed as a form of armor, a veneer which falls away to uncover the "baby" with a gun. For all the backwoods *politesse* and homemade existentialism which locate him in this particular time and place, The Misfit is in essence a variation on that enduring American type, the individualistic male whose violence both expresses and substitutes for inner incompleteness. Despite his assertion, he is not "doing all right by myself," but the only "hep" he might accept would be disembodied, intellectual—to have "known" whether or not Jesus raised the dead so that "I wouldn't be," as he at last admits, "like I am now." The messiness and disorder of life in the flesh, particularly the domestic flesh, is anathema to him: children make him "nervous," and the touch of a foolish old woman who sees him momentarily as "one of my children" triggers a visceral, defensive violence. If, as O'Connor said, "It is the extreme situation that best reveals what we are essentially," what is revealed in The Misfit is an anger and anguish never entirely assuaged by the "meanness" he visits on the world around him.

And what is revealed about the grandmother in *her* comparable moment of extremity? Taking the identification of The Misfit as "one of my babies" together with the gesture of reaching out to him as O'Connor says she in-

tended us to, we can see the grandmother adopting for the first time an archetypal female role, one that she has denied, but that has also been denied her, in the family context so fiercely limned in the earlier part of the story. If we wish to press that maternal gesture in the direction of O'Connor's declared Catholicism, we can see glimmer through the grandmother the figure of the Grand Mother, a momentary *imitatio Virginis*—Our Lady of Sorrows, the Hope of Criminals, and so on. However, as other critics have shown, if we ignore O'Connor's comments, it seems possible to see this as one last self-serving grasp at survival, or as an ironically threatening identification (all her other "children" are dead), or as an attempt to "adopt" The Misfit into her smothering, diminishing superficiality.

But the story itself has more to say of the grandmother: two other roles here get pressed on her in a kind of double epitaph, one by The Misfit, the other by the narrator. Her corpse is described with its legs crossed under it "like a child's and her face smiling up at the cloudless sky" just before The Misfit pronounces, "She would of been a good woman . . . if it had been somebody there to shoot her every minute of her life." Both "child" and "woman," of course, ignore the grandmother's own social self-identification, "lady," and at first appear so antithetically matched as to raise the suspicion of irony. The dissonance may at first seem reconcilable by noting the gap between the living and the dead, between childlike corpse and living "woman"—until we realize that both designations must be applied to the very moment before death. We can, with a small stretch, give the passage a Christian reading in which the grandmother, stripped to her essential being as a genuine "woman," has, in her recovery of simplicity, become again as a little child. Yet it can also be understood more darkly, to suggest that the recovery of one's genuine female self is a dangerous business indeed, likely to reduce one to a condition of double and final powerlessness, the child-like corpse.

However we interpret the ending of **"A Good Man,"** or indeed the tale as a whole, it seems to go on resonating in the imagination, perhaps the single story that has most compellingly captured that condition of modern American life where, in Boyle's words, "the safety net drops away" and we are suddenly confronted with an overwhelming violence, a violence that apparently chooses its victims randomly and before which they are helpless. That sense of impotence in the face of terror is the stuff of nightmares (one might note that, with terror lightened to "unpleasantness," it is also the stuff of the grandmother's daily life in the earlier part of the story), and as such it addresses some of our deepest fears. Such fears, as **"A Good Man"** itself implies, are hardly peculiar to women, yet it seems inevitable that the protagonist of such a story should be female, and that the prolonged confrontation with an armed male should end in her death. This much is all too familiar, yet O'Connor would have us note not simply the man's violent gesture—"The Misfit sprang back . . . and shot her three times through the chest"—but also the woman's motions, particularly those with which she begins and ends. Her opening gesture is an aggressive (but useless) "rattling the newspaper" at the bald head of "her only boy," who continues to ignore her; her final one is to reach out and touch on the shoulder the man she calls "one of my own children." He will certainly not ignore her, but the distance she has travelled in these twenty-odd pages places her with the figures of classic American stories—from Irving's Ichabod Crane, Melville's Benito Cereno, and Stephen Crane's Swede to those of Flannery O'Connor's contemporaries, Eudora Welty's Clytie, J. D. Salinger's Teddy, Ralph Ellison's "King of the Bingo Game"—whose initiations into a frightening world are both astonishing and lethal.

FURTHER READING

Criticism

Browning, Preston M., Jr. "A Good Man Is Hard to Find." In *Flannery O'Connor*, pp. 40-71. Carbondale: Southern Illinois University Press, 1974.

> Discusses the title story of *A Good Man Is Hard to Find* in the context of the entire volume.

Bryant, Hallman B. "Reading the Map in 'A Good Man Is Hard to Find.'" *Studies in Short Fiction* XVIII, No. 3 (Summer 1981): 301-07.

> Surveys the significant settings and place names in O'Connor's short story.

Desmond, John F. "Signs of the Times: Lancelot and The Misfit." *The Flannery O'Connor Bulletin* XVIII (1989): 91-8.

> Considers similarities between the anti-heroes in the fiction of Walker Percy and Flannery O'Connor.

DiRenzo, Anthony. "Grinning Devils and Ludicrous Saints: The Grotesque and the Dialectic between Satire and Sanctity." In *American Gargoyles: Flannery O'Connor and the Medieval Grotesque*, pp. 134-49, 153-62. Carbondale: Southern Illinois University Press, 1993.

> Compares O'Connor's use of the grotesque to medieval religious art.

Doxey, William S. "A Dissenting Opinion of Flannery O'Connor's 'A Good Man Is Hard to Find.'" *Studies in Short Fiction* X, No. 2 (1973): 199-204.

> Provides a structural analysis of O'Connor's short story. Doxey maintains that "the point-of-view shifts from the grandmother to the Misfit, and the reader is suddenly left holding the bag, as it were, or—to be more technical—without a focus of narration."

Eggenschwiler, David. "Demons and Neuroses." In *The Christian Humanism of Flannery O'Connor*, pp. 31-70. Detroit: Wayne State University Press, 1972.

> Discusses suffering and despair in O'Connor's stories, with reference to The Misfit.

Frieling, Kenneth. "Flannery O'Connor's Vision: The Violence of Revelation." In *The Fifties: Fiction, Poetry, Drama*, edited by Warren French, pp. 111-20. Deland, Fla.: Everett/Edwards, 1969.

> Examines the impact of violence and grace in "A Good Man Is Hard to Find."

Martin, Carter W. *The True Country: Themes in the Fiction of Flannery O'Connor*. Nashville: Vanderbilt University Press, 1968, 253 p.

> Examines recurrent themes in O'Connor's fiction, with references to "A Good Man Is Hard to Find."

McFarland, Dorothy Tuck. "A Good Man Is Hard to Find." In *Flannery O'Connor*, pp. 13-41. New York: Frederick Ungar Publishing Co., 1976.

> Examines the major themes of "A Good Man Is Hard to Find."

Mills, Jerry Leath. "Samburan Outside of Toombsboro: Conrad's Influence on 'A Good Man Is Hard to Find.'" *The South Atlantic Quarterly* 84, No. 2 (1985): 186-96.

> Finds parallels in structure and characterization between O'Connor's story and Joseph Conrad's novel *Victory*.

Orvell, Miles. "A Good Man Is Hard to Find." In *Invisible Parade: The Fiction of Flannery O'Connor*, pp. 130-36. Philadelphia: Temple University Press, 1972.

> Discusses the tragi-comic effect of O'Connor's story.

Renner, Stanley. "Secular Meaning in 'A Good Man Is Hard to Find.'" *College Literature* IX, No. 2 (Spring 1982): 123-32.

> Views O'Connor's story as a dramatization of the human condition.

Walters, Dorothy. "Excursions into Catastrophe." In *Flannery O'Connor*, pp. 63-70. Boston: Twayne Publishers, 1973.

> Presents a nihilistic interpretation of "A Good Man Is Hard to Find," concluding that "whether read as Christian testimony or a nihilistic document, the story is powerful in its impact."

Additional coverage of O'Connor's life and career is contained in the following sources published by Gale Research: *Authors and Artists for Young Adults*, Vol. 7; *Concise Dictionary of American Literary Biography*, 1941-1968; *Contemporary Authors*, Vols. 1-4 (rev. ed.); *Contemporary Authors New Revision Series*, Vols. 3, 41; *Contemporary Literary Criticism*, Vols. 1, 2, 3, 6, 10, 13, 15, 21, 66; *Dictionary of Literary Biography*, Vol. 2; *Dictionary of Literary Biography Yearbook: 1980*; *DISCovering Authors*; *Major 20th-Century Authors*; *Short Story Criticism*, Vol. 1; and *World Literature Criticism*.

Juan Carlos Onetti
1909–1994

Uruguayan novelist, short story and novella writer, editor, journalist, and translator.

INTRODUCTION

Onetti is widely considered to be among the finest and most innovative novelists and short fiction writers of Latin America. Commenting on the alienation and dissatisfaction of modern life, his works feature such novelties as self-referentiality, nonlinear representation of events, emphasis on subjectivity, multiple narrative layers, characters invented by other characters, and the creation of a fictional milieu called Santa María. Onetti achieved international distinction with the publication of *La vida breve* (*A Brief Life*), hailed as one of the most original novels of the 1950s to emerge from South America. Nevertheless, he remains, as James Polk of the *New York Times* noted, "probably the least-known giant among modern Latin American writers."

Biographical Information

Onetti was born in Montevideo. His education was interrupted frequently as a result of numerous relocations by his family, and he eventually dropped out of high school to pursue a bohemian lifestyle, supporting himself with a variety of jobs. Though his formal studies were ended, Onetti was an avid reader, favoring particularly the works of Knut Hamsun. In 1931 he completed *El pozo* (*The Pit*), though this novella wasn't published until 1939, after having been reworked. An early publication of his won a prize from the journal *Prensa* in 1933, and Onetti was subsequently encouraged by the appearance of the stories "El obstáculo" and "El posible Baldi" in the *Nación* in 1935 and 1936, respectively. He served as the managing editor of the influential weekly magazine *Marcha* from its inception in 1939 until 1941. The magazine lasted as an important voice within the Uruguayan cultural world for more than three decades, with Onetti as a notable contributor of essays and articles. In 1941 he became an editor for Reuters news in Montevideo and continued his duties for Reuters in Buenos Aires until 1954. During this period he also worked for the *Nación*, which printed the stories "Un sueño realizado" ("A Dream Come True") in 1942 and "Bienvenido, Bob" ("Welcome, Bob") in 1944. With *La vida breve*, published in 1950, Onetti became one of the originators of the contemporary Spanish-American novel and garnered recognition as a writer worthy of note in the international literary world. His first collection of short stories, *Un sueño realizado y otros cuentos*, appeared in 1951 and was followed three years later by the novella *Los adioses*. Around 1954 Onetti returned to Montevideo, where he concentrated on journalism, working for the newspaper *Acción*. Somewhat later he undertook the

role of director of municipal libraries in Montevideo. With the success of the novels *El astillero* (*The Shipyard*) and *Juntacadáveres* (*Junta, the Bodysnatcher*), Onetti became a more prominent literary figure and in 1962 was awarded the Premio Nacional de Literatura by the Uruguayan government for his body of writing. In the following years, his schedule included the travels and conferences typical of an internationally renowned author. However, in 1974 he suffered imprisonment by the government for three months for having served on the jury of a contest that honored a work of fiction deemed subversive. Frustrated by the country's dictatorship, Onetti abandoned Uruguay for Europe the following year, settling in Spain. In 1980 he received a nomination for the Nobel Prize in Literature from the Latin American PEN Club and was awarded the Premio Miguel de Cervantes Prize by the Spanish Ministerio de Cultura y Información. Onetti remained in Madrid until his death in 1994.

Major Works of Short Fiction

Creating an atmosphere of moral, physical, and psychological decay, Onetti wrote about characters—typically outsiders—who are isolated, disenchanted, and lonely. They mourn squandered opportunities, live in fear of death, or seek to escape the monotonous routine of their daily lives. These people are often pushed to the edge by society and live in a nightmare world of ruin and corruption that they try to escape through their imagination or the creation of dream worlds. Seldom given proper names by Onetti, these characters are identified by their occupation, psychological characteristics, or a particular aspect of their appearance. Usually little action occurs in Onetti's fiction. Plots tend to center on an event or decision, followed by testimonials from various characters whose observations relate to the preceding anecdote and simultaneously elucidate and muddle the story. Most of Onetti's fiction is open-ended: he offers no neat conclusions and some mysteries remain. Santa María serves as the setting of "Jacob y el otro" ("Jacob and the Other"), which is about a wrestler who takes on any opponent for a cash prize. One man—prodded by his pregnant fiancée, who wants money for their wedding—challenges the wrestler. The story is divided into parts that present narration from distinct characters' points of view. Each narrator relates the events in a different sequence, resulting in a puzzle that the reader must piece together in order to have a clear understanding of the actual chronological sequence of incidents and of the possible cause-effect relationships. The novella *El pozo* is the story of a man alone on the night of his fortieth birthday, writing his memoirs. He recollects his rape of a girl, his moral degradation, and tortuous nightly self-analysis. This confession signals the potential for choosing a different way of life, but at the close of the narrative the man's direction remains unknown. Onetti's dramatization of the protagonist's internal, subjective state in *El pozo* is regarded as the beginning of existential fiction in Latin America.

Critical Reception

Praised for their imaginativeness and originality, Onetti's works have been described as fundamentally ambiguous, fragmented, and complex. John Deredita has found that "melodrama . . . occasionally damages Onetti's shorter works," and notes that "critics reproach Onetti's thematic insistence, the lapses into rhetoric, the minute descriptive style that serves as the imitative form of boredom and that sometimes reproduces it in the reader." Furthermore, critics have accused Onetti of misogyny because his fictional women are almost always presented in an unflattering light, often as prostitutes or unfaithful wives. Despite these defects, Onetti's works have been favorably compared to those of Jean-Paul Sartre, James Joyce, Samuel Beckett, and especially William Faulkner, whose interest in layered narratives and imaginary settings was shared by Onetti. Referring to the arrival of modern society in the twentieth century, Carlos Fuentes has stated: "That civilization, far from providing happiness or a sense of identity or the discovery of common values, was a new alienation, a more profound fragmentation, a more troublesome loneliness. No one came to see this better or sooner than the great Uruguayan novelist, Juan Carlos Onetti."

PRINCIPAL WORKS

Short Fiction

El pozo [*The Pit*] (novella) 1931
Un sueño realizado y otros cuentos (short stories) 1951
Los adioses [*Goodbyes*] (novella) 1954; translated in *Goodbyes, and Other Stories*, 1990
Una tumba sin nombre [*A Nameless Tomb*] (novella) 1959
La cara de la desgracia [*The Face of Misfortune*] (novella) 1960
El infierno tan temido [*Dreaded Hell*] (short stories) 1962
Jacob y el otro; Un sueño realizado y otros cuentos [*Jacob and the Other; A Dream Come True, and Other Stories*] (short stories) 1965
La novia robada y otros cuentos [*The Stolen Bride*] (short stories) 1968
Tiempo de abrazar [*Time to Embrace*] (novella) 1974
Tan triste como ella y otros cuentos [*As Sad as She Is, and Other Stories*] (novella and short stories) 1976

*Also published as *Para una tumba sin nombre*.

Other Major Works

Tierra de nadie [*No Man's Land*] (novel) 1941
Para esta noche [*Tonight*] (novel) 1943
La vida breve [*A Brief Life*] (novel) 1950
El astillero [*The Shipyard*] (novel) 1961
Juntacadáveres [*Junta, the Bodysnatcher*] (novel) 1964
La muerte y la niña [*Death and the Girl*] (novel) 1973
Réquiem por Faulkner y otros artículos [*Requiem for Faulkner, and Other Articles*] (essays) 1975
Dejemos hablar al viento (novel) 1979
Cuando entonces [*When Then*] (novel) 1987

CRITICISM

Luis Harss and Barbara Dohmann (essay date 1966)

SOURCE: "Juan Carlos Onetti, or the Shadows on the Wall," in *Into the Mainstream: Conversations with Latin-American Writers*, Harper & Row, 1967, pp. 173-205.

[*Harss is a Chilean-born novelist, journalist, and critic. In the following excerpt from a study originally published by Harss in 1966 as* Los Nuestros *and subsequently translated with Dohmann, the critics survey Onetti's short fiction and, observing the miserable state of all his characters, note that* "his pessimism seems to have become almost generic."]

Onetti, an ardent Arltian [i.e. strongly influenced by the writer Roberto Arlt], belongs to a "lost" generation that came of age around 1940, when the intellectual life of the country was being reassessed against a background of demagoguery and political disenchantment, of totalitarianism in Europe, and nationalism—with pro-Axis sympathies—in Argentina. In Uruguay a reactionary government ruled the country from 1933 to 1942, eroding faith in democracy as the corruption lurking under the monotonous surface of bureaucratic stability became daily more obvious. There were many broken lives in those days. Onetti speaks of the nihilism of his generation—portrayed in massive detail in his second novel, *Tierra de Nadie (No Man's Land,* 1941)—as a delayed echo of the epidemic malaise of the twenties. But, of course, Onetti lived it as an endemic phenomenon. For him, it was the disillusionment and resulting individualism of an era in which he was one of those who fell by the wayside. . . .

A new type of human being, a creature of twilight, rootless, rancorous, frustrated, displaced, populated our big cities. He was not so much the Marxist underdog as the spiritual outlaw, the moral discard. Arlt had already drawn his prophetic portrait. Now Onetti followed suit, with the dour shrug of a man shouldering the burden of a sad responsibility. In a prefatory note to *Tierra de Nadie,* whose action takes place in the Buenos Aires of 1940, Onetti has said: "I paint a group of people who may seem exotic in Buenos Aires but are nevertheless representative of a generation. . . . The fact is that the most important country of the young South American continent has started to produce a type of morally indifferent individual who has lost his faith and all interest in his own fate." He adds, defining a bankrupt attitude conditioned by the surrounding indigence: "Let no one reproach the novelist for having undertaken the portrait of this human type in the same spirit of indifference."

In his first published work, *El Pozo (The Pit,* 1939), the gloomy protagonist, Eladio, a thinly veiled projection of the author, had already recorded his skepticism in regard to personal commitment, his phlegmatic unconcern for anything resembling direct action or involvement. With sad irony Eladio confesses his total lack of social consciousness, of "popular spirit." The tone, as in most of Onetti, is confessional. Why even bother to put pen to paper? wonders Eladio, thinking out loud for the author. The willful answer is in a kind of militant argument for self-expression. "It's true I don't know how to write," he admits. "But I write about myself." Eladio, with his apoplectic inhibitions, is the classic Outsider. He lives disconnected from the world, stranded within himself, adrift in his tiny corner on the borderline of humanity, without any possibility of joining the mainstream. He begins and ends in himself. Which is why his single ambition is "to write the story of a soul, all by itself, without any of the events it had to mix in whether it wanted to or not." Though, of course, whether he "wants to or not," he forms part of the unconscious community of the lonely, the diaspora of the estranged. Even in his alienation, or because of it, he is the representative of a time and place, a frame of mind, an epoch. It is this fact that gives his experiences

relevance and validity. To have realized this is Onetti's merit. In a literary scene still too often made up of inflated social canvases, painters of the soul like Onetti are a rarity. But, if only because in the last years they have been producing much of our best work, they have begun to seem inevitable. That our literature is gradually shifting its focus from object to subject, in appearance, perhaps, narrowing its perspectives, is actually a clear sign of our growing self-awareness and, of course, the price in pain and distress that we are paying for it. The price may be high, but, then, who can deny that the stakes are, too? Meditating on the world of solitary inner lives he has created out of what might pass for superfluous materials in the age of industrial waste, Onetti, a man who has never bargained, said in an interview in 1961, without immodesty: "All I want to express is the adventure of man.". . .

In Onetti's ordinarily middle-aged protagonists—his other selves—there is a desperate yearning for vanished youth, innocence and purity, corroded images to which they cling, rusted by time and undermined by memory. They live in the nonexistent past, in the shambles of approaching death and decay, as life passes them by. They have grown old without ever growing up, barely surviving or subsisting through the years, after some distant—and more or less nebulous—fall from grace into the sordid facts of life. Thus, we have Ana María in *El Pozo,* a joyless little sexpot who inspires a sad lust in the protagonist. His absurd love for her, which exists entirely in the sublimated realm of reverie, is a cynical front behind which he disguises feelings of guilt and remorse. It is nothing but an exorcism—an alibi. The fact is that he has once raped or in some way humiliated her—an impulse that in Onetti functions as a form of wish fulfillment—after which, for understandable reasons, their relations were discontinued. But in his vagaries the climactic act of violence repeats itself indefinitely with a high poetic charge, as if it had been an act of love. The switch is an attempt on Eladio's part to trick himself out of the trap he has set for himself. But it is too late. In Onetti a single moment of bad faith—or bad luck—derails a life forever. Perhaps because "love is marvelous and absurd, and incomprehensibly visits all kinds of souls. But absurd and marvelous people do not abound; and even those gifted with those qualities retain them only for a short time, in their early youth. Then they start accepting things and that's the end of them."

For Onetti, growing out of adolescence into adult life means compromising with impotence and despair. Hidden somewhere in the process is a loss that can never be made up. Says Onetti: "I think that happens to everybody." The sense of having strayed, of things left undone, opportunities missed, chances overlooked, is universal, says Onetti. He has always been haunted by it. The feeling is vague—a sort of chronic uneasiness. "Each person, out of convenience, even intellectual convenience, tries to pinpoint the cause of the trouble, to find something concrete and say: 'This is it.' Even if it isn't." The effect is numbing. But numbness is the human lot. Onetti defines his characters in terms of their omissions. "Because that's the way I am." In fact, in his early work . . . the characters are little more than episodes in his own mental processes. They are passing fancies that flicker in and out of existence like dream figures. Their sole reality is their subjective charge. And that defines their function. They are dreams dreamed by an author who in turn is dreamed by them. They have only a shadowy secondary—subsidiary—existence and no dramatic substance.

Passing himself off as his narrator is a favorite Onetti device. "I feel freer, more like myself, working this way," he says. Thus Eladio, an inchoate writer, is doubling for the author when he sits down to compose a page of his journal reflecting, as he puts it with heavy irony, that "a man ought to write the story of his life when he reaches the age of forty, especially if interesting things have happened to him." The point is, of course, that nothing has ever happened to him worth mentioning. And what little has happened is a lot less real or interesting than what he has imagined. Reality is tedious and destructive, never up to the high standards of fantasy. Perhaps in this notion lies the source of the narrator's sense of inferiority which his dreams compensate for, providing him with a means of working off his obscure grudge against the world. Because "facts are always empty." It is out of this sense of inadequacy that the author invents surrogate characters who in turn perpetuate themselves in an endless succession of other invented characters that are all his mirror images. "For the writer," says Onetti, "his world is the world. Otherwise he is cheating." What this amounts to in practice is that reading an Onetti book is a schizophrenic experience. The reader is in constant flux between the mind or perceptions of the narrator-protagonist and those of the author, the two being practically indistinguishable. Onetti's figments would cease to exist the moment no one looked at them. They are in the mind's eye and gain access to their borrowed reality only in so far as there is an onlooker to bear witness to them. That is why Onetti says he writes "for his characters." They are his inner inventory. Exposing and outlining himself in them is his way of offering himself through them. Even in their spuriousness, the subjective load they carry is a sign of his abiding affection for them. He has been accused of emotional poverty. The charge is not unfounded. He is not versatile with his emotions. . . .

La Vida Breve, which contains the germ of everything that followed in Onetti's subsequent work, is a long pregnancy that ends in the birth of a subject and a fictional world. Onetti seems to have caught a sudden—incomplete but ultimately lucid—glimpse of the whole road that lay ahead of him. Here, for the first time, we encounter Santa María, "a small town extending between a river and a settlement of Swiss laborers." Here, in the narrator's overactive imagination, we witness the birth of Díaz Grey, himself the narrator and central intelligence in later works. *La Vida Breve* is a dream-world that later becomes the real world. Dreams used symbolically, says Onetti, are a cheap device. For him they are not transparent Freudian metaphors subject to pat clinical interpretation but an added dimension of reality.

The protagonist, or figurehead, of *La Vida Breve,* Bransen, is a colorless minor employee in a publicity firm who, attempting to find a way out of the dreariness of his life, dreams himself into the person of Díaz Grey, a doctor he conjures up out of some vaporous literary reminiscence, presumably for a film script he has been commissioned to write for his friend Julio Stein. A chance meeting in the hallway of the rooming house where he lives supplies him with a third identity. A fourth—the author, multiplied, occasionally dissolved, in the roles he shares—complicates the strange cast of characters. Bransen's various split personalities are in constant tension, nourishing and starving each other as they compete for supremacy. There is doubt up to the end as to which will impose itself at the expense of the others. The center of the whirlpool—the eye of the storm—is a static tableau, a set piece of décor in which Bransen, in suspended animation, stages the drama: his room. The immutable setting, says Onetti, was "stolen" from a still life by Ivan Albright that depicts objects on a table, among them a pair of empty gloves that retain the shape of the hands that have been in them. Bransen inhabits this unchanging picture. From there he spins out his fantasies, which branch off in all directions in an intricate pattern of crisscrossing lines in which each intersection is a new starting point. The author, hovering over his shoulder, is an active participant in every story. In each, there is a woman who is all women and enacts the standard parts in the female repertory, appearing under the different guises of sister, wife, mistress, prostitute. The protagonist, in vicarious raptures, escapes from one life into another, improvising as he goes. But every apparent escape leads to a dead end.

Of all Bransen's surrogate creations, it is the doctor Díaz Grey (Dorian Gray?) who acquires the most depth and substance and gradually gains the upper hand over the others, finally supplanting the author himself. . . .

The creation, via Bransen, of Díaz Grey and his world committed Onetti to a task of years and heroic feats of concentration. It has always been a tenuous and unstable fiction that a moment's absentmindedness could obliterate. Already in *La Vida Breve,* says Onetti, "there are several attempts on the part of the narrator to keep Díaz Grey alive." The ubiquitous but incurably ephemeral doctor keeps slipping away from Bransen, who "sets him back up again, shelters him, damns him, puts him by the window to look out at the river. At a certain moment he says: 'So many days have gone by since I was last able to see Díaz Grey.' He has to bring him back to put him on his fated course again." A lot is at stake. Like God and His creatures in some eminently symbiotic scheme, Onetti and Díaz Grey depend on each other.

Evidence of this is **Un Sueño Realizado y Otros Cuentos (A Dream Fulfilled and Other Stories,** 1951), written between 1941 and 1949—or more or less simultaneously with *La Vida Breve*—and first published in the course of the years in the Buenos Aires newspaper *La Nación.* Here, amid a lot of peripheral stage machinery, we can see Onetti assembling and dismounting the props that support his framework. **Un Sueño Realizado** is setting and background for *La Vida Breve.* Onetti is projecting antecedents, plotting case histories, feeling his way into attitudes, customs, and habitats. People and faces are in uncertain suspense, shadows flashing on the screen and flickering off in the blink of an eyelash. We have no clear concept, no overall view, of the situation yet; but Onetti's main themes are all present. The hypocritical idealism of adolescence is exposed in **"Bienvenido, Bob"** (**"Welcome, Bob"**). The shabbiness of false hope—in this case a man who swindles his boss to fulfill his Danish wife's ruinous yearning to return to the land of her childhood—is portrayed in **"Esbjerg, en la Costa"** (**"Esbjerg, on the Coast"**). Again, there is the death of illusion on contact with reality, in the title story, **"Un Sueño Realizado."** And, most notably, there is our friend Díaz Grey—grown independent of his progenitor, Bransen—in a familiar dilemma: the recollection, from the unfathomable depths of age, of the one moment of possible redemption in his life, which he threw away when he betrayed the trust of the woman who had offered him her help and love (**"La Casa en la Arena"**— **"The House on the Sand"**). The retrospective view of Díaz Grey ties up some loose ends in his story, but actually raises more questions than it solves. The past, in Onetti, is mythologized. Remembrance is a distant vantage point in which old scenes recur full of problematic variations. In **"La Casa en la Arena"** we are told what actually happened, what the protagonist imagined had happened, what he wished had happened, and what may, for all we know, still be happening, all of these different phases of the experience superimposed as time holds still around them. Onetti does not want to crystallize his world; he wants it to remain fluid. Therefore his various accounts of events, even when they cover the same grounds, may not coincide. Facts in one book may contradict those given in another, or even elsewhere in the same book. Inconsistencies need not be accounted for. What remains unchanged is the atmosphere of loss and drift, resentment and cynicism, that absorbs his creatures with their vague urges, their flashes of hate toward others, their perverse fantasies and obscure qualms and regrets. They are fixtures in a closed circuit that seals off all escape routes and makes all conclusions foregone. The town is little more than an extension of their boredom, staleness, and misery. Everywhere there are "fat and badly dressed people." The settings are grubby bedrooms, sweaty bars, fetid back streets, or "any smelly office." The detailed description—sometimes ad nauseam—of the gestures and movements of minor characters thickens the paste, adding to the cumulative agony. Every twitch and contortion has its place in the system. Even as the protagonists reflect the author, the secondary characters enact the moods of the protagonists. They form overlapping images that act as objective correlatives of a single state of mind. "That's the way I am. The small detail in persons or situations is enormously important to me," says Onetti. The traits scattered among the surrounding human specters belong less to individual persons than they do to the ensemble, to the repertory of the book as a whole. Personifying the décor is a way of rendering it dynamic, humanizing it. Onetti's figments are never rounded persons; they are choreographic figures. He says he could never create the complete psychology of a Babbitt. Nor would he want to. He deals with a single emotional—almost abstract—type: the stranger. Often his characters are actually out-of-towners of vaguely foreign

genealogy; there is a predominance of Nordic or Germanic names that enhance this effect. They lead an erratic existence, "a grotesque life," married to flabby women, too big for their small lives, too small for their fantasies, straitjacketed by their past, eroded by "the quiet underhanded work of time."

A somewhat painful subject must be brought up in relation to Onetti: his style. Over the years it has gone through subtle but steady changes that throw considerable light on Onetti's intentions. In *El Pozo* the language was careless, straightforward, almost journalistic, in the Arltian manner—decidedly antiliterary. In *La Vida Breve* it had become more elliptical, but without taking on any added syntactical complications, retaining its aura of artlessness. In *Un Sueño Realizado*—as in *Tierra de Nadie* and, increasingly, in *Para Esta Noche*—there is more artifice. Onetti is echoing a master who has had an enormous influence on him: Faulkner. The influence is conscious and deliberate, and Onetti sees no reason to apologize for it. But it is sometimes embarrassing to the reader. *Un Sueño Realizado* is made of tortuously long and graceful Faulknerian sentences that contribute to the cloistered atmosphere of the book but, because of an excess of imitated mannerisms—intricate modifiers, pleomastic subclauses, redundant adjectival expanses—sometimes seem affected. Onetti loves the circular and static, perfectly suitable devices in a world of fates settled in advance, where every life is a sentence served backward, predestined and therefore in some sense tautological. The reiterative style is an integral part of the manic-depressive atmosphere. But in strong doses it can begin to seen like a noisy contrivance, more hysterical than inherent. In Faulkner accumulations of words add force and momentum to the story; in Onetti they too often merely distract and diffuse. Onetti admits and does not attempt to justify, his Faulknerian variations. He merely points out the obvious difference between his and Faulkner's conceptions of the world. Faulkner is a tragedian; Onetti, if one can coin a term, is a pathetician. He shares with Faulkner the use of a fictional site as his setting, a preoccupation for inner architectures with metaphysical overtones. Otherwise—above all, temperamentally—they have little in common. Their respective frames of reference are entirely different. And perhaps that is where the trouble lies. Faulkner's characters live outside him, in time and history; they are endowed with independent means of action and individual consciences. Onetti's characters are at once more intimate and more abstract. Living at such close quarters with their creator, they have become disembodied. The more said about them, the less real they seem. They are floating essences. Words bury them. Whether or not Onetti has overcome this danger is a matter we leave unresolved. The Faulknerian trance has had such a lasting hold over him that even today he claims that the best thing he ever wrote was a translation he did years ago of a story from *These 13.*

One of his works most damaged by contact with the Faulknerian mode was *Los Adioses,* an involuted chronicle of futility that ends in suicide. A moribund athlete— one of Onetti's melancholy maniacs—retires to die in Santa María. He rents a house on a knoll outside town, where he secludes himself, alternately receiving two apparently rival women who have an agreement to visit him separately. Letters, in the possession of the narrator (in this case not one of the protagonists but the owner of the general store, who keeps the refugees in supplies), subsequently reveal the women to be his wife—and a daughter by a previous marriage. The loneliness and essential selfishness of the suicidal impulse are the subject of the story. The protagonist, reduced to the last imaginable extreme, clings to the forlorn hope of privacy in death, because "he had only that, and did not want to share it." The language overloads a thin plot which, typically, unfolds at second hand, progressing through gossip, rumor, and indirection. The effect is somewhat hazy. The surprise ending—based on withheld information—does not seem implicit. Yet in a sense *Los Adioses* represents an advance over *La Vida Breve,* or at least a new phase in Onetti's work. The narrator, though not dispensed with, has been relegated to a secondary plane. The protagonists—whose impenetrable mystery ultimately remains intact—have at least a semblance of an objective existence outside him.

A considerable improvement in this vein, and one of Onetti's most readable books, because of a skillfully handled element of suspense in it, is *Una Tumba sin Nombre* (*A Nameless Tomb,* 1959), an enigma without a complete solution that generates some of the excitement of a good detective story (a genre the author is much addicted to; he says he wishes he could plot as well as Raymond Chandler). The setting, as usual, is Santa María. The subject is the moral corruption and consequent compunctions of an errant adolescent, Jorge Malabia, who pours out his guilt to a sympathetic listener, and chronicler: Díaz Grey. As Díaz Grey records it with bloodthirsty relish—picking up odds and ends to complete the picture from Tito Perotti, Jorge's roommate at the university, and spicing the racy mixture with his own acid speculations—it is a gory tale. It involves an amoral young woman, Rita, an ex-maid in the Malabia household, once the mistress of Marcos Bergner, the brother of Jorge's sister-in-law, Julita. Exploited, then abandoned, by Marcos, Rita has taken to whoring for a living in Buenos Aires, where Jorge meets her while studying at the university and sets up house with her. *Una Tumba sin Nombre,* with all due allowances for its Onettian vagaries, is a Bildungsroman. The occasion for Jorge's growth is his enslaving passion, which is at least partly self-imposed. As a child, the commentator reveals, Jorge used to spy on Marcos and Rita through the keyhole, fascinated by their lovemaking. It is his tormenting memories of Rita in intimate postures, become obsessive with time, that somehow make him feel entitled to possess her now, as if she had been destined for him. He picks her up, installs her among his belongings, and although he has a generous allowance of his own and he knows she is dying of tuberculosis, lives off her for months, completely abandoning his studies. A curious twist is the motivation Onetti provides for the melodrama. Rita, bound from the beginning to occupy the unmarked tomb of the title, attracts disaster and thrives on humiliation; she is one of the insulted and injured of the world. Jorge

turns out to be a sort of minor Raskolnikov. He acts out of gratuitous malice, pleased to imagine himself in the shoes of Rita's ex-pimp, Ambrosio, whose identity he borrows on the theory, as he tells Tito Perotti, that "I can never regret anything because whatever I do will have to be within the limits of human possibility." Of course—as we gather from the distortions and refractions out of which the story gradually takes shape—he learns better. His intellectual arrogance, his middle-class smugness, have led him into some of the cardinal sins on Onetti's list: hypocrisy, cynicism, and above all, the false pride that tempts the gods. His righteousness is a disguise for cowardice, his rebelliousness for conformity. Onetti—or Díaz Grey—does not blame him. He merely exposes him. Jorge has tried to find a way out; he has failed. His crime—the crime of phoniness—was in pretending he could win in the first place. Covering up his failure compounded it. The author's—or narrator's—verdict is dispassionate. Such is life. Jorge's defeat is everyone's defeat. As they filter through to us, the facts of the case remain somewhat enigmatic. We have to sift shifting points of view. Here Onetti has hit on a compromise formula he uses with varying success in his later books. Díaz Grey, the seeing eye, is only a partial witness. Sometimes there is none. Certain passages are told straight. Others are once, twice, or even three times removed behind layers of lenses. Díaz Grey, not quite emancipated from his creator, has become a sort of universal conscience, a father confessor and faceless guilt-bearer for others. His independence is strictly putative, conditional—a convenient assumption for narrative purposes, pending the author's suspension of belief in him, whereupon his fickle autonomy will instantly vanish. Which is what happens once he has provided the necessary angles and insights. Suddenly slight differentiations are abandoned. The author becomes the actor. He is directly involved when he qualifies his—or Díaz Grey's; here the two fuse—account of Jorge's adventures as a liberating experience for him, who, in living it down or, more precisely, writing it out, has gained the upper hand over at least one of life's "daily setbacks."

In *La Cara de la Desgracia* (*The Face of Misfortune,* 1960) we find Onetti making a clean breast of the things he will obviously never be entirely rid of. Written in an unusually polite and slick style for him, told directly in the first person, with its share of ambivalences and blackouts, it is another story of guilt and noncommunication. The setting is a resort somewhere in the coastal area of Santa María, where the protagonist, in retreat, searches his conscience over the recent death of his brother, declines responsibility for the brother's widow, and on the side conducts an intermittent love affair on the beach with a deaf girl—another nymphomaniac virgin—who pays for their love (a scandal against the order of things: the rules of mourning, human solidarity in suffering) with her life. The germ of *La Cara de la Desgracia* was a story called "La Larga Historia" ("The Long Affair") that Onetti had written many years before (in 1944). The lighter accent, the more flippant tone, cannot hide the fact that his standard themes appear in a more muddled form than usual. There are too many blind spots. But we strike a new note here. The narrator-protagonist is another of Onetti's dreamers; but, though as usual mortally wounded by life, he is no longer entirely the helpless victim of circumstance. He has begun to develop a strategy with which to fight back. He is an embryonic ancestor of the saintly sinner that appears in Onetti's later work, for whom criminal intent miraculously becomes a twisted form of faith and inner harmony. . . .

After *El Astillero* . . . , we have a pause which he fills with a mortuary exercise in Faulknerian craftsmanship, a collection of stories called *El Infierno tan Temido* (*The Hell We Dread,* 1962). We are back in a Santa María now so intensely felt that it is almost lost in the glare. Somehow it seems less credible than before. The verbal flood has become more convoluted as the author's backstage maneuverings become more devious and remote. Díaz Grey, Petrus, [from *El Astillero*], and other staples reappear, but in residual form. The foreground is occupied by marginal characters, sometimes outlandish visitors on their way through town, who flare into existence for a second, then recede into the surrounding vacuum. The language is of no help. The compliment of imitation Onetti pays his master sometimes verges on parody. Nevertheless, the characteristic Onettian mode is present. The best of the stories deals with the sad predicament of an aging lecher infatuated with a frivolous actress who succumbs to extracurricular temptations, elopes with one of them, then tortures her admirer for the rest of his life mailing him obscene photographs she has posed for in compromising postures, as if to get back at him for saddling her with his charity and forgiveness, intent on blaming him for her inability to atone for her own weakness and treachery.

Shifting the blame is also the topic of the rather careless and superficial *Tan Triste Como Ella* (*As Sad as She Is,* 1963), "a sketch that didn't quite come off," as Onetti says himself, recognizing its poverty, which gives it the distinction of being probably the worst thing he ever wrote. He committed the mistake, he says, of describing something—a marriage on the rocks—that had actually happened (to him? He has been married three or four times) and that therefore enslaved him to the facts, dampening his inventiveness. The story reads like a self-conscious love letter that soon dwindles into radio drama. A curious slip for a writer at such a late stage in his work. But Onetti has too little distance from his work to take an objective view of the results. He lacks judgment and perspective. . . .

[Onetti's] pessimism seems to have become almost generic. He is resigned, as Jorge in *Juntacadáveres,* to furnish his empty world with the shapes of his fictions, to create faces and gestures, needs and ambitions, and appropriate roles to which they can be appointed, the better to be sacrificed. The fate assigned each man is impersonal, he wrote in *La Vida Breve.* It can be fulfilled only in so far as it is the fate of all men. It does not allude to his true self, which is elsewhere, out of sight and circulation, a humble offering waiting to be put before the gods, who may choose to regard it as a small masterpiece or a penny dreadful.

On Onetti's literary style:

'I don't know how to write badly,' Chao reports Onetti as saying [Ramón Chao, *Onetti,* 1990]. This is not an empty boast, but the remark needs interpreting. Onetti writes wonderfully well, indeed never writes badly; but he often overwrites, his work is full of moments of old-fashioned fine writing, bids for easy lyricism or philosophy. His characters, so dedicated to perspective, are always trying to find out where they are, and they often lecture us about it. It is on these occasions that we read of 'an unproud enemy to pity', or 'the pale silent frenzy of putrefaction', or the 'apocryphal evocations' of 'the aroma of jasmines'; or that a character tells us, 'I examined my bravado, I began to doubt the sincerity of my hatred.' More often, Onetti's language is not easy but brilliantly risky, moving very suddenly from the laconic to the expansive, with an almost Joycean lift from the shabby into the poignant.

Michael Wood, "A Faint Sound of Rust," in The London Review of Books, *October 21, 1993.*

John F. Deredita (essay date 1971)

SOURCE: "The Shorter Works of Juan Carlos Onetti," in *Studies in Short Fiction,* Vol. VIII, No. 1, Winter, 1971, pp. 112-22.

[*In the following essay, Deredita discusses major motifs in Onetti's novellas and short stories.*]

For some twenty years after he published his first work, *El pozo* (*The Well,* 1939), Juan Carlos Onetti's reputation was confined to his native Uruguay and to Argentina. Born in 1909, he lived in Buenos Aires during most of the thirties, forties and early fifties, met the literary establishment there and published with major houses; but his books sold poorly, and he received scant critical attention. Except for a few critics and the coterie of Montevideo writers who felt his influence, the reading public seemed unprepared to follow his technical explorations or to recognize itself in the degraded world he was devising.

Wider recognition came in the sixties. Onetti won several distinctions, including the Uruguayan national literary prize in 1963. More important, as awareness spread of the rich new strain of Latin American fiction that had superseded the die-hard conventions of naturalism and sentimental folklore, critics began to name Onetti as a forerunner and a major participant in the movement. Two of them have discovered recently that *El pozo* fits neatly into their constructs as its starting point. Leo Pollmann, in his parallel study of the Latin American and French new novels [*Der Neue Roman in Frankreich and Lateinamerika,* 1969], detects an existentialist strain *sui generis* beginning haltingly with Roberto Arlt, Miguel Angel Asturias, and Eduardo Mallea, and he concludes that Onetti was the first in that line fully to unify form and content. Similarly, [in "Primitives and Creators," *The Times Literary Supplement,* November 14, 1968] Mario Vargas Llosa divides the history of the Latin American novel into a primitive form, culminating in Ciro Alegría and Asturias, which "constituted the subjectivization of a selected objective reality," and the authentically creative form, which began with *El pozo* and "consists in the objectivization of something subjective." Whatever rankings one prefers to make, it should be stressed that Onetti has contributed both to the novel (five to date) and to the shorter forms (six novellas and a dozen stories). *El pozo* itself would more properly be called a novella, although these commentators chose it to exemplify a trend in the novel. In the short pieces, Onetti brings some of his key symbols into close focus, and he has made explorations in self-conscious or reflexive narration, multiple point of view and, to some extent, language.

THE TWO AGES OF MAN

Onetti's "subjective something" consists in a pathetic and ironic recognition of human aging and decay, of life as tedious compromise, of the futility and necessity of illusion. Much of the décor of the dark tradition of modern fiction has found its way into his works, through literary cross-breeding and simply through his own affinity with the negative view of man's possibilities. Certainly his habitat, urban Uruguay and Argentina, has offered a natural setting for pessimism and considerations of marginality. Immigrant nations, barely pretending to be viable bourgeois states, they suffer their own version of Latin America's neocolonial malaise. While Onetti's fiction may be shown to reflect the individual alienation that results from deficient forms of social organization, its laws are not primarily social. The conflict takes place not between classes but between man and his fatally predetermined nature. Often the major battle of the conflict has taken place before the work begins, and the protagonist acts from a basic attitude of disillusionment. As in much literature of marginality, plot is usually subordinated to descriptive detail that emphasizes the drag of time. Typically, Onetti focuses upon an anti-hero in resentful estrangement from others, from political commitment and from any metaphysical sense. The characters tend toward atrophy and lack will. They spend their days and nights smoking insomniac on a bed, making routine trips to prostitutes, toying with seedy enterprises doomed from the start. Their prototype, Eladio Linacero of *El pozo,* bluntly sums up his lot in this way: "I feel that my life is nothing more than the passing of fractions of time, one after the other, like the sound of a clock, running water, coins being counted. I'm lying flat and time is passing."

Perception of this fate is the sign of maturity. There are two ages of man, naïve youth and the age of conformity. These are defined in the early story **"Bienvenido, Bob"** (**"Welcome, Bob"**; written in the early forties, collected in 1951), as a middle-aged narrator celebrates the initiation of a younger man into hopelessness. Ten years earlier, Bob had successfully blocked the narrator's effort to

marry his sister, on the grounds that he was too old for her. With the arrogance of "implacable youth," Bob twitted the narrator over his surrender to age and habit, and finally destroyed the courtship. Now Bob himself has aged, is known as Roberto, and has traded his confidence and personal promise for a routine of alcohol and gambling. Previously, the older man had the role of uncomfortable victim and was fascinated with his tormentor's nonchalance. Now he takes delight in recording the sadistic friendship he has struck up with Roberto, so as to observe him at last "sunken into the filthy life of men . . . tainted for good." The narrator has won the upper hand, and his obsessive game is to bait any nostalgia Roberto still has for the days of Bob. The taint of age was summed up by Bob when he told the narrator he would not permit the marriage: ". . . you are a mature man, that's to say a man undone, like all men your age who are not extraordinary. . . . You are an egoist; you are sensual in a dirty way. You are attached to miserable objects and it is the objects that lead you around. You are not going anywhere, you don't really want to." Just as the narrator was barred from recapturing some of his lost purity in the person of the young woman, maturity welcomes Bob with a vengeance.

One finds comparable pairings of the two ages everywhere in Onetti. They give structure to several other stories. Youth and age coincide in the heroine of **"Un sueño realizado"** (**"A Dream Come True"**), title story of the collection that includes **"Bienvenido, Bob."** The dreamer is in her fifties, but has the "air of a young girl from another century who had fallen asleep and was just now awakening, hardly aged but on the verge of catching up with her years at any moment, all of a sudden, and falling apart there in silence." She hires the narrator, a down-and-out director, to stage an apparently uneventful street scene she has dreamed, in which she takes the role of a young girl. At the end of the performance, given in an empty theater, she dies on stage. The scene juxtaposes her conflicting aspects, and the narrator's premonitory description is confirmed. The pathos of the woman's dream-like attempt to reverse time stands in contrast to the cynicism of the narrator and of the chief actor, both of whom have accepted the compromises of life.

A close inside view of a girl's thoughts and sensations as she moves toward her fall from innocence is provided in **"Mascarada"** (**"Masquerade"**; another early story collected only in 1962). Her mask is the thick make-up she has applied after deciding, a few hours before, to parade herself as a prostitute. Her motivation is never made clear, and this increases the sense of inevitability. She moves through a park full of onlookers who are watching a sleazy group of entertainers and then turn their attention to her. The entire story is limited to this walk with its foreseeable ending. Every movement and every image of the park has a metaphoric function and adds to the portrait of the young girl as she makes the transition from youth to experience, still uncomfortable under her painted face. The story is one of the finest examples of a functional application of the convoluted language Onetti adapted from Faulkner. At its best, this language of linked clauses, of qualifiers and amplifications spun out into lengthy periods, can refine sentiments and articulate nuances exhaustively. Here its wavy rhythmic patterns correspond to a reported interior monologue that objectifies the protagonist's movement and the chain of almost hallucinatory raw images she encounters on her walk.

THE FACE OF MISFORTUNE

Eve is predestined to bring about the loss of innocence and the arrival of sobering knowledge. In Onetti, *la desgracia*—the misfortune that causes a fall or relapse into disillusionment—tends to be centered in a woman and transmitted to the man who placed his hope in her. Male points of view reveal her as the instinctive vehicle of destiny. In **"Esbjerg, en la costa" ("Esbjerg, on the Coast,"** 1951), Kirsten, a Dane, began to long for her country. Her lover, Montes, caught up in her dimly articulated dream of recovering the past, tried to embezzle money for her passage from his employer, a bookie. He failed and is being made to repay the loss. Montes and Kirsten now make a daily routine of going to the harbor to watch departing ships, she a heavy figure with the "face of a statue in winter, the face of someone who fell asleep and didn't close her eyes in the rain." The bookie, who as narrator restrains excessive sentimentality, imagines that "when the ships' horns allow Montes to hear how she moves along the stones, dragging her men's shoes, the poor devil must feel that he is getting deeper into the night on the arm of misfortune." Kirsten's doggedness, as well as the details of her peasant frame and her shoes, may be seen to derive from some of Faulkner's women who carry out the designs of fate in similar ways.

[In *Literatura uruguaya del medio siglo,* 1966] Emir Rodríguez Monegal has described the hero of what he calls Onetti's "allegories" as "a solitary man with the illusion (always defrauded) of attaining the purity of an adolescent girl, with the inner certainty that to win her means to destroy her, to reveal her basic sordidness." This confrontation, with its mixed motives and its inevitable pull toward disaster, is sharply defined in the novella *La cara de la desgracia* (*The Face of Misfortune,* 1960). The narrator sizes up a young bicyclist at a beach resort. She postures and throws him a memorable glance. He realizes that the attraction he feels is a resurgence of his "old, unjust, almost always mistaken pity. There was no doubt that I loved her and wanted to protect her. I could not guess from what or against what. I wanted, furiously, to shield her from herself and from any danger. I had seen her unsure and defiant, I had seen her display a proud face of misfortune. That can last for a time, but it is always repaid prematurely, disproportionately." Forewarnings of this sort produce the somewhat overdeveloped climate of fatality of the novella. The narrator perceives a resemblance between the girl's expression and that of his brother at their last meeting before his recent suicide. The feeling of guilt for his brother's death complicates his attraction for the girl as he sees in her apparent hopelessness a chance for expiation. He is temporarily rejuvenated and freed from guilt after the seduction scene, which occurs in the woods at night. But the atmosphere of the encounter is strained. The girl appears remote and speaks haltingly in a hoarse voice. The man's intentions seem more ordinary than previously described in the narration. The incommunication is made grotesque by the later revelation that the girl was deaf.

Despite some obscurity in the narrator's version, it seems clear that he did not kill the girl, but the next morning he is accused of her murder and brought before her bruised remains. The face of misfortune, which had been "twisted in tears" after the anxious coupling of the night before, has taken a final form, described at length in the funereal voice and clinical jargon of a medical examiner. It is suggested that by deflowering the girl the narrator is the virtual agent of her death. He returns to indifference, telling the police, "The amusing thing is that you are mistaken. But that doesn't matter. Nothing matters, not even this." The novella lapses into the melodrama that occasionally damages Onetti's short works, but succeeds in its detailed presentation of the narrator's fascination. Each time he sees the girl, a cinematic slow pan in the description visualizes her movements and reproduces the eagerness of his staring.

Photographs record the face of misfortune in **"El infierno tan temido" ("Dreaded Hell,"** 1962, title story of a collection). The virgin eager for life was an actress, pointedly named Gracia, whose face was seen peering from theater posters "a little defiant, a little fascinated by the hope of convincing and being understood." Risso, a widower, married her, looking for purity and an ideal state. Instead of understanding, Gracia encountered tedious sexual insistence and Risso's repeated dictum: "Anything can happen and we'll always be happy and in love with each other." This set up a ritual of mediation in which she could express her feeling for Risso only in adultery. After they have separated, she goes on tour and begins to send him photos of herself with men. At first the photos continue the mediation, and Risso is almost caught up in it; but soon he cannot look at the photos that keep arriving. When other people in town begin receiving them, the nature of her revenge becomes clear. The progressive arrival of the photos forms the linear portion of the narrative, which is interspersed with flashbacks that describe the uncommunicative relationship. Even in the context of a story of revenge, human will is subordinated to situations. The ubiquitous third-person narrator describes both Risso's and Gracia's actions as responses to the circumstances in which they find themselves.

THE CREATIVE ILLUSION AND REFLEXIVITY

[In their *Into the Mainstream: Conversations with Latin-American Writers,* 1967] Luis Harss and Barbara Dohmann have observed that "to break the irreversible pattern of his life is the compulsive need of every Onetti character." Amid the paralysis and fatalism, attempts to escape through illusion are distorted by heavy irony. Love appears in perverse forms, or as the dull sensuality that underlies Risso's sentiments toward Gracia. Power, as in the case of **"Bienvenido, Bob,"** is reduced to the exercise of small-time sadism. Another means of escape continually entertained as a counter to the grim reality principle is artistic creation. This appears to be Onetti's compulsive need. He has explored it in a series of self-conscious or reflexive works both short and long, where debased artist-heroes and self-conscious narrators grope for a kind of salvation he once optimistically described in this way: "Creations justify man. . . . They lift him above his numbered days, perhaps with no need for further assistance, without a search for another faith." The creative hero's characteristic move is to annihilate his dwindled selfhood in fictive worlds, in what Brausen of the novel *La vida breve* calls "a short life, in which time did not suffice to compromise me, to age me or to make me regret."

The creative theme was first sketched in *El pozo*. The reflexive apparatus of the novella and its attention to the physical details of the character's current situation produce an oppressive sense of time. The entire text dramatizes Eladio Linacero's act of writing a confessional memoir on the eve of his fortieth birthday. The jagged, associational development of the text responds to his mental process. The flow of time, with its disintegrating effects, is evoked as Linacero listens to the sound of his own pacing about the room, in his decline into fatigue at the end of the night when he stops writing, and even in the layout of the novella in short fragments.

Like Dostoyevsky's underground man, from whom he is derived, Linacero has retired into the uncomfortable isolation of his furnished room because he is incapable of dealing with the world. His recollections comprise a series of disastrous personal encounters each of which involved an attempt to transcend self and to enter into communication with another. At age sixteen he attacked an older cousin who had never paid much attention to him. His marriage broke up when he saw that the young Ceci he married had become Cecilia, a woman "with a stinking practical sense." A flirtation with political activism ended as he came to see that middle-class intellectuals were parasites on the social movement. His response to estrangement has been to fabricate what he calls "dreams" or sometimes "adventures" having the consistency of pulp stories or B movies. The dreams are built out of the material of his experience, but in them he has an active role denied to him in real life, and his interpersonal defeats become simple triumphs. He does not write them down, but he keeps them catalogued in his memory. Defensively, he insists he is no mere dreamer, that he has "lived as much as anyone or more." But his testimony belies it. His only full experience occurs on the sublimated level of the adventures, and they are a flimsy mediation. In the last fragment, Linacero is stretched out on his cot, listening to the sounds of the city. His language traces an imagery of surrender to the night and to the flow of time, prefiguring death. Significantly, at this point his dreams are not proof against reality: he is too exhausted to conjure up his favorite, in which his cousin gives herself to him in an idyllic log cabin in Alaska.

Although Linacero says he has suitcases full of writings, he does not presume to be a writer. The novella's reflexive passages are largely given over to his excuses and ironic commentaries on the haphazard organization he is giving to the narrative. It is in these passages that Onetti's authorial presence may be discerned most clearly, diffident about his capacity ("I don't know how to write," says Linacero, "but I'm writing about myself") but at the same time presenting an anti-literary stance in opposition to the then current high-sounding fiction of Uruguay and Argentina. *El pozo* is expressly barbarous, designed to communicate bitter experience bitterly. Linacero's fantasies cannot be taken as seriously by the reader as they are by himself. Simple exercises in wish fulfillment, they are too easily dispersed by reality.

A somewhat more persuasive case for the possibility of imaginative sublimation—always within the fated context—is made in *La vida breve* (1950). A massive re-elaboration of the solipsistic world of *El pozo,* the novel deserves brief mention here not only because it develops the creative theme but because it marks the transition from Onetti's first period to his second group of works, most of which are set in the Faulknerian town sketched in *La vida breve* for the first time. As his surrogate in the novel was creating a filmscript set in the provincial Santa María, Onetti was preparing the locale for later works. Juan María Brausen's imaginative effort is an extension of the author's own. Its motivation is again the narrator's need to escape isolation and routine. In his lucid self-analysis, Brausen arrives at zero, discovering he is "nobody, really; a name, three words, a diminutive idea put together mechanically by my father." The narrative is thick with surface detail descriptive of the fragmentary consciousness Brausen seeks to reconstitute or submerge in a short life out of time. He embarks upon two short lives: an impersonation by which he enters into relations with a prostitute and the surrogate creature, Dr. Díaz Grey, the protagonist of the filmscript, whose experiences, as we see, spring from Brausen's own.

Notably, Brausen does not conjure up rosy sublimations, as in the case of Linacero, but existences almost as colorless as his original one, continuations of the self he hoped to shed. Proceeding by fluid movement from one level to another of his divided self, and by the accumulation of morbid detail on all levels, the novel reaches a resolution in which the protagonist effectively fades out of view and the narration is taken up by Díaz Grey. With its interpenetrating orders of reality and its divine analogy between creator Brausen and creature Díaz Grey (as well as implied creator Onetti), the novel seems worthy of some unimaginable Borges, long-winded enough to write a 390-page tome. In fact, there is reason to believe that Borges's speculations may have influenced Onetti's.

The aging Díaz Grey carries on in subsequent Onetti works as artist-narrator. The first of these is the story **"La casa en la arena"** ("The House in the Sand"; collected in *Un sueño realizado*). Díaz Grey is the reflector of a third-person narrative. The story material is presented as the obsessive recollection of an incident from his past in the drug racket. "His life, he himself, was no longer anything more than that recollection, the only one worth remembering and correcting, worth falsifying time and again." The invention of the incident stimulates the Doctor; it is a self-projection which makes his present more tolerable. In it he comes together with an idiot firebug called El Colorado and a woman named Molly in a beach chalet where they must keep out of circulation. The atmosphere is one of imprisonment. Díaz Grey and Molly have a chance to escape together, but he rejects it. Sufficient tension of plot is maintained to make **"La casa en la arena"** an example, as well as a parody, of the crime story; but any naïve response to the incident is discouraged by the device of filtering it through Díaz Grey's imagination. We see the fictionalized recollection as such, and its origin as the ineffectual doctor's compulsive self-projection. Its insubstantiality and his dependence on it become clear to him: "When Díaz Grey, in the office facing the plaza of the provincial town, engages in the game of recognizing himself in this memory, the only one, he is obliged to . . . suppose that his meticulous life, his own body deprived of lust, his bland beliefs, are symbols of the essential banality of the memory he has been careful to keep up for years." The passage recalls Díaz Grey's own fictionality and comments on the story as a meshing of two planes of reality, both dominated by the atmosphere of indifference.

Events are at an even greater remove in the novella *Para una tumba sin nombre* (*For a Nameless Tomb,* 1959). The multiple point of view of a series of unreliable testimonies is deployed to produce an unclear story. Díaz Grey, cast in the explicit role of a writer elaborating on supposedly true events, admits that what he finally had was "nothing, a hopeless confusion, a tale with no possible ending, of doubtful meaning, refuted by the very elements I had at hand to shape it." The ultimate refutation—his own position as fictive surrogate for the author—perforce escapes him. In any case, Díaz Grey writes the story once he has convinced himself that none of it is true. In his final note, he professes to have reached a modest triumph that distantly echoes Onetti's remark about creative activity: "All that matters is that when I finished writing, I was at peace, sure that I had achieved the most that can be expected from this kind of task: I had accepted a challenge, I had converted at least one of the daily defeats into victory."

He makes his points: detachment is required of the writer, there is a satisfaction in craftsmanship, and fiction is not life. Considerable portions of the novella are devoted to the investigation of storytelling. But Díaz Grey's aesthetic remove is also linked to the theme of human solidarity and indifference, around which the material of his story hovers. The incidents he has tried to piece together (adding "some deliberate lies" of his own to those of the witnesses) concern the exploitation of Rita, an ex-servant woman turned prostitute and beggar. A succession of laconic pimps lived off her work in Buenos Aires, among them Jorge Malabia, the Santa María society boy who is Díaz Grey's chief informant. The conflicting reports, complicated by additions and retractions, make it impossible to determine the exact nature of Rita, of her relationships with the men, and of their motivation. The overall picture that comes out of the accounts and Díaz Grey's inventions portrays a recognizable Onettian woman plodding in the path reserved to her by fate, accompanied by men who interpret their indifference as pity. The picture is distorted not only by the confusion of perspectives but by grotesque humor, much of it attached to the billygoat that Rita took with her daily as she solicited in a railroad station and which Malabia led to her

burial. Scapegoat, symbol of lust, evil, cuckoldry—it officiates in "its divine condition," and provides a partial opprobrium to the goings-on beyond Díaz Grey's detachment.

The author-character narcissism is most communicative when controlled by the distance between what is discernible as "Onetti" and his surrogate creators. When that distance is badly handled, the result may be a tone of self-indulgence and apology or a loss of coherence. This damages the long story **"La novia robada"** (**"The Stolen Bride,"** 1968). The title refers to the theft of the heroine from the tradition of would-be brides—Dickens' Miss Havisham, Faulkner's Miss Emily—confessed and apologized for at the beginning. The narrator continually addresses himself to Moncha, the heroine, and tells her that he is writing a letter, words for her ears only, although "many will be called to read them." This indicates the reader's subordinate place in the story. The narration is sentimental and strewn with cryptic references that reach beyond Moncha, apparently to an extra-literary woman she represents. There is more that the usual number of allusions to Onetti's earlier writings, limiting the readership to devotees. As an attempt to break out of the form of the short story, **"La novia robada"** fails. It reads as too private an expression, the record of an authorial whim.

The critics reproach Onetti's thematic insistence, the lapses into rhetoric, the minute descriptive style that serves as the imitative form of boredom and that sometimes reproduces it in the reader. The charges are often valid, but a defense might also be made of the variety of his short works. He is capable of evoking a mood, as in the uneventful **"Esbjerg, en la costa"**; but **"Un sueño realizado"** is sustained by forewarnings, suggestive symmetries and a pronounced ending. The lingering visualization heralded in *El pozo* forms an even more expressive part of *La cara de la desgracia*. Despite his narrators' frequent sameness of diction, there is variety in the narrative structures. Quite different effects emerge from the heated first-person of **"Bienvenido, Bob"** (sympathy for the human condition negatively expressed through a bilious narrator) and, say, the third-person of **"Mascarada"** (sympathy expressed through an ostensibly neutral account). Onetti's experiments in self-conscious form, particularly in the novellas, represent an awareness of the subtleties of fiction and a coming to terms with the vital implications of creativity.

Onetti's antiheroes proclaim that "nothing can be done," or, what seems more serious still, that "nothing is worth doing." Far from anguish, nausea, and even *détresse,* one can speak only of fatalism and resignation.

—Fernando Ainsa, "Juan Carlos Onetti: An Existential Allegory of Contemporary Man," in World Literature Today, Summer, 1994.

Joel C. Hancock (essay date 1973)

SOURCE: "Psychopathic Point of View: Juan Carlos Onetti's *Los adioses*," in *Latin American Literary Review*, Vol. II, No. 3, Fall-Winter, 1973, pp. 19-29.

[*In the following essay, Hancock assesses the mental state of the narrator of* Los adioses *in order to determine the reliability of his account.*]

In the now classic article "Point of View in Fiction" [*PMLA* 70 (1955)], Norman Friedman codifies four basic questions in his attempt to define the various modes a narrator has for transmitting his story to the reader: 1) who talks to the reader; 2) from what position regarding the story does he tell it; 3) what channels of information does the narrator use to convey the story to the reader; and, 4) at what distance does he place the reader from the story. These considerations are not only significant, but vital and essential to the appreciation of Juan Carlos Onetti's enigmatic novel, *Los adioses* [*The Goodbyes*] (1954), which is told from a seemingly traditional first person or "I"-as-witness vantage point. The point of view of this work must be studied with special care and attention, for only through a close analysis of this technique does the reader become aware of the narrator's psychopathic mental condition and its effect on the narration. The reader is faced with the challenge of trying to determine the actual facts and events of a story related by a deranged person. A serious examination of the psychopathic point of view and its many implications offers different impressions and, as a result, the possibility of new interpretations to the novel.

Certainly Onetti is not unique in employing the point of view of a mentally disturbed person. A noteworthy precedent in Spanish American literature is Ernesto Sábato's *El túnel* [*The Tunnel*] (1951) in which the narrator-protagonist is afflicted with a condition very similar to that of the narrator of *Los adioses*. There is an important difference, however, in the reader's reaction to the narration and his awareness of the narrator's problem. In *El túnel*, the mental problems of Juan Pablo Castel are apparent from the outset. In *Los adioses,* on the other hand, only the extremely perceptive reader is able to guard himself against the detail of distorted observations which pretend to be logical and accurate.

Critical appraisal of *Los adioses* is scarce; what is available is uneven and contradictory. Concerned primarily with presenting an overview of Onetti's total production, critics such as Mario Benedetti [*Literatura uruguaya del siglo XX,* 1963] and Luis Harss [*Los nuestros,* 1968] offer plot summaries and concentrate on relating Onetti's various works to each other, and thus their discussion of *Los adioses* is cursory and does not focus on the crucial elements. [In *Literatura uruguaya del medio siglo*] Emir Rodríguez Monegal also surveys themes and techniques in Onetti's works. Of particular interest, however, is his explicit identification of the narrator of *Los adioses* as a sick man: "Enfermo él también, y no sólo de los pulmones. . . ." ["Himself sick also, and not only of the lungs. . . ."].

The most comprehensive study of *Los adioses* is Wolfgang Luchting's excellent investigation of "reader participation" generated by the use of a special point of view ["El lector como protagonista de la novela: Onetti y *Los adioses,*" *Nueva Narrativa Hispanoamericana*, I, No. 2 (Septiembre 1971)]. Luchting attempts to establish which events actually took place; he does not analyze precisely why the point of view leads to such interpretational chaos (I shall comment on some of the interesting theories postulated in Luchting's article later).

The complexity and confusion of *Los adioses* lies not in the story itself, but in the manner in which the events are seen and interpreted by the narrator, the nameless owner of an *almacén* [general store] which serves as a gathering place for local townspeople. The novel opens with the arrival of a one-time basketball star who has come to the town to be treated for tuberculosis. As the ex-athlete steps into the store, the almacenero [storekeeper]—the narrator of the story—immediately expresses interest in the life of the newly arrived man and proceeds to describe, in great detail, what he knows and surmises about him. A reserved and standoffish person, the man—referred to as el hombre or el tipo—does not mix with his fellow patients or, for that matter, anyone else in the community. He lives for the delivery of the mail, specifically letters from two different sources. The correspondents turn out to be two women who come to the town to visit el hombre: la mujer [the woman], mother of a young son; and la muchacha [the girl]. The man appears to be cheered by the various visits of the two women. After la mujer and her child depart, the ex-athlete stays on with the younger girl, moving first into a chalet and later to the sanitarium for a more intensive treatment of his disease. The novel ends with the man's death.

These are, in outline, the factual details of the novel. Interpreted by the narrator's sick mind, however, the story is erotically intensified. The almacenero imagines the man has rejected his wife and child so he can involve himself in a lustful and illicit relationship with the younger girl. The narrator's anger and disgust are contagious, and soon everyone is criticizing el hombre for his "immorality." Toward the end of the novel, the truth of the situation is established. In the almacenero's possession is a letter revealing that the younger girl is the man's daughter; la mujer is, in fact, the "other woman."

How, precisely, is the narrator psychopathic? Suffering from a severe functional psychosis, an extreme case of paranoia, he is dominated by an idée fixe which on the surface seems very reasonable. The narrator is a megalomaniac, deluded with the grandiose idea—one which consumes a great deal of his emotional life and interest—that he has the power to predict, even control, people's lives. The moment he sees el hombre, the narrator feels compelled to make a judgment and boast: "Me hubieran bastado aquellos movimientos sobre la madera llena de tajos rellenados con grasa y mugre para saber que no iba a curarse. . . . En general, me basta verlos y no recuerdo haberme equivocado." ["Those movements on the wooden floor full of cracks packed with grease and grime would have been enough for me to know he would not be cured. . . . In general, I only have to see them, and I do not remember ever making a mistake."]

Once the prophecy is expressed and the man's fate mapped out, the almacenero is obsessed with the notion that it be fulfilled or executed. Indeed, all the storekeeper's time is devoted to speculation about the hombre, conjuring up visions of his every thought and move. His conjectures— cloaked in terminology such as "es posible" [it is possible], "tal vez" [perhaps], "lo supuse" [I supposed], or utilizing verbs in the conditional tense denoting "he might have"—soon become visions. He imagines and reconstructs the man's habits and activities. The reader must be aware of the storekeeper's pastime, and must constantly question whether the statements are really correct or mere suppositions. Because of the detail and elaborateness of the descriptions, it is easy to lose sight of what is fact or fancy. The reader is soon convinced of the validity of the thoughts or events, forgetting it is all material from the almacenero's imagination, even when incidents presented directly in dialogue contradict the narrators assessment of situations. At one point, for example, the storekeeper is informed that el hombre is happy and well on his way to recovery. To this the narrator responds: "El enfermero tenía razón y no me era posible decirle nada en contra; y, sin embargo, no llegaba a creer y ni siquiera sabía qué clase de creencia estaba en juego, qué artificio agregaba yo a lo que veía, qué absurda, desagradable esperanza me impedía conmoverme." ["The nurse was right and it wasn't possible for me to tell him anything against it; and, nevertheless, I did not quite believe it, nor did I even know what kind of belief was at stake, what contrivance I added to what I saw, what absurd unpleasant hope kept me from being moved."] He intends to abide by his earlier prediction, and most readers do not doubt him.

The almacenero's paranoid obsession with the life of the former basketball player becomes first a game and then a battle. This relationship, defined by the storekeeper, is warlike in nature; it is, specifically, a duel: "el habitual duelo nunca declarado: luchando él por hacerme desaparecer, por borrar el testimonio de fracaso y desgracia que yo me emperraba en dar; luchando yo por la dudosa victoria de convencerlo de que todo esto era cierto, enfermedad, separación, acabamiento." ["The never declared, habitual duel: he, fighting to make me disappear, to erase the testimony of failure and disgrace which I was determined to give; I, fighting for the dubious victory of convincing him that all this was true, sickness, separation, death."]

This competition, however, is unrecognized by el hombre, a fact which the storekeeper chooses to ignore. On the contrary, the narrator reads defiance into the man's words and gestures, and to emerge victor in the imagined war, he carefully plans his strategies. The storekeeper's most common tactics is to distort and fabricate evidence which will support his confabulations about the man's life. Occasionally, though, the almacenero breaks down and admits to distorting the information: "Porque, además, es cierto que yo estuve buscando modificaciones, fisuras y agregados, y

es cierto que llegué a inventarlos." ["Because, also, it is true I was looking for modifications, fissures and additions, and it is true I went so far as to invent them."] Ironically, because he is aware of his own propensity to alter facts, the almacenero is suspicious of what others tell him. In his typical fashion he conjectures about Andrade, the town real estate agent: "Andrade montaba en la bicicleta y regresaba vibroreando hasta su oficina o continuaba recorriendo las casas de la sierra que administraba, pensando en lo que había visto, en lo que era admisible deducir, en lo que podía mentir y contar." ["Andrade would ride his bicycle and wind back like a snake to his office or he would continue on to the houses on the hills which he administered, thinking about what he had seen, about what was admissible to deduce, about what he could lie or tell."] This description, intended to report the thoughts of another person, is, in fact, an exposé of the narrator himself.

The insistence on attributing to another person the thoughts belonging to himself is practiced frequently by the storekeeper. Projection, the transferring of one's own ideas to another, plays an important role in this thinking. Once we have identified it as a habit to which the narrator often resorts, we are provided with clearer insights into his personality and therefore the likelihood of new interpretations to the novel. When the almacenero discusses a person, or people in general, chances are he is defining himself. As he muses, for example, about the humdrum daily functions of certain people, the reader should recognize that the narrator is describing his own behavior: "Siempre habría casas y caminos, autos y surtidores de nafta, otra gente que está y respira, presiente, imagina, hace comida, se contempla tediosa y reflexiva, disimula y hace cálculos." ["There would always be houses and roads, cars and gasoline pumps, other people who are around and breathe, have premonitions, imagine, fix food, who are tedious and reflective in contemplation of themselves, who pretend and calculate."]

It is important to always be aware that the information and evaluation of el hombre is largely the storekeeper's projection. The entire speculation about the torrid affair between the younger girl and the ex-athlete, perhaps the basic subject of the book, could very well have resulted from the storekeeper's own sexual fantasies. He thinks of la muchacha in sexual terms the moment he first sees her, before he discovers why she has come to the town. Focusing first on her legs, then her skirt, she soon becomes a sexual object: "Pensé en la cara, excitada, alerta, hambrienta, asimilando, mientras ella apartaba las rodillas para cada amor definitivo y para parir." ["I thought of her face, excited, alert, hungry, assimilating, while she spread her knees for each definitive love and to give birth."] Once he learns the reason for her visit, he immediately envisions a carnal relationship between el hombre and the girl. Now the storekeeper is free with his descriptive labels; he uses strong adjectives which mirror his mind. He intimates that the girl behaves obscenely while the man, on the other hand, is immoral. But obscenity is in the mind of the storekeeper as he conjures wild visions of boudoir scenes: "Imaginaba la lujuria furtiva, los reclamos del hombre, las negativas, los compromisos y las furias despiadadas de la muchacha, sus posturas empeñosas, masculinas." ["I imagined the furtive lustfulness, the demands of the man, the rejections, the compromises and the merciless furies of the girl, her insistent, masculine postures."]

This almacenero is using the couple as a scapegoat, accusing them of imagined activities which he actually desires for himself. There are many incidents in the novel indicating that sexual matters weigh heavily on the storekeeper's mind. As he considers hosting holiday parties at the almacén, he thinks of the sexual frenzy in people's behavior during such festivities, equating it with insanity. While working at his New Year's party, he stares at a blonde woman and has lustful thoughts about her. When the older woman comes to town, much detail is imagined during alleged intimate moments with el hombre. His description is cushioned in sensational terminology:

> Y él golpeó, largo y sinuoso contra la puerta, avergonzado en la claridad estrecha del corredor que transitaban mucamas y las viejas señoritas que volvían del paseo digestivo por el parque; y estuvo, mientras esperaba, evocando nombres antiguos, de desteñida obscenidad, nombres que había inventado mucho tiempo atrás para una mujer que ya no existía. Hasta que ella vino y descorrió la llave, semidesnuda, exagerando el pudor y el sueño, sin anteojos ahora, y se alejó para volver a tirarse a la cama. El pudo ver la forma de los muslos, los pies descalzos, arrastrados, la boca abierta del niño dormido. Antes de avanzar pensó, volvió a descubrir, que el pasado no vale más que un sueño ajeno. [And he knocked, tall and sinuous against the door, ashamed in the narrow brightness of the hallway used by aides and old maids returning from their digestive walk through the park; and, as he waited, he evoked old names, of faded obscenity, names he had invented a long time ago for a woman who no longer existed. Finally she came and removed the latch, half naked, exaggerating her modesty and sleepiness, without her glasses now, and she turned away to stretch out again on the bed. He could see the shape of her thighs, her bare feet, dangling, the open mouth of the sleeping child. Before going on he thought, he discovered once again, that the past is worth no more than someone else's dream.]

It is logical to conclude that the narrator is ridding himself of his own lustful cravings by projecting them on other people, as he admits in the final sentence of this thought.

The almacenero's projections are a revelation of his own mental state. Thus, the storekeeper's analysis of el hombre is often a disguised self-disclosure. The rancor he attributes to the man, for example, is a part of his own being: "Yo insistía en examinarle los ojos, en estimar la calidad y la potencia del rencor que podía descubrírsele en el fondo: un rencor domesticado, hecho a la paciencia, definitivamente añadido." ["I insisted on examining his eyes, on estimating the nature and capacity of the rancor which could be discovered deep inside him: a domesticated rancor, developed through patience, definitely added."] So, too, when he interprets the male nurse's dislike of the ex-athlete, he is in reality defining his own hatred for the

man: "Se me ocurrió que el odio del enfermero, apenas tibio, empecinado, no podía haber nacido de la negativa del otro a las inyecciones propuestas por Gunz; que había en su origen una incomprensible humillación, una ofensa secreta." ["It occurred to me that the nurse's hatred, barely warm, unrelenting, could not have been caused by the refusal of the other to the injections prescribed by Gunz; that its origin was due to an incomprehensible humiliation, a secret offense."]

One of the most significant acts of projection, possibly a key to the storekeeper's personality and existence, can be observed in a remark he makes about other people. If interpreted as a self-revealing statement, we have a succinct description of the almacenero's thinking and behavior throughout the novel. It is a confession of his fabrication of stories about the consumptive and how everyone is convinced of their authenticity: "Estaba solo, y cuando la soledad nos importa somos capaces de cumplir todas las vilezas adecuadas para asegurarnos compañía, oídos y ojos que nos atiendan. Hablo de ellos, de los demás, no de mí." ["I was alone, and when loneliness is important to us we are capable of carrying out all the base deeds necessary to ensure us company, ears and eyes to attend to us. I'm talking about them, about the others, not myself."] But he protests too much in the last sentence, for at a later moment, comparing himself to the younger girl, he identifies the loneliness discussed above as being integral to his own personality: "Yo era el más débil de los dos, el equivocado; yo estaba descubriendo la invariada desdicha de mis quince años en el pueblo, el arrepentimiento de haber pagado como precio la soledad, el almacén, esta manera de no ser nada. Yo era minúsculo, sin significado, muerto." ["I was the weaker of the two, the mistaken one; I was discovering the constant unhappiness of my fifteen years in the town, the repentance of having paid as price the loneliness, the store, this way of not being anything. I was small, meaningless, dead."]

This declaration is shocking in its candor as well as its implications. The almacenero confesses to a depressing, negative situation: he is weak, unhappy, insignificant; he is devoid of life. The power he pretends to exert over people's destinies is a delusion. A possible explanation for his attitude and behavior toward the man can be inferred: despairing of his own condition, he projects it on el hombre and will have everyone believe the latter is small, meaningless, dead.

At times the storekeeper analyzes his own circumstance and occasionally advises himself to take a certain course of action. These brief moments of lucidity furnish the reader with important clues which might provide insight into determining what is fact and what is fiction. Is the almacenero's portrait of the ex-athlete fairly accurate? Or does it remain a mystery: the picture painted being that of the narrator himself? The preceding discussion, I feel, would support the second assumption.

A study of the narrator's relations with the people around him offers another means for exploring his psychopathic nature and his peculiar view of the ex-athlete. It is significant to note that only on very rare occasions is the store-keeper physically present in the man's environment—the hotel, the chalet, or the hospital. The data we receive is derived either from the narrator's fertile imagination or from accounts supplied by outsiders. The principal contributor is the enfermero, the male nurse of the hospital who spends his leisure moments at the store. For reasons unknown to the reader, the nurse, aware of the death wish, feeds the storekeeper with biased information that adds fuel to the hatred. In the following bit of gossip, for example, the enfermero hints that the man has a drinking problem—a rumor accepted later by all as a fact—and concludes his observations baiting the storekeeper with a pointed declaration: "El otro día compró media docena de botellas en el hotel y se las hizo llevar al chalet. Ahora sabemos para qué se encierra. Además, podía habérselas comprado a usted." ["The other day he bought half a dozen bottles at the hotel and had them delivered to the chalet. Now we know why he locks himself up. Anyway, he could have bought them from you."] The almacenero offers positive feedback to the nurse's dislike and ridicule of the sick man, and seems to encourage the practice: "Me reí un poco, para contentarlo, para demostrar que lo estaba escuchando." ["I laughed a little, to cheer him up, to show him I was listening."] And when the narrator takes a turn at derision, there is a reversal of roles in the reaction, corroborating our idea of the possibility of collusion: "El enfermero se puso a reír como si yo me hubiera burlado de alguien." ["The nurse started laughing as if I had made fun of someone."]

The conversations engaged in by the narrator also help us to discern what actually goes on in his mind. Mysterious and morbid topics are interspersed among the common and ordinary themes of a casual chat. In the following lines, for example, the storekeeper lists the subjects touched upon in a conversation with the nurse: "El enfermero y yo hablamos del granizo, de un misterio que podía sospecharse en la vida del dueño de El Pedregal, del envejecimiento y su fatalidad; hablamos de precios, de transportes, de aspectos de cadáveres, de mejorías engañosas, de los consuelos que acerca el dinero, de la inseguridad considerada como inseparable de la condición humana, de los cálculos que hicieron los Barroso sentados una tarde frente a un campo de trigo." ["The nurse and I talked about the hail-storm, about a mystery that could be suspected in the life of the owner of El Pedregal, about old age and its fatality; we talked about prices, transportation, the appearance of cadavers, deceiving improvements, the comforts money brings, insecurity considered as inseparable from the human condition, the calculations made by the Barrosos while sitting one day in front of a wheat field."] Hidden in this discussion are obvious references to el hombre, allusions which express the narrator's prejudices.

The storekeeper's use of language likewise reflects the mechanisms of his mind at work. Death and violence, for instance, are at times associated with elements of nature. Of particular interest are the descriptions of the ex-athlete. The narrator will frequently utilize strange but singularly expressive images in his portrayals. In the following passage, one of the last in the novel, the man is depicted with great detail: "Estaba envejecido y muerto, destruido, vaciándose; pero sin embargo, más joven que cualquier otra vez anterior, reproduciendo la cabeza que había enderezado en la almohada, en la adolescencia, al salir de la primera congestión. Convirtió en ruido su sonrisa y me tendió la mano; lo vi cruzar la puerta, atrevido, marcial, metiendo a empujones en el viento el sobretodo flotante que alguna vez le había ajustado en el pecho; lo vi arrastrar, ascendiendo, la luz de la linterna." ["He was aged and dead, destroyed, draining himself; but, nonetheless, younger than ever before, reproducing the head that he straightened out on the pillow, during adolescence, as he got over his first congestion. He turned his smile into noise and gave me his hand; I saw him crossing the doorway, daring, martial, pushing into the wind the floating overcoat that once was tight across the chest; I saw him drag, raising, the light of the lantern."]

Our attention immediately focuses on the antithetical concepts present in this visual description. We are informed the man is aged, but looking younger than ever; he is empty and destroyed, yet manages to smile and be cordial; he is brave and daring, but not strong enough to carry the lantern. Though this drawing may confuse the reader insofar as its contradictions, it is, however, the vision of a floating skeleton: the spectre of death. In summary, we are presented with the almacenero's death wish for the man, conveyed in vivid pictorial terms.

The narrator's relations with other characters in the novel are governed by his basically misanthropic nature. He mistrusts and despises everyone including the nurse and other members of the hospital staff. The younger girl, for example, is often a target of his merciless attacks. This hatred for her is equalled only by his feelings of hostility toward the ex-athlete. As already suggested, the almacenero resents her relationship with the man, and convinces himself and others of her immorality. Admitting, too, that his notions are gratuitous inventions, the narrator nonetheless fabricates a story about her and delineates her destiny: her life is to consist of a series of short-lived love affairs. For the time being, however, he is intent on seeing her defeated at this particular time, and the death of the man will insure it.

The almacenero's hatred of people is probably rooted in his fear of them. One expression of paranoia is apparent in his delusions of persecution. He suspects everyone of harming or trying to take advantage of him. If anyone is respectful or attentive, he supposes it is flattery: "También hablaba el enfermero, porque necesitaba adularme y había comprendido que el hombre me interesaba." ["The nurse was also talking, because he needed to flatter me, and he had understood that the man interested me."] If not adulation, he considers it mockery, and to this he is also very sensitive. He infers ridicule from words, looks, or actions. When the nurse suggests celebrating Christmas and New Year's holidays at the store, the almacenero suspects it was intended as a slight to him and his place. Once he sees the validity of the idea, he changes his mind and reflects that it was partially his notion too: "La idea fue del enfermero, aunque no del todo; y pienso, además, que él no creía en ella y que la propuso burlándose, no de mí ni del almacén, sino de la idea misma." ["It was the nurse's idea, though not entirely; and I also think that he didn't believe in it, but proposed it making fun, not of me or the store, but of the idea itself."] More serious is the occasion he thinks the ex-athlete intends to jeer him, for this is dangerous: "Apareció en la escalera, flaco, insomne, en camisa, con una peligrosa inclinación a la burla." ["He appeared at the stairs, skinny, sleepless, in shirt-sleeves, with a dangerous inclination toward mockery."]

Everyone, from anonymous customers to more important characters in the novel, seems to prey on the narrator. As he sees it, people are spying on his every move; customers are constantly fixing their states on him; certain stances or smiles are a challenge. The most extraordinary example of his persecutory paranoia is seen in his view of nature: "Salí al frío azul y gris, al viento que parecía no bajar de la sierra, sino formarse en las copas de los árboles del camino y atacarme desde allí, una vez y otra, casi a cada paso, enconado y jubiloso." ["I went out into the blue and gray cold, into the wind that seemed not to come down from the mountains, but appeared to gather in the branches of the trees along the road and attack me from there, once and again, almost at every step, frenzied and jubilant."]

This interpretation of nature—as joyful in its attempt to massacre the narrator—is another clear illustration of his mental state. The almacenero is a very sick man. He is convinced of his power to predict a person's fate, and seeing the fulfillment of his prophecy obsesses and controls him. Though rational and logical in appearance, his unbalanced intellect distorts reality. And just as the deranged mind perceives, so does it communicate with the same distortion. The reader of *Los adioses* should bear in mind this consideration as he attempts to analyze and interpret the novel.

At this point I would like to propose my own explanation of the outcome of the novel. In the previously cited article by Wolfgang Luchting, the critic paves the way for debate on possibilities of interpreting certain details found in the story. The suggestion—which he calls the "turn of the screw"—consists of speculating that the younger girl is not the ex-athlete's daughter after all. The man, proposes Luchting, lied to la mujer in order to maintain his relationship with both women. The first to respond to the idea was Onetti himself [in "Media vuelta de tuerca," in *Los adioses,* 1970]. Praising Luchting's discussion of "reader participation," the novelist nonetheless states that the article represents only "half a turn of the screw"—words which serve as the title to his remarks. To make matters more intriguing, Onetti adds that the "definitive interpretation"—and it is not his responsibility to present it—is still missing. The screw is still available for tightening.

My hypothesis is rooted in the psychopathic nature and behavior of the narrator as already described in this paper. The almacenero, feeling persecuted or threatened by others, is very capable of retaliating against his imagined offenders. He is calculating, cruel, and oriented in his thoughts toward violence. It is very likely that the storekeeper killed the ex-athlete. The contention that it was murder can be supported with evidence found in the novel itself. The man's death is attributed to suicide, but there is nothing in the text which conclusively proves this idea. On the other hand, there are facts pointing to the possibility of a homicide. Early in the novel the narrator implies he will see to it that his prophecy is fulfilled, resorting, if need, be, to violence: "Me sentía responsable del cumplimiento de su destino, obligado a la crueldad necesaria para evitar que se modificara la profecía, seguro de que bastaba recordarlo y recordar mi espontánea maldición para que él continuara acercándose a la catástrofe." ["I felt responsible for the fulfillment of his destiny, obligated to the cruelty necessary to avoid a modification of the prophecy, certain that it was enough to remember him and recall my spontaneous curse so he would continue getting closer to the catastrophe."]

The idea of homicide recurs at a later moment in the novel. Conversing with the nurse and the hospital aide, his faithful suppliers of gossip, the narrator is given the details of the first reunion of the man, the younger girl, and the mature woman—a meeting they call an "epilogue." The narrator muses on what the true epilogue may be like: "'Un epílogo,' pensaba yo, defendiéndome, 'un final para la discutible historia, tal como estos dos son capaces de imaginarlo'". ["'An epilogue,' I thought, defending myself, 'an ending to the debatable story, such as these two are capable of imagining it.'"] Moments later the aide voices the ending: "Habría que matarlo—decía la mucama—. Matarlo a él." ["He ought to be killed, the aide was saying. He should be killed."] After the nurse confirms the thought, the narrator confesses he cannot resist the idea either: "—Un hijo de por medio—confirmaba el enfermero; pero me sonreía dichoso, vengativo, seguro de mi imposibilidad de disentir." ["There's a child at stake, confirmed the nurse; but he smiled at me happy, vindictive, certain of the impossibility of my dissenting."]

There are sufficient motives to impel the storekeeper to the crime. The prophecy is not becoming a reality; the man has moved to the sanitarium and expects to be cured within six months. And when the almacenero discovers in the letters the true relationship of the man and the two women, proving him wrong again, he becomes enraged: "Sentí vergüenza y rabia, mi piel fue vergënza durante muchos minutos y dentro de ella crecían la rabia, la humillación, el viboreo de un orgullo atormentado." ["I felt shame and anger, my skin was shame for many minutes and inside it grew the anger, the humiliation, the crawling of a tormented pride."] Such a fury could have led the disturbed narrator to violence.

It is also interesting to observe the almacenero at the scene of the death. He is a renewed man, and he experiences the feeling of power once again: "Me sentía lleno de poder, como si el hombre y la muchacha, y también la mujer grande y el nino, hubieran nacido de mi voluntad para vivir lo que yo había determinado." ["I felt full of power, as if the man and the girl, and the older woman and the child also, had been born from my will in order to live what I had determined."] Shaken by the impact of the occurrence, he is, nonetheless, finally at peace: "Me senté en el diván, estremecido y en paz." ["I sat on the divan, shaken and in peace."]

Thus, the key to this reading lies in the psychopathic mind and behavior of the narrator. A close study of his point of view is essential for a clear understanding of *Los adioses*. The reader must maintain a proper perspective of the story, being always aware of the narrator's mental problems and consequent distortion of views. It should be remembered that he is rarely present at the scene of action; the account is the product of gossip sifted through an obsessed mind.

Onetti's narrative art is a response to the necessity of justifying existence, of overcoming the limitations of the human condition. Far from being a gratuitous aesthetic game, his work draws its narrative material from the empirical world and, above all, from subjective experiences.

—*Hugo J. Verani, "Juan Carlos Onetti," in* Latin American Writers, *Volume III, edited by Carlos A. Solé and Maria Isabel Abreu, 1989.*

M. Ian Adams (essay date 1975)

SOURCE: "Juan Carlos Onetti: Alienation and the Fragmented Image," in *Three Authors of Alienation: Bombal, Onetti, Carpentier,* University of Texas Press, 1975, pp. 38-80.

[*In the following excerpt, Adams studies* El pozo *with the intention of illustrating "how Onetti's artistic manipulation of the schizophrenic experience (or the experience of extreme alienation) produces a unique imagery and an unusual sensation for the reader of participation in an alienated world."*]

In addition to writing novels, Onetti has been a productive short-story writer. *Un sueño realizado y otros cuentos* was published in 1951. Another collection, *El infierno tan temido y otros cuentos,* came out in 1962. All of these are in *Cuentos completos,* published in 1967. Mario Benedetti has described the nature of Onetti's stories compared to his novels: "Onetti's stories show, as soon as they are compared to his novels, two notable differences: the obligatory restriction of material, which simplifies its dramatism, affirming it, and also the relative abandonment—the unconscious transfer—of the subjective burden that is borne by the protagonist in the novels and that generally is a limitation, at times a monotonous insistence of the narrator" [*Literatura uruguaya del siglo XX*].

Many of his works, however, fall into the territory between novel and short story. The relative complexity of theme and the quantity of subjective elements associated with it, as mentioned by Benedetti, seem to be reasonable criteria to separate short novels from short stories. Thus *El pozo,* although of few pages, is in Onetti's novelistic mode because of the presence of many themes and because of the subjective, ambiguous presentation of these themes. **"El infierno tan temido"** is structured around one action and its consequences and is very limited thematically. **"Jacob y el otro"** is of greater length than the other stories, but is again characterized by simplicity. A future action, a wrestling match, is the cause of all of the story's movement, and there are few complications of imagery or subjective content.

Complexity and ambiguity are the major characteristics of Onetti's novels. Emir Rodríguez Monegal, comparing him with his contemporaries, describes the difficulties and rewards of reading Onetti: "Anyone will notice the suspicious monotony of his figures, the unilaterality of descriptive method, the symbolism (at times excessive) of his actions and characters, the deliberately baroque development that obstructs the reading, the isolated traces of bad taste. But none of those in his category (urban and realist) attains the violence and lucidity of his declarations, the sure quality of his art, which overcomes superficial realism and moves with passion among symbols" [*Literatura uruguaya del medio siglo*].

Augmenting this complexity is, as Harss and Dohmann point out [in *Into the Mainstream*], Onetti's way of dealing with content. "He is less interested in arriving at the truth of a situation than in isolating its components—its alternatives—which are likely to yield as many falsehoods as facts." As will be seen in the discussion of *El pozo,* the reader must separate falsehoods from facts in order to understand the character of the protagonist and the nature of the problems facing him.

At the stylistic level much of Onetti's complexity is not original. It stems from the acknowledged influence of other writers, particularly Faulkner. Dos Passos has been important in influencing the structure of Onetti's earlier work, above all *Tierra de nadie.* The other major foreign influence has been Celine. Roberto Arlt, according to Harss and Dohmann, is also of importance.

Onetti's creation of a fictional geography would seem to be obviously due to Faulkner, but the major differences between Yoknapatawpha County and Santa María are indicative of the different goals of the authors. Faulkner gives his creation all the appearance of reality. More importantly, his use of location is centrifugal. He peoples his county with generations of families and explores its history from the beginning. His characters stand apart from one another and are united by their roots in the land and its history. Readers of Onetti know that Santa María is a creation, because they were present at its birth in *La vida breve,* where it is an invention of the main character, Brausen. The major difference is, however, that Onetti's world is centripetal. The external features serve only as a frame for internal chaos. All the characters fall toward this center point, and individuals do not stand out as they do in Faulkner. Onetti himself, in *Juntacadáveres,* has best described his typical character in Santa María: "He isn't a person; he is, like all the inhabitants of this strip of the river, a determined intensity of life molding itself in the form of his own mania, his own idiocy."

Alienation is a major feature of Onetti's internalized world. Mario Benedetti recognizes this when he states that "the dramatism of his fiction is derived precisely from a reiterated verification of alienation, from the forced incommunication endured by the protagonist and, therefore, by the author." Harss and Dohmann, writing of the main figure in *El pozo,* generalize on the importance of alienation in Onetti. "Even in his alienation, or because of it, he is representative of a time and place, a frame of mind, an epoch. It is this fact that gives his experiences relevance and validity. To have realized this is Onetti's merit."

Harss and Dohmann have also pointed out another aspect of alienation in Onetti. "What this amounts to in practice is that reading an Onetti book is a schizophrenic experience. The reader is in constant flux between the mind or perceptions of the narrator-protagonist and those of the author, the two being practically indistinguishable." They do not explore this aspect any further. In the discussion that follows, an attempt will be made to show how Onetti's artistic manipulation of the schizophrenic experience (or the experience of extreme alienation) produces a unique imagery and an unusual sensation for the reader of participation in an alienated world.

Due to the cohesiveness of Onetti's fictional world in terms of characters and content, with the exceptions of *Tierra de nadie* and *Para esta noche,* and also to the presence of recurring reworked themes, with the same people in different situations and stages of development, the procedure followed in this study will be to examine carefully a limited number of works, while attempting to show their relation to others, in terms of theme and technique. *El pozo,* because of its relative clarity and simplicity of themes, compared to their later ambiguity, and because of the importance critics have attached to it, will be studied first.

The protagonist of *El pozo,* Eladio Linacero, is one of the best examples in contemporary South American literature of the completely alienated man. Angel Rama considers the main theme of the novel to be "radical solitude." He divides this solitude into two aspects, physical and emotional. The protagonist is physically isolated, alone in a room, and he is emotionally isolated, having cut all ties with other human beings, according to Rama ["Origen de un novelista de una generación literaria," introduction to *El pozo*].

The story is, however, built not around the solitude of the protagonist but, rather, around his attempts at communication. The time elapsed, less than one day, is limited to how long it takes Linacero to write his first-person narrative. The author-protagonist gives the reader fragments of past and present personal history and an ostensibly complete picture of his emotional life.

Based on the nature of the attempts at communication, the novel divides itself into two parts. The first is concerned with the narrator's presentation of his present situation, the beginning of the act of writing, a statement of purpose that, as will be seen, is both aesthetic and emotional, and, finally, the first attempt at written communication, directed toward the reader. The second part is primarily a description of past frustrated attempts at communication with other people. In each case the hidden content of these efforts reveals more of the narrator's condition than he is aware of presenting. The result of the narrative is that Eladio Linacero reaches a crisis of self-hate, induced by a confrontation with his own existence. The novel ends at the moment of his maximum desperation.

It is evident from the foregoing synopsis that literary creation is an important theme in *El pozo,* and this fact has been noted by most of the critics who have studied the work. What is less evident is that the theme is shaped by and develops within the restrictions imposed upon it by the personality of the protagonist. Because extreme alienation is the outstanding characteristic of the narrator, *El pozo* provides a unique opportunity to examine the relations between alienation and literary creation.

The first paragraph of the novel indirectly introduces the theme of creation, in an unexpected context. "A while ago I was walking around the room and it suddenly occurred to me that I was seeing it for the first time. There are two cots, broken-down chairs without seats, sun-faded papers, months old, fixed in the window in place of glass." The room is important as the boundary of the narrator's physical solitude and as the setting for the entire story. It is also the only place left to the narrator in his retreat from the world. At the beginning of the narration, the room has been a fixture and a delimitation of his life for some time, to the point that he is no longer aware of its existence. Yet, upon starting an attempt at communication, he sees it again, with new perspective. The inference is that he is entering into a new relation with his surroundings, no matter how reduced they are, caused by the act of creation. This interpretation is supported by the first statement he makes about the act of writing, a page later. "I found a pencil and a pile of pamphlets under Lázaro's bed, and now nothing bothers me, neither the filth, nor the heat, nor the wretches in the patio. It is certain that I don't know how to write, but I'm writing about myself."

The quoted lines also illuminate a feature of the first paragraph of the story that will have meaning later and will be seen in other works by Onetti. The word *filth* describes the emotional impact of Linacero's environment, especially that of the room. Yet, in the already quoted first paragraph, when he is looking at the room as though it were for the first time, he does not generalize on what he sees. Instead he describes isolated parts, substituting them for a totality of vision.

This form of vision emerges more clearly in his first description of a person, a prostitute. "She was a small woman, with pointed fingers . . . I can't remember her face; I see only her shoulder chapped by the whiskers that had been rubbing it, always that shoulder, never the right one, the skin reddened and the fine-fingered hand pointing it out." Two fragments—fingers and a shoulder—serve to represent a human being. The narrator remembers nothing else about her.

The function and meaning of this type of vision do not become evident immediately. It is only through the additional information given by the narrator and through contrast with another kind of vision present in his dreams that the reader can begin to define their importance.

Before Linacero breaks the time sequence of the first section to describe a past event and the dream constructed around it, he talks about himself and his intentions with respect to what he is going to write. His self-description both directly and indirectly defines his alienation.

His reaction to a child playing in the mud and to the activities of people seen from his window shows several alienated attitudes. He says, "I realized that there really were people capable of feeling tenderness for that." The scene that provoked the response was banal but not repulsive. An underlying disgust for life is the obvious bias that explains the incongruity of the response. Linacero's lack of toleration of other viewpoints implies confidence in the correctness of his reaction. The possibility that he has been disillusioned by the failure of humanistic ideals is fairly well negated by the absence of repulsive elements in the scene. However, his disillusionment is implied by a value judgment in another description of people, "the wretches in the patio." At this point in the work, there is not enough evidence to assess the narrator's idealism, although the possibility of projection of his unhappiness and disgust to other people suggests itself. As the novel progresses, idealism is seen to be a veneer covering Linacero's radical irrational disgust with life.

Further motives for Linacero's efforts toward written communication are given. The next day will be his fortieth birthday. "I never would have imagined forty this way, alone and surrounded by filth, enclosed in a room. But this doesn't make me melancholic. Nothing more than a feeling of curiosity about life and a bit of admiration for its ability to always disconcert. I don't even have any tobacco." He obviously considers the birthday to be of importance as a personal dividing line and as a way of measuring his solitude. He implies disillusionment due to unfulfilled expectations, but he does not attach much importance to it. The description stresses his physical solitude and, at the same time, seems to show philosophical acceptance of his emotional alienation from life and his distrust of it. To claim curiosity would seem to mean that his removal of himself from life has not caused too much difficulty.

The last sentence—"I don't even have any tobacco"—is apparently a *non sequitur,* yet the negative relates it to the rest of the paragraph. Only in retrospect does its meaning become clear. At the end of *El pozo,* when Linacero has reached a state of total desperation, he gives another definition of himself. "I'm a solitary man who smokes any-

place in the city." The habit of smoking has become his only human action in the face of total alienation, withdrawal, desperation, and disgust. Thus, in the first part of the work, when he says he does not have any tobacco, it would seem that he is making a symbolic statement about the depth of his solitude that belies his more rational statement of philosophical fortitude. Other examples of the same technique of symbolic commentary that support this interpretation will be seen later.

Onetti often uses two levels of repeated actions: habitual actions and repeated meaningless actions. They have as a common ground repetition, but habitual actions are meaningful in that they reflect and define the existence of the person involved. Repeated meaningless actions are external to the character of the person but may have meaning in relation to the book. An example of habitual action is seen in *Los adioses*; the protagonist is most frequently seen in the act of drinking, and this act is his major connection with the narrator.

In addition to the function of these two types of action with respect to the description of characters, they also are major structural elements. In *Para una tumba sin nombre* the action of smoking a pipe is used to separate the narrative sections and to represent the narrator's periods of communication. It has a similar function in *La cara de la desgracia.* Habitual action is raised to the level of ritual in *Tan triste como ella,* where it is central to the understanding of the protagonist's suicide. When she can no longer struggle against the vegetation in her garden, life ceases to have meaning for her. In *El astillero* repeated meaningless action, reading former business transactions, becomes a defensive ploy in Larsen's fight to endure.

One of the significant differences between Onetti's novels and his short stories is the relative lack of repeated action patterns of both types in the latter. **"El infierno tan temido"** initially seems to be built around repetition, the sending of pornographic photographs, but the action is really cumulative rather than repetitive: it is the vengeance taken by the wife for damage done by her husband. The stories probably lack these patterns because they are concerned with one action and its immediate consequences, whereas the other works emphasize an expanding series of possibilities, conflicts, and ambiguities arising from any situation or action.

The aesthetic result of this technique is a fragmentation of the character or characters involved. The repetition destroys what would be a normal process of development and response, so that, instead of gaining recognition and familiarity with the literary figure through cumulative exposure, the reader is constantly thrown back to the uncertainty and ambiguity of his first contacts with the character. Onetti's frequent use of a narrator separated from the protagonist would also seem to indicate his intention to distance the reader from his characters. In effect this is planned alienation of the reader from the content of the work.

El pozo is atypical of Onetti's works in that the first-person narration has an immediacy and a directness not seen in most of the others. There are probably two reasons for this. First, it is an early work and Onetti had not yet developed the use of ambiguity and multiplicity of planes that characterize his later writing. *Tierra de nadie* and *Para esta noche* show a developing ability in the manipulation of these factors. *La vida breve* represents their full development. The second reason is the importance of the theme of communication in *El pozo*. The aforementioned tendencies and techniques would blunt the impact and restrict the development of this theme. *Para una tumba sin nombre* shows the application of these techniques to the theme of communication, with resultant complete ambiguity as to motives and content.

Communication is uppermost in Linacero's mind when he reaches what he calls "the point of departure" in his attempt to write. "But now I want to do something different. Something better than the story of the things that happened to me. I would like to write the story of a soul, of it alone, without the events in which it had to participate, wanting to or not. Or of dreams. From some nightmare, the most distant that I remember, to the adventures in the log cabin."

That these two artistic possibilities are of equal value to the narrator is obvious, but at first there does not seem to be any explanation as to why they should be equal. The first, "the story of a soul," free from the events in which it had to participate, is an undefinable and unobtainable goal, an artistic ideal. The other, the story of dreams, is, as the reader knows retrospectively, the essence of the emotional life of the narrator. Thus the second possibility is really a particularization or individualization of the first. That the narrator does not make the logical link is not important. In fact, he goes to the opposite extreme and tries to deny the role dreams play in his life. "What is curious is that, should anyone say of me that I'm a dreamer, it would annoy me. It's absurd. I've lived like everybody else." The reader has enough information to know that the narrator has not lived as described. The development of the story will show the untruth of his denial of being a dreamer.

Thus, before starting into the series of dreams to be related by Linacero, the reader should be aware that he cannot take the declarations and judgments of the narrator at face value but must instead search for evidence of other interpretations. Without this realization it would be impossible to interpret the relation of Eladio to the prostitute Ester, or to see the self-knowledge she forces on him, or to recognize his methods of evasion. If the scene with Ester were not interpreted correctly, Linacero's final state of desperation would be deprived of much of its meaning, because it then would not be greatly different from his state at the beginning.

As a literary device the deceitful narrator poses several problems. First of all, the reader must not have a sense of being manipulated by the author. Onetti avoids this problem by making deceit an integral part of the narrator's character and an essential part of the meaning of that which is narrated.

In terms of personality, Linacero's deceit becomes an external measure of his alienation. He can tell the reader about his solitude and isolation from humanity, but only through the discovery of his deceit is the reader able to judge Linacero's alienation from himself and his inability to exercise self-control even in an artistic creation.

Another problem is the possibility of excessive distancing of the reader from the character, with resultant loss of interest in the entire work. This possibility is also avoided because the detection and evaluation of the deceit become a necessity. Thus, although the reader is separated from the protagonist, he participates in the work because of the independent judgments he has to make.

Onetti uses the deceitful narrator, with significant variations, in other works. In *La cara de la desgracia* the reader, because of events, must decide if the narrator is telling the truth, but he must do so without any conclusive textual evidence. The meaning of the story changes completely, according to his decision. *Para una tumba sin nombre* has two narrators. The admission of deceit by one of them, Jorge Malabia, is made totally ambiguous because of conflicting lies by several persons.

A new dimension of Linacero's alienation is presented when he starts to tell what happened with Ana María. He places the adventure in the world of real events, "something that happened in the real world. . . ." This description of course implies a split emotional life, and it is the first evidence of a divided personality. Three of the narrated episodes—with Ana María, with Ester the prostitute, and with his wife—revolve around the relation between his dream world and the real world. It becomes apparent that the only satisfactory life he has takes place in his dream world. His attempts at communication fail because people either reject his dream world or see the true motives behind it that he is unwilling to accept. The division is so important that it is reflected by the novel's imagery. Each world is characterized by its way of looking at people and objects. Thus the description of the episode with Ana María is worthy of special attention for what it reveals about the "real world" and its relation to the imaginary one.

The first aspect of interest in this episode is another contradiction. It reaffirms the falsity of Linacero's denial of being a dreamer and his claim of having led a normal life. He says of his adolescence, "Even then I had nothing to do with anyone." This statement extends his solitude and alienation into childhood and suggests causes other than the philosophical rejection of the world implied in his introduction and presented again when he describes his failure with other people. It seems legitimate to infer the existence of the same irrational disgust with and rejection of life in adolescence that is present in Linacero's adulthood, as one can deduce from his reaction to the view from his room.

Two other features of the encounter with Ana María deserve attention. The first is the way she is described, and the second is the sexual content of the episode, both manifest and latent, and its relation to the dream of Ana María and "the log cabin."

When Linacero portrays Ana María, he describes only parts of her body: her arm, shoulder, and neck. He recognizes her "by her way of carrying an arm separated from her body." When he looks at her he sees only "nude arms and the nape of her neck." When he attacks Ana María he uses the same fragmented form of description. Her rage is shown by her breasts. "Only her chest, her huge breasts, were moving, desperate with rage and fatigue." Never is there any kind of description that allows a total vision of the girl.

It is obvious that the assault is sexual and yet Linacero disclaims any desire. "I never had, at any moment, the intention of violating her; I had no desire for her." However, he gives no reason for his actions, only indirectly suggesting a wish to humiliate. In his description, nevertheless, it is he who is humiliated. It seems reasonable to assume, given his age, that what he narrates is his sexual initiation and that, due to failure, humiliation, or totally unexplained reasons, he does not wish to, or cannot, reveal the true nature of the encounter.

Linacero's sexual desires toward Ana María do not become manifest until he describes the dream based on the encounter in real life. As a prologue to the dream he relates its content to Ana María in the "real world." "But now I don't have to lay stupid traps. She is the one who comes at night, without my calling her, without knowing where she comes from . . . Nude, she extends herself on the burlap covering of the bough bed." Sex is the only motive in the dream, but the initiative has been transferred to Ana María. Furthermore, the Eladio Linacero she offers herself to has no relation either to the adolescent who desired her but hid his desire from himself or to the solitary, alienated, withdrawn man writing in his room. The imagined Linacero is a gregarious man of action, the object of unreasoned sexual desire. Thus in both dream and reality Linacero presents a distorted image of himself. In the dream the image is changed by fantasy that would seem to be compensatory for an unacceptable reality. In reality it is changed by omission or misdirection in order to conceal his true nature and feelings from himself. In both cases the projected self-image indicates the irrational basis of his alienation.

Thus one aspect of Angel Rama's description of the function of dreams seems to be incorrect. He states, "If there is a dominant and original line running through the story, defining it, defining the character, it is this capacity for 'dreaming', removing himself from reality." At all levels of narration Linacero alters reality. The difference between the dreams and the "real world" lies in the method and degree of separation from reality, not in the separation itself.

Another major difference exists between Linacero's dreams and all other events. The fragmented vision resulting in incomplete images in his description of the real Ana María has already been noted. In the dream this type of vision is absent. Instead Linacero gives a complete description of Ana María's body. "From above, without gesture and without speaking to her, I look at her cheeks that are starting to flush, at the thousand drops shining on her body and moving with the flames of the fire, at her breasts that seem to quiver like a flickering candle agitated by silent steps. The girl's face has an open frank look, and, scarcely separating her lips, she smiles at me." The part of the body he isolates indicates his desire. "Slowly, still looking at her, I sit on the edge of the bed and fix my eyes on the black triangle, still shining from the storm. It is then, exactly, that the adventure begins." The sexual aspect of Linacero's fragmented vision is perfectly clear. When he is attempting to conceal his desire from himself and the reader, he fragments the body and describes parts that generally have no sexual interest. In the fantasized dream, where his desire is foremost, the body and its sexual attributes are completely described.

A point of coincidence between dreams and reality is seen when Linacero, after speaking about a woman with whom he has had sexual relations, generalizes about women. "A woman will be eternally closed to one, in spite of everything, if one does not possess her with the spirit of a violator." This is a projection of a wish from his dream world into the real world. Only in the former is he a man of action, a "violator." This projection shows, again, the confusion of self-image between dream world and real world. It also perhaps reveals a hidden wish not to communicate with women, as this concept of physical love precludes communication. A further indication of this desire appears when Hanka asks Linacero a question— why he thinks that he will never fall in love again—that to answer would require both communication and self-realization. Rather than respond he breaks his relation with her. In addition, his philosophical outlook toward both women and humanity in general radically changes. Significantly, he rejects the possibility of communication with women, allowing a good deal of hate and disgust to show. "Why, a few lines before, was I speaking of understanding? None of these filthy beasts are able to understand anything." In the same fashion he shows his basic dislike of humanity: ". . . but the truth is that there are no people like that, healthy as animals. There are only men and women who are animals." Both of these statements are a long way from the earlier viewpoints expressed, but they are more revealing of the truth of Linacero's nature in that they come in response to stimuli that activate the deeper levels of his being. What is now completely visible is an all-encompassing disgust toward life and other human beings.

Of the additional attempts at communication described by Linacero only one is central to further understanding of his character and alienation. The others—with his former wife and with Cordes—add to his frustration and push him toward partial self-realization and desolation. In his relation with Ester, the prostitute, he is forced to look at the real, and probably most important, function of his dreams. Angel Rama has described this function: "The pleasurable, erotic, content of these dreams is known; it nourishes the masturbatory episodes . . ." Rama does not, however, deal with the importance of Linacero's being confronted with this knowledge, beyond recognizing his rejection of the charge by the prostitute.

There is a great deal of similarity, in terms of structure and imagery, between Linacero's description of his relation with the prostitute and the earlier episode with Ana María. The reader again sees something that takes place in the "real world." After failure on this plane there is a dream, much abbreviated as compared to the one of "the log cabin," that changes the reality involved. The description of Ester is another example of fragmented vision. "But she seemed younger, and her arms, thick and white, stretched out, milky in the light of the café, as if, on sinking into life, she had raised her hands, desperately pleading for help, thrashing like a drowned person, and the arms had remained behind, distant in time, the arms of a young girl, separate from the large nervous body, which no longer existed." The same process is at work but in a more exaggerated fashion. Not only do the parts of the prostitute described have no sexual connotations, but also they are surprisingly related to an earlier state of purity. That this difficult association takes place due to emotional needs of the narrator is obvious, because it is totally divorced from the physical and emotional reality of the situation. Linacero again seems to be masking his sexual desires as he did in the description of his assault on Ana María. His wish not to pay Ester can be interpreted as a symptom of his evasion, in that the money would be an open declaration of sexual intent.

It is also significant that Linacero interrupts the narrative of the lowest point in his life, the sexual conquest of a whore, to talk about the highest point, his brief love for his former wife. He says, "There had been something marvelous created by us." He offers two generalities to cover the failure of love and his marriage. "Love is marvelous and absurd, and, incomprehensibly, it touches all classes of souls. But absurd marvelous people are rare, and they are that way only for a short time, in early youth. Afterward they begin to accept, and they are lost." The basic belief expressed here is in the destructive power of life and of experience. The state of purity referred to can exist only in early youth, when there has been no exposure to life and no adjustment of ideals to reality. Youth is also the time of sexual awakening. It is this awakening that lies behind the other generalization, which is again overlaid by the idea of a lost purity. "And if one marries a girl and one day wakes at the side of a woman, it is possible that one will understand, without disgust, the souls of violators of children and the drooling kindness of those old men who wait with chocolates at school street corners." Here, however, the only attraction of youth is sexual.

The idea of purity is the key to the explanation of the episode with Ester. After succeeding in going with her to a hotel without paying, Linacero attempts to talk to her, when she is dressing, about her dreams and to create one for her. She responds with disgust, telling him that she knows they serve as an introduction to masturbation. He does not deny the charge; instead, as he did with Hanka, he rejects the person. "She was a wretched woman, and it

was imbecilic to speak to her about this." He converts her into a dream, where she becomes completely pure and innocent. "At times I think about her, and there is an adventure in which Ester comes to visit me, or we unexpectedly meet, drinking and talking as good friends. She then tells me the things she dreams or imagines and they are always things of extraordinary purity, as simple as tales for children." The major modification is that she, in what she communicates as a dreamer, has taken over the role of Linacero. By giving her purity he has given it to himself. The inference is that the disgust felt by Ester was also felt by Linacero, and what he is trying to conceal is self-hate.

This interpretation is indirectly supported by the beginning of the paragraph following the one quoted above. Onetti uses a habitual action that has already acquired meaning to indicate the hidden reaction of Linacero. "I don't know what time it is. I've smoked so much that tobacco disgusts me." His definition of his essential life is that he is a solitary man who smokes. Repugnance for smoking symbolically means disgust with self and with life.

In addition to the indirect evidence discussed above, the last two episodes show a growing awareness on Linacero's part of his own self-hate. It is revealed directly but gradually. The first stage occurs when his roommate calls him a failure. Linacero only suggests his reaction. "But Lázaro doesn't know what he's saying when he screams 'failure' at me. He can't even suspect what that word means to me." Nevertheless, he does not expand on its meaning for him, instead making the reader guess what it might be. To be sensitive to failure can only indicate insecurity in terms of self-image and self-esteem.

In the episode with Cordes, Linacero for the first time in his narrative expresses a feeling of happiness and a belief that he is communicating. "It has been a long time since I felt so happy, free, talking with enthusiasm, tumultuously, without vacillation, sure of being understood, also listening with the same intensity, trying to foresee Cordes's thoughts." He tells Cordes a fantastic dream, and when he is not understood he has a violent reaction. "I'm sick of everything, do you understand, of people, of life, of proper verse. I go in a corner and imagine all that. That and dirty things, every night." This is at last the truth about himself, and its intensity can be explained only by the unwilling increase in self-awareness that has taken place through the narrative. Because of it he is partially able to assess his position in respect to himself and to others. His new perspective becomes evident when he compares himself to Lázaro, his roommate, for whom he has shown only disgust. "When all's said and done it's he who is the poet and dreamer. I'm a miserable man who turns at night toward the shadowed wall to think shoddy fantastic things."

Linacero's final statement about life carries the entire weight of the anguish that gradually reveals itself in the narrative. "This is night; he who couldn't feel it doesn't known it. Everything in life is shit, and now we're blind in the night, attentive and without comprehension." It is evident that, although he faces his condition more fully than before, he does not totally accept it and still desires communication with other human beings. It is a one-sided act of communication to extend, by the use of the first person plural, his condition onto humanity.

The picture of alienation that has emerged from the study of what the narrator relates and what can be seen behind his words is one of almost total withdrawal and isolation, made even more intense by repeated efforts at communication. The underlying causes of this alienation are rooted in the character of the narrator and are not due to any outside social pressures. The essence of Linacero's personality is an irrational disgust for all aspects of living. This disgust is coupled with self-hate that seems to arise from his adult sexual life. However, the origins of these features remain largely conjectural. Onetti has limited himself to presenting the condition without going into the causes of it.

The dominant technique used in the development of the protagonist's personality is that of the deceitful narrator. The reader, although distanced from Linacero, participates in the work because he has to make judgments about it that affect the meaning of the entire story.

Two other techniques were noted. One, the use of habitual or repeated action, does not play a very great role in *El pozo,* although several times the act of smoking carries the true meaning of what is being narrated. Of much more importance are the vision and visual images described by the narrator. A fragmented imagery is characteristic of all that he describes in the real world. The dream world contains coherent vision and imagery. The sexual aspect of this vision has been discussed, but its relation to the personality of Linacero was only indirectly dwelt upon. He obviously has a totally split personality in that his emotional life takes place in his imaginary world. His external "real world" personality is permeated by his fantasy self. Neither part functions satisfactorily. The visual fragmentation is schizophrenic, offering a broken surface with no depth coherence. An example of this depthless vision is the lack of sexual connotations of the parts of the female body described in the "real world." Only in the fantasy world is there something behind the imagery.

Thus, in order to convey the experience of extreme alienation, Onetti has created a schizoid form of vision and made it coincide with the split personality of the protagonist. On a different plane he has fragmented normal action patterns, emphasizing repeated or habitual actions. The result of this technique is to give the entire work a schizoid atmosphere. The personality of the protagonist is, however, the determinant for the techniques used to create alienation. This is not the case in many of the later works of Onetti, in which the personality becomes lost in a web of objects, actions, incongruous emotions, and partially understood symbolism. . . .

In addition to the other planes of imagery, there is a symbolic plane in *El pozo,* but it is weakly developed and serves only as background to the narrative. All the important action, real and imaginary, takes place in small en-closed areas. On the real plane this setting is indicative of the isolation of the protagonist, but in the imaginary world these enclosed areas, "the log cabin," above all, become indistinct sexual symbols. All the imagery related to the cabin has sexual overtones on an oneiric Freudian level.

The theme of artistic creation introduced at the beginning of *El pozo* is seen to be determined and formed by the personality of the narrator. The content of his dreams is a manifestation of emotions and desires that he conceals from himself in the real world. The dreams also serve as sexual stimulants. The reader is able to judge the extent of alienation by the schizoid form it forces upon the images and actions of the protagonist.

Sexuality in Onetti's works is, like all human relations in his writings, contaminated, another moment of domination, humiliation, or degradation. It is simply a kind of egoism which has little to do with pleasure. There is little eroticism in Onetti's texts, and sexuality is usually linked with violence, with violation or rape, never with love.

—Alfred J. Mac Adam, in **Modern Latin American Narratives,** *1977.*

Jack Murray (essay date 1983)

SOURCE: "Plot and Space in Juan Carlos Onetti's 'Tan Triste Como Ella,'" in *Symposium,* Vol. XXXVII, No. 1, Spring, 1983, pp. 68-83.

[*In the following excerpt, Murray aims to demonstrate that the meaning usually found in a story's plot has been transferred to the physical surroundings and space occupied by the main characters in "Tan triste como ella."*]

It has often been observed that Juan Carlos Onetti's unhappy lot is to represent trends before their time. He was writing fantastic stories before the fashion for the fantastic, New Novels before the New Novelists came along. While Onetti's penchant for setting yet-to-be vogues has doubtless created difficulties for him, for his admirers such a tendency denotes something positive and lasting: his broad and profound representativeness of what is typical and abiding in twentieth-century fiction. No one should be surprised that it could only be a South American, and specifically a *platense,* author who should possess this quality. In the cultural setting of Western literature, only writers from that part of the world seem able to combine intertextual currents and influences so diverse and unexpected as to be unlikely anywhere else. In the case of the object of the present study, Onetti's **"Tan triste como ella,"** for example, we must speak in the same breath of William Faulkner and Alain Robbe-Grillet.

The specific problem we wish to examine is both Onettian and typical of twentieth-century fiction: how is the story told when the events are fragmented and blurred, the viewpoint partial and obscured, and the authorly position toward the story's contents aloof and often uncomprehending? In other words, how do we answer the reader's question "What is happening?" or "What has happened?"

A review of Onetti's fiction shows that such blurring and fragmentation are typical. We find them as much in an earlier work like *Tierra de nadie* as in a recent one such as *Dejemos hablar al viento*. Because Onetti consistently uses similar techniques and authorly strategies in all his fiction, and also because all his works essentially exploit the same restricted repertory of themes, I shall concentrate on a single short story, **"Tan triste como ella,"** instead of a longer or better known work such as the renowned *Vida breve* or *El astillero*. Anything I say about this particular work will have a broad application to the rest of his fiction—particularly the problem of how, in Jonathan Culler's terms [presented in *The Pursuit of Signs*, 1981], a logic of signification becomes imposed upon the events of a story (especially when these events are fragmented). What I say about Onetti will be enlightening for other twentieth-century novelists in other times and lands.

When Ivonne Bordelois reviewed **"Tan triste"** [in *Cuadernos* 98 (1965)] shortly after its publication as the title piece for a collection of short stories in 1965, she noted how much the work reflected certain developments in European film and fiction of that period. (Presumably, she was thinking of the New Novel and its recent entry into film, *Last Year at Marienbad*.) She was more interested in the symbols found in **"Tan triste"** than in the plot, saying only that the latter seemed to consist of "una falsa venganza apoyada sobre celos falsos." She felt a shadowy impersonal force was pushing its characters on. Specifically, she noted Onetti's refusal to indulge in psychological dissections of character and his invocation of a modified symbolic mode that recalled medieval legend. And she suggested that he was leaving up to the reader the task of unraveling the meaning of the tale.

The last supposition is most assuredly true. All of Onetti's fiction might be described usefully as undergoing a constant process of "self-deconstruction," with the events not only fragmenting but with vital pieces of information actually being withheld from the reader [Enrique Anderson Imbert, in *Historia de la literatura hispanoamericana*, 1961]. Hence, the reader's task is to *reconstruct* the tale from the "disjecta membra." It will be my major argument that Onetti displaces the meaning of his story from the shattered events to the rigorously, if not exhaustively, observed space in which the story takes place. On this matter, it should come as no surprise that **"Tan triste,"** like most of Onetti's fiction, takes place in his equivalent of Faulkner's Yoknapatawpha County: Santa Maria. Imaginary space becomes the arena in which psychological truths are objectified and symbols attain concrete life.

Here is synopsis of what we may glean the story is about. A man, never named, is sick, perhaps dying, and has formed the obsessive conviction that his wife (also unnamed) has been unfaithful to him with a certain Mendel. (All the narrative tells us is that the woman went home once with a man a few months before her marriage but did not yield herself to him.) The husband claims to have a piece of evidence that will put Mendel in jail. Meanwhile, he has taken to staying away from home, not only during the day when he is at work but also for most of the night (with a succession of mistresses). He presents his wife with a revolver for her protection during his absences but, when it fails to fire, he throws it in the bottom of their bedroom closet. A side project of his is to remove the weed jungle in back of the house, cement it over, and install tanks in which to raise exotic fish. For this project he hires three workmen—two young men and their employer, a problematical man who in the past has falsely represented himself as a priest and architect. They are assigned to carry out their work in the husband's absence. The wife, who has already perceived this absence as spitefully directed against her, is especially dismayed at the destruction of the garden. She has been a dutiful housewife and mother until this point. Now she begins to debase herself both by abortive intimacies with the two young men and also by mutilating herself on the Jerusalem thorn hedge surrounding the garden. One day her husband returns and announces triumphantly that Mendel has been arrested, though without his personal intervention. The woman goes down to the garden to find the hedge has wilted and will no longer prick. She then goes up to the bedroom closet, takes the gun, and shoots herself in the mouth.

This shocking tale may be better understood if we see it as a fragmented and eroded version of the ancient motif of the Eaten Heart. The prototypical version is found in the *vida* of the Provençal troubadour Guillem de Cabestanh (c. 1190-1212). He fell in love with, and was loved in return by, Soremonda, wife of Raimon de Castel Rossillon. Raimon, learning of the affair, captured the troubadour, had him killed and served his heart to his wife in a stew, telling her what it was only after she had eaten it. In dismay over her unwitting deed and as reprisal for her husband's cruelty, she threw herself to her death from an adjoining window. The essential components of the story are three: crime (adultery), punishment (murder of the lover, entrapment of the wife), reprisal (the wife kills herself).

Here is what is left in **"Tan triste"** of those elements that appear so clear in the medieval version.

The crime. Because the story is told mainly from the wife's perspective, we see the husband's conviction over her infidelity as delusional. The story says only that she went home with a man before her marriage. But the reader's trust in the accuracy of her viewpoint is tested by a chance sentence in which she is described as erasing from her mind not only her husband but also Mendel: "Mendel: habia desaparecido junto con el hombre flaco (her husband) . . . Nunca habia estado con Mendel, nunca lo habia conocido ni le habia visto el cuerpo corto y musculoso." The description of Mendel's body is too precise for this denial not to read like an oblique confession of familiarity with him. Elsewhere, we see the husband trying to hear *again* the story of her meetings with Mendel. In the face of this uncertainty, the reader finds himself confronted by the enigma so typical of detective stories that Josefina Ludmer finds basic to Onetti's fiction—the lack of a sentence that says all [Ludmer, *Onetti, Los procesos de construcción del relato*, 1977]. But none of this explains away the irrational aspects of the husband's jealous behavior. For instance, he interprets his wife's having had a boy instead of the girl they were expecting (even to the point of having invested in a sizable layette in pink) as a further infidelity.

The punishment. The husband's efforts to have Mendel arrested by denouncing him to the police with an incriminating document prove to be unnecessary. Fate takes the matter out of his hands. One notes the wife's skepticism over his effectiveness here. As for the entrapment the husband sets up for her through the two young workmen in the garden, she at once goes along with it (as if to say: "if this is what you expect of me, then this you shall have") but she is not fooled into it. As we shall see, the only act of punishment that appears totally successful is the husband's perhaps fortuitous and unmotivated decision to have the garden cut down. This blow finds its mark.

The reprisal. The woman's suicide is as enigmatic as the infidelity. She seems only to be play-acting when she pulls the gun out of the closet and not to expect that it will fire, since it failed to fire for her husband before. But this effort does coincide with his crowing announcement that Mendel has been arrested.

Each of the three main elements in the tale, then, is puzzling or has broken down. Onetti deliberately obscures the main superstructure of the story in order to force the reader to apply even deeper readings.

First of all, of course, the story as I have told it may only be *apparent* and cover over another narrative stratagem. For example, we may be dealing with something like the subplot of a Clouzot or Hitchcock film: what the husband really wants to do is drive his wife to kill herself by hounding her with the false accusation that she has been unfaithful. Ivonne Bordelois invites this interpretive tactic when she speaks of false vengeance based on false jealousy. The accusation of adultery is a bogus plot that lures the woman into a fatal ambush. The episodes the ambush entails, from the woman's vantage point, do not seem related, appear arbitrary. First, the husband throws the gun in the closet. Then, he decides to remove the weed jungle and announces this to his weakly protesting wife. For this purpose, he calls in the three workmen.

This subplot suggests Bluebeard pretending to go away while leaving all the keys to the palace in his new wife's charge, telling her she may use all but one. [In *The Uses of Enchantment* (1977)] Bruno Bettelheim has seen the element of the forbidden room as a disguised version of the theme of infidelity. Both Bluebeard and Onetti's husband apparently think of the wife as curious, disposed to

infidelity, if not wanton. Neither is disappointed in his low esteem.

But why does the gun fire for the wife when it does not for the husband? And is he not too inept to bring off so complex a plot? Even on the level of subplot it would seem that Onetti has structured his story so that everything seems to fragment or remain in the air.

In order to see how the story has both logic and meaning we may usefully compare it with another mystery story as construed by Jacques Lacan: his famous analysis of Edgar Allan Poe's "The Purloined Letter" ["Le séminaire sur *La lettre volée*," in *Ecrits I*, 1966]. Culler has observed that the dynamic tension in a tale comes from the interplay between a logic of event and a logic of signification. This interplay generates meaning. In the Poe story Lacan shows that it is the movement of the letter that produces signification. A similar chain of meaning might be seen as emerging from both the main and the subplot of **"Tan triste"** as well. In this context, cutting down the garden is the most significant event, since it corresponds to the theft of the letter in Poe, a matter we shall investigate shortly in greater detail.

The relation between this tale and Onetti's is clearest if we consider Borges's stratagem in "La muerte y la brújula" as a point of transition. Here the detective (who, incidentally, is described by the author as taking himself for an Auguste Dupin) falls victim to his killer Red Scharlach because he reads a cunning logical design into Scharlach's random and spontaneous acts. The design falls into place when the detective is killed. This mortal outcome has a direct bearing upon **"Tan triste,"** since it shows that accidental events may produce the same logic and signification as ones that are carefully planned and perpetrated by a story's protagonists. While Onetti's story, in appearance, is the least structured of the three tales, it has the same fatal logic. The signification is more problematical, however, if only because there is no detective in the story to explain it all to us. It is now to this that we turn.

Plainly the actions in the story's plot do not speak for themselves or enlighten us as to what motivates the characters to act as they do. Moreover, the author offers the reader no psychological explanation for their behavior. The reader is therefore led to seek that explanation in other elements, and in his search he may well be attracted by the insistently intrusive spatial elements in the story. Indeed, Josefina Ludmer, among others, has sanctioned an investigation of these elements by pointing out how much topography offers a key to Onetti's writings. It is now my intention to show that, far more than the mechanics of plot or of meaning as generated through plot, it is space that projects the author's point, particularly since it provides an arena in which antagonistic forces are affirmed or enfeebled, compete with or flee from each other.

As in Robbe-Grillet's *La Jalousie*, the locus of the entire story is the house and the compound surrounding it. It consists of the hedge-bound garden, garden shed, garage, and house itself (we see only the downstairs kitchen, the stairs going up, the upstairs bedrooms with connecting hall, all in the back of the house facing the garden). This locus, however, is not an inert backdrop—something like what we would see on a stage—but provides the medium through which the psychological forces at work in the story achieve the recognizable outline of the classical male-female confrontation lying at the thematic center of Onetti's works. The confinement of the story to this one spatial setting not only emphasizes its restriction to the woman's vantage point but also reinforces the claustrophobic sense of her unending imprisonment within the house. The house is the place from which the husband seems almost continually to be away, the place in which the wife sits waiting for his return.

At first sight it would appear that the husband is in command of this space. He can order that the garden be destroyed. He may come in and go out of this space as he pleases. But the house and his money come from his wife. Hence, his commanding position may simply be empty swagger. The ambiguous and undermined title he has to the space is a correlative not only of his physical, moral, and even intellectual weakness but also of his wife's potential superiority over him. This purely virtual advantage possessed by the wife has meant that, for him, she has turned into a kind of evil genius haunting the place, poisoning his enjoyment of his powers, and driving him away. But she can hardly be said to be deliberately trying to eclipse her husband, if only because her upbringing in a paternalistic society has left her without any idea of how to assert herself or take the initiative and see the house as partially hers: she has been raised to believe it was her father's before, it is now her husband's (who has simply stepped into the father's place). The woman's confinement inside the paternally controlled home throughout her life has made her unaware of having any rights or power. She seems totally under her husband's sway, in this regard. Quite clearly we are in the thematic setting of the "woman question" dating at least back to Ibsen in modern literature.

The wife in Onetti's story, just like Brigida in "El árbol" by the Chilean author Maria Luisa Bombal, finds confinement to male-dominated space is to be sentenced to what Hernán Vidal calls its "rutina anestesiante y traicionera" [*Maria Luisa Bombal: La femineidad enajenada,* 1976]. Vidal sees the husband's paternalistic administration of property and money as setting up a tight hierarchical order in which everyone has a strictly limited and permanently assigned place. In the present instance, the woman in Onetti's story is to occupy herself with her duties in the kitchen and nursery and not concern herself with anything else. A system so rigid is bound to turn everyone into a mutilated stereotype. Exceeding the stereotype in any way is grounds for abject humiliation. While both Bombal's and Onetti's wife have been trained to submit to a paternalistic regime, Onetti's character is not so ready as Brigida to be convinced of the validity of her husband's negative assessment of her. But neither woman seems able to achieve individuation on her own, at least in a positive sense, and is limited to the closed space of home, a space that seems to be a correlate of the limitations of her own

mind. Almost in spite of themselves, both women are kept in a state of dependent infantilism imposed upon them by the seemingly male-dominated social order.

Onetti emphasizes the symbolic value of his use of space by having the woman in **"Tan triste"** try to escape her confinement by choosing, not the husband's garage door or the garden gate used by the workmen, but an attempt to find a way out through the resisting needles of the Jerusalem thorn hedge. Her inability to break free of this enclosure betrays a general inability to think of herself in autonomous terms. It does not seem to occur to her to be anything more than a wife and mother. It is only in the rather Emma Bovary-like activity of reading that she becomes able to articulate her feelings, but this is because they are spelled out for her by someone else in a book: "Figúrense ustedes el pesar creciente, el ansia de huir, la repugnancia impotente, la sumisión, el odio."

The house, then, is a place in which the struggle between husband and wife has reached a stand-off. Both are alienated from it: the husband, because it came to him from his wife, the wife, because the house has always been, and continues to be, the place of male domination. While each partner has a relative kind of power over the other, an equal weakness prevents this power from becoming dominant.

The wife's confinement within the house and the husband's absences from it underscore an even deeper level of conflict which spatial concepts help elucidate. If we imagine a pole with internalization at one extreme, externalization at the other, then we see that the wife and husband are situated at opposite poles. The husband's drive toward externalization may be seen not only in his absences from the house but also in his need to affirm himself through power in his world, to possess, to dominate. The wife's equivalent tendency toward internalization is expressed in her privatization of being in the face of alienation caused by her assigned role in life and also by her husband's aggressive behavior toward her.

In his efforts toward externalization the husband not only seeks to dominate the home but also to attain financial success in the world at large. The text pointedly expresses his effort to increase his domain outside the home in spatial terms: "se iba extendiendo, desde las nueve hasta las cinco, a través de oficinas de un local enorme." As for sexual self-affirmation, here we find a compulsive need to enlarge his area of conquest, partly in compensation for supposed failure in this domain at home. Yet all these efforts to assert himself in the business or sexual world tend to miss their mark as much as his efforts at home ("inútil" is an adjective frequently applied to the man). In the long run, his sense of alienation is unrelieved and he is brought back again to confront his own powerlessness to escape from it.

In Onetti the male's sexual crisis is almost always related to the parallel theme of death, just as it is in so much of modern literature. From the husband's viewpoint, the wife's growing from a girl into full maternal womanhood signals the passage of time and consequent mortality. He has been unable to halt this advance and retain his wife as a little girl fetish figure. Rubén Cotelo has noted, in Onetti's works, the presence of Nabokovian nymphets who retain medieval overtones of the female as depraved and corrupt. In such a figure, Cotelo claims, we see a perverse version of the Marian personage. She is not only related to sin and grace, however, but also serves as an extension of the myth of youth [Cotelo, "Cinco lecturas de Onetti," in *Onetti*, edited by Jorge Ruffinelli, 1973]. The husband clings to such a figure because she offers the fleeting impression of being a miraculous bulwark against time, although time corrodes the husband's body throughout the story in the form of (fatal?) sickness and visible signs of aging. Therefore, a relationship with the girl will always be characterized by what Aínsa has called "dolorismo" [*Las trampas de Onetti*, 1970]. As the husband puts it: "La muchacha, la casi mujer que puede ser contemplada con melancolia, con la sensación espantosa de que ya no es posible." Aínsa reminds us that ecstatic love for a virgin may not be repeated with the same girl. Once touched, she is already defiled and in full decomposition. As her husband tersely puts it: "El pelo se va, los dientes se pudren." One can only agree with M. R. Frankenthaler that the assumption of womanhood necessarily entails the fall of an ideal [*J. C. Onetti: La salvación por la forma*, 1977].

As in Maria Luisa Bombal's "El árol," the relationship has incestuous overtones, particularly since we are dealing with an older man marrying a younger girl. The husband seems to transfer all the blame for the defilement to the wife. Specifically, he seems to feel she has lost her capacity to symbolize innocence and youth and furthermore has deprived him of the possibility of renewing his fantasy (essentially a salvation fantasy) by failing to bear him a daughter. Hern Vidal, in discussing Bombal's story, sees transgression against the incest taboo as implicit in bourgeois marriage. This, in turn, leads to an ever greater degeneration, a loss in vitality, and an inability to renew order, once decay has set in.

In short, the husband feels he has lost control over his world when he sees his wife has grown into the fullness of womanhood. She has assumed those very qualities that he (and all normal males, he claims) are not looking for: "la que comprende, protege, mima, ayuda, endereza, corrige, mejora, apoya, aconseja, dirige y administra." Such qualities would denote a full person, a fellow being, a companion who shares his life with him. But woman in the plenitude of the human person the husband can only perceive as a challenging and alienating force. She not only threatens his masculinity; she brings out its pathetic vulnerability. Hence, we note the typical misogyny of the insecure male. In spatial terms, this means he is not in total control of his space.

The internalization I have attributed to the wife takes place when she can only withdraw inside herself in the face of such resistance against her integrity as a person. But the husband, restricted to the external, hence superficial, aspect of his world, perceives this move as a sexual turning

away from him. If she is now aloof from him, it can only be for sexual reasons. She has given herself to someone else. Seeing her retreat within herself as simple sexual infidelity, he lapses into self-pity and spiteful behavior. Such conduct is not without its masochistic side. His brooding over his wife's defection verges on delectation. He goads her to make further, and more painful, disclosures. But she has become totally inured to his supplications of this matter: "La frase no vendría."

On a far more primitive level, the woman's tendency to internalize may suggest to the husband a kind of voraciousness, possibly cannibalistic in nature. While it is true that he perceives his feelings toward his wife in the mode of jealousy, he also may fear being consumed, at least on a subconscious level, and must attempt to escape her. On this matter, we might well ponder the deeper implications of Raimon de Castel Rossillon making Soremonda eat his rival's heart. In a wry—and indeed ghastly—way, he seems to be recognizing the cannibalistic aspect of the woman's sexuality (inevitably one thinks, in this context, of certain female spiders or else of the nineteenth-century *femme-vampire*). In this light, the woman comes to appear as wild, primitive, and fatally cunning. She possesses a power for which the husband is no match, particularly in his present debilitated condition. If he is to be rid of her, it must be by clever and oblique means. It is here that he falls, perhaps unconsciously, on the expedient of cutting down the garden, an oblique strategy that eventually sends her to her death. Dimly, he senses that the garden is a correlate of her being, and, in destroying it, he robs her of her power in much the same way as people in more primitive societies shaved the heads of women suspected of witchcraft.

Josefina Ludmer has spoken of the *cut* that produces Onetti's fiction and the cutting down of the garden in **"Tan triste"** fits into this pattern. The garden comes to have meaning by being irreversibly altered. Or, as Ludmer puts it, the assassination of the thing gives rise to the sign. The cut, of course, figures in the Guillem de Cabestanh legend and even in "Bluebeard" (where it stands as a threat: the bride has seen the hacked up bodies of her predecessors in the forbidden room). The cut is the horrible awakening from a long sleep.

It is not until after the garden is gone that the woman realizes it has been the only place where she was ever happy ("desde la infancia no había tenido otra felicidad verdadera, sólida, aparte de los verdes arrebatados al jardin.") And she seems convinced that her husband has intuited this. The blow he strikes at the garden is really one he is striking at her.

As long as the garden existed, the woman could feel in some respects that time stood still. Left untouched, the garden would have permitted her to persevere in a world unchanged since childhood and to go on enjoying an undisturbed kind of innocence and narcissism. Hence, her internalization is not simply a strategy adopted against her husband's cruel mistreatment of her in marriage, but must be seen as a tendency surviving from childhood. In this context, we may consider her ongoing inclination to internalize as having, at least in part, the same goal as the husband's toward externalization: the arresting of time. But when such a disposition takes an inward direction, we must see it as autistic in character. Unfortunately, the very withdrawal that autism involves suggests the kind of ingesting of the external world that has so misled and frightened the husband.

For her own part, the woman's edenic image of the childhood garden entails not only free-growing grass but a sense of communion with a father who is totally unthreatening and never gets around to cutting it, thus declining to thwart her continuing bliss in the autistic realm. The security of this possibly incestuous (but never aggressive) relationship came to be associated with the taste of grass in the mouth, hence internalized through that orifice that ingests nourishment from the external world. Freud has spoken of this type of orality in infants as one of the first expressions of sexuality, the eventual aim being incorporation and identity. In the story, the traces of this primordial sexuality are seen in the woman's happy memory of going home with the man at the beginning of the story and her recollection of his taste and the happy sense of security it gave her. The same reassuring taste appears again during the recurrence of the dream at the end of the story, where it is explicitly associated with grass. Regrettably, the oral side of her sexuality has entirely different, and far more sinister, overtones for the woman's husband.

Perhaps the woman was first drawn to her husband because of his paternal aspect, imagining that the happy idyll first begun with her father and the garden would continue. Instead, she was plunged into the cruel world of the phallus which summarily ejected her from the "locus amoenus" where she had been the joyous center of a narcissistic realm. When we see her in the story, the objectification of her place in the world has produced so complete a sense of alienation in her that she cannot identify with what she has become in her husband's mind: the cunning, unfaithful wife ("putita astuta"), a person so threatening and perhaps frightening to him that he would want to kill her. While the garden still existed, she could escape inside herself from this horrible counterfeit being he would force upon her; cut down, she no longer can. In such a dilemma she disowns life itself: "Pero recordaba, aún ahora y con mayor fuerza, la sensación de estafa iniciada al final de la infancia . . . Nunca había sido consultada respecto a la vida que fue obligada a conocer y aceptar. Una sola pregunta anterior y habría rechazado, con horror equivalente, los intestinos y la muerte, la necesidad de la palabra para communicarse e intentar la comprensión ajena."

Josefina Ludmer has spoken of the problem that arises with the "phantom limb" after the cut and of the search for the prosthesis to take its place. For example, the woman continues to walk across the cement as if all the vegetation were still there. And we note a certain inconclusiveness, even impulsiveness, about her behavior after the garden is cut down that suggests the troubled effort to find something to replace it. The woman, a creature of internalization, tends mostly to withdraw—the autism of which

I have spoken. Hence, she does not fight back. Indeed, the anger she ought to be directing at her husband she directs at herself in various acts of self-flagellation. At times, she almost appears to be trying to conform to, and so confirm, her husband's loathing opinion of her.

The most obvious form of self-flagellation is the wife's daily self-mutilation on the Jerusalem thorn. The thorns, of course, must be understood as phallic: the organ epitomizing male domination is here transposed into something sharp that invites masochistic self-debasement. But throughout the story Onetti insists on the impotence that may beset the male. In the case of the thorn hedge, he has it go soft at the end so that, when the wife runs to it to tear her flesh again, she finds that "las espinas no tenían ya fuerza para herir y goteaban, apenas, leche, un agua viscosa y lenta, blancuzca, perezosa."

As for the three workmen—or "poceros"—they seem to represent three aspects of the male, and specifically of the woman's husband, from which she is alienated. In this context, her dealings with each constitute an enlightening parody of the main relationship in the story. The old man, in his complexity, raises more problems than we can deal with here, but at least we must point out that he offers the wife Christian fellowship at one point, a spiritual gift of the sort she could never expect from her husband. The giant well-digger appeals to her because his very size and huge muscularity are phallic, and she will devour him in the sort of raw sexual act the husband cravenly expects of her (she is especially aroused at the sight of the giant standing in a hole he is digging in the garden). He also appeals to her because of the emblematic piece of grass he characteristically chews upon or tucks over his ear. His attack of impotence at the crucial moment seems to epitomize a male failing which, in the husband, takes place on the psychological level. Specifically, we are dealing with the male's sense of powerlessness before the female's emasculating glance. Here she is the symbol of alterity for the male. In the case of the wife's sado-masochistic games with the younger well-digger, she is simply inverting her husband's treatment of her and, at the same time, reducing the love relationship to a brutal game of master and slave.

On a yet deeper level we come upon one of the most startling aspects of **"Tan triste"**: the true enforcers of the reign of the phallus and the consequent assassins turning against the wife are the women lurking in the background of the story. If I have correctly interpreted the underlying symbolism of the story, the efforts of the wife's mother to get the easy-going father to cut the grass must be seen as an effort on her part to impede her daughter's evolution toward individual identity. The husband's destruction of the garden, then, is but a pale copy of an idea coming from the female side. With respect to her marriage, her having begot a male rather than a female child not only suggests her willfulness and contrariness but, more perfidiously, has created a gap in the female chain of generations. The suggestion of an inter-generational chain of hatred on the female side is confirmed, finally, by the gun the woman kills herself with: it belonged to her husband's mother and grandmother (hence, its feminine mother-of-pearl decoration); it expressly would not fire for the husband, so that he presumably could not have used it directly on his wife; it does fire for her when she uses it on herself. Paradoxically, then, it is the female line that supports the reign of the phallus in the story, the abject subservience and depersonalization of woman, and even intervenes when the male stumbles in his role or loses his power. One notes the female recourse to technological substitutes for male muscle: the lawn mower, the gun. This perverse role of the female element in the story is perhaps the most sinister of its underlying horrors.

This final closing in upon the woman from every side leads us to the heart of the logic of signification in the story. The husband, as Onetti portrays him, cannot embody the avenging force that overcomes the wife because of a fundamental impotence. He therefore must leave all to chance: "el hombre solo creía en la desgracia en la fortuna, en la buena o en la mala suerte, en todo lo triste y alegre que puede caernos encima, lo merezcamos o no." It is on this point that the woman's superiority over the man shines through: "Ella creía saber algo más; pensaba en el destino, en errores y misterios, aceptaba la culpa y—al final—terminó admitiendo que vivir es culpa suficiente para que aceptemos el pago, recompensa o castigo." Awakening into consciousness, from her viewpoint, is awakening to guilt. And the woman's crime has at last been named: *vivir*.

The fetish-object has come to life. As a full person, the wife becomes the Other in her husband's world: the daunting presence of alterity, that living and judging glance that emasculates him, reduces him to impotence. This consuming, if unintended, aggression against him on the ontological level is so painful that he must displace it to the more manageable (and banal) level of sexual infidelity. We have seen how unconvinced the wife is by this stratagem, how ineffectual it turns out to be. The true dilemma lies elsewhere: in the presence of a consciousness behind the glance across the breakfast table. In spite of herself, the wife has driven her husband to wish this witness she is for him were dead. In this respect the entire story may be seen as the husband's wish-fulfillment, the hoped-for death being motivated by his perception of her living individuality as an assault against him. He leaves it to her (and the female line, as it turns out) to carry this wish out.

In **"Tan triste,"** we have found ourselves confronted by a particularly apt example of what Jonathan Culler perceives as the conflict between the logic of the structure of events and the logic of the structure of meaning. Culler quotes Peter Brook's statement that the relationship between fable (an ordering of events conceivable outside a particular telling) and its narrative forms is one of "suspicion and conjecture, a structure of undecidability." Culler adds: "This undecidability is the effect of the convergence of two narrative logics that do not give rise to a synthesis." In the present analysis of **"Tan triste,"** I have endeavored to show these two lines of logic by considering separately the fragmented story (or plot of events) and the psychological forces at work underneath as displaced to the spatial elements.

The fragmentation underscores the undecidability of the basic fable as construed through the narrative form (illustrated by my comparison of **"Tan triste"** with the motif of the Eaten Heart). Onetti seems to have stressed purposely the mystery story effect that the fragmentation procedure produces. Somewhat like Robbe-Grillet, he strews details along the path which virtually beg for analysis. Against the anonymity of the primary couple in the story, for example, we have the strange fact that their "rivals" have names beginning with "m": Mendel and Másam (to say nothing of Montero, a secondary character, or the mysterious "M. C." of the story's dedication). *Másam* invites all sorts of conjectural interpretations. There is also the fanciful association of *pOcerOs/pEcerAs* to intrigue us. Finally, the Argentine term for Jerusalem thorn—"cinacina"—is a reduplication that suggests the mirroring of the husband's and wife's mournful situation in the other's, reinforced by the comparison contained in the story's title and illustrating a phenomenon Ludmer has masterfully examined in *Vida breve*.

Yet, as demonstrated, the story nonetheless yields a signification and does so, first of all, through the same process at work in Poe's "Purloined Letter" and Borges' "La muerte y la brújula." In this respect, it is pertinent to show how many techniques Onetti might be seen to have borrowed from Faulkner. James Irby has seen significant traces of the Mississippian in his fiction: the intersection of different narrative planes, the use of an indirect narrator, the emphasis on gestures and signs, a static and obsessive conception of character, and, particularly, the fragmentation of the story so that it is seen from many different angles [Irby, *La influencia de William Faulkner en cuatro narradores hispanoamericanos,* thesis, 1956]. Like Faulkner, Onetti rejects the typical narrative sequence. The progression of the story often appears arbitrary, although the Uruguayan author shares the North American's view that fate is sealed before the story begins. But Onetti is more like Robbe-Grillet, in subjecting this random presentation to a masked, though calculated, intellectual order that the reader is invited to unravel. In this respect, he seems to anticipate the elegantly designed labyrinth of Julio Cortázar's *Rayuela*. At all events, the fragmentation technique appears to be a widely representative feature of twentieth-century writing.

As for what the signification of the story is, I have shown that the very process of degrading its episodes and facts to inconclusive enigmas causes the signification to be displaced elsewhere: in the case of **"Tan triste,"** to the spatial aspect. My analysis has shown the extraordinary results that can emerge from a strategy that Onetti has used repeatedly in his fiction, although nowhere more masterfully than in *Vida breve* in which a spatialization of Brausen's conflict gradually fills the whole novel.

Even through a shorter and perhaps lesser work like **"Tan triste como ella,"** Onetti manages to be broadly representative of what is characteristic of twentieth-century fiction. I have stressed the narrative, the structural, and the psychological aspects of this question. I might have stressed other aspects as well, particularly the spiritual, so apparent in the wife's prayers to the Virgin or the husband's irrational and obsessive search for salvation through young girls. It is in this framework that we must perceive the many pained relationships seen in Onetti's longer and better-known works that are mirrored in **"Tan triste como ella,"** since the doomed love relation between man and woman stands at the thematic center of his work. The man suffers from failure and impotence, the woman from being the scapegoat for what Onetti is fond of characterizing as *fracaso*. Few writers have succeeded as well as Onetti in displaying, in a profoundly unified and coherent picture, the sexual, psychological, and spiritual aspects of this confrontation. Onetti has succeeded in communicating so rich and complex a theme by his skillful use of what we have seen as a typical technique of fragmentation, causing traditional story elements to atrophy, while displacing the more profound impact of the story to the spatial dimension.

> Onetti's is a literature of subjectivity, about how we perceive and interpret, as we are perceived and interpreted by others. Through words we are capable of transforming others and being transformed by them, as so many fragments of perceptions and interpretations coalesce in order to create any given version of reality.
>
> —*Mary-Lee Sullivan, "Projection as a Narrative Technique in Juan Carlos Onetti's* Goodbyes," *Studies in Short Fiction, Summer, 1994.*

Mark Millington (essay date 1987)

SOURCE: "No Woman's Land: The Representation of Woman in Onetti," in *MLN,* Vol. 102, No. 2, March, 1987, pp. 358-77.

[*Millington is the author of* Reading Onetti: Language, Narrative, and the Subject *(1985). In the following excerpt, he examines the characterization and function of women in Onetti's fiction.*]

In Onetti we read a narrative of male subjectivity. It is a narrative founded on male characters' heterogeneity, incompleteness and difficulties. In a crucial sense, women characters barely exist—their containment within the categories of a male discourse is what constitutes them as well as what denies them. They have no independence of the male problematic, so that even the privileged, marginal women are to be understood as marginal to the male centre. The male value system maps the entire terrain of the narrative, his are the only coordinates. Hence women characters are given no intrinsic interest by the narrative.

But women are not therefore irrelevant, indeed they are an essential element in the structure of male experience in Onetti. The importance of women is that they are precisely different, and their difference defines and supports male identity and therefore also male power. A woman's location may be privileged within the discourse as that of an unorthodox outsider, or it may be derided as that of a futile conformist, but in neither case has the location any intrinsic interest for the male characters—there is no wish to occupy the woman's place. On the contrary, the woman is a marker, a token of what is happening to a male character. Hence, when the women characters are conformists they must be abandoned, when they are outsiders they can facilitate escape. Their meaning is thus defined by male movement in relation to them. And there is no reciprocity: women characters are functions, they help to articulate a male signifying system. As a result it is inevitable that women very rarely have their own concerns or problems in Onetti. Women never initiate action in Onetti's fiction with a view to changing their situations, but they frequently stimulate male characters to move, and it is that movement which creates the narrative dynamic of the fiction.

The characterization of women in Onetti is therefore essentialistic. Women occupy static positions and, with very rare exceptions, they are identified with functions. Hence their identities are homogeneous and largely stable, and that contrasts very markedly with male identity, which is conflictive, heterogeneous and problematic. This contrast in characterization between male and female is posited on underlying polarization: homogeneous/heterogeneous, passive/active and unconscious/conscious. Women are passive, with little or no awareness, and if they are aware of their difficulties they tend to take refuge from them in the past without considering undertaking any innovatory action. Their absence of consciousness is part of their basic characterization. Male characters, by contrast, can be active, and the important ones generally are. Their activity is founded on desire, and their desire is the propelling force of Onetti's narratives. Their desire is in turn founded on lack, on the incompleteness of the self and an awareness of this. Their activity is inextricably related to consciousness.

Women characters serve to help men to articulate their desire, and this takes two forms: negative and positive. In the negative form, the women characters help to define what it is men wish to reject—they are perceived as representing all that constricts men and creates their incompleteness. These are the non-privileged women in Onetti. In the positive form, the women characters seem to galvanize men into movement. They help to define the desire to alter and supplement the self, and thus stimulate action. This second type of woman character is the privileged sort and is more generally in evidence. These privileged women are outsiders, that is they have unofficial, nonsocial roles: they are not mothers, wives or daughters. The vital question to ask about them is: "What do men want of these women?" And the answer is that men have a desire not *for* them but *via* them. These privileged women assist in the formulation of male desire for a renewed self—they are not objects of desire in themselves, they are not the "truth of man." These women may suggest the possible attainment of an other self, an imaginary fulfilment, and so they are vehicles of male desire rather than its object.

Hence women characters are crucial signifiers in male discourse, but these are women as constituted by the male. In a very real sense women are outside these representations of them: the representations do not "mirror" or "reflect" a reality so much as help construct a certain sort of reality. The woman's status as a signifier in male discourse is clear from this key fact: there seems to be no need for emotional reciprocity in the relationships with women, there is no stress on love. The nature of relationships between men and the privileged women are not examined under a shared focus: what happens to the male is the crucial thing.

This stress on the male response to a relationship is linked to Onetti's reticence about sex. Sexual relationships are frequently implied in the narratives but there is a perennial silence about them. The narratives elide reference to sex, indeed there is little mention even of physical contact. This is the counterpart of the narratives' centering on the male, on his mind, emotions and needs. All that happens matters to him and that is the angle of representation in the narratives. This stress on the male perspective gives concrete sense to the notion that his desire is *via* the woman and for a (new) self. This male desire is essentially narcissistic. The male self matters, and the male seeks a new self-reflection through contact with certain women privileged by the male value system. The self-reflection sought is imaginary and ideal, and (not surprisingly) is never attained.

Onetti's is a discourse centred on and conterminous with a male problematic. The mastery and writing of the woman means that she has no independent concerns: male subjectivity and its ramifications not only dominate but are totally exclusive. Within this male discourse woman is different: she is positioned and given identity in relation to man, and this identity is more constricting than identity normally is. So woman has a certain significance for the male in terms of her position and her gender: her position helps to define and articulate male situations and movement; and her gender is significant in that she is other— to be a woman is to be outside the male domain, and therefore there can be no wish to occupy those positions she is represented as occupying. Her gender appears to make no other independent or intrinsic contribution—it is not male, it is other.

It might be possible to argue that within these male narratives women characters are little more than actants. That is, the female characters have little in excess of their attributes as functions. It is as if their functionality accounted for more or less the whole of their construction. There is certainly hardly ever any sign of that crucial heterogeneity of identity which is so frequent in the male characters and which renders them of interest as characters. All that is female in Onetti's narratives is more or less contained within the solid homogeneity of four roles, or four actantial functions: the wife, the prostitute, the girl and

the mad woman. Hence female characters figure for their *use* value—their use value for male characters. When the use is completed the female character can be dismissed, murdered or simply forgotten.

Rita in *Para una tumba sin nombre* (1959) is a prime example of female functionality. She is narrated by Godoy, Jorge (three times) and Tito, that is she figures in five distinct, male versions of a supposedly identical story. The point is that she has no existence independent of these narratives and they only coincide in a few details (her telling a story for money in a railway station accompanied by a goat). In fact the name "Rita" is a kind of hook on which different male characters (in Jorge's case three different stages of himself) can hang their own ideas. Their different ideologies totally reformulate the nature of "Rita", to such an extent that "Rita" can hardly be said to exist— there is no possible referent on which all these narratives could coincide. In other words, "Rita" is a signifier with shifting and contradictory signifieds according to the context in which it occurs. Hence even the grave which initially seemed to contain her body may contain that of another person or even nothing at all: it is a tomb without a name just as "Rita" is a woman without an identity. Essentially each male narrative tells us about its teller but not about its ostensible subject: "Rita" and the goat.

Tito, for example, is associated explicitly and forcefully with the orthodox values of Santa María. This is clear from his physical shape—he is emulating the obesity of his father, taking on the form of patriarchy—, and also from the fact that he is studying law, an obvious identification in Onetti's discourse with the status quo. Hence the sort of narrative that Tito tells about "Rita" attempts to marginalize her and bolster his own position. Tito casts "Rita" as a prostitute because this is illegal and thus allows him to avoid making any more profound sense of her. So her telling of stories in the railway station in order to deceive unsuspecting travellers into giving her money is seen by Tito as simply lying and worthy only of disdain. In telling his story, Tito implicitly reinforces his own ideological position within the traditional order of Santa María.

By contrast, Jorge tells a different sort of story about "Rita." In his first version, Jorge is attempting to perpetuate his own position as a rebel, as someone outside the order of Santa María, and "Rita" is used as part of that personal iconoclasm. For Jorge in this vein, "Rita" represents a bridge out of the legal world, out of the traditional values of his parents, and she is therefore invested with decisive value. Her telling of stories, far from being disdained, is seen as creative and part of the enterprise of disrupting, even of destroying, the constrictions of Santa María. In his second and third versions of the narrative, when Jorge is moving more and more towards the values of Santa María, he modifies his viewpoint on "Rita" and in doing so he domesticates and ultimately eliminates all that was previously seen as positive and rebellious about "Rita's" position. The point is not that his version of events finally coincides with that of Tito, but that his identity gradually changes and that, as a result, he attempts to eliminate the impression of himself created by his previous narratives.

"Rita" is therefore a function of male narratives in **Para una tumba sin nombre,** she is a polyvalent device. She is only what male characters make her, and any independent identity is not even an issue. The different ideologies tell us nothing about her—they obscure whatever truth might be supposed to attach to her. In this way, the male narratives are not so much miss-apprehensions as miss-appropriations, since they take her over. In the multiplicity and contradictions of the versions "Rita" disappears, and that invisibility is not untypical of female characters in Onetti.

"Rita" is a clear case of invisibility brought about by the multiplicity of uses to which she is put. Most female characters in Onetti are given one stable function, without that leading to anything like a high degree of visibility as we can see by looking at the four major functions in turn.

THE WIFE

The first function that I am going to consider is that of the wife. It must be stressed that there are fairly few wives in Onetti (for example, Cecilia in **El pozo** [1939], Beatriz in *Para esta noche* [1943], Gertrudis in *La vida breve* [1950], and señora Gálvez in *El astillero* [1961]), but their roles have similar implication in each of the narratives in which they appear. The existence of a wife is never associated with a family—Onetti's narratives do not include a familial dimension, so that what children there are appear independently for their connotative link with youth. . . . [The] overriding characteristic of the function of wives in Onetti is to create a sense of frustration and futility in male characters. Marriage stultifies and frustrates, it is a trap from which those male protagonists who are married try to escape. . . . The repetition, the growing old, the sense of a comfortable opting out of life, are all characteristic of the married protagonists, and are the immediate cause of the desire to move and to supplement the self for the loss suffered. This desire is always focused through the male consciousness, and the dismissal of the marriage and the constricting wife create the male superiority: his is the awareness, his the revulsion, and his the desire to act.

Indeed the male's urge to act is generally what inaugurates narrative in Onetti—it creates the breach which the narrative action will try to fill in, or repair. Failure to break out of the constrictions caused by an unproductive marriage leads to total defeat and the destruction of the individual, as shown by the case of Morasán in *Para esta noche*. To get out of marriage, out of the trap created by the ossified relationship with a wife, is to create some hope, some possibility of renewal. This hope of renewal in overcoming the obstruction of a wife is given particular force since it is precisely the negation of an official bond sanctioned by social norm. And it is crucial to note that Onetti's male protagonists achieve whatever it is they do achieve outside of marriage, and, more generally, outside of official, legal constraints. In Onetti, to abandon marriage is a positive value, an opening, and it is important to note that, as a result, no Onetti narrative finds its cul-

mination and closure in marriage. To that extent, Onetti is operating against cultural norms, where marriage is generally figured as a point of balance and fulfilment, even though his treatment of women generally displays much of the ideology of his cultural environment. In Onetti's discourse, marriage is inscribed as unequivocally negative, and the greater reality is always outside, in that vague, unofficial terrain his narratives seek to occupy. His discourse valorizes unofficial, even illegal bonds as alternatives to the bondage of the officially sanctioned bonds. And this is partly because relationships with women in Onetti are never viewed or experienced as permanent or even potentially so: they are means to a male end.

THE PROSTITUTE

This final point is also decisively true of the next female function in Onetti, that of the prostitute, where impermanence and male advantage are key defining features. The prostitute seems to represent the immediate and obvious alternative to marriage in Onetti. The prostitute is used in the search for something different from the restrictions of marriage and represents something like its reverse side. But this obvious alternative presents something of a paradox in that the prostitute is the official alternative, as Jane Gallop trenchantly puts it [in *Feminism and Psychoanalysis*, 1982]: "Prostitution for money has a place in the phallocentric sexual economy . . ." The point is that this otherness of the prostitute is an important part of the dominant order from which the male protagonists in Onetti seem to be trying to escape. Prostitution is a more or less sanctioned unorthodoxy and therefore has a somewhat equivocal status within the efforts of the protagonists to redefine themselves.

There are two features of the relationships with prostitutes which need to be pinpointed. Firstly, the relationship with them is essentially short; in no sense is the alternative to marriage seen as a potentially permanent liaison—the prostitute might help the protagonist at a particular moment, without there being anything to bind the two together for more than this functional effect. Secondly, the relationship with prostitutes is sometimes associated with fantasies of wishfulfilment, and this helps to locate the real significance of these relationships, since the alternative with the prostitute is frequently no more than a frustrated striving for an imaginary alternative which never materializes in any sustained way. In this respect the sanctioned nature of the unorthodoxy clearly also contributes to the failure to achieve some kind of comprehensive reorganization of experience.

The temporary nature of these relationships and their fantasy elements are both manifest in **El pozo** with Linacero and the prostitute Ester. The meeting between Linacero and Ester occurs in the period after he has left his wife and is leading a sort of marginal existence. It is important that for Linacero the liaison does not simply represent the possibility of sexual intercourse but also that of telling a story, which contains one of his recurrent fantasies about himself as an heroic adventurer, that is as an idealized, fulfilled being. Indeed, the intercourse and the story are closely connected in their significance, since he refuses to pay Ester for her services with money, preferring instead to pay her with the fantasy. The relationship with this alternative woman and the attempt to share his fantasy with her are part of a combined project to achieve self-fulfilment by breaking out of his past. But Ester cannot understand his story since the fantasy is essentially private—it cannot be shared. . . .

The Girl

The third function amongst the female characters is that of the girl. The girl is in early adolescence and seems always to possess certain crucial characteristics. Those characteristics can be defined in terms of certain major polarities: orthodox/unorthodox, legal/illegal, insider/outsider, and the girls are always privileged by association with the second term of these polarities. They are the focus of difference as gauged by the dominant values of the male characters. Their difference is centred on the fact that they are perceived as not having subscribed to the orthodoxies of the adult world, in that sense they are outsiders, they have not accepted adult (and, by implication, bourgeois) standards. There are one or two examples of girls who do come to subscribe to these despised standards (Nora in *Tierra de nadie* and Cecilia in *El pozo*), but these figures are simply dismissed from male interest once their symbolic value as outsider has ceased to exist.

More generally, girls act as markers for the adult male, as markers of what the male has lost, the price that has been paid by being an orthodox adult. The male desire which adopts the girls is a sign of this lack, of what has been lost. There is then an idealistic regression in the wish to possess the girl, in the desire to possess what is now seen to have been important in adolescence. And this idea of (re)possession is usually associated with sexual possession of the girl. . . .

In *Los adioses* (1954) one discovers a . . . sort of symbolic function in the girl associated with the basketball player. If one reads the novel ignoring the interpretative difficulty created by the narrator's equivocal position, then it is clear that there is a polarization between the girl and the woman, who is also associated with the basketball player. This polarization has meaning only in terms of the basketball player's life and his personal struggle with a premature death. With the woman, and adult, the man is a conformist; with the girl, an adolescent, the man refuses to play the game of the other adults. The narrator makes the girl's position as outsider absolutely clear:

> . . . no necesité mirarla para ver su cara, para convencerme de que la cara iba a estar, hasta la muerte en días luminosos y poblados, en noches semejantes a la que atravesábamos, enfrentando la segura, fatua, ilusiva aproximación de los hombres . . . la cara había sido hecha para enfrentar lo que los hombres representaban y distinguían . . .

Her symbolic status as other to men could hardly be more clearly formulated: she acts as a stimulus to the basketball player in his struggle against death, against the acceptance of the compromise which the other adults around him have all accepted—this is the sense of his relationship with the girl. His final commitment to the girl is consistent with his prior behaviour, but has all the idealistic and problematic overtones of Ossorio's commitment to Victoria since it is likewise made at the moment of dying.

It is clear from the cases of Victoria [in *Para esta noche*] and the girl in *Los adioses* that the girls acquiesce with male need. They play a willing, or at least passive, part in the attempt to alleviate the male problem. However, the reality of achieving fulfilment via the girl is far from clear—in both *Para esta noche* and *Los adioses* death curtails the life of the male protagonists leaving their affirmative commitment to the girls and what they represent in a somewhat problematic impasse. . . . [In relationships between an adult male and an adolescent girl in Onetti] the girl appears to be a vehicle, a means to an end. The girls may prompt a self-examination, or coincide with a pre-existent desire to return to an idealized past self, but the crucial factor is the difficulty for the male in achieving any lasting contact with the idea of a more real self. There is a strong element of regressive fantasy in this experience which is persistent but frustrated in different ways.

Perhaps the clearest example of the regressive fantasy focused on a girl is that of Linacero in *El pozo*. This novel is particularly revealing of the male desire for an other self and of the position of the girl as different from man in both gender and position. The relationship of Linacero with Ana María hinges on two encounters. The first encounter occurs in reality during Linacero's adolescence. It is New Year's Eve and Linacero leaves the adult world of dull celebrations and goes out into the garden. He meets Ana María and tricks her into entering the gardener's hut. He takes great pleasure in fooling her, and when inside tries to humiliate her more by pushing her to the floor in a kind of physical assault which he claims is not sexual. After the two emerge from the hut, Ana María shows her disdain for Linacero by spitting in his face and then running off. This act is a decisive judgment on Linacero and it also creates a sort of identity for him, precisely as inferior to Ana María—she has assumed the dominant position. It is as if by spitting at him she had assumed the male role (the spitting may be seen as a displaced ejaculation) and this disturbs Linacero: where his own actions towards Ana María had no sexual climax (or content, he claims), her actions towards him are quite the opposite.

This real encounter, with its unsatisfactory outcome for Linacero, leads him to construct another encounter, a fantasy, in later life in order to compensate. The second encounter seems to have a dual function. On the other hand, it is created to restore his position vis á vis Ana María, to reestablish her difference and inferiority; and on the other hand, it provides a means for creating a whole image of the self (a full identity) after the frustrations and repressions of marriage. This second encounter is explicitly sexual. Ana María comes to Linacero in the fantasy naked and he is clearly not threatened by her sexually:

... me siento en el borde de la cama y clavo los ojos
en el triángulo negro [de Ana María] ...

Miro el vientre de Ana María ... apenas redondeado
... A veces, siempre inmóvil, sin un gesto, creo ver
la pequeña ranura del sexo.

Ana María is decisively repositioned here in Linacero's
fantasy as the female: her belly is rounded, in other words
she has no penis. And this reinstatement restores Linacero
by implication to the role of power and security which he
lost in adolescence. That reinstatement also coincides with
the second aspect of Ana María's function, which is to
help mobilize an image of Linacero: the fantasy also contains an image of Linacero as an "adventurer", as a fulfilled, active self, which serves to supplement the less
than fulfilling experience of his marriage. Ana María is
therefore, like Victoria and the girl in *Los adioses,* a symbol of lost adolescent integrity. Hence the two encounters
together reveal the two basic motifs of the relationship
between adult males and adolescent girls in Onetti: in part,
the girl is an image or a reminder of what the male has
lost, and what he wishes to regain; and in part, the girl is
simply a vehicle, an other, who stands apart from the
orthodoxy which the males inhabit—her gender and her
position are different and inferior, and can be mobilized
within male thinking to define the male situation.

The Mad Woman

The fourth function of the female characters in Onetti is
that of the mad woman. This function is the least definite
and the least numerous of the four, but nonetheless it does
have some consistency. Madness is almost exclusively
associated with female characters in Onetti. Its major
examples are Beatriz in *Para esta noche,* Angélica Inés in
El astillero, Julita in *Juntacadáveres* and Moncha Insur-
ralde in **"La novia robada"** (1968). The only male character who is mad is Petrus in *El astillero,* and the reasons
for his madness seem to be roughly similar to those of the
female characters.

The common ground of all the mad characters is a resistance to, or a refusal of the shared reality of the sane
characters. Madness is a refusal to compromise, a refusal
to repress the truth. As a result of this refusal, the mad
characters inhabit private worlds in which they manage to
preserve something like an integral self. By refusing the
social game, they cling on to a certain sort of identity,
with childlike connotations, although this necessarily mar-
ginalizes them. The proximity to the meaning of the adolescent girl is apparent in this. The crucial point is that
their refusal is a withdrawal from the world, and is therefore passive. The male characters in Onetti who try to
resist the world do so in an active way, however fruitless
it proves to be. But the mad women are contemplative and
withdrawn, and so function as complementary figures to
the male protagonists—there are important shared motives,
but contrasted responses. . . .

[In **"Tan triste como ella"**] the female character is given
the function of wife, and her husband seems to react to

her as male characters in Onetti do react to wives: he
discovers that she has grown old and he loses interest in
her. But the familiarity of this state of affairs is registered
from an unusual angle, since it is the woman who is the
main focalized character. The estrangement that affects
their relationship is shown by concentrating on her, and
the story shows her collapse under the neglect of her
husband. Here for once an Onetti story shows the response
of a woman to one of the basic problems with which his
stories and novels deal. But in essence the position of the
woman in **"Tan triste como ella"** is analogous to that of
Julita [in *Juntacadáveres*]. She can find no satisfactory
alternative to married life (her extramarital sexual activities are unsuccessful) while the husband is active in his
professional and sexual life outside the home. In addition,
the woman here finds no temporary outlet in madness as
does Julita, but ultimately looks for a way out of the situation in suicide—that is the only real alternative to an
intolerable situation which Onetti's discourse seems to
allow a female character. So there is inscribed here the
same structure of relations and power as in Onetti's other
works, and that is also made manifest in the very title of
the story which actually refers to the husband rather than
to the woman who is apparently the focus of the story!

Onetti's fictional discourse is fundamentally posited on
the dominance of male characters. The male situation is
that of a post-Oedipal self-consciousness, when the knowledge of a prior acceptance of the dominant, patriarchal
order is formulated. The male characters struggle continually with their status as adults within the symbolic order,
and their struggles with that order frequently lead to projections of escape and fulfilment which are imaginary and
fleeting. The women characters figure within the male
struggle to achieve and perpetuate some solution to or
denial of the frustrations which they become acutely aware
of.

In fact, I would suggest that the roles of women characters
can be seen as part of the problem with which the male
characters are dealing. Their roles and positioning are a
mark of a crucial blind spot in Onetti's thinking. This is
a specific ideological foreclosure: the representation of
woman in Onetti's narratives constitutes a revealing contradiction. Male discourse and action marginalize woman
and fix her in a position very similar to that which the
male himself is attempting to resolve. The roles and positioning of women characters reiterate (as far as the discourse is concerned, in an entirely unproblematical way)
the very oppression which the male wishes to alleviate for
himself. The implicit, patriarchal power structure is not
overturned but is actually reinscribed in the representation
of women. And this ideological blindness, this contradiction, is never resolved. The unthinkable seems to be that
the experience of the male and the female could have
similarities, or that female subjection (as represented in
Onetti's narratives themselves) could be a more pressing
issue than male subjection. And this underlines the absence of any collective consciousness in Onetti, the heavy
concentration on isolated male subjectivity. The investigation of male subjectivity is in itself interesting enough,
but it produces this internal contradiction whereby the key

problem is simply displaced on to the woman and so perpetuated within male thinking. The subjection of woman within Onetti's representations is one sign of the absence of an explicit social or political dimension in the writing. Without confronting the possible social and political *causes* of the basic male dilemma, the texts of Onetti get locked into and return again and again to the same difficulties of how to cope with that dilemma. Hence the texts frequently repeat the same basic moves, and narrative dynamism becomes extremely attenuated since all seems to have been decided in advance. There is, within Onetti, a certain regime of repetition, which is a sign of the nature of the limits in his discourse.

This paradoxical subjection of women characters is one of the major impasses of Onetti's thinking. One might speculate that not until the hierarchy is reversed and woman is put into the superior position, that is, not until the specifically invisible problem of woman within Onetti's discourse is pushed into the foreground, will any progress be made beyond the repetition of the same male difficulties. For what alleviation of, or even liberation from their problems, can the male characters hope for if their acts and thinking are dependent on the subjection of women? The answer is that it could only be a male and highly partial alleviation or liberation, which had not broken with the basic structures that created the male dilemma in the first place. In this respect, we come up against one of the ideological closures in Onetti. My point is that the way Onetti represents woman (that is, creates a configuration of elements called "woman") is highly paradoxical, since it so places woman as to make man alone have meaning. And my purpose in emphasizing this point is to open the texts of Onetti on to the historical moment of his writing, to denaturalize this repeated treatment of women characters. It seems to me that to make the representation of women visible, to call attention to it, goes hand in hand with the need to see that Onetti is writing from within a particular, male dominated society and is conditioned by that. If his representation of women is not problematized it too easily takes on a natural, invisible status—it becomes an abstract, deracinated, neutral and imperceptible "fact". The ultimate rationale of this article is to see the productivity of Onetti's representation (it is a produced, cultural phenomenon) and to understand it as part of an historical process.

[Onetti's] characters are low-life brothel-haunters, drunks, frustrated artists, mediocre provincials. They are uprooted men with names like Larsen and Brausen, dreaming of distant places like Norway, and often haunted by faded youth and promise.

—*Jason Wilson, "River Plate Emptiness,"* in The Times Literary Supplement, *July 26, 1991.*

Eugene A. Maio (essay date 1989)

SOURCE: "Onetti's *Los adioses*: A Cubist Reconstruction of Reality," in *Studies in Short Fiction,* Vol. XXVI, No. 2, Spring, 1989, pp. 173-81.

[*In the following excerpt, Maio maintains that the challenges that* Los adioses *poses to readers are similar to those that a cubist work of art presents to viewers.*]

A careful reading of Juan Carlos Onetti's **Los adioses** (1954) reveals unmistakable affinities between the aesthetic goals and structures of cubism and the narrative structure of his fiction. The bond that unites Onetti's prose to modern painting is not based on a narrative prose style that constructs visual images through intricate word patterns. Rather, Onetti's narrative style, the way in which he tells a story, indicates a structure and a process that have much in common not only with cubism but also with the aesthetics of contemporary art in general. . . .

[In *Rococo to Cubism in Art and Literature,* 1960] Wylie Sypher writes that "technically cubism is a breakdown of three-dimensional space constructed from a fixed point of view: things exist in multiple relations to each other and change their appearance according to the point of view from which we see them." First worked out in painting, the reverberations of cubism were felt directly in sculpture and architecture, and indirectly in literature and music. Sypher writes that "cubism is an attempt to *conceive* the world in new ways, just as renaissance art was an attempt to conceive the world in new ways." Cubism is primarily an intellectual approach. The cubist painter breaks open the volumes of things by spreading objects upon shifting interrelated planes and therefore presents several faces of things simultaneously. The cubist discovers that an object—guitar, violin, sheet music—is a multiple reality that can be defined only by multiple images. It is for these reasons that Sypher concludes that "cubism is an art that expresses the condition of modern man who has been forced to live in a world where there are, as Whitehead put it, no longer any simple locations, where all relations are plural."

Cubism is a visual statement that art and life intersect, and the cubist underscores this conviction by the use of certain technical devices. As Sypher indicates, one is *collage,* the assimilation of fragments of reality—cord, cloth, newsprint—into the pictorial world. A second is *passage,* a breaking of contours "so that a form merges with the space about it or with other forms; planes or tones bleed into other planes and tones; outlines that coincide with other outlines, then suddenly reappear in new relations." A third is *montage,* in which two or more pictures or images are seen together in a compound image. "Based not on sequence but on counterpoint," says Sypher, "*montage* compels us to see things in multiple perspective, telescoping time and fixing representation in a spliced image like the flattened cubist perspective."

Certain formal structures in **Los adioses** closely parallel these techniques of the cubist reconstruction of reality. To begin with, Onetti does not comply with the traditional demand in fiction for an omniscient narrator who tells a story in a rationally ordered space-time system. Onetti entrusts his narration to a reporter who is neither omniscient nor reliable. The reporter, isolated behind the bar that creates his own secure alienation, cannot be an eyewitness of what the ex-basketball player says and does. Yet the reporter fills in the unknown with details created by his imagination, and therefore he reconstructs the protagonist's character out of his own fantasy. The reporter is assisted in the narration by a male nurse and a hotel maid who also embellish facts with imagination so that the history of the athlete/patient is an ambiguous mixture of reality and fantasy created by a trio of unreliable reporters governed not by truth and experience but by prejudice, imagination, hostility, suspicion, self-righteousness, and scorn. In cubist fashion, the "volume" of the protagonist's history is broken open by spreading information "upon shifting interrelated planes"—the voices of the bartender, nurse, and maid.

Near the end of *Los adioses* the narrator admits that his role as a reporter has been vitiated by his determination to force the characters to live the kind of life he determined. He says:

> Salí afuera y me apoyé en la baranda de la galería, temblando de frío, mirando las luces del hotel. Me bastaba anteponer mi reciente descubrimiento al principio de la historia, para que todo se hiciera sencillo y previsible. Me sentía lleno de poder, como si el hombre y la muchacha, y también la mujer y el niño, hubieran nacido de mi voluntad para vivir lo que yo había determinado.

> I went outside and leaned on the balcony railing, shivering in the cold, looking at the hotel lights. It would have been enough for me to put my recent discovery at the beginning of the story so that everything would have been simple and foreseeable. But I felt full of power as though the man and the young woman, as well as the older woman and the boy, had been born of my will to live out what I had determined.

It is now clear that the reported narrative is not a reliable account of what actually happened in the lives of the athlete/patient and the two women, but a reconstruction by a partial eyewitness whose story is part fact, part fantasy, intellectually scrutinized and rearranged to fit the narrator's suspicious, prejudicial, despotic point of view. He deliberately omits essential information about the identity of the two women so that the reader is misled into believing with the villagers that the athlete/patient is involved in a scandalous love affair. Even with the knowledge that the young woman is the basketball player's daughter, the reader is still left with the further ambiguity about whether the daughter's love is filial or incestuous.

Onetti, like Picasso, has shattered the traditional renaissance perspective: single point of view, logical structure, fully rounded characters. Onetti disassembles the narra-

tive point of view into a plurality of unreliable commentators, not witnesses, each of whom is governed by a particular bias. The result is a fragmentation of characters and actions whose reality changes arbitrarily depending upon whose perspective the reader adopts. "One effect of such fragmentation," writes Arthur Terry, "is to dispel the illusion that what we are reading is in some way a transcript of 'real events' and to confirm our sense of a text which is being created in accordance with its own internal laws" ["Onetti and the Meaning of Fiction: Notes on *La muerte y la niña*," in *Contemporary Latin American Fiction,* edited by Salvador Bacarisse, 1980].

In the process of re-constructing the ex-athlete's history, the narrator/creator displaces the reader's attention from narrative facticity and contextuality to the reporter's own emotional responses to the information he discovers and reports. In a veritable cubist *passage* the narration moves simultaneously on two superimposed planes: the plane of what the reader assumes is the story of the tubercular athlete's relations with two women and the plane of the narrator's emotional responses to the characters' actions which fragment and distort the historicity of the characters' lives. The shifting of these superimposed planes of reality and fantasy are responsible in large part for the ambiguity the reader experiences. *Los adioses* is similar to another work of Onetti's, *La muerte y la niña,* which Terry says "both defeats the reader's conventional expectations and confronts him with the possibility that the 'meaning' of the story may lie not so much in a paraphraseable content as in the actual activity he is compelled to pursue in his attempt to 'make sense' of the text."

The reader also discovers the effects of another displacement, this one in the use of time. The narration of what happens to the protagonist runs in a different time frame than the subjective commentary of the reporter. It soon becomes clear that the reader is not a witness to the pathetic disintegration of a once powerful athlete but a credulous victim of a trap skillfully contrived by the reporter/author/creator. The narrator is not reporting the sordid details of a love triangle but foisting upon the reader a life story as he thinks it ought to be and wants it to be. It is a story in which the characters have lost their autonomy, their credibility, their ability to be and to say who they are because their being and their activity are under the imperious control of an unscrupulous reporter who manipulates their lives in order to establish and to vindicate his supposed omniscience. The awareness of this contrived and manipulated sequence of events is confirmed by the almost exclusive use of verbs in the past tense. Such a ploy gives the reporter complete control of the narrative material in contrast to a narrative mode in the present tense, in which the narrator is limited, as is the reader, to watching an action unfold through a series of events whose outcome is still uncertain.

In *Los adioses* we eventually become aware that we are reading a novel about the apparent impossibility of writing a novel. We come to doubt the expertise of a narrator whose lack of integrity and veracity make it almost impossible for him to create a fictional world in which we vicariously experience recognizable human experiences. Instead of insights, we get suspicions; in lieu of understanding, we get ambiguity; in place of fiction, we get gamesmanship.

The narrator has disassembled the information he has gathered as bartender/postmaster/observer and re-assembled these pieces of information into a cubist *collage*. He collects fragments of characters and episodes and juxtaposes them in a frame that destroys their autonomy and identity. For instance, when the narrator first introduces the protagonist in the opening chapter, he actually constructs a *collage* of the athlete/patient composed of a suitcase, raincoat, shoulders, smile, hands, tickets and a glass of beer. These parts and pieces of a person—disembodied fragments—are assembled artfully in one-dimensional space.

To this *collage* of disembodied fragments the narrator adds his gratuitous speculations about the indifference and the apathy of the newly arrived patient. He says, for example, that the ex-athlete entered the general store "saludando sin sonreír porque su sonrisa no iba a ser creída" 'saying hello without smiling because his smile was not going to be believed.' The former basketball star is un-souled, despirited, reduced to mere physical dimensions. This flattening-out technique, a cubist destruction of fully rounded forms and three-dimensional space, is evident in the manner in which the reporter crowds people, events, and objects into a single dimension. Most of the characters are nameless and seem to be no more important than raincoats, beer glasses, taxis, letters, and dried sausages that clutter this *collage*. Characters and things co-exist in one-dimensional space, flattened out in an emotional ambush of hostility, degradation, and sordid alienation.

The treatment of time in **Los adioses** has affinities with the cubist technique of *passage,* the device in which planes and tones merge or bleed into other planes and tones. There are four time-frames in the novel: the remote past, the glory days of the basketball star; the proximate past, the last few weeks of the patient's stay in the sanatorium; the present, the interaction of the reporter with the athlete/patient, the women, the staff at the sanatorium; and the future, the dismal suicide of the athlete/patient. The reader never loses awareness of these four time-frames that are skillfully superimposed one upon another.

This *passage* of time-frames gives the reader the impression that the narrator is omniscient since he can move from one time-frame to another to establish the credibility of his powers of prophecy, introspection, and divination. This credibility is destroyed, however, once the reader realizes that another *passage* is at work, one in which fantasy bleeds into fact. The outline of what really took place and the outline of what the reporter imagined took place merge into one another so that the reader is left with distrust, mystery, and ambiguity. Very little of the narration recounts what actually took place in the life of the protagonist. Most of what the reporter narrates is an embellishment of partially known, partially related events.

The perimeter of the athlete's consciousness and the perimeter of the narrator's consciousness bleed into each other—become often indistinguishable—so that the reader is deceived into accepting what the narrator imagines the athlete/patient thinks and does is actually what the protagonist thinks and does.

An example of the narrator's deceptive narrative style shows the presence of a cubist *passage*. The bartender relates how the protagonist does not wear the hospital attire given to the patients in the sanatorium, but continues to wear his regular clothes—suit, tie and hat. Analyzing this behavior the narrator concludes that the protagonist is "empecinado, manteniendo su aire de soledad . . . defendiéndose con las ropas, el sombrero y los polvorientos zapatos de la aceptación de estar enfermo y separado" 'stubborn in maintaining his attitude of isolation . . . protecting himself with his clothes, his hat, and his dusty shoes from admitting that he is sick and alone.'

The reader is at first inclined to accept the narrator's diagnosis about the protagonist's psychological condition until he reads further and finds out that this diagnosis as well as others he makes about the athlete/patient is totally imagined. On learning from the nurse that the ex-athlete goes into the city to mail his letters, the narrator says, "Yo lo imaginaba, solitario y perezoso, mirando la iglesia como miraba la sierra desde el almacén, sin aceptarles un significado, casi para eliminarlos" 'I imagined him, alone and indolent, looking at the church as he looked at the mountain range from the grocery store without attributing to them any significance, even trying to obliterate them.' What the protagonist feels is not necessarily what the narrator imagines he feels. Once we remind ourselves that the narrator is not only unreliable but also egocentric, it is certainly plausible to conclude that the narrator may be projecting his own feelings of alienation and denial into the heart of the protagonist. What is true is that fact and fantasy have merged. On a deeper level, the subjectivity of the protagonist and that of the narrator have also merged to such an extent as to become at times indistinguishable. Through the process of a cubist *passage* a more encompassing subjectivity fuses the reader, author, narrator, and protagonist into a common, disconcerting awareness of ambiguity and mystery.

It seems fairly evident that Onetti casts doubt on the creative process itself, on the ability of a writer to create autonomous characters with an authentic reality undamaged by a narrator's biased subjectivity. In **Los adioses** the narrator has assumed a despotic role. He has overstepped his secondary role as an objective reporter, and by focusing the reader's attention primarily on his own interior monologues, the narrator becomes the protagonist who manipulates the other fictional characters into a reconstructed history of people and events that must conform to his own needs for omniscience. An ambiguous, shifting perspective that makes it difficult to decide who is the protagonist, or whose story is being narrated—that of the athlete/patient or that of the bartender—is yet another example of the use of *passage*.

The use of multiple narrators in *Los adioses* is a literary parallel to the cubist technique of *montage,* the device in which the artist forces the viewer to look at objects from multiple perspectives simultaneously. For instance, at the mid-point of the novel a triad of narrators is formed. The bartender is joined by the nurse and the maid in recounting the events in the life of the ex-athlete. As the narrator describes this colloquy: "Entonces, aquella misma tarde o semanas después, porque la precisión ya no importa, porque desde aquel momento yo no ví de ellos nada más que sus distintos estilos de fracaso, el enfermero y la mucama, la Reina, empezaron a contarme la historia del epílogo" 'Then, that very afternoon or weeks later, because accuracy is no longer important, because from that moment I saw in them nothing more than their distinct styles of failure, the nurse and the maid, the Queen, began to relate to me the history of the epilogue.'

The protagonist's daily routine is spliced into three frames: what he does at the general store, as observed by the bartender; what he does at the sanatorium, as observed by the nurse; and what he does at the hotel when visited by the two women, as observed by the maid. Each frame has a separate, exclusive witness, no one of which is reliable. The bartender admits as much when he comments: "Un epílogo, pensaba, yo, defendiéndome, un final para la discutible historia, tal como estos dos son capaces de imaginarlo" 'The epilogue, I thought, defending myself, an ending for a controvertible history, such as these two are capable of imagining it.'

The reader is already aware of how much of the bartender's narration is based on imagination. To that is added the imagined history contributed by the nurse and the maid. The resulting portrait of the protagonist is splintered into fact and fiction, left impaired by the ambiguous details offered by three unscrupulous and biased reporters. What Gabriel Josipovici says about the fiction of Alain Robbe-Grillet is equally applicable to Onetti's work: "As with a cubist painting, the reader is forced to move again and again over the material that is presented, trying to force it into a single vision, a final truth, but is always foiled by the resistant artifact" ["'But time will not relent': Modern Literature and the Experience of Time," in *The Modern English Novel,* edited by Gabriel Josipovici, 1976].

In producing this fictional *montage,* each of the narrators excises from its temporal and emotional context certain events in the lives of the protagonist and the two women, re-assembles these events to fit the emotional needs of the narrator, and thus presents to the reader a multiple perspective in which the characters lose their fully rounded autonomy, their individuality, and their integrity. The multiple narrators in *Los adioses* do not present a reliably objective account of the lives of the principal characters. In cubist fashion the perspective is displaced, twisted away from narrative accuracy toward subjective reactions to what these narrators observe. The anticipated focus on what these characters say and do gives way to an exaggerated subjectivity in which the narrator/creator displaces the protagonist as the central figure. Objectivity is further compromised by the substitution of a biased imagination

in place of reliable reporting. The arbitrary enlargement of the fictional history through creative imagination further reduces the fictional world to shadows and tones of diminishing reality.

If cubism, as Sypher argues, "is a study of the very techniques of representation—painting about the methods of painting, a report on the reality of art," then *Los adioses* is a study of the techniques of narration—fiction about the methods of fiction, an inquiry into the reality of narrative fiction. Like a Picasso canvas, Onetti's fiction is not an imitation of nature but an imposition upon nature of forms derived from the mind, a cubist reconstruction—multi-dimensional and ambiguous—that leads the reader into the inevitable feelings of skepticism and discomfort.

George R. McMurray   (essay date 1991)

SOURCE: A review of *Goodbyes and Stories,* in *Hispania,* Vol. LXXIV, No. 2, May, 1991, pp. 335-36.

[*McMurray is an American educator and critic who has published book-length studies of Jorge Luis Borges, Jose Donoso, and Gabriel García Márquez. In the following excerpt, McMurray offers a favorable review of* Goodbyes and Stories.]

Juan Carlos Onetti (1909) is Uruguay's best-known and most admired writer of fiction. Although he owes his reputation primarily to his novels, he is also the creator of some fine short stories. . . . [The translations in *Goodbyes and Stories*] succeed admirably in capturing the monotony and pessimism pervading the Uruguayan's bleak imaginary world. Like other Latin Americans of his generation, Onetti writes in a style replete with problems for the translator. These include a convoluted style reminiscent of Faulkner (a major influence) and an abundance of abstract nouns which, if not translated with care, can cloud meaning and lessen poetic effect. . . .

Onetti's works will likely satisfy only the sophisticated reader accustomed to deciphering ambiguous plots, shadowy characters, and fragmented structures. In one of the stories, **"The House of Sand,"** these elements become so dominant that, at least for this reader, aesthetic expectations remain unfulfilled. But most of the other stories are well worth the effort required to appreciate Onetti's tantalizing description of deceit, disillusionment, and decay.

The three most memorable pieces are **Goodbyes,** **"A Dream Come True,"** and **"The Image of Misfortune."** A tubercular ex-basketball player's last weeks of life supply the underpinnings of **Goodbyes,** in which the themes of impending death and renewed emotional attachments sustain dramatic interest up to the denouement. This tale is typical Onetti fare for its solitary, unnamed protagonist, sketchy relationships, and shifting points of view. In **"A Dream Come True"** a woman, perhaps deranged, pays a theater director to present a plotless play in an empty hall so that she might relive a moment of happiness experienced in a dream. Her demise in the final lines suggests the absurdity of both life and art. The most straightforward story of the collection, **"The Image of Misfortune,"** nevertheless ends on a note of ambiguity. Here the narrator's burden of responsibility for his brother's suicide is made heavier when he makes love to a fifteen-year-old deaf girl and soon thereafter learns that she has been found murdered. Detained by the police the following morning, he states his willingness to sign "whatever you want without even reading it."

Other stories especially worthy of mention are **"The Photograph Album,"** in which a series of pictures embody the essence of a love affair; **"Sad as She,"** an intriguing, fragmented chronicle of a failed marriage resulting from infidelity, aging, and the pressures of everyday living; and **"The Stolen Bride,"** about a mad widow who, like the woman in **"A Dream Come True,"** imposes her dream on reality—in this case her marriage to a dead man—shortly before she dies.

Written between 1941 and 1948, the tales of this volume convey many of the existential themes characteristic of post-World-War-II literature.

FURTHER READING

Criticism

Ainsa, Fernando. "Juan Carlos Onetti: An Existential Allegory of Contemporary Man." *World Literature Today* LXVIII, No. 3 (Summer 1994): 501-04.

> Reflects on Onetti's career, concluding: "Herein lies the true meaning of Onetti's work: to arrive at the crux of the individual's intimate solitude, at the metaphysical sadness of the human condition, through the progressive awareness of the uselessness of most human action and through the stripping away of all the trappings that surround us and create for us false dependencies on our surrounding reality."

Jones, Yvonne Perier. *The Formal Expression of Meaning in Juan Carlos Onetti's Narrative Art.* Cuernavaca, Mexico: Centro Intercultural de Documentacíon, 1971, 150 p.

> Focuses on Onetti's novels but briefly discusses his novellas.

Kadir, Djelal. *Juan Carlos Onetti.* Boston: Twayne Publishers, 1977, 160 p.

> Examines various aspects of Onetti's fiction, including characterization, plot, and narrative. Kadir's study contains discussion of the novellas *El pozo, Para una tumba sin nombre,* and *Los adioses.*

Millington, Mark. *Reading Onetti: Language, Narrative, and the Subject.* Liverpool: Francis Cairns, 1985, 345 p.

> Contains a chapter on each of the following novellas: *El pozo, Los adioses,* and *Para una tumba sin nombre.*

Richards, Katherine C. "Playing God: The Narrator in Onetti's *Los adioses.*" *Studies in Short Fiction* XXVI, No. 2 (Spring 1989): 163-71.

> Examines the authoritative position assumed by the narrator of *Los adioses.* Commenting on the conclusion of the narrator's account, Richards states: "The covert, unintended fictionalizing which we perceive in the earlier chapters has at last become an activity which the Narrator not only acknowledges but exalts."

Sullivan, Mary-Lee. "Projection as a Narrative Technique in Juan Carlos Onetti's *Goodbyes.*" *Studies in Short Fiction* XXXI, No. 3 (Summer 1994): 441-47.

> Comments on the readers' and narrator's projection of their private psychological states on the events that are related in *Goodbyes (Los adioses).* Sullivan observes that the interpretation "to which individual readers subscribe may well depend on their own capacities for projection or their own repertoire of fantasies."

Wood, Michael. "A Faint Sound of Rust." *London Review of Books* XV, No. 20 (21 October 1993): 20-1.

> A review of several works by Onetti, including the novellas *The Pit (El pozo)* and *Farewells (Los adioses),* interspersed with commentary on Onetti's life and literary accomplishment.

Thomas Nelson Page
1853–1922

American short story writer, novelist, essayist, and poet.

INTRODUCTION

Page is widely regarded as the most significant writer of the Southern plantation tradition. In the aftermath of the Civil War, Page penned nostalgic stories of a glamorous and harmonious plantation life, capturing the imagination of both Northern and Southern readers. For a war-worn nation disillusioned by the struggles of Reconstruction, Page popularized the myth of an antebellum South with vast, lush plantations, benevolent masters, happy-go-lucky blacks, beautiful belles, and gallant cavaliers. Part of the local color movement, Page faithfully recorded the minutiae of Southern life with meticulous attention to dress, local customs, setting, and speech. His sentimental stories are remarkable for their skillful use of a black narrator whose dialect, although nearly incomprehensible today, contributed to the charm and authenticity of his stories for his contemporary readers. The most important feature of his writing, however, was his reliance on the code of Southern heroism; in his most memorable and enduring collection of short stories, *In Ole Virginia; or Marse Chan, and Other Stories* (1887), Page created the Southern gentleman hero who exemplifies the virtues of honor, loyalty, military discipline, chivalry, patriotism, and devotion to an idealized lady. Other writers of the Southern plantation tradition, such as John Pendleton Kennedy, William Gilmore Simms, and John Esten Cooke, similarly employed the antebellum South and its code of heroism as a framework for literature, yet Page's oeuvre is recognized as the culmination of this tradition; the end of the gracious and noble social order is depicted by him as a loss to the entire nation. In portraying the vanished culture of the South as a lost Golden Age, his tales are, as one critic wrote, "the epitaph of a civilization."

Biographical Information

Page was born at Oakland Plantation, Hanover County, Virginia, in 1853, to John and Elizabeth Burnwell Nelson Page. The descendant of Thomas Nelson, the founder of Yorktown, Virginia; another Thomas Nelson, governor of Virginia and a signer of the Declaration of Independence; and John Page, a Revolutionary leader, Page was proud of his colonial ancestors, whom he saw as heroic figures embodying the solid virtues of aristocracy. His quiet childhood at Oakland ended with the Civil War, as Hanover County became the site of important battles; several of his stories written for children present the war through the eyes of a Southern boy. Page's father returned from the war to a ruined plantation, and his family, never prosperous, suffered poverty during the Reconstruction period. Page entered Washington College (now Washington and Lee College) in 1869 but left without graduating. He tu-

tored the children of his cousins, and when he had earned enough money, studied law at the University of Virginia and passed the bar in 1874. Settling in Richmond, he practiced law and wrote occasionally for newspapers. His first published piece, the dialect poem "Uncle Gabe's White Folks," appeared in 1877, and between 1884 and 1886 he sold his best-known stories to the *Century Magazine*. In 1886 he married Anne Seddon Bruce, who provided Page with a model of proper Southern womanhood. Her death two years later stunned him and deprived him of a valuable editor as well. In 1893 he married Florence Lathrop Field and retired from law to write and lecture full time. Established in Washington, D.C., Page wrote several novels, short stories, essays on Southern issues, and was elected to the American Academy of Arts and Letters in 1908. He became active in politics, and in 1913 Woodrow Wilson appointed him ambassador to Italy, where he served for six years. Page died at Oakland in 1922.

Major Works of Short Fiction

Page was prolific, writing poetry, novels, children's stories, sketches, essays, and literary criticism, but he is best known for his short stories. In these tales, as in all that he wrote, he espoused traditional Southern values and eulogized the Southern way of life before the Civil War. In "Marse Chan," his first and most acclaimed story, a former slave, now a servant, recounts the noble deeds of his former master and recalls the glorious days of a vanished era to a Northern visitor. The device of the black narrator and the themes of Southern heroism, tragic love, and reconciliation which Page employed in his first story reappear in the later stories "Meh Lady" and "Unc' Edinburg's Drowndin'." His short stories "Unc' Edinburg's Drowndin'" and "Ole 'Stracted" are significant contributions to the development of the local color movement for their strong evocation of place and their portrayal of Southern social and political attitudes before the Civil War. In 1887, these four stories, with the addition of "No Haid Pawn" and "Polly," were collected under the title *In Ole Virginia*, which Theodore Gross described as "the author's lasting contribution to American literature. . . . [His] major themes are formulated and fully realized in this first published work." Of his later short stories, only "Two Little Confederates," "The Burial of the Guns," "Little Darby," and "The Gentleman of the Black Stock" employed with success the themes that had served him so well in his early stories. The stories collected in *Under the Crust* and *The Land of the Spirit* represent a new direction for Page, for these non-Southern stories do not glorify a vanished past; rather, they protest social injustices and reveal his scorn for modern commercialism. Lacking the charm and local color of his plantation tales, his last stories had little contemporary appeal, and they are generally ignored today.

Critical Reception

Page was fortunate to write at an auspicious time for the local color movement. Nostalgia for the romantic Old South governed literary taste; Northerners were fascinated by the plantation civilization that they had destroyed, and Southerners were eager to justify and champion their former way of life. Accordingly, Page's chivalric tales of Southern heroes set in a glorious past found immediate acclaim. With the publication of *In Ole Virginia* and the lecture series he subsequently undertook to promote his stories and views, Page became the literary spokesman of the South. His editors were eager to publish what he sent them, and reviewers were largely appreciative of his work, commenting favorably on his depth of feeling and warmth of characterization. But as the local color movement surrendered to literary realism by the end of the century, Page's writing fell gradually into disfavor. His late stories, in which he experimented with new themes and techniques, were submitted to unreceptive editors, and he abandoned fiction-writing entirely by 1910. Although often overlooked today, Page remains an important figure in the history of Southern literature; contemporary Southern writers have noted the impact of his work on their own. As the novelist Grace King wrote in her memoirs: "It is hard to explain in simple terms what Thomas Nelson Page meant to us in the South at that time. He was the first Southerner to appear in print as a Southerner, and his stories, short and simple, written in Negro dialect, and, I

may say, Southern pronunciation, showed us with ineffable grace that although we were sore bereft, politically, we had now a chance in literature at least." In his time, Page was the most successful author of the plantation tradition, and the popular image of the Old South which he created in his best short stories endures today.

PRINCIPAL WORKS

Short Fiction

In Ole Virginia; or Marse Chan, and Other Stories 1887
Befo' de War: Echoes in Negro Dialect 1888
Two Little Confederates 1888
Among the Camps, or Young People's Stories of the War 1891
Elsket, and Other Stories 1891
The Burial of the Guns 1894
Pastime Stories 1894
The Old Gentleman of the Black Stock 1897
Santa Claus's Partner 1899
Bred in the Bone 1904
Under the Crust 1907
Tommy Trot's Visit to Santa Claus 1908
The Land of the Spirit 1913

Other Major Works

On Newfound River (novel) 1891
The Old South: Essays Social and Political (essays) 1892
Red Rock (novel) 1898
Gordon Keith (novel) 1903
The Negro: The Southerner's Problem (essays) 1904
The Coast of Bohemia (poetry) 1906
The Novels, Stories, Sketches, and Poems of Thomas Nelson Page: The Plantation Edition. 18 vols. (collected works) 1906-1912
The Old Dominion: Her Making and Her Manners (essays) 1908
Robert E. Lee, the Southerner (biography) 1908
John Marvel, Assistant (novel) 1909
Robert E. Lee, Man and Soldier (biography) 1911
Italy and the World War (essays) 1921
Dante and His Influence: Studies (criticism) 1923
Washington and Its Romance (essays) 1923
The Red Riders (novel) 1924

CRITICISM

The Nation (essay date 1887)

SOURCE: A review of *In Ole Virginia*, in *The Nation*, Vol. 45, No. 1160, September 22, 1887, p. 236.

[*In the following review of* In Ole Virginia, *the critic praises Page's creation of the Southern hero and use of Negro dialect.*]

Collectively, Mr. Page's tales entitled **In Ole Virginia** form an epic historical and tragic. After reading them we see one figure with the certainty and distinctness of actual vision. Called by no matter what name, that figure is always the same—a young man, exquisitely fine of nature, gentle, chivalrous, hot-blooded, at once the pink of courtesy, courage incarnate, and honor's self. He can think no evil, much less do it. Born to lordship, his life-path cut straight through gardens of roses that never fade almost before he comes to his own, his princedom is but an empty name: the roses are all thorns; he falls before the cannon's mouth, his dead fingers twined about his so-called country's flag. That is the beautiful figure by which, be it true to life or false, a capable story-teller has chosen to perpetuate the South that fought and died. That is the figure which vivifies all the incidents, serious, melodramatic, and comic, and illumines every picture of family and plantation life.

Mr. Page, like all who are notable in the rising host of Southern writers of fiction, does not recite the epic impersonally as an outside observer, nor does he put it in the mouth of a survivor of the ruling class. The glory of the master is told by the lips and in the language of the slave. There is nothing more curious or interesting in this creative literature of the New South than the apparently spontaneous and almost uniform choice of the negro and his dialect as the mediums best fitted to lay bare the heart of the Old South. The obvious reasons for the selection, such as greater opportunity afforded by it for picturesqueness, for novelty, and for eccentric humor, are not sufficient wholly to account for it. Nor is it convincing to remark flippantly that all the gentlemen perished in the war, or to attribute to the authors a desire to correct a widespread belief in the horrors of the past condition of servitude. The selection is not deliberate and calculated, but rather a strange, general impulse, in obeying which probably not one of the authors perceived any singular significance. The thoroughgoing abolitionist may discover here the hand of fate, retributive and compensatory. The tradition of splendor and supreme distinction is handed down by those upon whose labor they were founded, and for whose sake they were annihilated.

In Mr. Page's hands the negro dialect is an extraordinarily flexible and effective literary tool, By his apparently inexhaustible command of its vocabulary and phraseology, he has won special distinction, but in the writing of plain English he has yet much to learn. **"No Haid Pawn"** (which, being translated, means No Head Pond) is an effort which suggests limitation of ability. The idea of frightful crime and supernatural visitation in a setting of swamp, marsh, and jungle is too much for him, and he is further handicapped by a seeming fear of that latitude in English construction allowable for grace and force, and by a weakness in some fine points of English grammar. Any man, however, must have a peculiarly weird and fantastic vocabulary at his tongue's end to do justice to the subject of

"No Haid Pawn." The only example in the volume of a character not drawn in dialect, yet full of life and free, is that of the Colonel in **"Polly."** The author has so thoroughly imagined the hard-drinking, hard-riding, freely profane old planter, that the words exactly descriptive come to him with perfect ease and naturalness.

The Nation (essay date 1894)

SOURCE: A review of "Polly" and *The Burial of the Guns,* in *The Nation,* Vol. 59, No. 1539, December 27, 1894, p. 483.

[*In the following review, the critic derides the excessive sentimentality of "Polly," but praises the realism and feeling of "The Burial of the Guns" and "My Cousin Fanny."*]

Mr. Page's publishers have supplied a new example to the old adage concerning fine feathers and fine birds. They have put his short story **"Polly"** into a delicate cover of small folio form, and have printed it on paper with a glaze so high that, no matter at what angle the volume is held, it never leaves the print undisputed possession of the field of vision; and they have singled out for these distinctions a heroine who is not of the ilk of fair ones who are worth following under difficulties to the end of their fate. Polly is a young lady belonging south of Mason and Dixon's line; she has a choleric uncle breathing threats of disinheritance from a soft heart; and she has a lover who turns pale whenever he should, and has the facial play proper to his situation. She is also very fond of a drunken negro servant. She displays great variety of complexion herself, clasps her arms freely about her uncle's neck, and sets one wondering what in the world she will find to do with herself when, as in the course of nature she must, she leaves off "tears and sobs and caresses." If it is captious to pick flaws in a **"Christmas Recollection,"** as this story is further entitled, the apology therefor must be lack of a choice. One would fain point out niceties of style and narrative as an offset to lack of substance; but the query is how to do this when the English runs in general about in this wise: "So that although he did not take his degree, he had gotten the start which enabled him to complete his studies during the time he was taking care of his mother, which he did until her death, so that as soon as he was admitted to the bar he made his mark."

Much nearer the usual level of Mr. Page's excellence is the volume which takes its title, **The Burial of the Guns,** from the second of its six stories. Even at the risk of harping on an ungracious point, it is to be insisted that it is a pity to spoil a really eloquent and moving paragraph, descriptive of the rally of Confederate veterans in Richmond, on the occasion of the unveiling of a monument, with a climax so ill-worded as the following: "Not one of them all but was self-sustaining, sustained by the South, or had ever even for one moment thought in his direst extremity that he would have what was, undone." It would hardly be possible, even for a new Irving with a new *Rip,* to present more humanely or more in the spirit of a literary good Samaritan the remnants of dignity of character left to the battered drunkard who is the hero of this story, **"The Gray Jacket of 'No. 4.'"** The title story is, as one surmises, the history of an episode in the surrender of the forces of the Southern Confederacy. It tells well and touchingly of the bravery, loyalty, and spirit of self-sacrifice that animated the followers of that lost cause. **"Little Darby,"** too, reflects qualities of feeling and powers of action and endurance in its personages that amply make their peace with readers of any political dye. The finest skill in portrayal of character has, however, been reserved for **"My Cousin Fanny,"** a sketch in which effective realism, lightened by delicate irony and some very exquisite touches of feeling, has produced a woman's portrait of admirable lifelikeness and finish—always barring the imperfection already indicated.

Edwin Mims (essay date 1903)

SOURCE: "Thomas Nelson Page," in *Southern Writers: Biographical and Critical Sources, Volume II*, M. E. Church, 1903, pp. 120-51.

[*Mims, one of the first scholars of Southern literature, provides a contemporary assessment of Page's popularity and achievements.*]

Different from the poet and the critic is the romancer who finds in the past the inspiration of his art, and would fain preserve the traditions and legends of a bygone age. Mr. Page, by birth, training, temperament, is in thorough sympathy with the ante-bellum South, and in the new life springing up all about him he has endeavored to preserve what is most noteworthy in a civilization that seems to him "the sweetest, purest, and most beautiful ever lived." He would have us not "to forget the old radiance in the new glitter," believing with Burke that people will never look forward to posterity who never look backward to their ancestors. He is perhaps aware of the limitations of that life—not so much as the poet or the critic—but seeing it with something of modern breadth, he loves it, idealizes it, and would preserve it as a record of the past and as an inspiration for the future. He may not have occupied some one field as well as Cable or Harris or Craddock, but more than any of the other story-writers he has taken for his field no less than the life of the people of the whole South. Himself a typical Southern gentleman, modest, generous, well-bred, lover of good stories, he has, by his mastery of the short story and his gifts of humor and pathos, delineated the life of the people he loves so well.

If in the preceding paragraph I had substituted "Virginian" for "Southern," I should have been nearer the truth, perhaps, for it is always of Virginia that Mr. Page writes. The title of his most significant book is *In Ole Virginia,* and the background of nearly all his stories is in old Hanover. Attention has been recently called to the difference between the Southern States—between Georgia and Virginia, for instance, or Tennessee and South Carolina. The difference may be seen in the writings of Page and Harris. In the writings of the latter there is a raciness, a freshness that is almost American in its scope; in those of the former we are always in conservative, aristocratic Virginia. Indeed, he takes as much pride in his State as did any of his ancestors. . . .

His interest in the plantation life before the war found expression first in the many stories he told to his friends in the social circle in which he moved. Mr. Polk Miller, who knew him well at that time, says: "In the social circle he was a great favorite, and, having the ability to tell good negro stories, and his association being with that class of people whose parents had been large owners of slaves in Virginia, they kept him busy telling the humorous and pathetic side of negro life on the plantations. Every one testified to the naturalness and truthfulness of the negro character, and this led to his writing short stories from time to time."

All through his life he had shown a disposition to write. Like Cable and Harris, he began by writing for the newspapers. It was in the air then to write—those years from 1876 to 1880, that saw the emergence of a well-defined group of Southern writers. Of these, the leader was Irwin Russell. "It was the light of his genius," Page says, "shining through his dialect poems, that led my feet in the direction I have since tried to follow." His friend A. C. Gordon was also writing dialect poems, and Page's first efforts were in this direction, his poem "Uncle Gabe's White Folks" appearing in *Scribner's Magazine.*

His most distinctive work was to be the short story, and not poetry, and his first story was **"Marse Chan."**. . .

This deservedly popular story was sent in 1880 to *Scribner's Magazine,* where it remained for nearly four years without being published. In the meantime many of his friends advised him to give up the idea of writing and devote himself exclusively to the law. On the other hand, his wife encouraged him in his literary work. The story of their courtship is, I imagine, suggested in **"The Old Gentleman of the Black Stock."** She was Miss Anne Seddon Bruce, a niece of Hon. James A. Seddon, Secretary of War under Jefferson Davis.

"She was a very bright woman," says one who knew her well, "and as her father was one of the largest landowners and slaveholders in Virginia, she had a considerable knowledge, and doubtless contributed as much to her husband's store of negro comicalities as any one else. She was naturally solicitous of his popularity as a writer, and encouraged him to continue in that line of work."

When **"Marse Chan"** finally appeared it was received at once with universal praise. In quick succession Mr. Page wrote **"Unc' Edinburg's Drowndin',"** **"Meh Lady,"** **"Polly,"** **"Ole 'Stracted,"** all of which were published in the volume *In Ole Virginia* in 1887. This volume of short stories established his place in American letters, and is still his most characteristic work.

Mr. Page contributed to the popularity of his stories by public readings, given in all parts of the country. He and

Hopkinson Smith took Boston by storm, said a writer in the *Critic* a few years ago, and students of Yale and other universities gave him a hearty reception. In the cities of the South especially he was received with an enthusiasm rarely displayed. . . .

With his reputation established and his income augmented by receipts from books and readings, Page gradually gave up the practice of law. The death of his first wife is most tenderly referred to in the dedication of *Elsket and Other Stories*. In 1893 he was married to Mrs. Field, of Chicago. Since their marriage they have lived in Washington City. He has not taken his art any too seriously, nor has the writing of a book made him lean. He has had none of the struggles that Russell or Lanier had. He is, as Carlyle said of Scott, "a robust, thoroughly healthy man, and withal a very prosperous and victorious man. An eminently well-conditioned man, healthy in body, healthy in soul, we shall call him one of the healthiest of men."

And yet with all his ease and with the temptations that have come with a life of leisure, he has continued to write with much attention to his style, and always with a certain degree of "high seriousness." He is not a prolific writer; has taken pains to make his work as good as possible. The printers testify to his revision of his stories, even after they have appeared in magazine form. He has resorted to no sensational measures to acquire cheap notoriety.

I have already referred to the publication of his first volume, *In Ole Virginia,* in 1887. *Two Little Confederates* appeared in 1888, and *Among the Camps* in 1891—books that reveal one of the most charming elements in Mr. Page's character, his love for children. Their popularity is not difficult to understand, so thoroughly human are they, so different from the conventional juvenile books. In 1892 came *Elsket and Other Stories*; in 1894, *The Burial of the Guns*; in 1896, a series of political and social essays entitled *The Old South*; in 1898, *Red Rock, a Chronicle of Reconstruction*; and for the Christmas holidays, 1900, **"Santa Claus's Partner,"** a somewhat conventional Christmas story after the manner of Dickens. He is now at work on a new novel, and has promised short stories for the magazines. There is no reason why he should not continue to delight the wide reading public he has made for himself.

While in **"Elsket"** he has written with much power the tragic story of two Norwegian lovers, the most characteristic work that Mr. Page has done is his delineation of the life of the Southern people. I have already spoken of the way in which he was gradually led into literature, his genuine delight in a story, his early fondness for writing; but I doubt not that the most decided impulse has come from his desire to portray the life of the ante-bellum South and the heroism of Southern men and women during and since the war. In his paper on "Authorship in the South Before the War" he says: "The old South had no chronicler to tell its story in that spirit of sympathy from which alone come the lights and shadings on which depend perspective and real truth. It was for lack of a literature that it was left behind in the great race for outside favor, and

that in the supreme moment of existence it found itself arraigned at the bar of the world without an advocate and without defense." In an address delivered at Washington and Lee in 1887 he closed by appealing to the men of that institution to look forward to the true historian of the South. "What nobler task can be set himself than this: to preserve from oblivion or, worse, from misrepresentation a civilization which produced as its natural fruit Washington and Lee?" Mr. Page is not this true historian to whom he looks forward with prophetic gaze; nor is he, as he himself realizes, the artist to represent on a large scale the tremendous tragedy of the Civil War; his stories are but a "fragmentary record" of the life of the people he loves.

The best account of life in the South before the war is in **"Unc' Edinburg's Drowndin'."** The fox-hunting, dueling, Christmas celebrations, hospitality, chivalry, love-making—all are there, not in the nervous prose of his essay on "Social Life Before the War," but in the artistic words of the old negro who recalls it all from the haze of the past. In the preface to *Red Rock* we are made to feel that a glory has passed away from the earth. "Even the moonlight was richer and mellower before the war than it is now. . . . What an air suddenly comes in with them of old courts and polished halls! What an odor, as it were, of those gardens which Watteau painted floats in as they enter!" The same idea is expressed in the less poetical but more significant words: "Dem was good ole times, Marster; de best Sam ever see!" And again: "Dat wuz de een o' de ole time."

To all of which one may be allowed to ask if there is not too much of a glamour about the old plantations and too much of a halo about the heads of Southern gentlemen and gentlewomen. One wishes that now and then the romancer had used some of the sarcastic touches of Thackeray in dealing with the higher classes of English society, or that he would use some of the irony that Hawthorne shows in dealing with the Puritans. . . .

Mr. Page has some of the sensitiveness of the men about whom he writes—an almost fatal obstacle to insight. I hasten to say, however, that this is a failing of nearly all romantic writers. The same criticism has been passed upon Scott for his presentation of the Middle Ages. He does not see life as it is, he does not write with his eye on the object; but who would be without his enthusiasm for the age of chivalry? And the reader may be allowed to enjoy the idealization of ante-bellum life, and at the same time be aware of the fresh current of ideas of the new South. . . .

In Mr. Page's stories the political problems of [the civil war] and our minds rest upon the heroic men and women who bore the brunt of it all. We can never be too grateful to the writer who has given us the description of Marse Phil's charge "across de oat fiel'," or Little Darby's heroic cutting down of the tree while the bullets rain about him, or the devotion of the men to their guns and their colonel. And more moving than their bravery is the death that these sons of the South meet as they do their duty— Marse Chan, brought home in an ambulance by his faithful servant and put "to rest in de ole grabeyard (he done got he furlough);" Marse Phil, found amid the wreck and confusion of the battlefield and dying with the arms of his mother about him; Col. Gray, "falling at the head of his regiment on one of those great days which are the milestones of history."

It is no disparagement to the men to say that, whatever courage they displayed, it was less than that which the women showed; "hit 'peared like when it start the ladies wuz ambitiouser fir it 'n de mens." It would not be difficult to criticise the woman of the ante-bellum days as Mr. Page has described her—the gay and joyous Polly, "the tenderest-hearted little thing in the world," "de young mistis in de sky-blue robes," or the more dignified Miss Charlotte, "who look like she has done come down right from de top o' de blue sky an bring a piece o' it wid her." But these young women are transformed into such heroines as Meh Lady and Cousin Belle, the mother of Frank an' Willie, My Cousin Fanny, Blair Cary, who in times of storm and stress assume the heroic. Theirs is the loneliness of life on the old plantation, with none but the negroes and boys for company; the agony and pathos of death; the decline of once proud estates; the hard, coarse living they had to submit to; the insults of Northern soldiers; after the war the removal to cabins and the teaching of negro schools. It is in the delineation of these women that Mr. Page is at his best.

The favorite way Mr. Page has of presenting his stories is through some negro who in these latter days looks back to the good old days of slavery. He has realized with Irwin Russell and Joel Chandler Harris the literary capabilities of the negro—with a difference, however. Mr. Page delineates the negro only as he is identified with slavery; his thoughts never go beyond that relation; there is much wit and commonsense philosophy characteristic of an unconventional character, but none of the folklore, none of the legends peculiar to the negro race. He is an accessory to the white man, set up to see him as the author sees him. Mr. Harris, on the other hand, gives the negro a separate existence. In "Free Joe" especially he shows the latent life underneath the forms of slavery. It is a mistake to say that Page's characters are untrue to life. There are many such negroes living now, perfectly loyal sons of the Old South to whom the passing away of slavery was the destruction of all that was best in the world. There will be fewer and fewer as time passes and as the negro develops along lines indicated by such leaders as Booker Washington. It is fortunate that one so well fitted as Mr. Page has preserved this interesting type; if for no other reason, to offset the erroneous impressions made in *Uncle Tom's Cabin.*

Such a negro as I have indicated is the best possible character with which to present certain phases of Southern life. In his mouth the most exaggerated words seem justifiable. He cannot adjust himself to new conditions, to "free issue negroes" and "poor white trash." Uncle Sam has been over to the old place to water the graves of his dead master and mistress; Uncle Edinburg meets the writer at the depot and tells him of the Christmas of long ago, "the sho' 'nough tyah down Chris'mas"; Uncle Billy is cutting fishing poles for the sons of the finest of Southern women and the most chivalrous of Northern men.

The blending of humor and pathos which is one of the finest characteristics of Mr. Page is nowhere so evident as in the stories in his first volume. There is one passage that seems to me one of the best in his works, and, indeed, one of the best in American literature: the conclusion of **"Meh Lady,"** where Uncle Billy muses of the olden times as he sits in his cabin door: "An' dat night when de preacher was gone wid his wife an' Hannah done drapt off to sleep, I wuz settin' in der do' wid meh pipe, an' I heah 'em settin' dyah on de front steps, de voices soundin' low like bees an' de moon sort o' meltin' over de yard, an' I sort o' studyin', an' hit 'pear like de plantation live once mo', an' de ain' no mo' scufflin', an' de ole times come back ag'in, an' I heah meh kerridge horses stompin' in de stalls, an' de place all cleared up ag'in, an' fence all roun' de pasture, an' I smell de wet clover blossoms right good, an' Marse Phil an' Meh Lady done come, an' runnin' all roun' me, climbin' up on meh knees, runnin' callin' me Unc' Billy, an' pesterin' me to go fishin', whil' some'ow Meh Lady an' de Cun'l settin' dyah on de steps wid de voice hummin' low like water runnin' in de dark."

So far I have spoken of Mr. Page as a writer of short stories. A more difficult question arises when we consider him as a novelist. The passing from the short story to a really great novel is a task that few men have been able to achieve, perhaps not Kipling himself. That Mr. Page failed in *On New-found River* is generally conceded; that he came much nearer to it in *Red Rock* is as generally recognized. . . .

The concluding scene in *Red Rock,* representing the reconciliation of the two sections in the marriage of Ruth Welch and Steve Allen, suggests a most important phase of Mr. Page's work. While he has written with much enthusiasm, and at times with decided feeling, of the life of his people, he has never been bitter. He has had not a little to do with the fostering of the new national spirit that has been so characteristic of the last few years. His works in the hands of some Southerners have no doubt encouraged them in provincialism and conservatism; to the great majority they have served to keep alive the best memories of the past. To his Northern readers, ***In Ole Virginia*** and *Red Rock* have been a revelation of a life they have misunderstood and misrepresented. This national service rendered by him was fittingly recognized on October 23, 1901, when Yale University, in connection with her bicentennial celebration, conferred upon him the degree of Doctor of Literature.

The New York Times Book Review (essay date 1907)

SOURCE: A review of *The Plantation Edition,* in *The New York Times Book Review,* Vol. XII, No. 3, January 19, 1907, p. 27.

[*In this review occasioned by the publication of* The Plantation Edition, *the critic assesses Page's contribution to the literature of the South.*]

Since the appearance in the early eighties of **"Marse Chan,"** the first and best of his stories, Thomas Nelson Page has been the recognized interpreter of the South—the old South—to the rest of the country. Indeed, it would hardly be too much to say that most people of the younger generation who live north of Mason and Dixon's line have built their conception of what the South before the war was likely largely upon the foundation furnished by Mr. Page's writings. They might, to be honest, have done worse. For though Mr. Page has but a middling literary talent, though his pictures are colored and softened out of the bald truth by an inveterate sentimentality, that very sentimentality was partly characteristic of the life he has taken as his crude material.

He tells you—and glows as he tells—of gentlefolk such as a certain school in the South used to dream all gentlefolk should be; he exalts certain virtues and glosses over certain vices; he paints you the black folk, likewise, as the South likes to remember them; he conjures up before admiring eyes a life—a wonderfully appealing sort of life—that is dead, that in fact never quite was, though very nearly. And he does all this in such fashion as not to tread on the toes of people whose dream of life as it should be is quite different. More, he has actually won these people to share his own sentiment—popularized all over the country the antebellum Southern ideal of a civilization. Herein lies the value of his work in a large sense—not in any distinctly literary quality or special merit in the work itself. While the commercial North has been teaching the South thrift, Mr. Page has been showing the North the good and pleasant things about his fellow-Southerners. This taking the matter broadly and in the sum—for, of course, Mr. Page has not absolutely confined himself to the pleasant things. . . .

It is, of course, upon his short stories that Mr. Page's reputation must mainly rest, for his most distinct contribution to the world is the picture of the Virginia darky which those short stories contain. Right or wrong, to the world Mr. Page's Sam in **"Marse Chan"** is the Virginia darky, and always will be. And to those who knew him and appreciated him at least that darky and Sam are the same. The pity is that the difficulty of expressing in English letters the actual quality of Sam's talk was insurmountable. The letters you see on the printed page mean certain sounds to Mr. Page and other Virginians, and quite different sounds to residents of Boston and Chicago. And the idea of negro dialect in those cities is false accordingly. If Boston and Chicago must continue to cherish the false dialect forever, it is not Mr. Page's fault.

Outlook (essay date 1922)

SOURCE: A review of *Under the Crust,* in *Outlook,* Vol. 131, August 16, 1922, pp. 742-43.

[*In the excerpt below, the critic admires Page for his traditional values and his protest against vulgarity in* Under the Crust.]

[Page] has the American temperament and the American point of view; he believes instinctively in the best things, and he has the courage of a great hope. A Virginian of the Virginians, he has been the secretary and recorder of a form of social life which had the charm of lavish hospitality, of gracious manners, of a generous habit of life, and of a keen sense of personal dignity. Of that old order there are no more charming reports than **"Meh Lady"** and **"Marse Chan,"** nor are these unaffected and deeply human interpretations of a vanished social order likely to be surpassed in the future. They give one that sense of finality which comes only from those things which are so adequately done that the imagination rests content in them. Mr. Page has written other stories which show the same qualities of insight, sympathy, humor, pathos, easy command of the resources of the short story, but these tales which have become American classics may stand as representative of the finest portraiture of the old-time Virginia gentlefolk and of the relations they held with their family slaves.

The charm of that society lay largely in the absence of the commercial spirit, the emphasis on the arts of social intercourse, the chivalrous feeling for women. It was provincial in interest, content with its own standards, proud of its descent, and somewhat given to self-assertion; but it was brave, generous, gallant, and it did not count the cost when friends or convictions were at stake. No one has realized so clearly in art the latent idealism of this society, touched with a more delicate hand its finer qualities, or entered more sympathetically into its humor than Mr. Page; to the end of the story he will be one of the chief interpreters and recorders of the Old South.

In his later work Mr. Page has made his readers feel in different ways the vigor of this power of indignation, which is a forcible expression of his idealism. To the fine qualities which touched his imagination in the old social order he remains true in his later stories and essays. More than once he has attacked the pretension, waste, and vulgarity of the ultra-fashionable set with unsparing vigor of feeling and speech; in a period of extravagance, display, and moral laxity he has stood resolutely for the old-time and all-time qualities of a real social life—cleanness, refinement, honor, dignity, courage. For the cheap, self-constituted aristocracies of the day, the rank mushroom growths of a prolific soil, he has expressed the wholesome scorn of the man who hates vulgar shams and of the American who feels that the spirit of the country has been grossly caricatured by a horde of vulgarians. It is interesting to note the fact that American novelists have made common cause against these degraders of American standards and traditions; Mr. Howells, Mr. James, Mr. Wister, by portraiture, irony, invective, have stood, as Mr. Page has stood, for the Americanism which is not vulgarized by wealth nor perverted by leisure.

In the seven stories which make up the volume of short tales, *Under the Crust,* the discerning reader will find the characteristic idealism of Mr. Page expressing itself in delicate and sympathetic studies of men and women to whom commercialism exists only to be resisted, and who live in the world as if life were still a matter of the spirit and not a matter of physical luxury. **"Miss Godwin's Inheritance"** is a charming study of the supremacy of sentiment in a woman's heart, and in delicacy of perception and sensitiveness to the more elusive qualities of character is quite on a level with Mr. Page's best work. The portrait of an idealist in **"A Brother to Diogenes"** is in another and broader style, and gains in effectiveness by reason of the vastness and solitude of its background; while **"My Friend the Doctor"** is a personal study in a beautiful kind of altruism rather than a piece of fiction. It would be a mistake, however, to convey the impression that Mr. Page draws only the men and women who live by the heart; the vigor with which he can sketch an elemental man is strikingly shown in the dramatic study of **"A Goth."** The stories in this volume are not of equal excellence, but it contains work which Mr. Page has never surpassed.

Rosewell Page (essay date 1923)

SOURCE: "His War Experience," in *Thomas Nelson Page: A Memoir of a Virginia Gentleman,* Charles Scribner's Sons, 1923, pp. 31-42.

[*Rosewell Page, Page's younger brother, tells of Page's Civil War experiences and their influence on his writing.*]

Young Page's first experience of war was in the spring of 1861, when he saw his father and Ralph, the son of his brother's black mammy, ride off to join the Confederate army, and a few days later saw his uncle William ride off with Nat upon the same errand. He saw Nat brought home demented after the considerate order of the master allowing him to ride on the caisson across the Potomac was countermanded by another officer, and the wading the stream brought on an illness which left the faithful man bereft of his reason. . . .

Deep and lasting was the impression made upon the boy, and from that time he became and thought himself endowed with the powers and duties of manhood. He saw armies pass up and down the highway during the next four years, for "'Oakland' was in the track of the armies.". . .

The day after the battle of Fredericksburg young Page went with his uncle Robert Nelson, a clergyman, who had been for years before the war and was for many years after it a missionary in China, to find out about his dear ones who had been in that dreadful battle. The boy slept that night in the tent of his father, which was also that of his uncle, the chief of artillery, and heard of the mortal wound of his neighbor, Colonel Lewis Minor Coleman. There he saw the horrors of war in all their fullness—the dead being buried, the wounded being cared for, and the victorious army in possession of the field.

The boy's own experiences, and the constant reiteration and commemoration of the marches and battles of Lee's army in which those nearest to him indulged as they sat by the bright fires at "Oakland" and talked the night away,

like Goldsmith's broken soldier, deeply impressed the author of **"Marse Chan"** and of the *Life of Lee.*

His father and uncle, with often a visitor—for the whole white population of the neighborhood had been in the army—would recount the movements of the armies, the strategy of the generals, the bravery of the individuals, the causes of victory or defeat, until it was time for the boys to go to their books or to bed.

Thus the author of the stories dealing with the war, and of the biography of Lee, was informed by those who, like Æneas, had seen a great part of that war, or of that part which related to the movements of the armies in the great campaigns in Virginia.

Robert Underwood Johnson (essay date 1942)

SOURCE: "Thomas Nelson Page," in *Commemorative Tributes of the American Academy of Arts and Letters, 1905-1941,* Spiral Press, 1942, pp. 134-38.

[*Johnson, one of Page's editors at* The Century Magazine, *defines Page's contribution to American literature.*]

One day in 1881 there came to the editorial office of *Scribner's Monthly,* afterward the *Century Magazine,* the manuscript of a story destined to be of large significance in American fiction. It was a tale of Virginia during the Civil War and was entitled **"Marse Chan,"** and it was signed by a name not known to the editorial staff, that of Thomas Nelson Page. The editor-in-chief, Richard Watson Gilder, being then in Europe, as a matter of routine it was first submitted to the "reader," Mrs. Sophie Bledsoe Herrick, who (so to speak) "discovered" it and passed it on to the present writer with a warm recommendation that it be accepted. It proved to be a story of such obvious merits that it fell into the class of manuscript that, in the lingo of the editorial office, "accepts itself." It had but one fault of importance, that of redundancy, the action being retarded by a surplusage of interesting detail. This is a fault not only far from infrequent in young writers but fortunately one easy to remedy. With the consent of the author, excision was made of this digressive material— perhaps a third of the original manuscript—and I believe that none of the omitted portions was restored in the publication in book form of this and other stories by the same author. The narrative is wholly cast in negro dialect, which at that time was much in favor. The magazine had already on its accepted list a number of admirable examples of such stories by well-known writers and the obligation of precedence, and not a lack of appreciation of the tale itself, was the occasion of the delay of its publication for nearly three years.

When it did appear, in the *Century* for April, 1884, **"Marse Chan"** made a sensation. It was not only interesting in itself, as a well-told narrative, but it was typical of what may be called the "Southern literary invasion" which came in the twenty-five years that followed the Civil War. The

Southern writer of that period did not study life analytically but was content to report it objectively. Cable was perhaps the only one whose method was conspicuously dramatic. **"Marse Chan"** and Page's later stories had the Southern literary trait of straight-forward, felicitous narrative style, the somewhat leisurely current sweeping into a swifter climax. He may be considered as standing at the head of this group in pathos, humor and a convincing truthfulness. The local color of much American fiction has been challenged—often from a too matter-of-fact point of view—but no one has ever detected a forced or false note in the work of Thomas Nelson Page. This first story is among the foremost in the list of the best American short stories produced during the post-bellum renaissance. . . .

"Marse Chan" is typical of Page's works in two respects. First, in dealing with sectional prejudices, it has that fine quality, whether of a gentleman or an author, a generous candor, and, next, it has a tenderness that in the writer's attitude toward women amounts to chivalry. Page was not ashamed to portray love as a principle rather than a passion, and his sincerity enabled him to escape sentimentality. He made the most of the background of the Civil War and in a dignified way presented the devotion and sacrifice of the South without bitterness or vaunting. This was seen particularly in his second story of note, **"Meh Lady,"** the motive of which, the reconciliation of prejudiced foes, the present writer had the good fortune to suggest to him. His treatment of sectional questions is unexceptionable, despite the fact that his local traditions were sunned and watered in a soil of two centuries. He is the adequate exponent of Virginia aristocracy turned democrat. The hero of his youth was Robert E. Lee, to whom he paid the tribute of an admirable biography, and his ancestors of the Revolutionary period always seemed to be speaking through him.

This is not the place for a critical estimate of Page's numerous books. They have homogeneity rather than diversity, but they never fail of ease or charm of atmosphere, and while they make no presumption to profundity, they show no "variableness or shadow of turning" from the truth either of history or of human nature. They are indispensable to the understanding of the character of Virginia, which, with certain quite attractive traits of provinciality, is perhaps the most American State in the Union.

Hugh M. Gloster (essay date 1948)

SOURCE: "Backgrounds of Negro Fiction," in *Negro Voices in American Fiction,* Russell & Russell, 1948, pp. 3-22.

[Gloster claims that Page's writings are partially responsible for the South's success in curtailing the rights of black citizens.]

Among . . . post-bellum writers . . . Thomas Nelson Page stood out as the leading portrayer of what E. C. Stedman sentimentally termed "the unspeakable charm that lived

and died with the old South." In such volumes as *In Ole Virginia, or Marse Chan and Other Stories* (1887), *The Old South: Essays Social and Political* (1892), and *Social Life in Old Virginia* (1897), Page, adopting a condescending and smiling attitude, creates an appealing plantation scene. On a broad canvas he paints a stately mansion presided over by lovely ladies and gallant gentlemen who wear imported finery, enjoy horse-racing and other gentle diversions, and dispense prodigal hospitality. The attitude of these cavaliers toward their slaves is cordial, kindly, benign, and sometimes devoted. The contented bondmen appear proudly engaged as servants in the big house or as laborers in the fields. Near the quarters are prankish pickaninnies romping gleefully in youthful abandon and black veterans resting comfortably in their declining years. Particularly emphasized is the loyal relationship between the master and the servant, the mistress and the maid, and the Negro mammy and her charges. The slave receives commendatory treatment for showing courage, fortitude, and self-sacrifice in relieving the destitution and distress of the Southern aristocracy during and after the war. In general, however, the Negro is presented as a simple, contented, comic, credulous, picturesque, and sometimes philosophical character, gifted in singing, dancing, tale-telling, and reuniting estranged white lovers. Such, then, is the picture of the Southern plantation provided by Page, of whom Gaines says, in comparing him with Harris:

> The Virginian is, however, far more passionate in the maintenance of a hypothesis of departed glory, paints in more glowing colors, is uniformly more idealistic, descends less frequently—if ever—from the heights of romantic vision; in short, he expresses the supreme glorification of the old regime, he 'wrote the epitaph of a civilization.' [F. P. Gaines, in *The Southern Plantation,* 1927]

Despite obvious tricks of literary endearment, the sentimental plantation vogue sponsored by Page and his associates attracted an extensive reading public, including a large number of reconciled and kindly disposed Northerners, and literally submerged the limited pro-Negro literature of the time. "Abolitionism," as Gaines notes, "was swept from the field; it was more than routed, it was tortured, scalped, 'mopped up.'" During Reconstruction the plantation tradition gained as signal a victory in the literary wars as did *Uncle Tom's Cabin* in the ante-bellum period.

Page, however, was more than the retrospective romancer of a vanished civilization; he was also the partisan defender of the patriarchal South. In the latter capacity he helped to bring about disfranchisement and other restrictions applied to Negroes, who were portrayed as maladjusted or dangerous after emancipation. **"How Andrew Carried the Precinct,"** a short story which appears in *Pastime Stories* (1894), presents a mulatto politician who would have won an election over a white man if the latter's black servant had not intervened. *Red Rock* (1898), a novel, berates scalawags, carpetbaggers, Negro politicians, and Northern missionaries and idealizes Southern blue-bloods for nobility in adversity as well as in prosperity. In *Red Rock* Moses, a mixed-blood character depicted as the incarnation of the black peril, is eventually lynched after several crimes "sufficiently heinous to entitle him to be classed as one of the greatest scoundrels in the world." In "The Negro Question," an essay in *The Old South* (1892), Page marshals references in an effort to demonstrate that the black man, being unprogressive as well as mentally and socially inferior, is unprepared to assume the unlimited enjoyment of citizenship:

> These examples cited, if they establish anything, establish the fact that the Negro race does not possess, in any development which he has yet attained, the elements of character, the essential qualifications to conduct a government, even for himself, and that if the reins of government be intrusted to his unaided hands, he will fling reason to the winds and drive to ruin.

However, because he was convinced that schooling made freedmen more useful members of society, Page advocated elementary education for all Negroes and higher training for those who proved themselves worthy. He was particularly fond of Booker T. Washington, to whom he refers as "one who is possibly esteemed at the South the wisest and sanest man of color in the country, and who has, perhaps, done more than any other to carry out the ideas that the Southern well-wishers of his race believe to be the soundest and most promising of good results" [Thomas N. Page, *The Negro,* 1904]. The Negro in a superior position, however, was more than Page could tolerate:

> We have educated him; we have aided him; we have sustained him in all right directions. We are ready to continue our aid; but we will not be dominated by him. When we shall be, it is our settled conviction that we shall deserve the degradation to which we have sunk. [Thomas N. Page, *The Old South,* 1892]

Though demanding Anglo-Saxon supremacy, Page at least looked with favor upon Negroes like Booker T. Washington, felt that the two races could thrive in a system of social separation, and never attempted to excuse the Invisible Empire of responsibility for lawlessness.

Jay B. Hubbell   (essay date 1954)

SOURCE: "Thomas Nelson Page," in *The South in American Literature, 1607-1900,* Duke University Press, 1954, pp. 795-804.

[*Hubbell, a pioneer and leader in Southern literature studies, describes Page's relationship with his editor and literary advisors.*]

More than his fellow Southerners, the Virginian is regarded as a glorifier of times past, perhaps because—as a Virginian might reply to such a charge—his state has a longer and more magnificent past to boast of. Thomas Nelson Page was among the writers of the New South the stoutest defender of the old regime. Like most of the other

Virginian writers of fiction, he belonged to a family with a distinguished ancestry, and, like them, he gave his heroes and heroines a line of ancestors comparable to his own. The great days of the Nelsons and the Pages, however, had come in the last half of the eighteenth century. "Oakland" plantation in Hanover County, where he was born, was not a prosperous estate in the fifties. Hanover County, which is north of Richmond, lay directly in the path of invading Union armies, and it was fought over repeatedly by the soldiers of McClellan, Grant, and Lee. John Esten Cooke, to whom Hanover County was a familiar battleground, saw little that was romantic about the war; but Page, who was only twelve when the war ended, always saw it as a romantic Virginian epic age. He looked back upon the old regime as a near approach to the Golden Age and regarded Reconstruction as a betrayal of the state and the social class to which he belonged.

Page was a student at Washington College while General Lee was its president. After studying law at the University of Virginia, he practiced law for two years in Hanover County. Then at the age of twenty-three he gladly accepted a place in the office of a cousin, Henry T. Wickham, who was attorney for the Chesapeake and Ohio Railroad. Page was ambitious, eager for position and power, and not averse to seeing his name in print. Owning and operating a Virginia farm were not his ambition. In Richmond, where he had relatives and soon made many friends, he became known as a skilful raconteur. So impressed were some of his listeners with his stories of the old plantation and his command of the Negro dialect that they suggested that he ought to write them out and publish them. Irwin Russell's dialect poems, which were appearing in *Scribner's Monthly* in 1876, suggested a method. Page's **"Uncle Gabe's White Folks"** was published in the *Monthly* in April, 1877. Although his best work was to be done in prose rather than in verse, Page had thus early discovered his most effective mouthpiece in the faithful ex-slave who boasts of his old master's wealth and grandeur.

> "Fine ole place?" Yes, suh, 't is so;
>   An' mighty fine people my white folks war—
> But you ought ter 'a' seen it years ago,
>   When de Marster an' de Mistis lived up dyah;
> When de niggers 'd stan' all roun' de do',
> Like grains o' corn on the cornhouse flo'.
>
> "Live' mons'ous high?" Yes, Marster, yes;
>   D' cut 'n' onroyal 'n' gordly dash;
> Eat an' drink till you could n' res'.
>   My folks war n' none o' yo' po'-white-trash;
> Nor, suh, dey was of high degree—
> Dis heah nigger am quality!

In Page's stories the emphasis is upon the loyalty of the slave to a kindly master, of the planter to his state and to his code of honor, and upon the glorification of woman. Later he added the theme of sectional reconciliation. His chief characters belong to two classes: the great planters and the faithful house servants, who looked down on the field hands and the "po'-white trash." His best Negro characters—Sam of **"Marse Chan"** and Billy of **"Meh**

Lady"—are faithful ex-slaves. He did not treat the typical freedman with distinction, and his Negro women are on the whole inferior to his men. Rarely did he portray the numerous field hands or the Southern small farmers or the poorer whites.

In 1881 *Scribner's Monthly* accepted Page's offer to write an article on Yorktown for the centennial of Cornwallis's surrender. In 1881 also the magazine accepted his most famous story, **"Marse Chan,"** but the story remained unpublished until April, 1884, by which time the *Monthly* had become the *Century Magazine.* The editors were apparently fearful of printing so long a story written almost entirely in Negro dialect. It appears also that they found it necessary to delete certain passages which did not relate directly to the love story.

"Marse Chan" had its genesis in a letter, shown to Page by a friend, which was found on the body of an uneducated Georgia private killed in one of the great battles around Richmond. The letter was from his sweetheart, who told him that she had discovered that she loved him after all and added that if he could get a furlough and come home, she would marry him. She concluded: "Don't come without a furlough, for if you don't come honorable, I won't marry you." In theme and narrative method, as Page himself acknowledged, **"Marse Chan"** owes something to "Envion," a story which his friend Armistead C. Gordon had published in the *South-Atlantic* for July, 1880. The theme, however, continued to haunt Page until in 1894 he published **"Little Darby,"** which is essentially the same story, this time with Virginia poor-whites as the chief characters. He felt, as he wrote to Arthur H. Quinn, "that it was due to that class that I should testify with whatever power I might possess, to their devotion to the South."

In January, 1886, Page published in *Harper's* **"Unc' Edinburg's Drowndin',"** which he was inclined to think his best story. On December 31, 1885, Joel Chandler Harris wrote to Page that he would rather have written this story and **"Marse Chan"** than "everything else that has appeared since the War—or before the War, for that matter." Richard Watson Gilder also had high praise for **"Unc' Edinburg's Drowndin'."** In a letter to Page, January 19, 1886, he said: "I take off my hat to you for that. It is dramatically perfect, and in detail it is a most extraordinary reflection, through the mind and dialect of that old darky, of an interesting and complete society. It is an exquisite story."

In June, 1886, the *Century* published **"Meh Lady"** and paid Page two hundred and fifty dollars for it. Remembering Lessing's *Minna von Barnhelm,* Robert Underwood Johnson of the *Century* staff had suggested the love story of the Union soldier and the Virginia planter's daughter—a theme which was a conventional one in 1886. Page's handling of it, however, is far superior to that found in so many stories by Northern writers who had little understanding of Southern life. Page was doing his part to promote better relations between South and North, but it is perhaps significant that in **"Meh Lady"** the Union soldier turns out to be the son of a Virginia kinsman.

"Marse Chan," "Meh Lady," "Unc' Edinburg's Drowndin'," and three other stories were republished in book form in *In Ole Virginia* (1887). *Two Little Confederates,* the best of his stories for young people, appeared the next year. *The Burial of the Guns* followed in 1894. These books were widely read and were highly praised by Northern reviewers, but it was not until 1890 or after, that Page regarded his writing as being as important as his law practice. "Even now," he wrote in *The Old South* (1892), "the Southerner will not believe that a man can be a lawyer and an author." James Lane Allen had written to Page on October 16, 1889: "I cannot submit to the idea that you will allow the law or any other claim to separate you from literature. . . . I shall count it a loss if Southern literature is not to have from you some novels of Virginia life." Page had not found the writing of short stories particularly profitable, and he was already struggling with his first novel, *Red Rock,* which was not to be published until 1898.

The library at "Oakland" did not contain many new books, and Page was never a great reader. In his earlier years he was fond of Scott's historical romances, Cooper's Leather-Stocking Tales, and French romances. He was fond of Addison, Steele, and Goldsmith. His father's favorites were Pope, Goldsmith, and Boswell's life of Dr. Johnson. Page was little influenced by any writer of the North or the West. He read Poe and the romances of his father's friend, John Esten Cooke; but in later life he censured Cooke for seeing "the life of the South through the lenses of Scott, and his imitators." He acknowledged a debt to the dialect poems of Irwin Russell and the Virginia stories of his friend Armistead C. Gordon. To the pioneer work of the Virginia humorist, George W. Bagby, he confessed "an unending debt of gratitude," for Bagby, he said, had "opened his eyes to the beauty that lay at hand and whispered into his ear the charm that sang to his soul of the South" [Preface to Page's edition of *The Old Virginia Gentleman, and Other Sketches*]. But Bagby, though he loved Virginia no less than Page, was far more the realist, and it seems probable that some of the humorist's sketches—"Bacon and Greens," for instance—seemed to Page not only unromantic but also in poor taste.

In his Richmond period Page wrote comparatively little, but he revised with care the stories he published. Nearly everything he printed after *Red Rock* shows evidence of hasty writing and inadequate revision. He grew more reluctant to follow the suggestions of his literary advisers and publishers. His usual method in the earlier years was to tell his story to friends before he put it on paper. When the story was written down, he would read it aloud to a group of sympathetic listeners, watching carefully their reaction to every part of the story. In his later years he too often forgot the advice which he once gave to a nephew who wanted to write: "Write what you know about; write what you feel deeply as to; write as you feel; write simply, clearly, sincerely, and you will write strongly."

Like other writers of the New South, Page owed much to his Northern editors and publishers, especially Richard Watson Gilder, Robert Underwood Johnson, and Charles

Dudley Warner. On his frequent visits to New York he learned from them something about literary style and structure as well as about what the reading public wanted. Nevertheless, they found it necessary to revise and condense his stories, for Page, like Harris, when left to himself was more likely to write a sketch than a carefully plotted short story. His *Pastime Stories* (1894), written for the "Editor's Drawer" department of *Harper's Magazine,* are frankly anecdotes rather than orthodox short stories. Two of Page's most helpful literary advisers were Southern women: Mrs. Bessie Pascal Wright, an editorial reader for Harper & Brothers who as Mrs. T. P. O'Connor was to dedicate to Page her *My Beloved South* (1913), and Mrs. Sophia Bledsoe Herrick of the *Century* staff, who had served her apprenticeship on her father's *Southern Review* in the 1870's. Mrs. Herrick wrote to Page on August 29, 1885:

> There is a quality in your work, I think (if my thinking is worth anything to you)—which is like that in nobody's else. . . . If you only select your material wisely I do not think, in your own line, there is any one living who can touch you. But I sometimes think you do not quite see the limitations of your art. Art is not a literal transcript of nature. It must be true, not so much really, as ideally. And that requires the power of selection, the self restraint which can leave unsaid many good things. In **"Marse Chan"** the material was in excellent shape, it was a charming story. Where it had to be shortened I cut it with positive pain—it was so exquisite from beginning to end. In **"Meh Lady"** the form was not so good; the incidents & treatment were [in] no way inferior, but it lacked proportion & perspective. It was a little panoramic I think.

Gilder in a letter of January 19, 1886, pointed out a "grave defect" in Page's **"A Soldier of the Empire"**: ". . . there is no climax, therefore no story. It is too much like a story for a sketch, but *as* a story it lacks dramatic completeness such as all your other stories have had."

E. L. Burlingame, the editor of *Scribner's Magazine,* pointed out two defects in the first version of Page's **"No Haid Pawn."** Severing the head of a man being hanged seemed to the editor "unnecessarily repellent without increasing the force of the story." He asked: " . . . ought not the dimly suggested connection of the runaway negro & his booty with the climax, to be brought out just a shade more, for the sake of the average rather inattentive reader?" Another editor, Mrs. Mary Mapes Dodge, in accepting *Two Little Confederates* as a serial to be run in *St. Nicholas,* stipulated that the six introductory chapters should be condensed to a single instalment by "shortening the general descriptions, cutting the amusing hen-house episode. . . ." She added: ". . . the account of the Yankee raid . . . must necessarily be pruned for St. Nicholas. To leave it in entire, as it now reads, would quite prevent the story, I fear, from being the olive branch you desire it to be."

Of all the writers of the New South except Hayne, Page was the staunchest defender of the old regime. He disliked the phrase "New South" because it seemed to imply an invidious comparison with the Old South and a desertion of its ideals. In December, 1887, he wrote to William Hamilton Hayne, son of the poet: "The New South is in my judgment only the Old South with slavery gone and the fire of exaction on its back." Some of the essays and addresses in Page's *The Old South* (1892) are in effect replies to Grady's addresses on the New South. When compared with Cable's *The Silent South* (1885), Page's *The Negro* (1904), with its rather defiant subtitle, "The Southerner's Problem," seems today somewhat reactionary, even to Southerners.

Northern misconceptions of Southern life and character irritated Page, and much of his earlier work was designed to refute them. *Red Rock* (1898), in spite of his change of plan, was in effect a belated reply to *Uncle Tom's Cabin,* which had appeared forty-six years earlier. And yet Page found a large and sympathetic audience waiting for him in the North. He once told Edwin Mims that the city of Boston bought more of his books than the entire state of Virginia. Mrs. Annie Fields, widow of the Boston publisher, James T. Fields, wrote to Page from Venice in May, 1892: "I have been reading your **'Gray Jacket'** with my eyes full of tears." She added that her friend Sarah Orne Jewett had also read the story and "felt it deeply." Mrs. Stowe's famous brother, Henry Ward Beecher, shed tears when Mrs. T. P. O'Connor read **"Marse Chan"** to him. Thomas Wentworth Higginson, who had also shed tears over that story, wrote to Page in September, 1892: "I have been reading your *Old South* with much interest & occasional disagreement."

For some Northern readers, I suspect, **"Marse Chan"** and **"Unc' Edinburg's Drowndin'"** were stories of a vanished way of life so remote in time and space that they had a romantic charm. Or perhaps these stories recalled to readers in huge Northern cities memories of a simpler life they had known or heard their parents or grandparents speak of. . . .

To Page's Southern readers, **"Marse Chan," "Meh Lady,"** and *Red Rock* were not merely good stories but historical documents which justified the slave plantation and made the Lost Cause seem in many ways the right one. Mrs. Paul Hamilton Hayne wrote to Page on May 10, 1888, that she and her son William were following his literary career with keen interest. "Our sacred past," she said, "we felt to be safe in your keeping." Page's friend William W. Archer wrote from Richmond, May 27, 1887: ". . . you have been the first Virginian to catch the attention of the outside world, and force its audience [to listen] while you told the story truthfully and pathetically, of **Ole Virginia**. . . ." Molly Elliot Seawell spoke for other Virginia writers when she wrote to Page in December, 1888: "Every body who writes about Virginia now must follow your lead. . . ."

Page of course did not create the plantation literary legend. Before the Civil War Kennedy, Caruthers, Beverley Tucker, Cooke, Thackeray, and G. P. R. James had made the Virginia plantation a part of our literary tradition. Page, however, went far beyond most of them in idealizing the plantation life. . . . So far did Page carry the tendency to idealize the past that later Virginia writers reacted against him in his own lifetime. Mary Johnston's *Hagar* (1913) is a protest on the part of the New Woman of the South against the code of "Southern chivalry" which motivated Page's heroines. In *The Rivet in Grandfather's Neck* (1915) James Branch Cabell went so far as to burlesque the story of **"Meh Lady."**. . .

Page's stories and the point of view they represent are out of fashion now even in his native state. The pendulum has swung away from romance and sentiment. It is not the modern fashion to portray gentlemen and ladies or, perhaps one may even say, honest and decent persons in the upper class of any society. In a recent survey of contemporary Southern fiction a Southern scholar has shown that in twentieth-century novels by Southerners the gentleman plays a sorry role indeed [C. P. Lee, "Decline and Death of the Southern Gentleman," *Southwest Review,* XXXVI (Summer 1951)]. That there were Southern gentlemen worthy of admiration is evident to anyone who knows something about Southern history or who has read a life of General Lee or Lucius Q. C. Lamar or Susan Dabney Smedes's life of her father, Thomas Dabney. Not many will ever care to read or reread Page's novels, but at some time in the future perhaps, when readers of fiction have grown weary of stories of Southern perverts and degenerates, a few may turn back to Page's early dialect stories, which even Ellen Glasgow could praise as "firm and round and as fragrant as dried rose-leaves. . . ."

John R. Roberson (essay date 1957)

SOURCE: "The Manuscript of Page's 'Marse Chan,'" in *Studies in Bibliography, Papers of the Bibliographical Society of the University of Virginia,* Vol. 9, edited by Fredson Bowers, Bibliographical Society of the University of Virginia, 1957, pp. 259-62.

[*Roberson discusses the revisions made to "Marse Chan" before its publication in 1884 by the editors of* The Century Illustrated Monthly Magazine.]

Thomas Nelson Page's volume of short stories, *In Ole Virginia,* was first published in 1887. Page's autograph drafts of the six stories which constitute the book are contained in the collection of literary manuscripts given to the Alderman Library by Clifton Waller Barrett. I have collated the first and most famous of them, **"Marse Chan,"** as it appears in the manuscript, in *The Century Illustrated Monthly Magazine* for April, 1884, in the 1887 edition of *In Ole Virginia,* and in the Plantation Edition of Page's collected works (1906). The collation reveals that the editors of the *Century* made considerable revisions before the first publication, and that almost without exception Page let their changes stand when he brought out the story in book form. . . .

Page had a tendency, in his early days at least, to diffuseness. The greater part of the changes the editors of the *Century* made in the story were intended simply to shorten it. In the letter accepting **"Marse Chan,"** they wrote that they would like to omit some parts near the beginning which

they felt were "extraneous to the subject of the story . . . the relations of the young couple." Later Mrs. Sophia Bledsoe Herrick, of the *Century* staff wrote to Page, on August 29, 1885: "In '**Marse Chan**' the material was in excellent shape, it was a charming story. Where it had to be shortened I cut it with positive pain—it was so exquisite from beginning to end." But cut it she did.

Two incidents included in the manuscript were cut out entirely. One concerns the childhood of Marse Chan and Miss Anne, when a boy in their school dropped a slate pencil down Anne's dress, and Chan, to avenge her, put two hornets down the boy's back. Sam, the Negro narrator, says that Chan was whipped, but that he never told "huccome" he did it. Page noted in the margin of the manuscript, "This incident was cut out to shorten the story—T.N.P." The other omission concerns a time when a neighbor whipped Sam, and Chan sought out the man and thrashed him. Page noted, "This incident was cut out and was used in '**Edinburg's Drowndin'.**' T.N.P.". . .

There are a number of minor changes. Apparently the editors felt that Page's reproduction of the Negro dialect, no matter how faithful, would be unintelligible to northern readers if the pronunciations were too foreign to those to which they were accustomed, or the spellings too removed from conventional orthography. Consequently they modified a number of them. The very title of the story was changed from "Mahs Chan" to **"Marse Chan,"** a spelling which Page himself used afterwards. "Cyahn" became "Kyarnt," "Whahn yo come on dawg?" became "Whyn't you come on, dawg?" and "geahden" became "garden.". . .

In 1887 the firm of Charles Scribner's Sons brought out *In Ole Virginia, or Marse Chan and Other Stories*. The text is substantially the same as that which appeared in the *Century;* none of the omissions have been restored. The main changes concern the spelling of the Negro dialect. As has been remarked, the *Century* did not follow Page's spellings when they seemed likely to be unintelligible. Apparently Page went through the magazine version and corrected words he thought too untrue to Negro speech, and Scribner's used this marked *Century* as printer's copy. . . .

Consideration of the manuscript and three printed versions of **"Marse Chan"** lends support to two accepted facts about Page the artist. Magazine editors did him a great service in disciplining his creations. Page himself gave rather careful attention to the details of his transcription of the speech of the old Virginia Negro. Both facts contributed to make him one of the most successful dialect story writers of his day.

Edmund Wilson (essay date 1962)

SOURCE: "Novelists of the Post-War South," in *Patriotic Gore: Studies in the Literature of the American Civil War,* Oxford University Press, 1962, pp. 529-616.

[*Wilson, one of the nation's foremost literary critics, notes*

Page reading a book.

that Page's popularity derives from his ability to soothe the Northern conscience and to stir Southern pride.]

One can trace very clearly in the pages of the *Century* the modulating attitude of the North toward the South. The stories of the Virginian Thomas Nelson Page began appearing in the magazine in 1884, at the moment when the resentment against [George W.] Cable in the South was reaching its most rabid point. "It is hard to explain in simple terms," says Grace King in her memoirs already mentioned, "what Thomas Nelson Page meant to us in the South at that time. He was the first Southern writer to appear in print as a Southerner, and his stories, short and simple, written in Negro dialect, and, I may say, Southern pronunciation, showed us with ineffable grace that although we were sore bereft, politically, we had now a chance in literature at least." And Page was equally popular in the North. Having devastated the feudal South, the Northerners wanted to be told of its glamour, of its old-time courtesy and grace. That was what they had wanted of Cable. A rush of industrial development had come at the end of the war, and the cities of the North and the West, now the scene of so much energetic enterprise which rendered them uglier and harsher, were losing their old amenities; and

the Northerners wanted, besides, a little to make it up to the South for their wartime vituperation. They took over the Southern myth and themselves began to revel in it. This acceptance was to culminate in *Gone with the Wind*, the enormous success of which novel makes a curious counterbalance to that of *Uncle Tom's Cabin*. But it began in the *Century* of the eighties with the stories of Thomas Nelson Page. Though Page had been only twelve at the end of the Civil War, so had had little firsthand experience of the life of the old regime, he really invented for the popular mind Old Massa and Mistis and Meh Lady, with their dusky-skinned adoring retainers. The Northerners, after the shedding of so much blood, illogically found it soothing to be told that slavery had been not so bad, that the Negroes were a lovable but simple race, whose business was to work for the whites. And Page also struck in his stories a note of reconciliation that everybody wanted to hear: he cooked up romances between young Northern officers, as gentlemanly as any Southerner, and spirited plantation beauties who might turn out to be the young men's cousins and who in any case would marry them after the war. To Grace King he gave this advice when she talked to him of a novel which she could not get accepted: "Now I will tell you what to do; for I did it! . . . It is the easiest thing to do in the world. Get a pretty girl and name her Jeanne, that name always takes! Make her fall in love with a Federal officer and your story will be printed at once! The publishers are right; the public wants love stories. Nothing easier than to write them.". . .

The whole picture in Page has been blurred. [By 1898] nobody North or South wanted . . . to be shown the realities. Not only is Virginia before the war made to fuse with the colonial Virginia of [John Esten] Cooke and other writers, so that both hang in the past as a glamorous legend. The attitudes of the North and South themselves have now become somewhat blurred. Animosities must be forgotten; the old issues must be put to sleep with the chloroform of magazine prose.

In **"Two Little Confederates,"** a story for children, once popular both North and South, a Confederate boy is caught by Federal soldiers, who threaten to shoot him if he refuses to tell where his older brother is hiding. The boy faints, and when he comes to, he finds a "big dragoon" from Delaware tenderly caring for him and is told that they had not really meant to kill him. "The soldier gently set him on his feet, and before he let him go kissed him. 'I've got a curly-headed fellow at home, just the size of you,' he said softly. Frank saw that his eyes were moist. 'I hope you'll get safe back home,' he said." Later, Frank and his little chum find this soldier wounded and begging for water. "'Willy, it's my Yankee!' exclaimed Frank." But the Federal dies, to the anguish of Frank, before they can do anything for him. The Northerner's mother comes after the war to look for her son's body. Frank shows her the grave in the garden, and she stays several days with his family. Frank's mother commiserates with her: her older son has not come back. But for her the ending is happy, since the young man does later return, and the story is concluded by the mating of two lovers who have been alienated. It was hard to make the Civil War seem cosy, but Thomas Nelson Page did his best.

In another of his sentimental stories—**"The Gray Jacket of '4'"**—there is a very curious effort in this direction. He describes a parade of veterans on the occasion of the unveiling in Richmond of a monument to the Confederate dead, then comments upon it as follows: "Only a thousand or two of old or aging men riding or tramping along through the dust of the street, under some old flags, dirty and ragged and stained. But they represented the spirit of the South; they represented the spirit which when honor was in question never counted the cost; the spirit that had stood up for the South against overwhelming odds for four years, and until the South had crumbled and perished under the forces of war; the spirit that is the strongest guaranty to us to-day that the Union is and is to be; the spirit that, glorious in victory, had displayed a fortitude yet greater in defeat. They saw in every stain on those tattered standards the blood of their noblest, bravest, and best; in every rent a proof of their glorious courage and sacrifice." Compare this with the scene in *Dr. Sevier*—so offensive to Southern readers—in which Cable makes one of his characers look on while a company of Union soldiers marches in the streets of New York, and

the author declares that their "cause is just"—though "we of the South . . . cannot forget—and we would not." Cable—though with tender regret for the heroism of his fellow Southerners—has taken up a definite position: he has decided that the South was mistaken. But Page will not take up a position: he somehow, by ambiguous language, makes it appear that "the spirit of the South," which had "stood up against overwhelming odds . . . until the South had crumbled and perished," was "the strongest guaranty today . . . that the Union is and is to be." What did he mean by this? There was something perhaps of the prewar pride of the Roman days of the Republic that was common to North and South and has made Northerners claim Lee as a great American. If, however, Page means what he seems to say, it has certainly not proved to be true: that spirit is still resisting its enforced incorporation in the Union. But I believe that what Page was now doing was nothing more than applying soft poultices of words not merely to the suppurating wounds of the South but also to the feelings of guilt of the North; and in New England Thomas Wentworth Higginson, who had subsidized John Brown, served as colonel of a Negro regiment and been present at the burning of Jacksonville, had been weeping over Page's **"Marse Chan,"** the story of a faithful old Negro stricken by grief at the death of his master, who has fought for the Confederate cause.

Theodore L. Gross (essay date 1967)

SOURCE: "The Old South," in *Thomas Nelson Page*, Twayne Publishers, 1967, pp. 39-77.

[*Gross, Page's biographer, assesses three late stories in which Page illustrates the poignant aftermath of the Civil War.*]

"The Burial of the Guns," although a weak story, reveals most clearly Page's over-all attitude toward the South and the Civil War. The guns that are buried (by a company of Confederate soldiers) are of course Southern guns, and the burial is that of the South's hopes for ever winning the war. As Page describes these weapons, they seem almost human and animistic; they certainly are more human than the characters themselves. This observation is not surprising, for in **"The Burial of the Guns"** the author is not really interested in people or guns but in what they represent, in the concept that they dramatize. In this case, the guns symbolize the Southern honor and duty and loyalty—in a word, the Southern heroism—that have been overcome but not destroyed.

The loss of the guns is the loss of great dignity and power—almost, the reader is made to feel, a sexual power. It is a loss that is greater than that of human beings, more significant and transcending than that of human beings; and as Page extols this superhuman quality, he himself grows curiously inhuman: "Most of the men who were not killed were retaken before the day was over, with many guns; but the Cat was lost. She remained in enemy's hands and probably was being turned against her old comrades and lovers. The company was inconsolable. The death of comrades was too natural and common a thing to depress the men beyond what such occurrences necessarily did; but to lose a gun! It was like losing the old Colonel: it was worse: a gun was ranked as a brigadier: and the Cat was equal to a major-general. The other guns seemed lost without her . . .".

What counts is not so much the human beings who have been lost on the battlefield but the honor with which these human beings have fought and died. Page tells us of the effects of the Civil War—and they are certainly harrowing—but he never demonstrates dramatically the suffering of individual people; the result is experience rendered at second hand:

> The minds of the men seemed to go back to the time when they were not so alone, but were part of a great and busy army, and some of them fell to talking of the past, and the battles they had figured in, and of the comrades they had lost. They told them off in a slow and colorless way, as if it were all part of the great past as much as the dead they named. One hundred and nineteen times they had been in action. Only seventeen men were left of the eighty odd who had first enlisted in the battery, and of these four were at home crippled for life. Two of the oldest men had been among the half-dozen who had fallen in the skirmish just the day before. It looked tolerably hard to be killed that way after passing for four years through such battles as they had been in; and both had wives and children at home, too, and not a cent to leave them to their names. They agreed calmly that they'd have to "sort of look after them a little" if they ever got home. These were some of the things they talked about as they pulled their old worn coats about them, stuffed their thin, weather-stained hands in their ragged pockets to warm them, and squatted down under the breastwork to keep a little out of the wind.

What the reader witnesses in **"The Burial of the Guns"** is pathos evoked at the moment of death; and he is reminded, once again, of the great propensity that Page has for death in his fiction, the frequency with which he presents his Southern hero dying in the moment of a glory that is certain to vanish. In this tale, the guns are the hero; and before they are dropped into the water, before the troops disband, the Colonel utters what is really a prayer and a eulogy:

> My men, I cannot let you go so. We were neighbors when the war began—many of us, and some not here to-night; we have been more since then—comrades in arms; we have all stood for one thing—for Virginia and the South; we have all done our duty—tried to do our duty; we have fought a good fight, and now it seems to be over, and we have been overwhelmed by number, not whipped—and we are going home. We have the future before us—we don't know just what it will bring, but we can stand a good deal. We have proved it. Upon us depends the South in the future as in the past. You have done your duty in the past, you will not fail in the future. Go home and be honest, brave, self-sacrificing, God-fearing citizens, as you have been soldiers, and you need not fear for Virginia and

the South. The war may be over; but you will ever be ready to serve your country. The end may not be as we wanted it, prayed for it, fought for it; but we can trust God; the end in the end will be the best that could be; even if the South is not free she will be better and stronger that she fought as she did. Go home and bring up your children to love her, and though you may have nothing else to leave them, you can leave them the heritage that they are sons of men who were in Lee's army.

This speech, idealistic and biased, chauvinistic and parochial, can be duplicated by similar quotations from the most sophisticated Southern authors of the post-Civil War period. It indicates, for one thing, that Page was not always successful in keeping the detachment of which he perennially boasts in so many stories and essays, and it contradicts the assertion often made that local color-fiction was disinterested and unconcerned with political issues. The Colonel's speech depends for its effects on the assumption that words like *duty, honest, brave, self-sacrificing,* and *God-fearing* are meaningful to these unsuccessful soldiers after all that they have been through; it also implies that the abstractions are intrinsically more important than the soldiers whom the Colonel addresses. Although Page is unaware of his final effect, this dedication to abstractions has led, in a curious way, to the abdication of human relations, and the connection between the individual and Virginia or the South or honor has assumed transcendent significance.

The whites honor these abstractions in other whites and more importantly in the Negro. The faithful colored man knows this axiom of Southern heroism intuitively and so never insists on his freedom, never insists on being considered a human being. In a story like **"Burial of the Guns,"** the quality of idealism is strained to an extreme point so that it is difficult to conceive of the war as having been fought by individual people. At the end of the tale, which has concerned itself fundamentally with those moments after Appomattox when the guns must be buried, the soldiers include in the burial rites the names of the guns that they have used in combat. Those names—Matthew, Mark, Luke, John, The Eagle, and The Cat—are pointedly Christian. The implication is clear: the war these soldiers have fought has been not only religious in nature but also in the service of the highest possible cause in their lives—the honor of the South.

"Little Darby," a story in the same vein, retells the well-known anecdote that served as the source of **"Marse Chan."** But in **"Little Darby"** Page is closer to the original material than in the more compressed and suggestive early version: the girl's letter that warns the hero, "Don't come home without a furlough," takes on greater significance, and the individual families do not have the aristocratic bearing of those in **"Marse Chan"**—they are poor-whites. The serenity of Virginia, the threat of oncoming war, and the rival families recall those similar elements in **"Marse Chan"** and the other stories of *In Ole Virginia*; in **"Little Darby,"** however, Page intends to testify to the sectional loyalty of the lower classes during the Civil War. He attempts to demonstrate that heroism can exist among the poor as well as the rich, but in the process of writing the story he cannot avoid making class distinctions—Darby descends from a tradition of noble Englishmen, and his pedigree accounts for his courage during the war. Arthur Hobson Quinn, in a sympathetic estimation of Page's fiction, makes a similar point and reprints a long, significant letter that "explains the genesis of **'Little Darby'** and also of his earliest stories":

> I have no doubt that your estimate of the comparative merits of my short stories and of my novels is absolutely correct and I have a secret fear that my earlier stories, those in dialect, are superior in their appeal to any that I have written since. If I find you selecting **"Marse Chan"** and **"Meh Lady"** in preference to **"Edinburg's Drowndin'"** and **"Polly,"** I have no right to complain and it brings me to a reflection which I have always had: as to what is the secret of the success of the story or novel. Is it the theme or the art with which any theme, reasonably broad, is handled, or is it something growing out of the union of the two? Personally I have always estimated **"Edinburg's Drowndin'"** as possibly the broadest of my stories, at least as the one giving a reflection of the broadest current of the old Southern life, and so far as literary art is concerned, it seems to me at least on a par with the others. I think, therefore, it must be the unrelieved tragedy in **"Marse Chan"** or the fact that **"Meh Lady"** appealed to both sides, and was written to make this appeal, that has given them a prestige, if I may use so important a word, far beyond that of **"Edinburg's Drowndin'"** and **"Ole 'Stracted."** **"Little Darby,"** **"Run to Seed"** and **"Elsket,"** which you have signalized with the stamp of your imprimatur, I also think among the very best stories I have written. The first two of these appeal to me almost as much as the dialect stories. The first of these was written on precisely the same theme with **"Marse Chan"** and out of the consciousness that whereas the tragedy of **"Marse Chan"** was laid in the highest social rank, the incident which had given rise to it was based on a letter written by a poor girl, of much lower rank, to her lover, who like **"Marse Chan"** had found his death on the battle-field, and I felt somehow that it was due to that class that I should testify with whatever power I might possess, to their devotion to the South. If there is a difference it seems to me that it lies rather in the fact that readers estimate as more romantic a tragedy in the upper ranks of life than in lower, whereas, we know that rank has nothing to do with it. [Arthur Hobson Quinn, *American Fiction: An Historical and Critical Survey*, 1936]

In the early part of **"Little Darby,"** the pre-war South—and, more specifically, pre-war Virginia—is presented as a quiet, rural area. Political differences are the only cause for excitement, and the opposing political positions are made clear: they represent secession and national unity. Little Darby, whose family favors secession, is separated from Vashti, the girl he loves, because of the political differences of their families. When he enlists in the army, she does not permit herself to yield to him although she confesses her love to her mother. Page gives the situation the chivalric overtones that are present in his other fiction: like lovers in a courtly romance, the warrior leaves to defend his lady despite the fact that the lady rejects him.

But Darby is not so heroic in battle as those protagonists of the earlier stories in spite of Page's desire "to testify" to his "devotion to the South." He is described as a poor-white without breeding; and though the author brings compassion to his tale, he does not assume the same attitude of admiration that he maintains toward those Southern heroes who have a more aristocratic pedigree. Consequently, Little Darby is more credible and realistic though he is smaller in scope than the figures of *In Ole Virginia*. He is inconspicuous as a soldier—taciturn, loyal, brave, but largely unnoticed—and Page puts him into a company of common soldiers whom he describes with restraint: "The war was very different from what those who went into it expected it to be. Until it had gone on some time it seemed mainly marching and camping and staying in camp, quite uselessly as seemed to many, and drilling and doing nothing. Much of the time—especially later on—was given to marching and getting food; but drilling and camp duties at first took up most of it. This was especially hard on the poorer men, no one knew what it was to them. Some moped, some fell sick."

Equally successful is the description of the women who stayed at home and suffered appalling poverty. Once again the mood described is credible because it is not excessive:

> . . . the women of the district had a hungry time, and the war bore on them heavily as on everyone else, and as it went on they suffered more and more. Many a woman went day after day and week after week without even the small portion of coarse cornbread which was ordinarily her common fare. They called oftener and oftener at the houses of their neighbors who owned the plantations near them, and always received something; but as time went on the plantations themselves were stripped; the little things they could take with them when they went, such as eggs, honey, etc., were wanting, and to go too often without anything to give might make them seem like beggars, and that they were not. Their husbands were in the army fighting for the South, as well as those from the plantations, and they stood by this fact on the same level.

> The arrogant looks of the negroes were unpleasant, and in marked contrast to the universal graciousness of their owners. but they were slaves and they could afford to despise them. Only they must uphold their independence. Thus no one outside knew what the women of the district went through. When they wrote to their husbands or sons that they were in straits, it meant that they were starving. Such a letter meant all the more because they were used to hunger, but not to writing, and a letter meant perhaps days of thought and enterprise and hours of labor.

Against this bleak background, the simple action of the story rises. It turns upon the hero's demonstration of honor to his lady, a demonstration that is all the more impressive for the circumstances that surround it. The lady, Vashti, finally confesses her love to Darby and writes that his mother is ill, that "he ought to get a furlough and come home, and when he did she would marry him." The letter, however, contains one crucial proviso:

At the end of the letter, as if possibly she thought, in the greatness of her relief at her confession, that the temptation she held out might prove too great even for him, or possibly only because she was a woman, there was a postscript scrawled across the coarse, blue Confederate paper: "Don't come without a furlough; for if you don't come honorable I won't marry you." This, however, Darby scarcely read. His being was in the letter. It was only later that the picture of his mother ill and failing came to him, and it smote him in the midst of his happiness and clung to him afterward like a nightmare. It haunted him. She was dying.

Darby does not wait for his furlough; when he meets Vashti, her first word is "Darby," uttered in surprise and love for the returned hero. When the subsequent conversation reveals that he has returned to his dying mother without a leave, Vashti accuses him of being a coward and a deserter, of having forsaken his honor. Honor at this point is more important than Darby himself, who grows sick and delirious because of the rejection. Ultimately, he redeems himself by dying for the South and for his heartless Lady, thus accepting the grounds on which Vashti has denied him: he prevents Northern soldiers from shooting Vashti, who is in the process of burning a bridge to prevent the Northern company from concluding a raid. Darby drowns, a fitting martyr to the abstract glory that Vashti has demanded of him.

"Little Darby" is still another retelling of that stock sentimental situation in which the hero dies in battle for his lady; and its power relies upon the dedication of the two central figures to abstractions that transcend their own humanity. Neither Little Darby nor Vashti doubts for a moment that honor transcends their individual importance; and the popularity of this tale—as well as many others like it—assumes the reader's implication in the myth of heroism, the belief in such abstractions as honor and courage.

A third story, **"The Old Gentleman of the Black Stock"** (1894), is not concerned with the war; it develops, in a quiet and attractive manner, some of the author's favorite themes: the superiority of the country to the city, of the past to the present, of feeling to intellect. This tale, one of Page's most popular ones, is an autobiographical recounting of his first experiences in Richmond twenty years earlier. The young lawyer's uncertainty and lack of sophistication are well presented, and his sentimental love affair, though traditional and predictable, is restrained. Most effective, however, is the description of "the old gentleman of the black stock" through whom the central ideas become evident. His life has been an economic success but an emotional failure largely because of one great fault—selfishness. "I made one mistake, sir," he tells the narrator, "early in life, and it has lasted me ever since. I put Brains before everything, Intellect before Heart. It was all selfishness: that was the rock on which I split. I was a man of parts, sir, and I thought with my intellect I could do everything. But I could not."

The old man serves as the narrator's literary and moral mentor. Having sacrificed love for the acquisition of money and the "selflessness" of family life for his own personal goals, he has since depended on books for comfort. Through the "old gentleman of the black stock," Page expresses some of his own observations on literature:

I asked him about Carlyle and Emerson, for I was just then discovering them. He admitted the sincerity of both; but Carlyle he did not like.

"He is always ill-tempered and sour, and is forever sneering at others. He is Jeremiah, without his inspiration or his occasion," he said of him. "He is not a gentleman, sir, and has never forgiven either the world or himself for it."

"Do you think he writes well?" I demanded.

"Yes, sir, he writes vigorously,—I suppose you mean that,—but it is not English. I do not know just what to term it. It was a trick with him, a part of his pedantry. But when I want acerbity I prefer Swift."

Emerson he put on a much higher place than Carlyle; but though he admitted his sincerity, and ranked him as the first American literary man, he did not read him much.

"He is a kindly man," he said, "and has 'wrought in a sad sincerity.' But he preaches too much for me, and he is all texts. When I want preaching I go to church."

Books can never supplant the emotional loss that the old gentleman has suffered—"they forsake you," he complains as he dies, "or bore you"—and he warns the young lawyer to "cultivate the affections. Take an old man's word for it, that the men who are happy are those who love and are loved. Better love the meanest thing that lives than only yourself." The narrator takes the man's advice and marries the daughter of the woman whom the "old gentleman" had given up years before.

This sentimental tale was so popular in its time because it satisfies all the demands of the popular romance: it presents love lost in the "old gentleman of the black stock" and love redeemed in the young lawyer; it emphasizes the triumph of the heart over the head, for the young lawyer wins his young lady through self-sacrifice and devotion; and it offers a tribute to the purity and innocence of rural life, for both the hero and heroine have just come from the country.

"The Burial of the Guns," "Little Darby," and **"The Old Gentleman of the Black Stock"** appeared in 1894. Page did not publish another work of fiction until 1898 when *Red Rock*, his most important novel, appeared serially in *Scribner's Magazine*. The human comedy that he had traced in **"Run to Seed"** and *On Newfound River* surrendered to the more tragic, more poignant, vanished glory of **"The Burial of the Guns"** and **"Little Darby."** None of these stories was so impressive as those he first published, and they all suggest a deliquescence of the clear point of view and tone in **"Marse Chan"** and **"Meh Lady."**

In the period from 1894 to 1898 Page struggled with *Red Rock*; in this elaborate, ambitious novel—the finest one that he wrote—he seeks to offer his ultimate defense of the South before and after the Civil War. As a work of art *Red Rock* does not succeed, for in spite of his attempt to be dispassionate and fair to both the North and the South, the book grows inevitably tendentious. As a defense of the South during Reconstruction, however, it remains one of the most impressive fictional accounts of the period.

Kimball King (essay date 1969)

SOURCE: "Introduction," in *In Ole Virginia; or, Marse Chan, and Other Stories* by Thomas Nelson Page, University of North Carolina Press, 1969, pp. ix-xxxvi.

[*King argues that Page's development of the Southern plantation tradition presents a contradiction between intent and outcome; his panegyrics of the antebellum South inadvertently reveal the fatal weaknesses of the plantation system.*]

The appearance in 1887 of Thomas Nelson Page's first collection of short stories, **In Ole Virginia; or, Marse Chan and Other Stories,** marked a new era in the plantation literary tradition. . . .

While Page was the most effective author to extol the virtues of the Old South, a plantation tradition had flourished for decades before the young Virginia lawyer began to write. Page merely surpassed his predecessors in enhancing the image. The success of **In Ole Virginia** and the acceptance of Page's work by popular national magazines such as *Scribner's Monthly* was part of the phenomenon of local color writing which swept America in the two decades following the Civil War. The new "national consciousness" that the war produced somewhat paradoxically encouraged investigation of the recently unified country's component parts. Every area of America in the late nineteenth century soon boasted its share of local color writers. In the South the local color movement was especially significant. The region had produced so few important men of letters before the Civil War that their appearance in large numbers during the years immediately following was observed with startled interest. The war had stimulated the nation's interest in rediscovering this unique region, and periodical readers were surfeited with Southern materials. Even Northern authors found attractive qualities in ante-bellum Southern life, which they attempted to portray as romantically as any native might do.

To most of these readers and authors, a Southern backdrop was a pleasing embellishment to a romantic tale, for the South's downfall added a touch of pathos that moved sentimental readers. But to Thomas Nelson Page, the Southern defeat marked the death of an aristocratic ideal that his ancestors had defended since the earliest days of the colonies. He was only twelve years old when the Civil War ended, so that his recollections of Old Virginia were based on childhood experiences and anecdotes of his family and older friends. Consequently, his Southern stories were in part attempts to recapture his childhood, to discover his personal identity, and to place himself and his society in an historical context. Early in his life he developed a fascination for genealogy and took pride in the knowledge that one of his forebears, Thomas Nelson, had founded Yorktown and that a later Thomas Nelson had signed the Declaration of Independence. Another ancestor, John Page of Rosewell, was a friend of Thomas Jefferson, a United States congressman, and a governor of Virginia. Not surprisingly, the Nelsons and the Pages were accustomed to the exercise of community leadership, accepting the responsibilities as well as the privileges of power. Thus Thomas Nelson Page grew to manhood believing that the traditions of the past were still functional and that contemporary society could be strengthened by leaders who, like himself, revered the seasoned ideals of the ante-bellum South. Part of the task of any new leader would be to revitalize the ideal society that his Southern antecedents had envisioned.

It seems difficult today to understand how so many Americans, with such different traditions and principles, could accept Page's views. Possibly the reluctance of Americans to face up to the troubling discoveries of contemporary social injustice following the war gave impetus to his popularity, since his idealized view of the Old South reassured a nation that was weary of disharmony.

Writing in the years following the close of Reconstruction, Page was freer to explore new topics than his pre-Civil War predecessors. The ante-bellum Southern man of letters had been trapped by the necessity of defending slavery. After the war, however, a Southerner could write not merely in defense of his region but with the greater freedom of the historian. Indeed, most novelists and poets of the New South considered themselves historians—and they usually claimed impartiality when dealing with "facts." Page could sympathize with the Confederacy and at the same time show his disapproval of secession. He could eulogize the plantation system by recalling only its happiest aspects, since it was no longer necessary, or even possible, to argue for its continuance.

Page and other writers in the plantation literary tradition tended to overemphasize the differences in the Southern way of life before and after the war, asserting that the present way of living was vastly different from the ante-bellum world and thus increasing the Southerner's pride in his past and dramatizing his sense of victimization and self-sacrifice. Page's essays and stories, published under such titles as *In Ole Virginia, The Old Dominion,* and *The Old South,* described a civilization in which landlords abided by an almost medieval sense of *gentilesse,* women were exalted, and all the chivalric virtues prevailed. The wealth and power of the Virginia planter was magnified by Page's fictional representations, and his accounts of plantation life in the Tidewater country contained large elements of hyperbole. The prosperity of Virginia was in truth considerably diminished by the war, but Page made the passing of the old order an epic theme by stressing the polarity of past and present. His protagonists were typically those who had survived the war and were faced with the task of adjusting to a new and alien culture. Thus Old Sam, the faithful slave in Page's first story **"Marse Chan,"** refers to his happy life before the war as "de good ole times . . . de bes' Sam ever see." When Page wrote, the idyll had already ended. He and his characters attempted to invoke a world that lived only in memory, and nostalgia was, therefore, the dominant mood of Page's most successful stories. . . .

Page owed his literary success to his investigation of a romantic culture and era. Although there were local color writers in the deep South and in the mountain regions, too, before World War I, the dominant literary image of the South was provided by accounts of life in the Tidewater country. The romantic, sentimental writings of Page and other gentlemen-authors who defended the plantation system succeeded in molding the public's view of Dixie for many years. Northern and Western readers devoured accounts of the people they had recently defeated, insatiable for details of Southern heroism and nobility. Page made it easier for skeptical readers to accept his idealized portraits of Virginians by concentrating on the gallant struggles of his compatriots in the Reconstruction Era.

Although Page wished to exonerate slaveholders from charges of barbarism or caprice, he was not prepared to defend slavery as an institution. Perpetuating a myth is very different from advocating a working policy. Page was not an active racist and preferred to discuss aspects of Southern life that were not so controversial. He held up for approbation the best qualities of the Southerners, and the virtues of plantation life that he chose to depict—simplicity, loyalty, gentility, compassion—are generally revered by civilized people. The issue of Southern autonomy was dead for Page, but he was concerned that certain Southern qualities might be eradicated by nationalism. If the South could not be a separate entity, at least Southern ideals could infiltrate the new Union. Each of Page's major novels (*Red Rock, Gordon Keith,* and *John Marvel, Assistant*) concerns Southern "missionaries," Virginia gentlemen who proseletyze Southern ideals and convert Yankees in the process. Part of their doctrine was a distrust of industrialization, a repudiation of the bourgeois goals of capitalistic society, a belief that aristocratic paternalism could still combat the grosser aspects of democracy, and a wistful agrarianism. Such themes were especially relevant to the New South as it underwent absorption into the Union.

Page's writings about the South are panegyrics. Their special quality depends on our distance from a hallowed past. Where there is no hope of resurrecting a civilization, we can understand regretfully its value and significance. Page's heroes possess many traditional characteristics, but most often they are associated with grief, martyrdom, undeserved injury, endurance against all odds, compassion for their adversaries, and an unremitting sense of loss. Those who display such traits are not knights and ladies of the Old Dominion but unfortunates caught in the transition between the old world and the new. The antebellum characters are lovingly portrayed, but essentially they serve as foils to their less favored descendants—the fallen heroes dominate the stage as we watch their expulsion from Eden. However much Page may have worshipped the past, he was feverishly concerned with the present in his fiction; the people and conditions he best described establish him as an author of the New South. . . .

All of the stories in [*In Ole Virginia*] reflect the conservative literary influences of the Oakland library. The chivalrous atmosphere of Sir Walter Scott's romances are easily detected in the boyish escapades of Page's heroes, in the chaste behavior of his young girls, in the use of folk characters, sub-plots, and historical events. Allusions to Swift, Thackeray, Tennyson, and Arnold are also present in the works of Page, but his debt to these authors is superficial. Of more obvious importance are the Southern writers who preceded him. Reading Poe reinforced Page's tendency to idealize pure women and provided the Gothic atmosphere of **"No Haid Pawn."** Irwin Russell's "Christmas Night in the Quarters" and other dialect poems probably gave Page the inspiration for his own first poem, "Uncle Gabe's White Folks" (1876), and led to his heavy reliance on dialect in most of his short stories. Two other Virginia authors, George Bagby and Armistead Gordon, had explored the themes that Page would later develop more fully. Page's most significant literary borrowing was his reworking of Gordon's story, "Envion," in his own story, **"Marse Chan."** Gordon's story makes similar use of a nostalgic former slave's recollections of a happier era, but it is not nearly so well constructed or believable as Page's tale.

Certainly any discussion of Page's work must begin with a brief analysis of **"Marse Chan,"** since it was his first short story and, I believe, his most effective piece of writing. **"Marse Chan"** has more than historical value to the contemporary reader. It simultaneously displays both the charm and the inequities of the Old South, the admirable qualities and the fatal weakness of that society. Page revealed more in this story than he wished of the perilous nature of the old order. It is a eulogy to the past, but consciously or unconsciously the author included disturbing details that make his story deeper, and more interesting, than he probably intended.

The opening encounter of Page's traveler with the former slave is sensitively drawn. Sam's dignified and melancholy bearing wins the immediate admiration of the white man, and the atmosphere of lost grandeur and lingering gentility that provides a backdrop for the conversation between the two men appropriately frames the demise of a noble family. Page convinces us of the former slave's integrity as an individual and his disorientation in the New South. In this way the author has vindicated the Southern cause. What interests contemporary readers is the implicit message of Page's documented microcosm of Southern life. Sam does not understand, nor is it likely that his creator realized, the extent to which the slave has been victimized by the old order. Throughout **"Marse Chan"** we glimpse the best aspects of the Tidewater ideal; Page has selected materials that show his aristocratic society to advantage. Yet unconsciously he reveals the abrasive conflicts within that society which had doomed it.

The result is an increasing sense of irony, which at times divides us from the author but finally unites us with him in mutual feelings of sympathy and admiration for Old Sam. Page both pities the former slave and laments the changes that have extinguished the paternalism of the slavery system. Sam shares Page's lament, and we see a dispossessed old man without an identity of his own, shut off from the present, sustained only by memories of the dead. "Marse Chan" is, as Page had hoped, a faithful representation of the world of his childhood recollections. Yet in portraying the virtues of that world he also exposed its faults: the ambiguities and weaknesses of feudal life. Reading it we discover that our emotions are derived from different assumptions and attitudes than the author's. Page mourns for the past and its lost grandeur; we are saddened by the universal failings of mankind which could construct with pride a system doomed to the destruction of those who were a part of it.

Consider, for example, our first insight into Old Sam's attitudes when he scolds Marse Chan's aged dog. His behavior toward the dog attests to his loyal character and good nature as he lowers the fence rails for the old animal and mutters, "Jes' like white folks—think 'cuz you's white and I's black, I got to wait on yo' all de time." The dog has become a substitute master whom Sam rebukes but also serves. He must continue to express his ingrained sense of servitude.

The story Sam tells us is old-fashioned and chivalrous. Tom Channing is a romantic hero—loyal, pure, and protective; and his girl, Anne Chamberlin, is one of Page's many tomboys who are suddenly transformed into aloof beauties. In contrast to these attractive lovers is the antagonist, Colonel Chamberlin, who is a rarity in Page's fictional world—an irresponsible aristocrat. The presence of even one such hotheaded bigot, however, counters Page's Edenic vision of the old order. Perhaps to compensate for the Colonel's failure to live up to his responsibilities, Page forcefully illustrates Mr. Channing's sense of *noblesse oblige* in the Ham Fisher episode. Yet even here flaws in the plantation system are unwittingly exposed. We cannot forget that Channing ordered Ham to rescue the horses in a burning barn; and even though he loses his eyesight protecting Ham, Channing's power over life and death and the tragic consequences of his hasty decision are disturbing. Doubtless Page saw this episode as a classic illustration of the landowner's mixed burden of privilege and responsibility, the reciprocal loyalty of liege lord and vassal. The fact remains that the disaster resulted from Channing's impulsiveness and unquestioned authority. It is unlikely that Page considered the slaveholder's blindness as in any way representing a chastisement for an irresponsible command. Yet what he reveals are the latent dangers of the system he praises. To a modern reader Channing's loss of eyesight assumes symbolic connotations, representing the landowner's inability, because of the presence of slavery, to face the end of the plantation system or to perceive the destructive forces in his present way of life.

Another suggestion of internal stress in the story can be found in the father-son relationship. Marse Chan's attitudes conflict several times with the values of his father's generation, and we see that he comprehends some of the injustices and archaisms of the aristocratic life—as, for example, in his challenging his father's right to whip his slave. Any mention of the son's hostility toward the father is avoided, but the reader is aware that the plantation system, as well as the man who represents this system in the son's eyes, is vulnerable and can be challenged. Page fails, however, to question Marse Chan's motives in freeing his slave. Why, if Sam's life on the plantation was so carefree, would young Channing make the gesture of emancipation?

Another problem raised by Marse Chan's contact with the older generation is his behavior toward Colonel Chamberlin. The young Virginian emerges victorious over his older compatriot by repudiating an important ritual of the chivalric code—dueling. Here Mark Twain comes to mind, especially his treatment of dueling in the Grangerford episode of *Huckleberry Finn.* Page, however, was not satirizing dueling; he was suggesting a manly alternative. Marse Chan's action prefigures the behavior of Bayard Sartoris in Faulkner's *The Unvanquished,* when the latter walks unarmed into the office of his father's murderer and tells him to leave town, simultaneously protecting both his family's honor and avoiding needless bloodshed. Although Page affirmed the tradition of satisfied honor, he was, in fact, advocating a radical change in accepted chivalric behavior.

Marse Chan's later defense of Colonel Chamberlin's honor is disinterested heroism, since we know that he and Anne have already been estranged by the earlier duel, and he dies unrewarded, for his generosity is sacrificed to a cause he and his family had first opposed. Thus Page has created what is ultimately an ironic tale, and we are likely to question Sam's assertion that he is describing the good old days. The young hero's passing and the other deaths that follow symbolize the end of the old order.

Bereft of his master, Sam must retain his loyalty to a system that can no longer protect him. He has no present personal identity, and his most valid relationships to other people and places have been terminated. In his lifetime he has become an historical figure. One could argue that the immediate cause of the plantation system's end was the war and the Northern foes who conquered, but in reality the flaw was internal. The system's feudal ties and the subordination of one group to another within a static environment contained its own destruction. The South had looked back, not forward, and was thus unprepared to meet the demands of sudden change. "Marse Chan" provides us with an ideal view of a conservative Southerner's world, which Page's admirers recognized as a proper tribute to the South's former greatness; but the story also illustrates the fragile structure of ante-bellum life and its unrealistic demands upon the individual, black or white.

"Unc' Edinburg's Drowndin'" amplifies a theme Page used earlier in "Marse Chan"—the landlord's readiness to protect his slave at the risk of his own life. Here Marse George rescues Edinburg, his valet, from drowning, thereby exposing himself to pneumonia and eventually succumbing. The nostalgic tones of Old Sam in Page's first story are echoed here by Edinburg, who similarly exults in his owner's distinguished lineage and fine character and regrets the passing of gracious living. Although Page had already illustrated the Southern conception of *noblesse oblige* in the events that led to the blinding of Marse Chan's father, the selfless heroism of Marse George reiterates Page's view of the aristocrat as victim. The authors of the plantation tradition insisted that the privileged classes had been doomed by their excessive responsibilities to their dependents. They agreed that the war and Reconstruction, though painful, relieved the overburdened aristocrat; the black man and the poor white, they claimed, were the principal victims of the new order. Hence young Channing and Marse George go to their heavenly rewards while Sam and Edinburg are left to mourn for a lost way of life. Page deliberately undermined the abolitionists' claims that slaves were exploited by their owners and craved freedom from oppression. The former slave as narrator in both stories becomes the most convincing champion of the Old South.

If we can accept the shaky premise of these tales—that Sam and Edinburg are discontented with their new freedom, it becomes relatively easy for us to accept Page's romantic assessment of the past. In each case Page beckons us to enter the mind of appealing, vital Negro characters whose believability is established through first person narration. The apparent elimination of the authorial point of view is disarming, and the Negro portraiture seemed credible at the time *In Ole Virginia* was written, since most readers were unfamiliar with the feelings of real black men and women. Edinburg's delight in holiday festivities and his appreciation of social and religious rituals were engaging traits to readers primarily interested in the curiosities of a glamorous era. What Edinburg esteemed fascinated them as well, and the old man's nostalgic outbursts satisfied their own sentimental longings for an orderly, bountiful life. Here, twenty-one years after the war, political and moral issues seemed irrelevant.

Romantic contrivances such as the Romeo and Juliet theme were especially popular in local color fiction. The recently concluded war perhaps stressed the dangers of feuding. The source of dramatic action in four of the six stories in *In Ole Virginia* stems from the separation of young lovers by hostile families. Page, as I have mentioned, admired Poe and may have drawn on that writer for the themes of unrequited love and the untimely death of the young and deserving. Like him, Page evades the sexual aspects of love, and extols chaste relationships that are consummated only in spirit.

The unvaried plots and characterizations of Page's many stories result from his preoccupation with theme rather than events or people. The movement in **"Unc' Edinburg's Drowndin'"** is not dependent on the believable action of defined characters in a given situation. Rather, the author's concern is defining loyalty and honor and recording behavior that illustrates his theories. Sub-themes, little vignettes about Southern culture, are treated so thoroughly that they threaten to destroy the proportion of his

tale. Although the author, at one time at least (in a letter to A. H. Quinn), especially favored **"Unc' Edinburg's Drowndin'"** among his stories, Edinburg's elaborate treatises on rhetoric and debating would be more appropriate in a lighthearted evaluation of old-time politics than in a story of a young man's death. This may partly account for our inability to empathize with Marse George, whereas Marse Chan, in a better-planned, more economical work, captures our feelings and imagination. Still, as in each of the stories in this volume, Page has demonstrated in **"Unc' Edinburg's Drowndin'"** his own loyalty to the code, real or imagined, of his forebears. And the reader again may note the sacrifice of both black and white individuals to the "system."

The third story in this collection is also well known. **"Meh Lady"** is likewise a study of racial relationships and conflicts within the plantation system. Critics have generally recognized it as an archetypal formula story of the local color era, since it focuses on the marriage of a Southern girl to a Yankee. The formula was ridiculed by James Branch Cabell when he parodied Page's story in his novel, *The Rivet in Grandfather's Neck*. Like the legend of the last male heir which we find in **"Marse Chan,"** anecdotes about intersectional marriages were popular after the war, and some specific incidents may have influenced the author in developing the plot of **"Meh Lady."** What is most interesting about **"Meh Lady"** is Page's personal interpretation of the story's events and his exposure of additional aspects of the plantation system. The theme was suggested to Page by Robert Underwood Johnson, who had seen a performance of *Minna Von Barnhelm* in New York and wrote to Page that he might profitably adapt the plot to a Southern setting. Like Lessing's play—and like John W. De Forest's *Miss Ravenel's Conversion*—**"Meh Lady"** centers on a love affair between a young man and woman with conflicting loyalties. Page developed this theme to encompass loyalties of all kinds—of Southerners to the Confederacy, of a Northern officer to his regiment, of a widow to her deceased husband, of a mother and sister to the family's remaining son, of aristocrats to their social class, of masters to servants and servants to masters. The author was doubtless aware that he had molded the characters of Meh Lady and her mother, identified only as Mistis', to be so wise and morally courageous that they inspired in their servants a similar sense of responsibility. The cruelly wronged South, the indomitable Southern gentlewoman, and the faithful slave interact to create a moving story.

Again Page tells us more about his world than he perhaps suspected. The story is a paean to loyalty, but implicitly it bears testimony also to the vulnerability of the plantation world. For in **"Meh Lady"** traditional decorum has been shattered by the exigencies of war, and the relationship between Mistis' and her servant is subtly altered. Unc' Billy, the plantation vassal, must assume an increasing number of responsibilities that were formerly the prerogatives of the landlord. Raised as a household dependent, Unc' Billy must develop into a mature, protective adult, even while retaining a household servant's subordinate status. Mistis' must assume full responsibility for the plantation's management, while deriving part of her power and safety from her servant. As Unc' Billy describes the hardships endured on the plantation during the war, he marvels at the courage of Meh Lady and her mother. Page wished to demonstrate the strength of a group of women whom the rest of the world considered pampered and weak. We are not surprised by the inner toughness of these gentle ladies, for such a characteristic is consistent with the theory of *noblesse oblige.* Background and breeding have been put to the test and have triumphed—but it is an anxious victory. The author has made his heroines so vulnerable that it is hard to share his optimism for their future.

The unexpected arrival of a chivalrous knight is congruent with the romantic milieu of **"Meh Lady,"** but Page's unusual stroke is casting the dragon-slayer as a Yankee officer. We learn, to be sure, that Captain Wilton's mother was a Virginian, which in part accounts for his gentlemanly behavior, but Mistis' defenselessness is again manifest. She is saved only by the interference of an enemy who challenges the wishes of his own troops. A class sympathy binds the Southern ladies and the gentleman soldier. In Southern fiction, social compatibility frequently overcomes the outward expression of sectional hostility. Here, Mistis' undoubtedly reminds the young officer of his mother, and she in turn acknowledges his resemblance to her dead son.

Readers forgave the implausibility of **"Meh Lady"** and accepted Page's solution to the conflict between the states in symbolic terms. They agreed there must be a marriage, a reunion of the two sections; practical considerations were avoided. On such a symbolic level, however, it is important to remember that the Union officer returns to the soil of his ancestors and becomes a plantation owner and that his life is "reconstructed" in terms of the old plantation system—all with the approval of a former slave. Because Unc' Billy is forced to become a surrogate father and manager of the plantation after Mistis' death, it is fitting that he should eventually give the bride away in the story's sentimental climax. But we should note that after faithfully discharging his final responsibility Unc' Billy recedes gladly into the background as the plantation's new master takes over. Unc' Billy at the same time refused to welcome his rise in status or power, and preferred instead the days preceding emancipation. His concluding description of life on the plantation before the war is a classic expression of sentiment for the ante-bellum world. Along with Sam and Edinburg, Billy represents the conservative element of any population that resists major changes; these three are the traditional "white folks" Negroes of plantation literature. What makes them impressive as characters, and not simply stereotypes, is the author's warmth of characterization and his ability to create memorable individuals within the limits of a type.

"Ole 'Stracted" differs from the previous three stories in that it tells of former slaves who enjoy their new status as freedmen and lead productive, dignified lives. Ole 'Stracted, himself, though senile, is not treated as a comic figure; rather, his forgetfulness adds a touching and suspenseful element to the story. Furthermore, Ephraim and his wife are mature, unselfish people, who stoically face the thwarting of their modest attempts to earn a better living. The end of the story is contrived and sentimental, but the theme of rewarded kindness makes it effective. Indeed, Page displays a rare instance of sympathy for the difficult upward road of the free black man to security and self-respect.

The two previously unpublished stories Page included in the volume are generally less interesting than the four published earlier in magazines. **"No Haid Pawn"** reveals the influence of Poe in its intensely Gothic atmosphere. Page drew on Virginia's natural scenery, as he seldom did again, to create a savage mood. His descriptions of the crumbling mansion recall the forlorn house of Usher, and Poe's theme of premature burial is briefly recalled in the narrator's allusion to the malaria-stricken slaves who were thrown into the pond before they died. The superstition that men could be seen navigating coffins on No Haid Pawn on dark nights and that there were concealed stone torture chambers in the basement of the mansion add further Poesque touches. Significantly, the murderous plantation owner and his predecessors came from the deep South, were of French-Spanish ancestry, and spoke the Creole patois. Page stresses the fact that no Virginian from the neighboring plantations permitted any social contact with the inmates of No Haid Pawn. Whenever Page admits that atrocities were committed by slave-owners, he makes it clear that the offenders came from the deep South and were not Anglo-Saxons.

Unlike Poe, however, Page was unable to tell a story of pure horror; always he injected his usual defense of Southern institutions. Thus No Haid Pawn plantation was suspected of having been a hiding place for abolitionists working in the underground railway, and Page digresses from his narrative to criticize these once "dangerous" emissaries from the North. Nor did Page have the imaginative boldness of Poe. The gruesome details of **"No Haid Pawn"** are those of a schoolboy's nightmare. We are made apprehensive by what the narrator tells us but are hardly chilled to the bone. It should be noted, however, that **"No Haid Pawn"** was altered in Scribner's editorial rooms; E. L. Burlingame suggested that Page modify the horror in the story and stress the exotic local color atmosphere instead. He wrote to Page on January 8, 1887: "It seemed to me that one incident—the severing of the head at the hanging—was unnecessarily repellent without increasing the force of the story." At Burlingame's request Page generally emphasized the mysterious rather than the macabre in this story.

"Polly: A Christmas Recollection," written specifically for inclusion in **In Ole Virginia,** is even more unsatisfying than **"No Haid Pawn."** The political and social bias of the first four stories in this volume was evidence of the author's serious attempt to add a chapter to Southern honor. Sentimental elements were present but were not integral to the sober view of Southern problems he was presenting. In **"Ole 'Stracted"** and **"No Haid Pawn"** Page was experimenting as an artist with new materials. The former work is unpretentious and provides a dignified portrait of the freedman. The latter is ineffectual as a story, but Page's attempt to create an exotic setting is at least adventure-some, while **"Polly"** is the flimsiest excuse for entertaining a maudlin, unsophisticated audience. Its theme of romance thwarted by politics is overworked in a number of Page's stories. This time, the Whig Colonel's hostility toward his niece's lawyer beau because of the young man's association with the Locofoco party is too arbitrary for us to accept. And the elopement of the young couple is unexciting. The story offers no serious discussions of political attitudes, no believable emotions, no charm in the setting or situation. Furthermore, Page's not-so-funny descriptions of the Colonel's joking threats to sell his drunken slave, Drinkwater Torm, are offensive to modern readers.

In Ole Virginia, though its stories are not uniformly good, reveals Page's special anecdotal talents and is a significant document in the local color movement. Local color writing passed from public favor in the last decade of the nineteenth century; by 1900 popular novelists, though they frequently used some of the devices of the local colorists, were stressing historical romance over regionalism. The romantic novelists were more loyal to the genre per se than to any particular area. They found chivalric behavior in a variety of places and eras; the ante-bellum South, while well represented, no longer had a monopoly. Many popular writers in the first two decades of the century eclipsed Page's triumphs of the 1880's in terms of fame and profit. Yet they differed from the Virginia author in a significant way. They lacked his unshakable convictions about order and the paternalistic social contract, his intent to establish an image and to persuade the country to accept a Virginia aristocrat's view of the vanquished South.

Page was possibly the last serious Southern writer to defend all the tenets of the plantation tradition uncritically. Page completely identified with the Virginia aristocrat and felt that the members of his own class were best fitted for community leadership. Thus it was easier for him to please the reading public of his age, for he wholeheartedly believed in the plantation myth he portrayed. While subsequent popular writers employed the same devices and propagated the same view of an idealized world which had made his stories popular, they lacked the first-hand knowledge characteristic of Page's use of his locale.

The use of Page's attitude and technique seems especially noteworthy in books like Margaret Mitchell's *Gone with the Wind* (1936) or even to some extent in Stark Young's more sophisticated but still romantic *So Red the Rose* (1934). Ellen Glasgow, James Branch Cabell, and the Nashville Fugitive-Agrarians used plantation experiences in their works—but often for an ironic effect. Faulkner, Warren, Porter, and a multitude of very recent Southern artists absorbed certain aspects of Page's code—the emphasis on honor, the importance of land, the concern with racial attitudes—even while reacting violently against certain injustices in the system that the elegant Virginian had defended. Both Glasgow and Cabell recognized the disparity between Page's mythical view of life and the harsher world they knew from experience, but it remained for Faulkner's generation to find in Southern myths the ele-

ments of universal frustration and suffering that are the substance of important literature. Faulkner was awake to the inconsistencies and falsehoods of the past, but he was compassionate towards his Southern ancestors and did not concern himself with the repudiation of their superficial weaknesses. He exploited the disparity between the plantation ideal and its reality, emphasizing the shared suffering of individuals torn by conflicting values, and he looked at the plantation tradition in the light of the twentieth century—although he sympathized with the misguided attempts of its proponents to find order in the universe. Romantic elements in his works often remind us of Page's world.

Any student of Southern literature, or of American racial attitudes, for that matter, can learn much from the writings of Thomas Nelson Page. *In Ole Virginia* epitomizes the plantation literary tradition, and in its strengths and weaknesses it provides an excellent illustration of a once popular literary genre.

Theodore L. Gross (essay date 1971)

SOURCE: "Thomas Nelson Page and the Postbellum Writers," in *The Heroic Ideal in American Literature,* The Free Press, 1971, pp. 105-11.

[*Gross discusses the protagonist of "Marse Chan" as Page's most fully delineated Southern hero.*]

Nowhere in postbellum Southern literature is [the] formal perpetuation of Southern chauvinism more clearly articulated than in the fiction of Thomas Nelson Page; indeed Page's conception of character and place and time is controlled by his slavish dedication to an idealization of the code of Southern heroism. He fuses the sentimental literary tradition and the glorification of the Southern past, and gives them a special significance, a special poignance, in the postbellum period when the South is suffering what he felt was the ignominy of Reconstruction. By idealizing the historical South and transmuting it into a civilization that is parochial and self-sufficient and intensely chauvinistic, Page makes the various types in his fiction—the gentleman, the lady, the Negro servant, the poor white—distinctly Southern. Throughout the stories of *In Ole Virginia* (1887), essays such as "Social Life in Old Virginia Before the War" (1892) and "The Old South" (1889), and novels like *Red Rock* (1898), *Gordon Keith* (1903), and *John Marvel* (1909), Page has the types represent that vanished era when the South was essentially a static society; and once he defines the types for us, the ceremonial celebration of the Southern past follows inexorably. Page sees the code of Southern heroism in retrospect as the armature of a great and fallen civilization. More than any of the postbellum Southern authors, he raises the code to mythical proportions. His heroes must learn to live by the code—most of his stories are basically concerned with that process of learning; his Negroes admire only those whites who enforce the code; and his Ladies insist upon the hero's demonstration of the code before they submit themselves in marriage. Page adheres to the code so rigidly that his best fiction—the stories of *In Ole Virginia*—takes on the qualities of a narrow but quite forceful epic. One feels that his heroes and heroines, who are given ideal dimensions, are perpetuating the noble qualities of a great race. His worst fiction—protracted, rambling novels like *Gordon Keith* and *John Marvel*—uses the code as a substitute for characterization and plot development.

In **"Marse Chan,"** Page's first and best-known story, we can measure the degree to which this sentimental writer, who wanted his work "to bring about a better understanding between the North and the South," depends upon the code of Southern heroism: nowhere else in postbellum Southern literature are the various characteristics of the code so clearly dramatized and idealized than in this minor American classic.

The origins of **"Marse Chan"** are significant, for as Page remembers them in the Preface to his Collected Works, they prepare the reader for the mythical and sentimental world that he is entering; they condition the mind of the reader to a certain way of thinking:

> In the autumn of 1880 a letter was shown [to Page] which had been taken from the pocket of a dead private in a Georgia regiment on one of the battle-fields around Richmond. It was written in an illiterate hand on coarse blue Confederate paper, and was from a young girl in Georgia to her sweetheart. In it she told him that she had discovered since he left that she loved him, and that she did not know why she had been so cruel to him before he went away; that, in fact, she had loved him ever since they had gone to school together in the little school-house in the woods, when he had been so good to her and that now if he would get a furlough and come home she would marry him. This was all, except, of course, a postscript. As if fearful that such a temptation might prove too much even for the man she loved, across the blue Confederate paper were scrawled these words: "Don't come without a furlough; for if you don't come honorable, I won't marry you."

The soldier dies in battle—"he got his furlough through a bullet"—and Page remarks that the "idea took possession of me, and in about ten days I had written '**Marse Chan.**' This story was promptly accepted, but was not published until something over three years afterwards. It was then followed by the other stories in *In Ole Virginia*, and later by the remaining tales in this edition."

The ingredients of the Southern local color story—honor, loyalty, love, the dangers of battle, death, the evocative past that the hero and heroine have shared—are all present in this incident upon which **"Marse Chan"** is based; and they are completely compatible with Page's own interest in Southern literature and life. All that Page needs to convert life into literature is the proper and authentic point of view. In choosing the slave as narrator he gives his story its most memorable quality, a voice that is a haunting and convincing echo, which, like the chorus of Greek tragedy, judges and interprets as well as reports the tragedy. Furthermore, the Negro narrator frees Page from "the

necessity of being specific"; he is a spectator rather than a participant in the action, as Page's most through critic, Harriet Holman, has observed, and can "therefore relate the whole story without either obvious self-glorification or undue reticence." By using a Negro narrator, Page successfully creates his idyll, a sentimentalized past which no one can refute; for the Negro, romantic and superstitious and nostalgic, summons up that past with complete recall: he was there, and though at times he seems a bit of a voyeur with a phenomenal memory, he is credible as the witness of that vanished era of glory.

Sam, the Negro, tells his story to a white man, who may be Southern or Northern—we are never certain—who may be Page himself or the reader. This man meets the isolated Negro in the postbellum South—the time is the autumn of 1872—and sees a shattered, disoriented ex-slave who now is suffering the horrors of Reconstruction. Cleverly Page puts the reader in the position of the author as someone listening objectively to recorded history, a history that takes on special significance since Sam is the only survivor of the wasted plantation and now bears the burden of accuracy.

Although the general outline of the story has been given to him, Page wants the reader to feel the full pathos of his hero's death, and he provides a background—what is to be the archetypical background for all his Southern fiction—to Marse Chan's life. Seen from the point of view of the Negro Sam, this life is highly ritualistic and even mythical, as we follow the development of the Southern hero, the boy who will later defend a civilization, the innocent youth who must learn and adhere to the code of Southern heroism, which, in Page's eyes, is as impressive as that of any knight in King Arthur's court.

Chan's birth is a time of great festivity—"jes' like in de Chris'mas," the narrator reminds us—and Page makes it clear that this birth is holy and significant, like that of Christ; eventually we discover that the boy is a martyr to the Southern cause, someone crucified in a war that for Page was as religious and moral as it was civil. The father gives his infant son a body servant and elects the Negro boy Sam for that sacred role, thus promoting a love relationship between the two that stems from birth. Throughout childhood the white and Negro boys attend school together, although, as Sam quickly assures his listener, only Marse Chan studies. Sam assumes his servile condition; indeed he is proud of it and wears his slavery like a badge of honor and distinction. He is no rebellious, discontented slave but a servant happy to share his master's life, feeling that his own status is enhanced by his close relationship to Marse Chan. As he remembers the antebellum period he can picture it in only glowing terms: "Dem wuz good ole times, marster—de bes' Sam ever see. Dey wuz, in fac'! Niggers didn' hed nothin' 't all to do—hes' hed to 'ten' to de feedin' an' cleanin' de hosses, an' doin' what de marster tell 'em to do; an' when dey wuz sick, dey had things son't 'ten' out de house, an' de same doctor come to see 'em whar 'ten' to de white folks when dey wez po'ly. Dyar warn' no trouble nor nothin'."

Plantation life is described in its rural splendor, a fit setting for the development of the Southern hero. What we witness in this early part of the story is the moral education of a young boy, the tender details of his *Bildungsroman*. Marse Chan not only learns formally in the school but also discovers how a Southerner must act in society. His early romance with Anne Chamberlain, the daughter of his father's political rival, is marked by a chivalric, deferential attitude; his loyalty to his body servant is unwavering; his defense of his father's honor remains constant. Chivalry, loyalty, honor, heroism: these traits equip Chan for the duel which forms the central conflict of the story.

Chan's father is a Democrat and Anne Chamberlain's a Whig; though both are loyal Southerners and eventually will join forces against the North, Chan's father—like all of Page's sympathetic characters—is opposed to secession and the extreme political measures of the Whigs. He buys slaves that Chamberlain sells, thus embittering the conservative. When a barn burns and a Negro, in trying to save the horses, is trapped in the flames, old Marse Chan rescues the Negro; but in demonstrating his instinctive loyalty and love for one who has served him, he blinds himself. This episode is made more dramatic, as Arthur Hobson Quinn notes, "because of the narrator's complete absence of comment." To the slave, "the 'marster' had a right to send his slave into danger, but that implied a duty to save him in turn, even if it cost his owner his eyesight." His son, who has now learned the code of Southern heroism and who has adopted his father's political and social beliefs, carries on the family traditions; he challenges Chamberlain's political ideas and consequently challenges the man. Insults inevitably occur, for these men are Southern firebrands, and they meet in that ancient chivalric contest—the duel.

For Chan the duel takes on religious connotations. As the Negro narrator remarks, Chan "look like he did sometimes when he come out of church." He is fighting for honor, and honor for Page always has a religious dimension. Furthermore, the duel is not so frivolous as a modern reader might believe, for it grows out of the central political conflict between Southerners in antebellum times; it reflects the tensions that will inevitably lead to the Civil War and reminds us of the divergent political views of many Southerners. Aesthetically Page is imitating Scott's *Ivanhoe,* but he is grafting onto the duel a political and historical meaning of particular significance. Chamberlain, the Whig, misses his opponent and Chan generously fires in the air. But there is not resolution to the conflict between these feuding families and, as in the story of Romeo and Juliet, the victims are the lovers, who must remain apart.

Page attempts to weld realistic and romantic elements in his legend. The war would ordinarily give an historical validity to otherwise trivial, sentimental situations; but the Civil War that Page describes seems enjoyable or at least romantic rather than onerous—it is an adventure, almost a *jeu d'esprit*. It is certainly not the Civil War described by De Forest in *Lily Ravenel's Conversion from Secession to Loyalty* or by Stephen Crane in *The Red Badge of Cour-*

age. Marse Chan as a Southern hero is a boyhood projection, a fanciful surrogate that Page imagines for himself. "He 'peares ti like to go prowlin' around 'mon dem Yankees," the narrator says, "an' he use' to tek me wid im whenever he could. Yes, seh, he sut'n'y wuz a good sodjer! He didn' mine bullets no more 'n did mon drops o' rain. But I use' to be pow'ful skeered sometimes. It jest use 'to 'pear like fun to 'im."

Privately Chan grieves the loss of Anne Chamberlain in good chivalric fashion. His lady, like the lady of medieval legend—or of Scott's version of medieval legend—rebuffs him; the lover, though morbidly melancholy, does not question her judgment—she is, after all, a moral arbiter, an absolute spiritual criterion against which he measures his own inadequate self. Anne Chamberlain symbolizes Southern purity and innocence, qualities that are almost mystical and certainly beyond definition in Page's moral universe.

The conclusion of the story is sentimentally contrived but nevertheless poignant. Anne Chamberlain sends Chan a letter in which she confesses her love. Immediately after he has read the letter, Chan dies on the battle-field—heroically, of course—and his Negro body servant, loving him in death as well as in life, makes his coffin, places him in it, and takes him home. The Negro's love for his white master is the most moving aspect of **"Marse Chan,"** the aspect that gives the story its verisimilitude and uniqueness. The relationship between Anne Chamberlain and Marse Chan is more artificial because Page must keep his heroine so incredibly idealistic that she is finally not human. She loves Chan in death; in death she can even dare to be erotic: "Miss Ann she tuk de coffin in her arms an' kissed it, an' kissed Marse Chan, an' call 'im by the name, an' her darlin,' an ole missis lef' her crying in dyar tell some on 'em went in, an' found her alone faint on de flo'." She dies and thus remains pristine and innocent, her abstract attributes never threatened by the practicalities of the post-Civil-War South. She and her lover are buried together—"dey's bofe in en sleep side over de ole grabeyard at home"—sexually united in death. **"Marse Chan,"** although the intention is clearly unconscious on Page's part, is a minor example of the eroticism so many nineteenth-century American authors associated with death.

The only credible person in this story—and in those that follow—is the Negro. The other characters belong to a mythical past that cannot be realistically created because it is not real; it is Page's evocation, his "picture of a civilization which, once having sweetened the life of the South, has since then well-nigh perished from the earth." Page, as Jay B. Hubbell points out, "was among the first to see that the old life was passing away," and he is clearly responding to a deep need that he shared with other Southerners: "The later South wanted its heroes painted, not as provincial tobacco farmers but as heroes and Cavaliers. . . . There is just the difference between [Page's] Virginia and the real Virginia that one expects to find between a painting and a photograph. Certain details of the old life are dropped or barely mentioned; while others are emphasized in every possible manner."

The code of heroism reappears throughout Page's work. In **"Meh Lady"** he elaborates upon the desperate dignity of a Southern lady who preserves the family's plantation after her brother has died in the Civil War; in **"Ole 'Stracted"** he dramatizes the Negro's loyalty, his inability to adjust himself to a Reconstruction period in which his master no longer guides and protects him; in countless other stories—**"The Burial of the Guns," "Little Darby," "Bred in the Bone,"** and **"The Gentleman of the Black Stock"**—he illustrates the various manifestations of the code and how they sustained Southern civilization; in essays like "The Old South" and "The Old Dominion" he stresses the idyllic lives of his ancestors—history becomes the sentimental memory of someone scarcely interested in facts. Page's stories and essays form one of the clearest and most forceful statements of white supremacy in nineteenth-century Southern literature.

Harriet R. Holman   (essay date 1973)

SOURCE: "Magazine Editors and the Stories of Thomas Nelson Page's Late Flowering," in *Essays Mostly on Periodical Publishing in America,* Duke University Press, 1973, pp. 148-61.

[*Holman focuses on the non-Southern stories collected in* Under the Crust, *which found inhospitable magazine editors because they did not conform to Page's earlier local color stories of Southern chivalry.*]

Like his enemies, the stories a writer has trouble selling are one measure of the man; they also tell the reader of a later generation something of his time and place, and they make a useful gauge of his editors. The stories of Thomas Nelson Page's late flowering [published in *Under the Crust* (1908), included also in the collected Plantation Edition, and *The Land of the Spirit* (1913)] are a case in point. They consist of eleven atypical stories employing characters, settings, techniques, and themes significantly different from Page's earlier stories of planation life in antebellum piedmont Virginia. Consideration of these stories and the correspondence relating to them suggests that Page was more than a writer of local-color stories and that after his initial success his editors too often proved prescriptive rather than perceptive, wholly concerned with the preference of their readers, inhospitable to innovation, and consequently more aware of the day's marketplace than of either literary values or the future. A writer more greatly gifted than Page, or arrogant, or more aggressive in marketing what he wrote might have evaded their limitations without damage to himself, but that is speculation unrelated to consideration of these eleven non-Southern stories Page wrote to please himself.

The stories have been so generally ignored by critics and literary historians that some word on them is prerequisite for understanding what Page's editors found objectionable. All are social commentary verging upon protest, all attack man's inhumanity to man, and all imply criticism of whole castes, if not classes, in the American social structure. Though at first glance they appear mannered, dated, a little remote and genteel, they are close to the spirit of protesters like Veblen, young Garland, young Robert Herrick, and occasionally Frank Norris. They fall into three groups—five stories with New England settings, three strong stories which differ from each other and all his other fiction, and three stories with religious themes.

The New England stories are **"Miss Godwin's Inheritance,"** published in *Scribner's Magazine,* 1904; **"The New Lebanon Agent,"** originally called "The New Agent at Lebanon Station," *Ladies' Home Journal,* 1905; **"Leander's Light,"** first called "Naboth's Vineyard," *Century,* 1907; **"My Friend the Doctor,"** *Scribner's Magazine,* 1907; and **"The Bigot,"** *Scribner's Magazine,* 1910. Page knew New England. Though Maine was his summer home for thirty years and local citizens counted him one of their own, he made no pretense to write from the inner consciousness of the villagers, as the local-color writers had done. By thus admitting the limitations of his own perceptions and experience, he avoided the condescension of summer-visitor writers like Edith Wharton, who had irritated Mary Wilkins Freeman and other native New Englanders. As usual, he was too honest an observer to risk faking what he did not know. The intent of the early Southern stories was to evoke time, place, and mood through the particulars of local color; in these New England stories the intent was quiet revelation of character, with setting only incidental. They appear in a volume significantly titled *Under the Crust*. For Page the shift involved innovations in technique as well as subject-matter and, less obviously, in center of interest. **"The New Lebanon Agent,"** for example, is essentially objective. **"Miss Godwin's Inheritance,"** which Charles Scribner considered "perfectly charming, and as a piece of art almost perfect" [correspondences cited in this essay are located in the Thomas Nelson Page collections at Duke University or the University of Virginia], differs from Page's earlier stories in having as both narrator and center of interest the *simpatico* summer visitor. In these New England stories Page makes his criticism explicit through the words of characters like Lishy Dow's widow in **"My Friend the Doctor"** when righteous indignation moved her to tell the self-gratifying Mrs. Durer exactly what she was.

By use of a different technique in three strong stories—**"A Brother to Diogenes,"** *Scribner's Magazine,* 1906; **"The Goth,"** *Scribner's Magazine,* 1907; and **"The Outcast,"** in this country unpublished except in Page's *The Land of the Spirit* (1913)—Page leaves to the reader the responsibility for providing his own commentary. **"A Brother to Diogenes"** is essentially objective, that is, dramatic, with its central figure an unhappily materialistic man insensitive to the human values which Page believed sweeten life. The taut ending shows the story well made from the beginning. Page called it his California story because it evolved from a winter spent in Santa Barbara. "It contains some of my philosophy," he wrote his mother from Naples within sight of smoking volcano and unbelievably blue sea. That philosophy—the healing power of nature in mountain, field, and plain, coupled with the conviction that wealth limited to material things is ultimately poverty of spirit—is part of an agrarian revolt against the anonymity and increasing complexity of life that came with industrialization, thereby showing Page surprisingly akin to the Jack London of *Martin Eden,* the Booth Tarkington of the Growth trilogy, the Willa Cather of *O, Pioneers!,* the Ellen Glasgow of *The Voice of the People,* the Vanderbilt Fugitives, and the Maxwell Anderson of *High Tor.* By contrast, **"The Goth"** has its setting in Monte Carlo. This slice-of-life story of an international gambler given the cut direct by an acquaintance reads rather like a Richard Harding Davis story of fashionable society illustrated by Charles Dana Gibson; it happens to be a direct result of Page's reading a book on the psychology of compulsive gamblers at about the time he made two visits to Monte Carlo as an interested spectator in the winter of 1905-1906. Both this story and **"The Outcast"** demand that the reader produce his own commentary. **"The Outcast"** centers on a judge hearing the case of a prostitute accused of murder. In its dramatic presentation Page attempts to assess the basic responsibility for her situation, which by implication he attributes to her fatherless home. The situation clearly shows injustice, but Page did not demand what Brand Whitlock called instant reform. He was too good a lawyer, too knowledgeable in the ways of the world to expect that to work.

The final group of three stories is built around religious themes. **"The Stranger's Pew,"** published in *Scribner's Magazine* in 1910, an effective retelling of the familiar story of a coldly formal church whose members could not recognize Christ in the flesh, reflects Page's continuing disavowal of worldliness within the church. **"The Shepherd Who Watched by Night,"** Page's tribute to a brother who served as Episcopal rector in Virginia, Texas, and New York, is, he said [in the preface to *The Land of the Spirit*], "real enough to be a transcription of fact." Page never offered it to magazine editors, giving first rights instead to the Episcopal Church to use in raising funds for superannuated ministers. **"The Stable of the Inn,"** which appeared in *Scribner's Magazine* in 1912, is another affirmation of his religious commitment; derived from the Biblical account of the first Christmas, it is "to some extent based on the Golden Legend" [preface to *The Land of the Spirit*]. These religious stories are workmanlike examples of a kind rarely commanding the attention of scholars and critics. In subject-matter they bear some relation to the stories with which Henry Van Dyke had been instructing the multitudes, but they differ from his in being more restrained and comparatively sparse stylistically. Page claimed no literary excellence for them, but they had a certain appeal, as readers often reminded him.

However diversified the settings of these eleven stories, they have in common the subject of responsibility, which Page designated duty to God and man. As any reader who knows Page's earlier stories will recall, it was duty that sent Marse Chan to war, and duty that put iron into the soul of the old colonel who spiked his guns and sank them in the river before surrendering. The difference in emphasis, however, combined with new settings and experiments in technique, makes the later stories seem the work of another writer. The change, which was the basic cause of

the editors' disaffection, challenges the reader to reassess for himself both the earlier stories and the later. After all the intervening years, of course, it is not likely that Page would find a wide audience of admirers again, but the reader who judges these stories of his late flowering by any objective standards will recognize in them evidence of a control of material, a knowledge of men and the world, and a more encompassing compassion than could have been predicted from the local-color stories on which Page's reputation still rests.

His apprenticeship to editors made him properly hesitant about going counter to their recommendations. Moreover, never a man to ignore an obligation, Page did not forget that without the active encouragement of the editors who came to Richmond to talk with him after publication of **"Marse Chan"** he would never have developed into a writer. William Dean Howells and Richard Watson Gilder made recommendations for cutting the long manuscript that fifteen years later became *Red Rock* (1898). Gilder urged him to record for the nation the recollections of a child growing up within sound of the battlefields; that account became *Two Little Confederates,* first published in 1888 and never out of print since. Robert Underwood Johnson suggested the theme of **"Meh Lady."** Editors taught him to shape and control his stories and to see all about him materials with fresh appeal to readers.

But those lessons had been learned in 1884-1886. Ten years later, the lyric impulse stilled by his wife's early death, Page was a different man with something else to say. By choice and conviction always a Virginian, he had in the intervening years lost the limitations of provincial horizons. Legal work for business interests he served had taken him into Colorado mining country and some even more inaccessible areas of the Appalachians. He carried letters of introduction from editors when he went to London to confer with financial backers. There his good breeding and charm continued to provide opportunities for intellectual and social life which included lunch with Edmund Gosse and W. M. Rossetti, Gosse's literary At-Homes, an afternoon with Kipling in his Embankment rooms, a Sunday with Thomas Hardy at the salon of Mrs. Francis Jeune, diplomatic receptions, days in the galleries of Parliament to study the oratory of Parnell, the theater with redoubtable old Countess Burdett-Coutts, friendship with Ada Rehan and the violinist Johannes Wolfe, beefsteak suppers in the Green Room of the Lyceum Theatre with Sir Henry Irving and the Beerbohm Trees, and a walking tour through Norway with the Irish editor of the London *Sun.* As a Southerner only a generation away from war and reconstruction, he found British attitudes toward life more congenial than those prevailing among Americans in the industrial and urban North, but when the financial panic of 1891 ended his English negotiations, he returned immediately home to Richmond. He was a cosmopolitan who kept his native roots.

The crucial year for Page, however, was 1892, when he "lectured"—that is, he read his own stories—from Boston to Denver and Palm Beach. Everywhere except in the impoverished South he saw the kind of wealth that, properly used, could found great libraries or free gifted individuals for work in the service of humanity and art, and what he saw aroused him to a sense of urgency: men of vision must take into the new industrial era the old aristocratic ideals of responsible leadership and service for the common good. A year later in Chicago his marriage to Mrs. Henry Field introduced him to the world of her Bryan and Lathrop relatives, unmistakably a moneyed aristocracy meeting its responsibilities in a mushrooming metropolis; her uncle was credited with bringing the Columbian Exposition to Chicago, her cousin served as secretary to liberal governor John Peter Altgeld, her brother gave sacrificially to support cultural activities, and Mrs. Page herself gave the nucleus of paintings for the Chicago Art Institute. Because her family was actively involved in the business of the city, they could give Page a depth of awareness that he might not have achieved without them. It has generally escaped the attention of critics that a full decade before the Muckrakers began spectacular disclosures about the new robber barons, Page was working into his stories satirical portraits of individuals who assumed money to be the one final measure of value. More significantly, he was writing stories of little people engulfed by urban blight and ill-planned industrialization, victims of what Kimball King called "an affluent society which has lost the traditional virtues of an aristocracy" ["Satirical Portraits by Thomas Nelson Page," *Mississippi Quarterly,* XVIII (Spring 1965)]. So long as these portraits were embedded in stories of plantation society, nobody seemed to pay much attention.

But increasingly when this new Page turned from accounts of a vanished past, the magazine editors did not like the change. They based their objections sometimes upon the story, sometimes upon Page's reputation, sometimes upon his "strong" language, and sometimes upon the expectation of their readers. Of the eleven short stories which I have been able to identify as part of this late burgeoning, Page managed to peddle nine essentially unchanged for magazine publication and gave to his church first-publication rights to a tenth one; of an additional group of manuscripts written in a new, sparse style from about 1897 to 1911 on subjects too powerful or controversial for editors to touch, however, Page seems to have saved intact only **"The Outcast."**

By this time Page had small need to turn out pot-boilers, because he was receiving a steady stream of book royalties from Scribner's. Though his wife's wealth paid most of their household bills, he remained scrupulously self-supporting. His chief expense was subsidies for an astonishingly long list of unfortunates, many with no claim upon him except that they had nowhere else to turn. If financial pressures eventually caused Page to alter what he had written (as I can only surmise that in some cases they did) and if the pressures certainly caused him to publish poor material previously withheld, like **"The Old Planters,"** it was essentially because he would not allow his wife or anyone else to meet responsibilities he had assumed for cousins in reduced circumstances, sick lawyers, a succession of widows and orphans, and former slaves who had never belonged to his family.

Letters to and from editors constitute the best evidence about the reaction to new developments in Page's writing. Page wrote Gilder in 1897 to suggest that he was experimenting deliberately with a way of writing which differed from his customary method. Ordinarily, except when he was writing an anecdote of the kind which gave him the reputation of *raconteur par excellence,* he began with a sketchlike impression of character or scene, in subsequent drafts revising form and action into it, often over a period of years. He seems to have suggested to Gilder in this letter that he was trying a direct story line to fit subject matter different from his plantation stories: "It's all right about the story," he wrote after Gilder had rejected an unspecified manuscript.

> I am sorry it does not appeal to you; but that's the test in a way. . . . It is not homogeneous—not complete up close enough—and the episodes are episodes rather than segments of a well rounded and compact story. All this I know and shall remedy. But the *succinct, colorless, direct narrative is what I am after here, and the style was deliberately adopted. I want to try it, and it must go so or not at all.*
>
> [Page to Gilder, December 3, 1897]

This was probably the "novelette or Long Story" which Edward Bok had wanted to see but returned because the *Ladies' Home Journal* required "the predominance of the feminine" [Bok to Page, January 28, 1898].

Careful attention to background was "the color" that editors not only expected, but demanded from Page. When he did not give it to them, they rejected his work. A case in point is the urban novel, *The Untried Way,* on which he had been working for several years in the directly simple style appropriate to the subject. In rejecting it, E. L. Burlingame of *Scribner's Magazine* explained:

> I really do not think that the story would be successful, judged by your own standards and the standards of your previous work; and I cannot help thinking it likely that a re-reading after an interval may make you agree with me, at least with regard to the present form. It seems to me, frankly, bald and held down very close to the actions of the plot, without the color which you usually give (except perhaps in the first sketch of the hero in the opening chapter) and it affects me rather like the *scenario* of a story than like the story itself in your usual sense. If I did not know to the contrary, I should imagine it had been sketched out long ago with the intention of founding something upon it later; but I know that it is sometimes the effect when a warm colorist, in some sudden mood of reaction, keeps himself pretty rigidly in line. The experiment is always a hard one to try; and in this case I think the reader will not read as much into the result as you yourself had in mind in making the sketch.
>
> [Burlingame to Page, July 29, 1898]

It is significant that Burlingame, acting here in dual editorial roles, with this same letter both rejected the manuscript for *Scribner's Magazine* and accepted it for book publication by Charles Scribner's Sons if Page insisted.

"Marse Chan."
(A Tale of Old Virginia.)

One afternoon in the Autumn of 1872, I was riding leisurely down the sandy road that wound along the top of the watershed between two of the smaller rivers of Eastern Virginia, when I made a chance acquaintance with an old "nigger" as he proudly styled himself, with the close union of the comical and the pathetic which is so striking a characteristic of his race.

His narrative, which I have endeavored to reproduce in his own language, illustrated strikingly the loving fidelity to his old master so inexplicable to the outside world, and so touching to those who alone know and appreciate the negro at his true worth.

The road I was travelling, following the ridge for miles had just struck me as most significant of the characters of the race whose only avenue of communication with the outside world it had been. Their once splendid mansions now fast falling to decay appeared to view from time to time set back far from the road, in proud seclusion among groves

Manuscript page of "Marse Chan," Page's best-known short story.

But in this instance Page's literary judgement must have yielded to his quick pride. I found no manuscript of *The Untried Way* in the vast Thomas Nelson Page collections, in the Clifton Waller Barrett Library at the University of Virginia and in the William R. Perkins Library at Duke University. Apparently Page uncharacteristically destroyed it, or possibly he made subsequent use of it as foundation for *John Marvel* (1909) or, more probably, *Gordon Keith* (1903).

Magazine editors also gave Page trouble about all his other long manuscripts except *Red Rock* (1898). In these manuscripts he was writing of prostitution, mercenary marriages, the urban poor and conspicuous consumers of wealth, the staggering impact of alien migrations into the Anglo-Saxon culture of middle America, and of Southerners as corrupt politicians, money-grabbers, and the self-serving rievers and destroyers of a mountain mining town. No one, editors or reviewers, seems to have been bothered by his failure to grapple with the basics of economics and human relations, or by his offering as solution for all problems the domestic virtues of duty and compassionate brotherly love. What did bother the reviewers was exactly what his editors had objected to. "It is when the action of his stories changes to the North that we miss something of the charm of Mr. Page's earlier work," Herman Knickerbocker Vielé wrote in *The Bookman* [XVII (July 1903)], as if Virginia possessed inherent powers to cast charm upon unscrupulous business dealings and violent death. "There are many who can paint the railroad strikes of *John Marvel* or the speculation of *Gordon Keith*," Arthur Hobson Quinn later wrote regretfully; "no one but a Southern gentleman could have written *Red Rock* or '**Meh Lady**'" ["Mr. Page in Fiction and Poetry," *The Book News Monthly*, XXVIII (November 1909)].

Moreover, *John Marvel,* innocuous as that work now seems, was kept out of sight in English circulating libraries except when a patron specifically requested it. "God bless the smug souls of the English Circulating Libraries!" Page exploded to Charles Scribner.

> Are not they a choice lot? Think of [Elinor Glyn's] *Three Weeks* and George Moore and *Man and Superman* [Page after all belonged to the audiences that Shaw enjoyed shocking] and a few other choice morsels of pruriency and the way in which they turned them over their tongues, and smacked their greasy lips at their salacious taste, and then consider John Marvel *doubtful!*

> I should not mind anything but doubtful, but if it does not go head on against their whole position of smuggy bourgeois hypocrisy, it is nothing. . . .
>
> [Page to Scribner, March 12, 1910]

In effect, then, what his magazine editors and individual readers were demanding of Page was more Southern material of the kind he had been writing twenty years before. The notable exception was *Scribner's Magazine,* whose editors, though sometimes unenthusiastic about his finished product, made no effort to dictate what he wrote. Charles and Arthur Scribner had assembled an editorial staff in-

cluding W. C. Brownell, E. L. Burlingame, and Robert Bridges, whose perceptive awareness of many kinds of excellence established the liberal milieu which Maxwell Perkins later inherited. Unlike some others, they did not reject good work in favor of inferior. Perhaps it was because they were also editors for the publishing house, with an obligation to keep a successful novelist happy. More probably, simply because they were editors for Charles Scribner's Sons they had a less restricted vision of what literature and the world are in reality, and thus a clearer understanding of the editor's relationship to the writer.

Among other editors, S. S. McClure asked for a series of articles on race relations in the South, subsequently collected as *The Negro: The Southerner's Problem.* He also asked Page for stories, but turned down two of the New England group as "what you might call a Northern story, a field in which we get plenty of stories [McClure to Page, Feb. 27, 1904]," and Page vowed to send him no more. Nor could Page place with his usual editors an article on the education of poor country girls in the South—of vital concern to Page and his father before him—and so he sold "**A Neglected Class**" to *Good Housekeeping* at about half his usual rates. Yet at the same time a Southern plantation story, like "**Mam Lyddy's Recognition**," bought by Charles Belmont Davis at *Collier's,* commanded top prices.

The editor who most frequently transgressed against Page's sense of values was Robert Underwood Johnson, who combined with an infinite capacity for detail a remarkable insensitivity to persons, managing to create one uproar after another without any awareness of storms about to break upon his head. Because Johnson was one of the editors cordial to him in the early years, Page swallowed without comment such judgments as "though it is not a '**Marse Chan**,' and depends upon its interest rather than on its charm (a quality we hope to find in the Xmas story) we shall be glad to publish '**The New Lebanon Agent**'. . ." [Johnson to Page, May 13, 1904]. But the condescending cajolery of another letter proved too much for Page. "At the earliest moment practicable," Johnson wrote,

> we have read "**My Friend Naboth**," and Mr. Gilder desires me to say how we feel about it.

> We find it not a story, in the sense of dramatic movement and interplay, but a sketch—to be sure, complete and rounded out with your wonted geniality— a typical though not very vivid sketch of our time. Now, what we are always hoping you will do for your old friends of *The Century* is to send them a first-rate breathless story which we can say is among your very best. As we have said, this is a sketch rather than a story. We want to have you in *The Century*'s pages but we do not quite feel up to paying story prices for it. We do not like any more than you the bargaining side of literature, but unfortunately it is one that has to be fronted. . . .

> We hope that you will put it within our reach.
>
> [Johnson to Page, December 21, 1906]

Page fired off a reply by return mail:

As . . . you do not think it a story at all, but only a sketch, and not a very vivid sketch at that, I am going to get you to send it back to me, and see if I can't write "horse" plainly enough on it to have someone recognize the genus. . . .

This is the second piece of writing on paper that I have sent to *The Century* under the impression that it was a story, but which has been stamped sketch and returned to me. I do not in the least question the sincerity of your views about it, for I am conceited enough to believe that you would be reasonably glad to publish a "story" by me; and, of course, I know that what you call an acceptable story must be of more immediate value to you than what you call a sketch, and what I call a story, but I do not know just what constitutes the difference.

I would call "Rab and His Friends" [by Dr. John Brown] and "Posson Jone" [by George W. Cable] stories, as I did call **"A Brother to Diogenes"** a story, though none of these has in it what I understand by "dramatic movement and interplay," each of them being, in fact, but a story of one dog, or one man, in which is grouped or is attempting[?] to be grouped, a picture of a segment of life amid which the scene is placed.

Referring to some of the "authorities," I find that one Joseph Addison, himself a writer of sketches, defines a story as "the relation of an incident or minor event, a short narrative, a tale," while in a recently published authority of great weight I find that a story in the sense in which the term is used in literature is defined as "a narrative; a tale written in more or less imaginative style, especially a fictitious tale, shorter and less elaborate than a novel," while I find a sketch appears to have as an essential a brief, slight, or hasty delineation or composition. Now, I am afraid you read *The Century Dictionary* too much and Addison too little. I know that often a man is not a good judge of his own work, so I let pass the fact that I think **"My Friend Naboth,"** a name for which I shall substitute **"Leander's Light,"** a pretty good relation, I mean for me, of minor events in the life of an old Maine countryman and his sister. It was written with a view to showing that under their hard and repellant exterior there lies a deep vein of sentiment that makes them close kin to the rest of Anglo-Saxondom, to whom the love of home and family is the most vital and lasting of all principles.

[Page to Johnson, December 22, 1906]

Though neither Page nor his editors knew it then, Page had the future on his side, for the short story as written by Sherwood Anderson and all his literary descendants resembles more nearly Page's picture of a "segment of life" than Johnson's plotted "dramatic movement and interplay." In this matter, by insight or accident, the writer evidenced better judgment than his editors.

Johnson rejected **"The Stranger's Pew"** because it lacked "the novelty which the public would expect from you . . . admirable as it is in feeling and direction of purpose" [Johnson to Page, April 21, 1910]. Of course he and other editors meant novelty acceptable to them, not a shocker

like **"A Modern Brutus,"** later renamed **"The Outcast."** "Your story, 'A Modern Brutus,' is terribly impressive," wrote H. M. Alden from *Harper's Magazine.*

It does not read like a piece of fiction but like a strong narrative of fact. I do not think a story of this kind presented in this way will be kindly received by our readers. The sheer strength of the presentment seems to make it impossible. I am sorry that I must return it. . . .

[Alden to Page, January 12, 1910]

Similarly, Charles Belmont Davis returned it because

notwithstanding the power with which you have told this big story, we cannot believe it is the best *kind* of story for *Collier's.* . . . Certainly no charge of pruriency could be brought against this tale. . . . I can only hope you will send us something else that will come more within the scope of what we believe our readers want.

[Davis to Page, February 4, 1910]

No other magazine editor would publish it. In 1913, while clearing his desk before he went to serve as Ambassador to Rome, Page included it in **The Land of the Spirit,** a volume of short stories which was not republished as part of his collected edition. Three years later, to Page's distress, **"The Outcast"** was made into a movie with Mae Marsh in the lead; special preshowing to local clergymen to attest that it was a proper movie for a decent community were emphasized by screaming advertisements.

From about 1895 when he was writing *The Untried Way,* unpublished and now lost, editors again and again asked Page for stories, and what they bought again and again was material related in some fashion to the plantation stories that had brought him fame. Again and again, with such grace as was given to them, editors returned other materials to him with a variety of explanations: too stark, too bald, too lacking in warmth and color, too powerful, a sketch rather than a plotted story, or simply not what they wanted from him. Comparing what any one editor bought with what he rejected makes clear the fact that what they wanted of Page was Southern materials, Southern plantation material only. Johnson, who longed for another **"Marse Chan"** at bargain prices, bought **"The Old Planters,"** a derivative and rambling piece that Page had pulled from his files and rewritten, but he returned **"The New Lebanon Agent,"** which by any objective standards is better work, and S. S. McClure commissioned controversial articles on race relations in the South but turned down two quiet New England stories. The fact that few of these later stories of Page's have great appeal for the general reader of a later day is quite beside the point: The combined influence of the magazine editors was against change, experimentation, or innovation in form, content, or style.

This record of Page and his editors offers support for a theory by which Fred Lewis Pattee explained the plight of distinguished local colorists, like Mary Noailles Murfree, who in their later writing years were reduced to peddling stories from editor to editor. When Garland wrote Pattee that "the writer can't go on doing it over and over," Pattee philosophised, "And yet the reading public, or perhaps it is the publishers, brand their new writers with a herd mark and do not let them escape the ranch where they made their first appearance" [*Penn State Yankee,* 1953]. For Page, the record clearly shows, magazine editors with the notable exception of those at *Scribner's* did what they could to restrict him to plantation Virginia and the kind of stories he had been writing when first he came to their attention.

L. Moody Simms, Jr. (essay date 1975)

SOURCE: "Corra Harris on the Declining Influence of Thomas Nelson Page," in *Mississippi Quarterly,* Vol. XXVIII, No. 4, Fall, 1975, pp. 505-09.

[*Simms quotes at length an astute critic who recognized and identified the causes of Page's declining popularity and influence.*]

By the end of the nineteenth century, Thomas Nelson Page (1853-1922) was the chief spokesman of the plantation literary tradition. Achieving fame as a local-color writer of the New South, he depicted life in the Tidewater region of the Old Dominion both before and after the Civil War. Most of his essays, stories, and novels celebrate the chivalric ways of pre-Civil War Virginians and lament the passing of the antebellum order.

In a time when critical standards were not particularly high, Page enjoyed favorable criticism of even his poorer stories of the 1890s. His work also appealed to the popular reader of the day. According to Rosewell Page, *Red Rock,* published in 1898, sold more than one thousand copies and ranked fifth in a list of best sellers. In 1903, Page's *Gordon Keith* appeared on a similar list.

Page did not have any real difficulty selling almost everything he wrote until around 1906. By that time, he had witnessed the surrender of the local-color movement to a more realistic literary treatment of life. It was during the following year that a critic wrote unsentimentally about Page's "waning influence" in American literature ["The Waning Influence of Thomas Nelson Page," *Current Literature* 43 (August 1907)].

The critic was Corra Harris (1869-1935), a perceptive Southerner who was a regular contributor to the *Independent*. In her article on Page, Mrs. Harris maintained that "when an author ceases to produce, and begins to revise what he has already written, and when his publishers begin to offer 'complete' editions of his works for sale, it is safe to conclude that his career is closed, and that it is time to write his literary obituary, even if he is, like Page, in the prime of life."

Mrs. Harris believed that Page's influence on American letters was declining because he was committed to a phase of national life and idealism that Americans had largely outgrown. His aristocratic birth and breeding, she asserted, was the "hallmark of his genius"; "if he had been exactly the man he is, but with a humbler pedigree, he would never have written a line." But who in early twentieth-century America, asked Mrs. Harris, was concerned with the credentials of aristocracy?

> The notion that a man must have extraordinary intelligence in order to have genius is a common error. And Mr. Page's literary career proves it. He is not a man of brains, but of feelings and excellent prejudices. He has just enough sense to be a Southern aristocrat, and those who know for how much more breeding and mettle count than mere brains in this extraordinary compound will understand Mr. Page's advantages and limitations as a writer. The opinion expressed of Thomas Carlyle by one of Page's characters, the **"Old Gentleman of the Black Stock,"** is characteristic of the author's own point of view—"He is not a gentleman, sir, and he has never forgiven either the world or himself for it!" No shrewder comment was ever made upon the surly Scotchman, but it also indicates the intolerance and narrowness of an aristocrat's vision. So much of life lies beyond it.

Mrs. Harris did not question the essential fitness of Page for the literary endeavor he had undertaken and largely accomplished.

> Mr. Page is peculiarly qualified by the mettle of his spirit and even by the limitations of his mind to dramatize the period he has chosen in Southern life. There is the South, and there is the spirit of the South—two very different propositions. For, with all their creating and re-creating, the people of that section have never been able to make it in their magnificent image—not even before the war. Reality remained reality in spite of their best endeavors. And if there is one thing which a Southerner despises more than another, it is that dull, plebeian snub-nosed thing accepted by the rest of the world as reality. This is where Mr. Page comes in. He has interpreted what was at the time he wrote the *spirit* of the South, that armored and helmeted spirit which survived the defeats of the Civil War, riding unconquered and unconquerable through bereavements, poverty, and the unimaginable humiliation of the Reconstruction period. "Mars[e] Chan" "Meh Lady" and "Miss Thomasia" are like no real men and women, but they are created in the spiritual, mettlesome likeness of ten thousand who did live in the South at that time. This is the secret of Mr. Page's popularity. He delineated the immortal features of a heartbroken people in terms of personality sufficiently graceful and heroic to satisfy this lofty sense they had of themselves. The kind of mind he has is sensitized not to facts, but to the poetry of facts. Many a man has recorded more facts about Southern life even in stories, and received no thanks for his dulness. But Mr. Page, through some quality of his own nature, recognized that the one permanent thing in the South during this storm-and-stress period, covered in *Red Rock* and other stories, was its invincible spirituality, which was more patriotic than religious (tho not lacking in piety), and more personal than patriotic.

In Mrs. Harris' judgment, the stories mentioned above would become a lasting part of American literature for still another reason: "They are the *first* impressions of a period which contained the dramatic climax of a great event—the Civil War"; "all others have been modeled after them or inspired by them."

Even so, Mrs. Harris contended that Page's stories in the volume *In Ole Virginia* (1887), which crowned the first phase of his literary work, also marked the beginning of his decline.

> After writing them, he did as the rest have done who laid their scenes over the same ground—imitated himself. His later novels show but the faded charm of these earlier productions. And they are not well constructed. He crowds in too much material, and reaches conclusions more arbitrary than convincing. For example, the sequel is too much in the author's hands. And he achieves it as easily and as incredibly as any knight of old who ever went forth to ease himself of a vow.

Finally, Mrs. Harris attempted to account for the passing of Page's genius.

> It is as natural as it is curious. A country or a section may change so suddenly in its character and ambitions that an author who once portrayed the life of it can do so no longer. He has a sense of the dead rather than of the living. Homer would be sadly out of place in modern Greece. Now, something has happened in the South during the last ten years so radical and so overwhelming that what was true is now history, what was characteristic has become bombastic, and what were principles of living are mere sentimentalities connected with the *code duello* existence of the past. Whether this is due to the fact that a younger, less prejudiced generation has reached up, taken the book from Mr. Page's hand, read it, tested it, and laid it, down with strange indifference, or whether commercialism has rendered us too sordid to appreciate the ideality for which his writings stand, it is impossible to say. But the fact remains that the South has outgrown Mr. Page one way or the other. The spirit of the South dramatized in his books is no longer sufficiently related to this new spirit to command its interest and obeisance. This accounts in a great measure for the comparative failure of *Gordon Keith,* after the immense popularity of *Red Rock.* The scenes of both stories cover practically the same period of reconstruction, both are based upon the same ideals of unimpeachable honor, of courage in adversity, and of being gentle according to the length of one's pedigree. But it happens that *Gordon Keith* was published five years later, when even Mr. Page's readers had grown weary of the eternal psalm about antebellum greatness and post-bellum persecutions. Young people have an element of vulgarity in them which usually prevents their minds dwelling so exclusively upon their ancestors, and they have an element of the heroic in them which makes them tired of hearing about the most beautiful martyrs. This is not an evidence of decadence, but of returning strength. Thus, in the South they suddenly realized that Gordon Keith was a posthumous knight, the italics of a type of manhood no longer convenient to imitate. They had

become suddenly interested in something else, in the future, that challenging, immeasurable future upon the walls of which no grandfather's swords hang to claim it. Henceforth the novelist of Southern life must change his scene, bring it forward. And Mr. Page can no more do this than he can change his name and his genius. Both belong essentially to the past, and as a part of it they command respect, admiration, even reverence, but no longer absorbing interest.

By the turn of the twentieth century, Thomas Nelson Page had achieved fame as the creator of such works as "the Virginia classic," [Jay B. Hubbell, *Virginia Life in Fiction, American Literature,* 1922] *In Ole Virginia*; yet he had also become, as Mrs. Harris contended, something of an anachronism. *Gordon Keith* (1903) and Page's next novel, *John Marvel, Assistant* (1909), are weak, artificial novels of manners; neither of these later works extends or modifies the unique vision of *In Ole Virginia*. In her essay on Page's "waning influence," Corra Harris was the first critic to point out and account for in part the inadequacy of his vision for twentieth-century Americans in general and Southerners in particular.

Louis D. Rubin, Jr. (essay date 1975)

SOURCE: "Southern Literature and Southern Society," in *Southern Literary Study: Problems and Possibilities,* edited by Louis D. Rubin, Jr., and C. Hugh Holman, University of North Carolina Press, 1975, pp. 3-20.

[*Rubin, a leading scholar of Southern literature, argues that Page's "No Haid Pawn," like many Southern works, implicitly acknowledged the possibility of black insurrection.*]

Now ordinarily the fiction of Thomas Nelson Page might be the last place anyone would think to look for critical insights into what the antebellum South really thought about slavery, since Page's whole literary career would appear to have been based on the uncritical, eulogistic defense of the Old South. But Page was a writer, and what writers know, they know best *in* their fiction, not in what they say about what it means. "Never trust the artist," as D. H. Lawrence puts it. "Trust the tale." In the 1880s Page tried his hand at what then was a popular magazine genre, the ghost story. He wrote one entitled **"No Haid Pawn,"** and included it in his first book, *In Ole Virginia,* the volume that includes those classic and beautiful eulogies of the old regime, **"Marse Chan"** and **"Meh Lady."** The ghost story was based on a legend current in the antebellum Virginia neighborhood of Page's boyhood at Oakland. It involved a long-deserted plantation home in a swampy neck along the river. The slaves throughout the neighborhood were quick to tell how the old place was the abode of ghosts and spirits of various sorts, including those of a number of slaves who were stricken with typhus malaria and were buried, while still alive, alongside the pond, on which it was their wont at night to float in their coffins. None of the white children ever dared venture into the swamps and bogs of the abandoned place, where the ghost of a former owner was said to prowl. This man, who had come from the West Indies, had been a person of brutal temper and ungovernable passions, and his slaves had been very much afraid of him. Finally he had on one occasion hacked the head off a slave and displayed him before an open window to his terrified slaves. The authorities had intervened, the man had been arrested, tried, and sentenced to death, and hanged just at the rear of his own mansion, within sight of his crime. At the hanging something especially gruesome happened: the man's head was severed from his body. From that day onward, nobody went near No Haid Pawn. It was, Page says, "invested, to us, with unparalleled horror; and thus to us, no less than because the dikes had given way and the overflowed flats had turned again to swamp and jungle, it was explicable that No Haid Pawn was abandoned, and was now untrodden by any foot but that of its ghostly tenants."

Having set the scene, Page begins the ghost story proper. The narrator describes how he as a youth, home from boarding school, determined to go duck hunting in the No Haid Pawn area, and how as night approached the onset of a furious storm forced him to take shelter in the old mansion. He found an ancient bed and a fireplace, though he had no matches with which to start a fire. The storm raged on, and eventually he fell asleep. Several hours later he was awakened by a very peculiar sound, "like a distant call or halloo." Presently, hearing it come closer, he looked outside at the canal, and saw a boat, coffin-like, with a man standing upright in it and something lying in a lump or mass at the bow. Then as he waited, he heard the ground-floor door pushed open, and "a string of fierce oaths, part English and part Creole French," and then the sound of someone dragging a body up the steps and flinging his burden on the floor with a strange wild laugh. Then,

> For a moment there was not a sound, and then the awful silence and blackness were broken by a crash of thunder that seemed to tear the foundations asunder like a mighty earthquake, and the whole house, and the great swamp outside, were filled with a glare of vivid, blinding light. Directly in front of me, clutching with his upraised hand a long, keen, glittering knife, on whose blade a ball of fire seemed to play, stood a gigantic figure in the very flame of the lightning, and stretched at his feet lay, ghastly and bloody, a black and headless trunk.

> I staggered to the door and, tripping, fell prostrate over the sill.

With that the story **"No Haid Pawn"** ends, though a postscript informs us that the house, struck by lightning, burned to the water's edge and the river later reclaimed the spot and "all its secrets lay buried under its dark waters."

The ghost, of course, is supposedly the ghost of the West Indian owner who had decapitated the slave and had himself been hanged and decapitated, and in true "House of Usher" style the dead had come to life and the mansion had been destroyed. But Page was writing his story in the

1880s, when the old-fashioned pure ghost story, as Henry James later remarked in his preface to *The Turn of the Screw,* was no longer in fashion. So Page must have a rational explanation for what happened at No Haid Pawn, and he sets one up just before the narrative proper begins. The neighborhood had been disturbed at the time, he says, by the presence of Abolitionists. More than the usual number of slaves had run off until the Abolitionists had been discovered and had fled. All the slaves had been caught or had returned except for one, a Negro of brutal character, brought from the lower Mississippi, and who cursed in a strange dialect and laid claim to voodoo powers. Even so his owner had kept him because he was an expert butcher and first-rate boatman. It was suspected that many a missing hog in the neighborhood had found its way to his cabin. It turned out that this slave had been the leader in the secret meetings with the Abolitionists, and had disappeared for good when the intruders fled.

So what really was happening out at No Haid Pawn that night, we are supposed to infer, was that it was no ghost carrying a murdered human corpse who had reappeared in the haunted mansion, but the fugitive slave from the lower Mississippi, who had been living out there by himself all the while, subsisting on what he could find, depending on the place's reputation for his safety; and the "black and headless trunk" he carried in that night was that of a stolen hog.

There is not time here to do more than to suggest what this story can be made to reveal about the Old South and slavery. Page himself obviously sensed the connection. Of the appearance of the Abolitionists in the neighborhood he writes:

> It was as if the foundations of the whole social fabric were undermined. It was the sudden darkening of a shadow that always hung in the horizon. The slaves were in a large majority, and had they risen, though the final issue could not be doubted, the lives of every white on the plantations must have paid the forfeit. Whatever the right and wrong of slavery might have been, its existence demanded that no outside interference with it should be tolerated. So much was certain; self-preservation required this.

The very image, "foundations of the whole social fabric were undermined," is interesting. In the story he makes a point that the old house had been built by the slaves, that one of them "had been caught and decapitated between two of the immense foundation stones," that the rumor was that under the house were "solid rock chambers, which had been built for dungeons, and had served for purposes which were none the less awful because they were vague and indefinite." Before the young man enters the haunted mansion for shelter he finds himself standing under the very crossbeam from which the owner had once been hanged. It is important that the owner had not been from the neighborhood, but was from the West Indies, where slave revolts had wiped out the French planters, and that the fugitive slave was from the lower Mississippi. For whatever slavery might have been in Virginia, however much it may have been gentled there, nevertheless in the deep South it could be something horrible and very brutal, without any of the mitigating mildness that, as Page so often insisted in his other stories, characterized it in Virginia. The point is that the possibilities were always there in the institution, that it was only local custom that made of it in Virginia something more palatable than in the Deep South, and that even there it was possible, on a remote plantation, for a slaveowner to exercise "a brutal temper, inflamed by unbridled passions," for "a long period of license and debauchery." No matter what the daylight justification of slavery might be, there was, back there in the darkness, that awful knowledge. And always, in the background, was that fear of revolt and massacre.

In **"No Haid Pawn"** Page clearly tells more than he means to. For a ghost story requires horror, and Page had a ready-made subject. The picture that he gives of the white children growing up among the slaves on the plantation is not that of gentle old darkies telling quaint tales of the days when the animals talked like folks. He describes how the slaves would inform the children about evil spirits, ghosts, frightening and terrible things. Concerning the malaria that wiped out the slaves on the nearby plantation, the children were told of "the horrors of the pestilence of No Haid Pawn as a peculiar visitation," of "with bloodcurdling details the burial by scores, in a thicket just beside the pond, of the stricken 'befo' dee *daid,* honey, befo' dee *daid!*'" And more than that—I am not a psychologist and can only barely suggest what I feel is there—the story is an initiation story, in which a youth, coming toward his manhood, ventures out of the known into the darkness of a swamp blocked by vines and tangled branches, "a mire apparently bottomless," and stands under the gallows, "a heavy upright timber with an arm or cross-beam stretching from it, from which dangled a long chain, almost rusted away." This house was the place where "a long period of license and debauchery" had once taken place—perhaps you see what I am getting at.

Furthermore, it is important, I think, that as the boatman outside the house neared the building he gave a call. Here Page clearly means to suggest that not only was the fugitive slave hiding there in the swamp, but that he was signaling to someone. The inference would seem to be that other slaves were taking care of him. There was a possibility of a union between this man and the supposedly docile and contented slaves back on the plantations. In another piece of writing Page describes how the Southside Virginia insurrectionist Nat Turner hid out for several weeks before he was discovered; he remembered being told the story, he says, as a child, by one who had been there. The experience of **"No Haid Pawn"** comes from just that period in his life.

I shall speculate no more. Here is the story, **"No Haid Pawn,"** set in the middle of a book of stories which otherwise glorify the joys and delights of plantation life before the war, and which are designed to show how the black slaves were perfect retainers, humble, loyal, gentle, content with their lot, devoted to their owners. As for the

owners, we are given for model the Ole Marster in **"Marse Chan,"** who "didn' like nobody to sell niggers, and knowin' dat Cun'l Chahmb'lin wuz sellin' o' his, he writ and offered to buy his M'ria an' all her chil'en, 'cause she hed married our Zeek'yel." It is Thomas Nelson Page's tribute to the golden days before the Fall. But in it, seemingly unrelated to the life described in all the other stories, is this terrible tale of horror, guilt, fear, and depravity. "*In Ole Virginia,*" one commentator has written, "is pre-eminently the Virginia classic. Anyone who wants to understand the Virginia mind, and the persistence of certain attitudes into the twentieth century, should read it." And so they should, but along with **"Marse Chan"** and **"Meh Lady"** and **"Unc' Edinburg's Drowndin'"** they should read **"No Haid Pawn,"** for it has something to tell that none of the other stories has.

I have spent a long time, perhaps too much, on this one, lesser-known story by Thomas Nelson Page. My point is that there are many others like it, stories and poems by southern authors that are potential sources for better understanding of the society and culture out of which they were written. Page's fiction is not, perhaps, in the first rank even of southern literature, but it is the work of an honest and dedicated artist who wrote with skill and perception. And there are others like him. If only we will read their work imaginatively, and give to them the careful attention that we might not under other circumstances hesitate to give to other kinds of southern studies, we can learn a great deal about the society in which they lived. But we have to read them *as* stories and poems, as works of literature, if they are to instruct us with any authority.

Robert B. Downs (essay date 1977)

SOURCE: "Moonlight and Magnolia: Thomas Nelson Page's *In Ole Virginia,*" in *Books That Changed the South,* University of North Carolina Press, 1977, pp. 176-85.

[*Downs argues that Page showed no artistic growth as a writer and succeeded only in creating stereotypes, but he also states that Page's work is, nonetheless, important to understanding Southern literary history.*]

An eminent *Baltimore Sun* editor, Gerald W. Johnson, a native Tar Heel, declares that "the greatest enemy of the late confederacy was certainly not Ulysses S. Grant, or even William T. Sherman. . . . Far more lasting damage was done it by men whom the South adores: at the head of the list Stephen Collins Foster. . . . Deceivers of the same kind were orators of Henry Grady's school and a long procession of literary gents, beginning with John Pendleton Kennedy and culminating in Thomas Nelson Page" [*The Man Who Feels Left Behind,* 1961].

Johnson goes on to comment that these men "meant no harm and, to do them justice, they told no lies." Instead, they created a legend, "informing and irradiating the landscape but distorting the vision and paralyzing the will."

The myth, Johnson believes "is, in fact, a recrudescence of the Arthurian legend, of loyalty, love and derring-do all compact—in short, romance." It is no more substantial than the "dream stuff that composed the walls and towers of Camelot" [*The Man Who Feels Left Behind*]. Out of these traditions grew certain typically Southern characteristics, according to some caustic critics: ancestor worship, an exaggerated gallantry toward women, over-emphasis on honor, and a glorification of war. . . .

Page was not the first writer to extol the virtues of the Old South and to help create a romantic plantation tradition, but he was by all odds the most successful. . . .

The times were propitious for Page: local-color writers were at the height of their popularity, there was a widespread desire for reconciliation of the sections, and there was avid interest for rediscovering a unique region of the nation. In the introduction to a recent addition of *In Ole Virginia,* Kimball King observes that "Even Northern authors found attractive qualities in ante-bellum Southern life, which they attempted to portray as romantically as any native might do." King adds that Page's "idealized view of the Old South reassured a nation that was weary of disharmony.". . .

The literary device used by Page in **"Marse Chan"** and two other stories, *In Ole Virginia,* **"Meh Lady"** and **"Unc' Edinburg's Drowndin',"** is simple: an old Negro, sentimental in praise of the old days, tells a tale of handsome cavaliers and lovely ladies, stressing the love between master and slave. Page's biographer, Theodore L. Gross, suggests that the only credible person in **"Marse Chan"** and in the stories that follow is the Negro. "The other characters belong to a mythical past that cannot be realistically created because it is not real; it is the author's evocation," in Page's words, the "picture of a civilization which once having sweetened the life of the South has since then well-nigh perished from the earth" [Theodore L. Gross, *Thomas Nelson Page,* 1967]. . . .

"Meh Lady: A Story of the War," the third tale in *In Ole Virginia,* is narrated by another Negro slave, Billy, and again builds up into an epic tragedy. The central theme is reconciliation, with nostalgic glimpses of the South before, during, and after the Civil War. Paul H. Buck, in *The Road to Reunion,* concludes that "'Meh Lady' was a fresh creation in which the baser metals of sectional strife were transmuted into pure gold. A later generation may deem it insignificant but in the eighties it was one of the brightest ornaments of reconciliation" [Paul H. Back, *The Road to Reunion,* 1959]. Page himself states in the introduction to the collected edition of his writings that he "feels that he may without impropriety claim that with his devotion for the South, whose life he has tried faithfully to portray, and his pride in the Union, which he has rejoiced to see fully restored in his time, he has never wittingly written a line which he did not hope might tend to bring about a better understanding between the North and South, and finally lead to a more perfect Union" [Thomas Nelson Page, *The Novels, Stories, Sketches, and Poems,* 1906]. . . .

Critics are in general agreement that there was no growth in Page's work. His first story, **"Marse Chan,"** was his best, containing all the elements that made his writings celebrated. After this minor stroke of genius, Page could only repeat himself endlessly. The dramatic action in four of the six stories in *In Ole Virginia* centers around the theme of young lovers being separated by feuding families. Running through the stories, like a Greek tragedy, are unrequited love, the untimely death of the young and brave, and chaste sexual relationships consummated only in spirit. Page's chief characters belong to two classes—the masters of the great plantations and the faithful house servants, the latter contemptuous of field-hand blacks and poor white "trash." Sam in **"Marse Chan"** and Billy in **"Meh Lady,"** his two best known and most believable Negroes, are ex-slaves. The masses of people, the black field hands and Negro women, freed blacks, the small farmers, and poorer whites scarcely exist for Page.

Page's black heroes become stereotypes. Old Sam, for example, is an object of sympathy—dispossessed, lacking any identity of his own, and finding no alternative to the paternalism of the slave system. In effect—though the fact is never acknowledged by Page—Sam is a victim of the old order, unable to adjust to the new. Sam, in short, is a bewildered, disoriented ex-slave suffering the horrors of Reconstruction.

The heroic code appears again and again in Page's writings. In numerous short stories he shows how the code is manifested in a variety of situations how it has been the sustaining force in Southern civilization. The idyllic lives of the plantation owners are revealed in sentimental memory, mainly remote from historical fact, and white supremacy is always to the fore. Gross declares that "Page was so committed to certain political and social attitudes—and to the defense of the entire Southern way of life—that he was incapable of writing realistically. The code of Southern heroism stifled his imagination." In Page's later novels, when he aimed at realistic portrayals, Gross states that "the code was anachronistic and completely incompatible with the tensions of an industrial society." [Theodore L. Gross, *The Heroic Ideal in American Literature,* 1971]

A leading literary historian, Jay B. Hubbell, concludes that the kind of life depicted by Page belonged to a "Southern literary legend which pictures a Golden Age in the slaveholding South. Now the remarkable thing about this legend is that apart from the poor-whites it plays up the very same classes as the Northern legend: the great planters and the Negro slaves. Like the Northern legend, it practically ignores some four million yeomen farmers. They did not belong to the First Families. . . . In Virginia in 1860 in a population of over one million whites there were only 52,128 men who owned any slaves. There were only 114 who owned as many as one hundred. At least nineteen out of every twenty slaveholders was a yeoman, who held two or three slaves and worked in the tobacco fields beside them. The great planters were few in numbers, but it was from their class that as a rule the people chose their representatives in Congress and the General Assembly" [Jay B. Hubbell, *Virginia Life in Fiction,* 1922].

Viewed in the light of hard facts, therefore, Page's picture of the Old South was extremely limited, partial, one-sided, and sentimental.

Nevertheless, Page's panegyric descriptions would credit the Old South with virtually every advance in American culture and civilization: the leadership of its armies and navies, the establishment of a strong federal government, the opening up of the West, the christianizing of the Negro race, and the maintenance of white supremacy—"upon which all civilization seems now to depend." The South's "heroic fight" during the Civil War had "enriched the annals of the human race," Page continues, producing "a people whose fortitude in defeat has been even more splendid than their valor in war. It made men noble, gentle, and brave and women tender and pure and true." It was upon such fantasy that Page drew to picture a prewar Garden of Eden in the South and the postwar loss of that paradise.

Like a later Southern writer, the historian Ulrich B. Phillips, Page was convinced that the South had been misrepresented and misunderstood, especially by Northern historians, which may be cited as part of the reason for Page's chauvinism and elaborate defense of the South. His bitterness and extreme sensitivity are reflected in an essay entitled "The Want of a History of the Southern People," in which Page maintains that "there is no true history of the South. . . . By the world at large we are held to have been an ignorant, illiterate, cruel, semi-barbarous section of the American people, sunk in brutality and vice, who have contributed nothing to the advancement of mankind: a race of slave-drivers, who, to perpetuate human slavery, conspired to destroy the Union, and plunged the country into war." Persuaded that a conspiracy existed and a grave injustice had been done to his beloved section, Page became the South's champion, with the avowed purpose of setting the record straight. Unfortunately, Page did not possess the proper qualities to succeed in that aim. Hubbell notes that his conception of the Old South was "so idealized that he cannot see it in any other way even when he assumes the role of historian" [Hubbell, *Virginia Life*].

The plantation literary legend was not created by Page, as noted earlier. Before the Civil War, John Pendleton Kennedy, William Alexander Caruthers, Beverly Tucker, John Esten Cooke, William M. Thackeray, and G. P. R. James adopted the plantation as a locale for their romantic fiction. The popular conception pictured the South as one great plantation "open as an inn and rich as a castle," where gaiety, hospitality, and prosperity abounded. One American novelist, Mrs. E. D. E. N. Southworth, writes: "In the South, houses are almost palatial; social activity is ceaseless, cultured, idyllic; men are gallant, courtly— princely is the favorite adjective—prodigal in the uncalculating Southern fashion; the heroines are beyond description in beauty, sentimentality, and the ineffable sickliness from which the maid of romance often languishes" [*South Atlantic Quarterly* 30 (1931)].

Page's views on the Southern Negro and race problems in general have been a topic for considerable critical comment. His beliefs are set forth most explicitly in an essay,

"The Race Question." Therein, Page discusses racial differences between the Anglo-Saxon and the African Negro; contends that the master-slave relationship as it existed under slavery was not necessarily immoral, and had advantages for both whites and blacks; and insists that history demonstrates the Negro's innate inferiority. At the same time, Page claims that he has great affection for the Negro: "What has been stated has been said in no feeling of personal hostility, or even unfriendliness to the Negro, for I have no unfriendliness toward any Negro on earth; on the contrary, I have a feeling of real friendliness toward many of that race and am the well-wisher of the whole people." Page was especially resentful of the new, aggressive, freed Negroes who were insisting upon equality. His affections appear to have been limited to what he called the "old-time Negro," an ex-slave, content with his servile state, and demonstrating undying loyalty to his white master.

At the height of his career, Page received much critical acclaim in both North and South. An instance is Arthur Hobson Quinn's tribute, written in 1909: "In the renaissance of the South, Thomas Nelson Page played a most prominent part, not only in his poems, his novels, and his short stories, but also in the addresses he had made throughout the country, in which he deals directly with Southern life and character. . . . The quality which makes these short stories great is the surety with which the effect is reached" [*Georgia Review* (1966)].

But some years before Page's death in 1922, literary tastes had begun to change. Romance and sentiment were out, realism was in. Even in Virginia, such writers as James Branch Cabell, Ellen Glasgow, and Mary Johnston rejected, early in the present century, excessive claims for Southern heroism, manners, social customs, military accomplishments, and womanhood. Cabell went so far as to satirize Page's **"Meh Lady"** in *The River in Grandfather's Neck* (1915), and later expressed regret that "the ghost of Thomas Nelson Page still haunted everybody's conception of the South, keening in Negro dialect over the Confederacy's fallen glories" [Gross, *The Heroic Ideal*]. On the other hand, a revival of Page's attitude and style may be observed in Stark Young's romantic *So Red the Rose* and Margaret Mitchell's phenomenally popular *Gone with the Wind*. . . .

Page has few readers today, and, as Hubbell remarks, "not many will care to read or reread Page's novels." Nonetheless, Thomas Nelson Page has continued significance for the literary historian, as the creator of memorable stories evoking Southern plantation legends prior to the Civil War and of heroic myths of the Southern gentleman, the Southern lady, and the Southern way of life. These traditions persist nearly a century after Page wrote his first short story.

Lucinda H. MacKethan (essay date 1978)

SOURCE: "Thomas Nelson Page: The Plantation as Arcady," in *The Virginia Quarterly Review,* Vol. 54, No. 2, Spring, 1978, pp. 314-32.

[*MacKethan relates how Page created his Arcadian vision of the antebellum South from his conflicted awareness that the Old South was forever destroyed yet still a symbol of strength and pride for the New South.*]

Thomas Nelson Page, the elder son of a Virginia aristocrat living on a gracious plantation, could watch with pride as his father rode out in bright uniform and flowing cape to defend the Confederacy. Yet in later years, he would remember his father's homecoming even better than his grand departure. What was most vivid to his memory was the image of "his hand over his face, and his groan, 'I never expected to come home so.'" Out of such recollections, out of his sense of the discontinuity in memories of life before and after the Civil War, Page was to fashion for the South a definitive version of the dream of Arcady.

The cornerstone of Page's vision would be his dual focus of pride and loss; the strength of his fictional recreations of the Old South as Arcady would rest primarily in his ability to balance his belief in his idealizations with his awareness of threat and inevitable doom facing them. Nostalgia might win out over fatalism, yet the feeling that this golden world cast its glow from the center of impending peril is what makes its charm effective.

Growing up during the Civil War on a Virginia plantation, Page was quite naturally drawn to evaluating the quality of life before and after the war. That he would idealize the past was an inevitable consequence of the experiences which made up the most impressionable years of his life. Before the war he was the proud son of a slaveowning planter, taught by conservative parents to respect the old and suspect the new. His childhood was, by all accounts, remarkably carefree until the war intervened. He seems to have been provided with the opportunity to know all the pleasures of rural life while avoiding its hardships.

Page's fictionalized account of his own youthful adventures during the Civil War, recorded in the popular boys' book, ***Two Little Confederates,*** provides an intriguing glimpse of the atmosphere that was to mold Page's later concerns as a writer. The tale deals with the exploits of two youngsters who, like Thomas Nelson Page and his younger brother, Rosewell, lived out the Civil War on a Tidewater plantation. From idyllic pursuits of fishing, possum hunting, and squirrel shooting, the boys' energies are turned during the war to searching for deserters, hiding family heirlooms and Confederate officers from the Yankees, and, finally, to aiding their mother in the matter of sheer day-to-day survival as food supplies diminish and the defeat of the glorious Confederacy becomes an inevitability.

Page, in this nostalgic review of the war years that changed his own life so drastically, shows the two little confederates' romantic acceptance of the war as a kind of play world offering adventure and fame. Still, the effects of the defeat are not glossed over. Page recalls again his father's return from service after the fall of Richmond: "It seemed like a funeral. The boys were near

the steps, and their mother stood on the portico with her forehead resting against a pillar. . . . It *was* a funeral—the Confederacy was dead." The father's final gesture in this scene is worth special note. He turns to his last remaining slave, his body-servant Ralph, gives him his last dollar, and tells him he is free: "Ralph stood where he was for some minutes without moving a muscle. His eyes blinked mechanically. Then he looked at the door and at the windows above him. Suddenly he seemed to come to himself. Turning slowly, he walked solemnly out of the yard."

From what we learn of Page's early experiences in ***Two Little Confederates,*** we can grasp the artistic potential of his situation; he was in a very sensitive position to measure the impact of the destruction of the old world and the violent advent of the new. His imagination was steeped in experiences that he had shared or had heard recounted by old soldiers and old slaves. Yet without the pressure of upheaval that was provided by the war, it is doubtful that Page would have had the impetus to produce what has become the classic fictional account of the plantation myth. The war and its aftermath emphasized for Page the values of the old world just at the moment that they were disappearing, leaving him with a sense that the regime destroyed had a tragic grandeur and his childhood memories a special importance that should be captured for posterity. . . .

His first book was his masterpiece, an achievement never closely matched by his later works, which seldom sustain the unique blend of nostalgia, romance, and local color that is the highlight of the stories of ***In Ole Virginia.*** Yet the works which followed his masterpiece continued to gain a large and fairly sympathetic audience. In a collection of essays entitled *The Old South,* Page wrote an eloquent if also chauvinistic "history" of plantation civilization as it could be viewed only through the eyes of a Virginia aristocrat. When he turned to the novel form, he dealt best with cavalier heroes who had to make the transition to the modern world but who survived actually because they remained attached to the old values. During the last ten years of his life, Page devoted himself almost completely to public life, notably as United States ambassador to Italy, but his major achievement remained his early fictional evocations of the special world that was the South in enchanted times "befo' de wah."

. . . . .

The three aspects of the antebellum world which Page turned into staples of his Arcadia were the plantation locale itself with the great house at the center; the image of the Southern gentleman; and most important, the "old time" Negro, the slave or "servant" as Page calls him, through whose voice the Old South achieves mythic status. Taking up these points as they appear in Page's major works, we begin, as almost all of his descriptions of plantation life begin, with the planter's home, which was for Page the hub of the universe. It is of interest to note that most of Page's stories and novels, and the essays dealing with Southern culture as well, contain, near their beginning, a fairly thorough account of the home occupied by the hero or heroine, and at any time in the stories the threat of the loss of that home portends a tragedy of major proportions.

One of Page's most lyrical panegyrics to the Old South is entitled "Social Life in Old Virginia Before the War." The essay begins with a description of Oakland, his own boyhood home. With few alterations, Oakland could serve as the setting for almost all of Page's plantation stories. The striking quality of his description of the house is his orderly arrangement of the picturesque scene into a composite that contains all the elements which he cherished about the Old South. "Oakland" is notable for the plainness of its construction; there is a quaintness in its design, a "manliness" about its offices and quarters, a special dignity in the way it is set among historic oaks, and an ineffable grace showing through the orchards and gardens that flourish on the grounds. When Page called again on his memories of Oakland to provide the setting for *Two Little Confederates,* his description emphasized two qualities: an excellence based on simplicity and a beauty based on older and, by implication, surer standards: "It was not a handsome place, as modern ideas go, but down in Old Virginia, where the standard was different from the later one, it passed in the old times as one of the best plantations in all that region."

When we read any of Page's stories of the Old South, we are made aware that his locales are charged with special significance. Every story contains reference, often extended, to the homes of the leading characters. And it is through these descriptions that Page is establishing the credentials of his heroes—if they come from a fine plantation, they are almost invariably of high moral quality and deserve universal admiration. A study of the stories in Page's first volume, *In Ole Virginia,* reveals that the plantation homes described are uniformly designed to be outward and visible signs of the spirit of the people who settled the Southern region and created an aristocratic utopia out of a wilderness. In these early stories, the preservation of the old estates represents for those involved in it an effort to maintain the nation's only remaining stronghold of non-material values.

In Page's first story, **"Marse Chan,"** the white narrator, a stranger to the Southern locale he is visiting, is struck immediately by the atmosphere surrounding the "once splendid mansions" which seem to him, in their "proud seclusion," to indicate that "Distance was nothing to this people; time was of no consequence to them. They desired but a level path in life, and that they had, though the way was longer, and the outer world strode by them as they dreamed." The outer world is always somewhere beyond the settings that Page uses for the stories in *In Ole Virginia.* The pertinent action in most of them takes place before the Civil War, so that the serenity of the scene is not disturbed, although the sense of impending destruction is always present. It is of this world that Page's most famous narrative spokesman, the venerable Unc' Sam of **"Marse Chan,"** says: "Dem wuz good ole times, marster—de bes' Sam ever see!"

In the story **"Meh Lady,"** the sense of place is the strong motivating force by which a young Virginia belle and her

faithful retainers struggle to maintain a home constantly threatened by Yankees or carpetbaggers. To leave the plantation, it is implied, would be death. After the war Meh Lady's estate stands as a small, embattled island where the old values and sense of pride are being defended against the rude forces of change.

The story in *In Ole Virginia* which least meets with Page's idea of normal conditions of plantation life is **"No Haid Pawn."** The plantation with the weird name "No Haid Pawn" is the antithesis of Oakland and the estates described in Page's other stories. Page wants to show here what happens to the plantation ideal when unworthy beings attempt to imitate its concepts. No Haid Pawn was built by strangers to the area, men of Creole blood who "never made it their permanent home. Thus, no ties either of blood or friendship were formed with their neighbors, who were certainly openhearted enough to overcome anything but the most persistent unneighborliness."

Because they are not Anglo-Saxons reared in the Virginia manner, the owners of No Haid Pawn build a mansion totally out of keeping with what was expected from the true plantation house. An unhealthy atmosphere surrounds the place from the very beginning, and eventually, in what was probably an attempt to copy the fate of Poe's House of Usher, Page allows nature to reclaim what the evil Creoles forfeited by their lack of morality and their disdain for the customs of the community. In this respect, the story offers some interesting parallels to Faulkner's treatment of "Sutpen's Hundred" in *Absalom, Absalom!* In **"No Haid Pawn,"** Page experimented with a new kind of atmosphere and setting, yet he ended by re-emphasizing a cardinal principle applied to all his plantations; that is, the place reflects its owner and thus the true plantation will symbolize and proclaim the ethical superiority of its inhabitants.

. . . . .

The plantation, for Page, was the breeding ground for heroes. It provided the cornerstone "of a civilization so pure, so noble, that the world to-day holds nothing equal to it." All of Page's major characters exhibit the traits of feudal lords, and all of them are involved in a crusade to preserve an ideal way of life against the forces of inevitable change. Their threatened plantation homes are a symbol of their struggle, and perhaps of its futility. In any case, Page's plantation settings provide much more than mere scenery; they supply motivation and meaning for the works as a whole and are at the center of Page's design.

The Southern plantation owner's attitude toward his home resembles that of a feudal lord toward his domain. Two things are of utmost importance to this figure as Page presents him—his land and his honor. Both are sacred, and both are the exclusive possessions of a particular kind of human being whom Page names reverently "the Virginia gentleman." It is a title which he does not lightly bestow, for it belongs only to his small group of embattled chivalric heroes who try to maintain the virtues of the Old South while the rest of the nation and even much of the South itself are given over to materialism. In his home state before the war, Page declared, "To be a Virginia gentleman was the first duty."

In Ole Virginia, Red Rock, and *Gordon Keith* contain many representatives of the "gentleman" figure. Among the heroes that are portrayed in these works, there are two types: the old gentlemen who are conservative fathers, often stubborn authoritarians, gracious to ladies and guests but unbending in their opposition to anything that threatens the status quo, and the young gentlemen who must meet new challenges posed by a changing technological society.

In the stories that make up *In Ole Virginia,* there is not too much distinction made between what is expected of the young and of the old; fathers and sons alike are involved simply and wholeheartedly in exemplifying the charm and chivalry that characterized life in the Old South. Because few of the stories deal with the question of what behavior should be in a defeated "new" South, the gentlemen both old and young in the stories of Page's first collection live out their roles in a kind of King Arthur's Court that has many intriguing aspects but that does not often try to treat the problems facing different generations of "gentlemen" after the Civil War. . . .

Page's young aristocrats differ from their elders in breadth of experience but not in substance. From Marse Chan to Gordon Keith, they form a neat chain of similar young heroes waiting to put the code they have been taught to the tests that will prove them true Virginia gentlemen. In the plantation stories of *In Ole Virginia,* the young man usually dies in the course of performing some act connected with the ritual of earning this title. He will be remembered by a former slave who was his childhood companion and who sees "young master's" death as a blessing which saved the hero from having to cope with the postbellum world. . . .

Page had great difficulty in making any of his young aristocratic Southerners believable. While characterizing them as the worthy representatives of all that the Old South stood for, he still wanted to be able to show that they could function successfully as heroes in a materialistic age. Part of his problem, particularly in his novels, was that he was preaching a "creed outworn" to a generation increasingly interested in other things, but his inability to produce believable characters in much of his fiction was due to more than this. What we get in his gentlemanly portrayals in his novels are products of an environment rather than people with individual emotions or spontaneous ideas. Marse Chan and Marse George, in the stories of *In Ole Virginia,* generate a great deal more interest than Page's later heroes. However, this is not really because they are portrayed with more flexibility, but because they are seen through the eyes of Page's Negro narrators, who speak with much greater originality and emotion than does the stiff, omniscient gentleman-narrator of the novels.

. . . . .

The Negroes of *In Ole Virginia* are the most important figures that Page produced in his fiction. Not only are

they more lifelike than the white heroes he created, but also they carry the chief responsibility for making and proving his arguments about the benevolence of race relations in the Old South. This is not to say that the Negro as Page presents him is not a stereotype, but only that Page, in conceptualizing the Old South darky, felt free to be more imaginative and less dogmatic than he was with his Old South gentlemen, and the result is that his black men usually have much greater appeal than his whites. Page lost some of his inhibitions when he used the voice of the Negro to tell his tales. They still preach his personal philosophy, but they do so in a way that enlarges and to some degree changes our vision of the world that he wanted us to see.

Sam, the old black freedman who was companion and servant to Page's Marse Chan, expresses the crux of Southern race relations in refreshing terms; speaking to his master's dog, he says, "Yo' so sp'ilt yo' kyahn hardly walk. . . . Jus' like white folks—think 'cus you's white and I's black, I got to wait on yo' all de time." The old servant's pointed remark, however, is meant to be more of a joke on himself than a criticism of white attitudes, as his subsequent actions show. The dog is treated with all the respect and favor due a monarch, simply because he once belonged, as did Sam himself, to the beloved Marse Chan. The fact that Sam was, by the sheer fact of his black skin, a slave, does not bother him at all. Actually he longs pitifully for the time when "Niggers didn't hed nothin' 't all to do—jes' hed to 'ten to de feedin' an' cleanin' de hosses, an' doin what marster tell 'em to do."

Page's fiction was designed to dramatize his racial views, and his stories became in fact his most effective tool for displaying what he felt was the true case concerning the relationship between whites and blacks which had once existed and could again exist in the South. Francis Pendleton Gaines points out that Page's Negroes feel a "not incongruous dignity" at being included as members of the plantation family. Page's argument was that the slave enjoyed a secure place in life and a certain sense of status through his bondage. Only by being a slave could he participate in the exclusive world of the planter, yet his gratitude for the opportunity was nevertheless unbounded.

Such is the case with Sam when he is given to his young master in **"Marse Chan."** Sam relates with pride what was for him the greatest moment in his life, when "ole marster" singled him out: "An den he sez: 'Now Sam, from dis time you belong to yo' young Marse Channin'; I want you to tek keer on im ez long ez he lives. You are to be his boy from distime. . . .' An from dat time I was tooken in de house to be Marse Channin's body servant."

Page was trying to make the point in **"Marse Chan"** that it would have been better for Sam if slavery had never ended, but for the modern reader Sam's description of all the wonders of the old time cannot disguise the fact that his present misery is the direct result of his having been made, at birth, totally dependent on a way of life which could not save either him or itself from destruction. Of course, Sam sees nothing of this, and his account of his existence before the war is meant to be an uncritical defense of the old regime, one that would put to rout the image left by Harriet Beecher Stowe's Uncle Tom. This it managed to do more effectively than even Page could have hoped, as witnessed by the reported spectacle of the abolitionist, Thomas Wentworth Higginson, weeping over Sam's description of Marse Chan's untimely death.

There is more pathos in Marse Chan's death than simply the fact that it keeps him from being reconciled with his true love. He dies in a war that he opposed in order to defend a system already doomed. And in spite of his brotherly regard for Sam, and Sam's undying loyalty to him, he is unable to provide for his slave's future. The result is a pathetic figure whom Page devised in order to praise the Old South, but who also reveals, all unconsciously, the plantation's inherent weaknesses.

The situation of Unc' Billy in **"Meh Lady"** is not as pathetic as that of the other Negro narrators in *In Ole Virginia*: For him, the old world manages to be retained on his plantation through the auspices of a former Northern soldier (with Virginia ancestors, Page hastens to inform us) who returns after the war to win the hand of Meh Lady and restore her home to its earlier elegance. Viewing the reconciled pair of lovers, who represented for Page's readers an idyllic reunion of North and South, Unc Billy sits with "de moon sort o' meltin' over de yard," and thinks "hit 'pear like de plantation 'live once mo', an' de ain' no mo scuffin', an' de ole times done come back agin."

It is fitting that, at the wedding of Meh Lady and her lover, Billy takes the responsibility unasked when the minister requests someone to give the bride away. His reasoning is simple and yet full of dignity: "an' I don' know huccome 'twuz, but I think 'bout Marse Jeems an' Mistis when he ax me dat, an' Marse Phil, whar all dead, an' all de scufflin' we done been th'oo, an' how de chile ain' got nobody to teck her part now 'sep' jes' me; an' . . . I 'bleeged to speak up, I jes' step for'ard an' say: 'Old Billy.'" Although Billy achieves a great deal of stature in this scene, his explanation nevertheless borders on being an apology for his presumption, and Page is quick to put him back in his place as simple darky.

There is one story in *In Ole Virginia* which differs from the rest in its focus and its message. Although not told from a Negro's point of view, the central character is a Negro whose tragic situation is not minimized by any of Page's usual propaganda of white benevolence. "Ole 'Stracted," in the story of that title, is a former slave who had been sold many years before to help to pay off his master's debts. His wife and child were sold elsewhere, and the old black man lives only to be reunited with his master, who had promised to buy him back with his family. Though he has no memory of anything that has happened to him since the scale, he has made his way back to his plantation, which is now in ruins and is owned by "po-white trash." The old man's only identity is bound up in his belief that his master is coming for him. Thus he spends his time dreaming "of a great plantation, and fine carriages and horses, and a house with his wife and the boy."

Ole 'Stracted's hopeless fantasy is matched by the far more compelling dream of a young neighbor who turns out to be the old black man's son. Ephraim is a freedman trying with dignity against impossible odds to make a good living for his wife and family. In spite of the new sort of potential here there are still some of the standard biases. It is a poor white and certainly not a Southern gentleman who victimizes Ephraim, and Ole 'Stracted never considers freedom a favorable alternative to the idyllic conditions he knew as a slave—the point is never made that the plantation system was responsible for separating him from his family in the first place. But Ephraim is a different kind of Negro from those whom Page had treated sympathetically in his other stories.

Ephraim's dream, like his father's, is of a Southern Arcady, but his is based on a future which holds dignity and self-sufficiency for his family, while Ole 'Stracted's is based on his memories of a time when his master provided for him. Ephraim has a recurring vision "in which he saw corn stand so high and rank over his land that he could scarcely distinguish the stalk, and a stable and barn and a mule . . . and two cows which his wife would milk, and a green wagon driven by his boys . . .", in which, in short, he would be a prosperous farmer sustaining himself and his family through his own labors on his own land.

This dream is a simple one which involves all of Ephraim's energy and keeps his hopes alive. It is one which Page lets us feel Ephraim has every right to realize, and this is what makes **"Ole 'Stracted"** so different from the other stories of his first collection. Page's usual attitude toward the freedman is one of scorn concerning the "new issue nigger" who does not have the proper respect for the old values. He frequently advised that the freedman should turn to his master for guidance and remain dependent on the white man until some vague future time when his race might finally "deserve" to govern themselves. In this one story, however, he seems to admit the justice of a plan whereby the Negro could take his life into his own hands through owning and working his land.

Page's story, despite the sympathy it gives to Ephraim's dream, finally demonstrates that the young freedman's hopes are as futile as his father's belief that his master will find him. Ephraim and his wife do not own their land, and never in a lifetime of sweating in the fields and taking in washing could they hope to earn enough to buy it. Everything they can possibly raise goes to pay their rent to the white man who lives on the hill. Page has sympathy, but in the story, as well as in the essays he devoted to solving the "Negro Question," he has few practical ideas as to how the Negro could maintain his self-respect and achieve his dreams in a white man's world. Yet Page evidently could not bear the indictment of the old world that his story implied, so he got himself off the hook through a fortuitous, if improbable, coincidence of the kind that he uses to resolve most of the potentially tragic situations in his works. The money that Ole 'Stracted has saved to buy back his wife and son goes at his death to Ephraim, who discovers just in time that the feeble-minded old man is his father. Thus he can buy his land and make his dream come true.

Page's conclusion is not a solution but an evasion of the implications of his story. The most disturbing element about **"Ole 'Stracted"** is that it appears in the same volume with **"Marse Chan"** and **"Meh Lady,"** stories in which the Negroes themselves sing the praises of the system that causes all of the suffering in **"Ole 'Stracted."** Even Ole 'Stracted longs for the past, however; his energies have always been fixed on the idea that his master will save him, so he is incapable of doing anything to save himself.

The situation of the black man in Page's pastoral kingdom is ambiguous at best, though it was clearly the author's intention to depict plantation life as the ideal mode of existence for both master and slave. His black spokesmen are meant to illustrate that Negroes and whites, in the old and better world, were united in their pursuits and purposes. In taking this stand, Page carves an image of the white man as the hero of Arcady, dedicated to preserving a civilization perfect in its innocence and magnificent in its program for the good life. His Negroes, however, remain his most compelling creations, as characters lost in a new world and from their longings creating the myth of a world which fulfills their need for identity and purpose.

That Page never consciously explored the flaws of the Old South, that he failed to see the ambiguities of his own recreations of the plantation as an ideal world, is only too clear a fact. His intention was not to hide the sins of the past, for indeed, he was blind to them himself. What he hoped to accomplish was to challenge the practices of the present by comparing them in art to the customs of a simpler, more natural time. Thus his stories have the force of a pastoral rebuke, and they also have the even more compelling force of a dream. Page created out of his own deep convictions a romantic world whose charm at times overshadows the realist's demand for a counterbalancing acknowledgement of truths based purely on fact. We return from Page's fiction to the real world very much aware that his vision is marred, yet also aware that as dreams go, the one Page fashioned for the Old South was convincing enough to give force to a myth that has itself shaped many realities and outlasted many others.

J. V. Ridgely (essay date 1980)

SOURCE: "The New South: The Past Recaptured," in *Nineteenth-Century Literature,* University Press of Kentucky, 1980, pp. 89-111.

[Ridgely focuses on Page's attempts through literature and lectures to prove the rightness of the Southern Cause.]

Page's forte, like [Joel Chandler] Harris's, was the tale told in Negro dialect. However embarrassing (and sometimes difficult to comprehend) such a rendering of dialog

may seem to the reader of today, it was vital in giving the ring of "reality" to his favorite characters, the faithful black servants who knew—and would not give up—their places. The wide success of the book suggests how easily his readers could accept the doctrine of paternalism—though, in fact, ex-slaveholders had been shocked by the "uppity" attitudes of their former property.

The opening story of *In Ole Virginia,* one of the most popular he ever composed, is an epitome of Page's world—and his appeal. The central narrative of **"Marse Chan"** is framed by a well worn device: a lone traveler on horseback meets a stranger, asks a few perfunctory questions, and is rewarded with a long and stirring narrative. . . .

The story is an unabashed tear-jerker which gains its effect—if it succeeds at all—by the reader's willingness to accept the fundamental goodness of the world which Sam, the black man, recalls so elegiacally. Marse Chan was the heir of a great plantation owner; Sam had been assigned to him as body servant and they had grown up, like brothers, in close association. There appears to be no irony in Sam's words, and certainly none in Page's, as he describes the joys of the old order: "'Dem wuz good ole times, marster—de bes' Sam ever see! Dey wuz, in fac'! Niggers didn' hed nothing 't all to do—jes' hed to 'ten' to de feedin' an' cleanin' de hosses, an' doin' what de marster tell 'em to do; an' when dey wuz sick, dey had things sont 'em out de house, an' de same doctor come to see 'em whar 'ten' to de white folks when dey wuz po'ly. Dyar warn' no trouble nor nothin'.'". . .

Even northern readers like Mrs. Stowe's brother, Henry Ward Beecher, and Emily Dickinson's "mentor," Thomas Wentworth Higginson, gladly confessed that they had shed tears over the tale; and their watery response would seem no more than was appropriate to this calculatedly doleful tale of love cut short. Yet something else is at work in Page's story. The plot contained nearly every stereotype of the southern legend: the gallant young man who falls for his nation; the chilly but eventually faithful lady; the proud colonel; the duel; the well treated darky; the good times on the old plantation. Chan and his Miss Anne sprang out of a vanished time; their deaths symbolized the passing of a never-to-be-resurrected social order of grace and honor. Surely *these* were not the people whom the North had sworn to destroy. *They* had not created the slave system; they had only defended their homeland and their way of life. Had the South alone been at fault in the conflict in which such people had given their lives?

For all the derivative quality of his work, for all the choke in the voice when he spoke of the old régime, Page was writing what for him was sacred history. As late as 1887 he gave a famous address on "The Old South" at Washington and Lee University, which he had attended and where the great General of the Confederacy now had his shrine. He undertook, he told his auditors, to prove that "the New South is, in fact, simply the Old South with its energies directed into new lines." Reviewing the history of the slave trade, he charged that the North had hardly been guiltless and that actually it was southerners like

Thomas Jefferson who had fought to abolish it. The extinction of slavery seemed assured, Page said, but it "was prevented by the attitude of the Northern Abolitionists. Their furious onslaughts, accompanied by the illegal circulation of literature calculated to excite the negroes to revolt" caused the temper of the South to change. For Page the issue was quite clear: "The real fight was whether the conservative South should, with its doctrine of States' rights, of original State sovereignty, rule the country according to a literal reading of the Constitution, or whether the North should govern according to a more liberal construction, adapted, as it claimed, by necessity to the new and more advanced conditions of the nation." The South had a sacred duty to fight to maintain its institutions, which had produced "a civilization so pure, so noble, that the world to-day holds nothing equal to it." In a few paragraphs, Page summarized the South's case and demanded recognition of its unique achievement:

> After less than a generation it has become among friends and enemies the recognized field of romance.

> Its chief attribute was conservatism. Others were courage, fidelity, purity, hospitality, magnanimity, honesty, and truth.

> Whilst it proudly boasted itself democratic, it was distinctly and avowedly anti-radical—holding fast to those things which were proved, and standing with its conservatism a steadfast bulwark against all novelties and aggressions. . . .

> Slavery itself, which proved the spring of woes unnumbered, and which clogged the wheels of progress and withdrew the South from sympathy with the outer world, christianized a race and was the automatic balance-wheel between labor and capital which prevented, on the one hand, the excessive accumulation of wealth, with its attendant perils, and on the other hand prevented the antithesis of the immense pauper class which work for less than the wage of the slave without any of his incidental compensations.

After this traditional attack on northern economy, Page brought himself to endorse reconciliation, but only with the understanding that the Lost Cause be recognized as having been constitutionally sanctioned:

> No section of this country more absolutely, loyally, and heartily accepts the fact that slavery and secession can never again become practical questions in this land, than does that which a generation ago flung all its weight into the opposite scale. But to pretend that we did not have the legal, constitutional right to secede from the Union is to stultify ourselves in falsification of history.

> If any portion of this nation doubt the South's devotion to the Union, let it attempt to impair the Union. If the South is ever to be once more the leader of this nation, she must cherish the traditional glory of her former station, and prove to the world that her revolution was not a rebellion, but was fought for the principle

upon which she was established as her foundation-stone—the sacred right of self-government.

It is no wonder that, with the command of such rhetoric, Page was widely hailed as the keeper of the flame.

Lucinda H. MacKethan (essay date 1985)

SOURCE: "Plantation Fiction, 1865-1900," in *The History of Southern Literature,* edited by Louis D. Rubin, Jr., and others, Louisiana State University Press, 1985, pp. 209-18.

[*MacKethan comments on how Page unconsciously reveals the weaknesses of the plantation system through his use of black narrators who embody the tensions of the master-slave relationship.*]

The literary phenomenon of the Old South, centered in the image of plantation culture, was the creation of writers pursuing careers in a very different South, dubbed "new" in economic, social, and political as well as literary structures. Thomas Nelson Page, the most durable of the post-Civil War plantation romancers, might assert that "the New South is . . . simply the Old South with its energies directed into new lines"; however, it was solely the newness of those lines that encouraged postbellum admirers of the plantation to turn a defeated way of life into a substantial legend. The design of images for a popular literature stocked with belles and cavaliers, courtships and duels, mansions and cotton blossoms, and, at the heart of the scene, wistfully reminiscing darkies, had to await the actual demise of the plantation world.

A predilection for local color dominated literary tastes in the major popular magazines of the North immediately following the Civil War, but this new way of dealing fictionally with regional material, while it provided for minute attention to features of setting, speech, and quaint character, incorporated a sentimental rather than a critical vision of life in the Old South. Thus the plantation literature that arose from the ashes of the past had as its primary quality a tone of nostalgia evoking, without questioning, an aura of Camelot. What appeared was a vision of order and grace to communicate a new myth of a lost cause. For writers turning to the antebellum scene, the item second in importance to the nostalgic glow was the voice of the black slave, brought forward to authenticate a version of the plantation system as tragic Eden. Irwin Russell's banjo-picking darkie dancers, Thomas Nelson Page's uncles, and Joel Chandler Harris' Remus told their stories in convincing dialect to both a North and South ready to see slavery, once abolished, in a light that would facilitate reconciliation and make the Negro once again the Southerner's problem. . . .

For post-Civil War plantation fiction writers, the figure of the slave provided an acceptable nostalgic perspective and even more; transforming the slave laborer of the Old South into the loyal sustainer and mourner of times gone by paradoxically both expedited the New South's entry into the industrial mainstream of a national future and salvaged a revitalizing sense of its glorious past.

What has long been known as a "plantation school" of white Southern local-color writers, coming into being to vindicate a lost cause, was actually a very diverse group whose experience within regional patterns differed widely and provoked responses that contrasted as often as they converged. One point seems to be settled; the most important contribution to the fictional shape given to plantation themes was made by Thomas Nelson Page (1853-1922). Sherwood Bonner published "Gran'mammy tales" told in Negro dialect in Northern periodicals in the 1870s, and Uncle Remus was firmly ensconced in his plantation cabin by 1880. Although Page's popularity began slightly later and he acknowledged many sources, especially Russell and his fellow Virginian George W. Bagby, his work was to surpass all others in forming the image of the plantation best suited to Southern aims, Northern expectations, and his own idealistic predilections. As Grace King, an admiring follower in the field, wrote, he "showed us with uneffable grace" that "we had now a chance in literature at last." Page's staples, "marsters," "mistises," and faithful retainers, provided the outlines for many disciples. When the *Century* published Page's first and most famous story, **"Marse Chan,"** in 1884, the market had been tested and found eager for just what Page had prepared for it: a totally sincere, elegiac, uncritical rendering of the plantation scene as prose idyll, presented by black narrators who were the "chief 'pendence" of helpless owners and unable, in most cases, to survive their expulsion from Eden. . . .

The black narrators of Page's first book—Sam in **"Marse Chan,"** Billy in **"Meh Lady,"** and Edinburg in **"Unc' Edinburg's Drowndin'"**—bask in the reflected glories of white owners who give to them the only functions they will ever comprehend and the "bes' times" they will ever see. When Sam is made body servant to the infant Marse Chan, a structure is conferred that he wears proudly for life. Billy can engineer his lady's marriage to a former Union army colonel in the classic rendition of a plot device designed to signal happy sectional reconciliation, yet Billy is most content when "hit 'pear like de plantation 'live once mo'." And Edinburg is, like the other two slave characters, unappreciative of a freedom that only robs him of purpose. He mourns, "Dese heah free-issue niggers don' know what Christmas is." These characters were created to verify the simple beauty of the plantation and to reconstruct the image of the noble cavalier. Still, a modern audience perceives that their sad purposelessness in the postbellum present has been caused by a system that never granted them identity as human beings.

Page's black voices sometimes go beyond his conscious applications, exposing ironies within the system they exalt. Two stories of **In Ole Virginia** not told by former black servants reveal other facets of Page's restricted view of what slavery in the Old South actually meant. In **"No Haid Pawn,"** Page attempted a Poe-like ghost story in which a cruel West Indian planter sets up housekeeping in Virginia and is finally hanged for decapitating one of his

slaves. This operation of Southern justice comes too late for the slaves who have had to bear his viciousness. In **"Ole 'Stracted"** Page sympathizes with the plight of the freedman Ephraim who nurses a legitimate dream of owning his land. Ephraim's crazy old black neighbor turns out to be his father who, sold away from him and his mother by the creditors of a benevolent master, has come upon hard times. The old man has been driven "distracted" by the shock of this separation and by his frantic attempts to find his family and buy their freedom. Yet Page has the old man speak lovingly of his master and longingly of the good old days. He wants not to be free but to return home to the master, a phenomenon he explains by saying, "You know we growed up togerr?"

Page saw only the charm of master-slave relations that to him were secured by the honor and generosity of the Virginia cavalier tradition. Yet the grave deficiencies of the masters he created for **"No Haid Pawn"** and **"Ole 'Stracted"** have the inevitable effect of calling to judgment the system as a whole. Page's seeming blindness to such ironies was a disorder fostered by the atmosphere in which he lived and by the audience, both Northern and Southern, who actively encouraged his construction of a myth glorifying the Old South. A final irony is that, while Page did not acknowledge his black narrators as individuals apart from their masters' interests, he yet depended on the vitality of their individualized voices to convey his vision. They are his most memorable figures. . . .

To bring together Page's **In Ole Virginia**. Harris' *Uncle Remus: His Songs and His Sayings,* and Charles Chesnutt's *The Conjure Woman* is to take the full measure of the potential for complexity that inheres in the exploitation of the plantation scene. The ground shared by these three works indicates common features that their authors saw as requirements for fiction treating the Old South. All placed the slave narrator at the center of the plantation scheme, not only because he fulfilled local-color standards but also because he provided an air of veracity and more subtly a persuasive doctrine of master-slave relations. These black narrators are the most valuable creations of the fictions for which they provided voice, for they embody the tensions that, with varying degrees of awareness, their authors brought to bear on the plantation they envisioned.

Clyde N. Wilson (essay date 1991)

SOURCE: "Introduction," in *In Ole Virginia* by Thomas Nelson Page, edited by M. E. Bradford, J. S. Sanders & Company, 1991, pp. xi-xxi.

[*In this essay, Wilson reassesses Page's role in American literary history and argues against seeing Page as outdated and a racist defender of the ignoble plantation tradition.*]

In Ole Virginia is a memorable portrait of the Old South before its destruction and one of the small company of truly enduring achievements in nineteenth century American literature. Its author, Thomas Nelson Page, was the most popular and most representative Southern writer of his time and one of the few Southern writers of any time to achieve the fullest measure of recognition and worldly success in his own lifetime.

Page was born in 1853 at Oakland plantation in Hanover County, Virginia, the same county in which Patrick Henry and Henry Clay had been born. Four obvious influences can be seen in his origins.

First, an ancestral pedigree that reads like a roster of the First Families of Virginia. Second, a childhood spent in a region north of Richmond during the War between the States that was one of the most heavily fought-over areas of the continent. Third, reduced family circumstances, which gave a spur to industry and ambition. Fourth, a spinster lady relative (remembered in Page's sketch, **"My Cousin Fanny,"** in the 1894 collection *The Burial of the Guns*) who introduced him to literature and determined the direction of his aspirations.

Turning twelve two weeks after Appomattox, Page experienced the war at the most impressionable age, so that the heroism of the men in gray and the women who sustained them, and the hardships of the "Reconstruction" peace which followed, formed the central theme of his experience and thus of his writing. He is the premier interpreter in fiction of those Southern experiences for his generation.

Page knew directly the fall of fortunes entailed by defeat for Southerners, especially those of his class, in an irregular education, interspersed with periods as a tutor. He was able to attend Washington and Lee (then Washington College) for a time when General Lee was president, but could not stay long enough to graduate. After awhile, he was able to attend the University of Virginia Law School. Again he had to leave without graduating, although he enjoyed at Charlottesville a stimulating literary fellowship.

In 1872 he began a law practice in Richmond that was moderately successful and which he continued for some years, even after his literary career had begun to prosper. In 1886 he married Anne Seddon Bruce, whose pedigree equalled his and who is perhaps the model for "Anne" in **"Marse Chan."** She died suddenly a year and a half later at age twenty.

"Marse Chan," Page's first significant published fiction, appeared in 1884 in the popular *Century Magazine* of the Scribner publishing family. The editors liked the story but delayed publication for two years, apparently because of misgivings about the readability of the dialect. The doubts proved unfounded. When published, the story was immediately popular, and thereafter demand for Page's work on the part of the Northern reading public never ceased.

In 1887 his first book, *In Ole Virginia,* a collection of his earliest stories, appeared, to critical and popular acclaim. It remained his most popular and characteristic book.

"Marse Chan" has always been his best-loved story, and Page considered the second story in the volume, **"Unc' Edinburg's Drowndin',"** to be his best-crafted and most technically perfect tale.

By 1893 he was able to give up law practice and lecturing. He married into a very wealthy Northern family and established a home in Washington, a gentleman of means free to mingle in the highest society, enjoying fame, a Maine seaside cottage, membership in the best New York clubs, and extended European travel. He was a friend of Theodore Roosevelt and Woodrow Wilson.

From 1913 to 1917, during most of the World War I era, Page was, on Wilson's appointment, the American ambassador to Italy, a difficult assignment well-performed. He died in 1922 at Oakland where he had begun.

Even after achieving fame and prosperity, Page continued writing—stories, novels, dramas, poetry, history, social commentary. The collected "Plantation Edition" of his works, published by Scribner's, ran to eighteen volumes. *In Ole Virginia* was Volume 1. This continued productivity, along with occasional efforts to break out of his successful formula and topics, are sure signs of serious literary craftsmanship and dedication. Page must be taken as a serious writer, in spite of the fate of immense popularity in his lifetime followed by neglect afterward.

When asked about his literary career, he wrote, in what is surely a remarkably accurate and guileless writer's confession: "I think the principal thing after my liking for books, was my desire to see myself in print. Emulation of others, the desire to add to my poor income, and ambition afterwards played their part; but I think . . . the first motive was, to use a term for want of a better—vanity."

The fact that a Southern writer, an unequivocal defender and celebrator of the virtues of the South and its people, could enjoy such a successful career is a commentary, of course, on the period of American history in which Page flourished. To put a fine point on it, he could not have achieved such recognition, as Southern writers have learned the hard way in less hospitable eras, had he not been perceived to be performing a service for the North.

Page was fortunate to begin writing at a time when the North had become disillusioned with the failed and misguided crusade of Reconstruction and was experiencing a widespread if not universal impulse for reconciliation and healing of old wounds. Such a reconciliation was necessary if American society was to go on to a higher level of unity. Thus it was a period in which Southerners could receive some encouragement on the national literary scene, and there was an audience willing to believe that there had been, after all, some honor, heroism, and sincerity in the Lost Cause.

Page did not pioneer the fiction of sectional reconciliation, which had already become a familiar mode when he began to publish, but he did become its most successful practitioner. Reconciliation by inter-sectional marriage was a popular theme, holding out the promise of a restoration of pre-war civility, and nowhere more happily treated than by Page in **"Meh Lady: A Story of the War."**

For Northerners Page provided reassurance that sectional conflict was not intransigent, that the South had accepted restoration of the Union in good faith. For Southerners, he satisfied the desire to establish that they had not been dishonorable in their motives and conduct in the war and that the South had not really been the domain of diabolism of lurid abolitionist and Black Republican propaganda. Both sections got something from the bargain. Page is thus a central cultural figure in American history, in the restoration of that real Union that must rest, as John C. Calhoun had always argued, on consent rather than conquest.

It is customary in recent commentary to dwell impatiently on the alleged disservice Page did the South in casting its history into an attractive and comforting myth. But he performed an equal or greater service for the North, where the preponderance of his readers were, by assuaging its guilt—not guilt over abandonment of the blacks at the end of Reconstruction, as modern liberal historians urge, because there was no guilt about that—but guilt over having indulged in excesses of political fanaticism in the war against erring but honorable countrymen.

A central part of the reconciliation bargain was the North's willingness to leave the problem of race relations to the Southern States. The most recent school of historiography sees this as a kind of moral betrayal of a previous commitment to equality. But it is doubtful if there ever had been such a commitment, except on the part of a very small minority, and hatred of Southern whites had always been a stronger motive for reform than sympathy for Southern blacks. It might be more accurate to say that the North had concluded that it had been wrongheaded to seek anything more than the original war aims—preservation of the Union and economic hegemony.

What is likely to be most unsatisfactory to egalitarian readers of the later twentieth century is the skill and success with which Page incorporated the black people into his Southern myth (and I mean myth here as an imaginative conception formulating a social truth in a way that is not counter-factual but supra-factual).

In Ole Virginia is Virginia before and during the war, as remembered fondly by its black bondsmen after its destruction. Here Page showed his real skill as a writer and a defender of the South, for he portrays the plantation gentry through the eyes of its faithful retainers. He was not the first or only Southern writer to do so—Joel Chandler Harris and others were about the same mission—but he perhaps did it best.

Much can be said about this before we dismiss it as no more than an imposture upon black Americans. The bardic voice, the survivor of a vanished regime who remains to tell its story—a role which Page ascribed to the blacks—has been a post of honor in Western literature from time immemorial. The virtues of Page's white Virginians are not imaginable or possible without the context of black Virginians.

Further, a bit of historical perspective might remind us that Page's attitude toward the black people, if paternalistic, was admirable and moral given the parameters of his time. For the choice in late nineteenth century America, as unpalatable as the historical truth may be, was not between old Virginia paternalism and social and political equality. It was between old Virginia paternalism and the hard racism that can be seen, for instance, in the works of Thomas Dixon.

If it is true that race relations are today better in the South than in other parts of the United States, and many would agree that they are, then surely it has something to do with the world that Page portrayed and the realities that lay behind it. For Southerners white and black the South has been a place they have to live in, and a place that is on the whole worth preserving—not a political abstraction to divert attention from the contradictions and hypocrisies of American society at large.

Given the long record of the crimes, follies, and misfortunes of mankind, and the realities of his era, Page's position is eminently moral and constructive. He reconciled the South to a failed sacrifice that was as great as any ever undergone by a large group of Americans. (The war killed a quarter of the white men in the Southeastern States and set the South back three generations economically.) And he also provided some of the grounds for future incorporation of black and white in a once-more viable Southern society.

The South had to come to terms with the greatest bloodletting in American history and the defeat of cherished hopes. And with potential for racial conflict such as was unknown in the Northern and Western States until the 1960's. Page in response created an ideal fictional world, but faced with the circumstances of despair and insoluble conflict, idealism was a heroic and constructive response.

In a literary sense he kept alive the reality of black characters in mainstream American literature, and therefore kept open a vital line that stretches on to William Faulkner's Lucas Beauchamp in *Intruder in the Dust* and Dilsey in *The Sound and the Fury*. Faulkner's characters were created in a literary age that was "realistic" rather than "sentimental" like Page's, but the line of descent is real, nonetheless.

The voices that Page creates in his work, black and white, are authentic Southern voices. Public voices, perhaps, that do not say everything they know and feel, that tactfully treat some troublesome subjects, and that consciously dramatize themselves—all of which are things that Southerners, black and white, are wont to do in real life. But they are authentic voices, in their own terms.

No writer can entirely escape his age. Page's age was one of sentimentality, something which his audience and editors expected. As Jay B. Hubbell, one of the leading students of Southern literature, has put it, Page's picture of Ole Virginia is a painting, not a photograph. If he did not escape sentimentality, he did at times surmount it. Often his effects are not so much sentimental as truly poignant. How skillfully he surmounted the cheaper forms of sentiment can be proved by a comparison with some of the now-forgotten popular literature of the time, and by the fact that he created a painting that, though unmistakably of a certain period, will endure in its interest to later generations.

Southern writers that followed him inevitably rebelled against Page. One thinks, for instance, of his fellow Richmonders, James Branch Cabell and Ellen Glasgow. But the next generation rediscovered the path.

The plantation society presented by such twentieth century writers as William Faulkner in *The Unvanquished,* Caroline Gordon in *Penhally,* or Shelby Foote in *Jordan County,* is a tougher and more realistic and earthy and ambiguous world than Page's. But like Page, these writers surmount the limitations of their own period ("realism") to redeem rather than reject Southern history. They create a world that is essentially admirable, that offers us in place of cynicism and despair a glimpse of heroism and honor that is a model for later generations of Southerners. This, surely, owes something to the trails blazed by Page.

It is difficult to judge Page fairly because it is difficult to recover a clear view of the plantation, which has been subjected to so much positive (*Gone with the Wind*) and negative (*Roots*) romanticism, and which has become politicized as the abode of the ultimate horror of American history, slavery.

The plantation already had a long literary tradition when Page began to write, developed by such writers as John P. Kennedy and William Gilmore Simms in the antebellum era. The literary convention of the plantation was as old as American literature, because the plantation was as old as American history.

Despite the tendency of scholars to mistake literary traditions for life, the plantation was far more than a scene for fiction—it was a historical reality of immense importance, central to American history and a characteristically American institution. It was not a remote quaintness or peculiar evil on the fringes of society. It is quite safe to say that without the institution of the plantation, the whole first two centuries of American development would have been retarded and the course of American history would have been quite different. And not necessarily better if we eliminate all the positive benefits that accrued to American society from the class that produced Washington and Jefferson.

Strictly speaking, the plantation is defined as a large agricultural unit with a dependent labor force, engaged at least in part in the production of staple crops, such as tobacco, cotton, or sugar, for the world market. The plantation was already well established in Latin America and the Caribbean before it appeared in seventeenth century Virginia and Carolina. In North America it took on Anglo-Saxon and Protestant features and existed in the midst of a largely yeoman society, which gave it distinguishing characteristics.

The amount of attention historians have paid to the plantation and the moral and ideological passions that it has aroused belie their frequent tendency to minimize its importance or deny its centrality. For some modern historians, like Kenneth Stampp, the plantation was only a particularly ugly form of capitalism. Here we find a failure of historical imagination, an inability to conceive of a different society in its own terms or to understand any other way of life except as a defective form of Americanism.

Most historians, however, whatever their value judgments, understand that the plantation world was a unique form of society. One convincing formulation is given by the Italian historian Raimondo Luraghi in *The Rise and Fall of the Plantation South.* The South was a seignorial society, neither feudal nor capitalist, with its own social reality and its own ethics—and not merely a debased form of bourgeois society. It is this world that is the locale of Page's fiction.

Antebellum Southern writers who used the plantation as a scene for fiction had been romantics to a degree, but had never lost a certain earthy realism. In keeping with his era and the elegiac nature of his mission, Page progressed further along the road to sentiment. We should remember that this was what the Northern audience wanted. (Southerners were too poor to buy enough books to make any writer a success.) Even so, Page, like his predecessors, never quite loses touch with the reality that the plantation is first and foremost a working farm. We always know that crops have to be planted, flooded creeks crossed, provisions put up for the winter, horses cared for. In real life the ending does not always work out so happily as in **"Meh Lady,"** but the hardships portrayed in that story were very real and intimately known.

There is no need to over-emphasize Page's sentimentality. The seemingly improbable plot of **"Marse Chan,"** for instance, is, as Page explained in his introduction to the Plantation Edition, based on the real story of a soldier whose sweetheart had told him to come home only with honor, and who was killed shortly after. The real story involved a Georgia private and not an FFV, however.

Readers who want to read more of Page after *In Ole Virginia* might look at the story collection *The Burial of the Guns,* where they will find deft and realistic treatments of social issues. The title story concerns the war—heroism and pride in defeat. But the other stories are more contemporary: social hypocrisy and triumphant spinsterhood in **"My Cousin Fanny"**; alcoholism and postwar demoralization in **"The Gray Jacket of No. 4"**; deception and disappointed love in **"Miss Dangerlie's Roses"**; and the sufferings and courage of the poorest class of white Southerners in **"Little Darby."** None of these stories would satisfy an exponent of French naturalism, but given the standards and tastes of the time, they deal with social issues in an unflinching way.

Superficially, Page fits perfectly the prevailing historical stereotype of the Southern Bourbon. As misleadingly described in the works of C. Vann Woodward, the Bourbon was a member of the antebellum gentry who made his peace with Northern capital, uniting with the most exploitive elements of American society for his own profit, while diverting the South from its real problems by sentimentalizing its past.

Though this historical interpretation is widely accepted, it is not strictly true, in regard either to Page or to the politics of the leading class in the South after the war. Rather than aiding and abetting the vested interests of the age, Southerners quite often provided a leavening influence of old-fashioned liberalism in a rapacious, utilitarian society—which was a heritage of the plantation class and its preference for honor over profit, its distaste for ruthless individualism, and its purchase on the ethics of an earlier American republicanism that had been forgotten in the North.

Page's novel *Gordon Keith* (1903), though it is not a successful work of fiction, deals with the shallowness and vanity of modern New York society and its pursuit of wealth. And in *John Marvel, Assistant* (1909), he exhibits sympathetic interest in the plights of labor and of Jews. In the larger sense, he is a critic, not an abettor, of the abuses of the Gilded Age. Indeed, the planter class had always been the seat of American liberalism, ever since Mr. Jefferson had stood up to General Hamilton and his schemes.

The idea of the plantation rests most uneasily in the American consciousness. On the one hand, it has been determined to be the seat of all horror. On the other, it is inextricably tied to some of the highest moments and grandest personalities of American history. One suspects that most of the thousands of tourists who throng Mount Vernon and Monticello imagine them to be something like Ohio farms. But, of course, they are nothing of the kind; they are plantations, examples of the very society with which Page is concerned.

Americans are unable to deal with the plain fact that eight of our first twelve Presidents were the masters of plantations, not marginally but in their primary social identity, and resort to all sorts of subterfuges to thrust the fact from mind. But the essence of American nationality and American institutions lies in the plantation quite as much as in the New England town meeting, or more so. How do we reconcile this to the images that appear in *Roots* and a host of other less celebrated works?

It may be true that the plantation is something of another age and that it embodied evils that have now been happily surpassed; but that is not the whole story. Is it not better and truer to view the society that produced Washington and Jefferson and Lee in the light provided by Page than in the lurid colors of neoabolitionist melodrama?

And why is it, if the plantation is a place of horror, that even today its relics give us a sense of peace and order, of communion with the roots of our society and a better past, while the vast expanses of modern urban democracy and egalitarianism give us only a sense of unease? We approach here some profound regions of the American soul, however strenuously denied, of which Page is the artistic medium.

Page's world is indeed an idealistic world, not likely to satisfy such modern types as the pragmatist, the utilitarian, the ideologue, or the cynic. And it is true that at times in his work such qualities as honor, duty, courage, and sacrifice approach an unpersuasive abstraction. But not always.

For Page does present human qualities and aspirations and behaviors that really did exist at one time. We know that people with the virtues he portrays did live. The heroism in adversity, the tragic deaths by battle and fever, the extravagant chivalric gestures, the sensitive pride, the aristocratic ethics, the unswerving loyalty, the affections between masters and servants, all really did exist, no matter how much moderns may choose to disbelieve them. They can be abundantly documented, to the satisfaction of any honest observer, in the hard documentary record of thousands of Southern families. It is just that now historians prefer to emphasize other things.

For us Page has made, in fiction, a number of satisfying human characters, characters who give us hope in the potential of our nature and who are models that we badly need of grace, courage, and honor. They are far more persuasive and useful than any number of politicians' and social scientists' paeans to democracy and progress. In that sense, Page is not so outdated as some think, and in fact will never be outdated. And, as well, *In Ole Virginia* is full of just plain good tales, well told, which is what a book of stories should be.

FURTHER READING

Bibliography

Gross, Theodore L. "Thomas Nelson Page." *American Literary Realism, 1870-1910* 1 (Fall 1967): 90-2.
    Provides a selective annotated bibliography of criticism on Page's writing.

Biography

Gross, Theodore L. *Thomas Nelson Page*. New York: Twayne Publishers, 1967, 175 p.
    An important critical biography by a prominent Page scholar.

Page, Rosewell. *Thomas Nelson Page: A Memoir of a Virginia Gentleman*. New York: Charles Scribner's Sons, 1923, 220 p.

Page's younger brother recounts the writer's life in eulogistic fashion.

Criticism

Blackall, Jean Frantz. "Literary Allusion as Imaginative Event in *The Awkward Age*." *Modern Fiction Studies* 26, No. 2 (Summer 1980): 179-97.

Notes briefly Henry James's probable indebtedness in *The Awkward Age* to Page's short story "The Prisoners."

Gross, Theodore L. "Thomas Nelson Page: Creator of a Virginia Classic." *The Georgia Review* XX, No. 3 (Fall 1966): 338-51.

Evaluates themes of reconciliation, heroism, and loyalty. Gross also defines Page's place in American literature.

Holman, Harriet. *The Literary Career of Thomas Nelson Page.* Dissertation. Durham, N.C.: Duke University, 1947, 226 p.

An invaluable study of Page's fiction and literary career, with a discussion of his usual method of composition.

King, Kimball. "Satirical Portraits by Thomas Nelson Page." *Mississippi Quarterly* 18, No. 2 (Spring 1965): 74-81.

Explores Page's satire of upperclass greed and vanity in his late fiction, particularly his novels.

A review of *The Land of the Spirit*. *Literary Digest* 47, No. 16 (18 October 1913): 696, 698.

Comments on the seriousness of Page's themes, asserting that *The Land of the Spirit* is pervaded by "an implied arraignment of the Church for the terrible contrast between its spiritual ideals and its hypocrisy and frequent superficiality."

McCluskey, John. "Americanisms in the Writings of Thomas Nelson Page." *American Speech: A Quarterly of English Usage* 57, No. 1 (Spring 1982): 44-7.

Focuses on Page's contributions to the American lexicon, particularly his use of Southern dialect.

A review of *Under the Crust*. *The New York Times Book Review* XII, No. 50 (14 December 1907): 826.

Notes "a certain vital and human quality" in the stories of *Under the Crust*.

O'Brien, Kenneth. "Race, Romance, and the Southern Literary Tradition." In *Recasting: Gone with the Wind in American Culture*, edited by Darden Asbury Pyron, pp. 153-66. Miami: University Presses of Florida, 1983.

Compares Margaret Mitchell's exploration of the Southern plantation tradition to Page's development of the Southern romance.

Payne, William Morton. A review of *The Burial of the Guns*. *The Dial* 17, No. 203 (1 December 1894): 333.

Praises *Burial of the Guns* as heartwarming and irresistible.

Shiga Naoya
1883–1971

Japanese short story writer, novelist, critic, and essayist.

INTRODUCTION

Shiga was one of the most influential Japanese fiction writers of the Taishō period (1912–26). Despite his comparatively modest output of one novel, three novellas, and a few dozen short stories, he has had a significant impact on subsequent generations of writers and remains one of Japan's most revered literary figures of the twentieth century. Shiga was associated with the *Shirakaba* (White Birch) school, a group of writers united by their opposition to naturalism, a pessimistic and deterministic literary philosophy prevalent in Japan in the early part of the century. Shiga and the other *Shirakaba* members were humanistic in their outlook and tended to base their fiction on autobiographical material. These authors, known as I-novelists, became the narrator-protagonists of novels which focused on the hero's emotional development. Shiga's *An'ya Kōro* (*A Dark Night's Passing*) is considered a major I-novel, and many of his most-admired short stories are fictionalized accounts of events in his life. Paradoxically, by focusing narrowly on his own personal experiences, often to the exclusion of events from the larger world, Shiga was able to create stories that capture something of a larger, quintessentially Japanese, view of life; and he himself, isolative and introspective, was hailed as a "god of fiction."

Biographical Information

Shiga was born in Ishimaki, in the northern part of Honshū, Japan's largest island. His family belonged to the samurai class, but his father, a strongly independent man, embarked on a successful business career. He was employed as a banker in Ishimaki but took a position with a business firm in Tokyo and moved his family there when Shiga was three years old. They moved into their clan's residence, and from this point on Shiga was raised by his grandparents. Shiga deeply loved his grandparents—his grandmother doted on him, and, as he later attested, his grandfather was one of the most influential people in his life. When Shiga was thirteen his mother died. He later recounted her death and his father's subsequent remarriage in "Haha no hi to atarashii haha" ("My Mother's Death and the Coming of My New Mother"). Shiga and his stepmother were fortunate in having a mutually affectionate and respectful relationship. In contrast, Shiga's relationship with his father was increasingly discordant. In 1900 Shiga became a follower of the Christian evangelist Uchimura Kanzo and as a result began to espouse social causes. The following year he planned to join a protest against the Ashio Copper Mine, which was polluting a local river and poisoning the nearby residents; but his father, who had business dealings with the mining company, forbid his son to participate. Although Shiga eventually complied with his father's demands, this incident marked the beginning of an estrangement between the two. Another clash centered around Shiga's love affair with one of the family's servants and his declared intention to marry the girl. His father, proud of the family's distinguished ancestry, vehemently opposed such a match. He separated the two by removing the maid from the household, and Shiga's infatuation eventually cooled. Tensions were exacerbated by what Shiga's father considered his son's idle and aimless lifestyle. Shiga had consistently been a mediocre student, first at Gakushuin Elementary School and later at Tokyo Imperial University. While in college Shiga became interested in writing—an activity his father thought useless—and he and his friends founded the literary magazine *Shirakaba*, which gave rise to the group of writers of the same name. Shiga dropped out of college in 1908, much to his family's dismay, and entered what was to be the most productive period of his writing career. In 1912 he published the novella *Ōtsu junkichi*, based on his love affair with the family servant. The publication of the novella occasioned another dispute between father and son which resulted in Shiga's moving out of the family residence.

In addition to *Ōtsu junkichi,* Shiga produced several of his most famous short stories in the 1910s, including "Claudius's Journal," "Sebei's Gourds," "An Incident," and "Han's Crime." He also began work on *A Dark Night's Passing,* though the novel would not be completed until 1937. His marriage in 1914 to a widow who had a child precipitated a complete break from his family, and Shiga renounced his inheritance. However, after the birth of his second daughter in 1917 (the first had died shortly after birth the previous year), Shiga reconciled with his father, recording the reunion in his novella *Wakai (Reconciliation).* By the middle of the 1920s Shiga's productivity had markedly declined. He continued to work on *A Dark Night's Passing* throughout the decade, but after the novel's publication he produced little for the remainder of his life.

Major Works of Short Fiction

Many of Shiga's stories are autobiographical in origin, but the lines between fiction and reportage are frequently blurred in his works. Shiga has explained his technique of blending fact and fiction in his comments on the hero of *A Dark Night's Passing.* Shiga observed: "Kensaku the hero is by and large myself. I would say his actions approximate the things I would do, or would wish to do, or actually did, under the given circumstances." Thus, he may begin with an actual person (often himself) or event as his subject, but he then builds a fictional world around it. "An Incident," for example, is based on an actual accident that Shiga witnessed in which a young boy was run over by a streetcar. Around this account, he constructs a story told by a fictive narrator who focuses on the imaginary thoughts and impressions of the passengers on the streetcar. Also characteristic of much of Shiga's fiction is its psychologically probing quality. Whether he himself is clearly the narrator, as in *Reconciliation,* or the central figure is fabricated, as in "Han's Crime," he continually analyzes the psychological complexities of the protagonist. Shiga's stories are also noted for their careful structure, their precise detail, and evocative, poetic language.

Critical Reception

Shiga occupies a dominant position in modern Japanese fiction. As Donald Keene has noted, "No modern writer was more idolized than Shiga Naoya. A half-dozen writers were recognized as his disciples, and innumerable others were so greatly influenced by his writings as to recall Shiga on every page." Such prominent writers as Akutagawa Ryūnosuke, Tanizaki Junichiro, and Kawabata Yasunari have admired his work. Although some post-World War II critics have questioned the value and significance of his work, they concede that he remains an important figure, not only for his contribution to the development of the I-novel, but for his flawless style. Precise, compressed, and carefully controlled, Shiga's writing has been extolled

for its ability to convey complex psychological states through suggestion, implication, and allusion.

PRINCIPAL WORKS

Short Fiction

Ōtsu junkichi (novella) 1912
Wakai [*Reconciliation*] (novella) 1917
Yoru no hikari (short stories) 1918
Aru otoko, sono ane no shi [*A Certain Man and the Death of His Sister*] (novella) 1920
Haiiro no tsuki, Manreki akae (short stories) 1968
Shiga Naoya shū (short stories) 1969
The Paper Door and Other Stories (short stories) 1987

Other Major Works

An'ya Kōro [*A Dark Night's Passing*] (novel) 1937
Kamakura zakki (essays and poems) 1948
Yamabato (essays) 1951
Pōtorēto (essays) 1954
Shiga Naoya zenshū. 17 vols. (collected works) 1955-56

CRITICISM

Francis Mathy (essay date 1974)

SOURCE: "A Golden Ten" and "The Achievement of Shiga Naoya," in *Shiga Naoya,* Twayne Publishers, Inc., 1974, pp. 105-36; 165-75.

[*In the following excerpts from his book-length study of Shiga, Mathy analyzes eight of the author's most famous short stories and summarizes how his work differs from Western standards of great literature.*]

Shiga was hampered by a literary theory that inhibited the writing of fiction, but he could, when he wished, turn out a well-made story with an exemplary unity of structure. The unifying principle might be plot or character or even atmosphere or mood, but every element, every separate part of the story, was tailored to create this unity. In the present [essay] we will consider what we judge to be the best of these stories. Western readers and critics, while generally critical of his autobiographical works, have found these short stories of Shiga's more to their liking and have singled out several for particular praise, especially **"Han's Crime"** and **"Seibei's Gourds."** . . .

"The Old Man" (1911)

Shiga calls **"The Old Man"** an exercise in form, interesting and successful only as such. The inspiration for it came from a story by Bjørnstjerne Bjørnson (whose title he later forgot) in which the three most important events of one man's life—his baptism, marriage, and death and burial—are described by a priest who assisted at all three. "These three points of his life were simply described, but in such a way that the entire life of the man was made strangely palpable. I thought it extremely well done."

The old man, who is never named, is a successful businessman who loses his wife when he is fifty-four and his two children are already grown. With her death he suddenly seems years older. But several months later he marries again, a lady one year younger than his daughter. She so rejuvenates him that he appears to be even younger than before and plunges into a round of youthful activities. He starts going to Sumo matches again, takes his wife to plays, and even goes to enjoy the waters of a mountain spa.

Two years later he retires from his company and becomes adviser to an oil firm, but leaves this too when the recommendations of a young engineer, two years behind his son in college, are accepted in preference to his. He is now sixty-five.

Since his second wife is childless, they adopt the daughter of his son and lavish affection upon her. After leaving the oil firm he spends his time building and tearing down houses, at great financial loss—which, however, he can well afford. His wife dies of tuberculosis and he returns their adopted child to her real parents. Now at sixty-nine he is alone again and lonely.

He takes to frequenting geisha houses and finally sets up one of the youngest girls, the same age as his oldest granddaughter, as his mistress, in a house he has built for her and which he promises to turn over to her completely after three years. They live very happily together. He is not disturbed by the fact that she has a young lover, and he feels no jealousy or resentment when she gives birth to her lover's child. At the end of the contracted three years the mistress herself proposes another year's extension, and when this year too passes, a second extension. He is pleased to the point of tears. This year she gives birth to her lover's second child. When he proposes still another year's extension, she gladly consents. He now feels ready for death and prays that it will come quickly, and it does. He catches cold and this develops into influenza. She joins the family circle of children and grandchildren at his deathbed, doing what she can to nurse him. He dies a peaceful death at the age of seventy-five. In his will he leaves her enough property to enable her to raise her two children.

Four months later, on the cushion where the old man formerly sat, now sits the young father of her children. In the alcove behind him is a large portrait of the old man, sitting ceremoniously in his formal dress.

Whatever Shiga may have thought of **"The Old Man,"** it is certainly more than an exercise in form. This picture of an old man gradually coming to terms with old age and death is permeated with a warm humanity that elevates the story to a level of universal significance. Though the subject invites sentimentality, Shiga's spare style is always well in control; the story never becomes sentimental.

The pathos of growing old is presented through the skillfully selected details. The sad frustration that a man who is still active experiences upon retirement, for example, is felt in the old man's frenzied building and rebuilding of houses with no prospect of financial gain. When he decides to set up a geisha, he recalls a story he heard in his youth of a certain geisha, who, given the choice between a patron forty-five years old and one seventy-two, chose the latter since he would not be around so long. Hearing the story, he had pitied the old man from his heart. Now he finds himself in that same position and he marvels at the rapid passage of the years.

In the new house with his mistress, surrounded by all new furniture, he feels as if he were still in his twenties or thirties. Yet when he sits across from her and observes her soft, well-fleshed hands, he does not dare let her see his own wizened hands, mere bones covered over with dry skin. He grieves that his arms no longer have the strength to enclose her in a powerful embrace, and that an old man's spirit does not grow old with the rest of him.

Transcending the pathos, however, is a sense of mature ripeness, a feeling that ripeness is all. The man in his old age has grown gentle and understanding—witness the attitude he takes toward his mistress's lover and their children. He has grown to understand and be considerate of others. Shiga gives us sufficient view of him as he was in the past to let it be seen that he was not always this way. Finally, his death at the end gives the impression of completeness and fulfillment rather than of tragedy.

It is remarkable that Shiga, still a young man, should have had such a profound understanding of an old man's psychology; and it is regrettable that he regarded this kind of story as a mere exercise in composition, somehow outside the range of his proper talent.

The central theme of **"The Old Man"** is the central theme of most of Shiga's work—that nature is best, that one should entrust oneself to its processes, finding there rest and contentment. The reason the old man's death is not tragic is that it is the culmination of a natural process to which he, at the end at least, has committed himself entirely.

"The Razor" (1910)

"The Razor" is the product of the same morbid imagination that was found at work in **"Confused Head,"** published five months later, and in **"For Grandmother,"** which came out the following year. Shiga states that the starting point for this story was the feeling of threat everyone experiences in the barber's chair. But it is probably more exact to say that the story originated in the feeling of threat that he himself experienced in his unsettled life at this time.

"**The Razor**" is a study in mood and atmosphere. What could possibly drive a respectable barber, who has probably never injured anyone in his life before, to sink his razor into the throat of an unsuspecting client? The excellence of the story lies in the high degree of plausibility the author is able to lend to this action.

Yoshisaburo is a young barber who has inherited his barber shop by marrying the daughter of its former proprietor, who has since died. As the story begins, he is in bed with a bad cold just before a holiday when he can expect many clients to come in. His two skilled assistants have just left him, and their replacements are not dependable. As he burns with fever in his bed, everything he sees and hears contributes to a growing impatience and sense of frustration. The very room in which he lies seems sick with fever. The anxious solicitude of his well-intentioned wife but makes him the more fretful. Rising from his bed, he hones and strops a razor that has been brought to him for sharpening; but its owner soon returns to report that it still will not cut, and he has a second try at it.

> After he had honed the blade, he began to strop it. It seemed as if the stagnant air of the room were set in motion by the sound of the razor against the strop. Yoshisaburo was able to control his shaking hand, and to strop with some kind of rhythm. But still it did not go well. Then the nail which his wife had pounded into the pillar suddenly fell out. The strop came flying down and wrapped itself several times around the blade.

He takes the razor out to the shop and continues working on it. The last client has left when a young man of twenty-two or so rushes in and asks for a shave. Though he is dressed in a new kimono and appears to be very conceited, Yoshisaburo can tell immediately that he is only a day laborer putting on airs. Yoshisaburo is all the more disgusted when he learns that the man is on his way to a brothel.

Yoshisaburo begins to shave him. But the blade will not cut properly, his hand is shaking, and his nose has begun to run. Inside the house the baby is crying. Yoshisaburo is further irritated by the insensitivity of his client: he sits there composed while the dull razor scrapes painfully over his skin. The barber does his best to give him a clean shave, but with little success. He becomes first angry, then discouraged.

> He felt like breaking down and crying. Body and spirit were completely worn out. His fever-swollen eyes were moist and felt as if they were about to melt away of fever.

> He did the throat, then the cheeks, then the chin, then the forehead, then back to the soft portion of the throat. This last part, no matter how carefully he worked, he could not do as he wished. He scraped and scraped, but with little effect. His patience was near the breaking point; an urge came over him to pare it off, skin and all. He looked at the face before him with its rough-

grained skin, pores filled with grease, and the urge became all the stronger. The young man in the meantime had fallen asleep. His head was swung back, his mouth wide open, revealing a set of ill-matched dirty teeth.

> Yoshisaburo was so tired that he could hardly stand. He felt as if poison had been poured into every joint. He wanted to stop and lie down. Enough! This was enough! So he decided again and again. But with the force of inertia, he kept on his struggle with each individual stubborn hair.

At this point the blade chances to cut into the flesh. Yoshisaburo feels all his lethargy and fatigue suddenly depart. As he watches, the skin where the blade has entered changes from a milky white to a pale crimson until finally red blood rises to the surface. A globule of dark red blood swells and then breaks, and the blood falls away in a trickle. At this point Yoshisaburo is seized by a kind of frenzy.

> The frenzy took a very strong hold of him. His breath became shorter and shorter. It seemed as if all of him, body and spirit, were being sucked into that wound. Try as he would, he could no longer control the impulse. He regripped the razor so that the tip pointed downward and with lightning speed plunged it into the throat until the blade was completely embedded in flesh. The young man did not so much as shudder.

> Yoshisaburo, almost in a faint, fell into the chair beside him. His tautness suddenly relaxed. But the heavy fatigue returned and he fell asleep, a deep, deathlike sleep. The night too was deathly still. All movement had come to a stop; everything was fallen into a deep sleep. The mirror alone, from three different angles, coldly surveyed the scene.

"**The Razor**," as mentioned above, has the aim of making this highly unlikely murder seem plausible. With a selection of detail characteristic of Shiga at his best, everything in the story builds up to this climax and makes it seem inevitable. There is no other statement and only the minimum of characterization needed to achieve the effect. Though lacking in depth, the story is a triumph of craftsmanship.

"My Mother's Death and the Coming of My New Mother" (1912)

This is one of the finest pieces Shiga ever wrote, one in which his celebrated style appears to greatest advantage. The story is divided into seven sections. The first four record the events revolving about the death of Shiga's mother on August 30, 1895.

In the summer of his thirteenth year, Shiga was in summer camp at the sea when he received a letter from his grandfather telling him that his mother was going to have another child. He was so pleased at the news that he spent all of his pocket money to buy a set of shell combs and hairpin to give her as a kind of "reward." When he gets home, his mother is not feeling well and in the weeks that follow she goes from bad to worse and finally dies, the baby with her.

The last three sections tell of the coming of his new mother. Two months after the death of his mother, Shiga's father begins to look around for a new wife. His grandmother shows him a picture of one of the women under consideration and asks his opinion. She is pleasantly surprised at his answer: "Fine as long as she has a good heart." The match is soon arranged, and Shiga waits eagerly for the coming of his new mother, who is very young and much more beautiful than his real mother.

Soon it is the day of the wedding, and Shiga awkwardly takes his part in the ceremonies. He even does a traditional dance at the reception that follows. He is disgusted when his father, who has had too much to drink, tells one of the geisha present that she is the loveliest woman in the room.

The next day the boy self-consciously goes through his morning routine of washing and dressing, and then goes to greet his new mother. He is filled with joy as he speaks to her alone for the first time. That night, after he has already gone to bed, his father sends a maid to ask if he wouldn't like to sleep beside his mother. He goes to their room. His father is in an unusually fine mood and keeps repeating that "after all, children are a man's greatest treasure." After his father has gone to sleep, he talks with his mother for a while and then goes back to sleep with his grandparents. His grandmother questions him about the conversation in the other room, but he pretends to be asleep and lies there quietly relishing a feeling of deep joy.

In the days that follow he is pleased that everyone is all praise for his new mother, and his real mother's death recedes quickly into the past. He accompanies his mother and grandmother on their rounds of the relatives, and feels a gentle pride when he sees men turn in the street to take a second look as they pass. In the years that follow, his mother gives birth to a boy and three girls.

Of the composition of this story, Shiga writes:

> I wrote of the events of my childhood exactly as they had taken place. I was able to finish this piece in one night. The boy that appears here is certainly sentimental, but the writing is not, a fact that greatly pleased me. Whenever I am asked to name a favorite among my writings, I often pick this one. If stories that have been completed only after great labor usually display a perfection proportionate to the pain that gave them birth, there is another perfection to be found in those that have flowed effortlessly from the author's pen. It appears that the writer is often fonder of the latter.

The reader will agree that the writing is not sentimental, and he too may very well select this story as one of his favorites. Here are to be found the elements of Shiga's most accomplished style: feeling that is deep and immediate, but conveyed indirectly through well-chiseled dialogue and masterful selection of detail; expression that is economical, precise, rich in nuance and suggestion.

Two parallel scenes will serve as illustration. The first is that of the morning after his real mother's death, and the second, the morning after his new mother's arrival.

The night before his mother's death Shiga had sat in her room with his father, his grandparents, his great-grandmother, his uncle, and the doctor, watching her breathing grow less and less frequent until it stopped altogether. The account of the following morning begins as follows:

> The next morning when I went to light an incense stick, there was no one in the room. I silently lifted the white cloth covering her face and looked at her. I was surprised to see around her mouth a kind of froth, such as one sometimes sees on the mouth of a crab. "She's still alive!" I thought, and I ran to the veranda to tell my grandmother.

> My grandmother came and looked. "It's just the air coming out," she explained, wiping the lips gently with a piece of paper.

> I put all the shell jewelry I had bought for her at Enoshima into her coffin.

> The sound of the hammer nailing down the coffin lid was almost too painful to bear.

> They lowered the coffin into the hole, and I thought, "It's all over!" The thud of clods of clay thrown down on the coffin echoed in my heart.

> "Okay?" asked the man who had been standing by impatiently with shovel and hoe, and without so much as a nod to us, he began noisily to fill in the hole. "Even if she did come back to life, she'd never be able to get out," I thought.

Though Shiga never tells us that he was grief-stricken at his mother's death, his sorrow is made powerfully present by the details he selects as significant. The time covered in this brief passage is considerable (presumably his mother was not buried the day after her death), but with a few well-executed strokes of the pen he is able to intimate the whole complex of grief from death to burial of one who has seen a loved one depart this world. This prose has the texture and concentration of poetry.

With the same economy of detail is portrayed the thirteen-year-old boy's pleasure at meeting his mother for the first time in his home. The previous passage was a description of the wedding ceremony and reception. The next section begins:

> The next morning when I got up, my mother was already puttering around the house. I washed my face at the washstand on the veranda, but I could not bring myself to blow my nose in my hand as I usually did.

> After I had washed my face, I got the handkerchief [that he had been asked to give her] and went to look for her. She was doing something in the dark room

next to the parlor. I handed the handkerchief to her, stammering an explanation.

"Thank you," answered my beautiful mother, looking at me affectionately. This was the first chance we had had to speak to each other alone.

After I had given her the handkerchief, I hopped on one leg down the veranda to the student's room, not that I had any reason to go there.

In this passage too there is no need for him to tell us how he felt. His actions reveal this better than words could.

The parallelism of these two passages, one revealing the boy's great sorrow and the other his equally great joy, is part of the thematic structure of this well-made story, which has for its basic theme the rhythm of nature with its elemental waves of joy and sorrow, life and death. The structure is very well suited to the theme, since it too follows a wave pattern, moving from joy-life to sorrow-death to joy-life again and ending with the suggestion of sorrow-death to come. Section 1 begins on a crest of joy-life, as the boy joyfully anticipates the birth of a brother or sister. From Section 2, in which his mother has become ill, to Section 3, in which she dies, and Section 4, in which she is buried, the wave descends into a trough of death and sorrow. With Section 5, in which is made the arrangement for the new marriage, the wave begins to rise again, through the wedding scene in Section 6, to the crest in Section 7, in which the new mother enters the home and in the years that follow gives birth to a boy and three girls. At the conclusion the wave is already receding. The boy's mother tells him that this last childbirth has been the hardest. He answers, "Now that you are growing older, your constitution is not as strong as it used to be," thinking as he speaks that even his mother, who had once been so young and beautiful, had already arrived at the stage of life where this could be said.

Life, this story suggests, consists basically in this ever-continuing alternation of moments of life and moments of death. Shiga entrusts himself to this natural rhythm, floating along with the tide, ready to accept whatever it will bring, whether sorrow or joy, life or death. This is especially evident in the rapid transition from sorrow at his real mother's death to joy at the coming of his new mother, a transition that is accomplished in the following brief passage:

[My mother's death] was, after all, the first irrevocable event in my life. My grandmother and I often wept together in the bath. But before a hundred days had passed, I was already looking forward with joyful anticipation to the coming of my new mother.

Another short piece written in the same year, **"Recollections of My Mother's Death and of her Tabi,"** elaborates further upon Shiga's feelings of sorrow and regret at the death of his mother. It begins with a brief account of his mother's death and the events leading up to it, in much the same words as the earlier story, and then goes on to recall an incident that took place about a year or so before her death, an incident which had caused her great pain.

One evening his mother comes to the room where he is working and tries to hand him his *tabi*. Absorbed in what he is doing, he ignores her. Since she is busy with her own work, she does not wait, but puts the *tabi* on his head and walks out. He gets angry and runs after her, shouting loudly his annoyance. She is taken aback at his outburst and gazes at him sadly. Even then he does not desist. The piece ends as follows:

Long afterward I heard from my father that I was often the cause of my mother's weeping. She complained to him that because of my grandmother's overindulgent love, I was so spoiled that she could do nothing with me. According to that, I seem to have given her much grief. But I remember nothing of it. Only this little incident of the *tabi* remains in my memory. I tried to imagine what my mother must have felt. She must have been very sad.

It was only a little out of my way to return from school by way of Aoyama Cemetery. So I occasionally stopped to visit her grave. And I often recalled the *tabi* incident. Each time I bowed to the grave and apologized to her in my heart.

The grief Shiga felt at his mother's death is powerfully presented in the image of the schoolboy bowed in apology before her grave. The tragedy of a boy so young losing his mother is deepened first of all by the feelings of regret for having hurt her so often, and then by the painful realization that of so many incidents that must have occurred, this one of the *tabi* is the only one he can remember.

"The Just Ones" (1912)

Both **"The Just Ones"** and **"An Incident,"** published a year later, tell of a child hit by a streetcar and of the consequences of the accident. Shiga himself points out the difference between the two stories:

"The Just Ones" takes as its theme the inflated pride of three men who have done what they thought was right and just, and the sad dissatisfaction that overtakes them when their justice is not rewarded. **"An Incident"** has a more direct feeling. It depicts the joy felt when a child, hit by a streetcar, emerges unharmed.

Three laborers working on the streetcar tracks in the Nihonbashi section of Tokyo are suddenly startled by a woman's cry and look up from their work in time to see a streetcar pressing down upon a little girl walking in the middle of the tracks, her back to it. Only after he has hit the child does the driver remember to apply his emergency brake, which brings the car to an immediate stop. Too late. The child is dead.

A crowd quickly gathers. The police arrive on the scene, also the streetcar-line supervisor. The latter prompts the driver and the conductor to say that the girl had rushed out in front of the streetcar so suddenly that there was not time to apply the emergency brake. Not so, cry out the three workmen, after a hurried consultation. There was plenty of time to apply the brake. The driver lost his presence of mind.

The three workers go along to the police station to present their eyewitness testimony. The supervisor tries to get them to change their story, reminding them that they work for the same company. Despite the implied threat to their jobs, however, they become only the more insistent.

Upon leaving the police station hours later, they experience a strange exhilaration, a pleasant excitement. They walk aimlessly about town, rehearsing among themselves the details of the incident. In their feeling of pride and achievement, they are tempted to stop passersby and ask, "Don't you recognize us?" "Wrong is always wrong," they assure each other. "We only did what we had to do." "The nerve of that guy—expecting that just because we work for the streetcar company we would go along with his story." They are immensely pleased with themselves and expect that their virtue will be rewarded.

But the reward is not forthcoming. The streets are no different from before; their virtue goes unrecognized. As they walk on, they begin to feel let down. A passing ricksha coolie yells at them to get out of the way, and they resent the insult to their dignity. Their pleasantly high spirits slowly ebb away and are replaced by a growing sense of irritation.

They find themselves again at the site of the accident, but no sign of it remains. This seems strange. They feel somehow deprived and angry, as if an injustice has been done them. The policeman in the police box is a young rookie who, of course, was not on duty at the time of the accident. To make matters worse, he glares at them suspiciously.

Only then does the realization hit them that they may now be out of jobs. The youngest of the three thinks of his aged grandmother waiting for him in their gloomy house. Their spirits grow more and more unsettled, and they decide to go somewhere for a drink.

They make their way to the second floor of a café where a number of people are eating and drinking. They still cannot leave the topic, and self-consciously begin discussing it again in voices loud enough to be overheard. Customers and waitresses gather around them to hear the details.

The story by now has become greatly exaggerated. The girl's head and arms were smashed to bloody pulp. The mother went berserk with grief. Their audience reacts with appropriate expressions of horror and concern. Drinking all the while, the workers go on to give a detailed account of the police interrogation, and speculate on what the morning paper will have to say about the incident. By now everyone in the place has stopped his own conversation to listen to them. For the first time

since leaving the police station they experience a measure of real satisfaction.

But this does not last long. Their auditors begin to drift away until the three are left to themselves. Although it is already midnight, they keep on drinking, growing dissatisfied and angry as before. The realization that they will be fired from their jobs is now uppermost in their minds. One of the three goes home and the other two, after a few more drinks, decide to go to a brothel. In their separate rickshas each recounts the incident once again to the driver. Their loud, drunken voices echo loudly in the silent streets. The rickshas reach the place of the accident. The older man would stop and have still another look, but the younger urges the drivers on.

Shiga in this story shows a deep knowledge of human nature and profound psychological insight. There is perhaps no one who has not experienced a like exhilaration at a good action performed and subsequent disappointment when tangible reward is not immediately forthcoming, and finally horror when he realizes the dread consequences which in his brash goodwill he had not stopped to take into account.

In this story too every detail is just right in achieving the desired effect and nothing is superfluous. So exactly is the focus of the story on the reaction of the three men that the reader is not even told the results of the police investigation. He never learns if the driver and the streetcar company are held responsible for the accident.

Shiga's skill in presenting scenes of great emotion without lapsing into sentimentality is again seen in his skillful description of the mother's grief:

> The young mother turned pale and lifted her eyes heavenward. She was unable to speak. She approached her daughter once, but then took her stand a short distance away and looked upon the scene as if completely detached from it. Even when the policemen pulled the small, blood-covered body from under the streetcar, she watched them with an eerie coldness as if she were looking at something distant and unconnected with her. Occasionally her empty and lusterless eyes looked sadly and nervously beyond the crowd in the direction of her home in the distance.

"An Incident" (1913)

Shiga tells this story in the first person. He professes it to be an almost exact account of an accident that he himself was witness to. But, as we shall see, it is not the accident itself that is of central interest in the story.

It is a hot, humid, breezeless afternoon in late July. Shiga sits at the front of a streetcar which rumbles along with monotonous rhythm down the nearly deserted street. The heat is so stifling that he has not even the energy to look at the magazine in his hand. With him in the car and also suffering from the heat are a young man with the insignia of an electric company on his cap, and a stern and forbidding expression on his face as he sits half asleep; two students sitting with their legs spread far apart, their bare feet black with grime and sweat—an unpleasant sight to behold; a large man of over forty, perhaps a petty official of some kind or a junior clerk, dressed in a Western suit with a dirty imitation-Panama hat pushed to the back of his head, chin resting on his stick and eyes staring vacantly ahead. A fat woman of about forty, with a red, sweaty face, boards the car. In one hand she carries a parasol; with the other she is wiping the sweat from her throat with a moist towel. Some of the passengers look up at her listlessly, but the others continue in their drowsy, disinterested state. The passengers are too overcome by the heat to pay any attention to each other. Burdened each with his private cares, they sit there insentient, as if they have forgotten where they are going and for what purpose.

A butterfly flies in through the window and flutters about the car for a while, giving the author a momentary sense of relief. It comes to rest on an advertisement for a play and looks very beautiful there.

The author is startled from his reverie by the cry of the driver, and he raises his head in time to see a little boy about to cross the street in the path of the streetcar. The boy is running at full speed, unaware of his danger. The driver applies his brake and the streetcar slows down. Even so, the boy and the streetcar are on a collision course. As the author looks on, the boy disappears under the windshield and there is a thud. The streetcar moves ahead a few more feet, then comes to a stop. The author has a moment of severe shock, followed by a feeling of tremendous relief and joy when he hears the boy sobbing loudly.

In no time a crowd gathers. The young man from the electric company takes the boy in his arms and scolds him roundly. The boy, still crying loudly, tries to get out of his embrace and begins to pummel him with his tiny fists. The other passengers try to console the boy, and they examine him for injuries. Fortunately, the front guard of the streetcar has saved him from being hurt: he has not a single scratch. Someone points out that the boy has wet his pants, and everyone bursts out laughing. The laugh becomes still louder when they see that the young man from the electric company is also wet where the boy has pressed against him. The young man, in retaliation, taps the boy a couple of times on the head with his chin, and the boy begins to sob again.

The mother arrives on the scene. She is over forty, dark-skinned, and ugly. She takes the boy from the young man, gives him a ferocious stare, then slaps him several times. He cries still louder. She draws him to her and shakes him severely. At this point the young man steps forward and tells her that she is the one that is really to blame, and they have an exchange of words.

The story ends as follows:

> The clerk, standing somewhat apart from the others, began to walk about in excitement, muttering to himself. Then seeing that the driver had already returned to his

seat, he stood in front of him on the street and said, "Good thing it worked," tapping the front guard of the streetcar with his cane. "It couldn't have worked better. This must be the first time since those guards came into use that such a thing has happened." These words were still not sufficient to give adequate expression to his pleasurable feeling of excitement. He seemed to want to say more, but the right words would not come. Besides, the driver was unresponsive.

By this time the crowd had largely dispersed. Most of the people had returned to their houses and were looking on from there. The mother was thanking the conductor profusely. The child, mouth and nose buried in the mother's large breasts, which hung down in an unsightly manner, was now still.

The young man and the clerk reboarded the car. The mother picked up the boy's clogs and started for home. The streetcar began to move again.

The young man removed his jacket and then his shirt, which was wet with urine, exposing his light skin and well-fleshed shoulders. He crumpled the shirt where it was wet and energetically began to wipe his stomach. It was pleasant to watch the rippling movement of his arm and chest muscles. He suddenly lifted his head and met my gaze. (I was sitting across from him.)

"He really fixed me," he said, laughing. The excited and forbidding expression he had previously worn had vanished from his face, and his countenance was now pleasant, good-natured, and sparklingly alive.

At the back of the streetcar the fat woman of about forty was talking to the clerk, who made reply with great earnestness and many gestures. The two students had also begun to converse. The passengers, who before the accident had been half asleep, overcome by the heat, now all had lively expressions on their faces. I too was enjoying a pleasant feeling of exhilaration. Suddenly I noticed that the innocent butterfly, which had fastened itself to the play advertisement, had taken its departure.

Most significant in the story is the contrast between the atmosphere in the streetcar before the accident and after. At the beginning is felt the heat, the humidity, the lethargy, the monotony, the general oppressiveness of the day. The passengers, of course, experience all this, but even nature seems to feel it. The streets are deserted. The leaves of the fig trees are dried and curled in, and covered with dust. The streetcar tracks stretch out ahead like two streams of mercury. The streetcar itself rumbles along in monotonous rhythm. But when the streetcar gets under way again after the accident, the passengers have forgotten the heat and everything accompanying it. They sit chatting vivaciously, with lively expressions on their faces, and the author too is "enjoying a pleasant feeling of exhilaration."

The contrast is more than one of atmosphere. The passengers, as a result of the accident, become human. At the beginning they occupy each his own isolated world. That this isolation is something ugly can be seen from the unfavorable impression each makes upon the author.

It is concern for the child that first brings out their humanity. When the streetcar comes to a sudden stop, the first one to stir into action from his lethargy is the young man from the electric company. He rushes out and grabs the child. The others follow him, and each one, except for the author who remains an onlooker throughout, plays his role in ministering to the boy. They feel a common relief in ascertaining that he is unharmed. This relief is intensified into the even deeper feeling of a common humanity when they discover that he has wet himself and the young man. The author calls the laugh that follows this discovery "a laugh of relief." It is the signal that completes the passengers' transformation into "brothers." When they return to the car, they look at each other with fresh eyes, and experience a bond of comradeship. They are now able to converse with each other congenially, and even the author, who has remained most distant from the action, is changed. The earlier unpleasant impression of his fellow passengers has disappeared.

Thus, the theme of this deceptively simple story is nothing less than the rediscovery of common brotherhood and of the innate goodness of man, and the joy at being given fresh evidence of it. Shiga implies as much when he states that he was moved to write this story when he saw the joy of these good-natured people at the child's escape from death.

"An Incident," therefore, is not a simple, artless account of an accident that the author was witness to. Short as it is, it is a fine piece of art. To say and imply so much in so few words is beyond the power of all but the finest writers. This story too is an example of Shiga's style at its best.

We cannot leave this piece without pointing out that the Shiga Naoya that appears in a work such as this is quite a different person from the self-centered monster of **"Ōtsu Junkichi"** and his other autobiographical stories. The side of Shiga that appears in **"An Incident"**—warmhearted, concerned with others, appreciative of the humanity of man wherever it is to be found—too seldom appears in the latter. One wonders if it was not an overscrupulous honesty, a fear of painting himself the least bit better than he actually was, that is responsible for the dreary picture of him that emerges in his other work. Where most autobiographical writers tend to use their works as a kind of apology for self, Shiga Naoya seems to have done just the opposite.

"Claudius's Journal" (1912)

"Claudius's Journal" was inspired by a particularly inept performance of the role of Hamlet in a Japanese production of the play that Shiga went to see. So bad was the actor who played Hamlet that Shiga found himself sympathizing rather with Claudius. What finally moved him to write the story was the discovery that no proof of Claudi-

us's guilt is offered in the play other than the dubious word of the ghost. Before beginning to write, Shiga made a careful study of Tsubouchi's translation of *Hamlet* to make certain that his story would be consistent at every point with the play.

In Shiga's version, Claudius is a very sensitive and good man who has loved Gertrude from before her marriage to his brother. At the start he has a warm feeling also for her son and wishes nothing more than to win his understanding and his love. Claudius's only fault is marrying too soon after his brother's death, thereby inviting misunderstanding and criticism.

Claudius sees Hamlet's attitude toward him change suddenly (the day after the ghost's appearance) from resentment to hatred. He cannot accept Polonius's view that Ophelia is responsible for the change. He doesn't want to hate Hamlet, if only for the sake of his wife. He recognizes Hamlet's great talent and fine character. Perhaps, he thinks, the players will be able to divert him from his grief.

Claudius realizes that he is so sensitive to criticism that even when innocent he soon begins to look and act as if he were guilty of what people accuse him of. Thus when the players act out the murder scene before him and he discerns that Hamlet suspects him of murdering his brother, he cannot help looking and even feeling guilty, though he is not.

In his mind Claudius accuses Hamlet of wishing to be the protagonist of a stupid tragedy and to cast him in the role of villain. "He seems to have come into this world to perform a tragedy. His education was for the sole purpose of constructing the plot, and his philosophy serves to make it seem plausible."

Claudius tries to suppress the ill will toward Hamlet that rises spontaneously in his heart, but he is finally unsuccessful. He hates him now from the bottom of his heart. He sends him to England and arranges to have him killed, since it is either Hamlet's death or his own. When word reaches him that Hamlet is dead, he is filled with a premonition of still more evil to come.

Here the journal ends, but Shiga asserts in a postscript that "the fate of this Claudius is not necessarily the same as in the play *Hamlet*."

This story is a tour de force, interesting because of its unusual, and yet to some extent plausible, interpretation of Shakespeare's play. It is interesting too because of the insight it gives us into Shiga's psychology, since it is evident that he identifies himself with Claudius.

In *Reconciliation* and elsewhere [can be] seen Shiga's high evaluation of all that is natural: his belief that man at any given moment can only do what comes naturally to him; that philosophy, ideals, rational thought can have little real influence on man's action. The following sentiments of Claudius give eloquent expression to this belief:

My great defect is that my entire being is sometimes irresistibly attracted to a passing emotion and I lose my balance of spirit. It is not seldom that an early morning dream will upset that balance for an entire day. I am not the least bit afraid of what people may think of me. I know that there are more than a few that hate me. As long as I am dealing with such objective reality, I am not the least perturbed. I am not a coward in such matters. But there are certain feelings that steal into my heart and try to ensnare me, and in their presence my own heart becomes the most terrifying of all things. . . .

Isn't it only natural that I was not overwhelmingly saddened by my brother's death? To say that it is natural is splendid justification, at least as far as I am concerned. . . . Losing the brother that had been with me since childhood was certainly sad. But greater still was my joy. My heart is free. I cannot control it with my thought. I was certainly not pleased at this. But there is nothing I can do about it, is there? At the same time I suffer very much because of this condition. In this respect there is nothing that I have less control over than my heart. At this moment I stand more in fear of the uncontrollable movement of my heart than of Hamlet, who is trying to kill me.

In this story, therefore, Shiga—in the character of Claudius—gives expression to his own psychological state, that especially of the difficult years before the reconciliation with his father. From the point of view of craftsmanship and general literary excellence, this story is inferior to the others already considered in this [essay].

"Seibei's Gourds" (1912)

Seibei is a twelve-year-old schoolboy whose one all-consuming interest is gourds. He has cultivated this interest to the point where he can discover potential beauty in ordinary gourds that others, even gourd-collectors of less discerning eye, would pass over as uninteresting. After school he wanders about town in search of new gourds for his collection, and at home he spends all his time treating and polishing his gourds, until they become objects of rare beauty.

But in this practical, no-nonsense world, such an esoteric art is not likely to find much appreciation. A typical reaction is that of his father's friend, who, seeing that Seibei passes over the old, gnarled, peculiarly formed gourds that generally attract collectors in favor of ordinary, even, and symmetrical ones, remarks to the father, "Your son seems to like only the ordinary ones," and advises Seibei that "there's no use just collecting lots of those things. It's not the quantity that counts, after all. You ought to find one or two really unusual ones." The father's own negative reaction is reflected in his reply to the friend: "Can you imagine a boy his age spending all his time playing with gourds!"

The most vehement reaction, however, is that of Seibei's teacher. Seibei had found one very ordinary-looking gourd that he was particularly fond of and spent much time working on. He kept it with him always, even taking it to

school and polishing it under his desk during class. A teacher caught him at it during ethics class. Now this teacher was always extolling the classic code of the samurai and considered gourd-collecting an effeminate pastime. So, naturally, he confiscated the gourd, after heaping much abuse on poor Seibei's head. Still not content, he paid a visit to Seibei's home that evening before Seibei's father had gotten back from work, and announced to the greatly embarrassed mother that this was the responsibility of the family. "It's the duty of parents to keep such things from happening."

When the father heard about it, he gave Seibei a thorough beating, shouting: "You're no good! At this rate you'll never get anywhere in the world. I ought to throw you out into the street where you belong!" Then with a hammer he smashed to pieces every one of Seibei's gourds.

The day after this incident the teacher gave the confiscated gourd to one of the school janitors. This janitor, hard pressed for money, took the gourd to the local curio shop, expecting to get only a few sen for it. Surprised to find the curio dealer willing to give him five yen, the shrewd janitor began to haggle and finally walked out of the shop with fifty yen in his pocket, the equivalent of a year's wages. Little did he realize that the curio dealer, shrewder still, would sell the gourd to a wealthy collector for six hundred yen.

The story ends as follows:

Seibei is now completely taken up with painting. Now that he has found a new occupation he no longer harbors any resentment toward the teacher or even toward his father, who smashed more than ten of his precious gourds.

But his father has already begun to find fault with his painting.

Even without Shiga's admission that his motive in writing this story was "resentment toward my father, who expressed such great displeasure at my writing fiction," it is immediately evident that Seibei and his gourds are a literary symbol for Shiga and his writing, especially if one adverts to the time of the story's composition, December of the year Shiga left home. Here Shiga succeeds in giving objective form to his feelings of resentment toward his father, in a story which has the even symmetry and simple beauty of one of Seibei's gourds.

The story can also be read as a parable illustrating the essence of Shiga's art. Seibei has a keen eye for selecting his gourds, and the gourds he selects are invariably simple and ordinary ones. Shiga likewise has an eye for fastening upon the significant elements of ordinary human experience. Both prefer the simple and natural to the striking and unusual. After securing his gourds, Seibei works untiringly at them until their simple beauty becomes manifest to the eye capable of apprehending it. So Shiga, eschewing ornament and exaggeration, orders the elements of ordinary experience until their beauty becomes manifest.

Unfortunately, a story as simple as this loses very much in even the best translation, since its excellence depends so much upon its use of language. The setting of the scene, the limning of the characters, and the unfolding of the action are all done with great economy. The words are almost all concrete. The sentences are short and have a crisp ring to them. There are few adjectives; the main burden of meaning is carried by the verbs. Despite the wealth of nuance, there is no fuzziness anywhere.

The structure of the story is tight. We have seen the ending. The beginning runs parallel to it:

> This is a story about a boy named Seibei and about his gourds. Afterward Seibei gave up the gourds and found something to replace them: he took up painting. He is now as absorbed in his new hobby as he had once been in his gourds.

With such clarity of structure we know always in what direction the story is moving.

The character of Seibei is most fully developed, but the other characters are also clearly conceived. The father does not understand his son or even try to do so. His ordinary norm of judgment is obvious in his criticism of Seibei: "You'll never get anywhere in the world." He is not uninterested in gourds, but in assessing their worth he is only too ready to rely upon the opinions of "experts." The Bakin gourd which he praises as "a real beauty" Seibei had found to be a big and clumsy monstrosity. When Seibei expresses his opinion, his father silences him with his authority: "You don't know what you're talking about, so you'd better shut up!" (Shiga states that the introduction of a Bakin gourd into the story was the result of the following incident: "Just before I went to Onomichi Father asked me what kind of a man I thought I'd become if I spent my life as a writer. I answered that Bakin had also been a writer but had written only stupid stories. I knew that he liked Bakin and had often read *Eight Dogs*. The fact is that I had almost no acquaintance with Bakin's work. . . .")

The teacher is not too different from the father, but is even more ignorant. His world is far removed from the world of art. He is not only not interested in gourds—unlike the father—but even becomes incensed that Seibei should be interested in them. His bullying of Seibei's mother reveals not only his own crudeness and lack of culture but also the mother's weakness before the authority of the teacher. Even the school janitor—in just one line—is given a vivid characterization: "[When he was offered five yen for the gourd] the janitor was surprised, but being quite a shrewd man, he answered coolly, 'I certainly wouldn't sell it for that.'"

"Han's Crime" (1913)

The story begins with a succinct account of the crime:

> It was a very strange incident. A young Chinese juggler by the name of Han in the course of a performance

severed his wife's carotid artery with one of his knives. The young woman died on the spot and Han was immediately arrested.

The body of the story consists of the examining judge's interrogation of the director of the theater, of Han's assistant in his juggling act, and finally of Han himself. The question is to decide whether the killing was deliberate murder or merely manslaughter.

The director testifies that Han's act is very difficult and requires steady nerves, complete concentration, and even a certain kind of intuitive sense. He cannot say whether the killing was intended or not.

The assistant tells the judge what he knows about Han and his wife. Han's behavior was always correct. He had become a Christian the previous year and always seemed to be reading Christian literature. Both Han and his wife were kind and gentle, very good to their friends and acquaintances, and never quarreled with others. Between themselves, however, it was another matter. They could be very cruel to each other. They had had a child, born prematurely, that had died soon after birth. Since its death their relationship had become strained. Han never raised his hand against his wife, but he always looked at her with angry eyes. He had confided to the assistant that his love for her had died but that he had no real grounds for a divorce. The assistant thinks that it was to overcome his hatred for her that Han had taken to reading the Bible and collections of Christian sermons. The wife could not leave Han because she would never have been able to find anyone else to marry her and she would have been unable to make her own living. The assistant admits that at the moment of the accident the thought had flashed through his mind, "He's gone and killed her," but now he is not so certain. It may have been because of his knowledge of Han's hatred for her that this thought had entered his head. He concludes his testimony by stating that after the incident Han dropped to his knees and prayed for some time in silence.

Interrogated next by the judge, Han admits that he had stopped loving his wife when the child was born, since he knew that it was not his. The child had died smothered by its mother's breasts and Han does not know whether this was accidental or not, though his wife had told him it was. Han thinks that she never really loved him. After the child's death she would observe him "with a cold, cruel look in her eyes" as he gradually went to pieces. "She never showed a flicker of sympathy as she saw me struggling in agony to escape into a better, truer sort of existence."

Han never considered leaving his wife because of his ideals: he wanted to behave in such a way as not to be in the wrong. When asked if he had ever thought of killing her, he admits that at first he often used to think how nice it would be if she were dead. Then, the night before the incident, the thought of killing her had occurred to him but never reached the point of decision. They had had a quarrel because supper was not ready when it should have been. He spent a sleepless night, visited by many nightmarish thoughts, but the idea of killing his wife gradually faded and he "was overcome by the sad, empty feeling that follows a nightmare." He realized that he was too weakhearted to achieve a better life than the one he had.

The next day he was physically exhausted, but the idea of killing no longer occurred to him. He did not even think of that evening's performance. But when the time came to take up his knives to begin his act, he found himself without his usual control. The first two knives did not miss their mark by far, but the third knife lodged itself in his wife's throat. At that moment Han felt that he had done it on purpose. To deceive the witnesses of the scene, he made a pretense of being grief-stricken and fell to his knees in prayer. He was certain that he could make others believe it was an accident.

But then he began to doubt that he had done it on purpose. Perhaps he had only thought he had done so because of his reflections of the previous night. The more he thought about it, the less certain he was about the actuality. It was at this point that he realized that his best defense would be admission of the truth. Since he himself did not know whether he was guilty or innocent, no one else could possibly know either. When the judge asks him if he feels any sorrow for her death, Han admits candidly that he does not, that he never imagined that her death would bring him such a sense of happiness. After this testimony the judge hands down a verdict of not guilty.

"Han's Crime," like **"Seibei's Gourds,"** is a skillful objectification of Shiga's state of mind at the time of its writing. The story was written in the brief period between his release from the hospital after his accident and his departure for Kinosaki. Leisurely reflection at Kinosaki upon the implications of his encounter with death was to drastically change his attitude toward life and to mark a turning point in his work—away from the posture of confrontation and self-assertion to one of harmony and reconciliation. It is therefore ironical that in the person of Han, Shiga should have sung his most triumphant song of self.

Han suffers greatly from the hypocrisy forced upon him in having to live with a wife he despises. He is a man of unusual intelligence, great sensitivity, and an "overwhelming desire to enter into a truer sort of life." His feelings the night before the event are certainly those of Shiga himself at the time when he was determined to "mine" what was in him.

> . . . I was more worked up than I had ever been. Of late I had come to realize with anger and grief that I had no real life of my own. At night when I went to bed, I could not get to sleep but lay there in an excited state with all kinds of things passing through my mind. I was aware of living in a kind of a daze, powerless to reach out with firm determination to the objects of my longing and equally powerless to drive away from me the sources of my displeasure. I came to see that this life of suspension and indecision was all owing to my relationship with my wife. I could see no light in my future, though the longing for light was still aflame. It would never die out but would continue smoldering

pitifully. I was in danger of dying of the poison of this displeasure and suffering. When the poison reached a certain concentration I would die. I would become a corpse among the living. I was nearing that point now. Still, I was doing my best not to succumb. Then the thought came: if only she would die! That filthy, unpleasant thought kept running through my mind. "In fact, why don't you kill her? Don't worry about what happens after that. You'll probably be sent to prison. But life in prison would be immeasurably better than the life you are leading now. Besides, that will be another day. When that day comes, you'll be able to break through somehow. You may have to throw yourself again and again against the obstacles and with no success. But then your true life will be to continue hurling yourself against whatever is in your way until you finally die of the effort."

Kobayashi Hideo, in an early essay on Shiga Naoya (1929), cites the latter portion of the above passage as an excellent statement of

> the basic form of Shiga's thought, or, more accurately, the norm of his action. He is never aware of the gap separating thought and action. Or else, if he does occasionally seem to take cognizance of it, it is only when his thought has not yet come ripe, and even then passion unfailingly jumps in to bridge the gap. For Shiga, to think is already to act, and to act is to think. To such a nature doubt and regret are equally absurd.

At the end of Han's confession, the judge asks him, "Aren't you the least bit grieved at your wife's death?" and Han replies frankly: "Not the least. Even in moments when I hated her most, I never imagined it would be so pleasant to speak of her death." Whether by chance or design, Han has triumphed and entered into what he feels is "a truer sort of life." This note of personal triumph was never again to be sounded so loudly and clearly in Shiga's work. . . .

But if **"Han's Crime"** is an excellent expression of Shiga's state of mind at the time of its writing, it is not for this reason that it is one of the finest stories of modern Japanese literature. The excellence of **"Han's Crime"** is due rather to the abundant life and individuality Shiga was able to give to the characters of Han and his wife, to the interest and tight unity of the plot, and to the masterful use of language.

. . . . .

In Western writers we are accustomed to look for and to find some kind of idealism and intellectual content. Even the lyrical poets are passionately devoted to one or another ideal—such as love between man and woman, justice, peace, individual and social goals—and find the spring of their lyricism therein. In Shiga, however, there is but one idea, one ideal: follow nature; and this ideal is not so much conceived and striven toward as something instinctive. "Follow instinct and all will be well." Fortunately, Shiga's instincts were basically healthy and constructive, perhaps because of the channeling they received during the long apprenticeship under Uchimura Kanzo, but ordinarily this would seem to be a disastrous path for a man to walk, disastrous at least for society if not for the man himself.

In Shiga there is but one idea, one ideal: follow nature; and this ideal is not so much conceived and striven toward as something instinctive.

—Francis Mathy

It is not only Shiga's creative work that is lacking in intellectual content—i.e., ideas of any kind—but even his diaries and recorded conversations. The latter would not give us the impression that he was a learned man. What we find expressed in them—besides comment upon himself, his activity, his likes and dislikes, and his family and friends—are subjective impressions. The best of these are aesthetic judgments, as often on art as on literature; the worst are irresponsible comments on people, events, and situations. Though he lived through one of the periods of greatest change in Japanese history, very little of this change is reflected in his work and only a little more in his diaries and conversations. He might as well have been a medieval monk taking refuge from the complications of the world in a secluded hermitage close to nature.

Since there was from the first so little of human experience to harmonize, one might be tempted to question the significance of the harmony and peace the writer finally achieved, and to find in the finished Shiga something of the quality of the Japanese dwarf tree (*bonsai*). While admiring the beauty of its form and the skill and patience that have gone into its making, one might still consider it something monstrous and prefer to it the less aesthetic lines of the naturally growing tree with its greater impression of life and wholesomeness. Did not Shiga, one may ask, give too narrow an interpretation to nature and so end up frustrating it? Did he not prune it to fit too constricted an area? Are not the elements he rejected or merely overlooked—human relations, individual and social goals, conscious striving for moral growth—part of nature too? Isn't Nakamura Mitsuo correct in calling Shiga's writing a literature of adolescence? Such a complete trust in intuition and impulse, Nakamura points out, is characteristic of early adolescence and generally comes to an end when the youth finally confronts the real world, the world of objective reality. For Shiga this confrontation did not take place until after the Yamashina affair when for the first time he admitted another person, his wife, into his thinking; and thereafter he found it almost impossible to write. Near the end of his study of Shiga, Nakamura makes the following summation:

> In his work from the beginning, Shiga was either the narrator completely outside the action of his story,

taking the attitude of a mere observer, or else he was the hero with other characters having no more existence than was necessary to give coloration to the hero's feelings. The result in either case was that he never really presented himself in the context of an external reality.

> Since he did not view himself as exposed to the air of the outside world, he never took hold of his objective self. During his youth, when the image of the self of everyday life was in agreement with his ethical conceptions, this weak point never emerged to view. That was because for him the complications of the inner self presented to his spirit a drama that substituted for external event.

> But when the inner drama of self was played out and maturity finally arrived, it arrived in a form that was fatal to him as a writer, absorbed as he had been in an unlimited affirmation of self and indifference to the outside world. Maturity for him meant old age. When the struggle within self comes to an end . . . the ordinary person shifts his interest from the inner world to the outer. But Shiga, perhaps because the struggle had been so intense, no longer had the strength to do this. It was too prodigious a task to observe and analyze self and to attempt to gain possession of self through action in the external world. . . . On the one hand, his spirit was worn out from the very earnest interior battle he had waged, and on the other, he was now too accustomed to the ease of ignoring the existence of others. He no longer had interest in anything except what concerned himself or his family.

Nakamura is equally harsh in his criticism of Shiga's major work, *Journey Through Dark Night*. Because of the special character of the hero, or rather because of his lack of character, writes Nakamura, the novel has the same narrow monotony one finds in private exhibitions of secondrate Impressionistic painters. "When compared to foreign novels, of course, but even in the light of the ideals that have nurtured the development of the Japanese modern novel, this long novel—which I am tempted to call 'non-literature'—is surprisingly stunted, the expression of a very special world." Then Nakamura quotes Masamune Hakucho's well-known remark: "If *Journey Through Dark Night* is the highest peak of modern Japanese literature, then modern Japanese literature is a very low range indeed."

But all of the above criticism may not be entirely just. It is based upon the premise that literature must always be mimetic, the imitation of reality in the Aristotelian sense. Is this necessarily so? Western literature, it is true, has been predominantly mimetic since the time when Aristotle gained the upper hand over Plato. But could there possibly exist another kind of literature that is not mimetic, a literature that takes hold of reality in an altogether different way? . . .

At the beginning of the century the poet and essayist Kitamura Tokoku lamented that Japanese literature seemed doomed to sing forever of flower, snow, and moon, and could not rise to the richness of either comedy or tragedy;

that it was outstanding in elegance and refinement but greatly deficient in seriousness and sublimity. It is this same realization that has moved the postwar novelists to try to throw off the influence of Shiga Naoya and break new paths.

But if the traditional Eastern approach to literature is limited in its ability to grasp and represent the fullness of reality, the Western mimetic approach also has its limitations. While it has produced a literature rich in the horizontal insight into the nature of being in all its relationships, the vertical insight into the fullness of the being of the present moment has remained largely undeveloped. The Romantics and the Symbolists sought to cultivate and express this vertical line, but for lack of an audience ready to receive non-conceptual verbal communication (an audience such as was created in Japan through the asceticism of the Ways) their highest flights ended in confusion rather than enlightenment. Again, the twentieth-century novelists have attempted to break up sequences of time and place and thereby achieve a simultaneity of presentation that would give enriched expression to the present reality, but these attempts too have not on the whole been successful. Joyce's *Finnegan's Wake,* one of the best examples of this kind of novel, is unintelligible without a key.

The point, therefore, is not which of these two approaches to literature—mimetic or ecstatic—is the better. Each is good but incomplete. Rather than censure Shiga for not possessing the virtues that are found in abundance in Western literature, it seems wiser to imbibe from him the elements in which our own literature is deficient. It is at this point that real cultural interchange can take place. It is for this reason that we dare to assert that the writing of Shiga Naoya has its place in world literature.

Makoto Ueda (essay date 1976)

SOURCE: "Shiga Naoya," in *Modern Japanese Writers and the Nature of Literature,* Stanford University Press, 1976, pp. 85-110.

[*In the excerpt below, Makoto examines Shiga's literary aesthetic through a survey of his fictional and autobiographical writings.*]

More than most other contemporary Japanese novelists of importance, Shiga Naoya (1883-1971) seems to have been fond of writing about his own works. When the first collection of his prose was published in 1928, he wrote a postscript explaining the motive and intent of each work included in it. He did the same for the nine-volume *Collected Works of Shiga Naoya* (1937-38), and for the five-volume *Library of Shiga Naoya's Writings* (1954-55), so that today's readers have the author's notes on virtually all his fiction. The works themselves also throw a good deal of light on his attitude toward literature, because many of them have a writer, often identifiable as Shiga, for their principal character. This is true of his only full-length novel, *Voyage Through the Dark Night,* as well as of his

three novelettes, **Ōtsu Junkichi, Reconciliation,** and *A Certain Man: His Sister's Death*. Then there are such literary essays of his as "Notes in My Leatherbound Box," "Rhythm," "Notebook of a Green Youth," and "On the Appreciation of Art," which directly touch on the art of writing or problems in aesthetics. When all these are put together, Shiga's views on the nature of literature emerge with unmistakable clarity.

In writing about his own works, Shiga was preoccupied above all with the question of their factuality. In almost every instance, he wanted to tell his readers to what extent the work was fictional. As it turned out, a large number of his stories were based on his own experience; many of them, indeed, purported to be faithful records of actual events. For instance, of his story called **"Influenza"** he said, "I wrote down the facts as they were," and of **"At Kinosaki,"** "This too is a story that tells what actually happened." As for his methods of composition, he said of a story entitled **"Morning, Noon, Evening"**: "In a relaxed frame of mind I wrote down the day's happenings as they actually occurred." When a certain critic made some derogatory remarks about his novelette **Reconciliation,** Shiga defended himself by saying that it was true to fact. He had written it, he said, not to present a moral thesis but to vent a "more immediate sentiment" of his—namely, "the joy of having arrived at a reconciliation [with my father] after a long period of estrangement." He concluded: "I simply kept on writing down the facts as they were, without any artifice, and I ended up producing a work of art. That is the strength of this work." Underlying all these comments is Shiga's idea that literature is in the last analysis a record of events that actually took place in the author's life. A literary work, he thought, should be autobiographical in the strict sense of the word; that is, it should be a conscious effort at self-revelation.

To Shiga the difference between fiction and nonfiction was minimal. Indeed, to carry his views to their logical conclusion, there would not seem much need for writing fiction at all, since the facts of daily life could be most satisfactorily presented in the form of a diary, an autobiography, or an essay.

—Makoto Ueda

To Shiga, then, the difference between fiction and nonfiction was minimal. Indeed, to carry his views to their logical conclusion, there would not seem much need for writing fiction at all, since the facts of daily life could be most satisfactorily presented in the form of a diary, an autobiography, or an essay. And to a certain extent Shiga himself found this to be the case. Of the seventeen-volume *Collected Works of Shiga Naoya* (the 1955-56 edition, in which each volume has roughly the same number of pages), nine volumes are devoted to his works of non-fiction—essays, diaries, and personal letters. Among his stories, too, there are a considerable number that border on nonfiction. In the case of **"Harvest Bugs,"** Shiga himself did not know which category it belonged to, and he remarked that this was characteristic of his work in general. In the case of another prose piece, he had first entitled it "Kusatsu Spa, an Essay" and sent it off to a publisher. But when it came back for proofreading he changed it into a short story by simply erasing "an Essay" from the title. It is difficult to think of any other major writer in modern Japan who could have done such a thing.

The fact remains, however, that Shiga was primarily a novelist, not an essayist or a diarist. His main creative energy went into writing works of fiction—a novel, three novelettes, and a sizable number of short stories, which include such obviously imaginative tales as **"Han's Crime," "Claudius' Diary,"** and **"Akanishi Kakita."** Why did he think fiction was the best mode in which to record the facts of his own daily existence? His answer can be found in his notes on *Voyage Through the Dark Night*. "Kensaku, the hero, is by and large myself," he wrote. "I would say his actions approximate the things I would do, or would wish to do, or actually did, under the given circumstances." The prime function of a diary, like most other genres of personal nonfiction, was to record only what one actually did. A work of fiction, on the other hand, could present what one "would do, or would wish to do" in various imaginary situations. It described man not only as he had been or was, but as he might be or might want himself to be.

Likewise, in Shiga's view, a novel presents facts not only as they are but also as the novelist imagines they are or as he would wish them to be. He might, indeed, write down things contrary to actual fact, if they seemed imaginatively more convincing to him. Once, on devising a scene for a short story, Shiga placed the moon in a geographically impossible position, but knowingly let the description stand because that was the way he had long visualized the scene in his mind. At another time he described a certain temple in Nara from memory and later discovered the description was wrong in many details. But again he left it intact, for the same reason. In a more striking instance, Shiga consciously created an imaginary incident and placed it among other events that were obviously autobiographical. Later, he was amused to hear his sister say that she remembered the incident well. "My sister had no reason to tell a lie about that [incident]," he observed. "It had floated most naturally into my imagination, and because of that naturalness it was recalled to my sister's memory as a fact." Shiga also tells of instances in which his imagination seemed to sense an event before it actually happened, despite the fact that he had no foreknowledge of the circumstances. On one occasion, he was writing a short story and was trying to visualize a scene in which a barber kills his customer with a razor [**"The Razor"**]. By coincidence, one of his next-door neighbors committed suicide with a razor just about the same time. On another occasion, he wrote a short story about a boy who was hit by a streetcar and narrowly escaped death [**"An Incident"**]. That same evening Shiga himself was hit by a streetcar and was seriously injured. All these instances seemed to him to substantiate his idea that some imaginary facts are just as valuable as, or even more valuable than, actual facts.

What kinds of facts, whether actual or imaginary, are most suitable for a work of fiction? Ordinary facts would not do; they would merely provide material for a chat, or for a popular novel at best. "A story that can be told in a chat," Shiga once said, "should be told in a chat. Only a story with something in it that could not be told in a chat could be made into a work of literature." Shiga did not elaborate on what that "something" was. But other writings of his show clearly enough what he meant. For instance, there is the revealing anecdote about the way he welcomed a close friend who had just returned from a year-long trip to Europe and North America. His wife showered the friend with "Welcome home!" and other such greetings. But Shiga did not utter a word of welcome; he did not even make the customary bow. It had always been this way between him and that friend of his, Shiga explained; he did not know why it should be so, but he felt "it was most natural." In the same essay, Shiga cites another instance, this time involving two naval officers who had been close friends since childhood. One of the officers had been shipwrecked and had barely managed to survive; the other officer, welcoming him at a naval station, said just one word, "Hi!"—and smiled. Shiga, after telling this anecdote, muses that such a scene would never occur in a work of popular fiction. Popular fiction described an event according to common sense, visualizing it as an average person would; when two intimate friends met after a long interval, they would greet each other effusively. Fiction above the popular level was different: it presented an event in the way the author thought most "natural." A serious writer of fiction presented men and women who behaved themselves more "naturally" than the average person; he presented facts that were more "natural" than facts usually were. A "naturally" conceived fact was one that, even though it had never existed in reality, would strike a person as being true and real, as had been the case with Shiga's sister.

Exactly what did Shiga mean by the word "natural"? The obvious answer, as we have seen, was that he used it to mean the opposite of "commonsense" or "conventionally accepted." When he said literature presented "natural" facts, he implied that it revealed facts ordinarily hidden beneath the surface of conventional appearances. At a deeper level, however, the term assumed a more positive value for him. To be "natural" meant to be true to nature. A person who behaved "naturally" was not a mere eccentric who pays little attention to conventional norms; he was a person who, having awakened to his innermost nature, was trying to return to it. When Shiga said a work of fiction presented things that he would do or would wish to do, he meant the things that were most natural to him in this sense. With such a creed, a writer of fiction becomes a seeker after his own and others' true nature.

Shiga must have arrived at this conclusion fairly early in his career as a novelist. An entry in his diary dated May 27, 1911, reads as follows:

The mission of art is to achieve a deeper understanding of nature's beauty. The mission, to put it another way, is to observe nature with an artistic mind, a mind bent on discovering beauty. Therefore, the kind of nature that the average person sees does not make art when it is reproduced. One must have a deep, deep understanding of nature. But men have become more and more forgetful of nature and are creating art out of art alone. Thereupon, men arise who cry, "Return to nature!" Art, when it is forgetful of nature, degrades itself. Degraded art is, I feel, like the expressionless face of a lovely princess born of a noble family.

Thirty-eight years later, he was still emphasizing the importance of "nature" as the source of literature and art. "I am still of the opinion," he said, "that the one thing man can certainly depend on is this 'nature.' There have been various literary and art movements, but I cannot think of any alternative other than to follow the trail of nature." The question of where this trail led is more of a philosophical than a literary one. We should pursue it, nevertheless, since it affected Shiga's concept of literature by influencing his definition of artistic imitation.

Shiga's answer seems to center on the word "wisdom." As against some of his literary colleagues, who tended to see human nature as founded on sexual drives, he believed that man possessed a kind of instinctive wisdom so deep-seated that it sometimes overrode even his sexual impulses. It was almost an animal instinct, an instinct that maintained man's physical and mental health. In **"Film Preview in the Morning,"** another of his autobiographical pieces, Shiga called it "the law of nature." The narrator of the story, obviously Shiga himself, is walking along the street with a male dog of his called Yone, when a neighborhood dog, a female, happens to come by. Yone becomes excited and goes up to her, but calmly leaves on discovering that her mating season has passed. The narrator is impressed to see that dogs act according to "the law of nature." He recalls a film, *The Charterhouse of Parma,* that he saw a week ago. The film's characters had become embroiled in a tragic crime of passion. "In the world of dogs a male would never kill a female for love, no matter how much they were at odds," Shiga wrote. "But in the human world, men have been known to kill women for precisely this. Man, by his wisdom, should be able to avoid such senseless tragedies." Man has impulses; Shiga would not deny that. Yet man has wisdom also, instinctive wisdom given him by nature for his own health and survival. Shiga advised that every man be attentive to it, understand it, and follow it; this was the way to return to nature. A work of art should present a man doing just that, under the specific circumstances in which he happened to have been placed. In short, a novel should describe a "wise" man.

Shiga's idea of a "wise" man is further clarified by two of the short stories written by the novelist-hero of *Reconciliation.* One of them is about a man who, though basically a decent enough fellow, is a chronic philanderer. Once, when his wife is away from home for an extended period, a maid in his household becomes pregnant. He has had nothing to do with the maid, but he has no way of proving it. When the maid's condition can escape his wife's notice no longer, he simply says to her, "I've had nothing to do with the maid, you know." The wife takes his word for it, fully believing in his integrity. At this point the narrator cuts in and says: "Both the husband and the wife were wise. Tragedy missed its last chance to feast on them." Another story in the same series is about a young man and a young woman, both postal workers, who fall in love and have an affair, though the norms of contemporary society prohibit any such thing. The local postmaster dismisses them both, terming their love affair shameless and scandalous. The young man's parents, however, have no hesitation in allowing the two lovers to marry; indeed, they are more than delighted to give them their blessing. The narrator likes this story because it showed the opposite of what usually happens: no tragedy takes place, because the parents are sensible people. There is no doubt that the narrator-hero of *Reconciliation* is Shiga himself. He, too, believed that people have this wisdom buried in their innermost selves, and that many tragedies occur unnecessarily because it goes unrecognized. But wise people, like the married couple in the first story and the parents in the second, make the best use of it that circumstances allow.

Many of Shiga's own stories depict such people. Explaining the theme of his lone full-length novel, he said: "Everybody, wise or foolish, has misfortunes that are due to fate; it is impossible to avoid them. Yet one should wish to tide oneself over them as wisely as possible. That is the theme of *Voyage Through the Dark Night.*" The novel's hero, Kensaku, suffers two misfortunes that he was powerless to prevent: his incestuous birth and his wife's rape (though Shiga preferred to call the latter incident adultery). Shiga's three novelettes, which he once compared to three branches of a tree, combine to tell the story of how a man, in trying to be faithful to his inner feelings, arrives at a tragic clash with his father because of their basic difference in personality, and how he eventually reaches a reconciliation with the latter in a way acceptable to them both. The same type of hero appears in many of Shiga's short stories; his progress is always from disaster to recovery. The theme is obvious in **"Mother's Death and the New Mother," "Seibei's Gourds," "An Incident," "Han's Crime," "At Kinosaki," "Influenza," "Tree Frogs," "Morning, Noon, Evening," "The Dog,"** and many more. In some stories, like **"The Razor," "Claudius' Diary,"** and **"Kuniko,"** the disaster part is heavily emphasized. In others, like **"A Snowy Day," "The Fires,"** and **"Yajima Ryūdō,"** a more peaceful mood prevails, since the protagonist has completely recovered from a disaster as the story begins. Also falling into the last category are many short prose pieces that deal with animals, birds, and insects—**"Dragonflies," "Harvest Bugs," "Kuma," "Insects and Birds," "Cats," "White-Eyes, Bulbuls, and a Bat," "Animal Sketches," "On Sparrows,"** etc. It is hardly surprising that Shiga, who recognized true wisdom in dogs, was so much at ease with so many other members of the animal kingdom.

Shiga's adverse criticism of certain literary works can also be explained in terms of this highly individual view of human nature. He did not like *Othello, Hamlet,* or *Romeo and Juliet* because they were, in his opinion, tragedies caused by human folly. He felt that, in each case, the tragedy could have been averted if the protagonists had been "wiser" in the sense already discussed. He also disliked naturalist writers, because the characters they described had nothing beautiful about them. In an obvious reference to them he said: "It is hazardous to health to be frequently exposed to the ugliness and folly in human life." For the same reason, Shiga was careful enough not to read those pages of the daily newspaper that reported on murders, burglaries, rapes, and frauds. He did not like Stendhal's *The Charterhouse of Parma* because, he thought, its hero differed little from the kind of delinquent one read about in newspapers. "At all events," he said, "we should take a little more severe attitude toward a person who conducts his life without wisdom or anything of that sort, and who, driven by his instinctive impulses, brings tragedy upon others and becomes the cause of all sorts of misfortunes."

Shiga's idea of artistic imitation thus assumes a didactic character. Literature should be factual, he believed, but that did not mean a writer should present all facts indiscriminately. Some facts were more "factual," more "natural," and therefore more convincing than others. Autobiographical facts were an important source of material for fiction, but only insofar as they resulted from the natural, instinctive behavior of the person in question. Events that took place as a result of social and moral convention were less valuable; even though they might actually have happened, they were less convincing than "natural" events that existed only in imagination. These "natural" events and facts were characterized, according to Shiga, by the "wisdom" that lay behind them. This "wisdom" was of a specific kind, a kind that had its roots deep down in man's biological nature and served to maintain his physical and mental health. Fundamentally, man was a wise being. It followed that a novel, if it was to be as factual as possible, should prove him to be so. In this way, the reader would be awakened to the fundamental wisdom lying dormant within himself.

Ultimately, Shiga's theory of literature is limited in the same way as his view of human nature. Even if it be granted that man has some basic animal wisdom such as Shiga recognized, it may be argued that he was being too optimistic. When he said that "Hi!" was enough to greet a really close friend, was he not attributing too much to human powers of communication? When he advised men to emulate dogs, which know when and when not to mate, was he not assuming too easily that man's sexual urge is basically controllable? He never seems to have visualized himself in an extreme situation; certainly, few of his heroes have been in them. To be born of an incestuous mother, to have one's wife raped, to live with a stubborn, domineering father—these are lesser disasters than, say, to be born crippled, to be born of an insane mother, or to have one's marriage forcibly broken up. Shiga's characters are never faced with such agonizing choices as either eating human flesh or starving to death. His theory seems reasonable enough as long as it maintains that literature must be true to fundamental human nature. But to make

wisdom, or anything resembling it, the very essence of human nature seems a little far-fetched. Inevitably, much of his fiction seems far-fetched as well, as far as its philosophical implications are concerned.

If a novel's primary purpose is to depict the life of a man who, having met with a catastrophic misfortune, recovers from it by his innate "wisdom," it seems that the novelist would do well to become such a man himself. To be sure, he can draw on hearsay (as Shiga himself did in **"The Righteous"**) or a newspaper story (as he did in **"Sasaki's Case"**). He will be on safer ground, however, if he writes directly out of his own experience—safer, because he knows his own fundamental nature better than anyone else knows it. How he will instinctively feel or act in a given situation is unpredictable, at times even to himself; better, then, to have the experience before writing about it. It follows that there are two prerequisites for being a novelist: first, one must be somewhat disaster-prone, whether by circumstances or by character; second, one must have the physical and mental vigor to rebound from a disaster. There is sufficient evidence to show that Shiga thought this was so.

Shiga's concept of the artist as a disaster-prone person is best expressed in his short story **"Kuniko."** The heroine, named Kuniko, is married to a playwright who is suffering from writer's block because his family life is too peaceful. She of course likes things to be that way; she cannot understand how he could sit at his desk and work if his home were not peaceful. Her husband, however, thinks of himself as having been rotting "like a peach" during those peaceful years. Finally he starts having an affair with a flighty young actress. When the affair is picked up by the newspapers as a juicy piece of scandal, news of it reaches his wife. The happy atmosphere of the household is completely shattered. At the same time, however, the playwright regains interest in his craft and begins work on a large-scale play. Kuniko, on the other hand, is utterly crushed by this turn of events. Having lost all hope of saving her marriage, she commits suicide.

While it would be rash to identify Kuniko's husband completely with Shiga, there is no doubt that Shiga was similarly exercised by the basic predicament of the artist's personal life. In fact, he said as much in an earlier essay. "When the day is windy, cloudy, and chilly," he wrote, "the weather alone is enough to fill people's minds with gloom. This is natural. On such a day, however, a novelist is seized by a desire—a desire more intense than an ordinary person's—to express that gloom in a work of fiction. And when he succeeds in expressing it well, he feels happy." Kuniko, then, is a victim of this unfortunate antinomy lying between the artist's happiness and the ordinary man's. The average person is happy when the weather is pleasant; the artist is happy when the weather is rough, because it is then that he can be creative.

Why does an unhappy personal life stimulate the writer to write, while a happy life does not? Shiga's answer, as might be expected, is that an unhappy man has a stronger motive for expressing himself, suffering as he does from frustrations that he cannot contain. A person may be unhappy because he believes he is right but few people sympathize with him; he therefore appeals to their sympathy in words. Shiga cites several instances of unhappy people who vented their frustrations through literary composition. In one instance, a college student is moved to write a novel when he violently disagrees with the minister of his church, who regards adultery as on a level with murder. In another, a young writer, when told about the checkered life of a certain geisha, thinks little of it. But when he hears his brother, who has also heard the gossip about her, retell it with emphasis on the geisha's depraved nature, he becomes thoroughly irritated, and begins to think of transforming the gossip into a work of literature. Shiga also gives an instance from his own life: he once saw *Hamlet* staged at a Tokyo theater, and was repelled by the scheming, heartless, selfish behavior of its hero—so much so, in fact, that he was moved to write a short story, **"Claudius' Diary."** All these cases support Shiga's view that creative writing functions as an emotional purge. The motive for writing a novel is to find an outlet for one's hatred, anger, and frustration, including the frustration of being treated unjustly. A peaceful life, devoid of these emotions, offers no such motive.

Characteristically, however, Shiga thought of creative writing as something that, while it might help to relieve tension, did not necessarily restore mental equilibrium. Venting one's frustrations in the form of a novel did not remove the cause of the frustrations. Literature was, after all, an inferior substitute for life, not life itself. The cause of one's unhappiness has to be dealt with and overcome in the sphere of one's actual life; this was as true of novelists as of ordinary people. But there was a clear distinction between a poet and a novelist in this respect. "A poet is emotional and tends to destroy his personal life," he observed, "like Baudelaire, Verlaine, Rimbaud, etc. But this would never do in the case of a novelist. . . . Poets and novelists are both men of letters, but there is a good deal of temperamental difference between them." Hence Shiga disliked a novelist who was like a poet—that is, a novelist who did not rebound from a misfortune. For instance, he did not like Tanaka Hidemitsu (1912-49), because the latter showed "no spirit of prose literature" and was completely overcome by his own misfortunes. He also did not like Tanaka's idol, Dazai Osamu, because he thought Dazai was a weak man who adopted a conceited pose to hide his weakness. "However hard I tried, I just could not bring myself to sympathize with Dazai's love suicide," he wrote. "If he had to die, why didn't he die alone?" He liked a novelist who was strong enough to die alone or, better, a novelist who refused to die in the face of disaster. A novelist, he thought, should have enough vitality to rebound from any misfortune he might have to face. Most of the artist-heroes in Shiga's stories have such vitality and do rebound from their misfortunes. The most striking example is the young novelist-hero of *Reconciliation,* who has a violent clash with his father and is disinherited as a result. The novelist, however, does not yield to defeatism; he is determined to fight on, and even imagines a scene in which he engages in a mortal duel with his father. The same can be said of Kensaku, the novelist-hero of *Voyage Through the Dark Night,* who prompts his half-brother to say of his character: ". . . you are strong. You have a strong self that enables you to do whatever you want to do. . . . You always have a focal point inside yourself, and all your indicators are always ready to point to it." It is this strong ego, this "focal point," that enables Kensaku to survive two major disasters. The protagonist of **"Han's Crime,"** who can also be called an artist, actually kills his wife because he can think of no other way to ensure his own survival. Because of his will to survive as a playwright, the playwright-hero of **"Kuniko"** also causes his wife's death, though not so directly. The Shiga-like narrator of **"At Kinosaki"** first longs for the peace of death, but regains his desire for life when he recalls the strong natural instinct for survival that he showed when caught in a traffic accident. The strong, vigorous character that Shiga demanded of a novelist is further illustrated by his diary entry for January 9, 1926, which is a kind of New Year's resolution:

> This year, I want to lead a vigorous life, in every sense of the word. I want to live in a positive frame of mind. No tearful complaints. No grumbling, slandering, or nagging. No flattering, no overconscientious acceptance of tiresome duties. I will love my wife and children. I will love them, without doting upon them. I must avoid, as much as possible, doing the sort of thing that I know will make me unhappy later on. I will make my living as a writer this year. I want to be free, natural, honest, vigorous, and carefree.

If this seems to present an image of an ideal man rather than an ideal novelist, that is consistent with Shiga's idea of a novelist. For Shiga, the ultimate goal in life was to become a man of moral strength. This was a logical conclusion for a writer who considered literature as at best an inferior substitute for life. Problems in life had to be solved in the realm of life; the solutions offered by art were, in the final analysis, no more than substitutes for real solutions, dreams that might or might not be fulfilled. The artist, Shiga thought, should not be a mere dreamer; he had to have vigor and strength to make his dreams come true in real life. He had to lead a "vigorous life" in a "positive frame of mind."

Shiga actually seems to have attained the goal he set for himself. The protagonists of his later works (say, after 1928), easily identifiable as Shiga, are by and large "free, natural, honest, vigorous, and carefree" persons. In fact, they are so vigorous and carefree that they hardly ever allow anything untoward to happen. When it does, it rarely amounts to more than a ripple on calm waters. In **"Kuma,"** for example, the "disaster" that befalls the hero is that his family dog goes astray for a few days. In **"Morning, Noon, Evening,"** it is that the hero's eldest daughter, who is recovering from a cold, goes to visit her grandmother on a chilly day without first asking his permission. In **"Film Preview in the Morning,"** the worst inconvenience suffered by the narrator is that the film he saw, *The Charterhouse of Parma,* was not to his liking and that the theater was poorly heated. In other stories— **"Harvest Bugs," "Sunday," "Typhoon," "Rabbit,"**

"Cats," "My Youngest Child," and "Kusatsu Spa," to name a few—hardly anything happens to disturb the equilibrium of the hero's mind. It seems that, as time progressed, Shiga succeeded in establishing his own and his family's well-being on such a firm basis that no serious misfortune could ever befall them again. Inevitably, given his view of literature, he lost the urge to write; he had no frustrations to vent, no disasters to rebound from. He wrote less and less frequently, his yearly production dwindling to fewer than five short prose pieces—normally two, one, or none—after 1928. Very likely he could not have cared less. "I have felt," he once said, "the important thing for me to do is to spend this unrepeatable life of mine in the best way possible. The fact that I have written works of fiction is of only secondary importance."

In Shiga's view, then, the ideal novelist is an inactive novelist, a writer who feels no urge to write. For if he remains active, he is forced to lead an ambivalent existence, keeping a delicate balance between his disaster-prone character and his strength to recover from disasters. If he is too disaster-prone, he will make a good poet (like Verlaine) but a bad novelist (like Dazai). If his character is too wholesome, he will hardly meet with any real misfortunes, and will therefore have little motive for writing a novel. In his younger days Shiga managed to keep this balance, and produced some fine pieces of literature as a result. But as he got older he lost it, and remained largely inactive as a writer. For most other writers this development would have constituted a painful setback. For Shiga, it was progress.

William F. Sibley (essay date 1979)

SOURCE: Introduction to *The Shiga Hero,* University of Chicago Press, 1979, pp. 1-34.

[*In the following excerpt, Sibley argues that the narrator of Shiga's stories is a distinct persona that, while often serving as the author's alter-ego, is separate from him. He names this figure the "Shiga hero."*]

Shiga Naoya (1883-1971) wrote a fairly large number of short stories, many pieces that are still shorter and essentially nonfiction, a few narratives of intermediate length (so-called *chūhen shōsetsu*), and only a single full-length novel, entitled *An'ya kōro,* which has been translated by Edwin McClellan as *A Dark Night's Passing.* In spite of the modest quantity of his works that would be considered by conventional Anglo-American standards belles-lettres or "serious literature," in his own country Shiga has at various times over the past sixty years been exalted as a master craftsman of the modern literature and a special spokesman for the genius of the nation (*bungaku no kamisama,* "the lord of literature," is the journalistic tag he was given late in his career), and has alternately been excoriated, particularly in the years after the Second World War, as one of those most responsible for the stunting of modern Japanese fiction.

In an often cited sweeping comment on much of modern Japanese fiction, Kobayashi Hideo stated, "Since Tayama Katai learned from Maupassant the literary value of daily life itself, no writer has succeeded as well as Shiga has in boldly, even violently, wresting from his own life a work of art; no one has adhered so scrupulously as he has to the approach of the personal novel [*shishōsetsu*], in which the logic of everyday life becomes the logic of literary creation."

Less grandiosely, Akutagawa Ryūnosuke, a contemporary, greatly admired Shiga for his ability to write what Akutagawa called "stories without stories" (*hanashi no nai hanshi*). But he too takes on an almost reverential tone when he further observes, "Shiga Naoya is the purest writer among us. His works are first and foremost those of a man who lives a fine life . . . by which I mean a morally spotless life."

As if in reply to Akutagawa's homage, Dazai Osamu wrote of Shiga some twenty-five years later, "What everyone says is so 'fine' in his works amounts to nothing more than the man's conceit, the courage of a bully. . . . If he writes that he has farted it will be published in large print, and we are supposed to read this with the utmost solemnity. What nonsense!"

Looking at Shiga's works themselves, one finds the most prominent, recurring themes to be obsessive memories of childhood; fantasies of murder and parricide, sometimes acted out on the stage of the narrative, elsewhere imagined by the narrator or the central character through evident substitutions; a deeply ambivalent attraction to alternately protective and destructive older women; and ultimately, the incest wish and the death wish, which appear in various partially displaced or sublimated forms. The evidence of his relatively slender œuvre, the only evidence of interest, leads one to the conclusion that, whatever Shiga was as a man, as a writer he has been neither so banal and literal-minded as Kobayashi's remarks (contrary to his intention) would suggest, nor so "pure" as Akutagawa would have us believe, nor finally so consumed with self-importance, relentlessly self-involved though his writing surely is, as Dazai's diatribe makes him out to be.

Shiga is an author who (to paraphrase William Gass on D. H. Lawrence [in *Fiction and the Figures of Life,* 1968]) wrote of nothing, in story, tract or letter, ever, but himself. "Anything can be made into fiction," Shiga himself once commented. "Whether a particular subject turns into a story or novel, an essay, biography, or diary depends entirely on the author's attitude as he writes rather than on the material itself." The interchangeability of such different genres in Shiga's mind, not excluding even biography, is a clear expression of the subjectivism bordering on solipsism that characterizes all of his writing. He has indeed been both canonized and castigated as the most successful (in Kobayashi's view) and most intransigent (in the eyes of his detractors) practitioner of those curious subgenres that so dominate Japanese literary-historical treatments of the first half of the twentieth century: the *shishōsetsu* ("I novel" or, better, in Henri Peyre's more broadly based terminology, "personal fiction" [*Literature and Sincerity*, 1963]) and the *shinkyō shōsetsu* ("the novel of mental states"). . . .

If Shiga did indeed start from the doubtful premise that, in Kobayashi's words, the "logic of everyday life" may serve as "the logic of literary creation," he has carried this formula to its often illogical conclusion. It hardly requires a trained psychologist to recognize that on a deeper level of reality our days are filled at least as much with irrational impulses and inchoate emotions as with orderly social intercourse and articulate thoughts. It is this sort of reality, bound up with and triggered by the external trivia of "everyday life" but having a separate life of its own, that Shiga has taken as his prime subject. Like various other writers both in Japan and the West, he has arrived independently at a wholly intuitive kind of psychoanalytical consciousness. And yet the "anything" that, in his above-quoted remark, Shiga asserted could serve as what Henry James called the "germ" of a story or novel, suggests a randomness that, as we shall see, does not obtain in the subject matter of his fiction.

Whatever the subject, when his "attitude" has determined that his work is to be fiction (that is, a *shōsetsu*), the focus is most often inward and backward, introspective and retrospective. As is the case with all deeply subjective fiction, much of Shiga's raw material is unmistakably rooted in his own inner experience, we may conclude; for he could scarcely know another's mind so thoroughly. But one may not find very interesting or particularly germane the dubious game of correlating closely the outward events of his life with the representation of psychological effects supposedly produced by them, the game so vigorously played by the biographical critics. His own words on several occasions invite a good deal of skepticism on this score: "It is hard to capture one's own psychology with some measure of accuracy. No matter how much one may grasp of the psychological states that arise in one's mind, there is always something that slips away. Then there are other things which one naturally does not want to touch. . . . Dreams, at least, are completely honest. But they are also sometimes treacherous."

> **Dreams and elusive "psychological states"—moods, feelings, impulses, are what is most real in Shiga's fiction, together with concrete impressions, the sights and sounds that are fused with these things**.
>
> —*William F. Sibley*

Dreams and elusive "psychological states"—moods, feelings, impulses, are finally what is most real in Shiga's fiction, together with concrete impressions, the sights and sounds that are fused with these things. Attempts to tie this intangible stuff directly to what we "know" about his life and times are not entirely convincing. And one need not make some facile identification between Shiga and his hero Kensaku to see in the latter's misgivings about psychological self-expression toward the end of *An'ya kōro* some of Shiga's own thoughts on the subject: "At first Kensaku proposed to write down in detail the mental states he had experienced since coming to this mountain retreat. But his preliminary deliberations left him unsatisfied. The thoughts that had ruled him until recently were purely chimerical. And if he tried to write truthfully about the change he had since undergone, it would no doubt sound equally vague and illusory. He concluded that he did not know how to write about such things."

The problem, then, is how to convey in an at least partially objectified form "purely chimerical thoughts," "vague and illusory" mental states. Unlike his hero in this instance, Shiga does of course eventually succeed in giving some outward form to his inner experience. He does this through vivid concrete images ("objective correlatives," in Eliot's much overquoted phrase, later repudiated by himself), detailed descriptions of dreams (nature's contribution to the process of visual objectification), and in general through the elaboration of a restricted symbolic vocabulary that includes elements borrowed from various established lexicons, fixed idioms that are frequently invoked in a sense peculiar to Shiga, even occasional neologisms.

That Shiga was in a general way ·a writer of personal fiction is borne out by a common-sense reading of the works and need not be confirmed by protracted exercises in biographical criticism of the most literal-minded kind. . . . [The] recurring events that form the narrative kernel of most of his major works are in any case most often non-events, rooted in "chimerical thoughts" whose actual occurrence in Shiga's mind are unknowable. That he also wished to become a "psychological" novelist is attested to by such passages as those quoted above, though the works themselves do not always fit obviously into this category and show ample traces of Shiga's self-doubts about this approach to writing fiction. What distinguishes Shiga from several other Japanese writers who, in the first decades of the century, set about writing various kinds of both personal and psychological fiction is his motive for undertaking the project in the first place, and the transparency with which, both in the works and outside, the motive is revealed. In a story entitled *Wakai* (*Reconciliation,* 1917), Shiga's hero, who is himself a writer, describes a kind of autotherapy which he has practiced in his works behind a thin veil of fiction: "I would write about [my own problems] from the point of view of the impersonal author. . . . Through putting down on paper various unpleasant events which might well occur in my own life . . . I hoped to prevent them from actually happening to me. As I set down each episode I would imagine that I had escaped acting out an identical situation myself." And after he had completed a large portion of his major works, Shiga reminisced: "It strikes me that in those years there was something pathological in me [as well as in my writing]. Lately, my interest in sick states has diminished. But I still cannot deny that one derives a certain élan from such sickness—an excitement which permits one to experience and to express things not accessible under normal conditions of sanity." These words cast considerable light both on Shiga's idiosyncratic practice of the craft of fiction and on what might be called his ulterior motives for writing in the first place. . . .

It is above all, and in some cases nothing but, style which, as "incitement pleasure," draws the reader into Shiga's works. Shiga's indifference to the larger formal features of narrative craft is often striking. Apart from the special vocabulary and the terse, rhythmical style which he has painstakingly created, there are few formally satisfying elements in his works, a minimum of well-constructed plot, dramatic incident, "big scenes," and sustained dialogue. If one's perspective stresses such larger formal attributes of the genre, as does that of Edward Seidensticker in his discussion of Shiga, one would no doubt agree with him that Shiga's only successful works have been a handful of short stories. But, as Seidensticker himself has pointed out, the modern Japanese temperament has not yielded many sturdily built novels laid out on a grand scale in the classic nineteenth century European manner.

Early in his career (1911), Shiga wrote in his diary, "I always manage to grasp the details of things but have little capacity for understanding the whole. I suppose it is enough if a writer captures life's details, but it bothers me a bit to think that I haven't got the whole. And yet, it sometimes seems to me that the whole is not to be understood in any case. . . . And I also wonder if, should I ever come to grasp the whole, or allow myself to apply to it some facile conceptualization, I would not in the process be stopped dead in my tracks." In addition to being personal, subjective, and often intuitively psychoanalytical (with an eye to autotherapy), Shiga's approach to fiction is, then, also highly fragmentary. In an effort to grasp some of the "whole" which eluded Shiga, or which, as the foregoing diary entry would imply, he deliberately eschewed, one would want to emphasize those elements in his individual works that contribute to some unity linking all of them. Chief among these, beyond the consistent surface of his well-honed style, is surely the single central character who, in one guise or another, appears in nearly all of Shiga's stories and novels, and whose viewpoint, with occasional interventions by the omniscient author, predominates in the great majority of his narratives.

This character is given a number of different names in the various works where he appears, and often speaks to us directly in the first person. We encounter him at several different stages in his life and in a variety of social roles. But in his inner life he is recognizably the same figure throughout Shiga's works. Although one need not be concerned with exact correlations and literal identifications, this created character and the microcosm he inhabits can no doubt be closely associated with the creating author and his world. By analogy with the "method" described in the above-quoted passage from *Wakai,* we may choose to imagine that Shiga projects what enters his consciousness onto this single character, sometimes in an unusually direct fashion. But to escape from the ironclad assumptions

about these matters that prevail in the Japanese critical climate, it is necessary to belabor the point, as one would not feel obliged to do when speaking of such Western personal novelists as the Lawrence of *Sons and Lovers,* say, or Proust. And so it will be useful to refer to Shiga's recurring protagonist in all cases (except for two early, openly confessional stories) as the Shiga hero, to distinguish this persona, alter ego, surrogate, etc., from Shiga's "real self," who is unknowable.

We recognize the Shiga hero precisely because his inner identity is always shifting. He is most often portrayed in the act of transforming his view of himself, of others close to him and of his immediate surroundings, social and natural. But the reader comes to discern certain patterns in these subjective transformations and, in large outline, a kind of cycle that recurs with inexorable regularity.

There are of course numerous subordinate characters, who are revealed to us from the hero's point of view and who take on a provisional reality through him. Also vivid images and wonderfully spare settings, often drawn from the realms of dreams and nature, which sometimes fulfill roles as important as the characters'. But it is first and foremost the single figure of the Shiga hero, both constant and protean, that gives some unity to the individual works and the entire œuvre. We come to depend on him for our bearings in the often amorphous world of Shiga's fiction.

Hiroaki Sato (essay date 1987)

SOURCE: "The Knife Thrower's Bad Aim," in *The New York Times Book Review,* April 5, 1987, p. 16.

[*In the following review, Sato offers a favorable assessment of Shiga's collection* The Paper Door and Other Stories.]

Naoya Shiga (1883-1971) was once described as "a god of fiction." Such an accolade might be a little excessive, even if the characterization were confined to his country, Japan. But he did write a number of short stories that are nearly perfect in their simplicity, directness and mastery of subject matter.

Take **"The Razor."** It begins: "Yoshisaburo, of the Tatsudoko in Azabu-Roppongi, a man almost never ill, took to his bed with a very bad cold. The Festival of the Autumn Equinox being close at hand, it was a very busy time for his barbershop." Yoshisaburo has a well-earned reputation for honing razors and shaving. He takes pride in these skills. So, when a regular customer sends a maid to leave a razor to be sharpened, Yoshisaburo is both unable to decline the request and unwilling to let either of his two new apprentices do the work. In his feverish state, and despite his wife's worried admonitions, he struggles to strop the razor in his bed. The maid picks up the razor but late in the evening returns it as not adequately sharpened. Awakened from his sleep, Yoshisaburo stubbornly tries to sharpen the razor once again. Just then, a young man, on his way to have fun at a nearby brothel, drops by for a quick shave. The senior apprentice is already out to see a girl in the neighborhood. The story unfolds inexorably, with mounting tension, and ends in a blood-letting. It is a masterpiece.

"Han's Crime" is told equally well. Again, the story opens with a few effective sentences: "In an unusual incident, a young Chinese juggler called Han severed his wife's carotid artery during a performance with a knife the size of a carver. The young wife died on the spot. Han was immediately arrested." This opening is followed by two brief paragraphs describing Han's knife-throwing performance before an audience of 300. Then the story moves abruptly to a courtroom, where the judge interrogates three men. First comes the owner-manager of the troupe with which Han performs. He is asked if throwing large knives at a board 12 feet away to form an outline of someone standing in front of it is "particularly difficult." He says he doesn't think it is for a performer with "experience [and] instinctive skill." In that case, was what happened "a deliberate act"? No, he doesn't think so, because every performance cannot be expected to come off "with a machinelike precision."

Next comes the stagehand who has known Han and his wife since they joined the troupe. He is asked about their personalities. He says Han is a gentle soul, a recent Christian convert who not long ago began reading collections of sermons in English (in his youth, Mr. Shiga studied Christianity intensely with the famous Christian teacher Kanzo Uchimura). Han's wife was a good person, too. But, the stagehand adds, they weren't getting along well since the death of their baby shortly after birth. Finally, it is Han's turn. His testimony, which takes up the rest of the story, is straightforward, but searching and intelligent. In the end, as he completes his testimony, he becomes a liberated man. Here, Mr. Shiga constructs a psychological drama that is extraordinary in the simplicity of its narrative structure and in the depth of its intellectual honesty.

Another well-told story is **"The Shopboy's God,"** a tale of a chance encounter between a poor shopboy who craves the tasty tuna sushi he can't afford and an aristocrat who craves the same thing but can't muster the courage to go to a cheap restaurant patronized by commoners. The story ends in a manner akin to John Fowles's *French Lieutenant's Woman,* though in a far less portentous fashion; here the author intrudes to suggest an alternative ending but withdraws it.

> **Shiga's stress on being truthful, emotionally or otherwise, at times makes his stories uncomfortably confessional.**
>
> —*Hiroaki Sato*

In spite of such masterfully told stories, calling Mr. Shiga the "god of fiction" could be misleading, because much of

the literature he created is heavily autobiographical. As he explained in a note on his only novel, *A Dark Night's Passing,* Mr. Shiga's main concern was the plausibility of his characters as measured against his own self. It was also the predominant concern of most Japanese writers of serious fiction in the early part of this century, when he began writing; these writers were interested in establishing a "modern self."

Mr. Shiga's effort to be true to himself makes some of his stories read like excerpts from a diary or personal, reflective accounts. Of the 17 stories in *The Paper Door,* all of them rendered competently into English by Lane Dunlop, at least six fall in this category. In fact, one is even dated precisely; it ends with the sentence, "This incident took place on October 16, 1945." Entitled **"A Gray Moon,"** it tells of the narrator's encounter with a young man on the brink of starvation on a crowded train.

Mr. Shiga's stress on being truthful, emotionally or otherwise, at times makes his stories uncomfortably confessional. **"A Memory of Yamashina"** and **"Infatuation"** are his attempts to recount, without much effort to dramatize it, his affair with a young woman and its effect on his wife. When he did try to fictionalize the affair—as in **"Kuniko,"** another story contained in this anthology—the result was rather inept. No wonder his wife is said to have refused to read his work after **"Kuniko."**

However, Mr. Shiga's brand of realism also produced several superb vignettes. **"As Far as Abashiri,"** a description of the author's brief acquaintance with a young mother traveling to the northern end of Japan on a train, and **"At Kinosaki,"** a meditative piece on the meanings of death, are justly celebrated.

Edward Fowler (essay date 1988)

SOURCE: "Shiga Naoya: The Hero as Sage," in *The Rhetoric of Confession: Shishōsetsu in Early Twentieth-Century Japanese Fiction,* University of California Press, 1988, pp. 187-247.

[*In the following excerpt, Fowler surveys Shiga's novellas, particularly* Wakai. *He then goes on to contend that Shiga "depopulates" his fiction, showing his main characters in relative isolation in order to better explore the nature of personal experience.*]

Both the power and the limitations of Shiga's confessional rhetoric are revealed perhaps most plainly in the "*Wakai* trilogy" (*Wakai sanbusaku*): *Ōtsu Junkichi* (*Ōtsu Junkichi,* 1912), *Wakai* (*Reconciliation,* 1917), and *Aru otoko, sono ane no shi* (*A certain man and the death of his sister,* 1920). It is united loosely by the theme of the hero's troubled relationship with his father. In *Ōtsu Junkichi,* the first-person narrator (a would-be writer) chronicles his ambivalent feelings toward his friend's sister, his special relationship with his grandmother, who raised him since he was an infant, and finally his unsuccessful attempt to marry a housemaid in the face of family opposition. The father remains in the background, although his presence is continually felt—most keenly when the narrator discovers that he was behind the maid's removal from the house. In *Wakai* the father again is very much in the background until the end. The first-person narrator merely informs the reader of a long estrangement without dwelling on the causes; his concern is rather with his own efforts to write about the estrangement. The reconciliation, initiated by the narrator's ritualistic apology, comes so abruptly that reader is not wholly convinced by the claim that it will last. It is only with *Aru otoko,* narrated by the Shiga hero's younger brother, that the reader gains some insight into the nature of the conflict, although he is encouraged by its fictional veneer (obvious to anyone even casually acquainted with the oeuvre) to disregard the content as autobiographical truth. This attempt by an author to guide the reading of a text as fiction is a crucial issue. . . .

A few comments about the trilogy's other two narratives are in order before we begin our discussion of *Wakai.* *Ōtsu Junkichi* was the first Shiga story to be published in a large-circulation, general-interest magazine (as well as the first for which he, at age twenty-nine, received payment); nearly all Shiga's previous stories had appeared in the coterie magazine *Shirakaba.* Not only was it a daring story for its time, thematizing a young man's rebellion (albeit a largely fruitless one) against family oppression, it was instrumental in making available the Shiga style to a wide audience. Ozaki Kazuo, one of Shiga's first disciples, discovered the story in 1916 and later had this to say about it:

> If I had not read *Ōtsu Junkichi,* I might never have become a writer. . . . It taught me that a *shōsetsu,* which I had thought of only as an entertaining mixture of fact and fiction, need not be that at all, and that if one had a grievance against one's father, then one should be bold enough to air it. . . . The language also took me by surprise. I had never encountered its like before. It was as though nothing came between the reader and the events described. . . . Reading this and other of Shiga's stories, I found that language actually disappears when it performs its function flawlessly.

Ozaki articulates here what has been suggested throughout this study: the *shōsetsu's* mission is to tell the "truth" about lived experience. Ozaki further argues that Shiga's language is particularly qualified to tell the truth, because it can convey the author's message, unadulterated, through a supposedly transparent medium. The cult of sincerity has already firmly taken hold. Honda Shūgo, comparing *Ōtsu Junkichi* with Sōseki's *Sore kara* (*And then,* 1909), which also treats a generational clash between father and son, concedes the novelistic superiority of the latter but claims that Shiga succeeds, especially in the story's second half, in removing the fictional "barriers" that separate reader and hero in Sōseki's text. "*Sore kara* enlightens the reader with its culture and insight," Honda concludes, "but *Ōtsu Junkichi* is the story that moves him."

The suggestion here of course is that Shiga's transparent, "fictionless" language of the heart comes through to the reader in a way that Sōseki's rational, "fictional" language cannot. Honda never tells us just how he distinguishes between the two languages, but it is clear that the styles of the two texts differ in fundamental ways. There is an ill-defined relationship between the hero as actor and as observer in *Ōtsu Junkichi* that undercuts any analytical or ironic perspective. The letter to a friend that ends the story (dated 30 August 1907), while providing an outlet for the hero's pent-up rage against his father, offers no background whatsoever to the generational conflict. The hero gives us no assessment, moreover, of the intervening five years between the story time and the narrative present, which would appear to coincide with the year of publication (1912). The lack of clues about the hero's present attitude leads us to believe that the hero has some reason to suppress it, although such an argument of course makes little sense in the context of a "fictionalized" narrative.

Ōtsu Junkichi, then, the story that immortalized Shiga's "rebellion" against his father, contains in fact little more than a few angry words about an apparition that readers never come to know. Most of the hero's rebellious behavior is aimed at his grandmother, whom he "loves and yet cannot help despising" for being such a dominant force in his life. The text is important, however, if only because it introduces us to the conflicting emotions with which the Shiga hero struggles so mightily in *Wakai.*

A word also on *Aru otoko,* which is easily the most penetrating statement in the trilogy on what Shiga calls "the riddle that the existence of a father poses to his son." Yet it has never been as highly regarded as the other two stories. Criticism of it invariably takes the form that one scholar voices when he acknowledges the narrator's disinterested appraisal of both the Shiga hero and his father but concludes that this very aloofness deprives the story of the poignancy and stark sense of reality so manifest in *Wakai.* Another scholar puts it even more succinctly: unlike *Ōtsu Junkichi* and *Wakai, Aru otoko* is "made up" (*tsukurareta shōsetsu*).

It is one thing for a literary scholar to conclude that a story is "made up," but Shiga has a way of letting even a casual reader know he has crossed the autobiographical line into the realm of "fabrication." He cues the reader, by fictionalization of the more obvious sort, to expect a retelling of the father-son conflict that, however incisive, cannot incriminate the real-life models. Once he has done so, he is then free to make his penetrating and sometimes devastating analysis of the conflict.

Shiga takes great pains to insure that the distance he imposes between subject and real-life model is plain for all to see. First, conscious perhaps that a mere switch from first- to third-person narrator will not sufficiently distance the hero, given the easy identification of *kare* with *watakushi,* he employs a separate first-person narrator (the hero Yoshiyuki's younger brother) to relate the story of his fictional alter ego. Second, he presents the hero in ways that often contradict previous portrayals. For example, Yoshiyuki in *Aru otoko* has an elder sister (and a brother-in-law who causes a scandal in his father's business), while the narrator-hero in *Ōtsu Junkichi* and *Wakai* has none. Yoshiyuki's mother dies when he is eight, while the narrator's mother in **"Haha no shi to atarashii haha"** (**"The death of my mother and my new mother,"** 1912) dies when the narrator is twelve. Yoshiyuki injures himself seriously when he falls out of a tree during an excursion to the country and recovers in Yugawara, a spa on the Pacific coast, while the narrator of **"Kinosaki nite"** (**"At Kinosaki,"** 1917) is injured when he is hit by a train in Tokyo and recovers in Kinosaki, a spa on the Japan Sea coast. Yoshiyuki and his father never achieve a reconciliation, while the hero in *Wakai* does. The list goes on.

It is the author's hope, one suspects, that the reader, recognizing that many incidents in *Aru otoko* do not agree with what he knows about the Shiga hero from earlier, more "authentic" accounts, will not equate the relationship between father and son, as it is somewhat harshly depicted in this text, with the actual one between the real-life models. In particular, by composing a tragic conclusion that obviously contradicts the "facts" as they are recorded in *Wakai*, Shiga hints that the bitter confrontations leading up to the hero's permanent departure from home are also mere figments of the author. Whether or not they are in fact is beside the point. The hidden message of *Aru otoko* is that they are, and the reader is less inclined to ascribe even those segments that are not blatantly "false" (insofar as they do not contradict previous narratives) to specific events or circumstances in the author's life. "Fabrication" and the distance it imposes, it would seem, is indispensible for truly cogent character analysis in Shiga's autobiographical fiction. And yet, as *Wakai*'s success makes abundantly clear, such analysis is not nearly as highly prized as the sense of authorial presence generated by the latter text.

Aru otoko is not without its limitations as a fictional text. A long parenthetical commentary that the narrator makes on one of his brother's letters is headed by a curious remark: "The author comments:" (*sakusha iu*). It is surely significant that the "speaker" here identifies himself not as the younger brother (*otōto iu*) or as "this writer" (*hissha iu*) but as "the author" and that he does so, moreover, in the plain, uninflected verb form, the only such use in the entire story. It is hard to believe that this self-conscious expression is a mere slip of the pen. Shiga had opportunities to make corrections when he anthologized the story, first serialized in a newspaper, in later editions of his writings. More likely, it is an example of Shiga's unwillingness to suppress completely his consciousness of the composition process in the interest of establishing an autonomous fictional time. Foregrounding the narrator's consciousness of writing rather then letting the drama unfold is of course a trademark of Shiga's and many other *shishōsetsu* writers' prose. It is indeed one of the conventions that gives the *shishōsetsu* its aura of authenticity. More than any event depicted in the fictive time frame, the simple refrain, "I now write," is the single most important statement that Shiga as author can make. This same attitude surely informs the ending of **"Kozō no kamisama."** At certain crucial points in Shiga's writing, then,

narrative representation takes second place to the recorder's self-conscious presentation of himself in the process of writing. This consciousness is most fully realized in *Wakai*.

Although *Wakai* is considered a sequel to *Ōtsu Junkichi,* a ten-year hiatus separates the events described in the two works. The narrator in *Wakai,* moreover, writes of a reconciliation that has just taken place (and of certain events preceding it), whereas the narrator in *Ōtsu Junkichi* writes of an estrangement as it stood in the (apparently) distant past. We have noted the unexplained gap between the narrator as actor and the narrator as recorder in *Ōtsu Junkichi*; in *Wakai* the two roles intertwine. We can only assume that the *Ōtsu Junkichi* narrator has actually become the writer he says he aspired to be; the *Wakai* narrator's professional status, meanwhile, is clear from the beginning. Indeed it soon becomes evident that the *Wakai* narrator has staked his writing career on the outcome of the events he describes. He is so obsessed with recording his relationship with his father that we cannot help viewing the reconciliation, which ends a decade-long rift, as a professional as much as a moral necessity.

Wakai chronicles four visits that the narrator-hero (also named Junkichi) makes from his home in Abiko, outside Tokyo, to his father's home in the city in 1917, from 31 July (the anniversary of his first daughter's death) to 30 August (the anniversary of his mother's death and the day of reconciliation). It concludes with his completion of a manuscript, inspired by recent events, in mid-September. This six- or seven-week period makes up the story's narrative time frame and it literally frames the story, occupying the first two and last six chapters. The intervening eight chapters, which bisect the four visits, chronicle incidents in previous years related to the hero's conflict with his father and his futile efforts to write about them, as well as the death of one infant daughter and birth of another. A third time frame, mentioned perfunctorily at the very end, sets the manuscript's composition time during the first half of September; it thus overlaps the final two weeks of the story's first narrative frame.

We are obliged to dwell at first on certain shortcomings and inconsistencies in *Wakai,* but we must ultimately acknowledge the spell that it undeniably casts over its readers. In order to understand more fully Shiga's verbal sorcery, we shall look beyond the story's thematic content (which Masamune Hakuchō describes with some justification as a sentimental tearjerker the likes of which might appear in any popular magazine) to its singular mode of presentation. Nakamura Mitsuo has written that readers of Shiga can be divided into two groups: believers and nonbelievers. This is an apt description, however ironic in intent, of the hold Shiga's prose has over its admirers. Nakamura goes on to suggest that the "believers" engage in a simple act of faith when they recognize Shiga "the man" behind his writing, but we must emphasize that this faith springs from a clearly (although perhaps not readily) identifiable technique of presentation that we have referred to as his "invisible" style, without which no myth of authorial presence would arise.

Although Shiga's brand of realism is founded on this distinctive "presence" and on a narrative that seemingly parallels the ebb and flow of life, we find in *Wakai* a number of curiously improbable events that might well have no place in a story that strictly conformed to the laws of verisimilitude: the hero's "conversation" with his dead grandfather during a visit to the family cemetery, the imagined reconciliation with his father described as part of an unfinished composition, and the hallucinatory sighting of his father hurrying away from the Tokyo house to avoid meeting him (just as he had once contemplated leaving his Kyoto house before his father made an unwelcome visit two years earlier). The impact of these unusual, even eerie, scenes would be greatly lessened were they not grounded in the utter reality of the narrator's seemingly corporeal "presence" in the text.

Of the conflict itself, *Wakai* offers extensive yet guarded treatment. We get neither the hero's case against the father nor the father's against the hero, in contrast to, say, Kafka's *Letter to His Father,* in which we get both. The hero depicts the rift to the last as a clash of roles rather than personalities. Juxtaposed with two other episodes in which human will plays but a small role—the death of one daughter and the birth of the other—the rift becomes a kind of fait accompli, much like a natural catastrophe or an act of God, or simply part of the landscape. Shiga met with criticism early on for his failure to probe in any depth the breach between father and son. But he casts his work in a way that militates against an in-depth analysis of the breach. The hero is the Shiga persona, bound by the author's self-imposed rules of propriety and by the image delineated in previous texts. The author clearly feels a responsibility to that image and not to the full disclosure of his private life. The details of the discordant father-son relationship remain part of the impenetrable core behind the hero's facade of candor.

Yet a contradictory urge to tell all, which the hero continually suppresses, pervades *Wakai*. Again and again he counters this urge by deferring to a moral code, calculated to exhibit the author-sage's integrity and with it the rightness of the story itself, which effectively sabotages outright confession. We learn in the second chapter, for example, that the hero must turn in a manuscript to a certain magazine by 19 August for publication the following month. Although determined to write about his father, he finds the task far more difficult than he ever imagined.

> I was on very bad terms with Father. This was a product in part, no doubt, of the complex tangle of emotions that divides any father and son, but I believed that my enmity arose from a fundamental discord between us. I did not hesitate to speak ill of him to others. I could not bring myself, however, to show my hostility on paper. I did not wish to give public vent to my private grudge. Not only would I then feel sorry for him, I feared that doing so would tarnish my writing.

With less than a week left, the hero finally abandons his project and dashes off an "imaginary" story he planned to have published a month later in another magazine.

"I did not wish to give public vent to my private grudge." The narrator's message, repeated like a refrain a number of times in the story, is clear: writing from the "imagination" is easy; telling the "truth" is difficult. Shiga is betting, one feels, that the refrain requires no explanation, that the reader will be satisfied merely with the hero's "candid" admission of his inability to be completely candid about his personal affairs. To display sincerity while suppressing the story: Shiga observes this formula to the end.

In the next chapter, the hero recalls with chagrin the words of his father in reference to himself: "Never again will I shed a tear for that rogue, no matter what happens to him." He further recalls that "a certain attitude" he had adopted toward his father precipitated this grim remark and that he cannot blame his father for feeling the way he did. The hero gives the reader no further details; yet is it not this very reticence that underwrites Shiga's acclaimed "realism"? By implying that any further revelation will be extremely awkward, the narrator-hero makes the best possible case for his own honesty and for the story's authenticity. If his tale were indeed a mere invention, the reader might well reason, the hero could just as easily flaunt as hide such painful incidents, since, as fictions, they would lose their capacity to incriminate. In a literary culture that defined realism specifically in terms of authorial "presence" rather than in terms of verisimilitude, Shiga actually gained more credibility by making a show of reticence than he ever would have by making a "full" confession, which would in any event always run the risk of criticism for being incomplete.

Having used his "imagination" as a stopgap, the hero once again confronts the task of completing his previously abandoned manuscript in time for the next deadline, only a month later than the first. Once again he rejects the temptation to tell all and merely comments on the dangers of making revelations not thoroughly pondered beforehand.

> When writing about actual events, I was often sorely tempted to put down everything I could think of. All sorts of incidents would come to mind, and I would want to record every last one of them. All were in fact connected in some way with my subject. Yet . . . I would inevitably encounter difficulties when trying to link them together and end up . . . having to cut out most of what I had wished to write about. This was especially true when it came to writing about Father. I could not begin to chronicle all the bitter arguments we had had.

This one brief passage would seem to overturn the thesis, argued by so many commentators, that Shiga's writings exemplify the unity of art and life. Indeed, . . . the unity of life and art for Shiga actually means the death of art. For what is the narrator saying here if not that the gap between them is in fact unbridgeable? The author-sage is nothing if not a disciplined editor who is alert to the dangers of his profession. Thus, he recognizes the futility of recording all that he has experienced and the necessity of arranging what is left after "cutting out" the rest. Shiga's sincerity under these circumstances can never mean "candor"; at most it implies a recognition of his own vagueness and is necessarily one step removed from the spontaneity we normally associate with the word. The author presents it to us as a locked vessel that contains however no secrets, only the enigma of itself.

At the middle of *Wakai* comes a well-known section in which the narrator considers his past attempts to write about his father. Its central position is no accident, one feels, for it marks a turning point in the hero's consciousness. It deserves quoting at length.

> I don't know how many times in the last half dozen years I planned a story about the breach with Father, but the plans ended in failure every time. . . . I would always lose heart when I thought of the tragedy in real life that its publication would inevitably cause. I became especially distraught when I imagined the dark shadow it would cast on relations with Grandmother. When I was in Matsue three years ago, I composed a long narrative in hopes of keeping just such a tragedy from befalling me. . . . My object in writing down every unpleasant incident that could possibly occur between me and Father was to prevent them from actually happening. . . . In the climactic scene . . . I imagined father and son coming to blows at last, and I pondered the matter of who would kill whom. But then, at the height of these imagined hostilities, an entirely different scene suddenly appeared before my eyes in which the two of them embraced each other and burst into tears. . . .

> I elected not to use this conclusion, however. It was not something to be decided on in advance. There was no telling how things would end until my writing had actually progressed that far. How wonderful it would be, though, I thought, if things would really turn out that way by so writing.

> . . . I commenced writing, but made little headway. . . . Still I could not help feeling that the denouement I had conjured up, almost unconsciously, would someday actually unfold between Father and myself. I thought it entirely possible for such a scene to occur at a time when relations between us had reached their lowest ebb. I could not be sure, of course. Yet even if there was no telling how things would end until I had reached that point myself, I believed that there dwelt in both Father and me something that could effect just such a complete turnabout. I said as much to my wife and to a friend.

This incantatory passage foreshadows, of course, the final reconciliation. It also voices the narrator's extremely complex position on the relationship between life and art, which, as posited here, harbors an insoluble dilemma. The hero wishes to prevent unpleasant incidents from happening between him and his father by writing them down beforehand, as if to cast a salutary spell on their relations. This formula proves unworkable, however. When he actually puts pen to paper, he finds that he makes little headway. He rationalizes his decision not to resolve the conflict in advance by arguing that "there was no telling how things would end until my writing had actually progressed

that far." But in fact he cannot complete the story that he claims only needs writing down to turn out as planned. Clearly, imagination is not enough. The hero must be guided by experience. He can only hope that the scene he conjured up three years earlier will one day take place; perhaps *then* he can write about it. Thus the subtle but unmistakable change of focus in the last paragraph. What he at first says about his story—that "there was no telling how things would end *until my writing had actually progressed that far*"—in fact holds true for his own life: "there was no telling how things would end *until I had reached that point myself.*" He can neither write nor act, and he is left with telling others close to him about the imagined denouement, as if to prevent it from dissipating completely. Having failed to turn art into life, he must wait for life to progress to the stage where it can someday serve his art.

Thwarted in his efforts to address the conflict in a fictional retelling, the hero later attempts to address it more directly in a letter to his father. The attempt is, however, doomed from the start, because his feelings are still too unstable to be pinned down by words. The failure to set down his all too volatile emotions on paper proves to be a blessing in disguise, however, since it prompts him to meet with his father face to face and to let emotions take him where they may. He is no longer bent on appealing to reason, as there are, he discovers, no "reasons," no natural explanation, for the rift.

The hero has already attempted to reason with his father some eighteen months or so earlier. Although this attempt presages in some ways the later, successful reconciliation (it features the same preliminaries, such as nervous instructions from his stepmother on how to behave, and the same somber exchange between the two principals), it ends in complete failure. Rationally speaking, he is not at fault and therefore has no reason to feel contrite, and he says so to his father, only to be promptly dismissed from the house. During his 30 August visit, he wisely airs his grievances to his stepmother in a kind of dress rehearsal before confronting his father. She asks him to put reason aside, to forget just this once who is to blame for the past and simply say that he is sorry. The hero resists at first, but then decides, as he did in the case of his aborted manuscript, that it is impossible to plan the outcome in advance. "Emotions have a momentum of their own," he tells his stepmother. "Who knows, I might find myself less hostile than I had anticipated."

Life has now indeed progressed to the stage where it can serve art: the hero having given up his attachment to reason, the long-awaited reconciliation can take place in all its formality and ceremony. And once it has transpired, his urge to finish the story begun in Matsue withers away. Now he must find something else to write about in time for the mid-September deadline. That "something else" turns out to be this very story, which he begins soon after.

We have noted the criticism Shiga received for avoiding any frank discussion of the breach. Shiga was by no means unaware of the criticism and rebutted it on several occasions. . . . Defending *Wakai* in an essay entitled "Kuchi-biru ga samui" (1922), he emphasizes that his purpose was to describe the joy of the reconciliation, rather than to dwell on unharmonious familial relations.

> *Wakai* does not focus on a "theme"; it is the product of a more direct, immediate inspiration. That is its strength, and that is what appeals to readers. . . . *The best thing about it is that simply recording the facts, without alteration or embellishment, has made it a work of art.* . . . I noted more than once right in the story that I could not begin to chronicle the cause of the discord. . . . Do the critics simply not understand how I felt? They ask why I failed to explain the causes. I ask the critics: how was I able to depict the reconciliation so well without even mentioning them? (emphasis added).

Effective the story may be—but not because the author has somehow succeeded in "recording the facts, without alteration or embellishment." Shiga's essay overlooks entirely the narrator's function as editor, self-charged, as is pointed out in the story itself, with the responsibility of "cutting out" the many potentially embarrassing incidents he might have recorded indiscriminately.

In an unpublished manuscript, Shiga further denounces critics who regard his reticence as a defect:

> How odd, I thought. They refuse to understand my silence about the causes of the estrangement even though they know that author and hero are one and the same person.

> I realized only too well that, in chronicling the reconciliation, I would first have to suffer the pain of recording the estrangement. That was only logical. And yet I could not bring myself to write about its causes. I simply couldn't. So I wrote instead about the violence of the breach. And I think that the story succeeded on those terms.

Even here, in a manuscript that never saw the light of print, Shiga is curiously reticent about his reticence. He regards the right to silence as natural and conceives of the writer and the reader of a *shishōsetsu* as bound by a special contract. Shiga implies that the reader, recognizing the author-hero equation and dutifully respecting the feelings of those close to the author, should not ask the latter to probe too deeply into personal matters that would only cause embarrassment to himself and his family.

The author who tells his readers to limit their expectations, however, is guilty of a double standard. He invites the reader into his world while leaving the door only half open, insisting that the reader identify with him uncritically. Of course, this is easier to do when, as is the case in *Wakai,* he elects not to question the moral position of either side in a dispute. It is no coincidence that the estrangement between father and son, presented without explanation in *Wakai,* is more akin to a motiveless act, resembling a natural calamity over which the hero has no control and for which he cannot be censured. Any concern

about the characters' motivations is misguided, the author seems to reason, since those motivations were never subjected to any moral scrutiny in the first place. The author is interested only in the hero's reaction to events, and he employs the variety of strategies we have noted to lead the reader's interest in the same direction as his own.

Those who do not accept the recorder-witness contract as Shiga defines it will no doubt feel deprived of the human interaction that forms the core of fictional narrative in the west. And yet, even though it lacks any truly dramatic confrontation, *Wakai* has the power to move its readers, as many critics attest, when it describes an event that can indeed be thought of as a natural calamity: namely, the sudden and fatal illness of the hero's infant daughter, described in the work's fifth and sixth chapters. Masamune Hakuchō notes that even Shiga, whose writing, he claims, normally exudes a certain dilettantism, manages to convey extreme tension when he stands at the crossroads of destiny and confronts so grave an event as the death of his child. We are reminded once again of the importance to literature of the Buddhist articulation of man's subordination to the forces of nature: the four "trials" of birth, aging, sickness, and death (*shō-rō-byō-shi*). The question of character or personality or will would seem irrelevant to experience in which personal volition is of no account. This "digression," which one critic likens to the large, tumorlike growth commonly seen on cherry- or pine-tree trunks, makes a greater impact on the reader than the final reconciliation scene does. Here, because of their utter futility, personalized emotions are out of place, and in their stead is the more generalized pathos of the human condition. The same holds true for the tenth chapter, added when *Wakai* first appeared in book form, which describes the birth of the hero's second daughter. These segments succeed precisely because they treat events on which the conflict of character has no bearing, as it finally must on a confrontation between father and son. They succeed so well, in fact, that one is tempted to conclude that *Wakai* treats birth and death more significantly than it does the hero's celebrated rift.

The segments take on an unexpected importance, moreover, because the author has succumbed to the influence of traditional narrative. What might have been edited out in the interest of emplotment is here left to gather its own momentum, as if in defiance of an overall unity. The narrator chronicles the baby's illness with no hint of the outcome, with the result that the narrative "present" regresses to a period conterminous with the events themselves. The reader is inexorably drawn in. In chapter 6, the narrator informs readers that the child died before he actually describes her death, but the announcement, again in defiance of plot, seems intended expressly to defuse the tension that has built up during the course of the previous and by far the story's longest chapter.

Because the narrative denies readers a panoramic perspective and draws them into the time frame of "recollected" events in the eight middle chapters, one feels as if far more than a week has elapsed between the story time in chapter 2 (16 August) and that in chapter 11 (23 August).

There is no particular sense of pastness about events in the presumably "retrospective" chapters or of presentness about the more recent events narrated in chronological order in chapters 1-2 and 11-16. The reader experiences crises as they are remembered, sharing the hero's emotional highs and lows with little anticipation of a final denouement. Although the reconciliation remains the high point in **Wakai,** it is finally but one of several climactic moments that punctuate the text. One event does not have priority over another in the way one might expect in a conventionally emplotted narrative. As one scholar suggests, the structure of **Wakai** recalls an *uta monogatari,* with its alternating prose passages providing a background for poems that vary the emotional intensity without necessarily leading the narrative anywhere.

We noted earlier in our discussion that Shiga purposefully casts **Wakai** in such a way as to defy an in-depth analysis of the breach. From the very beginning, the hero is at pains to demonstrate that no appeal to reason will resolve it, since it is itself rooted in wildly contradictory emotions that the hero is at a loss to grasp or describe—thus, the difficulties he encounters composing his long story and later writing to his father.

Once we understand this, queries about the father-son conflict as depicted in **Wakai** lose their relevance. It is precisely because the rift has no clearly definable causes that no premeditated action can bring about a reconciliation. Narrative fiction's inexorable logic of cause and effect is replaced in **Wakai** by juxtapositions of the rage and sympathy that the hero feels toward his father, the one seemingly inciting the other, throughout the text. That rift and reconciliation are rooted in the same tumultuous cluster of emotions, requiring no change of heart and therefore no atonement, is apparent from the hero's awareness of his own conciliatory feelings in the midst of his deepest anger. In the text's opening pages, before his first furtive visit to the Tokyo house on 31 July, the hero visits his daughter's grave in the family plot in nearby Aoyama. There, in the story's most intimate and startling scene, he "converses" with the spirit of his deceased grandfather, asking him whether he should visit the house to see his ailing grandmother. The encouraging answer that wells up in his heart surprises the hero both for its spontaneity and for its complete lack of reproach toward a man for whom the hero thought he felt only hatred. The confusion of emotions is also apparent from the altogether gruff manner in which the hero "apologizes" to his father in chapter 13. In his excitement he speaks as if out of anger, despite the promise to his stepmother to behave civilly. Yet the tone is entirely natural, he insists. "Looking back on it, I believe that it was the only appropriate tone possible, given our relationship."

Shiga's seeming unwillingness to probe the conflict in depth paradoxically forced him to write what was surely a very different story than he had planned when first taking up his pen in early September, for it in fact focuses far more on the breach than on the reconciliation. In doing so, he has produced a form of writing similar to what we know in the west as a "self-begetting novel," in which the writ-

er's preoccupation with creating a story becomes itself the "story" one reads. Whether or not we wish to think of **Wakai** as a novel, there is no question of its affinity with a species of twentieth-century western fiction that treats its own production. The word "affinity" is used advisedly here, for the dissimilarities are perhaps more readily apparent than the similarities. (One has only to think of the divergent notions of self, time, space, and metaphysics in **Wakai** and, say, *Nausea,* to realize the vastly different fictive worlds that Junkichi and Roquentin inhabit.) Yet the bond unmistakably exists and is worthy of attention, as it will enable us to assign new meaning to the word "unique," which is so often attached to *shishōsetsu.* The author struggling to write and thematizing his very struggle: a rather commonplace subject in recent decades. In 1917, however, it was not, in Japan or the west. Shiga experimented gingerly with the subject; it would be left to Kasai Zenzō to bring it to fruition.

Let us reconsider **Wakai,** then, with this "affinity" in mind. We recall that the work comprises three time frames. It is the third time frame, mentioned ever so casually a few lines from the end, that gives us pause. Why must the hero inform his readers that he decided to record the reconciliation and include the writing of it as part of the narrative? It is because, as he suggests in the long reflective passage in chapter 7 quoted above, his relationship with his father is inseparable from the writing about it. We have seen that he cannot write at all about the rift without having achieved a reconciliation, yet he cannot achieve that reconciliation without having attempted to write about the rift. This dilemma of using art to solve the difficulties of life while at the same time waiting for life's experience to motivate his art can only be resolved by another paradox. The hero discovers, on the eve of reconciliation, that he can will neither the discord nor its resolution. He can only prepare himself mentally to accommodate both. The surprise ending to the rough draft described in chapter 7 materializes almost literally in chapter 13, not because he so designs it but because he finds himself at the mercy of *both* art and life. He cannot author his story according to a particular plan any more than he can live his life according to one. Indeed, success comes only when he forfeits the role of author and lets the writing—and events—take their own course. Writing, seemingly powerless to address the rift, becomes itself in due time the source of harmony. Thus, **Wakai** itself becomes as much the story of writing as it is the story of reconciliation.

With **Wakai** we realize that Shiga, for reasons of discretion and simply of temperament, had little interest in dramatic character interaction. And yet it is no less successful a text for that fact. Excepting such blatant attempts at fictionalization as **Aru otoko, sono ane no shi,** which allow him some freedom in analyzing human relations (although at the cost of forfeiting his hallmark of "sincerity"), Shiga typically dispenses with character analysis in favor of depopulating his stories, entirely. In fact, he seems to feel least constrained, psychologically and artistically, in settings inhabited only by himself, creatures of nature, and characters who appear, if at all, merely as part of the landscape. Only in such settings, virtually devoid of human society, does he seem truly at liberty to depict personal experience without compunction.

Such a strategy may be anathema to narrative fiction; yet it resulted in an important part of the Shiga oeuvre: the *shinkyō shōsetsu*, those (usually) brief sketches in which the author-sage explores his inner landscape in a setting virtually stripped of people and props. No celebration of self emerges from this most introspective of *shishōsetsu* forms, however. Isolated from society, the hero accommodates himself to forces in nature that reduce to insignificance the autonomous, individuated ego. It is ironic yet revealing of the so-called "I-novel" that its acknowledged master should have arrived at such an enigmatic view of self.

"Horibata no sumai" (1925) is typical of the *shinkyō shōsetsu* in that the hero appears on a nearly empty stage, engaging in only one very brief exchange with another character. The story describes an alley cat's raid on a neighbor's chicken coop and the cat's eventual capture and extermination. The narrator-hero sets the stage for solitary meditation in the very first sentence: "I lived alone one summer in Matsue." Exhausted by life in the city and by the constant dealings with people there, the hero resolves to lead an existence, at its most basic level, in the small provincial town of Matsue. Here his companions are "the insects and birds, the fish and the water, the grass and the sky—and, finally, other human beings." Over and above its depiction of a man who shuns active engagement with his surroundings, **"Horibata no sumai"** can be read as a metaphor for the Shiga hero's reluctance to become a dramatic character in his writing. The author-sage's brief encounter with the neighbor who owns the chicken coop is purely explanatory in function, a mere formal exchange. The chickens and their plight are at issue here, not the two people who converse.

Shiga seems to feel least constrained, psychologically and artistically, in settings inhabited only by himself, creatures of nature, and characters who appear, if at all, merely as part of the landscape. Only in such settings, virtually devoid of human society, does he seem truly at liberty to depict personal experience without compunction.

—Edward Fowler

An even purer example of the hero depicted in contemplative isolation is **"Kinosaki nite"** (**"At Kinosaki,"** 1917), which is in its own way a masterpiece. The story chronicles the author's three-week sojourn at a well-known spa on the Japan Sea coast after being hit by a train in Tokyo. During the course of his convalescence, the narrator-hero witnesses all varieties of death—natural, murderous, accidental—that affect the small creatures he happens to see:

a bee outside his inn window, a rat in a stream, a water lizard sunning itself on a rock. He communes solely with the natural world, and all other human beings recede into the background. Identifying to an extraordinary degree with the ego-denying forces of nature, he experiences something akin to total self-dissolution—not in any negative or nihilistic sense but in a very positive one, as several critics have noted, in which life is no longer opposed to death.

Reflecting on his accident while convalescing at Kinosaki, the hero faces an insoluble dilemma: how to cope with his mortality? If the occasion for a life-and-death struggle arises, should he yield to his new-found desire for self-extinction that results from a thoroughgoing identification with nature, or should he follow his animal instinct for self-preservation? The hero faces a dilemma of another sort as well: how to continue writing when recent experience has so wrenched him that he can no longer identify with his heroes' frames of mind? Thus he ponders, in addition to the future of his existence, the future of his attempts at narrative. Having written **"Han no hanzai"** (**"Han's crime,"** 1913), the story of a Chinese juggler's impulsive wife-slaying narrated from the juggler's point of view, he is now seized with the desire to write of the wife, dead and quiet in her grave, from the wife's point of view. "I would call the story 'The Murdered Wife of Han.' I never did write it, but the urge was there. I was dismayed to find, moreover, that my feelings had strayed very far from those of the hero of a long narrative I was writing."

The long narrative, of course, is *Tokitō Kensaku*, the precursor of *An'ya kōro* that Shiga finally abandoned, having found himself no longer in tune with his hero. It comes as no surprise, then, when we learn that Shiga's difficulty writing *Tokitō Kensaku* in fact resulted in the first of several fallow periods, which finally ended three years later with the publication of this very story. Shiga at last regains momentum as a writer by avoiding the familial conflicts that had plagued him and by depicting himself in **"Kinosaki nite"** as a totally isolated being. When all conflict is erased, the hero is at liberty to engage in the pensive musings that are the *shinkyō shōsetsu*'s core. As in **"Horibata no sumai,"** the hero sets the stage for solitary meditation in the very first sentence: "I . . . traveled alone to Kinosaki Hot Spring to convalesce." He is absorbed in himself and his immediate surroundings, his sensibility the measure of all things. Only on such a deserted stage, free from external challenges, does the Shiga hero fulfill most completely the role of sage. In a story without dialogue, the hero is already halfway to the world of eternal silence.

"Kinosaki nite" has little of the self-righteous tone that often mars Shiga's first-person narratives, however. One does not get the feeling that the hero has tried to manipulate his material simply to bolster his image as a moral arbiter; on the contrary, he gains credibility by refusing to rationalize his situation. Having quelled the desire to demonstrate his moral authority, he devotes himself to a much profounder exploration of experience, and in doing so emerges as a far more sympathetic character. The author-sage, now a truly noble figure, attains this heightened consciousness with surprising ease in **"Kinosaki nite."** He attains it with difficulty, but with even greater effect, in Shiga's only extended narrative, *An'ya kōro.*

Marilyn Jeanne Miller (essay date 1989)

SOURCE: A review of *The Paper Door and Other Stories,* in *World Literature Today,* Vol. 63, No. 1, Winter, 1989, p. 166.

[*In the review below, Miller admires the "truthfulness" of the pieces in this collection of Shiga's stories.*]

Shiga, a member of the White Birch Movement (*Shirakabaha*), which was the most articulate group of writers advocating realism in fiction, absorbed the tenets of Western realism and married it to traditional Japanese esthetics and subjects. Like Natsume Sōseki, Shiga was interested in the subtleties of human psychology and human relationships. His realism never degenerated into the excesses of the *watakushi-shōsetsu* or I-novel, because he was always aware of his craft, his own subjectivity, his own imagination, and their influence on the writing and the story it created. In Shiga's work, as aptly demonstrated in story after story in **The Paper Door,** there is a strong tension between the truth of experience and the truth that arises out of the storytelling, the act of creation, the writing's own logic.

Shiga's awareness of the complexity inherent in writing and telling a "realistic" story is what makes him a force in Japanese literary history.

—Marilyn Jeanne Miller

Always frank about the experiential basis for his stories, Shiga created in his fiction an authenticity that validates for any reader the reality of the author's perceptions. Still, it was Shiga himself who reminded the reader that although every writer is dependent on experiences for materials, it is "the depth with which a writer portrays that experience that is the issue." Shiga himself subtly reminds the reader of his own vision's limitations, the untrustworthiness of his story, which is its very fictionality. Take, for instance, the piece **"The Shopboy's God,"** which ends with the writer laying down his pen when "actually he'd thought of ending the story" another way; but "the writer came to feel that such an ending would be somewhat cruel to the shopboy." Offering an alternative ending is a rather common modern plot device, but in 1919 it was a bit more inventive. More to the point, such a statement, while showing the author's sense of the reality of his own characters, an almost Jamesian sense of a character's "life of his own," also reminds the reader

of the author's power over that character, of the creative process behind the story.

Based on Shiga's own observations of a shopboy, the tale convinces the reader easily as to its truthfulness; yet Shiga deliberately undercuts that naïveté in order to create in the reader a trust in the teller's sense of fitness about what should be told. Shiga's awareness of the complexity inherent in writing and telling a "realistic" story is what makes him a force in Japanese literary history.

Shigekazu Ando (essay date 1993)

SOURCE: "The Destiny of Hamlet in Modern Japan: Concerning *The Diary of Claudius* by Shiga Naoya," in *Comparative Literature Studies,* Vol. 30, No. 4, 1993, pp. 351-60.

[*In the essay below, Shigekazu suggests that Shiga's revision of Shakespeare's* Hamlet *in "The Diary of Claudius" illustrates significant differences between Japanese and Western literary modernism.*]

D. H. Lawrence writes on *Hamlet* in his brilliant essay *Twilight in Italy* (1916):

> I had always felt an aversion from Hamlet: a creeping, unclean thing he seems, on the stage, whether he is Forbes Robertson or anyone else. His nasty porking and sniffing at his mother, his setting traps for the King, his conceited perversion with Ophelia make him always intolerable. The character is repulsive in its conception, based on self-dislike and a spirit of disintegration.

Lawrence sees in *Hamlet* a thesis about corruption in the flesh and the individual's conscious revolt from it. It is this consciousness that makes Hamlet frenzied, for he cannot admit that his flesh is corrupted too. Thus, in this essay Lawrence interprets the theme of *Hamlet* as the struggle between the *being* of the flesh and the *not-being* of the spirit.

This interpretation came from Lawrence's impression of an Italian performance of the play he saw in Garda, Italy. The actor playing Hamlet, Enrico Persevalli, seems to have disappointed and exasperated Lawrence. We may pause to ask why. Is Lawrence's response positioned in modernism? And how? Does his aversion come from his feelings towards a typical young hero of the Western world? Hamlet is a prototype of the young heroes in modern European literature such as Julien Sorel, young Werther, and Raskolnikov. These heroes inherit the Greek tragic-heroic quality of Hamlet's prototype, Orestes. But the next generation, as seen from the example of Lawrence, tends to think of Hamlet as comical or farcical. From this tendency, Hamlet is deformed into various types of young men, every one of them an anti-hero, and anti-Hamlet.

Similar anti-heroism also appeared in Japan, as a response to the country's earliest complete presentation of Hamlet, amid the influence of intercultural exchanges between the Western world and that of Japan. Shiga Naoya presented the first example, and more were to come.

Shiga Naoya (1883-1971), one of the greatest Japanese novelists of modern times, wrote **"The Diary of Claudius"** in 1912. Claudius is, of course, Hamlet's antagonist in the tragedy. He is not the hero, but the anti-hero—a villain's part—in Shakespeare's *Hamlet*. But after he saw the play for the first time, Shiga reversed his sympathy. His response was so acute and persistent that before long he wrote **"The Diary."**

How Shiga came to relate to the tragedy he has told us himself. In 1911, at the grand opening of Teikoku Gekijo [The Imperial Theater], *Hamlet* was the premiere performance. The company was the Bungei Kyokai [The Literary Society], directed by Tsubouchi Shoyo, who was also the translator. So far *Hamlet* had been adapted and performed by various groups, such as the Women Player's Company at the Misakiza, the Kodanji's Company at the Meijiza, and the Bungei Kyokai at Misakiza. But now, for the first time, *Hamlet* was to be performed for the audience at full length. Even at this early stage, the tragedy of Hamlet had caught the attention of the Japanese public. Take, for example, Mori Ogai, who contributed numerous theatrical reviews to various publications. On reviewing Tsubouchi's play *Kiri Hitoha* [*A Paulownia Leaf*] in 1904, Ogai compared Hamlet's world view to that of Katagiri Katsumoto's and Ophelia's drowning to that of Kagero's. Undoubtedly, Hamlet was already recognizable as a heroic character by ordinary theater-goers of those days, and presumably by Shiga Naoya as well, even before he had seen the performance at Teikoku Gekijo.

This performance featured Doi Shunsho as Hamlet. Doi had a good career as a Shakespearean player. Five years before, he had played Hamlet with the same company and the same director. But the character of Hamlet ended up disgusting Shiga Naoya. Repelled by this disgust, Shiga sympathized with Claudius, played by Togi Tetteki. Shiga went on to read the play, translated by Tsubouchi Shoyo, very carefully, and the experience confirmed his conclusion that Hamlet's tragedy and heroism were baseless and irrelevant. Hence his **"Diary of Claudius."**

Writes Shiga in his "Sosaku Yodan" ["Reminiscences of My Writing Career"]:

> I consumed much labor in writing **"The Diary of Claudius."** I got the motive for writing it when seeing a *Hamlet* performed by Bungei Kyokai. So distasteful was the lightness (frivolousness) of Hamlet as played by Doi Shunsho that I was turned rather to sympathize with Claudius, played by Togi Tetteki. Moreover, I found that not a single objective piece of evidence concerning King Hamlet's murder exists in the play except for the words of the Ghost, which gave me another motive for writing my story. I had a lot of trouble making the work conform with the context of *Hamlet,* since my Claudius is derived from the play and I did not want to be at odds with it. I read Dr. Tsubouchi's translation of *Hamlet* very carefully. But

even this intense reading did not change my early opinion on Hamlet's character as represented by Doi Shunsho. Years later I saw a film featuring the English actor Forbes Robertson and it was then that I, for the first time, felt able to sympathize with Hamlet's feelings. To lose one's father and see one's mother remarried to an uncle one loathes, is enough for a sensitive young man to frame such a tragedy, as long as his imagination goes. Ophelia, pathetic in herself, lacks the strength to console Hamlet in his melancholy. Her femininity is certainly most impressive. Then I thought I could also write a "Diary of Hamlet," and actually started writing it while I live in Abiko—to no avail, though.

It is significant that Shiga, the representative novelist of modern Japan, rejected the characterization of Hamlet and accepted the one of Claudius. In their opposition there is an opposition of literary attitudes.

In another essay, "Concerning the Diary of Claudius,—to Funaki Shigeo-kn—," Shiga reveals that he wanted to assault *Hamlet,* for the play seemed to him rather comical or farcical. He thought that if he wrote the figure of Claudius from an anti-Hamlet perspective, it would be more realistic. Shiga wanted to write about his own feeling, rather than Hamlet's truth. In his essay, he explains that he wanted to express his own psychological experience. That is to say, in the **"Diary,"** Shiga uses Claudius's own feelings to describe his own inner psychology.

Below, I summarize Shiga's diary when he was writing **"The Diary of Claudius,"** between February 19 and October 7, 1912:

> *February 19* (Mon.) Saw Hamlet. [Bungei Kyokai's performance]

> *March 4* (Mon.) I was sort of resentful. Home around eleven p.m. Jotted down the following: There are two selves in me which are inclined to draw away from each other. Now I have to try to bring them as close as possible. If I leave them with this tendency as it is, it might in time become impossible to restore them anymore.

> "Keep going ahead, but no need to do much," I say to myself. Not doing much is all right. But when you don't go ahead at all and feel nonchalant about it, that's when things are going wrong. Eventually I must get far enough ahead of the others so that they cannot catch up with me, and grow big enough, too. I'll try with all my might in this "Hamlet."

> Perhaps the truth about my character is like this: I am able to allow two opposite things to harmonize inside me—though I may suffer from the contradiction sometimes. My reflective self, etc. Nevertheless, each of these two is as true as the other. And to let them harmonize mutually might as well mean to make them compromise with each other at the expense of distorting some reality of both sides, which is a debased thing to do. How horrible!

March 9 (Sat.)—Night, read *Hamlet.* To my great pleasure, I found that there are no objective grounds at all for the tragedy to exist. Let my "Claudius" be widely read, and the tragedy of Hamlet will turn out to be absolutely pointless. The audience would no longer take it seriously. Read till four o'clock, and to bed.

March 10 (Sun.) Finished reading *Hamlet,* I can feel no sympathy for young Hamlet at all. **"The Diary of Claudius"** will be my title. Let the content be governed by itself, I will write arbitrarily, without dates. I tried to write a little, but made little progress.

March 11 (Mon.) Started writing at 1:00 p.m., and finished three days' portion of **"The Diary of Claudius."** So I was very excited and had no sleep during the night.

March 14 (Thurs.)—Night, finished the primary plot of **"The Diary of Claudius."**

March 15 (Fri.)—Read the **"The Diary of Claudius"** to Mr. Arishima. Although nothing is disappointing about it, I need to rewrite it at least twice.

June 3 (Mon.)—Begin rewriting **"The Diary of Claudius"** at 1:00 a.m., finishing eight pages or so by daybreak. I am exhausted. To become a fairly good work, this one perhaps still needs another rewriting in a month or so.

June 4 (Tues.)—Home and finished the 2nd Impre. of **"The Diary of Claudius."**

August 3 (Sat.)—Read **"The Diary of Claudius."** May present it for publication in the September issue of *Shirakaba.*

August 16 (Fri.)—Night, wrote a little of **"Claudius."**

August 20 (Tues.)—Home to find what I had expected unexecuted and the door was locked, too. I was very angry. In such a mood I stayed up all night and almost finished **"Claudius."**

August 23 (Fri.) Finished **"The Diary of Claudius."**

August 27 (Tues.) Proofread most of **"Claudius."**

October 7 (Mon.)—My **Ōtsu Junkichi** is favorably received for its sincerity in a lot of reviews. **"Claudius"** is also generally approved.

In these diary entries, edited to reconstruct the details, we can see how Shiga suffered from the labor of composition. It took nine months.

Surveying these materials, we can connect **"The Diary of Claudius"** with **Ōtsu Junkichi,** Shiga's short novel. He worked on both simultaneously. The latter was going to develop into *Tokito Kensasku,* the original writing of *Anya Koro.* Therefore, the former work has a close relation with *Anya Koro,* and, hence, with **Wakai.**

Shiga Naoya wrote *Anya Koro* [*A Dark Night's Passing,* 1921-37], one of the masterpieces of modern Japanese literature. This is a story of a man's search for love and true human relationships outside the traditional Japanese family organization. *Anya Koro* presents the ideal of a moral life. One of its themes is mutual understanding and harmony between the individual and nature. If discord strikes, human beings should endeavor to reconcile relationships, especially that with nature. Since this is the most important problem in modern Japanese literature, *Anya Koro* is regarded as the highest peak of modern Japanese literature. Shiga was called *shosetsunokamisama* ("god of fiction") from the Taisho to the Showa periods, and remains one of the most revered of modern Japanese writers.

The Japanese Naturalists of the Meiji period with their theory of autobiographical writing present one of the central problems in the criticism of modern Japanese literature. The main question of their controversy was how to acquire the fictional techniques of the orthodox European novel. Most modern Japanese writers struggle to produce a European literature in their own land, language, nature, and climate. In particular, they strive to achieve individualism, egotism, and citizenship, in modern Western ideas. But the Western impact in the Meiji and Taisho periods was as strong as it was difficult to clarify. Western notions of love, freedom, the self, or literary utopias may be no less complicated when abruptly transplanted into Japanese literary culture than Eastern notions of quietism, social conformity, the not-self, or a "concrete" literature are when transplanted into the West.

What shall we say if we compare Tokito Kensaku, the hero of *Anya Koro,* with Hamlet? Hamlet is a product of the English Renaissance, but he is also the typical hero for European young men. Kensaku also is the young hero in the modern Japanese world and is essentially a universal figure. But there is a great difference of characterization. The difference reflects the large difference between the modern European and the modern Japanese worlds. To close the difference, Shiga cannot but reject Hamlet, the Western hero. But the difference between the two characters is also the difference between Japan and Western modernism, and in this sense Tokito Kensaku is the modern Japanese "Hamlet." What, then, is the essential difference between Shakespeare and Shiga?

To answer this question, let us compare the final scenes of *Hamlet* and *Anya Koto.* Each signifies the final solution to the thematic problems of its respective work. Hamlet, Claudius, Gertrude, and Laertes all die; but in Shakespeare's dramaturgy their deaths imply the restoration of order. By contrast, Tokito Kensaku, "the Eastern Hamlet," roves the sacred mountain and achieves a reconciliation between human beings and nature, which has been against his destiny. Obviously, while the clean sweep of destiny—or rather "bloody sweep"—solves Hamlet's problems, Shiga finds this idea unacceptable, even in the name of justice.

Reconciliation had been an abiding idea for Shiga since the beginning of his career. It is an idea fermented, as it were, by his experience of discord, though. For Shiga, discord occurred between the self and the patriarchal circle of Japanese family institutions. The discord is apparently, if not essentially, analogous to the one occurring in the case of the Danish royal family—namely, between Hamlet and Claudius. Strangely enough, the causes of discord in both cases are rather analogous, too. In Shiga's case, sometimes it is sexual and moral (in *Ōtsu Junkichi* and in *Anya Koro*); sometimes the discord is caused by patriarchal authority and public morality (in *Wakai*, in **"A Man and His Older Sister's Death"**); sometimes it is due to incest (in *Anya Koro*). In *Hamlet* these causes are fatal, but in Shiga they must be solved by reconciliation. It is thus only natural that Shiga should feel a strong aversion to Hamlet's psychology. He had to write **"The Diary of Claudius"** to produce an anti-Hamlet work, so that he might sustain his own truth within himself.

With "The Diary of Claudius," Shiga manifests his anti-heroism. This work was the forerunner of a series of Japanese anti-heroic Hamlet variations.

—*Shigekazu Ando*

With **"The Diary of Claudius,"** Shiga manifests his anti-heroism. This work was the forerunner of a series of Japanese anti-heroic Hamlet variations, to which I will refer later. And dramatically, with **"The Diary,"** Shiga's creation of the young Japanese hero was in the making during the same period. As we have seen in his diary entries, while Shiga was toiling over **"The Diary,"** he was also writing *Ōtsu Junkichi*. Both were published on September 1, 1912. The character of Ōtsu Junkichi was to develop into Tokito Kensaku through *Wakai* [*Reconciliation*] (1917) and *Anya Koro*.

What is most remarkable is that Shiga reconciled himself with Hamlet. This is even more remarkable if one knows that Shiga made Tokito Kensaku embody Hamlet, and that this Hamlet abides in Tokito Kensaku. To know what happened to Shiga, let us remember the citation from *"Sosaku Yodan"* given earlier.

"Years later," Shiga says, "I, for the first time, felt able to sympathize with Hamlet's sentiment. . . . Then I thought I could also write a 'Diary of Hamlet,' and actually had started writing it in Abiko—to no avail, though." The unsuccessful draft of **"The Diary of Hamlet"** remains. An episode of wrestling, depicting the unhappy relationship between Hamlet as a little boy and his uncle Claudius, was transplanted to *Anya Koro* as an episode in Tokito Kensaku's childhood, the antagonist becoming his father. I cite it below from **"The Diary of Hamlet"** to compare with its counterpart in *Anya Koro*.

As a child Hamlet's memory of his uncle was not a pleasant one even from the very beginning. Early one afternoon—in his uncle's room, Hamlet jumped up to wrestle with the uncle while the latter remained seated. Hamlet was fond of wrestling. In those days he slept lying between his grandparents. Every night, before going to sleep, he would wrestle with Grandpa in the bed. Eventually Grandpa would give way to him. He thought he wrestled really well. But the uncle did not let down his defenses for Hamlet as Grandpa would do. Again and again he got on his feet to rush at him. At last the uncle tied him up by the hands. And by the feet. Then leaving him bound on the floor unheeded, the uncle turned away to face his desk. Hamlet struggled to free his hands and feet. He struggled to no avail. He had been playful at first. But now he turned serious. He hated his uncle from the bottom of his heart. Looking at the heaving outline of the uncle's shoulders, soon his eyes were full of tears of vexation. His former opinion of his uncle was rooted up completely. He hated the fellow as an enemy. (Do not say, "Oh, so simple!" provided that intensity has thinned down since, my feelings certainly have remained unchanged until this day.) Hamlet felt something swelling up from his chest. He tightened his lips. But, however he tried to restrain it, it still escaped from his nostrils. Finally he burst out crying. Claudius turned around quickly in surprise. "Silly fellow. All you had to do was ask me to untie you," he said with a strained laugh, and set Hamlet's hands and feet free.

The following passage is taken from "Prologue: The Hero's Reminiscences" in *Anya Koro*. It shows how Kensaku wrestled with his father, exactly the way Hamlet did with Claudius:

He said suddenly, "Would you like to wrestle with me, Kensaku?" I merely nodded. But my excitement and pleasure must have been pitifully apparent. He remained seated, "Come on, then," he said, and held out his hands. I jumped up and rushed at him. He pushed me away easily. "Say, you're not bad." I was elated. I braced myself, lowered my head, then charged again. All I wanted was to hear him say what a brave and strong boy I was. I don't think I cared very much whether I won or lost. I had never played like this with him before. I was taut with excitement. It was as though my entire body had gained a new strength from such unexpected pleasure, and no matter how often he pushed me away, I kept on hurling myself at him. But not once did he let down his defenses for me. Once more I charged. "How about this?" he said, and shoved me back hard. Surprised, I fell backward on the floor with a big thump. I lay still for a moment, stunned breathless. Then I felt a touch of anger. I jumped up and faced him, readying myself for another charge. But the man I now saw seemed suddenly to have changed. "It's all over," he said, smiling in a strange, tight away. "Not yet," I said. "So you won't give up, eh?" "Of course not." Very quickly I found myself on the floor again, this time pinned down under his knee. "Now will you give up?" he said. I said nothing. "All right, then." He undid his sash, then with the other tied my ankles. I couldn't move at all. "Say you've had enough and I'll untie you."

I looked at him coldly. The warmth that I had felt toward him only moments before was now all gone. The activity had exhausted him, and his face was pale and strained. He was breathing heavily. As he turned away to face his desk, I stared at his heaving shoulders with hate. Soon the outline of his back became blurred; then I burst out crying. He turned around quickly in surprise. "All right, all right. Silly fellow, all you had to do was ask me to untie you.". . .

I began to be ashamed of having shown such open animosity. Yet I could not bring myself to trust him entirely.

Since the time Shiga wrote **"The Diary of Claudius,"** he had transformed Shakespeare's archetypal Western young hero in Japan. And despite his anti-heroism, he even combined Hamlet with Tokito Kensaku in *Anya Koro,* as we have seen. As a result, he has achieved the outstanding characterization of an archetypal Japanese young hero. We may call Tokito Kensaku the Japanese Hamlet.

At any rate, Shiga failed to create his version of Hamlet, or Hamlet failed to establish himself through literature in a far eastern world. Why did they fail? This is an important problem in studying modern Japanese literature. If Shakespeare's Hamlet stands as one of the milestones at the beginning of Western modernity, the Japanese Hamlet occurs along the current of Japanese modernism which is three centuries younger than Western modernity and is burdened with accumulated western enlightenment, democracy, naturalism, and so on. Undaunted, Japan tries to learn from Western cultures. But so does the Western world try to learn from Japan. That is why, when Japanese writers attempted to transfer the methods of modern European fiction and create modern Japanese literature, their projects collapsed halfway and changed the quality of Japanese fiction. Bridging the gap between the Western and the Eastern worlds, between Hamlet and Tokito Kensaku, and between the West and the East in modernization: such is the destiny of the modern Japanese writer.

FURTHER READING

Criticism

Hisaaki Yamanouchi. "The Rivals: Shiga Naoya and Akutagawa Ryūnosuke." In *The Search for Authenticity in Modern Japanese Literature,* pp. 82-106. Cambridge: Cambridge University Press, 1978.
> Includes an assessment of the autobiographical elements of *Ōtsu Junkichi* and "The Diary of Claudius."

Keene, Donald. "Shiga Naoya (1883-1971)." In *Dawn to the West: Japanese Literature of the Modern Era, Volume I: Fiction,* pp. 458-70. New York: Holt, Rinehart and Winston, 1984.
> Biographical and critical introduction to the author and his major works.

Kohl, Stephen W. "Shiga Naoya and the Literature of Experience." *Monumenta Nipponica* 32, No. 2 (Summer 1977): 211-17.
> Investigates the stories "Manazuru" and "The Ashen Moon," concentrating on how Shiga conveys the subjective experiences of the characters.

Sylvia Townsend Warner
1893–1978

English novelist, short story writer, poet, translator, editor, and biographer.

INTRODUCTION

Warner's stories present variations on a number of overlapping themes revolving around the attempt to understand human nature in all its complexity. Her fiction variously addresses the relationship between art and life, the contrast between appearance and reality, and the sordidness, follies, and extraordinary moments of everyday life. While often thematically linked, Warner's stories range from lengthy, full narratives to sketch-like treatments in which considerations of plot have been replaced by a concern for conveying the intensity and ambiguousness that typify many human experiences.

Biographical Information

Warner was born to a schoolmaster and his wife in Harrow borough, Middlesex county, and educated at home. Her study of music was interrupted by the outbreak of World War I, at which time she helped raise money for the Red Cross and assisted in the settling of Belgian refugees in Harrow. In 1915 Warner went to work in a munitions factory. A few years later she moved to London, where she pursued a career as a musicologist, serving on the editorial committee for *Tudor Church Music*, a ten-volume project. Appearing in 1925, her first collection of poetry was followed by best-selling novels in the next two years. From 1927 on Warner supported herself by her writing. Her first short story, "The Maze," was published in 1928 and two more were included in the same volume as her third novel, *The True Heart*. Warner's books were even more popular in America than in England. She was treated like a celebrity during a visit to New York in 1929 and formed friendships with prominent women in American literary circles, including Dorothy Parker, Elinor Wylie, Anne Parrish, and Jean Untermeyer. In the mid-1930s Warner joined the Communist party and began to write for the *Left Review*. Supporting the Republican side in the Spanish civil war, she led appeals for the Committee for Spanish Medical Aid, visited Spain for the committee, and participated in rallies and demonstrations. During her literary career, Warner compiled ten collections of short stories, many of which originally appeared in *The New Yorker*, and one more volume was published posthumously. Warner died in 1978.

Major Works of Short Fiction

The stories of *The Salutation* are essentially plotless evocations of character and place. Warner's characters, com-

monly from the working class, are either failures or unhappy individuals. She depicts their flaws without judgment and avoids sentimentality. Written in a vein similar to that of *The Salutation*, *More Joy in Heaven, and Other Stories* satirizes the upper class and organized religion, while offering more portraits of people lost in the shuffle of society, such as the elderly and poor. Evincing Warner's political sympathies and commitment, *A Garland of Straw, and Other Stories* shows the hideousness of war, the smugness of bourgeois and chauvinistic individuals, the innocence of the young and uninformed, and the anti-Semitism of the Fascists. Here Warner also protests England's noninterventionist policy regarding the Spanish civil war and its failure to respond to the threat of Nazism. Similarly, in *The Museum of Cheats* she portrays the effects of war on the people of England, but also emphasizes the betrayals to which women are particularly vulnerable, living in fear of the men in their lives. The stories of *Winter in the Air, and Other Stories* are character studies featuring, for example, a soldier returned from the war, a mother tending to children left fatherless by the war, and a woman who moves to London seeking anonymity in the wake of abandonment by her husband. Demonstrating Warner's knack for the absurd and whimsical, "But at the

Stroke of Midnight" from *The Innocent and the Guilty* tells of a man who is so insensitive and oblivious that he realizes that his wife is gone only because dinner has not been set out. It never crosses his mind that his wife, who has assumed a new identity, intends never to return to him. His wife is eventually forced back to her old life, but only long enough for her and her husband to be carried off in a flood. Toward the end of her career, Warner wrote tales set in Elfland—a world of fairies, elves, werewolves, and other fantastical creatures—using this imaginary realm to comment indirectly on human behavior and society.

Critical Reception

Though Warner's short stories have generally been well received by readers, they have not attracted the longer, in-depth analyses that her novels have garnered. Commentators have observed that Warner successfully ennobles lowly protagonists rather than pitying or idealizing them. Similarly, critics note that Warner expressed compassion for unfortunate characters without becoming maudlin. In contrast, some of her stories with political content are perceived to be heavy-handed, and reviewers have objected to Warner's single-minded emphasis on social consequences at the expense of commentary about the morality of behavior such as adultery or prostitution. Nevertheless, feminist critics have generally been drawn to the satirical and political content of her work. Reviewing *The Museum of Cheats,* but summing up the sentiments of many readers, a commentator in *The Times Literary Supplement* stated: "Miss Warner is highly skilled as a writer in this medium [the short story], equally graceful and expert in handling farce or tragedy, the sordid or the purely funny. Her wit is delicate and precise, and her observation acute, so that a few lines are sufficient to create a character, whether it be an odious child, an obstinate lover, or a dreadful old woman who was popularly supposed to have eaten her husband. There is nothing portentous or bludgeoning about the style; and . . . the author is at her best when she is most absurd or fantastic."

PRINCIPAL WORKS

Short Fiction

A Moral Ending, and Other Stories 1931
More Joy in Heaven, and Other Stories 1935
The Cat's Cradle Book 1940
†*A Garland of Straw, and Other Stories* 1943
The Museum of Cheats 1947
Winter in the Air, and Other Stories 1955
A Spirit Rises 1962
‡*A Stranger with a Bag, and Other Stories* 1966
The Innocent and the Guilty: Stories 1971
The Kingdoms of Elfin 1977
One Thing Leading to Another, and Other Stories 1984

*Enlarged as *The Salutation* (1932).
†Republished as *A Garland of Straw: Twenty-Eight Stories* (1943).
‡Republished as *Swans on an Autumn River* (1966).

Other Major Works

The Espalier (poetry) 1925
Lolly Willowes; or, The Loving Huntsman (novel) 1926
Mr. Fortune's Maggot (novel) 1927
Time Importuned (poetry) 1928
The True Heart (novel) 1929
Opus 7 (poetry) 1931
Summer Will Show (novel) 1936
After the Death of Don Juan (novel) 1938
The Corner That Held Them (novel) 1948
Jane Austen (criticism) 1951
The Flint Anchor (novel) 1954
"Women as Writers" (lecture) February, 1959; published in *Journal of the Royal Society of Arts*, May, 1959
T. H. White: A Biography (biography) 1967
King Duffus, and Other Poems (poetry) 1968
§*Azrael, and Other Poems* (poetry) 1978
Scenes of Childhood (semiautobiographical sketches) 1981
Collected Poems (poetry) 1983
Letters (correspondence) 1983

§Republished as *Twelve Poems* (1980).

CRITICISM

Jane Spence Southron (essay date 1940)

SOURCE: "Catabasis," in *The New York Times Book Review*, October 20, 1940, p. 24.

[*In the following review, Southron claims that in* The Cat's Cradle *Warner is "at her most beguiling best."*]

"Our unhappiness transcended our egoism, and by degrees by a complicated process of advances and withdrawals, exchange of looks, fusion of silences, we fell deeply in love with each other. After that she lived with me . . . and now my whole life was transfigured, full of entertainment and delight. . . . Naturally, there was a good deal of talk about it—embassies always gossip." Which tells the story.

To begin with, you could hardly fail, even were no name attached, to recognize the writer. And, to proceed, the love affair was on the plane where the infrequent literary-human Alices meet in gentle, far too rare felicity; one party to the blissful, amorous interlude being a young embassy attaché, and the other—you have guessed it!—a cat. A Siamese, but no ordinary Siamese. "Beautiful, sensitive, unappreciated . . . an exquisite storyteller, in the purest, most classical tradition of narrative." His Schéhérazade, the attaché called her.

It was Haru who made it mockingly clear that the folk tales that have been told, with variations, all over the globe from time immemorial need no ethnological explanation; having been murmured to children in their cradles, in the one language that is "catholic, explicit, unvarying"; of which "every child picks up an inkling"— cat. These are the tales on which the kittens of all the ages have been brought up by their nursing mothers. They are the cat's diploma as universal nursemaid.

Here, following a thirty-two-page introduction, which sets the scene and authoritatively clinches the argument, are sixteen of the tales collected by the attaché from his large family of cats of all degrees of gentility or female rascaldom. Bluebeard figures in one; but through a long-forgotten daughter. The Marquisate of Carabas and Odin's birds crop up in others. But these, and the rest, are subtler, far less obvious than the cosmopolitan human folklore stories which had their distant origin in the cat world; and, since they are direct from source, their dispassionate, feline objectivity has suffered neither taint nor dilution.

Literature has surely much for which to thank the young attaché and his unconventional, chance-met feminine collaborator (not the cat), who are among the few grown-up humans—perhaps the only ones unless we may include Mr. Hartman, who supplied the captivating illustrations— who can, today, talk cat. It is distressing to consider what a loss man has suffered, these thousands of years, through not having retained, beyond babyhood, the ability to speak and understand it.

We very greatly fear that what the attaché and his admiring assistant dreaded will happen. The "editor" will be accused of having made the stories up. But let not this reviewer, at any rate, be guilty of the antireal enormities forecast by the two enthusiasts, who were far from underrating the difficulty of establishing the projected book's claim to be regarded "as a serious work of scholarship." Let us eschew such words as delicacy, fragrant, fantasy and such a phrase as "ideal for cat-lovers," to quote only a few of the anticipated verbalisms that sent shudders through the collector and his adviser. Let it not be said, as they did, that only scholars of Chinese, "accustomed to a tonal language," could be expected to understand the "fine shades of meaning" in the cat-talk.

Enough that here is a banquet of stories (fables, parables, what you will) to suit the most fastidious of literary epicures; salted, spiced and sauced with irony, satire and ghostly, evanescent wit. The menu card may suggest, here and there, a reminiscent dish, but savoring it you find it wholly new.

In short, *The Cat's Cradle-Book* is Sylvia Townsend Warner at her most beguiling best; using, invariably, the one right word, presenting outrageous situations with cool detachment; delighting you with her artistry and giving you furiously to think, with her deadly indictments.

Besides all this, it is a gem of bookmaking.

The Times Literary Supplement (essay date 1943)

SOURCE: A review of *A Garland of Straw*, in *The Times Literary Supplement*, No. 2165, July 31, 1943, p. 365.

[*The critic offers a mixed assessment of the stories in* A Garland of Straw.]

There have been several unusually interesting volumes of short stories in recent months. In most of them the stories represented the output of a longer period of time than that following the outbreak of war, so the war itself, while it has for obvious practical reasons given a fillip to the short-story form (and to verse) as a relatively unleisured means of expression, cannot alone account for the frequency of such volumes of late. But the fact is that, in this matter of types and casts of literature as of so much else, war-time conditions have only intensified the state of things before the war. For practising or potential writers of fiction of all sorts, one must assume, prolonged imaginative concentration has for some time seemed altogether too arduous, demanding greater sacrifices than they could or would make; the sense of catastrophe, after all, was too pressing. So the short story, just because it was short, offered opportunities that the novel put out of reach.

That, no doubt, is a mechanistic explanation which leaves more to be said. (It is not only the short space of time in which a poem can be composed, for instance, that accounts for the flowering of verse in war-time.) But it should not be ignored in considering the imaginative impulse or the quality of a collection of short stories at the present time by one of our serious novelists. Miss Sylvia Townsend Warner's volume, [*A Garland of Straw*] a collection of twenty-seven stories written between 1936 and 1942, is a case in point. As a novelist this author has fine precision of statement, a beautiful coolness of tone and a gift of fancy that is almost always kept free from the merely whimsical, and these qualities she has also exhibited in the past in her short stories. They are not absent from *A Garland of Straw*. Let it be confessed, however, that Miss Warner's subtlest or most engaging characteristics appear only in a minority of the tales in the volume. These are delicately individual pieces of work, some of them very good indeed, and they make up for the disappointment she leaves elsewhere. Nevertheless, the greater number of the tales, many of them apparently written in the first place for the *New Yorker*, illustrate all too plainly the restricted uses of mere brevity as an aid to expression. Here, among other sketches of war for the American reader, is a light invention about evacuee children, a near-tragedy of the cigarette shortage, the tale of a house which looked as if it had been blitzed but had only been occupied by some soldiers, the drama of a home beautiful threatened by a time-bomb in the neighbourhood. All are skilfully enough done but are of no great consequence.

A few of the stories not concerned with the war are on the sentimental side, others are inclined to indulge a somewhat trivial humour. But the good stories remain, some grim, some gay, a few both at the same time, and among them are two or three that are very funny indeed. **"The**

Language of Flowers" describes, in a wicked little series of imaginary letters, how in 1938 the Office of Works sent flowers from Kensington Palace garden to be planted on the grave of Queen Victoria's governess, Baroness Lehzen, at Bückeburg. **"Plutarco Roo"** tells of a Mexican pastry-cook's apprentice with a taste for ecclesiastical art who found a steady market for his ideals. **"The Song of Songs"** introduces in Mr. Pitfield the most reliable, the most versatile, the most gentlemanly of tenors with no music in his soul. All three tales raise at least two guffaws to the page.

But it is the serious stories, not all of them evoked by an image of catastrophe to come or in our midst, that give the truest measure of Miss Warner's talent. One is not always sure, perhaps, of the justice of her anger or pity—not sure, that is, of the aptness of her means of communication; the cool, cutting edge of her irony is sometimes more drastically surgical than she seems to intend. In the very brief **"In the Hour of Our Death,"** for instance, does she not overdo the heartless sanctimoniousness of the clergyman son whose clergyman father is dying? Her judgment is faultless, on the other hand, in **"The Level-Crossing,"** in which one of a small party of soldiers billeted upon the keeper and his niece, a dumb, disfigured girl, brings himself for a pitying, half-horrified moment to the point of wanting to marry her. Two of the stories with the war for background stand out from the rest. One is **"Apprentice,"** which is set in a brothel for German officers in occupied Poland and which tells how a ten-year-old representative of the victors, the flaxen-haired Lili, watched a Polish boy die of cold and hunger. The other is **"A Red Carnation,"** in which something of the cold, bitter antiquity of Spain pierces the hide of a romantic German youth sent there with his unit to fight and to die. In both stories Miss Warner is passionately hard, perceptive and truthful.

Diana Trilling (essay date 1943)

SOURCE: A review of *A Garland of Straw,* in *The Nation,* New York, Vol. 157, No. 15, October 9, 1943, pp. 414-15.

[In the following excerpt, Trilling claims Warner is "an accomplished practitioner of her craft," but finds fault with artistic practices of the generation of writers to which Warner belongs.]

In writing last week about Eudora Welty's latest volume of short stories I said that somewhere between Chekhov and Katherine Mansfield the short story had got off its trolley, and I suggested that it was Miss Mansfield who was in large part responsible for the exaggerated subjectivity which has so variously corrupted modern short fiction. The line of descent from Miss Mansfield to Miss Welty may not always be easy to trace: the family resemblance is more a matter of the carriage of the head than of feature for feature. But in a writer like Sylvia Townsend Warner the connection can be seen more readily. Miss Warner is less talented perhaps, and less ambitious, than

Miss Welty, but she is an accomplished practitioner of her craft and more typical of her literary generation. Twenty-eight of her stories, many of them familiar from having appeared in the *New Yorker,* have been gathered in *A Garland of Straw*. They are an interesting sampling of the thin brew of sensibility which has been so largely our nourishment in English and American short fiction since Miss Mansfield separated the flesh from the bone of Chekhov.

I use the word sensibility in its frankly pejorative connotation; obviously, sensibility under control is as necessary to a writer as an ear to a musician. But just as, in the case of Miss Welty, a too great subjectivity manifests itself in too great a preoccupation with fine prose, in Miss Warner a too great subjectivity manifests itself in an overdependence upon her private and special awarenesses. This is what I mean by sensibility, the delusion that an author's fugitive insights and sensitivities and symbolical observations will carry, in a piece of fiction, the full weight with which they are charged in the writer's own experience. They never do. Actually, they reduce the stature of a story to the size of the smallest elements that compose it—and this despite the fact that there is always implicit, in oversubjective writing, an author's emotion of superiority to his environment and his fellowman.

Sylvia Townsend Warner lives in a more politically conscious world than Miss Mansfield. Many of her stories are concerned with politics, war, and "issues"; one has the impression, however, that the bigger the issue the smaller and more personal the symbol by which Miss Warner communicates her indignation, and that the cause itself is actually secondary to the triumphant play of Miss Warner's creativity about it. For instance, a story called **"Apprentice,"** in intent one of the serious stories in *A Garland of Straw,* deals with the way Nazism can corrupt people. **"Apprentice"** is set in occupied Poland and is the story of a little girl who lives under the protection of a German *Gauleiter.* In the midst of starvation Lili has plenty to eat, and she elaborates a wonderful game in which, standing above the public road, she dangles bits of food on a string for the starving passersby to jump for. But one young Polish boy resists her temptations, and Lili becomes maddened with the need to break his independent spirit. On a particularly cold day she dangles a cinnamon bun before the boy; he is so hungry that he jumps for it, and Lili jerks the string out of his reach just as the boy falls dead of cold and hunger. Thinking, "It must be really terrible to die like that," Lili pulls up the bun and eats it.

Well, a story like this, it seems to me, defeats its purpose. Primarily concerned to assert the rightness of her own feelings, Miss Warner luxuriates in her scorn of the child Lili; in consequence, Lili becomes an incredible little monster instead of a credible little human being. And in consequence of Lili's monstrosity, Miss Warner's whole indictment of Nazism exposes itself as a contrivance.

Of course, not all Miss Warner's stories show such a flagrant discrepancy between purpose and method. Some are merely sketches or anecdotes ("**The Trumpet Shall Sound,**" "**To Cool the Air**"); some are frankly fragmentary ("**Rainbow Villa,**" "**Setteragic On**"). But the least of them mingles with the most ambitious without the reader being aware of a disturbing difference in kind because, having a common point of departure in sensibility, they all sacrifice permanent meaningfulness to the fleeting triumphs and self-justifications of the creative moment. Although Miss Warner is willing to be far more humanly fallible than Katherine Mansfield would ever have wished to be, and although her prevailing temper is neither ecstatic nor pitying but acidulous, her stories are unmistakably fledglings from "The Dove's Nest."

I have used Miss Warner as an instance of one of the major faults of a whole literary school; in fairness I should also point out that she has a liveliness and flavor which put her in a class quite apart from most of the writers represented in such a collection as Martha Foley's *The Best American Short Stories, 1943.*

James Hilton (essay date 1947)

SOURCE: "Stories to Be Long Remembered: Sylvia Townsend Warner, a Deceptively Blithe Spirit," in *New York Herald Tribune Weekly Book Review,* March 23, 1947, p. 4.

[*In the following review, Hilton praises* The Museum of Cheats, *adding that, to fully enjoy the stories, "one must listen as well as read."*]

Sylvia Townsend Warner, still best known as the author of *Lolly Willowes* and *Mr. Fortune's Maggot,* has collected a score or so of stories into a volume called, after prevalent fashion, from one of them, *The Museum of Cheats.* The title is also of a fashion: it puzzles rather than explains, incites more than invites, and in a literary world wary of face-value, it fools best by not fooling at all. Thus, in the name-story, the Museum is a real Museum and the Cheats are real Cheats. But being told that, you are no nearer to guessing what the story is about: indeed, there are readers who might still feel a need to guess when they had finished, They might conclude, after a re-reading, that it is just a story about a Museum of Cheats.

More successful, to my mind, are some of the other stories. There is one called "**The House with the Lilacs**" which, on the surface is a simple anecdote about a family who continually wish they had bought, when house hunting, a different house, but they hunted so much that they cannot recall where the lost paragon was though the most exact and curious details about it have lingered in memory. Not such a simple anecdote though: for the construction, to a writer who analyzes it clinically, is a small miracle of craftsmanship: while to the reader who reads it sensitively, the mood it puts him in may well seem an equal miracle after so few pages. It could be said, as of once-heard music by Delius, that one remembers it long after forgetting it.

There are other items in this collection that deserve mention: "**Major Bruce and Mrs. Conway**" (a few pages, brilliantly insufficient, about an American man and an Englishwoman who are not in the least like Babbitt and Mrs. Miniver: "**Story of a Patron**" a fantastic yarn about a retired policeman who paints primitives); and "**To Come So Far**" (a neat piece of bone-surgery on the skeleton of a marriage). In all of these appear Miss Warner's distinguishing qualities; an eye for the detail of English life, a prose that exactly matches the thought, both being quick, sharp, polished and sometimes pert; antiquarianism and folk-lore draped a little consciously, but in the main with elegance; and a complete absence of the pugilistic qualities so much admired in merchandised fiction—punch, snap, hit, smash, and what have you. Miss Warner does not even come to grips with a situation: one rather pictures her at the beginning of any story hovering over its general theme like a deceptively blithe spirit, wondering how she will haunt.

Since the material of this volume deals mainly with recent English years, it is of interest to note how far in the background Miss Warner keeps the war—or, alternatively, how deep are the undertones when for a change she lets it come to the front. Her English folk are plausibly preoccupied with all the harassments of their time—conscription and rations, fuel shortage and billeting, mountainous red tape and multiple interferences of officialdom—yet beyond all this they seem to have wise eccentric roots in the English past, and to derive strength from them—uneasily, perhaps, because it is 1947.

In the last of these stories Miss Warner writes: "It was one of those pull-down bells that answer from the depths of the house long after one has pulled—like dropping a stone down a deep well." The simile would suit *The Museum of Cheats* collection; it pulls down the bells, but to enjoy the performance one must listen as well as read.

Eunice S. Holsaert (essay date 1947)

SOURCE: "Tidbits in Acid," in *The New York Times,* Section 7, March 23, 1947, p. 16.

[*In the review below, Holsaert gives a favorable assessment of the stories in* The Museum of Cheats, *saying that Warner's "skilled guidance" allows ordinary characters to be "unexpectedly entertaining."*]

Miss Warner is one of that handful of English and American women writers who manage to be by turns compassionate and scathing without their syntax becoming ruffled or their taste affected by the moral climate of which they write. Less vibrant and evocative than Elizabeth Bowen, and not such a reformer at heart as Elizabeth Parsons, the touchstone of Miss Warner's gifts seems to be her level acceptance of people as they are.

It would be difficult, indeed, to choose the best from this collection of twenty-two short stories [*The Museum of*

Cheats]. Perhaps the title entry, which is also the longest in the book, represents her antic fantasy, shrewd commentary and silken satire at its most rounded. At any rate, the two-and-a-half centuries that she encompasses in the forty pages of **"Museum of Cheats"** certainly are populated by a great many of those unostentatious eccentrics, defiant clerks and strong-willed women who under this author's skilled guidance prove to be unexpectedly entertaining.

Another mood, **"Boors Carousing,"** is an incisive study of a self-serving author and a genteel lady tippler. There is a group of tales about agreeably demented people that manages to tell a good deal about the inner tensions and stresses of our society. This reader must openly admit to an admiring fondness for the mildly schizophrenic ex-policeman who enjoys brief fame as a "Genuine English Primitive" painter in the pages of **"Story of a Patron."** A real affection is also possible for vague Mrs. Finch, who, in **"The House with the Lilacs,"** embarrasses her family by fantasying about houses she's never seen, and for Rosie Flounders' war-time adventures. Among other wisely acid tidbits is **"Poor Mary,"** an account of an unwanted female that reminds one of rather somber Dorothy Parker, and **"The Cold,"** which gives a self-righteous, middle-class dowager much the same treatment that Saki often accorded her more elevated sisters.

Elizabeth Jennings   (essay date 1955)

SOURCE: A review of *Winter in the Air, and Other Stories,* in *The Spectator,* Vol. 195, No. 6652, December 23, 1955, p. 877.

[*In the following excerpt, Jennings finds that the stories in* Winter in the Air *reflect Warner's perceptivity about people and her strong sense of place.*]

Winter in the Air, by Sylvia Townsend Warner, is a very impressive book indeed. Every story shows sensitiveness in the good sense—that is, awareness of all the possibilities of a character or a situation, swiftness in reaching the honest conclusion. Miss Townsend Warner is, above all, interested in what people *feel* when they find themselves in certain situations—a woman returning to the place where she has been happily in love (**"Hee-Haw!"**); a boy almost, but not quite, embarking on his first love affair (**"Evan"**); a miserable, egotistical woman living in reduced circumstances (**"Under New Management"**); a writer discovering that a young man who has died was writing in the same manner as, but better than, himself (**"Absalom, My Son"**); a woman reconciling herself to an incompatible marriage (**"A Kitchen Knife"**). Perhaps the finest story in the book, however, is **"The Children's Grandmother."** This is an extraordinarily moving account of how a grandmother, who has lost all but one of her own children in early childhood, feels towards her grandchildren. 'What she felt for them I could not determine. Unless there be a kind of love that can exist without a breath of tenderness, it was not love. It was too

passionate for affection. It had nothing in common with the wistful doting of old age.'

As well as being immensely perceptive about people, Miss Townsend Warner has also an unusually strong sense of place. Everywhere, the environment of her characters is beautifully depicted.

Sara Henderson Hay   (essay date 1956)

SOURCE: "Brief, Poetic, Probing Stories," in *New York Herald Tribune Book Review,* February 26, 1956, p. 1.

[*In the following review, Hay praises* Winter in the Air, and Other Stories, *calling it "rewarding and stimulating."*]

Charlton Mackrell, impaled on the shaft of Sylvia Townsend Warner's fine irony, was a gentleman who, "in seeing both sides of a question, giving the Devil his due, stating the other man's case, allowing that to err is human, and never committing himself to any opinion till he had made quite sure there were no signs of error or prejudice about it . . . had attained eminence both as a judge of Shorthorn cattle and as a literary critic." This pleasant baiting brings to mind an apposite statement made by a certain writer a few weeks ago, who remarked that he believed the most valuable criticism to be highly opinionated, personal, emotional and biased. Somewhere between these nice exaggerations, the reviewer attempts to maintain a delicate balance: the short stories in Miss Warner's latest book, **Winter in the Air,** are, quite objectively, impeccable in craftsmanship and thoroughly enjoyable reading.

Since her first novel, *Lolly Willowes* (which, if I remember correctly, was the initial selection of the new-born Book of the Month Club back in 1926), Sylvia Townsend Warner has produced some fourteen volumes of prose and poetry. Her prose has much of poetry in it, as a matter of fact—the vividness and accuracy of sensory impression. For example: ". . . she remembered the colors of the parched landscape, at once violent and pale, and how strongly everything had smelled; the mown field where they had taken their supper one evening and everything they ate tasted of warm figs because of the intense, figlike sweetness of the cut clover, cooked all day in the blazing heat. . . ." And the poet's ability to bring together disparate elements into a graphic image, as in this description of a sleeping cat: "Like a frond of weed in the depth of ocean an ear stirred, but the cat did not wake . . . it deepened the profundity of its slumber, as though the intensity of her gaze were pushing against it like a tide. . . ." And the capacity to condense into a few lines or phrases the enormous pathos or meanness or dignity of human personality: and the gift of seeing in the commonplaces of existence those signs and symbols of things not in the least ordinary.

Such dualities are eminently suited to the short story, and to the type of short story which Miss Warner does superlatively well—the brief, sharply focused incident or series of incidents delineating and making clear a character and a history, in a manner which is subtle, subjective, often complex but not avantgarde Arty. The eighteen stories in *Winter in the Air* are on a variety of subjects, some poignant, some humorous, some grisly, some gay; gently, or not so gently, probing and trenchant. In **"A Kitchen Knife"** the humble tool which on impulse a young wife purloins from her neighbor's scullery is the symbol of the means by which she severs herself from her miserable pretenses and illusions. In **"Under New Management"** there appears the aging spinster, Miss St. John, a Permanent among the inferior Transients of the Peacock Hotel, who has developed the capacity to be disagreeable to a fine art; a figure which, for all the author's unrelenting detail she still allows its tragic pitiableness. In **"Absalom, My Son"** a celebrated writer recognizes both his triumphant relief and his shamed grief that a young unknown imitator of his has died at the age of twenty-six, and would never write another book to match or surpass him.

In all the stories the author's technical skill is evident but never obtrusive; her insight and sensitive perception, coupled with her extraordinary ability to describe and illuminate, give her characters an intense reality. And her genuine compassion removes far from them the root of bitterness. *Winter in the Air* is a rewarding and stimulating book; short stories which, as is not always the case, can be re-read with fresh pleasure.

Dachine Rainer (essay date 1956)

SOURCE: "Humor and Irony," in *Commonweal,* Vol. LXIV, No. 1, April 6, 1956, pp. 33-4.

[*In the following review, Rainer acknowledges Warner's technical skills but finds* Winter in the Air, and Other Stories *lacking in imagination.*]

A great deal has happened to both literary taste and to Miss Warner's talent since 1926 when her *Lolly Willowes* was the first Book-of-the-Month Club selection. Not only have standards for the minor novelist fallen into a grave decline, and Gresham's Law seen them give way to the sentimentality of Rumer Godden or the pretentious trash of Wouk, but the exciting experimentation or relative daring of writers has, with little exception, been self-expurgated during the last couple of decades, so that their current work or the work of their successors seems archaic and stratified. It has not been a glorious road from *Lolly Willowes* to *Winter in the Air.*

Certainly by her earlier standards this collection of short stories, most of them reprinted from the *New Yorker,* indicates a decided thinning of a very substantial gift; however, by comparison with much of what passes for the art of fiction, it is work of a very high order indeed. Miss Warner seldom fails to illuminate an aspect of experience, but she equally seldom succeeds in exalting us by the uniqueness of her vision or the grandeur of her attempt.

Her characters, scrupulously portrayed, with an amused faintly contemptuous air—she is detached from the human condition, not identified with it, except for the first story which conveys a certain anguish—have a sameness, not necessarily arising from any real similarity, but from Miss Warner's square and unadorned approach. There is a plethora of the middle-aged, middle-class in either outlook or actuality, and even the young frequently seem tired and somewhat seedy; many of the stories occur during the War, or Post-War, and their atmosphere is, understandably, one of apathy and deprivation, occasionally relieved from dullness only by the author's humor and ironic detachment.

Her humor, sophistication, perception, and, above all, her preoccupation with craftsmanship, however orthodox, are all to be highly commended, and I do not mean to say this in a methodical or off-hand manner; they are indeed rare. Her passions, and, consequently, the degree to which she establishes rapport with her characters are limited by control and refinement in a typically English manner. Detachment, polish, and a faint, but unmistakable, upperclass allegiance cling to her as to that much underrated and equally cultivated writer, Somerset Maugham; Miss Warner's is a more complicated manner, but her preoccupations and her fluid style alike are reminiscent of the older writer, and like him, she fails in achieving a major status through an absence of ambition. For the minor novelist, like the minor painter, it is the scope of the work, all things being equal, that is decisive. These stories are created on a very circumscribed canvas; they are superbly executed, but Miss Warner is—at least in this collection—simply not concerned with larger moral issues or with an enraptured or highly imaginative approach to her art.

William Arrowsmith (essay date 1956)

SOURCE: "News from Mojave," in *The Hudson Review,* Vol. IX, No. 3, Autumn, 1956, pp. 479-80.

[*In the following excerpt from a review of* Winter in the Air, *Arrowsmith describes Warner as being "an almost flawless writer" within a narrow range of fiction.*]

Within severe limits, Miss Sylvia Townsend Warner is an almost flawless writer, and *Winter in the Air* is an astonishingly sustained collection of a score of short stories. It is rare to find delicacy so untroubled by the fear of preciousness, and fastidiousness so capable of emotional, rather than verbal or atmospheric, precision. She is incapable of real power and these stories are innocent of ideas, but all worked up out of a scrupulous literacy and a fine eye, invariably particular and minor, but with the right power of the minor that flows from a good imagination, poised for the particular. She likes the lambent touch, an eloping girl in a vulgar bakery who speaks to a cat as though to a bridesmaid, the dying matriarch with the pride of dead children, the flickering of sexual antennae between an old tart and a schoolboy. And the language is exactly equal to the attempt: close, controlled, ripe with precision more than passion, deceptively discursive before falling to its true resolution, an effortless surprised rightness. The emotions she invokes are peripheral, but she gets her power by hinting of their real relation to the remembered center—nostalgia backed by love, arrogant eccentricity leaning on loss, sudden shocking revelation calmed back into the common pattern of life, and rightly claimed. But always the minor: wit rather than humor; loss more than tragedy; the quiet surrender, not the noisy triumph; irony, regret, wry conquest, autumn, disappointment, well-bred endurance. Such perfection of the minor is a blessing, though I confess I found the perch through twenty stories a little too much rare air, and giving perilously little purchase to American hands and the American liking for the big guns of the novel, however botched.

Frederic E. Faverty (essay date 1962)

SOURCE: "Stories with Mood and a Sense of Place," in *Chicago Sunday Tribune Magazine of Books,* March 18, 1962, p. 5.

[*In the following review of* A Spirit Rises, *Faverty appreciates Warner's ability to create an atmosphere in which the elements of her story seem believable.*]

In the title story of this collection [*A Spirit Rises*] a little girl is held enchanted as her father reads poetry to her on a rainy afternoon. Readers will be similarly held by some of these 14 stories, for Sylvia Warner is a practiced craftsman.

She is skilled first of all in evoking an atmosphere. The cadenced language of the title story fits the mood of reverie and nostalgia as an old lady is swept back into her childhood and feels herself secure again in her father's arms.

Along with mood goes a pronounced sense of place, so that some of the tales almost become local color stories. And the place is usually the industrial midlands of England, where one dismal town shades off into another, until the last loses itself in the moors.

Yet to these bleak streets and that harsh air the natives cannot wait to return, tho they be in Paris or on the Italian Riviera. Miss Warner achieves her realistic effects not by an inventory, as some novelists like Balzac do, but by selection of significant details.

The range of the author's interests also is impressive. She writes with authority of a doctor's daily rounds [**"The Locum Tenens"**], the ills he diagnoses, the medicines he prescribes. On music she is even more solidly informed. In **"On Living for Others"** everything is seen thru the eyes of a composer and is described in terms relating to music.

Whether the story deals with a dressmaker, a fortune teller, a landlady, a nun, a tramp, or a factory worker, Miss

Warner is able to build up a background against which the characters seem real and credible.

In each story the situation is a dramatic one. The character is caught in an hour of crisis: the landlady at the point of suicide, the doctor in a sentimental mood when he is almost drawn into marriage and a return to the grimy town of his origin. With a deft touch or two Miss Warner gives life to her characters: Bell Kirby "with her grating Midlands accent," Melissa Robinson with her gluttonous interest in nothing but her own cooking.

Some of the stories, like **"The Old Nun,"** are mere sketches. None of them has any plot. They are best classified as character studies, paintings of mood or place, dramatic incidents. In effectiveness they range from the rather thin **"Youth and the Lady"** to the memorable **"The Locum Tenens."**

Hallie Burnett (essay date 1962)

SOURCE: "The Indecisive Denouement," in *The Saturday Review,* (New York), Vol. 45, No. 16, April 21, 1962, p. 30.

[*In the following review, Burnett pronounces Warner's style in the stories of* A Spirit Rises *lucid and graceful.*]

Since it is the sharpest and briefest form in dramatic literature, and since there is room in the short story for humor or pathos, realism or symbolism, it has, as shown by Sylvia Townsend Warner in *A Spirit Rises,* something for everyone.

Take the story **"Barnby Robinson,"** where the wrongdoer in a triangle becomes the victim in an unforeseen way. At the beginning the situation is conventional enough: a playwright is leaving home for another woman, an actress, and a sad little scene takes place between him and the patient wife he forsakes. "On both their parts it was an expedient not to look at each other," we are told, and here, as always, Miss Warner shows us both her hands; no tricks up her sleeves. Yet as the story progresses we become increasingly disturbed by the very qualities we have admired in the wife, until these lead her, finally, to act as a monstrous hand of justice. After that the "other woman" has her revenge; and no doubt if the story were to be continued another paragraph the tables would be turned again, quite as effectively.

In **"In a Shaken House"** we see a familiar Katherine Mansfield-type character, Miss Turner, inspecting a furnished bed-sitting-room-and-kitchenette, which happens to be beside the railroad tracks. "Nobody ever notices the trains after the first week," says the owner of the house; and indeed this is so. But wait, now. Where Katherine Mansfield might have shown Miss Turner as a fortuneteller being cast out by a "good family" and growing from youth to middle age; where she might have even provided the final ironic touch of a brother who comes to Miss

Turner to have his own fortune read, hoping she will predict the early demise of their stepmother, we go on from there. For the fate of this Miss Turner is more than an ironic justification of her choice of a profession; the small, almost unnoticed subplot produces a final trap, ending the story on a note of impending disaster.

In **"A Dressmaker"** there is a memorable application of the Chekhovian method for presenting incidental character vividly to the eye of the reader—as when the Honorable Mrs. Benson appears at the dressmaker's rooms, first to order and then to model her magnificent ball gowns—but turns out, unfortunately, to be quite mad.

"The Snow Guest" tells about a young adolescents jealousy of his mother's sentimental urge to shelter an escaped convict; but, true to Miss Warner's probing view of life, the mother has the last word.

The title story is a delicately bitter vignette in which Ellie, the daughter of a teacher who is remembered with reverence by his pupils, reveals the tragedy of her own life to one of them. She was, she says, "her father's Cinderella, [who] went barefoot like the cobbler's child in the adage."

There is a variety of other fine stories in this book, all but two of which have appeared in *The New Yorker*—but no matter. These are tales that can be reread, if only for the delight of observing Miss Warner's lucid prose and savoring the grace of her one-step-beyond endings—in the style of the best short story writers today. For if some part of each story always seems left for the future to resolve, the immediate objectives are concluded tidily enough, and it is unlikely that any reader will leave the collection unsatisfied.

John Updike (essay date 1966)

SOURCE: A review of *Swans on an Autumn River*, in *The Critic as Artist: Essays on Books 1920-1970*, edited by Gilbert A. Harrison, Liveright Publishing, 1972, pp. 333-39.

[*In the following review, which was originally published in* The New Republic *in 1966, Updike comments on the "genius" of Warner's writing.*]

The stories of Sylvia Townsend Warner stick up from *The New Yorker*'s fluent fiction-stream with a certain stony air of mastery. They are granular and adamant and irregular in shape. The prose has a much-worked yet abrasive texture of minute juxtaposition and compounded accuracies. Candles are lit in an antique shop, and "The polished surfaces reflected the little flames with an intensification of their various colors—amber in satinwood, audit ale in mahogany, dragon's blood in tortoise shell." Two old ladies reminisce: "They talked untiringly about their girlhood—about the winters when they went skating, the summers when they went boating, the period when they were so very pious, the period when they were pious no longer

and sent a valentine to the curate: the curate blushed, a crack rang out like a pistol shot and Hector Gillespie went through the ice, the fox terriers fought under old Mrs. Bulliver's chair, the laundry ruined the blue voile, the dentist cut his throat in Century Wood, Claude Hopkins came back from Cambridge with a motorcar and drove it at thirty miles an hour with flames shooting out behind, Addie Carew was married with a wasp under her veil." How particular, yet how inclusive and shapely in this catalogue! Though Miss Warner can be trivial in her effects and vague in her intentions, she rarely lacks concreteness. On every page there is something to be seen or smelled or felt.

In *Repetition*, Kierkegaard, who had considerable fabling powers, interrupted his narrative to write: "If I were to pursue in detail the moods of the young man as I learned to know them, not to speak of including in a poetical manner a multitude of irrelevant matters—salons, wearing apparel, beautiful scenery, relatives and friends—this story might be drawn out to yard lengths. That, however, I have no inclination to do. I eat lettuce, it is true, but I eat only the heart; the leaves, in my opinion, are fit for swine." Contrariwise, Miss Warner's appetite for the leaves of circumstance is excellent. One story in this collection ("**An Act of Reparation**") is basically a recipe for oxtail stew; several others (**"Happiness," "The View of Rome"**) are like architectural drawings of houses with people sketched in for scale. The furniture in her fiction is always vivacious and in her stories about Mr. Edom's antique shop, not included in this collection, *objects* dominate. The grit of factuality scintillates for her and she inhales the world's rank melancholy as if it were ambrosial perfume. Churches especially arouse her olfactory relish:

> Candles were burning, some before this image, some before that. They gave a sort of top-dressing of warmth to the building, but basically it was as cold as river mud, and under a glazing of incense it smelt of poverty.

In another church, the preserved corpse of a local saint is wonderingly detailed:

> What extraordinary gloves—so thin that the nails, long and rather dirty, showed through. . . . She looked at the face. It had blue glass eyes, to match the blue dress. One of them projected from the face, squeezed out by the shrivelling socket into which it had been fitted. It seemed to stare at her with alarm. The other eye was still in place, and placid.

The story containing the placid glass eye, **"Fenella,"** and others such as **"Healthy Landscape with Dormouse"** and **"Total Loss"** pursue a steadily deepening drabness with a remorseless exhilaration. The septuagenarian Miss Warner's continued health as a writer of fiction is a testimonial to her iron diet. She has the spiritual digestion of a goat, and a ravenous eye for unpleasantness.

Between her firm particulars and the overbrooding Olympian forbearance of tone there is, sometimes, an unexpected vacuum. Her sense of form, of direction, is erratic, which is to say she has no prejudices about her material. Her endings are often weak—abrupt and enigmatic (**"A Stranger with a Bag," "Their Quiet Lives"**), sentimental (**"Happiness"**), crowded and vague (**"Johnnie Brewer"**). Here, where an author normally gathers his matter to a point in a final phrase or word, a dominant that will reverberate backward through the fabric of imagery, Miss Warner wanders off in the middle of the measure, or goes on a measure too long, or comes down hard on a note so wrong we doubt our ears. As I read these bound stories I had the impression that some were better when I first read them in *The New Yorker*. A little research proved it to be so.

"The View of Rome" is a generally charming story about an old engraver recovering from a nearly fatal illness. He is very anxious to return to his home and in order to secure early release from the hospital pretends that his cat, Hattie, is a stepniece coming from the Isle of Wight to nurse him. Though rather lightweight, the story gathers substance from the many sharp small touches ("The clock, with its light hopping gait, like a robin's, ticked on"), the persuasive limning of a gentle old bachelor (Miss Warner makes herself quite at home in male minds), and its articulation of a kind of joy, the joy of domestic possession, not often dramatized. I enjoyed rereading it until the last sentences, which went: "God is an Oriental potentate, unaffectedly lavish and sumptuous. He would not think it extravagant to heap up all these apples into a cenotaph for a Rural Dean. Here was no need for jam pots. They could stay in the attic." The apples, we know, are lying all about, and making jam of them has preoccupied the hero in the hospital, and we have been told of the Dean who died of a wasp sting incurred at a Harvest Festival. But those last two sentences, besides choppily cutting across the preceding grand strophes about God as an Oriental potentate, bring some unlooked-for words to the fore. Jam pots? Attic? The house's attic has not been previously mentioned, and abruptly occupies the position of a keystone. It is bewildering, and dulling. *The New Yorker* version, in place of these last two sentences, has: "There was no call for jam pots here." Surely this is better: "call" for "need," "here" for "attic," and the simpler phrasing permits the potentate-lavish-extravagant-cenotaph conceit to sound the conclusive chord in this wry fugue of mortality and gratitude.

Miss Warner thought well enough of **"Swans on an Autumn River"** to name her collection after it. It tells of Norman Repton, overweight and sixty-nine, attending a congress of sanitary engineers in Dublin. He has never been in Ireland, though when he was young it had represented romance to him. He sightsees confusedly, overeats in a restaurant, and, while feeding bread to some swans on a river and angrily fending off hungry seagulls, dies of a heart attack. Some women waiting for a bus and a *garda* directing traffic witness his death. The book version ends with the paragraph:

> The *garda* who had left his place amid the traffic, now came up to where Norman Repton lay motionless. After a momentary hesitation, as though he were hastily

summoning up something he had learned, he knelt beside him. The women drew closer together, and one of them pulled her coat about her, as though she had suddenly became conscious of the cold. Presently the *garda* looked up. "Will one of you ladies go across to the hotel," he said, "and ask them to telephone for the ambulance?" Two women detached themselves from the group and hurried across the road, arguing in whisper.

The New Yorker version is the same, until:

> Presently, the *garda* got up from his knees. Looking gravely down at the figure on the pavement, he pulled off his cap and crossed himself. The action unloosed a flutter of hands, a murmur of sound, among those waiting for the bus, as though it had stirred a dovecote.

Now, this at least gives us a vivid image in which Ireland, an exotic Catholic land, and birds, whose aloof beauty and sordid hunger have lured the hero to his death, intersect. The ending Miss Warner has chosen to preserve in her book is totally centrifugal, a burst of irrelevancies. Of what significance is the mechanical request for an ambulance? Who are the two women who go to telephone, and what if they argue "in whispers"? Whispers have nothing to do with Norman Repton, and though neither ending is quite satisfactory, it is Miss Warner's that confirms our suspicion that this story is aimless. It is an insistently ugly story whose ugliness has not been shaped to any purpose. We do not know enough about Repton to feel his terminal fight with the seagulls as anything more than the irritable fit of a choleric man. The editorial process that brought two endings into being is not at issue; either *The New Yorker* version is the original one, later revised, or it is a revision prompted by the magazine and finally discarded. In either case, Miss Warner has expressed her old-fashioned preference for events over gestures. The two women walking across the road to the telephone, however flat and irrelevant as an image, are, as an event, more world-engaging and, as it were, negotiable. In an artistic age of credit manipulation, Miss Warner deals in quaintly hard cash.

Her stories tend to convince us in process and baffle us in conclusion; they are not rounded with meaning but lift jaggedly toward new, unseen, developments. **"Healthy Landscape with Dormouse"** presents with unblinking clairvoyance a miserably married and (therefore) unrepentantly mischievous young woman, Belinda. The story's locale is Belinda's consciousness, but instead of ending there the story leaps out of her head and concludes on a village street. Some suddenly introduced bus passengers have seen Belinda and her husband fight and jump into a car: "They ran to the car, leaped in, drove away. Several quick-witted voices exclaimed, 'Take the number! Take the number!' But the car went so fast, there wasn't time." It suggests a Mack Sennett comedy; it suggests furthermore an almost compulsive need, in Miss Warner's work, for witnesses. Her world is thoroughly social, like those rings of Hades where the sinners, frozen into eternal postures, must stare at each other. **"A Stranger with a Bag"**

Dust jacket for Warner's 1943 collection of short stories.

and **"A Long Night"** make the act of onlooking centrally dramatic; and the excellent **"A Jump Ahead"** ends with the narrator understanding what he has seen: his ex-wife preparing to die of leukemia.

The very best story in the book, and a masterpiece, is **"A Love Match."** It too is a story of witnessing: a brother and sister, Justin and Celia, love incestuously in a small English town and finally, killed by a stray bomb while in bed together, are discovered. The witnesses, the men who find their bodies, agree upon a fiction:

> Then young Foe spoke out. "He must have come in to comfort her. That's my opinion." The others concurred.

The tale, with its congenial mixture of the Gothic and the pedestrian, excites her prose to a fine vividness:

> The rescue workers . . . followed the trail of bricks and rubble upstairs and into a bedroom whose door slanted from its hinges. A cold air met them; looking up, they saw the sky. The floor was deep in rubble; bits of broken masonry, clots of brickwork, stood up from it like rocks on a beach. A dark bulk crouched on the hearth, and was part of the chimney stack, and a torrent

of slates had fallen on the bed, crushing the two bodies that lay there.

The first act of love, the initial violation of this most sacred taboo, is beautifully described and justified as an incident within the horror and fatalism and hysteria of the First World War. Their quiet life and smoldering secret allegorize England between the wars. Framed by monstrous cataclysms, the diffident gallantry and fuddling ordinariness of the nation, personified by an incestuous couple, are seen as somehow monstrous—the cozy sibling idyll of Victorian mythology gone mad. The historical context is indicated; twenty years of truce pass in terms of private social strategies and public social movements. Justin arranges the dusty items of a dead eccentric's military collection; Celia interests herself in the poor, in Communism. They make a few friends and sometimes attend church.

> There was a nice, stuffy pitch-pine St. Cuthbert's near by, and at judicious intervals they went there for evensong—thereby renewing another bond of childhood: the pleasure of hurrying home on a cold evening to eat baked potatoes hot from the oven.

The odors and occupations of *inter-bella* England, evoking Miss Warner's full vocabulary of flowers and foods and architectures, are suffused with the blameless decadence of the central situation. The story moves with unforced symbolism to the level of epic statement. Incest is civilization's ultimate recourse:

> Loving each other criminally and sincerely, they took pains to live together and to safeguard their happiness from injuries of their own infliction or from outside.

Of course, no touch of implied condemnation, or of undue compassion, intrudes upon the perfect sympathy with which this scandalous marriage is chronicled. Miss Warner's genius is an uncannily equable openness to human data, and beneath her refined witchery lies a strange freshness one can only call, in praise, primitive.

Robert Emmet Long (essay date 1971)

SOURCE: A review of *The Innocent and the Guilty,* in *The Saturday Review* (New York), Vol. 54, No. 18, May 1, 1971, pp. 41-2.

[*In the following excerpt, Long comments on the "sophistication" and "imagination" of Warner's stories in* The Innocent and the Guilty.]

Sylvia Townsend Warner, who is now in her late seventies, has had a long, distinguished career. Her stories practically glisten with craftsmanship, and her imagination has a quality of urbanity that is present in all the tales in *The Innocent and the Guilty,* regardless of how different the scenes and characters are.

In **"The Perfect Setting"** Miss Warner has an opportunity for satire on manners and social types. To the garden of the late poet Oswald Corbett come a number of admirers, including Mrs. Bugler, who has gone through Corbett's manuscripts examining every watermark; Father Garment, S. J., who has discovered a latent Catholicism in Corbett's "Three Odes to Ovid," and Professor Mackenzie, who has translated Corbett's poems into Lallan. Another devotee wants to tape-record the owls in the garden. But the principal seeker is a journalist named Bannerman, whose interest in Corbett has to do with sales. The situation that develops between Bannerman and Corbett's widow is observed with a wry irony and understatement. The same is true of **"Bruno,"** in which a well-to-do Scottish gentleman in his sixties returns to settle in at his family estate with a nineteen-year-old companion named Bruno, "a lissome hearthrug cat." The social complications that result lead to a farcical *dénouement.*

Yet Miss Warner's sophistication operates at almost any level. In **"But at the Stroke of Midnight"** drab Lucy Ridpath leaves her husband and takes on the identity of a frivolous cousin who has recently died. The reader is caught up in her experience, and yet looks on helplessly, restrained by the author's detachment. **"The Quality of Mercy,"** about an alcoholic middle-aged woman, is already a classic and will probably be included in anthologies for years to come.

Sylvia Townsend Warner with Val Warner and Michael Schmidt (interview date 1975)

SOURCE: "Sylvia Townsend Warner: 1893-1978: A Celebration," edited by Claire Harman, in *PN Review,* Vol. 8, No. 3, 1981, pp. 35-7.

[In the following interview, which was conducted in 1975, Warner discusses her writing career and political views.]

[Sylvia Townsend Warner]: When did I begin to write? I was led away by paper. I'm always led away by blank paper. We had a great many photographs in our work, black and white photographs of manuscripts, and there were always some throw-aways. And the white was the most beautiful smooth white photographic paper and nobody wanted it, and I wanted it, and having collected it by degrees I thought, 'I must do something about all this handsome paper—I think I'll write a poem.' So I started writing poems on this handsome paper.

My first book was *The Espalier,* and that came out in, I think, 1925. After Chatto and Windus had seen my poems (they were sent there by David Garnett who liked them) and they said tentatively, 'You don't think you could write a novel, do you?' and I, with exasperating brightness, said, 'I've written a novel, but it isn't worth anything. I only did it to amuse myself in the evenings when I had nothing better to do.' And that was *Lolly Willowes.* And except that Charles Prentice wanted me to rewrite the ending, I didn't get to alter it much. I could have altered it more.

I never thought of being a professional writer. I never thought of being a professional anything, to tell the truth. I just slopped along like Mrs Warcornisher's English Lady, you know, doing one thing at one time and another at another.

[Warner and Schmidt]: *When did your political activities begin?*

I'm trying to remember. I think it was in 1933. . . . I know what influenced me and what influenced almost all the people of my generation more than anything was the Reichstag Fire trial. Extraordinary courage and enterprise and *poise* of Dimitrov. And that was very well reported in *The Times* and made me interested in contemporary politics. And that of course made me immediately interested in the doings of the Black Shirts, and *that's* how I came to meet the people in *Left Review* and eventually to do some writing. That's how I met Edgell [Rickword].

The *Left Review* I should say began about 1934. We went to Spain in 1936, to Barcelona. We had the greatest difficulty in getting across the frontier but everything went smoothly after that. And then the next year, with Valentine Ackland, I went to the Congress of anti-Fascist writers which had been scheduled to be held in Madrid before the war broke out, but in 1937 they still held the Congress; and a very fine Congress it was.

I wrote a few articles about life in wartime Spain and got them in where I could simply as propaganda. And of course by that time it was getting rather hard to get in any propaganda because the English authorities and respectables were clamping down on freelance journalists who had anything to say in favour of the Republic. I had a great deal to say. . . . I've never seen people who I admired more. I never again saw a country I loved as much as I loved Spain. A most ungainly country to love, but it's extraordinarily beautiful. I've never been back—I said I wouldn't go back till Franco was dead and the old brute is still hanging on.

The experience affected my writing to the extent that I wrote *After the Death of Don Juan,* which is definitely a political novel—at least perhaps I should say it's a political fable. It's very rare to get now, but I think it's an extremely good story because I took the Mozart subject as my framework but continued it into the Spain of this day and age. The trouble was it was published in 1938 and in not a very large edition and was soon swamped in the circumstances of the time.

Would you describe yourself as a Communist or an anarchist?

I was a Communist, but I always find anarchists very easy to get on with. I think that's because, if the English turn to the left at all, they are natural anarchists. They are not orderly enough to be good Communists and they're too refractory to be good Communists. I became a Communist simply because I was against the Government but that of course is not a suitable frame of mind for a Communist for very long. But you can go on being an anarchist for the rest of your life, as far as I can see, and doing very well. You've always got something to be anarchic about—your life is one long excitement. And anarchists are the most *charming* people!

Summer Will Show is very much a political novel too.

That *sounds* communist, but I think at that date for anybody of intelligence, that was the only way for them to go. When I wrote that book I had the most interesting time because I thought I ought to do a little research and so I poked up from the London Library books about that date written from the Orleanist point of view and then the Monarchist point of view, and the Socialist point of view and then casual memoirs, and *nothing* agreed with anything else.

Did your political commitments affect the reception of your work?

Oh, it affected it very badly. I usually had two or three amazingly good reviews, but I never had reviews from the sort of reviewers that *sell* books. I've never produced a bestseller. I sell very well to *The New Yorker,* that's my only claim to being a bestseller. They were providential. I began writing for them as the result of a dare because we had an American friend staying with us and I was telling her of some absurd thing which had happened in the village and she said, 'You really ought to write that for *The New Yorker.*' I said, 'Ba Pooh! I can't write for *The New Yorker.* People who write for *The New Yorker* are a special race—they are like nothing else. *I* couldn't write for *The New Yorker*!' And she said, 'Oh write it; I think they'd take it.' I said, 'Bet you they wouldn't!' She said, 'Well, try it!' I said, 'I bet you £5 that they won't take it.' And they did, so I had to forfeit the £5. But on the whole, it was a good bargain.

I'm now concentrating on an entirely different new kind of short story and have been for the last three years because I suddenly looked round on my career and thought, 'Good God, I've been understanding the human heart for all these decades. Bother the human heart, I'm tired of the human heart. I'm tired of the human race. I want to write about something entirely different.' And my first story in my new vein was called **"Something Entirely Different."** It was a study of the problems of changelings. It was about a human child that was taken into Elfinland and what became of him, and also what became of the elfin child who was planted in the human child's cradle and had to grow up in a small Scotch village. I found that so engrossing and I kept on making the most delightful discoveries of great social importance. I discovered that no well-bread fairy would ever *dream* of flying; they leave that to the servants. When one has discovered some truth of that sort, it's *so* reviving, it's such fun. And I don't want to write a respectable, realistic story ever again!

But of course there was a great deal of fantasy in your novels too, in Lolly Willowes *for example.*

Yes, it put its ugly face out in *Lolly Willowes*, didn't it? I think that I've always been interested in the supernatural in its social aspects, partly reading Pitcairn's Law Trials

of Scotland. It's by far the best record of the activities of witches and witchhunters in Scotland and written in the most beautiful Scotch, and I enjoyed reading that. And I suppose I went on from there. Of course I was very much influenced by old Margaret Murray's book, *The God of the Witches*. She was a surprising old lady—looked *exactly* like Queen Victoria. . . .

Isn't there some incompatability between political anarchism and formalism in writing?

I dare say there is. I remember a passage in Walt Whitman where someone or other is accusing him of being inconsistent and he says, 'Am I inconsistent? Well, I *am* inconsistent. Within me I contain millions!'

I'm more at home with seventeenth-century poetry than with any other. I'm a very great admirer of Dryden, because Dryden can say anything. He makes the most ridiculous statements and he can always bring them off. The line in 'The Hind and the Panther' that I particularly like—it's the last line of a section: 'The Lady of the spotted-muff began.' Now that is a line which is purely nonsensical and yet Dryden is so stately in his control of the medium and so sublime that one hears it almost with awe. When that line comes, one is merely delighted: Here is a splendid line.

Dryden has much more meat to him than Pope. I'm always attached to Marvell. I'm devoted to Defoe, and I'm fairly well at home with the Russians. I was very lucky: my mother liked reading aloud and she only read aloud the books which she liked herself and so it was that I heard the whole of *War and Peace* read to me before I was fourteen. Thackeray doesn't stand up to time so well. My passion for Flaubert and Stendhal, particularly for Stendhal, has never wavered. Stendhal is a very interesting Romantic because he's satirical. He's being intensely Romantic with half of him and there's a small cold beady eye which is fixed on the Romantic Stendhal saying, 'My God! What antics will this man get up to next?' I like inconsistencies in authors; I think I like inconsistencies in any creative work.

At the moment, I think the novel is falling to pieces, but I don't know how it will pull itself together again. Of course, it may be a varying form. It's been around for a very long time. I'm quite sure that the biography is an up-and-coming form, that much more in the way of biography will happen, partly because there's such a demand for it. Think how people seized on Boswell when Boswell's *Diaries* were put out. . . .

What are you working on at the moment?

I'm working on those short stories. I'm not working on anything else. And I'm steadily refusing to write an autobiography.

Why's that?

Because I'm too imaginative.

Do you still write poems?

Oh yes, usually just when I'm about to pack or catch a train or have someone to stay. Always at inconvenient moments like that. And I revise them endlessly, endlessly. I revise everything that I do.

Gabriele Annan (essay date 1977)

SOURCE: "The Not So Little People," in *The Times Literary Supplement,* January 14, 1977, p. 25.

[*In this review, Annan describes Warner's prose as "poetic and . . . mystical."*]

What is named on the label is found in the jar: [the stories in *Kingdoms of Elfin*] really are fairy stories and fourteen of the sixteen have appeared in *The New Yorker* where they must have glittered with a strange unearthly light among the wife-swappings on Martha's Vineyard, the examinations of social diseases, and the advertisements for Bergdorf Goodman. The elfin kingdoms over or underlie (mostly under, because they tend to be subterranean) Europe, and their inhabitants share the traditionally accepted characteristics of their human counterparts. Thus the elfins of the Kingdom of Wirre Gedanken in the Harz Mountains are given to metaphysical speculation; on the English side of the Scottish border the fairies are comparatively uncouth and deplorably indifferent to physical comfort; in Elfhame on the Scottish side they are natural theologians; in Ireland they see ghosts, and so on. These are not accidental clichés. You might not think them clichés at all, because they are handled so wittily and unexpectedly: but I think they are and are meant to be, and that the whole book is an attack on accepted thinking.

When the stories were appearing one by one the author needed to slip all the basic facts about her fairy cosmos into each one to give the reader his bearings. Now that the stories are collected together this repetition of information is irritating, though it helps to fix it in the reader's mind. Here are the main points: fairies are about four-fifths the size of a human being, not small enough to lie in a cowslip bell as the English poets made out; they can fly, but only the lower orders do it: among well-bred fairies flying is considered "servile and *infra dig*". Well-bred fairies hardly breed at all, but they are fond of babies, which is why they have to steal human changelings; all fairies have push-button invisibility; they live for hundreds of years, not aging at all; aging is considered disgusting, so the changelings are thrown out into the natural world when they begin to go grey. Fairies are elegant, ceremonious and cool. They have no conscience, no sense of obligation, no need for consistency. Most important of all, they have no souls and no immortality: "when they die they are dead: it is as simple as that".

The Peris of Persia, the stones of Carnac, the Greek gods, Morgan le Fay and King Arthur are part of elfin history. Their present is a picturesque past, set somewhere between the twelfth and seventeenth centuries: a feudal time with many small courts. All the fairies are princes, or courtiers, or their servants; there is no fairy bourgeoisie, and Miss Townsend Warner is not much interested in social criticism. Nor is she interested in the occult, as some modern writers of supernatural tales are. She turns the supernatural upside down: her fairies are not merely sweetly reasonable but sweetly rational, and her jokes—ironical, dry and sly—are jokes against religion, against superstition, gullibility, clericalism and priggishness.

Yet her book is not a dry Voltairian satire. It is poetic, and the poetry comes not only from the fastidious elfin magic of her prose, but also from a feeling for nature which could, perhaps, be called mystical (certainly it is more mystical than ecological). Her most famous work, *Lolly Willowes* (1926), a novel about an upper-middle-class girl turning into a witch, was a compound of nature mysticism and rationalism with the emphasis on the former. Here it is the other way around, but the combination either way is typically Georgian. One is reminded of David Garnett's *Lady into Fox* and of the Arthurian novels of T. H. White, whose biography Miss Townsend Warner wrote. She will be eighty-five this year, so her Georgianism is real, not retro.

William Jay Smith (essay date 1977)

SOURCE: A review of *Kingdoms of Elfin,* in *The New York Times Book Review,* March 27, 1977, pp. 6-7.

[*In the following review, Smith says that while Warner is dextrous and sharp in her presentation of the elfin world to the reader, behind it all "the reader senses the author's fundamental skepticism."*]

This collection of tales [*Kingdoms of Elfin*] by Sylvia Townsend Warner is, to say the least, cause for celebration. Issued on the fiftieth anniversary of the publication of her novel *Lolly Willowes,* the first book ever chosen by the Book-of-the-Month Club, it has all the freshness, wit, originality of perception and clarity of insight that have won for her rhythmical prose so many admirers over so long a time. It offers us an unforgettable journey through time and space, a cast of truly fantastic characters and an impressive and seemingly unending display of verbal fireworks.

Sylvia Townsend Warner's fairyland kingdoms will no doubt be likened to the imaginary realms of J. R. R. Tolkien in *The Lord of the Rings.* They may attract many of the same readers and even inspire a similar cult, but they are essentially different. It is Tolkien's contention that good fairy tales are concerned with "the *adventures* of men in the Perilous Realm or upon its shadowy marches. Naturally so; for if elves are true, and really exist independently of our tales about them, then this also is certainly true: elves are not primarily concerned with us, nor we with them. Our fates are sundered, and our paths seldom meet. Even upon the borders of Faërie we encounter them only at some chance crossing of the ways."

Genuine fairy tales must be presented as absolutely true. Because they deal with marvels, they cannot tolerate "any frame or machinery suggesting that the whole story in which they occur is a figment or illusion." The magic in the tales, Tolkien insists, can never be made fun of. Yet Sylvia Townsend Warner appears to do just that: She wishes her reader to enjoy her enjoyment of the enchantment, and irony in her work is omnipresent.

The stories in **Kingdoms of Elfin** are not genuine fairy tales, in the sense that the author chooses not to move *through* the looking-glass, but rather to hold that glass up over a long period of history to an imaginary world and to the real world beside it. She maneuvers the glass with such dexterity that the effect is at times dizzying. But the sharpness of detail offered is so great that the reader at the same time feels that he knows exactly where he is and where he will be going next.

Not everything is languorous and lovely in these elfin kingdoms; ugliness and cruelty exist "like dirt in the crevices of an artichoke," presented in the completely matter-of-fact manner of folk tales. The climax of **"The Revolt at Brocéliande"** is a fight between the two court eunuchs, who enter the ring spurred like roosters, egged on by the Master of the Werewolves. In all the bizarre detail, it is the exquisite verbal invention throughout that holds our attention. Since she is dealing with winged creatures, Sylvia Townsend Warner enjoys playing with the notion of flight: Elfins of good breeding do not fly, but assert their hereditary claim to go about on foot as though they were mortals. She plays also with the elfin rejection of the immortality of the soul. But behind all the occult learning that these stories demonstrate, the reader senses the author's fundamental skepticism.

In their intermingling of myth and everyday reality and their playful creation of imaginary worlds, these stories call to mind the moral tales of Jules Laforgue. And as with Laforgue, the moral is in the telling, in the music of language itself and in the perceptions of the human condition that are delivered in passing as from a flashing mirror. They will not be to everyone's liking. Their hothouse atmosphere, their lapidary sheen and their supreme artifice may be too much for those accustomed only to the rough tall tales of the American past or to the confessional alphabet-adventure soup of the moment. Some will find, as did Edwin Muir many years ago, that no matter how well Sylvia Townsend Warner does what she sets out to do, the finished work has a note of falsity to it. Others will delight in every aspect of her aphoristic style—beside which Tolkien seems the clumsiest of writers—and find her superbly wrought tales, however indirect their approach, the achievement of a fine writer and a wise woman.

David Williams (essay date 1979)

SOURCE: "Your Elf," in *Punch,* Vol. 277, August 1, 1979, p. 181.

[*In the following excerpt from a review of* The Kingdoms of Elfin, *Williams praises Warner's prose as "a delight."*]

Sylvia Townsend Warner was variously gifted. In *The Corner that Held Them* she wrote one of the finest novels to appear in this country since the war. She wrote also a magnificent biography of T. H. White, tragic author of *The Once and Future King.* But primarily she was, like White himself, a fantasist.

I'm not a Hobbit-man, not a Watership-down-man, not even a Narnia-man. These fantastics are too long, too self-important, too axe-grinding. But Sylvia Townsend Warner's otherworldliness is far different from these.

For a start, her prose is always a delight—sharp, crisp, unflagging, and often very funny. In England she never got her due, but America recognised her worth, and fourteen of the sixteen stories in her last collection **Kingdoms of Elfin**—she died a year or two back in her eighties—appeared first in the *New Yorker.*

Her various elfland hideouts are all nonmoral places, yet somehow never trivial. Her detail is richly inventive and surprising—but surprising in an assured way that commands instant acceptance. Her elfland creatures are small and green and have wings. These wings though are generally held to be bad form, and flying hours are kept to a minimum. Uncontrollable tail-spins and crash-landings are not unknown. They play three-handed whist, knit a lot, and eat well. At the same time they can become nonchalantly murderous if overworld beings start interfering. Time, most terrifying of dimensions, doesn't exist for them, and a Lecturer in Rhetoric at the University of Aberdeen who gets pulled underground finds that his watch stops instantly.

In addition this author can be highly indelicate, but always in a most delicate way: such a change from the routine crapulous bawdy which novelists now reach for in deference to passing fashion.

Glen Cavaliero (essay date 1981)

SOURCE: "The Short Stories," in "Sylvia Townsend Warner 1893-1978: A Celebration," edited by Claire Harman, in *PN Review,* Vol. 8, No. 3, 1981, p. 45.

[*In the following essay, Cavaliero lauds Warner's literary skill and "ability to celebrate the singular without declining into singularity."*]

Sylvia Townsend Warner may have been neglected by the critics, but her work was not unread. For over forty years her short stories appeared in *The New Yorker,* giving her a world-wide reputation; over one hundred and fifty of them appeared in published collections. Clearly she found them an appropriate medium for her gifts.

Those gifts included a talent for the telling phrase; similes that illuminated and did not distract; an eye for strangeness and incongruity; a detailed knowledge of the practicalities of daily life; the power to generalise informatively, an apparent inability to waste words, and a tart, unjudging awareness of the quirks and perversities of human nature. Also, an essential skill, she knew how to secure attention.

> 'Mary Glasscastle would have stayed quietly in his memory's cold storage if she had not been murdered.'

> 'Each warehouse along the London Thames has its staff of cats, half a dozen of them or more, heavy and redoubtable, hunters like William Rufus.'

> 'Private charity still persists in England though mostly it is practised in the disorderly, hole-and-corner style recommended by Jesus.'

The adroit, personal cadence and controlled aplomb betoken a confidence that becomes reciprocal. Nor are the stories in one mould; at the end one often finds oneself facing in a direction opposite to that in which one had set out. A good example is **"During a Winter Night,"** which gives a soberly ironical account of an overworked mother and land-lady whose preparations for suicide are interrupted by the need to save her lonely lodger from a similar attempt. The coincidence only serves to reinforce the desperation which the plot defines: the story ends, 'The kettle boiled and boiled away while she stood weeping for misery and mortification and defeat.' These are not just straight-forward *contes* with a sting in the tail, nor are they primarily expressions of mood or feeling: they owe as little to Mansfield as to Maugham.

The stories fall into four distinguishable groups. The ones collected in *The Salutation* (1932) and *More Joy in Heaven* (1935) are rather folksy and derivative; the shades of T. F. Powys and A. E. Coppard hang about them. The Second World War produced a shift in style and tone. *A Garland of Straw* (1943) and *The Museum of Cheats* (1947) are caustic, sometimes frivolous; on occasion anger degenerates into a sneer. But as pictures of civilian life in wartime these stories compare illuminatingly with those of Elizabeth Bowen. Instead of the haunted London of the Blitz one is made aware of provincial England, beset as much by inconveniences as hazards. Food shortages, the upending of taboos, the disparity between the war and the response it ordinarily evokes, are what interest Sylvia Townsend Warner. Few writers have such a feeling for the long littleness of life and such a flair for making its dissection entertaining.

In *Winter in the Air* (1955), *A Spirit Rises* (1962) and *A Stranger with a Bag* (1964) her command is absolute. She has a sure eye for local detail and historical tradition, as well as for the motives individual people have for living as they do. An unlaboured irony colours many of the tales, usually in the shape of recovery from disaster. '**Idenborough**' provides an instance of this. Accompanied by her second husband, a wife revisits the small country town in which she had for two nights been unfaithful to her first one. The cause of the visit is fortuitous, and shows the

author's mastery of the comedy of accidentals. Next, the reason for Amabel's emotion is broken to us, her happy acceptance that the town no longer looks as it did turning to dismay on her realising that it was another Idenborough she had visited before. Bedfordshire, not Oxfordshire: happiness has blinded her now as then. Her feelings of inadequacy resolve themselves into an affirmation of the past moment. 'It existed by her secrecy; to speak of it would be to dismiss it, like the small crystal world of a bubble, into common air. Any infidelity but that.' The tragi-comedy is further emphasised by the loving detail with which the second Idenborough is set before us. The author's architectural sense is very sure.

But by the time of *The Innocent and the Guilty* (1971) it was clear that she was getting a shade weary of writing in this mode, and her two efforts to portray the world of contemporary youth do not ring true. It is therefore not surprising, given this weariness and her own refusal to regulate her talents, that she should in the last years of her life embark on an entirely new venture. *Kingdoms of Elfin* (1977) was not her first essay in systematic fantasy (*The Cat's Cradle Book* had preceded it by over a decade) but in it she put the art to novel use. The fairy courts and kingdoms she describes so minutely are not so much commentaries on, or correctives to, our own world as parallel to it, involved in it, and sharing many of its habits and limitations. The tales provide a gloss on human institutions, and are delightfully free from knowingness and whimsy; they succeed in making the fairies creatures of fantasy in every meaning of the term. It is as though Sylvia Townsend Warner was producing an imaginative commentary on her own achievement, that of one who could celebrate the singular without declining into singularity. It is a gift as heartening as it is rare; and nowhere is it more in evidence than in her stories. She illuminates her subject matter from odd angles, adapting reality without transfiguring it. This most traditional of writers was at heart a modernist, fusing imagination with wit and lacing the result with her own particular blend of fantasy and tolerant good sense.

Shirley Toulson (essay date 1984)

SOURCE: A review of *One Thing Leading to Another, and Other Stories*, in *British Book News*, July, 1984, p. 427.

[*In the following review, Toulson calls* One Thing Leading to Another, and Other Stories *"a good collection" that includes some characters who showcase Warner "at her sharpest and funniest."*]

Sylvia Townsend Warner, a prolific poet and novelist, was at her best in the sympathetic creation of eccentric and slightly dotty characters. She is probably most widely known for *Lolly Willowes,* first published in 1925 and reissued by The Women's Press in 1978, the year of her death. Lolly is a sad, wispy, lonely person, the conventional maiden aunt, half-crazed by her isolation and inability to build herself a satisfactory life in society. The twenty stories here, selected and edited by Susanna Pinney, are woven round several such figures: Helen Logie, the priests' housekeeper in the title story, who having once accidentally made curry with snuff, amuses herself thereafter in seeing how far she can go, undetected, in using bizarre ingredients in her cooking; Mary Daker, who reacts so strongly against her neighbours' commendation that she is 'always the same' the she provokes them into burning her effigy on the Guy Fawkes' bonfire; the garrulous Miss Belforest, who is compelled to read aloud every notice she sees. The extraordinary thing about all these lost and apparently limited people is that they are far more fully realized as human beings than the well-established members of society who try to do good to them.

Sylvia Townsend Warner is at her sharpest and funniest in her portrayal of these well-meaning busybodies. There is Mrs Pansy Carrington, measuring the time she spends with a lively and intelligent old lady in miserly quarter hours, and Mrs Camden, the rural vicar's wife, who makes blind, conventual steps to persuade a totally scatty family to take part in the life of the village at the very time that the pregnant wife is attempting to shoot her exasperatingly ridiculous husband.

The stories in which these individuals appear are the best of a good collection [*One Thing Leading to Another, and Other Stories*], which also includes two groups of tales. One is centred on the orderly Mr Edom and his disorderly antique shop, the other on the slightly Pre-Raphaelite and utterly odd Finch family with their two pert little daughters and ailing son. Less successful are the four fairy stories that end the collection. Sylvia Townsed Warner wrote a biography of T. H. White, and in these tales she uses fairies as he used the Arthurian legends, to comment on human affairs. Although they are well worked out, and often quite witty, they fail because her sympathies are always with people rather than ideas, and it is for her characters that she will always be remembered.

Anne Duchêne (essay date 1984)

SOURCE: "Witty and Well-Mannered," in *The Times Literary Supplement*, No. 4247, August 24, 1984, p. 953.

[*In the following review, Duchêne describes Warner's prose as "witty, warmhearted, [and] well-mannered," but questions the selection and editing of the stories in* One Thing Leading to Another.]

"There's been another horrid murder by Teddy Bears": a well-bred female voice disturbs the Sunday quiet ("as though the words had been etched in dry-point on the silence") of a hotel lounge, and thus the little joke, heard or imagined, becomes the nucleus of another story by Sylvia Townsend Warner. As, in the uncharacteristically laborious title story here, does a cook's mistaking snuff

for curry; or, in a story dated shortly before Warner's death, a woman's sewing a "Widow's quilt" after seeing one in the American Museum in Bath.

Those who like to see the grain of sand working in the oyster of a story-teller's mind are splendidly served when another story is prefaced by a letter from the author to her friend George Plank in 1963, which uncovers the story's genesis. An American, she writes, has left a somewhat sumptuous hat, of Piccadilly provenance, in the antique shop of her woman friend; they have kept it piously, and put it outside, accessible but safe from cats, whenever they leave home; she would like to wear it herself, but her friend says this would "make her conspicuous" ("What other purpose has a hat?"); if it is unclaimed at Christmas, she will send it to George Plank.

This engendered a story, **"Some Effects of a Hat",** which appeared in the *New Yorker* a year later, about an American's leaving a similar hat in the home of a spinster (more exactly a weaver, of tweeds) in a Devonshire village; about her trying it on herself, with some pleasure—"instead of resembling a sheep, she resembled a goat"—and how it gives rise to rumour and thence to violence in the village, so that she flees (after having precipitately but sensibly sold up her home, because this author never forgets the practicalities of life) to her unknown cousins in Derbyshire, one of whom, in no time at all, and with every promise of happiness, she marries.

The tiny incident is transmuted, by the storyteller's authority, into a story shimmering with humour and pain, carrying all the blithe inconsequence of chance, which forges its own logic. Unhappily, this is the only time when editorial reticence is breached by Susanna Pinney, who thanks no fewer than three of her publishers for their "help and advice" but does not say why such a large corporate effort was required, nor anything about the unpublished work still remaining, from which she had drawn seven of the twenty stories here. Of the thirteen published stories, eleven appeared in the *New Yorker,* whose urbane contours coincided comfortably with the author's, and all of them appeared between 1944 and 1977, in the last thirty years of her life. Presumably the unpublished ones date from this period too, but the editor does not confirm this.

Dates are of little significance, however, where there is no evolutionary change, and all the stories might equally well have come from the previous two decades of the author's writing life. For just over half a century, Sylvia Townsend Warner wrote a witty, warm-hearted, well-mannered prose which never assumed greater significance than the giving—or more exactly, as she made it seem, the sharing—of a good deal of quiet enjoyment. (What might seem to us now the most "contemporary" of these stories, with a heavy charge of menace under its blandness, appeared in *Lilliput* in 1948.) She was happiest in the liberating latitudes of eccentricity, or when she could tilt some well-fleshed verisimilitude gently over into the unlikely, or perhaps beyond that into the fantastic; but she was a modest exotic, and her taste for the improbable was always tempered by good humour, good taste and good will. Lolly

Willowes, her first full-length heroine, back in the 1920s, might quite placidly turn into a witch, but cannot be conceived of as riding a camel in English lanes, for instance, or any of the other arrogant excesses to which fiercer writers like Rose Macaulay put ladies of similar ilk.

The one appreciable shift in her focus came late in life, when she succumbed to the temptations of mere fancifulness, which notably beset English writers in the genteel tradition; but even then, her rather tiresome four-foot elves, or Elfins, as she called them, remain paramortals, as serenely incisive as her humans. Four Elfin stories conclude this book; only one appeared in the *New Yorker* (it would be interesting to know if the others were rejected, or never submitted). Admirers may persuade themselves of an allegorical aftertaste in these stories—some familiar resonance, say, when Tamarind sets out to find and serve the philosophical author of "Grub's Exposition of the Limited" but ends at the feet of a gnomically vacuous peasant Grub. Less determined readers may simply find them a sad sign of declining imaginative powers.

With the recent publication of *Scenes of Childhood* and of her letters, there is evidently an elegant conspiracy afoot to remind us of Sylvia Townsend Warner. Rightly so; this collection lies too much under the *New Yorker*'s seal of approval, but her vision was both sharper and broader than this may suggest. If we are to keep her in perspective, though, we do need rather more information than we are given here about what is "selected", and how it is "edited".

Robert Crossley (essay date 1985)

SOURCE: "A Long Day's Dying: The Elves of J. R. R. Tolkien and Sylvia Townsend Warner," in *Death and the Serpent: Immortality in Science Fiction and Fantasy,* edited by Carl B. Yoke and Donald M. Hassler, Greenwood Press, 1985, pp. 57-70.

[*In the excerpt below, Crossley compares the elfin worlds of Warner and J. R. R. Tolkien.*]

Among the folklore traditions on the origin of elves is the notion that they are the lost children of Adam and Lilith, born before the fall in Eden and therefore exempt from the punishment of death, but born as well outside the framework of redemption and therefore also disenfranchised from the promise of a life beyond the end of the world. One paradox of the "fortunate fall" for human beings is that while the penalty for original sin is heavy, the unanticipated gift of a second life is a measure of the extraordinary bounty of the Creator towards his creatures. But for the elves this paradox is less happy. Their imaginative appeal for both folk audiences and sophisticated readers has always been connected with their apparent superiority to the contingencies of the world, their freedom from human responsibility and human sorrow. In their enviable longevity the elves are emblems of what human beings feel they have lost—life without interruption, life unlimited. In

his catalogue of elfin antiquities in *The Faerie Queene,* Spenser supposes the fairies to be the creation of Prometheus, and he names the first of their race "Elf, to weet, / 'Quick.'" Spenser's imaginary etymology calls to mind the opposition between the quick and the dead and invites nostalgia for a prelapsarian version of ourselves, a species noble, perpetually young, quick with life.

And yet the elves, spared the human penance of mortality, are not quite immortal. They are simply long-lived, bounded by the limits of created nature. They belong to the world, to its mutability, its finitude, its ultimate decay and end. Because elves are superhuman but not supernatural, their long life is also a protracted dying. What Milton's Adam foresaw for himself and Eve after their fall has even sharper pertinence for the elves. In his moment of deepest despair in *Paradise Lost,* Adam interprets God's suspension of the immediate sentence of death not as an act of mercy but as an excruciation:

> no sudden, but a slow-pac't evil,
> A long day's dying to augment our pain.

There is an antidote for Adam's despair. Under the instruction of the angel Michael he learns that his pain will be productive and that death will lead to transfiguration. In the words of Milton's God:

> so Death becomes
> His final remedy, and after Life
> Tri'd in sharp tribulation, and refin'd
> By Faith and faithful works, to second Life,
> Wak't in the renovation of the just,
> Resigns him up with Heav'n and Earth renew'd.

The elves, however, find neither remedy nor consolation for their slow-paced dying. Because their nature is more than human while their destiny remains less than human, they are at once the richest embodiment and the most profound critique of the human fantasy of longevity. The elves give the ancient cautionary maxim of *momento mori* (Remember that you must die) a renewed claim on our imaginations.

Of the many literary treatments of the elves, few since Spenser's have made them anything more than decorative aids to the establishment of fantastic "atmosphere." Still fewer writers have invested their elves with the psychological complexity that would reveal them as paradoxical reflections of the human wish for immortality. The notable twentieth-century exceptions are J. R. R. Tolkien and Sylvia Townsend Warner. From different perspectives and motives and with quite different kinds of sympathy, Tolkien's *Silmarillion* and Warner's **Kingdoms of Elfin** explore and amplify the paradoxes implied in the human attraction toward elves.

Tolkien and Warner make an unlikely pair. It is doubtful that either knew the other's work, although they were almost exact contemporaries. Their temperaments and literary sensibilities were so opposite—he melancholic and tardy, she nimble and social; he Catholic and pious, she latitudinarian and worldly; he with a taste for the austere myths of the North, she drawn to Shelley and Proust—that it is hard to imagine them approving either the form or the motive for each other's fantastic fiction. And there may have been an even sturdier obstacle to sympathy. Dustjacket photographs of the elderly Tolkien are so familiar that it is easy to forget that his history of the elves is the product of his youth. While his desire to perfect *The Silmarillion* lasted sixty years as his rewriting became habitual and finally self-defeating, the nature of his elves was fashioned and fixed when Tolkien was in his twenties. They are endowed with the seriousness with which youth takes its inventions, and the author clung to that youthful vision even as he aged through its revisions.

Warner's elfins, conceived the year before Tolkien's death, are a different matter altogether. Even their name suggests an ironic amusement Tolkien would not have permitted himself. *Kingdoms of Elfin* collects stories that belong to old ages. When she began writing them for the *New Yorker,* Warner was in her eighties, and they have that freedom from gravity which is one of the privileges of age. Warner drafted her stories quickly, assuredly, and with an aesthetic detachment so clinical and comic that there is no mistaking that her point of view is resolutely human. The cockeyed charm of her sophisticated elfins, who are always self-absorbed and snobbish, often daffy, rarely heroic, makes a revealing contrast with the grave dignity and sorrow of Tolkien's prehistoric elves.

Perhaps the issue of elven longevity was bound to be perceived differently from the vantages of youth and age. The young Tolkien—for whom there would never be enough time to compose and finish his stories—must have felt the pull of longevity as an irresistible fantasy, even as his Catholicism pulled him another way toward resignation to mortality and the hope for immortality. . . .

Warner seems hardly ambivalent at all about her elfins, probably because she was as nearly free as one can be from ambivalence about her own mortality. She can be ironic about elfin longevity because she had accepted her own brevity. In a letter of condolence written just before her eighty-second birthday, she acknowledged her good luck in having gotten a slightly larger than usual measure of life. Though moved by the suffering of others, she is self-possessed about her own approaching death; her protests are political, not personal. The tone here is a lovely combination of sympathetic understanding, acquiescence, and celebration—as good an introduction to *Kingdoms of Elfin* as one could wish:

> What is man's chief end? Death, I suppose, since we practice for it every night. I understand your resentment at the death of people you love. I feel even angrier at the death of those who are cut short; . . . even more for the young who go down into the pit in battles of the Somme. *That* is intolerable. I was brought up to think it a sin to waste bread, and I have lived all my life in a world that wastes life. When you shall hear the sudden surly bell, don't, I beg you, be angry on my behalf. Remember all the nets that

didn't catch me, all the lies that didn't trap me, all the tar-babies I didn't get stuck on.

Out of two such different experiences of mortality as Tolkien's and Warner's, it is not remarkable to discover two markedly distinctive attitudes towards elves and elfins.

What Tolkien discovered in shaping the chronicles of the elves is that to desire the abolition of death is to desire something inhuman. His elves are, to be sure, images of a wishful humanity, the human spirit in an exalted condition. But in their inability to die, they are also sadly inhuman. Their paradoxical condition is to be something like angelic zombies. They may suffer and mourn, but not die; they may know pain but not release. They are inconsolable.

Sylvia Townsend Warner wrote the stories set in Elfhame on borrowed time, as a passage in **"Winged Creatures"** makes beautifully clear:

> The measure of our mortal days is more or less threescore and ten. The lover cries out for a moment to be eternal, the astronomer would like to see a comet over again, but he knows this is foolish, as the lover knows his mistress will outlive her lustrous eyes and die round about the time he does. Our years, long or short, are told on the same plainfaced dial.

During the years of writing *Kingdoms of Elfin,* mortality was very much on Warner's mind, not just because of her advanced years but because of an immediate experience of loss. A few years before she started exploring the elfin kingdoms, her lifelong, intimate companion Valentine Ackland died. "I am in a new country and she is the compass I travel by," Warner wrote on the evening when Valentine's coffin was taken from the house [*Letters*]. In succeeding months she found herself bored, deprived, in pain, but not disabled. She discovered a way, as did Tolkien, of transmuting experience through the distancing mode of fantasy. Her "new country" she named Elfhame.

The elfin stories run hot and cold: they are eagerly detailed studies of elfin anthropology (a paradoxical but appropriate term), but they are also aloof, even cruel, taxonomies of elfin psychology and morality. The elfins are elegant, cultivated, shrewd—but petulant, selfish, blasé, too. The author scrutinizes them with a mixture of indulgence and genial contempt. Warner's correspondence about these stories while they were in draft tells a lot about their motives. Enclosing a copy of **"The Five Black Swans"** to Marchette and Joy Chute, she writes, "Oh, how I long to give it learned footnotes, and references. There is such heartless happiness in scholarship." Later, she sends three new stories to Ian Parsons: "All in Warner's late manner. . . . I myself enjoy them passionately. It is such a relief to escape from the human heart which I was growing rather too familiar with." To Bea Howe she confesses a fantasy that she would like being reincarnated as an astronomer: "Writing about Elfins is the nearest I can get to the abstract, but astronomy would be abstracteder. It would be a form of thinking, with intensity, about nothing." Answering some questions from David Garnett, she speculates that her elfins rarely fall in love because "longevity keeps them cool-blooded." And she dreams of a second installment: "I am still finding out more about them. If I am spared, I may do another volume. There are three stories already—and a heavenly amount of research involved." Passionate enjoyment of cold-blooded creatures, escape from the human to the abstract, the heartless delights of research, intense thinking about nothing, the picture that emerges is marvelously honest and revealing. The fantasies of *Kingdoms of Elfin* are valedictory and therapeutic: an imaginative taming of the grief that has been and a serene preparation for the death that is to be.

"The One and the Other," the initial story of changelings, is typical of the mood and manner of *Kingdoms of Elfin*. The one is a human baby stolen from a baker's wife and transported to Elfhame where its blood is exchanged for elfin ichor to lengthen its life; the child is named Tiffany and brought up in the royal court as a plaything of the elfins. The other is the elfin child who, its wings extirpated and its ichor diluted with an elixir of mortality, is left for the baker's wife to rear. He is reluctantly christened Adam by a dubious minister who suspects the curiously placid infant to be an elfin, "a soulless being between Heaven and Hell and of no interest to either." In Elfhame Tiffany grows up to become the Queen's gigolo and has little else to do but join in the sterile routines, the endless games of billiards and golf, the rituals of etiquette that comprise the daily round of aristocratic life in elfindom. When at last his hair begins to gray—the emblem of a mortality that transfusions of ichor cannot wash out—he ceases to amuse his hosts and is expelled from Elfhame to spend his declining years in the mortal world.

Meanwhile, Adam grows up thinking himself human but tormented by passions he cannot understand. In particular, he is morbidly fascinated with dying; he studies epitaphs, practices dissection on animals, even fancies himself the Angel of Death after hearing a sermon on the text, "For as in Adam all die." When he attends a Rosicrucian lecture on the magnetic air that supposedly makes sylphs immortal, he defines his special vocation: "He was a compendium of deaths. Death, then, must be his proper study. To understand death, he must approach it through its opposite: the incapacity to die. He must catch a fairy, draw blood from it, identify that special element of magnetic air." Here Warner discloses what is probably her governing motive for the elfin stories: to come to terms with death by exploring its alternative.

"The One and the Other" culminates in a meeting of the opposites. On a walking tour of Scotland, Adam stops at an inn where the aged Tiffany, ill and delirious, shouts during the night of his longing to return to Elfhame. Guessing, wrongly, that Tiffany is an elfin traveling incognito, Adam slips into Tiffany's bedroom and, as the old man raves quietly in his fever, bleeds him. To his chagrin, chemical analysis yields no trace of magnetism. But Adam has bungled the phlebotomy, and as he hunches over the test tubes pondering the scientific problem, Tiffany slowly

bleeds to death in his bed. Adam is sorry to conclude that his experiment was based on a mistaken premise, though he feels nothing for his victim: "So the poor wretch was not a fairy; and the bedding would have to be paid for. But if the body could be got to the anatomists in Edinburgh, thought Adam, taking heart again, I shall about break even." In his final acts and words Adam displays the real ethos of the elfins, which Warner elaborates in the succeeding tales. Adam has all the carelessness, the ethical obtuseness, the immunity to sympathy that make her elfins seem so utterly *other*. For Adam, as for all Warner's elfins, death is an intellectual dilemma, intriguing at a distance, distasteful close up, but never touching. That elfins are inhuman is expected; that they should be inhumane is chilling. Warner's sympathies do not lie with the elfin temperament, but in understanding elfins as human opposites she invites a richer appreciation for, a deeper contentment with the human condition.

Throughout *Kingdoms of Elfin* the Swiftian tone Warner liked to claim is more evident in her depiction of elfin societies than in her occasional arch glimpses into human institutions. This is not to depreciate her sharp eye for human folly; on clergymen, scholars, and other kinds of mountebanks she can be mercilessly amusing. But it is her Park Avenue elfins (inevitably, one imagines *these* elfins subscribing to the *New Yorker* to read about themselves) whom Warner finds insufferable, precisely because they do not suffer enough. The only elfins she is drawn to are those who find the enforced gaiety and complacency of Elfhame unbearable: the elfin heretics, exiles, dissidents, misfits, eccentrics, visionaries, and kooks who are always the memorable characters in each story.

There is, for instance, in **"Castor and Pollux"** an apostate elfin named Hamlet who causes scandal by founding a "Society for Unregulated Speculation" in which he enjoys taking the affirmative on such subversive propositions as "That Mortals Are More Interesting Than Elfins" and, more damagingly, "That Elfins Are Not Interesting." In one of her most delicate fictions, **"Elphenor and Weasel,"** Warner has an elfin choose to remain among humans because he finds that mortality *is* more interesting than longevity: "Mortals packed more variety into their brief lives—perhaps because they knew them to be brief. There was always something going on and being taken seriously." Most impressive and hilarious, there is the titular character in **"The Late Sir Glamie."** Following a suitably lengthened and distinguished life, the elfin Sir Glamie has the bad taste to keep materializing after his death, thereby affronting the most cherished elfin belief: that they do not have souls.

While the elfins consider the human faith in an afterlife a vulgar but understandable superstition, given our wretched condition, Sir Glamie's posthumous career embarrasses them. He keeps reappearing unpredictably—at one time lurking in a chandelier during spring cleaning, at other times inhabiting corridors and causing soufflés to collapse—and reviving old questions among the elfins about whether *homo sapiens* is, after all, a race apart or a race akin. They try hard to pretend not to notice the apparition, but Sir Glamie makes himself a nuisance to both the etiquette and metaphysics of the elfins. "Most painful of all was the threat to the calm negation on which all Elfindom reposes," Warner explains. If Sir Glamie's ghost is acknowledged, "fear of an awaiting life after death would rush in, and Elfins sink to the level of mortals."

Warner loves inflicting discomfort on her elfins, for their calmness proceeds from a different source than her own. Her ability to contemplate death with nearly impersonal detachment comes from looking at the experience head-on, neither minimizing nor sentimentalizing it. The elfins have only negative composure, achieved by averting their eyes. Warner's creatures are too passionless and trivial to be convincing sinners or to bear the weight of the ethical and epic struggles Tolkien imposes on his elves. They also differ from Tolkien's elves in that they do not have even a qualified immortality; although they last longer than we do, they do not endure until the world's end. With a life span of a millennium or so, Warner's elfins feel immensely superior to human beings. Their longevity does not fill them with the burdensome regret of the elves of *The Silmarillion,* but it does make them vain and self-satisfied—and a little frightened, for they construct a variety of distractions and taboos designed to prevent them from thinking much about their own deaths.

One elfin taboo that must have given Warner mischievous pleasure in describing is their "particular reprobation of demonstrable old age." Elfins who succumb to the sudden physical decline that precedes their death are expected to retire discreetly "rather than affront society with the spectacle of their decay." The elfin horror of aging provokes some of the most inspired silliness in *Kingdoms of Elfin*; Warner, after all, undertook the research for her biography of T. H. White in her seventies, began her elfin stories in her eighties, and delighted in making a spectacle of her old age. If there is any one of her dissidents who comes close to being Warner's persona, it must be the ancient Queen Alionde in **"Winged Creatures,"** who discomfits her courtiers by violating the prescription for elderly elfins. I know no reason to believe that Warner ever concealed her exact age or smelled bad or glowed in the dark, but in every other respect this splendidly declarative description sounds like a self-portrait and a manifesto:

> Queen Alionde had felt no call to go into retirement. She brandished her old age and insisted on having it acknowledged. No one knew how old she was. There had been confidential bowerwomen, Chancellors sworn to secrecy who knew, but they were long since dead. Her faculties remained in her like rats in a ruin. She never slept. She spoke the language of a forgotten epoch, mingling extreme salacity with lofty euphemisms and punctilios of grammar. She was long past being comical, and smelled like bad haddock. Some said she was phosphorescent in the dark. She found life highly entertaining.

Unlike Tolkien's elves, this one disdains consolation. Alionde flaunts her age and enjoys her mortality with thoroughly human, Warneresque élan. Warner's elfins

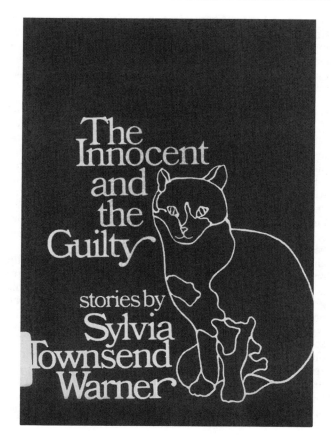

Dust jacket for a collection of Warner's short stories which was published in 1971. All of the stories in this collection were written when the author was in her seventies.

become attractive only when they adopt human poses, mortal longings, mundane heresies. The paradox here is that these opposites attract us at the very moments when, peering closely, we catch glimpses of ourselves.

A few final words by way of postscript, eulogy, epitaph. There may be significance in this symmetry: while Warner dreamed of larding her elfin stories with learned footnotes, in fact she just kept on writing them with apparent effortlessness, with neither notes nor introductions nor any external proppings. While Tolkien dreamed of perfecting his imaginary history of the elves, he could never relinquish his passion for annotation long enough to finish the story. Warner could let go; Tolkien could not. Their attitudes toward mortality seem somehow bound up in their habits of composition. Tolkien's biographer [Humphrey Carpenter] has suggested that he could not allow his fiction to be completed because he was unable to bear the prospect of having no creation left to do. One might go further and propose that Tolkien's fictional world, even more emphatically than his elves, needed a measure of indeterminacy; its unfinished state was a way of bridging personal mortality with the spiritual immortality he hoped for. One may certainly read "Leaf by Niggle"—the story that more than any other is Tolkien's authentic spiritual autobiography—as an *apologia* for the value of unfinished books and lives. The niggling artist, in the fiction, never finishes his big picture, but he finds himself at last achieving heaven painfully after passing through the purgatorial workhouse. And the landscape of heaven becomes the incomplete painting on which Niggle can lavish his painstaking attention eternally.

For Warner, too, work was heavenly, but without a hint of the penitential and purgatorial dilemma that divided Tolkien. She liked finishing things and she celebrated endings. Her biography has not yet been written, but her published letters are full of the satisfactions of a writer who regularly dispatches yet another completed piece of work to the *New Yorker*. Her life looks like a tapestry of endings and fresh starts. Not all the endings are happy, but each of them is to be acknowledged, pronounced true, embraced, and then surrendered to the adventure of a new beginning. Warner was much more tentative than Tolkien about spiritual immortality and therefore more content with her personal mortality. One token of Tolkien's discontent is the one-word epitaph he chose to have inscribed on his gravestone: Beren. It is the name of the unique human hero in *The Silmarillion* who returns from death. Tolkien worried whether people would think it a sentimental inscription; for me, the sentiment implied is protest. The only appropriate epitaph for Warner is very different in spirit and sentiment. It is the one she composed for an old drunken lady, a neighbor of hers, whose impulsiveness and worldliness Warner relished: "If there is a heaven, I am sure she went there like a cork from a champagne bottle."

Barbara Brothers (essay date 1989)

SOURCE: "Writing against the Grain: Sylvia Townsend Warner and the Spanish Civil War," in *Women's Writing in Exile*, edited by Mary Lynn Broe and Angela Ingram, University of North Carolina Press, 1989, pp. 351-68.

[*In the following excerpt, Brothers examines Warner's contributions to the body of literature inspired by the Spanish Civil War.*]

Sylvia Townsend Warner is an exile from the pages of literary history, her contributions unmarked even in Gilbert and Gubar's *Norton Anthology of Literature by Women*. Her politics labeled radical in the social text of the twentieth century and her poetic and fictional forms conservative in the Modernist canonical text, she is known by epithet—a *lady* communist, as Stephen Spender sarcastically dismissed her, and a *communist* writer who contributed to the *Left Review*, as those who purport to write the literary histories of the Spanish Civil War and the 1930s list her. Like other women writers of the 1930s denied authority in the arena of politics and war, she is denied authorship. Even apologists for the leftist writers of the 1930s view such women as dupes of the temporarily deceived. Ghettoized by the social text as *communist* and resegregated as *lady,* Warner is unnamed in twentieth-century literary history as well. Whatever social value is

accorded to political commitment, such commitment is proclaimed by the academic, critical establishment, worshipers of the idol of Modernism, to be the antithesis of literary value. Like the adjective *woman, political* effaces the category *writer* to which the adjectives are applied.

I have limited this essay to Warner's contributions to the literature of the Spanish Civil War, though she published a significant body of literature from 1925 to 1978 informed by the issues of gender and class. Warner wrote short stories, poems, a novel—*After the Death of Don Juan*— . . . and essays that depicted the people of Spain, the spirit of the republican struggle, the fascist invaders, and the British "gentlemen and their ladies" who supported the Nationalist side, actively or through nonintervention. Opposed to fascism and the institutional oppression of the poor, minorities, and women, she worked on behalf of the Loyalist cause, visited Spain twice during the war, and "wrote as much as anybody did about the war," [Valentine Cunningham, *Spanish Front: Writers on the Civil War,* 1986]. . . .

Why Warner and others like her were against the British government is clear from the pages of *Left Review*. Over and over again those writers of the 1930s who, like Warner, joined the Communist party repeated their ideals—"democratic liberty, anti-Fascism, and peace" and a literature that expressed the lives of those whose voices had not been heard [Cecil Day Lewis in his "English Writers and a People's Front," *Left Review,* October, 1936].

Though Warner never considered herself an anarchist, she told Elizabeth Wade in 1936, "It [anarchy] ought to be the political theory of heaven" (*Letters*). In her view the Spanish and the people of Barcelona, in particular, were more anarchist than communist in spirit. Warner perceived that the problem with anarchism was that it lacked the necessary organization to effect change, and during the 1930s Warner could still believe that Marxist communism provided the plan by which people could take charge of their own destinies and be governed by policies that allowed the masses an opportunity for growth and expression. But communism was to become just another of the "taskmasters who enforced ignorance on [the people]" (*Letters*), another patriarchal institution in its oppression of the many for the benefit of the few.

That the British government that signed the Non-Intervention Pact was not truly neutral—hypocritically supporting the rich and powerful while impeding the efforts of the working class who wished to aid the Spanish republican cause—is the point of Warner's story **"With the Nationalists."** Mr. Semple, "a business man upon a business errand," has no trouble securing a visa from his government, the same government that attempted to refuse visas for writers to attend the Madrid Congress because cultural reasons were suspect. The collusion of state, church, and business is depicted in the details of the journey of Mr. Semple, a shipping man. He secures help in making the right contacts from the senior partner of a firm that deals in church and table wines. He crosses the Spanish border from Portugal with a German businessman in a Mercedes-

Benz driven by one of the British nonintervention observers: "Herr Beinlein exposed his project for opening, quite soon, an automobile works in Spain, . . . and though Mr. Semple did not go so far as to offer Herr Beinlein a donation towards this project, he thought about doing so; for as a patriot he could not be unaware of storm-clouds on Britain's horizon, and it seemed to him there was much to be said for placing a little nest-egg abroad" (*A Garland of Straw*). That those who went to Spain to defeat the republic did so for economic exploitation and to play war games could not be clearer; the English business and German military social hour in the hotel in which no Spaniards are allowed breaks up when Semple "insults" two swarthy Italian generals by mistaking them for Spanish generals. Warner ends with an indictment of the Spanish church: a parade tomorrow of Moorish troops will end when the archbishop of Salamanca presents "them *all* with medals of the Sacred Heart."

Like the other stories in *A Garland of Straw,* "**With the Nationalists**" exposes the hatred and petty tyranny of fascism. That fascism, for Warner, is one man despising another man, one woman asserting her will over another woman, one human claiming superiority over another human is depicted in the opening story from which the volume takes its title. Miss Woodley hallucinates about the children she never had as she spends her days committed to a "home." Her sister had prevented her from marrying a man beneath her station—a man with madness in his family. Kitty visits Miss Woodley, "an insatiable ravening of triumph" upon her face. Warner leaves no question as to who is mad and to the irony of appearance and names.

Interspersing the stories of the Spanish Civil War among those with World War II as their setting, Warner makes the wars seem like one war with fascism, as those from the Left perceived might be the case. But their governments did not heed them, and the non-intervention agreement allowed the Germans free rein; Janet Flanner cites Hermann Göring's testifying at the Nuremburg trials to sending "his young fliers in rotation to Franco's war so that they could try their wings in a sort of rehearsal."

Warner satirizes the contemporary scare of the "Red Menace" in two of the stories in *A Garland of Straw*. In "**A Red Carnation**," a young and innocent German soldier discovers not communist troops, which his government had portrayed as the enemy, nor the romantic Spain of his daydreams, but the stench and hatred of the poor. For Warner, poverty and ignorance were the real enemies not only of the Spanish people but of the young and working class of all nationalities. In another story, Warner depicts the English fear of the communists and the hypocrisy, smugness, ignorance, and power of the aristocrats in England who admired and curried favor with the German fascists. A mother writes to a friend to protest the schoolmistress's attempts to raise money for educational supplies for Spain: "I happened to discover that that Miss Hopgood was actually attempting to send *chemicals* to the Spanish Reds, passing them off as coloured inks and mathematical instruments for schools (as if people of that

sort cared two-pence for education!) and it was all being got up as a tribute . . . to some Bolshevist schoolmaster" ("**The Language of Flowers,**" in *A Garland of Straw*). Instead, government officials and elected members of Parliament make arrangements to send flowers to be placed on the grave of the German governess of Queen Victoria as a "*simple,* peaceful gesture, recalling how much the two nations have in common." Mendelssohn's grave was originally suggested because his Elijah was so popular, but, of course, he was "racially ineligible."

The "racially ineligible," the economically disfranchised, and the others consigned to rap at the back door of the castle are Warner's subjects. Her view of history and of persons through the "pantry window" enabled her to challenge received opinion and to portray her characters as individuals and not stereotypes. Except for a few of the stories in *A Garland of Straw* in which her characters become mouthpieces for the ideas she is attacking or supporting, Warner's fictions of social protest are not marred by the perspective so often objected to in the leftist writers of the 1930s. Warner's view of history did not arise out of the guilt Virginia Woolf identified in "The Leaning Tower" and to which many admitted. Nor was Warner an ideologue, turning as did W. H. Auden, Aldous Huxley, and others to some other "god" when that of communism and socialism failed. Although she issued a plea for "Art for Man's sake," literature with "an underlying morality, a resolute understanding and intolerance of social conditions" ("Underlying Morality"), the right subject or theme with no sense of art is only propaganda in Warner's view (see "Competition"). Warner treated her partisan choice of subjects and themes with ironic wit; she accepted human weakness but was intolerant of hypocrisy. She was not a sentimental romanticist. In content and form—her stories most often blend social realism and comic fantasy—she wrote against the grain. But the writers of social and literary history are uncomfortable with the idea that a woman should be taken seriously in matters of politics and social justice. Thus "critical fashion," as Arnold Rattenbury states, has either "mostly disguised this blatant fact [Warner's political commitment to the others of society] or blatantly ignored this author."

FURTHER READING

Criticism

Forbes, Nancy. A review of *One Thing Leads to Another. The New York Times Book Review* (11 November 1984): 32.
      Positive assessment of Warner's posthumous collection.

Kiely, Benedict. "The Sky and the River and Man." *The New York Times Book Review* (6 February 1966): 4, 28.
      Enthusiastic endorsement of Warner's literary skills. Observing that Warner had published quite a bit to-date, Kiely states: "This is reason to be grateful. Whether she writes on the putting-to sleep of a favorite cat or on a case of quite respectable middle-class incest, she displays

always that irony, that ruthless coolness, that clear sight, that style."

Maxwell, William. "Sylvia Townsend Warner and *The New Yorker*." *PN Review* 8, No. 3 (1981): 44-5.
    Personal reminisces of Warner's editor.

"Wit and Fancy." *The Times Literary Supplement*, No. 2380 (13 September 1947): 461.
    Brief review of *The Museum of Cheats* in which the critic identifies Warner as a practitioner of a newer type of short story that eschews "the neatly tailored and explicit endings, the tidily rounded situations of the popular short story."

Additional coverage of Warner's life and career is contained in the following sources published by Gale Research: *Contemporary Authors*, Vols. 61-64, 77-80; *Contemporary Authors New Revision Series*, Vol. 16; *Contemporary Literary Criticism*, Vols. 7, 19; *Dictionary of Literary Biography*, Vols. 34, 139; and *Major 20th-Century Writers*.

Appendix:

Select Bibliography of General Sources on Short Fiction

BOOKS OF CRITICISM

Allen, Walter. *The Short Story in English*. New York: Oxford University Press, 1981, 413 p.

Aycock, Wendell M., ed. *The Teller and the Tale: Aspects of the Short Story* (Proceedings of the Comparative Literature Symposium, Texas Tech University, Volume XIII). Lubbock: Texas Tech Press, 1982, 156 p.

Averill, Deborah. *The Irish Short Story from George Moore to Frank O'Connor*. Washington, D.C.: University Press of America, 1982, 329 p.

Bates, H. E. *The Modern Short Story: A Critical Survey*. Boston: Writer, 1941, 231 p.

Bayley, John. *The Short Story: Henry James to Elizabeth Bowen*. Great Britain: The Harvester Press Limited, 1988, 197 p.

Bennett, E. K. *A History of the German Novelle: From Goethe to Thomas Mann*. Cambridge: At the University Press, 1934, 296 p.

Bone, Robert. *Down Home: A History of Afro-American Short Fiction from Its Beginning to the End of the Harlem Renaissance*. Rev. ed. New York: Columbia University Press, 1988, 350 p.

Bruck, Peter. *The Black American Short Story in the Twentieth Century: A Collection of Critical Essays*. Amsterdam: B. R. Grüner Publishing Co., 1977, 209 p.

Burnett, Whit, and Burnett, Hallie. *The Modern Short Story in the Making*. New York: Hawthorn Books, 1964, 405 p.

Canby, Henry Seidel. *The Short Story in English*. New York: Henry Holt and Co., 1909, 386 p.

Current-García, Eugene. *The American Short Story before 1850: A Critical History*. Twayne's Critical History of the Short Story, edited by William Peden. Boston: Twayne Publishers, 1985, 168 p.

Flora, Joseph M., ed. *The English Short Story, 1880-1945: A Critical History*. Twayne's Critical History of the Short Story, edited by William Peden. Boston: Twayne Publishers, 1985, 215 p.

Foster, David William. *Studies in the Contemporary Spanish-American Short Story*. Columbia, Mo.: University of Missouri Press, 1979, 126 p.

George, Albert J. *Short Fiction in France, 1800-1850*. Syracuse, N.Y.: Syracuse University Press, 1964, 245 p.

Gerlach, John. *Toward an End: Closure and Structure in the American Short Story*. University, Ala.: The University of Alabama Press, 1985, 193 p.

Hankin, Cherry, ed. *Critical Essays on the New Zealand Short Story*. Auckland: Heinemann Publishers,

1982, 186 p.

Hanson, Clare, ed. *Re-Reading the Short Story*. London: MacMillan Press, 1989, 137 p.

Harris, Wendell V. *British Short Fiction in the Nineteenth Century*. Detroit: Wayne State University Press, 1979, 209 p.

Huntington, John. *Rationalizing Genius: Ideological Strategies in the Classic American Science Fiction Short Story*. New Brunswick: Rutgers University Press, 1989, 216 p.

Kilroy, James F., ed. *The Irish Short Story: A Critical History*. Twayne's Critical History of the Short Story, edited by William Peden. Boston: Twayne Publishers, 1984, 251 p.

Lee, A. Robert. *The Nineteenth-Century American Short Story*. Totowa, N. J.: Vision / Barnes & Noble, 1986, 196 p.

Leibowitz, Judith. *Narrative Purpose in the Novella*. The Hague: Mouton, 1974, 137 p.

Lohafer, Susan. *Coming to Terms with the Short Story*. Baton Rouge: Louisiana State University Press, 1983, 171 p.

Lohafer, Susan, and Clarey, Jo Ellyn. *Short Story Theory at a Crossroads*. Baton Rouge: Louisiana State University Press, 1989, 352 p.

Mann, Susan Garland. *The Short Story Cycle: A Genre Companion and Reference Guide*. New York: Greenwood Press, 1989, 228 p.

Matthews, Brander. *The Philosophy of the Short Story*. New York, N.Y.: Longmans, Green and Co., 1901, 83 p.

May, Charles E., ed. *Short Story Theories*. Athens, Oh.: Ohio University Press, 1976, 251 p.

McClave, Heather, ed. *Women Writers of the Short Story: A Collection of Critical Essays*. Englewood Cliffs, N. J.: Prentice-Hall, 1980, 171 p.

Moser, Charles, ed. *The Russian Short Story: A Critical History*. Twayne's Critical History of the Short Story, edited by William Peden. Boston: Twayne Publishers, 1986, 232 p.

New, W. H. *Dreams of Speech and Violence: The Art of the Short Story in Canada and New Zealand*. Toronto: The University of Toronto Press, 1987, 302 p.

Newman, Frances. *The Short Story's Mutations: From Petronius to Paul Morand*. New York: B. W. Huebsch, 1925, 332 p.

O'Connor, Frank. *The Lonely Voice: A Study of the Short Story*. Cleveland: World Publishing Co., 1963, 220 p.

O'Faolain, Sean. *The Short Story*. New York: Devin-Adair Co., 1951, 370 p.

Orel, Harold. *The Victorian Short Story: Development and Triumph of a Literary Genre*. Cambridge: Cambridge University Press, 1986, 213 p.

O'Toole, L. Michael. *Structure, Style and Interpretation in the Russian Short Story*. New Haven: Yale University Press, 1982, 272 p.

Pattee, Fred Lewis. *The Development of the American Short Story: An Historical Survey*. New York: Harper and Brothers Publishers, 1923, 388 p.

Peden, Margaret Sayers, ed. *The Latin American Short Story: A Critical History*. Twayne's Critical History of the Short Story, edited by William Peden. Boston: Twayne Publishers, 1983, 160 p.

Peden, William. *The American Short Story: Continuity and Change, 1940-1975*. Rev. ed. Boston: Houghton Mifflin Co., 1975, 215 p.

Reid, Ian. *The Short Story*. The Critical Idiom, edited by John D. Jump. London: Methuen and Co., 1977, 76 p.

Rhode, Robert D. *Setting in the American Short Story of Local Color, 1865-1900*. The Hague: Mouton, 1975, 189 p.

Rohrberger, Mary. *Hawthorne and the Modern Short Story: A Study in Genre*. The Hague: Mouton and Co., 1966, 148 p.

Shaw, Valerie. *The Short Story: A Critical Introduction*. London: Longman, 1983, 294 p.

Stephens, Michael. *The Dramaturgy of Style: Voice in Short Fiction*. Carbondale, Ill.: Southern Illinois University Press, 1986, 281 p.

Stevick, Philip, ed. *The American Short Story, 1900-1945: A Critical History*. Twayne's Critical History of the Short Story, edited by William Peden. Boston: Twayne Publishers, 1984, 209 p.

Summers, Hollis, ed. *Discussion of the Short Story*. Boston: D. C. Heath and Co., 1963, 118 p.

Vannatta, Dennis, ed. *The English Short Story, 1945-1980: A Critical History*. Twayne's Critical History of the Short Story, edited by William Peden. Boston: Twayne Publishers, 1985, 206 p.

Voss, Arthur. *The American Short Story: A Critical Survey*. Norman, Okla.: University of Oklahoma Press, 1973, 399 p.

Walker, Warren S. *Twentieth-Century Short Story Explication: New Series, Vol. 1: 1989-1990*. Hamden, Conn.: Shoe String, 1993, 366 p.

Ward, Alfred C. *Aspects of the Modern Short Story: English and American*. London: University of London Press, 1924, 307 p.

Weaver, Gordon, ed. *The American Short Story, 1945-1980: A Critical History*. Twayne's Critical History of the Short Story, edited by William Peden. Boston: Twayne Publishers, 1983, 150 p.

West, Ray B., Jr. *The Short Story in America, 1900-1950*. Chicago: Henry Regnery Co., 1952, 147 p.

Williams, Blanche Colton. *Our Short Story Writers*. New York: Moffat, Yard and Co., 1920, 357 p.

Wright, Austin McGiffert. *The American Short Story in the Twenties*. Chicago: University of Chicago Press, 1961, 425 p.

CRITICAL ANTHOLOGIES

Atkinson, W. Patterson, ed. *The Short-Story*. Boston: Allyn and Bacon, 1923, 317 p.

Baldwin, Charles Sears, ed. *American Short Stories*. New York, N.Y.: Longmans, Green and Co., 1904, 333 p.

Charters, Ann, ed. *The Story and Its Writer: An Introduction to Short Fiction*. New York: St. Martin's Press, 1983, 1239 p.

Current-García, Eugene, and Patrick, Walton R., eds. *American Short Stories: 1820 to the Present*. Key Editions, edited by John C. Gerber. Chicago: Scott, Foresman and Co., 1952, 633 p.

Fagin, N. Bryllion, ed. *America through the Short Story*. Boston: Little, Brown, and Co., 1936, 508 p.

Frakes, James R., and Traschen, Isadore, eds. *Short Fiction: A Critical Collection*. Prentice-Hall English Literature Series, edited by Maynard Mack. Englewood Cliffs, N.J.: Prentice-Hall, 1959, 459 p.

Gifford, Douglas, ed. *Scottish Short Stories, 1800-1900*. The Scottish Library, edited by Alexander Scott. London: Calder and Boyars, 1971, 350 p.

Gordon, Caroline, and Tate, Allen, eds. *The House of Fiction: An Anthology of the Short Story with Commentary*. Rev. ed. New York: Charles Scribner's Sons, 1960, 469 p.

Greet, T. Y., et. al. *The Worlds of Fiction: Stories in Context*. Boston, Mass.: Houghton Mifflin Co., 1964, 429 p.

Gullason, Thomas A., and Caspar, Leonard, eds. *The World of Short Fiction: An International Collection*. New York: Harper and Row, 1962, 548 p.

Havighurst, Walter, ed. *Masters of the Modern Short Story*. New York: Harcourt, Brace and Co., 1945, 538 p.

Litz, A. Walton, ed. *Major American Short Stories*. New York: Oxford University Press, 1975, 823 p.

Matthews, Brander, ed. *The Short-Story: Specimens Illustrating Its Development*. New York: American Book Co., 1907, 399 p.

Menton, Seymour, ed. *The Spanish American Short Story: A Critical Anthology*. Berkeley and Los Angeles: University of California Press, 1980, 496 p.

Mzamane, Mbulelo Vizikhungo, ed. *Hungry Flames, and Other Black South African Short Stories*. Longman African Classics. Essex: Longman, 1986, 162 p.

Schorer, Mark, ed. *The Short Story: A Critical Anthology*. Rev. ed. Prentice-Hall English Literature Series, edited by Maynard Mack. Englewood Cliffs, N. J.: Prentice-Hall, 1967, 459 p.

Simpson, Claude M., ed. *The Local Colorists: American Short Stories, 1857-1900*. New York: Harper and Brothers Publishers, 1960, 340 p.

Stanton, Robert, ed. *The Short Story and the Reader*. New York: Henry Holt and Co., 1960, 557 p.

West, Ray B., Jr., ed. *American Short Stories*. New York: Thomas Y. Crowell Co., 1959, 267 p.

Short Story Criticism Indexes

Literary Criticism Series
Cumulative Author Index

SSC Cumulative Nationality Index
SSC Cumulative Title Index

How to Use This Index

The main references

Calvino, Italo
1923-1985.....CLC 5, 8, 11, 22, 33, 39,
73; SSC 3

list all author entries in the following Gale Literary Criticism series:

BLC = *Black Literature Criticism*
CLC = *Contemporary Literary Criticism*
CLR = *Children's Literature Review*
CMLC = *Classical and Medieval Literature Criticism*
DA = *DISCovering Authors*
DAB = *DISCovering Authors: British*
DAC = *DISCovering Authors: Canadian*
DC = *Drama Criticism*
HLC = *Hispanic Literature Criticism*
LC = *Literature Criticism from 1400 to 1800*
NCLC = *Nineteenth-Century Literature Criticism*
PC = *Poetry Criticism*
SSC = *Short Story Criticism*
TCLC = *Twentieth-Century Literary Criticism*
WLC = *World Literature Criticism, 1500 to the Present*

The cross-references

See also CANR 23; CA 85-88;
obituary CA 116

list all author entries in the following Gale biographical and literary sources:

AAYA = *Authors & Artists for Young Adults*
AITN = *Authors in the News*
BEST = *Bestsellers*
BW = *Black Writers*
CA = *Contemporary Authors*
CAAS = *Contemporary Authors Autobiography Series*
CABS = *Contemporary Authors Bibliographical Series*
CANR = *Contemporary Authors New Revision Series*
CAP = *Contemporary Authors Permanent Series*
CDALB = *Concise Dictionary of American Literary Biography*
CDBLB = *Concise Dictionary of British Literary Biography*
DAM = *DISCovering Authors: Modules*
       DRAM: Dramatists Module; *MST: Most-Studied Authors Module;*
       MULT: Multicultural Authors Module; *NOV: Novelists Module;*
       POET: Poets Module; *POP: Popular Fiction and Genre Authors Module*
DLB = *Dictionary of Literary Biography*
DLBD = *Dictionary of Literary Biography Documentary Series*
DLBY = *Dictionary of Literary Biography Yearbook*
HW = *Hispanic Writers*
JRDA = *Junior DISCovering Authors*
MAICYA = *Major Authors and Illustrators for Children and Young Adults*
MTCW = *Major 20th-Century Writers*
NNAL = *Native North American Literature*
SAAS = *Something about the Author Autobiography Series*
SATA = *Something about the Author*
YABC = *Yesterday's Authors of Books for Children*

Literary Criticism Series
Cumulative Author Index

Andrade, Mario de 1893-1945 ..... **TCLC 43**

Andreae, Johann V(alentin)
1586-1654 .... **LC 32**
See also DLB 164

Andreas-Salome, Lou 1861-1937 ... **TCLC 56**
See also DLB 66

Andrewes, Lancelot 1555-1626 .... **LC 5**
See also DLB 151

Andrews, Cicily Fairfield
See West, Rebecca

Andrews, Elton V.
See Pohl, Frederik

Andreyev, Leonid (Nikolaevich)
1871-1919 .... **TCLC 3**
See also CA 104

Andric, Ivo 1892-1975 .... **CLC 8**
See also CA 81-84; 57-60; CANR 43;
DLB 147; MTCW

Angelique, Pierre
See Bataille, Georges

Angell, Roger 1920- .... **CLC 26**
See also CA 57-60; CANR 13, 44

Angelou, Maya
1928- .... **CLC 12, 35, 64, 77; BLC; DA;**
DAB; DAC
See also AAYA 7; BW 2; CA 65-68;
CANR 19, 42; DAM MST, MULT,
POET, POP; DLB 38; MTCW; SATA 49

Annensky, Innokenty Fyodorovich
1856-1909 .... **TCLC 14**
See also CA 110

Anon, Charles Robert
See Pessoa, Fernando (Antonio Nogueira)

Anouilh, Jean (Marie Lucien Pierre)
1910-1987 ...... **CLC 1, 3, 8, 13, 40, 50**
See also CA 17-20R; 123; CANR 32;
DAM DRAM; MTCW

Anthony, Florence
See Ai

Anthony, John
See Ciardi, John (Anthony)

Anthony, Peter
See Shaffer, Anthony (Joshua); Shaffer,
Peter (Levin)

Anthony, Piers 1934- .... **CLC 35**
See also AAYA 11; CA 21-24R; CANR 28;
DAM POP; DLB 8; MTCW; SAAS 22;
SATA 84

Antoine, Marc
See Proust, (Valentin-Louis-George-Eugene-)
Marcel

Antoninus, Brother
See Everson, William (Oliver)

Antonioni, Michelangelo 1912- ..... **CLC 20**
See also CA 73-76; CANR 45

Antschel, Paul 1920-1970
See Celan, Paul
See also CA 85-88; CANR 33; MTCW

Anwar, Chairil 1922-1949 .... **TCLC 22**
See also CA 121

Apollinaire, Guillaume .. **TCLC 3, 8, 51; PC 7**
See also Kostrowitzki, Wilhelm Apollinaris
de
See also DAM POET

Appelfeld, Aharon 1932- .... **CLC 23, 47**
See also CA 112; 133

Apple, Max (Isaac) 1941- .... **CLC 9, 33**
See also CA 81-84; CANR 19; DLB 130

Appleman, Philip (Dean) 1926- ..... **CLC 51**
See also CA 13-16R; CAAS 18; CANR 6,
29

Appleton, Lawrence
See Lovecraft, H(oward) P(hillips)

Apteryx
See Eliot, T(homas) S(tearns)

Apuleius, (Lucius Madaurensis)
125(?)-175(?) .... **CMLC 1**

Aquin, Hubert 1929-1977 .... **CLC 15**
See also CA 105; DLB 53

Aragon, Louis 1897-1982 .... **CLC 3, 22**
See also CA 69-72; 108; CANR 28;
DAM NOV, POET; DLB 72; MTCW

Arany, Janos 1817-1882 .... **NCLC 34**

Arbuthnot, John 1667-1735 .... **LC 1**
See also DLB 101

Archer, Herbert Winslow
See Mencken, H(enry) L(ouis)

Archer, Jeffrey (Howard) 1940- .... **CLC 28**
See also AAYA 16; BEST 89:3; CA 77-80;
CANR 22, 52; DAM POP;
INT CANR-22

Archer, Jules 1915- .... **CLC 12**
See also CA 9-12R; CANR 6; SAAS 5;
SATA 4, 85

Archer, Lee
See Ellison, Harlan (Jay)

Arden, John 1930- .... **CLC 6, 13, 15**
See also CA 13-16R; CAAS 4; CANR 31;
DAM DRAM; DLB 13; MTCW

Arenas, Reinaldo
1943-1990 .... **CLC 41; HLC**
See also CA 124; 128; 133; DAM MULT;
DLB 145; HW

Arendt, Hannah 1906-1975 .... **CLC 66**
See also CA 17-20R; 61-64; CANR 26;
MTCW

Aretino, Pietro 1492-1556 .... **LC 12**

Arghezi, Tudor .... **CLC 80**
See also Theodorescu, Ion N.

Arguedas, Jose Maria
1911-1969 .... **CLC 10, 18**
See also CA 89-92; DLB 113; HW

Argueta, Manlio 1936- .... **CLC 31**
See also CA 131; DLB 145; HW

Ariosto, Ludovico 1474-1533 .... **LC 6**

Aristides
See Epstein, Joseph

Aristophanes
450B.C.-385B.C. .... **CMLC 4; DA;**
DAB; DAC; DC 2
See also DAM DRAM, MST

Arlt, Roberto (Godofredo Christophersen)
1900-1942 .... **TCLC 29; HLC**
See also CA 123; 131; DAM MULT; HW

Armah, Ayi Kwei 1939- .... **CLC 5, 33; BLC**
See also BW 1; CA 61-64; CANR 21;
DAM MULT, POET; DLB 117; MTCW

Armatrading, Joan 1950- .... **CLC 17**
See also CA 114

Arnette, Robert
See Silverberg, Robert

Arnim, Achim von (Ludwig Joachim von
Arnim) 1781-1831 .... **NCLC 5**
See also DLB 90

Arnim, Bettina von 1785-1859 .... **NCLC 38**
See also DLB 90

Arnold, Matthew
1822-1888 ..... **NCLC 6, 29; DA; DAB;**
DAC; PC 5; WLC
See also CDBLB 1832-1890; DAM MST,
POET; DLB 32, 57

Arnold, Thomas 1795-1842 ...... **NCLC 18**
See also DLB 55

Arnow, Harriette (Louisa) Simpson
1908-1986 .... **CLC 2, 7, 18**
See also CA 9-12R; 118; CANR 14; DLB 6;
MTCW; SATA 42; SATA-Obit 47

Arp, Hans
See Arp, Jean

Arp, Jean 1887-1966 .... **CLC 5**
See also CA 81-84; 25-28R; CANR 42

Arrabal
See Arrabal, Fernando

Arrabal, Fernando 1932- ... **CLC 2, 9, 18, 58**
See also CA 9-12R; CANR 15

Arrick, Fran .... **CLC 30**
See also Gaberman, Judie Angell

Artaud, Antonin (Marie Joseph)
1896-1948 .... **TCLC 3, 36**
See also CA 104; 149; DAM DRAM

Arthur, Ruth M(abel) 1905-1979 .... **CLC 12**
See also CA 9-12R; 85-88; CANR 4;
SATA 7, 26

Artsybashev, Mikhail (Petrovich)
1878-1927 .... **TCLC 31**

Arundel, Honor (Morfydd)
1919-1973 .... **CLC 17**
See also CA 21-22; 41-44R; CAP 2;
CLR 35; SATA 4; SATA-Obit 24

Asch, Sholem 1880-1957 .... **TCLC 3**
See also CA 105

Ash, Shalom
See Asch, Sholem

Ashbery, John (Lawrence)
1927- ...... **CLC 2, 3, 4, 6, 9, 13, 15, 25,**
41, 77
See also CA 5-8R; CANR 9, 37;
DAM POET; DLB 5, 165; DLBY 81;
INT CANR-9; MTCW

Ashdown, Clifford
See Freeman, R(ichard) Austin

Ashe, Gordon
See Creasey, John

Ashton-Warner, Sylvia (Constance)
1908-1984 .... **CLC 19**
See also CA 69-72; 112; CANR 29; MTCW

Asimov, Isaac
1920-1992 . . . **CLC 1, 3, 9, 19, 26, 76, 92**
See also AAYA 13; BEST 90:2; CA 1-4R;
137; CANR 2, 19, 36; CLR 12;
DAM POP; DLB 8; DLBY 92;
INT CANR-19; JRDA; MAICYA;
MTCW; SATA 1, 26, 74

Astley, Thea (Beatrice May)
1925- . . . . **CLC 41**
See also CA 65-68; CANR 11, 43

Aston, James
See White, T(erence) H(anbury)

Asturias, Miguel Angel
1899-1974 . . . . **CLC 3, 8, 13; HLC**
See also CA 25-28; 49-52; CANR 32;
CAP 2; DAM MULT, NOV; DLB 113;
HW; MTCW

Atares, Carlos Saura
See Saura (Atares), Carlos

Atheling, William
See Pound, Ezra (Weston Loomis)

Atheling, William, Jr.
See Blish, James (Benjamin)

Atherton, Gertrude (Franklin Horn)
1857-1948 . . . . **TCLC 2**
See also CA 104; DLB 9, 78

Atherton, Lucius
See Masters, Edgar Lee

Atkins, Jack
See Harris, Mark

Attaway, William (Alexander)
1911-1986 . . . . **CLC 92; BLC**
See also BW 2; CA 143; DAM MULT;
DLB 76

Atticus
See Fleming, Ian (Lancaster)

Atwood, Margaret (Eleanor)
1939- . . . . . **CLC 2, 3, 4, 8, 13, 15, 25, 44,
84; DA; DAB; DAC; PC 8; SSC 2; WLC**
See also AAYA 12; BEST 89:2; CA 49-52;
CANR 3, 24, 33; DAM MST, NOV,
POET; DLB 53; INT CANR-24; MTCW;
SATA 50

Aubigny, Pierre d'
See Mencken, H(enry) L(ouis)

Aubin, Penelope 1685-1731(?) . . . . **LC 9**
See also DLB 39

Auchincloss, Louis (Stanton)
1917- . . . . . . **CLC 4, 6, 9, 18, 45; SSC 22**
See also CA 1-4R; CANR 6, 29;
DAM NOV; DLB 2; DLBY 80;
INT CANR-29; MTCW

Auden, W(ystan) H(ugh)
1907-1973 . . . . . . **CLC 1, 2, 3, 4, 6, 9, 11,
14, 43; DA; DAB; DAC; PC 1; WLC**
See also AAYA 18; CA 9-12R; 45-48;
CANR 5; CDBLB 1914-1945;
DAM DRAM, MST, POET; DLB 10, 20;
MTCW

Audiberti, Jacques 1900-1965 . . . . . . **CLC 38**
See also CA 25-28R; DAM DRAM

Audubon, John James
1785-1851 . . . . **NCLC 47**

Auel, Jean M(arie) 1936- . . . . **CLC 31**
See also AAYA 7; BEST 90:4; CA 103;
CANR 21; DAM POP; INT CANR-21

Auerbach, Erich 1892-1957 . . . . **TCLC 43**
See also CA 118

Augier, Emile 1820-1889 . . . . **NCLC 31**

August, John
See De Voto, Bernard (Augustine)

Augustine, St. 354-430 . . . . . . **CMLC 6; DAB**

Aurelius
See Bourne, Randolph S(illiman)

Aurobindo, Sri 1872-1950 . . . . **TCLC 63**

Austen, Jane
1775-1817 . . . . . **NCLC 1, 13, 19, 33, 51;
DA; DAB; DAC; WLC**
See also CDBLB 1789-1832; DAM MST,
NOV; DLB 116

Auster, Paul 1947- . . . . **CLC 47**
See also CA 69-72; CANR 23, 52

Austin, Frank
See Faust, Frederick (Schiller)

Austin, Mary (Hunter)
1868-1934 . . . . **TCLC 25**
See also CA 109; DLB 9, 78

Autran Dourado, Waldomiro
See Dourado, (Waldomiro Freitas) Autran

Averroes 1126-1198 . . . . **CMLC 7**
See also DLB 115

Avicenna 980-1037 . . . . **CMLC 16**
See also DLB 115

Avison, Margaret 1918- . . . . **CLC 2, 4; DAC**
See also CA 17-20R; DAM POET; DLB 53;
MTCW

Axton, David
See Koontz, Dean R(ay)

Ayckbourn, Alan
1939- . . . . **CLC 5, 8, 18, 33, 74; DAB**
See also CA 21-24R; CANR 31;
DAM DRAM; DLB 13; MTCW

Aydy, Catherine
See Tennant, Emma (Christina)

Ayme, Marcel (Andre) 1902-1967 . . . **CLC 11**
See also CA 89-92; CLR 25; DLB 72

Ayrton, Michael 1921-1975 . . . . **CLC 7**
See also CA 5-8R; 61-64; CANR 9, 21

Azorin . . . . **CLC 11**
See also Martinez Ruiz, Jose

Azuela, Mariano
1873-1952 . . . . **TCLC 3; HLC**
See also CA 104; 131; DAM MULT; HW;
MTCW

Baastad, Babbis Friis
See Friis-Baastad, Babbis Ellinor

Bab
See Gilbert, W(illiam) S(chwenck)

Babbis, Eleanor
See Friis-Baastad, Babbis Ellinor

Babel, Isaak (Emmanuilovich)
1894-1941(?) . . . . . . **TCLC 2, 13; SSC 16**
See also CA 104

Babits, Mihaly 1883-1941 . . . . **TCLC 14**
See also CA 114

Babur 1483-1530 . . . . **LC 18**

Bacchelli, Riccardo 1891-1985 . . . . . **CLC 19**
See also CA 29-32R; 117

Bach, Richard (David) 1936- . . . . **CLC 14**
See also AITN 1; BEST 89:2; CA 9-12R;
CANR 18; DAM NOV, POP; MTCW;
SATA 13

Bachman, Richard
See King, Stephen (Edwin)

Bachmann, Ingeborg 1926-1973 . . . . . **CLC 69**
See also CA 93-96; 45-48; DLB 85

Bacon, Francis 1561-1626 . . . . **LC 18, 32**
See also CDBLB Before 1660; DLB 151

Bacon, Roger 1214(?)-1292 . . . . . . **CMLC 14**
See also DLB 115

Bacovia, George . . . . **TCLC 24**
See also Vasiliu, Gheorghe

Badanes, Jerome 1937- . . . . **CLC 59**

Bagehot, Walter 1826-1877 . . . . **NCLC 10**
See also DLB 55

Bagnold, Enid 1889-1981 . . . . **CLC 25**
See also CA 5-8R; 103; CANR 5, 40;
DAM DRAM; DLB 13, 160; MAICYA;
SATA 1, 25

Bagritsky, Eduard 1895-1934 . . . . . **TCLC 60**

Bagrjana, Elisaveta
See Belcheva, Elisaveta

Bagryana, Elisaveta . . . . **CLC 10**
See also Belcheva, Elisaveta
See also DLB 147

Bailey, Paul 1937- . . . . **CLC 45**
See also CA 21-24R; CANR 16; DLB 14

Baillie, Joanna 1762-1851 . . . . **NCLC 2**
See also DLB 93

Bainbridge, Beryl (Margaret)
1933- . . . . **CLC 4, 5, 8, 10, 14, 18, 22, 62**
See also CA 21-24R; CANR 24;
DAM NOV; DLB 14; MTCW

Baker, Elliott 1922- . . . . **CLC 8**
See also CA 45-48; CANR 2

Baker, Nicholson 1957- . . . . **CLC 61**
See also CA 135; DAM POP

Baker, Ray Stannard 1870-1946 . . . **TCLC 47**
See also CA 118

Baker, Russell (Wayne) 1925- . . . . . . **CLC 31**
See also BEST 89:4; CA 57-60; CANR 11,
41; MTCW

Bakhtin, M.
See Bakhtin, Mikhail Mikhailovich

Bakhtin, M. M.
See Bakhtin, Mikhail Mikhailovich

Bakhtin, Mikhail
See Bakhtin, Mikhail Mikhailovich

Bakhtin, Mikhail Mikhailovich
1895-1975 . . . . **CLC 83**
See also CA 128; 113

Bakshi, Ralph 1938(?)- . . . . **CLC 26**
See also CA 112; 138

Bakunin, Mikhail (Alexandrovich)
1814-1876 . . . . **NCLC 25**

Baldwin, James (Arthur)
1924-1987 ...... **CLC 1, 2, 3, 4, 5, 8, 13,
15, 17, 42, 50, 67, 90; BLC; DA; DAB;
DAC; DC 1; SSC 10; WLC**
See also AAYA 4; BW 1; CA 1-4R; 124;
CABS 1; CANR 3, 24;
CDALB 1941-1968; DAM MST,
NOV, POP; DLB 2, 7, 33; DLBY 87;
MTCW; SATA 9; SATA-Obit 54

Ballard, J(ames) G(raham)
1930- .... **CLC 3, 6, 14, 36; SSC 1**
See also AAYA 3; CA 5-8R; CANR 15, 39;
DAM NOV, POP; DLB 14; MTCW

Balmont, Konstantin (Dmitriyevich)
1867-1943 .... **TCLC 11**
See also CA 109

Balzac, Honore de
1799-1850 .... **NCLC 5, 35, 53; DA;
DAB; DAC; SSC 5; WLC**
See also DAM MST, NOV; DLB 119

Bambara, Toni Cade
1939-1995 ...... **CLC 19, 88; BLC; DA;
DAC**
See also AAYA 5; BW 2; CA 29-32R; 150;
CANR 24, 49; DAM MST, MULT;
DLB 38; MTCW

Bamdad, A.
See Shamlu, Ahmad

Banat, D. R.
See Bradbury, Ray (Douglas)

Bancroft, Laura
See Baum, L(yman) Frank

Banim, John 1798-1842 .... **NCLC 13**
See also DLB 116, 158, 159

Banim, Michael 1796-1874 ...... **NCLC 13**
See also DLB 158, 159

Banks, Iain
See Banks, Iain M(enzies)

Banks, Iain M(enzies) 1954- .... **CLC 34**
See also CA 123; 128; INT 128

Banks, Lynne Reid .... **CLC 23**
See also Reid Banks, Lynne
See also AAYA 6

Banks, Russell 1940- .... **CLC 37, 72**
See also CA 65-68; CAAS 15; CANR 19,
52; DLB 130

Banville, John 1945- .... **CLC 46**
See also CA 117; 128; DLB 14; INT 128

Banville, Theodore (Faullain) de
1832-1891 .... **NCLC 9**

Baraka, Amiri
1934- .... **CLC 1, 2, 3, 5, 10, 14, 33;
BLC; DA; DAC; DC 6; PC 4**
See also Jones, LeRoi
See also BW 2; CA 21-24R; CABS 3;
CANR 27, 38; CDALB 1941-1968;
DAM MST, MULT, POET, POP;
DLB 5, 7, 16, 38; DLBD 8; MTCW

Barbauld, Anna Laetitia
1743-1825 .... **NCLC 50**
See also DLB 107, 109, 142, 158

Barbellion, W. N. P. .... **TCLC 24**
See also Cummings, Bruce F(rederick)

Barbera, Jack (Vincent) 1945- ...... **CLC 44**
See also CA 110; CANR 45

Barbey d'Aurevilly, Jules Amedee
1808-1889 .... **NCLC 1; SSC 17**
See also DLB 119

Barbusse, Henri 1873-1935 .... **TCLC 5**
See also CA 105; DLB 65

Barclay, Bill
See Moorcock, Michael (John)

Barclay, William Ewert
See Moorcock, Michael (John)

Barea, Arturo 1897-1957 .... **TCLC 14**
See also CA 111

Barfoot, Joan 1946- .... **CLC 18**
See also CA 105

Baring, Maurice 1874-1945 .... **TCLC 8**
See also CA 105; DLB 34

Barker, Clive 1952- .... **CLC 52**
See also AAYA 10; BEST 90:3; CA 121;
129; DAM POP; INT 129; MTCW

Barker, George Granville
1913-1991 .... **CLC 8, 48**
See also CA 9-12R; 135; CANR 7, 38;
DAM POET; DLB 20; MTCW

Barker, Harley Granville
See Granville-Barker, Harley
See also DLB 10

Barker, Howard 1946- .... **CLC 37**
See also CA 102; DLB 13

Barker, Pat(ricia) 1943- .... **CLC 32, 94**
See also CA 117; 122; CANR 50; INT 122

Barlow, Joel 1754-1812 .... **NCLC 23**
See also DLB 37

Barnard, Mary (Ethel) 1909- .... **CLC 48**
See also CA 21-22; CAP 2

Barnes, Djuna
1892-1982 ... **CLC 3, 4, 8, 11, 29; SSC 3**
See also CA 9-12R; 107; CANR 16; DLB 4,
9, 45; MTCW

Barnes, Julian 1946- .... **CLC 42; DAB**
See also CA 102; CANR 19; DLBY 93

Barnes, Peter 1931- .... **CLC 5, 56**
See also CA 65-68; CAAS 12; CANR 33,
34; DLB 13; MTCW

Baroja (y Nessi), Pio
1872-1956 .... **TCLC 8; HLC**
See also CA 104

Baron, David
See Pinter, Harold

Baron Corvo
See Rolfe, Frederick (William Serafino
Austin Lewis Mary)

Barondess, Sue K(aufman)
1926-1977 .... **CLC 8**
See also Kaufman, Sue
See also CA 1-4R; 69-72; CANR 1

Baron de Teive
See Pessoa, Fernando (Antonio Nogueira)

Barres, Maurice 1862-1923 .... **TCLC 47**
See also DLB 123

Barreto, Afonso Henrique de Lima
See Lima Barreto, Afonso Henrique de

Barrett, (Roger) Syd 1946- .... **CLC 35**

Barrett, William (Christopher)
1913-1992 .... **CLC 27**
See also CA 13-16R; 139; CANR 11;
INT CANR-11

Barrie, J(ames) M(atthew)
1860-1937 .... **TCLC 2; DAB**
See also CA 104; 136; CDBLB 1890-1914;
CLR 16; DAM DRAM; DLB 10, 141,
156; MAICYA; YABC 1

Barrington, Michael
See Moorcock, Michael (John)

Barrol, Grady
See Bograd, Larry

Barry, Mike
See Malzberg, Barry N(athaniel)

Barry, Philip 1896-1949 .... **TCLC 11**
See also CA 109; DLB 7

Bart, Andre Schwarz
See Schwarz-Bart, Andre

Barth, John (Simmons)
1930- ...... **CLC 1, 2, 3, 5, 7, 9, 10, 14,
27, 51, 89; SSC 10**
See also AITN 1, 2; CA 1-4R; CABS 1;
CANR 5, 23, 49; DAM NOV; DLB 2;
MTCW

Barthelme, Donald
1931-1989 ...... **CLC 1, 2, 3, 5, 6, 8, 13,
23, 46, 59; SSC 2**
See also CA 21-24R; 129; CANR 20;
DAM NOV; DLB 2; DLBY 80, 89;
MTCW; SATA 7; SATA-Obit 62

Barthelme, Frederick 1943- .... **CLC 36**
See also CA 114; 122; DLBY 85; INT 122

Barthes, Roland (Gerard)
1915-1980 .... **CLC 24, 83**
See also CA 130; 97-100; MTCW

Barzun, Jacques (Martin) 1907- .... **CLC 51**
See also CA 61-64; CANR 22

Bashevis, Isaac
See Singer, Isaac Bashevis

Bashkirtseff, Marie 1859-1884 ... **NCLC 27**

Basho
See Matsuo Basho

Bass, Kingsley B., Jr.
See Bullins, Ed

Bass, Rick 1958- .... **CLC 79**
See also CA 126; CANR 53

Bassani, Giorgio 1916- .... **CLC 9**
See also CA 65-68; CANR 33; DLB 128;
MTCW

Bastos, Augusto (Antonio) Roa
See Roa Bastos, Augusto (Antonio)

Bataille, Georges 1897-1962 .... **CLC 29**
See also CA 101; 89-92

Bates, H(erbert) E(rnest)
1905-1974 ...... **CLC 46; DAB; SSC 10**
See also CA 93-96; 45-48; CANR 34;
DAM POP; DLB 162; MTCW

Bauchart
See Camus, Albert

Baudelaire, Charles
1821-1867 .... **NCLC 6, 29, 55; DA;
DAB; DAC; PC 1; SSC 18; WLC**
See also DAM MST, POET

Baudrillard, Jean 1929- .... **CLC 60**

Baum, L(yman) Frank 1856-1919 . . . **TCLC 7**
See also CA 108; 133; CLR 15; DLB 22;
JRDA; MAICYA; MTCW; SATA 18

Baum, Louis F.
See Baum, L(yman) Frank

Baumbach, Jonathan 1933- . . . . . . **CLC 6, 23**
See also CA 13-16R; CAAS 5; CANR 12;
DLBY 80; INT CANR-12; MTCW

Bausch, Richard (Carl) 1945- . . . . . . **CLC 51**
See also CA 101; CAAS 14; CANR 43;
DLB 130

Baxter, Charles 1947- . . . . **CLC 45, 78**
See also CA 57-60; CANR 40; DAM POP;
DLB 130

Baxter, George Owen
See Faust, Frederick (Schiller)

Baxter, James K(eir) 1926-1972 . . . . **CLC 14**
See also CA 77-80

Baxter, John
See Hunt, E(verette) Howard, (Jr.)

Bayer, Sylvia
See Glassco, John

Baynton, Barbara 1857-1929 . . . . . **TCLC 57**

Beagle, Peter S(oyer) 1939- . . . . **CLC 7**
See also CA 9-12R; CANR 4, 51;
DLBY 80; INT CANR-4; SATA 60

Bean, Normal
See Burroughs, Edgar Rice

Beard, Charles A(ustin)
1874-1948 . . . . **TCLC 15**
See also CA 115; DLB 17; SATA 18

Beardsley, Aubrey 1872-1898 . . . . . **NCLC 6**

Beattie, Ann
1947- . . . . **CLC 8, 13, 18, 40, 63; SSC 11**
See also BEST 90:2; CA 81-84; CANR 53;
DAM NOV, POP; DLBY 82; MTCW

Beattie, James 1735-1803 . . . . **NCLC 25**
See also DLB 109

Beauchamp, Kathleen Mansfield 1888-1923
See Mansfield, Katherine
See also CA 104; 134; DA; DAC;
DAM MST

Beaumarchais, Pierre-Augustin Caron de
1732-1799 . . . . **DC 4**
See also DAM DRAM

Beaumont, Francis
1584(?)-1616 . . . . **LC 33; DC 6**
See also CDBLB Before 1660; DLB 58, 121

Beauvoir, Simone (Lucie Ernestine Marie
Bertrand) de
1908-1986 . . . . **CLC 1, 2, 4, 8, 14, 31, 44,
50, 71; DA; DAB; DAC; WLC**
See also CA 9-12R; 118; CANR 28;
DAM MST, NOV; DLB 72; DLBY 86;
MTCW

Becker, Carl 1873-1945 . . . . **TCLC 63:**
See also DLB 17

Becker, Jurek 1937- . . . . **CLC 7, 19**
See also CA 85-88; DLB 75

Becker, Walter 1950- . . . . **CLC 26**

Beckett, Samuel (Barclay)
1906-1989 . . . . . . **CLC 1, 2, 3, 4, 6, 9, 10,
11, 14, 18, 29, 57, 59, 83; DA; DAB;
DAC; SSC 16; WLC**
See also CA 5-8R; 130; CANR 33;
CDBLB 1945-1960; DAM DRAM, MST,
NOV; DLB 13, 15; DLBY 90; MTCW

Beckford, William 1760-1844 . . . . **NCLC 16**
See also DLB 39

Beckman, Gunnel 1910- . . . . **CLC 26**
See also CA 33-36R; CANR 15; CLR 25;
MAICYA; SAAS 9; SATA 6

Becque, Henri 1837-1899 . . . . **NCLC 3**

Beddoes, Thomas Lovell
1803-1849 . . . . **NCLC 3**
See also DLB 96

Bedford, Donald F.
See Fearing, Kenneth (Flexner)

Beecher, Catharine Esther
1800-1878 . . . . **NCLC 30**
See also DLB 1

Beecher, John 1904-1980 . . . . **CLC 6**
See also AITN 1; CA 5-8R; 105; CANR 8

Beer, Johann 1655-1700 . . . . **LC 5**

Beer, Patricia 1924- . . . . **CLC 58**
See also CA 61-64; CANR 13, 46; DLB 40

Beerbohm, Henry Maximilian
1872-1956 . . . . **TCLC 1, 24**
See also CA 104; DLB 34, 100

Beerbohm, Max
See Beerbohm, Henry Maximilian

Beer-Hofmann, Richard
1866-1945 . . . . **TCLC 60**
See also DLB 81

Begiebing, Robert J(ohn) 1946- . . . . . **CLC 70**
See also CA 122; CANR 40

Behan, Brendan
1923-1964 . . . . **CLC 1, 8, 11, 15, 79**
See also CA 73-76; CANR 33;
CDBLB 1945-1960; DAM DRAM;
DLB 13; MTCW

Behn, Aphra
1640(?)-1689 . . . . . . **LC 1, 30; DA; DAB;
DAC; DC 4; PC 13; WLC**
See also DAM DRAM, MST, NOV, POET;
DLB 39, 80, 131

Behrman, S(amuel) N(athaniel)
1893-1973 . . . . **CLC 40**
See also CA 13-16; 45-48; CAP 1; DLB 7,
44

Belasco, David 1853-1931 . . . . **TCLC 3**
See also CA 104; DLB 7

Belcheva, Elisaveta 1893- . . . . **CLC 10**
See also Bagryana, Elisaveta

Beldone, Phil "Cheech"
See Ellison, Harlan (Jay)

Beleno
See Azuela, Mariano

Belinski, Vissarion Grigoryevich
1811-1848 . . . . **NCLC 5**

Belitt, Ben 1911- . . . . **CLC 22**
See also CA 13-16R; CAAS 4; CANR 7;
DLB 5

Bell, James Madison
1826-1902 . . . . **TCLC 43; BLC**
See also BW 1; CA 122; 124; DAM MULT;
DLB 50

Bell, Madison (Smartt) 1957- . . . . . . **CLC 41**
See also CA 111; CANR 28

Bell, Marvin (Hartley) 1937- . . . . **CLC 8, 31**
See also CA 21-24R; CAAS 14;
DAM POET; DLB 5; MTCW

Bell, W. L. D.
See Mencken, H(enry) L(ouis)

Bellamy, Atwood C.
See Mencken, H(enry) L(ouis)

Bellamy, Edward 1850-1898 . . . . . . **NCLC 4**
See also DLB 12

Bellin, Edward J.
See Kuttner, Henry

Belloc, (Joseph) Hilaire (Pierre)
1870-1953 . . . . **TCLC 7, 18**
See also CA 106; DAM POET; DLB 19,
100, 141; YABC 1

Belloc, Joseph Peter Rene Hilaire
See Belloc, (Joseph) Hilaire (Pierre)

Belloc, Joseph Pierre Hilaire
See Belloc, (Joseph) Hilaire (Pierre)

Belloc, M. A.
See Lowndes, Marie Adelaide (Belloc)

Bellow, Saul
1915- . . . . . . **CLC 1, 2, 3, 6, 8, 10, 13, 15,
25, 33, 34, 63, 79; DA; DAB; DAC;
SSC 14; WLC**
See also AITN 2; BEST 89:3; CA 5-8R;
CABS 1; CANR 29, 53;
CDALB 1941-1968; DAM MST, NOV,
POP; DLB 2, 28; DLBD 3; DLBY 82;
MTCW

Belser, Reimond Karel Maria de 1929-
See Ruyslinck, Ward
See also CA 152

Bely, Andrey . . . . **TCLC 7; PC 11**
See also Bugayev, Boris Nikolayevich

Benary, Margot
See Benary-Isbert, Margot

Benary-Isbert, Margot 1889-1979 . . . **CLC 12**
See also CA 5-8R; 89-92; CANR 4;
CLR 12; MAICYA; SATA 2;
SATA-Obit 21

Benavente (y Martinez), Jacinto
1866-1954 . . . . **TCLC 3**
See also CA 106; 131; DAM DRAM,
MULT; HW; MTCW

Benchley, Peter (Bradford)
1940- . . . . **CLC 4, 8**
See also AAYA 14; AITN 2; CA 17-20R;
CANR 12, 35; DAM NOV, POP;
MTCW; SATA 3

Benchley, Robert (Charles)
1889-1945 . . . . **TCLC 1, 55**
See also CA 105; DLB 11

Benda, Julien 1867-1956 . . . . **TCLC 60**
See also CA 120

Benedict, Ruth 1887-1948 . . . . **TCLC 60**

Benedikt, Michael 1935- . . . . **CLC 4, 14**
See also CA 13-16R; CANR 7; DLB 5

Benet, Juan 1927-............. **CLC 28**
See also CA 143

Benet, Stephen Vincent
1898-1943 .... **TCLC 7; SSC 10**
See also CA 104; DAM POET; DLB 4, 48,
102; YABC 1

Benet, William Rose 1886-1950 ... **TCLC 28**
See also CA 118; DAM POET; DLB 45

Benford, Gregory (Albert) 1941-.... **CLC 52**
See also CA 69-72; CANR 12, 24, 49;
DLBY 82

Bengtsson, Frans (Gunnar)
1894-1954 .... **TCLC 48**

Benjamin, David
See Slavitt, David R(ytman)

Benjamin, Lois
See Gould, Lois

Benjamin, Walter 1892-1940..... **TCLC 39**

Benn, Gottfried 1886-1956........ **TCLC 3**
See also CA 106; DLB 56

Bennett, Alan 1934-..... **CLC 45, 77; DAB**
See also CA 103; CANR 35; DAM MST;
MTCW

Bennett, (Enoch) Arnold
1867-1931 .... **TCLC 5, 20**
See also CA 106; CDBLB 1890-1914;
DLB 10, 34, 98, 135

Bennett, Elizabeth
See Mitchell, Margaret (Munnerlyn)

Bennett, George Harold 1930-
See Bennett, Hal
See also BW 1; CA 97-100

Bennett, Hal .... **CLC 5**
See also Bennett, George Harold
See also DLB 33

Bennett, Jay 1912-................ **CLC 35**
See also AAYA 10; CA 69-72; CANR 11,
42; JRDA; SAAS 4; SATA 41, 87;
SATA-Brief 27

Bennett, Louise (Simone)
1919- .... **CLC 28; BLC**
See also BW 2; CA 151; DAM MULT;
DLB 117

Benson, E(dward) F(rederic)
1867-1940 .... **TCLC 27**
See also CA 114; DLB 135, 153

Benson, Jackson J. 1930-......... **CLC 34**
See also CA 25-28R; DLB 111

Benson, Sally 1900-1972 .... **CLC 17**
See also CA 19-20; 37-40R; CAP 1;
SATA 1, 35; SATA-Obit 27

Benson, Stella 1892-1933........ **TCLC 17**
See also CA 117; DLB 36, 162

Bentham, Jeremy 1748-1832 ..... **NCLC 38**
See also DLB 107, 158

Bentley, E(dmund) C(lerihew)
1875-1956 .... **TCLC 12**
See also CA 108; DLB 70

Bentley, Eric (Russell) 1916-....... **CLC 24**
See also CA 5-8R; CANR 6; INT CANR-6

Beranger, Pierre Jean de
1780-1857 .... **NCLC 34**

Berendt, John (Lawrence) 1939-.... **CLC 86**
See also CA 146

Berger, Colonel
See Malraux, (Georges-)Andre

Berger, John (Peter) 1926- ...... **CLC 2, 19**
See also CA 81-84; CANR 51; DLB 14

Berger, Melvin H. 1927-.......... **CLC 12**
See also CA 5-8R; CANR 4; CLR 32;
SAAS 2; SATA 5, 88

Berger, Thomas (Louis)
1924- .... **CLC 3, 5, 8, 11, 18, 38**
See also CA 1-4R; CANR 5, 28, 51;
DAM NOV; DLB 2; DLBY 80;
INT CANR-28; MTCW

Bergman, (Ernst) Ingmar
1918- .... **CLC 16, 72**
See also CA 81-84; CANR 33

Bergson, Henri 1859-1941....... **TCLC 32**

Bergstein, Eleanor 1938-.......... **CLC 4**
See also CA 53-56; CANR 5

Berkoff, Steven 1937-............. **CLC 56**
See also CA 104

Bermant, Chaim (Icyk) 1929- ...... **CLC 40**
See also CA 57-60; CANR 6, 31

Bern, Victoria
See Fisher, M(ary) F(rances) K(ennedy)

Bernanos, (Paul Louis) Georges
1888-1948 .... **TCLC 3**
See also CA 104; 130; DLB 72

Bernard, April 1956- .... **CLC 59**
See also CA 131

Berne, Victoria
See Fisher, M(ary) F(rances) K(ennedy)

Bernhard, Thomas
1931-1989 .... **CLC 3, 32, 61**
See also CA 85-88; 127; CANR 32;
DLB 85, 124; MTCW

Berriault, Gina 1926-............. **CLC 54**
See also CA 116; 129; DLB 130

Berrigan, Daniel 1921-............. **CLC 4**
See also CA 33-36R; CAAS 1; CANR 11,
43; DLB 5

Berrigan, Edmund Joseph Michael, Jr.
1934-1983
See Berrigan, Ted
See also CA 61-64; 110; CANR 14

Berrigan, Ted.................... **CLC 37**
See also Berrigan, Edmund Joseph Michael,
Jr.
See also DLB 5

Berry, Charles Edward Anderson 1931-
See Berry, Chuck
See also CA 115

Berry, Chuck .... **CLC 17**
See also Berry, Charles Edward Anderson

Berry, Jonas
See Ashbery, John (Lawrence)

Berry, Wendell (Erdman)
1934- .... **CLC 4, 6, 8, 27, 46**
See also AITN 1; CA 73-76; CANR 50;
DAM POET; DLB 5, 6

Berryman, John
1914-1972 ...... **CLC 1, 2, 3, 4, 6, 8, 10,**
13, 25, 62
See also CA 13-16; 33-36R; CABS 2;
CANR 35; CAP 1; CDALB 1941-1968;
DAM POET; DLB 48; MTCW

Bertolucci, Bernardo 1940-........ **CLC 16**
See also CA 106

Bertrand, Aloysius 1807-1841 .... **NCLC 31**

Bertran de Born c. 1140-1215..... **CMLC 5**

Besant, Annie (Wood) 1847-1933 ... **TCLC 9**
See also CA 105

Bessie, Alvah 1904-1985.......... **CLC 23**
See also CA 5-8R; 116; CANR 2; DLB 26

Bethlen, T. D.
See Silverberg, Robert

Beti, Mongo................. **CLC 27; BLC**
See also Biyidi, Alexandre
See also DAM MULT

Betjeman, John
1906-1984 ... **CLC 2, 6, 10, 34, 43; DAB**
See also CA 9-12R; 112; CANR 33;
CDBLB 1945-1960; DAM MST, POET;
DLB 20; DLBY 84; MTCW

Bettelheim, Bruno 1903-1990 ...... **CLC 79**
See also CA 81-84; 131; CANR 23; MTCW

Betti, Ugo 1892-1953 .... **TCLC 5**
See also CA 104

Betts, Doris (Waugh) 1932-.... **CLC 3, 6, 28**
See also CA 13-16R; CANR 9; DLBY 82;
INT CANR-9

Bevan, Alistair
See Roberts, Keith (John Kingston)

Bialik, Chaim Nachman
1873-1934 .... **TCLC 25**

Bickerstaff, Isaac
See Swift, Jonathan

Bidart, Frank 1939-.............. **CLC 33**
See also CA 140

Bienek, Horst 1930-............. **CLC 7, 11**
See also CA 73-76; DLB 75

Bierce, Ambrose (Gwinett)
1842-1914(?) .... **TCLC 1, 7, 44; DA;**
DAC; SSC 9; WLC
See also CA 104; 139; CDALB 1865-1917;
DAM MST; DLB 11, 12, 23, 71, 74

Biggers, Earl Derr 1884-1933 ..... **TCLC 65**
See also CA 108

Billings, Josh
See Shaw, Henry Wheeler

Billington, (Lady) Rachel (Mary)
1942- .... **CLC 43**
See also AITN 2; CA 33-36R; CANR 44

Binyon, T(imothy) J(ohn) 1936- .... **CLC 34**
See also CA 111; CANR 28

Bioy Casares, Adolfo
1914- ... **CLC 4, 8, 13, 88; HLC; SSC 17**
See also CA 29-32R; CANR 19, 43;
DAM MULT; DLB 113; HW; MTCW

Bird, Cordwainer
See Ellison, Harlan (Jay)

Bird, Robert Montgomery
1806-1854 .... **NCLC 1**

Birney, (Alfred) Earle
1904- .... **CLC 1, 4, 6, 11; DAC**
See also CA 1-4R; CANR 5, 20;
DAM MST, POET; DLB 88; MTCW

Bishop, Elizabeth
1911-1979 . . . . . . **CLC 1, 4, 9, 13, 15, 32; DA; DAC; PC 3**
See also CA 5-8R; 89-92; CABS 2; CANR 26; CDALB 1968-1988; DAM MST, POET; DLB 5; MTCW; SATA-Obit 24

Bishop, John 1935-. . . . . **CLC 10**
See also CA 105

Bissett, Bill 1939-. . . . . **CLC 18; PC 14**
See also CA 69-72; CAAS 19; CANR 15; DLB 53; MTCW

Bitov, Andrei (Georgievich) 1937-. . . **CLC 57**
See also CA 142

Biyidi, Alexandre 1932-
See Beti, Mongo
See also BW 1; CA 114; 124; MTCW

Bjarme, Brynjolf
See Ibsen, Henrik (Johan)

Bjornson, Bjornstjerne (Martinius)
1832-1910 . . . . **TCLC 7, 37**
See also CA 104

Black, Robert
See Holdstock, Robert P.

Blackburn, Paul 1926-1971 . . . . . . **CLC 9, 43**
See also CA 81-84; 33-36R; CANR 34; DLB 16; DLBY 81

Black Elk 1863-1950 . . . . **TCLC 33**
See also CA 144; DAM MULT; NNAL

Black Hobart
See Sanders, (James) Ed(ward)

Blacklin, Malcolm
See Chambers, Aidan

Blackmore, R(ichard) D(oddridge)
1825-1900 . . . . **TCLC 27**
See also CA 120; DLB 18

Blackmur, R(ichard) P(almer)
1904-1965 . . . . **CLC 2, 24**
See also CA 11-12; 25-28R; CAP 1; DLB 63

Black Tarantula, The
See Acker, Kathy

Blackwood, Algernon (Henry)
1869-1951 . . . . **TCLC 5**
See also CA 105; 150; DLB 153, 156

Blackwood, Caroline 1931-1996 . . . **CLC 6, 9**
See also CA 85-88; 151; CANR 32; DLB 14; MTCW

Blade, Alexander
See Hamilton, Edmond; Silverberg, Robert

Blaga, Lucian 1895-1961 . . . . **CLC 75**

Blair, Eric (Arthur) 1903-1950
See Orwell, George
See also CA 104; 132; DA; DAB; DAC; DAM MST, NOV; MTCW; SATA 29

Blais, Marie-Claire
1939-. . . . . **CLC 2, 4, 6, 13, 22; DAC**
See also CA 21-24R; CAAS 4; CANR 38; DAM MST; DLB 53; MTCW

Blaise, Clark 1940-. . . . . **CLC 29**
See also AITN 2; CA 53-56; CAAS 3; CANR 5; DLB 53

Blake, Nicholas
See Day Lewis, C(ecil)
See also DLB 77

Blake, William
1757-1827 . . . . **NCLC 13, 37, 57; DA; DAB; DAC; PC 12; WLC**
See also CDBLB 1789-1832; DAM MST, POET; DLB 93, 163; MAICYA; SATA 30

Blake, William J(ames) 1894-1969 . . . **PC 12**
See also CA 5-8R; 25-28R

Blasco Ibanez, Vicente
1867-1928 . . . . **TCLC 12**
See also CA 110; 131; DAM NOV; HW; MTCW

Blatty, William Peter 1928-. . . . . **CLC 2**
See also CA 5-8R; CANR 9; DAM POP

Bleeck, Oliver
See Thomas, Ross (Elmore)

Blessing, Lee 1949-. . . . . **CLC 54**

Blish, James (Benjamin)
1921-1975 . . . . **CLC 14**
See also CA 1-4R; 57-60; CANR 3; DLB 8; MTCW; SATA 66

Bliss, Reginald
See Wells, H(erbert) G(eorge)

Blixen, Karen (Christentze Dinesen)
1885-1962
See Dinesen, Isak
See also CA 25-28; CANR 22, 50; CAP 2; MTCW; SATA 44

Bloch, Robert (Albert) 1917-1994 . . . **CLC 33**
See also CA 5-8R; 146; CAAS 20; CANR 5; DLB 44; INT CANR-5; SATA 12; SATA-Obit 82

Blok, Alexander (Alexandrovich)
1880-1921 . . . . **TCLC 5**
See also CA 104

Blom, Jan
See Breytenbach, Breyten

Bloom, Harold 1930-. . . . . **CLC 24**
See also CA 13-16R; CANR 39; DLB 67

Bloomfield, Aurelius
See Bourne, Randolph S(illiman)

Blount, Roy (Alton), Jr. 1941-. . . . . . **CLC 38**
See also CA 53-56; CANR 10, 28; INT CANR-28; MTCW

Bloy, Leon 1846-1917. . . . . **TCLC 22**
See also CA 121; DLB 123

Blume, Judy (Sussman) 1938-. . . **CLC 12, 30**
See also AAYA 3; CA 29-32R; CANR 13, 37; CLR 2, 15; DAM NOV, POP; DLB 52; JRDA; MAICYA; MTCW; SATA 2, 31, 79

Blunden, Edmund (Charles)
1896-1974 . . . . **CLC 2, 56**
See also CA 17-18; 45-48; CAP 2; DLB 20, 100, 155; MTCW

Bly, Robert (Elwood)
1926-. . . . . **CLC 1, 2, 5, 10, 15, 38**
See also CA 5-8R; CANR 41; DAM POET; DLB 5; MTCW

Boas, Franz 1858-1942. . . . . **TCLC 56**
See also CA 115

Bobette
See Simenon, Georges (Jacques Christian)

Boccaccio, Giovanni
1313-1375 . . . . **CMLC 13; SSC 10**

Bochco, Steven 1943-. . . . . **CLC 35**
See also AAYA 11; CA 124; 138

Bodenheim, Maxwell 1892-1954 . . . **TCLC 44**
See also CA 110; DLB 9, 45

Bodker, Cecil 1927-. . . . . **CLC 21**
See also CA 73-76; CANR 13, 44; CLR 23; MAICYA; SATA 14

Boell, Heinrich (Theodor)
1917-1985 . . . . **CLC 2, 3, 6, 9, 11, 15, 27, 32, 72; DA; DAB; DAC; SSC 23; WLC**
See also CA 21-24R; 116; CANR 24; DAM MST, NOV; DLB 69; DLBY 85; MTCW

Boerne, Alfred
See Doeblin, Alfred

Boethius 480(?)-524(?) . . . . **CMLC 15**
See also DLB 115

Bogan, Louise
1897-1970 . . . . **CLC 4, 39, 46, 93; PC 12**
See also CA 73-76; 25-28R; CANR 33; DAM POET; DLB 45; MTCW

Bogarde, Dirk . . . . **CLC 19**
See also Van Den Bogarde, Derek Jules Gaspard Ulric Niven
See also DLB 14

Bogosian, Eric 1953-. . . . . **CLC 45**
See also CA 138

Bograd, Larry 1953-. . . . . **CLC 35**
See also CA 93-96; SAAS 21; SATA 33

Boiardo, Matteo Maria 1441-1494 . . . . **LC 6**

Boileau-Despreaux, Nicolas
1636-1711 . . . . **LC 3**

Bojer, Johan 1872-1959. . . . . **TCLC 64**

Boland, Eavan (Aisling) 1944-. . . **CLC 40, 67**
See also CA 143; DAM POET; DLB 40

Bolt, Lee
See Faust, Frederick (Schiller)

Bolt, Robert (Oxton) 1924-1995 . . . . **CLC 14**
See also CA 17-20R; 147; CANR 35; DAM DRAM; DLB 13; MTCW

Bombet, Louis-Alexandre-Cesar
See Stendhal

Bomkauf
See Kaufman, Bob (Garnell)

Bonaventura. . . . . **NCLC 35**
See also DLB 90

Bond, Edward 1934-. . . . . . . **CLC 4, 6, 13, 23**
See also CA 25-28R; CANR 38; DAM DRAM; DLB 13; MTCW

Bonham, Frank 1914-1989. . . . . **CLC 12**
See also AAYA 1; CA 9-12R; CANR 4, 36; JRDA; MAICYA; SAAS 3; SATA 1, 49; SATA-Obit 62

Bonnefoy, Yves 1923-. . . . . **CLC 9, 15, 58**
See also CA 85-88; CANR 33; DAM MST, POET; MTCW

Bontemps, Arna(ud Wendell)
1902-1973 . . . . **CLC 1, 18; BLC**
See also BW 1; CA 1-4R; 41-44R; CANR 4, 35; CLR 6; DAM MULT, NOV, POET; DLB 48, 51; JRDA; MAICYA; MTCW; SATA 2, 44; SATA-Obit 24

Booth, Martin 1944-. . . . . **CLC 13**
See also CA 93-96; CAAS 2

Booth, Philip 1925-. . . . . **CLC 23**
See also CA 5-8R; CANR 5; DLBY 82

Booth, Wayne C(layson) 1921- . . . . . **CLC 24**
See also CA 1-4R; CAAS 5; CANR 3, 43;
DLB 67

Borchert, Wolfgang 1921-1947 . . . . . **TCLC 5**
See also CA 104; DLB 69, 124

Borel, Petrus 1809-1859. . . . . **NCLC 41**

Borges, Jorge Luis
1899-1986 . . . **CLC 1, 2, 3, 4, 6, 8, 9, 10,**
13, 19, 44, 48, 83; DA; DAB; DAC;
HLC; SSC 4; WLC
See also CA 21-24R; CANR 19, 33;
DAM MST, MULT; DLB 113; DLBY 86;
HW; MTCW

Borowski, Tadeusz 1922-1951. . . . . . **TCLC 9**
See also CA 106

Borrow, George (Henry)
1803-1881 . . . . **NCLC 9**
See also DLB 21, 55, 166

Bosman, Herman Charles
1905-1951 . . . . **TCLC 49**

Bosschere, Jean de 1878(?)-1953. . . **TCLC 19**
See also CA 115

Boswell, James
1740-1795 . . . . . . **LC 4; DA; DAB; DAC;**
WLC
See also CDBLB 1660-1789; DAM MST;
DLB 104, 142

Bottoms, David 1949-. . . . . **CLC 53**
See also CA 105; CANR 22; DLB 120;
DLBY 83

Boucicault, Dion 1820-1890. . . . . . **NCLC 41**

Boucolon, Maryse 1937(?)-
See Conde, Maryse
See also CA 110; CANR 30, 53

Bourget, Paul (Charles Joseph)
1852-1935 . . . . **TCLC 12**
See also CA 107; DLB 123

Bourjaily, Vance (Nye) 1922- . . . . **CLC 8, 62**
See also CA 1-4R; CAAS 1; CANR 2;
DLB 2, 143

Bourne, Randolph S(illiman)
1886-1918 . . . . **TCLC 16**
See also CA 117; DLB 63

Bova, Ben(jamin William) 1932- . . . . **CLC 45**
See also AAYA 16; CA 5-8R; CAAS 18;
CANR 11; CLR 3; DLBY 81;
INT CANR-11; MAICYA; MTCW;
SATA 6, 68

Bowen, Elizabeth (Dorothea Cole)
1899-1973 . . . . . . **CLC 1, 3, 6, 11, 15, 22;**
SSC 3
See also CA 17-18; 41-44R; CANR 35;
CAP 2; CDBLB 1945-1960; DAM NOV;
DLB 15, 162; MTCW

Bowering, George 1935-. . . . . **CLC 15, 47**
See also CA 21-24R; CAAS 16; CANR 10;
DLB 53

Bowering, Marilyn R(uthe) 1949-. . . **CLC 32**
See also CA 101; CANR 49

Bowers, Edgar 1924- . . . . **CLC 9**
See also CA 5-8R; CANR 24; DLB 5

Bowie, David . . . . **CLC 17**
See also Jones, David Robert

Bowles, Jane (Sydney)
1917-1973 . . . . **CLC 3, 68**
See also CA 19-20; 41-44R; CAP 2

Bowles, Paul (Frederick)
1910- . . . . **CLC 1, 2, 19, 53; SSC 3**
See also CA 1-4R; CAAS 1; CANR 1, 19,
50; DLB 5, 6; MTCW

Box, Edgar
See Vidal, Gore

Boyd, Nancy
See Millay, Edna St. Vincent

Boyd, William 1952-. . . . . . . **CLC 28, 53, 70**
See also CA 114; 120; CANR 51

Boyle, Kay
1902-1992 . . . . . **CLC 1, 5, 19, 58; SSC 5**
See also CA 13-16R; 140; CAAS 1;
CANR 29; DLB 4, 9, 48, 86; DLBY 93;
MTCW

Boyle, Mark
See Kienzle, William X(avier)

Boyle, Patrick 1905-1982. . . . . **CLC 19**
See also CA 127

Boyle, T. C. 1948-
See Boyle, T(homas) Coraghessan

Boyle, T(homas) Coraghessan
1948- . . . . **CLC 36, 55, 90; SSC 16**
See also BEST 90:4; CA 120; CANR 44;
DAM POP; DLBY 86

Boz
See Dickens, Charles (John Huffam)

Brackenridge, Hugh Henry
1748-1816 . . . . **NCLC 7**
See also DLB 11, 37

Bradbury, Edward P.
See Moorcock, Michael (John)

Bradbury, Malcolm (Stanley)
1932-. . . . . **CLC 32, 61**
See also CA 1-4R; CANR 1, 33;
DAM NOV; DLB 14; MTCW

Bradbury, Ray (Douglas)
1920- . . . . **CLC 1, 3, 10, 15, 42; DA;**
DAB; DAC; WLC
See also AAYA 15; AITN 1, 2; CA 1-4R;
CANR 2, 30; CDALB 1968-1988;
DAM MST, NOV, POP; DLB 2, 8;
INT CANR-30; MTCW; SATA 11, 64

Bradford, Gamaliel 1863-1932. . . . . **TCLC 36**
See also DLB 17

Bradley, David (Henry, Jr.)
1950- . . . . **CLC 23; BLC**
See also BW 1; CA 104; CANR 26;
DAM MULT; DLB 33

Bradley, John Ed(mund, Jr.)
1958-. . . . . **CLC 55**
See also CA 139

Bradley, Marion Zimmer 1930-. . . . . **CLC 30**
See also AAYA 9; CA 57-60; CAAS 10;
CANR 7, 31, 51; DAM POP; DLB 8;
MTCW

Bradstreet, Anne
1612(?)-1672 . . . . . . **LC 4, 30; DA; DAC;**
PC 10
See also CDALB 1640-1865; DAM MST,
POET; DLB 24

Brady, Joan 1939- . . . . **CLC 86**
See also CA 141

Bragg, Melvyn 1939- . . . . **CLC 10**
See also BEST 89:3; CA 57-60; CANR 10,
48; DLB 14

Braine, John (Gerard)
1922-1986 . . . . **CLC 1, 3, 41**
See also CA 1-4R; 120; CANR 1, 33;
CDBLB 1945-1960; DLB 15; DLBY 86;
MTCW

Brammer, William 1930(?)-1978 . . . . **CLC 31**
See also CA 77-80

Brancati, Vitaliano 1907-1954. . . . . **TCLC 12**
See also CA 109

Brancato, Robin F(idler) 1936-. . . . . **CLC 35**
See also AAYA 9; CA 69-72; CANR 11,
45; CLR 32; JRDA; SAAS 9; SATA 23

Brand, Max
See Faust, Frederick (Schiller)

Brand, Millen 1906-1980. . . . . **CLC 7**
See also CA 21-24R; 97-100

Branden, Barbara . . . . **CLC 44**
See also CA 148

Brandes, Georg (Morris Cohen)
1842-1927 . . . . **TCLC 10**
See also CA 105

Brandys, Kazimierz 1916-. . . . . **CLC 62**

Branley, Franklyn M(ansfield)
1915-. . . . . **CLC 21**
See also CA 33-36R; CANR 14, 39;
CLR 13; MAICYA; SAAS 16; SATA 4,
68

Brathwaite, Edward Kamau 1930-. . . **CLC 11**
See also BW 2; CA 25-28R; CANR 11, 26,
47; DAM POET; DLB 125

Brautigan, Richard (Gary)
1935-1984 . . . . **CLC 1, 3, 5, 9, 12, 34, 42**
See also CA 53-56; 113; CANR 34;
DAM NOV; DLB 2, 5; DLBY 80, 84;
MTCW; SATA 56

Brave Bird, Mary 1953-
See Crow Dog, Mary
See also NNAL

Braverman, Kate 1950- . . . . **CLC 67**
See also CA 89-92

Brecht, Bertolt
1898-1956 . . . . . . **TCLC 1, 6, 13, 35; DA;**
DAB; DAC; DC 3; WLC
See also CA 104; 133; DAM DRAM, MST;
DLB 56, 124; MTCW

Brecht, Eugen Berthold Friedrich
See Brecht, Bertolt

Bremer, Fredrika 1801-1865 . . . . . **NCLC 11**

Brennan, Christopher John
1870-1932 . . . . **TCLC 17**
See also CA 117

Brennan, Maeve 1917-. . . . . **CLC 5**
See also CA 81-84

Brentano, Clemens (Maria)
1778-1842 . . . . **NCLC 1**
See also DLB 90

Brent of Bin Bin
See Franklin, (Stella Maraia Sarah) Miles

Brenton, Howard 1942-. . . . . **CLC 31**
See also CA 69-72; CANR 33; DLB 13;
MTCW

Breslin, James 1930-
See Breslin, Jimmy
See also CA 73-76; CANR 31; DAM NOV;
MTCW

Breslin, Jimmy . . . . CLC 4, 43
See Breslin, James
See also AITN 1

Bresson, Robert 1901- . . . . CLC 16
See also CA 110; CANR 49

Breton, Andre
1896-1966 . . . . . CLC 2, 9, 15, 54; PC 15
See also CA 19-20; 25-28R; CANR 40;
CAP 2; DLB 65; MTCW

Breytenbach, Breyten 1939(?)- . . CLC 23, 37
See also CA 113; 129; DAM POET

Bridgers, Sue Ellen 1942- . . . . CLC 26
See also AAYA 8; CA 65-68; CANR 11,
36; CLR 18; DLB 52; JRDA; MAICYA;
SAAS 1; SATA 22

Bridges, Robert (Seymour)
1844-1930 . . . . TCLC 1
See also CA 104; CDBLB 1890-1914;
DAM POET; DLB 19, 98

Bridie, James . . . . TCLC 3
See also Mavor, Osborne Henry
See also DLB 10

Brin, David 1950- . . . . CLC 34
See also CA 102; CANR 24;
INT CANR-24; SATA 65

Brink, Andre (Philippus)
1935- . . . . CLC 18, 36
See also CA 104; CANR 39; INT 103;
MTCW

Brinsmead, H(esba) F(ay) 1922- . . . . CLC 21
See also CA 21-24R; CANR 10; MAICYA;
SAAS 5; SATA 18, 78

Brittain, Vera (Mary)
1893(?)-1970 . . . . CLC 23
See also CA 13-16; 25-28R; CAP 1; MTCW

Broch, Hermann 1886-1951 . . . . TCLC 20
See also CA 117; DLB 85, 124

Brock, Rose
See Hansen, Joseph

Brodkey, Harold (Roy) 1930-1996 . . CLC 56
See also CA 111; 151; DLB 130

Brodsky, Iosif Alexandrovich 1940-1996
See Brodsky, Joseph
See also AITN 1; CA 41-44R; 151;
CANR 37; DAM POET; MTCW

Brodsky, Joseph . . CLC 4, 6, 13, 36, 50; PC 9
See also Brodsky, Iosif Alexandrovich

Brodsky, Michael Mark 1948- . . . . . CLC 19
See also CA 102; CANR 18, 41

Bromell, Henry 1947- . . . . CLC 5
See also CA 53-56; CANR 9

Bromfield, Louis (Brucker)
1896-1956 . . . . TCLC 11
See also CA 107; DLB 4, 9, 86

Broner, E(sther) M(asserman)
1930- . . . . CLC 19
See also CA 17-20R; CANR 8, 25; DLB 28

Bronk, William 1918- . . . . CLC 10
See also CA 89-92; CANR 23; DLB 165

Bronstein, Lev Davidovich
See Trotsky, Leon

Bronte, Anne 1820-1849 . . . . NCLC 4
See also DLB 21

Bronte, Charlotte
1816-1855 . . . . NCLC 3, 8, 33; DA;
DAB; DAC; WLC
See also AAYA 17; CDBLB 1832-1890;
DAM MST, NOV; DLB 21, 159

Bronte, Emily (Jane)
1818-1848 . . . . NCLC 16, 35; DA; DAB;
DAC; PC 8; WLC
See also AAYA 17; CDBLB 1832-1890;
DAM MST, NOV, POET; DLB 21, 32

Brooke, Frances 1724-1789 . . . . LC 6
See also DLB 39, 99

Brooke, Henry 1703(?)-1783 . . . . LC 1
See also DLB 39

Brooke, Rupert (Chawner)
1887-1915 . . . . TCLC 2, 7; DA; DAB;
DAC; WLC
See also CA 104; 132; CDBLB 1914-1945;
DAM MST, POET; DLB 19; MTCW

Brooke-Haven, P.
See Wodehouse, P(elham) G(renville)

Brooke-Rose, Christine 1926- . . . . . . CLC 40
See also CA 13-16R; DLB 14

Brookner, Anita
1928- . . . . CLC 32, 34, 51; DAB
See also CA 114; 120; CANR 37;
DAM POP; DLBY 87; MTCW

Brooks, Cleanth 1906-1994 . . . . . CLC 24, 86
See also CA 17-20R; 145; CANR 33, 35;
DLB 63; DLBY 94; INT CANR-35;
MTCW

Brooks, George
See Baum, L(yman) Frank

Brooks, Gwendolyn
1917- . . . . . . CLC 1, 2, 4, 5, 15, 49; BLC;
DA; DAC; PC 7; WLC
See also AITN 1; BW 2; CA 1-4R;
CANR 1, 27, 52; CDALB 1941-1968;
CLR 27; DAM MST, MULT, POET;
DLB 5, 76, 165; MTCW; SATA 6

Brooks, Mel . . . . CLC 12
See also Kaminsky, Melvin
See also AAYA 13; DLB 26

Brooks, Peter 1938- . . . . CLC 34
See also CA 45-48; CANR 1

Brooks, Van Wyck 1886-1963 . . . . . . CLC 29
See also CA 1-4R; CANR 6; DLB 45, 63,
103

Brophy, Brigid (Antonia)
1929-1995 . . . . CLC 6, 11, 29
See also CA 5-8R; 149; CAAS 4; CANR 25,
53; DLB 14; MTCW

Brosman, Catharine Savage 1934- . . . . CLC 9
See also CA 61-64; CANR 21, 46

Brother Antoninus
See Everson, William (Oliver)

Broughton, T(homas) Alan 1936- . . . CLC 19
See also CA 45-48; CANR 2, 23, 48

Broumas, Olga 1949- . . . . CLC 10, 73
See also CA 85-88; CANR 20

Brown, Charles Brockden
1771-1810 . . . . NCLC 22
See also CDALB 1640-1865; DLB 37, 59,
73

Brown, Christy 1932-1981 . . . . CLC 63
See also CA 105; 104; DLB 14

Brown, Claude 1937- . . . . CLC 30; BLC
See also AAYA 7; BW 1; CA 73-76;
DAM MULT

Brown, Dee (Alexander) 1908- . . CLC 18, 47
See also CA 13-16R; CAAS 6; CANR 11,
45; DAM POP; DLBY 80; MTCW;
SATA 5

Brown, George
See Wertmueller, Lina

Brown, George Douglas
1869-1902 . . . . TCLC 28

Brown, George Mackay
1921-1996 . . . . CLC 5, 48
See also CA 21-24R; 151; CAAS 6;
CANR 12, 37; DLB 14, 27, 139; MTCW;
SATA 35

Brown, (William) Larry 1951- . . . . . . CLC 73
See also CA 130; 134; INT 133

Brown, Moses
See Barrett, William (Christopher)

Brown, Rita Mae 1944- . . . . . CLC 18, 43, 79
See also CA 45-48; CANR 2, 11, 35;
DAM NOV, POP; INT CANR-11;
MTCW

Brown, Roderick (Langmere) Haig-
See Haig-Brown, Roderick (Langmere)

Brown, Rosellen 1939- . . . . CLC 32
See also CA 77-80; CAAS 10; CANR 14, 44

Brown, Sterling Allen
1901-1989 . . . . CLC 1, 23, 59; BLC
See also BW 1; CA 85-88; 127; CANR 26;
DAM MULT, POET; DLB 48, 51, 63;
MTCW

Brown, Will
See Ainsworth, William Harrison

Brown, William Wells
1813-1884 . . . . NCLC 2; BLC; DC 1
See also DAM MULT; DLB 3, 50

Browne, (Clyde) Jackson 1948(?)- . . . CLC 21
See also CA 120

Browning, Elizabeth Barrett
1806-1861 . . . . . NCLC 1, 16; DA; DAB;
DAC; PC 6; WLC
See also CDBLB 1832-1890; DAM MST,
POET; DLB 32

Browning, Robert
1812-1889 . . . . NCLC 19; DA; DAB;
DAC; PC 2
See also CDBLB 1832-1890; DAM MST,
POET; DLB 32, 163; YABC 1

Browning, Tod 1882-1962 . . . . CLC 16
See also CA 141; 117

Brownson, Orestes (Augustus)
1803-1876 . . . . NCLC 50

Bruccoli, Matthew J(oseph) 1931- . . CLC 34
See also CA 9-12R; CANR 7; DLB 103

Bruce, Lenny . . . . CLC 21
See also Schneider, Leonard Alfred

Bruin, John
See Brutus, Dennis

Brulard, Henri
See Stendhal

Byron, George Gordon (Noel)
1788-1824 ..... **NCLC 2, 12; DA; DAB;**
DAC; PC 16; WLC
See also CDBLB 1789-1832; DAM MST,
POET; DLB 96, 110

C. 3. 3.
See Wilde, Oscar (Fingal O'Flahertie Wills)

Caballero, Fernan 1796-1877..... **NCLC 10**

Cabell, James Branch 1879-1958 ... **TCLC 6**
See also CA 105; DLB 9, 78

Cable, George Washington
1844-1925 .... **TCLC 4; SSC 4**
See also CA 104; DLB 12, 74; DLBD 13

Cabral de Melo Neto, Joao 1920-... **CLC 76**
See also CA 151; DAM MULT

Cabrera Infante, G(uillermo)
1929- .... **CLC 5, 25, 45; HLC**
See also CA 85-88; CANR 29;
DAM MULT; DLB 113; HW; MTCW

Cade, Toni
See Bambara, Toni Cade

Cadmus and Harmonia
See Buchan, John

Caedmon fl. 658-680............. **CMLC 7**
See also DLB 146

Caeiro, Alberto
See Pessoa, Fernando (Antonio Nogueira)

Cage, John (Milton, Jr.) 1912- ..... **CLC 41**
See also CA 13-16R; CANR 9;
INT CANR-9

Cain, G.
See Cabrera Infante, G(uillermo)

Cain, Guillermo
See Cabrera Infante, G(uillermo)

Cain, James M(allahan)
1892-1977 .... **CLC 3, 11, 28**
See also AITN 1; CA 17-20R; 73-76;
CANR 8, 34; MTCW

Caine, Mark
See Raphael, Frederic (Michael)

Calasso, Roberto 1941- .... **CLC 81**
See also CA 143

Calderon de la Barca, Pedro
1600-1681 .... **LC 23; DC 3**

Caldwell, Erskine (Preston)
1903-1987 .... **CLC 1, 8, 14, 50, 60;**
SSC 19
See also AITN 1; CA 1-4R; 121; CAAS 1;
CANR 2, 33; DAM NOV; DLB 9, 86;
MTCW

Caldwell, (Janet Miriam) Taylor (Holland)
1900-1985 .... **CLC 2, 28, 39**
See also CA 5-8R; 116; CANR 5;
DAM NOV, POP

Calhoun, John Caldwell
1782-1850 .... **NCLC 15**
See also DLB 3

Calisher, Hortense
1911- .... **CLC 2, 4, 8, 38; SSC 15**
See also CA 1-4R; CANR 1, 22;
DAM NOV; DLB 2; INT CANR-22;
MTCW

Callaghan, Morley Edward
1903-1990 ..... **CLC 3, 14, 41, 65; DAC**
See also CA 9-12R; 132; CANR 33;
DAM MST; DLB 68; MTCW

Callimachus
c. 305B.C.-c. 240B.C........ **CMLC 18**

Calvino, Italo
1923-1985 ..... **CLC 5, 8, 11, 22, 33, 39,**
73; SSC 3
See also CA 85-88; 116; CANR 23;
DAM NOV; MTCW

Cameron, Carey 1952- .... **CLC 59**
See also CA 135

Cameron, Peter 1959-............. **CLC 44**
See also CA 125; CANR 50

Campana, Dino 1885-1932........ **TCLC 20**
See also CA 117; DLB 114

Campanella, Tommaso 1568-1639 .... **LC 32**

Campbell, John W(ood, Jr.)
1910-1971 .... **CLC 32**
See also CA 21-22; 29-32R; CANR 34;
CAP 2; DLB 8; MTCW

Campbell, Joseph 1904-1987 .... **CLC 69**
See also AAYA 3; BEST 89:2; CA 1-4R;
124; CANR 3, 28; MTCW

Campbell, Maria 1940-....... **CLC 85; DAC**
See also CA 102; NNAL

Campbell, (John) Ramsey
1946- .... **CLC 42; SSC 19**
See also CA 57-60; CANR 7; INT CANR-7

Campbell, (Ignatius) Roy (Dunnachie)
1901-1957 .... **TCLC 5**
See also CA 104; DLB 20

Campbell, Thomas 1777-1844 .... **NCLC 19**
See also DLB 93; 144

Campbell, Wilfred .... **TCLC 9**
See also Campbell, William

Campbell, William 1858(?)-1918
See Campbell, Wilfred
See also CA 106; DLB 92

Campion, Jane................... **CLC 95**
See also CA 138

Campos, Alvaro de
See Pessoa, Fernando (Antonio Nogueira)

Camus, Albert
1913-1960 .... **CLC 1, 2, 4, 9, 11, 14, 32,**
63, 69; DA; DAB; DAC; DC 2; SSC 9;
WLC
See also CA 89-92; DAM DRAM, MST,
NOV; DLB 72; MTCW

Canby, Vincent 1924-............. **CLC 13**
See also CA 81-84

Cancale
See Desnos, Robert

Canetti, Elias
1905-1994 .... **CLC 3, 14, 25, 75, 86**
See also CA 21-24R; 146; CANR 23;
DLB 85, 124; MTCW

Canin, Ethan 1960-............... **CLC 55**
See also CA 131; 135

Cannon, Curt
See Hunter, Evan

Cape, Judith
See Page, P(atricia) K(athleen)

Capek, Karel
1890-1938 ...... **TCLC 6, 37; DA; DAB;**
DAC; DC 1; WLC
See also CA 104; 140; DAM DRAM, MST,
NOV

Capote, Truman
1924-1984 ...... **CLC 1, 3, 8, 13, 19, 34,**
38, 58; DA; DAB; DAC; SSC 2; WLC
See also CA 5-8R; 113; CANR 18;
CDALB 1941-1968; DAM MST, NOV,
POP; DLB 2; DLBY 80, 84; MTCW

Capra, Frank 1897-1991........... **CLC 16**
See also CA 61-64; 135

Caputo, Philip 1941-.............. **CLC 32**
See also CA 73-76; CANR 40

Card, Orson Scott 1951- .... **CLC 44, 47, 50**
See also AAYA 11; CA 102; CANR 27, 47;
DAM POP; INT CANR-27; MTCW;
SATA 83

Cardenal, Ernesto 1925-..... **CLC 31; HLC**
See also CA 49-52; CANR 2, 32;
DAM MULT, POET; HW; MTCW

Cardozo, Benjamin N(athan)
1870-1938 .... **TCLC 65**
See also CA 117

Carducci, Giosue 1835-1907...... **TCLC 32**

Carew, Thomas 1595(?)-1640........ **LC 13**
See also DLB 126

Carey, Ernestine Gilbreth 1908- .... **CLC 17**
See also CA 5-8R; SATA 2

Carey, Peter 1943-............. **CLC 40, 55**
See also CA 123; 127; CANR 53; INT 127;
MTCW

Carleton, William 1794-1869...... **NCLC 3**
See also DLB 159

Carlisle, Henry (Coffin) 1926-...... **CLC 33**
See also CA 13-16R; CANR 15

Carlsen, Chris
See Holdstock, Robert P.

Carlson, Ron(ald F.) 1947-........ **CLC 54**
See also CA 105; CANR 27

Carlyle, Thomas
1795-1881 .. **NCLC 22; DA; DAB; DAC**
See also CDBLB 1789-1832; DAM MST;
DLB 55; 144

Carman, (William) Bliss
1861-1929 .... **TCLC 7; DAC**
See also CA 104; DLB 92

Carnegie, Dale 1888-1955 .... **TCLC 53**

Carossa, Hans 1878-1956........ **TCLC 48**
See also DLB 66

Carpenter, Don(ald Richard)
1931-1995 .... **CLC 41**
See also CA 45-48; 149; CANR 1

Carpentier (y Valmont), Alejo
1904-1980 .... **CLC 8, 11, 38; HLC**
See also CA 65-68; 97-100; CANR 11;
DAM MULT; DLB 113; HW

Carr, Caleb 1955(?)-............... **CLC 86**
See also CA 147

Carr, Emily 1871-1945........... **TCLC 32**
See also DLB 68

Carr, John Dickson 1906-1977 ...... **CLC 3**
See also CA 49-52; 69-72; CANR 3, 33;
MTCW

Carr, Philippa
See Hibbert, Eleanor Alice Burford

Carr, Virginia Spencer 1929- . . . . . . **CLC 34**
See also CA 61-64; DLB 111

Carrere, Emmanuel 1957- . . . . **CLC 89**

Carrier, Roch 1937- . . . . . **CLC 13, 78; DAC**
See also CA 130; DAM MST; DLB 53

Carroll, James P. 1943(?)- . . . . **CLC 38**
See also CA 81-84

Carroll, Jim 1951- . . . . **CLC 35**
See also AAYA 17; CA 45-48; CANR 42

Carroll, Lewis . . . . **NCLC 2, 53; WLC**
See also Dodgson, Charles Lutwidge
See also CDBLB 1832-1890; CLR 2, 18;
DLB 18, 163; JRDA

Carroll, Paul Vincent 1900-1968. . . . **CLC 10**
See also CA 9-12R; 25-28R; DLB 10

Carruth, Hayden
1921- . . . . . . **CLC 4, 7, 10, 18, 84; PC 10**
See also CA 9-12R; CANR 4, 38; DLB 5,
165; INT CANR-4; MTCW; SATA 47

Carson, Rachel Louise 1907-1964 . . . **CLC 71**
See also CA 77-80; CANR 35; DAM POP;
MTCW; SATA 23

Carter, Angela (Olive)
1940-1992 . . . . . . **CLC 5, 41, 76; SSC 13**
See also CA 53-56; 136; CANR 12, 36;
DLB 14; MTCW; SATA 66;
SATA-Obit 70

Carter, Nick
See Smith, Martin Cruz

Carver, Raymond
1938-1988 . . . **CLC 22, 36, 53, 55; SSC 8**
See also CA 33-36R; 126; CANR 17, 34;
DAM NOV; DLB 130; DLBY 84, 88;
MTCW

Cary, Elizabeth, Lady Falkland
1585-1639 . . . . **LC 30**

Cary, (Arthur) Joyce (Lunel)
1888-1957 . . . . **TCLC 1, 29**
See also CA 104; CDBLB 1914-1945;
DLB 15, 100

Casanova de Seingalt, Giovanni Jacopo
1725-1798 . . . . **LC 13**

Casares, Adolfo Bioy
See Bioy Casares, Adolfo

Casely-Hayford, J(oseph) E(phraim)
1866-1930 . . . . **TCLC 24; BLC**
See also BW 2; CA 123; DAM MULT

Casey, John (Dudley) 1939- . . . . **CLC 59**
See also BEST 90:2; CA 69-72; CANR 23

Casey, Michael 1947- . . . . **CLC 2**
See also CA 65-68; DLB 5

Casey, Patrick
See Thurman, Wallace (Henry)

Casey, Warren (Peter) 1935-1988 . . . **CLC 12**
See also CA 101; 127; INT 101

Casona, Alejandro . . . . **CLC 49**
See also Alvarez, Alejandro Rodriguez

Cassavetes, John 1929-1989 . . . . **CLC 20**
See also CA 85-88; 127

Cassill, R(onald) V(erlin) 1919- . . **CLC 4, 23**
See also CA 9-12R; CAAS 1; CANR 7, 45;
DLB 6

Cassirer, Ernst 1874-1945 . . . . **TCLC 61**

Cassity, (Allen) Turner 1929- . . . **CLC 6, 42**
See also CA 17-20R; CAAS 8; CANR 11;
DLB 105

Castaneda, Carlos 1931(?)- . . . . **CLC 12**
See also CA 25-28R; CANR 32; HW;
MTCW

Castedo, Elena 1937- . . . . **CLC 65**
See also CA 132

Castedo-Ellerman, Elena
See Castedo, Elena

Castellanos, Rosario
1925-1974 . . . . **CLC 66; HLC**
See also CA 131; 53-56; DAM MULT;
DLB 113; HW

Castelvetro, Lodovico 1505-1571 . . . . **LC 12**

Castiglione, Baldassare 1478-1529 . . . **LC 12**

Castle, Robert
See Hamilton, Edmond

Castro, Guillen de 1569-1631 . . . . **LC 19**

Castro, Rosalia de 1837-1885 . . . . . **NCLC 3**
See also DAM MULT

Cather, Willa
See Cather, Willa Sibert

Cather, Willa Sibert
1873-1947 . . . . **TCLC 1, 11, 31; DA;
DAB; DAC; SSC 2; WLC**
See also CA 104; 128; CDALB 1865-1917;
DAM MST, NOV; DLB 9, 54, 78;
DLBD 1; MTCW; SATA 30

Catton, (Charles) Bruce
1899-1978 . . . . **CLC 35**
See also AITN 1; CA 5-8R; 81-84;
CANR 7; DLB 17; SATA 2;
SATA-Obit 24

Catullus c. 84B.C.-c. 54B.C. . . . . . **CMLC 18**

Cauldwell, Frank
See King, Francis (Henry)

Caunitz, William J. 1933- . . . . **CLC 34**
See also BEST 89:3; CA 125; 130; INT 130

Causley, Charles (Stanley) 1917- . . . . . **CLC 7**
See also CA 9-12R; CANR 5, 35; CLR 30;
DLB 27; MTCW; SATA 3, 66

Caute, David 1936- . . . . **CLC 29**
See also CA 1-4R; CAAS 4; CANR 1, 33;
DAM NOV; DLB 14

Cavafy, C(onstantine) P(eter)
1863-1933 . . . . **TCLC 2, 7**
See also Kavafis, Konstantinos Petrou
See also CA 148; DAM POET

Cavallo, Evelyn
See Spark, Muriel (Sarah)

Cavanna, Betty . . . . **CLC 12**
See also Harrison, Elizabeth Cavanna
See also JRDA; MAICYA; SAAS 4;
SATA 1, 30

Cavendish, Margaret Lucas
1623-1673 . . . . **LC 30**
See also DLB 131

Caxton, William 1421(?)-1491(?) . . . . . **LC 17**

Cayrol, Jean 1911- . . . . **CLC 11**
See also CA 89-92; DLB 83

Cela, Camilo Jose
1916- . . . . **CLC 4, 13, 59; HLC**
See also BEST 90:2; CA 21-24R; CAAS 10;
CANR 21, 32; DAM MULT; DLBY 89;
HW; MTCW

Celan, Paul . . . . . . **CLC 10, 19, 53, 82; PC 10**
See also Antschel, Paul
See also DLB 69

Celine, Louis-Ferdinand
. . . . **CLC 1, 3, 4, 7, 9, 15, 47**
See also Destouches, Louis-Ferdinand
See also DLB 72

Cellini, Benvenuto 1500-1571 . . . . **LC 7**

Cendrars, Blaise . . . . **CLC 18**
See also Sauser-Hall, Frederic

Cernuda (y Bidon), Luis
1902-1963 . . . . **CLC 54**
See also CA 131; 89-92; DAM POET;
DLB 134; HW

Cervantes (Saavedra), Miguel de
1547-1616 . . . . **LC 6, 23; DA; DAB;
DAC; SSC 12; WLC**
See also DAM MST, NOV

Cesaire, Aime (Fernand)
1913- . . . . **CLC 19, 32; BLC**
See also BW 2; CA 65-68; CANR 24, 43;
DAM MULT, POET; MTCW

Chabon, Michael 1965(?)- . . . . **CLC 55**
See also CA 139

Chabrol, Claude 1930- . . . . **CLC 16**
See also CA 110

Challans, Mary 1905-1983
See Renault, Mary
See also CA 81-84; 111; SATA 23;
SATA-Obit 36

Challis, George
See Faust, Frederick (Schiller)

Chambers, Aidan 1934- . . . . **CLC 35**
See also CA 25-28R; CANR 12, 31; JRDA;
MAICYA; SAAS 12; SATA 1, 69

Chambers, James 1948-
See Cliff, Jimmy
See also CA 124

Chambers, Jessie
See Lawrence, D(avid) H(erbert Richards)

Chambers, Robert W. 1865-1933. . . **TCLC 41**

Chandler, Raymond (Thornton)
1888-1959 . . . . **TCLC 1, 7; SSC 23**
See also CA 104; 129; CDALB 1929-1941;
DLBD 6; MTCW

Chang, Jung 1952- . . . . **CLC 71**
See also CA 142

Channing, William Ellery
1780-1842 . . . . **NCLC 17**
See also DLB 1, 59

Chaplin, Charles Spencer
1889-1977 . . . . **CLC 16**
See also Chaplin, Charlie
See also CA 81-84; 73-76

Chaplin, Charlie
See Chaplin, Charles Spencer
See also DLB 44

Chapman, George 1559(?)-1634 . . . . . . **LC 22**
See also DAM DRAM; DLB 62, 121

Cox, William Trevor   1928- ... **CLC 9, 14, 71**
See also Trevor, William
See also CA 9-12R; CANR 4, 37;
DAM NOV; DLB 14; INT CANR-37;
MTCW

Coyne, P. J.
See Masters, Hilary

Cozzens, James Gould
1903-1978 .... **CLC 1, 4, 11, 92**
See also CA 9-12R; 81-84; CANR 19;
CDALB 1941-1968; DLB 9; DLBD 2;
DLBY 84; MTCW

Crabbe, George   1754-1832...... **NCLC 26**
See also DLB 93

Craddock, Charles Egbert
See Murfree, Mary Noailles

Craig, A. A.
See Anderson, Poul (William)

Craik, Dinah Maria (Mulock)
1826-1887 .... **NCLC 38**
See also DLB 35, 163; MAICYA; SATA 34

Cram, Ralph Adams   1863-1942.... **TCLC 45**

Crane, (Harold) Hart
1899-1932 .... **TCLC 2, 5; DA; DAB;**
DAC; PC 3; WLC
See also CA 104; 127; CDALB 1917-1929;
DAM MST, POET; DLB 4, 48; MTCW

Crane, R(onald) S(almon)
1886-1967 .... **CLC 27**
See also CA 85-88; DLB 63

Crane, Stephen (Townley)
1871-1900 .... **TCLC 11, 17, 32; DA;**
DAB; DAC; SSC 7; WLC
See also CA 109; 140; CDALB 1865-1917;
DAM MST, NOV, POET; DLB 12, 54,
78; YABC 2

Crase, Douglas   1944- .... **CLC 58**
See also CA 106

Crashaw, Richard   1612(?)-1649...... **LC 24**
See also DLB 126

Craven, Margaret
1901-1980 .... **CLC 17; DAC**
See also CA 103

Crawford, F(rancis) Marion
1854-1909 .... **TCLC 10**
See also CA 107; DLB 71

Crawford, Isabella Valancy
1850-1887 .... **NCLC 12**
See also DLB 92

Crayon, Geoffrey
See Irving, Washington

Creasey, John   1908-1973......... **CLC 11**
See also CA 5-8R; 41-44R; CANR 8;
DLB 77; MTCW

Crebillon, Claude Prosper Jolyot de (fils)
1707-1777 .... **LC 28**

Credo
See Creasey, John

Creeley, Robert (White)
1926- ..... **CLC 1, 2, 4, 8, 11, 15, 36, 78**
See also CA 1-4R; CAAS 10; CANR 23, 43;
DAM POET; DLB 5, 16; MTCW

Crews, Harry (Eugene)
1935- .... **CLC 6, 23, 49**
See also AITN 1; CA 25-28R; CANR 20;
DLB 6, 143; MTCW

Crichton, (John) Michael
1942- .... **CLC 2, 6, 54, 90**
See also AAYA 10; AITN 2; CA 25-28R;
CANR 13, 40; DAM NOV, POP;
DLBY 81; INT CANR-13; JRDA;
MTCW; SATA 9, 88

Crispin, Edmund .... **CLC 22**
See also Montgomery, (Robert) Bruce
See also DLB 87

Cristofer, Michael   1945(?)- .... **CLC 28**
See also CA 110; DAM DRAM; DLB 7

Croce, Benedetto   1866-1952 ...... **TCLC 37**
See also CA 120

Crockett, David   1786-1836 .... **NCLC 8**
See also DLB 3, 11

Crockett, Davy
See Crockett, David

Crofts, Freeman Wills
1879-1957 .... **TCLC 55**
See also CA 115; DLB 77

Croker, John Wilson   1780-1857 .. **NCLC 10**
See also DLB 110

Crommelynck, Fernand   1885-1970 .. **CLC 75**
See also CA 89-92

Cronin, A(rchibald) J(oseph)
1896-1981 .... **CLC 32**
See also CA 1-4R; 102; CANR 5; SATA 47;
SATA-Obit 25

Cross, Amanda
See Heilbrun, Carolyn G(old)

Crothers, Rachel   1878(?)-1958..... **TCLC 19**
See also CA 113; DLB 7

Croves, Hal
See Traven, B.

Crow Dog, Mary .... **CLC 93**
See also Brave Bird, Mary

Crowfield, Christopher
See Stowe, Harriet (Elizabeth) Beecher

Crowley, Aleister................... **TCLC 7**
See also Crowley, Edward Alexander

Crowley, Edward Alexander   1875-1947
See Crowley, Aleister
See also CA 104

Crowley, John   1942-.............. **CLC 57**
See also CA 61-64; CANR 43; DLBY 82;
SATA 65

Crud
See Crumb, R(obert)

Crumarums
See Crumb, R(obert)

Crumb, R(obert)   1943-............ **CLC 17**
See also CA 106

Crumbum
See Crumb, R(obert)

Crumski
See Crumb, R(obert)

Crum the Bum
See Crumb, R(obert)

Crunk
See Crumb, R(obert)

Crustt
See Crumb, R(obert)

Cryer, Gretchen (Kiger)   1935-...... **CLC 21**
See also CA 114; 123

Csath, Geza   1887-1919.......... **TCLC 13**
See also CA 111

Cudlip, David   1933- .... **CLC 34**

Cullen, Countee
1903-1946 ...... **TCLC 4, 37; BLC; DA;**
DAC
See also BW 1; CA 108; 124;
CDALB 1917-1929; DAM MST, MULT,
POET; DLB 4, 48, 51; MTCW; SATA 18

Cum, R.
See Crumb, R(obert)

Cummings, Bruce F(rederick)   1889-1919
See Barbellion, W. N. P.
See also CA 123

Cummings, E(dward) E(stlin)
1894-1962 ...... **CLC 1, 3, 8, 12, 15, 68;**
DA; DAB; DAC; PC 5; WLC 2
See also CA 73-76; CANR 31;
CDALB 1929-1941; DAM MST, POET;
DLB 4, 48; MTCW

Cunha, Euclides (Rodrigues Pimenta) da
1866-1909 .... **TCLC 24**
See also CA 123

Cunningham, E. V.
See Fast, Howard (Melvin)

Cunningham, J(ames) V(incent)
1911-1985 .... **CLC 3, 31**
See also CA 1-4R; 115; CANR 1; DLB 5

Cunningham, Julia (Woolfolk)
1916- .... **CLC 12**
See also CA 9-12R; CANR 4, 19, 36;
JRDA; MAICYA; SAAS 2; SATA 1, 26

Cunningham, Michael   1952- .... **CLC 34**
See also CA 136

Cunninghame Graham, R(obert) B(ontine)
1852-1936 .... **TCLC 19**
See also Graham, R(obert) B(ontine)
Cunninghame
See also CA 119; DLB 98

Currie, Ellen   19(?)-............... **CLC 44**

Curtin, Philip
See Lowndes, Marie Adelaide (Belloc)

Curtis, Price
See Ellison, Harlan (Jay)

Cutrate, Joe
See Spiegelman, Art

Czaczkes, Shmuel Yosef
See Agnon, S(hmuel) Y(osef Halevi)

Dabrowska, Maria (Szumska)
1889-1965 .... **CLC 15**
See also CA 106

Dabydeen, David   1955- .... **CLC 34**
See also BW 1; CA 125

Dacey, Philip   1939- .... **CLC 51**
See also CA 37-40R; CAAS 17; CANR 14,
32; DLB 105

Dagerman, Stig (Halvard)
1923-1954 .... **TCLC 17**
See also CA 117

Dahl, Roald
1916-1990 . . . . . . **CLC 1, 6, 18, 79; DAB; DAC**
See also AAYA 15; CA 1-4R; 133;
CANR 6, 32, 37; CLR 1, 7, 41;
DAM MST, NOV, POP; DLB 139;
JRDA; MAICYA; MTCW; SATA 1, 26,
73; SATA-Obit 65

Dahlberg, Edward 1900-1977 . . . **CLC 1, 7, 14**
See also CA 9-12R; 69-72; CANR 31;
DLB 48; MTCW

Dale, Colin . . . . **TCLC 18**
See also Lawrence, T(homas) E(dward)

Dale, George E.
See Asimov, Isaac

Daly, Elizabeth 1878-1967 . . . . **CLC 52**
See also CA 23-24; 25-28R; CAP 2

Daly, Maureen 1921- . . . . **CLC 17**
See also AAYA 5; CANR 37; JRDA;
MAICYA; SAAS 1; SATA 2

Damas, Leon-Gontran 1912-1978 . . . **CLC 84**
See also BW 1; CA 125; 73-76

Dana, Richard Henry Sr.
1787-1879 . . . . **NCLC 53**

Daniel, Samuel 1562(?)-1619 . . . . **LC 24**
See also DLB 62

Daniels, Brett
See Adler, Renata

Dannay, Frederic 1905-1982 . . . . . . **CLC 11**
See also Queen, Ellery
See also CA 1-4R; 107; CANR 1, 39;
DAM POP; DLB 137; MTCW

D'Annunzio, Gabriele
1863-1938 . . . . **TCLC 6, 40**
See also CA 104

Danois, N. le
See Gourmont, Remy (-Marie-Charles) de

d'Antibes, Germain
See Simenon, Georges (Jacques Christian)

Danticat, Edwidge 1969- . . . . **CLC 94**
See also CA 152

Danvers, Dennis 1947- . . . . **CLC 70**

Danziger, Paula 1944- . . . . **CLC 21**
See also AAYA 4; CA 112; 115; CANR 37;
CLR 20; JRDA; MAICYA; SATA 36,
63; SATA-Brief 30

Da Ponte, Lorenzo 1749-1838 . . . . **NCLC 50**

Dario, Ruben
1867-1916 . . . . **TCLC 4; HLC; PC 15**
See also CA 131; DAM MULT; HW;
MTCW

Darley, George 1795-1846 . . . . **NCLC 2**
See also DLB 96

Darwin, Charles 1809-1882 . . . . . . **NCLC 57**
See also DLB 57, 166

Daryush, Elizabeth 1887-1977 . . . . **CLC 6, 19**
See also CA 49-52; CANR 3; DLB 20

Dashwood, Edmee Elizabeth Monica de la
Pasture 1890-1943
See Delafield, E. M.
See also CA 119

Daudet, (Louis Marie) Alphonse
1840-1897 . . . . **NCLC 1**
See also DLB 123

Daumal, Rene 1908-1944 . . . . **TCLC 14**
See also CA 114

Davenport, Guy (Mattison, Jr.)
1927- . . . . **CLC 6, 14, 38; SSC 16**
See also CA 33-36R; CANR 23; DLB 130

Davidson, Avram 1923-
See Queen, Ellery
See also CA 101; CANR 26; DLB 8

Davidson, Donald (Grady)
1893-1968 . . . . **CLC 2, 13, 19**
See also CA 5-8R; 25-28R; CANR 4;
DLB 45

Davidson, Hugh
See Hamilton, Edmond

Davidson, John 1857-1909 . . . . **TCLC 24**
See also CA 118; DLB 19

Davidson, Sara 1943- . . . . **CLC 9**
See also CA 81-84; CANR 44

Davie, Donald (Alfred)
1922-1995 . . . . **CLC 5, 8, 10, 31**
See also CA 1-4R; 149; CAAS 3; CANR 1,
44; DLB 27; MTCW

Davies, Ray(mond Douglas) 1944- . . **CLC 21**
See also CA 116; 146

Davies, Rhys 1903-1978 . . . . **CLC 23**
See also CA 9-12R; 81-84; CANR 4;
DLB 139

Davies, (William) Robertson
1913-1995 . . . . . **CLC 2, 7, 13, 25, 42, 75,**
91; DA; DAB; DAC; WLC
See also BEST 89:2; CA 33-36R; 150;
CANR 17, 42; DAM MST, NOV, POP;
DLB 68; INT CANR-17; MTCW

Davies, W(illiam) H(enry)
1871-1940 . . . . **TCLC 5**
See also CA 104; DLB 19

Davies, Walter C.
See Kornbluth, C(yril) M.

Davis, Angela (Yvonne) 1944- . . . . . . **CLC 77**
See also BW 2; CA 57-60; CANR 10;
DAM MULT

Davis, B. Lynch
See Bioy Casares, Adolfo; Borges, Jorge
Luis

Davis, Gordon
See Hunt, E(verette) Howard, (Jr.)

Davis, Harold Lenoir 1896-1960 . . . . **CLC 49**
See also CA 89-92; DLB 9

Davis, Rebecca (Blaine) Harding
1831-1910 . . . . **TCLC 6**
See also CA 104; DLB 74

Davis, Richard Harding
1864-1916 . . . . **TCLC 24**
See also CA 114; DLB 12, 23, 78, 79;
DLBD 13

Davison, Frank Dalby 1893-1970 . . . **CLC 15**
See also CA 116

Davison, Lawrence H.
See Lawrence, D(avid) H(erbert Richards)

Davison, Peter (Hubert) 1928- . . . . . **CLC 28**
See also CA 9-12R; CAAS 4; CANR 3, 43;
DLB 5

Davys, Mary 1674-1732 . . . . **LC 1**
See also DLB 39

Dawson, Fielding 1930- . . . . **CLC 6**
See also CA 85-88; DLB 130

Dawson, Peter
See Faust, Frederick (Schiller)

Day, Clarence (Shepard, Jr.)
1874-1935 . . . . **TCLC 25**
See also CA 108; DLB 11

Day, Thomas 1748-1789 . . . . **LC 1**
See also DLB 39; YABC 1

Day Lewis, C(ecil)
1904-1972 . . . . . . **CLC 1, 6, 10; PC 11**
See also Blake, Nicholas
See also CA 13-16; 33-36R; CANR 34;
CAP 1; DAM POET; DLB 15, 20;
MTCW

Dazai, Osamu . . . . **TCLC 11**
See also Tsushima, Shuji

de Andrade, Carlos Drummond
See Drummond de Andrade, Carlos

Deane, Norman
See Creasey, John

de Beauvoir, Simone (Lucie Ernestine Marie
Bertrand)
See Beauvoir, Simone (Lucie Ernestine
Marie Bertrand) de

de Brissac, Malcolm
See Dickinson, Peter (Malcolm)

de Chardin, Pierre Teilhard
See Teilhard de Chardin, (Marie Joseph)
Pierre

Dee, John 1527-1608 . . . . **LC 20**

Deer, Sandra 1940- . . . . **CLC 45**

De Ferrari, Gabriella 1941- . . . . **CLC 65**
See also CA 146

Defoe, Daniel
1660(?)-1731 . . . . **LC 1; DA; DAB; DAC;**
WLC
See also CDBLB 1660-1789; DAM MST,
NOV; DLB 39, 95, 101; JRDA;
MAICYA; SATA 22

de Gourmont, Remy(-Marie-Charles)
See Gourmont, Remy (-Marie-Charles) de

de Hartog, Jan 1914- . . . . **CLC 19**
See also CA 1-4R; CANR 1

de Hostos, E. M.
See Hostos (y Bonilla), Eugenio Maria de

de Hostos, Eugenio M.
See Hostos (y Bonilla), Eugenio Maria de

Deighton, Len . . . . **CLC 4, 7, 22, 46**
See also Deighton, Leonard Cyril
See also AAYA 6; BEST 89:2;
CDBLB 1960 to Present; DLB 87

Deighton, Leonard Cyril 1929-
See Deighton, Len
See also CA 9-12R; CANR 19, 33;
DAM NOV, POP; MTCW

Dekker, Thomas 1572(?)-1632 . . . . **LC 22**
See also CDBLB Before 1660;
DAM DRAM; DLB 62

Delafield, E. M. 1890-1943 . . . . **TCLC 61**
See also Dashwood, Edmee Elizabeth
Monica de la Pasture
See also DLB 34

de la Mare, Walter (John)
1873-1956 .... **TCLC 4, 53; DAB; DAC;**
SSC 14; WLC
See also CDBLB 1914-1945; CLR 23;
DAM MST, POET; DLB 162; SATA 16

Delaney, Franey
See O'Hara, John (Henry)

Delaney, Shelagh 1939- .... **CLC 29**
See also CA 17-20R; CANR 30;
CDBLB 1960 to Present; DAM DRAM;
DLB 13; MTCW

Delany, Mary (Granville Pendarves)
1700-1788 .... **LC 12**

Delany, Samuel R(ay, Jr.)
1942- .... **CLC 8, 14, 38; BLC**
See also BW 2; CA 81-84; CANR 27, 43;
DAM MULT; DLB 8, 33; MTCW

De La Ramee, (Marie) Louise 1839-1908
See Ouida
See also SATA 20

de la Roche, Mazo 1879-1961 ...... **CLC 14**
See also CA 85-88; CANR 30; DLB 68;
SATA 64

Delbanco, Nicholas (Franklin)
1942- .... **CLC 6, 13**
See also CA 17-20R; CAAS 2; CANR 29;
DLB 6

del Castillo, Michel 1933- .... **CLC 38**
See also CA 109

Deledda, Grazia (Cosima)
1875(?)-1936 .... **TCLC 23**
See also CA 123

Delibes, Miguel .... **CLC 8, 18**
See also Delibes Setien, Miguel

Delibes Setien, Miguel 1920-
See Delibes, Miguel
See also CA 45-48; CANR 1, 32; HW;
MTCW

DeLillo, Don
1936- ..... **CLC 8, 10, 13, 27, 39, 54, 76**
See also BEST 89:1; CA 81-84; CANR 21;
DAM NOV, POP; DLB 6; MTCW

de Lisser, H. G.
See De Lisser, Herbert George
See also DLB 117

De Lisser, Herbert George
1878-1944 .... **TCLC 12**
See also de Lisser, H. G.
See also BW 2; CA 109

Deloria, Vine (Victor), Jr. 1933-.... **CLC 21**
See also CA 53-56; CANR 5, 20, 48;
DAM MULT; MTCW; NNAL; SATA 21

Del Vecchio, John M(ichael)
1947- .... **CLC 29**
See also CA 110; DLBD 9

de Man, Paul (Adolph Michel)
1919-1983 .... **CLC 55**
See also CA 128; 111; DLB 67; MTCW

De Marinis, Rick 1934- .... **CLC 54**
See also CA 57-60; CAAS 24; CANR 9, 25,
50

Dembry, R. Emmet
See Murfree, Mary Noailles

Demby, William 1922- ...... **CLC 53; BLC**
See also BW 1; CA 81-84; DAM MULT;
DLB 33

Demijohn, Thom
See Disch, Thomas M(ichael)

de Montherlant, Henry (Milon)
See Montherlant, Henry (Milon) de

Demosthenes 384B.C.-322B.C. .... **CMLC 13**

de Natale, Francine
See Malzberg, Barry N(athaniel)

Denby, Edwin (Orr) 1903-1983 ..... **CLC 48**
See also CA 138; 110

Denis, Julio
See Cortazar, Julio

Denmark, Harrison
See Zelazny, Roger (Joseph)

Dennis, John 1658-1734 .... **LC 11**
See also DLB 101

Dennis, Nigel (Forbes) 1912-1989 .... **CLC 8**
See also CA 25-28R; 129; DLB 13, 15;
MTCW

De Palma, Brian (Russell) 1940-.... **CLC 20**
See also CA 109

De Quincey, Thomas 1785-1859 ... **NCLC 4**
See also CDBLB 1789-1832; DLB 110; 144

Deren, Eleanora 1908(?)-1961
See Deren, Maya
See also CA 111

Deren, Maya .... **CLC 16**
See also Deren, Eleanora

Derleth, August (William)
1909-1971 .... **CLC 31**
See also CA 1-4R; 29-32R; CANR 4;
DLB 9; SATA 5

Der Nister 1884-1950 .... **TCLC 56**

de Routisie, Albert
See Aragon, Louis

Derrida, Jacques 1930-........ **CLC 24, 87**
See also CA 124; 127

Derry Down Derry
See Lear, Edward

Dersonnes, Jacques
See Simenon, Georges (Jacques Christian)

Desai, Anita 1937- ...... **CLC 19, 37; DAB**
See also CA 81-84; CANR 33, 53;
DAM NOV; MTCW; SATA 63

de Saint-Luc, Jean
See Glassco, John

de Saint Roman, Arnaud
See Aragon, Louis

Descartes, Rene 1596-1650 .... **LC 20**

De Sica, Vittorio 1901(?)-1974 ..... **CLC 20**
See also CA 117

Desnos, Robert 1900-1945 .... **TCLC 22**
See also CA 121; 151

Destouches, Louis-Ferdinand
1894-1961 .... **CLC 9, 15**
See also Celine, Louis-Ferdinand
See also CA 85-88; CANR 28; MTCW

Deutsch, Babette 1895-1982 .... **CLC 18**
See also CA 1-4R; 108; CANR 4; DLB 45;
SATA 1; SATA-Obit 33

Devenant, William 1606-1649 .... **LC 13**

Devkota, Laxmiprasad
1909-1959 .... **TCLC 23**
See also CA 123

De Voto, Bernard (Augustine)
1897-1955 .... **TCLC 29**
See also CA 113; DLB 9

De Vries, Peter
1910-1993 .... **CLC 1, 2, 3, 7, 10, 28, 46**
See also CA 17-20R; 142; CANR 41;
DAM NOV; DLB 6; DLBY 82; MTCW

Dexter, John
See Bradley, Marion Zimmer

Dexter, Martin
See Faust, Frederick (Schiller)

Dexter, Pete 1943-............ **CLC 34, 55**
See also BEST 89:2; CA 127; 131;
DAM POP; INT 131; MTCW

Diamano, Silmang
See Senghor, Leopold Sedar

Diamond, Neil 1941- .... **CLC 30**
See also CA 108

Diaz del Castillo, Bernal 1496-1584 .. **LC 31**

di Bassetto, Corno
See Shaw, George Bernard

Dick, Philip K(indred)
1928-1982 .... **CLC 10, 30, 72**
See also CA 49-52; 106; CANR 2, 16;
DAM NOV, POP; DLB 8; MTCW

Dickens, Charles (John Huffam)
1812-1870 ...... **NCLC 3, 8, 18, 26, 37,**
50; DA; DAB; DAC; SSC 17; WLC
See also CDBLB 1832-1890; DAM MST,
NOV; DLB 21, 55, 70, 159, 166; JRDA;
MAICYA; SATA 15

Dickey, James (Lafayette)
1923- .... **CLC 1, 2, 4, 7, 10, 15, 47**
See also AITN 1, 2; CA 9-12R; CABS 2;
CANR 10, 48; CDALB 1968-1988;
DAM NOV, POET, POP; DLB 5;
DLBD 7; DLBY 82, 93; INT CANR-10;
MTCW

Dickey, William 1928-1994 ...... **CLC 3, 28**
See also CA 9-12R; 145; CANR 24; DLB 5

Dickinson, Charles 1951-.......... **CLC 49**
See also CA 128

Dickinson, Emily (Elizabeth)
1830-1886 .... **NCLC 21; DA; DAB;**
DAC; PC 1; WLC
See also CDALB 1865-1917; DAM MST,
POET; DLB 1; SATA 29

Dickinson, Peter (Malcolm)
1927- .... **CLC 12, 35**
See also AAYA 9; CA 41-44R; CANR 31;
CLR 29; DLB 87, 161; JRDA; MAICYA;
SATA 5, 62

Dickson, Carr
See Carr, John Dickson

Dickson, Carter
See Carr, John Dickson

Diderot, Denis 1713-1784 .... **LC 26**

Didion, Joan 1934-..... **CLC 1, 3, 8, 14, 32**
See also AITN 1; CA 5-8R; CANR 14, 52;
CDALB 1968-1988; DAM NOV; DLB 2;
DLBY 81, 86; MTCW

Dietrich, Robert
See Hunt, E(verette) Howard, (Jr.)

Dillard, Annie 1945-............ CLC 9, 60
See also AAYA 6; CA 49-52; CANR 3, 43;
DAM NOV; DLBY 80; MTCW;
SATA 10

Dillard, R(ichard) H(enry) W(ilde)
1937-...................... CLC 5
See also CA 21-24R; CAAS 7; CANR 10;
DLB 5

Dillon, Eilis 1920-1994............ CLC 17
See also CA 9-12R; 147; CAAS 3; CANR 4,
38; CLR 26; MAICYA; SATA 2, 74;
SATA-Obit 83

Dimont, Penelope
See Mortimer, Penelope (Ruth)

Dinesen, Isak....... CLC 10, 29, 95; SSC 7
See also Blixen, Karen (Christentze
Dinesen)

Ding Ling......................... CLC 68
See also Chiang Pin-chin

Disch, Thomas M(ichael) 1940-... CLC 7, 36
See also AAYA 17; CA 21-24R; CAAS 4;
CANR 17, 36; CLR 18; DLB 8;
MAICYA; MTCW; SAAS 15; SATA 54

Disch, Tom
See Disch, Thomas M(ichael)

d'Isly, Georges
See Simenon, Georges (Jacques Christian)

Disraeli, Benjamin 1804-1881 .. NCLC 2, 39
See also DLB 21, 55

Ditcum, Steve
See Crumb, R(obert)

Dixon, Paige
See Corcoran, Barbara

Dixon, Stephen 1936-..... CLC 52; SSC 16
See also CA 89-92; CANR 17, 40; DLB 130

Dobell, Sydney Thompson
1824-1874 .... NCLC 43
See also DLB 32

Doblin, Alfred .... TCLC 13
See also Doeblin, Alfred

Dobrolyubov, Nikolai Alexandrovich
1836-1861 .... NCLC 5

Dobyns, Stephen 1941-............. CLC 37
See also CA 45-48; CANR 2, 18

Doctorow, E(dgar) L(aurence)
1931-..... CLC 6, 11, 15, 18, 37, 44, 65
See also AITN 2; BEST 89:3; CA 45-48;
CANR 2, 33, 51; CDALB 1968-1988;
DAM NOV, POP; DLB 2, 28; DLBY 80;
MTCW

Dodgson, Charles Lutwidge 1832-1898
See Carroll, Lewis
See also CLR 2; DA; DAB; DAC;
DAM MST, NOV, POET; MAICYA;
YABC 2

Dodson, Owen (Vincent)
1914-1983 .... CLC 79; BLC
See also BW 1; CA 65-68; 110; CANR 24;
DAM MULT; DLB 76

Doeblin, Alfred 1878-1957........ TCLC 13
See also Doblin, Alfred
See also CA 110; 141; DLB 66

Doerr, Harriet 1910- .... CLC 34
See also CA 117; 122; CANR 47; INT 122

Domecq, H(onorio) Bustos
See Bioy Casares, Adolfo; Borges, Jorge
Luis

Domini, Rey
See Lorde, Audre (Geraldine)

Dominique
See Proust, (Valentin-Louis-George-Eugene-)
Marcel

Don, A
See Stephen, Leslie

Donaldson, Stephen R. 1947-...... CLC 46
See also CA 89-92; CANR 13; DAM POP;
INT CANR-13

Donleavy, J(ames) P(atrick)
1926- .... CLC 1, 4, 6, 10, 45
See also AITN 2; CA 9-12R; CANR 24, 49;
DLB 6; INT CANR-24; MTCW

Donne, John
1572-1631 .... LC 10, 24; DA; DAB;
DAC; PC 1
See also CDBLB Before 1660; DAM MST,
POET; DLB 121, 151

Donnell, David 1939(?)-........... CLC 34

Donoghue, P. S.
See Hunt, E(verette) Howard, (Jr.)

Donoso (Yanez), Jose
1924- .... CLC 4, 8, 11, 32; HLC
See also CA 81-84; CANR 32;
DAM MULT; DLB 113; HW; MTCW

Donovan, John 1928-1992 .... CLC 35
See also CA 97-100; 137; CLR 3;
MAICYA; SATA 72; SATA-Brief 29

Don Roberto
See Cunninghame Graham, R(obert)
B(ontine)

Doolittle, Hilda
1886-1961 ..... CLC 3, 8, 14, 31, 34, 73;
DA; DAC; PC 5; WLC
See also H. D.
See also CA 97-100; CANR 35; DAM MST,
POET; DLB 4, 45; MTCW

Dorfman, Ariel 1942-.... CLC 48, 77; HLC
See also CA 124; 130; DAM MULT; HW;
INT 130

Dorn, Edward (Merton) 1929-... CLC 10, 18
See also CA 93-96; CANR 42; DLB 5;
INT 93-96

Dorsan, Luc
See Simenon, Georges (Jacques Christian)

Dorsange, Jean
See Simenon, Georges (Jacques Christian)

Dos Passos, John (Roderigo)
1896-1970 ...... CLC 1, 4, 8, 11, 15, 25,
34, 82; DA; DAB; DAC; WLC
See also CA 1-4R; 29-32R; CANR 3;
CDALB 1929-1941; DAM MST, NOV;
DLB 4, 9; DLBD 1; MTCW

Dossage, Jean
See Simenon, Georges (Jacques Christian)

Dostoevsky, Fedor Mikhailovich
1821-1881 ...... NCLC 2, 7, 21, 33, 43;
DA; DAB; DAC; SSC 2; WLC
See also DAM MST, NOV

Doughty, Charles M(ontagu)
1843-1926 .... TCLC 27
See also CA 115; DLB 19, 57

Douglas, Ellen .... CLC 73
See also Haxton, Josephine Ayres;
Williamson, Ellen Douglas

Douglas, Gavin 1475(?)-1522....... LC 20

Douglas, Keith 1920-1944 .... TCLC 40
See also DLB 27

Douglas, Leonard
See Bradbury, Ray (Douglas)

Douglas, Michael
See Crichton, (John) Michael

Douglass, Frederick
1817(?)-1895 .... NCLC 7, 55; BLC; DA;
DAC; WLC
See also CDALB 1640-1865; DAM MST,
MULT; DLB 1, 43, 50, 79; SATA 29

Dourado, (Waldomiro Freitas) Autran
1926-.................... CLC 23, 60
See also CA 25-28R; CANR 34

Dourado, Waldomiro Autran
See Dourado, (Waldomiro Freitas) Autran

Dove, Rita (Frances)
1952-............. CLC 50, 81; PC 6
See also BW 2; CA 109; CAAS 19;
CANR 27, 42; DAM MULT, POET;
DLB 120

Dowell, Coleman 1925-1985........ CLC 60
See also CA 25-28R; 117; CANR 10;
DLB 130

Dowson, Ernest (Christopher)
1867-1900 .... TCLC 4
See also CA 105; 150; DLB 19, 135

Doyle, A. Conan
See Doyle, Arthur Conan

Doyle, Arthur Conan
1859-1930 .... TCLC 7; DA; DAB;
DAC; SSC 12; WLC
See also AAYA 14; CA 104; 122;
CDBLB 1890-1914; DAM MST, NOV;
DLB 18, 70, 156; MTCW; SATA 24

Doyle, Conan
See Doyle, Arthur Conan

Doyle, John
See Graves, Robert (von Ranke)

Doyle, Roddy 1958(?)-............ CLC 81
See also AAYA 14; CA 143

Doyle, Sir A. Conan
See Doyle, Arthur Conan

Doyle, Sir Arthur Conan
See Doyle, Arthur Conan

Dr. A
See Asimov, Isaac; Silverstein, Alvin

Drabble, Margaret
1939- .... CLC 2, 3, 5, 8, 10, 22, 53;
DAB; DAC
See also CA 13-16R; CANR 18, 35;
CDBLB 1960 to Present; DAM MST,
NOV, POP; DLB 14, 155; MTCW;
SATA 48

Drapier, M. B.
See Swift, Jonathan

Drayham, James
See Mencken, H(enry) L(ouis)

Drayton, Michael 1563-1631........ LC 8

Dreadstone, Carl
See Campbell, (John) Ramsey

Dreiser, Theodore (Herman Albert)
1871-1945 ...... **TCLC 10, 18, 35; DA;**
DAC; WLC
See also CA 106; 132; CDALB 1865-1917;
DAM MST, NOV; DLB 9, 12, 102, 137;
DLBD 1; MTCW

Drexler, Rosalyn 1926- .... **CLC 2, 6**
See also CA 81-84

Dreyer, Carl Theodor 1889-1968.... **CLC 16**
See also CA 116

Drieu la Rochelle, Pierre(-Eugene)
1893-1945 .... **TCLC 21**
See also CA 117; DLB 72

Drinkwater, John 1882-1937..... **TCLC 57**
See also CA 109; 149; DLB 10, 19, 149

Drop Shot
See Cable, George Washington

Droste-Hulshoff, Annette Freiin von
1797-1848 .... **NCLC 3**
See also DLB 133

Drummond, Walter
See Silverberg, Robert

Drummond, William Henry
1854-1907 .... **TCLC 25**
See also DLB 92

Drummond de Andrade, Carlos
1902-1987 .... **CLC 18**
See also Andrade, Carlos Drummond de
See also CA 132; 123

Drury, Allen (Stuart) 1918-........ **CLC 37**
See also CA 57-60; CANR 18, 52;
INT CANR-18

Dryden, John
1631-1700 .... **LC 3, 21; DA; DAB;**
DAC; DC 3; WLC
See also CDBLB 1660-1789; DAM DRAM,
MST, POET; DLB 80, 101, 131

Duberman, Martin 1930-.......... **CLC 8**
See also CA 1-4R; CANR 2

Dubie, Norman (Evans) 1945-...... **CLC 36**
See also CA 69-72; CANR 12; DLB 120

Du Bois, W(illiam) E(dward) B(urghardt)
1868-1963 ...... **CLC 1, 2, 13, 64; BLC;**
DA; DAC; WLC
See also BW 1; CA 85-88; CANR 34;
CDALB 1865-1917; DAM MST, MULT,
NOV; DLB 47, 50, 91; MTCW; SATA 42

Dubus, Andre 1936-.... **CLC 13, 36; SSC 15**
See also CA 21-24R; CANR 17; DLB 130;
INT CANR-17

Duca Minimo
See D'Annunzio, Gabriele

Ducharme, Rejean 1941- .... **CLC 74**
See also DLB 60

Duclos, Charles Pinot 1704-1772 ..... **LC 1**

Dudek, Louis 1918- .... **CLC 11, 19**
See also CA 45-48; CAAS 14; CANR 1;
DLB 88

Duerrenmatt, Friedrich
1921-1990 ...... **CLC 1, 4, 8, 11, 15, 43**
See also CA 17-20R; CANR 33;
DAM DRAM; DLB 69, 124; MTCW

Duffy, Bruce (?)-................. **CLC 50**

Duffy, Maureen 1933- .... **CLC 37**
See also CA 25-28R; CANR 33; DLB 14;
MTCW

Dugan, Alan 1923-.............. **CLC 2, 6**
See also CA 81-84; DLB 5

du Gard, Roger Martin
See Martin du Gard, Roger

Duhamel, Georges 1884-1966 .... **CLC 8**
See also CA 81-84; 25-28R; CANR 35;
DLB 65; MTCW

Dujardin, Edouard (Emile Louis)
1861-1949 .... **TCLC 13**
See also CA 109; DLB 123

Dumas, Alexandre (Davy de la Pailleterie)
1802-1870 .... **NCLC 11; DA; DAB;**
DAC; WLC
See also DAM MST, NOV; DLB 119;
SATA 18

Dumas, Alexandre
1824-1895 .... **NCLC 9; DC 1**

Dumas, Claudine
See Malzberg, Barry N(athaniel)

Dumas, Henry L. 1934-1968 ..... **CLC 6, 62**
See also BW 1; CA 85-88; DLB 41

du Maurier, Daphne
1907-1989 .... **CLC 6, 11, 59; DAB;**
DAC; SSC 18
See also CA 5-8R; 128; CANR 6;
DAM MST, POP; MTCW; SATA 27;
SATA-Obit 60

Dunbar, Paul Laurence
1872-1906 ...... **TCLC 2, 12; BLC; DA;**
DAC; PC 5; SSC 8; WLC
See also BW 1; CA 104; 124;
CDALB 1865-1917; DAM MST, MULT,
POET; DLB 50, 54, 78; SATA 34

Dunbar, William 1460(?)-1530(?) .... **LC 20**
See also DLB 132, 146

Duncan, Lois 1934-.............. **CLC 26**
See also AAYA 4; CA 1-4R; CANR 2, 23,
36; CLR 29; JRDA; MAICYA; SAAS 2;
SATA 1, 36, 75

Duncan, Robert (Edward)
1919-1988 .... **CLC 1, 2, 4, 7, 15, 41, 55;**
PC 2
See also CA 9-12R; 124; CANR 28;
DAM POET; DLB 5, 16; MTCW

Duncan, Sara Jeannette
1861-1922 .... **TCLC 60**
See also DLB 92

Dunlap, William 1766-1839 .... **NCLC 2**
See also DLB 30, 37, 59

Dunn, Douglas (Eaglesham)
1942- .... **CLC 6, 40**
See also CA 45-48; CANR 2, 33; DLB 40;
MTCW

Dunn, Katherine (Karen) 1945-..... **CLC 71**
See also CA 33-36R

Dunn, Stephen 1939- .... **CLC 36**
See also CA 33-36R; CANR 12, 48, 53;
DLB 105

Dunne, Finley Peter 1867-1936.... **TCLC 28**
See also CA 108; DLB 11, 23

Dunne, John Gregory 1932-........ **CLC 28**
See also CA 25-28R; CANR 14, 50;
DLBY 80

Dunsany, Edward John Moreton Drax
Plunkett 1878-1957
See Dunsany, Lord
See also CA 104; 148; DLB 10

Dunsany, Lord. .... **TCLC 2, 59**
See also Dunsany, Edward John Moreton
Drax Plunkett
See also DLB 77, 153, 156

du Perry, Jean
See Simenon, Georges (Jacques Christian)

Durang, Christopher (Ferdinand)
1949- .... **CLC 27, 38**
See also CA 105; CANR 50

Duras, Marguerite
1914-1996 .. **CLC 3, 6, 11, 20, 34, 40, 68**
See also CA 25-28R; 151; CANR 50;
DLB 83; MTCW

Durban, (Rosa) Pam 1947-........ **CLC 39**
See also CA 123

Durcan, Paul 1944-............ **CLC 43, 70**
See also CA 134; DAM POET

Durkheim, Emile 1858-1917 ...... **TCLC 55**

Durrell, Lawrence (George)
1912-1990 .... **CLC 1, 4, 6, 8, 13, 27, 41**
See also CA 9-12R; 132; CANR 40;
CDBLB 1945-1960; DAM NOV; DLB 15,
27; DLBY 90; MTCW

Durrenmatt, Friedrich
See Duerrenmatt, Friedrich

Dutt, Toru 1856-1877........... **NCLC 29**

Dwight, Timothy 1752-1817...... **NCLC 13**
See also DLB 37

Dworkin, Andrea 1946- .... **CLC 43**
See also CA 77-80; CAAS 21; CANR 16,
39; INT CANR-16; MTCW

Dwyer, Deanna
See Koontz, Dean R(ay)

Dwyer, K. R.
See Koontz, Dean R(ay)

Dylan, Bob 1941- ...... **CLC 3, 4, 6, 12, 77**
See also CA 41-44R; DLB 16

Eagleton, Terence (Francis) 1943-
See Eagleton, Terry
See also CA 57-60; CANR 7, 23; MTCW

Eagleton, Terry .... **CLC 63**
See also Eagleton, Terence (Francis)

Early, Jack
See Scoppettone, Sandra

East, Michael
See West, Morris L(anglo)

Eastaway, Edward
See Thomas, (Philip) Edward

Eastlake, William (Derry) 1917-..... **CLC 8**
See also CA 5-8R; CAAS 1; CANR 5;
DLB 6; INT CANR-5

Eastman, Charles A(lexander)
1858-1939 .... **TCLC 55**
See also DAM MULT; NNAL; YABC 1

Eberhart, Richard (Ghormley)
1904- .... **CLC 3, 11, 19, 56**
See also CA 1-4R; CANR 2;
CDALB 1941-1968; DAM POET;
DLB 48; MTCW

Eberstadt, Fernanda 1960-......... **CLC 39**
See also CA 136

Echegaray (y Eizaguirre), Jose (Maria Waldo)
1832-1916 .... **TCLC 4**
See also CA 104; CANR 32; HW; MTCW

Echeverria, (Jose) Esteban (Antonino)
1805-1851 .... **NCLC 18**

Echo
See Proust, (Valentin-Louis-George-Eugene-)
Marcel

Eckert, Allan W. 1931- .... **CLC 17**
See also AAYA 18; CA 13-16R; CANR 14,
45; INT CANR-14; SAAS 21; SATA 29;
SATA-Brief 27

Eckhart, Meister 1260(?)-1328(?) .. **CMLC 9**
See also DLB 115

Eckmar, F. R.
See de Hartog, Jan

Eco, Umberto 1932-........... **CLC 28, 60**
See also BEST 90:1; CA 77-80; CANR 12,
33; DAM NOV, POP; MTCW

Eddison, E(ric) R(ucker)
1882-1945 .... **TCLC 15**
See also CA 109

Edel, (Joseph) Leon 1907-...... **CLC 29, 34**
See also CA 1-4R; CANR 1, 22; DLB 103;
INT CANR-22

Eden, Emily 1797-1869 .... **NCLC 10**

Edgar, David 1948-.............. **CLC 42**
See also CA 57-60; CANR 12;
DAM DRAM; DLB 13; MTCW

Edgerton, Clyde (Carlyle) 1944- .... **CLC 39**
See also AAYA 17; CA 118; 134; INT 134

Edgeworth, Maria 1768-1849... **NCLC 1, 51**
See also DLB 116, 159, 163; SATA 21

Edmonds, Paul
See Kuttner, Henry

Edmonds, Walter D(umaux) 1903- .. **CLC 35**
See also CA 5-8R; CANR 2; DLB 9;
MAICYA; SAAS 4; SATA 1, 27

Edmondson, Wallace
See Ellison, Harlan (Jay)

Edson, Russell .... **CLC 13**
See also CA 33-36R

Edwards, Bronwen Elizabeth
See Rose, Wendy

Edwards, G(erald) B(asil)
1899-1976 .... **CLC 25**
See also CA 110

Edwards, Gus 1939-.............. **CLC 43**
See also CA 108; INT 108

Edwards, Jonathan
1703-1758 .... **LC 7; DA; DAC**
See also DAM MST; DLB 24

Efron, Marina Ivanovna Tsvetaeva
See Tsvetaeva (Efron), Marina (Ivanovna)

Ehle, John (Marsden, Jr.) 1925-.... **CLC 27**
See also CA 9-12R

Ehrenbourg, Ilya (Grigoryevich)
See Ehrenburg, Ilya (Grigoryevich)

Ehrenburg, Ilya (Grigoryevich)
1891-1967 .... **CLC 18, 34, 62**
See also CA 102; 25-28R

Ehrenburg, Ilyo (Grigoryevich)
See Ehrenburg, Ilya (Grigoryevich)

Eich, Guenter 1907-1972 .... **CLC 15**
See also CA 111; 93-96; DLB 69, 124

Eichendorff, Joseph Freiherr von
1788-1857 .... **NCLC 8**
See also DLB 90

Eigner, Larry...................... **CLC 9**
See also Eigner, Laurence (Joel)
See also CAAS 23; DLB 5

Eigner, Laurence (Joel) 1927-1996
See Eigner, Larry
See also CA 9-12R; 151; CANR 6

Einstein, Albert 1879-1955 .... **TCLC 65**
See also CA 121; 133; MTCW

Eiseley, Loren Corey 1907-1977 ..... **CLC 7**
See also AAYA 5; CA 1-4R; 73-76;
CANR 6

Eisenstadt, Jill 1963- .... **CLC 50**
See also CA 140

Eisenstein, Sergei (Mikhailovich)
1898-1948 .... **TCLC 57**
See also CA 114; 149

Eisner, Simon
See Kornbluth, C(yril) M.

Ekeloef, (Bengt) Gunnar
1907-1968 .... **CLC 27**
See also CA 123; 25-28R; DAM POET

Ekelof, (Bengt) Gunnar
See Ekeloef, (Bengt) Gunnar

Ekwensi, C. O. D.
See Ekwensi, Cyprian (Odiatu Duaka)

Ekwensi, Cyprian (Odiatu Duaka)
1921- .... **CLC 4; BLC**
See also BW 2; CA 29-32R; CANR 18, 42;
DAM MULT; DLB 117; MTCW;
SATA 66

Elaine........................ **TCLC 18**
See also Leverson, Ada

El Crummo
See Crumb, R(obert)

Elia
See Lamb, Charles

Eliade, Mircea 1907-1986 .... **CLC 19**
See also CA 65-68; 119; CANR 30; MTCW

Eliot, A. D.
See Jewett, (Theodora) Sarah Orne

Eliot, Alice
See Jewett, (Theodora) Sarah Orne

Eliot, Dan
See Silverberg, Robert

Eliot, George
1819-1880 ..... **NCLC 4, 13, 23, 41, 49;
DA; DAB; DAC; WLC**
See also CDBLB 1832-1890; DAM MST,
NOV; DLB 21, 35, 55

Eliot, John 1604-1690 .... **LC 5**
See also DLB 24

Eliot, T(homas) S(tearns)
1888-1965 ..... **CLC 1, 2, 3, 6, 9, 10, 13,
15, 24, 34, 41, 55, 57; DA; DAB; DAC;
PC 5; WLC 2**
See also CA 5-8R; 25-28R; CANR 41;
CDALB 1929-1941; DAM DRAM, MST,
POET; DLB 7, 10, 45, 63; DLBY 88;
MTCW

Elizabeth 1866-1941............. **TCLC 41**

Elkin, Stanley L(awrence)
1930-1995 ...... **CLC 4, 6, 9, 14, 27, 51,
91; SSC 12**
See also CA 9-12R; 148; CANR 8, 46;
DAM NOV, POP; DLB 2, 28; DLBY 80;
INT CANR-8; MTCW

Elledge, Scott..................... **CLC 34**

Elliott, Don
See Silverberg, Robert

Elliott, George P(aul) 1918-1980..... **CLC 2**
See also CA 1-4R; 97-100; CANR 2

Elliott, Janice 1931-.............. **CLC 47**
See also CA 13-16R; CANR 8, 29; DLB 14

Elliott, Sumner Locke 1917-1991 ... **CLC 38**
See also CA 5-8R; 134; CANR 2, 21

Elliott, William
See Bradbury, Ray (Douglas)

Ellis, A. E........................ **CLC 7**

Ellis, Alice Thomas................ **CLC 40**
See also Haycraft, Anna

Ellis, Bret Easton 1964-........ **CLC 39, 71**
See also AAYA 2; CA 118; 123; CANR 51;
DAM POP; INT 123

Ellis, (Henry) Havelock
1859-1939 .... **TCLC 14**
See also CA 109

Ellis, Landon
See Ellison, Harlan (Jay)

Ellis, Trey 1962-................. **CLC 55**
See also CA 146

Ellison, Harlan (Jay)
1934- .... **CLC 1, 13, 42; SSC 14**
See also CA 5-8R; CANR 5, 46;
DAM POP; DLB 8; INT CANR-5;
MTCW

Ellison, Ralph (Waldo)
1914-1994 .... **CLC 1, 3, 11, 54, 86;
BLC; DA; DAB; DAC; WLC**
See also BW 1; CA 9-12R; 145; CANR 24,
53; CDALB 1941-1968; DAM MST,
MULT, NOV; DLB 2, 76; DLBY 94;
MTCW

Ellmann, Lucy (Elizabeth) 1956-.... **CLC 61**
See also CA 128

Ellmann, Richard (David)
1918-1987 .... **CLC 50**
See also BEST 89:2; CA 1-4R; 122;
CANR 2, 28; DLB 103; DLBY 87;
MTCW

Elman, Richard 1934-............. **CLC 19**
See also CA 17-20R; CAAS 3; CANR 47

Elron
See Hubbard, L(afayette) Ron(ald)

Eluard, Paul.................. **TCLC 7, 41**
See also Grindel, Eugene

Elyot, Sir Thomas 1490(?)-1546 ..... **LC 11**

Elytis, Odysseus 1911-1996..... **CLC 15, 49**
See also CA 102; 151; DAM POET; MTCW

Emecheta, (Florence Onye) Buchi
1944-.............. **CLC 14, 48; BLC**
See also BW 2; CA 81-84; CANR 27;
DAM MULT; DLB 117; MTCW;
SATA 66

Emerson, Ralph Waldo
1803-1882 ..... **NCLC 1, 38; DA; DAB;**
DAC; WLC
See also CDALB 1640-1865; DAM MST,
POET; DLB 1, 59, 73

Eminescu, Mihail 1850-1889..... **NCLC 33**

Empson, William
1906-1984 .... **CLC 3, 8, 19, 33, 34**
See also CA 17-20R; 112; CANR 31;
DLB 20; MTCW

Enchi Fumiko (Ueda) 1905-1986.... **CLC 31**
See also CA 129; 121

Ende, Michael (Andreas Helmuth)
1929-1995 .... **CLC 31**
See also CA 118; 124; 149; CANR 36;
CLR 14; DLB 75; MAICYA; SATA 61;
SATA-Brief 42; SATA-Obit 86

Endo, Shusaku 1923-..... **CLC 7, 14, 19, 54**
See also CA 29-32R; CANR 21;
DAM NOV; MTCW

Engel, Marian 1933-1985......... **CLC 36**
See also CA 25-28R; CANR 12; DLB 53;
INT CANR-12

Engelhardt, Frederick
See Hubbard, L(afayette) Ron(ald)

Enright, D(ennis) J(oseph)
1920-................... **CLC 4, 8, 31**
See also CA 1-4R; CANR 1, 42; DLB 27;
SATA 25

Enzensberger, Hans Magnus
1929-..................... **CLC 43**
See also CA 116; 119

Ephron, Nora 1941-.......... **CLC 17, 31**
See also AITN 2; CA 65-68; CANR 12, 39

Epsilon
See Betjeman, John

Epstein, Daniel Mark 1948- .... **CLC 7**
See also CA 49-52; CANR 2, 53

Epstein, Jacob 1956- .... **CLC 19**
See also CA 114

Epstein, Joseph 1937-............. **CLC 39**
See also CA 112; 119; CANR 50

Epstein, Leslie 1938- .... **CLC 27**
See also CA 73-76; CAAS 12; CANR 23

Equiano, Olaudah
1745(?)-1797 .... **LC 16; BLC**
See also DAM MULT; DLB 37, 50

Erasmus, Desiderius 1469(?)-1536.... **LC 16**

Erdman, Paul E(mil) 1932- .... **CLC 25**
See also AITN 1; CA 61-64; CANR 13, 43

Erdrich, Louise 1954-.......... **CLC 39, 54**
See also AAYA 10; BEST 89:1; CA 114;
CANR 41; DAM MULT, NOV, POP;
DLB 152; MTCW; NNAL

Erenburg, Ilya (Grigoryevich)
See Ehrenburg, Ilya (Grigoryevich)

Erickson, Stephen Michael 1950-
See Erickson, Steve
See also CA 129

Erickson, Steve .... **CLC 64**
See also Erickson, Stephen Michael

Ericson, Walter
See Fast, Howard (Melvin)

Eriksson, Buntel
See Bergman, (Ernst) Ingmar

Ernaux, Annie 1940- .... **CLC 88**
See also CA 147

Eschenbach, Wolfram von
See Wolfram von Eschenbach

Eseki, Bruno
See Mphahlele, Ezekiel

Esenin, Sergei (Alexandrovich)
1895-1925 .... **TCLC 4**
See also CA 104

Eshleman, Clayton 1935-........... **CLC 7**
See also CA 33-36R; CAAS 6; DLB 5

Espriella, Don Manuel Alvarez
See Southey, Robert

Espriu, Salvador 1913-1985........ **CLC 9**
See also CA 115; DLB 134

Espronceda, Jose de 1808-1842... **NCLC 39**

Esse, James
See Stephens, James

Esterbrook, Tom
See Hubbard, L(afayette) Ron(ald)

Estleman, Loren D. 1952- .... **CLC 48**
See also CA 85-88; CANR 27; DAM NOV,
POP; INT CANR-27; MTCW

Eugenides, Jeffrey 1960(?)-........ **CLC 81**
See also CA 144

Euripides c. 485B.C.-406B.C. .... **DC 4**
See also DA; DAB; DAC; DAM DRAM,
MST

Evan, Evin
See Faust, Frederick (Schiller)

Evans, Evan
See Faust, Frederick (Schiller)

Evans, Marian
See Eliot, George

Evans, Mary Ann
See Eliot, George

Evarts, Esther
See Benson, Sally

Everett, Percival L. 1956-......... **CLC 57**
See also BW 2; CA 129

Everson, R(onald) G(ilmour)
1903-....................... **CLC 27**
See also CA 17-20R; DLB 88

Everson, William (Oliver)
1912-1994 .... **CLC 1, 5, 14**
See also CA 9-12R; 145; CANR 20; DLB 5,
16; MTCW

Evtushenko, Evgenii Aleksandrovich
See Yevtushenko, Yevgeny (Alexandrovich)

Ewart, Gavin (Buchanan)
1916-1995 .... **CLC 13, 46**
See also CA 89-92; 150; CANR 17, 46;
DLB 40; MTCW

Ewers, Hanns Heinz 1871-1943 ... **TCLC 12**
See also CA 109; 149

Ewing, Frederick R.
See Sturgeon, Theodore (Hamilton)

Exley, Frederick (Earl)
1929-1992 .... **CLC 6, 11**
See also AITN 2; CA 81-84; 138; DLB 143;
DLBY 81

Eynhardt, Guillermo
See Quiroga, Horacio (Sylvestre)

Ezekiel, Nissim 1924-............. **CLC 61**
See also CA 61-64

Ezekiel, Tish O'Dowd 1943-....... **CLC 34**
See also CA 129

Fadeyev, A.
See Bulgya, Alexander Alexandrovich

Fadeyev, Alexander............... **TCLC 53**
See also Bulgya, Alexander Alexandrovich

Fagen, Donald 1948-.............. **CLC 26**

Fainzilberg, Ilya Arnoldovich 1897-1937
See Ilf, Ilya
See also CA 120

Fair, Ronald L. 1932-............. **CLC 18**
See also BW 1; CA 69-72; CANR 25;
DLB 33

Fairbairns, Zoe (Ann) 1948- .... **CLC 32**
See also CA 103; CANR 21

Falco, Gian
See Papini, Giovanni

Falconer, James
See Kirkup, James

Falconer, Kenneth
See Kornbluth, C(yril) M.

Falkland, Samuel
See Heijermans, Herman

Fallaci, Oriana 1930-............. **CLC 11**
See also CA 77-80; CANR 15; MTCW

Faludy, George 1913-............. **CLC 42**
See also CA 21-24R

Faludy, Gyoergy
See Faludy, George

Fanon, Frantz 1925-1961..... **CLC 74; BLC**
See also BW 1; CA 116; 89-92;
DAM MULT

Fanshawe, Ann 1625-1680.......... **LC 11**

Fante, John (Thomas) 1911-1983 ... **CLC 60**
See also CA 69-72; 109; CANR 23;
DLB 130; DLBY 83

Farah, Nuruddin 1945-....... **CLC 53; BLC**
See also BW 2; CA 106; DAM MULT;
DLB 125

Fargue, Leon-Paul 1876(?)-1947 ... **TCLC 11**
See also CA 109

Farigoule, Louis
See Romains, Jules

Farina, Richard 1936(?)-1966 .... **CLC 9**
See also CA 81-84; 25-28R

Farley, Walter (Lorimer)
1915-1989 .... **CLC 17**
See also CA 17-20R; CANR 8, 29; DLB 22;
JRDA; MAICYA; SATA 2, 43

Fitzgerald, Zelda (Sayre)
1900-1948 .... **TCLC 52**
See also CA 117; 126; DLBY 84

Flanagan, Thomas (James Bonner)
1923- .... **CLC 25, 52**
See also CA 108; DLBY 80; INT 108;
MTCW

Flaubert, Gustave
1821-1880 .... **NCLC 2, 10, 19; DA;**
DAB; DAC; SSC 11; WLC
See also DAM MST, NOV; DLB 119

Flecker, Herman Elroy
See Flecker, (Herman) James Elroy

Flecker, (Herman) James Elroy
1884-1915 .... **TCLC 43**
See also CA 109; 150; DLB 10, 19

Fleming, Ian (Lancaster)
1908-1964 .... **CLC 3, 30**
See also CA 5-8R; CDBLB 1945-1960;
DAM POP; DLB 87; MTCW; SATA 9

Fleming, Thomas (James) 1927- .... **CLC 37**
See also CA 5-8R; CANR 10;
INT CANR-10; SATA 8

Fletcher, John 1579-1625 ...... **LC 33; DC 6**
See also CDBLB Before 1660; DLB 58

Fletcher, John Gould 1886-1950 ... **TCLC 35**
See also CA 107; DLB 4, 45

Fleur, Paul
See Pohl, Frederik

Flooglebuckle, Al
See Spiegelman, Art

Flying Officer X
See Bates, H(erbert) E(rnest)

Fo, Dario 1926- .... **CLC 32**
See also CA 116; 128; DAM DRAM;
MTCW

Fogarty, Jonathan Titulescu Esq.
See Farrell, James T(homas)

Folke, Will
See Bloch, Robert (Albert)

Follett, Ken(neth Martin) 1949- .... **CLC 18**
See also AAYA 6; BEST 89:4; CA 81-84;
CANR 13, 33; DAM NOV, POP;
DLB 87; DLBY 81; INT CANR-33;
MTCW

Fontane, Theodor 1819-1898 ..... **NCLC 26**
See also DLB 129

Foote, Horton 1916- .... **CLC 51, 91**
See also CA 73-76; CANR 34, 51;
DAM DRAM; DLB 26; INT CANR-34

Foote, Shelby 1916- .... **CLC 75**
See also CA 5-8R; CANR 3, 45;
DAM NOV, POP; DLB 2, 17

Forbes, Esther 1891-1967 .... **CLC 12**
See also AAYA 17; CA 13-14; 25-28R;
CAP 1; CLR 27; DLB 22; JRDA;
MAICYA; SATA 2

Forche, Carolyn (Louise)
1950- .... **CLC 25, 83, 86; PC 10**
See also CA 109; 117; CANR 50;
DAM POET; DLB 5; INT 117

Ford, Elbur
See Hibbert, Eleanor Alice Burford

Ford, Ford Madox
1873-1939 .... **TCLC 1, 15, 39, 57**
See also CA 104; 132; CDBLB 1914-1945;
DAM NOV; DLB 162; MTCW

Ford, John 1895-1973 .... **CLC 16**
See also CA 45-48

Ford, Richard 1944- .... **CLC 46**
See also CA 69-72; CANR 11, 47

Ford, Webster
See Masters, Edgar Lee

Foreman, Richard 1937- .... **CLC 50**
See also CA 65-68; CANR 32

Forester, C(ecil) S(cott)
1899-1966 .... **CLC 35**
See also CA 73-76; 25-28R; SATA 13

Forez
See Mauriac, Francois (Charles)

Forman, James Douglas 1932- ...... **CLC 21**
See also AAYA 17; CA 9-12R; CANR 4,
19, 42; JRDA; MAICYA; SATA 8, 70

Fornes, Maria Irene 1930- ...... **CLC 39, 61**
See also CA 25-28R; CANR 28; DLB 7;
HW; INT CANR-28; MTCW

Forrest, Leon 1937- .... **CLC 4**
See also BW 2; CA 89-92; CAAS 7;
CANR 25, 52; DLB 33

Forster, E(dward) M(organ)
1879-1970 ..... **CLC 1, 2, 3, 4, 9, 10, 13,**
15, 22, 45, 77; DA; DAB; DAC; WLC
See also AAYA 2; CA 13-14; 25-28R;
CANR 45; CAP 1; CDBLB 1914-1945;
DAM MST, NOV; DLB 34, 98, 162;
DLBD 10; MTCW; SATA 57

Forster, John 1812-1876 .... **NCLC 11**
See also DLB 144

Forsyth, Frederick 1938- ...... **CLC 2, 5, 36**
See also BEST 89:4; CA 85-88; CANR 38;
DAM NOV, POP; DLB 87; MTCW

Forten, Charlotte L. .... **TCLC 16; BLC**
See also Grimke, Charlotte L(ottie) Forten
See also DLB 50

Foscolo, Ugo 1778-1827 .... **NCLC 8**

Fosse, Bob .... **CLC 20**
See also Fosse, Robert Louis

Fosse, Robert Louis 1927-1987
See Fosse, Bob
See also CA 110; 123

Foster, Stephen Collins
1826-1864 .... **NCLC 26**

Foucault, Michel
1926-1984 .... **CLC 31, 34, 69**
See also CA 105; 113; CANR 34; MTCW

Fouque, Friedrich (Heinrich Karl) de la Motte
1777-1843 .... **NCLC 2**
See also DLB 90

Fourier, Charles 1772-1837 ...... **NCLC 51**

Fournier, Henri Alban 1886-1914
See Alain-Fournier
See also CA 104

Fournier, Pierre 1916- .... **CLC 11**
See also Gascar, Pierre
See also CA 89-92; CANR 16, 40

Fowles, John
1926- ...... **CLC 1, 2, 3, 4, 6, 9, 10, 15,**
33, 87; DAB; DAC
See also CA 5-8R; CANR 25; CDBLB 1960
to Present; DAM MST; DLB 14, 139;
MTCW; SATA 22

Fox, Paula 1923- .... **CLC 2, 8**
See also AAYA 3; CA 73-76; CANR 20,
36; CLR 1; DLB 52; JRDA; MAICYA;
MTCW; SATA 17, 60

Fox, William Price (Jr.) 1926- ..... **CLC 22**
See also CA 17-20R; CAAS 19; CANR 11;
DLB 2; DLBY 81

Foxe, John 1516(?)-1587 .... **LC 14**

Frame, Janet .... **CLC 2, 3, 6, 22, 66**
See also Clutha, Janet Paterson Frame

France, Anatole .... **TCLC 9**
See also Thibault, Jacques Anatole Francois
See also DLB 123

Francis, Claude 19(?)- .... **CLC 50**

Francis, Dick 1920- .... **CLC 2, 22, 42**
See also AAYA 5; BEST 89:3; CA 5-8R;
CANR 9, 42; CDBLB 1960 to Present;
DAM POP; DLB 87; INT CANR-9;
MTCW

Francis, Robert (Churchill)
1901-1987 .... **CLC 15**
See also CA 1-4R; 123; CANR 1

Frank, Anne(lies Marie)
1929-1945 .... **TCLC 17; DA; DAB;**
DAC; WLC
See also AAYA 12; CA 113; 133;
DAM MST; MTCW; SATA 87;
SATA-Brief 42

Frank, Elizabeth 1945- .... **CLC 39**
See also CA 121; 126; INT 126

Frankl, Viktor E(mil) 1905- .... **CLC 93**
See also CA 65-68

Franklin, Benjamin
See Hasek, Jaroslav (Matej Frantisek)

Franklin, Benjamin
1706-1790 ..... **LC 25; DA; DAB; DAC**
See also CDALB 1640-1865; DAM MST;
DLB 24, 43, 73

Franklin, (Stella Maraia Sarah) Miles
1879-1954 .... **TCLC 7**
See also CA 104

Fraser, (Lady) Antonia (Pakenham)
1932- .... **CLC 32**
See also CA 85-88; CANR 44; MTCW;
SATA-Brief 32

Fraser, George MacDonald 1925- .... **CLC 7**
See also CA 45-48; CANR 2, 48

Fraser, Sylvia 1935- .... **CLC 64**
See also CA 45-48; CANR 1, 16

Frayn, Michael 1933- ...... **CLC 3, 7, 31, 47**
See also CA 5-8R; CANR 30;
DAM DRAM, NOV; DLB 13, 14;
MTCW

Fraze, Candida (Merrill) 1945- ..... **CLC 50**
See also CA 126

Frazer, J(ames) G(eorge)
1854-1941 .... **TCLC 32**
See also CA 118

Frazer, Robert Caine
See Creasey, John

Frazer, Sir James George
See Frazer, J(ames) G(eorge)

Frazier, Ian 1951-............... **CLC 46**
See also CA 130

Frederic, Harold 1856-1898...... **NCLC 10**
See also DLB 12, 23; DLBD 13

Frederick, John
See Faust, Frederick (Schiller)

Frederick the Great 1712-1786...... **LC 14**

Fredro, Aleksander 1793-1876..... **NCLC 8**

Freeling, Nicolas 1927-........... **CLC 38**
See also CA 49-52; CAAS 12; CANR 1, 17, 50; DLB 87

Freeman, Douglas Southall
1886-1953.................. **TCLC 11**
See also CA 109; DLB 17

Freeman, Judith 1946-........... **CLC 55**
See also CA 148

Freeman, Mary Eleanor Wilkins
1852-1930............ **TCLC 9; SSC 1**
See also CA 106; DLB 12, 78

Freeman, R(ichard) Austin
1862-1943.................. **TCLC 21**
See also CA 113; DLB 70

French, Albert 1943-............. **CLC 86**

French, Marilyn 1929-...... **CLC 10, 18, 60**
See also CA 69-72; CANR 3, 31; DAM DRAM, NOV, POP; INT CANR-31; MTCW

French, Paul
See Asimov, Isaac

Freneau, Philip Morin 1752-1832.. **NCLC 1**
See also DLB 37, 43

Freud, Sigmund 1856-1939....... **TCLC 52**
See also CA 115; 133; MTCW

Friedan, Betty (Naomi) 1921-...... **CLC 74**
See also CA 65-68; CANR 18, 45; MTCW

Friedlander, Saul 1932-........... **CLC 90**
See also CA 117; 130

Friedman, B(ernard) H(arper)
1926-........................ **CLC 7**
See also CA 1-4R; CANR 3, 48

Friedman, Bruce Jay 1930-.... **CLC 3, 5, 56**
See also CA 9-12R; CANR 25, 52; DLB 2, 28; INT CANR-25

Friel, Brian 1929-........... **CLC 5, 42, 59**
See also CA 21-24R; CANR 33; DLB 13; MTCW

Friis-Baastad, Babbis Ellinor
1921-1970.................. **CLC 12**
See also CA 17-20R; 134; SATA 7

Frisch, Max (Rudolf)
1911-1991..... **CLC 3, 9, 14, 18, 32, 44**
See also CA 85-88; 134; CANR 32; DAM DRAM, NOV; DLB 69, 124; MTCW

Fromentin, Eugene (Samuel Auguste)
1820-1876.................. **NCLC 10**
See also DLB 123

Frost, Frederick
See Faust, Frederick (Schiller)

Frost, Robert (Lee)
1874-1963..... **CLC 1, 3, 4, 9, 10, 13, 15, 26, 34, 44; DA; DAB; DAC; PC 1; WLC**
See also CA 89-92; CANR 33; CDALB 1917-1929; DAM MST, POET; DLB 54; DLBD 7; MTCW; SATA 14

Froude, James Anthony
1818-1894................. **NCLC 43**
See also DLB 18, 57, 144

Froy, Herald
See Waterhouse, Keith (Spencer)

Fry, Christopher 1907-....... **CLC 2, 10, 14**
See also CA 17-20R; CAAS 23; CANR 9, 30; DAM DRAM; DLB 13; MTCW; SATA 66

Frye, (Herman) Northrop
1912-1991................. **CLC 24, 70**
See also CA 5-8R; 133; CANR 8, 37; DLB 67, 68; MTCW

Fuchs, Daniel 1909-1993........ **CLC 8, 22**
See also CA 81-84; 142; CAAS 5; CANR 40; DLB 9, 26, 28; DLBY 93

Fuchs, Daniel 1934-.............. **CLC 34**
See also CA 37-40R; CANR 14, 48

Fuentes, Carlos
1928-...... **CLC 3, 8, 10, 13, 22, 41, 60; DA; DAC; HLC; WLC**
See also AAYA 4; AITN 2; CA 69-72; CANR 10, 32; DAM MST, MULT, NOV; DLB 113; HW; MTCW

Fuentes, Gregorio Lopez y
See Lopez y Fuentes, Gregorio

Fugard, (Harold) Athol
1932-.... **CLC 5, 9, 14, 25, 40, 80; DC 3**
See also AAYA 17; CA 85-88; CANR 32; DAM DRAM; MTCW

Fugard, Sheila 1932-............. **CLC 48**
See also CA 125

Fuller, Charles (H., Jr.)
1939-................ **CLC 25; BLC; DC 1**
See also BW 2; CA 108; 112; DAM DRAM, MULT; DLB 38; INT 112; MTCW

Fuller, John (Leopold) 1937-....... **CLC 62**
See also CA 21-24R; CANR 9, 44; DLB 40

Fuller, Margaret.............. **NCLC 5, 50**
See also Ossoli, Sarah Margaret (Fuller marchesa d')

Fuller, Roy (Broadbent)
1912-1991................. **CLC 4, 28**
See also CA 5-8R; 135; CAAS 10; CANR 53; DLB 15, 20; SATA 87

Fulton, Alice 1952-............... **CLC 52**
See also CA 116

Furphy, Joseph 1843-1912....... **TCLC 25**

Fussell, Paul 1924-............... **CLC 74**
See also BEST 90:1; CA 17-20R; CANR 8, 21, 35; INT CANR-21; MTCW

Futabatei, Shimei 1864-1909...... **TCLC 44**

Futrelle, Jacques 1875-1912...... **TCLC 19**
See also CA 113

Gaboriau, Emile 1835-1873...... **NCLC 14**

Gadda, Carlo Emilio 1893-1973.... **CLC 11**
See also CA 89-92

Gaddis, William
1922-..... **CLC 1, 3, 6, 8, 10, 19, 43, 86**
See also CA 17-20R; CANR 21, 48; DLB 2; MTCW

Gaines, Ernest J(ames)
1933-........ **CLC 3, 11, 18, 86; BLC**
See also AAYA 18; AITN 1; BW 2; CA 9-12R; CANR 6, 24, 42; CDALB 1968-1988; DAM MULT; DLB 2, 33, 152; DLBY 80; MTCW; SATA 86

Gaitskill, Mary 1954-............. **CLC 69**
See also CA 128

Galdos, Benito Perez
See Perez Galdos, Benito

Gale, Zona 1874-1938............ **TCLC 7**
See also CA 105; DAM DRAM; DLB 9, 78

Galeano, Eduardo (Hughes) 1940-... **CLC 72**
See also CA 29-32R; CANR 13, 32; HW

Galiano, Juan Valera y Alcala
See Valera y Alcala-Galiano, Juan

Gallagher, Tess 1943-.... **CLC 18, 63; PC 9**
See also CA 106; DAM POET; DLB 120

Gallant, Mavis
1922-...... **CLC 7, 18, 38; DAC; SSC 5**
See also CA 69-72; CANR 29; DAM MST; DLB 53; MTCW

Gallant, Roy A(rthur) 1924-....... **CLC 17**
See also CA 5-8R; CANR 4, 29; CLR 30; MAICYA; SATA 4, 68

Gallico, Paul (William) 1897-1976... **CLC 2**
See also AITN 1; CA 5-8R; 69-72; CANR 23; DLB 9; MAICYA; SATA 13

Gallo, Max Louis 1932-........... **CLC 95**
See also CA 85-88

Gallois, Lucien
See Desnos, Robert

Gallup, Ralph
See Whitemore, Hugh (John)

Galsworthy, John
1867-1933...... **TCLC 1, 45; DA; DAB; DAC; SSC 22; WLC 2**
See also CA 104; 141; CDBLB 1890-1914; DAM DRAM, MST, NOV; DLB 10, 34, 98, 162

Galt, John 1779-1839............ **NCLC 1**
See also DLB 99, 116, 159

Galvin, James 1951-.............. **CLC 38**
See also CA 108; CANR 26

Gamboa, Federico 1864-1939...... **TCLC 36**

Gandhi, M. K.
See Gandhi, Mohandas Karamchand

Gandhi, Mahatma
See Gandhi, Mohandas Karamchand

Gandhi, Mohandas Karamchand
1869-1948.................. **TCLC 59**
See also CA 121; 132; DAM MULT; MTCW

Gann, Ernest Kellogg 1910-1991.... **CLC 23**
See also AITN 1; CA 1-4R; 136; CANR 1

Garcia, Cristina 1958-............ **CLC 76**
See also CA 141

Garcia Lorca, Federico
1898-1936 ... **TCLC 1, 7, 49; DA; DAB;**
DAC; DC 2; HLC; PC 3; WLC
See also CA 104; 131; DAM DRAM, MST,
MULT, POET; DLB 108; HW; MTCW

Garcia Marquez, Gabriel (Jose)
1928- .... **CLC 2, 3, 8, 10, 15, 27, 47, 55,**
68; DA; DAB; DAC; HLC; SSC 8; WLC
See also AAYA 3; BEST 89:1, 90:4;
CA 33-36R; CANR 10, 28, 50;
DAM MST, MULT, NOV, POP;
DLB 113; HW; MTCW

Gard, Janice
See Latham, Jean Lee

Gard, Roger Martin du
See Martin du Gard, Roger

Gardam, Jane 1928- .... **CLC 43**
See also CA 49-52; CANR 2, 18, 33;
CLR 12; DLB 14, 161; MAICYA;
MTCW; SAAS 9; SATA 39, 76;
SATA-Brief 28

Gardner, Herb(ert) 1934- .... **CLC 44**
See also CA 149

Gardner, John (Champlin), Jr.
1933-1982 ..... **CLC 2, 3, 5, 7, 8, 10, 18,**
28, 34; SSC 7
See also AITN 1; CA 65-68; 107;
CANR 33; DAM NOV, POP; DLB 2;
DLBY 82; MTCW; SATA 40;
SATA-Obit 31

Gardner, John (Edmund) 1926- ..... **CLC 30**
See also CA 103; CANR 15; DAM POP;
MTCW

Gardner, Miriam
See Bradley, Marion Zimmer

Gardner, Noel
See Kuttner, Henry

Gardons, S. S.
See Snodgrass, W(illiam) D(e Witt)

Garfield, Leon 1921- .... **CLC 12**
See also AAYA 8; CA 17-20R; CANR 38,
41; CLR 21; DLB 161; JRDA; MAICYA;
SATA 1, 32, 76

Garland, (Hannibal) Hamlin
1860-1940 .... **TCLC 3; SSC 18**
See also CA 104; DLB 12, 71, 78

Garneau, (Hector de) Saint-Denys
1912-1943 .... **TCLC 13**
See also CA 111; DLB 88

Garner, Alan 1934- .... **CLC 17; DAB**
See also AAYA 18; CA 73-76; CANR 15;
CLR 20; DAM POP; DLB 161;
MAICYA; MTCW; SATA 18, 69

Garner, Hugh 1913-1979 .... **CLC 13**
See also CA 69-72; CANR 31; DLB 68

Garnett, David 1892-1981 .... **CLC 3**
See also CA 5-8R; 103; CANR 17; DLB 34

Garos, Stephanie
See Katz, Steve

Garrett, George (Palmer)
1929- .... **CLC 3, 11, 51**
See also CA 1-4R; CAAS 5; CANR 1, 42;
DLB 2, 5, 130, 152; DLBY 83

Garrick, David 1717-1779 .... **LC 15**
See also DAM DRAM; DLB 84

Garrigue, Jean 1914-1972 .... **CLC 2, 8**
See also CA 5-8R; 37-40R; CANR 20

Garrison, Frederick
See Sinclair, Upton (Beall)

Garth, Will
See Hamilton, Edmond; Kuttner, Henry

Garvey, Marcus (Moziah, Jr.)
1887-1940 .... **TCLC 41; BLC**
See also BW 1; CA 120; 124; DAM MULT

Gary, Romain .... **CLC 25**
See also Kacew, Romain
See also DLB 83

Gascar, Pierre .... **CLC 11**
See also Fournier, Pierre

Gascoyne, David (Emery) 1916- .... **CLC 45**
See also CA 65-68; CANR 10, 28; DLB 20;
MTCW

Gaskell, Elizabeth Cleghorn
1810-1865 .... **NCLC 5; DAB**
See also CDBLB 1832-1890; DAM MST;
DLB 21, 144, 159

Gass, William H(oward)
1924- ... **CLC 1, 2, 8, 11, 15, 39; SSC 12**
See also CA 17-20R; CANR 30; DLB 2;
MTCW

Gasset, Jose Ortega y
See Ortega y Gasset, Jose

Gates, Henry Louis, Jr. 1950- ..... **CLC 65**
See also BW 2; CA 109; CANR 25, 53;
DAM MULT; DLB 67

Gautier, Theophile
1811-1872 .... **NCLC 1; SSC 20**
See also DAM POET; DLB 119

Gawsworth, John
See Bates, H(erbert) E(rnest)

Gay, Oliver
See Gogarty, Oliver St. John

Gaye, Marvin (Penze) 1939-1984 ... **CLC 26**
See also CA 112

Gebler, Carlo (Ernest) 1954- .... **CLC 39**
See also CA 119; 133

Gee, Maggie (Mary) 1948- .... **CLC 57**
See also CA 130

Gee, Maurice (Gough) 1931- .... **CLC 29**
See also CA 97-100; SATA 46

Gelbart, Larry (Simon) 1923- ... **CLC 21, 61**
See also CA 73-76; CANR 45

Gelber, Jack 1932- .... **CLC 1, 6, 14, 79**
See also CA 1-4R; CANR 2; DLB 7

Gellhorn, Martha (Ellis) 1908- .. **CLC 14, 60**
See also CA 77-80; CANR 44; DLBY 82

Genet, Jean
1910-1986 ... **CLC 1, 2, 5, 10, 14, 44, 46**
See also CA 13-16R; CANR 18;
DAM DRAM; DLB 72; DLBY 86;
MTCW

Gent, Peter 1942- .... **CLC 29**
See also AITN 1; CA 89-92; DLBY 82

Gentlewoman in New England, A
See Bradstreet, Anne

Gentlewoman in Those Parts, A
See Bradstreet, Anne

George, Jean Craighead 1919- ...... **CLC 35**
See also AAYA 8; CA 5-8R; CANR 25;
CLR 1; DLB 52; JRDA; MAICYA;
SATA 2, 68

George, Stefan (Anton)
1868-1933 .... **TCLC 2, 14**
See also CA 104

Georges, Georges Martin
See Simenon, Georges (Jacques Christian)

Gerhardi, William Alexander
See Gerhardie, William Alexander

Gerhardie, William Alexander
1895-1977 .... **CLC 5**
See also CA 25-28R; 73-76; CANR 18;
DLB 36

Gerstler, Amy 1956- .... **CLC 70**
See also CA 146

Gertler, T. .... **CLC 34**
See also CA 116; 121; INT 121

Ghalib .... **NCLC 39**
See also Ghalib, Hsadullah Khan

Ghalib, Hsadullah Khan 1797-1869
See Ghalib
See also DAM POET

Ghelderode, Michel de
1898-1962 .... **CLC 6, 11**
See also CA 85-88; CANR 40;
DAM DRAM

Ghiselin, Brewster 1903- .... **CLC 23**
See also CA 13-16R; CAAS 10; CANR 13

Ghose, Zulfikar 1935- .... **CLC 42**
See also CA 65-68

Ghosh, Amitav 1956- .... **CLC 44**
See also CA 147

Giacosa, Giuseppe 1847-1906 ...... **TCLC 7**
See also CA 104

Gibb, Lee
See Waterhouse, Keith (Spencer)

Gibbon, Lewis Grassic .... **TCLC 4**
See also Mitchell, James Leslie

Gibbons, Kaye 1960- .... **CLC 50, 88**
See also CA 151; DAM POP

Gibran, Kahlil
1883-1931 .... **TCLC 1, 9; PC 9**
See also CA 104; 150; DAM POET, POP

Gibran, Khalil
See Gibran, Kahlil

Gibson, William
1914- .... **CLC 23; DA; DAB; DAC**
See also CA 9-12R; CANR 9, 42;
DAM DRAM, MST; DLB 7; SATA 66

Gibson, William (Ford) 1948- ... **CLC 39, 63**
See also AAYA 12; CA 126; 133;
CANR 52; DAM POP

Gide, Andre (Paul Guillaume)
1869-1951 .... **TCLC 5, 12, 36; DA;**
DAB; DAC; SSC 13; WLC
See also CA 104; 124; DAM MST, NOV;
DLB 65; MTCW

Gifford, Barry (Colby) 1946- .... **CLC 34**
See also CA 65-68; CANR 9, 30, 40

Gilbert, W(illiam) S(chwenck)
1836-1911 .... **TCLC 3**
See also CA 104; DAM DRAM, POET;
SATA 36

Gordon, Adam Lindsay
1833-1870 .... NCLC 21

Gordon, Caroline
1895-1981 ... CLC 6, 13, 29, 83; SSC 15
See also CA 11-12; 103; CANR 36; CAP 1;
DLB 4, 9, 102; DLBY 81; MTCW

Gordon, Charles William 1860-1937
See Connor, Ralph
See also CA 109

Gordon, Mary (Catherine)
1949- .... CLC 13, 22
See also CA 102; CANR 44; DLB 6;
DLBY 81; INT 102; MTCW

Gordon, Sol 1923- .... CLC 26
See also CA 53-56; CANR 4; SATA 11

Gordone, Charles 1925-1995 ...... CLC 1, 4
See also BW 1; CA 93-96; 150;
DAM DRAM; DLB 7; INT 93-96;
MTCW

Gorenko, Anna Andreevna
See Akhmatova, Anna

Gorky, Maxim .... TCLC 8; DAB; WLC
See also Peshkov, Alexei Maximovich

Goryan, Sirak
See Saroyan, William

Gosse, Edmund (William)
1849-1928 .... TCLC 28
See also CA 117; DLB 57, 144

Gotlieb, Phyllis Fay (Bloom)
1926- .... CLC 18
See also CA 13-16R; CANR 7; DLB 88

Gottesman, S. D.
See Kornbluth, C(yril) M.; Pohl, Frederik

Gottfried von Strassburg
fl. c. 1210- .... CMLC 10
See also DLB 138

Gould, Lois .... CLC 4, 10
See also CA 77-80; CANR 29; MTCW

Gourmont, Remy (-Marie-Charles) de
1858-1915 .... TCLC 17
See also CA 109; 150

Govier, Katherine 1948- .... CLC 51
See also CA 101; CANR 18, 40

Goyen, (Charles) William
1915-1983 .... CLC 5, 8, 14, 40
See also AITN 2; CA 5-8R; 110; CANR 6;
DLB 2; DLBY 83; INT CANR-6

Goytisolo, Juan
1931- .... CLC 5, 10, 23; HLC
See also CA 85-88; CANR 32;
DAM MULT; HW; MTCW

Gozzano, Guido 1883-1916 .... PC 10
See also DLB 114

Gozzi, (Conte) Carlo 1720-1806 .. NCLC 23

Grabbe, Christian Dietrich
1801-1836 .... NCLC 2
See also DLB 133

Grace, Patricia 1937- .... CLC 56

Gracian y Morales, Baltasar
1601-1658 .... LC 15

Gracq, Julien .... CLC 11, 48
See also Poirier, Louis
See also DLB 83

Grade, Chaim 1910-1982 .... CLC 10
See also CA 93-96; 107

Graduate of Oxford, A
See Ruskin, John

Graham, John
See Phillips, David Graham

Graham, Jorie 1951- .... CLC 48
See also CA 111; DLB 120

Graham, R(obert) B(ontine) Cunninghame
See Cunninghame Graham, R(obert)
B(ontine)
See also DLB 98, 135

Graham, Robert
See Haldeman, Joe (William)

Graham, Tom
See Lewis, (Harry) Sinclair

Graham, W(illiam) S(ydney)
1918-1986 .... CLC 29
See also CA 73-76; 118; DLB 20

Graham, Winston (Mawdsley)
1910- .... CLC 23
See also CA 49-52; CANR 2, 22, 45;
DLB 77

Grahame, Kenneth
1859-1932 .... TCLC 64; DAB
See also CA 108; 136; CLR 5; DLB 34, 141;
MAICYA; YABC 1

Grant, Skeeter
See Spiegelman, Art

Granville-Barker, Harley
1877-1946 .... TCLC 2
See also Barker, Harley Granville
See also CA 104; DAM DRAM

Grass, Guenter (Wilhelm)
1927- ..... CLC 1, 2, 4, 6, 11, 15, 22, 32,
49, 88; DA; DAB; DAC; WLC
See also CA 13-16R; CANR 20;
DAM MST, NOV; DLB 75, 124; MTCW

Gratton, Thomas
See Hulme, T(homas) E(rnest)

Grau, Shirley Ann
1929- .... CLC 4, 9; SSC 15
See also CA 89-92; CANR 22; DLB 2;
INT CANR-22; MTCW

Gravel, Fern
See Hall, James Norman

Graver, Elizabeth 1964- .... CLC 70
See also CA 135

Graves, Richard Perceval 1945- .... CLC 44
See also CA 65-68; CANR 9, 26, 51

Graves, Robert (von Ranke)
1895-1985 ...... CLC 1, 2, 6, 11, 39, 44,
45; DAB; DAC; PC 6
See also CA 5-8R; 117; CANR 5, 36;
CDBLB 1914-1945; DAM MST, POET;
DLB 20, 100; DLBY 85; MTCW;
SATA 45

Graves, Valerie
See Bradley, Marion Zimmer

Gray, Alasdair (James) 1934- ...... CLC 41
See also CA 126; CANR 47; INT 126;
MTCW

Gray, Amlin 1946- .... CLC 29
See also CA 138

Gray, Francine du Plessix 1930-.... CLC 22
See also BEST 90:3; CA 61-64; CAAS 2;
CANR 11, 33; DAM NOV;
INT CANR-11; MTCW

Gray, John (Henry) 1866-1934 .... TCLC 19
See also CA 119

Gray, Simon (James Holliday)
1936- .... CLC 9, 14, 36
See also AITN 1; CA 21-24R; CAAS 3;
CANR 32; DLB 13; MTCW

Gray, Spalding 1941- .... CLC 49
See also CA 128; DAM POP

Gray, Thomas
1716-1771 ...... LC 4; DA; DAB; DAC;
PC 2; WLC
See also CDBLB 1660-1789; DAM MST;
DLB 109

Grayson, David
See Baker, Ray Stannard

Grayson, Richard (A.) 1951- .... CLC 38
See also CA 85-88; CANR 14, 31

Greeley, Andrew M(oran) 1928- .... CLC 28
See also CA 5-8R; CAAS 7; CANR 7, 43;
DAM POP; MTCW

Green, Anna Katharine
1846-1935 .... TCLC 63
See also CA 112

Green, Brian
See Card, Orson Scott

Green, Hannah
See Greenberg, Joanne (Goldenberg)

Green, Hannah .... CLC 3
See also CA 73-76

Green, Henry .... CLC 2, 13
See also Yorke, Henry Vincent
See also DLB 15

Green, Julian (Hartridge) 1900-
See Green, Julien
See also CA 21-24R; CANR 33; DLB 4, 72;
MTCW

Green, Julien .... CLC 3, 11, 77
See also Green, Julian (Hartridge)

Green, Paul (Eliot) 1894-1981...... CLC 25
See also AITN 1; CA 5-8R; 103; CANR 3;
DAM DRAM; DLB 7, 9; DLBY 81

Greenberg, Ivan 1908-1973
See Rahv, Philip
See also CA 85-88

Greenberg, Joanne (Goldenberg)
1932- .... CLC 7, 30
See also AAYA 12; CA 5-8R; CANR 14,
32; SATA 25

Greenberg, Richard 1959(?)- .... CLC 57
See also CA 138

Greene, Bette 1934- .... CLC 30
See also AAYA 7; CA 53-56; CANR 4;
CLR 2; JRDA; MAICYA; SAAS 16;
SATA 8

Greene, Gael .... CLC 8
See also CA 13-16R; CANR 10

Greene, Graham
    1904-1991 .... **CLC 1, 3, 6, 9, 14, 18, 27,
    37, 70, 72; DA; DAB; DAC; WLC**
    See also AITN 2; CA 13-16R; 133;
    CANR 35; CDBLB 1945-1960;
    DAM MST, NOV; DLB 13, 15, 77, 100,
    162; DLBY 91; MTCW; SATA 20

Greer, Richard
    See Silverberg, Robert

Gregor, Arthur   1923- .... **CLC 9**
    See also CA 25-28R; CAAS 10; CANR 11;
    SATA 36

Gregor, Lee
    See Pohl, Frederik

Gregory, Isabella Augusta (Persse)
    1852-1932 .... **TCLC 1**
    See also CA 104; DLB 10

Gregory, J. Dennis
    See Williams, John A(lfred)

Grendon, Stephen
    See Derleth, August (William)

Grenville, Kate   1950- .... **CLC 61**
    See also CA 118; CANR 53

Grenville, Pelham
    See Wodehouse, P(elham) G(renville)

Greve, Felix Paul (Berthold Friedrich)
    1879-1948
    See Grove, Frederick Philip
    See also CA 104; 141; DAC; DAM MST

Grey, Zane   1872-1939 .... **TCLC 6**
    See also CA 104; 132; DAM POP; DLB 9;
    MTCW

Grieg, (Johan) Nordahl (Brun)
    1902-1943 .... **TCLC 10**
    See also CA 107

Grieve, C(hristopher) M(urray)
    1892-1978 .... **CLC 11, 19**
    See also MacDiarmid, Hugh; Pteleon
    See also CA 5-8R; 85-88; CANR 33;
    DAM POET; MTCW

Griffin, Gerald   1803-1840 .... **NCLC 7**
    See also DLB 159

Griffin, John Howard   1920-1980.... **CLC 68**
    See also AITN 1; CA 1-4R; 101; CANR 2

Griffin, Peter   1942- .... **CLC 39**
    See also CA 136

Griffiths, Trevor   1935- .... **CLC 13, 52**
    See also CA 97-100; CANR 45; DLB 13

Grigson, Geoffrey (Edward Harvey)
    1905-1985 .... **CLC 7, 39**
    See also CA 25-28R; 118; CANR 20, 33;
    DLB 27; MTCW

Grillparzer, Franz   1791-1872...... **NCLC 1**
    See also DLB 133

Grimble, Reverend Charles James
    See Eliot, T(homas) S(tearns)

Grimke, Charlotte L(ottie) Forten
    1837(?)-1914
    See Forten, Charlotte L.
    See also BW 1; CA 117; 124; DAM MULT,
    POET

Grimm, Jacob Ludwig Karl
    1785-1863 .... **NCLC 3**
    See also DLB 90; MAICYA; SATA 22

Grimm, Wilhelm Karl   1786-1859 .. **NCLC 3**
    See also DLB 90; MAICYA; SATA 22

Grimmelshausen, Johann Jakob Christoffel
    von   1621-1676 .... **LC 6**

Grindel, Eugene   1895-1952
    See Eluard, Paul
    See also CA 104

Grisham, John   1955- .... **CLC 84**
    See also AAYA 14; CA 138; CANR 47;
    DAM POP

Grossman, David   1954- .... **CLC 67**
    See also CA 138

Grossman, Vasily (Semenovich)
    1905-1964 .... **CLC 41**
    See also CA 124; 130; MTCW

Grove, Frederick Philip .... **TCLC 4**
    See also Greve, Felix Paul (Berthold
    Friedrich)
    See also DLB 92

Grubb
    See Crumb, R(obert)

Grumbach, Doris (Isaac)
    1918- .... **CLC 13, 22, 64**
    See also CA 5-8R; CAAS 2; CANR 9, 42;
    INT CANR-9

Grundtvig, Nicolai Frederik Severin
    1783-1872 .... **NCLC 1**

Grunge
    See Crumb, R(obert)

Grunwald, Lisa   1959- .... **CLC 44**
    See also CA 120

Guare, John   1938- .... **CLC 8, 14, 29, 67**
    See also CA 73-76; CANR 21;
    DAM DRAM; DLB 7; MTCW

Gudjonsson, Halldor Kiljan   1902-
    See Laxness, Halldor
    See also CA 103

Guenter, Erich
    See Eich, Guenter

Guest, Barbara   1920- .... **CLC 34**
    See also CA 25-28R; CANR 11, 44; DLB 5

Guest, Judith (Ann)   1936- .... **CLC 8, 30**
    See also AAYA 7; CA 77-80; CANR 15;
    DAM NOV, POP; INT CANR-15;
    MTCW

Guevara, Che .... **CLC 87; HLC**
    See also Guevara (Serna), Ernesto

Guevara (Serna), Ernesto   1928-1967
    See Guevara, Che
    See also CA 127; 111; DAM MULT; HW

Guild, Nicholas M.   1944- .... **CLC 33**
    See also CA 93-96

Guillemin, Jacques
    See Sartre, Jean-Paul

Guillen, Jorge   1893-1984 .... **CLC 11**
    See also CA 89-92; 112; DAM MULT,
    POET; DLB 108; HW

Guillen, Nicolas (Cristobal)
    1902-1989 .... **CLC 48, 79; BLC; HLC**
    See also BW 2; CA 116; 125; 129;
    DAM MST, MULT, POET; HW

Guillevic, (Eugene)   1907- .... **CLC 33**
    See also CA 93-96

Guillois
    See Desnos, Robert

Guillois, Valentin
    See Desnos, Robert

Guiney, Louise Imogen
    1861-1920 .... **TCLC 41**
    See also DLB 54

Guiraldes, Ricardo (Guillermo)
    1886-1927 .... **TCLC 39**
    See also CA 131; HW; MTCW

Gumilev, Nikolai Stephanovich
    1886-1921 .... **TCLC 60**

Gunesekera, Romesh............... **CLC 91**

Gunn, Bill .... **CLC 5**
    See also Gunn, William Harrison
    See also DLB 38

Gunn, Thom(son William)
    1929- .... **CLC 3, 6, 18, 32, 81**
    See also CA 17-20R; CANR 9, 33;
    CDBLB 1960 to Present; DAM POET;
    DLB 27; INT CANR-33; MTCW

Gunn, William Harrison   1934(?)-1989
    See Gunn, Bill
    See also AITN 1; BW 1; CA 13-16R; 128;
    CANR 12, 25

Gunnars, Kristjana   1948-.......... **CLC 69**
    See also CA 113; DLB 60

Gurganus, Allan   1947-............. **CLC 70**
    See also BEST 90:1; CA 135; DAM POP

Gurney, A(lbert) R(amsdell), Jr.
    1930- .... **CLC 32, 50, 54**
    See also CA 77-80; CANR 32;
    DAM DRAM

Gurney, Ivor (Bertie)   1890-1937... **TCLC 33**

Gurney, Peter
    See Gurney, A(lbert) R(amsdell), Jr.

Guro, Elena   1877-1913........... **TCLC 56**

Gustafson, Ralph (Barker)   1909-.... **CLC 36**
    See also CA 21-24R; CANR 8, 45; DLB 88

Gut, Gom
    See Simenon, Georges (Jacques Christian)

Guterson, David   1956-............. **CLC 91**
    See also CA 132

Guthrie, A(lfred) B(ertram), Jr.
    1901-1991 .... **CLC 23**
    See also CA 57-60; 134; CANR 24; DLB 6;
    SATA 62; SATA-Obit 67

Guthrie, Isobel
    See Grieve, C(hristopher) M(urray)

Guthrie, Woodrow Wilson   1912-1967
    See Guthrie, Woody
    See also CA 113; 93-96

Guthrie, Woody.................... **CLC 35**
    See also Guthrie, Woodrow Wilson

Guy, Rosa (Cuthbert)   1928-........ **CLC 26**
    See also AAYA 4; BW 2; CA 17-20R;
    CANR 14, 34; CLR 13; DLB 33; JRDA;
    MAICYA; SATA 14, 62

Gwendolyn
    See Bennett, (Enoch) Arnold

H. D. .... **CLC 3, 8, 14, 31, 34, 73; PC 5**
    See also Doolittle, Hilda

H. de V.
    See Buchan, John

Haavikko, Paavo Juhani
  1931- .... **CLC 18, 34**
  See also CA 106

Habbema, Koos
  See Heijermans, Herman

Hacker, Marilyn
  1942- .... **CLC 5, 9, 23, 72, 91**
  See also CA 77-80; DAM POET; DLB 120

Haggard, H(enry) Rider
  1856-1925 .... **TCLC 11**
  See also CA 108; 148; DLB 70, 156;
  SATA 16

Hagiwara Sakutaro 1886-1942 .... **TCLC 60**

Haig, Fenil
  See Ford, Ford Madox

Haig-Brown, Roderick (Langmere)
  1908-1976 .... **CLC 21**
  See also CA 5-8R; 69-72; CANR 4, 38;
  CLR 31; DLB 88; MAICYA; SATA 12

Hailey, Arthur 1920- .... **CLC 5**
  See also AITN 2; BEST 90:3; CA 1-4R;
  CANR 2, 36; DAM NOV, POP; DLB 88;
  DLBY 82; MTCW

Hailey, Elizabeth Forsythe 1938-... **CLC 40**
  See also CA 93-96; CAAS 1; CANR 15, 48;
  INT CANR-15

Haines, John (Meade) 1924- .... **CLC 58**
  See also CA 17-20R; CANR 13, 34; DLB 5

Hakluyt, Richard 1552-1616 .... **LC 31**

Haldeman, Joe (William) 1943-..... **CLC 61**
  See also CA 53-56; CANR 6; DLB 8;
  INT CANR-6

Haley, Alex(ander Murray Palmer)
  1921-1992 .... **CLC 8, 12, 76; BLC; DA;
  DAB; DAC**
  See also BW 2; CA 77-80; 136; DAM MST,
  MULT, POP; DLB 38; MTCW

Haliburton, Thomas Chandler
  1796-1865 .... **NCLC 15**
  See also DLB 11, 99

Hall, Donald (Andrew, Jr.)
  1928- .... **CLC 1, 13, 37, 59**
  See also CA 5-8R; CAAS 7; CANR 2, 44;
  DAM POET; DLB 5; SATA 23

Hall, Frederic Sauser
  See Sauser-Hall, Frederic

Hall, James
  See Kuttner, Henry

Hall, James Norman 1887-1951 ... **TCLC 23**
  See also CA 123; SATA 21

Hall, (Marguerite) Radclyffe
  1886-1943 .... **TCLC 12**
  See also CA 110; 150

Hall, Rodney 1935- .... **CLC 51**
  See also CA 109

Halleck, Fitz-Greene 1790-1867 .. **NCLC 47**
  See also DLB 3

Halliday, Michael
  See Creasey, John

Halpern, Daniel 1945- .... **CLC 14**
  See also CA 33-36R

Hamburger, Michael (Peter Leopold)
  1924- .... **CLC 5, 14**
  See also CA 5-8R; CAAS 4; CANR 2, 47;
  DLB 27

Hamill, Pete 1935-............... **CLC 10**
  See also CA 25-28R; CANR 18

Hamilton, Alexander
  1755(?)-1804 .... **NCLC 49**
  See also DLB 37

Hamilton, Clive
  See Lewis, C(live) S(taples)

Hamilton, Edmond 1904-1977....... **CLC 1**
  See also CA 1-4R; CANR 3; DLB 8

Hamilton, Eugene (Jacob) Lee
  See Lee-Hamilton, Eugene (Jacob)

Hamilton, Franklin
  See Silverberg, Robert

Hamilton, Gail
  See Corcoran, Barbara

Hamilton, Mollie
  See Kaye, M(ary) M(argaret)

Hamilton, (Anthony Walter) Patrick
  1904-1962 .... **CLC 51**
  See also CA 113; DLB 10

Hamilton, Virginia 1936-.......... **CLC 26**
  See also AAYA 2; BW 2; CA 25-28R;
  CANR 20, 37; CLR 1, 11, 40;
  DAM MULT; DLB 33, 52;
  INT CANR-20; JRDA; MAICYA;
  MTCW; SATA 4, 56, 79

Hammett, (Samuel) Dashiell
  1894-1961 .... **CLC 3, 5, 10, 19, 47;
  SSC 17**
  See also AITN 1; CA 81-84; CANR 42;
  CDALB 1929-1941; DLBD 6; MTCW

Hammon, Jupiter
  1711(?)-1800(?) ... **NCLC 5; BLC; PC 16**
  See also DAM MULT, POET; DLB 31, 50

Hammond, Keith
  See Kuttner, Henry

Hamner, Earl (Henry), Jr. 1923- ... **CLC 12**
  See also AITN 2; CA 73-76; DLB 6

Hampton, Christopher (James)
  1946-....................... **CLC 4**
  See also CA 25-28R; DLB 13; MTCW

Hamsun, Knut .... **TCLC 2, 14, 49**
  See also Pedersen, Knut

Handke, Peter 1942- .. **CLC 5, 8, 10, 15, 38**
  See also CA 77-80; CANR 33;
  DAM DRAM, NOV; DLB 85, 124;
  MTCW

Hanley, James 1901-1985 ... **CLC 3, 5, 8, 13**
  See also CA 73-76; 117; CANR 36; MTCW

Hannah, Barry 1942- .... **CLC 23, 38, 90**
  See also CA 108; 110; CANR 43; DLB 6;
  INT 110; MTCW

Hannon, Ezra
  See Hunter, Evan

Hansberry, Lorraine (Vivian)
  1930-1965 ...... **CLC 17, 62; BLC; DA;
  DAB; DAC; DC 2**
  See also BW 1; CA 109; 25-28R; CABS 3;
  CDALB 1941-1968; DAM DRAM, MST,
  MULT; DLB 7, 38; MTCW

Hansen, Joseph 1923-............. **CLC 38**
  See also CA 29-32R; CAAS 17; CANR 16,
  44; INT CANR-16

Hansen, Martin A. 1909-1955..... **TCLC 32**

Hanson, Kenneth O(stlin) 1922- .... **CLC 13**
  See also CA 53-56; CANR 7

Hardwick, Elizabeth 1916- .... **CLC 13**
  See also CA 5-8R; CANR 3, 32;
  DAM NOV; DLB 6; MTCW

Hardy, Thomas
  1840-1928 ..... **TCLC 4, 10, 18, 32, 48,
  53; DA; DAB; DAC; PC 8; SSC 2; WLC**
  See also CA 104; 123; CDBLB 1890-1914;
  DAM MST, NOV, POET; DLB 18, 19,
  135; MTCW

Hare, David 1947- .... **CLC 29, 58**
  See also CA 97-100; CANR 39; DLB 13;
  MTCW

Harford, Henry
  See Hudson, W(illiam) H(enry)

Hargrave, Leonie
  See Disch, Thomas M(ichael)

Harjo, Joy 1951- .... **CLC 83**
  See also CA 114; CANR 35; DAM MULT;
  DLB 120; NNAL

Harlan, Louis R(udolph) 1922-..... **CLC 34**
  See also CA 21-24R; CANR 25

Harling, Robert 1951(?)- .... **CLC 53**
  See also CA 147

Harmon, William (Ruth) 1938-..... **CLC 38**
  See also CA 33-36R; CANR 14, 32, 35;
  SATA 65

Harper, F. E. W.
  See Harper, Frances Ellen Watkins

Harper, Frances E. W.
  See Harper, Frances Ellen Watkins

Harper, Frances E. Watkins
  See Harper, Frances Ellen Watkins

Harper, Frances Ellen
  See Harper, Frances Ellen Watkins

Harper, Frances Ellen Watkins
  1825-1911 .... **TCLC 14; BLC**
  See also BW 1; CA 111; 125; DAM MULT,
  POET; DLB 50

Harper, Michael S(teven) 1938- ... **CLC 7, 22**
  See also BW 1; CA 33-36R; CANR 24;
  DLB 41

Harper, Mrs. F. E. W.
  See Harper, Frances Ellen Watkins

Harris, Christie (Lucy) Irwin
  1907-....................... **CLC 12**
  See also CA 5-8R; CANR 6; DLB 88;
  JRDA; MAICYA; SAAS 10; SATA 6, 74

Harris, Frank 1856-1931........ **TCLC 24**
  See also CA 109; 150; DLB 156

Harris, George Washington
  1814-1869 .... **NCLC 23**
  See also DLB 3, 11

Harris, Joel Chandler
  1848-1908 .... **TCLC 2; SSC 19**
  See also CA 104; 137; DLB 11, 23, 42, 78,
  91; MAICYA; YABC 1

Harris, John (Wyndham Parkes Lucas)
  Beynon 1903-1969
  See Wyndham, John
  See also CA 102; 89-92

Harris, MacDonald................. **CLC 9**
  See also Heiney, Donald (William)

Heller, Joseph
1923- .... **CLC 1, 3, 5, 8, 11, 36, 63; DA;**
DAB; DAC; WLC
See also AITN 1; CA 5-8R; CABS 1;
CANR 8, 42; DAM MST, NOV, POP;
DLB 2, 28; DLBY 80; INT CANR-8;
MTCW

Hellman, Lillian (Florence)
1906-1984 ...... **CLC 2, 4, 8, 14, 18, 34,**
44, 52; DC 1
See also AITN 1, 2; CA 13-16R; 112;
CANR 33; DAM DRAM; DLB 7;
DLBY 84; MTCW

Helprin, Mark 1947- ..... **CLC 7, 10, 22, 32**
See also CA 81-84; CANR 47; DAM NOV,
POP; DLBY 85; MTCW

Helvetius, Claude-Adrien
1715-1771 .... **LC 26**

Helyar, Jane Penelope Josephine 1933-
See Poole, Josephine
See also CA 21-24R; CANR 10, 26;
SATA 82

Hemans, Felicia 1793-1835 ...... **NCLC 29**
See also DLB 96

Hemingway, Ernest (Miller)
1899-1961 .... **CLC 1, 3, 6, 8, 10, 13, 19,**
30, 34, 39, 41, 44, 50, 61, 80; DA; DAB;
DAC; SSC 1; WLC
See also CA 77-80; CANR 34;
CDALB 1917-1929; DAM MST, NOV;
DLB 4, 9, 102; DLBD 1; DLBY 81, 87;
MTCW

Hempel, Amy 1951- .... **CLC 39**
See also CA 118; 137

Henderson, F. C.
See Mencken, H(enry) L(ouis)

Henderson, Sylvia
See Ashton-Warner, Sylvia (Constance)

Henley, Beth .... **CLC 23; DC 6**
See also Henley, Elizabeth Becker
See also CABS 3; DLBY 86

Henley, Elizabeth Becker 1952-
See Henley, Beth
See also CA 107; CANR 32; DAM DRAM,
MST; MTCW

Henley, William Ernest
1849-1903 .... **TCLC 8**
See also CA 105; DLB 19

Hennissart, Martha
See Lathen, Emma
See also CA 85-88

Henry, O. .... **TCLC 1, 19; SSC 5; WLC**
See also Porter, William Sydney

Henry, Patrick 1736-1799 .... **LC 25**

Henryson, Robert 1430(?)-1506(?).... **LC 20**
See also DLB 146

Henry VIII 1491-1547 .... **LC 10**

Henschke, Alfred
See Klabund

Hentoff, Nat(han Irving) 1925- ..... **CLC 26**
See also AAYA 4; CA 1-4R; CAAS 6;
CANR 5, 25; CLR 1; INT CANR-25;
JRDA; MAICYA; SATA 42, 69;
SATA-Brief 27

Heppenstall, (John) Rayner
1911-1981 .... **CLC 10**
See also CA 1-4R; 103; CANR 29

Herbert, Frank (Patrick)
1920-1986 ...... **CLC 12, 23, 35, 44, 85**
See also CA 53-56; 118; CANR 5, 43;
DAM POP; DLB 8; INT CANR-5;
MTCW; SATA 9, 37; SATA-Obit 47

Herbert, George
1593-1633 .... **LC 24; DAB; PC 4**
See also CDBLB Before 1660; DAM POET;
DLB 126

Herbert, Zbigniew 1924- .... **CLC 9, 43**
See also CA 89-92; CANR 36;
DAM POET; MTCW

Herbst, Josephine (Frey)
1897-1969 .... **CLC 34**
See also CA 5-8R; 25-28R; DLB 9

Hergesheimer, Joseph
1880-1954 .... **TCLC 11**
See also CA 109; DLB 102, 9

Herlihy, James Leo 1927-1993 ...... **CLC 6**
See also CA 1-4R; 143; CANR 2

Hermogenes fl. c. 175- .... **CMLC 6**

Hernandez, Jose 1834-1886 ...... **NCLC 17**

Herodotus c. 484B.C.-429B.C.... **CMLC 17**

Herrick, Robert
1591-1674 ..... **LC 13; DA; DAB; DAC;**
PC 9
See also DAM MST, POP; DLB 126

Herring, Guilles
See Somerville, Edith

Herriot, James 1916-1995 .... **CLC 12**
See also Wight, James Alfred
See also AAYA 1; CA 148; CANR 40;
DAM POP; SATA 86

Herrmann, Dorothy 1941- .... **CLC 44**
See also CA 107

Herrmann, Taffy
See Herrmann, Dorothy

Hersey, John (Richard)
1914-1993 .... **CLC 1, 2, 7, 9, 40, 81**
See also CA 17-20R; 140; CANR 33;
DAM POP; DLB 6; MTCW; SATA 25;
SATA-Obit 76

Herzen, Aleksandr Ivanovich
1812-1870 .... **NCLC 10**

Herzl, Theodor 1860-1904 .... **TCLC 36**

Herzog, Werner 1942- .... **CLC 16**
See also CA 89-92

Hesiod c. 8th cent. B.C.- .... **CMLC 5**

Hesse, Hermann
1877-1962 .... **CLC 1, 2, 3, 6, 11, 17, 25,**
69; DA; DAB; DAC; SSC 9; WLC
See also CA 17-18; CAP 2; DAM MST,
NOV; DLB 66; MTCW; SATA 50

Hewes, Cady
See De Voto, Bernard (Augustine)

Heyen, William 1940- .... **CLC 13, 18**
See also CA 33-36R; CAAS 9; DLB 5

Heyerdahl, Thor 1914- .... **CLC 26**
See also CA 5-8R; CANR 5, 22; MTCW;
SATA 2, 52

Heym, Georg (Theodor Franz Arthur)
1887-1912 .... **TCLC 9**
See also CA 106

Heym, Stefan 1913- .... **CLC 41**
See also CA 9-12R; CANR 4; DLB 69

Heyse, Paul (Johann Ludwig von)
1830-1914 .... **TCLC 8**
See also CA 104; DLB 129

Heyward, (Edwin) DuBose
1885-1940 .... **TCLC 59**
See also CA 108; DLB 7, 9, 45; SATA 21

Hibbert, Eleanor Alice Burford
1906-1993 .... **CLC 7**
See also BEST 90:4; CA 17-20R; 140;
CANR 9, 28; DAM POP; SATA 2;
SATA-Obit 74

Hichens, Robert S. 1864-1950..... **TCLC 64**
See also DLB 153

Higgins, George V(incent)
1939- .... **CLC 4, 7, 10, 18**
See also CA 77-80; CAAS 5; CANR 17, 51;
DLB 2; DLBY 81; INT CANR-17;
MTCW

Higginson, Thomas Wentworth
1823-1911 .... **TCLC 36**
See also DLB 1, 64

Highet, Helen
See MacInnes, Helen (Clark)

Highsmith, (Mary) Patricia
1921-1995 .... **CLC 2, 4, 14, 42**
See also CA 1-4R; 147; CANR 1, 20, 48;
DAM NOV, POP; MTCW

Highwater, Jamake (Mamake)
1942(?)- .... **CLC 12**
See also AAYA 7; CA 65-68; CAAS 7;
CANR 10, 34; CLR 17; DLB 52;
DLBY 85; JRDA; MAICYA; SATA 32,
69; SATA-Brief 30

Highway, Tomson 1951-...... **CLC 92; DAC**
See also CA 151; DAM MULT; NNAL

Higuchi, Ichiyo 1872-1896....... **NCLC 49**

Hijuelos, Oscar 1951- ...... **CLC 65; HLC**
See also BEST 90:1; CA 123; CANR 50;
DAM MULT, POP; DLB 145; HW

Hikmet, Nazim 1902(?)-1963....... **CLC 40**
See also CA 141; 93-96

Hildesheimer, Wolfgang
1916-1991 .... **CLC 49**
See also CA 101; 135; DLB 69, 124

Hill, Geoffrey (William)
1932- .... **CLC 5, 8, 18, 45**
See also CA 81-84; CANR 21;
CDBLB 1960 to Present; DAM POET;
DLB 40; MTCW

Hill, George Roy 1921- .... **CLC 26**
See also CA 110; 122

Hill, John
See Koontz, Dean R(ay)

Hill, Susan (Elizabeth)
1942- .... **CLC 4; DAB**
See also CA 33-36R; CANR 29;
DAM MST, NOV; DLB 14, 139; MTCW

Hillerman, Tony 1925-............ **CLC 62**
See also AAYA 6; BEST 89:1; CA 29-32R;
CANR 21, 42; DAM POP; SATA 6

Hillesum, Etty 1914-1943 . . . . TCLC 49
See also CA 137

Hilliard, Noel (Harvey) 1929- . . . . . . CLC 15
See also CA 9-12R; CANR 7

Hillis, Rick 1956- . . . . CLC 66
See also CA 134

Hilton, James 1900-1954 . . . . TCLC 21
See also CA 108; DLB 34, 77; SATA 34

Himes, Chester (Bomar)
1909-1984 . . . . CLC 2, 4, 7, 18, 58; BLC
See also BW 2; CA 25-28R; 114; CANR 22;
DAM MULT; DLB 2, 76, 143; MTCW

Hinde, Thomas . . . . CLC 6, 11
See also Chitty, Thomas Willes

Hindin, Nathan
See Bloch, Robert (Albert)

Hine, (William) Daryl 1936- . . . . CLC 15
See also CA 1-4R; CAAS 15; CANR 1, 20;
DLB 60

Hinkson, Katharine Tynan
See Tynan, Katharine

Hinton, S(usan) E(loise)
1950- . . . . CLC 30; DA; DAB; DAC
See also AAYA 2; CA 81-84; CANR 32;
CLR 3, 23; DAM MST, NOV; JRDA;
MAICYA; MTCW; SATA 19, 58

Hippius, Zinaida . . . . TCLC 9
See also Gippius, Zinaida (Nikolayevna)

Hiraoka, Kimitake 1925-1970
See Mishima, Yukio
See also CA 97-100; 29-32R; DAM DRAM;
MTCW

Hirsch, E(ric) D(onald), Jr. 1928- . . . CLC 79
See also CA 25-28R; CANR 27, 51;
DLB 67; INT CANR-27; MTCW

Hirsch, Edward 1950- . . . . CLC 31, 50
See also CA 104; CANR 20, 42; DLB 120

Hitchcock, Alfred (Joseph)
1899-1980 . . . . CLC 16
See also CA 97-100; SATA 27;
SATA-Obit 24

Hitler, Adolf 1889-1945 . . . . TCLC 53
See also CA 117; 147

Hoagland, Edward 1932- . . . . CLC 28
See also CA 1-4R; CANR 2, 31; DLB 6;
SATA 51

Hoban, Russell (Conwell) 1925- . . CLC 7, 25
See also CA 5-8R; CANR 23, 37; CLR 3;
DAM NOV; DLB 52; MAICYA;
MTCW; SATA 1, 40, 78

Hobbs, Perry
See Blackmur, R(ichard) P(almer)

Hobson, Laura Z(ametkin)
1900-1986 . . . . CLC 7, 25
See also CA 17-20R; 118; DLB 28;
SATA 52

Hochhuth, Rolf 1931- . . . . CLC 4, 11, 18
See also CA 5-8R; CANR 33;
DAM DRAM; DLB 124; MTCW

Hochman, Sandra 1936- . . . . CLC 3, 8
See also CA 5-8R; DLB 5

Hochwaelder, Fritz 1911-1986 . . . . . . CLC 36
See also CA 29-32R; 120; CANR 42;
DAM DRAM; MTCW

Hochwalder, Fritz
See Hochwaelder, Fritz

Hocking, Mary (Eunice) 1921- . . . . . CLC 13
See also CA 101; CANR 18, 40

Hodgins, Jack 1938- . . . . CLC 23
See also CA 93-96; DLB 60

Hodgson, William Hope
1877(?)-1918 . . . . TCLC 13
See also CA 111; DLB 70, 153, 156

Hoeg, Peter 1957- . . . . CLC 95
See also CA 151

Hoffman, Alice 1952- . . . . CLC 51
See also CA 77-80; CANR 34; DAM NOV;
MTCW

Hoffman, Daniel (Gerard)
1923- . . . . CLC 6, 13, 23
See also CA 1-4R; CANR 4; DLB 5

Hoffman, Stanley 1944- . . . . CLC 5
See also CA 77-80

Hoffman, William M(oses) 1939- . . . CLC 40
See also CA 57-60; CANR 11

Hoffmann, E(rnst) T(heodor) A(madeus)
1776-1822 . . . . NCLC 2; SSC 13
See also DLB 90; SATA 27

Hofmann, Gert 1931- . . . . CLC 54
See also CA 128

Hofmannsthal, Hugo von
1874-1929 . . . . TCLC 11; DC 4
See also CA 106; DAM DRAM; DLB 81,
118

Hogan, Linda 1947- . . . . CLC 73
See also CA 120; CANR 45; DAM MULT;
NNAL

Hogarth, Charles
See Creasey, John

Hogarth, Emmett
See Polonsky, Abraham (Lincoln)

Hogg, James 1770-1835 . . . . NCLC 4
See also DLB 93, 116, 159

Holbach, Paul Henri Thiry Baron
1723-1789 . . . . LC 14

Holberg, Ludvig 1684-1754 . . . . LC 6

Holden, Ursula 1921- . . . . CLC 18
See also CA 101; CAAS 8; CANR 22

Holderlin, (Johann Christian) Friedrich
1770-1843 . . . . NCLC 16; PC 4

Holdstock, Robert
See Holdstock, Robert P.

Holdstock, Robert P. 1948- . . . . CLC 39
See also CA 131

Holland, Isabelle 1920- . . . . CLC 21
See also AAYA 11; CA 21-24R; CANR 10,
25, 47; JRDA; MAICYA; SATA 8, 70

Holland, Marcus
See Caldwell, (Janet Miriam) Taylor
(Holland)

Hollander, John 1929- . . . . . . CLC 2, 5, 8, 14
See also CA 1-4R; CANR 1, 52; DLB 5;
SATA 13

Hollander, Paul
See Silverberg, Robert

Holleran, Andrew 1943(?)- . . . . CLC 38
See also CA 144

Hollinghurst, Alan 1954- . . . . CLC 55, 91
See also CA 114

Hollis, Jim
See Summers, Hollis (Spurgeon, Jr.)

Holly, Buddy 1936-1959 . . . . TCLC 65

Holmes, John
See Souster, (Holmes) Raymond

Holmes, John Clellon 1926-1988 . . . . CLC 56
See also CA 9-12R; 125; CANR 4; DLB 16

Holmes, Oliver Wendell
1809-1894 . . . . NCLC 14
See also CDALB 1640-1865; DLB 1;
SATA 34

Holmes, Raymond
See Souster, (Holmes) Raymond

Holt, Victoria
See Hibbert, Eleanor Alice Burford

Holub, Miroslav 1923- . . . . CLC 4
See also CA 21-24R; CANR 10

Homer
c. 8th cent. B.C.- . . . . . CMLC 1, 16; DA;
DAB; DAC
See also DAM MST, POET

Honig, Edwin 1919- . . . . CLC 33
See also CA 5-8R; CAAS 8; CANR 4, 45;
DLB 5

Hood, Hugh (John Blagdon)
1928- . . . . CLC 15, 28
See also CA 49-52; CAAS 17; CANR 1, 33;
DLB 53

Hood, Thomas 1799-1845 . . . . NCLC 16
See also DLB 96

Hooker, (Peter) Jeremy 1941- . . . . . . CLC 43
See also CA 77-80; CANR 22; DLB 40

hooks, bell . . . . CLC 94
See also Watkins, Gloria

Hope, A(lec) D(erwent) 1907- . . . . CLC 3, 51
See also CA 21-24R; CANR 33; MTCW

Hope, Brian
See Creasey, John

Hope, Christopher (David Tully)
1944- . . . . CLC 52
See also CA 106; CANR 47; SATA 62

Hopkins, Gerard Manley
1844-1889 . . . . NCLC 17; DA; DAB;
DAC; PC 15; WLC
See also CDBLB 1890-1914; DAM MST,
POET; DLB 35, 57

Hopkins, John (Richard) 1931- . . . . . . CLC 4
See also CA 85-88

Hopkins, Pauline Elizabeth
1859-1930 . . . . TCLC 28; BLC
See also BW 2; CA 141; DAM MULT;
DLB 50

Hopkinson, Francis 1737-1791 . . . . . . LC 25
See also DLB 31

Hopley-Woolrich, Cornell George 1903-1968
See Woolrich, Cornell
See also CA 13-14; CAP 1

Horatio
See Proust, (Valentin-Louis-George-Eugene-)
Marcel

Horgan, Paul (George Vincent O'Shaughnessy)
1903-1995 .... CLC 9, 53
See also CA 13-16R; 147; CANR 9, 35;
DAM NOV; DLB 102; DLBY 85;
INT CANR-9; MTCW; SATA 13;
SATA-Obit 84

Horn, Peter
See Kuttner, Henry

Hornem, Horace Esq.
See Byron, George Gordon (Noel)

Hornung, E(rnest) W(illiam)
1866-1921 .... TCLC 59
See also CA 108; DLB 70

Horovitz, Israel (Arthur) 1939- ..... CLC 56
See also CA 33-36R; CANR 46;
DAM DRAM; DLB 7

Horvath, Odon von
See Horvath, Oedoen von
See also DLB 85, 124

Horvath, Oedoen von 1901-1938 ... TCLC 45
See also Horvath, Odon von
See also CA 118

Horwitz, Julius 1920-1986 .... CLC 14
See also CA 9-12R; 119; CANR 12

Hospital, Janette Turner 1942- ..... CLC 42
See also CA 108; CANR 48

Hostos, E. M. de
See Hostos (y Bonilla), Eugenio Maria de

Hostos, Eugenio M. de
See Hostos (y Bonilla), Eugenio Maria de

Hostos, Eugenio Maria
See Hostos (y Bonilla), Eugenio Maria de

Hostos (y Bonilla), Eugenio Maria de
1839-1903 .... TCLC 24
See also CA 123; 131; HW

Houdini
See Lovecraft, H(oward) P(hillips)

Hougan, Carolyn 1943- .... CLC 34
See also CA 139

Household, Geoffrey (Edward West)
1900-1988 .... CLC 11
See also CA 77-80; 126; DLB 87; SATA 14;
SATA-Obit 59

Housman, A(lfred) E(dward)
1859-1936 ...... TCLC 1, 10; DA; DAB;
DAC; PC 2
See also CA 104; 125; DAM MST, POET;
DLB 19; MTCW

Housman, Laurence 1865-1959 ..... TCLC 7
See also CA 106; DLB 10; SATA 25

Howard, Elizabeth Jane 1923- ... CLC 7, 29
See also CA 5-8R; CANR 8

Howard, Maureen 1930- ..... CLC 5, 14, 46
See also CA 53-56; CANR 31; DLBY 83;
INT CANR-31; MTCW

Howard, Richard 1929- ...... CLC 7, 10, 47
See also AITN 1; CA 85-88; CANR 25;
DLB 5; INT CANR-25

Howard, Robert Ervin 1906-1936 ... TCLC 8
See also CA 105

Howard, Warren F.
See Pohl, Frederik

Howe, Fanny 1940- .... CLC 47
See also CA 117; SATA-Brief 52

Howe, Irving 1920-1993 .... CLC 85
See also CA 9-12R; 141; CANR 21, 50;
DLB 67; MTCW

Howe, Julia Ward 1819-1910 ..... TCLC 21
See also CA 117; DLB 1

Howe, Susan 1937- .... CLC 72
See also DLB 120

Howe, Tina 1937- .... CLC 48
See also CA 109

Howell, James 1594(?)-1666 .... LC 13
See also DLB 151

Howells, W. D.
See Howells, William Dean

Howells, William D.
See Howells, William Dean

Howells, William Dean
1837-1920 .... TCLC 7, 17, 41
See also CA 104; 134; CDALB 1865-1917;
DLB 12, 64, 74, 79

Howes, Barbara 1914-1996 .... CLC 15
See also CA 9-12R; 151; CAAS 3;
CANR 53; SATA 5

Hrabal, Bohumil 1914- .... CLC 13, 67
See also CA 106; CAAS 12

Hsun, Lu
See Lu Hsun

Hubbard, L(afayette) Ron(ald)
1911-1986 .... CLC 43
See also CA 77-80; 118; CANR 52;
DAM POP

Huch, Ricarda (Octavia)
1864-1947 .... TCLC 13
See also CA 111; DLB 66

Huddle, David 1942- .... CLC 49
See also CA 57-60; CAAS 20; DLB 130

Hudson, Jeffrey
See Crichton, (John) Michael

Hudson, W(illiam) H(enry)
1841-1922 .... TCLC 29
See also CA 115; DLB 98, 153; SATA 35

Hueffer, Ford Madox
See Ford, Ford Madox

Hughart, Barry 1934- .... CLC 39
See also CA 137

Hughes, Colin
See Creasey, John

Hughes, David (John) 1930- .... CLC 48
See also CA 116; 129; DLB 14

Hughes, Edward James
See Hughes, Ted
See also DAM MST, POET

Hughes, (James) Langston
1902-1967 ..... CLC 1, 5, 10, 15, 35, 44;
BLC; DA; DAB; DAC; DC 3; PC 1;
SSC 6; WLC
See also AAYA 12; BW 1; CA 1-4R;
25-28R; CANR 1, 34; CDALB 1929-1941;
CLR 17; DAM DRAM, MST, MULT,
POET; DLB 4, 7, 48, 51, 86; JRDA;
MAICYA; MTCW; SATA 4, 33

Hughes, Richard (Arthur Warren)
1900-1976 .... CLC 1, 11
See also CA 5-8R; 65-68; CANR 4;
DAM NOV; DLB 15, 161; MTCW;
SATA 8; SATA-Obit 25

Hughes, Ted
1930- .... CLC 2, 4, 9, 14, 37; DAB;
DAC; PC 7
See also Hughes, Edward James
See also CA 1-4R; CANR 1, 33; CLR 3;
DLB 40, 161; MAICYA; MTCW;
SATA 49; SATA-Brief 27

Hugo, Richard F(ranklin)
1923-1982 .... CLC 6, 18, 32
See also CA 49-52; 108; CANR 3;
DAM POET; DLB 5

Hugo, Victor (Marie)
1802-1885 .... NCLC 3, 10, 21; DA;
DAB; DAC; WLC
See also DAM DRAM, MST, NOV, POET;
DLB 119; SATA 47

Huidobro, Vicente
See Huidobro Fernandez, Vicente Garcia

Huidobro Fernandez, Vicente Garcia
1893-1948 .... TCLC 31
See also CA 131; HW

Hulme, Keri 1947- .... CLC 39
See also CA 125; INT 125

Hulme, T(homas) E(rnest)
1883-1917 .... TCLC 21
See also CA 117; DLB 19

Hume, David 1711-1776............. LC 7
See also DLB 104

Humphrey, William 1924- .... CLC 45
See also CA 77-80; DLB 6

Humphreys, Emyr Owen 1919- ..... CLC 47
See also CA 5-8R; CANR 3, 24; DLB 15

Humphreys, Josephine 1945- .... CLC 34, 57
See also CA 121; 127; INT 127

Huneker, James Gibbons
1857-1921 .... TCLC 65
See also DLB 71

Hungerford, Pixie
See Brinsmead, H(esba) F(ay)

Hunt, E(verette) Howard, (Jr.)
1918- .... CLC 3
See also AITN 1; CA 45-48; CANR 2, 47

Hunt, Kyle
See Creasey, John

Hunt, (James Henry) Leigh
1784-1859 .... NCLC 1
See also DAM POET

Hunt, Marsha 1946- .... CLC 70
See also BW 2; CA 143

Hunt, Violet 1866-1942 .... TCLC 53
See also DLB 162

Hunter, E. Waldo
See Sturgeon, Theodore (Hamilton)

Hunter, Evan 1926- .... CLC 11, 31
See also CA 5-8R; CANR 5, 38;
DAM POP; DLBY 82; INT CANR-5;
MTCW; SATA 25

Hunter, Kristin (Eggleston) 1931- ... CLC 35
See also AITN 1; BW 1; CA 13-16R;
CANR 13; CLR 3; DLB 33;
INT CANR-13; MAICYA; SAAS 10;
SATA 12

James, Dynely
See Mayne, William (James Carter)

James, Henry Sr. 1811-1882 . . . . . NCLC 53

James, Henry
1843-1916 . . . . . . **TCLC 2, 11, 24, 40, 47,**
64; DA; DAB; DAC; SSC 8; WLC
See also CA 104; 132; CDALB 1865-1917;
DAM MST, NOV; DLB 12, 71, 74;
DLBD 13; MTCW

James, M. R.
See James, Montague (Rhodes)
See also DLB 156

James, Montague (Rhodes)
1862-1936 . . . . **TCLC 6; SSC 16**
See also CA 104

James, P. D. . . . . **CLC 18, 46**
See also White, Phyllis Dorothy James
See also BEST 90:2; CDBLB 1960 to
Present; DLB 87

James, Philip
See Moorcock, Michael (John)

James, William 1842-1910 . . . . . **TCLC 15, 32**
See also CA 109

James I 1394-1437 . . . . **LC 20**

Jameson, Anna 1794-1860 . . . . **NCLC 43**
See also DLB 99, 166

Jami, Nur al-Din 'Abd al-Rahman
1414-1492 . . . . **LC 9**

Jandl, Ernst 1925- . . . . **CLC 34**

Janowitz, Tama 1957- . . . . **CLC 43**
See also CA 106; CANR 52; DAM POP

Japrisot, Sebastien 1931- . . . . **CLC 90**

Jarrell, Randall
1914-1965 . . . . **CLC 1, 2, 6, 9, 13, 49**
See also CA 5-8R; 25-28R; CABS 2;
CANR 6, 34; CDALB 1941-1968; CLR 6;
DAM POET; DLB 48, 52; MAICYA;
MTCW; SATA 7

Jarry, Alfred
1873-1907 . . . . **TCLC 2, 14; SSC 20**
See also CA 104; DAM DRAM

Jarvis, E. K.
See Bloch, Robert (Albert); Ellison, Harlan
(Jay); Silverberg, Robert

Jeake, Samuel, Jr.
See Aiken, Conrad (Potter)

Jean Paul 1763-1825 . . . . **NCLC 7**

Jefferies, (John) Richard
1848-1887 . . . . **NCLC 47**
See also DLB 98, 141; SATA 16

Jeffers, (John) Robinson
1887-1962 . . . . **CLC 2, 3, 11, 15, 54; DA;**
DAC; WLC
See also CA 85-88; CANR 35;
CDALB 1917-1929; DAM MST, POET;
DLB 45; MTCW

Jefferson, Janet
See Mencken, H(enry) L(ouis)

Jefferson, Thomas 1743-1826 . . . . **NCLC 11**
See also CDALB 1640-1865; DLB 31

Jeffrey, Francis 1773-1850 . . . . **NCLC 33**
See also DLB 107

Jelakowitch, Ivan
See Heijermans, Herman

Jellicoe, (Patricia) Ann 1927- . . . . . . **CLC 27**
See also CA 85-88; DLB 13

Jen, Gish . . . . **CLC 70**
See also Jen, Lillian

Jen, Lillian 1956(?)-
See Jen, Gish
See also CA 135

Jenkins, (John) Robin 1912- . . . . **CLC 52**
See also CA 1-4R; CANR 1; DLB 14

Jennings, Elizabeth (Joan)
1926- . . . . **CLC 5, 14**
See also CA 61-64; CAAS 5; CANR 8, 39;
DLB 27; MTCW; SATA 66

Jennings, Waylon 1937- . . . . **CLC 21**

Jensen, Johannes V. 1873-1950 . . . . **TCLC 41**

Jensen, Laura (Linnea) 1948- . . . . . . **CLC 37**
See also CA 103

Jerome, Jerome K(lapka)
1859-1927 . . . . **TCLC 23**
See also CA 119; DLB 10, 34, 135

Jerrold, Douglas William
1803-1857 . . . . **NCLC 2**
See also DLB 158, 159

Jewett, (Theodora) Sarah Orne
1849-1909 . . . . **TCLC 1, 22; SSC 6**
See also CA 108; 127; DLB 12, 74;
SATA 15

Jewsbury, Geraldine (Endsor)
1812-1880 . . . . **NCLC 22**
See also DLB 21

Jhabvala, Ruth Prawer
1927- . . . . **CLC 4, 8, 29, 94; DAB**
See also CA 1-4R; CANR 2, 29, 51;
DAM NOV; DLB 139; INT CANR-29;
MTCW

Jibran, Kahlil
See Gibran, Kahlil

Jibran, Khalil
See Gibran, Kahlil

Jiles, Paulette 1943- . . . . **CLC 13, 58**
See also CA 101

Jimenez (Mantecon), Juan Ramon
1881-1958 . . . . **TCLC 4; HLC; PC 7**
See also CA 104; 131; DAM MULT,
POET; DLB 134; HW; MTCW

Jimenez, Ramon
See Jimenez (Mantecon), Juan Ramon

Jimenez Mantecon, Juan
See Jimenez (Mantecon), Juan Ramon

Joel, Billy . . . . **CLC 26**
See also Joel, William Martin

Joel, William Martin 1949-
See Joel, Billy
See also CA 108

John of the Cross, St. 1542-1591 . . . . **LC 18**

Johnson, B(ryan) S(tanley William)
1933-1973 . . . . **CLC 6, 9**
See also CA 9-12R; 53-56; CANR 9;
DLB 14, 40

Johnson, Benj. F. of Boo
See Riley, James Whitcomb

Johnson, Benjamin F. of Boo
See Riley, James Whitcomb

Johnson, Charles (Richard)
1948- . . . . **CLC 7, 51, 65; BLC**
See also BW 2; CA 116; CAAS 18;
CANR 42; DAM MULT; DLB 33

Johnson, Denis 1949- . . . . **CLC 52**
See also CA 117; 121; DLB 120

Johnson, Diane 1934- . . . . **CLC 5, 13, 48**
See also CA 41-44R; CANR 17, 40;
DLBY 80; INT CANR-17; MTCW

Johnson, Eyvind (Olof Verner)
1900-1976 . . . . **CLC 14**
See also CA 73-76; 69-72; CANR 34

Johnson, J. R.
See James, C(yril) L(ionel) R(obert)

Johnson, James Weldon
1871-1938 . . . . **TCLC 3, 19; BLC**
See also BW 1; CA 104; 125;
CDALB 1917-1929; CLR 32;
DAM MULT, POET; DLB 51; MTCW;
SATA 31

Johnson, Joyce 1935- . . . . **CLC 58**
See also CA 125; 129

Johnson, Lionel (Pigot)
1867-1902 . . . . **TCLC 19**
See also CA 117; DLB 19

Johnson, Mel
See Malzberg, Barry N(athaniel)

Johnson, Pamela Hansford
1912-1981 . . . . **CLC 1, 7, 27**
See also CA 1-4R; 104; CANR 2, 28;
DLB 15; MTCW

Johnson, Samuel
1709-1784 . . . . . **LC 15; DA; DAB; DAC;**
WLC
See also CDBLB 1660-1789; DAM MST;
DLB 39, 95, 104, 142

Johnson, Uwe
1934-1984 . . . . **CLC 5, 10, 15, 40**
See also CA 1-4R; 112; CANR 1, 39;
DLB 75; MTCW

Johnston, George (Benson) 1913- . . . **CLC 51**
See also CA 1-4R; CANR 5, 20; DLB 88

Johnston, Jennifer 1930- . . . . **CLC 7**
See also CA 85-88; DLB 14

Jolley, (Monica) Elizabeth
1923- . . . . **CLC 46; SSC 19**
See also CA 127; CAAS 13

Jones, Arthur Llewellyn 1863-1947
See Machen, Arthur
See also CA 104

Jones, D(ouglas) G(ordon) 1929- . . . . **CLC 10**
See also CA 29-32R; CANR 13; DLB 53

Jones, David (Michael)
1895-1974 . . . . **CLC 2, 4, 7, 13, 42**
See also CA 9-12R; 53-56; CANR 28;
CDBLB 1945-1960; DLB 20, 100; MTCW

Jones, David Robert 1947-
See Bowie, David
See also CA 103

Jones, Diana Wynne 1934- . . . . **CLC 26**
See also AAYA 12; CA 49-52; CANR 4,
26; CLR 23; DLB 161; JRDA; MAICYA;
SAAS 7; SATA 9, 70

Jones, Edward P. 1950- . . . . **CLC 76**
See also BW 2; CA 142

Jones, Gayl 1949-......... **CLC 6, 9; BLC**
See also BW 2; CA 77-80; CANR 27;
DAM MULT; DLB 33; MTCW

Jones, James 1921-1977.... **CLC 1, 3, 10, 39**
See also AITN 1, 2; CA 1-4R; 69-72;
CANR 6; DLB 2, 143; MTCW

Jones, John J.
See Lovecraft, H(oward) P(hillips)

Jones, LeRoi .... **CLC 1, 2, 3, 5, 10, 14**
See also Baraka, Amiri

Jones, Louis B. .... **CLC 65**
See also CA 141

Jones, Madison (Percy, Jr.) 1925- ... **CLC 4**
See also CA 13-16R; CAAS 11; CANR 7;
DLB 152

Jones, Mervyn 1922- .... **CLC 10, 52**
See also CA 45-48; CAAS 5; CANR 1;
MTCW

Jones, Mick 1956(?)- .... **CLC 30**

Jones, Nettie (Pearl) 1941-........ **CLC 34**
See also BW 2; CA 137; CAAS 20

Jones, Preston 1936-1979 .... **CLC 10**
See also CA 73-76; 89-92; DLB 7

Jones, Robert F(rancis) 1934-....... **CLC 7**
See also CA 49-52; CANR 2

Jones, Rod 1953- .... **CLC 50**
See also CA 128

Jones, Terence Graham Parry
1942- .... **CLC 21**
See also Jones, Terry; Monty Python
See also CA 112; 116; CANR 35; INT 116

Jones, Terry
See Jones, Terence Graham Parry
See also SATA 67; SATA-Brief 51

Jones, Thom 1945(?)- .... **CLC 81**

Jong, Erica 1942-...... **CLC 4, 6, 8, 18, 83**
See also AITN 1; BEST 90:2; CA 73-76;
CANR 26, 52; DAM NOV, POP; DLB 2,
5, 28, 152; INT CANR-26; MTCW

Jonson, Ben(jamin)
1572(?)-1637 ...... **LC 6, 33; DA; DAB;**
DAC; DC 4; WLC
See also CDBLB Before 1660;
DAM DRAM, MST, POET; DLB 62,
121

Jordan, June 1936-......... **CLC 5, 11, 23**
See also AAYA 2; BW 2; CA 33-36R;
CANR 25; CLR 10; DAM MULT,
POET; DLB 38; MAICYA; MTCW;
SATA 4

Jordan, Pat(rick M.) 1941-........ **CLC 37**
See also CA 33-36R

Jorgensen, Ivar
See Ellison, Harlan (Jay)

Jorgenson, Ivar
See Silverberg, Robert

Josephus, Flavius c. 37-100 ...... **CMLC 13**

Josipovici, Gabriel 1940-........ **CLC 6, 43**
See also CA 37-40R; CAAS 8; CANR 47;
DLB 14

Joubert, Joseph 1754-1824 .... **NCLC 9**

Jouve, Pierre Jean 1887-1976 ...... **CLC 47**
See also CA 65-68

Joyce, James (Augustine Aloysius)
1882-1941 ...... **TCLC 3, 8, 16, 35, 52;**
DA; DAB; DAC; SSC 3; WLC
See also CA 104; 126; CDBLB 1914-1945;
DAM MST, NOV, POET; DLB 10, 19,
36, 162; MTCW

Jozsef, Attila 1905-1937......... **TCLC 22**
See also CA 116

Juana Ines de la Cruz 1651(?)-1695 ... **LC 5**

Judd, Cyril
See Kornbluth, C(yril) M.; Pohl, Frederik

Julian of Norwich 1342(?)-1416(?) .... **LC 6**
See also DLB 146

Juniper, Alex
See Hospital, Janette Turner

Junius
See Luxemburg, Rosa

Just, Ward (Swift) 1935-........ **CLC 4, 27**
See also CA 25-28R; CANR 32;
INT CANR-32

Justice, Donald (Rodney) 1925- .. **CLC 6, 19**
See also CA 5-8R; CANR 26; DAM POET;
DLBY 83; INT CANR-26

Juvenal c. 55-c. 127 .... **CMLC 8**

Juvenis
See Bourne, Randolph S(illiman)

Kacew, Romain 1914-1980
See Gary, Romain
See also CA 108; 102

Kadare, Ismail 1936- .... **CLC 52**

Kadohata, Cynthia. .... **CLC 59**
See also CA 140

Kafka, Franz
1883-1924 .... **TCLC 2, 6, 13, 29, 47, 53;**
DA; DAB; DAC; SSC 5; WLC
See also CA 105; 126; DAM MST, NOV;
DLB 81; MTCW

Kahanovitsch, Pinkhes
See Der Nister

Kahn, Roger 1927- .... **CLC 30**
See also CA 25-28R; CANR 44; SATA 37

Kain, Saul
See Sassoon, Siegfried (Lorraine)

Kaiser, Georg 1878-1945 .... **TCLC 9**
See also CA 106; DLB 124

Kaletski, Alexander 1946-......... **CLC 39**
See also CA 118; 143

Kalidasa fl. c. 400- .... **CMLC 9**

Kallman, Chester (Simon)
1921-1975 .... **CLC 2**
See also CA 45-48; 53-56; CANR 3

Kaminsky, Melvin 1926-
See Brooks, Mel
See also CA 65-68; CANR 16

Kaminsky, Stuart M(elvin) 1934-... **CLC 59**
See also CA 73-76; CANR 29, 53

Kane, Paul
See Simon, Paul

Kane, Wilson
See Bloch, Robert (Albert)

Kanin, Garson 1912-............. **CLC 22**
See also AITN 1; CA 5-8R; CANR 7;
DLB 7

Kaniuk, Yoram 1930-............. **CLC 19**
See also CA 134

Kant, Immanuel 1724-1804 ...... **NCLC 27**
See also DLB 94

Kantor, MacKinlay 1904-1977 ...... **CLC 7**
See also CA 61-64; 73-76; DLB 9, 102

Kaplan, David Michael 1946- ...... **CLC 50**

Kaplan, James 1951- .... **CLC 59**
See also CA 135

Karageorge, Michael
See Anderson, Poul (William)

Karamzin, Nikolai Mikhailovich
1766-1826 .... **NCLC 3**
See also DLB 150

Karapanou, Margarita 1946-....... **CLC 13**
See also CA 101

Karinthy, Frigyes 1887-1938...... **TCLC 47**

Karl, Frederick R(obert) 1927-..... **CLC 34**
See also CA 5-8R; CANR 3, 44

Kastel, Warren
See Silverberg, Robert

Kataev, Evgeny Petrovich 1903-1942
See Petrov, Evgeny
See also CA 120

Kataphusin
See Ruskin, John

Katz, Steve 1935-................ **CLC 47**
See also CA 25-28R; CAAS 14; CANR 12;
DLBY 83

Kauffman, Janet 1945-............ **CLC 42**
See also CA 117; CANR 43; DLBY 86

Kaufman, Bob (Garnell)
1925-1986 .... **CLC 49**
See also BW 1; CA 41-44R; 118; CANR 22;
DLB 16, 41

Kaufman, George S. 1889-1961..... **CLC 38**
See also CA 108; 93-96; DAM DRAM;
DLB 7; INT 108

Kaufman, Sue .... **CLC 3, 8**
See also Barondess, Sue K(aufman)

Kavafis, Konstantinos Petrou 1863-1933
See Cavafy, C(onstantine) P(eter)
See also CA 104

Kavan, Anna 1901-1968...... **CLC 5, 13, 82**
See also CA 5-8R; CANR 6; MTCW

Kavanagh, Dan
See Barnes, Julian

Kavanagh, Patrick (Joseph)
1904-1967 .... **CLC 22**
See also CA 123; 25-28R; DLB 15, 20;
MTCW

Kawabata, Yasunari
1899-1972 ..... **CLC 2, 5, 9, 18; SSC 17**
See also CA 93-96; 33-36R; DAM MULT

Kaye, M(ary) M(argaret) 1909-..... **CLC 28**
See also CA 89-92; CANR 24; MTCW;
SATA 62

Kaye, Mollie
See Kaye, M(ary) M(argaret)

Kaye-Smith, Sheila 1887-1956..... **TCLC 20**
See also CA 118; DLB 36

Kaymor, Patrice Maguilene
See Senghor, Leopold Sedar

Kazan, Elia 1909- .... **CLC 6, 16, 63**
See also CA 21-24R; CANR 32

Kazantzakis, Nikos
1883(?)-1957 .... **TCLC 2, 5, 33**
See also CA 105; 132; MTCW

Kazin, Alfred 1915- .... **CLC 34, 38**
See also CA 1-4R; CAAS 7; CANR 1, 45;
DLB 67

Keane, Mary Nesta (Skrine) 1904-1996
See Keane, Molly
See also CA 108; 114; 151

Keane, Molly .... **CLC 31**
See also Keane, Mary Nesta (Skrine)
See also INT 114

Keates, Jonathan 19(?)- .... **CLC 34**

Keaton, Buster 1895-1966 .... **CLC 20**

Keats, John
1795-1821 .... **NCLC 8; DA; DAB;**
DAC; PC 1; WLC
See also CDBLB 1789-1832; DAM MST,
POET; DLB 96, 110

Keene, Donald 1922- .... **CLC 34**
See also CA 1-4R; CANR 5

Keillor, Garrison .... **CLC 40**
See also Keillor, Gary (Edward)
See also AAYA 2; BEST 89:3; DLBY 87;
SATA 58

Keillor, Gary (Edward) 1942-
See Keillor, Garrison
See also CA 111; 117; CANR 36;
DAM POP; MTCW

Keith, Michael
See Hubbard, L(afayette) Ron(ald)

Keller, Gottfried 1819-1890 ...... **NCLC 2**
See also DLB 129

Kellerman, Jonathan 1949- .... **CLC 44**
See also BEST 90:1; CA 106; CANR 29, 51;
DAM POP; INT CANR-29

Kelley, William Melvin 1937- ...... **CLC 22**
See also BW 1; CA 77-80; CANR 27;
DLB 33

Kellogg, Marjorie 1922- .... **CLC 2**
See also CA 81-84

Kellow, Kathleen
See Hibbert, Eleanor Alice Burford

Kelly, M(ilton) T(erry) 1947- ...... **CLC 55**
See also CA 97-100; CAAS 22; CANR 19,
43

Kelman, James 1946- .... **CLC 58, 86**
See also CA 148

Kemal, Yashar 1923- .... **CLC 14, 29**
See also CA 89-92; CANR 44

Kemble, Fanny 1809-1893 .... **NCLC 18**
See also DLB 32

Kemelman, Harry 1908- .... **CLC 2**
See also AITN 1; CA 9-12R; CANR 6;
DLB 28

Kempe, Margery 1373(?)-1440(?) ..... **LC 6**
See also DLB 146

Kempis, Thomas a 1380-1471 .... **LC 11**

Kendall, Henry 1839-1882 .... **NCLC 12**

Keneally, Thomas (Michael)
1935- ..... **CLC 5, 8, 10, 14, 19, 27, 43**
See also CA 85-88; CANR 10, 50;
DAM NOV; MTCW

Kennedy, Adrienne (Lita)
1931- .... **CLC 66; BLC; DC 5**
See also BW 2; CA 103; CAAS 20; CABS 3;
CANR 26, 53; DAM MULT; DLB 38

Kennedy, John Pendleton
1795-1870 .... **NCLC 2**
See also DLB 3

Kennedy, Joseph Charles 1929-
See Kennedy, X. J.
See also CA 1-4R; CANR 4, 30, 40;
SATA 14, 86

Kennedy, William 1928-... **CLC 6, 28, 34, 53**
See also AAYA 1; CA 85-88; CANR 14,
31; DAM NOV; DLB 143; DLBY 85;
INT CANR-31; MTCW; SATA 57

Kennedy, X. J. .... **CLC 8, 42**
See also Kennedy, Joseph Charles
See also CAAS 9; CLR 27; DLB 5;
SAAS 22

Kenny, Maurice (Francis) 1929-.... **CLC 87**
See also CA 144; CAAS 22; DAM MULT;
NNAL

Kent, Kelvin
See Kuttner, Henry

Kenton, Maxwell
See Southern, Terry

Kenyon, Robert O.
See Kuttner, Henry

Kerouac, Jack ..... **CLC 1, 2, 3, 5, 14, 29, 61**
See also Kerouac, Jean-Louis Lebris de
See also CDALB 1941-1968; DLB 2, 16;
DLBD 3; DLBY 95

Kerouac, Jean-Louis Lebris de 1922-1969
See Kerouac, Jack
See also AITN 1; CA 5-8R; 25-28R;
CANR 26; DA; DAB; DAC; DAM MST,
NOV, POET, POP; MTCW; WLC

Kerr, Jean 1923-.................. **CLC 22**
See also CA 5-8R; CANR 7; INT CANR-7

Kerr, M. E. .... **CLC 12, 35**
See also Meaker, Marijane (Agnes)
See also AAYA 2; CLR 29; SAAS 1

Kerr, Robert .... **CLC 55**

Kerrigan, (Thomas) Anthony
1918- .... **CLC 4, 6**
See also CA 49-52; CAAS 11; CANR 4

Kerry, Lois
See Duncan, Lois

Kesey, Ken (Elton)
1935- ...... **CLC 1, 3, 6, 11, 46, 64; DA;**
DAB; DAC; WLC
See also CA 1-4R; CANR 22, 38;
CDALB 1968-1988; DAM MST, NOV,
POP; DLB 2, 16; MTCW; SATA 66

Kesselring, Joseph (Otto)
1902-1967 .... **CLC 45**
See also CA 150; DAM DRAM, MST

Kessler, Jascha (Frederick) 1929-.... **CLC 4**
See also CA 17-20R; CANR 8, 48

Kettelkamp, Larry (Dale) 1933- .... **CLC 12**
See also CA 29-32R; CANR 16; SAAS 3;
SATA 2

Key, Ellen 1849-1926 .... **TCLC 65**

Keyber, Conny
See Fielding, Henry

Keyes, Daniel 1927-.... **CLC 80; DA; DAC**
See also CA 17-20R; CANR 10, 26;
DAM MST, NOV; SATA 37

Keynes, John Maynard
1883-1946 .... **TCLC 64**
See also CA 114; DLBD 10

Khanshendel, Chiron
See Rose, Wendy

Khayyam, Omar
1048-1131 .... **CMLC 11; PC 8**
See also DAM POET

Kherdian, David 1931-............ **CLC 6, 9**
See also CA 21-24R; CAAS 2; CANR 39;
CLR 24; JRDA; MAICYA; SATA 16, 74

Khlebnikov, Velimir .... **TCLC 20**
See also Khlebnikov, Viktor Vladimirovich

Khlebnikov, Viktor Vladimirovich 1885-1922
See Khlebnikov, Velimir
See also CA 117

Khodasevich, Vladislav (Felitsianovich)
1886-1939 .... **TCLC 15**
See also CA 115

Kielland, Alexander Lange
1849-1906 .... **TCLC 5**
See also CA 104

Kiely, Benedict 1919-.......... **CLC 23, 43**
See also CA 1-4R; CANR 2; DLB 15

Kienzle, William X(avier) 1928-.... **CLC 25**
See also CA 93-96; CAAS 1; CANR 9, 31;
DAM POP; INT CANR-31; MTCW

Kierkegaard, Soren 1813-1855.... **NCLC 34**

Killens, John Oliver 1916-1987..... **CLC 10**
See also BW 2; CA 77-80; 123; CAAS 2;
CANR 26; DLB 33

Killigrew, Anne 1660-1685........... **LC 4**
See also DLB 131

Kim
See Simenon, Georges (Jacques Christian)

Kincaid, Jamaica 1949- ... **CLC 43, 68; BLC**
See also AAYA 13; BW 2; CA 125;
CANR 47; DAM MULT, NOV;
DLB 157

King, Francis (Henry) 1923- ..... **CLC 8, 53**
See also CA 1-4R; CANR 1, 33;
DAM NOV; DLB 15, 139; MTCW

King, Martin Luther, Jr.
1929-1968 .... **CLC 83; BLC; DA; DAB;**
DAC
See also BW 2; CA 25-28; CANR 27, 44;
CAP 2; DAM MST, MULT; MTCW;
SATA 14

King, Stephen (Edwin)
1947- .... **CLC 12, 26, 37, 61; SSC 17**
See also AAYA 1, 17; BEST 90:1;
CA 61-64; CANR 1, 30, 52; DAM NOV,
POP; DLB 143; DLBY 80; JRDA;
MTCW; SATA 9, 55

King, Steve
See King, Stephen (Edwin)

King, Thomas 1943-......... **CLC 89; DAC**
See also CA 144; DAM MULT; NNAL

Lee, Willy
See Burroughs, William S(eward)

Lee-Hamilton, Eugene (Jacob)
1845-1907 . . . . **TCLC 22**
See also CA 117

Leet, Judith 1935- . . . . **CLC 11**

Le Fanu, Joseph Sheridan
1814-1873 . . . . **NCLC 9; SSC 14**
See also DAM POP; DLB 21, 70, 159

Leffland, Ella 1931- . . . . **CLC 19**
See also CA 29-32R; CANR 35; DLBY 84;
INT CANR-35; SATA 65

Leger, Alexis
See Leger, (Marie-Rene Auguste) Alexis
Saint-Leger

Leger, (Marie-Rene Auguste) Alexis
Saint-Leger 1887-1975. . . . . . . **CLC 11**
See also Perse, St.-John
See also CA 13-16R; 61-64; CANR 43;
DAM POET; MTCW

Leger, Saintleger
See Leger, (Marie-Rene Auguste) Alexis
Saint-Leger

Le Guin, Ursula K(roeber)
1929- . . . . . . **CLC 8, 13, 22, 45, 71; DAB;**
DAC; SSC 12
See also AAYA 9; AITN 1; CA 21-24R;
CANR 9, 32, 52; CDALB 1968-1988;
CLR 3, 28; DAM MST, POP; DLB 8, 52;
INT CANR-32; JRDA; MAICYA;
MTCW; SATA 4, 52

Lehmann, Rosamond (Nina)
1901-1990 . . . . **CLC 5**
See also CA 77-80; 131; CANR 8; DLB 15

Leiber, Fritz (Reuter, Jr.)
1910-1992 . . . . **CLC 25**
See also CA 45-48; 139; CANR 2, 40;
DLB 8; MTCW; SATA 45;
SATA-Obit 73

Leimbach, Martha 1963-
See Leimbach, Marti
See also CA 130

Leimbach, Marti . . . . **CLC 65**
See also Leimbach, Martha

Leino, Eino . . . . **TCLC 24**
See also Loennbohm, Armas Eino Leopold

Leiris, Michel (Julien) 1901-1990 . . . **CLC 61**
See also CA 119; 128; 132

Leithauser, Brad 1953- . . . . **CLC 27**
See also CA 107; CANR 27; DLB 120

Lelchuk, Alan 1938- . . . . **CLC 5**
See also CA 45-48; CAAS 20; CANR 1

Lem, Stanislaw 1921- . . . . **CLC 8, 15, 40**
See also CA 105; CAAS 1; CANR 32;
MTCW

Lemann, Nancy 1956- . . . . **CLC 39**
See also CA 118; 136

Lemonnier, (Antoine Louis) Camille
1844-1913 . . . . **TCLC 22**
See also CA 121

Lenau, Nikolaus 1802-1850 . . . . . . **NCLC 16**

L'Engle, Madeleine (Camp Franklin)
1918- . . . . **CLC 12**
See also AAYA 1; AITN 2; CA 1-4R;
CANR 3, 21, 39; CLR 1, 14; DAM POP;
DLB 52; JRDA; MAICYA; MTCW;
SAAS 15; SATA 1, 27, 75

Lengyel, Jozsef 1896-1975. . . . . **CLC 7**
See also CA 85-88; 57-60

Lennon, John (Ono)
1940-1980 . . . . **CLC 12, 35**
See also CA 102

Lennox, Charlotte Ramsay
1729(?)-1804 . . . . **NCLC 23**
See also DLB 39

Lentricchia, Frank (Jr.) 1940- . . . . . . **CLC 34**
See also CA 25-28R; CANR 19

Lenz, Siegfried 1926- . . . . **CLC 27**
See also CA 89-92; DLB 75

Leonard, Elmore (John, Jr.)
1925- . . . . **CLC 28, 34, 71**
See also AITN 1; BEST 89:1, 90:4;
CA 81-84; CANR 12, 28, 53; DAM POP;
INT CANR-28; MTCW

Leonard, Hugh. . . . . **CLC 19**
See also Byrne, John Keyes
See also DLB 13

Leonov, Leonid (Maximovich)
1899-1994 . . . . **CLC 92**
See also CA 129; DAM NOV; MTCW

Leopardi, (Conte) Giacomo
1798-1837 . . . . **NCLC 22**

Le Reveler
See Artaud, Antonin (Marie Joseph)

Lerman, Eleanor 1952- . . . . **CLC 9**
See also CA 85-88

Lerman, Rhoda 1936- . . . . **CLC 56**
See also CA 49-52

Lermontov, Mikhail Yuryevich
1814-1841 . . . . **NCLC 47**

Leroux, Gaston 1868-1927 . . . . **TCLC 25**
See also CA 108; 136; SATA 65

Lesage, Alain-Rene 1668-1747 . . . . . . **LC 28**

Leskov, Nikolai (Semyonovich)
1831-1895 . . . . **NCLC 25**

Lessing, Doris (May)
1919- . . . . . **CLC 1, 2, 3, 6, 10, 15, 22, 40,**
94; DA; DAB; DAC; SSC 6
See also CA 9-12R; CAAS 14; CANR 33;
CDBLB 1960 to Present; DAM MST,
NOV; DLB 15, 139; DLBY 85; MTCW

Lessing, Gotthold Ephraim
1729-1781 . . . . **LC 8**
See also DLB 97

Lester, Richard 1932- . . . . **CLC 20**

Lever, Charles (James)
1806-1872 . . . . **NCLC 23**
See also DLB 21

Leverson, Ada 1865(?)-1936(?) . . . . **TCLC 18**
See also Elaine
See also CA 117; DLB 153

Levertov, Denise
1923- . . . . . . **CLC 1, 2, 3, 5, 8, 15, 28, 66;**
PC 11
See also CA 1-4R; CAAS 19; CANR 3, 29,
50; DAM POET; DLB 5, 165;
INT CANR-29; MTCW

Levi, Jonathan. . . . . **CLC 76**

Levi, Peter (Chad Tigar) 1931- . . . . . **CLC 41**
See also CA 5-8R; CANR 34; DLB 40

Levi, Primo
1919-1987 . . . . **CLC 37, 50; SSC 12**
See also CA 13-16R; 122; CANR 12, 33;
MTCW

Levin, Ira 1929- . . . . **CLC 3, 6**
See also CA 21-24R; CANR 17, 44;
DAM POP; MTCW; SATA 66

Levin, Meyer 1905-1981 . . . . **CLC 7**
See also AITN 1; CA 9-12R; 104;
CANR 15; DAM POP; DLB 9, 28;
DLBY 81; SATA 21; SATA-Obit 27

Levine, Norman 1924- . . . . **CLC 54**
See also CA 73-76; CAAS 23; CANR 14;
DLB 88

Levine, Philip 1928-. . **CLC 2, 4, 5, 9, 14, 33**
See also CA 9-12R; CANR 9, 37, 52;
DAM POET; DLB 5

Levinson, Deirdre 1931-. . . . . **CLC 49**
See also CA 73-76

Levi-Strauss, Claude 1908- . . . . **CLC 38**
See also CA 1-4R; CANR 6, 32; MTCW

Levitin, Sonia (Wolff) 1934- . . . . **CLC 17**
See also AAYA 13; CA 29-32R; CANR 14,
32; JRDA; MAICYA; SAAS 2; SATA 4,
68

Levon, O. U.
See Kesey, Ken (Elton)

Lewes, George Henry
1817-1878 . . . . **NCLC 25**
See also DLB 55, 144

Lewis, Alun 1915-1944. . . . . **TCLC 3**
See also CA 104; DLB 20, 162

Lewis, C. Day
See Day Lewis, C(ecil)

Lewis, C(live) S(taples)
1898-1963 . . . . . **CLC 1, 3, 6, 14, 27; DA;**
DAB; DAC; WLC
See also AAYA 3; CA 81-84; CANR 33;
CDBLB 1945-1960; CLR 3, 27;
DAM MST, NOV, POP; DLB 15, 100,
160; JRDA; MAICYA; MTCW;
SATA 13

Lewis, Janet 1899- . . . . **CLC 41**
See also Winters, Janet Lewis
See also CA 9-12R; CANR 29; CAP 1;
DLBY 87

Lewis, Matthew Gregory
1775-1818 . . . . **NCLC 11**
See also DLB 39, 158

Lewis, (Harry) Sinclair
1885-1951 . . . . . **TCLC 4, 13, 23, 39; DA;**
DAB; DAC; WLC
See also CA 104; 133; CDALB 1917-1929;
DAM MST, NOV; DLB 9, 102; DLBD 1;
MTCW

Lewis, (Percy) Wyndham
1884(?)-1957 . . . . TCLC 2, 9
See also CA 104; DLB 15

Lewisohn, Ludwig 1883-1955. . . . . . TCLC 19
See also CA 107; DLB 4, 9, 28, 102

Leyner, Mark 1956- . . . . CLC 92
See also CA 110; CANR 28, 53

Lezama Lima, Jose 1910-1976 . . . CLC 4, 10
See also CA 77-80; DAM MULT;
DLB 113; HW

L'Heureux, John (Clarke) 1934- . . . . CLC 52
See also CA 13-16R; CANR 23, 45

Liddell, C. H.
See Kuttner, Henry

Lie, Jonas (Lauritz Idemil)
1833-1908(?) . . . . TCLC 5
See also CA 115

Lieber, Joel 1937-1971. . . . . CLC 6
See also CA 73-76; 29-32R

Lieber, Stanley Martin
See Lee, Stan

Lieberman, Laurence (James)
1935- . . . . CLC 4, 36
See also CA 17-20R; CANR 8, 36

Lieksman, Anders
See Haavikko, Paavo Juhani

Li Fei-kan 1904-
See Pa Chin
See also CA 105

Lifton, Robert Jay 1926- . . . . CLC 67
See also CA 17-20R; CANR 27;
INT CANR-27; SATA 66

Lightfoot, Gordon 1938- . . . . CLC 26
See also CA 109

Lightman, Alan P. 1948- . . . . CLC 81
See also CA 141

Ligotti, Thomas (Robert)
1953- . . . . CLC 44; SSC 16
See also CA 123; CANR 49

Li Ho 791-817. . . . . PC 13

Liliencron, (Friedrich Adolf Axel) Detlev von
1844-1909 . . . . TCLC 18
See also CA 117

Lilly, William 1602-1681 . . . . LC 27

Lima, Jose Lezama
See Lezama Lima, Jose

Lima Barreto, Afonso Henrique de
1881-1922 . . . . TCLC 23
See also CA 117

Limonov, Edward 1944- . . . . CLC 67
See also CA 137

Lin, Frank
See Atherton, Gertrude (Franklin Horn)

Lincoln, Abraham 1809-1865 . . . . . NCLC 18

Lind, Jakov . . . . CLC 1, 2, 4, 27, 82
See Landwirth, Heinz
See also CAAS 4

Lindbergh, Anne (Spencer) Morrow
1906- . . . . CLC 82
See also CA 17-20R; CANR 16;
DAM NOV; MTCW; SATA 33

Lindsay, David 1878-1945 . . . . TCLC 15
See also CA 113

Lindsay, (Nicholas) Vachel
1879-1931 . . . TCLC 17; DA; DAC; WLC
See also CA 114; 135; CDALB 1865-1917;
DAM MST, POET; DLB 54; SATA 40

Linke-Poot
See Doeblin, Alfred

Linney, Romulus 1930- . . . . CLC 51
See also CA 1-4R; CANR 40, 44

Linton, Eliza Lynn 1822-1898. . . . NCLC 41
See also DLB 18

Li Po 701-763 . . . . CMLC 2

Lipsius, Justus 1547-1606 . . . . LC 16

Lipsyte, Robert (Michael)
1938- . . . . CLC 21; DA; DAC
See also AAYA 7; CA 17-20R; CANR 8;
CLR 23; DAM MST, NOV; JRDA;
MAICYA; SATA 5, 68

Lish, Gordon (Jay) 1934- . . CLC 45; SSC 18
See also CA 113; 117; DLB 130; INT 117

Lispector, Clarice 1925-1977 . . . . . . CLC 43
See also CA 139; 116; DLB 113

Littell, Robert 1935(?)- . . . . CLC 42
See also CA 109; 112

Little, Malcolm 1925-1965
See Malcolm X
See also BW 1; CA 125; 111; DA; DAB;
DAC; DAM MST, MULT; MTCW

Littlewit, Humphrey Gent.
See Lovecraft, H(oward) P(hillips)

Litwos
See Sienkiewicz, Henryk (Adam Alexander
Pius)

Liu E 1857-1909 . . . . TCLC 15
See also CA 115

Lively, Penelope (Margaret)
1933- . . . . CLC 32, 50
See also CA 41-44R; CANR 29; CLR 7;
DAM NOV; DLB 14, 161; JRDA;
MAICYA; MTCW; SATA 7, 60

Livesay, Dorothy (Kathleen)
1909- . . . . CLC 4, 15, 79; DAC
See also AITN 2; CA 25-28R; CAAS 8;
CANR 36; DAM MST, POET; DLB 68;
MTCW

Livy c. 59B.C.-c. 17 . . . . CMLC 11

Lizardi, Jose Joaquin Fernandez de
1776-1827 . . . . NCLC 30

Llewellyn, Richard
See Llewellyn Lloyd, Richard Dafydd
Vivian
See also DLB 15

Llewellyn Lloyd, Richard Dafydd Vivian
1906-1983 . . . . CLC 7, 80
See Llewellyn, Richard
See also CA 53-56; 111; CANR 7;
SATA 11; SATA-Obit 37

Llosa, (Jorge) Mario (Pedro) Vargas
See Vargas Llosa, (Jorge) Mario (Pedro)

Lloyd Webber, Andrew 1948-
See Webber, Andrew Lloyd
See also AAYA 1; CA 116; 149;
DAM DRAM; SATA 56

Llull, Ramon c. 1235-c. 1316 . . . . . CMLC 12

Locke, Alain (Le Roy)
1886-1954 . . . . TCLC 43
See also BW 1; CA 106; 124; DLB 51

Locke, John 1632-1704 . . . . LC 7
See also DLB 101

Locke-Elliott, Sumner
See Elliott, Sumner Locke

Lockhart, John Gibson
1794-1854 . . . . NCLC 6
See also DLB 110, 116, 144

Lodge, David (John) 1935- . . . . CLC 36
See also BEST 90:1; CA 17-20R; CANR 19,
53; DAM POP; DLB 14; INT CANR-19;
MTCW

Loennbohm, Armas Eino Leopold 1878-1926
See Leino, Eino
See also CA 123

Loewinsohn, Ron(ald William)
1937- . . . . CLC 52
See also CA 25-28R

Logan, Jake
See Smith, Martin Cruz

Logan, John (Burton) 1923-1987 . . . . . CLC 5
See also CA 77-80; 124; CANR 45; DLB 5

Lo Kuan-chung 1330(?)-1400(?) . . . . . . LC 12

Lombard, Nap
See Johnson, Pamela Hansford

London, Jack . . TCLC 9, 15, 39; SSC 4; WLC
See also London, John Griffith
See also AAYA 13; AITN 2;
CDALB 1865-1917; DLB 8, 12, 78;
SATA 18

London, John Griffith 1876-1916
See London, Jack
See also CA 110; 119; DA; DAB; DAC;
DAM MST, NOV; JRDA; MAICYA;
MTCW

Long, Emmett
See Leonard, Elmore (John, Jr.)

Longbaugh, Harry
See Goldman, William (W.)

Longfellow, Henry Wadsworth
1807-1882 . . . . . NCLC 2, 45; DA; DAB;
DAC
See also CDALB 1640-1865; DAM MST,
POET; DLB 1, 59; SATA 19

Longley, Michael 1939- . . . . CLC 29
See also CA 102; DLB 40

Longus fl. c. 2nd cent. - . . . . CMLC 7

Longway, A. Hugh
See Lang, Andrew

Lonnrot, Elias 1802-1884 . . . . NCLC 53

Lopate, Phillip 1943- . . . . CLC 29
See also CA 97-100; DLBY 80; INT 97-100

Lopez Portillo (y Pacheco), Jose
1920- . . . . CLC 46
See also CA 129; HW

Lopez y Fuentes, Gregorio
1897(?)-1966 . . . . CLC 32
See also CA 131; HW

Lorca, Federico Garcia
See Garcia Lorca, Federico

Maniere, J.-E.
  See Giraudoux, (Hippolyte) Jean

Manley, (Mary) Delariviere
      1672(?)-1724 . . . . LC 1
  See also DLB 39, 80

Mann, Abel
  See Creasey, John

Mann, (Luiz) Heinrich   1871-1950. . . TCLC 9
  See also CA 106; DLB 66

Mann, (Paul) Thomas
      1875-1955 . . . . TCLC 2, 8, 14, 21, 35, 44,
                        60; DA; DAB; DAC; SSC 5; WLC
  See also CA 104; 128; DAM MST, NOV;
      DLB 66; MTCW

Mannheim, Karl   1893-1947 . . . . . . TCLC 65

Manning, David
  See Faust, Frederick (Schiller)

Manning, Frederic   1887(?)-1935 . . . TCLC 25
  See also CA 124

Manning, Olivia   1915-1980 . . . . . . CLC 5, 19
  See also CA 5-8R; 101; CANR 29; MTCW

Mano, D. Keith   1942- . . . . CLC 2, 10
  See also CA 25-28R; CAAS 6; CANR 26;
      DLB 6

Mansfield, Katherine
      . . TCLC 2, 8, 39; DAB; SSC 9, 23; WLC
  See also Beauchamp, Kathleen Mansfield
  See also DLB 162

Manso, Peter   1940- . . . . CLC 39
  See also CA 29-32R; CANR 44

Mantecon, Juan Jimenez
  See Jimenez (Mantecon), Juan Ramon

Manton, Peter
  See Creasey, John

Man Without a Spleen, A
  See Chekhov, Anton (Pavlovich)

Manzoni, Alessandro   1785-1873 . . NCLC 29

Mapu, Abraham (ben Jekutiel)
      1808-1867 . . . . NCLC 18

Mara, Sally
  See Queneau, Raymond

Marat, Jean Paul   1743-1793 . . . . LC 10

Marcel, Gabriel Honore
      1889-1973 . . . . CLC 15
  See also CA 102; 45-48; MTCW

Marchbanks, Samuel
  See Davies, (William) Robertson

Marchi, Giacomo
  See Bassani, Giorgio

Margulies, Donald. . . . . CLC 76

Marie de France   c. 12th cent. -. . . . CMLC 8

Marie de l'Incarnation   1599-1672 . . . . LC 10

Mariner, Scott
  See Pohl, Frederik

Marinetti, Filippo Tommaso
      1876-1944 . . . . TCLC 10
  See also CA 107; DLB 114

Marivaux, Pierre Carlet de Chamblain de
      1688-1763 . . . . LC 4

Markandaya, Kamala . . . . CLC 8, 38
  See also Taylor, Kamala (Purnaiya)

Markfield, Wallace   1926- . . . . CLC 8
  See also CA 69-72; CAAS 3; DLB 2, 28

Markham, Edwin   1852-1940 . . . . . TCLC 47
  See also DLB 54

Markham, Robert
  See Amis, Kingsley (William)

Marks, J
  See Highwater, Jamake (Mamake)

Marks-Highwater, J
  See Highwater, Jamake (Mamake)

Markson, David M(errill)   1927- . . . . CLC 67
  See also CA 49-52; CANR 1

Marley, Bob. CLC 17
  See also Marley, Robert Nesta

Marley, Robert Nesta   1945-1981
  See Marley, Bob
  See also CA 107; 103

Marlowe, Christopher
      1564-1593 . . . . . LC 22; DA; DAB; DAC;
                          DC 1; WLC
  See also CDBLB Before 1660;
      DAM DRAM, MST; DLB 62

Marmontel, Jean-Francois
      1723-1799 . . . . LC 2

Marquand, John P(hillips)
      1893-1960 . . . . CLC 2, 10
  See also CA 85-88; DLB 9, 102

Marquez, Gabriel (Jose) Garcia
  See Garcia Marquez, Gabriel (Jose)

Marquis, Don(ald Robert Perry)
      1878-1937 . . . . TCLC 7
  See also CA 104; DLB 11, 25

Marric, J. J.
  See Creasey, John

Marrow, Bernard
  See Moore, Brian

Marryat, Frederick   1792-1848 . . . . NCLC 3
  See also DLB 21, 163

Marsden, James
  See Creasey, John

Marsh, (Edith) Ngaio
      1899-1982 . . . . CLC 7, 53
  See also CA 9-12R; CANR 6; DAM POP;
      DLB 77; MTCW

Marshall, Garry   1934- . . . . CLC 17
  See also AAYA 3; CA 111; SATA 60

Marshall, Paule
      1929- . . . . CLC 27, 72; BLC; SSC 3
  See also BW 2; CA 77-80; CANR 25;
      DAM MULT; DLB 157; MTCW

Marsten, Richard
  See Hunter, Evan

Marston, John   1576-1634 . . . . LC 33
  See also DAM DRAM; DLB 58

Martha, Henry
  See Harris, Mark

Martial   c. 40-c. 104 . . . . PC 10

Martin, Ken
  See Hubbard, L(afayette) Ron(ald)

Martin, Richard
  See Creasey, John

Martin, Steve   1945- . . . . CLC 30
  See also CA 97-100; CANR 30; MTCW

Martin, Valerie   1948- . . . . CLC 89
  See also BEST 90:2; CA 85-88; CANR 49

Martin, Violet Florence
      1862-1915 . . . . TCLC 51

Martin, Webber
  See Silverberg, Robert

Martindale, Patrick Victor
  See White, Patrick (Victor Martindale)

Martin du Gard, Roger
      1881-1958 . . . . TCLC 24
  See also CA 118; DLB 65

Martineau, Harriet   1802-1876. . . . NCLC 26
  See also DLB 21, 55, 159, 163, 166;
      YABC 2

Martines, Julia
  See O'Faolain, Julia

Martinez, Jacinto Benavente y
  See Benavente (y Martinez), Jacinto

Martinez Ruiz, Jose   1873-1967
  See Azorin; Ruiz, Jose Martinez
  See also CA 93-96; HW

Martinez Sierra, Gregorio
      1881-1947 . . . . TCLC 6
  See also CA 115

Martinez Sierra, Maria (de la O'LeJarraga)
      1874-1974 . . . . TCLC 6
  See also CA 115

Martinsen, Martin
  See Follett, Ken(neth Martin)

Martinson, Harry (Edmund)
      1904-1978 . . . . CLC 14
  See also CA 77-80; CANR 34

Marut, Ret
  See Traven, B.

Marut, Robert
  See Traven, B.

Marvell, Andrew
      1621-1678 . . . . . . LC 4; DA; DAB; DAC;
                           PC 10; WLC
  See also CDBLB 1660-1789; DAM MST,
      POET; DLB 131

Marx, Karl (Heinrich)
      1818-1883 . . . . NCLC 17
  See also DLB 129

Masaoka Shiki. . . . . TCLC 18
  See also Masaoka Tsunenori

Masaoka Tsunenori   1867-1902
  See Masaoka Shiki
  See also CA 117

Masefield, John (Edward)
      1878-1967 . . . . CLC 11, 47
  See also CA 19-20; 25-28R; CANR 33;
      CAP 2; CDBLB 1890-1914; DAM POET;
      DLB 10, 19, 153, 160; MTCW; SATA 19

Maso, Carole   19(?)- . . . . CLC 44

Mason, Bobbie Ann
      1940- . . . . CLC 28, 43, 82; SSC 4
  See also AAYA 5; CA 53-56; CANR 11,
      31; DLBY 87; INT CANR-31; MTCW

Mason, Ernst
  See Pohl, Frederik

Mason, Lee W.
  See Malzberg, Barry N(athaniel)

Mason, Nick   1945- . . . . CLC 35

Mason, Tally
  See Derleth, August (William)

Mass, William
See Gibson, William

Masters, Edgar Lee
1868-1950 ...... TCLC 2, 25; DA; DAC;
PC 1
See also CA 104; 133; CDALB 1865-1917;
DAM MST, POET; DLB 54; MTCW

Masters, Hilary 1928- .... CLC 48
See also CA 25-28R; CANR 13, 47

Mastrosimone, William 19(?)- ...... CLC 36

Mathe, Albert
See Camus, Albert

Matheson, Richard Burton 1926- ... CLC 37
See also CA 97-100; DLB 8, 44; INT 97-100

Mathews, Harry 1930- .... CLC 6, 52
See also CA 21-24R; CAAS 6; CANR 18,
40

Mathews, John Joseph 1894-1979... CLC 84
See also CA 19-20; 142; CANR 45; CAP 2;
DAM MULT; NNAL

Mathias, Roland (Glyn) 1915- ...... CLC 45
See also CA 97-100; CANR 19, 41; DLB 27

Matsuo Basho 1644-1694 .... PC 3
See also DAM POET

Mattheson, Rodney
See Creasey, John

Matthews, Greg 1949- .... CLC 45
See also CA 135

Matthews, William 1942- .... CLC 40
See also CA 29-32R; CAAS 18; CANR 12;
DLB 5

Matthias, John (Edward) 1941- ...... CLC 9
See also CA 33-36R

Matthiessen, Peter
1927- .... CLC 5, 7, 11, 32, 64
See also AAYA 6; BEST 90:4; CA 9-12R;
CANR 21, 50; DAM NOV; DLB 6;
MTCW; SATA 27

Maturin, Charles Robert
1780(?)-1824 .... NCLC 6

Matute (Ausejo), Ana Maria
1925- .... CLC 11
See also CA 89-92; MTCW

Maugham, W. S.
See Maugham, W(illiam) Somerset

Maugham, W(illiam) Somerset
1874-1965 .... CLC 1, 11, 15, 67, 93;
DA; DAB; DAC; SSC 8; WLC
See also CA 5-8R; 25-28R; CANR 40;
CDBLB 1914-1945; DAM DRAM, MST,
NOV; DLB 10, 36, 77, 100, 162; MTCW;
SATA 54

Maugham, William Somerset
See Maugham, W(illiam) Somerset

Maupassant, (Henri Rene Albert) Guy de
1850-1893 ..... NCLC 1, 42; DA; DAB;
DAC; SSC 1; WLC
See also DAM MST; DLB 123

Maupin, Armistead 1944- .... CLC 95
See also CA 125; 130; DAM POP; INT 130

Maurhut, Richard
See Traven, B.

Mauriac, Claude 1914- .... CLC 9
See also CA 89-92; DLB 83

Mauriac, Francois (Charles)
1885-1970 .... CLC 4, 9, 56
See also CA 25-28; CAP 2; DLB 65;
MTCW

Mavor, Osborne Henry 1888-1951
See Bridie, James
See also CA 104

Maxwell, William (Keepers, Jr.)
1908- .... CLC 19
See also CA 93-96; DLBY 80; INT 93-96

May, Elaine 1932- .... CLC 16
See also CA 124; 142; DLB 44

Mayakovski, Vladimir (Vladimirovich)
1893-1930 .... TCLC 4, 18
See also CA 104

Mayhew, Henry 1812-1887 ...... NCLC 31
See also DLB 18, 55

Mayle, Peter 1939(?)- .... CLC 89
See also CA 139

Maynard, Joyce 1953- .... CLC 23
See also CA 111; 129

Mayne, William (James Carter)
1928- .... CLC 12
See also CA 9-12R; CANR 37; CLR 25;
JRDA; MAICYA; SAAS 11; SATA 6, 68

Mayo, Jim
See L'Amour, Louis (Dearborn)

Maysles, Albert 1926- .... CLC 16
See also CA 29-32R

Maysles, David 1932- .... CLC 16

Mazer, Norma Fox 1931- .... CLC 26
See also AAYA 5; CA 69-72; CANR 12,
32; CLR 23; JRDA; MAICYA; SAAS 1;
SATA 24, 67

Mazzini, Guiseppe 1805-1872 .... NCLC 34

McAuley, James Phillip
1917-1976 .... CLC 45
See also CA 97-100

McBain, Ed
See Hunter, Evan

McBrien, William Augustine
1930- .... CLC 44
See also CA 107

McCaffrey, Anne (Inez) 1926- ...... CLC 17
See also AAYA 6; AITN 2; BEST 89:2;
CA 25-28R; CANR 15, 35; DAM NOV,
POP; DLB 8; JRDA; MAICYA; MTCW;
SAAS 11; SATA 8, 70

McCall, Nathan 1955(?)- .... CLC 86
See also CA 146

McCann, Arthur
See Campbell, John W(ood, Jr.)

McCann, Edson
See Pohl, Frederik

McCarthy, Charles, Jr. 1933-
See McCarthy, Cormac
See also CANR 42; DAM POP

McCarthy, Cormac 1933- ..... CLC 4, 57, 59
See also McCarthy, Charles, Jr.
See also DLB 6, 143

McCarthy, Mary (Therese)
1912-1989 ... CLC 1, 3, 5, 14, 24, 39, 59
See also CA 5-8R; 129; CANR 16, 50;
DLB 2; DLBY 81; INT CANR-16;
MTCW

McCartney, (James) Paul
1942- .... CLC 12, 35
See also CA 146

McCauley, Stephen (D.) 1955- ..... CLC 50
See also CA 141

McClure, Michael (Thomas)
1932- .... CLC 6, 10
See also CA 21-24R; CANR 17, 46;
DLB 16

McCorkle, Jill (Collins) 1958- ...... CLC 51
See also CA 121; DLBY 87

McCourt, James 1941- .... CLC 5
See also CA 57-60

McCoy, Horace (Stanley)
1897-1955 .... TCLC 28
See also CA 108; DLB 9

McCrae, John 1872-1918 .... TCLC 12
See also CA 109; DLB 92

McCreigh, James
See Pohl, Frederik

McCullers, (Lula) Carson (Smith)
1917-1967 .... CLC 1, 4, 10, 12, 48; DA;
DAB; DAC; SSC 9; WLC
See also CA 5-8R; 25-28R; CABS 1, 3;
CANR 18; CDALB 1941-1968;
DAM MST, NOV; DLB 2, 7; MTCW;
SATA 27

McCulloch, John Tyler
See Burroughs, Edgar Rice

McCullough, Colleen 1938(?)- ...... CLC 27
See also CA 81-84; CANR 17, 46;
DAM NOV, POP; MTCW

McDermott, Alice 1953- .... CLC 90
See also CA 109; CANR 40

McElroy, Joseph 1930- .... CLC 5, 47
See also CA 17-20R

McEwan, Ian (Russell) 1948- ... CLC 13, 66
See also BEST 90:4; CA 61-64; CANR 14,
41; DAM NOV; DLB 14; MTCW

McFadden, David 1940- .... CLC 48
See also CA 104; DLB 60; INT 104

McFarland, Dennis 1950- .... CLC 65

McGahern, John
1934- .... CLC 5, 9, 48; SSC 17
See also CA 17-20R; CANR 29; DLB 14;
MTCW

McGinley, Patrick (Anthony)
1937- .... CLC 41
See also CA 120; 127; INT 127

McGinley, Phyllis 1905-1978 ...... CLC 14
See also CA 9-12R; 77-80; CANR 19;
DLB 11, 48; SATA 2, 44; SATA-Obit 24

McGinniss, Joe 1942- .... CLC 32
See also AITN 2; BEST 89:2; CA 25-28R;
CANR 26; INT CANR-26

McGivern, Maureen Daly
See Daly, Maureen

McGrath, Patrick 1950- .... CLC 55
See also CA 136

McGrath, Thomas (Matthew)
1916-1990 .... CLC 28, 59
See also CA 9-12R; 132; CANR 6, 33;
DAM POET; MTCW; SATA 41;
SATA-Obit 66

McGuane, Thomas (Francis III)
1939- . . . . **CLC 3, 7, 18, 45**
See also AITN 2; CA 49-52; CANR 5, 24,
49; DLB 2; DLBY 80; INT CANR-24;
MTCW

McGuckian, Medbh 1950- . . . . **CLC 48**
See also CA 143; DAM POET; DLB 40

McHale, Tom 1942(?)-1982 . . . . . . **CLC 3, 5**
See also AITN 1; CA 77-80; 106

McIlvanney, William 1936- . . . . **CLC 42**
See also CA 25-28R; DLB 14

McIlwraith, Maureen Mollie Hunter
See Hunter, Mollie
See also SATA 2

McInerney, Jay 1955- . . . . **CLC 34**
See also AAYA 18; CA 116; 123;
CANR 45; DAM POP; INT 123

McIntyre, Vonda N(eel) 1948- . . . . . **CLC 18**
See also CA 81-84; CANR 17, 34; MTCW

McKay, Claude
. . . . **TCLC 7, 41; BLC; DAB; PC 2**
See also McKay, Festus Claudius
See also DLB 4, 45, 51, 117

McKay, Festus Claudius 1889-1948
See McKay, Claude
See also BW 1; CA 104; 124; DA; DAC;
DAM MST, MULT, NOV, POET;
MTCW; WLC

McKuen, Rod 1933- . . . . **CLC 1, 3**
See also AITN 1; CA 41-44R; CANR 40

McLoughlin, R. B.
See Mencken, H(enry) L(ouis)

McLuhan, (Herbert) Marshall
1911-1980 . . . . **CLC 37, 83**
See also CA 9-12R; 102; CANR 12, 34;
DLB 88; INT CANR-12; MTCW

McMillan, Terry (L.) 1951- . . . . **CLC 50, 61**
See also BW 2; CA 140; DAM MULT,
NOV, POP

McMurtry, Larry (Jeff)
1936- . . . . **CLC 2, 3, 7, 11, 27, 44**
See also AAYA 15; AITN 2; BEST 89:2;
CA 5-8R; CANR 19, 43;
CDALB 1968-1988; DAM NOV, POP;
DLB 2, 143; DLBY 80, 87; MTCW

McNally, T. M. 1961- . . . . **CLC 82**

McNally, Terrence 1939- . . . **CLC 4, 7, 41, 91**
See also CA 45-48; CANR 2;
DAM DRAM; DLB 7

McNamer, Deirdre 1950- . . . . **CLC 70**

McNeile, Herman Cyril 1888-1937
See Sapper
See also DLB 77

McNickle, (William) D'Arcy
1904-1977 . . . . **CLC 89**
See also CA 9-12R; 85-88; CANR 5, 45;
DAM MULT; NNAL; SATA-Obit 22

McPhee, John (Angus) 1931- . . . . . . **CLC 36**
See also BEST 90:1; CA 65-68; CANR 20,
46; MTCW

McPherson, James Alan
1943- . . . . **CLC 19, 77**
See also BW 1; CA 25-28R; CAAS 17;
CANR 24; DLB 38; MTCW

McPherson, William (Alexander)
1933- . . . . **CLC 34**
See also CA 69-72; CANR 28;
INT CANR-28

Mead, Margaret 1901-1978 . . . . **CLC 37**
See also AITN 1; CA 1-4R; 81-84;
CANR 4; MTCW; SATA-Obit 20

Meaker, Marijane (Agnes) 1927-
See Kerr, M. E.
See also CA 107; CANR 37; INT 107;
JRDA; MAICYA; MTCW; SATA 20, 61

Medoff, Mark (Howard) 1940- . . . **CLC 6, 23**
See also AITN 1; CA 53-56; CANR 5;
DAM DRAM; DLB 7; INT CANR-5

Medvedev, P. N.
See Bakhtin, Mikhail Mikhailovich

Meged, Aharon
See Megged, Aharon

Meged, Aron
See Megged, Aharon

Megged, Aharon 1920- . . . . **CLC 9**
See also CA 49-52; CAAS 13; CANR 1

Mehta, Ved (Parkash) 1934- . . . . **CLC 37**
See also CA 1-4R; CANR 2, 23; MTCW

Melanter
See Blackmore, R(ichard) D(oddridge)

Melikow, Loris
See Hofmannsthal, Hugo von

Melmoth, Sebastian
See Wilde, Oscar (Fingal O'Flahertie Wills)

Meltzer, Milton 1915- . . . . **CLC 26**
See also AAYA 8; CA 13-16R; CANR 38;
CLR 13; DLB 61; JRDA; MAICYA;
SAAS 1; SATA 1, 50, 80

Melville, Herman
1819-1891 . . . . . **NCLC 3, 12, 29, 45, 49;
DA; DAB; DAC; SSC 1, 17; WLC**
See also CDALB 1640-1865; DAM MST,
NOV; DLB 3, 74; SATA 59

Menander
c. 342B.C.-c. 292B.C. . . . . **CMLC 9; DC 3**
See also DAM DRAM

Mencken, H(enry) L(ouis)
1880-1956 . . . . **TCLC 13**
See also CA 105; 125; CDALB 1917-1929;
DLB 11, 29, 63, 137; MTCW

Mercer, David 1928-1980 . . . . **CLC 5**
See also CA 9-12R; 102; CANR 23;
DAM DRAM; DLB 13; MTCW

Merchant, Paul
See Ellison, Harlan (Jay)

Meredith, George 1828-1909 . . . **TCLC 17, 43**
See also CA 117; CDBLB 1832-1890;
DAM POET; DLB 18, 35, 57, 159

Meredith, William (Morris)
1919- . . . . **CLC 4, 13, 22, 55**
See also CA 9-12R; CAAS 14; CANR 6, 40;
DAM POET; DLB 5

Merezhkovsky, Dmitry Sergeyevich
1865-1941 . . . . **TCLC 29**

Merimee, Prosper
1803-1870 . . . . **NCLC 6; SSC 7**
See also DLB 119

Merkin, Daphne 1954- . . . . **CLC 44**
See also CA 123

Merlin, Arthur
See Blish, James (Benjamin)

Merrill, James (Ingram)
1926-1995 . . . . **CLC 2, 3, 6, 8, 13, 18, 34,
91**
See also CA 13-16R; 147; CANR 10, 49;
DAM POET; DLB 5, 165; DLBY 85;
INT CANR-10; MTCW

Merriman, Alex
See Silverberg, Robert

Merritt, E. B.
See Waddington, Miriam

Merton, Thomas
1915-1968 . . **CLC 1, 3, 11, 34, 83; PC 10**
See also CA 5-8R; 25-28R; CANR 22, 53;
DLB 48; DLBY 81; MTCW

Merwin, W(illiam) S(tanley)
1927- . . . **CLC 1, 2, 3, 5, 8, 13, 18, 45, 88**
See also CA 13-16R; CANR 15, 51;
DAM POET; DLB 5; INT CANR-15;
MTCW

Metcalf, John 1938- . . . . **CLC 37**
See also CA 113; DLB 60

Metcalf, Suzanne
See Baum, L(yman) Frank

Mew, Charlotte (Mary)
1870-1928 . . . . **TCLC 8**
See also CA 105; DLB 19, 135

Mewshaw, Michael 1943- . . . . **CLC 9**
See also CA 53-56; CANR 7, 47; DLBY 80

Meyer, June
See Jordan, June

Meyer, Lynn
See Slavitt, David R(ytman)

Meyer-Meyrink, Gustav 1868-1932
See Meyrink, Gustav
See also CA 117

Meyers, Jeffrey 1939- . . . . **CLC 39**
See also CA 73-76; DLB 111

Meynell, Alice (Christina Gertrude Thompson)
1847-1922 . . . . **TCLC 6**
See also CA 104; DLB 19, 98

Meyrink, Gustav . . . . **TCLC 21**
See also Meyer-Meyrink, Gustav
See also DLB 81

Michaels, Leonard
1933- . . . . **CLC 6, 25; SSC 16**
See also CA 61-64; CANR 21; DLB 130;
MTCW

Michaux, Henri 1899-1984 . . . . . . **CLC 8, 19**
See also CA 85-88; 114

Michelangelo 1475-1564 . . . . **LC 12**

Michelet, Jules 1798-1874 . . . . **NCLC 31**

Michener, James A(lbert)
1907(?)- . . . . **CLC 1, 5, 11, 29, 60**
See also AITN 1; BEST 90:1; CA 5-8R;
CANR 21, 45; DAM NOV, POP; DLB 6;
MTCW

Mickiewicz, Adam 1798-1855 . . . . . **NCLC 3**

Middleton, Christopher 1926- . . . . . . **CLC 13**
See also CA 13-16R; CANR 29; DLB 40

Middleton, Richard (Barham)
1882-1911 . . . . **TCLC 56**
See also DLB 156

Middleton, Stanley 1919-........ **CLC 7, 38**
See also CA 25-28R; CAAS 23; CANR 21,
46; DLB 14

Middleton, Thomas
1580-1627 .... **LC 33; DC 5**
See also DAM DRAM, MST; DLB 58

Migueis, Jose Rodrigues 1901-..... **CLC 10**

Mikszath, Kalman 1847-1910 ..... **TCLC 31**

Miles, Josephine
1911-1985 .... **CLC 1, 2, 14, 34, 39**
See also CA 1-4R; 116; CANR 2;
DAM POET; DLB 48

Militant
See Sandburg, Carl (August)

Mill, John Stuart 1806-1873 ..... **NCLC 11**
See also CDBLB 1832-1890; DLB 55

Millar, Kenneth 1915-1983 .... **CLC 14**
See also Macdonald, Ross
See also CA 9-12R; 110; CANR 16;
DAM POP; DLB 2; DLBD 6; DLBY 83;
MTCW

Millay, E. Vincent
See Millay, Edna St. Vincent

Millay, Edna St. Vincent
1892-1950 ...... **TCLC 4, 49; DA; DAB;
DAC; PC 6**
See also CA 104; 130; CDALB 1917-1929;
DAM MST, POET; DLB 45; MTCW

Miller, Arthur
1915- .... **CLC 1, 2, 6, 10, 15, 26, 47, 78;
DA; DAB; DAC; DC 1; WLC**
See also AAYA 15; AITN 1; CA 1-4R;
CABS 3; CANR 2, 30;
CDALB 1941-1968; DAM DRAM, MST;
DLB 7; MTCW

Miller, Henry (Valentine)
1891-1980 .... **CLC 1, 2, 4, 9, 14, 43, 84;
DA; DAB; DAC; WLC**
See also CA 9-12R; 97-100; CANR 33;
CDALB 1929-1941; DAM MST, NOV;
DLB 4, 9; DLBY 80; MTCW

Miller, Jason 1939(?)- .... **CLC 2**
See also AITN 1; CA 73-76; DLB 7

Miller, Sue 1943-................ **CLC 44**
See also BEST 90:3; CA 139; DAM POP;
DLB 143

Miller, Walter M(ichael, Jr.)
1923- .... **CLC 4, 30**
See also CA 85-88; DLB 8

Millett, Kate 1934-............... **CLC 67**
See also AITN 1; CA 73-76; CANR 32, 53;
MTCW

Millhauser, Steven 1943-....... **CLC 21, 54**
See also CA 110; 111; DLB 2; INT 111

Millin, Sarah Gertrude 1889-1968 .. **CLC 49**
See also CA 102; 93-96

Milne, A(lan) A(lexander)
1882-1956 .... **TCLC 6; DAB; DAC**
See also CA 104; 133; CLR 1, 26;
DAM MST; DLB 10, 77, 100, 160;
MAICYA; MTCW; YABC 1

Milner, Ron(ald) 1938-...... **CLC 56; BLC**
See also AITN 1; BW 1; CA 73-76;
CANR 24; DAM MULT; DLB 38;
MTCW

Milosz, Czeslaw
1911- ... **CLC 5, 11, 22, 31, 56, 82; PC 8**
See also CA 81-84; CANR 23, 51;
DAM MST, POET; MTCW

Milton, John
1608-1674 ...... **LC 9; DA; DAB; DAC;
WLC**
See also CDBLB 1660-1789; DAM MST,
POET; DLB 131, 151

Min, Anchee 1957-............... **CLC 86**
See also CA 146

Minehaha, Cornelius
See Wedekind, (Benjamin) Frank(lin)

Miner, Valerie 1947-............. **CLC 40**
See also CA 97-100

Minimo, Duca
See D'Annunzio, Gabriele

Minot, Susan 1956- .... **CLC 44**
See also CA 134

Minus, Ed 1938-................. **CLC 39**

Miranda, Javier
See Bioy Casares, Adolfo

Mirbeau, Octave 1848-1917....... **TCLC 55**
See also DLB 123

Miro (Ferrer), Gabriel (Francisco Victor)
1879-1930 .... **TCLC 5**
See also CA 104

Mishima, Yukio
...... **CLC 2, 4, 6, 9, 27; DC 1; SSC 4**
See also Hiraoka, Kimitake

Mistral, Frederic 1830-1914 ...... **TCLC 51**
See also CA 122

Mistral, Gabriela............ **TCLC 2; HLC**
See also Godoy Alcayaga, Lucila

Mistry, Rohinton 1952-...... **CLC 71; DAC**
See also CA 141

Mitchell, Clyde
See Ellison, Harlan (Jay); Silverberg, Robert

Mitchell, James Leslie 1901-1935
See Gibbon, Lewis Grassic
See also CA 104; DLB 15

Mitchell, Joni 1943-.............. **CLC 12**
See also CA 112

Mitchell, Margaret (Munnerlyn)
1900-1949 .... **TCLC 11**
See also CA 109; 125; DAM NOV, POP;
DLB 9; MTCW

Mitchell, Peggy
See Mitchell, Margaret (Munnerlyn)

Mitchell, S(ilas) Weir 1829-1914 .. **TCLC 36**

Mitchell, W(illiam) O(rmond)
1914- .... **CLC 25; DAC**
See also CA 77-80; CANR 15, 43;
DAM MST; DLB 88

Mitford, Mary Russell 1787-1855.. **NCLC 4**
See also DLB 110, 116

Mitford, Nancy 1904-1973........ **CLC 44**
See also CA 9-12R

Miyamoto, Yuriko 1899-1951 ..... **TCLC 37**

Mo, Timothy (Peter) 1950(?)-...... **CLC 46**
See also CA 117; MTCW

Modarressi, Taghi (M.) 1931-...... **CLC 44**
See also CA 121; 134; INT 134

Modiano, Patrick (Jean) 1945-..... **CLC 18**
See also CA 85-88; CANR 17, 40; DLB 83

Moerck, Paal
See Roelvaag, O(le) E(dvart)

Mofolo, Thomas (Mokopu)
1875(?)-1948 .... **TCLC 22; BLC**
See also CA 121; DAM MULT

Mohr, Nicholasa 1935-...... **CLC 12; HLC**
See also AAYA 8; CA 49-52; CANR 1, 32;
CLR 22; DAM MULT; DLB 145; HW;
JRDA; SAAS 8; SATA 8

Mojtabai, A(nn) G(race)
1938-.............. **CLC 5, 9, 15, 29**
See also CA 85-88

Moliere
1622-1673 ..... **LC 28; DA; DAB; DAC;
WLC**
See also DAM DRAM, MST

Molin, Charles
See Mayne, William (James Carter)

Molnar, Ferenc 1878-1952........ **TCLC 20**
See also CA 109; DAM DRAM

Momaday, N(avarre) Scott
1934- ..... **CLC 2, 19, 85, 95; DA; DAB;
DAC**
See also AAYA 11; CA 25-28R; CANR 14,
34; DAM MST, MULT, NOV, POP;
DLB 143; INT CANR-14; MTCW;
NNAL; SATA 48; SATA-Brief 30

Monette, Paul 1945-1995......... **CLC 82**
See also CA 139; 147

Monroe, Harriet 1860-1936....... **TCLC 12**
See also CA 109; DLB 54, 91

Monroe, Lyle
See Heinlein, Robert A(nson)

Montagu, Elizabeth 1917-........ **NCLC 7**
See also CA 9-12R

Montagu, Mary (Pierrepont) Wortley
1689-1762 .... **LC 9; PC 16**
See also DLB 95, 101

Montagu, W. H.
See Coleridge, Samuel Taylor

Montague, John (Patrick)
1929-.................... **CLC 13, 46**
See also CA 9-12R; CANR 9; DLB 40;
MTCW

Montaigne, Michel (Eyquem) de
1533-1592 ...... **LC 8; DA; DAB; DAC;
WLC**
See also DAM MST

Montale, Eugenio
1896-1981 .... **CLC 7, 9, 18; PC 13**
See also CA 17-20R; 104; CANR 30;
DLB 114; MTCW

Montesquieu, Charles-Louis de Secondat
1689-1755 .... **LC 7**

Montgomery, (Robert) Bruce 1921-1978
See Crispin, Edmund
See also CA 104

Montgomery, L(ucy) M(aud)
1874-1942 .... **TCLC 51; DAC**
See also AAYA 12; CA 108; 137; CLR 8;
DAM MST; DLB 92; JRDA; MAICYA;
YABC 1

Newman, Edwin (Harold) 1919- .... CLC 14
See also AITN 1; CA 69-72; CANR 5

Newman, John Henry
1801-1890 .... NCLC 38
See also DLB 18, 32, 55

Newton, Suzanne 1936- .... CLC 35
See also CA 41-44R; CANR 14; JRDA;
SATA 5, 77

Nexo, Martin Andersen
1869-1954 .... TCLC 43

Nezval, Vitezslav 1900-1958 ...... TCLC 44
See also CA 123

Ng, Fae Myenne 1957(?)- .... CLC 81
See also CA 146

Ngema, Mbongeni 1955- .... CLC 57
See also BW 2; CA 143

Ngugi, James T(hiong'o) .... CLC 3, 7, 13
See also Ngugi wa Thiong'o

Ngugi wa Thiong'o 1938- ...... CLC 36; BLC
See also Ngugi, James T(hiong'o)
See also BW 2; CA 81-84; CANR 27;
DAM MULT, NOV; DLB 125; MTCW

Nichol, B(arrie) P(hillip)
1944-1988 .... CLC 18
See also CA 53-56; DLB 53; SATA 66

Nichols, John (Treadwell) 1940- .... CLC 38
See also CA 9-12R; CAAS 2; CANR 6;
DLBY 82

Nichols, Leigh
See Koontz, Dean R(ay)

Nichols, Peter (Richard)
1927- .... CLC 5, 36, 65
See also CA 104; CANR 33; DLB 13;
MTCW

Nicolas, F. R. E.
See Freeling, Nicolas

Niedecker, Lorine 1903-1970. ... CLC 10, 42
See also CA 25-28; CAP 2; DAM POET;
DLB 48

Nietzsche, Friedrich (Wilhelm)
1844-1900 .... TCLC 10, 18, 55
See also CA 107; 121; DLB 129

Nievo, Ippolito 1831-1861 .... NCLC 22

Nightingale, Anne Redmon 1943-
See Redmon, Anne
See also CA 103

Nik. T. O.
See Annensky, Innokenty Fyodorovich

Nin, Anais
1903-1977 ...... CLC 1, 4, 8, 11, 14, 60;
SSC 10
See also AITN 2; CA 13-16R; 69-72;
CANR 22, 53; DAM NOV, POP; DLB 2,
4, 152; MTCW

Nishiwaki, Junzaburo 1894-1982 .... PC 15
See also CA 107

Nissenson, Hugh 1933- .... CLC 4, 9
See also CA 17-20R; CANR 27; DLB 28

Niven, Larry .... CLC 8
See also Niven, Laurence Van Cott
See also DLB 8

Niven, Laurence Van Cott 1938-
See Niven, Larry
See also CA 21-24R; CAAS 12; CANR 14,
44; DAM POP; MTCW

Nixon, Agnes Eckhardt 1927- ...... CLC 21
See also CA 110

Nizan, Paul 1905-1940 .... TCLC 40
See also DLB 72

Nkosi, Lewis 1936- .... CLC 45; BLC
See also BW 1; CA 65-68; CANR 27;
DAM MULT; DLB 157

Nodier, (Jean) Charles (Emmanuel)
1780-1844 .... NCLC 19
See also DLB 119

Nolan, Christopher 1965- .... CLC 58
See also CA 111

Noon, Jeff 1957- .... CLC 91
See also CA 148

Norden, Charles
See Durrell, Lawrence (George)

Nordhoff, Charles (Bernard)
1887-1947 .... TCLC 23
See also CA 108; DLB 9; SATA 23

Norfolk, Lawrence 1963- .... CLC 76
See also CA 144

Norman, Marsha 1947- .... CLC 28
See also CA 105; CABS 3; CANR 41;
DAM DRAM; DLBY 84

Norris, Benjamin Franklin, Jr.
1870-1902 .... TCLC 24
See also Norris, Frank
See also CA 110

Norris, Frank
See Norris, Benjamin Franklin, Jr.
See also CDALB 1865-1917; DLB 12, 71

Norris, Leslie 1921- .... CLC 14
See also CA 11-12; CANR 14; CAP 1;
DLB 27

North, Andrew
See Norton, Andre

North, Anthony
See Koontz, Dean R(ay)

North, Captain George
See Stevenson, Robert Louis (Balfour)

North, Milou
See Erdrich, Louise

Northrup, B. A.
See Hubbard, L(afayette) Ron(ald)

North Staffs
See Hulme, T(homas) E(rnest)

Norton, Alice Mary
See Norton, Andre
See also MAICYA; SATA 1, 43

Norton, Andre 1912- .... CLC 12
See also Norton, Alice Mary
See also AAYA 14; CA 1-4R; CANR 2, 31;
DLB 8, 52; JRDA; MTCW

Norton, Caroline 1808-1877 ...... NCLC 47
See also DLB 21, 159

Norway, Nevil Shute 1899-1960
See Shute, Nevil
See also CA 102; 93-96

Norwid, Cyprian Kamil
1821-1883 .... NCLC 17

Nosille, Nabrah
See Ellison, Harlan (Jay)

Nossack, Hans Erich 1901-1978 ..... CLC 6
See also CA 93-96; 85-88; DLB 69

Nostradamus 1503-1566 .... LC 27

Nosu, Chuji
See Ozu, Yasujiro

Notenburg, Eleanora (Genrikhovna) von
See Guro, Elena

Nova, Craig 1945- .... CLC 7, 31
See also CA 45-48; CANR 2, 53

Novak, Joseph
See Kosinski, Jerzy (Nikodem)

Novalis 1772-1801 .... NCLC 13
See also DLB 90

Nowlan, Alden (Albert)
1933-1983 .... CLC 15; DAC
See also CA 9-12R; CANR 5; DAM MST;
DLB 53

Noyes, Alfred 1880-1958 .... TCLC 7
See also CA 104; DLB 20

Nunn, Kem 19(?)- .... CLC 34

Nye, Robert 1939- .... CLC 13, 42
See also CA 33-36R; CANR 29;
DAM NOV; DLB 14; MTCW; SATA 6

Nyro, Laura 1947- .... CLC 17

Oates, Joyce Carol
1938- ...... CLC 1, 2, 3, 6, 9, 11, 15, 19,
33, 52; DA; DAB; DAC; SSC 6; WLC
See also AAYA 15; AITN 1; BEST 89:2;
CA 5-8R; CANR 25, 45;
CDALB 1968-1988; DAM MST, NOV,
POP; DLB 2, 5, 130; DLBY 81;
INT CANR-25; MTCW

O'Brien, Darcy 1939- .... CLC 11
See also CA 21-24R; CANR 8

O'Brien, E. G.
See Clarke, Arthur C(harles)

O'Brien, Edna
1936- ... CLC 3, 5, 8, 13, 36, 65; SSC 10
See also CA 1-4R; CANR 6, 41;
CDBLB 1960 to Present; DAM NOV;
DLB 14; MTCW

O'Brien, Fitz-James 1828-1862... NCLC 21
See also DLB 74

O'Brien, Flann........ CLC 1, 4, 5, 7, 10, 47
See also O Nuallain, Brian

O'Brien, Richard 1942- .... CLC 17
See also CA 124

O'Brien, Tim 1946- .... CLC 7, 19, 40
See also AAYA 16; CA 85-88; CANR 40;
DAM POP; DLB 152; DLBD 9;
DLBY 80

Obstfelder, Sigbjoern 1866-1900... TCLC 23
See also CA 123

O'Casey, Sean
1880-1964 ...... CLC 1, 5, 9, 11, 15, 88;
DAB; DAC
See also CA 89-92; CDBLB 1914-1945;
DAM DRAM, MST; DLB 10; MTCW

O'Cathasaigh, Sean
See O'Casey, Sean

Ochs, Phil 1940-1976 .... CLC 17
See also CA 65-68

O'Connor, Edwin (Greene)
1918-1968 .... CLC 14
See also CA 93-96; 25-28R

Owen, Wilfred (Edward Salter)
    1893-1918 ...... **TCLC 5, 27; DA; DAB;**
                                DAC; WLC
    See also CA 104; 141; CDBLB 1914-1945;
    DAM MST, POET; DLB 20

Owens, Rochelle 1936-.............. **CLC 8**
    See also CA 17-20R; CAAS 2; CANR 39

Oz, Amos 1939- ... **CLC 5, 8, 11, 27, 33, 54**
    See also CA 53-56; CANR 27, 47;
    DAM NOV; MTCW

Ozick, Cynthia
    1928-........ **CLC 3, 7, 28, 62; SSC 15**
    See also BEST 90:1; CA 17-20R; CANR 23;
    DAM NOV, POP; DLB 28, 152;
    DLBY 82; INT CANR-23; MTCW

Ozu, Yasujiro 1903-1963 .... **CLC 16**
    See also CA 112

Pacheco, C.
    See Pessoa, Fernando (Antonio Nogueira)

Pa Chin .... **CLC 18**
    See also Li Fei-kan

Pack, Robert 1929-............... **CLC 13**
    See also CA 1-4R; CANR 3, 44; DLB 5

Padgett, Lewis
    See Kuttner, Henry

Padilla (Lorenzo), Heberto 1932-... **CLC 38**
    See also AITN 1; CA 123; 131; HW

Page, Jimmy 1944-............... **CLC 12**

Page, Louise 1955-............... **CLC 40**
    See also CA 140

Page, P(atricia) K(athleen)
    1916-........ **CLC 7, 18; DAC; PC 12**
    See also CA 53-56; CANR 4, 22;
    DAM MST; DLB 68; MTCW

Page, Thomas Nelson 1853-1922.... **SSC 23**
    See also CA 118; DLB 12, 78; DLBD 13

Paget, Violet 1856-1935
    See Lee, Vernon
    See also CA 104

Paget-Lowe, Henry
    See Lovecraft, H(oward) P(hillips)

Paglia, Camille (Anna) 1947-....... **CLC 68**
    See also CA 140

Paige, Richard
    See Koontz, Dean R(ay)

Pakenham, Antonia
    See Fraser, (Lady) Antonia (Pakenham)

Palamas, Kostes 1859-1943 .... **TCLC 5**
    See also CA 105

Palazzeschi, Aldo 1885-1974 .... **CLC 11**
    See also CA 89-92; 53-56; DLB 114

Paley, Grace 1922-.... **CLC 4, 6, 37; SSC 8**
    See also CA 25-28R; CANR 13, 46;
    DAM POP; DLB 28; INT CANR-13;
    MTCW

Palin, Michael (Edward) 1943-..... **CLC 21**
    See also Monty Python
    See also CA 107; CANR 35; SATA 67

Palliser, Charles 1947-............ **CLC 65**
    See also CA 136

Palma, Ricardo 1833-1919........ **TCLC 29**

Pancake, Breece Dexter 1952-1979
    See Pancake, Breece D'J
    See also CA 123; 109

Pancake, Breece D'J .... **CLC 29**
    See also Pancake, Breece Dexter
    See also DLB 130

Panko, Rudy
    See Gogol, Nikolai (Vasilyevich)

Papadiamantis, Alexandros
    1851-1911 .... **TCLC 29**

Papadiamantopoulos, Johannes 1856-1910
    See Moreas, Jean
    See also CA 117

Papini, Giovanni 1881-1956...... **TCLC 22**
    See also CA 121

Paracelsus 1493-1541............. **LC 14**

Parasol, Peter
    See Stevens, Wallace

Parfenie, Maria
    See Codrescu, Andrei

Parini, Jay (Lee) 1948- .... **CLC 54**
    See also CA 97-100; CAAS 16; CANR 32

Park, Jordan
    See Kornbluth, C(yril) M.; Pohl, Frederik

Parker, Bert
    See Ellison, Harlan (Jay)

Parker, Dorothy (Rothschild)
    1893-1967 .... **CLC 15, 68; SSC 2**
    See also CA 19-20; 25-28R; CAP 2;
    DAM POET; DLB 11, 45, 86; MTCW

Parker, Robert B(rown) 1932-...... **CLC 27**
    See also BEST 89:4; CA 49-52; CANR 1,
    26, 52; DAM NOV, POP;
    INT CANR-26; MTCW

Parkin, Frank 1940-.............. **CLC 43**
    See also CA 147

Parkman, Francis, Jr.
    1823-1893 .... **NCLC 12**
    See also DLB 1, 30

Parks, Gordon (Alexander Buchanan)
    1912-................ **CLC 1, 16; BLC**
    See also AITN 2; BW 2; CA 41-44R;
    CANR 26; DAM MULT; DLB 33;
    SATA 8

Parnell, Thomas 1679-1718 .... **LC 3**
    See also DLB 94

Parra, Nicanor 1914-........ **CLC 2; HLC**
    See also CA 85-88; CANR 32;
    DAM MULT; HW; MTCW

Parrish, Mary Frances
    See Fisher, M(ary) F(rances) K(ennedy)

Parson
    See Coleridge, Samuel Taylor

Parson Lot
    See Kingsley, Charles

Partridge, Anthony
    See Oppenheim, E(dward) Phillips

Pascoli, Giovanni 1855-1912 ..... **TCLC 45**

Pasolini, Pier Paolo
    1922-1975 .... **CLC 20, 37**
    See also CA 93-96; 61-64; DLB 128;
    MTCW

Pasquini
    See Silone, Ignazio

Pastan, Linda (Olenik) 1932- ...... **CLC 27**
    See also CA 61-64; CANR 18, 40;
    DAM POET; DLB 5

Pasternak, Boris (Leonidovich)
    1890-1960 ...... **CLC 7, 10, 18, 63; DA;**
                          DAB; DAC; PC 6; WLC
    See also CA 127; 116; DAM MST, NOV,
    POET; MTCW

Patchen, Kenneth 1911-1972 ... **CLC 1, 2, 18**
    See also CA 1-4R; 33-36R; CANR 3, 35;
    DAM POET; DLB 16, 48; MTCW

Pater, Walter (Horatio)
    1839-1894 .... **NCLC 7**
    See also CDBLB 1832-1890; DLB 57, 156

Paterson, A(ndrew) B(arton)
    1864-1941 .... **TCLC 32**

Paterson, Katherine (Womeldorf)
    1932-..................... **CLC 12, 30**
    See also AAYA 1; CA 21-24R; CANR 28;
    CLR 7; DLB 52; JRDA; MAICYA;
    MTCW; SATA 13, 53

Patmore, Coventry Kersey Dighton
    1823-1896 .... **NCLC 9**
    See also DLB 35, 98

Paton, Alan (Stewart)
    1903-1988 ...... **CLC 4, 10, 25, 55; DA;**
                              DAB; DAC; WLC
    See also CA 13-16; 125; CANR 22; CAP 1;
    DAM MST, NOV; MTCW; SATA 11;
    SATA-Obit 56

Paton Walsh, Gillian 1937-
    See Walsh, Jill Paton
    See also CANR 38; JRDA; MAICYA;
    SAAS 3; SATA 4, 72

Paulding, James Kirke 1778-1860.. **NCLC 2**
    See also DLB 3, 59, 74

Paulin, Thomas Neilson 1949-
    See Paulin, Tom
    See also CA 123; 128

Paulin, Tom...................... CLC 37
    See also Paulin, Thomas Neilson
    See also DLB 40

Paustovsky, Konstantin (Georgievich)
    1892-1968 .... **CLC 40**
    See also CA 93-96; 25-28R

Pavese, Cesare
    1908-1950 ..... **TCLC 3; PC 13; SSC 19**
    See also CA 104; DLB 128

Pavic, Milorad 1929-............. **CLC 60**
    See also CA 136

Payne, Alan
    See Jakes, John (William)

Paz, Gil
    See Lugones, Leopoldo

Paz, Octavio
    1914-....... **CLC 3, 4, 6, 10, 19, 51, 65;**
                          DA; DAB; DAC; HLC; PC 1; WLC
    See also CA 73-76; CANR 32; DAM MST,
    MULT, POET; DLBY 90; HW; MTCW

Peacock, Molly 1947-............. **CLC 60**
    See also CA 103; CAAS 21; CANR 52;
    DLB 120

Peacock, Thomas Love
    1785-1866 .... **NCLC 22**
    See also DLB 96, 116

Peake, Mervyn 1911-1968 .... **CLC 7, 54**
    See also CA 5-8R; 25-28R; CANR 3;
    DLB 15, 160; MTCW; SATA 23

Pirandello, Luigi
1867-1936 ...... TCLC 4, 29; DA; DAB;
DAC; DC 5; SSC 22; WLC
See also CA 104; DAM DRAM, MST

Pirsig, Robert M(aynard)
1928- .... CLC 4, 6, 73
See also CA 53-56; CANR 42; DAM POP;
MTCW; SATA 39

Pisarev, Dmitry Ivanovich
1840-1868 .... NCLC 25

Pix, Mary (Griffith) 1666-1709 ...... LC 8
See also DLB 80

Pixerecourt, Guilbert de
1773-1844 .... NCLC 39

Plaidy, Jean
See Hibbert, Eleanor Alice Burford

Planche, James Robinson
1796-1880 .... NCLC 42

Plant, Robert 1948- .... CLC 12

Plante, David (Robert)
1940- .... CLC 7, 23, 38
See also CA 37-40R; CANR 12, 36;
DAM NOV; DLBY 83; INT CANR-12;
MTCW

Plath, Sylvia
1932-1963 ..... CLC 1, 2, 3, 5, 9, 11, 14,
17, 50, 51, 62; DA; DAB; DAC; PC 1;
WLC
See also AAYA 13; CA 19-20; CANR 34;
CAP 2; CDALB 1941-1968; DAM MST,
POET; DLB 5, 6, 152; MTCW

Plato
428(?)B.C.-348(?)B.C..... CMLC 8; DA;
DAB; DAC
See also DAM MST

Platonov, Andrei .... TCLC 14
See also Klimentov, Andrei Platonovich

Platt, Kin 1911- .... CLC 26
See also AAYA 11; CA 17-20R; CANR 11;
JRDA; SAAS 17; SATA 21, 86

Plautus c. 251B.C.-184B.C.......... DC 6

Plick et Plock
See Simenon, Georges (Jacques Christian)

Plimpton, George (Ames) 1927-..... CLC 36
See also AITN 1; CA 21-24R; CANR 32;
MTCW; SATA 10

Plomer, William Charles Franklin
1903-1973 .... CLC 4, 8
See also CA 21-22; CANR 34; CAP 2;
DLB 20, 162; MTCW; SATA 24

Plowman, Piers
See Kavanagh, Patrick (Joseph)

Plum, J.
See Wodehouse, P(elham) G(renville)

Plumly, Stanley (Ross) 1939- ...... CLC 33
See also CA 108; 110; DLB 5; INT 110

Plumpe, Friedrich Wilhelm
1888-1931 .... TCLC 53
See also CA 112

Poe, Edgar Allan
1809-1849 .... NCLC 1, 16, 55; DA;
DAB; DAC; PC 1; SSC 1, 22; WLC
See also AAYA 14; CDALB 1640-1865;
DAM MST, POET; DLB 3, 59, 73, 74;
SATA 23

Poet of Titchfield Street, The
See Pound, Ezra (Weston Loomis)

Pohl, Frederik 1919- .... CLC 18
See also CA 61-64; CAAS 1; CANR 11, 37;
DLB 8; INT CANR-11; MTCW;
SATA 24

Poirier, Louis 1910-
See Gracq, Julien
See also CA 122; 126

Poitier, Sidney 1927-............. CLC 26
See also BW 1; CA 117

Polanski, Roman 1933- .... CLC 16
See also CA 77-80

Poliakoff, Stephen 1952- .... CLC 38
See also CA 106; DLB 13

Police, The
See Copeland, Stewart (Armstrong);
Summers, Andrew James; Sumner,
Gordon Matthew

Polidori, John William
1795-1821 .... NCLC 51
See also DLB 116

Pollitt, Katha 1949-............. CLC 28
See also CA 120; 122; MTCW

Pollock, (Mary) Sharon
1936- .... CLC 50; DAC
See also CA 141; DAM DRAM, MST;
DLB 60

Polo, Marco 1254-1324 .... CMLC 15

Polonsky, Abraham (Lincoln)
1910- .... CLC 92
See also CA 104; DLB 26; INT 104

Polybius c. 200B.C.-c. 118B.C.... CMLC 17

Pomerance, Bernard 1940-.... CLC 13
See also CA 101; CANR 49; DAM DRAM

Ponge, Francis (Jean Gaston Alfred)
1899-1988 .... CLC 6, 18
See also CA 85-88; 126; CANR 40;
DAM POET

Pontoppidan, Henrik 1857-1943 ... TCLC 29

Poole, Josephine .... CLC 17
See also Helyar, Jane Penelope Josephine
See also SAAS 2; SATA 5

Popa, Vasko 1922-1991 .... CLC 19
See also CA 112; 148

Pope, Alexander
1688-1744 ...... LC 3; DA; DAB; DAC;
WLC
See also CDBLB 1660-1789; DAM MST,
POET; DLB 95, 101

Porter, Connie (Rose) 1959(?)- ..... CLC 70
See also BW 2; CA 142; SATA 81

Porter, Gene(va Grace) Stratton
1863(?)-1924 .... TCLC 21
See also CA 112

Porter, Katherine Anne
1890-1980 ...... CLC 1, 3, 7, 10, 13, 15,
27; DA; DAB; DAC; SSC 4
See also AITN 2; CA 1-4R; 101; CANR 1;
DAM MST, NOV; DLB 4, 9, 102;
DLBD 12; DLBY 80; MTCW; SATA 39;
SATA-Obit 23

Porter, Peter (Neville Frederick)
1929- .... CLC 5, 13, 33
See also CA 85-88; DLB 40

Porter, William Sydney 1862-1910
See Henry, O.
See also CA 104; 131; CDALB 1865-1917;
DA; DAB; DAC; DAM MST; DLB 12,
78, 79; MTCW; YABC 2

Portillo (y Pacheco), Jose Lopez
See Lopez Portillo (y Pacheco), Jose

Post, Melville Davisson
1869-1930 .... TCLC 39
See also CA 110

Potok, Chaim 1929-....... CLC 2, 7, 14, 26
See also AAYA 15; AITN 1, 2; CA 17-20R;
CANR 19, 35; DAM NOV; DLB 28, 152;
INT CANR-19; MTCW; SATA 33

Potter, Beatrice
See Webb, (Martha) Beatrice (Potter)
See also MAICYA

Potter, Dennis (Christopher George)
1935-1994 .... CLC 58, 86
See also CA 107; 145; CANR 33; MTCW

Pound, Ezra (Weston Loomis)
1885-1972 ..... CLC 1, 2, 3, 4, 5, 7, 10,
13, 18, 34, 48, 50; DA; DAB; DAC; PC 4;
WLC
See also CA 5-8R; 37-40R; CANR 40;
CDALB 1917-1929; DAM MST, POET;
DLB 4, 45, 63; MTCW

Povod, Reinaldo 1959-1994 .... CLC 44
See also CA 136; 146

Powell, Adam Clayton, Jr.
1908-1972 .... CLC 89; BLC
See also BW 1; CA 102; 33-36R;
DAM MULT

Powell, Anthony (Dymoke)
1905- .... CLC 1, 3, 7, 9, 10, 31
See also CA 1-4R; CANR 1, 32;
CDBLB 1945-1960; DLB 15; MTCW

Powell, Dawn 1897-1965 .... CLC 66
See also CA 5-8R

Powell, Padgett 1952-............. CLC 34
See also CA 126

Power, Susan..................... CLC 91

Powers, J(ames) F(arl)
1917- .... CLC 1, 4, 8, 57; SSC 4
See also CA 1-4R; CANR 2; DLB 130;
MTCW

Powers, John J(ames) 1945-
See Powers, John R.
See also CA 69-72

Powers, John R. .... CLC 66
See also Powers, John J(ames)

Powers, Richard (S.) 1957- .... CLC 93
See also CA 148

Pownall, David 1938-............. CLC 10
See also CA 89-92; CAAS 18; CANR 49;
DLB 14

Powys, John Cowper
1872-1963 .... CLC 7, 9, 15, 46
See also CA 85-88; DLB 15; MTCW

Powys, T(heodore) F(rancis)
1875-1953 .... TCLC 9
See also CA 106; DLB 36, 162

Prager, Emily 1952-............. CLC 56

Raine, Kathleen (Jessie) 1908- ... **CLC 7, 45**
See also CA 85-88; CANR 46; DLB 20;
MTCW

Rainis, Janis 1865-1929 .... **TCLC 29**

Rakosi, Carl.................... **CLC 47**
See also Rawley, Callman
See also CAAS 5

Raleigh, Richard
See Lovecraft, H(oward) P(hillips)

Raleigh, Sir Walter 1554(?)-1618 .... **LC 31**
See also CDBLB Before 1660

Rallentando, H. P.
See Sayers, Dorothy L(eigh)

Ramal, Walter
See de la Mare, Walter (John)

Ramon, Juan
See Jimenez (Mantecon), Juan Ramon

Ramos, Graciliano 1892-1953 ..... **TCLC 32**

Rampersad, Arnold 1941-......... **CLC 44**
See also BW 2; CA 127; 133; DLB 111;
INT 133

Rampling, Anne
See Rice, Anne

Ramsay, Allan 1684(?)-1758 .... **LC 29**
See also DLB 95

Ramuz, Charles-Ferdinand
1878-1947 .... **TCLC 33**

Rand, Ayn
1905-1982 ...... **CLC 3, 30, 44, 79; DA;**
DAC; WLC
See also AAYA 10; CA 13-16R; 105;
CANR 27; DAM MST, NOV, POP;
MTCW

Randall, Dudley (Felker)
1914- .... **CLC 1; BLC**
See also BW 1; CA 25-28R; CANR 23;
DAM MULT; DLB 41

Randall, Robert
See Silverberg, Robert

Ranger, Ken
See Creasey, John

Ransom, John Crowe
1888-1974 .... **CLC 2, 4, 5, 11, 24**
See also CA 5-8R; 49-52; CANR 6, 34;
DAM POET; DLB 45, 63; MTCW

Rao, Raja 1909- .... **CLC 25, 56**
See also CA 73-76; CANR 51; DAM NOV;
MTCW

Raphael, Frederic (Michael)
1931- .... **CLC 2, 14**
See also CA 1-4R; CANR 1; DLB 14

Ratcliffe, James P.
See Mencken, H(enry) L(ouis)

Rathbone, Julian 1935- .... **CLC 41**
See also CA 101; CANR 34

Rattigan, Terence (Mervyn)
1911-1977 .... **CLC 7**
See also CA 85-88; 73-76;
CDBLB 1945-1960; DAM DRAM;
DLB 13; MTCW

Ratushinskaya, Irina 1954- .... **CLC 54**
See also CA 129

Raven, Simon (Arthur Noel)
1927- .... **CLC 14**
See also CA 81-84

Rawley, Callman 1903-
See Rakosi, Carl
See also CA 21-24R; CANR 12, 32

Rawlings, Marjorie Kinnan
1896-1953 .... **TCLC 4**
See also CA 104; 137; DLB 9, 22, 102;
JRDA; MAICYA; YABC 1

Ray, Satyajit 1921-1992 .... **CLC 16, 76**
See also CA 114; 137; DAM MULT

Read, Herbert Edward 1893-1968.... **CLC 4**
See also CA 85-88; 25-28R; DLB 20, 149

Read, Piers Paul 1941- ...... **CLC 4, 10, 25**
See also CA 21-24R; CANR 38; DLB 14;
SATA 21

Reade, Charles 1814-1884 .... **NCLC 2**
See also DLB 21

Reade, Hamish
See Gray, Simon (James Holliday)

Reading, Peter 1946- .... **CLC 47**
See also CA 103; CANR 46; DLB 40

Reaney, James 1926- .... **CLC 13; DAC**
See also CA 41-44R; CAAS 15; CANR 42;
DAM MST; DLB 68; SATA 43

Rebreanu, Liviu 1885-1944 .... **TCLC 28**

Rechy, John (Francisco)
1934- .... **CLC 1, 7, 14, 18; HLC**
See also CA 5-8R; CAAS 4; CANR 6, 32;
DAM MULT; DLB 122; DLBY 82; HW;
INT CANR-6

Redcam, Tom 1870-1933 .... **TCLC 25**

Reddin, Keith................. **CLC 67**

Redgrove, Peter (William)
1932- .... **CLC 6, 41**
See also CA 1-4R; CANR 3, 39; DLB 40

Redmon, Anne.................... **CLC 22**
See also Nightingale, Anne Redmon
See also DLBY 86

Reed, Eliot
See Ambler, Eric

Reed, Ishmael
1938- ... **CLC 2, 3, 5, 6, 13, 32, 60; BLC**
See also BW 2; CA 21-24R; CANR 25, 48;
DAM MULT; DLB 2, 5, 33; DLBD 8;
MTCW

Reed, John (Silas) 1887-1920 ...... **TCLC 9**
See also CA 106

Reed, Lou........................ **CLC 21**
See also Firbank, Louis

Reeve, Clara 1729-1807 .... **NCLC 19**
See also DLB 39

Reich, Wilhelm 1897-1957........ **TCLC 57**

Reid, Christopher (John) 1949-..... **CLC 33**
See also CA 140; DLB 40

Reid, Desmond
See Moorcock, Michael (John)

Reid Banks, Lynne 1929-
See Banks, Lynne Reid
See also CA 1-4R; CANR 6, 22, 38;
CLR 24; JRDA; MAICYA; SATA 22, 75

Reilly, William K.
See Creasey, John

Reiner, Max
See Caldwell, (Janet Miriam) Taylor
(Holland)

Reis, Ricardo
See Pessoa, Fernando (Antonio Nogueira)

Remarque, Erich Maria
1898-1970 .... **CLC 21; DA; DAB; DAC**
See also CA 77-80; 29-32R; DAM MST,
NOV; DLB 56; MTCW

Remizov, A.
See Remizov, Aleksei (Mikhailovich)

Remizov, A. M.
See Remizov, Aleksei (Mikhailovich)

Remizov, Aleksei (Mikhailovich)
1877-1957 .... **TCLC 27**
See also CA 125; 133

Renan, Joseph Ernest
1823-1892 .... **NCLC 26**

Renard, Jules 1864-1910 .... **TCLC 17**
See also CA 117

Renault, Mary............... **CLC 3, 11, 17**
See also Challans, Mary
See also DLBY 83

Rendell, Ruth (Barbara) 1930- .. **CLC 28, 48**
See also Vine, Barbara
See also CA 109; CANR 32, 52;
DAM POP; DLB 87; INT CANR-32;
MTCW

Renoir, Jean 1894-1979........... **CLC 20**
See also CA 129; 85-88

Resnais, Alain 1922-.............. **CLC 16**

Reverdy, Pierre 1889-1960 .... **CLC 53**
See also CA 97-100; 89-92

Rexroth, Kenneth
1905-1982 ...... **CLC 1, 2, 6, 11, 22, 49**
See also CA 5-8R; 107; CANR 14, 34;
CDALB 1941-1968; DAM POET;
DLB 16, 48, 165; DLBY 82;
INT CANR-14; MTCW

Reyes, Alfonso 1889-1959 .... **TCLC 33**
See also CA 131; HW

Reyes y Basoalto, Ricardo Eliecer Neftali
See Neruda, Pablo

Reymont, Wladyslaw (Stanislaw)
1868(?)-1925 .... **TCLC 5**
See also CA 104

Reynolds, Jonathan 1942- .... **CLC 6, 38**
See also CA 65-68; CANR 28

Reynolds, Joshua 1723-1792 .... **LC 15**
See also DLB 104

Reynolds, Michael Shane 1937- .... **CLC 44**
See also CA 65-68; CANR 9

Reznikoff, Charles 1894-1976 .... **CLC 9**
See also CA 33-36; 61-64; CAP 2; DLB 28,
45

Rezzori (d'Arezzo), Gregor von
1914- .... **CLC 25**
See also CA 122; 136

Rhine, Richard
See Silverstein, Alvin

Rhodes, Eugene Manlove
1869-1934 .... **TCLC 53**

R'hoone
See Balzac, Honore de

Rhys, Jean
      1890(?)-1979 .... **CLC 2, 4, 6, 14, 19, 51;**
                                          SSC 21
      See also CA 25-28R; 85-88; CANR 35;
      CDBLB 1945-1960; DAM NOV; DLB 36,
      117, 162; MTCW

Ribeiro, Darcy 1922- .... **CLC 34**
      See also CA 33-36R

Ribeiro, Joao Ubaldo (Osorio Pimentel)
      1941- .... **CLC 10, 67**
      See also CA 81-84

Ribman, Ronald (Burt) 1932- .... **CLC 7**
      See also CA 21-24R; CANR 46

Ricci, Nino 1959- .... **CLC 70**
      See also CA 137

Rice, Anne 1941- .... **CLC 41**
      See also AAYA 9; BEST 89:2; CA 65-68;
      CANR 12, 36, 53; DAM POP

Rice, Elmer (Leopold)
      1892-1967 .... **CLC 7, 49**
      See also CA 21-22; 25-28R; CAP 2;
      DAM DRAM; DLB 4, 7; MTCW

Rice, Tim(othy Miles Bindon)
      1944- .... **CLC 21**
      See also CA 103; CANR 46

Rich, Adrienne (Cecile)
      1929- .... **CLC 3, 6, 7, 11, 18, 36, 73, 76;**
                                          PC 5
      See also CA 9-12R; CANR 20, 53;
      DAM POET; DLB 5, 67; MTCW

Rich, Barbara
      See Graves, Robert (von Ranke)

Rich, Robert
      See Trumbo, Dalton

Richard, Keith .... **CLC 17**
      See also Richards, Keith

Richards, David Adams
      1950- .... **CLC 59; DAC**
      See also CA 93-96; DLB 53

Richards, I(vor) A(rmstrong)
      1893-1979 .... **CLC 14, 24**
      See also CA 41-44R; 89-92; CANR 34;
      DLB 27

Richards, Keith 1943-
      See Richard, Keith
      See also CA 107

Richardson, Anne
      See Roiphe, Anne (Richardson)

Richardson, Dorothy Miller
      1873-1957 .... **TCLC 3**
      See also CA 104; DLB 36

Richardson, Ethel Florence (Lindesay)
      1870-1946
      See Richardson, Henry Handel
      See also CA 105

Richardson, Henry Handel .... **TCLC 4**
      See also Richardson, Ethel Florence
      (Lindesay)

Richardson, John
      1796-1852 .... **NCLC 55; DAC**
      See also DLB 99

Richardson, Samuel
      1689-1761 ...... **LC 1; DA; DAB; DAC;**
                                          WLC
      See also CDBLB 1660-1789; DAM MST,
      NOV; DLB 39

Richler, Mordecai
      1931- .... **CLC 3, 5, 9, 13, 18, 46, 70;**
                                          DAC
      See also AITN 1; CA 65-68; CANR 31;
      CLR 17; DAM MST, NOV; DLB 53;
      MAICYA; MTCW; SATA 44;
      SATA-Brief 27

Richter, Conrad (Michael)
      1890-1968 .... **CLC 30**
      See also CA 5-8R; 25-28R; CANR 23;
      DLB 9; MTCW; SATA 3

Ricostranza, Tom
      See Ellis, Trey

Riddell, J. H. 1832-1906 .... **TCLC 40**

Riding, Laura .... **CLC 3, 7**
      See also Jackson, Laura (Riding)

Riefenstahl, Berta Helene Amalia 1902-
      See Riefenstahl, Leni
      See also CA 108

Riefenstahl, Leni .... **CLC 16**
      See also Riefenstahl, Berta Helene Amalia

Riffe, Ernest
      See Bergman, (Ernst) Ingmar

Riggs, (Rolla) Lynn 1899-1954 .... **TCLC 56**
      See also CA 144; DAM MULT; NNAL

Riley, James Whitcomb
      1849-1916 .... **TCLC 51**
      See also CA 118; 137; DAM POET;
      MAICYA; SATA 17

Riley, Tex
      See Creasey, John

Rilke, Rainer Maria
      1875-1926 .... **TCLC 1, 6, 19; PC 2**
      See also CA 104; 132; DAM POET;
      DLB 81; MTCW

Rimbaud, (Jean Nicolas) Arthur
      1854-1891 ..... **NCLC 4, 35; DA; DAB;**
                                  DAC; PC 3; WLC
      See also DAM MST, POET

Rinehart, Mary Roberts
      1876-1958 .... **TCLC 52**
      See also CA 108

Ringmaster, The
      See Mencken, H(enry) L(ouis)

Ringwood, Gwen(dolyn Margaret) Pharis
      1910-1984 .... **CLC 48**
      See also CA 148; 112; DLB 88

Rio, Michel 19(?)- .... **CLC 43**

Ritsos, Giannes
      See Ritsos, Yannis

Ritsos, Yannis 1909-1990..... **CLC 6, 13, 31**
      See also CA 77-80; 133; CANR 39; MTCW

Ritter, Erika 1948(?)- .... **CLC 52**

Rivera, Jose Eustasio 1889-1928... **TCLC 35**
      See also HW

Rivers, Conrad Kent 1933-1968...... **CLC 1**
      See also BW 1; CA 85-88; DLB 41

Rivers, Elfrida
      See Bradley, Marion Zimmer

Riverside, John
      See Heinlein, Robert A(nson)

Rizal, Jose 1861-1896.......... **NCLC 27**

Roa Bastos, Augusto (Antonio)
      1917- .... **CLC 45; HLC**
      See also CA 131; DAM MULT; DLB 113;
      HW

Robbe-Grillet, Alain
      1922- .... **CLC 1, 2, 4, 6, 8, 10, 14, 43**
      See also CA 9-12R; CANR 33; DLB 83;
      MTCW

Robbins, Harold 1916-............ **CLC 5**
      See also CA 73-76; CANR 26; DAM NOV;
      MTCW

Robbins, Thomas Eugene 1936-
      See Robbins, Tom
      See also CA 81-84; CANR 29; DAM NOV,
      POP; MTCW

Robbins, Tom .... **CLC 9, 32, 64**
      See also Robbins, Thomas Eugene
      See also BEST 90:3; DLBY 80

Robbins, Trina 1938- .... **CLC 21**
      See also CA 128

Roberts, Charles G(eorge) D(ouglas)
      1860-1943 .... **TCLC 8**
      See also CA 105; CLR 33; DLB 92;
      SATA 88; SATA-Brief 29

Roberts, Kate 1891-1985 .... **CLC 15**
      See also CA 107; 116

Roberts, Keith (John Kingston)
      1935- .... **CLC 14**
      See also CA 25-28R; CANR 46

Roberts, Kenneth (Lewis)
      1885-1957 .... **TCLC 23**
      See also CA 109; DLB 9

Roberts, Michele (B.) 1949-....... **CLC 48**
      See also CA 115

Robertson, Ellis
      See Ellison, Harlan (Jay); Silverberg, Robert

Robertson, Thomas William
      1829-1871 .... **NCLC 35**
      See also DAM DRAM

Robinson, Edwin Arlington
      1869-1935 .... **TCLC 5; DA; DAC; PC 1**
      See also CA 104; 133; CDALB 1865-1917;
      DAM MST, POET; DLB 54; MTCW

Robinson, Henry Crabb
      1775-1867 .... **NCLC 15**
      See also DLB 107

Robinson, Jill 1936-.............. **CLC 10**
      See also CA 102; INT 102

Robinson, Kim Stanley 1952- ...... **CLC 34**
      See also CA 126

Robinson, Lloyd
      See Silverberg, Robert

Robinson, Marilynne 1944-........ **CLC 25**
      See also CA 116

Robinson, Smokey................. **CLC 21**
      See also Robinson, William, Jr.

Robinson, William, Jr. 1940-
      See Robinson, Smokey
      See also CA 116

Robison, Mary 1949- .... **CLC 42**
      See also CA 113; 116; DLB 130; INT 116

Rod, Edouard 1857-1910 .... **TCLC 52**

Roddenberry, Eugene Wesley 1921-1991
See Roddenberry, Gene
See also CA 110; 135; CANR 37; SATA 45;
SATA-Obit 69

Roddenberry, Gene . . . . **CLC 17**
See also Roddenberry, Eugene Wesley
See also AAYA 5; SATA-Obit 69

Rodgers, Mary 1931- . . . . **CLC 12**
See also CA 49-52; CANR 8; CLR 20;
INT CANR-8; JRDA; MAICYA;
SATA 8

Rodgers, W(illiam) R(obert)
1909-1969 . . . . **CLC 7**
See also CA 85-88; DLB 20

Rodman, Eric
See Silverberg, Robert

Rodman, Howard 1920(?)-1985 . . . . . **CLC 65**
See also CA 118

Rodman, Maia
See Wojciechowska, Maia (Teresa)

Rodriguez, Claudio 1934- . . . . **CLC 10**
See also DLB 134

Roelvaag, O(le) E(dvart)
1876-1931 . . . . **TCLC 17**
See also CA 117; DLB 9

Roethke, Theodore (Huebner)
1908-1963 . . . . . . **CLC 1, 3, 8, 11, 19, 46;
PC 15**
See also CA 81-84; CABS 2;
CDALB 1941-1968; DAM POET; DLB 5;
MTCW

Rogers, Thomas Hunton 1927- . . . . . **CLC 57**
See also CA 89-92; INT 89-92

Rogers, Will(iam Penn Adair)
1879-1935 . . . . **TCLC 8**
See also CA 105; 144; DAM MULT;
DLB 11; NNAL

Rogin, Gilbert 1929- . . . . **CLC 18**
See also CA 65-68; CANR 15

Rohan, Koda . . . . **TCLC 22**
See also Koda Shigeyuki

Rohmer, Eric . . . . **CLC 16**
See also Scherer, Jean-Marie Maurice

Rohmer, Sax . . . . **TCLC 28**
See also Ward, Arthur Henry Sarsfield
See also DLB 70

Roiphe, Anne (Richardson)
1935- . . . . **CLC 3, 9**
See also CA 89-92; CANR 45; DLBY 80;
INT 89-92

Rojas, Fernando de 1465-1541 . . . . . . **LC 23**

**Rolfe, Frederick (William Serafino Austin
Lewis Mary)** 1860-1913 . . . . . . **TCLC 12**
See also CA 107; DLB 34, 156

Rolland, Romain 1866-1944 . . . . . . **TCLC 23**
See also CA 118; DLB 65

Rolvaag, O(le) E(dvart)
See Roelvaag, O(le) E(dvart)

Romain Arnaud, Saint
See Aragon, Louis

Romains, Jules 1885-1972 . . . . **CLC 7**
See also CA 85-88; CANR 34; DLB 65;
MTCW

Romero, Jose Ruben 1890-1952 . . . **TCLC 14**
See also CA 114; 131; HW

Ronsard, Pierre de
1524-1585 . . . . **LC 6; PC 11**

Rooke, Leon 1934- . . . . **CLC 25, 34**
See also CA 25-28R; CANR 23, 53;
DAM POP

Roper, William 1498-1578 . . . . **LC 10**

Roquelaure, A. N.
See Rice, Anne

Rosa, Joao Guimaraes 1908-1967 . . . **CLC 23**
See also CA 89-92; DLB 113

Rose, Wendy 1948- . . . . **CLC 85; PC 13**
See also CA 53-56; CANR 5, 51;
DAM MULT; NNAL; SATA 12

Rosen, Richard (Dean) 1949- . . . . **CLC 39**
See also CA 77-80; INT CANR-30

Rosenberg, Isaac 1890-1918 . . . . . . **TCLC 12**
See also CA 107; DLB 20

Rosenblatt, Joe . . . . **CLC 15**
See also Rosenblatt, Joseph

Rosenblatt, Joseph 1933-
See Rosenblatt, Joe
See also CA 89-92; INT 89-92

Rosenfeld, Samuel 1896-1963
See Tzara, Tristan
See also CA 89-92

Rosenthal, M(acha) L(ouis) 1917- . . . **CLC 28**
See also CA 1-4R; CAAS 6; CANR 4, 51;
DLB 5; SATA 59

Ross, Barnaby
See Dannay, Frederic

Ross, Bernard L.
See Follett, Ken(neth Martin)

Ross, J. H.
See Lawrence, T(homas) E(dward)

Ross, Martin
See Martin, Violet Florence
See also DLB 135

Ross, (James) Sinclair
1908- . . . . **CLC 13; DAC**
See also CA 73-76; DAM MST; DLB 88

Rossetti, Christina (Georgina)
1830-1894 . . . . . **NCLC 2, 50; DA; DAB;
DAC; PC 7; WLC**
See also DAM MST, POET; DLB 35, 163;
MAICYA; SATA 20

Rossetti, Dante Gabriel
1828-1882 . . . . **NCLC 4; DA; DAB;
DAC; WLC**
See also CDBLB 1832-1890; DAM MST,
POET; DLB 35

Rossner, Judith (Perelman)
1935- . . . . **CLC 6, 9, 29**
See also AITN 2; BEST 90:3; CA 17-20R;
CANR 18, 51; DLB 6; INT CANR-18;
MTCW

Rostand, Edmond (Eugene Alexis)
1868-1918 . . . . . . **TCLC 6, 37; DA; DAB;
DAC**
See also CA 104; 126; DAM DRAM, MST;
MTCW

Roth, Henry 1906-1995 . . . . **CLC 2, 6, 11**
See also CA 11-12; 149; CANR 38; CAP 1;
DLB 28; MTCW

Roth, Joseph 1894-1939 . . . . **TCLC 33**
See also DLB 85

Roth, Philip (Milton)
1933- . . . . . . **CLC 1, 2, 3, 4, 6, 9, 15, 22,
31, 47, 66, 86; DA; DAB; DAC; WLC**
See also BEST 90:3; CA 1-4R; CANR 1, 22,
36; CDALB 1968-1988; DAM MST,
NOV, POP; DLB 2, 28; DLBY 82;
MTCW

Rothenberg, Jerome 1931- . . . . **CLC 6, 57**
See also CA 45-48; CANR 1; DLB 5

Roumain, Jacques (Jean Baptiste)
1907-1944 . . . . **TCLC 19; BLC**
See also BW 1; CA 117; 125; DAM MULT

Rourke, Constance (Mayfield)
1885-1941 . . . . **TCLC 12**
See also CA 107; YABC 1

Rousseau, Jean-Baptiste 1671-1741 . . . **LC 9**

Rousseau, Jean-Jacques
1712-1778 . . . . . **LC 14; DA; DAB; DAC;
WLC**
See also DAM MST

Roussel, Raymond 1877-1933 . . . . . **TCLC 20**
See also CA 117

Rovit, Earl (Herbert) 1927- . . . . **CLC 7**
See also CA 5-8R; CANR 12

Rowe, Nicholas 1674-1718 . . . . **LC 8**
See also DLB 84

Rowley, Ames Dorrance
See Lovecraft, H(oward) P(hillips)

Rowson, Susanna Haswell
1762(?)-1824 . . . . **NCLC 5**
See also DLB 37

Roy, Gabrielle
1909-1983 . . . . . **CLC 10, 14; DAB; DAC**
See also CA 53-56; 110; CANR 5;
DAM MST; DLB 68; MTCW

Rozewicz, Tadeusz 1921- . . . . **CLC 9, 23**
See also CA 108; CANR 36; DAM POET;
MTCW

Ruark, Gibbons 1941- . . . . **CLC 3**
See also CA 33-36R; CAAS 23; CANR 14,
31; DLB 120

Rubens, Bernice (Ruth) 1923- . . . **CLC 19, 31**
See also CA 25-28R; CANR 33; DLB 14;
MTCW

Rudkin, (James) David 1936- . . . . . . **CLC 14**
See also CA 89-92; DLB 13

Rudnik, Raphael 1933- . . . . **CLC 7**
See also CA 29-32R

Ruffian, M.
See Hasek, Jaroslav (Matej Frantisek)

Ruiz, Jose Martinez . . . . **CLC 11**
See also Martinez Ruiz, Jose

Rukeyser, Muriel
1913-1980 . . . . . . **CLC 6, 10, 15, 27; PC 12**
See also CA 5-8R; 93-96; CANR 26;
DAM POET; DLB 48; MTCW;
SATA-Obit 22

Rule, Jane (Vance) 1931- . . . . **CLC 27**
See also CA 25-28R; CAAS 18; CANR 12;
DLB 60

Rulfo, Juan 1918-1986 . . . . **CLC 8, 80; HLC**
See also CA 85-88; 118; CANR 26;
DAM MULT; DLB 113; HW; MTCW

Runeberg, Johan 1804-1877 . . . . . . **NCLC 41**

Runyon, (Alfred) Damon
1884(?)-1946 . . . . **TCLC 10**
See also CA 107; DLB 11, 86

Rush, Norman 1933- . . . . **CLC 44**
See also CA 121; 126; INT 126

Rushdie, (Ahmed) Salman
1947- . . . . . . **CLC 23, 31, 55; DAB; DAC**
See also BEST 89:3; CA 108; 111;
CANR 33; DAM MST, NOV, POP;
INT 111; MTCW

Rushforth, Peter (Scott) 1945- . . . . . **CLC 19**
See also CA 101

Ruskin, John 1819-1900 . . . . **TCLC 63**
See also CA 114; 129; CDBLB 1832-1890;
DLB 55, 163; SATA 24

Russ, Joanna 1937- . . . . **CLC 15**
See also CA 25-28R; CANR 11, 31; DLB 8;
MTCW

Russell, George William 1867-1935
See A. E.
See also CA 104; CDBLB 1890-1914;
DAM POET

Russell, (Henry) Ken(neth Alfred)
1927- . . . . **CLC 16**
See also CA 105

Russell, Willy 1947- . . . . **CLC 60**

Rutherford, Mark . . . . **TCLC 25**
See also White, William Hale
See also DLB 18

Ruyslinck, Ward 1929- . . . . **CLC 14**
See also Belser, Reimond Karel Maria de

Ryan, Cornelius (John) 1920-1974 . . . **CLC 7**
See also CA 69-72; 53-56; CANR 38

Ryan, Michael 1946- . . . . **CLC 65**
See also CA 49-52; DLBY 82

Rybakov, Anatoli (Naumovich)
1911- . . . . **CLC 23, 53**
See also CA 126; 135; SATA 79

Ryder, Jonathan
See Ludlum, Robert

Ryga, George 1932-1987 . . . . . **CLC 14; DAC**
See also CA 101; 124; CANR 43;
DAM MST; DLB 60

S. S.
See Sassoon, Siegfried (Lorraine)

Saba, Umberto 1883-1957 . . . . **TCLC 33**
See also CA 144; DLB 114

Sabatini, Rafael 1875-1950 . . . . **TCLC 47**

Sabato, Ernesto (R.)
1911- . . . . **CLC 10, 23; HLC**
See also CA 97-100; CANR 32;
DAM MULT; DLB 145; HW; MTCW

Sacastru, Martin
See Bioy Casares, Adolfo

Sacher-Masoch, Leopold von
1836(?)-1895 . . . . **NCLC 31**

Sachs, Marilyn (Stickle) 1927- . . . . . **CLC 35**
See also AAYA 2; CA 17-20R; CANR 13,
47; CLR 2; JRDA; MAICYA; SAAS 2;
SATA 3, 68

Sachs, Nelly 1891-1970 . . . . **CLC 14**
See also CA 17-18; 25-28R; CAP 2

Sackler, Howard (Oliver)
1929-1982 . . . . **CLC 14**
See also CA 61-64; 108; CANR 30; DLB 7

Sacks, Oliver (Wolf) 1933- . . . . **CLC 67**
See also CA 53-56; CANR 28, 50;
INT CANR-28; MTCW

Sade, Donatien Alphonse Francois Comte
1740-1814 . . . . **NCLC 47**

Sadoff, Ira 1945- . . . . **CLC 9**
See also CA 53-56; CANR 5, 21; DLB 120

Saetone
See Camus, Albert

Safire, William 1929- . . . . **CLC 10**
See also CA 17-20R; CANR 31

Sagan, Carl (Edward) 1934- . . . . **CLC 30**
See also AAYA 2; CA 25-28R; CANR 11,
36; MTCW; SATA 58

Sagan, Francoise . . . . **CLC 3, 6, 9, 17, 36**
See also Quoirez, Francoise
See also DLB 83

Sahgal, Nayantara (Pandit) 1927- . . . **CLC 41**
See also CA 9-12R; CANR 11

Saint, H(arry) F. 1941- . . . . **CLC 50**
See also CA 127

St. Aubin de Teran, Lisa 1953-
See Teran, Lisa St. Aubin de
See also CA 118; 126; INT 126

Sainte-Beuve, Charles Augustin
1804-1869 . . . . **NCLC 5**

**Saint-Exupery, Antoine (Jean Baptiste Marie
Roger) de**
1900-1944 . . . . **TCLC 2, 56; WLC**
See also CA 108; 132; CLR 10; DAM NOV;
DLB 72; MAICYA; MTCW; SATA 20

St. John, David
See Hunt, E(verette) Howard, (Jr.)

Saint-John Perse
See Leger, (Marie-Rene Auguste) Alexis
Saint-Leger

Saintsbury, George (Edward Bateman)
1845-1933 . . . . **TCLC 31**
See also DLB 57, 149

Sait Faik . . . . **TCLC 23**
See also Abasiyanik, Sait Faik

Saki . . . . **TCLC 3; SSC 12**
See also Munro, H(ector) H(ugh)

Sala, George Augustus . . . . **NCLC 46**

Salama, Hannu 1936- . . . . **CLC 18**

Salamanca, J(ack) R(ichard)
1922- . . . . **CLC 4, 15**
See also CA 25-28R

Sale, J. Kirkpatrick
See Sale, Kirkpatrick

Sale, Kirkpatrick 1937- . . . . **CLC 68**
See also CA 13-16R; CANR 10

Salinas, Luis Omar 1937- . . . **CLC 90; HLC**
See also CA 131; DAM MULT; DLB 82;
HW

Salinas (y Serrano), Pedro
1891(?)-1951 . . . . **TCLC 17**
See also CA 117; DLB 134

Salinger, J(erome) D(avid)
1919- . . . . . . **CLC 1, 3, 8, 12, 55, 56; DA;
DAB; DAC; SSC 2; WLC**
See also AAYA 2; CA 5-8R; CANR 39;
CDALB 1941-1968; CLR 18; DAM MST,
NOV, POP; DLB 2, 102; MAICYA;
MTCW; SATA 67

Salisbury, John
See Caute, David

Salter, James 1925- . . . . **CLC 7, 52, 59**
See also CA 73-76; DLB 130

Saltus, Edgar (Everton)
1855-1921 . . . . **TCLC 8**
See also CA 105

Saltykov, Mikhail Evgrafovich
1826-1889 . . . . **NCLC 16**

Samarakis, Antonis 1919- . . . . **CLC 5**
See also CA 25-28R; CAAS 16; CANR 36

Sanchez, Florencio 1875-1910 . . . . . **TCLC 37**
See also HW

Sanchez, Luis Rafael 1936- . . . . **CLC 23**
See also CA 128; DLB 145; HW

Sanchez, Sonia 1934- . . . **CLC 5; BLC; PC 9**
See also BW 2; CA 33-36R; CANR 24, 49;
CLR 18; DAM MULT; DLB 41;
DLBD 8; MAICYA; MTCW; SATA 22

Sand, George
1804-1876 . . . . **NCLC 2, 42, 57; DA;
DAB; DAC; WLC**
See also DAM MST, NOV; DLB 119

Sandburg, Carl (August)
1878-1967 . . . . **CLC 1, 4, 10, 15, 35; DA;
DAB; DAC; PC 2; WLC**
See also CA 5-8R; 25-28R; CANR 35;
CDALB 1865-1917; DAM MST, POET;
DLB 17, 54; MAICYA; MTCW; SATA 8

Sandburg, Charles
See Sandburg, Carl (August)

Sandburg, Charles A.
See Sandburg, Carl (August)

Sanders, (James) Ed(ward) 1939- . . . **CLC 53**
See also CA 13-16R; CAAS 21; CANR 13,
44; DLB 16

Sanders, Lawrence 1920- . . . . **CLC 41**
See also BEST 89:4; CA 81-84; CANR 33;
DAM POP; MTCW

Sanders, Noah
See Blount, Roy (Alton), Jr.

Sanders, Winston P.
See Anderson, Poul (William)

Sandoz, Mari(e Susette)
1896-1966 . . . . **CLC 28**
See also CA 1-4R; 25-28R; CANR 17;
DLB 9; MTCW; SATA 5

Saner, Reg(inald Anthony) 1931- . . . . **CLC 9**
See also CA 65-68

Sannazaro, Jacopo 1456(?)-1530 . . . . . . **LC 8**

Sansom, William
1912-1976 . . . . **CLC 2, 6; SSC 21**
See also CA 5-8R; 65-68; CANR 42;
DAM NOV; DLB 139; MTCW

Santayana, George 1863-1952 . . . . . **TCLC 40**
See also CA 115; DLB 54, 71; DLBD 13

Santiago, Danny . . . . CLC 33
See also James, Daniel (Lewis)
See also DLB 122

Santmyer, Helen Hoover
1895-1986 . . . . CLC 33
See also CA 1-4R; 118; CANR 15, 33;
DLBY 84; MTCW

Santos, Bienvenido N(uqui)
1911-1996 . . . . CLC 22
See also CA 101; 151; CANR 19, 46;
DAM MULT

Sapper . . . . TCLC 44
See also McNeile, Herman Cyril

Sappho   fl. 6th cent. B.C.- . . . . CMLC 3; PC 5
See also DAM POET

Sarduy, Severo   1937-1993 . . . . CLC 6
See also CA 89-92; 142; DLB 113; HW

Sargeson, Frank   1903-1982 . . . . CLC 31
See also CA 25-28R; 106; CANR 38

Sarmiento, Felix Ruben Garcia
See Dario, Ruben

Saroyan, William
1908-1981 . . . . . CLC 1, 8, 10, 29, 34, 56;
DA; DAB; DAC; SSC 21; WLC
See also CA 5-8R; 103; CANR 30;
DAM DRAM, MST, NOV; DLB 7, 9, 86;
DLBY 81; MTCW; SATA 23;
SATA-Obit 24

Sarraute, Nathalie
1900- . . . . CLC 1, 2, 4, 8, 10, 31, 80
See also CA 9-12R; CANR 23; DLB 83;
MTCW

Sarton, (Eleanor) May
1912-1995 . . . . CLC 4, 14, 49, 91
See also CA 1-4R; 149; CANR 1, 34;
DAM POET; DLB 48; DLBY 81;
INT CANR-34; MTCW; SATA 36;
SATA-Obit 86

Sartre, Jean-Paul
1905-1980 . . . . CLC 1, 4, 7, 9, 13, 18, 24,
44, 50, 52; DA; DAB; DAC; DC 3; WLC
See also CA 9-12R; 97-100; CANR 21;
DAM DRAM, MST, NOV; DLB 72;
MTCW

Sassoon, Siegfried (Lorraine)
1886-1967 . . . . CLC 36; DAB; PC 12
See also CA 104; 25-28R; CANR 36;
DAM MST, NOV, POET; DLB 20;
MTCW

Satterfield, Charles
See Pohl, Frederik

Saul, John (W. III)   1942- . . . . CLC 46
See also AAYA 10; BEST 90:4; CA 81-84;
CANR 16, 40; DAM NOV, POP

Saunders, Caleb
See Heinlein, Robert A(nson)

Saura (Atares), Carlos   1932- . . . . CLC 20
See also CA 114; 131; HW

Sauser-Hall, Frederic   1887-1961 . . . . CLC 18
See also Cendrars, Blaise
See also CA 102; 93-96; CANR 36; MTCW

Saussure, Ferdinand de
1857-1913 . . . . TCLC 49

Savage, Catharine
See Brosman, Catharine Savage

Savage, Thomas   1915- . . . . CLC 40
See also CA 126; 132; CAAS 15; INT 132

Savan, Glenn   19(?)- . . . . CLC 50

Sayers, Dorothy L(eigh)
1893-1957 . . . . TCLC 2, 15
See also CA 104; 119; CDBLB 1914-1945;
DAM POP; DLB 10, 36, 77, 100; MTCW

Sayers, Valerie   1952- . . . . CLC 50
See also CA 134

Sayles, John (Thomas)
1950- . . . . CLC 7, 10, 14
See also CA 57-60; CANR 41; DLB 44

Scammell, Michael . . . . CLC 34

Scannell, Vernon   1922- . . . . CLC 49
See also CA 5-8R; CANR 8, 24; DLB 27;
SATA 59

Scarlett, Susan
See Streatfeild, (Mary) Noel

Schaeffer, Susan Fromberg
1941- . . . . CLC 6, 11, 22
See also CA 49-52; CANR 18; DLB 28;
MTCW; SATA 22

Schary, Jill
See Robinson, Jill

Schell, Jonathan   1943- . . . . CLC 35
See also CA 73-76; CANR 12

Schelling, Friedrich Wilhelm Joseph von
1775-1854 . . . . NCLC 30
See also DLB 90

Schendel, Arthur van   1874-1946 . . . TCLC 56

Scherer, Jean-Marie Maurice   1920-
See Rohmer, Eric
See also CA 110

Schevill, James (Erwin)   1920- . . . . . . CLC 7
See also CA 5-8R; CAAS 12

Schiller, Friedrich   1759-1805 . . . . NCLC 39
See also DAM DRAM; DLB 94

Schisgal, Murray (Joseph)   1926- . . . . . CLC 6
See also CA 21-24R; CANR 48

Schlee, Ann   1934- . . . . CLC 35
See also CA 101; CANR 29; SATA 44;
SATA-Brief 36

Schlegel, August Wilhelm von
1767-1845 . . . . NCLC 15
See also DLB 94

Schlegel, Friedrich   1772-1829 . . . . NCLC 45
See also DLB 90

Schlegel, Johann Elias (von)
1719(?)-1749 . . . . LC 5

Schlesinger, Arthur M(eier), Jr.
1917- . . . . CLC 84
See also AITN 1; CA 1-4R; CANR 1, 28;
DLB 17; INT CANR-28; MTCW;
SATA 61

Schmidt, Arno (Otto)   1914-1979 . . . . CLC 56
See also CA 128; 109; DLB 69

Schmitz, Aron Hector   1861-1928
See Svevo, Italo
See also CA 104; 122; MTCW

Schnackenberg, Gjertrud   1953- . . . . . CLC 40
See also CA 116; DLB 120

Schneider, Leonard Alfred   1925-1966
See Bruce, Lenny
See also CA 89-92

Schnitzler, Arthur
1862-1931 . . . . TCLC 4; SSC 15
See also CA 104; DLB 81, 118

Schopenhauer, Arthur
1788-1860 . . . . NCLC 51
See also DLB 90

Schor, Sandra (M.)   1932(?)-1990 . . . CLC 65
See also CA 132

Schorer, Mark   1908-1977 . . . . CLC 9
See also CA 5-8R; 73-76; CANR 7;
DLB 103

Schrader, Paul (Joseph)   1946- . . . . . CLC 26
See also CA 37-40R; CANR 41; DLB 44

Schreiner, Olive (Emilie Albertina)
1855-1920 . . . . TCLC 9
See also CA 105; DLB 18, 156

Schulberg, Budd (Wilson)
1914- . . . . CLC 7, 48
See also CA 25-28R; CANR 19; DLB 6, 26,
28; DLBY 81

Schulz, Bruno
1892-1942 . . . . TCLC 5, 51; SSC 13
See also CA 115; 123

Schulz, Charles M(onroe)   1922- . . . . CLC 12
See also CA 9-12R; CANR 6;
INT CANR-6; SATA 10

Schumacher, E(rnst) F(riedrich)
1911-1977 . . . . CLC 80
See also CA 81-84; 73-76; CANR 34

Schuyler, James Marcus
1923-1991 . . . . CLC 5, 23
See also CA 101; 134; DAM POET; DLB 5;
INT 101

Schwartz, Delmore (David)
1913-1966 . . . CLC 2, 4, 10, 45, 87; PC 8
See also CA 17-18; 25-28R; CANR 35;
CAP 2; DLB 28, 48; MTCW

Schwartz, Ernst
See Ozu, Yasujiro

Schwartz, John Burnham   1965- . . . . CLC 59
See also CA 132

Schwartz, Lynne Sharon   1939- . . . . . CLC 31
See also CA 103; CANR 44

Schwartz, Muriel A.
See Eliot, T(homas) S(tearns)

Schwarz-Bart, Andre   1928- . . . . CLC 2, 4
See also CA 89-92

Schwarz-Bart, Simone   1938- . . . . CLC 7
See also BW 2; CA 97-100

Schwob, (Mayer Andre) Marcel
1867-1905 . . . . TCLC 20
See also CA 117; DLB 123

Sciascia, Leonardo
1921-1989 . . . . CLC 8, 9, 41
See also CA 85-88; 130; CANR 35; MTCW

Scoppettone, Sandra   1936- . . . . CLC 26
See also AAYA 11; CA 5-8R; CANR 41;
SATA 9

Scorsese, Martin   1942- . . . . CLC 20, 89
See also CA 110; 114; CANR 46

Scotland, Jay
See Jakes, John (William)

Scott, Duncan Campbell
1862-1947 . . . . TCLC 6; DAC
See also CA 104; DLB 92

Shaw, George Bernard
1856-1950 ... **TCLC 3, 9, 21; DA; DAB; DAC; WLC**
See also Shaw, Bernard
See also CA 104; 128; CDBLB 1914-1945; DAM DRAM, MST; DLB 10, 57; MTCW

Shaw, Henry Wheeler
1818-1885 .... **NCLC 15**
See also DLB 11

Shaw, Irwin 1913-1984...... **CLC 7, 23, 34**
See also AITN 1; CA 13-16R; 112; CANR 21; CDALB 1941-1968; DAM DRAM, POP; DLB 6, 102; DLBY 84; MTCW

Shaw, Robert 1927-1978 .... **CLC 5**
See also AITN 1; CA 1-4R; 81-84; CANR 4; DLB 13, 14

Shaw, T. E.
See Lawrence, T(homas) E(dward)

Shawn, Wallace 1943- .... **CLC 41**
See also CA 112

Shea, Lisa 1953-................ **CLC 86**
See also CA 147

Sheed, Wilfrid (John Joseph)
1930- .... **CLC 2, 4, 10, 53**
See also CA 65-68; CANR 30; DLB 6; MTCW

Sheldon, Alice Hastings Bradley
1915(?)-1987
See Tiptree, James, Jr.
See also CA 108; 122; CANR 34; INT 108; MTCW

Sheldon, John
See Bloch, Robert (Albert)

Shelley, Mary Wollstonecraft (Godwin)
1797-1851 .... **NCLC 14; DA; DAB; DAC; WLC**
See also CDBLB 1789-1832; DAM MST, NOV; DLB 110, 116, 159; SATA 29

Shelley, Percy Bysshe
1792-1822 .... **NCLC 18; DA; DAB; DAC; PC 14; WLC**
See also CDBLB 1789-1832; DAM MST, POET; DLB 96, 110, 158

Shepard, Jim 1956-................ **CLC 36**
See also CA 137

Shepard, Lucius 1947- .... **CLC 34**
See also CA 128; 141

Shepard, Sam
1943- .... **CLC 4, 6, 17, 34, 41, 44; DC 5**
See also AAYA 1; CA 69-72; CABS 3; CANR 22; DAM DRAM; DLB 7; MTCW

Shepherd, Michael
See Ludlum, Robert

Sherburne, Zoa (Morin) 1912-...... **CLC 30**
See also AAYA 13; CA 1-4R; CANR 3, 37; MAICYA; SAAS 18; SATA 3

Sheridan, Frances 1724-1766........ **LC 7**
See also DLB 39, 84

Sheridan, Richard Brinsley
1751-1816 .... **NCLC 5; DA; DAB; DAC; DC 1; WLC**
See also CDBLB 1660-1789; DAM DRAM, MST; DLB 89

Sherman, Jonathan Marc.......... **CLC 55**

Sherman, Martin 1941(?)- .... **CLC 19**
See also CA 116; 123

Sherwin, Judith Johnson 1936-... **CLC 7, 15**
See also CA 25-28R; CANR 34

Sherwood, Frances 1940-......... **CLC 81**
See also CA 146

Sherwood, Robert E(mmet)
1896-1955 .... **TCLC 3**
See also CA 104; DAM DRAM; DLB 7, 26

Shestov, Lev 1866-1938 .... **TCLC 56**

Shevchenko, Taras 1814-1861 .... **NCLC 54**

Shiel, M(atthew) P(hipps)
1865-1947 .... **TCLC 8**
See also CA 106; DLB 153

Shields, Carol 1935-......... **CLC 91; DAC**
See also CA 81-84; CANR 51

Shiga, Naoya 1883-1971... **CLC 33; SSC 23**
See also CA 101; 33-36R

Shilts, Randy 1951-1994 .... **CLC 85**
See also CA 115; 127; 144; CANR 45; INT 127

Shimazaki, Haruki 1872-1943
See Shimazaki Toson
See also CA 105; 134

Shimazaki Toson................. **TCLC 5**
See also Shimazaki, Haruki

Sholokhov, Mikhail (Aleksandrovich)
1905-1984 .... **CLC 7, 15**
See also CA 101; 112; MTCW; SATA-Obit 36

Shone, Patric
See Hanley, James

Shreve, Susan Richards 1939-...... **CLC 23**
See also CA 49-52; CAAS 5; CANR 5, 38; MAICYA; SATA 46; SATA-Brief 41

Shue, Larry 1946-1985............ **CLC 52**
See also CA 145; 117; DAM DRAM

Shu-Jen, Chou 1881-1936
See Lu Hsun
See also CA 104

Shulman, Alix Kates 1932- ...... **CLC 2, 10**
See also CA 29-32R; CANR 43; SATA 7

Shuster, Joe 1914- .... **CLC 21**

Shute, Nevil.................... **CLC 30**
See also Norway, Nevil Shute

Shuttle, Penelope (Diane) 1947- ..... **CLC 7**
See also CA 93-96; CANR 39; DLB 14, 40

Sidney, Mary 1561-1621 .... **LC 19**

Sidney, Sir Philip
1554-1586 ..... **LC 19; DA; DAB; DAC**
See also CDBLB Before 1660; DAM MST, POET; DLB 167

Siegel, Jerome 1914-1996 .... **CLC 21**
See also CA 116; 151

Siegel, Jerry
See Siegel, Jerome

Sienkiewicz, Henryk (Adam Alexander Pius)
1846-1916 .... **TCLC 3**
See also CA 104; 134

Sierra, Gregorio Martinez
See Martinez Sierra, Gregorio

Sierra, Maria (de la O'LeJarraga) Martinez
See Martinez Sierra, Maria (de la O'LeJarraga)

Sigal, Clancy 1926-................ **CLC 7**
See also CA 1-4R

Sigourney, Lydia Howard (Huntley)
1791-1865 .... **NCLC 21**
See also DLB 1, 42, 73

Siguenza y Gongora, Carlos de
1645-1700 .... **LC 8**

Sigurjonsson, Johann 1880-1919... **TCLC 27**

Sikelianos, Angelos 1884-1951 .... **TCLC 39**

Silkin, Jon 1930- .... **CLC 2, 6, 43**
See also CA 5-8R; CAAS 5; DLB 27

Silko, Leslie (Marmon)
1948- .... **CLC 23, 74; DA; DAC**
See also AAYA 14; CA 115; 122; CANR 45; DAM MST, MULT, POP; DLB 143; NNAL

Sillanpaa, Frans Eemil 1888-1964... **CLC 19**
See also CA 129; 93-96; MTCW

Sillitoe, Alan
1928- .... **CLC 1, 3, 6, 10, 19, 57**
See also AITN 1; CA 9-12R; CAAS 2; CANR 8, 26; CDBLB 1960 to Present; DLB 14, 139; MTCW; SATA 61

Silone, Ignazio 1900-1978 .... **CLC 4**
See also CA 25-28; 81-84; CANR 34; CAP 2; MTCW

Silver, Joan Micklin 1935- .... **CLC 20**
See also CA 114; 121; INT 121

Silver, Nicholas
See Faust, Frederick (Schiller)

Silverberg, Robert 1935- .... **CLC 7**
See also CA 1-4R; CAAS 3; CANR 1, 20, 36; DAM POP; DLB 8; INT CANR-20; MAICYA; MTCW; SATA 13

Silverstein, Alvin 1933- .... **CLC 17**
See also CA 49-52; CANR 2; CLR 25; JRDA; MAICYA; SATA 8, 69

Silverstein, Virginia B(arbara Opshelor)
1937-..................... **CLC 17**
See also CA 49-52; CANR 2; CLR 25; JRDA; MAICYA; SATA 8, 69

Sim, Georges
See Simenon, Georges (Jacques Christian)

Simak, Clifford D(onald)
1904-1988 .... **CLC 1, 55**
See also CA 1-4R; 125; CANR 1, 35; DLB 8; MTCW; SATA-Obit 56

Simenon, Georges (Jacques Christian)
1903-1989 .... **CLC 1, 2, 3, 8, 18, 47**
See also CA 85-88; 129; CANR 35; DAM POP; DLB 72; DLBY 89; MTCW

Simic, Charles 1938-... **CLC 6, 9, 22, 49, 68**
See also CA 29-32R; CAAS 4; CANR 12, 33, 52; DAM POET; DLB 105

Simmel, Georg 1858-1918 .... **TCLC 64**

Simmons, Charles (Paul) 1924-.... **CLC 57**
See also CA 89-92; INT 89-92

Simmons, Dan 1948-............. **CLC 44**
See also AAYA 16; CA 138; CANR 53; DAM POP

Snow, C(harles) P(ercy)
1905-1980 . . . . **CLC 1, 4, 6, 9, 13, 19**
See also CA 5-8R; 101; CANR 28;
CDBLB 1945-1960; DAM NOV; DLB 15,
77; MTCW

Snow, Frances Compton
See Adams, Henry (Brooks)

Snyder, Gary (Sherman)
1930- . . . . **CLC 1, 2, 5, 9, 32**
See also CA 17-20R; CANR 30;
DAM POET; DLB 5, 16, 165

Snyder, Zilpha Keatley 1927- . . . . . . **CLC 17**
See also AAYA 15; CA 9-12R; CANR 38;
CLR 31; JRDA; MAICYA; SAAS 2;
SATA 1, 28, 75

Soares, Bernardo
See Pessoa, Fernando (Antonio Nogueira)

Sobh, A.
See Shamlu, Ahmad

Sobol, Joshua . . . . **CLC 60**

Soderberg, Hjalmar 1869-1941 . . . . **TCLC 39**

Sodergran, Edith (Irene)
See Soedergran, Edith (Irene)

Soedergran, Edith (Irene)
1892-1923 . . . . **TCLC 31**

Softly, Edgar
See Lovecraft, H(oward) P(hillips)

Softly, Edward
See Lovecraft, H(oward) P(hillips)

Sokolov, Raymond 1941- . . . . **CLC 7**
See also CA 85-88

Solo, Jay
See Ellison, Harlan (Jay)

Sologub, Fyodor . . . . **TCLC 9**
See also Teternikov, Fyodor Kuzmich

Solomons, Ikey Esquir
See Thackeray, William Makepeace

Solomos, Dionysios 1798-1857 . . . **NCLC 15**

Solwoska, Mara
See French, Marilyn

Solzhenitsyn, Aleksandr I(sayevich)
1918- . . . . . . **CLC 1, 2, 4, 7, 9, 10, 18, 26,
34, 78; DA; DAB; DAC; WLC**
See also AITN 1; CA 69-72; CANR 40;
DAM MST, NOV; MTCW

Somers, Jane
See Lessing, Doris (May)

Somerville, Edith 1858-1949 . . . . . . **TCLC 51**
See also DLB 135

Somerville & Ross
See Martin, Violet Florence; Somerville,
Edith

Sommer, Scott 1951- . . . . **CLC 25**
See also CA 106

Sondheim, Stephen (Joshua)
1930- . . . . **CLC 30, 39**
See also AAYA 11; CA 103; CANR 47;
DAM DRAM

Sontag, Susan 1933- . . . **CLC 1, 2, 10, 13, 31**
See also CA 17-20R; CANR 25, 51;
DAM POP; DLB 2, 67; MTCW

Sophocles
496(?)B.C.-406(?)B.C. . . . . **CMLC 2; DA;
DAB; DAC; DC 1**
See also DAM DRAM, MST

Sordello 1189-1269 . . . . **CMLC 15**

Sorel, Julia
See Drexler, Rosalyn

Sorrentino, Gilbert
1929- . . . . **CLC 3, 7, 14, 22, 40**
See also CA 77-80; CANR 14, 33; DLB 5;
DLBY 80; INT CANR-14

Soto, Gary 1952- . . . . **CLC 32, 80; HLC**
See also AAYA 10; CA 119; 125;
CANR 50; CLR 38; DAM MULT;
DLB 82; HW; INT 125; JRDA; SATA 80

Soupault, Philippe 1897-1990 . . . . . . **CLC 68**
See also CA 116; 147; 131

Souster, (Holmes) Raymond
1921- . . . . **CLC 5, 14; DAC**
See also CA 13-16R; CAAS 14; CANR 13,
29, 53; DAM POET; DLB 88; SATA 63

Southern, Terry 1924(?)-1995 . . . . **CLC 7**
See also CA 1-4R; 150; CANR 1; DLB 2

Southey, Robert 1774-1843 . . . . **NCLC 8**
See also DLB 93, 107, 142; SATA 54

Southworth, Emma Dorothy Eliza Nevitte
1819-1899 . . . . **NCLC 26**

Souza, Ernest
See Scott, Evelyn

Soyinka, Wole
1934- . . . . **CLC 3, 5, 14, 36, 44; BLC;
DA; DAB; DAC; DC 2; WLC**
See also BW 2; CA 13-16R; CANR 27, 39;
DAM DRAM, MST, MULT; DLB 125;
MTCW

Spackman, W(illiam) M(ode)
1905-1990 . . . . **CLC 46**
See also CA 81-84; 132

Spacks, Barry 1931- . . . . **CLC 14**
See also CA 29-32R; CANR 33; DLB 105

Spanidou, Irini 1946- . . . . **CLC 44**

Spark, Muriel (Sarah)
1918- . . . . . **CLC 2, 3, 5, 8, 13, 18, 40, 94;
DAB; DAC; SSC 10**
See also CA 5-8R; CANR 12, 36;
CDBLB 1945-1960; DAM MST, NOV;
DLB 15, 139; INT CANR-12; MTCW

Spaulding, Douglas
See Bradbury, Ray (Douglas)

Spaulding, Leonard
See Bradbury, Ray (Douglas)

Spence, J. A. D.
See Eliot, T(homas) S(tearns)

Spencer, Elizabeth 1921- . . . . **CLC 22**
See also CA 13-16R; CANR 32; DLB 6;
MTCW; SATA 14

Spencer, Leonard G.
See Silverberg, Robert

Spencer, Scott 1945- . . . . **CLC 30**
See also CA 113; CANR 51; DLBY 86

Spender, Stephen (Harold)
1909-1995 . . . . . . **CLC 1, 2, 5, 10, 41, 91**
See also CA 9-12R; 149; CANR 31;
CDBLB 1945-1960; DAM POET;
DLB 20; MTCW

Spengler, Oswald (Arnold Gottfried)
1880-1936 . . . . **TCLC 25**
See also CA 118

Spenser, Edmund
1552(?)-1599 . . . . **LC 5; DA; DAB; DAC;
PC 8; WLC**
See also CDBLB Before 1660; DAM MST,
POET; DLB 167

Spicer, Jack 1925-1965 . . . . . . **CLC 8, 18, 72**
See also CA 85-88; DAM POET; DLB 5, 16

Spiegelman, Art 1948- . . . . **CLC 76**
See also AAYA 10; CA 125; CANR 41

Spielberg, Peter 1929- . . . . **CLC 6**
See also CA 5-8R; CANR 4, 48; DLBY 81

Spielberg, Steven 1947- . . . . **CLC 20**
See also AAYA 8; CA 77-80; CANR 32;
SATA 32

Spillane, Frank Morrison 1918-
See Spillane, Mickey
See also CA 25-28R; CANR 28; MTCW;
SATA 66

Spillane, Mickey . . . . **CLC 3, 13**
See also Spillane, Frank Morrison

Spinoza, Benedictus de 1632-1677 . . . . **LC 9**

Spinrad, Norman (Richard) 1940- . . . **CLC 46**
See also CA 37-40R; CAAS 19; CANR 20;
DLB 8; INT CANR-20

Spitteler, Carl (Friedrich Georg)
1845-1924 . . . . **TCLC 12**
See also CA 109; DLB 129

Spivack, Kathleen (Romola Drucker)
1938- . . . . **CLC 6**
See also CA 49-52

Spoto, Donald 1941- . . . . **CLC 39**
See also CA 65-68; CANR 11

Springsteen, Bruce (F.) 1949- . . . . . . **CLC 17**
See also CA 111

Spurling, Hilary 1940- . . . . **CLC 34**
See also CA 104; CANR 25, 52

Spyker, John Howland
See Elman, Richard

Squires, (James) Radcliffe
1917-1993 . . . . **CLC 51**
See also CA 1-4R; 140; CANR 6, 21

Srivastava, Dhanpat Rai 1880(?)-1936
See Premchand
See also CA 118

Stacy, Donald
See Pohl, Frederik

Stael, Germaine de
See Stael-Holstein, Anne Louise Germaine
Necker Baronn
See also DLB 119

**Stael-Holstein, Anne Louise Germaine Necker
Baronn** 1766-1817 . . . . **NCLC 3**
See also Stael, Germaine de

Stafford, Jean 1915-1979 . . . **CLC 4, 7, 19, 68**
See also CA 1-4R; 85-88; CANR 3; DLB 2;
MTCW; SATA-Obit 22

Stafford, William (Edgar)
1914-1993 . . . . **CLC 4, 7, 29**
See also CA 5-8R; 142; CAAS 3; CANR 5,
22; DAM POET; DLB 5; INT CANR-22

Staines, Trevor
See Brunner, John (Kilian Houston)

Stowe, Harriet (Elizabeth) Beecher
1811-1896 . . . . . **NCLC 3, 50; DA; DAB;
DAC; WLC**
See also CDALB 1865-1917; DAM MST,
NOV; DLB 1, 12, 42, 74; JRDA;
MAICYA; YABC 1

Strachey, (Giles) Lytton
1880-1932 . . . . **TCLC 12**
See also CA 110; DLB 149; DLBD 10

Strand, Mark 1934- . . . . . . **CLC 6, 18, 41, 71**
See also CA 21-24R; CANR 40;
DAM POET; DLB 5; SATA 41

Straub, Peter (Francis) 1943- . . . . . . **CLC 28**
See also BEST 89:1; CA 85-88; CANR 28;
DAM POP; DLBY 84; MTCW

Strauss, Botho 1944- . . . . **CLC 22**
See also DLB 124

Streatfeild, (Mary) Noel
1895(?)-1986 . . . . **CLC 21**
See also CA 81-84; 120; CANR 31;
CLR 17; DLB 160; MAICYA; SATA 20;
SATA-Obit 48

Stribling, T(homas) S(igismund)
1881-1965 . . . . **CLC 23**
See also CA 107; DLB 9

Strindberg, (Johan) August
1849-1912 . . . . . . **TCLC 1, 8, 21, 47; DA;
DAB; DAC; WLC**
See also CA 104; 135; DAM DRAM, MST

Stringer, Arthur 1874-1950 . . . . . . **TCLC 37**
See also DLB 92

Stringer, David
See Roberts, Keith (John Kingston)

Strugatskii, Arkadii (Natanovich)
1925-1991 . . . . **CLC 27**
See also CA 106; 135

Strugatskii, Boris (Natanovich)
1933- . . . . **CLC 27**
See also CA 106

Strummer, Joe 1953(?)- . . . . **CLC 30**

Stuart, Don A.
See Campbell, John W(ood, Jr.)

Stuart, Ian
See MacLean, Alistair (Stuart)

Stuart, Jesse (Hilton)
1906-1984 . . . . **CLC 1, 8, 11, 14, 34**
See also CA 5-8R; 112; CANR 31; DLB 9,
48, 102; DLBY 84; SATA 2;
SATA-Obit 36

Sturgeon, Theodore (Hamilton)
1918-1985 . . . . **CLC 22, 39**
See also Queen, Ellery
See also CA 81-84; 116; CANR 32; DLB 8;
DLBY 85; MTCW

Sturges, Preston 1898-1959 . . . . . . **TCLC 48**
See also CA 114; 149; DLB 26

Styron, William
1925- . . . . **CLC 1, 3, 5, 11, 15, 60**
See also BEST 90:4; CA 5-8R; CANR 6, 33;
CDALB 1968-1988; DAM NOV, POP;
DLB 2, 143; DLBY 80; INT CANR-6;
MTCW

Suarez Lynch, B.
See Bioy Casares, Adolfo; Borges, Jorge
Luis

Su Chien 1884-1918
See Su Man-shu
See also CA 123

Suckow, Ruth 1892-1960 . . . . **SSC 18**
See also CA 113; DLB 9, 102

Sudermann, Hermann 1857-1928 . . **TCLC 15**
See also CA 107; DLB 118

Sue, Eugene 1804-1857 . . . . **NCLC 1**
See also DLB 119

Sueskind, Patrick 1949- . . . . **CLC 44**
See also Suskind, Patrick

Sukenick, Ronald 1932- . . . . . **CLC 3, 4, 6, 48**
See also CA 25-28R; CAAS 8; CANR 32;
DLBY 81

Suknaski, Andrew 1942- . . . . **CLC 19**
See also CA 101; DLB 53

Sullivan, Vernon
See Vian, Boris

Sully Prudhomme 1839-1907 . . . . . . **TCLC 31**

Su Man-shu . . . . **TCLC 24**
See also Su Chien

Summerforest, Ivy B.
See Kirkup, James

Summers, Andrew James 1942- . . . . . **CLC 26**

Summers, Andy
See Summers, Andrew James

Summers, Hollis (Spurgeon, Jr.)
1916- . . . . **CLC 10**
See also CA 5-8R; CANR 3; DLB 6

Summers, (Alphonsus Joseph-Mary Augustus)
Montague 1880-1948 . . . . **TCLC 16**
See also CA 118

Sumner, Gordon Matthew 1951- . . . . **CLC 26**

Surtees, Robert Smith
1803-1864 . . . . **NCLC 14**
See also DLB 21

Susann, Jacqueline 1921-1974 . . . . . . **CLC 3**
See also AITN 1; CA 65-68; 53-56; MTCW

Su Shih 1036-1101 . . . . **CMLC 15**

Suskind, Patrick
See Sueskind, Patrick
See also CA 145

Sutcliff, Rosemary
1920-1992 . . . . **CLC 26; DAB; DAC**
See also AAYA 10; CA 5-8R; 139;
CANR 37; CLR 1, 37; DAM MST, POP;
JRDA; MAICYA; SATA 6, 44, 78;
SATA-Obit 73

Sutro, Alfred 1863-1933 . . . . **TCLC 6**
See also CA 105; DLB 10

Sutton, Henry
See Slavitt, David R(ytman)

Svevo, Italo . . . . **TCLC 2, 35**
See also Schmitz, Aron Hector

Swados, Elizabeth (A.) 1951- . . . . **CLC 12**
See also CA 97-100; CANR 49; INT 97-100

Swados, Harvey 1920-1972 . . . . **CLC 5**
See also CA 5-8R; 37-40R; CANR 6;
DLB 2

Swan, Gladys 1934- . . . . **CLC 69**
See also CA 101; CANR 17, 39

Swarthout, Glendon (Fred)
1918-1992 . . . . **CLC 35**
See also CA 1-4R; 139; CANR 1, 47;
SATA 26

Sweet, Sarah C.
See Jewett, (Theodora) Sarah Orne

Swenson, May
1919-1989 . . . . **CLC 4, 14, 61; DA; DAB;
DAC; PC 14**
See also CA 5-8R; 130; CANR 36;
DAM MST, POET; DLB 5; MTCW;
SATA 15

Swift, Augustus
See Lovecraft, H(oward) P(hillips)

Swift, Graham (Colin) 1949- . . . . **CLC 41, 88**
See also CA 117; 122; CANR 46

Swift, Jonathan
1667-1745 . . . . . . **LC 1; DA; DAB; DAC;
PC 9; WLC**
See also CDBLB 1660-1789; DAM MST,
NOV, POET; DLB 39, 95, 101; SATA 19

Swinburne, Algernon Charles
1837-1909 . . . . . . **TCLC 8, 36; DA; DAB;
DAC; WLC**
See also CA 105; 140; CDBLB 1832-1890;
DAM MST, POET; DLB 35, 57

Swinfen, Ann . . . . **CLC 34**

Swinnerton, Frank Arthur
1884-1982 . . . . **CLC 31**
See also CA 108; DLB 34

Swithen, John
See King, Stephen (Edwin)

Sylvia
See Ashton-Warner, Sylvia (Constance)

Symmes, Robert Edward
See Duncan, Robert (Edward)

Symonds, John Addington
1840-1893 . . . . **NCLC 34**
See also DLB 57, 144

Symons, Arthur 1865-1945 . . . . **TCLC 11**
See also CA 107; DLB 19, 57, 149

Symons, Julian (Gustave)
1912-1994 . . . . **CLC 2, 14, 32**
See also CA 49-52; 147; CAAS 3; CANR 3,
33; DLB 87, 155; DLBY 92; MTCW

Synge, (Edmund) J(ohn) M(illington)
1871-1909 . . . . **TCLC 6, 37; DC 2**
See also CA 104; 141; CDBLB 1890-1914;
DAM DRAM; DLB 10, 19

Syruc, J.
See Milosz, Czeslaw

Szirtes, George 1948- . . . . **CLC 46**
See also CA 109; CANR 27

Tabori, George 1914- . . . . **CLC 19**
See also CA 49-52; CANR 4

Tagore, Rabindranath
1861-1941 . . . . **TCLC 3, 53; PC 8**
See also CA 104; 120; DAM DRAM,
POET; MTCW

Taine, Hippolyte Adolphe
1828-1893 . . . . **NCLC 15**

Talese, Gay 1932- . . . . **CLC 37**
See also AITN 1; CA 1-4R; CANR 9;
INT CANR-9; MTCW

Tallent, Elizabeth (Ann) 1954- ..... **CLC 45**
See also CA 117; DLB 130

Tally, Ted 1952- .... **CLC 42**
See also CA 120; 124; INT 124

Tamayo y Baus, Manuel
1829-1898 .... **NCLC 1**

Tammsaare, A(nton) H(ansen)
1878-1940 .... **TCLC 27**

Tan, Amy 1952- .... **CLC 59**
See also AAYA 9; BEST 89:3; CA 136;
DAM MULT, NOV, POP; SATA 75

Tandem, Felix
See Spitteler, Carl (Friedrich Georg)

Tanizaki, Jun'ichiro
1886-1965 ...... **CLC 8, 14, 28; SSC 21**
See also CA 93-96; 25-28R

Tanner, William
See Amis, Kingsley (William)

Tao Lao
See Storni, Alfonsina

Tarassoff, Lev
See Troyat, Henri

Tarbell, Ida M(inerva)
1857-1944 .... **TCLC 40**
See also CA 122; DLB 47

Tarkington, (Newton) Booth
1869-1946 .... **TCLC 9**
See also CA 110; 143; DLB 9, 102;
SATA 17

Tarkovsky, Andrei (Arsenyevich)
1932-1986 .... **CLC 75**
See also CA 127

Tartt, Donna 1964(?)- .... **CLC 76**
See also CA 142

Tasso, Torquato 1544-1595 .... **LC 5**

Tate, (John Orley) Allen
1899-1979 .... **CLC 2, 4, 6, 9, 11, 14, 24**
See also CA 5-8R; 85-88; CANR 32;
DLB 4, 45, 63; MTCW

Tate, Ellalice
See Hibbert, Eleanor Alice Burford

Tate, James (Vincent) 1943- ... **CLC 2, 6, 25**
See also CA 21-24R; CANR 29; DLB 5

Tavel, Ronald 1940- .... **CLC 6**
See also CA 21-24R; CANR 33

Taylor, C(ecil) P(hilip) 1929-1981... **CLC 27**
See also CA 25-28R; 105; CANR 47

Taylor, Edward
1642(?)-1729 ... **LC 11; DA; DAB; DAC**
See also DAM MST, POET; DLB 24

Taylor, Eleanor Ross 1920- .... **CLC 5**
See also CA 81-84

Taylor, Elizabeth 1912-1975 ... **CLC 2, 4, 29**
See also CA 13-16R; CANR 9; DLB 139;
MTCW; SATA 13

Taylor, Henry (Splawn) 1942- ...... **CLC 44**
See also CA 33-36R; CAAS 7; CANR 31;
DLB 5

Taylor, Kamala (Purnaiya) 1924-
See Markandaya, Kamala
See also CA 77-80

Taylor, Mildred D. .... **CLC 21**
See also AAYA 10; BW 1; CA 85-88;
CANR 25; CLR 9; DLB 52; JRDA;
MAICYA; SAAS 5; SATA 15, 70

Taylor, Peter (Hillsman)
1917-1994 ..... **CLC 1, 4, 18, 37, 44, 50,
71; SSC 10**
See also CA 13-16R; 147; CANR 9, 50;
DLBY 81, 94; INT CANR-9; MTCW

Taylor, Robert Lewis 1912- .... **CLC 14**
See also CA 1-4R; CANR 3; SATA 10

Tchekhov, Anton
See Chekhov, Anton (Pavlovich)

Teasdale, Sara 1884-1933 .... **TCLC 4**
See also CA 104; DLB 45; SATA 32

Tegner, Esaias 1782-1846 .... **NCLC 2**

Teilhard de Chardin, (Marie Joseph) Pierre
1881-1955 .... **TCLC 9**
See also CA 105

Temple, Ann
See Mortimer, Penelope (Ruth)

Tennant, Emma (Christina)
1937- .... **CLC 13, 52**
See also CA 65-68; CAAS 9; CANR 10, 38;
DLB 14

Tenneshaw, S. M.
See Silverberg, Robert

Tennyson, Alfred
1809-1892 .... **NCLC 30; DA; DAB;
DAC; PC 6; WLC**
See also CDBLB 1832-1890; DAM MST,
POET; DLB 32

Teran, Lisa St. Aubin de .... **CLC 36**
See also St. Aubin de Teran, Lisa

Terence 195(?)B.C.-159B.C. ...... **CMLC 14**

Teresa de Jesus, St. 1515-1582 ...... **LC 18**

Terkel, Louis 1912-
See Terkel, Studs
See also CA 57-60; CANR 18, 45; MTCW

Terkel, Studs .... **CLC 38**
See also Terkel, Louis
See also AITN 1

Terry, C. V.
See Slaughter, Frank G(ill)

Terry, Megan 1932- .... **CLC 19**
See also CA 77-80; CABS 3; CANR 43;
DLB 7

Tertz, Abram
See Sinyavsky, Andrei (Donatevich)

Tesich, Steve 1943(?)- .... **CLC 40, 69**
See also CA 105; DLBY 83

Teternikov, Fyodor Kuzmich 1863-1927
See Sologub, Fyodor
See also CA 104

Tevis, Walter 1928-1984 .... **CLC 42**
See also CA 113

Tey, Josephine .... **TCLC 14**
See also Mackintosh, Elizabeth
See also DLB 77

Thackeray, William Makepeace
1811-1863 .... **NCLC 5, 14, 22, 43; DA;
DAB; DAC; WLC**
See also CDBLB 1832-1890; DAM MST,
NOV; DLB 21, 55, 159, 163; SATA 23

Thakura, Ravindranatha
See Tagore, Rabindranath

Tharoor, Shashi 1956- .... **CLC 70**
See also CA 141

Thelwell, Michael Miles 1939- ..... **CLC 22**
See also BW 2; CA 101

Theobald, Lewis, Jr.
See Lovecraft, H(oward) P(hillips)

Theodorescu, Ion N. 1880-1967
See Arghezi, Tudor
See also CA 116

Theriault, Yves 1915-1983 .... **CLC 79; DAC**
See also CA 102; DAM MST; DLB 88

Theroux, Alexander (Louis)
1939- .... **CLC 2, 25**
See also CA 85-88; CANR 20

Theroux, Paul (Edward)
1941- .... **CLC 5, 8, 11, 15, 28, 46**
See also BEST 89:4; CA 33-36R; CANR 20,
45; DAM POP; DLB 2; MTCW;
SATA 44

Thesen, Sharon 1946- .... **CLC 56**

Thevenin, Denis
See Duhamel, Georges

Thibault, Jacques Anatole Francois
1844-1924
See France, Anatole
See also CA 106; 127; DAM NOV; MTCW

Thiele, Colin (Milton) 1920- .... **CLC 17**
See also CA 29-32R; CANR 12, 28, 53;
CLR 27; MAICYA; SAAS 2; SATA 14,
72

Thomas, Audrey (Callahan)
1935- .... **CLC 7, 13, 37; SSC 20**
See also AITN 2; CA 21-24R; CAAS 19;
CANR 36; DLB 60; MTCW

Thomas, D(onald) M(ichael)
1935- .... **CLC 13, 22, 31**
See also CA 61-64; CAAS 11; CANR 17,
45; CDBLB 1960 to Present; DLB 40;
INT CANR-17; MTCW

Thomas, Dylan (Marlais)
1914-1953 ... **TCLC 1, 8, 45; DA; DAB;
DAC; PC 2; SSC 3; WLC**
See also CA 104; 120; CDBLB 1945-1960;
DAM DRAM, MST, POET; DLB 13, 20,
139; MTCW; SATA 60

Thomas, (Philip) Edward
1878-1917 .... **TCLC 10**
See also CA 106; DAM POET; DLB 19

Thomas, Joyce Carol 1938- .... **CLC 35**
See also AAYA 12; BW 2; CA 113; 116;
CANR 48; CLR 19; DLB 33; INT 116;
JRDA; MAICYA; MTCW; SAAS 7;
SATA 40, 78

Thomas, Lewis 1913-1993 .... **CLC 35**
See also CA 85-88; 143; CANR 38; MTCW

Thomas, Paul
See Mann, (Paul) Thomas

Thomas, Piri 1928- .... **CLC 17**
See also CA 73-76; HW

Thomas, R(onald) S(tuart)
1913- .... **CLC 6, 13, 48; DAB**
See also CA 89-92; CAAS 4; CANR 30;
CDBLB 1960 to Present; DAM POET;
DLB 27; MTCW

Thomas, Ross (Elmore) 1926-1995 .. **CLC 39**
See also CA 33-36R; 150; CANR 22

Thompson, Francis Clegg
See Mencken, H(enry) L(ouis)

Thompson, Francis Joseph
1859-1907 .... **TCLC 4**
See also CA 104; CDBLB 1890-1914;
DLB 19

Thompson, Hunter S(tockton)
1939- .... **CLC 9, 17, 40**
See also BEST 89:1; CA 17-20R; CANR 23,
46; DAM POP; MTCW

Thompson, James Myers
See Thompson, Jim (Myers)

Thompson, Jim (Myers)
1906-1977(?) .... **CLC 69**
See also CA 140

Thompson, Judith .... **CLC 39**

Thomson, James 1700-1748 ...... **LC 16, 29**
See also DAM POET; DLB 95

Thomson, James 1834-1882 ...... **NCLC 18**
See also DAM POET; DLB 35

Thoreau, Henry David
1817-1862 ..... **NCLC 7, 21; DA; DAB;
DAC; WLC**
See also CDALB 1640-1865; DAM MST;
DLB 1

Thornton, Hall
See Silverberg, Robert

Thucydides c. 455B.C.-399B.C. .... **CMLC 17**

Thurber, James (Grover)
1894-1961 .... **CLC 5, 11, 25; DA; DAB;
DAC; SSC 1**
See also CA 73-76; CANR 17, 39;
CDALB 1929-1941; DAM DRAM, MST,
NOV; DLB 4, 11, 22, 102; MAICYA;
MTCW; SATA 13

Thurman, Wallace (Henry)
1902-1934 .... **TCLC 6; BLC**
See also BW 1; CA 104; 124; DAM MULT;
DLB 51

Ticheburn, Cheviot
See Ainsworth, William Harrison

Tieck, (Johann) Ludwig
1773-1853 .... **NCLC 5, 46**
See also DLB 90

Tiger, Derry
See Ellison, Harlan (Jay)

Tilghman, Christopher 1948(?)- ..... **CLC 65**

Tillinghast, Richard (Williford)
1940- .... **CLC 29**
See also CA 29-32R; CAAS 23; CANR 26,
51

Timrod, Henry 1828-1867 ...... **NCLC 25**
See also DLB 3

Tindall, Gillian 1938- .... **CLC 7**
See also CA 21-24R; CANR 11

Tiptree, James, Jr. .... **CLC 48, 50**
See also Sheldon, Alice Hastings Bradley
See also DLB 8

Titmarsh, Michael Angelo
See Thackeray, William Makepeace

**Tocqueville, Alexis (Charles Henri Maurice
Clerel Comte)** 1805-1859 ..... **NCLC 7**

Tolkien, J(ohn) R(onald) R(euel)
1892-1973 ...... **CLC 1, 2, 3, 8, 12, 38;
DA; DAB; DAC; WLC**
See also AAYA 10; AITN 1; CA 17-18;
45-48; CANR 36; CAP 2;
CDBLB 1914-1945; DAM MST, NOV,
POP; DLB 15, 160; JRDA; MAICYA;
MTCW; SATA 2, 32; SATA-Obit 24

Toller, Ernst 1893-1939 .... **TCLC 10**
See also CA 107; DLB 124

Tolson, M. B.
See Tolson, Melvin B(eaunorus)

Tolson, Melvin B(eaunorus)
1898(?)-1966 .... **CLC 36; BLC**
See also BW 1; CA 124; 89-92;
DAM MULT, POET; DLB 48, 76

Tolstoi, Aleksei Nikolaevich
See Tolstoy, Alexey Nikolaevich

Tolstoy, Alexey Nikolaevich
1882-1945 .... **TCLC 18**
See also CA 107

Tolstoy, Count Leo
See Tolstoy, Leo (Nikolaevich)

Tolstoy, Leo (Nikolaevich)
1828-1910 ...... **TCLC 4, 11, 17, 28, 44;
DA; DAB; DAC; SSC 9; WLC**
See also CA 104; 123; DAM MST, NOV;
SATA 26

Tomasi di Lampedusa, Giuseppe 1896-1957
See Lampedusa, Giuseppe (Tomasi) di
See also CA 111

Tomlin, Lily .... **CLC 17**
See also Tomlin, Mary Jean

Tomlin, Mary Jean 1939(?)-
See Tomlin, Lily
See also CA 117

Tomlinson, (Alfred) Charles
1927- .... **CLC 2, 4, 6, 13, 45**
See also CA 5-8R; CANR 33; DAM POET;
DLB 40

Tonson, Jacob
See Bennett, (Enoch) Arnold

Toole, John Kennedy
1937-1969 .... **CLC 19, 64**
See also CA 104; DLBY 81

Toomer, Jean
1894-1967 ...... **CLC 1, 4, 13, 22; BLC;
PC 7; SSC 1**
See also BW 1; CA 85-88;
CDALB 1917-1929; DAM MULT;
DLB 45, 51; MTCW

Torley, Luke
See Blish, James (Benjamin)

Tornimparte, Alessandra
See Ginzburg, Natalia

Torre, Raoul della
See Mencken, H(enry) L(ouis)

Torrey, E(dwin) Fuller 1937- .... **CLC 34**
See also CA 119

Torsvan, Ben Traven
See Traven, B.

Torsvan, Benno Traven
See Traven, B.

Torsvan, Berick Traven
See Traven, B.

Torsvan, Berwick Traven
See Traven, B.

Torsvan, Bruno Traven
See Traven, B.

Torsvan, Traven
See Traven, B.

Tournier, Michel (Edouard)
1924- .... **CLC 6, 23, 36, 95**
See also CA 49-52; CANR 3, 36; DLB 83;
MTCW; SATA 23

Tournimparte, Alessandra
See Ginzburg, Natalia

Towers, Ivar
See Kornbluth, C(yril) M.

Towne, Robert (Burton) 1936(?)- .... **CLC 87**
See also CA 108; DLB 44

Townsend, Sue 1946- .. **CLC 61; DAB; DAC**
See also CA 119; 127; INT 127; MTCW;
SATA 55; SATA-Brief 48

Townshend, Peter (Dennis Blandford)
1945- .... **CLC 17, 42**
See also CA 107

Tozzi, Federigo 1883-1920 .... **TCLC 31**

Traill, Catharine Parr
1802-1899 .... **NCLC 31**
See also DLB 99

Trakl, Georg 1887-1914 .... **TCLC 5**
See also CA 104

Transtroemer, Tomas (Goesta)
1931- .... **CLC 52, 65**
See also CA 117; 129; CAAS 17;
DAM POET

Transtromer, Tomas Gosta
See Transtroemer, Tomas (Goesta)

Traven, B. (?)-1969 .... **CLC 8, 11**
See also CA 19-20; 25-28R; CAP 2; DLB 9,
56; MTCW

Treitel, Jonathan 1959- .... **CLC 70**

Tremain, Rose 1943- .... **CLC 42**
See also CA 97-100; CANR 44; DLB 14

Tremblay, Michel 1942- ...... **CLC 29; DAC**
See also CA 116; 128; DAM MST; DLB 60;
MTCW

Trevanian .... **CLC 29**
See also Whitaker, Rod(ney)

Trevor, Glen
See Hilton, James

Trevor, William
1928- .... **CLC 7, 9, 14, 25, 71; SSC 21**
See also Cox, William Trevor
See also DLB 14, 139

Trifonov, Yuri (Valentinovich)
1925-1981 .... **CLC 45**
See also CA 126; 103; MTCW

Trilling, Lionel 1905-1975 .... **CLC 9, 11, 24**
See also CA 9-12R; 61-64; CANR 10;
DLB 28, 63; INT CANR-10; MTCW

Trimball, W. H.
See Mencken, H(enry) L(ouis)

Tristan
See Gomez de la Serna, Ramon

Tristram
See Housman, A(lfred) E(dward)

Trogdon, William (Lewis) 1939-
See Heat-Moon, William Least
See also CA 115; 119; CANR 47; INT 119

Trollope, Anthony
1815-1882 ..... **NCLC 6, 33; DA; DAB;
DAC; WLC**
See also CDBLB 1832-1890; DAM MST,
NOV; DLB 21, 57, 159; SATA 22

Trollope, Frances 1779-1863 ..... **NCLC 30**
See also DLB 21, 166

Trotsky, Leon 1879-1940 .... **TCLC 22**
See also CA 118

Trotter (Cockburn), Catharine
1679-1749 .... **LC 8**
See also DLB 84

Trout, Kilgore
See Farmer, Philip Jose

Trow, George W. S. 1943- .... **CLC 52**
See also CA 126

Troyat, Henri 1911- .... **CLC 23**
See also CA 45-48; CANR 2, 33; MTCW

Trudeau, G(arretson) B(eekman) 1948-
See Trudeau, Garry B.
See also CA 81-84; CANR 31; SATA 35

Trudeau, Garry B. .... **CLC 12**
See also Trudeau, G(arretson) B(eekman)
See also AAYA 10; AITN 2

Truffaut, Francois 1932-1984. ...... **CLC 20**
See also CA 81-84; 113; CANR 34

Trumbo, Dalton 1905-1976 .... **CLC 19**
See also CA 21-24R; 69-72; CANR 10;
DLB 26

Trumbull, John 1750-1831 .... **NCLC 30**
See also DLB 31

Trundlett, Helen B.
See Eliot, T(homas) S(tearns)

Tryon, Thomas 1926-1991 .... **CLC 3, 11**
See also AITN 1; CA 29-32R; 135;
CANR 32; DAM POP; MTCW

Tryon, Tom
See Tryon, Thomas

Ts'ao Hsueh-ch'in 1715(?)-1763. ...... **LC 1**

Tsushima, Shuji 1909-1948
See Dazai, Osamu
See also CA 107

Tsvetaeva (Efron), Marina (Ivanovna)
1892-1941 .... **TCLC 7, 35; PC 14**
See also CA 104; 128; MTCW

Tuck, Lily 1938- .... **CLC 70**
See also CA 139

Tu Fu 712-770. .... **PC 9**
See also DAM MULT

Tunis, John R(oberts) 1889-1975 ... **CLC 12**
See also CA 61-64; DLB 22; JRDA;
MAICYA; SATA 37; SATA-Brief 30

Tuohy, Frank .... **CLC 37**
See also Tuohy, John Francis
See also DLB 14, 139

Tuohy, John Francis 1925-
See Tuohy, Frank
See also CA 5-8R; CANR 3, 47

Turco, Lewis (Putnam) 1934- ... **CLC 11, 63**
See also CA 13-16R; CAAS 22; CANR 24,
51; DLBY 84

Turgenev, Ivan
1818-1883 .... **NCLC 21; DA; DAB;
DAC; SSC 7; WLC**
See also DAM MST, NOV

Turgot, Anne-Robert-Jacques
1727-1781 .... **LC 26**

Turner, Frederick 1943- .... **CLC 48**
See also CA 73-76; CAAS 10; CANR 12,
30; DLB 40

Tutu, Desmond M(pilo)
1931- .... **CLC 80; BLC**
See also BW 1; CA 125; DAM MULT

Tutuola, Amos 1920- ... **CLC 5, 14, 29; BLC**
See also BW 2; CA 9-12R; CANR 27;
DAM MULT; DLB 125; MTCW

Twain, Mark
..... **TCLC 6, 12, 19, 36, 48, 59; SSC 6;
WLC**
See also Clemens, Samuel Langhorne
See also DLB 11, 12, 23, 64, 74

Tyler, Anne
1941- .... **CLC 7, 11, 18, 28, 44, 59**
See also AAYA 18; BEST 89:1; CA 9-12R;
CANR 11, 33, 53; DAM NOV, POP;
DLB 6, 143; DLBY 82; MTCW; SATA 7

Tyler, Royall 1757-1826. .... **NCLC 3**
See also DLB 37

Tynan, Katharine 1861-1931 .... **TCLC 3**
See also CA 104; DLB 153

Tyutchev, Fyodor 1803-1873 ..... **NCLC 34**

Tzara, Tristan .... **CLC 47**
See also Rosenfeld, Samuel
See also DAM POET

Uhry, Alfred 1936- .... **CLC 55**
See also CA 127; 133; DAM DRAM, POP;
INT 133

Ulf, Haerved
See Strindberg, (Johan) August

Ulf, Harved
See Strindberg, (Johan) August

Ulibarri, Sabine R(eyes) 1919- ..... **CLC 83**
See also CA 131; DAM MULT; DLB 82;
HW

Unamuno (y Jugo), Miguel de
1864-1936 .... **TCLC 2, 9; HLC; SSC 11**
See also CA 104; 131; DAM MULT, NOV;
DLB 108; HW; MTCW

Undercliffe, Errol
See Campbell, (John) Ramsey

Underwood, Miles
See Glassco, John

Undset, Sigrid
1882-1949 .... **TCLC 3; DA; DAB;
DAC; WLC**
See also CA 104; 129; DAM MST, NOV;
MTCW

Ungaretti, Giuseppe
1888-1970 .... **CLC 7, 11, 15**
See also CA 19-20; 25-28R; CAP 2;
DLB 114

Unger, Douglas 1952- .... **CLC 34**
See also CA 130

Unsworth, Barry (Forster) 1930- .... **CLC 76**
See also CA 25-28R; CANR 30

Updike, John (Hoyer)
1932- ...... **CLC 1, 2, 3, 5, 7, 9, 13, 15,
23, 34, 43, 70; DA; DAB; DAC; SSC 13;
WLC**
See also CA 1-4R; CABS 1; CANR 4, 33,
51; CDALB 1968-1988; DAM MST,
NOV, POET, POP; DLB 2, 5, 143;
DLBD 3; DLBY 80, 82; MTCW

Upshaw, Margaret Mitchell
See Mitchell, Margaret (Munnerlyn)

Upton, Mark
See Sanders, Lawrence

Urdang, Constance (Henriette)
1922- .... **CLC 47**
See also CA 21-24R; CANR 9, 24

Uriel, Henry
See Faust, Frederick (Schiller)

Uris, Leon (Marcus) 1924- .... **CLC 7, 32**
See also AITN 1, 2; BEST 89:2; CA 1-4R;
CANR 1, 40; DAM NOV, POP; MTCW;
SATA 49

Urmuz
See Codrescu, Andrei

Urquhart, Jane 1949- .... **CLC 90; DAC**
See also CA 113; CANR 32

Ustinov, Peter (Alexander) 1921- .... **CLC 1**
See also AITN 1; CA 13-16R; CANR 25,
51; DLB 13

Vaculik, Ludvik 1926- .... **CLC 7**
See also CA 53-56

Valdez, Luis (Miguel)
1940- .... **CLC 84; HLC**
See also CA 101; CANR 32; DAM MULT;
DLB 122; HW

Valenzuela, Luisa 1938- ... **CLC 31; SSC 14**
See also CA 101; CANR 32; DAM MULT;
DLB 113; HW

Valera y Alcala-Galiano, Juan
1824-1905 .... **TCLC 10**
See also CA 106

Valery, (Ambroise) Paul (Toussaint Jules)
1871-1945 .... **TCLC 4, 15; PC 9**
See also CA 104; 122; DAM POET; MTCW

Valle-Inclan, Ramon (Maria) del
1866-1936 .... **TCLC 5; HLC**
See also CA 106; DAM MULT; DLB 134

Vallejo, Antonio Buero
See Buero Vallejo, Antonio

Vallejo, Cesar (Abraham)
1892-1938 .... **TCLC 3, 56; HLC**
See also CA 105; DAM MULT; HW

Valle Y Pena, Ramon del
See Valle-Inclan, Ramon (Maria) del

Van Ash, Cay 1918- .... **CLC 34**

Vanbrugh, Sir John 1664-1726 ...... **LC 21**
See also DAM DRAM; DLB 80

Van Campen, Karl
See Campbell, John W(ood, Jr.)

Vance, Gerald
See Silverberg, Robert

Vance, Jack .... **CLC 35**
See also Vance, John Holbrook
See also DLB 8

Von Rachen, Kurt
See Hubbard, L(afayette) Ron(ald)

von Rezzori (d'Arezzo), Gregor
See Rezzori (d'Arezzo), Gregor von

von Sternberg, Josef
See Sternberg, Josef von

Vorster, Gordon 1924- . . . . **CLC 34**
See also CA 133

Vosce, Trudie
See Ozick, Cynthia

Voznesensky, Andrei (Andreievich)
1933- . . . . **CLC 1, 15, 57**
See also CA 89-92; CANR 37;
DAM POET; MTCW

Waddington, Miriam 1917- . . . . **CLC 28**
See also CA 21-24R; CANR 12, 30;
DLB 68

Wagman, Fredrica 1937- . . . . **CLC 7**
See also CA 97-100; INT 97-100

Wagner, Richard 1813-1883. . . . . . . **NCLC 9**
See also DLB 129

Wagner-Martin, Linda 1936- . . . . **CLC 50**

Wagoner, David (Russell)
1926- . . . . **CLC 3, 5, 15**
See also CA 1-4R; CAAS 3; CANR 2;
DLB 5; SATA 14

Wah, Fred(erick James) 1939- . . . . . . **CLC 44**
See also CA 107; 141; DLB 60

Wahloo, Per 1926-1975 . . . . **CLC 7**
See also CA 61-64

Wahloo, Peter
See Wahloo, Per

Wain, John (Barrington)
1925-1994 . . . . **CLC 2, 11, 15, 46**
See also CA 5-8R; 145; CAAS 4; CANR 23;
CDBLB 1960 to Present; DLB 15, 27,
139, 155; MTCW

Wajda, Andrzej 1926-. . . . . **CLC 16**
See also CA 102

Wakefield, Dan 1932-. . . . . **CLC 7**
See also CA 21-24R; CAAS 7

Wakoski, Diane
1937- . . . . . **CLC 2, 4, 7, 9, 11, 40; PC 15**
See also CA 13-16R; CAAS 1; CANR 9;
DAM POET; DLB 5; INT CANR-9

Wakoski-Sherbell, Diane
See Wakoski, Diane

Walcott, Derek (Alton)
1930- . . . . **CLC 2, 4, 9, 14, 25, 42, 67, 76;
BLC; DAB; DAC**
See also BW 2; CA 89-92; CANR 26, 47;
DAM MST, MULT, POET; DLB 117;
DLBY 81; MTCW

Waldman, Anne 1945- . . . . **CLC 7**
See also CA 37-40R; CAAS 17; CANR 34;
DLB 16

Waldo, E. Hunter
See Sturgeon, Theodore (Hamilton)

Waldo, Edward Hamilton
See Sturgeon, Theodore (Hamilton)

Walker, Alice (Malsenior)
1944- . . . . **CLC 5, 6, 9, 19, 27, 46, 58;
BLC; DA; DAB; DAC; SSC 5**
See also AAYA 3; BEST 89:4; BW 2;
CA 37-40R; CANR 9, 27, 49;
CDALB 1968-1988; DAM MST, MULT,
NOV, POET, POP; DLB 6, 33, 143;
INT CANR-27; MTCW; SATA 31

Walker, David Harry 1911-1992. . . . **CLC 14**
See also CA 1-4R; 137; CANR 1; SATA 8;
SATA-Obit 71

Walker, Edward Joseph 1934-
See Walker, Ted
See also CA 21-24R; CANR 12, 28, 53

Walker, George F.
1947- . . . . **CLC 44, 61; DAB; DAC**
See also CA 103; CANR 21, 43;
DAM MST; DLB 60

Walker, Joseph A. 1935- . . . . **CLC 19**
See also BW 1; CA 89-92; CANR 26;
DAM DRAM, MST; DLB 38

Walker, Margaret (Abigail)
1915- . . . . **CLC 1, 6; BLC**
See also BW 2; CA 73-76; CANR 26;
DAM MULT; DLB 76, 152; MTCW

Walker, Ted. **CLC 13**
See also Walker, Edward Joseph
See also DLB 40

Wallace, David Foster 1962- . . . . **CLC 50**
See also CA 132

Wallace, Dexter
See Masters, Edgar Lee

Wallace, (Richard Horatio) Edgar
1875-1932 . . . . **TCLC 57**
See also CA 115; DLB 70

Wallace, Irving 1916-1990 . . . . . . **CLC 7, 13**
See also AITN 1; CA 1-4R; 132; CAAS 1;
CANR 1, 27; DAM NOV, POP;
INT CANR-27; MTCW

Wallant, Edward Lewis
1926-1962 . . . . **CLC 5, 10**
See also CA 1-4R; CANR 22; DLB 2, 28,
143; MTCW

Walley, Byron
See Card, Orson Scott

Walpole, Horace 1717-1797. . . . . **LC 2**
See also DLB 39, 104

Walpole, Hugh (Seymour)
1884-1941 . . . . **TCLC 5**
See also CA 104; DLB 34

Walser, Martin 1927-. . . . . **CLC 27**
See also CA 57-60; CANR 8, 46; DLB 75,
124

Walser, Robert
1878-1956 . . . . **TCLC 18; SSC 20**
See also CA 118; DLB 66

Walsh, Jill Paton. . . . . **CLC 35**
See also Paton Walsh, Gillian
See also AAYA 11; CLR 2; DLB 161;
SAAS 3

Walter, Villiam Christian
See Andersen, Hans Christian

Wambaugh, Joseph (Aloysius, Jr.)
1937- . . . . **CLC 3, 18**
See also AITN 1; BEST 89:3; CA 33-36R;
CANR 42; DAM NOV, POP; DLB 6;
DLBY 83; MTCW

Ward, Arthur Henry Sarsfield 1883-1959
See Rohmer, Sax
See also CA 108

Ward, Douglas Turner 1930-. . . . . . . **CLC 19**
See also BW 1; CA 81-84; CANR 27;
DLB 7, 38

Ward, Mary Augusta
See Ward, Mrs. Humphry

Ward, Mrs. Humphry
1851-1920 . . . . **TCLC 55**
See also DLB 18

Ward, Peter
See Faust, Frederick (Schiller)

Warhol, Andy 1928(?)-1987. . . . . . . **CLC 20**
See also AAYA 12; BEST 89:4; CA 89-92;
121; CANR 34

Warner, Francis (Robert le Plastrier)
1937- . . . . **CLC 14**
See also CA 53-56; CANR 11

Warner, Marina 1946- . . . . **CLC 59**
See also CA 65-68; CANR 21

Warner, Rex (Ernest) 1905-1986. . . . **CLC 45**
See also CA 89-92; 119; DLB 15

Warner, Susan (Bogert)
1819-1885 . . . . **NCLC 31**
See also DLB 3, 42

Warner, Sylvia (Constance) Ashton
See Ashton-Warner, Sylvia (Constance)

Warner, Sylvia Townsend
1893-1978 . . . . **CLC 7, 19; SSC 23**
See also CA 61-64; 77-80; CANR 16;
DLB 34, 139; MTCW

Warren, Mercy Otis 1728-1814. . . **NCLC 13**
See also DLB 31

Warren, Robert Penn
1905-1989 . . . . **CLC 1, 4, 6, 8, 10, 13, 18,
39, 53, 59; DA; DAB; DAC; SSC 4; WLC**
See also AITN 1; CA 13-16R; 129;
CANR 10, 47; CDALB 1968-1988;
DAM MST, NOV, POET; DLB 2, 48,
152; DLBY 80, 89; INT CANR-10;
MTCW; SATA 46; SATA-Obit 63

Warshofsky, Isaac
See Singer, Isaac Bashevis

Warton, Thomas 1728-1790. . . . . **LC 15**
See also DAM POET; DLB 104, 109

Waruk, Kona
See Harris, (Theodore) Wilson

Warung, Price 1855-1911. . . . . **TCLC 45**

Warwick, Jarvis
See Garner, Hugh

Washington, Alex
See Harris, Mark

Washington, Booker T(aliaferro)
1856-1915 . . . . **TCLC 10; BLC**
See also BW 1; CA 114; 125; DAM MULT;
SATA 28

Washington, George 1732-1799. . . . . . **LC 25**
See also DLB 31

Wassermann, (Karl) Jakob
1873-1934 . . . . **TCLC 6**
See also CA 104; DLB 66

Wasserstein, Wendy
1950- . . . . **CLC 32, 59, 90; DC 4**
See also CA 121; 129; CABS 3; CANR 53;
DAM DRAM; INT 129

Waterhouse, Keith (Spencer)
1929- . . . . **CLC 47**
See also CA 5-8R; CANR 38; DLB 13, 15;
MTCW

Waters, Frank (Joseph)
1902-1995 . . . . **CLC 88**
See also CA 5-8R; 149; CAAS 13; CANR 3,
18; DLBY 86

Waters, Roger 1944- . . . . **CLC 35**

Watkins, Frances Ellen
See Harper, Frances Ellen Watkins

Watkins, Gerrold
See Malzberg, Barry N(athaniel)

Watkins, Gloria 1955(?)-
See hooks, bell
See also BW 2; CA 143

Watkins, Paul 1964- . . . . **CLC 55**
See also CA 132

Watkins, Vernon Phillips
1906-1967 . . . . **CLC 43**
See also CA 9-10; 25-28R; CAP 1; DLB 20

Watson, Irving S.
See Mencken, H(enry) L(ouis)

Watson, John H.
See Farmer, Philip Jose

Watson, Richard F.
See Silverberg, Robert

Waugh, Auberon (Alexander) 1939- . . **CLC 7**
See also CA 45-48; CANR 6, 22; DLB 14

Waugh, Evelyn (Arthur St. John)
1903-1966 . . . . . . **CLC 1, 3, 8, 13, 19, 27,
44; DA; DAB; DAC; WLC**
See also CA 85-88; 25-28R; CANR 22;
CDBLB 1914-1945; DAM MST, NOV,
POP; DLB 15, 162; MTCW

Waugh, Harriet 1944- . . . . **CLC 6**
See also CA 85-88; CANR 22

Ways, C. R.
See Blount, Roy (Alton), Jr.

Waystaff, Simon
See Swift, Jonathan

Webb, (Martha) Beatrice (Potter)
1858-1943 . . . . **TCLC 22**
See also Potter, Beatrice
See also CA 117

Webb, Charles (Richard) 1939- . . . . . . **CLC 7**
See also CA 25-28R

Webb, James H(enry), Jr. 1946- . . . . **CLC 22**
See also CA 81-84

Webb, Mary (Gladys Meredith)
1881-1927 . . . . **TCLC 24**
See also CA 123; DLB 34

Webb, Mrs. Sidney
See Webb, (Martha) Beatrice (Potter)

Webb, Phyllis 1927- . . . . **CLC 18**
See also CA 104; CANR 23; DLB 53

Webb, Sidney (James)
1859-1947 . . . . **TCLC 22**
See also CA 117

Webber, Andrew Lloyd . . . . **CLC 21**
See also Lloyd Webber, Andrew

Weber, Lenora Mattingly
1895-1971 . . . . **CLC 12**
See also CA 19-20; 29-32R; CAP 1;
SATA 2; SATA-Obit 26

Webster, John
1579(?)-1634(?) . . . . . . **LC 33; DA; DAB;
DAC; DC 2; WLC**
See also CDBLB Before 1660;
DAM DRAM, MST; DLB 58

Webster, Noah 1758-1843 . . . . **NCLC 30**

Wedekind, (Benjamin) Frank(lin)
1864-1918 . . . . **TCLC 7**
See also CA 104; DAM DRAM; DLB 118

Weidman, Jerome 1913- . . . . **CLC 7**
See also AITN 2; CA 1-4R; CANR 1;
DLB 28

Weil, Simone (Adolphine)
1909-1943 . . . . **TCLC 23**
See also CA 117

Weinstein, Nathan
See West, Nathanael

Weinstein, Nathan von Wallenstein
See West, Nathanael

Weir, Peter (Lindsay) 1944- . . . . **CLC 20**
See also CA 113; 123

Weiss, Peter (Ulrich)
1916-1982 . . . . **CLC 3, 15, 51**
See also CA 45-48; 106; CANR 3;
DAM DRAM; DLB 69, 124

Weiss, Theodore (Russell)
1916- . . . . **CLC 3, 8, 14**
See also CA 9-12R; CAAS 2; CANR 46;
DLB 5

Welch, (Maurice) Denton
1915-1948 . . . . **TCLC 22**
See also CA 121; 148

Welch, James 1940- . . . . **CLC 6, 14, 52**
See also CA 85-88; CANR 42;
DAM MULT, POP; NNAL

Weldon, Fay
1933- . . . . **CLC 6, 9, 11, 19, 36, 59**
See also CA 21-24R; CANR 16, 46;
CDBLB 1960 to Present; DAM POP;
DLB 14; INT CANR-16; MTCW

Wellek, Rene 1903-1995 . . . . **CLC 28**
See also CA 5-8R; 150; CAAS 7; CANR 8;
DLB 63; INT CANR-8

Weller, Michael 1942- . . . . **CLC 10, 53**
See also CA 85-88

Weller, Paul 1958- . . . . **CLC 26**

Wellershoff, Dieter 1925- . . . . **CLC 46**
See also CA 89-92; CANR 16, 37

Welles, (George) Orson
1915-1985 . . . . **CLC 20, 80**
See also CA 93-96; 117

Wellman, Mac 1945- . . . . **CLC 65**

Wellman, Manly Wade 1903-1986 . . **CLC 49**
See also CA 1-4R; 118; CANR 6, 16, 44;
SATA 6; SATA-Obit 47

Wells, Carolyn 1869(?)-1942 . . . . . . **TCLC 35**
See also CA 113; DLB 11

Wells, H(erbert) G(eorge)
1866-1946 . . . . **TCLC 6, 12, 19; DA;
DAB; DAC; SSC 6; WLC**
See also AAYA 18; CA 110; 121;
CDBLB 1914-1945; DAM MST, NOV;
DLB 34, 70, 156; MTCW; SATA 20

Wells, Rosemary 1943- . . . . **CLC 12**
See also AAYA 13; CA 85-88; CANR 48;
CLR 16; MAICYA; SAAS 1; SATA 18,
69

Welty, Eudora
1909- . . . . . . **CLC 1, 2, 5, 14, 22, 33; DA;
DAB; DAC; SSC 1; WLC**
See also CA 9-12R; CABS 1; CANR 32;
CDALB 1941-1968; DAM MST, NOV;
DLB 2, 102, 143; DLBD 12; DLBY 87;
MTCW

Wen I-to 1899-1946 . . . . **TCLC 28**

Wentworth, Robert
See Hamilton, Edmond

Werfel, Franz (V.) 1890-1945 . . . . . . **TCLC 8**
See also CA 104; DLB 81, 124

Wergeland, Henrik Arnold
1808-1845 . . . . **NCLC 5**

Wersba, Barbara 1932- . . . . **CLC 30**
See also AAYA 2; CA 29-32R; CANR 16,
38; CLR 3; DLB 52; JRDA; MAICYA;
SAAS 2; SATA 1, 58

Wertmueller, Lina 1928- . . . . **CLC 16**
See also CA 97-100; CANR 39

Wescott, Glenway 1901-1987 . . . . **CLC 13**
See also CA 13-16R; 121; CANR 23;
DLB 4, 9, 102

Wesker, Arnold 1932- . . **CLC 3, 5, 42; DAB**
See also CA 1-4R; CAAS 7; CANR 1, 33;
CDBLB 1960 to Present; DAM DRAM;
DLB 13; MTCW

Wesley, Richard (Errol) 1945- . . . . . . **CLC 7**
See also BW 1; CA 57-60; CANR 27;
DLB 38

Wessel, Johan Herman 1742-1785 . . . . **LC 7**

West, Anthony (Panther)
1914-1987 . . . . **CLC 50**
See also CA 45-48; 124; CANR 3, 19;
DLB 15

West, C. P.
See Wodehouse, P(elham) G(renville)

West, (Mary) Jessamyn
1902-1984 . . . . **CLC 7, 17**
See also CA 9-12R; 112; CANR 27; DLB 6;
DLBY 84; MTCW; SATA-Obit 37

West, Morris L(anglo) 1916- . . . . . **CLC 6, 33**
See also CA 5-8R; CANR 24, 49; MTCW

West, Nathanael
1903-1940 . . . . . **TCLC 1, 14, 44; SSC 16**
See also CA 104; 125; CDALB 1929-1941;
DLB 4, 9, 28; MTCW

West, Owen
See Koontz, Dean R(ay)

West, Paul 1930- . . . . **CLC 7, 14**
See also CA 13-16R; CAAS 7; CANR 22,
53; DLB 14; INT CANR-22

Williams, John A(lfred)
1925- .... **CLC 5, 13; BLC**
See also BW 2; CA 53-56; CAAS 3;
CANR 6, 26, 51; DAM MULT; DLB 2,
33; INT CANR-6

Williams, Jonathan (Chamberlain)
1929- .... **CLC 13**
See also CA 9-12R; CAAS 12; CANR 8;
DLB 5

Williams, Joy 1944- .... **CLC 31**
See also CA 41-44R; CANR 22, 48

Williams, Norman 1952- .... **CLC 39**
See also CA 118

Williams, Sherley Anne
1944- .... **CLC 89; BLC**
See also BW 2; CA 73-76; CANR 25;
DAM MULT, POET; DLB 41;
INT CANR-25; SATA 78

Williams, Shirley
See Williams, Sherley Anne

Williams, Tennessee
1911-1983 ..... **CLC 1, 2, 5, 7, 8, 11, 15,
19, 30, 39, 45, 71; DA; DAB; DAC;
DC 4; WLC**
See also AITN 1, 2; CA 5-8R; 108;
CABS 3; CANR 31; CDALB 1941-1968;
DAM DRAM, MST; DLB 7; DLBD 4;
DLBY 83; MTCW

Williams, Thomas (Alonzo)
1926-1990 .... **CLC 14**
See also CA 1-4R; 132; CANR 2

Williams, William C.
See Williams, William Carlos

Williams, William Carlos
1883-1963 .... **CLC 1, 2, 5, 9, 13, 22, 42,
67; DA; DAB; DAC; PC 7**
See also CA 89-92; CANR 34;
CDALB 1917-1929; DAM MST, POET;
DLB 4, 16, 54, 86; MTCW

Williamson, David (Keith) 1942- .... **CLC 56**
See also CA 103; CANR 41

Williamson, Ellen Douglas 1905-1984
See Douglas, Ellen
See also CA 17-20R; 114; CANR 39

Williamson, Jack .... **CLC 29**
See also Williamson, John Stewart
See also CAAS 8; DLB 8

Williamson, John Stewart 1908-
See Williamson, Jack
See also CA 17-20R; CANR 23

Willie, Frederick
See Lovecraft, H(oward) P(hillips)

Willingham, Calder (Baynard, Jr.)
1922-1995 .... **CLC 5, 51**
See also CA 5-8R; 147; CANR 3; DLB 2,
44; MTCW

Willis, Charles
See Clarke, Arthur C(harles)

Willy
See Colette, (Sidonie-Gabrielle)

Willy, Colette
See Colette, (Sidonie-Gabrielle)

Wilson, A(ndrew) N(orman) 1950- .. **CLC 33**
See also CA 112; 122; DLB 14, 155

Wilson, Angus (Frank Johnstone)
1913-1991 .. **CLC 2, 3, 5, 25, 34; SSC 21**
See also CA 5-8R; 134; CANR 21; DLB 15,
139, 155; MTCW

Wilson, August
1945- .... **CLC 39, 50, 63; BLC; DA;
DAB; DAC; DC 2**
See also AAYA 16; BW 2; CA 115; 122;
CANR 42; DAM DRAM, MST, MULT;
MTCW

Wilson, Brian 1942- .... **CLC 12**

Wilson, Colin 1931- .... **CLC 3, 14**
See also CA 1-4R; CAAS 5; CANR 1, 22,
33; DLB 14; MTCW

Wilson, Dirk
See Pohl, Frederik

Wilson, Edmund
1895-1972 .... **CLC 1, 2, 3, 8, 24**
See also CA 1-4R; 37-40R; CANR 1, 46;
DLB 63; MTCW

Wilson, Ethel Davis (Bryant)
1888(?)-1980 .... **CLC 13; DAC**
See also CA 102; DAM POET; DLB 68;
MTCW

Wilson, John 1785-1854 .... **NCLC 5**

Wilson, John (Anthony) Burgess 1917-1993
See Burgess, Anthony
See also CA 1-4R; 143; CANR 2, 46; DAC;
DAM NOV; MTCW

Wilson, Lanford 1937- .... **CLC 7, 14, 36**
See also CA 17-20R; CABS 3; CANR 45;
DAM DRAM; DLB 7

Wilson, Robert M. 1944- .... **CLC 7, 9**
See also CA 49-52; CANR 2, 41; MTCW

Wilson, Robert McLiam 1964- ..... **CLC 59**
See also CA 132

Wilson, Sloan 1920- .... **CLC 32**
See also CA 1-4R; CANR 1, 44

Wilson, Snoo 1948- .... **CLC 33**
See also CA 69-72

Wilson, William S(mith) 1932- ..... **CLC 49**
See also CA 81-84

Winchilsea, Anne (Kingsmill) Finch Counte
1661-1720 .... **LC 3**

Windham, Basil
See Wodehouse, P(elham) G(renville)

Wingrove, David (John) 1954- ...... **CLC 68**
See also CA 133

Winters, Janet Lewis .... **CLC 41**
See also Lewis, Janet
See also DLBY 87

Winters, (Arthur) Yvor
1900-1968 .... **CLC 4, 8, 32**
See also CA 11-12; 25-28R; CAP 1;
DLB 48; MTCW

Winterson, Jeanette 1959- .... **CLC 64**
See also CA 136; DAM POP

Winthrop, John 1588-1649 .... **LC 31**
See also DLB 24, 30

Wiseman, Frederick 1930- .... **CLC 20**

Wister, Owen 1860-1938 .... **TCLC 21**
See also CA 108; DLB 9, 78; SATA 62

Witkacy
See Witkiewicz, Stanislaw Ignacy

Witkiewicz, Stanislaw Ignacy
1885-1939 .... **TCLC 8**
See also CA 105

Wittgenstein, Ludwig (Josef Johann)
1889-1951 .... **TCLC 59**
See also CA 113

Wittig, Monique 1935(?)- .... **CLC 22**
See also CA 116; 135; DLB 83

Wittlin, Jozef 1896-1976 .... **CLC 25**
See also CA 49-52; 65-68; CANR 3

Wodehouse, P(elham) G(renville)
1881-1975 ... **CLC 1, 2, 5, 10, 22; DAB;
DAC; SSC 2**
See also AITN 2; CA 45-48; 57-60;
CANR 3, 33; CDBLB 1914-1945;
DAM NOV; DLB 34, 162; MTCW;
SATA 22

Woiwode, L.
See Woiwode, Larry (Alfred)

Woiwode, Larry (Alfred) 1941-... **CLC 6, 10**
See also CA 73-76; CANR 16; DLB 6;
INT CANR-16

Wojciechowska, Maia (Teresa)
1927- .... **CLC 26**
See also AAYA 8; CA 9-12R; CANR 4, 41;
CLR 1; JRDA; MAICYA; SAAS 1;
SATA 1, 28, 83

Wolf, Christa 1929- .... **CLC 14, 29, 58**
See also CA 85-88; CANR 45; DLB 75;
MTCW

Wolfe, Gene (Rodman) 1931-....... **CLC 25**
See also CA 57-60; CAAS 9; CANR 6, 32;
DAM POP; DLB 8

Wolfe, George C. 1954- .... **CLC 49**
See also CA 149

Wolfe, Thomas (Clayton)
1900-1938 ..... **TCLC 4, 13, 29, 61; DA;
DAB; DAC; WLC**
See also CA 104; 132; CDALB 1929-1941;
DAM MST, NOV; DLB 9, 102; DLBD 2;
DLBY 85; MTCW

Wolfe, Thomas Kennerly, Jr. 1931-
See Wolfe, Tom
See also CA 13-16R; CANR 9, 33;
DAM POP; INT CANR-9; MTCW

Wolfe, Tom **CLC 1, 2, 9, 15, 35, 51**
See also Wolfe, Thomas Kennerly, Jr.
See also AAYA 8; AITN 2; BEST 89:1;
DLB 152

Wolff, Geoffrey (Ansell) 1937- ..... **CLC 41**
See also CA 29-32R; CANR 29, 43

Wolff, Sonia
See Levitin, Sonia (Wolff)

Wolff, Tobias (Jonathan Ansell)
1945- .... **CLC 39, 64**
See also AAYA 16; BEST 90:2; CA 114;
117; CAAS 22; DLB 130; INT 117

Wolfram von Eschenbach
c. 1170-c. 1220 .... **CMLC 5**
See also DLB 138

Wolitzer, Hilma 1930- .... **CLC 17**
See also CA 65-68; CANR 18, 40;
INT CANR-18; SATA 31

Wollstonecraft, Mary 1759-1797...... **LC 5**
See also CDBLB 1789-1832; DLB 39, 104,
158

SSC Cumulative Nationality Index

Title Index

City Life (Barthelme) **2**:30-5, 37-9

"A City of Churches" (Barthelme) **2**:37, 39, 41, 54

"The City of Dreadful Night" (Henry) **5**:188, 197

"City of London Churches" (Dickens) **17**:123

"A City of the Dead, a City of the Living" (Gordimer) **17**:171, 174, 191

"Civil War" (O'Flaherty) **6**:262, 274

Claire Lenoir (Villiers de l'Isle Adam) **14**:376

The Clairvoyant (Gass) **12**:148

"Clancy in the Tower of Babel" (Cheever) **1**:107

"Clara" (O'Brien) **10**:333

"Clara Milich" (Turgenev)
   See "Klara Milich"

"Clarence" (Harte) **8**:222, 251-52

"Clarissa" (Morand) **22**:156-57, 165, 168

Claudine à l'école (*Claudine at School*) (Colette) **10**:269

Claudine at School (Colette)
   See *Claudine à l'école*

"Claudius' Diary" (Shiga)
   See "Kurōdiasu no nikki"

"Claudius' Journal" (Shiga)
   See "Kurōdiasu no nikki"

"Clave para un amor" (Bioy Casares) **17**:58

"Clay" (Joyce) **3**:205, 209, 211, 221-22, 226, 233-34, 237, 247

"A Clean, Well-Lighted Place" (Hemingway) **1**:216, 230, 232, 237-38

"The Cleaner's Story" (Sansom) **21**:83

"The Clear Track" (O'Hara) **15**:289

"A Cleared Path" (Gilman) **13**:141-42

"The Clemency of the Court" (Cather) **2**:96, 100, 103, 105

"Clementina" (Cheever) **1**:100, 107

"Clementine" (Caldwell) **19**:56

"The Clerk's Quest" (Moore)
   See "Tóir Mhic Uí Dhíomasuigh"

"The Clerk's Tale" (Pritchett) **14**:271

"The Clever Little Trick" (Zoshchenko) **15**:404

"A Clever-Kids Story" (Beattie) **11**:6, 15-16

The Clicking of Cuthbert (Wodehouse) **2**:344, 354

"The Climber" (Mason) **4**:3

"The Cloak" (Gogol)
   See "The Overcoat"

"The Clock" (Baudelaire)
   See "L'horloge"

"Clone" (Cortazar) **7**:69-71

"Clorinda Walks in Heaven" (Coppard) **21**:27

Clorinda Walks in Heaven (Coppard) **21**:7-8, 15

Closed All Night (Morand)
   See *Fermé la nuit*

"Closed Space" (Beckett) **16**:123, 126

"Clothe the Naked" (Parker) **2**:275, 280-81, 286

"Cloud, Castle, Lake" (Nabokov) **11**:108-09, 127

The Cloven Viscount (Calvino)
   See *Il visconte dimezzato*

"Clowns in Clover" (Gordimer) **17**:153

"The Club Bedroom" (Auchincloss) **22**:10

"Le club des hachichins" (Gautier) **20**:16, 23-5, 31

The Club of Queer Trades (Chesterton) **1**:120, 122, 139

"Clytie" (Welty) **1**:466, 468, 471, 481, 495

"The Coach House" (Chekhov) **2**:128

"The Cobweb" (Saki) **12**:296

"Cock Crow" (Gordon) **15**:123-24, 126

"Cock-a-Doodle-Doo!" (Melville) **1**:295, 298, 303, 305, 322; **17**:363

"Cockadoodledoo" (Singer) **3**:358

"Cockroaches" (Schulz) **13**:333-34

"Cocky Olly" (Pritchett) **14**:300

"Coco" (Maupassant) **1**:275

"The Cocoons" (Ligotti) **16**:282-84

"Coda" (Selby) **20**:253, 255-57

"Un coeur simple" ("A Simple Heart") (Flaubert) **11**:37, 45-6, 54-6, 58-66, 70-1, 80-1, 84, 87, 91, 94, 96-9, 101, 103

"Un coeur simple" (Maupassant) **1**:286

"The Coice of a Bride" (Hoffmann)
   See "Die Brautwahl"

"The Cold" (Warner) **23**:370

"Cold Autumn" (Bunin) **5**:115-16

"A Cold, Calculating Thing" (O'Hara) **15**:252

"A Cold Day" (Saroyan) **21**:143

"The Cold House" (O'Hara) **15**:258, 265

"Cold Print" (Campbell) **19**:61-2, 64, 66, 71-3, 81, 88, 90-1

Cold Print (Campbell) **19**:66, 70-2, 80, 87, 90

"Colic" (O'Flaherty) **6**:271

"Collaboration" (Collier) **19**:98, 114

Collages (Nin) **10**:305-06, 308

Collected Ghost Stories (James) **16**:227, 230-32, 239, 241, 246, 249, 251, 255

The Collected Short Stories of Conrad Aiken (Aiken) **9**:9, 12, 28, 41

The Collected Stories (Babel) **16**:6, 8, 11, 14, 17, 19, 21, 25, 35, 41, 59

The Collected Stories (Boyle) **16**:155

Collected Stories (Garcia Marquez) **8**:182-84

Collected Stories (Lavin) **4**:174

Collected Stories (Lessing) **6**:196, 218-19

Collected Stories (Malamud)
   See *The Stories of Bernard Malamud*

Collected Stories (Mansfield) **9**:281

The Collected Stories (McGahern) **17**:318, 322

Collected Stories (O'Connor) **5**:398

The Collected Stories (Price) **22**:384-85, 388

Collected Stories (Pritchett) **14**:301

The Collected Stories (Trevor) **21**:260-61, 264

Collected Stories I (Spark) **10**:359-60, 368

Collected Stories: 1939-1976 (Bowles) **3**:65, 68-9

The Collected Stories of Caroline Gordon (Gordon) **15**:137-38, 141

The Collected Stories of Colette (Colette) **10**:280, 291

The Collected Stories of Hortense Calisher (Calisher) **15**:7-8, 15, 19, 21

The Collected Stories of Isaac Bashevis Singer (Singer) **3**:383-84

The Collected Stories of Katherine Anne Porter (Porter) **4**:347, 351, 358, 361

The Collected Stories of Louis Auchincloss (Auchincloss) **22**:52-3

The Collected Stories of Peter Taylor (Taylor) **10**:389

The Collected Stories Of Seán O'Faoláin (O'Faolain) **13**:313

Collected Stories of William Faulkner (Faulkner) **1**:151, 161-62, 177, 181

The Collected Tales of A. E. Coppard (Coppard) **21**:18

Collected Works (Bunin) **5**:99

Collected Works (Walser) **20**:339

Collected Works of Henry Lawson (Lawson) **18**:210

Collected Writings (Bierce) **9**:75

"The Collection" (Pritchett) **14**:296, 298

"The Collector" (Auchincloss) **22**:13

"Collector of Innocents" (Auchincloss) **22**:49

"Collectors" (Carver) **8**:11, 19

"Le collier" (Maupassant) **1**:259

"Colloquy" (Jackson) **9**:252

"The Colloquy of Monos and Una" (Poe) **1**:401-02

Le Colonel Chabert (Balzac) **5**:8, 18, 24-7

The Colonel Has No One to Write Him (Garcia Marquez)
   See *El colonel no tiene quien le escribe*

"Colonel Julian" (Bates) **10**:117

Colonel Julian, and Other Stories (Bates) **10**:115-17

El colonel no tiene quien le escribe (*The Colonel Has No One to Write Him*; *No One Writes to the Colonel*) (Garcia Marquez) **8**:162, 185, 192-97

"Colonel Starbottle for the Plaintiff" (Harte) **8**:229

"Colonel Starbottle's Client" (Harte) **8**:216, 245

"The Colonel's Awakening" (Dunbar) **8**:121, 127, 131, 148

"The Colonel's Foundation" (Auchincloss) **22**:53

"The Colonel's Lady" (Maugham) **8**:366, 380

"The Colonel's 'Nigger Dog'" (Harris) **19**:182

"El coloquio de los perros" ("The Dialogue of the Dogs"; *The Dogs' Colloguy*) (Cervantes) **12**:4, 8, 14-16, 21, 24, 26-8, 33-4, 37-8,

"Colorado" (Beattie) **11**:4-5, 7, 17

"Colour and Line" ("Line and Colour") (Babel) **16**:22, 27, 59

"The Colour Out of Space" (Lovecraft) **3**:261, 263, 267-69, 274, 281, 290-91

Columba (Merimee) **7**:276-77, 280-83, 290, 294-95, 300-05, 308

"Come Again Tomorrow" (Gordimer) **17**:165

"Come Along, Marjorie" (Spark) **10**:355-57, 359, 365, 370

Come Along with Me (Jackson) **9**:254

Come Back, Dr. Caligari (Barthelme) **2**:26-9, 31, 37-9, 46, 49, 51

"Come on a Coming" (Dixon) **16**:208

"Come On Back" (Gardner) **7**:224-25, 227-28, 235, 240-41

"Come Out the Wilderness" (Baldwin) **10**:2-3, 5, 7-9

La Comédie humaine (*The Human Comedy*) (Balzac) **5**:6-13, 16-17, 19-20, 26-33, 43, 48

"Les comédiens sans le savoir" (Balzac) **5**:31

"Comedy Evening" (Walser) **20**:353

"A Comedy in Rubber" (Henry) **5**:158

"Comedy Is Where You Die and They Don't Bury You Because You Can Still Walk" (Saroyan) **21**:144

"The Comedy of War" (Harris) **19**:183

"The Comet" (Schulz)
   See "Kometa"

"The Comforts of Home" (O'Connor) **1**:343-44, 351, 353, 365

"Coming Apart" (Walker) **5**:412-14

"Coming, Aphrodite!" (Cather) **2**:91-2, 95, 104, 111-12

"Coming, Eden Bower!" (Cather) **2**:111-12, 114

Title Index

Title Index

Title Index

Title Index

Title Index

ISBN 0-7876-0755-X